2001

HISTORIC DOCUMENTS
OF
2001

2001

HISTORIC DOCUMENTS

OF

2001

Cumulative Index, 1997–2001

CQ PRESS

A Division of Congressional Quarterly Inc.

Historic Documents of 2001

Editors: Martha Gottron, John Felton, Bruce Maxwell
Production and Associate Editor: Kerry V. Kern
Indexer: Victoria Agee

CQ Press
A Division of Congressional Quarterly Inc.
1255 22nd Street, N.W., Suite 400
Washington, D.C. 20037
202-729-1900 (in Washington, D.C.); 866-4CQ-PRESS (866-427-7737) toll-free
www.cqpress.com

The Library of Congress cataloged the first issue of this title as follows:

Historic documents. 1972—
      Washington. Congressional Quarterly Inc.

      1. United States—Politics and government—1945– —Yearbooks.
2. World politics—1945– —Yearbooks. I. Congressional Quarterly Inc.

E839.5H57   917.3'03'9205   72-97888

ISBN 1-56802-724-9
ISSN 0892-080X

PREFACE

Throughout history major transformations in world affairs generally have resulted from wars, economic crises, or major political events, such as elections and revolutions. In 2001 nineteen men armed with boxcutters and motivated by a zealous hatred of the United States managed to precipitate what appeared to be the greatest upheaval in the world since the collapse of the Soviet Union a decade earlier. The nineteen men were terrorists allegedly sponsored by the al Qaeda network based in Afghanistan and headed by wealthy Saudi Arabian exile Osama bin Laden. On a beautiful late summer day, September 11, they hijacked four airliners on the East Coast and deliberately flew two of them into the twin World Trade Center towers in New York City and a third into the Pentagon just outside Washington; the fourth plane crash-landed in rural Pennsylvania, its intended target unknown. The World Trade Center towers—a symbol of American economic might—collapsed from the impact, killing approximately 3,000 people. Nearly 200 people died at the Pentagon, the headquarters of American military power. Even greater damage was done to the cherished belief held by many Americans that they were safe from the cares of the rest of the world, protected by the vast oceans and the nation's $300 billion defense budget. Suddenly, Americans were frightened, as the terrorists had meant them to be.

The consequences of September 11 were far reaching. Afraid to travel, many Americans shunned the airplanes that had become a major convenience of the modern area, sending the travel industry into a depression. Stock markets tumbled, as did consumer confidence; unemployment rose and the overall economy, already struggling from recessionary pressures, fell further. The initial shock of September 11 had barely begun to dull when, in late September and early October, envelopes containing deadly anthrax spores arrived at news media offices and on Capitol Hill. For a while, it appeared that terrorists might be using biological weapons, as well as hijacked airplanes, to try to bring the world's economic and military superpower to its knees.

President George W. Bush, who had taken office eight months earlier following a disputed election and had been struggling to gain a foothold for his presidency, quickly seized the initiative. In a fiery speech to Congress and the nation on September 20 Bush declared that the United States was at war with

---

How to Use This Book

The documents are arranged in chronological order. If you know the approximate date of the report, speech, statement, court decision, or other document you are looking for, glance through the titles for that month in the table of contents.

If the table of contents does not lead you directly to the document you want, turn to the index at the end of the book. There you may find references not only to the particular document you seek but also to other entries on the same or a related subject. The index in this volume is a five-year cumulative index of *Historic Documents* covering the years 1997–2001. There is a separate volume, *Historic Documents Index, 1972–1999*, which may also be useful.

The introduction to each document is printed in italic type. The document itself, printed in roman type, follows the spelling, capitalization, and punctuation of the original or official copy. Where the full text is not given, omissions of material are indicated by the customary ellipsis points.

Internet URL addresses noting where the documents have been obtained appear at the end of each introduction. If documents were not available on the Internet, this also has been noted.

"evil" forces who sought to destroy democracy and the values of "progress and pluralism, tolerance and freedom." The president called for a global coalition to defeat all terrorist networks "of global reach," starting with the al Qaeda network in Afghanistan and the Taliban government that had sheltered it. In numerous other speeches later in the year, Bush placed a stark choice before the rest of the world: "Either you are for us or you are against us," he said. Despite the intensity of this rhetoric, Bush was careful to say that the United States was not at war with Islam, but with bin Laden and other extremists who used their own interpretations of Islam to justify a hatred of Western values.

Given the choice Bush offered, most of the world chose to side with the United States. The vast majority of world leaders condemned the September 11 attacks; among them were some countries that long had been hostile toward Washington, including Iran, Libya, and Syria. Dozens of countries also offered some form of direct support for Bush's campaign against global terrorism: freezing the bank accounts of terrorist groups, arresting suspected members of terrorist cells, or agreeing to help the United States root out the terrorists in Afghanistan. Some of these allies were among Washington's closest friends, notably Great Britain and other members of the NATO alliance, which for the first time in its fifty-two-year history invoked a treaty clause declaring that an attack on one alliance member obligated other nations to come to its defense.

Perhaps even more important, for the long term, were the decisions by several nonallies to offer concrete support to the United States. Chief among these was Russian president Vladimir Putin, who on September 24 said he would allow the use of Russian air space for U.S. "humanitarian" flights into Afghanistan and would agree to the U.S. use of military bases in the Central Asian republics that had once been part of the Soviet Union. Putin's support eased a simmering dispute between the United States and Russia over arms control issues and, more significantly, seemed to move Russia closer to the West than ever before. By the end of the year Russia and the U.S.-led NATO alliance were declaring the start of a "new relationship." China also announced its cooperation and sent intelligence agents to Washington with information about bin Laden's al Qaeda network. That move by Beijing eased a relationship that had been battered earlier in the year by a dispute over a U.S. spy plane that crash-landed in Chinese territory. These suddenly pro-U.S. positions by Russia and China were not entirely altruistic. Both had long battled what they described as Islamist terrorism within their own borders, and the U.S.-declared war against global terrorism offered them a degree of international cover for repressive actions that had enraged human rights advocates.

Of all the world's leaders, perhaps none was put in a more difficult position by the events of September 11 than Pakistan's military president, General Pervez Musharraf. Pakistan had helped the fanatic Islamist faction known as the Taliban come to power in Afghanistan in 1995 and had been its protector ever since. In a speech to his nation on September 19, Musharraf acknowledged that Pakistan faced a "very critical situation," by which he meant a choice between siding with its Western ally, the United States, or its Islamist client in Afghanistan, the Taliban, which had wide support within Pakistan. To Western eyes, the choice might not have seemed a difficult one. But Musharraf's dilemma mirrored that of many leaders in Muslim countries, who had allowed fundamentalist Islamist factions to flourish as a relief valve for disenfranchised, impoverished masses with no other source of hope. Musharraf made it clear that he was choosing the United States over the Taliban. His choice prompted street demonstrations and brought denunciations from some Islamist leaders, but the protests quickly faded and posed no immediate threat to Pakistani stability. Even so, Musharraf faced yet more difficulty in December when Pakistan-supported guerrillas fighting India's control of Kashmir attacked the Indian parliament building in New Delhi, killing four security officers and a gardener. The two countries, both equipped with nuclear weapons, rushed thousands of troops to the border and, at the end of the year, were threatening war against each other. President Bush called on both sides to "stand down" from their confrontation.

The threat of war on the Indian subcontinent emerged as the United States was attempting to wrap up the antiterrorism war that Bush had promised in Afghanistan. That war had opened on October 7, when U.S. planes and a British submarine unleashed bombs and missiles against military targets in Afghanistan. The fighting in Afghanistan quickly became a one-sided affair, as the world's greatest military power used the full scale of its high-technology weaponry to pound Taliban and al Qaeda fighters, who were armed with little more than assault rifles and who traveled by foot, on horseback, and aboard Toyota pickup trucks. Having terrorized their country and thereby lost public support, the Taliban had few allies other than bin Laden's al Qaeda fighters, most of whom were Arabs or Pakistanis. By the end of November the Taliban had been driven from their home base of Kandahar in southern Afghanistan. An undetermined number of Taliban and al Qaeda fighters were killed, while thousands laid down their weapons and faded into the population or kept their weapons and headed to the mountains. At year's end the U.S. military and its allies in Afghanistan were bombing mountain caves in eastern Afghanistan, hoping to flush out the remnants of bin Laden's al Qaeda network, including bin Laden himself, who had disappeared.

To take the place of the defeated Taliban, the United Nations convened an assembly of leaders of Afghanistan's various factions. On December 6 the leaders signed an agreement establishing an interim government headed by a respected tribal leader, Hamid Karzai. Karzai took office December 22 and faced the monumental task of running a country that had been at war for two decades, was still deeply divided along tribal and ethnic lines, and had virtually no domestic resources for economic recovery. The United Nations planned a reconstruction program with an estimated ten-year cost of more than $10 billion; the U.S. war against the Taliban and al Qaeda had cost slightly more than $6 billion in just the first three months.

The September 11 terrorist attacks and the subsequent war offered Bush an opportunity to demonstrate qualities of leadership that he had shown only infrequently during the early stages of his presidency. Until September 11 the president could boast of only one unqualified victory on domestic policy: congressional approval of most of a $1.6 trillion tax cut that had been the centerpiece of his 2000 election campaign. Many of Bush's other priorities had stalled in Congress, especially after the defection of Vermont senator James Jeffords from the Republican Party gave Democrats the leadership the Senate. During the late summer Bush was facing the prospect of contentious political battles over spending priorities.

The political dynamic in Washington changed dramatically after September 11, when the president declared that he had found a "mission" in defeating terrorism and rallied the country to his side. Congress overwhelmingly approved a resolution giving the president nearly open-ended authority to conduct an antiterrorism war. With little dissent, Congress also passed a bill, called the USA Patriot Act, that gave law enforcement agencies wide latitude to use wiretaps and other previously controversial investigative methods against suspected terrorists in the United States. The FBI arrested more than 1,200 foreign-born men and held hundreds of them indefinitely for violating immigration regulations and other crimes. Only one detainee was charged with participating in the September 11 terrorist plot: Zacarias Moussaoui, a French citizen of Moroccan descent, who had told a flight instructor in Minnesota that he wanted to learn how to fly large jets but not how to land them.

Attempting to reassure Americans that the home front would be protected against terrorists, Bush on September 20 appointed former Pennsylvania governor Tom Ridge to head a White House Office of Homeland Security. Ridge had barely started work when he faced what initially appeared to be a major terrorist threat in the form of anthrax-laden envelopes delivered to several East Coast media offices and to the offices of two Democratic senators. Letters in some of the envelopes made explicit references to the September 11 attacks, raising fears that terrorists were attacking the United States on a broad front. Public anxieties were heightened when government agencies and medical authorities gave confusing, and sometimes contradictory, advice about anthrax and how to combat it. Eventually, five people died and eighteen people became ill from exposure to anthrax; they were the first U.S. victims ever of what the government called bioterrorism. By the end of the year no further anthrax attacks were known to have occurred, and law enforcement agencies had concluded that the letters probably were the work of one or more disgruntled Americans, not of a foreign terrorist organization.

Although other events of the year seemed pale in comparison, they nonetheless were likely to have long-lasting if perhaps less terrifying consequences. Just as the economy appeared to be climbing out of recession, Enron, the innovative energy company that had quickly grown to be the seventh largest corporation in the United States, suddenly went bankrupt in December, stranding its shareholders and wiping out the pensions of many of its 21,000 employees. As the year ended it was becoming glaringly apparent that the company had been too innovative in its attempts to escape the realities of the marketplace.

As predicted, the Bush administration began to undo several of the programs and policies that its Democratic predecessor had promoted. Bush's first action as president was to sign an executive order barring federal funds to any international family planning organization that provided or promoted abortion. The action reinstated a policy enacted during the administration of Republican Ronald Reagan but reversed by Bill Clinton in one of his first acts as president. In a slap at his Democratic presidential opponent, Al Gore, Bush also pulled the United States out of international negotiations to implement the Kyoto Protocol, a treaty mandating steps to reduce the causes of global warming. Gore had been active in promoting the treaty, which was opposed by most major U.S. industries. The administration also appeared to be poised to seriously weaken, if not overturn outright, many of Clinton's environmental protection measures and federal gun control laws. On several other issues, however, Bush disappointed his supporters and carried forward with Clinton administration policies that he had been urged to abandon. Among these were retaining tough new standards for arsenic levels in drinking water and a decision to allow federal funding of embryonic stem cell research.

Both federal and international health organizations continued to issue warnings about the dangers of smoking. In the United States the surgeon general issued the first-ever federal call to action to reduce obesity, which was the second leading cause, next to smoking, of preventable death and disease in the United States. Meanwhile, the AIDS pandemic continued to expand into new corners of the world even as world leaders began to show a new commitment to trying to stop its spread. Already these three conditions had killed millions more people both in the United States and elsewhere than armed terrorists anywhere in the world.

These are only some of the topics of national and international interest chosen by the editors for *Historic Documents of 2001*. This edition marks the thirtieth volume of a Congressional Quarterly project that began with *Historic Documents of 1972*. The purpose of the series is to give students, librarians, journalists, scholars, and others convenient access to documents on a wide range of topics that set forth some of the most important issues of the year. In our judgment, the official statements, news conferences, speeches, special studies, and court decisions presented here will be of lasting interest.

Each document is preceded by an introduction that provides context and background material and, when relevant, an account of continuing developments during the year. We believe these introductions will become increasingly useful as memories of current events fade.

John Felton and Martha Gottron

CONTENTS

January

Richard Gephardt, the minority leader of the House of Representatives, and Tom Daschle, the minority leader of the Senate.

March

April

May

(GOI), the Palestine Liberation Organization (PLO), and the Palestinian Authority (PA) refer to written submissions that those agencies gave the committee.

July

August

September

Amendment guarantees the right of an individual to own a gun subject to limited, narrowly tailored exceptions.

November

CONTENTS

December

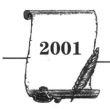

January

DEFENSE DEPARTMENT ON USS *COLE* ATTACK
January 9, 2001

The Pentagon determined in January that the entire military chain of command—and not any individual—should be held responsible for security lapses that may have contributed to the vulnerability of a U.S. warship bombed three months earlier in Yemen. The USS Cole, *a navy destroyer refueling at the port of Aden, Yemen, was attacked October 12, 2000, by two men who piloted a small boat next to the ship and then ignited a large quantity of explosives. Seventeen sailors were killed in the explosion (as were the two terrorists), and forty-two sailors were wounded. (*Cole *bombing, Historic Documents of 2000, p. 861)*

U.S. officials attributed the attack on the Cole *to the al Qaeda terrorist network headed by wealthy Saudi Arabian exile Osama bin Laden. Almost exactly eleven months after the* Cole *bombing, terrorists allegedly associated with bin Laden's network hijacked four commercial jets on the east coast of the United States and flew two of them into the World Trade Center towers in New York City and a third plane into the Pentagon near Washington; the fourth plane crashed near Pittsburgh. An estimated 3,000 people died in the September 11 attacks—the worst terrorist incident in U.S. history—and the World Trade Center towers were destroyed, along with several neighboring buildings.* (Terrorist attacks, p. 614)

Attack on the Cole

The bombing of the Cole *was the latest of a series of terrorist attacks against U.S. government targets in the Middle East. Terrorists had bombed U.S. diplomatic and military compounds in Lebanon in 1983, killing hundreds of people, and an apartment complex in Saudi Arabia in 1996, killing nineteen. Bombers also struck the U.S. embassies in Kenya and Tanzania in 1998, killing twelve Americans and more than two hundred Africans.* (Lebanon bombings, Historic Documents of 1983, p. 993; Saudi Arabia bombing, Historic Documents of 1996, p. 672; Embassy bombings, Historic Documents of 1998, p. 555)

The Cole, *which was heavily damaged by the bombing, was carried back to the United States on a large transport ship to a repair facility in Mississippi. The ship was put afloat at a repair dock on September 14, 2001, but was not expected to return to its home port of Norfolk, Virginia, until the spring of 2002.*

After the bombing, the Pentagon launched two separate inquiries to determine whether any action or inaction by U.S. officials could have contributed to the Cole's *vulnerability. One inquiry, by the navy, was focused solely on whether the ship's captain and/or crew should be held responsible. The other inquiry had a broader goal of determining whether failures elsewhere in the U.S. military and intelligence services might have exposed the* Cole *to heightened risks of a terrorist attacks.*

Navy Inquiry

The navy's inquiry into the Cole *bombing involved a series of reviews at progressively higher levels of the service. The first review was conducted in October and November 2000 by an unidentified captain of the Fifth Fleet, based in Bahrain. His findings, dated November 27, 2000 (but not released until the following January), were then reviewed by Admiral Charles W. Moore Jr., commander of the navy forces in the central command; then by Admiral Robert J. Natter, commander of the navy's Atlantic fleet; and then by Admiral Vernon Clark, the chief of naval operations, who had the final say in the matter.*

The original investigating officer argued that the Cole's *commanding officer, Commander Kirk S. Lippold, should be held responsible for failing to implement fully a required security plan that he had filed before the* Cole *entered the port of Aden. The captain said Lippold had carried out only half of the sixty-two steps (known as "force protection measures") required for ships entering an area, such as Yemen, where the terrorism threat was considered moderate to high.*

Most of the steps that Lippold did not take were irrelevant to the security situation the Cole *faced as it docked in Yemen, the investigating captain said. But, he added, twelve of those steps were critical actions that—if they had been taken—"might have prevented the suicide boat attack or mitigated its effects." Among the most important steps: the crew should have been given more information about the potential for terrorist action in Yemen; duty officers should have been stationed on the bridge, where they might have been able to observe activity in the port area near the* Cole, *rather than on the quarter-deck; all unauthorized boats should have been kept away from the* Cole; *and all boats approaching the* Cole *should have been identified and inspected.*

As the investigating officer's report headed up the chain of command, aspects of it repeatedly were overturned, first by Moore, then by Natter, and finally by Clark. All three admirals rejected the investigating captain's key assessment that the Cole *bombing might have been averted if Commander Lippold had carried out all security measures. All three senior admirals also concluded that Lippold had taken appropriate precautions given the in-*

telligence information available to him—information that in retrospect clearly was inadequate. "We cannot use 20–20 hindsight to penalize a commanding officer for not knowing in advance what has [since] become common knowledge, that a determined, well-armed and well-financed terrorist cell was operating in the port of Aden," Moore said in his report. Clark added that Lippold had received information that discussed the possible threat of terrorism on land in Yemen but did not mention a possible threat at sea or even in the Aden harbor.

Although he declined to take punitive action against Lippold, Clark said he was "not completely satisfied" with the commander's performance prior to the attack. Clark said Lippold entered Aden harbor not knowing several important facts about the situation his ship would encounter, such as how the refueling was to be accomplished and whether the Yemeni authorities were to provide any security assistance. "I am troubled that he took no steps to resolve these uncertainties prior to pulling into port," Clark said.

On a broader level, Clark said the Cole incident "revealed weaknesses in our force projection plan." In particular, he said it had become clear that the navy gave ship commanders "inadequate guidance" on understanding and carrying out the plans for protecting their ships. Clark solicited suggestions from all senior navy commanders for steps to improve that guidance.

Defense Department Inquiry

The broader Pentagon inquiry into the Cole bombing was headed by retired admiral Harold W. Gehman and retired army general William W. Crouch. The Pentagon on January 9 released a five-page executive summary of their report; the much-longer full report was classified and not released to the public.

Gehman and Crouch noted that the Pentagon had made "significant improvements" in efforts to protect U.S. military installations since the 1996 bombing in Saudi Arabia. But, they said, the Cole bombing had demonstrated "a seam in the fabric" of Pentagon programs to protect its forces. That seam, or weakness, showed up when ships, aircraft, and land vehicles were in transit from one point to another.

The general thrust of the report was that the U.S. military and related agencies needed to become more "proactive" in detecting terrorist threats and then stopping them from being carried out. In the past, the military had been in a "purely defensive mode" in reacting to terrorism, the report said.

Many of the report's recommendations involved operational matters, such as improved procedures for alerting unit commanders to possible threats in a given region. More generally, the report argued that the government needed to "reprioritize" its intelligence-gathering operations to focus more attention on terrorism, which had emerged as a persistent threat to the United States only after the end of the cold war a decade earlier. In addition, the report made a strong pitch for the military services to devote more resources to training their forces to combat terrorism.

Although Gehman and Crouch did not focus their report on assessing individual responsibility for any failures in the Cole *case, they did appear to argue that officials much senior to Lippold should have been the ones to determine what threats existed in the Aden port. Commanders of individual units "do not have time or resources to focus on a series of locations while in transit," Gehman and Crouch said. Rather, they argued, the commander of each armed service (known as the "component commander") in each regional theater of operations should have the "mindset" and the "resources" to ensure that U.S. forces in that region have adequate protection. In the case of the* Cole, *the component commander was Admiral Moore, the naval commander in the Persian Gulf. Gehman and Crouch recommended that component commanders have full-time staff officers dedicated to protecting U.S. forces while in transit.*

The navy and Pentagon inquiries were concluded early in January, and Defense Secretary William S. Cohen announced a final disposition of them on January 19, the last full day in office for him and the rest of the administration of President Bill Clinton. Cohen said he concluded that the entire military leadership should be held responsible for any failures in the Cole *case. Cohen said that conclusion had been endorsed by General Henry H. Shelton, the chairman of the Joint Chiefs of Staff.*

"We have, in fact, identified accountability through the chain of command, all the way from the central commander [the head of the U.S. Central Command, which supervises U.S. forces in the Middle East], right up through the secretary of the navy, the chairman of the Joint Chiefs, and myself," Cohen said. Referring to the navy and Pentagon reports on the Cole *bombing, he added: "I think that we have pointed out that we didn't do all that needed to be done."*

The Pentagon's decision not to punish Lippold, or any other officers, for failures to prevent the Cole *attack was criticized by some on Capitol Hill. John W. Warner, R-Va., chairman of the Senate Armed Services Committee and a former secretary of the navy, was perhaps the most critical. At a committee hearing May 3, Warner suggested that the navy had abandoned its standard policy of holding commanding officers accountable for mistakes. "Military personnel in positions of responsibility must be accountable for their actions or failure to act, if we are to maintain the order and discipline essential to successful military operations," Warner told Shelton and Clark. In response, Shelton said that "everybody in the chain of command could have done better." But, he added, "there was no dereliction [of duty] and there was certainly no criminal intent or any criminal actions or anything else that warranted punishment."*

Investigating the Terrorists

Yemeni authorities in late 2000 and early 2001 detained eight suspects in connection with the bombing and were searching for another man, Mohammed Omar al-Harazi, who was suspected of supervising the operation on behalf of bin Laden. The government had hoped to begin trying the suspects in 2001 but delayed a trial at the request of the United States, which wanted more time to pursue the investigation in hopes of establishing bin Laden's responsibility.

For nearly a year, U.S. and Yemeni officials clashed over several important aspects of the investigation, most of which were related to Washington's desire for a broad examination of anti-U.S. groups in Yemen and throughout the Middle East that might have contributed to the Cole *bombing. The United States requested, and the Yemeni government rejected, permission for FBI agents to interview the arrested suspects, as well as local government and military officials. FBI agents investigating the case left Yemen in mid-June 2001, after the Yemeni government arrested nine men said to have been plotting an attack against the Americans. A U.S. official said the arrested men had possessed small weapons, grenades, and documents indicating they were planning such an attack. The FBI agents returned to work in late August.*

Relations between the United States and Yemen suddenly improved after the September 11 terrorist attacks in New York and Washington. Seeking support from Arab countries for its war in Afghanistan against bin Laden and his associates, the George W. Bush administration in October and November offered the Yemeni government U.S. aid and military training. Yemeni president Ali Abdullah Saleh, in turn, allowed FBI agents to interview the Cole *suspects and several witnesses.*

U.S. investigators worked during 2001 to establish a definite link between bin Laden's organization and the Cole *bombing. The best evidence may have come from bin Laden himself. A videotape circulated in the Middle East during the late summer showed bin Laden reciting a poem praising the bombing of the* Cole. *News reports late in the year also indicated that Yemeni authorities had uncovered a letter written by bin Laden in 1997 describing plans for an attack against a U.S. warship in Yemen. U.S. officials said that letter might have been referring to a failed attack in January 2000 against another destroyer,* The Sullivans.

Following is the text of the unclassified executive summary of a classified report prepared by a Department of Defense commission that examined the circumstances surrounding the October 12, 2000, bombing of the USS Cole *in the port of Aden, Yemen. The Pentagon released the executive summary January 9, 2001.*

The document was obtained from the Internet at http:// www.defenselink.mil/pubs/cole20010109.html.

Executive Summary

Since the attack on Khobar Towers in June 1996, the Department of Defense (DoD) has made significant improvements in protecting its service members, mainly in deterring, disrupting and mitigating terrorist attacks on installations. The attack on USS COLE (DDG 67), in the port of Aden, Yemen, on 12 October 2000, demonstrated a seam in the fabric of efforts to protect our forces, namely in-transit forces. Our review was focused on finding ways to improve the US policies and practices for deterring, disrupting and mitigating terrorist attack on US forces in transit.

1. Overseas Presence since the End of the Cold War

Our review was based on the premise that worldwide presence and continuous transit of ships, aircraft and units of the United States military support the engagement elements of both the National Security Strategy and the National Military Strategy and are in the nation's best interest. The US military is conducting overseas operations in a new post-Cold War world environment characterized by unconventional and transnational threats. Operating in this new world exposes US forces to terrorist attacks and requires a major effort in force protection. This major effort will require more resources and, in some cases, a better use of existing resources for protecting transiting units. The net result of our recommendations is a form of operational risk management applied at both the national and operational levels to balance the benefits with the risks of overseas operations. We determined that the "fulcrum" of this balance is usually the Unified Commander-in-Chief's (CINC) Service Component Commander; therefore, a significant number of our recommendations are designed to improve that commander's AT/FP antiterrorism/force protection (AT/FP) capabilities.

We organized our findings at both the national and operational levels into the five functional areas of organization, antiterrorism/force protection, intelligence, logistics and training.

2. National Level Policies and Practices

Conducting engagement activities (including those by transiting forces) in higher threat areas in support of the National Security Strategy and National Military Strategy requires completely coordinated priorities, policies and oversight at all levels. The pervasive and enduring threat calls for some adjustments to national level policies and procedures.

2.a. Organization

Unity of effort among the offices and agencies in the DoD providing resources, policy, oversight and direction is critical to truly gain the initiative over a very adaptive, persistent, patient and tenacious terrorist. This unity of effort extends also to the coordination of engagement activities across US Government agencies, including developing the security capabilities of host nations to help protect US forces and balancing the range and frequency of activities among all agencies.

2.b. Antiterrorism/Force Protection

In force protection, we identified seven national level policy and procedural improvements to better support AT/FP for transiting units. We have five of the seven that address additional resources and two that address procedural changes. They are covered in the findings.

2.c. Intelligence

Intelligence priorities and resources have shifted from Cold War focus to new and emerging threats only at the margins. We, like other commissions before us, recommend the reprioritization of resources for collection and analysis, including human intelligence and signal intelligence, against the terrorist. Intelligence production must be refocused and tailored to overwatch transiting units to mitigate the terrorist threat. Furthermore, an increase in counterintelligence (CI) resources dedicated to combating terrorism and development of clearer CI assessment standards is required.

2.d. Logistics

Logistics practices and policies can impact force protection if imaginatively applied. We believe the current level of Combat Logistics Force oilers is sufficient to support the refueling and logistics requirements of the national strategy. The regional logistics support structure must provide the Component Commander the opportunity and flexibility to adapt operational patterns to minimize exposure to threats.

2.e. Training

We believe most firmly that the US military must create an integrated system of training that produces a unit that is clearly and visibly ready, alert and capable. To achieve this level of AT/FP proficiency, AT/FP training must be elevated to the same priority as primary mission training. The level of competence with which units execute force protection must be the same level for which primary combat skills are executed; and we must develop and resource credible deterrence standards; deterrence specific tactics, techniques and procedures; and defensive equipment packages.

3. Operational Level Lessons Learned

The links between national policies/resources and individual transiting units are the geographic Unified CINCs and their Component Commanders. Transiting units do not have time or resources to focus on a series of locations while in transit, requiring these units to rely on others to support their efforts to deter, disrupt and mitigate terrorist attacks. We think it is the Component Commander who has the operational war-fighting mindset for the region and is capable of controlling the resources to fight the fight and tailor specific AT/FP measures to protect transiting units. Below we identify operational level recommendations in the areas of antiterrorism/force protection, intelligence, logistics, and training for improving AT/FP support to transiting units.

3.a. Antiterrorism/Force Protection

First, we must get out of the purely defensive mode by proactively applying AT/FP techniques and assets to detect and deter terrorists. Second, transfer of transiting units between and within theaters must be better coordinated.

Third, a discrete operation risk management model should be adopted and utilized in AT/FP planning and execution.

3.b. Intelligence

Independent transiting units must be better trained and resourced to provide appropriate requests for information to force intelligence organizations to be responsive to the transiter's AT/FP requirements.

3.c. Logistics

While classifying the logistics request and diplomatic clearance request processes is not practical, implementation of the recommendations in this Report is required to mitigate the AT/FP effects of public knowledge of movements.

3.d. Training

Predeployment training regimes must include deterrence tactics, techniques and procedures; deterrence AT/FP measures specific to the area of operation; and equipment rehearsals.

The AT/FP training provided to unit commanding officers and force protection officers and the tools necessary to sustain an AT/FP training program needs increased attention.

In summary, we found Component Commanders are the fulcrum of a balance with the benefits of engagement on one side and the associated risks/costs on the other side. Our review suggests there is much we can do to help the field commander reach the proper balance. Taken as a whole, the Commission's recommendations are intended to enhance the tools available to commanders in making this balance.

Unclassified Findings and Recommendations Summary

Organizational

Finding: Combating terrorism is so important that it demands complete unity of effort at the level of the Office of the Secretary of Defense.

- *Recommendation:* Secretary of Defense develop an organization that more cohesively aligns policy and resources within DoD to combat terrorism and designate an Assistant Secretary of Defense (ASD) to oversee these functions.

Finding: The execution of the engagement element of the National Security Strategy lacks an effective, coordinated interagency process, which results in a fragmented engagement program that may not provide optimal support to in-transit units.

- *Recommendation:* Secretary of Defense support an interagency process to provide overall coordination of US engagement.

Finding: DoD needs to spearhead an interagency, coordinated approach to developing non-military host nation security efforts in order to enhance force protection for transiting US forces.

- *Recommendation:* Secretary of Defense coordinate with Secretary of State to develop an approach with shared responsibility to enhance host nation security capabilities that result in increased security for transiting US forces.

Antiterrorism/Force Protection (AT/FP)

Finding: Service manning policies and procedures that establish requirements for full-time Force Protection Officers and staff billets at the Service Component level and above will reduce the vulnerability of in-transit forces to terrorist attacks.

- *Recommendation:* Secretary of Defense direct the Services to provide Component Commanders with full-time force protection officers and staffs that are capable of supporting the force protection requirements of transiting units.

Finding: Component Commanders need the resources to provide in-transit units with temporary security augmentation of various kinds.

- *Recommendation:* Secretary of Defense direct the Services to resource Component Commanders to adequately augment units transiting through higher-threat areas.

Finding: Service AT/FP programs must be adequately manned and funded to support threat and physical vulnerability assessments of ports, airfields and inland movement routes that may be used by transiting forces.

- *Recommendation:* Secretary of Defense direct the Chairman of the Joint Chiefs of Staff, the CINCs and the Services to identify and resource manning and funding requirements to perform quality assessments of routes and sites used by transiting forces in support of Component Commanders.

Finding: The Chairman of the Joint Chiefs of Staff Combating Terrorism Readiness Initiative Fund is a responsive and relevant program designed to fund execution-year emergent and emergency antiterrorism/force protection physical security requirements. To optimize the program, Combating Terrorism Readiness Initiative Fund initiatives must be coordinated with Service programming for a commitment of life-cycle costs, and the Combating Terrorism Readiness Initiative Fund must fund the transition period.

Recommendations:

- The Chairman of the Joint Chiefs of Staff Combating Terrorism Readiness Initiative Fund should be increased to cover the period prior to which a Service program can fund the remaining life-cycle costs.
- Secretary of Defense direct the Services to establish a formal link to the Chairman of the Joint Chiefs of Staff Combating Terrorism Readiness

Initiative Fund to ensure that initiatives receive a commitment for fol-
low-on programming.

Finding: More responsive application of currently available military equipment, commercial technologies, and aggressive research and development
can enhance the AT/FP and deterrence posture of transiting forces.

- *Recommendation:* Secretary of Defense direct the Services to initiate
  a major unified effort to identify near-term AT/FP equipment and
  technology requirements, field existing solutions from either military
  or commercial sources, and develop new technologies for remaining
  requirements.

Finding: The Geographic Commander in Chief [CINC] should have the sole
authority for assigning the threat level for a country within his area of
responsibility.

Recommendations:

- Secretary of Defense direct that the Geographic CINCs be solely responsible for establishing the threat level within the appropriate area of responsibility with input from DIA [Defense Intelligence Agency].
- Secretary of Defense coordinate with Secretary of State, where possible,
  to minimize conflicting threat levels between the Department of Defense
  and the Department of State.
- Secretary of Defense designate an office or agency responsible for setting
  the threat level for Canada, Mexico, Russia, and the United States.

Finding: AT/FP will be enhanced by improvements to the THREATCON
[Threat Conditions] system.

Recommendations:

- Secretary of Defense change the term "THREATCONs" to "Alert States,"
  "FP Conditions," or some other term.
- Secretary of Defense direct the CINCs and Services to give Component
  Commanders the responsibility and resources to direct tailored force
  protection measures to be implemented at specific sites for in-transit
  units.
- Secretary of Defense direct that the AT/FP plan and the particular mea-
  sures that are triggered by a specific THREATCON be classified.

Finding: The CJCS Standing Rules of Engagement for US forces are adequate
against the terrorist threat.

- *Recommendation:* Make no changes to the SROE.

Finding: We need to shift transiting units from an entirely reactive posture to
a posture that more effectively deters terrorist attacks.

- *Recommendation:* Secretary of Defense direct the CINCs and Services to
  have Component Commanders identify proactive techniques and assets
  to deter terrorists.

Finding: The amount of AT/FP emphasis that units in-transit receive prior to or during transfer between CINCs can be improved.

- *Recommendation:* Secretary of Defense direct the CINCs and Services to have Component Commanders ensure unit situational awareness by providing AT/FP briefings to transiting units prior to entry into higher threat level areas in the gaining Geographic CINC's AOR.

Finding: Intra-theater transiting units require the same degree of attention as other transiting units to deter, disrupt and mitigate acts of terrorism.

- *Recommendation:* Secretary of Defense direct Geographic CINCs and Component Commanders to reassess current procedures to ensure that AT/FP principles enumerated in this Report are applied to intra-theater transiting units.

Finding: Using operational risk management standards as a tool to measure engagement activities against risk to in-transit forces will enable commanders to determine whether to suspend or continue engagement activities.

- *Recommendation:* Secretary of Defense direct the CINCs to adopt and institutionalize a discrete operational risk management model to be used in AT/FP planning and execution.

Finding: Incident response must be an integral element of AT/FP planning.

- *Recommendation:* Secretary of Defense direct the Geographic CINCs to identify theater rapid incident response team requirements and integrate their utilization in contingency planning for in-transit units, and the Services to organize, train, and equip such forces.

Intelligence

Finding: In-transit units require intelligence support tailored to the terrorist threat in their immediate area of operations. This support must be dedicated from a higher echelon (tailored production and analysis).

- *Recommendation:* Secretary of Defense reprioritize intelligence production to ensure that in-transit units are given tailored, focused intelligence support for independent missions.

Finding: If the Department of Defense is to execute engagement activities related to the National Security Strategy with the least possible level of risk, then Services must reprioritize time, emphasis, and resources to prepare the transiting units to perform intelligence preparation of the battlespace–like processes and formulate intelligence requests for information to support operational decision points.

- *Recommendation:* Secretary of Defense direct the Services to ensure forces are adequately resourced and trained to make maximum use of intelligence processes and procedures, including priority information requests and requests for information to support intelligence preparation of the battlespace for in-transit unit antiterrorism/force protection.

Finding: DoD does not allocate sufficient resources or all-source intelligence analysis and collection in support of combating terrorism.

Recommendations:

- Secretary of Defense reprioritize all-source intelligence collection and analysis personnel and resources so that sufficient emphasis is applied to combating terrorism. Analytical expertise must be imbedded, from the national, CINC, and Component Command levels, to the joint task force level.
- Secretary of Defense reprioritize terrorism-related human intelligence and signals intelligence resources.
- Secretary of Defense reprioritize resources for the development of language skills that support combating terrorism analysis and collection.

Finding: Service counterintelligence programs are integral to force protection and must be adequately manned and funded to meet the dynamic demands of supporting in-transit forces.

- *Recommendation:* Secretary of Defense ensure DoD counterintelligence organizations are adequately staffed and funded to meet counterintelligence force protection requirements.

Finding: Clearer DoD standards for threat and vulnerability assessments, must be developed at the joint level and be common across Services and commands.

Recommendations:

- Secretary of Defense standardize counterintelligence assessments and increase counterintelligence resources.
- Secretary of Defense direct DoD-standard requirements for the conduct of threat and vulnerability assessments for combating terrorism.
- Secretary of Defense direct the production of a DoD-standard Counterintelligence Collection Manual for combating terrorism.

Logistics

Finding: While classifying the diplomatic clearance and logistics requirement process may improve the operational security of transiting units, it is not practical due to the commercial nature of the process.

- *Recommendation:* None. Implementing proactive AT/FP measures identified in this report mitigate the effect of public knowledge of US military ship and aircraft visits.

Finding: The combination of the Combat Logistics Force and the Department of Defense worldwide logistics network is sufficient to meet current operations and has the collateral benefit of supporting the engagement component of the National Security Strategy and National Military Strategy.

- *Recommendation:* None. The current level of Combat Logistics Force oilers is sufficient to support the refueling and logistics requirements of the national strategy.

Finding: CINCs/Component Commanders can enhance force protection for transiting forces when the Component Commanders are included in the logistics planning and contract award process.

- *Recommendation:* Secretary of Defense direct the Chairman of the Joint Chiefs of Staff and the Services to update respective logistics doctrine to incorporate AT/FP considerations for transiting units.

Finding: Local providers of goods, services, and transportation must be employed and evaluated in ways that enhance the AT/FP posture of the in-transit unit.

- *Recommendation:* Secretary of Defense direct the Defense Logistics Agency and the Services to incorporate AT/FP concerns into the entire fabric of logistics support.

Training

Finding: Military Services must accomplish AT/FP training with a degree of rigor that equates to the unit's primary mission areas.

Recommendations:

- Secretary of Defense direct the Services to develop rigorous tactics, techniques, and procedures with measurable standards for AT/FP training and develop training regimens that will integrate AT/FP into unit-level training plans and pre-deployment exercises.
- Secretary of Defense direct the Services to elevate AT/FP training to the equivalent of a primary mission area and provide the same emphasis afforded combat tasks in order to instill a force protection mindset into each Service.

Finding: Better force protection is achieved if forces in transit are trained to demonstrate preparedness to deter acts of terrorism.

Recommendations:

- Secretary of Defense direct the Services to develop and resource credible deterrence standards, deterrence-specific tactics, techniques, and procedures and defensive equipment packages for all forms of transiting forces.
- Secretary of Defense direct the Services to ensure that pre-deployment training regimes include deterrence tactics, techniques, and procedures and AT/FP measures specific to the area of operation and equipment rehearsals.

Finding: DoD must better support commanders' ability to sustain their anti-terrorism/force protection program and training regimens.

Recommendations:

- Secretary of Defense direct the Chairman of the Joint Chiefs of Staff to publish a single source document that categorizes all of the existing

AT/FP training literature, plans and tactics, techniques, and procedures for use by the Services (on both classified and unclassified versions) (short term).

- Secretary of Defense direct the Chairman of the Joint Chiefs of Staff to consolidate and develop a single repository for all AT/FP lessons learned. This database should be accessible to unit commanders in the classified and unclassified mode (long term).
- Secretary of Defense direct the Chairman of the Joint Chiefs of Staff to continually update training tools, capture lessons and trends and aid Commanders in sustaining meaningful AT/FP training programs.

Finding: DoD and Service guidance on the content of AT/FP Level III training must be more definitive if commanders at the O-5 and O-6 levels are to execute their AT/FP responsibilities.

- *Recommendation:* Secretary of Defense direct more rigorous Level III AT/FP training requirements for each Service.

Finding: Service Level II AT/FP Training must produce a force protection officer capable of supervising unit training and acting as the subject matter expert for the commander in transit.

Recommendations:

- Secretary of Defense direct the Services to establish more rigorous training standards for unit-level Force Protection Officers.
- Secretary of Defense direct the Services to increase the emphasis and resources devoted to producing qualified Force Protection Officers through Level II training.

ENERGY COMMISSION REPORT ON RUSSIAN NUCLEAR WEAPONS
January 10, 2001

A task force of prominent political leaders and national security experts concluded early in 2001 that urgent new steps were needed to prevent terrorists and other opponents of the United States from acquiring nuclear weapons and materials that were poorly protected in Russia. Insecure Russian nuclear weapons posed "the most urgent unmet national security threat to the United States," the task force said in a report made public January 10, 2001. The panel was headed by former Senate Majority Leader Howard Baker, a Tennessee Republican, and Lloyd Cutler, a Democrat who was one of Washington's most prominent attorneys.

Despite that warning, the new administration of President George W. Bush initially proposed budget cutbacks for some of the more than thirty U.S. programs that were intended to safeguard nuclear facilities in Russia. The administration then conducted a lengthy policy review that ultimately endorsed most of the programs but did not support major spending increases that the Baker-Cutler panel had proposed. By year's end Congress had approved a limited expansion of funding for the Russia nuclear programs, which generally had broad bipartisan support.

The issue took on a new urgency following the September 11, 2001, terrorist attacks against the World Trade Center towers in New York City and the Pentagon. Politicians from across the political spectrum—along with experts on foreign affairs and national security—expressed heightened concerns that well-organized terrorist groups might be able to buy or steal nuclear weapons from Russia and use them against the United States or its allies. Several reports late in the year indicated that Osama bin Laden, the accused mastermind behind the September 11 attacks, had tried to acquire nuclear weapons for his al Qaeda terrorist network. (September 11 attacks and aftermath, pp. 614, 624, 663)

U.S.-Russia Nuclear Programs

After the collapse of the Soviet Union in late 1991, worldwide concerns arose about the security of the nearly 30,000 nuclear bombs and warheads that Moscow had built during the cold war. The new Russian government (which succeeded the Soviet state) took control of most of the weapons, but an estimated 5,000 weapons were in the hands of new governments in Belarus, Kazakhstan, and Ukraine. In addition to these weapons, the Soviet Union had developed more than 600 tons of weapons-grade fissile material—plutonium and highly enriched uranium; that amount was enough to produce another 40,000-some nuclear weapons. The Soviet Union also left behind an estimated 32,000 tons of chemical weapons (mostly nerve gases) and a large quantity of highly potent biological weapons, such as anthrax.

During the Soviet era, most of these weapons and materials were tightly controlled and guarded by the military. But with the collapse of rigid Soviet authority, Russia and other former Soviet republics lacked the manpower and money to guarantee the security of these dangerous items. Large quantities of weapons-grade materials were stored in flimsy, unlocked, and unguarded warehouses. Moreover, tens of thousands of nuclear engineers and scientists were left unemployed or were forced to go months without being paid.

Under the leadership of Senators Sam Nunn, D-Ga., and Richard G. Lugar, R-Ind., Congress in November 1991 gave the U.S. Defense Department $400 million to help Russia and the three other former Soviet republics dismantle unneeded nuclear weapons and protect those that were to remain in the Russian arsenal. This Nunn-Lugar initiative, formally known as the Cooperative Threat Reduction Program, ultimately helped pay for the destruction or removal to Russia of all nuclear weapons held by Belarus, Kazakhstan, and Ukraine. The program was made possible by a remarkable degree of cooperation between Washington and Moscow, which for nearly five decades had pointed thousands of nuclear weapons at one another. Russian officials— sometimes grudgingly, other times eagerly—allowed U.S. weapons experts into many of the former Soviet Union's most secret defense facilities.

With Russian cooperation, Congress gradually expanded the Nunn-Lugar program during the 1990s, adding components run by the U.S. energy and state departments to improve the physical security at Russian nuclear facilities and to provide useful employment for thousands of Russian scientists and engineers. By the end of 2000 the three U.S. agencies had spent a combined total of more than $4 billion on some thirty programs involving Russian nuclear security. Specific achievements of the Nunn-Lugar programs included: a program to purchase from Russia and convert to civilian use 500 tons of highly enriched uranium, enough to produce about 20,000 nuclear weapons; the dismantling of more than 6,000 strategic (long-range) nuclear bombs and missile warheads, along with hundreds of bombers and missiles that carried these weapons; the 1997 purchase from Moldova of twenty-one MIG-29C warplanes capable of carrying nuclear weapons; and the installation of improved security measures at more than 100 Russian facilities where nuclear weapons and supplies were stored or manufactured. The United States also helped Russia begin dismantling its arsenal of chemical weapons.

In at least two cases, the United States made emergency purchases of nuclear materials that were considered in imminent danger of theft or diversion. In 1994 U.S. agents removed 1,300 pounds of highly enriched uranium (enough to make at least twenty nuclear weapons) from Kazakhstan. Representatives of the Iranian government reportedly had tried to buy the material for that country's nuclear weapons program. In 1998 the United States removed about twenty pounds of highly enriched uranium from the nation of Georgia, where it reportedly had been the target of terrorist groups.

Despite these successes, some officials and experts in both Washington and Moscow criticized the Nunn-Lugar programs. U.S. critics complained that Russia hampered the programs by imposing bureaucratic delays and denying U.S. officials needed access to key nuclear facilities. A handful of conservatives also charged that the programs wasted money that should have been spent upgrading the U.S. military and that Russia should have carried more of the financial burden. Nationalist politicians in Russia objected to what they called U.S. "interference" with that nation's military.

In a series of reports from the mid-1990s through 2001, the General Accounting Office (GAO) said the Nunn-Lugar programs were succeeding in reducing the threat of Russian nuclear weapons or supplies falling into the hands of terrorists. But the GAO found numerous management problems—both in Washington and in Russia—that had delayed and undermined the effectiveness of the programs. Among other things, the GAO argued that the Department of Energy (DoE) was spending too much money in the United States on designs and plans for projects that were to be carried out in Russia. The GAO and other critics also argued that U.S. agencies and Congress had created too many programs with similar purposes, each program needing its own staff and budget.

Baker-Cutler Report

Partly in response to criticisms of Nunn-Lugar programs, Secretary of Energy Bill Richardson in February 2000 appointed a bipartisan task force to examine seven of the DoE's major programs in the former Soviet Union. Chaired by Baker and Cutler, the panel included Nunn and fifteen other prominent politicians and experts on national security issues. The other members were Graham T. Alison, director of the Belfer Center at Harvard University's Kennedy School of Government; Andrew Athy, an attorney; J. Brian Atwood, president of Citizens International; David Boren, president of the University of Oklahoma and a former senator; Lynn Davis, senior fellow at the RAND Corporation; Butler Derrick, an attorney and former House member; Susan Eisenhower, president of the Eisenhower Institute; Lee Hamilton, director of the Woodrow Wilson Center and a former House member; Robert I. Hanfling, an advisor to a management consulting firm; Gary Hart, an attorney and former senator; Daniel Mayers, an attorney; Jim McClure, an attorney and former senator; Alan Simpson, a lobbyist and former senator; David Skaggs, an official of the Aspen Institute and a former House member; and John Tuck, an attorney and former undersecretary of the DoE.

The panel members visited Russia in July 2000 and interviewed dozens of Russian and U.S. government officials and nongovernment experts. The panel's report was made public on January 10, 2001, during the closing days of the administration of President Bill Clinton.

In general, the task force commended the Nunn-Lugar programs, saying they had made a significant contribution to reducing the prospect that former Soviet nuclear weapons or materials would fall into the hands of terrorists or "rogue" states, such as Iraq or North Korea, that were opposed to U.S. interests around the world. Bureaucratic and political obstacles still hampered several of the programs but could be reduced or eliminated if U.S. and Russian leaders assigned a high priority to such an effort, the panel said.

However, the task force argued that most of the major U.S. programs suffered from two overall problems that hampered their effectiveness: a severe shortage of funds and a lack of high-level coordination. As an example of inadequate budgets, the task force pointed to the DoE's Material Protection, Control, and Accounting Program. Under way since 1994, this program provided funding, supplies, and technical expertise to help the Russian government improve security at 252 laboratories, storage facilities, and other sites where nuclear weapons and weapons-grade materials were located. By the end of 2000 this program had made partial or complete security upgrades at 115 facilities housing only about one-third of the estimated 603 tons of weapons-grade nuclear material in Russia. The program's budget was $174 million in fiscal year 2001—an amount the Baker-Cutler panel said was substantially less than needed to complete the work in a timely manner.

The task force offered what it called a "strategic plan" for improving and speeding up the Nunn-Lugar programs in Russia. Overall, the panel called for spending about $30 billion on the effort during a period of eight to ten years—an "insignificant" amount when compared with what the United States spent to build its nuclear arsenal during the cold war. As priorities, the panel suggested "drastically" reducing the number of buildings where nuclear materials were stored in Russia, accelerating a program to buy Russia's enormous supply of highly enriched uranium, giving new emphasis to several programs intended to eliminate excess plutonium produced by Russian nuclear reactors, and reducing the overall size of the Russian nuclear complex while continuing to provide useful jobs for the country's nuclear engineers and scientists. The panel also called for improved coordination of U.S. programs in Russia, perhaps through the naming of a senior White House official with the authority over all the agencies operating those programs.

To highlight the importance of its findings, the panel flatly stated: "The most urgent unmet national security threat to the United States today is the danger that weapons of mass destruction or weapons-usable material in

Russia could be stolen or sold to terrorists or hostile nation states and used against American troops abroad or citizens at home."

Baker and Cutler presented their panel's findings to the Senate Foreign Relations Committee during a hearing March 28. Asked to defend the alarming tone of the report, Baker told the committee: "I do not mean to be unduly philosophical or psychological about it, but it really boggles my mind that there could be 40,000 nuclear weapons, or maybe 80,000, in the former Soviet Union, poorly controlled and poorly stored, and that the world is not in a near state of hysteria about the danger. But it is a function of the human mind that after you live with something for a while, you sort of get used to it."

Bush Administration Actions

Despite the bipartisan warnings of the Baker-Cutler panel, officials of the new Bush administration gave mixed reactions to the report. Secretary of State Colin Powell—apparently reflecting the views of diplomats who long had supported the weapons-reduction programs in Russia—said he agreed "entirely" with the report. But Secretary of Defense Donald H. Rumsfeld—apparently reflecting views of some conservatives who had criticized the programs—argued that U.S. subsidies for such efforts freed up money for the Russian government to spend on modernizing aspects of its armed forces, including improved intercontinental ballistic missiles.

At least initially, Rumsfeld's views held sway within the administration, which early in 2001 took two steps that were widely seen in Washington as playing down the importance of the Russian nuclear security programs. First, in late March the White House announced a "review" of all the programs to determine which ones to keep and which to cut. The review was overseen by members of the National Security Council staff, who had been critical of the programs in the past. Then in April President Bush sent an amended budget to Congress that called for spending cuts in several of the Russia programs, including ones—such as the DoE's program to improve security at weapons storage facilities—that had broad support on Capitol Hill. Bush proposed cutting the budget for that program to $139 million in fiscal year 2002; that request was $34 million below the fiscal 2001 level and nearly $80 million less than what Clinton had proposed.

The administration's plans met a mixed reaction on Capitol Hill. Some members who had been angered by Russian sales to Iran of weapons and nuclear power plants supported the cutbacks or even called for an indefinite halt to all U.S. aid to Russia. A group of twenty-nine House members sent Bush a letter in mid-March demanding a suspension of aid until Russia stopped selling military supplies to Iran. But supporters of the aid programs expressed concerns that Bush was reversing the position he took during the 2000 election campaign favoring increased aid for nuclear security programs in Russia. Senator Pete Domenici, R-N.M., chairman of the Budget Committee and a key supporter of the programs, said he feared the administration "intends to take an axe to some of the key programs currently involved in addressing the threat" of insecure Russian nuclear weapons.

White House officials revealed in mid-June that preliminary results of the policy review found most of the Russian programs to be effective and well managed. But, the officials told reporters, the administration would move to reorganize several programs, including a lagging effort to destroy more than thirty tons of weapons-grade plutonium in Russia and a controversial program, the Nuclear Cities Initiative, which was intended to provide jobs for tens of thousands of scientists in several cities where the Soviet government had based much of the country's nuclear research. Critics in Congress said both programs were inordinately expensive and had faltered because of Russia's lack of cooperation.

The September 11 terrorist attacks against the World Trade Center towers and the Pentagon heightened public and political interest in the Russia programs—especially when news reports indicated that suspected terrorist Osama bin Laden had tried to buy or steal fissile materials or nuclear weapons. According to the reports, representatives of bin Laden's al Qaeda organization had worked in Russia, at least since 1998, to obtain materials and technology for nuclear weapons. Some reports also said bin Laden appeared to be trying to build a "dirty bomb"—a device based on conventional explosives (such as dynamite) but laced with radioactive material that would contaminate a large area. A Pakistani newspaper quoted bin Laden in November as saying that his organization had chemical and nuclear weapons and would use them if attacked by the United States. Most Western experts discounted his claim about nuclear weapons but said it was possible that al Qaeda had acquired at least a small quantity of chemical weapons.

With the administration review still under way, Congress attempted to strike a balance between supporters and critics of the Russian program. The fiscal 2002 appropriations bill (PL 107-66) for the DoE essentially kept funding for most programs at the previous year's levels, which represented an increase over the Bush request. Then, in December, Congress added $120 million to those programs as part of a supplemental appropriations measure attached to the fiscal 2002 Department of Defense funding bill (PL 107-177). The net effect was to provide a substantial increase for the Russia programs, though one that was far short of the major new effort called for by the Baker-Cutler panel.

The White House released a summary of the final conclusions of its policy review on December 27. The review found that most of the U.S. programs in Russia "are focused on priority tasks, and are well-managed," a White House statement said. The statement added that Bush intended to expand four of the programs, including the core DoE program on storage of Russian nuclear materials. However, the statement offered no specific figures for future budgets, which were expected to be announced early in 2002.

> *Following are excerpts from the executive summary and the conclusions and recommendations sections of "A Report Card on the Department of Energy's Nonproliferation Programs with Russia," issued January 10, 2001, by the Secretary of Energy Advisory Board.*

The document was obtained from the Internet at http:// www.hr.doe.gov/seab/rusrpt.pdf.

Introduction

Since the breakup of the Soviet Union, we have witnessed the dissolution of an empire having over 40, 000 nuclear weapons, over a thousand metric tons of nuclear materials, vast quantities of chemical and biological weapons materials, and thousands of missiles. This Cold War arsenal is spread across 11 time zones and lacks the Cold War infrastructure that provided the control and financing necessary to assure that chains of command remain intact and nuclear weapons and materials remain securely beyond the reach of terrorists and weapons-proliferating states. This problem is compounded by the existence of thousands of weapons scientists who, not always having the resources necessary to adequately care for their families, may be tempted to sell their expertise to countries of proliferation concern.

In order to assess the Department of Energy's part of current U.S. efforts to deal with this critical situation, in February 2000 Secretary of Energy Bill Richardson asked former Senate Majority Leader Howard Baker and former White House Counsel Lloyd Cutler to co-chair a bipartisan task force to review and assess DOE's nonproliferation programs in Russia and to make recommendations for their improvement. After nine months of careful examination of current DOE programs and consideration of related nonproliferation policies and programs of the U.S. Government, the Task Force reached the following conclusions and recommendations.

1. *The most urgent unmet national security threat to the United States today is the danger that weapons of mass destruction or weapons-usable material in Russia could be stolen and sold to terrorists or hostile nation states and used against American troops abroad or citizens at home.*

   This threat is a clear and present danger to the international community as well as to American lives and liberties.

2. *Current nonproliferation programs in the Department of Energy, the Department of Defense, and related agencies have achieved impressive results thus far, but their limited mandate and funding fall short of what is required to address adequately the threat.*

   The Task Force applauds and commends Secretary Richardson, his predecessors and colleagues for their dedication, commitment and hard work in seeking to address this issue. The cooperation of the Russian Federation has also been a critical and significant factor in the work carried out to date.

   But the Task Force concludes that the current budget levels are inadequate and the current management of the U.S. Government's response is too diffuse. The Task Force believes that the existing scope and management of the U.S. programs addressing this threat leave an unacceptable risk of failure and the potential for catastrophic consequences.

3. *The new President and leaders of the 107th Congress face the urgent national security challenge of devising an enhanced response proportionate to the threat.*

The enhanced response should include: a net assessment of the threat; a clear achievable mission statement; the development of a strategy with specific goals and measurable objectives; a more centralized command of the financial and human resources required to do the job; and an identification of criteria for measuring the benefits for Russia, the United States, and the entire world.

The Task Force offers one major recommendation to the President and the Congress. **The President, in consultation with Congress and in cooperation with the Russian Federation, should quickly formulate a strategic plan to secure and/or neutralize in the next eight to ten years all nuclear weapons-usable material located in Russia and to prevent the outflow from Russia of scientific expertise that could be used for nuclear or other weapons of mass destruction.** Accomplishing this task will be regarded by future generations as one of the greatest contributions the United States and Russia can make to their long-term security and that of the entire world.

While emphasizing that enhanced efforts are needed from the U. S., the Task Force underscores that enhanced efforts are also required from Russia. Ultimately, Russia will be responsible for securing its remaining nuclear arsenal. If this program is conceived in full cooperation with the Russian Federation, is adequately financed, and is implemented as part of a growing, open and transparent partnership, then the Task Force believes that Russia should be positioned to take over any work remaining at the end of the eight to ten year period. If Russia is not prepared for such a partnership, then full success will not be achieved.

Bearing this in mind, the Task Force report outlines an enhanced national Security program as described above. This program could be carried out for less than one percent of the U.S. defense budget, or up to a total of $30 billion over the next eight to ten years. The Russian Government would, of course, be expected to make a significant contribution commensurate with its own financial ability. The national security benefits to U.S. citizens from securing and/or neutralizing the equivalent of more than 80,000 nuclear weapons and potential nuclear weapons would constitute the highest return on investment in any current U.S. national security and defense program. The new President should press other major powers such as the European Union, Japan and Canada to assume a fair share of the costs of these efforts designed also to enhance the security of these countries. Contributions from other countries could significantly reduce U.S. costs.

Background

As two former adversaries adapting to the end of the Cold War, the United States and Russia both have a responsibility to examine and address the dangers posed by the massive nuclear arsenal built up over the past five decades.

In Russia, this review must examine the many dangers and challenges posed by the more than 40,000 nuclear weapons produced by the former Soviet Union and the large quantities of highly enriched uranium (HEU) and plutonium that could be used to make more than 40,000 additional nuclear weapons.

Important steps have already been taken with many ambitious milestones being met over the past decade. Former President Bush negotiated and President Clinton implemented what some have called the "contract of the century" with President Yeltsin. Under this agreement, the U.S. is purchasing 500 metric tons of HEU removed from former Soviet nuclear weapons, and this material is being converted to low enriched uranium fuel that is then used in civilian power reactors. To date, more than 110 metric tons of HEU, enough to build some 5,000 nuclear weapons, have been blended down and rendered impotent for nuclear weapons use. In its blended-down form, this material has been delivered to the international market to fuel civilian power reactors. Through close cooperation among the U. S., Russia, and other countries of the former Soviet Union, we have also succeeded in eliminating strategic nuclear arsenals left in Ukraine, Kazakhstan, and Belarus—preventing the potential emergence of three major new nuclear weapon states. The elimination of these arsenals has greatly increased U.S. and international security, particularly since these nuclear weapons were mounted on strategic intercontinental ballistic missiles aimed at the United States.

Since the Nunn-Lugar legislative initiative of 1991 [PL 102-228, the "Soviet Nuclear Threat Reduction Act of 1991," sponsored by Senators Sam Nunn and Richard Lugar] the U.S. Government has established an array of threat reduction programs in both the Departments of Defense and Energy to assist in dismantling Russian nuclear and other weapons of mass destruction and to improve significantly the security of such weapons and materials. Together, these programs have helped to protect, secure, and begin disposition of strategic weapons delivery systems as well as hundreds of metric tons of nuclear weapons-usable material—preventing the emergence of a virtual "Home Depot" for would-be proliferators. Additional work, under the aegis of the Department of State, has addressed what is known as the 'brain drain problem' both in Russia and other countries of the former Soviet Union through programs such as the International Science and Technology Center (ISTC) Program. This program, together with DOE's Initiatives for Proliferation Prevention and its Nuclear Cities Initiative, has helped to redirect weapons scientists and engineers from defense work to civilian employment.

These U.S. programs have reduced the threat of diversion of nuclear weapons materials. To the best of our knowledge, no nuclear weapons or quantity of nuclear weapons-usable material have been successfully stolen and exported, while many efforts to steal weapons-usable material have been intercepted by Russian and international police operations.

Much more remains to be done, however. The Task Force observes that while we know a good deal about the size and state of the Russian weapons complex, there is still much that we do not know. More than 1,000 metric tons of HEU and at least 150 metric tons of weapons-grade plutonium exist in the

Russian weapons complex. Most of the cases involving the successful seizure and recovery of stolen nuclear weapons-usable material have occurred on the western border of Russia. The southern border is less secure. Materials may be diverted through centuries old trade routes along Russia's mountainous border. In addition, many of the Russian nuclear sites remain vulnerable to insiders determined to steal enough existing material to make several nuclear weapons and to transport these materials to Iran, Iraq, or Afghanistan. At some sites, one well-placed insider would be enough. The Task Force was advised that buyers from Iraq, Iran and other countries have actively sought nuclear weapons-usable material from Russian sites.

In a worst-case scenario, a nuclear engineer graduate with a grapefruit-sized lump of HEU or an orange-sized lump of plutonium, together with material otherwise readily available in commercial markets, could fashion a nuclear device that would fit in a van like the one the terrorist Yosif parked in the World Trade Center in 1993 [Ramzi Ahmad Yosif was convicted in 1997 of master-minding the 1993 bombing, which killed six people]. The explosive effects of such a device would destroy every building in the Wall Street financial area and would level lower Manhattan.

In confronting this danger, the Russian Government has recognized that theft of nuclear weapons or nuclear weapons-usable material threatens Moscow or St. Petersburg as surely as it threatens Washington, DC or New York. Chechen terrorists have already threatened to spread radioactive material around Moscow; if they were armed with a nuclear device, the situation would be much worse. Success in countering this threat to both nations rests on a bedrock of shared vital interests.

The Threat Today

Russia today wrestles with a weakened ability to protect and secure its Cold War legacy. A number of factors have come together to present an immediate risk of theft of potential weapons of mass destruction: delays in payments to guards at nuclear facilities; breakdowns in command structures, including units that control weapons or guard weapons-usable material; and inadequate budgets for protection of stockpiles and laboratories housing thousands of potential nuclear weapons. Such threats are not hypothetical. Consider the following:

- In late 1998, conspirators at a Ministry of Atomic Energy (MinAtom) facility in Chelyabinsk [in west-central Russia] were caught attempting to steal fissile material of a quantity just short of that needed for one nuclear device. The head of MinAtom's nuclear material accounting confirmed the attempted theft and warned that, had the attempt been successful, it would have caused "significant damage to the Russian State."

- Early in 1998, the mayor of Krasnoyarsk-45, a closed Russian "nuclear city" [in south-central Russia] that stores enough HEU for hundreds of nuclear weapons, wrote to Krasnoyarsk Governor Alexander Lebed warning that a social explosion in his city was unavoidable unless urgent action was taken. Nuclear scientists and other workers in the city remained unpaid for several months, and basic medical supplies could not be purchased. General Lebed, a former National Security Advisor to President Yeltsin, had earlier proposed to Moscow that his region take responsibility for the nuclear forces and facilities on its territory, pay salaries for these military officers and atomic workers, and take command of the structures. The Russian Government has never agreed to the proposal.

- In December 1998, an employee at Russia's premier nuclear weapons laboratory in Sarov (formerly Arzamas-16) was arrested for espionage and charged with attempting to sell documents on nuclear weapons designs to agents of Iraq and Afghanistan for $3 million. The regional head of the Federal Security Bureau, when reporting the case, confirmed that this was not the first case of nuclear theft at Sarov [in western Russia] and explained that such thefts were the result of the "very difficult financial position" of workers at such defense enterprises.

- In January 2000, Federal Security Bureau agents arrested four sailors at the nuclear submarine base in Vilyuchinsk-3 on the Kamchatka Peninsula [in far eastern Russia] with a stash of precious metals and radioactive material they had stolen from an armored safe in their nuclear submarine. After the sailors' arrest, investigators discovered at their homes additional stashes of stolen radioactive material and submarine components containing gold, platinum, silver, and palladium.

These are a sample of dozens of actual incidents. Imagine if such material were successfully stolen and sold to a terrorist like Osama bin Laden, who reportedly masterminded the bombings of the U.S. embassies in Kenya and Tanzania [the bombings in August 1998 killed more than 200 people] and is the chief suspect in the recent attack on the U.S. destroyer Cole [terrorists bombed the USS Cole in October 2000 when it was docked at the port of Aden, Yemen; seventeen U.S. sailors were killed in the explosion].

Democracies like ours are inherently messy, frequently distracted, and often bogged down in partisanship. Our government historically finds it difficult to mobilize without the catalyst of an actual incident. The new President and leaders of the 107th Congress face no larger challenge than to mobilize the nation to precautionary action before a major disaster strikes.

Assessing Current DOE
Nonproliferation Programs

The Task Force had the benefit of briefings by both government and non-government experts and reviews of written materials. Members of the Task Force also visited seven sites in Russia in July 2000, reviewing DOE programs and meeting with 13 organizations over the course of a week. The Task Force was able to visit only a few sites of the vast nuclear complex, and it recognizes that those sites were probably in better economic and physical condition than others in the complex. The dire state of those sites gave the Task Force members cause for grave concern about the overall condition of the Russian nuclear complex.

The Task Force applauds the accomplishments of current DOE programs and related programs of other U.S. Government agencies. The Task Force commends in particular the dedication to duty exhibited by the hundreds of DOE and national laboratory employees involved in these programs. The Task Force was also impressed by the high quality of cooperation extended by most of DOE's Russian counterparts during the course of its visit to Russia. Both MinAtom and the Russian Navy provided access to all of the facilities requested, as well as some additional sites that were thought to be inaccessible. Despite difficulties in the overall implementation of the DOE programs, the Task Force found Russia's cooperation to be a significant and positive factor. The United States and the Soviet Union competed in creating nuclear weapons of mass destruction; now the U.S. and Russia are cooperating to dismantle them. The Task Force believes that the record of progress demonstrates it is far better for the United States to be on the inside working with Russia than on the outside with no capability to affect Russia's actions.

However, the Task Force finds very disturbing the ongoing Russian trade with Iran in dual-use nuclear technology and missile technology ["dual use" items can be used for civilian or military purposes] and Russia's apparent intention to supply new conventional weapons systems to Iran. Despite the fact that these issues have been raised with Russia at the highest levels of both governments, the problem has not yet been resolved. The Task Force views the failure to resolve these issues as very serious and believes the lack of satisfactory resolution will increase the difficulties inherent in continued cooperation with Russia and in carrying out the Task Force's recommendations. While the Task Force affirms that the DOE nonproliferation programs are unequivocally in the U.S. national security interest, the Task Force is particularly concerned that if Russian cooperation with Iran continues in a way that compromises nuclear nonproliferation norms, it will inevitably have a major adverse effect on continued cooperation in a wide range of other ongoing nonproliferation programs. Among other consequences, there will be little support in Congress and the Executive Branch for the major new initiatives the Task Force is recommending.

Unquestionably, much has been accomplished by the array of programs now Being operated by DOE and other U.S. Government agencies. Nonetheless, the Task Force believes it is time for the U.S. Government to perform a risk assessment based on input from all relevant agencies to estimate the total magnitude of the threat posed to U.S. national security. The Task Force also believes there is a strong need to create greater synergies among the existing nonproliferation programs, hence its call for government-wide coordination of the current programs and direct White House involvement.

The Task Force Specifically Finds . . .

1. By and large, current DOE programs are having a significant and positive effect. The strategic plan recommended by the Task Force should review the needs of each of these programs and, where appropriate, provide for a substantial increase in funding. Expansions of program

scope and increases in funding, however, must take careful account of the pace at which funds can usefully be expended in each individual program.

2. The strategic plan and the associated budgets should identify specific goals and measurable objectives for each program, as well as provide criteria for success and an exit strategy. These should be factored into the five-year budget plan currently being developed for the National Nuclear Security Administration [an agency of the Energy Department].

3. A major obstacle to further expansion and success of current programs is the continuation of differences between the U.S. and Russia over transparency and access. As a condition for a substantially expanded program, the U.S. and Russia should agree at a high level on the degree of transparency needed to assure that U.S.-funded activity has measurable impacts on program objectives and that U.S. taxpayer dollars are being spent as intended.

4. Given the gravity of the existing situation and the nature of the challenge before us, it is imperative that the President establish a high-level leadership position in the White House with responsibility for policy and budget coordination for threat reduction and nonproliferation programs across the U.S. Government. The President should appoint a person of stature who commands the respect and attention of relevant Cabinet officers and Congressional leaders to lead this program.

5. The U.S. administration of these programs should seek to eliminate any unnecessary and overly restrictive controls that hamper swift and efficient action. To overcome potential impediments that often arise from "business as usual" practices within the Russian and U.S. bureaucracies, DOE and related agencies should take practical steps, including further enlargement of the DOE team working with the U.S. Ambassador in Moscow, to ensure the most efficient on-the-ground implementation of the programs in Russia.

6. It is imperative to mobilize the sustained interest and concern of the Congress. The Task Force urges the Congress to consider the creation of a joint Committee on weapons of mass destruction, nuclear safety and nonproliferation, modeled after the former Joint Committee on Atomic Energy. Creation of such a Committee would ensure that the issues receive adequate high-level attention and that Member and staff expertise is developed and preserved. . . .

Recommendations

The new President, in consultation with Congress and in cooperation with the Russian Federation, should quickly:

- **Formulate a strategic plan** to secure and/or neutralize in the next eight to ten years all nuclear weapons-usable material located in Russia and to pre-vent the outflow from Russia of scientific expertise that could be used for nuclear or other weapons of mass destruction;

- **Identify specific goals and measurable objectives** within the strategic plan and associated budgets for each program, as well as provide criteria for success and an exit strategy;
- **Accelerate the pace and increase funding** for specific programs in coordination with the strategic plan;
- Reach agreement with the Russian Federation at the highest level on **acceptable measures transparency and access;**
- Improve coordination within the U.S. Government by establishing a **high-level leadership position in the White House;** and
- **Focus public and congressional attention** on this critical issue.

The Task Force emphasizes that Russian consultation and collaboration will be key to success in accomplishing these goals.

Proposed Strategic Plan to Accomplish the Task

The major Task Force recommendation to the President and Congress is to formulate a strategic plan to secure and/ formulate a strategic plan to secure and/or neutralize in the next eight to ten years all nuclear weapons-usable material located in Russia and to prevent the outflow from Russia of scientific expertise that could be used for nuclear or other weapons of mass destruction. Recognizing that the President will wish to examine many options, this report outlines a proposed strategic plan with goals and measurable objectives to eliminate the danger of inadequate controls over weapons of mass destruction and weapons usable materials. The Task Force recognizes that the quantities of excess weapons-usable material in Russia are so large that they cannot be completely eliminated even within an eight to ten year period. This is specially true of the plutonium stockpile, elimination of which is directly linked to the progress of U.S. efforts to eliminate its own excess plutonium. This proposed plan is designed to bring all the material under effective control, to reduce drastically the threat posed by such materials, and to reach a position where Russia can take over any remaining work at the end of the eight to ten year period. Consultation and collaboration with Russia will be critical to success. The proposed strategic plan follows.

1. *Secure Russian nuclear weapons and material* by:
   - drastically shrinking the number of buildings where such material is held and consolidating material to secure central storage facilities;
   - accelerating security and accounting upgrades for the remaining buildings in use;
   - assisting the Russians as they identify, tag, and seal all their warheads and materials to facilitate development of a reliable list of where everything is located, and subsequently following up with the more complex job of measuring all of the material;
   - developing a high-intensity plan to return HEU from Soviet-built research reactors, primarily in Eastern Europe, to Russia for downblending and disposition; and

- developing a plan, after a joint U. S.-Russian examination of the extent of the threat, to be implemented by DOE and DOD, to minimize potential proliferation threats posed by decommissioned Russian general-purpose submarines and their fuel.

2. *Eliminate excess Russian HEU* by:
   - demilitarizing all remaining excess Russian HEU through a program of U.S. investment in expanded capacity for down-blending [the process of mixing, or "blending," highly-enriched uranium so that it can no longer be used for nuclear weapons[in Russia. The resultant LEU [low-enriched uranium], which would not be nuclear weapons usable, could remain in Russia but would be sold onto international markets only with consent of both the United States and Russia.
   - accelerating purchase of the approximately 400 metric tons of HEU remaining to be down-blended under the current HEU agreement, while ensuring that the material not flood or depress the world market. This could require the Russian or the U.S. Government to hold the material for an indefinite period of time.

   These two major steps would be augmented if agreements are reached on:
   - the total size of the existing Russian stockpile, after an appropriate audit (fashioned on DOE's ongoing audit of past U.S. HEU production and current stock-piles); and
   - the degree of transparency needed to assure that no additional HEU is being produced.

3. *Manage excess Russian plutonium*, accelerating existing disposition commitments and emphasizing safe and secure storage, by:
   - storing up to 50 metric tons of plutonium at Mayak [a new U.S.-financed facility in west-central Russia for storage of plutonium no longer needed for civilian or military purposes], depending on progress on the nuclear storage facility now under construction with U.S. assistance (the first wing is scheduled to open in 2002);
   - storing the additional material not contained in weapons in either additional wings to be constructed at Mayak or in other highly secure sites (such as facilities fashioned from the empty concrete rooms at Krasnoyarsk-26)[a nuclear weapons facility in south-central Russia]; and/ or
   - eliminating up to 100 metric tons of Russian plutonium by blending fuel as mixed oxide fuel and burning it in civilian reactors or immobilizing it with high-level waste, as the U.S. and Russia have agreed for an initial 34 metric tons. A "swap" of excess military plutonium with Western European countries, in exchange for civilian plutonium already being burned as mixed oxide fuel in these countries, would accelerate this process. Alternatively, the U.S. could purchase excess plutonium from Russia, with the U.S. either storing the plutonium or paying for it to be immobilized as waste.

   In addition, the United States and Russia should reinvigorate their efforts to:

- halt additional plutonium production in a verifiable manner; and
- inventory the total stockpile (similar to the U.S. inventory completed by DOE some years ago).

4. *Downsize the nuclear complex*, building on existing Russian plans and accomplishments, by:
   - facilitating Russian efforts to accelerate the shutdown of its weapons assembly, component fabrication, and materials production facilities, ensuring that the highest-value targets for cooperation are identified;
   - funding "contract research" using existing DOE research and development funds aimed at spurring new technologies for use in cleaning up the U.S. weapons complex. For example, Russian nuclear scientists could be funded to develop efficient, low-cost environmental technologies;
   - working with Russia to ensure nuclear weapons scientists and workers are provided financial incentives for early retirement from the weapons complex;
   - overhauling foreign and domestic lending practices to new businesses in the nuclear cities, seeking ways to extend credit at rates below the Russian market rate to promising small businesses employing former weapons specialists; and
   - enhancing communication between the municipalities and the weapons institutes or facilities that are co-located with them in order to increase efficiency in the expenditure of resources.

5. *Plan for Russian financing of sustainable security by:*
   - seeking specific commitments from Russia to fund adequate levels of security and accounting for its nuclear material and maintenance of a slimmed-down nuclear complex;
   - exploring, in consultation with Russian officials, an array of concepts for developing new revenue streams for financing nuclear security projects in an accountable and transparent manner; and
   - developing a detailed agenda for the transition, which includes identifying specific goals.

The Task Force believes it is quite feasible for the Russian Federation and the United States to carry out together an intensive, well-conceived and well-funded strategic plan as outlined above over the next eight to ten years. If the strategic plan is conceived in full cooperation with the Russians, is adequately financed, and carried out as part of a growing and transparent partnership, the Task Force believes that Russia should be positioned to take over any work remaining at the end of the eight to ten year period.

U.S. ARMY REPORT ON NO GUN RI INCIDENT
January 11, 2001

The United States Army acknowledged January 11, 2001, that some South Korean civilians were killed by the U.S. military in July 1950 during the early stages of the Korean War. But the army insisted that any such killings were not deliberate and had not been ordered by senior officers. President Bill Clinton expressed "regret" about the killings and announced plans to build a $1 million memorial to the victims and to establish a $750,000 scholarship fund for South Korean students, as gestures of U.S. concern.

U.S. and South Korean authorities had conducted an extensive investigation into claims, made by South Korean survivors, that American soldiers and pilots had shot and killed several hundred civilians in late July 1950, just one month after a massive North Korean force invaded South Korea. The killings were said to have taken place near the village of No Gun Ri, about 100 miles southwest of Seoul.

Information about the No Gun Ri incident first reached a worldwide audience in September 1999 when the Associated Press (AP) published an extensive report—based largely on recollections by army veterans and some Korean survivors—estimating that as many as several hundred civilians were killed. The AP reported that poorly trained U.S. troops, who had just arrived in South Korea from occupation duty in postwar Japan, believed that North Korean forces had infiltrated the thousands of refugees fleeing the fighting. The Associated Press was awarded the Pulitzer Prize in 2000 for its report, but several other news organizations attacked the credibility of key sources cited by the AP, including some of the army veterans who claimed to have participated in the killings. (Historic Documents of 1999, p. 552)

The Investigation

The No Gun Ri issue presented a dilemma for the Clinton administration. On one hand, the wide publicity ensuing from the AP report made it imperative that the United States take some action to address a situation that had been ignored, and possibly covered up, for nearly a half century.

*On the other hand, the administration clearly did not want to do anything
that would diminish the overall accomplishments of U.S. servicemen who
fought in Korea, especially the more than 36,000 who died during the conflict. In releasing the report, Defense Secretary William S. Cohen reflected
the administration's desire to put the No Gun Ri incident in context: "Innocent Korean civilians died as a result of the war forced upon our two countries, and we should never forget them, as we should never forget the brave
soldiers who fought to defend freedom."*

*Even before the AP publicized the matter, the army had conducted two
cursory investigations that turned up no evidence of any U.S. involvement
in killings at No Gun Ri. Following the AP report, the Pentagon acknowledged that those investigations had been inadequate. Cohen ordered a full
inquiry on September 30, 1999, the day after the AP report was published.
Assisting the army was a committee of eight "experts," including former
senior U.S. diplomats and military officers, as well as academics and writ-
ers. The South Korean government conducted its own investigation.*

*U.S. and South Korean investigators worked separately, but coopera-
tively, according to the report. The U.S. team said it reviewed more than
1 million pages of documents from the National Archives and about 45,000
containers of film—including aerial reconnaissance photographs that apparently had never been examined. U.S. investigators also interviewed
nearly 200 former U.S. servicemen, while the Korean team interviewed several dozen Korean survivors of the attacks—some of whom had been young
children at the time.*

*The army report noted that the passage of time had dimmed the memo-
ries of those involved. By 1999 and 2000, when they were interviewed,
many of the U.S. servicemen were in their seventies or eighties and could
offer only hazy recollections of events, even dramatic events, that occurred
when they were young men. Nearly all officers, who were older than the
troops in 1950, had since died. Moreover, U.S. military records contained
no information about the alleged killings, and some documents that might
have shed light on the incidents could not be found. Aerial photographs of
the general vicinity offered little help, and experts came to conflicting conclusions about one photograph taken of the general scene about ten days
after the alleged shootings.*

*The army probe was narrowly focused on alleged incidents in the area
around No Gun Ri between July 26 and 29, 1950. It did not examine allegations, reported by the AP and other news organizations in late 1999 and
early 2000, of other U.S. military killings of Korean civilians during the
early stages of the war. The senior Pentagon official who oversaw the investigation, Charles Cragin, principal deputy undersecretary of defense for
personnel and readiness, said no further inquiries into other alleged killings were planned.*

Key Findings

*The core of the report was an examination of the circumstances sur-
rounding two incidents that allegedly took place in the vicinity of No Gun*

Ri: the aerial bombing and/or machine-gun strafing on July 26, 1950, of several hundred Korean refugees congregated on a set of railroad tracks, and then the shooting, starting later that day and possibly lasting for several days, of dozens or even hundreds of refugees who had gathered beneath a large railroad bridge nearby.

The incidents occurred in the midst of a confusing and dangerous situation one month after the start of the Korean War, when thousands of heavily armed North Korean troops streamed across the dividing line between the two Koreas and quickly overwhelmed defending South Korean forces. The United States, with the support of Australia and other allies, sent ground and air forces to confront the North Korean advance—but as of late July the North Koreans were still on the march south. The war ended three years later in a stalemate, with North Korean forces having been driven back to a line near the original boundary along the 38th parallel.

The U.S. military unit allegedly involved in both aspects of the killings near No Gun Ri was the 2nd Battalion of the 7th Cavalry Regiment of the 1st Cavalry Division—itself a unit of the U.S. Eighth Army, the principal American fighting force in South Korea at the time. Before it was sent to Korea, the 1st Cavalry Division had been serving in Japan on post–World War II occupation duty. According to the No Gun Ri investigative report, the division was undermanned, lacked adequate equipment and supplies for combat, and few of its troops had any combat experience or training. Many of the 1st Division's noncommissioned officers had been transferred to another unit that was sent earlier to Korea, depriving the division of critical leadership during a highly stressful period. The division's remaining leaders had "limited proven experience in combat," the report said.

The 2nd Battalion arrived in Korea on July 20 and moved to the front lines, near No Gun Ri, on July 24. There, the battalion confronted a bewildering scene: North Korean forces pressing steadily southward; American forces retreating, often in disarray; and thousands of civilian refugees fleeing their homes, generally crowding with their ox-drawn carts onto the same roads the U.S. Army was trying to use for military operations. American troops had learned at the outset of the war that North Korean soldiers often disguised themselves as civilian refugees, then, once behind allied lines, produced hidden weapons and attacked the allied forces.

On the evening of July 25, according to the army report, the 2nd Battalion began a "disorganized and undisciplined withdrawal" from the frontline sector where it had been stationed—apparently in the mistaken belief that it was in danger of being overwhelmed by a North Korean attack. The unit spent much of the following day, July 26, trying to collect weapons and equipment lost in the retreat and to locate some 200 troops who had disappeared.

During the afternoon of July 26, as the battalion was attempting to reorganize, a group of several dozen—and possibly several hundred—Korean refugees gathered on a railroad track near a high overpass outside No Gun Ri. Several survivors told the South Korean investigative team that American troops had ordered them out of their villages nearby and onto the railroad tracks. Further, some said American troops at the scene used radios to call in an air strike, which occurred shortly afterward. The 2nd Battalion was the only army unit located in the area at the time. The army report expressed strong doubt that troops had ordered the refugees from their villages, in part because doing so would have worsened a refugee situation that already was hampering U.S. military operations. Further, the army report rejected the contention that U.S. troops called in air strikes, noting that ordinary soldiers did not have radio contact with the command posts that controlled air operations.

Thirty-four Korean survivors told investigators that one or two U.S. warplanes arrived on the scene and attacked the refugees gathered on the railroad tracks. Some survivors said the planes had dropped bombs, while others described strafing by machine guns. The survivors described injuries they received from bullets or bombs, and they said an unknown number of people, possibly more than 100, were killed.

The army investigative team said it could find no evidence to support the survivors' claims about the air attack. U.S. Air Force and Navy records made no mention of air missions over the No Gun Ri area on July 26, and surviving pilots who had flown missions in Korea during that time period adamantly denied any attacks on civilians. An aerial photograph taken of the railroad tracks on August 6 proved inconclusive. One analyst consulted by the army team detected some evidence of strafing, while other experts found no such evidence.

Based on all the available evidence, the army report concluded that "strafing may have occurred near No Gun Ri in the last week of July 1950 and could have injured or killed Korean civilians." But, the report added, "any such strikes were not deliberate attacks on Korean civilians." An accidental attack on the civilians could have resulted from such factors as the misidentification of a target, the lack of reliable communications, or "the fluid nature of the battlefield," the report said.

The original AP report had described an even more dramatic event starting later on July 26: U.S. troops ordered several hundred Korean refugees into two tunnels beneath a large railroad bridge near the site of the alleged air attack, then fired at the refugees with rifles, machine guns, and mortars, killing an estimated 50 to 150 of them over a period that might have lasted four days. The AP report and subsequent news accounts quoted former U.S. soldiers who said they had participated in the shooting. One, Edward Daily, vividly described shooting into the group of refugees and hearing "the frightful screams of women and children, crying out with pain and fear."

The report of the army investigation concluded that "an unknown number of Korean civilians" were injured and killed by small-arms fire in the vicinity of No Gun Ri during the last week of July 1950. The shootings occurred at several locations in the area, the report said, not just at the railroad bridge where most of the Korean survivors had placed the incident. The army panel said some U.S. veterans recalled shooting toward (but not necessarily directly at) Korean civilians—either in response to what they believed to be hostile fire from North Korean troops who had infiltrated the refugee throng or as a warning to the refugees to stay away from the American positions.

The army report said three of the veterans who had described the shootings to the AP probably were not even on the scene at the time. One of the three was Daily, who, according to army records, was assigned to a different unit and could not have been present. The report said Daily could not explain the discrepancy between his memory and army records. Daily for years had attended 2nd Battalion reunions and had talked repeatedly about the No Gun Ri killings. As a result, the army panel said, his accounts could have "contaminated" the memories of other veterans.

The Korean survivors gave various accounts of what happened at the No Gun Ri railway bridge, but common themes were that dozens of them were crowded in terror under the bridge, that U.S. troops fired repeatedly at them, and that many of them recalled hiding behind stacks of bodies.

Because of the discrepancies in the accounts of the former U.S. servicemen and the Korean survivors, the army panel said it could not determine exactly what happened at No Gun Ri, nor could it answer such questions as how long the shooting lasted, who did the shooting, or how many people were injured or killed. But the panel did draw some firm conclusions from the evidence it uncovered: "The firing was a result of hostile fire seen or received from civilian positions or [was] fire directed over their heads or near them to control their movement. The deaths and injuries of civilians, wherever they occurred, were an unfortunate tragedy inherent to war and not a deliberate killing."

Further, the panel rejected the suggestion—made most notably by Daily—that army officers had ordered their troops to fire at the civilians. At least four army documents issued at the general time of the No Gun Ri incident discussed controlling the flow of Korean refugees and suggested that refugees who crossed battle lines should be considered as enemies. Even so, the panel said it concluded from available information that "U.S. commanders did not issue oral or written orders to shoot and kill Korean civilians during the last week of July 1950 in the vicinity of No Gun Ri."

Some of the outside experts who advised the army panel suggested that, even if the shootings had not been ordered specifically, senior commanders ultimately were responsible for what happened at No Gun Ri. Retired Marine Lt. Gen. Bernard Trainor said in a letter to Cohen that "a failure of leadership" played a role in the incident. "My conclusion is that the American command was responsible for the loss of innocent civilian life in or around No Gun Ri," Trainor said. "At the very least, it failed to control the fire of its subordinate units and personnel. At the worst, it ordered the firing."

The army panel said it could not determine with any accuracy how many civilians had been killed in the vicinity of No Gun Ri during late July 1950. The original AP report had concluded that "hundreds" of people were killed, and the South Korean investigation team cited a figure of 248, apparently based on claims made by survivors to local officials. The army panel made only one attempt to come up with a figure of its own: Citing information from 27 Korean survivors who mentioned specific family members or friends who had been killed, the panel said the number in those accounts totaled "approximately 70 dead." In any event, the panel said it believed the actual number killed was less than the 248 cited by the Korean team. One important basis for that conclusion was the aerial photograph of the No Gun Ri bridge area dated August 6, 1950, which showed no bodies or mass graves, contradicting statements by some of the Korean survivors that dozens of bodies remained unburied for weeks after the shootings.

Korean Reaction

Representatives of the Korean survivors expressed dismay at the army report and Clinton's statement. "There is no fig leaf large enough for the U.S. Army high command to hide behind," said Chung Koo-do, a spokesman for the survivors, whose younger brother and sister died in the shootings. Chung and others said they had hoped the United States would formally apologize for the killings and would identify officers responsible for ordering the shootings, which Chung described as a "carefully coordinated operation." Because it failed to identify who ordered the shootings, Chung said, the army report "can't be construed as anything other than a Pentagon attempt to whitewash the massacre."

South Korean president Kim Dae-jung telephoned President Clinton to thank him for expressing "regret" about the killings, and the chairman of the South Korean investigating team asked his fellow citizens to accept the U.S. findings. "It isn't completely satisfactory, but in the beginning, the Americans did not even acknowledge the existence" of the No Gun Ri incident, said Ahn Byung Woo. "Now, they are acknowledging it, and the American president has even expressed his regret."

Following is the executive summary of the "No Gun Ri Review" conducted by the Office of the Inspector General of the U.S. Department of the Army and released January 11, 2001, by the Department of Defense.

The document was obtained from the Internet at http:// www.army.mil/nogunri/BookCoverJan01Summary.pdf.

Introduction

Following the release of the Associated Press story concerning the matter on September 29, 1999, the United States (U.S.) and the Republic of Korea (ROK) initiated independent, but cooperative, reviews of the incident at No Gun Ri. This story brought to the forefront the earlier efforts of Korean citizens to secure an official inquiry into their claims surrounding certain events that occurred in the vicinity of No Gun Ri, including the firing upon Korean refugees at the double railroad overpass and an air strike on the railroad track.

Over the last year, the U.S. Review Team has conducted an exhaustive factual review by examining over a million documents from the National Archives, conducting interviews with approximately 200 American witnesses, and analyzing the interview transcripts and oral statements of approximately 75 Korean witnesses. The U.S. Review Team also closely examined press reports, aerial imagery, and other forensic examination results. This U.S. Report reflects the U.S. Review Team's factual findings based upon all the evidence available on the incident.

Unfortunately, the passage of 50 years greatly reduces the possibility that we will ever know all of the facts surrounding this particular event. A large number of factors, including but not limited to trauma, age, and the media, influenced the recollection of Korean and U.S. witnesses. By comparing and contrasting all of these available information sources, the U.S. Review Team has developed a clearer picture of the events that occurred in the vicinity of No Gun Ri in July 1950. The findings of the U.S. Review Team have been organized into several key issues, which describe the Team's conclusions regarding what occurred at No Gun Ri based upon all the information available half a century later.

I. Background—The Korean Account

The Korean villagers stated that on July 25, 1950, U.S. soldiers evacuated approximately 500 to 600 villagers from their homes in Im Gae Ri and Joo Gok Ri. The villagers said the U.S. soldiers escorted them towards the south. Later that evening, the American soldiers led the villagers near a riverbank at Ha Ga Ri and ordered them to stay there that night. During the night, the villagers witnessed a long parade of U.S. troops and vehicles moving towards Pusan.

On the morning of July 26, 1950, the villagers continued south along the Seoul-Pusan road. According to their statements, when the villagers reached the vicinity of No Gun Ri, U.S. soldiers stopped them at a roadblock and ordered the group onto the railroad tracks, where the soldiers searched them and their personal belongings. The Koreans state that, although the soldiers found no prohibited items (such as weapons or other military contraband), the soldiers ordered an air attack upon the villagers via radio communications with U.S. aircraft. Shortly afterwards, planes flew over and dropped bombs and fired machine guns, killing approximately 100 villagers on the railroad tracks. Those villagers who survived sought protection in a small culvert underneath the railroad tracks. The U.S. soldiers drove the villagers out of the culvert and into the larger double tunnels nearby (this report subsequently refers to these tunnels as the "double railroad overpass"). The Koreans state that the U.S. soldiers then fired into both ends of the tunnels over a period of four days (July 26-29, 1950), resulting in approximately 300 additional deaths.

II. Department of Defense Review Directives

On September 30, 1999, the Secretary of Defense directed the Secretary of the Army to lead a review to determine "the full scope of the facts surrounding these [No Gun Ri] press reports." On October 25, 1999, the Secretary of the

Army directed The Inspector General to conduct a thorough review of the allegations, pursue every reasonable lead to determine the facts, and then prepare and submit a report of the findings with regard to the allegations.

The Office of the Secretary of Defense established a Steering Group chaired by the Under Secretary of Defense (Personnel and Readiness) to oversee the conduct of the review. In addition, the Secretary of Defense invited eight distinguished Americans, who are not affiliated with the Department of Defense, to advise on the conduct of the review based upon their expertise in academia, journalism, the Korean War, and U.S. -ROK relations.

III. Department of the Army
Inspector General Review Effort

The Inspector General developed a four-phase concept plan: Preparation; Research and Interviews; Review and Analysis; and Production of the Final Report. The Inspector General then formed the No Gun Ri Review Team (U.S. Review Team) into a Research Team and an Interview Team. The research effort, led by an Army historian, began in October 1999. The Research Team consisted of Department of the Army military and civilian members augmented by a United States Air Force research team, an imagery analyst, a Korean linguist, and professional research assistants from the U.S. Army Corps of Engineers. The researchers examined over one million pages of text from the National Archives and other repositories and approximately 45,000 containers of United States Air Force reconnaissance film.

The interview process started on December 29, 1999, after the Interview Team located former soldiers assigned to the major combat units that passed through the Yongdong-Hwanggan area in mid-to late July 1950. The Interview Team and Air Force researchers culled through over 7,375 names to locate and interview approximately 200 U.S. veterans. While every effort was made to make this a comprehensive sample, the U.S. Review Team had no power to compel a witness to grant an interview and no authority to issue subpoenas or to grant immunity. In fact, eleven veterans contacted by the U.S. Review Team declined to be interviewed. The U.S. Review Team did review, however, the published accounts of some witnesses who declined to be interviewed by the Team.

IV. U.S. and ROK Cooperation

The Department of the Army and the Department of Defense worked in close cooperation with the representatives of the government of the Republic of Korea who were conducting a parallel review of the allegations. Members from the U.S. Review Team, the Republic of Korea Investigation Team (ROK Review Team), and government officials from both countries met on approximately a dozen occasions in both the United States and Korea, to include the Secretary of the Army's meetings with President Kim Dae-Jung and Minister of National Defense Cho Song-Tae in January 2000. The U.S. Review Team provided the ROK Review Team with copies of all relevant documents and other information discovered in the course of the review in support of the ROK's parallel investigation. On two occasions, the U.S. Review Team supported working visits by a ROK Review Team researcher to the National Archives in College Park, Maryland. The U.S. Review Team provided full access to, and funded the reproduction costs of, any materials already gathered by the U.S. researchers. No information was withheld.

V. Organization of the U.S. Report

The U.S. Review Team conducted this review and prepared this report fully aware of the political, military, and emotional significance of the allegations. This report is not intended as a point-by-point response to the media and Korean accounts. The report presents an independent assessment of the facts derived directly from an exhaustive review of primary and secondary sources, the statements of U.S. veterans and Koreans, ballistic and pathology forensics, and imagery analysis. . . .

VI. Findings

Given the challenge of ascertaining facts a half century after their occurrence, the U.S. Review Team made findings when possible, identified possibilities, and noted when the evidence was not sufficient to identify a possibility or reach a finding about what may have occurred at No Gun Ri in July 1950 based upon an analysis of available information. A summary of its factual findings has been organized into several key issues. These issues were identified and developed in coordination with the Office of the Secretary of Defense Steering Group, U.S. Outside Experts, and counterparts from the Republic of Korea.

A. Key Issue 1: Condition of U.S. Forces in July 1950

Background. U.S. soldiers were young, under-trained, under-equipped, and unprepared for the fight they would wage against the North Korean People's Army (NKPA). The soldiers of the Army of Occupation in Japan functioned primarily as a constabulary in a conquered land and not as combat-ready warfighters.

Their lack of combat preparedness was a direct result of deficiencies in training, equipment, structure, personnel strength, and leadership. Proper training areas were not available to conduct more than small-unit training. Classes for critical specialties such as maintenance and communications were also inadequate. Most of their equipment, including ammunition, was of World War II vintage, and had been poorly stored and maintained. The three infantry regiments in the 1st Cavalry Division had only two of the three battalions normally assigned. Likewise, each regiment lacked its authorized tank company, and the division artillery battalions contained only two of the normal three firing batteries. In response to a requirement to bring the 24th Infantry Division up to strength prior to that division's departure for Korea, the 1st Cavalry Division transferred nearly 800 men, most of them from the top four senior non-commissioned officer grades, to the 24th. This loss of non-commissioned officers with whom the soldiers had trained weakened the cohesion of the division and significantly reduced the number of leaders with combat experience at the small-unit level.

Finding. Based on the documentary evidence, as well as the statements by U.S. veterans, the U.S. Review Team concluded that most American units and soldiers were not adequately prepared for the combat conditions that they confronted in Korea in June and July 1950. No experience or training equipped them to deal with an aggressive enemy that employed both conventional and guerilla warfare tactics or with a large refugee population, which the enemy was known to have infiltrated. Shortages of experienced Non-commissioned officers, along with inadequate equipment and doctrine, made it difficult for individuals or units to adapt to these conditions.

B. Key Issue 2: U.S. and ROK Refugee Control Policies

Background. The U.S. troops were completely unprepared for the stark reality of dealing with the numerous, uncontrolled refugees who clogged the roads and complicated the battlefield to an unexpected degree. Early on in the war, U.S. forces encountered the NKPA practice of infiltrating soldiers dressed as civilians among large refugee concentrations. Once behind American lines, these infiltrated soldiers would then conduct guerilla-style combat operations against American rear-area units and activities.

In late July 1950, the ROK government and the Eighth U.S. Army Headquarters issued refugee control policies to protect the U.S. and ROK forces from NKPA infiltration and attacks from the rear. Additionally, these policies were aimed at reducing the adverse impact of large refugee concentrations on main supply routes, which stymied the U.S. and UN troops' ability to rush ammunition forward and evacuate casualties to the rear. These U.S. and ROK refugee policies depended heavily upon the constant presence of, and coordination with, the ROK National Police to handle the uncontrolled refugee population.

Despite comments attributed to Major General Gay, the 1st Cavalry Division Commander, that he would not employ the Korean National Police in his division's area of operations, his refugee policy directive of July 23, 1950, made the National Police responsible for handling refugees. The movement of civilians and refugees in the 1st Cavalry Division area was restricted to specific hours and for specific purposes by a limited number of people, and the National Police were responsible for enforcing the policy.

On July 26, 1950, the Eighth U.S. Army Korea (EUSAK), in coordination with the ROK government, established and disseminated a plan to control refugee movement which:

- precluded movement of refugees across battle lines at all times, prohibited evacuation of villages without general officer approval, and established a National Police responsibility,
- prescribed procedures for Korean National Police to clear desired areas and routes,
- strictly precluded Korean civilian movement during the hours of darkness, and
- established requirements for disseminating the policy.

The Eighth Army's policy was intended to deny the NKPA their widely used infiltration tactic while also safeguarding civilians by prohibiting refugees from crossing *battle lines* (battle lines are the areas where there is contact with the enemy or contact is about to occur). The policy did not state that refugees could not cross *friendly lines* and contains instructions for the handling of refugees in friendly areas (friendly lines are the forward troop positions not in contact with the enemy). The policy emphasized the Korean government's responsibility for the control and screening of refugees to provide for their welfare. Nothing in this policy was intended to put refugees at risk.

Most veterans from the 7th Cavalry Regiment interviewed by the U.S. Review Team were enlisted men during the Korean War and did not receive copies of policies from higher headquarters. In general, most U.S. veterans remembered warnings that there were North Korean infiltrators among the refugees. The veterans who remembered more specific details about refugee control remembered specific actions to be taken; for example, keep refugees off the roads, do not let refugees pass, or search refugees and let them pass.

Finding. From its study of the refugee control policies in effect during the last week of July 1950, the U.S. Review Team found that the Eighth U.S. Army published, in coordination with the ROK government, refugee control policies that reflected two predominant concerns: (1) protecting U.S. and ROK troops from the danger of NKPA soldiers infiltrating U.S.–ROK lines; and (2) precluding uncontrolled refugee movements from impeding flows of supplies and troops. The published 1st Cavalry Division refugee control policy dated July 23, 1950, reflected the same two concerns. The task of keeping innocent civilians out of harm's way was left entirely to ROK authorities. By implication, these policies also protected refugees by attempting to ensure they were not in harm's way.

C. Key Issue 3: Tactical Situation July 22-29, 1950

Background. The 1st Cavalry Division relieved the 24th Infantry Division northwest of Yongdong on July 22, 1950. The 7th Cavalry Regiment of the 1st Cavalry Division arrived in Pohangdong, Korea, on July 22, 1950, and the 2nd Battalion, 7th Cavalry Regiment, moved forward to the Yongdong area. With friendly forces outnumbered by the NKPA, the Eighth Army developed a strategy to withdraw behind the last defensible terrain feature, the Naktong River. As events developed, the 1st Cavalry Division withdrew from Yongdong through a series of delaying actions in accordance with the Eighth Army strategy and to avoid a threatened envelopment. On the evening of July 25, 1950, the 7th Cavalry Regiment was supporting the 5th Cavalry Regiment in positions east of Yongdong.

Sometime during the night of July 25, the 7th Cavalry received a report that a breakthrough had occurred in the sector to the 7th Cavalry Regiment's north.

Finding. The U.S. Review Team found that, in the early morning hours of July 26, 1950, the 2nd Battalion of the 7th Cavalry Regiment, without specific orders but believing they were being enveloped, conducted a disorganized and undisciplined withdrawal from a position east of Yongdong to the vicinity of No Gun Ri. They spent the remaining hours of July 26 until late into that night recovering abandoned personnel and equipment from the area where the air strike and machine-gun firing on Korean refugees is alleged to have occurred. On July 26, 1950, at 9: 30 at night, 119 men were still unaccounted for. It will probably never be possible to reconstruct the activities of the scattered soldiers of the 2nd Battalion.

The U.S. Review Team determined that the 1st Battalion, 7th Cavalry Regiment, arrived in the vicinity of No Gun Ri in the afternoon of July 26, 1950. They relieved the 2nd Battalion, 5th Cavalry Regiment, and established their position east of the 2nd Battalion, 7th Cavalry Regiment.

The U.S. Review Team found that there was repeated contact reported between the 7th Cavalry and enemy forces in the vicinity of No Gun Ri on July 27 and July 28. The records indicate by this time that the 7th Cavalry had been told that there were no friendly forces to the west and south of No Gun Ri (i. e. back toward Yongdong). The 2nd Battalion, 7th Cavalry, reported an enemy column on the railroad tracks on July 27, which they fired upon. On July 29, the battalion withdrew as the NKPA advanced.

The U.S. Review Team concluded that based on the available evidence, the 7th Cavalry Regiment was under attack, as they believed, between July 27 and July 29, 1950, when in position near No Gun Ri.

D. Key Issue 4: Assembly and Movement of Villagers

Background. The U.S. and ROK policy in July 1950 stated generally that Korean civilians should not evacuate their villages. The U.S. Review Team could not determine the reasons why the refugees gathered in Im Gae Ri, but this gathering of refugees was probably not the result of any U.S. action. Some witnesses stated that the Americans told them that they were being moved for their safety. Some U.S. veterans remember escorting refugees from villages, but these veterans cannot remember the villages' names or the dates the evacuations occurred. Therefore, the U.S. Review Team cannot rule out the possibility that U.S. soldiers told the villagers at Im Gae Ri to evacuate the village.

While the U.S. Review Team cannot rule out the possibility that the villagers were moved, there was no sound military reason for soldiers to travel approximately three miles off their designated movement route to the village of Im Gae Ri during a hasty withdrawal for the purpose of encouraging an additional 400 refugees onto the already crowded roads and further aggravating the congested conditions. It is also unlikely that the soldiers would have performed this evacuation given the widespread knowledge and fear of North Korean infiltrators believed to be present in refugee concentrations.

Some 7th Cavalry Regiment veterans recalled displacing South Koreans from unknown villages on unknown dates. The U.S. Review Team found that the 7th Cavalry Regiment was not in the vicinity of Im Gae Ri on July 25 based upon official records of the Regiment's positions. Some veterans of the 5th Cavalry Regiment indicated that they evacuated or escorted Korean civilians from unknown villages in late July and early August 1950. A patrol from the 5th Cavalry Regiment may have told the villagers who had assembled at Im Gae Ri to leave.

Finding. The U.S. Review Team could not determine the reasons why the refugees gathered in Im Gae Ri, but the U.S. Review Team concluded that this gathering of refugees was probably not the result of U.S. action. Based on some of the available evidence, the U.S. Review Team cannot rule out the possibility that U.S. soldiers told the villagers at Im Gae Ri to evacuate the village, but the soldiers who did so were not from the 7th Cavalry Regiment.

E. Key Issue 5: Air Strikes in the Vicinity of No Gun Ri

Background. Korean witnesses describe an air strike/strafing around noon on July 26, 1950 on the railroad tracks. The Korean witnesses describe the effects of machine gun fire and explosions.

The U.S. Review Team could not locate any records to substantiate the occurrence of an air strike/strafing incident in the vicinity of No Gun Ri around noon on July 26, 1950. While there are mission reports for July 26, 1950, that could not be located, the missions can be accounted for through other reports. The only documented USAF air strike in the immediate vicinity of the Hwanggan area occurred southwest of No Gun Ri on July 27. This air strike was a friendly fire incident in which a F-80 accidentally strafed the 1st Battalion, 7th Cavalry Regiment's command post at 7: 15 in the morning. The strafing destroyed two U.S. trucks but claimed no lives. . . .

No U.S. Air Force veteran that the U.S. Review Team interviewed participated in, or had any knowledge of anyone participating in, the strafing of civilians in the vicinity of No Gun Ri in late July 1950. U.S. Air Force interviewees vividly recalled stern verbal policies implemented to prevent the attack of non-combatants.

The Navy discovered no evidence of naval aircraft operating in the vicinity of No Gun Ri on July 26 or 27. However, on July 28, Navy aircraft from the USS Valley Forge were directed into the area and attacked a railroad tunnel occupied by enemy troops and other targets forward of the 7th Cavalry in the direction of Yongdong with bombs and machine guns.

The Defense Intelligence Agency found 8th Tactical Reconnaissance Squadron photographs of the No Gun Ri area dated August 6 and September 19, 1950. The Air Force Team showed these photographs to four retired photo interpreters of national reputation, all of whom agree that the photographs show no signs of bombing or strafing on the railroad tracks. A NIMA photo interpreter maintains that some patterns near the tracks approximately 350 yards from the double railroad overpass show "an imagery signature of probable strafing" but no bomb damage. The location of the probable strafing is in the same relative location identified by the Korean witnesses as that location where they were strafed.

Finding. An exhaustive search of U.S. Air Force and U.S. Navy records and interviews with U.S. pilots did not identify an air strike in the No Gun Ri area on July 26, 1950. The number of Korean witness statements describing the strafing and the photograph interpretation by NIMA does not permit the U.S. Review Team to exclude the possibility that U.S. or allied aircraft might have hit civilian refugees in the vicinity of No Gun Ri during an air strike/strafing on

July 26, 1950. On July 27, 1950, an air strike did in fact occur on the 1st Battalion, 7th Cavalry's position near No Gun Ri that both the Air Force and Army recorded in official documents. On July 28, there was also an air strike on NKPA forces near 1st Battalion, 7th Cavalry Regiment. Assuming Korean civilians were near the positions of these strikes, they could have been injured.

The U.S. Review Team concluded that strafing may have occurred near No Gun Ri in the last week of July 1950 and could have injured or killed Korean civilians but that any such air strikes were not deliberate attacks on Korean civilians. The U.S. Review Team concluded that any air strikes/strafing occurring on July 26 took place under the same conditions as the air strikes/strafing on July 27, specifically an accidental air strike/strafing caused by the misidentification of targets and not a pre-planned strike. An accidental air strike/strafing could have happened due to several factors: target misidentification, lack of reliable communications, absence of a Tactical Air Control Party in the 7th Regiment, and the fluid nature of the battlefield. It was not a pre-planned strike on civilian refugees.

F. Key Issue 6: Ground Fire in the Vicinity of No Gun Ri

Background. Some U.S. and Korean witness statements indicate that U.S. ground forces fired toward refugees in the vicinity of No Gun Ri during the period July 26-29, 1950, as discussed below. According to the Korean description of the events on July 26, 1950, refugees were strafed or bombed on the railroad tracks. Some fled the area or hid in ditches and others went into the double railroad overpass tunnel where they were fired upon from different locations for a period of up to four days, with the heaviest fire occurring on July 26 (which was the first day they report spending in the double railroad overpass).

In interviews, some U.S. veterans stated they saw or heard firing of various types including machine-gun, mortar, artillery, and rifle fire, near unidentified individuals in civilian clothing outside the tunnels/bridges in the vicinity of No Gun Ri. Only a few veterans interviewed by the U.S. Review Team stated they fired toward civilians in the vicinity of No Gun Ri. Two veterans fired over the heads of or into the ground in front to keep the civilians pinned down or to prevent them from moving. Several other veterans stated they either received hostile fire from, or saw hostile fire coming from, the civilian positions in the double railroad overpass and elsewhere. They also stated that they returned fire, or observed fire being returned, on the civilian positions as a response to the hostile fire they received or observed. Some veterans also remember intermittent NKPA and U.S. artillery and mortar fires.

Official records indicate that the NKPA attacked the 7th Cavalry on July 27 and 28, and the 7th Cavalry employed every means at its disposal to defend itself, including the use of small-arms fire, mortars, and artillery.

Finding. Although the U.S. Review Team cannot determine what happened near No Gun Ri with certainty, it is clear, based upon all available evidence, that an unknown number of Korean civilians were killed or injured by the effects of small-arms fire, artillery and mortar fire, and strafing that preceded or coincided with the NKPA's advance and the withdrawal of U.S. forces in the vicinity of No Gun Ri during the last week of July 1950. These Korean deaths and injuries occurred at different locations in the vicinity of No Gun Ri and were not concentrated exclusively at the double railroad overpass.

Some U.S. veterans describe fire that lasted for a few to 60 minutes. Some Korean witnesses describe fire day and night on the tunnel for as long as four days. Because Korean estimates of the length of time they spent in the tunnel are so inconsistent, the U.S. Review Team drew no conclusion about the amount of time they spent in the tunnel.

The firing was a result of hostile fire seen or received from civilian positions or fire directed over their heads or near them to control their movement. The deaths and injuries of civilians, wherever they occurred, were an unfortunate tragedy inherent to war and not a deliberate killing.

G. Key Issue 7: Issuance of Orders to Fire on Refugees

Background. To determine if soldiers or pilots were issued orders to attack and fire on refugees in the vicinity of No Gun Ri, the Review Team reviewed documents and conducted interviews with Army and Air Force veterans. Based upon the available evidence, which included the statements of veterans, documents, and the absence of documents, the U.S. Review Team concluded that U.S. commanders did not issue oral or written orders to fire on refugees in the vicinity of No Gun Ri between July 25 and 29, 1950.

Pilots were not ordered to attack and kill civilian refugees in the vicinity of No Gun Ri. Air strikes in the vicinity of No Gun Ri on July 26 were either the result of a misidentification of a target or an accident as discussed above. No USAF veteran that the U.S. Review Team interviewed participated in, or had any knowledge of anyone participating in, the strafing of civilians in the vicinity of No Gun Ri in late July 1950. U.S. Air Force interviewees vividly recalled stern verbal policies implemented to prevent the attack of non-combatants. In interviews, pilots stated that they sought out targets such as tanks, trucks, moving troops, and groups of men in uniform. Pilots fired when they were told a target was hostile and fired back when fired upon.

The U.S. Review Team found two documents that refer to an unknown Army request to the Air Force and the Navy to strafe civilian or refugee columns. The first reference is in a memorandum by COL T. C. Rogers, Fifth Air Force ADVON (Korea), dated 25 July 1950. The second reference is a Naval Activity Summary for the same date from the Aircraft Carrier Valley Forge. The U.S. Review Team could not find any originating request from the Army that prompted these two references. The Rogers' memorandum actually recommends that civilians not be attacked unless they are definitely known to be North Korean soldiers or have committed hostile acts. The Navy document stated that the first pass over personnel would be a non-firing run to identify if civilians were present. If the target was determined to be hostile, a firing run would follow.

Soldiers were not ordered to attack and kill civilian refugees in the vicinity of No Gun Ri. The veterans interviewed said that deadly force was not authorized against civilian refugees who posed no threat to the unit, and they were not given orders to shoot and kill civilian refugees in the vicinity of No Gun Ri. However, the U.S. Review Team found that soldiers who were in the vicinity of No Gun Ri were given an order to stop civilians and not to let them pass their position. Some soldiers did believe if civilian refugees did not stop, they could use deadly force to prevent them from passing.

Several other veterans stated they observed firing at the civilians in response to perceived hostile fire from the positions near the double railroad overpass and elsewhere. Based on veterans' interviews, the U.S. Review Team found that soldiers believed that they could take action in self-defense against civilians; that is, if they were fired upon or if they saw actions that indicated hostile intent. Some veterans said they observed firing in the direction of the double railroad overpass in response to fire from that location. Return fire in this case would have been an action in self-defense, and no orders were required. Two veterans fired over the heads of civilians, or into the ground in front to keep the civilians pinned down or prevent them from moving. The U.S. soldiers were repeatedly warned that North Korean soldiers wore civilian clothing over their uniforms in order to infiltrate U.S. positions. The U.S. soldiers were also told that North Korean soldiers would hide within refugee columns.

In interviews with the U.S. Review Team, several veterans stated that they assumed there was an order to fire on civilians because artillery and mortar fires were used that may have hit civilians. These veterans had no information to support their assertions. When interviewed, the veterans said they did not know who gave the order, they did not hear the order, they did not know when the order was given, and they personally did not receive the order. Former officers of the 2nd Battalion, 7th Cavalry Regiment, that the U.S. Review Team interviewed remain adamant that the battalion commander issued no order to fire on refugees at any time.

There are references that appear to authorize firing on Korean civilians in Army records. The first reference was an abbreviated message that appeared in an 8th Cavalry Regiment message log dated 10: 00 AM on July 24, 1950, that stated: "No refugees to cross the frontline. Fire everyone trying to cross the lines. Use discretion in case of women and children." The U.S. Review Team found no similar entry in the records of the 1st Cavalry Division, its other two regiments (the 5th and 7th Cavalry Regiments), or in the records of units subordinate to the 8th Cavalry Regiment. The U.S. Review Team found no evidence that the 8th Cavalry message was transmitted to the 5th or 7th Cavalry Regiments or any other subordinate element of the division. In interviews, U.S. veterans in the vicinity of No Gun Ri do not recall instructions to fire on civilian refugees. The 7th Cavalry Regiment was the unit in the vicinity of No Gun Ri on July 26. By July 26, 1950, the last elements of the 8th Cavalry Regiment were withdrawing from the vicinity of No Gun Ri to the division rear near Hwanggan.

The refugee control policy set by the 1st Cavalry Division Commander in his order of July 23, 1950, titled "Control of Refugee Movement" makes no mention of the use of force by soldiers. It stated: "Municipal authorities, local police and the National Police will enforce this directive." The U.S. Review Team concluded that the 8th Cavalry Regiment log entry did not constitute a 1st Cavalry Division order to fire upon Korean civilians at No Gun Ri.

The second reference was a 25th Infantry Division Commander's memorandum to commanders issued on July 27, 1950. On July 25, 1950, the 25th ID Activities Report stated: "Refugees and Korean Civilians were ordered out of the combat zone in order to eliminate possible serious traffic problems and to aid in blocking the infiltration of North Korean Forces through the lines. These instructions were passed to the civilians through the Korean Police." The July 27, 1950, memo to Commanders reads: "Korean police have been directed to remove all civilians from the area between the blue lines shown on the attached overlay and report the evacuation has been accomplished. All civilians seen in this area are to be considered as enemy and action taken accordingly." The area "between the blue lines" was in front of the 25th Infantry Division's main line of defense, an area about to be occupied by the enemy. Two things are clear: actions had been taken in conjunction with the Korean National Police to clear the civilians out of the danger area, and those actions were intended to ensure that noncombatants would not find themselves in harm's way when the advancing NKPA subsequently made contact along the Division's front. After the area was cleared, anyone caught in civilian clothes and suspected of being an enemy agent was to be turned over to the Counter-Intelligence Corps immediately and not to the Korean Police. There is nothing to suggest any summary measures were considered against refugees or people dressed like refugees. The 25th Infantry Division was not located in the vicinity of No Gun Ri during the last week of July 1950.

Finding. Based upon the available evidence, and despite some conflicting statements and misunderstandings, the U.S. Review Team concluded that U.S. commanders did not issue oral or written orders to shoot and kill Korean civilians during the last week of July 1950 in the vicinity of No Gun Ri.

A veteran stated that soldiers could have misunderstood the order not to let refugees pass or to stop refugees. Some veterans did believe that if a civilian would not stop, they could use deadly force to prevent civilians from passing.

Some veterans stated that there was an order to shoot civilians at No Gun Ri but had no information to support their assertions. These soldiers did not know who gave the order, did not hear the order, did not know when the order was given, and personally did not receive the order. As a result, the U.S. Review Team concluded that these veterans assumed that an order was given because artillery and mortars were fired. The U.S. Review Team also considered media statements quoting veterans who claimed that an order to shoot Korean civilians was given at No Gun Ri. The U.S. Review Team was unable to confirm these reports because the witnesses either were not at No Gun Ri at the time or refused to speak to the U.S. Army.

Although the U.S. Review Team found four references (entry in the 8th Cavalry Regiment Message Log, 25th Infantry Division Commander's order, Colonel Rogers' memorandum, and an extract from the U.S. Navy's Aircraft Carrier Valley Forge Activity Summary) discussing actions against civilians, it did not find evidence of an order given to soldiers by a U.S. commander, orally or in writing, to kill Korean civilians in the vicinity of No Gun Ri in the last week of July 1950.

H. Key Issue 8: Number of Korean Deaths and Injuries

Background. After taking the statements of U.S. veterans and securing the professional evaluation of the August 6, 1950, aerial reconnaissance photograph by the National Imagery and Mapping Agency and the Armed Forces Institute of Pathology, the U.S. Review Team asked the ROK Review Team to provide information on the number of casualties. The U.S. Review Team's research revealed no official records of refugee deaths or injuries in the vicinity of No Gun Ri between July 26 and July 29, 1950.

The initial Associated Press articles reported hundreds of people killed. Korean witness estimates range between 60 -100 dead in the double tunnel and 50 -150 dead or injured from strafing/bombing. Several U.S. veterans describe a lower number of dead or injured civilians. The soldiers did not check the areas where civilians came under fire to determine whether there were dead bodies, and some estimates appear to be guesswork or to be based on recollections not related to No Gun Ri.

At three different meetings, ROK officials reported an unverified number of 248 casualties, which they stated was provided to them by the Yongdong County Office. But the ROK Review Team acknowledges that the estimated figure of 248 is not considered factual and will have to be substantiated by an additional investigation at some future date by the ROK government.

Finding. Based on the available evidence, the U.S. Review Team is unable to determine the number of Korean civilians who were killed or injured in the vicinity of No Gun Ri. During their investigation, the ROK Review Team reported that the Korean survivors' organization claimed an unverified number of 248 South Korean civilians killed, injured, or missing in the vicinity of No Gun Ri between July 25 and 29, 1950. This report was recorded by the Yongdong County Office. The ROK Steering Group, at a ROK-U.S. Steering Group meeting on December 6–7, 2000, in Seoul, ROK, reiterated the claim of 248 casualties.

The actual number of Korean casualties cannot be derived from the U.S. veteran statements and Korean witness statements. The U.S. Team believes that number to be lower than the Korean claim. An aerial reconnaissance photograph of the No Gun Ri area taken on August 6, 1950, shows no indication of human remains or mass graves in the vicinity of the No Gun Ri double railroad overpass. Korean burial customs, farming in the area, lack of reliable information, wartime disruptions of the countryside, and the passage of time preclude an accurate determination of the numbers involved.

Conclusion

During late July 1950, Korean civilians were caught between withdrawing U.S. forces and attacking enemy forces. As a result of U.S. actions during the Korean War in the last week of July 1950, Korean civilians were killed and injured in the vicinity of No Gun Ri. The U.S. Review Team did not find that the Korean deaths and injuries occurred exactly as described in the Korean account. To appraise these events, it is necessary to recall the circumstances of the period. U.S. forces on occupation duty in Japan, mostly without training for, or experience in, combat were suddenly ordered to join ROK forces in defending against a determined assault by well-armed and well-trained NKPA forces employing both conventional and guerilla warfare tactics. The U.S. troops had to give up position after position. In the week beginning July 25, 1950, the 1st Cavalry Division, withdrawing from Yongdong toward the Naktong River, passed through the vicinity of No Gun Ri. Earlier, roads and trails in South Korea had been choked with civilians fleeing south. Disguised NKPA soldiers had mingled with these refugees. U.S. and ROK commanders had published a policy designed to limit the threat from NKPA infiltrators, to protect U.S. forces from attacks from the rear, and to prevent civilians from interfering with the flow of supplies and troops. The ROK National Police were supposed to control and strictly limit the movements of innocent refugees.

In these circumstances, especially given the fact that many of the U.S. soldiers lacked combat-experienced officers and Non-commissioned officers, some soldiers may have fired out of fear in response to a perceived enemy threat without considering the possibility that they might be firing on Korean civilians.

Neither the documentary evidence nor the U.S. veterans' statements reviewed by the U.S. Review Team support a hypothesis of deliberate killing of Korean civilians. What befell civilians in the vicinity of No Gun Ri in late July 1950 was a tragic and deeply regrettable accompaniment to a war forced upon unprepared U.S. and ROK forces.

PRESIDENT'S ECONOMIC REPORT, ECONOMIC ADVISERS' REPORT
January 12, 2001

In his last economic report to Congress, delivered a week before he left office, President Bill Clinton hailed the eight years of prosperity and economic progress that had marked his two terms in office. During his presidency, some 22 million jobs were created, unemployment and inflation were low, and the federal government began to run a budget surplus for the first time in thirty years.

But for more than a year before Clinton left the White House, the economy had been demonstrating clear signs of slowing. The final months of 2000 were marked by falling stock prices, tumbling business profits, and increasing numbers of workers laid off from their jobs. By the time Republican George W. Bush was sworn in as president on January 20, 2001, the longest recorded expansion in U.S. history was drawing to a close and economic growth was slowing in much of the rest of the world as well.

Still, the United States might have escaped a recession had it not been for the events of September 11, when terrorists flew three highjacked commercial airliners into the World Trade Center in New York and the Pentagon in suburban Washington—not coincidentally the two most prominent symbols of American economic and military might. The attacks had a devastating effect on the travel and tourism industries around the world, causing huge revenue losses and widespread layoffs. By the end of the year, a sudden drop in the economy had also wiped out the year's federal budget surplus, which had already been eroded by diminishing tax revenues during the early stages of a recession. (Post-attack economy, p. 663)

Clinton's Final Economic Report

Bill Clinton gained the presidency in 1992 largely because voters blamed the first President Bush for not paying enough attention to the economy, which was still feeling the lingering effects of a recession during 1990 and 1991. Unemployment in that election year stood at 7.5 percent, the highest rate in nearly ten years, and the federal budget deficit was $290 billion. During Clinton's presidency unemployment fell to its lowest levels in thirty *years, the budget deficit turned into a sizable and growing surplus, productivity growth rates quickened, real income increased, net worth increased even more, and inflation remained low.*

In its report to Congress, released January 12, Clinton's Council of Economic Advisers (CEA) attributed the expansion to three mutually reinforcing factors that coincided in the 1990s to create the "new economy": technological innovation, better business management, and federal fiscal discipline. The high-tech sector grew exponentially as businesses and consumers rushed to take advantage of the new opportunities created by innovations in computer hardware and software, telecommunications, and information processing technology. In 1999, according to the CEA, business spending on information technology equipment and software accounted for more than 11 percentage points of the 14 percent real growth in total equipment and software spending by business.

At the same time, the other sectors of the economy began to find ways to use the new technologies to streamline their operations and work more efficiently, thus producing more with less labor. The Clinton administration managed to prod and push Congress into agreeing to tax and spending limits that put the budget deficit on a downward course. Declining federal budget deficits helped to keep interest rates down and spurred private investment both at home and abroad, creating new markets, which in turn allowed for more growth.

The economic picture during the Clinton years was mixed overseas, however. The world's number two and three economies—Japan and Germany—were sluggish during most of the 1990s; Japan, in fact, suffered periodic recessions following the collapse in 1991 of its "bubble economy," which was based largely on speculative investments in an overheated real estate market. Financial crises in Mexico in 1994–1995 and in East Asia in 1997–1998 had widespread implications for developing countries worldwide, affecting countries as diverse as Argentina and Russia. China, which was transforming its economy from communism to a mixture of socialism and capitalism, was one of the few major countries that experienced sustained economic growth throughout the decade. (Japanese economy, p. 304; Asian financial crisis, Historic Documents of 1998, p. 532)

Ominous Signs

Clinton's economic advisers painted a cautiously optimistic picture for 2001 and beyond. "Core inflation remains low, inventories in most industries remain lean in relation to sales, and the outlook for the economy remains good," they said. The advisers projected that the gross domestic product would rise 3.2 percent during the year and stay at about that level through 2007. A key factor, the advisers said, would be the rate of growth in productivity. If productivity continued to grow at an annual level of 3 percent or more, they said, economic growth could continue.

Despite such optimism, no one expected the surging U.S. economy of the 1990s to last forever, and during the election year of 2000 early warning signs portended a slowdown. In fact, the Federal Reserve Board and most

*economists suggested that the nation should hope for a "soft landing"—
a slowly weakening economy, followed by a brief recession, and then a
steady recovery—rather than a sudden crash.*

*Perhaps the most visible sign of trouble had been the swoon of high tech-
nology stocks on Wall Street during much of 2000. Following a banner year
in 1999, stocks of computer manufacturers, software developers, telecommunications firms, and especially Internet startup companies were ham-
mered in 2000. In many cases, investors were simply correcting for their
earlier overenthusiasm in buying stocks of companies that showed lots of
promise but had yet to demonstrate any prospect of turning a profit. But
many analysts said the collapse of computer industry stock prices also
reflected a deeper concern that economic growth was on the downhill slide.*

*Whether it was a self-fulfilling prophecy or not, final figures for 2000
showed that those concerns were justified. Real gross domestic product, the
value of all the goods and services produced in the United States, grew at an
overall rate of 4.1 percent in 2000, but the economy slowed markedly in the
second half of the year. In the fourth quarter the economy grew at a rate of
1.4 percent, the worst quarterly growth since 1995, the last time the economy flirted with a recession.*

*Trends were mixed in 2001. First quarter figures released April 27
showed that the gross domestic product had grown by 2 percent, apparently
fueled by consumer spending. This result was significantly better than during the fourth quarter of 2000 and better than many forecasters had predicted. Even so, investors clearly were concerned, and Wall Street sagged
during March, when the Dow-Jones Industrial Average plummeted by more
than 800 points in a single week.*

*In Washington, political leaders began the customary process of assess-
ing blame. Speaking to reporters and then to a gathering of chambers of
commerce, Bush on March 15 expressed concern that "a lot of Americans'
portfolios have been affected" by the steep slide in stock prices. But the president insisted he had a recipe for a cure: a proposed $1.6 trillion tax cut plan
he had presented to Congress. Bush insisted that cutting taxes would stimulate the economy by encouraging investment and spending. "To create economic growth and opportunity, we must put money back into the hands of
the people who buy goods and create jobs," he said in his speech to a joint
session of Congress on February 27. (Bush speech, p. 171)*

*Democrats laid at least some of the blame for the sagging economy di-
rectly on Bush, who they said was "talking down" the economy to build support for his tax cut. Democrats also noted statements by many economists,
including by Bush's own Treasury secretary, Paul H. O'Neill, that the tax
plan would have little immediate economic impact because most of the cuts
would not go into effect for several years. Congress addressed that concern
by adding to Bush's plan an immediate "tax rebate" of up to $300 for indi-
viduals, $500 for single parents, and $600 for married couples. Congress
approved a $1.35 trillion, ten-year tax cut on May 26 and Bush signed it
into law (PL 107-16) on June 7. The rebate checks arrived in mailboxes dur-*

ing the late summer, but most analysts said the $39 billion worth of new spending money would have only limited impact on the country's $10 trillion economy. (Tax cut, p. 400)

While the political bantering was getting underway in Washington, the Federal Reserve Board launched an aggressive attempt to use monetary policy to ensure that the economy had a soft landing. On January 3 the board began cutting its target for the federal funds interest rate, the interest rate financial institutions charge each other on overnight loans. The first cut was 0.5 percent (or 50 basis points), moving the federal funds rate from 6.50 percent, where it had been for much of 2000, to 6.0 percent. During the course of the year, the board lowered the rate ten more times, bringing the federal funds rate to 1.75 percent on December 11, its lowest point in forty years.

The Slowdown

The slowdown came in the second quarter, and it appeared to be the hoped-for soft landing. Adjusted for inflation, growth in the April-June period was just 0.3 percent, which basically was no growth at all. Still, many economists had been expecting much worse, and they viewed the statistic as an indication that the economy had reached its low point and would now begin to grow.

Economists offered many explanations for the slowdown. One specific they pointed to was an increase in energy prices, which had begun to rise late in 2000, eroding consumer and business confidence. These concerns were heightened by a brief but severe "energy crisis" in California, where an ill-planned deregulation of the energy industries, coupled with other factors, had sent wholesale energy prices soaring, even as supply failed to keep pace with demand. A series of six one-day energy blackouts in California had captured the nation's attention and spawned unfounded fears of a broader energy crisis. (Energy crisis, p. 331)

The first half of the year saw the emergence of the typical economic cycle in a downturn: retail sales weakened; profits declined, causing investors to pull out of the stock market, thereby reducing the amount of money available for business investment; and manufacturing companies in turn cut back on production in hopes of being able to get rid of inventories.

Production cutbacks, of course, meant layoffs, which eroded consumer confidence even further. Early in the year some of the nations' best known companies pared back employment, in some cases by the tens of thousands. Among the big names shedding jobs were Montgomery Ward, General Motors, Lucent Technologies, Sara Lee, Whirlpool, Aetna, Chase Manhattan, Goodyear Tire and Rubber, Dell Computer, and Nortel Networks. Many firms delayed layoffs as long as possible, hoping that the downturn would be short. Moreover, employers had painful memories of the tight labor market in the late 1990s, when a "full employment economy" had cut the unemployment rate to historic lows and given workers increased bargaining power. As an alternative to layoffs, firms cut back on overtime and used temporary employees as much as possible. Many thousands of the jobs "lost" to layoffs were held by overseas workers of U.S.-based multinational corporations or were buy-outs of employees nearing retirement who accepted generous early retirement packages.

Unemployment, which in 1999 had reached a thirty-year record low of 4.2 percent, gradually rose to 4.5 percent in July 2001 and then to 4.9 percent in August. Most of the job loss came in the manufacturing sector, which shed 1 million workers between the early summer of 2000 and the summer of 2001; by the latter date, fewer people worked in U.S. manufacturing plants than at any time since 1964. On a regional basis, the Midwest and the South were hardest hit by the manufacturing slowdown.

Global Slowdown

The slowing of the U.S. economy—by far the world's largest—had an almost automatic effect on the rest of the world. Most European economies grew less than 2 percent overall in 2001, about the same as the United States and well below initial forecasts. By mid-year Japan had slipped back into recession after being in the economic doldrums for the last decade. Singapore was also in recession, and with the U.S. and other export markets contracting, growth was down in virtually every other major Asian economy except China. Mexico fell into recession in April. Brazil was suffering from high interest rates. Argentina, which had been in recession for three years, fell into deep economic and political turmoil at the end of the year and appeared on the verge of the largest overseas loan default in world history. (Japan's economic problems, p. 304)

This "synchronized" downturn, affecting nearly the entire world simultaneously, developed in part because of the trend known as globalization: the growing interdependence of all nations through international trade and investment. The globalized economy at the turn of the century was more sensitive than ever before to both upswings and downswings in one or two major economies. But if the overall trend was obvious, the exact causes were not always clear. Even Federal Reserve Board Chairman Alan Greenspan was forced to admit to a congressional committee in June that "we don't yet fully understand all the elements" that made the world's economies affect each other more than they once did.

One factor was thought to be world trade, which in 2000 accounted for 25 percent of world economic output—double the percentage in 1970. Much of that trade involved the United States, and the countries most affected by the slowdown were among America's largest trading partners. Globalization of finance and investment was another factor. The same major investors were involved in all major stock and bond markets, while the same banks were lending in all the major economies. According to conventional wisdom, economic events in one country tended to cause investors and lenders to reduce their exposure not only in that country but elsewhere. Economists also cited the increase of multinational corporations as a factor. When a multinational was doing well, it tended to expand investment and employment in all its sectors. Conversely, when it sustained a loss in one country, it tended to pull back everywhere. As the multinationals ex-panded and contracted, so did their suppliers, sending ripple effects deeper into each affected country's economy.

In this context, some economists and policymakers were uncertain about the factors that might fuel a global resurgence. The last time the U.S. econ-omy was in recession, in 1990–1991, Japan's economy was still growing; together with the strong German and emerging Asian economies, Japan provided an engine that helped drive the U.S. recovery. "At this point, the formula for global recovery has got to be more complex than simply provid-ing modest tax and interest rate cuts to the U.S. economy," Jeffrey E. Garten, dean of Yale University's School of Management, told the Washington Post *in July. "The complacency shown by the political leaders I find really dangerous."*

Bush insisted he was not complacent, and by Labor Day he began shifting his focus from education—which he had previously called his top priority—to the economy. In a speech to a union group in Wisconsin on September 3, Bush said he was worried about rising unemployment and its effect on families. "I'm concerned our economy is not as good as it should be," he said, calling growth "anemic." Just eight days later, the terrorist attacks in New York and Washington made even the "anemic" term seem optimistic.

> *Following are the text of President Bill Clinton's last economic report to Congress and excerpts from chapter 1 of the Annual Re-port of the Council of Economic Advisers, both released Janu-ary 12, 2001.*

> **The documents were obtained from the Internet at http:// w3.access.gpo.gov/eop/index.html.**

ECONOMIC REPORT OF THE PRESIDENT

To the Congress of the United States:

I am pleased to report that the American economy today is strong. We are enjoying the longest economic expansion ever recorded, with more than 22 million new jobs since 1993, the lowest unemployment rate in 30 years, the lowest female unemployment rate in 40 years, the lowest Hispanic and African-American unemployment rates ever recorded, and the highest home ownership rate on record.

This economic expansion has been not only unusually long, but also broad and deep. For the first time in decades, wages are rising at all income levels. We have the lowest child poverty in 20 years and the lowest poverty rate for single mothers ever recorded. Since 1993 the median family income has gone up more than $6,000, and for African-American families it has risen even more. The number of families who own stock has grown by 40 percent.

Our current economic strength is the result not of chance, but of a choice the American people made 8 years ago. At that time, 10 million of our fellow citizens were out of work. Interest rates were high. The Federal budget deficit was $290 billion and rising. And the Federal debt had quadrupled in the previous 12 years, imposing a crushing burden on our economy and on our children.

The American people chose to change direction, and empowered by that choice, Vice President Gore and I put in place a new economic strategy: fiscal discipline, greater investment in our people, and expanded trade. The result of that three-part strategy has been 8 years of prosperity and progress. Continuing with this proven strategy is the best way to keep that prosperity and progress going.

The Administration's Economic Agenda

Our strategy has been based, first and foremost, on a commitment to fiscal discipline. By first cutting and then eliminating the deficit, we have helped to create a virtuous cycle of lower interest rates, greater investment, more jobs, higher productivity, and higher wages. In the process we have gone from the largest deficits in history to the largest surpluses in history. We have extended the life of the Medicare trust fund to 2025—when I was elected President, it was scheduled to go bankrupt in 1999. And we have paid off $362.5 billion in debt.

Second, our strategy has focused on investing more in education, health care, and science and technology, to strengthen our people's capacity to make the most of the new opportunities of the 21st century. We have doubled funding for Head Start, provided after-school opportunities and mentoring to more than a million young people, and begun putting 100,000 new, well-trained teachers in the early grades to lower class size. These investments, combined with an insistence on high standards for all students and accountability for results, have helped improve student achievement nationwide: reading, math, and SAT scores are all up. And with the largest expansion of college aid since the G.I. Bill, more students than ever are going on to college.

We have also invested in our people through targeted tax relief, to help Americans meet the challenges of work and child rearing. Last year alone, our HOPE Scholarship and Lifetime Learning tax credits helped 10 million families pay for college. Our expansion of the Earned Income Tax Credit will help 15 million families work their way toward the middle class. And 25 million families will get a $500 child tax credit. The typical American family today is paying a lower share of its income in Federal income taxes than at any time during the past 35 years.

Since 1993 we have increased funding for long-term research and development—investments that lead to more economic growth, more high-wage jobs, more cures for diseases, and a cleaner environment. Funding for the National Institutes of Health, for instance, has nearly doubled over the past 7 years.

Meanwhile we have continued to make important investments in our Nation's communities. Our Empowerment Zone tax credits are bringing new business and new jobs to our hardest pressed communities, from the inner cities to Appalachia to the Mississippi Delta to Native American communities. With the help of 100,000 more community police officers funded for our streets, and commonsense measures such as the Brady law and the assault weapons ban that keep guns out of the wrong hands, crime has fallen to a 26-year low. Under the State Children's Health Insurance Program, 2 million previously uninsured children now have health coverage.

Third, our economic strategy has focused on opening markets around the world. Today, with more than 300 new trade agreements in place, including the North American Free Trade Agreement and the Uruguay Round agreements, American workers and firms are competing in more markets than ever before, and our economy is stronger for it.

Continuing Our Economic Strategy

Last year we took important new actions to secure our economic future, guided by the same three-part strategy. We normalized trade with China, a move that will open China's markets to American products from wheat to cars to consulting services. It will also ensure that American companies will be better able to sell goods in China without having to move factories or investments there. Congress also passed, and I signed, a 2001 budget that maintains our commitment to fiscal discipline. Under this new budget we will continue to pay down the debt. If we stay on this path, we can make America debt-free by 2012 for the first time since Andrew Jackson was President in 1835, thereby keeping interest rates low and prosperity going strong.

The 2001 budget also continues our strategy of investing in our people. It includes the largest-ever increase in funding for the National Science Foundation and major increases in funding for education. A new, $1.2 billion investment will help thousands of school districts make emergency repairs and renovations to our children's classrooms. We have increased by 25 percent the funding dedicated to our goal of hiring 100,000 new, highly qualified teachers, to reduce class size. We have nearly doubled funding for after-school programs to help more than 1.3 million students, while increasing support for teacher training and for turning around failing schools. And to open the doors of college even wider, we have increased the maximum Pell grant to an all-time high of $3,750—up nearly $1,500 since 1993.

The new budget also includes our historic New Markets and Renewal Communities Initiative, the most significant effort ever to help hard-pressed communities lift themselves up through entrepreneurship and access to new capital. With our New Markets tax credit, 40 Empowerment Zones, and 40 renewal communities, this initiative will spur billions in private investment in communities that have not yet shared in our great economic revival.

This is a unique moment in U.S. history, a time of unrivaled prosperity and progress, with few internal crises or external threats. We have the responsibility to use our good fortune wisely. If we maintain our current economic strategy, we can sustain our prosperity, expand the circle of opportunity, meet the long-term challenges of this new century, and provide our children the chance to live their dreams.

William J. Clinton
The White House
January 2001

THE ANNUAL REPORT OF THE COUNCIL OF ECONOMIC ADVISERS

The Making of the New Economy

Over the last 8 years the American economy has transformed itself so radically that many believe we have witnessed the creation of a New Economy. This *Report* presents evidence of fundamental and unanticipated changes in economic trends that justify this claim. In the 1990s, after two decades of disappointing performance, the economy enjoyed one of its most prosperous periods ever. Strong and rising growth in real gross domestic product (GDP), declining and then very low unemployment, and a low, stable core inflation rate characterize the long expansion. Even though growth moderated in the second half of 2000, the achievements of the past 8 years remain impressive.

From the first quarter of 1993 through the third quarter of 2000, real GDP grew at an average annual rate of 4.0 percent—46 percent faster than the average from 1973 to 1993. This exceptional growth reflects both strong job creation and increased productivity growth. Americans are working in record numbers: the number of payroll jobs has increased by more than 22 million since January 1993, and in 2000 the share of the population employed reached its highest level on record. Also in 2000 the unemployment rate dipped to 3.9 percent, the lowest level in a generation. Unemployment rates for African Americans and Hispanic Americans were the lowest since separate statistics for these groups were first collected in the early 1970s.

Americans are not only working more; they are also working smarter. The economy has rapidly become more productive. Since the beginning of 1993, output per hour in the nonfarm business sector has grown at an average rate of 2.3 percent per year, compared with an average of 1.4 percent per year for the previous 20 years. Even more remarkably, since the fourth quarter of 1995 productivity growth has averaged 3 percent per year. This acceleration in productivity has produced higher incomes and greater wealth. From 1993 to 1999, the real income of the median household grew more than in any period of similar length in the last 30 years. Meanwhile the value of corporate stocks has nearly trebled, even after taking into account the downward adjustment in stock prices during 2000.

These income gains have also been widely shared: even incomes at the bottom of the distribution have risen rapidly. Disadvantaged groups have seen their situation improve markedly. The overall poverty rate declined to

11.8 percent in 1999 (the most recent year for which data are available), its lowest level since 1979 and 3.3 percentage points below the rate in 1993. The poverty rate for African Americans was 23.6 percent in 1999—still too high, but far below the 1993 level of 33.1 percent. The poverty rates for Hispanic Americans and elderly Americans have also fallen sharply. . . .

The Economy from 1973 to 1993

The remarkable economic trends of the 1990s took many by surprise. They represent a distinct change from the 1970s and 1980s, decades in which the economy was plagued by persistent inflation, periodically high unemployment, slow growth in productivity, rising inequality, and large Federal budget deficits. Stagflation was an unwelcome phenomenon of the 1970s, as two major oil shocks were followed by simultaneous inflation and recession. The massive and costly recession of the early 1980s and the collapse of oil prices in 1986 broke the back of the very high inflation rates that had emerged in the late 1970s. But as unemployment fell below 6 percent in the late 1980s, core inflation started to climb again. Between 1973 and 1993, GDP growth received a boost from the large numbers of women and baby-boomers entering the work force. But at the same time, persistently slow productivity growth (averaging less than half of what it had been during the preceding 25 years) kept GDP growth in check.

These trends affected the incidence of poverty. In the 1960s and early 1970s, poverty had been declining as economic progress gradually raised the incomes of those at the bottom. The nationwide poverty rate, which had stood at 22.2 percent in 1960, fell to 11.1 percent in 1973. But the combination of slow productivity growth and a relatively slack labor market likely played a role in ending this improvement, dragging down household incomes, especially for the poorest. The poverty rate continued to fluctuate, falling during expansions in the business cycle and rising during contractions. However, throughout the 1980s it never fell lower than 12.8 percent, far above the low of the early 1970s. And by 1993 poverty had risen to 15.1 percent, almost matching the 1983 level of 15.2 percent, its worst since the 1960s.

Federal budget deficits had become commonplace in the 1970s, but they increased rapidly in the 1980s in the presence of a fiscal policy based on overly optimistic budget forecasts. Efforts to restore fiscal discipline in 1990 failed because of a weakening economy, and deficits grew worse rather than better, reaching almost $300 billion in fiscal 1992. By the end of fiscal 1981, publicly held Federal debt had fallen to 25.8 percent of GDP. By the end of fiscal 1993 it had almost doubled, to 49.5 percent.

Given these problems, few believed in 1993 that the U.S. economy could achieve and sustain low unemployment rates, moderate inflation, or robust productivity growth, let alone all three. The Federal Government seemed incapable of balancing its budget, and there was little to suggest that U.S. incomes could grow more rapidly than those in other major industrial countries. Yet in the years that followed, all of these seemingly improbable events occurred—and at the same time.

What Makes the Economy New?

The U.S. economy today displays several exceptional features. The first is its strong rate of productivity growth. Since 1995 the trend rate of productivity growth has been more than double that of the 1973-95 period. A second is its unusually low levels of both inflation and unemployment. In the past, low levels of unemployment have usually meant sharply rising inflation. Yet despite an unemployment rate that has been close to (and at times below) 4 percent for 2 years, core inflation has remained in the 2 to 3 percent range. A third is the disappearance of Federal budget deficits. Federal fiscal policy often becomes more expansionary as a period of economic growth is sustained, yet in the past 8 years the structural budget balance has moved steadily from a massive deficit to a large surplus. A fourth is the strength of the U.S. economy's performance relative to other industrial economies. As a world technological leader, the United States might have been expected to grow more slowly than countries that can benefit from imitating the leader's technological advances. Yet over the second half of the 1990s, the United States continued to enjoy both the highest income per capita and the fastest income growth of the major industrial nations. These developments reveal profound changes in economic trends that justify the term "New Economy."

Three interrelated factors lie behind these extraordinary economic gains: technological innovation, organizational changes in businesses, and public policy. Information technology has long been important to the economy. But in the early 1990s a number of simultaneous advances in information technology—computer hardware, software, and telecommunications—allowed these new technologies to be combined in ways that sharply increased their economic potential.

In part to realize this potential, entrepreneurs instituted widespread changes in business organizations, reconfiguring their existing businesses and starting new ones. These changes included new production methods and human resource management practices, new types of relationships with suppliers and customers, new business strategies (with some firms expanding the scope of their enterprises through mergers and acquisitions, and others streamlining them to best utilize core competencies), and new forms of finance and compensation.

Public policy was the third driving force. This Administration embraced policies and strategies based on fiscal discipline, investing in people and technologies, opening new markets at home and abroad, and developing an institutional framework that supported continued global integration. Together these created an environment in which the new technologies and organizational changes could flourish.

The interactions among these three factors have created a virtuous cycle in which developments in one area reinforce and stimulate developments in another. The result is an economic system in which the whole is greater than the sum of its parts. New technologies have created opportunities for organizational innovations, and these innovations in turn have engendered demand for these technologies and others still newer. The increased growth prompted by the new technologies helped the Federal Government restrain its spending growth and boosted its revenue; the resulting smaller budget deficits (and later surpluses) have helped keep interest rates down, encouraging further investment in new technologies. Economic policies directed toward promoting competition have prodded firms to adopt the new technologies, spurring other firms to innovate or be left behind. Policies aimed at opening foreign markets have increased earnings in the U.S. technology sector, leading to yet more innovation, including innovation in information technologies, which have lowered barriers to trade and investment still further. These market-opening policies have also allowed U.S. producers to become more productive, by expanding the variety of key inputs available to them.

This Report defines the New Economy by the extraordinary gains in performance—including rapid productivity growth, rising incomes, low unemployment, and moderate inflation—that have resulted from this combination of mutually reinforcing advances in technologies, business practices, and economic policies.

Sustaining the Virtuous Cycle

Americans can be gratified by the achievements of the last 8 years, but we must not become complacent. The economy has been performing well for so long now that there is a danger of taking growth for granted. There are good reasons to believe that the long-term trend rate of productivity growth has increased relative to the post-1973 trend, and many new technologies do not yet appear to have exhausted their potential for further improvements. On the other hand, more moderate economic growth is projected for 2001 and beyond. . . .

In addition, it would be a grave error to assume that the economy has been so transformed that the basic rules of economics no longer apply. The potential for faster growth exists, but demand cannot run ahead of supply without the danger of rising inflation. The economy also remains susceptible to cyclical fluctuations. Indeed, the rewards of the New Economy are associated with increased risk, since the economy depends more heavily than before on financial markets, which remain volatile.

Abandoning the public policies that have helped transform the economy would also be a mistake. The current prosperity certainly reflects, above all, the efforts of the private sector, but it would be wrong—and dangerous—to ignore the contribution of policy. In particular, it would be risky to put aside the policies that have helped us move from huge budget deficits to large surpluses and have laid the groundwork for the capital formation that has been so important in stimulating growth. It would be just as dangerous to undermine the policies that have supported the investments in people and technologies that are the keys to advancing productivity. It would be folly to abandon the efforts to increase competition in markets at home and abroad, because it is this competition that helped create a domestic business environment in which entrepreneurs can flourish and a global economy from which all Americans can benefit. Finally, the government should continue its efforts to ensure that prosperity is more widely shared, because this is something the private sector will not automatically accomplish on its own. . . .

Information Technology and the New Economy

Spending on information technology has clearly played a leading role in the recent acceleration of economic growth. Although this sector remains a fairly small part of the economy—its share of GDP was an estimated 8.3 percent in 2000—it accounted for almost one-third of all output growth between 1995 and 1999. Even more remarkable, in 1999 business spending on information technology equipment and software was responsible for more than 11 percentage points of the 14 percent real growth in total equipment and software spending by business. The information technology sector is also one that has seen a surge in innovation. To be sure, the computer, the cell phone, optical fibers, lasers, and the Internet had all been invented before the mid-1990s. But over the course of that decade, a series of innovations in computer hardware and software and in telecommunications took place that has allowed for new and complementary interactions among these technologies on an unprecedented scale—a dramatic example of which is the emergence and increasing commercial use of the World Wide Web.

There is a broad consensus that information technology has been important in the recent surge in economic performance. But the role of developments beyond this sector remains more controversial. One view of the recent economic transformation identifies the New Economy narrowly with the production and use of information technology. Some proponents of this view argue that performance in the rest of the economy has simply followed previous trends, or that the recent strong economic growth has boosted it only temporarily.

Although the innovation and diffusion of information technology have clearly been important, the broader definition of the New Economy adopted in this *Report* more accurately conveys the pervasiveness of the recent economic changes. A growing body of evidence now shows that the widespread application of information technologies has stimulated remarkable improvements in production processes and other business practices outside the information technology sector. But innovations in information technology and its use have not been the only source of such change. Indeed, there has been a surge in innovation in other technologies as well. Together with supportive public policies, these changes have fundamentally transformed the economy. An examination of recent productivity growth supports this view.

The New Trend in Productivity Growth

Productivity is now growing considerably faster than it did over the 20 years after 1973. What can be said about the sources of this acceleration? Two simple analyses help to answer this question. The first estimates the contributions to growth in aggregate private nonfarm business productivity from each of the different sources of that growth, such as increases in the amount of capital per worker. The second uses data on output and employment by industry to pinpoint the areas of economic activity where the acceleration has taken place.

Sources of Growth: Capital, Labor Quality, and Total Factor Productivity

A standard model of economic growth allows us to estimate how various sources have contributed to the recent acceleration of productivity. [P]roductivity, measured as output per hour in the private nonfarm business sector, accelerated in the late 1990s. Its growth rate rose from an annual average of 1.4 percent before 1995 to an annual average of 3.0 percent from 1995 through 2000. The total acceleration from the first period to the second is thus slightly more than 1.6 percentage points. . . . The first question to ask about this total acceleration is how much, if any, of it is the result of business cycle effects and how much is structural.

Productivity Growth and the Business Cycle

Productivity growth varies over the course of the business cycle, typically speeding up in the early stages of booms and slowing or even turning negative in slumps. But changes in productivity also have an underlying structural, or trend, component. There is no foolproof way to tease apart these cyclical and structural components in the productivity changes one actually observes. The increase in productivity growth after 1995, however, is noteworthy in that it occurred at a time when the economy already was enjoying a high rate of resource utilization. Sharp increases in productivity have usually occurred in economies recovering from recession. By contrast, since 1995 the U.S. economy has followed a steeper productivity trend, which started well after the 1990-91 recession was over.

Statistical estimates suggest that almost none of the acceleration in productivity after 1995 has been cyclical. . . . From 1995 through 2000, the cyclical component of productivity edged up only slightly relative to its trend, so that actual productivity grew only slightly faster (by 0.04 percentage point) than structural productivity. As of the third quarter of 2000, the cyclical component of productivity was still above trend, suggesting that actual productivity growth is likely to fall below trend growth over the next year or so, as GDP growth moderates. But the estimates indicate that there has been a structural acceleration in productivity since 1995 of slightly less than 1.6 percentage points. . . .

The fact of a shift in the trend of structural productivity growth does not tell us how permanent that shift will turn out to be. All one can say is that the post-1995 acceleration does not appear to be associated with the normal business cycle variation of productivity. Whether the structural trend that emerged in 1995-2000 will continue for many more years, or whether structural productivity growth will moderate sooner, remains uncertain. We could be observing not a long-term shift to a faster productivity growth rate but simply a shift to a higher level of productivity, with faster growth for a while followed by a return to the pre-1995 trend. Or we may be witnessing the opportunity for faster trend growth over a longer time span. . . .

Contributors to the Structural Productivity Acceleration

In general, a structural acceleration in productivity can come from an increase in any of the following four sources of growth or their combination:

- growth in the amount of capital per worker-hour throughout the economy (capital deepening)
- improvements in the measurable skills of the work force, or labor quality
- total factor productivity (TFP) growth in computer-producing industries, and
- TFP growth in other industries.

TFP growth is the increase in aggregate output over and above that due to increases in the quantities of capital or labor inputs. For example, TFP growth may result when a firm redesigns its production line in a way that increases output while keeping the same number of machines, materials, and workers as before.

Capital investment has been extremely strong during the current expansion. Particularly after 1995, investment in computers and software responded markedly to robust economic growth, low real interest rates, a strong stock market, and rapidly falling computer prices. [I]nvestment in information technologies added slightly more than 0.6 percentage point to the increase in structural productivity growth after 1995. Because the rate of investment in capital goods other than computer hardware and software slowed during that period, the contribution of overall capital deepening to increased productivity growth was only about 0.4 percentage point, or roughly 24 percent of the post-1995 acceleration of structural productivity.

The Bureau of Labor Statistics measures labor quality in terms of the education, gender, and experience of the work force. Using statistical methods, the Bureau determines differences in earnings paid to workers with different characteristics and infers that these relative wage differences reflect relative productivity differences. Measured in this way, labor quality has risen as the education and skills of the work force have increased. Because that increase occurred at about the same rate before and after 1995, however, the contribution of labor quality to the recent acceleration in productivity has been negligible.

The rate of growth in TFP in computer-producing industries has been rising. Computer prices have been falling as technological improvements are adopted and made available commercially. The decline in prices was particularly marked from 1997 to 1999. Calculations based on these price changes indicate that computer manufacturing accounts for about 0.2 percentage point, or about 11 percent, of the acceleration in structural productivity.

The final contribution comes from accelerating TFP in the economy outside the computer-producing industries. The contribution of this "non- computer sector TFP" category is calculated as a residual; it captures the extent to which technological change and other business and workplace improvements outside the computer sector have boosted productivity growth since 1995. This factor accounts for about 1.0 percentage point of the acceleration in productivity, or about 63 percent of the total. (The percentages do not sum to 100 because of rounding.) This implies that improvements in the ways capital and labor are used throughout the economy are central to the recent acceleration in productivity. Some of these gains have likely resulted as firms learn to apply innovative information technology to their particular business and production methods.

Productivity Increases by Sector and Industry

The figures reported above indicate that both the more widespread use of information technology and improvements in business practices have boosted productivity growth. Data on productivity growth by industry provide a further means of exploring this idea. If the story is correct, these data should show, for example, an acceleration in productivity in wholesale and retail trade as a result of improvements in distribution and supply chain management. Improvements would also be expected in financial and business services, both of which are heavy users of information technology. . . .

Striking evidence of improvements in distribution and in the management of the supply chain comes from wholesale and retail trade, both of which experienced much faster productivity growth after 1995. In 1999 these industries accounted for 25 percent of full-time equivalent employees in private industry. Output in these industries increased significantly without corresponding increases in employment.

Data for financial institutions as a group also show an acceleration in productivity after 1995, supporting the view that these heavy users of information technology have performed well. Within financial institutions, however, this observation holds true only for nondepository institutions and brokers. Banks and other depository institutions experienced a reduction in productivity growth after 1995. The insurance industry also experienced an acceleration in productivity, reversing what had previously been negative productivity growth.

The services sector showed an acceleration in productivity, but this sector still experienced negative productivity growth after 1995. Business services shifted from negative to positive productivity growth, as did personal services. Health services, the largest industry in this sector, reduced its rate of productivity decline.

On balance, the pattern of productivity growth by industry is consistent with (although it does not prove) the view that improved business practices and more-productive use of information technology have played an important role in the acceleration of productivity. In addition, some of the gain in productivity is presumably associated with capital deepening. . . .

Learning from the New Productivity Trends

The breakdown of the sources of accelerated productivity and the analysis of industry data suggest three important lessons:

- The information technology sector itself has provided a direct boost to productivity growth. Part of the recent surge in productivity is the direct result of productivity growth within this sector.
- The spread of information technology throughout the economy has been a major factor in the acceleration of productivity through capital deepening. Increasingly, companies have been eager and able to buy powerful computers at relatively low prices. The rapid advances in computer technology, together with favorable economic conditions, have fueled a computer and software investment boom.
- Outside the information technology sector, organizational innovations and better ways of applying information technology are boosting the productivity of skilled workers. A variety of changes that go beyond the direct application of new computer technology, including structural changes in private businesses and more effective use of worker skills, have further boosted productivity.

What accounts for the changes revealed in this productivity analysis? Answering this question requires moving behind the aggregate and industry numbers to consider three sets of complementary developments: changes within the information technology sector, changes in other sectors, and changes in economic policy.

Innovations in the
Information Technology Sector

Dramatic developments occurred within the information technology sector in the 1990s, particularly in the second half of the decade, when the pace of innovation accelerated. . . .

The process by which new information technologies are created in the United States has undergone a number of major changes that have transformed the ways in which such innovation occurs. In much of the postwar period, defense spending was a major driver of innovation, and the Federal budget was a more important source of R&D funding than it is today. Innovation, however, was undertaken predominantly by large manufacturers, and the U.S. economy was less integrated with the international economy than it is today. That situation has changed considerably. . . . Four developments in particular deserve mention: changes in the competitive environment, changes in organizational structures, changes in compensation and finance, and innovations in complementary technologies.

Growing Competition

The information technology sector is being driven by heightened competition in an increasingly deregulated economy in which international trade plays an ever-growing role. These pressures foster the creation and adoption of new technologies, especially in the private sector, which has begun to play a greater role in innovation since the end of the Cold War. When businesses bring innovations to market, their rivals are given strong incentives to innovate as well. In the area of information technology, the firm that is the first to gain market acceptance for a new type of product often gets to set the standard for that product, and therefore is most likely to capture the lion's share of the market. The innovating firm can then exploit its early success, to develop the next generation of technology and products. The prospect of second-generation success thus raises the premium on rapid innovation.

For firms to have strong financial incentives to innovate, there must be strong demand for such innovation from other firms in other industries. Almost 70 percent of all information technology products are purchased by the wholesale and retail trade, finance, and telecommunications industries. Competition in these industries (often on a global level) encourages them to seek out new technologies to improve their own productivity. Unlike in some other countries, in which barriers to entry, pricing restrictions, and other business restrictions restrain competition, in the United States competitive pressures are generally strong. Deregulation in finance and telecommunications has helped create an increasingly competitive environment.

The number of new firms in the information technology sector is a measure of the incentives and opportunity to innovate—and the figures paint a dramatic picture. Between 1990 and 1997 the number of information technology firms more than doubled. Many innovations have come from talented individuals in small startup companies that are willing to take risks.

Organizational Changes

Competitive pressures have increased the importance of introducing new products and processes quickly. Yet the know-how required to create these products has become more complex and more dispersed. Today it is rarely cost-effective for a single firm to control an entire innovation process. As a result, businesses have altered the organizational structures within which innovation takes place.

A smaller fraction of R&D now takes place within large, integrated companies. Small firms are responsible for an increasing share of the Nation's industrial research. Collaboration between innovating firms has become commonplace, as the dramatic growth in interfirm technology alliances in the 1990s demonstrates. Furthermore, today's innovations increasingly draw upon scientific knowledge, much of which is developed by universities and national laboratories. To take advantage of this science base, private firms are now performing more basic research than ever before. And because proximity to these universities and national laboratories matters—by improving a firm's chances of capturing spillovers and of hiring high-quality researchers—innovation today is often characterized by geographic concentration into high-technology clusters such as Silicon Valley, California. In these clusters and elsewhere, many new firms, free of the constraints often imposed in large, established corporations, continually enter the market with new technologies and innovative business ideas.

Innovations in Compensation and Finance

New methods of financing have evolved to address the needs of new entrants and of R&D in the information technology sector. Traditionally, firms have used their physical plant and equipment as collateral for financing. But the unique challenges of promoting innovation in sectors where much of the know-how is based on intangible capital, plus the considerable risks involved in financing high-technology companies, have generated new institutional arrangements. Venture capital, in particular, has played a crucial role, supplying funds and providing management know-how and connections for entrepreneurs. Initial public offerings (IPOs) have also been instrumental. The information technology sector has made extensive use of new compensation mechanisms that provide incentives to talented workers and managers. For example, stock options enable firms to attract and retain talent while passing some risk on to workers. The vibrant stock market has also been important, allowing venture capitalists to cash out more easily through IPOs and enabling workers holding stock options to boost their earnings. In an important sense, success has generated success, as venture capitalists score big and then use their augmented capital to seek out new profit opportunities.

The excitement over the technology revolution drove technology stocks to extraordinary heights in the spring of 2000, although they have retreated since then. The volatility in technology equity markets can be disruptive to companies seeking new funding, but investors' willingness to take risks and the availability of financial resources for successful entrepreneurs continue to make U.S. financial markets important contributors to the New Economy. Even after the recent decline in the technology sector, price-earnings ratios remain high. This indicates that investors are still willing to take a chance on companies with low current earnings but the potential for rapid future growth.

New Complementarities

The changes in the information technology sector have been both cumulative and complementary. Innovations in one area have created demands in another. Breakthroughs in communications and data compression techniques, for instance, generate demand for improved software and for more powerful computers. Complementarities operate on both the supply and the demand sides. In particular, the falling costs associated with the use of computers have made certain types of research feasible for the first time—the mapping of the human genome, for instance, was made feasible by computers. Information technology is becoming increasingly important in the development of new treatment options, and the Food and Drug Administration uses computers to streamline the analysis and approval of new drugs. Demand is particularly powerful when it generates positive feedback through network effects. E-mail, for example, becomes increasingly useful as more people use it.

The evidence suggests, then, that a number of factors have combined to create a uniquely favorable climate for entrepreneurs. These factors include a growing demand for new and improved technologies (spurred by intense domestic and global competition and technological complementarities), the improved capacity of reorganized firms and networks to supply the new technologies, and innovations in thriving financial markets.

Innovation Throughout the Economy

Simply buying and installing new technology does not automatically increase productivity, profitability, or job creation. Yet some views of the New Economy reveal a kind of naive technological determinism that ignores the vital role of complementary changes in production and business practices. Companies throughout the U.S. economy have been radically transformed by new technologies that enable entire product networks to become more efficient, effective, and integrated. [A] few of the most important changes are noted here, including changes in production, inventory and supply management, customer relations, and corporate structure.

New Production Methods

Innovations in information technology have generated many changes in manufacturing processes. New technologies permit workers to analyze data and make detailed adjustments to production lines on the plant floor, boosting productivity, improving quality, and lowering costs. The availability of data, often on a real-time basis, allows for continuous performance evaluation that can improve efficiency. Workers who have access to information technology can be empowered with more decisionmaking responsibility. In addition, the new technology allows organizations to disseminate information and coordinate their activities more easily, resulting in less hierarchical organizational structures. In turn, these new structures may reduce costs and further increase efficiency. Finally, as in the information technology sector itself, innovations in the way workers are compensated can help firms achieve greater productivity gains from new technology, spurring further innovation in compensation and finance. Studies suggest that worker performance improves when incentives are tied more closely to performance. Stock options have become more common as a method of attracting, retaining, and rewarding employees.

Changes in Inventory
and Supply Chain Management

Firms typically hold inventories as a cushion against uncertainties. Producers keep excess raw materials and other inputs on hand to prevent shortages on the production line, for example, and stores maintain inventories to meet fluctuations in demand. The need for inventories springs in part from incomplete information about demand. For this reason, technologies that improve the dissemination of information enable companies to react more promptly to market signals and to economize on inventories (by sharing point-of-sale data, for example). Indeed, aggregate inventory-to-sales ratios have fallen significantly since the early 1990s.

The new information technologies have also changed the nature of relationships between firms and their suppliers. Procurement practices have changed radically, as firms become linked to suppliers through Internet-based business-to-business marketplaces. This capability allows businesses to streamline procurement activities, lower transactions costs, improve the management of supplier relationships, and even engage in collaborative product design. "Just-in-time" delivery, facilitated by a more efficient transportation network including both surface and aviation infrastructure, has been instrumental in allowing firms to reduce inventories and lower costs while continuing to provide essential services to producers and consumers.

New Relationships with Customers

Information technologies give firms the ability to develop richer, more targeted relationships with their customers. Firms are able to tailor marketing and product design more precisely to customer needs. Customers, in turn, are able to find and compare the products that most closely match their preferences. Scanner data from retail stores allow companies to monitor which items are selling and which are not. This information can be transmitted back to manufacturers, who can then adjust their production schedules. This avoids stockouts and surplus inventory. The information from scanners can also be used for marketing. Customers who have purchased outdoor adventure products, for example, can be sent information on related gear or travel opportunities that they may wish to purchase.

Shifting Corporate Boundaries

Markets allocate resources efficiently by setting prices, expanding choices, and encouraging competition. But in situations where pricing and writing contracts is costly and difficult, where uncertainty is high, and where information is difficult to come by, some activities may be more efficiently undertaken within the firm than in the marketplace. Transactions costs thus affect the make-or-buy decision, which determines where the firm's boundaries end and the market begins. Information technologies can radically change where these boundaries should be drawn, and this sets in motion both centrifugal and centripetal forces. An example of the latter is the large number of recent mergers, some motivated by the belief on the part of some firms that new technology allows the span of organization to be extended. [B]oth the number and the value of mergers and acquisitions have moved to new heights as firms seek to capitalize on both efficiency gains and increased market power. On the other hand, many small firms may be able to benefit by specializing in a few core activities. This can lead companies to spin off parts of their operations—an example of centrifugal forces at work. . . .

SURGEON GENERAL'S REPORT ON YOUTH VIOLENCE
January 17, 2001

The surgeon general of the United States warned Americans not to be lulled into complacency by official statistics showing a decline in the incidence of serious youth violence. Despite downward trends in measures such as arrest records and victimization data, surveys showed no change in the proportion of young people who said they had committed physically injurious and potentially lethal acts of violence. "This is no time to let down our guard on youth violence," Surgeon General David Satcher said at a news conference releasing the report. "Even so," he added, "our success in developing knowledge and tools to prevent serious violence gives us reason for optimism."

The surgeon general's report, issued January 17, 2001, was the first of several government reports released during the year that focused on the scope and causes of youth violence and possible ways to reduce it. In April and again in December the Federal Trade Commission reported on the progress—or lack of it—made by various sectors of the entertainment industry in meeting their own standards on marketing violent adult entertainment to children. The Justice Department in April released an assessment of how many localities in the country were afflicted with youth gangs. In May the governor of Colorado released the first independent study of the shootings at Columbine High School, in which two students massacred thirteen people before taking their own lives. (Columbine report, p. 347; Historic Documents of 1999, p. 179)

Continuing Epidemic of Youth Violence

Between 1983 and 1993 the United States was plagued by a crime wave that was notable for its violence and for the youth of its offenders. By 1999 youth homicide, robbery, and arrest rates had all dropped below their rates in 1983, largely due to a decrease in the use of guns in serious crime. Aggravated assaults, however, were still 70 percent higher than they had been in 1983, dropping only 24 percent from the peak rates recorded in 1994.

Moreover, surveys of teenagers themselves showed that for every youth arrested in the late 1990s, at least ten had engaged in some sort of violent behavior that could have seriously injured or killed another person. According to the report, the number of violent acts committed by high school seniors rose by nearly 50 percent over the 1980s and 1990s, similar to the trend in arrests for violent crimes. But unlike youth arrests, the number of nonfatal violent incidents and the proportion of high school seniors involved in them remained at the peak levels.

Under Satcher's guidance, researchers in three agencies—the Centers for Disease Control and Prevention, the National Institutes of Health, and the Substance Abuse and Mental Health Services Administration—examined the causes of youth violence and effective ways to prevent it. The research focused on children from approximately age ten through age eighteen or, roughly, fifth graders through twelfth graders. According to the report, violence among children fell into two general paths—violent behavior that emerged before the onset of puberty and violent behavior that emerged afterward. Although most violent behavior ended with the transition to adulthood, research showed that children who exhibited violent behavior before their teenage years were at greater risk of "persistent, even lifelong involvement in violent behavior."

The report identified twenty-seven specific intervention programs that it said had proven effective in preventing youth violence. It also challenged what it said were several false notions about youth violence, including the common myths that African American and Hispanic youths were more likely to be involved in violence than other racial and ethnic groups and that a new youthful breed of "superpredators" was menacing the United States. In fact, the report said, although more black and Hispanic youths were arrested on homicide charges, surveys showed that race and ethnicity had little bearing on the overall proportion of nonfatal youth violence. Moreover, there was no evidence showing that the violent youths during the peak crime wave years of the early 1990s were any more vicious or more frequent offenders than violent youths in earlier years.

The report said risk factors for youth violence existed in every area of life and included childhood involvement in serious but not necessarily violent crime, being male, substance abuse, physical aggression, poverty, antisocial parents, ties to antisocial or delinquent peers as adolescents, and belonging to gangs. The more risk factors a child encountered, the more likely the child was to become violent, the report said. The importance of specific risk factors was likely to change depending on the age of the child at risk. Substance use was a stronger risk factor at age nine than at age fourteen, for example.

The report said that scientists had identified only two protective factors that buffered specific risk factors: the child's commitment to school and his or her intolerance of "deviance." The report said the most effective intervention programs addressed both individual risks and environmental conditions, including building individuals skills and competencies, improving the social climate of schools, and changing the type and level of involvement in peer groups.

Spread of Gang Activity

A related report, sponsored by the Justice Department's Office of Juvenile Justice and Delinquency Prevention, attempted to determine the growth of youth gangs in the United States and found that gang activity had spread extensively—from nineteen states in the 1970s to all fifty states and the District of Columbia by 1998. The states with the most cities reporting youth gang activity in 1998 were California (363 cities), Illinois (261), Texas (156), Florida (125), and Ohio (86). Of those five states, only California and Illinois had reported a high number of cities with gang activities in the 1970s. The study also found that gang activity, once largely a big-city phenomenon, was now evident in smaller cities, towns, and villages.

The report's author, Walter B. Miller, focused his study on "traditional area-based adolescent and young adult street gangs," ages twelve to twenty-four, whose crimes included assault and predation. Not included were motorcycle gangs, hate or ideological gangs, prison gangs, or other primarily adult gangs, including drug syndicates and organized crime.

The report made no attempt to recommend how gangs might be prevented or controlled, but it offered comment on several reasons often given to explain the growth of gang activity. Growth of the drug trade and immigration were two of the more prevalent explanations cited, but the report said that while these factors no doubt contributed to gang activity, their effects were probably exaggerated. Nor was there much evidence supporting the theory that gang activity spread when local gangs migrated to other areas. Although intercity migration was common, according to one study Miller quoted, it was not the original cause of gang problems in two-thirds of the 800 cities surveyed.

The report said that the increase of female-headed households appeared to be linked to an increase in gang membership. The report also attributed the spread of gang activity in part to government antipoverty policies of the 1960s, which encouraged youth gangs in poor neighborhoods to abandon their criminal practices and to take a leading role in community improvement. Although these efforts were largely unsuccessful, they lent an air of legitimacy and acceptance of gangs and the gang lifestyle, which the report said was still embedded in the ghetto subculture. The report also said that the advent of "gangsta rap," with its explicit language about sex and violence and its glorification of the gang lifestyle, was an incentive for children and adolescents particularly in ghetto and barrio communities to join gangs.

Media and Youth

The surgeon general's report on youth violence found that exposure to violence in the media could increase "aggressive behavior" in children in the short term, but that the long-term effects of exposure were "relatively small."

Nonetheless, it said, "research to date justifies sustained efforts to curb the adverse effects of media violence on youths."

One of those efforts was an attempt to persuade the entertainment industry to stop marketing to children movies, music recordings, and computer games containing violence. In September 2000 the Federal Trade Commission (FTC) released a report lambasting all three segments of the industry for violating their own standards that gave parents some guidance about the content of the products. (Marketing violent entertainment, Historic Documents of 2000, p. 729)

In follow-up reports released in April and December 2001, the FTC said that the movie and video game industries were making "commendable progress" in limiting marketing of violent and sexually explicit violence to children. In its December report, the FTC reviewed teen magazines and previews shown before G- and PG-rated movies and found no advertising for violent adult movies. (G-rated movies were deemed suited for a general audience including children, while PG-rated movies were deemed suitable for children with parental guidance.) The FTC also said movie ads were routinely displaying ratings and the reasons for the ratings. The agency said the video game industry had made similar strides.

The FTC still found the music industry wanting. The agency acknowledged that record companies had made progress with parental advisory labels on albums, but charged that the industry "continued to advertise explicit content recordings in most popular teen venues in all media." Hilary Rosen, president of the Recording Industry Association of America, said the industry was making "tremendous progress."

Senator Joseph I. Lieberman, D-Conn., a longtime critic of the entertainment industry's marketing to children, disagreed with Rosen, saying that the recording companies "have repeated excuses for their ongoing inaction that sound more and more like a broken record trying to defend a broken system." Nonetheless, Lieberman said, he would postpone action on legislation he introduced to tighten federal regulation of the entertainment industry's marketing operations. "Marketing self-regulation is working—which was my hope all along—and there is not pressing need for government standard setting," he said.

Following are excerpts from the executive summary of a study entitled "Youth Violence: Report of the Surgeon General," released January 17, 2001.

The document was obtained from the Internet at http://www .surgeongeneral.gov/library/youthviolence/youvioreport .htm.

Youth violence is a high-visibility, high-priority concern in every sector of U.S. society. No community, whether affluent or poor, urban, suburban, or rural, is immune from its devastating effects. In the decade extending from roughly 1983 to 1993, an epidemic of violent, often lethal behavior broke out in this country, forcing millions of young people and their families to cope with injury, disability, and death. This epidemic left lasting scars on victims, perpetrators, and their families and friends. It also wounded entire communities and, in ways not yet fully understood, the United States as a whole.

Since 1993, when the epidemic peaked, youth violence has declined significantly nationwide, as signaled by downward trends in arrest records, victimization data, and hospital emergency room records. But the problem has not been resolved. Another key indicator of violence—youths' confidential reports about their violent behavior—reveals no change since 1993 in the proportion of young people who have committed physically injurious and potentially lethal acts. Moreover, arrests for aggravated assault have declined only slightly and in 1999 remained nearly 70 percent higher than pre-epidemic levels. In 1999, there were 104,000 arrests of people under age 18 for a serious violent crime—robbery, forcible rape, aggravated assault, or homicide. Of these, 1,400 were for homicides committed by adolescents and, on occasion, even younger children. But viewing homicide arrests as a barometer of all youth violence is quite misleading, as is judging the success of violence prevention efforts solely on the basis of reductions in homicides.

Arrest records give only a partial picture of youth violence. For every youth arrested in any given year in the late 1990s, at least 10 were engaged in some form of violent behavior that could have seriously injured or killed another person, according to the several national research surveys in which youths report on their own behavior. Thus, despite reductions in the lethality of violence and consequent arrests, the number of adolescents involved in violent behavior remains disconcertingly high, underscoring the urgency of this report.

This is no time for complacency. The epidemic of lethal violence that swept the United States from 1983 to 1993 was fueled in large part by easy access to weapons, notably firearms. If the sizable numbers of youths still involved in violence today begin carrying and using weapons as they did a decade ago, this country may see a resurgence of the lethal violence that characterized the violence epidemic.

To address the troubling presence of violence in the lives of U.S. youths, the Administration and Congress urged the Surgeon General to develop a report on youth violence, with particular focus on the scope of the problem, its causes, and how to prevent it. Surgeon General Dr. David Satcher requested three agencies, all components of the Department of Health and Human Services, to share lead responsibility for preparing the report. The agencies are the Centers for Disease Control and Prevention (CDC), the National Institutes of Health (NIH), and the Substance Abuse and Mental Health Services Administration (SAMHSA).

Under Dr. Satcher's guidance, these agencies established a Planning Board comprising individuals with expertise in diverse disciplines and professions involved in the study, treatment, and prevention of youth violence. The Planning Board also enlisted individuals representing various Federal departments, including particularly the Department of Justice (juvenile crime aspects of youth violence), the Department of Education (school safety issues), and the Department of Labor (the association between youth violence and youth employment, and out-of-school youth). Invaluable assistance was obtained as well from individual citizens who have founded and operate nonprofit organizations designed to meet the needs of troubled and violent youths. Most important, young people themselves accepted invitations to become involved in the effort. All of these persons helped to plan the report and participated in its prepublication reviews.

This report—the first Surgeon General's report on youth violence—is a product of extensive collaboration. It reviews a massive body of research on where, when, and how much youth violence occurs, what causes it, and which of today's many preventive strategies are genuinely effective. Like other reports from the Surgeon General, this report reviews existing knowledge to provide scientifically derived bases for action at all levels of society. Suggesting whether and how the areas of opportunity listed in the final chapter might lend themselves to policy development to reduce youth violence is beyond the report's purview.

Report Perspectives

Focus on Violence by Youths

The research described here focuses on physical assault by a youth that carries a significant risk of injuring or killing another person. It includes a wealth of studies into the many individual, family, school, peer group, and community factors associated with serious violence—aggravated assault, robbery, rape, and homicide—in the second decade of life, when most such violence emerges. Thus, the young people who are the focus of this report are principally children and adolescents from about age 10 through high school. Appropriate interventions during as well as before this period stand a good chance of helping redirect violent young people toward healthy and constructive adult lives. The window of opportunity for effective interventions opens early and rarely, if ever, closes.

The Developmental Perspective

This report views violence from a developmental perspective. To understand why some young people become involved in violence and some do not, it examines how youths' personal characteristics interact over time with the social contexts in which they live. This perspective considers a range of risks over the life course, from prenatal factors to factors influencing whether patterns of violent behavior in adolescence will persist into adulthood. The developmental perspective has enabled scientists to identify two general onset trajectories of violence: one in which violent behaviors emerge before puberty, and one in which they appear after puberty. The early-onset trajectory shows stronger links between childhood factors and persistent, even lifelong involvement in violent behavior. Identifying such pathways to violence can help researchers target interventions to the periods in development where they will be most effective. . . .

Myths about Youth Violence

An important reason for making research findings widely available is to challenge false notions and misconceptions about youth violence. Ten myths about violence and violent youth are listed and debunked. Examples of these myths include:

Myth: Most future offenders can be identified in early childhood.
Myth: Child abuse and neglect inevitably lead to violent behavior later in life.
Myth: African American and Hispanic youths are more likely to become involved in violence than other racial or ethnic groups.
Myth: A new, violent breed of young superpredators threatens the United States.
Myth: Getting tough with juvenile offenders by trying them in adult criminal courts reduces the likelihood that they will commit more crimes.
Myth: Nothing works with respect to treating or preventing violent behavior.
Myth: Most violent youths will end up being arrested for a violent crime.

These false ideas are intrinsically dangerous. Assumptions that a problem does not exist or failure to recognize the true nature of a problem can obscure the need for informed policy or for interventions. An example is the conventional wisdom in many circles that the epidemic of youth violence so evident in the early 1990s is over. Alternatively, myths may trigger public fears and lead to inappropriate or misguided policies that result in inefficient or counterproductive use of scarce public resources. An example is the current policy of waiving or transferring young offenders into adult criminal courts and prisons.

Major Research Findings and Conclusions

This report reviews a vast, multidisciplinary, and often controversial research literature. In the process, it seeks to clarify the discrepancies between official records of youth violence and young people's own reports of their violent behaviors. It identifies factors that increase the risk, or statistical probability, that a young person will gravitate toward violence and reviews studies that have begun to identify developmental pathways that may lead a young person into a violent lifestyle. Also explored is a less well developed area of research—the factors that seem to protect youths from the effects of exposure to risk factors for violence. Finally, the report reviews research on the effectiveness of specific strategies to reduce and prevent youth violence.

The most important conclusion of this report is that youth violence is not an intractable problem. We now have the knowledge and tools needed to reduce or even prevent much of the most serious youth violence, with the added benefit of reducing less dangerous, but still serious problem behaviors and promoting healthy development. Scientists from many disciplines, working in a variety of settings with public and private agencies, are generating needed information and putting it to use in designing, testing, and evaluating intervention programs. However, after years of effort and massive expenditures of public and private resources, the search for solutions to the issue of youth violence remains an enormous challenge. Some traditional as well as seemingly innovative approaches to reducing and preventing youth violence have failed to deliver on their promise, and successful approaches are often eclipsed by random violent events such as the school shootings that have occurred in recent years in communities throughout the country. Thus, the most urgent need is a national resolve to confront the problem of youth violence systematically, using research-based approaches, and to correct damaging myths and stereotypes that interfere with the task at hand. . . .

Trends in Youth Violence

Two distinctly different, complementary ways of measuring violence are used by scientists—official reports and self-reports. Official arrest data are an obvious means of determining the extent of youth violence, and a surge in arrests for violent crimes marked the epidemic of youth violence between 1983 and 1993. Arrests were driven largely by the rapid proliferation of firearms use by adolescents engaging in violent acts and the likelihood that violent confrontations would—as they did—produce serious or lethal injuries. Today, with fewer young people carrying weapons, including guns, to school and elsewhere, violent encounters are less likely to result in homicide and serious injury and therefore are less likely to draw the attention of police. By 1999, arrest rates for homicide, rape, and robbery had all dropped below 1983 rates. Arrest rates for aggravated assault, however, were nearly 70 percent higher than they were in 1983, having declined only 24 percent from the peak rates in 1994.

Youth violence can also be measured on the basis of confidential reporting by youths themselves. Confidential surveys find that 13 to 15 percent of high school seniors report having committed an act of serious violence in recent years (1993 to 1998). These acts typically do not come to the attention of police, in part because they are less likely than in years past to involve firearms. Over the past two decades, the number of violent acts by high school seniors increased nearly 50 percent, a trend similar to that found in arrests for violent crimes. But neither this incident rate nor the proportion of high school seniors involved in violence has declined in the years since 1993—they remain at peak levels. In the aggregate, the best available evidence from multiple sources indicates that youth violence is an ongoing national problem, albeit one that is largely hidden from public view.

Major Findings and Conclusions

1. The decade between 1983 and 1993 was marked by an epidemic of increasingly lethal violence that was associated with a large rise in the use of firearms and involved primarily African American males. There was a

modest rise in the proportion of young persons involved in other forms of serious violence.

2. Since 1994, a decline in homicide arrests has reflected primarily the decline in use of firearms. There is some evidence that the smaller decline in nonfatal serious violence is also attributable to declining firearm use.

3. By 1999, arrest rates for violent crimes—with the exception of aggravated assault—had fallen below 1983 levels. Arrest rates for aggravated assault remain almost 70 percent higher than they were in 1983, and this is the offense most frequently captured in self-reports of violence.

4. Despite the present decline in gun use and in lethal violence, the self-reported proportion of young people involved in nonfatal violence has not dropped from the peak years of the epidemic, nor has the proportion of students injured with a weapon at school declined.

5. The proportion of schools in which gangs are present continued to increase after 1994 and has only recently (1999) declined. However, evidence shows that the number of youths involved with gangs has not declined and remains near the peak levels of 1996.

6. Although arrest statistics cannot readily track firearm use in specific serious crimes other than homicide, firearm use in violent crimes declined among persons of all ages between 1993 and 1997.

7. The steep rise and fall in arrest rates for homicide over the past two decades have been matched by similar, but less dramatic changes in some of the other indicators of violence, including arrest rates for all violent crimes and incident rates from victims' self-reports. This pattern is not matched by arrests for selected offenses, such as aggravated assault, or incident rates and prevalence rates from offenders' self-reports.

8. Young men—particularly those from minority groups—are disproportionately arrested for violent crimes. But self-reports indicate that differences between minority and majority populations and between young men and young women may not be as large as arrest records indicate or conventional wisdom holds. Race/ethnicity, considered in isolation from other life circumstances, sheds little light on a given child's or adolescent's propensity for engaging in violence.

9. Schools nationwide are relatively safe. Compared to homes and neighborhoods, schools have fewer homicides and nonfatal injuries. Youths at greatest risk of being killed in school-associated violence are those from a racial or ethnic minority, senior high schools, and urban school districts.

Pathways to Youth Violence

Viewed from a developmental perspective, violence stems from a complex interaction of individuals with their environment at particular times in their lives. Longitudinal research has enabled investigators to describe the emergence of violence in terms of two (and possibly more) life-course trajectories. In the early-onset trajectory, violence begins before puberty, whereas in the late-onset trajectory it begins after puberty, at about age 13. These two trajectories offer insights into the likely course, severity, and duration of violence over the life span and have practical implications for the timing of intervention programs and strategies. Some research has examined the co-occurrence of serious violence and other problems, including drug use and mental disorders, and some has looked at factors associated with the cessation of youth violence or its continuation into adulthood. Both of these areas need—and warrant—more study.

Major Findings and Conclusions

1. There are two general onset trajectories for youth violence—an early one, in which violence begins before puberty, and a late one, in which violence begins in adolescence. Youths who become violent before about age 13 generally commit more crimes, and more serious crimes, for a longer time. These young people exhibit a pattern of escalating violence through childhood, and they sometimes continue their violence into adulthood.

2. Most youth violence begins in adolescence and ends with the transition into adulthood.

3. Most highly aggressive children or children with behavioral disorders do not become serious violent offenders.

4. Surveys consistently find that about 30 to 40 percent of male youths and 15 to 30 percent of female youths report having committed a serious violent offense by age 17.

5. Serious violence is part of a lifestyle that includes drugs, guns, precocious sex, and other risky behaviors. Youths involved in serious violence often commit many other types of crimes and exhibit other problem behaviors, presenting a serious challenge to intervention efforts. Successful interventions must confront not only the violent behavior of these young people, but also their lifestyles, which are teeming with risk.

6. The differences in patterns of serious violence by age of onset and the relatively constant rates of individual offending have important implications for prevention and intervention programs. Early childhood programs that target at-risk children and families are critical for preventing the onset of a chronic violent career, but programs must also be developed to combat late-onset violence.

7. The importance of late-onset violence prevention is not widely recognized or well understood. Substantial numbers of serious violent offenders emerge in adolescence without warning signs in childhood. A comprehensive community prevention strategy must address both onset patterns and ferret out their causes and risk factors.

Risk and Protective Factors

Extensive research in recent decades has sought to identify various personal characteristics and environmental conditions that either place children and adolescents at risk of violent behavior or that seem to protect them from the effects of risk. Risk and protective factors can be found in every area of life. Exerting different effects at different stages of development, they tend to appear in clusters, and they appear to gain strength in numbers. These risk probabilities apply to groups, not to individuals. Although risk factors are not necessarily causes, a central aim of the public health approach to youth violence is to identify these predictors and to determine when in the life course they typically come into play. Armed with such information, researchers are better equipped to design well-timed, effective preventive programs. Identifying and understanding how protective factors operate is potentially as important to preventing and stopping violence as identifying and understanding risk factors. Several protective factors have been proposed, but to date only two have been found to buffer the effects of exposure to specific risks for violence: an intolerant attitude toward deviance, including violence, and commitment to school. Protective factors warrant, and are beginning to receive, more research attention.

Major Findings and Conclusions

1. Risk and protective factors exist in every area of life—individual, family, school, peer group, and community. Individual characteristics interact in complex ways with people and conditions in the environment to produce violent behavior.
2. Risk and protective factors vary in predictive power depending on when in the course of development they occur. As children move from infancy to early adulthood, some risk factors will become more important and others less important. Substance use, for example, is a much stronger risk factor at age 9 than it is at age 14.
3. The strongest risk factors during childhood are involvement in serious but not necessarily violent criminal behavior, substance use, being male, physical aggression, low family socioeconomic status or poverty and antisocial parents—all individual or family attributes or conditions.
4. During adolescence, the influence of family is largely supplanted by peer influences. The strongest risk factors are weak ties to conventional peers, ties to antisocial or delinquent peers, belonging to a gang, and involvement in other criminal acts.
5. Risk factors do not operate in isolation—the more risk factors a child or young person is exposed to, the greater the likelihood that he or she will become violent. Risk factors can be buffered by protective factors, however. An adolescent with an intolerant attitude toward deviance, for example, is unlikely to seek or be sought out by delinquent peers, a strong risk factor for violence at that age.
6. Given the strong evidence that risk factors predict the likelihood of future violence, they are useful for identifying vulnerable populations that may benefit from intervention efforts. Risk markers such as race or ethnicity are frequently confused with risk factors; risk markers have no causal relation to violence.
7. No single risk factor or combination of factors can predict violence with unerring accuracy. Most young people exposed to a single risk factor will not become involved in violent behavior; similarly, many young people exposed to multiple risks will not become violent. By the same

token, protective factors cannot guarantee that a child exposed to risk will not become violent.

Preventing Youth Violence

Research clearly demonstrates that prevention programs and strategies can be effective against both early- and late-onset forms of violence in general populations of youths, high-risk youths, and even youths who are already violent or seriously delinquent. Chapter 5 highlights 27 specific youth violence prevention programs that are not only effective at preventing youth violence but cost-effective as well. In a number of cases, the long-term financial benefits of prevention are substantially greater than the costs of the programs. These promising findings indicate that youth violence prevention has an important role to play in overall efforts to provide a safe environment for youths.

Despite these positive findings, current research on youth violence prevention has important limitations. For example, relatively little is known about the scientific effectiveness of hundreds of youth violence programs currently in use in schools and communities in the United States. This situation invites concern because in the past, many well-intentioned youth violence prevention programs were found to have been ineffective or to have had negative effects on youths. Even less is known about the best strategies for implementing effective programs on a national scale without compromising their results.

Major Findings and Conclusions

1. A number of youth violence intervention and prevention programs have demonstrated that they are effective; assertions that "nothing works" are false.
2. Most highly effective programs combine components that address both individual risks and environmental conditions, particularly building individual skills and competencies, parent effectiveness training, improving the social climate of the school, and changes in type and level of involvement in peer groups.
3. Rigorous evaluation of programs is critical. While hundreds of prevention programs are being used in schools and communities throughout the country, little is known about the effects of most of them.
4. At the time this report was prepared, nearly half of the most thoroughly evaluated strategies for preventing violence had been shown to be ineffective—and a few were known to harm participants.
5. In schools, interventions that target change in the social context appear to be more effective, on average, than those that attempt to change individual attitudes, skills, and risk behaviors.
6. Involvement with delinquent peers and gang membership are two of the most powerful predictors of violence, yet few effective interventions have been developed to address these problems.
7. Program effectiveness depends as much on the quality of implementation as on the type of intervention. Many programs are ineffective not because their strategy is misguided, but because the quality of implementation is poor.

A Vision for the Future

The most important conclusion of this report is that an array of intervention programs with well-documented effectiveness is now in place to reduce and prevent youth violence. Such programs are the outcome of a large body of research that has examined the paths and trajectories that lead some youths toward lives marred by violence. Multiple studies have identified and examined specific risk factors—personal and environmental features of young people's lives that heighten the statistical probability of their engaging in violent behaviors. Research has also begun to identify protective factors that appear to buffer the effects of exposure to risk. While this information has been accumulating, researchers, youth service practitioners, and others have been actively engaged in designing, implementing, and evaluating a variety of interventions to reduce and prevent the occurrence of youth violence. The best of these interventions target specific populations of young people, as defined by particular constellations of risk and life experience.

Chapter 6 highlights courses of action for the Nation to consider. Given the focus of the report, particular emphasis is placed on consideration of research opportunities and needs. Although effective interventions exist today, only through continued research will all intervention programs be shown to meet a standard of effectiveness—or be discarded. Although the research options and other courses of action suggested here are not formal policy recommendations, they offer a vision that may inform the generation of policies that will build on information we possess today. They are intended for policy makers, service and treatment providers, individuals affiliated with the juvenile justice system, researchers, and, most important, the people of the United States. This vision for the future is presented with the hope that it will engage an expanding number of citizens in the challenge of redressing the problem of youth violence. The following are possible courses of action:

- Continue to build the science base.
- Accelerate the decline in gun use by youths in violent encounters.
- Facilitate the entry of youths into effective intervention programs rather than incarcerating them.
- Disseminate model programs with incentives that will ensure fidelity to original program design when taken to scale.
- Provide training and certification programs for intervention personnel.
- Improve public awareness of effective interventions.
- Convene youths and families, researchers, and private and public organizations for a periodic youth violence summit.
- Improve Federal, state, and local strategies for reporting crime information and violent deaths.

BILL CLINTON'S FAREWELL
TO THE PRESIDENCY
January 18, 2001

Most U.S. presidents fade quickly into the background after leaving the White House, but not Bill Clinton, one of the most dynamic and controversial presidents in American history. Clinton continued making news for weeks after stepping out of the presidency. That much of the news involved controversial actions during his final hours in office somehow seemed to fit right into the context of his presidency, which was plagued by scandal and bitter partisan political turmoil.

As the final hours of his presidency ticked away, Clinton took several steps to write his own version of his legacy. On January 18, 2001, he made a televised address to the nation touting the accomplishments of his eight years in office and subtly attempting to influence the agenda of his successor, George W. Bush. On January 19, his last full day in office, Clinton cleared away the final debris from the unsuccessful effort by congressional Republicans two years earlier to remove him from office; he signed a plea-bargain agreement with federal prosecutors acknowledging he had lied to a grand jury investigating aspects of his affair with a White House intern. Finally, just before handing the presidency over to Bush on January 20, Clinton issued dozens of pardons, one of which created a new storm of controversy in the succeeding days. Other controversies swirled over the Clinton family's decision to take nearly $200,000 worth of items given him as president and unsubstantiated allegations by Bush aides that some Clinton staff members had vandalized White House offices. Clinton stoutly defended his pardons, and all the controversies eventually blew away—but not before the former president's legion of critics, and many of his friends, had one more opportunity to argue heatedly about his stormy tenure in office.

Clinton ultimately disappeared from the front pages as 2001 wore on and as the nation turned its attention to Bush's political agenda and then the aftermath of the September 11 terrorist attacks in New York City and Washington. As he began the process of writing his memoirs and raising money for his presidential library in Little Rock, the most often-mentioned politician named Clinton was his wife, Hillary Rodham Clinton, beginning her term of office as the junior senator from New York. She was the first First Lady ever elected to public office. (Terrorist attacks, p. 614; Clinton Senate election, Historic Documents of 2000, p. 906)

Clinton's Farewell Address

Rarely a man of few words, Clinton's farewell speech on January 18 was one of the shortest major addresses of his presidency, taking less than ten minutes on prime-time television. Speaking from the Oval Office, Clinton clearly was trying to shape how he would be viewed in history and to influence important decisions in the months after he left office.

The first part of the speech address was a recapitulation of Clinton's successes as president. Reciting a litany of statistics he had frequently used in political campaigns, Clinton proudly claimed that "America has done well" during his tenure, with millions of new jobs, low unemployment and inflation, the longest economic expansion in history, increased federal aid for education at all levels, and an end to the welfare system.

While never referring directly or indirectly to Bush, Clinton had advice on foreign policy and budget matters for his successor. On the world stage, he said, the United States had become the leader of the "forces of freedom and peace" in places such as Bosnia and Kosovo and should not shirk that responsibility. This was widely seen as a subtle rebuke to Bush's campaign statements calling for a reduced U.S. role in peacekeeping operations and what Bush derided as "nation-building" in those places. Domestically, Clinton suggested that the new president should rethink the central plank of his campaign platform: a giant tax cut weighted heavily in favor of high-income taxpayers and businesses. Clinton argued that "fiscal responsibility" should be the government's first priority. "If we choose wisely, we can pay down the debt, deal with the retirement of the baby boomers, invest more in our future and provide tax relief," he said.

Clinton also appeared to be attempting to revise the conventional view of his position on one of the most important trends of the late twentieth century: globalization, the increasing economic interdependence of nations as a result of international investment and free trade. Throughout his presidency Clinton was by far the world's most prominent exponent of globalization, urging and in some cases practically coercing other countries to open their economies to international trade and investment. But globalization became progressively controversial in the late 1990s, as questions were raised about whether the rich, industrialized countries (most prominently, the United States) benefited far more than poor nations and their citizens. Clinton had acknowledged this criticism in a major speech at the University of Warwick in England just a month earlier, and he borrowed some of the language from that speech in his farewell address. He noted that the expansion of free trade "hasn't fully closed the gap between those of us who live on the cutting edge of the global economy and the billions around the world who live on the knife's edge of survival." Global poverty, he added, "is a powder keg that could be ignited by our indifference." (Clinton at G-8 summit, Historic Documents of 2000, p. 477)

*Finally, Clinton held out a promise—his critics would say a threat—
that he would not entirely disappear from the national stage once he left the
presidency. "My days in this office are nearly through," he said. "But my
days of service, I hope, are not." He said nothing specific about what he
meant, adding only that he would be proud simply to be called a "citizen."*

Plea-Bargain Agreement

*As he offered his farewell address, Clinton surely was aware that he
would be the focus of at least one more major news story before leaving the
White House. For weeks he and his attorneys had been negotiating with
Robert Ray, the special prosecutor who was concluding the lengthy and
expensive investigations into several alleged wrongdoings by Clinton, his
wife, and associates. Ray, who inherited the investigations from former independent counsel Kenneth W. Starr, had held out the prospect of seeking an
indictment, once Clinton left office, for misleading statements Clinton had
made during a grand jury testimony about his affair with former White
House intern Monica S. Lewinsky. Clinton's affair with Lewinsky, and his
attempts to cover it up, had been at the center of his 1998 impeachment by
the House of Representatives—an impeachment the Senate refused to sustain the following year when it acquitted him.* (Impeachment, Historic Documents of 1999, p. 15)

*In an agreement announced January 19, Clinton confessed that he had
lied when he denied to the grand jury that he and Lewinsky had been engaged in an affair. "I tried to walk a fine line between acting lawfully and
testifying falsely, but I now recognize that I did not fully accomplish this
goal and that certain of my responses to questions about Ms. Lewinsky were
false," he said in a statement. In exchange for that admission—one Clinton
had long refused to make—Ray said he would not seek an indictment of
Clinton and that the investigation of the president "is now concluded." He
added: "May history and the American people judge that it has been concluded justly."*

*Ray in October sent his final report on the Lewinsky scandal to a three-
judge panel that supervised his investigation. The judges withheld publication of the report until January 2002 to give Clinton and others a chance to
respond to it. Ray had announced in September 2000 that he was concluding an investigation into participation by Clinton and his wife in a failed
Arkansas land deal known as Whitewater. Ray had not sought charges
against the Clintons in that case.* (Whitewater report, Historic Documents of
2000, p. 762)

*In a separate but related agreement with the Committee on Professional
Conduct of the Arkansas Supreme Court, Clinton accepted a five-year suspension of his law license in that state and a $25,000 fine, to be paid the
Arkansas Bar Association. This agreement spared Clinton the humiliation
of having his license revoked by the authorities in his home state, where he
had served for eight years as governor before becoming president.*

*Clinton's agreement with Ray won praise from most of his friends and
political foes, with both sides claiming it demonstrated the correctness of*

their positions during the painful impeachment process. Rep. Henry J. Hyde, R-Ill., who as chairman of the Judiciary Committee had been a leader in the impeachment drive, said the agreement "vindicates the House impeachment proceeding and reaffirms that our actions were in defense of the rule of law rather than merely a political initiative." The senior Democrat on Hyde's committee, John Conyers Jr. of Michigan, expressed relief at the end of "this long national farce of an extramarital affair." Even so, some of Clinton's staunchest critics could not bring themselves to acknowledge an end to the Lewinsky scandal. Among them, Rep. Dan Burton, R-Ind., complained that Clinton had "received preferential treatment."

Controversial Pardons

National relief over the long-delayed conclusion to the Lewinsky scandal was short-lived, replaced within a day by a new political uproar over Clinton's last-minute pardons, which wiped out guilt and punishment and restored legal status to the pardoned persons. This outburst of indignation against Clinton lasted at least two months before fading away. In the meantime, however, much of the residual public sympathy toward Clinton dissipated, and even some of his most loyal friends and admirers were left shaking their heads at Clinton's ability to step out of one scandal into another.

On Inauguration Day, January 20, Clinton's staff announced that the president had issued pardons to 176 people; the number was later raised to 177, which brought to 258 the number he had issued during his last month in office. This was the largest number issued by any modern president at the end of his term; however, Clinton pardoned fewer people during the entire course of his presidency than did most of his recent predecessors.

Most of the initial attention focused on a handful of pardons, those for former CIA director John Deutch, who had been forced to resign because he violated regulations for protecting classified information; Henry Cisneros, former secretary of housing and urban development, who had pleaded guilty to lying to the FBI about his payments to a former mistress; Susan McDougal, a friend of the Clintons who was convicted of fraud charges in the Whitewater case and had been imprisoned for refusing to say whether Clinton had spoken the truth when he testified during her trial; Clinton's half-brother, Roger, who had been convicted on federal narcotics charges; and Patricia Hearst Shaw, a member of the family that owned the Hearst newspaper chain who had participated in a 1974 bank robbery after she was kidnapped by a group of political radicals.

Media attention quickly shifted to one pardon that had received little notice in the initial flurry of reports: that of Marc Rich, a wealthy New York commodities trader who had been indicted in 1983 on tax evasion and tax fraud charges and had fled to Switzerland, where he had lived ever since, renouncing his U.S. citizenship. Clinton also pardoned a Rich associate, Pincus Green.

The Rich pardon generated controversy for several reasons. First, it was one of about thirty pardons that Clinton granted without submitting the

*cases to the Justice Department for a standard review. Key justice lawyers
learned about the proposed pardon of Rich only a few hours before Clinton
signed the papers, and they said they were not told that Rich was a fugitive.
Moreover, it became clear that Rich's case advanced to the White House only
because of his extraordinary connections. His lawyer at the time was Jack
Quinn, who had been White House counsel in Clinton's first term. Among
those advocating a pardon, according to news reports, were Israeli prime
minister Ehud Barak and Spain's King Juan Carlos; the king reportedly
acted in response to an appeal from Israeli officials. Also lobbying on Rich's
behalf were his former wife, Denise Rich, who had donated hundreds of
thousands of dollars to Democratic Party candidates (including Hillary
Clinton's Senate race) and had contributed $450,000 to the fund for Clin-
ton's presidential library.*

*Congressional Republicans and Democrats alike denounced the Rich par-
don. Committees in both branches of Congress launched investigations into
the matter, with a focus on whether Clinton had acted in response to Denise
Rich's contributions and other pressures. Mary Jo White, the U.S. district
attorney in New York City whose office had indicted Rich in 1983, also
opened a preliminary criminal investigation into the pardon issue.*

*The one leading Republican who professed no interest in the matter was
President Bush, who said he preferred to "move on" with his presidency.
Some Democrats suggested Bush feared that a prolonged investigation of the
pardon would lead to renewed inquiries into controversial pardons issued
by his father, George H. Bush, during his presidency. The senior Bush had
pardoned oil industry executive Armand Hammer, who had been convicted
of making illegal contributions to former president Richard M. Nixon; he
also had pardoned former defense secretary Caspar Weinberger and other
Reagan administration officials involved in the 1986–1987 abuse-of-power
scandal known as the Iran-contra affair.*

The New York Times *on February 18 published an op-ed column by Clinton defending the Rich pardon and citing "legal and foreign policy reasons"
in support of it. Among those reasons, Clinton said, Rich should have been
indicted on civil, rather than criminal, charges. Clinton noted that his pardon was conditioned on Rich's agreement to waive a statute of limitations
on possible civil charges. Clinton also said the pardon had been supported
by prominent Israeli officials and by three "distinguished Republican attorneys." The attorneys were Leonard Garment, who had been a senior aide
to Nixon; Lewis Libby, the chief of staff for Vice President Dick Cheney;
and William Bradford Reynolds, a senior Justice Department official under
President Ronald Reagan. All three had represented Rich in his past efforts
to suppress the charges against him, but all three denied having played any
role in Clinton's pardon.*

*At one of several congressional hearings on the issue, conducted March 1
by the House Government Reform Committee, three of Clinton's senior aides
testified that they had urged Clinton not to pardon Rich. The aides said they
had assumed Clinton would not grant the pardon, only to discover at the last
minute—late on January 19 or early on January 20—that Clinton was de-*

termined to proceed. One of the aides, White House counsel Beth Nolan, suggested that a telephone call on Rich's behalf from Israeli leader Barak had been a "significant" factor in persuading the president to grant the pardon. (Barak reportedly had been impressed by Rich's donations to charitable causes in Israel and by his unspecified help to the Israeli intelligence service.) Nevertheless, John Podesta, Clinton's chief of staff, said he was convinced that Clinton's decision, whether it was "wise or unwise," was made "on the merits of the case" and not because of influences such as Denise Rich's contributions.

The political furor over the Rich pardon eventually died down, largely because even those most infuriated by the matter realized that nothing could be done to reverse what Clinton had done. Under the Constitution, the president has the sole power to issue pardons, and there is no established procedure for Congress or succeeding presidents to overturn them. Even so, the damage to Clinton's already frayed reputation had been done. That damage could be reversed, or sustained, only with the judgments of history.

Following is the text of President Bill Clinton's farewell address, which he made to a national television audience January 18, 2001, two days before leaving the presidency.

The document was obtained from the Internet at http://clinton6.nara.gov/2001/01/2001-01-18-farewell-address-by-the-president-to-the-nation.html.

My fellow citizens, tonight is my last opportunity to speak to you from the Oval Office as your President. I am profoundly grateful to you for twice giving me the honor to serve—to work for you and with you to prepare our nation for the 21st century.

And I'm grateful to Vice President Gore, to my Cabinet Secretaries, and to all those who have served with me for the last eight years.

This has been a time of dramatic transformation, and you have risen to every new challenge. You have made our social fabric stronger, our families healthier and safer, our people more prosperous. You, the American people, have made our passage into the global information age an era of great American renewal.

In all the work I have done as President—every decision I have made, every executive action I have taken, every bill I have proposed and signed, I've tried to give all Americans the tools and conditions to build the future of our dreams in a good society, with a strong economy, a cleaner environment, and a freer, safer, more prosperous world.

I have steered my course by our enduring values—opportunity for all, responsibility from all, a community of all Americans. I have sought to give America a new kind of government, smaller, more modern, more effective, full of ideas and policies appropriate to this new time, always putting people first, always focusing on the future.

Working together, America has done well. Our economy is breaking records, with more than 22 million new jobs, the lowest unemployment in 30 years, the highest home ownership ever, the longest expansion in history.

Our families and communities are stronger. Thirty-five million Americans have used the Family Leave law; 8 million have moved off welfare. Crime is at a 25-year low. Over 10 million Americans receive more college aid, and more people than ever are going to college. Our schools are better. Higher standards, greater accountability and larger investments have brought higher test scores and higher graduation rates.

More than 3 million children have health insurance now, and more than 7 million Americans have been lifted out of poverty. Incomes are rising across the board. Our air and water are cleaner. Our food and drinking water are safer. And more of our precious land has been preserved in the continental United States than at any time in a hundred years.

America has been a force for peace and prosperity in every corner of the globe. I'm very grateful to be able to turn over the reins of leadership to a new President with America in such a strong position to meet the challenges of the future.

Tonight I want to leave you with three thoughts about our future. First, America must maintain our record of fiscal responsibility. Through our last four budgets we've turned record deficits to record surpluses, and we've been able to pay down $600 billion of our national debt, on track to be debt-free by the end of the decade for the first time since 1835. Staying on that course will bring lower interest rates, greater prosperity, and the opportunity to meet our big challenges. If we choose wisely, we can pay down the debt, deal with the retirement of the baby boomers, invest more in our future, and provide tax relief.

Second, because the world is more connected every day, in every way, America's security and prosperity require us to continue to lead in the world. At this remarkable moment in history, more people live in freedom than ever before. Our alliances are stronger than ever. People all around the world look to America to be a force for peace and prosperity, freedom and security.

The global economy is giving more of our own people and billions around the world the chance to work and live and raise their families with dignity. But the forces of integration that have created these good opportunities also make us more subject to global forces of destruction—to terrorism, organized crime and narco trafficking, the spread of deadly weapons and disease, the degradation of the global environment.

The expansion of trade hasn't fully closed the gap between those of us who live on the cutting edge of the global economy and the billions around the world who live on the knife's edge of survival. This global gap requires more than compassion; it requires action. Global poverty is a powder keg that could be ignited by our indifference.

In his first inaugural address, Thomas Jefferson warned of entangling alliances. But in our times, America cannot, and must not, disentangle itself from the world. If we want the world to embody our shared values, then we must assume a shared responsibility.

If the wars of the 20th century, especially the recent ones in Kosovo and Bosnia, have taught us anything, it is that we achieve our aims by defending our values, and leading the forces of freedom and peace. We must embrace boldly and resolutely that duty to lead—to stand with our allies in word and deed, and to put a human face on the global economy, so that expanded trade benefits all peoples in all nations, lifting lives and hopes all across the world.

Third, we must remember that America cannot lead in the world unless here at home we weave the threads of our coat of many colors into the fabric of one America. As we become ever more diverse, we must work harder to unite around our common values and our common humanity. We must work harder to overcome our differences, in our hearts and in our laws. We must treat all our people with fairness and dignity, regardless of their race, religion, gender or sexual orientation, and regardless of when they arrived in our country; always moving toward the more perfect union of our founders' dreams.

Hillary, Chelsea, and I join all Americans in wishing our very best to the next President, George W. Bush, to his family and his administration, in meeting these challenges, and in leading freedom's march in this new century.

As for me, I'll leave the presidency more idealistic, more full of hope than the day I arrived, and more confident than ever that America's best days lie ahead.

My days in this office are nearly through, but my days of service, I hope, are not. In the years ahead, I will never hold a position higher or a covenant more sacred than that of President of the United States. But there is no title I will wear more proudly than that of citizen.

Thank you. God bless you, and God bless America.

PRESIDENT GEORGE W. BUSH'S INAUGURAL ADDRESS
January 20, 2001

George W. Bush took the oath of office as the nation's forty-third president on January 20, 2001, a little more than a month after he was declared the winner in the closest and most divisive presidential election in modern history. Bush, whose father, George, had taken the same oath of office twelve years earlier, became only the second son of a former president to become the chief executive. The first was John Quincy Adams, son of the nation's second president, John Adams.

In his relatively brief inaugural address, Bush emphasized the themes of "civility" and "character"—an obvious attempt to set aside the scandals that had plagued predecessor Bill Clinton, who sat on the inaugural dais outside the Capitol just a few feet from Bush. "I will live by these principles: to advance my convictions with civility, to pursue the public interest with courage, to speak for greater justice and compassion, to call for responsibility and try to live it as well," Bush said. (Clinton farewell address, p. 86)

The new president made only a vague reference to the unusual route by which he had reached the pinnacle of American political power. In the presidential election the previous November 7, Democrat Al Gore had won 500,000 more popular votes than had Republican Bush, and Gore led in the all-important electoral college, with the results uncertain in just one state, Florida, where Bush led by a few hundred votes. After thirty-six days of lawsuits and bitter partisan warfare, the Supreme Court, by a 5–4 majority, blocked Gore's attempt to continue counting disputed votes in Florida, thereby ensuring Bush would gain the presidency. Chief Justice William H. Rehnquist, who had voted with the majority, administered the oath of office to Bush.

While millions of Americans may have believed Bush had no legitimate right to be taking the oath of office (and several thousand angry protesters on the fringe of the inaugural crowd shouted slogans such as "hail to the thief"), the majesty of the nation's political system prevailed in the end. Bush himself noted in his opening sentence that "the peaceful transfer of au-

thority is rare in history, yet common in our country." Even more power-ful than Bush's words was the presence of Gore, who, Bush acknowledged, had accepted the outcome with "grace." (Presidential election, Historic Documents of 2000, p. 1025)

Inaugural Address

Delivered in a foggy gloom characteristic of many January days in Washington, Bush's fourteen-minute speech was uncharacteristically lofty. It was a sharp contrast to his standard political rhetoric, which he report-edly liked to keep simple and direct—reflecting what many said was his own view of himself. As a two-term governor of Texas and then as a presi-dential candidate, Bush had deliberately communicated with the public in commonplace language and portrayed himself as a man of "Middle Amer-ica," despite his upbringing in a wealthy, patrician family from New En-gland. Members of that family, along with others in the Republican Party establishment, were close at hand as Bush assumed the presidency. Among them were his father, George; and mother, Barbara; his brother Jeb, the gov-ernor of Florida; Dick Cheney, the new vice president, who had served as his father's defense secretary and had managed the transition on Bush's behalf; and James A. Baker III, his father's secretary of state, who had led Bush's legal team in Florida's postelection skirmishing.

As had most of his predecessors, Bush used his inaugural address as a sermon to inspire the American public and to reassure the country's over-seas allies, not as a litany of concrete legislative proposals. Bush offered more specifics in his address delivered to a joint session of Congress on Feb-ruary 27. (Bush's address to Congress p. 171)

A "born-again" Christian, Bush laced his speech with numerous religious references, a prelude to his later legislative proposal for federal aid to "faith-based" charities that help the poor and downtrodden. Indeed, much of the president's speech focused on the need for Americans to help each other. Bush in his campaign had called himself a "compassionate conservative," and he used variations of the word compassion *four times in his address. "America, at its best, is compassionate," he said. "In the quiet of American conscience, we know that deep, persistent poverty is unworthy of the na-tion's promise." But he also made it clear that he had in mind the efforts of individuals and private groups and was not proposing new government programs. "Government has great responsibilities for public safety and public health, for civil rights and common schools. Yet compassion is the work of a nation, not just a government," he said.* (Faith-based proposal, p. 132)

Expanding on this theme, Bush seemed to echo, in different words, the fa-mous call of John F. Kennedy in his inaugural address forty years earlier that Americans "ask not what your country can do for you—ask what you can do for your country." In Bush's formulation, that call appeared as: "What you do is as important as anything government does. I ask you to seek a common good beyond your comfort; to defend needed reforms against easy attacks; to serve your nation, beginning with your neighbor. I ask you to be citizens, not spectators; citizens, not subjects; responsible citizens, building communities of service and a nation of character."

Except in times of war or other foreign crises, inaugural addresses generally do not dwell on foreign policy, and so Bush devoted only seven sentences of his speech to nondomestic matters. Alluding to his campaign pledge for increased military spending and a defensive system against ballistic missile attacks, Bush said simply: "We will build our defenses beyond challenge, lest weakness invite challenge." And to reassure allies concerned by some of his campaign positions that seemed to portend a reduced U.S. role in world affairs, Bush said that "America remains engaged in the world by history and by choice, shaping a balance of power that favors freedom." As additional reassurance that he did not see the United States as a superpower free to act entirely on its own volition, Bush said: "We will show purpose without arrogance."

Bush did not mention the one challenge that, to his shock and dismay, would come to dominate his presidency just eight months later: terrorism. All of the president's domestic and foreign policy priorities would pale in the face of a war against terrorism following attacks on September 11 against the World Trade Center towers in New York City and the Pentagon that killed approximately 3,000 people. (Terrorist attacks, p. 614)

The hundreds of thousands of spectators gathered along the West Front of the Capitol and the Mall interrupted Bush's inaugural address with applause fourteen times. The biggest cheer, sparked by the Republican members of Congress on the platform near Bush, followed his promise to "reduce taxes." That was reference to the central promise of his campaign: a massive cut in individual income tax rates.

Assembling a Cabinet

In selecting the key officials who would manage his presidency, Bush made some historic appointments in terms of racial and ethnic diversity, but, more important from a political point of view, he tried to balance the interests of the competing conservative and moderate wings of his Republican Party. The most visible cabinet selection was that of Colin Powell, the first African American to be secretary of state. Powell was a retired army general who had been chairman of the Joint Chiefs of Staff under Bush's father. In terms of Republican Party politics, Powell generally was considered a moderate. To balance Powell's views, Bush named Donald Rumsfeld, a favorite of hard-line conservatives, as secretary of defense. Rumsfeld had held that post a quarter century earlier under President Gerald Ford and had spent the intervening period in private industry. Bush named as his national security adviser Condoleezza Rice, an African American woman who had served on his father's National Security Council staff.

In the immediate aftermath of the Florida electoral standoff, Bush and his staff had talked about adding a "bipartisan" flavor to the cabinet by including an unspecified number of prominent Democrats. After several Democrats declined positions and Republicans opposed accommodating too many partisan adversaries, the number of Democrats in the cabinet turned out to be one: Norman Y. Mineta, as secretary of transportation. Mineta had been a respected House member from California for many years and had served as secretary of commerce at the end of the Clinton presidency; he had been the first Asian American to hold a cabinet post. Bush invited one other prominent Democratic holdover from the Clinton administration to remain on the job indefinitely, CIA director George J. Tenet. Tenet's job was no longer considered a cabinet-level post, however, as it had been when Bush's father held it in the 1970s.

The Senate confirmed Powell, Rumsfeld, and four other cabinet members (Spencer Abraham as energy secretary, Donald I. Evans as commerce secretary, Roderick R. Paige as education secretary, and Ann M. Veneman as agriculture secretary) in a brief ceremony shortly after Bush's inauguration.

Just about every new president in recent decades had made at least one high-level appointment that stirred controversy and produced a confirmation fight in the Senate. Bush was no exception. The political lightening rod early in his administration turned out to be John Ashcroft. A former governor of Missouri and senator from that state, Ashcroft had been defeated for reelection to the Senate the previous November by a dead man: Governor Mel Carnahan, who was killed in a plane crash shortly before the election. Carnahan's widow, Jean, had agreed to serve if her husband won the election, and a majority of the state's voters seemed to prefer that arrangement to sending Ashcroft back to the Senate. Bush then selected Ashcroft as his attorney general, a choice that reinforced the president-elect's right flank within the Republican Party but outraged many liberals, feminists, African Americans, and others who long had been at odds with the former senator.

The partisan fight over Ashcroft's nomination quickly centered around his views on abortion and gun control laws, both of which he had vigorously opposed as a senator, and his actions in the 1999 Senate battle over Clinton's nomination of Ronnie White, a black justice on the Missouri Supreme Court, to be a federal district court judge. Ashcroft had opposed White as a judicial "activist," and the Republican-led Senate rejected the nomination along party lines. Some Democrats suggested that Ashcroft had opposed White because of his race, a charge Ashcroft denied. The Senate on February 1 confirmed Ashcroft by a 58–42 vote. Eight Democrats joined all fifty Republicans in supporting the nomination, while forty-two Democrats were opposed. It was the closest vote on the nomination of an attorney general since 1925, when the Senate rejected Calvin Coolidge's choice of Charles B. Warren for the post.

Two other Bush nominees also faced controversy. Linda Chavez, nominated to be labor secretary, was strongly opposed by the AFL-CIO on grounds that she did not support worker rights. She withdrew on January 8 after media reports that she had improperly aided an illegal immigrant. Bush replaced her with Elaine L. Chao, a former government official and wife of Senator Mitch McConnell, R-Ky. Gale A. Norton, a former Colorado attorney general nominated as interior secretary, was opposed by representatives of

environmental groups. Norton had worked for a conservative legal founda-
tion that fought many environmental laws and regulations, and her record
in Colorado led environmentalists to argue that she would eagerly turn fed-
eral lands controlled by the Interior Department over to mining and timber
companies. The Senate confirmed Norton on January 30 by a 75–24 vote,
with Democrats casting all the "no" votes.

> *Following is the text of the inaugural address delivered Janu-*
> *ary 20, 2001, by George W. Bush after he took the oath of office as*
> *the forty-third president of the United States.*

> **The document was obtained from the Internet at http://**
> **www.whitehouse.gov/news/inaugural-address.html.**

President Clinton, distinguished guests and my fellow citizens, the peaceful transfer of authority is rare in history, yet common in our country. With a
simple oath, we affirm old traditions and make new beginnings.

As I begin, I thank President Clinton for his service to our nation.

And I thank Vice President Gore for a contest conducted with spirit and
ended with grace.

I am honored and humbled to stand here, where so many of America's leaders have come before me, and so many will follow.

We have a place, all of us, in a long story—a story we continue, but whose
end we will not see. It is the story of a new world that became a friend and lib-
erator of the old, a story of a slave-holding society that became a servant of
freedom, the story of a power that went into the world to protect but not possess, to defend but not to conquer.

It is the American story—a story of flawed and fallible people, united
across the generations by grand and enduring ideals.

The grandest of these ideals is an unfolding American promise that everyone belongs, that everyone deserves a chance, that no insignificant person
was ever born.

Americans are called to enact this promise in our lives and in our laws. And
though our nation has sometimes halted, and sometimes delayed, we must follow no other course.

Through much of the last century, America's faith in freedom and democracy was a rock in a raging sea. Now it is a seed upon the wind, taking root in
many nations.

Our democratic faith is more than the creed of our country, it is the inborn
hope of our humanity, an ideal we carry but do not own, a trust we bear and
pass along. And even after nearly 225 years, we have a long way yet to travel.

While many of our citizens prosper, others doubt the promise, even the justice, of our own country. The ambitions of some Americans are limited by failing schools and hidden prejudice and the circumstances of their birth. And

sometimes our differences run so deep, it seems we share a continent, but not a country.

We do not accept this, and we will not allow it. Our unity, our union, is the serious work of leaders and citizens in every generation. And this is my solemn pledge: I will work to build a single nation of justice and opportunity.

I know this is in our reach because we are guided by a power larger than ourselves who creates us equal in His image.

And we are confident in principles that unite and lead us onward.

America has never been united by blood or birth or soil. We are bound by ideals that move us beyond our backgrounds, lift us above our interests and teach us what it means to be citizens. Every child must be taught these principles. Every citizen must uphold them. And every immigrant, by embracing these ideals, makes our country more, not less, American.

Today, we affirm a new commitment to live out our nation's promise through civility, courage, compassion and character.

America, at its best, matches a commitment to principle with a concern for civility. A civil society demands from each of us good will and respect, fair dealing and forgiveness.

Some seem to believe that our politics can afford to be petty because, in a time of peace, the stakes of our debates appear small.

But the stakes for America are never small. If our country does not lead the cause of freedom, it will not be led. If we do not turn the hearts of children toward knowledge and character, we will lose their gifts and undermine their idealism. If we permit our economy to drift and decline, the vulnerable will suffer most.

We must live up to the calling we share. Civility is not a tactic or a sentiment. It is the determined choice of trust over cynicism, of community over chaos. And this commitment, if we keep it, is a way to shared accomplishment.

America, at its best, is also courageous.

Our national courage has been clear in times of depression and war, when defending common dangers defined our common good. Now we must choose if the example of our fathers and mothers will inspire us or condemn us. We must show courage in a time of blessing by confronting problems instead of passing them on to future generations.

Together, we will reclaim America's schools, before ignorance and apathy claim more young lives.

We will reform Social Security and Medicare, sparing our children from struggles we have the power to prevent. And we will reduce taxes, to recover the momentum of our economy and reward the effort and enterprise of working Americans.

We will build our defenses beyond challenge, lest weakness invite challenge.

We will confront weapons of mass destruction, so that a new century is spared new horrors.

The enemies of liberty and our country should make no mistake: America remains engaged in the world by history and by choice, shaping a balance of power that favors freedom. We will defend our allies and our interests. We will show purpose without arrogance. We will meet aggression and bad faith with resolve and strength. And to all nations, we will speak for the values that gave our nation birth.

America, at its best, is compassionate. In the quiet of American conscience, we know that deep, persistent poverty is unworthy of our nation's promise.

And whatever our views of its cause, we can agree that children at risk are not at fault. Abandonment and abuse are not acts of God, they are failures of love.

And the proliferation of prisons, however necessary, is no substitute for hope and order in our souls.

Where there is suffering, there is duty. Americans in need are not strangers, they are citizens, not problems, but priorities. And all of us are diminished when any are hopeless.

Government has great responsibilities for public safety and public health, for civil rights and common schools. Yet compassion is the work of a nation, not just a government.

And some needs and hurts are so deep they will only respond to a mentor's touch or a pastor's prayer. Church and charity, synagogue and mosque lend our communities their humanity, and they will have an honored place in our plans and in our laws.

Many in our country do not know the pain of poverty, but we can listen to those who do.

And I can pledge our nation to a goal: When we see that wounded traveler on the road to Jericho, we will not pass to the other side.

America, at its best, is a place where personal responsibility is valued and expected.

Encouraging responsibility is not a search for scapegoats, it is a call to conscience. And though it requires sacrifice, it brings a deeper fulfillment. We find the fullness of life not only in options, but in commitments. And we find that children and community are the commitments that set us free.

Our public interest depends on private character, on civic duty and family bonds and basic fairness, on uncounted, unhonored acts of decency which give direction to our freedom.

Sometimes in life we are called to do great things. But as a saint of our times has said, every day we are called to do small things with great love. The most important tasks of a democracy are done by everyone.

I will live and lead by these principles: to advance my convictions with civility, to pursue the public interest with courage, to speak for greater justice and compassion, to call for responsibility and try to live it as well.

In all these ways, I will bring the values of our history to the care of our times.

What you do is as important as anything government does. I ask you to seek a common good beyond your comfort; to defend needed reforms against easy attacks; to serve your nation, beginning with your neighbor. I ask you to be citizens: citizens, not spectators; citizens, not subjects; responsible citizens, building communities of service and a nation of character.

Americans are generous and strong and decent, not because we believe in ourselves, but because we hold beliefs beyond ourselves. When this spirit of citizenship is missing, no government program can replace it. When this spirit is present, no wrong can stand against it.

After the Declaration of Independence was signed, Virginia statesman John Page wrote to Thomas Jefferson: "We know the race is not to the swift nor the battle to the strong. Do you not think an angel rides in the whirlwind and directs this storm?"

Much time has passed since Jefferson arrived for his inauguration. The years and changes accumulate. But the themes of this day he would know: our nation's grand story of courage and its simple dream of dignity.

We are not this story's author, who fills time and eternity with his purpose. Yet his purpose is achieved in our duty, and our duty is fulfilled in service to one another.

Never tiring, never yielding, never finishing, we renew that purpose today, to make our country more just and generous, to affirm the dignity of our lives and every life.

This work continues. This story goes on. And an angel still rides in the whirlwind and directs this storm.

God bless you all, and God bless America.

ARROYO ON HER INAUGURATION
AS PHILIPPINE PRESIDENT
January 20, 2001

"People Power" surfaced again during 2001 as a significant force in public life in the Philippines, forcing a president from office but failing to topple his successor. But there was an important difference from the first emergence of people power in 1986, when massive public protests forced a corrupt dictator, Ferdinand Marcos, to abandon the presidential palace in Manila after he attempted to steal an election. This time, in January 2001, the protests were against an elected president who still had substantial public support and was not even halfway into his six-year term. Public anger at President Joseph Estrada's corruption—and the very real possibility that he might be able to get away with it—boiled over into the streets of Manila and cost Estrada support among key constituencies, including the military. Vice President Gloria Macapagal Arroyo took the oath of office as president on January 20, 2001, even as Estrada was still holed up in the presidential palace. Weeks later, when Estrada was arrested on corruption charges, his supporters tried, but failed, to use similar public protests to try to force Arroyo out of office. (Marcos ouster, Historic Documents of 1986, p. 307)

This political theater took place in the context of deepening economic woes in the Philippines, which had missed out on much of the boom in the rest of East Asia during the 1980s and 1990s and then was buffeted by the Asian financial crisis of 1997–1998. Unable to attract substantial foreign investment and with few domestic resources other than its 73 million people, the Philippines struggled along with an economy based largely on subsistence agriculture, with a few pockets of high-tech industry susceptible to the turbulent winds of the global economy. In 2001 the official employment rate was about 11 percent (but real unemployment probably was much higher) and per capita income was just $1,000, among the lowest in East Asia. (Asian financial crisis, Historic Documents of 1998, p. 722)

As if political and economic troubles were not enough, late in the year the Philippines appeared headed for involvement in the Bush administration's international campaign to root out Islamic terrorist groups in the wake of the September 11 attacks against the United States. Bush laid plans in November and December to provide military equipment and training for Philippine forces battling insurgent groups in the southern part of the country. One of the groups was said to have links to Osama bin Laden's al Qaeda network, which Bush blamed for the September 11 attacks. (Terrorist attacks, pp. 614, 624)

People Power II

Joseph Estrada had been an actor in low-budget movies, often portraying tough-talking gangsters and policemen who helped the poor. Such roles won him wide popularity among the millions of impoverished Filipinos, who then flocked to the polls when the actor-turned-politician ran for the presidency in 1998. Estrada won an overwhelming victory, becoming the country's third successive elected president; the first was Corazon Aquino, whose electoral victory Marcos had tried to overturn in 1986, and the second was Fidel Ramos, a former military chief elected in 1992.

It soon became evident that Estrada was more interested in the social aspects of the presidency than in public policy. Local newspapers reported that Estrada partied and gambled late into the night, drank excessively, and was accompanied by numerous women other than his wife. Many Filipinos reportedly found this roguish behavior charming, but the president's personal life took on a different cast in October 2000 when a provincial governor, who was a long-time friend, accused Estrada of accepting $8 million in bribes from illegal gambling syndicates and about $2.7 million in kickbacks from local tobacco taxes. Estrada denied the charges, but his accuser, Luis Singson, produced evidence backing his complaints, and opposition legislators filed an impeachment resolution in the lower house of parliament. Arroyo, an opposition leader who had been elected as Estrada's vice president as part of a coalition, quickly resigned her position in his cabinet (but not the vice presidency), and several dozen other legislators quit the ruling coalition as well. The lower house voted on November 13, 2000, to impeach Estrada on bribery charges. The Senate, narrowly controlled by Estrada's allies, began a trial on December 8.

Evidence introduced during the trial made it apparent that Singson's charges against Estrada were just the tip of an iceberg of corruption. Prosecutors said Estrada had illegally accepted $63.5 million from kickbacks, bribes, insider-trading deals, and other corrupt dealings with business associates. But on January 16, 2001, the Senate, on an 11–10 vote, refused to authorize a review of Estrada's bank records, a step necessary to prove the charges against him.

Opposition senators quit in disgust and the country's influential Roman Catholic primate, Cardinal Jaime Sin, urged people to gather at a Manila shrine that had been the focal point of the people power protests against Marcos nearly fourteen years earlier (the protests were called "Edsa," after the road where they occurred). Thousands of people heeded the cardinal's call, surging through the streets with a demand that Estrada resign. The demonstrations continued for two more days, then on January 19 military *leaders and most cabinet members broke with Estrada and told him they were throwing their support to Arroyo. Word of those defections set off wild celebrations in the streets, but Estrada refused to step down and made a televised appeal for new elections, promising not to be a candidate. Even that last-minute ploy failed to sway the crowds or the political establishment, which laid plans for Arroyo to assume the presidency the next day.*

Huge crowds assembled early on January 20 for the inauguration of Arroyo, which took place at the Edsa shrine. In her inaugural address, Arroyo pledged to "change the character of our politics" by doing away with the "personality and patronage" features that had dominated in the past. Arroyo said elimination of poverty would be her first priority. That statement clearly was intended to overcome the conviction among many Filipinos that the country's ruling classes had turned against Estrada simply because he had championed the poor. Arroyo also sought to contrast herself to Estrada, saying that "the presidency is not a position to be enjoyed. It is a position where one must work very hard."

After Arroyo took the oath of office, a crowd estimated at more than 70,000 people headed toward the presidential palace, where Estrada was still ensconced with several hundred supporters and was demanding a pardon and five more days in power. When those demands were refused and protesters broke through police barricades surrounding the palace, Estrada left through a back door (just as Marcos had in 1986), boarded a waiting barge on the Pasig River, and eventually made his way to his private residence outside Manila.

The high drama of Estrada's hasty departure from the palace did not end the 2001 chapter of Filipino people power, however. Refusing to give up, Estrada filed a claim with the Supreme Court that he was still the president because he had not resigned and was therefore immune from criminal prosecution. The Supreme Court rejected that claim in two rulings. Immediately after the second ruling on April 3, prosecutors indicted Estrada on charges that he had taken about $82 million worth of bribes and other payoffs while in office. Estrada was arrested April 25, and for days afterwards thousands of his supporters surrounded the presidential palace demanding that the charges against him be dropped and that Arroyo step aside. Four people were killed in rioting on May 1, leading Arroyo to declare a "state of rebellion" that gave police extraordinary powers. Arroyo lifted that order after five days, when the protests quieted.

The next major challenge for Arroyo was the May 14 election for thirteen open seats in the twenty-four-seat Senate, the upper chamber of the legislature that had been controlled by Estrada loyalists. Parties loyal to Arroyo won eight of the open seats, giving her a slight working majority, but not the overwhelming victory she had wanted as a mandate. Among the anti-Arroyo senators elected was Luisa Ejercito, Estrada's wife.

Arroyo's background, coupled with her firm actions during her early weeks in office, helped reassure business leaders and international observers who were unnerved by the frequency of mass protests in the Philippines. Arroyo was the daughter of one of the country's early elected presidents, Diosdado

Macapagal, who served from 1961 to 1965 and was defeated for reelection by Marcos. She studied economics at Georgetown University in Washington, D.C., becoming a friend of fellow student Bill Clinton. Arroyo served in a subcabinet post during the Aquino administration, then was elected to the Senate in 1992 and ran as Estrada's vice presidential candidate in a coalition in 1998.

Rebellions in the South

In addition to economic malaise, one of the persistent challenges facing Arroyo was an assortment of Islam-based guerrilla movements on Mindanao and other islands in the southern Philippines. The islands were home to nearly all the 4 million Muslim Filipinos, who were a small minority in the overwhelmingly Roman Catholic country. Two groups had fought for the independence of Mindanao from the rest of the country. One, the Moro National Liberation Front (MNLF), had signed a peace agreement with the government in 1996 and laid down its arms after three decades of fighting in which more than 100,000 people were killed; a faction of that group, the Moro Islamic Liberation Front, had continued to fight even while engaging in periodic negotiations with the Estrada administration. A third rebel group, Abu Sayyaf ("Father of the Sword" in Arabic), had taken up arms against the government in 1991 on Basilan Island, southwest of Mindanao.

Arroyo had to deal with crises involving both the Moro Islamic Liberation Front and the Abu Sayyaf guerrillas during her first few months in office. Abu Sayyaf posed the first dilemma, in May, when it kidnapped twenty people, including three Americans, from a resort. This appeared to be a repeat of the group's kidnapping in April 2000 of twenty-one tourists from a resort in Malaysia. In the previous case, Abu Sayyaf held the tourists captive on the Philippine island of Jolo for several months, eventually freeing them in return for a ransom variously reported as $20–25 million, paid by the Libyan government. Philippine officials said the guerrillas used the money to buy weapons and even a small fleet of speedboats. The guerrillas demanded ransom again in 2001, but when it was not forthcoming they claimed to have beheaded one of the captives, Guillermo Sobero of Corona, California. Two other Americans, missionaries Gracia and Martin Burnham of Wichita, Kansas, and a Filipino remained in captivity throughout the rest of 2001 while the government tried unsuccessfully to locate the Abu Sayyaf rebels.

In the meantime, Arroyo stepped up negotiations with the Moro Islamic Liberation Front. A tentative peace agreement was reached in June, with Libya acting as the mediator; the government and rebels on August 7 signed a formal cease-fire mediated by Malaysia. That peace process was threatened briefly in late November, when elements of the supposedly defunct MNLF staged attacks on Jolo Island, also southwest of Mindanao. Those attacks reportedly were precipitated by the group's former leader, Nur Misauri, who had been serving as the appointed governor of an "autonomous" region of Mindanao and objected to the government's plans for an election. More than 100 people were killed in clashes between government forces and guerrillas loyal to Misauri, according to news reports. Misauri was captured in late November, and several thousand government troops landed on Jolo to suppress the insurgency.

The clashes on Jolo Island occurred as Arroyo was in Washington, D.C., for meetings with President Bush, whose attention had been drawn to the Philippines because of persistent reports linking the Abu Sayyaf group to terrorist leader bin Laden. Abu Sayyaf's founder, Abuarak Abubakar Janjalani, reportedly received financial support in the 1990s from bin Laden's brother-in-law, Muhammad Jamal Khalifa; U.S. intelligence agencies said Khalifa, in turn, had ties to the terrorists who bombed the World Trade Center in 1995. (World Trade Center bombing, Historic Documents of 1995, p. 176)

In a meeting at the White House on November 20, Bush promised Arroyo more than $90 million in military aid to help battle the Abu Sayyaf guerrillas. Bush reportedly offered to send U.S. combat forces to the Philippines, as well, but Arroyo rebuffed the offer, citing legal and political obstacles to such a move. The United States had controlled the Philippines from 1898 until after World War II and had maintained two major military bases there until 1992, when the Philippine government refused to renew the leases. Despite Arroyo's refusal of the offer, Bush said the United States "will cooperate in any way she suggests in getting rid of Abu Sayyaf."

Bush and Arroyo ultimately settled on a compromise: the United States would send Army Special Forces units to the Philippines to train the local military in counterinsurgency tactics. Special forces officers arrived in the southern Philippines in December to arrange plans for the training mission, which was expected to begin in January 2002 with about 100 troops.

The U.S. soldiers were to be armed and were to accompany Philippine troops on patrols but were not to engage in actual combat except in defense, Pentagon officials said. Admiral Dennis C. Blair, commander of U.S. forces in the Pacific region, called the mission the "largest and most comprehensive" U.S. military operation in Asia in many years—but the Bush administration and Philippine officials insisted they had no plans to expand the mission or its role.

> *Following are excerpts from a speech delivered January 20, 2001, by Gloria Macapagal Arroyo after taking the oath of office as president of the Philippines.*
>
> **The document was obtained from the Internet at http:// www.kgma.org/speech.html.**

In all humility, I accept the presidency of the Republic. I do so with both trepidation and a sense of awe.

Trepidation, because it is now, as the good book says, a time to heal and a time to build. The task is formidable, and so I pray that we will all be one, one in our priorities, one in our values and commitments and one because of

EDSA 2001 [EDSA is the acronym for Epifanio de los Santos, a ring road around Manila that was the site of demonstrations leading to the ouster of President Ferdinand Marcos in 1986; it had since become the popular term for "People Power" revolt against Marcos.

Sense of awe, because of the Filipino has done it again on the hallowed ground of EDSA.

People power and the "oneness" of will and vision have made a new beginning possible. I cannot, therefore, at this point, but recall Ninoy Aquino's words: "I have carefully weighed the virtues and the faults of the Filipino, and I have come to the conclusion that he is worth dying for." [Benigno Aquino was an opposition leader assassinated in 1983.]

As we break from the past in our quest for a new Philippines, the unity, the Filipino's sense of history, and his unshakable faith in the Almighty that prevailed in EDSA '86 and EDSA 2001 will continue to guide and inspire us. . . .

I am certain that pride will reign supreme as they recall the heroism and sacrifices and prayers of Jaime Cardinal Sin, former Presidents Corazon Aquino and Fidel Ramos, the legislators who fought the good fight in Congress, the leaders whose principles were beyond negotiation, the witnesses in the impeachment trial who did not count the cost of testifying, the generals in the Armed Forces and the Philippine National Police, and the Filipino out there who stood up to be counted in these troubled times.

The Filipino, crises and all, is truly worth living and dying for.

But pray, where do we go from here?

Jose Rizal, the first to articulate self-determination in a free society [Rizal led Philippine resistance to Spanish rule in the late 1800s], provides the answer.

Rizal counseled the Filipino to lead a life of commitment. He must think national, go beyond self.

A stone is worthless, Rizal wrote, if it is not part of an edifice.

We are the stones, and the Philippines is our edifice.

On many occasions I have given my views on what our program of government should be. This is not the time or place to repeat them all. However, I can tell you that they converge on four core beliefs.

1. We must be bold in our national ambitions, so that our challenge must be that within this decade, we will win the fight against poverty.
2. We must improve moral standards in government and society, in order to provide a strong foundation for good governance.
3. We must change the character of our politics, in order to create fertile ground for true reforms. Our politics of personality and patronage must give way to a new politics of party programs and process of dialogue with the people.
4. Finally, I believe in leadership be example. We should promote solid traits such as work ethic and a dignified lifestyle, matching action to rhetoric, performing rather that grandstanding.

The first of my core beliefs pertains to the elimination of (poverty). This is our unfinished business from the past. It dates back to the creation of our

Republic, whose seeds were sown in the revolution launched in 1896 by the plebeian Andres Bonifacio. It was an unfinished revolution, for to this day, (poverty remains our national problem). We need to complete what Andres Bonifacio began. The ultimate solution to (poverty) has both a political and an economic aspect. Let me first talk about the political aspect.

In doing so, I will refer to one of my core beliefs, that of the need for new politics. Politics and political power as traditionally practiced and used in the Philippines are among the roots of the social and economic inequities that characterize our national problems. Thus, to achieve true reforms, we need to outgrow our traditional brand of politics based on patronage and personality. Traditional politics is the politics of the status quo. It is a structural part of our problem.

We need to promote a new politics of true party programs and platforms, of an institutional process of dialogue with our citizenry. This new politics is the politics of genuine reform. It is a structural part of the solution.

We have long accepted the need to level the playing field in business and economics. Now, we must accept the need to level the playing field in politics as well. We have long aspired to be a world class economy. Now, we must also aspire to develop a world class political system, one in tune with the 21st century.

The world of the 21st century that our youth will inherit is truly a new economy, where relentless forces such as capital market flows and advances in information and communications technology create both peril and opportunity.

To tap the opportunities, we need an economic philosophy of transparency and private enterprise, for these are the catalysts that [nurture] the entrepreneurial spirit to be globally competitive.

To extend the opportunities to our rural countryside, we must create a modernized and socially equitable agricultural sector.

To address the perils, we must give a social bias to balance our economic development, and these are embodied in safety nets for sectors affected by globalization, and safeguards for our environment.

To ensure that our gains are not dissipated through corruption, we must improve [moral standards]. As we do so, we create fertile ground for good governance based on a sound moral foundation, a philosophy of transparency, and an ethic of effective implementation.

Considering the divisions of today, our commitment will entail a lot of sacrifices among us all, as work to restore the dignity and pre-eminence of the Filipino.

Join me therefore as we begin to tear down the walls that divide. Let us build an edifice of peace, progress, and economic stability.

People power has dramatized the Filipino's capacity for greatness.

I ask for your support and prayers. Together, we will light the healing and cleansing flame.

This we owe to the Philippines. This we owe to every Filipino.

Thank you and may the good Lord bless us all.

UN SCIENTIFIC PANEL ON GLOBAL WARMING
January 22, 2001

International scientists issued new warnings during 2001 that human activities—especially the burning of coal, petroleum products, and other fossil fuels—were contributing to an increase in temperatures known as "global warming." Despite a firmer consensus among scientists on the issue, the new administration of President George W. Bush pulled the United States out of international negotiations on a treaty mandating steps to reduce the causes of global warming.

Many scientists had argued since the early 1980s that the burning of fossil fuels, which produced carbon dioxide (CO_2), helped caused a "greenhouse effect" by trapping heat in the Earth's atmosphere. The greenhouse effect, these scientists said, had contributed to a perceived increase in global temperatures during the past century of about 1 degree Fahrenheit and probably would force temperatures substantially higher during the twenty-first century; the result would be significant changes in the world climate, including a worsening of droughts, floods, and storms. A minority of scientists, along with many industry groups, rejected this theory and said any warming of the global climate was due more to natural causes than to human activity; these global warming skeptics also suggested that future climate changes would not be severe.

In 1997 the United States joined 150 other nations in negotiating a treaty, the Kyoto Protocol on Climate Change, that committed them to legally binding reductions in emissions of greenhouse gases; for the United States, that meant returning its greenhouse gas emissions to the 1990 level by 2012, in effect a 30 percent reduction. Most major U.S. industries staunchly opposed the Kyoto treaty, saying it would undermine the economy by forcing drastic changes in energy consumption. President Bill Clinton, who generally approved the treaty, never submitted it to the Senate for approval, but the Senate in 1998 put itself on record as opposing the treaty. Negotiations in November 2000 failed to produce agreement on technical details needed to implement the Kyoto treaty. After Bush withdrew the United States from talks on the issue, two sets of negotiations during 2001 resulted in a landmark agreement on carrying out the Kyoto mandates. (Framework convention, Historic Documents of 1992, p. 499; Kyoto treaty, Historic Documents of 1997, p. 859; Kyoto implementing negotiations, Historic Documents of 2000, p. 337)

International Panel Report

Global warming arose as an international scientific and political issue because climatologists and other experts had raised a warning about the effects of accumulations in the atmosphere of carbon dioxide and other "greenhouse gases." The United Nations in 1988 established an international panel of several hundred scientists, the Intergovernmental Panel on Climate Change, to review the evidence and draw conclusions that could help national policymakers make decisions. The panel issued several reports during the 1990s, including one in 1995 that found a "discernable human influence" on global warming and predicted that the average global surface temperature could rise by 6.3 degrees Fahrenheit by 2100. The 1995 report helped set the stage for adoption of the Kyoto Protocol in 1997.

The scientific panel reviewed the evidence again during 2000, with two "working groups" tackling separate but related questions. One group examined the causes of global warming and how much temperatures could expect to change over the next century; the other group examined specific climate changes that could result from global warming.

The working group on temperature changes convened in Shanghai in January 2001 and released its findings January 22. The report said that new research and computer models had given the panel "a greater understanding of climate change" and had led it to adjust upwards its estimate of how much temperatures had risen in the previous century and its projection of increases during the twenty-first century. During the twentieth century, the panel said, temperatures had risen by about 1.1 degree Fahrenheit (or 0.6 degree Celsius). The rising temperatures could help explain such recent phenomena (primarily in the northern hemisphere) as the retreat of mountain glaciers, a noticeable reduction in annual snow and ice cover, and an increase in severe weather patterns, the panel said. During the twenty-first century average temperatures could increase by another 2.5 to 10.4 degrees Fahrenheit (or 1.4 to 5.8 degrees Celsius). Both the low and high parts of that range were significantly above estimates the panel had made just six years earlier. The panel said it was likely that the greatest temperature increases would occur during the winter in the northern regions of North America and in northern and central Asia. (As a point of comparison, scientists said global temperatures at the end of the twentieth century were about 9 degrees Fahrenheit higher than during the most recent ice age about 10,000 to 15,000 years ago.)

The panel also said it had found "new and stronger evidence that most of the observed warming of the last fifty years is attributable to human activities," principally the burning of coal, oil, and gasoline. Deforestation—which reduced the natural absorption of CO_2—was another significant factor. Natural phenomena, such as sun spots and volcanic eruptions, *likely were responsible for only "small amounts" of global warming, the panel said.*

Summarizing the report, Robert Watson, an American scientist working as an adviser to the World Bank, said: "We see changes in climate, we believe we humans are involved, and we're projecting future climate changes much more significant over the next 100 years than the last 100 years." Such findings "should sound alarm bells in every national capital and in every local community," said Klaus Töpfer, executive director of the UN's environment program.

The second working group met in Geneva, Switzerland, in February and issued its report February 19. That report reviewed the effects of global warming during the twentieth century and projected the impact on humans and natural systems of the even more extensive global warming expected during the twenty-first century. During the past century, the report said, global warming had been at least partly responsible for such phenomena as shrinking glaciers and thawing permafrost, reduced ice cover on lakes and rivers, longer growing seasons in mid- to high latitudes, declines of some animal and plant populations, and the earlier flowering of trees and emergence of insects in the spring.

For the twenty-first century, the panel said global warming is likely to lead to substantial changes in climate, such as higher maximum temperatures, with more hot days and more heat waves, over nearly all land areas; higher minimum temperatures, with fewer cold days and cold waves, over nearly all land areas; and more intense "precipitation events" (torrential rain storms, for example) over many areas. Many natural systems would be subject to increased stress, including glaciers and polar ice caps, temperate forests, mountain ecosystems, and coral reefs.

These changes, in turn, could have major consequences for humans, such as more heat-induced deaths among the elderly and urban poor, reduced crop production in some areas and enhanced crop production in others, and more frequent and severe floods in low-lying coastal areas and landslides in upland areas. The panel gave probability ranges for all its estimates, noting that some consequences of global warming appeared to be more likely than others and would have variable affects on different regions of the world. Moreover, the panel said some societies would be more able than others to adapt to changes caused by global warming. In general, it suggested that developing countries—already stressed by population growth, poverty, and depletion of natural resources such as water and forests—would suffer more than developed countries in terms of loss of life and reduced economic growth The panel's chairman, James J. McCarthy of Harvard University, gave this blunt summary: "Most of the Earth's people will be on the losing side."

Although the UN reports represented the consensus views of hundreds of respected scientists from around the world, some critics were not impressed by the findings. One of the most vocal was S. Fred Singer, professor emeritus of environmental science at the University of Virginia and former director of the U.S. Weather Bureau's Satellite Service. Singer rejected the findings of the UN panel and told the Washington Post *that the panel's second report "is based on shaky science and is designed to present only the worst possible cases in order to scare politicians and the population and pressure the [Bush] administration into signing the Kyoto Protocol."*

National Research Council Report

In preparation for President Bush's first trip to Europe in mid-June, the White House in May asked the National Academy of Science for a report on the current status of scientific research into global warming. The academy's National Research Council then convened a committee of eleven specialists on atmospheric science, chaired by Ralph Cicerone, chancellor of the University of California at Irvine. Several of the committee members had previously expressed skepticism about aspects of global warming, including its causes. The committee worked from a series of questions posed by the White House, some of which appeared to stem from a skepticism that global warming was a serious problem.

Released on June 6, that committee's report essentially supported the findings of the UN panel. In particular, the committee agreed with the UN panel that global temperatures had risen and that the global climate changes "are likely mostly due to human activities," especially increased emissions of greenhouse gases. The latter conclusion, the committee said, "accurately reflects the current thinking of the scientific community." The committee offered only one mild criticism of the UN panel's work: a suggestion that the UN panel needed to state the "caveats" to its conclusions more clearly.

Bush and key cabinet officials discussed the National Academy of Science study at a meeting on June 5. The president's national security adviser, Condoleezza Rice, said senior officials had been educating themselves and "grappling with the issue" for weeks.

The academy's report generated predictable reactions on Capitol Hill, where members on both sides of the global warming issue had been maneuvering to influence policies of the new administration. Senator John Kerry, a Democrat from Massachusetts who had called for more U.S. action to combat global warming, said the report "confirms in stark terms the reality that many of us had accepted a considerable amount of time ago and refutes an effort by the White House to seek some sort of escape hatch from that reality." By contrast, Senator Chuck Hagel, R-Neb., a staunch opponent of the Kyoto Protocol, said the report "is certainly not a prescription for the drastic measures required" by that treaty.

Bush Announces New U.S. Policy

With his previously stated views doubting the reality of global warming having been rebuffed by leading scientists, Bush turned to a new strategy, which he announced at the White House June 11. Flanked by Vice President Dick Cheney and key cabinet members, Bush emphasized the still uncertain elements of research into global warming and vigorously attacked the Kyoto Protocol.

Bush acknowledged that the National Academy of Science report said that the increased concentrations of greenhouse gases in the atmosphere were "due in large part to human activity." But he added that the report "tells us that we do not know how much effect natural fluctuations in climate may have had on warming. We do not know how much our climate could, or will change in the future. We do not know how fast change will occur, or even how some of our actions could impact."

Bush acknowledged that the United States was the single largest producer of greenhouse gases, saying that the United States accounted for about 20 percent of the world total (the most recent government figures, for 1997, had put the U.S. contribution at 24 percent). Even so, he said, the remaining 80 percent came from other countries, including developing countries such as China and India that had been exempted from the mandatory emission reductions of the Kyoto Protocol.

"Kyoto is, in many ways, unrealistic," Bush said, adding that the treaty's targets for reducing emissions were "arbitrary, and not based on science." For the United States, "complying with those mandates would have a negative economic impact, with layoffs of workers and price increases for consumers."

Having rejected the Kyoto treaty as "not sound public policy," Bush offered no specific alternatives beyond pledging that the administration "will be creative" and would emphasize continued economic growth and "market-based incentives" for curbing greenhouse gas emissions. To help answer remaining questions, Bush announced creation of the National Climate Change Technology Initiative, which he said would "strengthen research" at universities and other scientific centers into means of measuring climate change and developing demonstration projects for "cutting-edge technologies" into alternative energy sources.

As with all other policy statements on the issue, Bush's new position generated expected reactions. Environmental groups and scientists who had warned of global warming dangers expressed dismay that Bush was proposing further delay in action to curb greenhouse gas emissions so more studies could be conducted. "There will be deep uncertainty in the climate future for a long time," Michael E. Schlesinger, director of climate research at the University of Illinois at Urbana-Champaign told the New York Times. "But if you wait until [the uncertainty] diminished to some threshold that you assign, and then learn that the problem is severe, it may be too late to do anything about it." Representatives of industry groups that had opposed the Kyoto treaty said they were pleased by Bush's stance.

The White House on July 13 announced a series of research projects that it said were to be included in the Bush initiative. They included a $120 million, three-year project managed by NASA to research basic science questions involved in global warming; a $25 million Energy Department agreement with the Nature Conservancy to study the potential impact on global warming of land use and forestry practices, using plots in Belize and Brazil as examples; and a "debt for forest" swap under which the Treasury

Department would erase $14 million of El Salvador's debt to the United States in return for forest conservation in that country. Both the energy and treasury programs had been in the planning stages for some time. Even as it announced these programs, the administration sent Congress a fiscal 2002 budget that cut U.S. aid to other countries for programs to combat greenhouse gas emissions.

Agreement on Kyoto Ratification

By removing the biggest player from the negotiating table, Bush's withdrawal of the United States from the Kyoto Protocol made it easier for other countries to settle issues that long had plagued efforts to put final touches on the treaty. The 1997 negotiations that led to the Kyoto treaty had left unresolved key issues, most notably how each country should be given credit for reducing its greenhouse gas emissions. The treaty required about forty industrialized countries to curb their emissions by 2012. Negotiations at The Hague, Netherlands, in November 2000 failed to settle the unresolved issues, and so new talks were convened in mid-July in Bonn, Germany. A U.S. representative attended but did not participate in the negotiations.

In Bonn representatives of 178 countries that had signed the Kyoto treaty reached a complex series of agreements on July 23 settling most of the remaining issues on how to enforce it. In general, the agreement involved a complex series of tradeoffs intended to make it easier for key countries, especially Japan, to meet their targets. Environmental advocates said the agreement weakened the original Kyoto treaty, but they acknowledged that political leaders were having difficulty accepting the changes needed to cut greenhouse gas emissions.

The agreement allowed industrialized countries to gain credit for the presence of forests and croplands, called "carbon sinks" because they absorb huge quantities of carbon dioxide. Many European nations—which had led the world in curbing greenhouse gas emissions—had opposed giving credits for carbon sinks; they said it would allow countries to appear to meet their emissions targets without actually cutting emissions. Similarly, the agreement allowed industrialized countries to gain credit for emissions cuts by investing in clean-air projects in developing countries or by buying emission credits from other countries. For example, Japan could buy credits for reduced emissions from Russia and the Ukraine, both of which had reduced industrial production, and thereby reduced greenhouse gas emissions, because of economic decline during the 1990s. (Russian economy, p. 254)

Under the Bonn agreement, the Kyoto treaty would take effect—and thus become legally binding on signatory nations—once it had been ratified by fifty-five nations, including nations that had generated at least 55 percent of the industrialized world's carbon dioxide emissions in 1990. In effect, that provision meant the treaty would have to be ratified by Britain, Canada, Germany, and Japan, which together accounted for nearly all of the 55 percent minimum. Of those nations, Japan was seen as the key because it had lagged behind in the reduction of greenhouse gases.

Despite the progress of the Bonn talks, several important details were still unresolved, and further negotiations were convened in Marrakech, Morocco, in late October. White House officials had said the United States would present a new proposal at those talks, but the administration delayed any action on the issue after the September 11 terrorist attacks against targets in New York and Washington. (Terrorist attacks, pp. 614, 624)

The Marrakech negotiations focused on technical details, notably how to implement the trading of emissions credits. An agreement reached on November 10 settled those details, enabling the United Nations to announce that the Kyoto Protocol was a finished product ready for ratification by member nations. Olivier Deleuze, chief delegate at the talks for the European Union, said the agreement "saved" the Kyoto Protocol. "The Kyoto process is now irreversible," he said. By the end of 2001, more than forty countries had ratified the treaty, but Romania was the only one on the list of industrialized countries required to reduce greenhouse gas emissions by 2012. A review of progress toward ratification was planned for the UN's World Summit on Sustainable Development to be held in Johannesburg, South Africa, in August 2002.

Following are excerpts from the "Summary for Policymakers," released January 22, 2001, in Shanghai, China, by the Working Group 1 of the Intergovernmental Panel on Climate Change.

The document was obtained from the Internet at http://www.ipcc.ch/pub/spm22-01.pdf.

The Third Assessment Report of Working Group I of the Intergovernmental Panel on Climate Change (IPCC) builds upon past assessments and incorporates new results from the past five years of research on climate change. Many hundreds of scientists from many countries participated in its preparation and review.

This Summary for Policymakers (SPM), which was approved by IPCC member governments in Shanghai in January 2001, describes the current state of understanding of the climate system and provides estimates of its projected future evolution and their uncertainties. . . .

An increasing body of observations gives a collective picture of a warming world and other changes in the climate system.

Since the release of the Second Assessment Report (SAR), additional data from new studies of current and palaeoclimates, improved analysis of data sets, more rigorous evaluation of their quality, and comparisons among data from different sources have led to greater understanding of climate change.

The global average surface temperature has increased over the 20th century by about 0.6°C. [1 degree Celsius equals 1.08 degree Fahrenheit.]

- The global average surface temperature (the average of near surface air temperature over land, and sea surface temperature) has increased since 1861. Over the 20th century the increase has been 0.6 ± 0.2°C. This value is about 0.15°C larger than that estimated by the SAR for the period up to 1994, owing to the relatively high temperatures of the additional years (1995 to 2000) and improved methods of processing the data. These numbers take into account various adjustments, including urban heat island effects. The record shows a great deal of variability; for example, most of the warming occurred during the 20th century, during two periods, 1910 to 1945 and 1976 to 2000.
- Globally, it is very likely [defined as a 90 to 99 percent change] that the 1990s was the warmest decade and 1998 the warmest year in the instrumental record, since 1861.
- New analyses of proxy data [such as examinations of polar cap ice cores] for the Northern Hemisphere indicate that the increase in temperature in the 20th century is likely [defined as a 66 to 90 percent change] to have been the largest of any century during the past 1,000 years. It is also likely that, in the Northern Hemisphere, the 1990s was the warmest decade and 1998 the warmest year. Because less data are available, less is known about annual averages prior to 1,000 years before present and for conditions prevailing in most of the Southern Hemisphere prior to 1861.
- On average, between 1950 and 1993, night-time daily minimum air temperatures over land increased by about 0.2°C per decade. This is about twice the rate of increase in daytime daily maximum air temperatures (0.1°C per decade). This has lengthened the freeze-free season in many mid-and high latitude regions. The increase in sea surface temperature over this period is about half that of the mean land surface air temperature.

Temperatures have risen during the past four decades in the lowest 8 kilometres of the atmosphere.

- Since the late 1950s (the period of adequate observations from weather balloons), the overall global temperature increases in the lowest 8 kilometres of the atmosphere and in surface temperature have been similar at 0.1°C per decade.
- Since the start of the satellite record in 1979, both satellite and weather balloon measurements show that the global average temperature of the lowest 8 kilometres of the atmosphere has changed by + 0.05 ± 0.10°C per decade, but the global average surface temperature has increased significantly by + 0.15 ± 0.05°C per decade. The difference in the warming rates is statistically significant. This difference occurs primarily over the tropical and sub-tropical regions.
- The lowest 8 kilometres [4.8 miles] of the atmosphere and the surface are influenced differently by factors such as stratospheric ozone depletion, atmospheric aerosols, and the El Niño phenomenon. Hence, it is physically plausible to expect that over a short time period (e.g., 20 years)

there may be differences in temperature trends. In addition, spatial sampling techniques can also explain some of the differences in trends, but these differences are not fully resolved.

Snow cover and ice extent have decreased.

- Satellite data show that there are very likely to have been decreases of about 10% in the extent of snow cover since the late 1960s, and ground-based observations show that there is very likely to have been a reduction of about two weeks in the annual duration of lake and river ice cover in the mid-and high latitudes of the Northern Hemisphere, over the 20th century.
- There has been a widespread retreat of mountain glaciers in non-polar regions during the 20th century.
- Northern Hemisphere spring and summer sea-ice extent has decreased by about 10 to 15% since the 1950s. It is likely that there has been about a 40% decline in Arctic sea-ice thickness during late summer to early autumn in recent decades and a considerably slower decline in winter sea-ice thickness.

Global average sea level has risen and ocean heat content has increased.

- Tide gauge data show that global average sea level rose between 0.1 and 0.2 metres during the 20th century.
- Global ocean heat content has increased since the late 1950s, the period for which adequate observations of sub-surface ocean temperatures have been available.

Changes have also occurred in other important aspects of climate.

- It is very likely that precipitation has increased by 0.5 to 1% per decade in the 20th century over most mid- and high latitudes of the Northern Hemisphere continents, and it is likely that rainfall has increased by 0.2 to 0.3% per decade over the tropical (10°N to 10°S) land areas. Increases in the tropics are not evident over the past few decades. It is also likely that rainfall has decreased over much of the Northern Hemisphere subtropical (10°N to 30°N) land areas during the 20th century by about 0.3% per decade. In contrast to the Northern Hemisphere, no comparable systematic changes have been detected in broad latitudinal averages over the Southern Hemisphere. There are insufficient data to establish trends in precipitation over the oceans.
- In the mid-and high latitudes of the Northern Hemisphere over the latter half of the 20th century, it is likely that there has been a 2 to 4% increase in the frequency of heavy precipitation events. Increases in heavy precipitation events can arise from a number of causes, e.g., changes in atmospheric moisture, thunderstorm activity and large-scale storm activity.
- It is likely that there has been a 2% increase in cloud cover over mid-to high latitude land areas during the 20th century. In most areas the trends relate well to the observed decrease in daily temperature range.

- Since 1950 it is very likely that there has been a reduction in the frequency of extreme low temperatures, with a smaller increase in the frequency of extreme high temperatures.
- Warm episodes of the El Niño-Southern Oscillation (ENSO) phenomenon (which consistently affects regional variations of precipitation and temperature over much of the tropics, sub-tropics and some mid-latitude areas) have been more frequent, persistent and intense since the mid-1970s, compared with the previous 100 years.
- Over the 20th century (1900 to 1995), there were relatively small increases in global land areas experiencing severe drought or severe wetness. In many regions, these changes are dominated by inter-decadal and multi-decadal climate variability, such as the shift in ENSO towards more warm events.
- In some regions, such as parts of Asia and Africa, the frequency and intensity of droughts have been observed to increase in recent decades.

Some important aspects of climate appear not to have changed.
- A few areas of the globe have not warmed in recent decades, mainly over some parts of the Southern Hemisphere oceans and parts of Antarctica.
- No significant trends of Antarctic sea-ice extent are apparent since 1978, the period of reliable satellite measurements.
- Changes globally in tropical and extra-tropical storm intensity and frequency are dominated by inter-decadal to multi-decadal variations, with no significant trends evident over the 20th century. Conflicting analyses make it difficult to draw definitive conclusions about changes in storm activity, especially in the extra-tropics.
- No systematic changes in the frequency of tornadoes, thunder days, or hail events are evident in the limited areas analysed.

Emissions of greenhouse gases and aerosols due to human activities continue to alter the atmosphere in ways that are expected to affect the climate.

Changes in climate occur as a result of both internal variability within the climate system and external factors (both natural and anthropogenic [caused by human activity]). The influence of external factors on climate can be broadly compared using the concept of radiative forcing [a measure of the influence a factor has in altering the balance of incoming and outgoing energy in the Earth-atmosphere system, and is an index of the importance of the factor as a potential climate change mechanism. It is expressed in Watts per square metre (Wm^{-2})]. A positive radiative forcing, such as that produced by increasing concentrations of greenhouse gases, tends to warm the surface. A negative radiative forcing, which can arise from an increase in some types of aerosols (microscopic airborne particles) tends to cool the surface. Natural factors, such as changes in solar output or explosive volcanic activity, can also cause radiative forcing. Characterisation of these climate forcing agents and their changes over time is required to understand past climate changes in the context of natural variations and to project what climate changes could lie ahead. . . .

Concentrations of atmospheric greenhouse gases and their radiative forcing have continued to increase as a result of human activities.

- The atmospheric concentration of carbon dioxide (CO_2) has increased by 31% since 1750. The present CO_2 concentration has not been exceeded during the past 420,000 years and likely not during the past 20 million years. The current rate of increase is unprecedented during at least the past 20,000 years.
- About three-quarters of the anthropogenic emissions of CO_2 to the atmosphere during the past 20 years is due to fossil fuel burning. The rest is predominantly due to land-use change, especially deforestation.
- Currently the ocean and the land together are taking up about half of the anthropogenic CO_2 emissions. On land, the uptake of anthropogenic CO_2 very likely exceeded the release of CO_2 by deforestation during the 1990s.
- The rate of increase of atmospheric CO_2 concentration has been about 1.5 ppm (0.4%) per year over the past two decades. During the 1990s the year to year increase varied from 0.9 ppm (0.2%) to 2.8 ppm (0.8%). A large part of this variability is due to the effect of climate variability (e.g., El Niño events) on CO_2 uptake and release by land and oceans. [ppm (parts per million) or ppb (parts per billion) is the ratio of the number of greenhouse gas molecules to the total number of molecules of dry air. For example: 300 ppm means 300 molecules of a greenhouse gas per million molecules of dry air.]
- The atmospheric concentration of methane (CH_4) has increased by 1060 ppb (151%) since 1750 and continues to increase. The present CH_4 concentration has not been exceeded during the past 420,000 years. The annual growth in CH_4 concentration slowed and became more variable in the 1990s, compared with the 1980s. Slightly more than half of current CH_4 emissions are anthropogenic (e.g., use of fossil fuels, cattle, rice agriculture and landfills). In addition, carbon monoxide (CO) emissions have recently been identified as a cause of increasing CH_4 concentration.
- The atmospheric concentration of nitrous oxide (N_2O) has increased by 46 ppb (17%) since 1750 and continues to increase. The present N_2O concentration has not been exceeded during at least the past thousand years. About a third of current N_2O emissions are anthropogenic (e.g., agricultural soils, cattle feed lots and chemical industry).
- Since 1995, the atmospheric concentrations of many of those halocarbon gases that are both ozone-depleting and greenhouse gases (e.g., $CFCl_3$ and CF_2Cl_2), are either increasing more slowly or decreasing, both in response to reduced emissions under the regulations of the Montreal Protocol and its Amendments [the 1987 Montreal Protocol banned the use of chlorofluorocarbons and other gases that deplete the Earth's ozone layer]. Their substitute compounds (e.g., CHF_2Cl and CF_3CH_2F)

and some other synthetic compounds (e.g., perfluorocarbons (PFCs) and sulphur hexafluoride (SF_6)) are also greenhouse gases, and their concentrations are currently increasing.

- The radiative forcing due to increases of the well-mixed greenhouse gases from 1750 to 2000 is estimated to be 2.43 Wm^2: 1.46 Wm^2 from CO_2; 0.48 Wm^2 from CH_4; 0.34 Wm^2 from the halocarbons; and 0.15 Wm^2 from N_2O.

- The observed depletion of the stratospheric ozone (O_3) layer from 1979 to 2000 is estimated to have caused a negative radiative forcing (<0.15 Wm^2). Assuming full compliance with current halocarbon regulations, the positive forcing of the halocarbons will be reduced as will the magnitude of the negative forcing from stratospheric ozone depletion as the ozone layer recovers over the 21st century.

- The total amount of O_3 in the troposphere is estimated to have increased by 36% since 1750, due primarily to anthropogenic emissions of several O_3-forming gases. This corresponds to a positive radiative forcing of 0.35 Wm^2. O_3 forcing varies considerably by region and responds much more quickly to changes in emissions than the long-lived greenhouse gases, such as CO_2. . . .

Confidence in the ability of models to project future climate has increased.

Complex physically-based climate models are required to provide detailed estimates of feedbacks and of regional features. Such models cannot yet simulate all aspects of climate (e.g., they still cannot account fully for the observed trend in the surface-troposphere temperature difference since 1979) and there are particular uncertainties associated with clouds and their interaction with radiation and aerosols. Nevertheless, confidence in the ability of these models to provide useful projections of future climate has improved due to their demonstrated performance on a range of space and time-scales.

- Understanding of climate processes and their incorporation in climate models have improved, including water vapour, sea-ice dynamics, and ocean heat transport.

- Some recent models produce satisfactory simulations of current climate without the need for non-physical adjustments of heat and water fluxes at the ocean-atmosphere interface used in earlier models.

- Simulations that include estimates of natural and anthropogenic forcing reproduce the observed large-scale changes in surface temperature over the 20th century. However, contributions from some additional processes and forcings may not have been included in the models. Nevertheless, the large-scale consistency between models and observations can be used to provide an independent check on projected warming rates over the next few decades under a given emissions scenario.

- Some aspects of model simulations of ENSO, monsoons and the North Atlantic Oscillation, as well as selected periods of past climate, have improved.

There is new and stronger evidence that most of the warming observed over the last 50 years is attributable to human activities.

The SAR [Second Assessment Report of 1995] concluded: "The balance of evidence suggests a discernible human influence on global climate". That report also noted that the anthropogenic signal was still emerging from the background of natural climate variability. Since the SAR, progress has been made in reducing uncertainty, particularly with respect to distinguishing and quantifying the magnitude of responses to different external influences. Although many of the sources of uncertainty identified in the SAR still remain to some degree, new evidence and improved understanding support an updated conclusion.

- There is a longer and more closely scrutinised temperature record and new model estimates of variability. The warming over the past 100 years is very unlikely [described as a 1 to 10 percent change] to be due to internal variability alone, as estimated by current models. Reconstructions of climate data for the past 1,000 years also indicate that this warming was unusual and is unlikely to be entirely natural in origin.
- There are new estimates of the climate response to natural and anthropogenic forcing, and new detection techniques have been applied. Detection and attribution studies consistently find evidence for an anthropogenic signal in the climate record of the last 35 to 50 years.
- Simulations of the response to natural forcings alone (i.e., the response to variability in solar irradiance and volcanic eruptions) do not explain the warming in the second half of the 20th century. However, they indicate that natural forcings may have contributed to the observed warming in the first half of the 20th century.
- The warming over the last 50 years due to anthropogenic greenhouse gases can be identified despite uncertainties in forcing due to anthropogenic sulphate aerosol and natural factors (volcanoes and solar irradiance). The anthropogenic sulphate aerosol forcing, while uncertain, is negative over this period and therefore cannot explain the warming. Changes in natural forcing during most of this period are also estimated to be negative and are unlikely [described as a 10 to 33 percent change] to explain the warming.
- Detection and attribution studies comparing model simulated changes with the observed record can now take into account uncertainty in the magnitude of modelled response to external forcing, in particular that due to uncertainty in climate sensitivity.
- Most of these studies find that, over the last 50 years, the estimated rate and magnitude of warming due to increasing concentrations of greenhouse gases alone are comparable with, or larger than, the observed warming. Furthermore, most model estimates that take into account both greenhouse gases and sulphate aerosols are consistent with observations over this period.

- The best agreement between model simulations and observations over the last 140 years has been found when all the above anthropogenic and natural forcing factors are combined. These results show that the forcings included are sufficient to explain the observed changes, but do not exclude the possibility that other forcings may also have contributed.

In the light of new evidence and taking into account the remaining uncertainties, most of the observed warming over the last 50 years is likely to have been due to the increase in greenhouse gas concentrations.

Furthermore, it is very likely that the 20th century warming has contributed significantly to the observed sea level rise, through thermal expansion of sea water and widespread loss of land ice. Within present uncertainties, observations and models are both consistent with a lack of significant acceleration of sea level rise during the 20th century.

Human influences will continue to change atmospheric composition throughout the 21st century.

Models have been used to make projections of atmospheric concentrations of greenhouse gases and aerosols, and hence of future climate, based upon emissions scenarios from the IPCC Special Report on Emission Scenarios (SRES). . . .

Greenhouse gases:
- Emissions of CO_2 due to fossil fuel burning are virtually certain [described as a greater than 99 percent chance] to be the dominant influence on the trends in atmospheric CO_2 concentration during the 21st century.
- As the CO_2 concentration of the atmosphere increases, ocean and land will take up a decreasing fraction of anthropogenic CO_2 emissions. The net effect of land and ocean climate feedbacks as indicated by models is to further increase projected atmospheric CO_2 concentrations, by reducing both the ocean and land uptake of CO_2. . . .
- Changing land use could influence atmospheric CO_2 concentration. Hypothetically, if all of the carbon released by historical land-use changes could be restored to the terrestrial biosphere over the course of the century (e.g., by reforestation), CO_2 concentration would be reduced by 40 to 70 ppm. . . .
- Reductions in greenhouse gas emissions and the gases that control their concentration would be necessary to stabilise radiative forcing. For example, for the most important anthropogenic greenhouse gas, carbon cycle models indicate that stabilisation of atmospheric CO_2 concentrations at 450, 650 or 1,000 ppm would require global anthropogenic CO_2 emissions to drop below 1990 levels, within a few decades, about a century, or about two centuries, respectively, and continue to decrease steadily thereafter. Eventually CO_2 emissions would need to decline to a very small fraction of current emissions.

Aerosols

- The SRES scenarios include the possibility of either increases or decreases in anthropogenic aerosols (e.g., sulphate aerosols, biomass aerosols, black and organic carbon aerosols) depending on the extent of fossil fuel use and policies to abate polluting emissions. In addition, natural aerosols (e.g., sea salt, dust and emissions leading to the production of sulphate and carbon aerosols) are projected to increase as a result of changes in climate.

Radiative forcing over the 21st century

- For the SRES illustrative scenarios, relative to the year 2000, the global mean radiative forcing due to greenhouse gases continues to increase through the 21st century, with the fraction due to CO_2 projected to increase from slightly more than half to about three quarters. The change in the direct plus indirect aerosol radiative forcing is projected to be smaller in magnitude than that of CO_2.

Global average temperature and sea level are projected to rise under all IPCC SRES scenarios.

In order to make projections of future climate, models incorporate past, as well as future emissions of greenhouse gases and aerosols. Hence, they include estimates of warming to date and the commitment to future warming from past emissions.

Temperature

- The globally averaged surface temperature is projected to increase by 1.4 to 5.8°C over the period 1990 to 2100. These results are for the full range of 35 SRES scenarios, based on a number of climate models .
- Temperature increases are projected to be greater than those in the SAR, which were about 1.0 to 3.5°C based on the six [1992] scenarios. The higher projected temperatures and the wider range are due primarily to the lower projected sulphur dioxide emissions in the SRES scenarios relative to the [1992] scenarios.
- The projected rate of warming is much larger than the observed changes during the 20th century and is very likely to be without precedent during at least the last 10,000 years, based on palaeoclimate data.
- By 2100, the range in the surface temperature response across the group of climate models run with a given scenario is comparable to the range obtained from a single model run with the different SRES scenarios.
- On timescales of a few decades, the current observed rate of warming can be used to constrain the projected response to a given emissions scenario despite uncertainty in climate sensitivity. This approach suggests that anthropogenic warming is likely to lie in the range of 0.1 to 0.2°C per decade over the next few decades. . . .
- Based on recent global model simulations, it is very likely that nearly all land areas will warm more rapidly than the global average, particularly

those at northern high latitudes in the cold season. Most notable of these is the warming in the northern regions of North America, and northern and central Asia, which exceeds global mean warming in each model by more than 40%. In contrast, the warming is less than the global mean change in south and southeast Asia in summer and in southern South America in winter.

- Recent trends for surface temperature to become more El Niño-like in the tropical Pacific, with the eastern tropical Pacific warming more than the western tropical Pacific, with a corresponding eastward shift of precipitation, are projected to continue in many models.

Precipitation

- Based on global model simulations and for a wide range of scenarios, global average water vapour concentration and precipitation are projected to increase during the 21st century. By the second half of the 21st century, it is likely that precipitation will have increased over northern mid-to high latitudes and Antarctica in winter. At low latitudes there are both regional increases and decreases over land areas. Larger year to year variations in precipitation are very likely over most areas where an increase in mean precipitation is projected. . . .

El Niño

- Confidence in projections of changes in future frequency, amplitude, and spatial pattern of El Niño events in the tropical Pacific is tempered by some shortcomings in how well El Niño is simulated in complex models. Current projections show little change or a small increase in amplitude for El Niño events over the next 100 years.
- Even with little or no change in El Niño amplitude, global warming is likely to lead to greater extremes of drying and heavy rainfall and increase the risk of droughts and floods that occur with El Niño events in many different regions.

Monsoons

- It is likely that warming associated with increasing greenhouse gas concentrations will cause an increase of Asian summer monsoon precipitation variability. Changes in monsoon mean duration and strength depend on the details of the emission scenario. The confidence in such projections is also limited by how well the climate models simulate the detailed seasonal evolution of the monsoons.

Thermohaline circulation

- Most models show weakening of the ocean thermohaline circulation [the combined effects of temperature and salinity] which leads to a reduction of the heat transport into high latitudes of the Northern Hemisphere. However, even in models where the thermohaline circulation weakens, there is still a warming over Europe due to increased greenhouse gases. The current projections using climate models do not exhibit a complete shut-down of the thermohaline circulation by 2100. Beyond 2100, the thermohaline circulation could completely, and possibly irreversibly, shut-down in either hemisphere if the change in radiative forcing is large enough and applied long enough.

Snow and ice

- Northern Hemisphere snow cover and sea-ice extent are projected to decrease further.
- Glaciers and ice caps are projected to continue their widespread retreat during the 21st century.
- The Antarctic ice sheet is likely to gain mass because of greater precipitation, while the Greenland ice sheet is likely to lose mass because the increase in runoff will exceed the precipitation increase.
- Concerns have been expressed about the stability of the West Antarctic ice sheet because it is grounded below sea level. However, loss of grounded ice leading to substantial sea level rise from this source is now widely agreed to be very unlikely during the 21st century, although its dynamics are still inadequately understood, especially for projections on longer time-scales.

Sea level

- Global mean sea level is projected to rise by 0.09 to 0.88 metres [a meter is about 39.4 inches] between 1990 and 2100, for the full range of SRES scenarios. [This projected increase was less than the panel had estimated in 1995, primarily because of improved computer models.]

Anthropogenic climate change will persist for many centuries.

- Emissions of long-lived greenhouse gases (i.e., CO_2, N_2O, PFCs, SF_6) have a lasting effect on atmospheric composition, radiative forcing and climate. For example, several centuries after CO_2 emissions occur, about a quarter of the increase in CO_2 concentration caused by these emissions is still present in the atmosphere.
- After greenhouse gas concentrations have stabilised, global average surface temperatures would rise at a rate of only a few tenths of a degree per century rather than several degrees per century as projected for the 21st century without stabilisation. The lower the level at which concentrations are stabilised, the smaller the total temperature change.
- Global mean surface temperature increases and rising sea level from thermal expansion of the ocean are projected to continue for hundreds of years after stabilisation of greenhouse gas concentrations (even at present levels), owing to the long timescales on which the deep ocean adjusts to climate change.
- Ice sheets will continue to react to climate warming and contribute to sea level rise for thousands of years after climate has been stabilised. Climate models indicate that the local warming over Greenland is likely to be one to three times the global average. Ice sheet models project that a local warming of larger than 3°C, if sustained for millennia, would lead to

virtually a complete melting of the Greenland ice sheet with a resulting sea level rise of about 7 metres. A local warming of 5.5°C, if sustained for 1000 years, would be likely to result in a contribution from Greenland of about 3 metres to sea level rise.

- Current ice dynamic models suggest that the West Antarctic ice sheet could contribute up to 3 metres to sea level rise over the next 1000 years, but such results are strongly dependent on model assumptions regarding climate change scenarios, ice dynamics and other factors.

Further action is required to address remaining gaps in information and understanding.

Further research is required to improve the ability to detect, attribute and understand climate change, to reduce uncertainties and to project future climate changes. In particular, there is a need for additional systematic and sustained observations, modeling and process studies. A serious concern is the decline of observational networks. . . .

PRESIDENT BUSH ON FUNDING OF ABORTION COUNSELING ABROAD
January 22, 2001

On his first full day in office, President George W. Bush fired the opening salvo in what many expected to be a running war on abortion throughout his presidency, signing an order to restore a Reagan-era policy that barred federal funds from going to international family planning agencies that used their own money to perform or promote abortions overseas. The symbolic action came on the twenty-eighth anniversary of Roe v. Wade, *in which the Supreme Court established the constitutional right of women to abortion. It also came eight years to the day after President Bill Clinton had lifted the restriction.*

The reinstitution of the so-called Mexico City Policy was only one of several signals Bush sent in the early days of his presidency indicating that his administration would do what it could to reduce the incidence of abortion in the United States, if not make it illegal outright. Even before being inaugurated, Bush named two staunch abortion foes to key cabinet positions, nominating former Missouri senator John Ashcroft to become attorney general and Wisconsin governor Tommy G. Thompson to become secretary of health and human services. In short order Bush reiterated his campaign pledge to nominate judges "who strictly interpret the Constitution," a code phrase meaning opposition to abortion, and he repeated his opposition to the use of aborted fetal tissue in stem cell research. (Stem cell research, p. 539)

Bush's actions did not surprise anyone—he had long opposed abortion except in cases of rape or incest or to save the life of the mother. But coming one after the other at the beginning of his presidency, when he had been expected to keep the focus on tax cuts and his education initiative, the moves made clear that the dynamics of the volatile abortion debate had changed dramatically. Antiabortion activists now had a powerful ally in the White House, who was able to influence the direction and shape of the abortion debate with nominations to judgeships and key executive branch positions, executive orders, regulations, and proposed legislation. Pro-choice advo-

cates, who had been able to count on similar help when Bill Clinton was in the White House, were now likely to look to the Senate to block legislation and nominees they found unacceptable.

Neither side expected the Bush administration to make an all-out assault on Roe v. Wade. *Bush himself had said that he did not think there were enough votes in either the House or Senate to enact a constitutional amendment banning abortion. Nor was the public likely to support such a move. National opinion polls showed that about three-fifths of Americans supported a woman's right to choose, while about two-fifths wanted to ban abortion. Instead, the president's efforts "are going to focus immediately on those things we can get done," said White House spokesman Ari Fleischer.*

In addition to restoring the Mexico City Policy, the Bush administration indicated it might review the safety of the abortion pill RU-486, which the Food and Drug Administration had just approved for use in September 2000 after sixteen years of study. Perhaps more disturbing to pro-choice advocates were various proposals that would have the effect of making a human fetus a person in the eyes of the law. Treating a fetus like a person legally could put the fetus's interests in direct conflict with the interests of the mother, and women's right activists portrayed such attempts as a "backdoor" approach to overturning Roe v. Wade. *As the year progressed, many women's groups also grew wary of Bush administration proposals in several other areas affecting women's reproductive rights, including additional funding for sexual abstinence programs.* (Abstinence programs, p. 456; RU-486, Historic Documents of 2000, p. 781)

The battle began almost immediately as women's rights groups joined civil rights groups, gun control advocates, and others to try to defeat Ashcroft's nomination as attorney general. The former governor of Missouri and U.S. senator had made opposition to abortion a focal point of his political career, and pro-choice groups questioned whether he could fairly enforce laws that he personally did not believe in. On February 1, 2001, the Senate confirmed Ashcroft, 58–42—the closest vote confirming a cabinet nominee in decades. Thompson's nomination was far less controversial, and he was confirmed unanimously.

Reinstating the Mexico City Policy

The United States had prohibited international family planning agencies from using federal funds to provide abortions overseas since 1973. Under the Mexico City Policy, established by President Ronald Reagan at a U.S. population conference in Mexico City in 1984 and continued through the administration of the first George Bush, those family planning agencies were also barred from receiving federal funds if they used their own money to perform abortions or provide information about them. Women's rights activists referred to the policy as the "global gag rule," arguing that it was a denial of free speech to the agencies and prevented their clients from receiving information about abortions, even if they were legal in their own country.

Clinton lifted the ban when he took office in January 1993, and for the rest of his presidency social conservatives in Congress tried to attach language reinstating the Mexico City Policy to annual foreign aid appropriations. In 1997 conservatives tried to force Clinton to give in on the ban by blocking funding to repay back dues the United States owed to the United Nations, a plan to reorganized foreign policy agencies, and additional credit for the International Monetary Fund. The latter two issues were resolved in 1998, but it was not until 1999 that Clinton finally agreed to accept reinstatement of the Mexico City Policy in return for funding for the UN dues. (UN dues, Historic Documents of 1999, p. 700)

In 2000 it was the Republicans' turn to back down. To avoid an election-year confrontation with Clinton, they heeded his veto threat and removed the restrictions from the annual aid bill and approved increased funding for international family planning. But release of the $425 million in international family planning aid was delayed until February 15, 2001, when conservatives hoped that a Republican would be in the White House.

In his brief memorandum restoring the Mexico City Policy, Bush said it was his "conviction that taxpayer funds should not be used to pay for abortions or advocate or actively promote abortion, either here or abroad." A clarifying statement issued by the White House press secretary said that Bush was "committed to maintaining" the $425 million funding level and that the restrictions would not prevent the agencies from treating injuries or illnesses caused by abortions.

Pro-choice advocates in the House and Senate tried unsuccessfully to overturn the reinstatement of the Mexico City Policy. The House International Relations Committee added language lifting the restrictions to legislation reauthorizing the State Department. But after a major lobbying effort by the Bush administration, the full House voted, 218–210, to restore the ban. The Senate did not complete action on that measure before the end of the session. The Senate, however, did vote to repeal the policy as part of the annual foreign aid appropriations bill. After Bush threatened to veto the measure, Senate Democrats backed down, agreeing to drop the repeal in exchange for additional funding for the United Nations Fund for Population Activities.

Granting Legal Status
to the "Unborn Child"

In other congressional action on abortion in 2001, the House passed legislation making it a federal crime to harm or kill a fetus during the commission of any one of sixty-eight federal crimes or crimes under military law. The same penalty would apply for harm or death to a fetus as to a person, although the death penalty would not be permitted. Supporters of the bill said it had been narrowly drawn to exempt pregnant women and doctors who performed abortions. Opponents, however, charged that the legislation would give legal standing to a fetus for the first time, thereby undermining the constitutional right to abortion. The House measure passed comfortably, by a vote of 252–172, but the Senate took no action before the end of the year. The House in 1999 had passed a similar measure, which also died in the Senate.

In early July it was reported that the Bush administration had drafted a new policy to allow states to define a fetus as a person eligible for medical coverage under the Children's Health Insurance Program (CHIP). The CHIP program, created in 1997, provided a wide range of health care services for children. In most states the program was open to children whose family incomes were up to twice the poverty rate. A family of four was considered poor if its income was under $17,650 a year. (Health insurance, p. 710)

The administration claimed the policy would allow states to pay for prenatal care for mothers who were not eligible for Medicaid or CHIP. "This will increase access to prenatal care for pregnant women, the ultimate goal being healthier babies and healthier children," a spokesman for the Department of Health and Human Services said. Pro-choice advocates, however, saw the proposed policy as yet another attempt to grant legal status to the fetus as a person. A better alternative, they said, would be to extend CHIP coverage to pregnant women. Two states, New Jersey and Rhode Island, had already received waivers from the federal government to cover pregnant women under their CHIP programs.

Anthrax and Other Threats

On December 5 federal agents arrested Clayton Lee Waagner in Cincinnati, Ohio, and charged him with mailing hundreds of letters to abortion clinics warning that the enclosed packets contained anthrax. The powder contained in the letters turned out to be harmless. Abortion clinics were often targets of threats and violent acts by antiabortion extremists, but the anthrax scare was especially alarming given the real deaths caused by anthrax in the wake of the terrorist attacks in September. (Homeland security, p. 637)

Waagner, who in February had escaped from prison where he was serving a sentence for crimes involving firearms and car theft, called himself an antiabortion "warrior" in the "army of God." The mailings to some 280 clinics contained the powdery substance and a warning that read, "You have chosen a profession, which profits from the senseless murder of millions of innocent children each year. We are going to kill you. This is your notice. Stop now or die."

Earlier in the year, the alleged killer of a doctor who performed abortions was arrested in western France and later extradited to the United States. James Charles Kopp was wanted in connection with the October 1998 shooting of Barnett A. Slepian in his home near Buffalo, New York. Slepian was killed by a shot from a high-powered rifle fired through the window of his kitchen while he was fixing dinner with his wife. Attorney General Ashcroft promised an aggressive prosecution of both men. (Antiabortion violence, Historic Documents of 1998, p. 809)

Following is the text of "Memorandum for the Administrator of the United States Agency for International Development," signed by President George W. Bush on January 22, 2001, reinstating a prohibition on federal funds to any international family planning agency that used its own funds to perform or promote abortions.

The document was obtained from the Internet at http:// www.whitehouse.gov/news/releases/20010123-5.html.

SUBJECT: Restoration of the Mexico City Policy

The Mexico City Policy announced by President Reagan in 1984 required nongovernmental organizations to agree as a condition of their receipt of federal funds that such organizations would neither perform nor actively promote abortion as a method of family planning in other nations. This policy was in effect until it was rescinded on January 22, 1993.

It is my conviction that taxpayer funds should not be used to pay for abortions or advocate or actively promote abortion, either here or abroad. It is therefore my belief that the Mexico City Policy should be restored. Accordingly, I hereby rescind the "Memorandum for the Acting Administrator of the Agency for International Development, Subject: AID Family Planning Grants/Mexico City Policy," dated January 22, 1993, and I direct the Administrator of the United States Agency for International Development to reinstate in full all of the requirements of the Mexico City Policy in effect on January 19, 1993.

GEORGE W. BUSH

PRESIDENT BUSH ON FAITH-BASED AND COMMUNITY INITIATIVES
January 29, 2001

President George W. Bush moved quickly to fulfill his campaign promise to allow faith-based groups to accept direct federal funding for providing a wide range of social service programs. Little more than a week after his inauguration, the new president called for a broad federal effort to encourage and support the hundreds of faith-based organizations that incorporated religious beliefs into their service programs. "Government cannot be replaced by charities, but it can welcome them as partners instead of resenting them as rivals," the new president said February 1 at a National Prayer Breakfast in Washington.

To create this new partnership, Bush on January 29, 2001, signed two executive orders, one creating a White House office to coordinate the effort and the other setting up centers in five Cabinet departments to eliminate regulatory barriers that kept faith-based groups from providing social services such as drug treatment and prisoner rehabilitation programs. On January 30 he outlined a set of legislative proposals including a series of tax incentives to encourage charitable giving and an expansion of "charitable choice," making federal funds directly available to religious organizations that provided faith-based social services.

The federal government had a long history of funding groups with religious affiliations, such as Catholic Charities, that provided social services in a secular setting without any overt religious content. The proposal to permit religious groups to receive federal funds directly for providing programs with religious content released a flood of criticism, much of it from unexpected quarters, that caught the new administration offguard and kept the initiative from getting very far off the ground. The House passed a bill in July by a narrow margin, but Democratic leaders in the Senate said they were in no hurry to take it up. In August the director of the White House Office of Faith-Based and Community Initiatives announced he was leaving after only seven months in the post. John J. DiIulio Jr. cited personal reasons for his departure, but he was reportedly also frustrated by the opposition he encountered.

Although the president continued to tout the proposal, little more happened on it after the September 11 terrorist attacks on the Pentagon and the World Trade Center. In December the White House was reported to be working with key legislators on scaled-back legislation, but no measure was forthcoming before the year ended. (Terrorist attacks, p. 164)

A Cornerstone of Compassionate Conservatism

A born-again Christian who had received substantial political support from conservative religious groups in his presidential campaign, Bush had both personal and political reasons for proposing faith-based solutions to the nation's social problems. During his campaign, he frequently lauded programs such as Teen Challenge and Victory Fellowship, which used Christian teachings to motivate teens and others to get off and stay off drugs, as the kinds of effective programs that often had more success than traditional approaches. He promised that if elected, he would direct more support to such groups both by promoting greater private charitable donations and by directing federal funding to social service programs operated by faith-based and other grassroots community organizations.

On January 29, at a ceremony attended by religious leaders from a broad range of faiths, Bush signed two executive orders. The first created the White House Office of Faith-Based and Community Initiatives to coordinate and oversee implementation of federal policy regarding faith-based groups. Bush appointed DiIulio, a political science professor at the University of Pennsylvania, to head that office. He also named Stephen Goldsmith, a former mayor of Indianapolis, as chairman of a new national advisory board to work with faith-based, nonprofit, and volunteer organizations and to advise the president on issues related to the initiative. Goldsmith served as Bush's chief domestic policy adviser during his presidential election campaign.

The second executive order set up centers in the departments of Education, Health and Human Services, Housing and Community Development, Justice, and Labor to identify and eliminate regulatory, contracting, and other obstacles that made small religious and secular organizations reluctant to work with government. In a joint report released in August, these five centers said their investigation had found a "widespread bias" in their agencies against faith-based and community organizations, including regulations that were "needlessly burdensome administrative creations." It also said the agencies had virtually ignored the charitable choice laws already enacted, doing little to encourage participation from faith-based and community organizations.

On January 30 Bush outlined his legislative proposals, which included relatively noncontroversial tax incentives to spur greater private and corporate charitable giving. The chief incentive would extend the income tax deduction for charitable contributions to the more than 80 million taxpayers who did not itemize their returns. He also asked that the limit on corporate charitable deductions be raised from 10 percent of a company's taxable income to 15 percent, and that taxpayers over age 59 be permitted to withdraw money from their Individual Retirement Accounts without penalty for charitable contributions.

The heart of Bush's legislative proposals, and the one that was to run into the most trouble, was his call to expand charitable choice, which explicitly allowed religious groups to take federal money for specific social services without having to remove the religious or spiritual content from their programs. Faith-based groups that received federal funding would be exempt from laws prohibiting job discrimination, but they could not discriminate against clients on the basis of religion, require clients to convert or participate in religious services, or use the federal funding to provide religious instruction. "We will not fund the religious activities of any group," Bush said January 29, "but when people of faith provide social services, we will not discriminate against them. As long as there are secular alternatives, faith-based charities should be able to compete for funding on an equal basis and in a manner that does not cause them to sacrifice their mission."

An Outpouring of Opposition

During his election campaign, Bush's promise to expand government funding of faith-based social service programs roused comparatively little controversy. His Democratic opponent, Vice President Al Gore, had a similar plank in his platform. Moreover, Congress had already approved charitable choice for four major federal programs, all with little controversy. The first charitable choice program was included in the 1996 welfare overhaul measure (PL 104-193) and allowed faith-based groups to compete for funding from the Temporary Assistance for Needy Families programs. Congress subsequently included charitable choice provisions in three other measures: the 1998 Community Services Block Grant Program (PL 105-285); the Children's Health Act (PL 106-310); and the Community Renewal Tax Relief Act of 2000 (PL 106-554). In the latter two laws, faith-based groups were authorized to apply for drug abuse and treatment grant programs.

But as a top priority of the new administration, the charitable choice proposal provoked an outpouring of opposition from all points of the political and religious spectrum. Groups such as Americans United for Separation of Church and State and the American Civil Liberties Union argued that none of the safeguards provided in charitable choice were strong enough to overcome the First Amendment's restrictions on government establishment of religion. Several constitutional challenges to the already enacted charitable choice programs were wending their way through the court system, but the Supreme Court had yet to rule on any of them. Liberals were also concerned that charitable choice could lead to less funding for government social programs.

Civil rights groups and some religious organizations were opposed to what they said amounted to subsidized hiring discrimination. Exempting faith-based groups from the employment discrimination protections of the 1964 Civil Rights Act as well as from state and local antidiscrimination provisions, they argued, meant that these groups could refuse to hire people who did not share their religious beliefs. Senator Joseph Lieberman, D-Conn., the Democratic vice presidential nominee in 2000 and initially a supporter of charitable choice, was one of several lawmakers concerned about the exemption. In a March 1 speech Lieberman said the exemption could "effectively give federally funded workplaces far greater leeway to discriminate than their privately funded counterparts."

Lieberman and others were also concerned that religious groups that believed homosexuality was a sin could use the exemption to discriminate against gays and lesbians. Those fears were heightened in early July when the Washington Post *reported that in return for the Salvation Army's support of charitable choice legislation pending in the House, the Bush administration had promised to issue a regulation specifically exempting faith-based groups from complying with state and local laws barring discrimination against gays. The Salvation Army, which was opposed to homosexuality, said it was primarily concerned about having to pay domestic-partner benefits. Within hours of the* Post *report, the White House said it would not pursue the regulation, but the incident hardened opposition in Congress among Democrats and moderate Republicans.*

Criticisms also came from a broad range of religious leaders who warned that faith-based organizations might lose their independence and autonomy if they accepted federal funding and submitted to federal oversight. Others worried that the government would prefer one religion over another or that the government might fund organizations that were outside the religious mainstream, such as the Church of Scientology, which operated a drug abuse program, or the Nation of Islam, which was known for its work with young African American men. Still others worried about the potential for fraud. Senator Peter G. Fitzgerald, R-Ill., said some people might set up "fly-by-night" religious charities to take advantage of federal funding under charitable choice. "The church and state issue doesn't bother me as much as the potential for fraud," he said. Evangelist Pat Robertson may have offered the most succinct summation. "This thing could be a real Pandora's box," he said on his February 20 "700 Club" broadcast.

Even one of the main architects of compassionate conservatism, Marvin Olasky, complained about the plan. He noted that "Teen Challenge" and some of the other groups that Bush had offered as models for charitable choice would be ineligible for federal funding because they required conversion as a condition for receiving services. "If the federal government puts out the welcome mat for some religious groups and tells others to 'opt out,' it is preferring one religious belief over another," Olasky said. "This is exactly the type of religious discrimination that the First Amendment is designed to prevent."

With Republican legislators quietly telling them charitable choice was a dead issue unless some changes were made, the Bush administration agreed to several changes to the pending House measure. As passed on July 19 by a vote of 233-198, the legislation extended charitable choice to several more social programs than Bush had originally proposed, including juvenile delinquency and crime prevention programs, housing and community de-

velopment grants, and child care programs, but required recipients of direct aid to separate religious activities from social services. To reach groups that could not or were unwilling to divorce religious messages from their social service programs, the measure allowed federal agencies to use their funds to issue vouchers for services to individuals in need, who could use the vouchers to obtain faith-based services. Critics complained that the voucher system was a back-door way to give federal aid to groups that proselytized, since the ban on proselytizing and other religious activities applied only to groups that accepted direct funding. Because of budget constraints, the House measure also cut back substantially on Bush's proposed tax incentives.

The measure then stalled in the Senate, where Majority Leader Tom Daschle, D-S.D., and Lieberman both made it clear that they would kill any bill that preempted antidiscrimination laws. "We can't move backwards on the progress we've made on discrimination in this country," Daschle told reporters July 19.

Following are the texts of two executive orders, signed by President George W. Bush and released January 29, 2001, creating the Office of Faith-Based and Community Initiatives in the White House and setting up similar centers in five cabinet-level departments with the purpose of eliminating barriers to participation in the federal social service safety net to faith-based and grassroots charitable organizations.

The documents were obtained from the Internet at http:// www.whitehouse.gov/news/releases/20010129-2.html; http://www.whitehouse.gov/news/releases/200101293.html.

ESTABLISHMENT OF WHITE HOUSE OFFICE OF FAITH-BASED AND COMMUNITY INITIATIVES

By the authority vested in me as President of the United States by the Constitution and the laws of the United States of America, and in order to help the Federal Government coordinate a national effort to expand opportunities for faith-based and other community organizations and to strengthen their capacity to better meet social needs in America's communities, it is hereby ordered as follows

Section 1. Policy. Faith-based and other community organizations are indispensable in meeting the needs of poor Americans and distressed neighborhoods. Government cannot be replaced by such organizations, but it can and should welcome them as partners. The paramount goal is compassionate results, and private and charitable community groups, including religious ones, should have the fullest opportunity permitted by law to compete on a level playing field, so long as they achieve valid public purposes, such as curbing crime, conquering addiction, strengthening families and neighborhoods, and overcoming poverty. This delivery of social services must be results oriented and should value the bedrock principles of pluralism, nondiscrimination, evenhandedness, and neutrality.

Sec. 2. Establishment. There is established a White House Office of Faith-Based and Community Initiatives (White House OFBCI) within the Executive Office of the President that will have lead responsibility in the executive branch to establish policies, priorities, and objectives for the Federal Government's comprehensive effort to enlist, equip, enable, empower, and expand the work of faith-based and other community organizations to the extent permitted by law.

Sec. 3. Functions. The principal functions of the White House OFBCI are, to the extent permitted by law: (a) to develop, lead, and coordinate the Administration's policy agenda affecting faith-based and other community programs and initiatives, expand the role of such efforts in communities, and increase their capacity through executive action, legislation, Federal and private funding, and regulatory relief;

(b) to ensure that Administration and Federal Government policy decisions and programs are consistent with the President's stated goals with respect to faith-based and other community initiatives;

(c) to help integrate the President's policy agenda affecting faith-based and other community organizations across the Federal Government;

(d) to coordinate public education activities designed to mobilize public support for faith-based and community nonprofit initiatives through volunteerism, special projects, demonstration pilots, and public-private partnerships;

(e) to encourage private charitable giving to support faith-based and community initiatives;

(f) to bring concerns, ideas, and policy options to the President for assisting, strengthening, and replicating successful faith-based and other community programs;

(g) to provide policy and legal education to State, local, and community policymakers and public officials seeking ways to empower faith-based and other community organizations and to improve the opportunities, capacity, and expertise of such groups;

(h) to develop and implement strategic initiatives under the President's agenda to strengthen the institutions of civil society and America's families and communities;

(i) to showcase and herald innovative grassroots nonprofit organizations and civic initiatives;

(j) to eliminate unnecessary legislative, regulatory, and other bureaucratic barriers that impede effective faith-based and other community efforts to solve social problems;

(k) to monitor implementation of the President's agenda affecting faith-based and other community organizations; and

(1) to ensure that the efforts of faith-based and other community organizations meet high standards of excellence and accountability.

Sec. 4. Administration. (a) The White House OFBCI may function through established or ad hoc committees, task forces, or interagency groups.

(b) The White House OFBCI shall have a staff to be headed by the Assistant to the President for Faith-Based and Community Initiatives. The White House OFBCI shall have such staff and other assistance, to the extent permitted by law, as may be necessary to carry out the provisions of this order. The White House OFBCI operations shall begin no later than 30 days from the date of this order.

(c) The White House OFBCI shall coordinate with the liaison and point of contact designated by each executive department and agency with respect to this initiative.

(d) All executive departments and agencies (agencies) shall cooperate with the White House OFBCI and provide such information, support, and assistance to the White House OFBCI as it may request, to the extent permitted by law.

(e) The agencies' actions directed by this Executive Order shall be carried out subject to the availability of appropriations and to the extent permitted by law.

Sec. 5. Judicial Review. This order does not create any right or benefit, substantive or procedural, enforceable at law or equity by a party against the United States, its agencies or instrumentalities, its officers or employees, or any other person.

GEORGE W. BUSH
The White House
January 29, 2001.

AGENCY RESPONSIBILITIES WITH RESPECT TO FAITH-BASED AND COMMUNITY INITIATIVES

By the authority vested in me as President by the Constitution and the laws of the United States of America, and in order to help the Federal Government coordinate a national effort to expand opportunities for faith-based and other community organizations and to strengthen their capacity to better meet social needs in America's communities, it is hereby ordered as follows:

Section 1. Establishment of Executive Department Centers for Faith-Based and Community Initiatives. (a) The Attorney General, the Secretary of Education, the Secretary of Labor, the Secretary of Health and Human Services, and the Secretary of Housing and Urban Development shall each establish within their respective departments a Center for Faith-Based and Community Initiatives (Center).

(b) Each executive department Center shall be supervised by a Director, appointed by the department head in consultation with the White House Office of Faith-Based and Community Initiatives (White House OFBCI).

(c) Each department shall provide its Center with appropriate staff, administrative support, and other resources to meet its responsibilities under this order.

(d) Each department's Center shall begin operations no later than 45 days from the date of this order.

Sec. 2. Purpose of Executive Department Centers for Faith-Based and Community Initiatives. The purpose of the executive department Centers will be to coordinate department efforts to eliminate regulatory, contracting, and other programmatic obstacles to the participation of faith-based and other community organizations in the provision of social services.

Sec. 3. Responsibilities of Executive Department Centers for Faith-Based and Community Initiatives. Each Center shall, to the extent permitted by law: (a) conduct, in coordination with the White House OFBCI, a department-wide audit to identify all existing barriers to the participation of faith-based and other community organizations in the delivery of social services by the department, including but not limited to regulations, rules, orders, procurement, and other internal policies and practices, and outreach activities that either facially discriminate against or otherwise discourage or disadvantage the participation of faith-based and other community organizations in Federal programs;

(b) coordinate a comprehensive departmental effort to incorporate faith-based and other community organizations in department programs and initiatives to the greatest extent possible;

(c) propose initiatives to remove barriers identified pursuant to section 3(a) of this order, including but not limited to reform of regulations, procurement, and other internal policies and practices, and outreach activities;

(d) propose the development of innovative pilot and demonstration programs to increase the participation of faith-based and other community organizations in Federal as well as State and local initiatives; and

(e) develop and coordinate department outreach efforts to disseminate information more effectively to faith-based and other community organizations with respect to programming changes, contracting opportunities, and other department initiatives, including but not limited to Web and Internet resources.

Sec. 4. Additional Responsibilities of the Department of Health and Human Services and the Department of Labor Centers. In addition to those responsibilities described in section 3 of this order, the Department of Health and Human Services and the Department of Labor Centers shall, to the extent permitted by law: (a) conduct a comprehensive review of policies and practices affecting existing funding streams governed by so-called "Charitable Choice" legislation to assess the department's compliance with the requirements of Charitable Choice; and (b) promote and ensure compliance with existing Charitable Choice legislation by the department, as well as its partners in State and local government, and their contractors.

Sec. 5. Reporting Requirements. (a) Report. Not later than 180 days after the date of this order and annually thereafter, each of the five executive department Centers described in section 1 of this order shall prepare and submit a report to the White House OFBCI.

(b) Contents. The report shall include a description of the department's efforts in carrying out its responsibilities under this order, including but not limited to:

(1) a comprehensive analysis of the barriers to the full participation of faith-based and other community organizations in the delivery of social services identified pursuant to section 3(a) of this order and the proposed strategies to eliminate those barriers; and

(2) a summary of the technical assistance and other information that will be available to faith-based and other community organizations regarding the program activities of the department and the preparation of applications or proposals for grants, cooperative agreements, contracts, and procurement.

(c) Performance Indicators. The first report, filed 180 days after the date of this order, shall include annual performance indicators and measurable objectives for department action. Each report filed thereafter shall measure the department's performance against the objectives set forth in the initial report.

Sec. 6. Responsibilities of All Executive Departments and Agencies. All executive departments and agencies (agencies) shall: (a) designate an agency employee to serve as the liaison and point of contact with the White House OFBCI; and

(b) cooperate with the White House OFBCI and provide such information, support, and assistance to the White House OFBCI as it may request, to the extent permitted by law.

Sec. 7. Administration and Judicial Review. (a) The agencies' actions directed by this Executive Order shall be carried out subject to the availability of appropriations and to the extent permitted by law.

(b) This order does not create any right or benefit, substantive or procedural, enforceable at law or equity against the United States, its agencies or instrumentalities, its officers or employees, or any other person.

GEORGE W. BUSH
The White House
January 29, 2001.

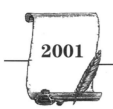

February

REPORTS ON U.S. SPACECRAFT LANDING ON ASTEROID
February 12 and 14, 2001

A U.S. spacecraft, NEAR Shoemaker, *capped an extraordinarily success-ful career by landing on an asteroid near Earth on February 12, 2001. The pinpoint landing was the first by any spacecraft on any small object in space. The event was doubly unusual because* NEAR Shoemaker *had been built to orbit—but not land on—the asteroid known as Eros.*

During its orbit of Eros, and then its bonus landing, NEAR Shoemaker *sent back more than 160,000 images that scientists said would provide a rich source of information about the origins of the solar system and about the makeup of asteroids that orbit the Sun near Earth. Among other things, scientists said the information might some day help people on Earth avert the crash-landing of a large asteroid or meteor.*

The success of NEAR Shoemaker *was a scientific and political plus for the National Aeronautics and Space Administration (NASA), which had come under wide criticism for its management of two major missions to Mars that failed in late 1999. NASA officials had spent much of 2000 redesigning plans for future space missions, especially those to Mars.* (Mars mission fail-ures, Historic Documents of 2000, p. 88)

NEAR Shoemaker's *Mission*

The spacecraft that landed on Eros had a two-part name: NEAR *was the acronym for Near Earth Asteroid Rendezvous, and* Shoemaker *honored famed planetary geologist and asteroid expert Eugene Shoemaker, who died in 1997. NASA launched* NEAR Shoemaker *in February 1996, with a goal of reaching Eros three years later. The craft was the first product of NASA's "faster, better, cheaper" philosophy featuring slimmed-down, tightly fo-cused unmanned space probes, rather than the mammoth, expensive space missions of the previous three decades. The Applied Physics Laboratory of Johns Hopkins University built* NEAR Shoemaker *and managed the entire mission; it was the first time NASA turned an entire mission over to an outside contractor. The craft and its mission cost $224 million, less than* *budgeted and a fraction of the multibillion- dollar cost of most major space missions.*

NEAR Shoemaker's early career in space was a series of near-disasters that offered no hint of the craft's later successes. Immediately after launch, NASA temporarily lost radio contact with the craft because of a problem at a receiving station on Earth. In late December 1998, as it neared Eros, NEAR Shoemaker's engine suddenly stopped, sending the craft spinning helplessly for more than a day. After the engine restarted, the spacecraft shot wildly off course and sped past its intended orbit around Eros. Ultimately, NASA was able to maneuver the craft into a much longer course that took it back to a low orbit around Eros starting on February 14, 2000—a year behind schedule.

Eros itself runs an oval-shaped orbit around the Sun just outside the Mars orbit. In February 2001 Eros was nearly 200 million miles from Earth. Shaped something like a russet potato, Eros is about twenty-one miles long, an average of about eight miles wide, and eight miles thick. It is the largest asteroid near Earth, and its orbit of the Sun offered a unique opportunity for the type of mission NASA envisioned.

For one year, NEAR Shoemaker circled Eros 230 times, at one point within about three miles of the surface but generally at a distance of between 30 and 200 miles . During its orbit, NEAR Shoemaker took more than 160,000 images (photographs and other scientific readings) that were radioed back to Earth. NASA scientists said they received about ten times as much information from the spacecraft as they had hoped for during the mission.

Landing on Eros

As NEAR Shoemaker neared the scheduled end of its mission in early 2001, NASA and Johns Hopkins officials decided to add a maneuver the spacecraft had not been designed to accomplish: a landing on Eros. Intended strictly for orbiting, NEAR Shoemaker had no landing gear to absorb the shock of encountering a rocky surface. The craft also was running low on fuel to power its engine for a slow descent to the surface. Despite these major obstacles, officials hoped the descent would enable NEAR Shoemaker to take a final series of close-up photographs and scientific readings of Eros.

Mirroring its performance during its orbit of Eros, NEAR Shoemaker exceeded all expectations during a slow descent to the surface February 12. In a series of five maneuvers over a period of more than four hours, the craft slipped out of orbit, headed toward the asteroid, and touched down at a speed of about four miles per hour—an amazingly slow speed for space travel. The descent was complicated by the fact that Eros is not a stationary target; it rotates on its own axis about once every five hours as it moves through space

During the final three miles of its descent, NEAR Shoemaker took sixty-nine detailed photographs. The final photograph sent to Earth was taken at 394 feet above the surface and showed features as small as a golf ball.

NASA officials later determined that NEAR Shoemaker landed safely on the tips of two of its four solar panels and the bottom edge of the spacecraft

body. To the amazement of mission engineers and scientists, NEAR Shoemaker *continued sending signals back to Earth even after landing. Jumping
at the chance to get even more information, the mission's team then directed
the craft's gamma-ray spectrometer to examine the area immediately
around the landing site for data on the composition of Eros's surface. This
was the first close-up observation by such an instrument of any planetary
body other than Earth.*

*NASA's three Deep Space Network antennas in the United States, Aus-
tralia, and Spain had been scheduled to stop receiving signals from* NEAR
Shoemaker *on February 14. Because the craft was still sending radio messages, NASA authorized a ten-day extension on use of the antennas, and
then another four-day extension. By the time the last signals were received
on February 28, the* NEAR Shoemaker *staff had received seven days worth
of information from the craft's gamma-ray spectrometer. NASA officials
planned no further communications with the spacecraft but did not rule out
a future check on its signals from Eros.*

Learning about Eros

Scientists associated with the NEAR Shoemaker *mission expected that it
would take them many years to examine all the data retrieved from Eros.
Even so, they said they were thrilled by the amount and quality of information they examined just before and after the mission ended.*

The most important fact that NEAR Shoemaker *discovered about Eros
was its basic composition. Eros proved to be a giant rock, pockmarked with
craters and covered with thousands of boulders and layers of dirt and dust.
This finding surprised many scientists who had expected that Eros would
turn out to be a "conglomerate"—basically a pile of boulders and other space
rubble kept together only by gravity.*

NEAR Shoemaker's *data also showed that the bottoms of many craters
and other depressions on Eros are covered with very fine particles, similar
to dust or sand, creating a smooth surface effect that scientists call "ponds."
On Earth, this ponding would result from the action of water and wind. But
Eros has no water or wind, and so scientists were developing theories about
how dust settled on the asteroid.*

The first scientific paper resulting from the NEAR Shoemaker *mission,
published in the April 20 edition of* Science *magazine, speculated that relentless bombardment of Eros by debris from space probably caused most of
the asteroid's physical features, including its thousands of craters.*

Another paper, published in the September 27 issue of Nature, *gave the
first report of a detailed map of Eros. Based on information from that
map, the report's authors concluded that most of the large rocks on Eros
(those larger than fifteen meters across) had been ejected from one crater
that was formed when a large meteor or comet hit Eros, possibly a billion
years ago. "This observation is helping us start answering questions about
how things work on the surface of an asteroid," said Peter Thomas, an
astronomy researcher at Cornell University and an author of the report in*
Nature.

A Help for Advance Planning?

In addition to providing data to help scientists understand the composition and history of a large asteroid relatively close to Earth, NASA officials said, the NEAR Shoemaker *mission might eventually turn out to be of enormous practical value. At some point in the future, a large asteroid similar to Eros will be on a collision course with Earth. Such a collision could have devastating consequences, as did the presumed crash off Mexico's Yucatan peninsula of a large object (an asteroid, comet, or meteor) 65 million years ago that dramatically changed the Earth's climate and killed off the dinosaurs.*

An even more devastating collision may have occurred 250 million years ago, according to a NASA-funded study reported in the February 23 issue of Science. *A team led by Luann Becker of the University of Washington at Seattle reported research on soil samples in China, Hungary, and Japan indicating that the impact on Earth of a large comet or asteroid may have triggered a series of climate changes, tidal waves, volcanic eruptions, and other consequences that killed most life on Earth. Scientists have estimated that 90 percent of all marine species and 70 percent of all land species perished during these events, which took place over a period of tens of thousands of years—ending the Permian geological period and initiating the Triassic period. At sedimentary boundaries between these two periods, researchers found concentrations of complex carbon molecules called buckminsterfullernes (after the scientist and inventor Buckminster Fuller) containing a mixture of argon and helium gases. These molecules are formed outside the solar system and, according to researchers, likely reached Earth aboard a large comet or meteor that hit just before the geological and climactic events that destroyed most life on the planet. New forms of life then emerged during the Triassic period.*

Using information gained from the study of Eros, scientists and engineers might be able to plot the best strategy for heading off a similar collision in the future—possibly by sending rockets or electronic rays capable of destroying the asteroid or nudging it into a different course, thus avoiding Earth. Scientists will have a long wait before they can put this knowledge to use, however. Eros itself is not expected to pose any possible danger to Earth for at least 1.5 million years, and no other sizable asteroids appear to be headed toward Earth in the foreseeable future.

More Planets Discovered

Reports from astronomers issued during 2001 raised to nearly eighty the number of planets discovered orbiting stars relatively near the solar system. None of the planets discovered so far exhibit all or even many of the characteristics thought to be necessary to sustain life as known on Earth. Even so, the discoveries encouraged further scientific research into the age-old question of whether life might be present somewhere other than on Earth. (Previous planet discoveries, Historic Documents of 1999, p. 173)

In January, a team lead by Geoffrey W. Marcy of the University of Cali-

fornia at Berkeley reported finding two planetary systems. In one, a gigantic object thought to be about seventeen times the size of Jupiter (the monster planet in Earth's solar system) orbits the star HD168443 in the constellation Serpens. That object, which could be a planet or some other unknown mass, is accompanied by a planet about seven times as large as Jupiter. This system is about 123 light years away from Earth (a light year is 6 trillion miles). Marcy's team also reported finding a system of two large planets orbiting the star Gliese 876 in the constellation Aquarius, about 15 light years from Earth. One planet is about half the mass of Jupiter and the other is about twice the size of Jupiter.

Later in the year NASA reported that research teams had discovered eight more planets in various systems, some of which have circular orbits around a star. A circular orbit is needed to ensure a narrow range of temperature fluctuations on a planet—a factor thought necessary for the development and sustenance of life. One finding was especially intriguing to scientists. In August a team including Marcy and other astronomers reported locating a second large planet orbiting the star 47 Ursae Majoris in the Big Dipper constellation, also known as Ursa Major. Like a companion planet discovered around that star several years earlier, this planet is gaseous (as is Jupiter) and has a circular orbit. To date, this is the only case—other than our own solar system—in which two planets have been found in circular orbits around one star. Researchers said it was possible that smaller planets also have circular orbits around the star but are too small or are not in position to be observed on Earth.

> *Following are portions of two press releases from the Applied Physics Laboratory of Johns Hopkins University in Laurel, Maryland. The first, dated February 12, 2001, announced the safe landing on Eros of the* NEAR Shoemaker *spacecraft. The second, dated February 14, reported some of the details of early data received from the spacecraft.*
>
> **The documents were obtained from the Internet at http:// near.jhuapl.edu/news/flash/01feb12_8.html; http://near .jhuapl.edu/news/flash/01feb14_1.html.**

TOUCHDOWN OF NASA'S *NEAR SHOEMAKER*

Today, at 3:01:52 P.M. EST, NASA's *NEAR [Near Earth Asteroid Rendezvous] Shoemaker* spacecraft traveled its last mile, cruising to the surface of asteroid Eros at a gentle 4 mph (1.9 meters per second)—finally coming to rest after its 2-billion-mile journey.

Cheers and congratulations filled the Mission Operations Center at the Johns Hopkins University Applied Physics Laboratory (APL) in Laurel, Md., which built the spacecraft and manages the mission for NASA, when NEAR Mission Director Robert Farquhar announced, "I'm happy to say the spacecraft is safely on the surface of Eros."

The last image snapped by *NEAR Shoemaker* was a mere 394 feet (120 meters) from the asteroid's surface and covered a 20-foot (6-meter) area. As *NEAR Shoemaker* touched down it began sending a beacon, assuring the team that the small spacecraft had landed gently. The signal was identified by radar science data, and about an hour later was locked onto by NASA's Deep Space Network antennas, which will monitor the spacecraft until Feb. 14.

NEAR Shoemaker's final descent started with an engine burn at 10:31 A.M. (EST) that nudged the spacecraft toward Eros from about 16 miles (26 kilometers) away. Then four braking maneuvers brought the spacecraft to rest on the asteroid's surface in an area just outside a saddle-shaped depression, Himeros. When it touched down, *NEAR Shoemaker* became the first spacecraft ever to land, or even attempt to land on an asteroid. The success was sweetened by the fact that *NEAR Shoemaker* was not designed as a lander.

The spacecraft spent the last year in a close-orbit study of asteroid 433 Eros, a near-Earth asteroid that is currently 196 million miles (316 million kilometers) from Earth. During that time it collected 10 times more data than originally planned and completed all its science goals before attempting its descent to the asteroid.

DATA COLLECTED BY
NEAR SHOEMAKER

The *NEAR Shoemaker* spacecraft's historic soft landing on asteroid 433 Eros Feb. 12 turned out to be a mission planner's dream—providing NEAR team members with more scientific and engineering information than they ever expected from the carefully designed series of descent maneuvers.

"We put the first priority on getting high-resolution images of the surface and the second on putting the spacecraft down safely—and we got both," says NEAR Mission Director Dr. Robert Farquhar of the Johns Hopkins University Applied Physics Laboratory in Laurel, Md., which manages the Near Earth Asteroid Rendezvous (NEAR) mission for NASA. "This could not have worked out better."

Two days after a set of five de-orbit and braking maneuvers brought it to the surface of Eros, *NEAR Shoemaker* is still communicating with the NEAR team at the Applied Physics Lab. The spacecraft gently touched down at 3:01:52 P.M. EST on Monday, ending a journey of more than 2 billion miles (3.2 billion kilometers) and a full year in orbit around the large space rock.

Yesterday the NEAR mission operations team disabled a redundant engine firing that would have been activated had it been necessary to adjust the spacecraft's orientation in order to receive telemetry from it. But because *NEAR Shoemaker* landed with such a favorable orientation, and telemetry has already been received, it was no longer necessary to move the spacecraft from its resting place.

Mission operators say the touchdown speed of less than 4 miles per hour (between 1.5 and 1.8 meters per second) may have been one of the slowest planetary landings in history. They also have a better picture of what happened in the moments after the landing: What they originally thought was the spacecraft bouncing may have been little more than short hop or "jiggle" on the surface; the thrusters were still firing when the craft hit the surface, but cut off on impact; and *NEAR Shoemaker* came down only about 650 feet (200 meters) from the projected landing site.

"It essentially confirmed that all the mathematical models we proposed for a controlled descent would work," says Dr. Bobby Williams, NEAR navigation team leader at NASA's Jet Propulsion Laboratory. "You never know if they'll work until you test them, and this was like our laboratory. The spacecraft did what we expected it to do, and everyone's real happy about that."

NEAR Shoemaker snapped 69 detailed pictures during the final three miles (five kilometers) of its descent, the highest resolution images ever obtained of an asteroid. The camera delivered clear pictures from as close as 394 feet (120 meters) showing features as small as one centimeter across. The images also included several things that piqued the curiosity of NEAR scientists, such as fractured boulders, a football-field sized crater filled with dust, and a mysterious area where the surface appears to have collapsed.

"These spectacular images have started to answer the many questions we had about Eros," says Dr. Joseph Veverka, NEAR imaging team leader from Cornell University in Ithaca, N.Y., "but they also revealed new mysteries that we will explore for years to come."

NEAR Shoemaker launched on Feb. 17, 1996—the first in NASA's Discovery Program of low-cost, scientifically focused planetary missions—and became the first spacecraft to orbit an asteroid on Feb. 14, 2000. The car-sized spacecraft gathered 10 times more data during its orbit than originally planned, and completed all the mission's science goals before Monday's controlled descent.

"NEAR has raised the bar," says Dr. Stamatios M. Krimigis, head of the Applied Physics Laboratory's Space Department. "The Laboratory is very proud to manage such a successful mission and work with such a strong team of partners from industry, government and other universities. This team had no weak links—not only did we deliver a spacecraft in 26 months, we were ready to launch a month early, and that efficiency continued through five years of operations. This is what the Discovery Program is designed to do."

FBI DIRECTOR FREEH ON THE ARREST OF A SPY IN THE RANKS
February 20, 2001

Robert Philip Hanssen, a senior FBI counterintelligence agent, was arrested on February 18, 2001, and charged two days later with espionage against the United States. On July 6 Hanssen pleaded guilty to fifteen counts of spying on behalf of the former Soviet Union and Russia. FBI Director Louis J. Freeh said Hanssen had done "exceptionally grave" damage to national security by giving more than six thousand pages of highly classified information to the Soviet intelligence agency, the KGB, and the Russian successor agency, the SVR.

Hanssen allegedly received about $1.4 million from Moscow for his espionage work, which began in 1979 and continued periodically until the day he was arrested. By pleading guilty, Hanssen avoided the death penalty. He spent the last six months of 2001 giving detailed information about his activities to federal officials. Hanssen was scheduled to be sentenced early in 2002 to a term of life in prison without the possibility of parole.

Intelligence experts said Hanssen was the most important spy caught among U.S. officials since Aldrich Ames, a senior CIA official who was apprehended in 1994 after nine years of selling U.S. secrets to Moscow. Ames and Hanssen both gave Moscow information about Russian agents whom had worked for the United States; at least two of those agents were executed when their identities were exposed. Perhaps of greater long-term damage, Hanssen also gave Russian authorities substantial information about American electronic espionage capabilities. Some experts said the loss of such classified information could have compromised much of the nation's intelligence-gathering efforts, and even some aspects of national security decision making, during the 1980s and 1990s. (Ames case, Historic Documents of 1994, p. 475)

A Mole's Life

For years many U.S. intelligence officials and experts had suspected that the Soviet Union had succeeded in planting one or more espionage agents—

or "moles"—in high-level government positions. The 1994 arrest and guilty plea of Ames, a senior counterintelligence official at the CIA, appeared to confirm those suspicions. Even so, the Ames arrest left unexplained some apparent leaks of sensitive U.S. intelligence information, but subsequent efforts to find other moles were unsuccessful.

Hanssen appeared to be an unlikely candidate as a Russian spy in the FBI's ranks—making him ideal for the role. Deeply religious and intensely patriotic, from all appearances, Hanssen was known by his coworkers as a hard-working, colorless bureaucrat with few friends; newspapers reported that FBI colleagues referred to him as "the mortician."

In fact, Hanssen led a secret life in which he avidly collected hard-core pornography and lavished cash, jewelry, and other gifts on a former stripper. As a counterintelligence agent, trained to combat espionage against the United States, he knew how to disguise his activities from his FBI colleagues. Even Hanssen's Russian contacts never met him or knew who he was, Freeh said; Hanssen used several pseudonyms for his work, including "B," "Ramon Garcia," "Jim Baker," and "G. Robertson."

A former accountant and police officer in Chicago, Hanssen joined the FBI in 1976. Two years later he was assigned to the bureau's New York office, where he helped develop a new computer system that kept track of counterintelligence information. According to court documents filed by federal prosecutors, Hanssen on one occasion in 1979 provided secret information to Soviet Union's military intelligence agency, the GRU. Two years later he was transferred to Washington as a special agent in the FBI's intelligence division. He was sent back to New York in 1985 to manage a unit of agents who spied on the Soviet Union's mission to the United Nations. Shortly after taking on that assignment, Hanssen passed a treasure trove of classified information to a senior KGB agent in Washington, including the identities of three KGB agents who were working as double agents on behalf of the United States. Hanssen's information apparently corroborated information that CIA official Ames had provided early in 1985, and two of the double agents later were sent back to Moscow and executed.

Hanssen returned to Washington in 1987 and for the next eight years held senior posts in various FBI units devoted to countering Soviet espionage. Hanssen provided numerous documents, many of them detailing what the FBI knew about Moscow's espionage against the United States. In 1989 he gave the KGB information that foiled a U.S. investigation of alleged espionage against the United States by Felix S. Bloch, a State Department diplomat serving in Vienna. Bloch was forced out of the State Department in 1990 but never charged with a crime.

After the collapse of the Soviet Union at the end of 1991, Hanssen curtailed his espionage work for Moscow, possibly out of concern about the chaotic state of the Russian government that succeeded the Soviet regime. The FBI in 1995 assigned Hanssen as its liaison official in the State Department's Office of Foreign Missions, which dealt with diplomatic posts of foreign governments in the United States. He resumed his contacts with the Russians in 1999—reportedly because he was impressed by

Russian president Boris Yeltsin's naming of former KGB official Vladimir Putin as his prime minister. (Putin rise to power, Historic Documents of 1999, p. 917)

In messages to his Russian contacts, Hanssen offered several reasons for his actions against his country, including the excitement of engaging in espionage and the low regard in which he held many of his colleagues and government agencies (including the FBI). In one letter that the FBI said was written in 2000, Hanssen also declared his loyalty to the Russian contacts he had never met but whom he seemed to regard as friends: "One might propose that I am either insanely brave or quite insane. I'd answer neither. I'd say, insanely loyal."

In 1997, if not earlier, Hanssen became concerned that his FBI colleagues might have begun to suspect him. He repeatedly searched FBI computer files for information linking him to espionage. The Washington Post *reported that Hanssen's brother-in-law, also an FBI agent, had told the bureau as early as 1990 that he suspected Hanssen of spying for the Soviet Union, but the bureau reportedly did not investigate the tip.*

A Russian intelligence source in late 2000 gave U.S. officials documents that enabled the FBI to pinpoint Hanssen as an espionage agent. The FBI mounted an around-the-clock surveillance of Hanssen, including wiretaps on his home and office telephones, and in January 2001 transferred him to bureau headquarters so he could be more closely monitored.

Early on a Sunday evening, February 18, Hanssen dropped a bag containing classified documents at a park in a Virginia suburb outside Washington; hidden nearby was a bag for him containing $50,000. FBI agents arrested Hanssen as he left the bag of documents. Two days later Freeh and Attorney General John Ashcroft announced that Hanssen had been charged with espionage. On May 16 a federal grand jury indicted Hanssen on twenty-one espionage counts. After more than a month of negotiations between U.S. prosecutors and Hanssen's attorneys, Hanssen on July 6 pleaded guilty to fifteen counts and agreed to give detailed information about his actions in exchange for a sentence of life in prison. The government dropped six other charges as part of the plea bargain. Several of the charges against Hanssen carried the death penalty, and many senior U.S. officials—reportedly including Ashcroft and Defense Secretary Donald H. Rumsfeld—favored pursuing that penalty to make an "example" of Hanssen. Other officials, however, prevailed with the argument that getting Hanssen to testify about his espionage was more important to the government than the satisfaction of putting him to death. The plea bargain also enabled prosecutors to avoid taking the case to trial, where embarrassing information about the government might have been made public.

Under the plea bargain, Hanssen agreed to turn over to the government whatever remained of the $1.43 million worth of cash, diamonds, and deposits in a Moscow bank that he had received for his espionage work. Hanssen's wife, who reportedly was unaware of the extent of his activities and had cooperated with investigators, was allowed to keep the family home and draw some of her husband's pension.

Hanssen's Damage

In their original affidavit supporting the charges against Hanssen, federal prosecutors said he had given Russian agents more than twenty packages of material, including more than six thousand pages of documents. Freeh told reporters on February 20 that during his career Hanssen had access to "some of the most sensitive and highly classified information in the United States government." Hanssen's espionage "represents the most traitorous actions imaginable" and had caused damage to the United States that was "exceptionally grave," Freeh said.

According to federal court documents and news reports, Hanssen's disclosures of classified materials included a detailed description of U.S. strategic weapons, U.S. intelligence reports on the Soviet strategic arsenal, and numerous documents about U.S. counterintelligence programs, including the identities of nine Soviet agents who had spied on behalf of the United States, and the existence of an eavesdropping tunnel underneath the new Soviet embassy in Washington. Hanssen also gave the KGB numerous details of the secret information that the United States had been able to collect about the Soviet Union through satellites and interceptions of electronic communications. Officials and intelligence experts outside the government said no other FBI agent had ever betrayed as much information to a foreign power, and that, among recent espionage cases, only Ames had given as much damaging information to the Russians.

James Bamford, who had written extensively about U.S. intelligence programs, told the Washington Post that Hanssen's espionage might have been especially damaging to the work of the National Security Agency (NSA), which monitors telephone and other electronic communications in foreign countries. "It takes years and years for an agency like the NSA to get to that position [of successfully monitoring governments such as the Soviet Union], and then to have someone just give it all away is devastating, especially when you don't know it," Bamford said. "We could be making a lot of defense decisions, like how to design this torpedo or warhead, based on false assumptions provided by the Russians."

One month after Hanssen's arrest, the United States and Russia engaged in a tit-for-tat retaliation that briefly damaged relations between the two countries. Secretary of State Colin Powell on March 21 gave Russian ambassador Yuri Ushakov a list of four Russian diplomats ordered to leave the United States immediately. U.S. officials said another forty or so Russians—all of them alleged to be intelligence agents—would be ordered to leave during the course of the year. The Russian government responded two days later by expelling four American diplomats and promising to match future U.S. expulsions on a one-for-one basis.

During the course of 2001 the FBI put in place several new security precautions intended to make it difficult for an agent such as Hanssen to pass *secret information to foreign governments. Among the new procedures were requirements that all counterintelligence agents take periodic polygraph tests and that agents routinely look for and report to superiors cases in which other agents looked at case files without authorization.*

Attorney General Ashcroft on May 9 appointed a seven-member commission, headed by former FBI and CIA director William Webster, to review the FBI's internal security procedures and make recommendations for improvements. The panel had not finished its work by the end of 2001. Robert Mueller, who took over from Freeh as FBI director in August, announced a broad reorganization of the bureau in December; officials said the shake-up was only partly in response to problems uncovered by the Hanssen case.

An Intelligence Failure?

The FBI and other intelligence agencies had barely recovered from the storm of publicity about the Hanssen case when they were buffeted by consequences of the September 11 terrorist attacks against targets in New York and Washington. Several members of Congress and intelligence experts from outside the government charged that government agencies should have been able to detect signs of the planned attacks. Perhaps the most outspoken was Richard C. Shelby of Alabama, the senior Republican on the Senate Intelligence Committee, who complained of a "stunning intelligence failure." (Terrorist attacks, pp. 614, 624)

During the three months after the attacks, the House and Senate intelligence committees debated whether and how to launch investigations into why U.S. agencies had no advance warning of the attacks. The House panel at first adopted a provision, in its fiscal 2002 intelligence authorization bill (HR 2883), establishing an independent commission with subpoena powers to conduct such an investigation. But panel members and House Republican leaders later had second thoughts, and on October 5 the full House voted to water down that provision by deleting the subpoena powers and giving the commission a broader mandate to examine possible improvements in the intelligence services without focusing on the September 11 attacks. Ultimately, the two intelligence panels agreed to drop the idea of mandating a commission. Instead, congressional leaders suggested that any investigations into intelligence failures preceding the September 11 attacks be put off at least until 2002.

Following is the text of a statement made February 20, 2001, by Louis J. Freeh, director of the Federal Bureau of Investigation, announcing that senior FBI agent Robert Philip Hanssen had been arrested and charged with committing espionage against the United States on behalf of the former Soviet Union and Russia.

The document was obtained from the Internet at http://www.fbi.gov/pressrel/pressrel01/freeh022001.htm.

Sunday night [February 18] the FBI arrested Robert Philip Hanssen who has been charged with committing espionage. Hanssen is a Special Agent of the FBI with a long career in counterintelligence.

The investigation that led to these charges is the direct result of the long-standing FBI/CIA efforts, ongoing since the Aldrich Ames case, to identify additional foreign penetrations of the United States Intelligence Community. The investigation of Hanssen was conducted by the FBI in partnership with the CIA, the Department of State, and, of course, the Justice Department.

The complaint alleges that Hanssen conspired to and did commit espionage for Russia and the former Soviet Union. The actions alleged date back as far as 1985 and, with the possible exception of several years in the 1990s, continued until his arrest on Sunday. He was arrested while in the process of using a "dead drop" to clandestinely provide numerous classified documents to his Russian handler.

It is alleged that Hanssen provided to the former Soviet Union and subsequently to Russia substantial volumes of highly classified information that he acquired during the course of his job responsibilities in counterintelligence. In return, he received large sums of money and other remuneration. The complaint alleges that he received over $600,000.

The full extent of the damage done is yet unknown because no accurate damage assessment could be conducted without jeopardizing the investigation. We believe it was exceptionally grave.

The criminal conduct alleged represents the most traitorous actions imaginable against a country governed by the Rule of Law. As difficult as this moment is for the FBI and for the country, I am immensely proud of the men and women who conducted this investigation. Their actions represent counterintelligence at its very best and under the most difficult and sensitive of circumstances. Literally, Hanssen's colleagues and coworkers at the FBI conducted this investigation and did so quietly, securely and without hesitation. Much of what these men and women did remains undisclosed but their success and that of their CIA counterparts represents unparalleled expertise and dedication to both principle and mission.

The complaint alleges that Hanssen, using the code name "Ramon," engaged in espionage by providing highly classified information to the KGB and its successor agency, the SVR, using encrypted communications, dead drops, and other clandestine techniques. The information he is alleged to have provided compromised numerous human sources, technical operations, counterintelligence techniques, sources and methods, and investigations, including the Felix Bloch investigation.

The affidavit alleges that Hanssen voluntarily became an agent of the KGB in 1985 while assigned to the intelligence division at the FBI field office in New York City as supervisor of a foreign counterintelligence squad. Hanssen allegedly began spying for the Soviets in 1985 when, in his first letter to the KGB, he volunteered information that compromised several sensitive techniques. He also independently disclosed the identity of two KGB officials who, first compromised by Aldrich Ames, had been recruited by the U.S.

Government to serve as "agents in place" at the Soviet Embassy in Washington. When these two KGB officials returned to Moscow, they were tried and convicted on espionage charges and executed.

Hanssen subsequently was assigned to a variety of national security posts that legitimately provided him access to classified information relating to the former Soviet Union and Russia. As a result of these assignments within the FBI, Hanssen gained access to some of the most sensitive and highly classified information in the United States Government. To be very clear on this issue, at no time was he authorized to communicate information to agents of the KGB/SVR. Nor can there be any doubt that he was keenly aware of the gravity of his traitorous actions. He later wrote to his KGB handler, speaking about the severity with which U.S. laws punishes his alleged actions, and acknowledging ". . . I know far better than most what minefields are laid and the risks."

Hanssen was detailed to the Office of Foreign Missions at the Department of State from 1995 to 2000. The complaint, however, does not allege any compromises by him at the State Department. In one letter to his Russian handlers, Hanssen complains about lost opportunities to alert them that the FBI had discovered the microphone hidden at the State Department, known then by the FBI but apparently not by Hanssen as being monitored by a Russian intelligence officer. In this assignment, however, Hanssen did continue to have access to sensitive FBI information as he remained assigned to the FBI's National Security Division and routinely dealt with sensitive and classified matters.

For many years, the CIA and FBI have been aggressively engaged in a sustained analytical effort to identify foreign penetrations of the Intelligence Community. That effort is complemented by substantial FBI proactive investigation of foreign service intelligence officers here and by the critical work done by the CIA. Because of these coordinated efforts, the FBI was able to secure original Russian documentation of an American spy who appeared to the FBI to be Hanssen—a premise that was soon to be confirmed when Hanssen was identified by the FBI as having clandestinely communicated with Russian intelligence officers.

As alleged in the complaint, computer forensic analysis, substantial covert surveillance, court authorized searches and other sensitive techniques revealed that Hanssen has routinely accessed FBI records and clandestinely provided those records and other classified information to Russian intelligence officers. As alleged, he did so using a variety of sophisticated means of communication, encryption, and dead drops.

Further, the complaint alleges that Hanssen, using his training and experience to protect himself from discovery by the FBI, never met face-to-face with his Russian handlers, never revealed to them his true identity or where he worked, constantly checked FBI records for signs he and the drop sites he was using were being investigated, refused any foreign travel to meet with the Russians, and even declined to accept any "trade craft." Hanssen never displayed outward signs that he was receiving large amounts of unexplained cash. He was, after all, a trained counterintelligence specialist. For these reasons, the FBI learned of his true identity before the Russians; they are learning of it only now. Even without knowing who he was or where he worked, Hanssen's value to the Russians was clear both by the substantial sums of money paid and the prestigious awards given to their own agents for Hanssen's operation.

While this arrest represents a counterintelligence investigative success, the complaint alleges that Hanssen located and removed undetected from the FBI substantial quantities of information that he was able to access as a result of his assignments. None of the internal information or personnel security measures in place alerted those charged with internal security to his activities. In short, the trusted insider betrayed his trust without detection.

While the risk that an employee of the United States Government will betray his country can never be eliminated, there must be more that the FBI can do to protect itself from such an occurrence. I have asked Judge William H. Webster, and he has graciously agreed, to examine thoroughly the internal security functions and procedures of the FBI and recommend improvements. Judge Webster is uniquely qualified as a former FBI Director, CIA Director and Director of Central Intelligence to undertake this review. This is particularly timely as we move to the next generation of automation to support the FBI's information infrastructure. Judge Webster and anyone he selects to assist him will have complete access and whatever resources are necessary to complete this task. He will report directly to the Attorney General and me and we will share his report with the National Security Council and Congress. I intend to act swiftly on his recommendations.

Before concluding, I would like to take this opportunity to thank Director of Central Intelligence George Tenet for the cooperation and assistance of his agency in this investigation. Through our cooperative efforts, the FBI and CIA were able to learn the true identity of "Ramon" and the FBI was able to conduct a solid investigation. Our joint efforts over the last several years and specifically in this case should give pause to those contemplating betrayal of the Nation's trust. Without the current unprecedented level of trust and cooperation between the CIA and FBI, making this case would not have been possible. Nor would many other intelligence and counterintelligence accomplishments that routinely but quietly contribute to the security of this Nation.

Through Attorney General John Ashcroft, I would like to thank the Department of Justice and the U.S. Attorney's Office for the Eastern District of Virginia. The level of support and expertise from Acting Deputy Attorney General Robert Mueller, Counsel for Intelligence Policy Frances Fragos Townsend, U.S. Attorney Helen Fahey and Assistant United States Attorney Randy Bellows is superb. We particularly appreciate the unhesitating leadership and support of Attorney General Ashcroft from the moment he took office.

Director Tenet and I have briefed the intelligence committees of Congress because of the clear national security implications.

As Director of the FBI, I am proud of the courageous men and women of the FBI who each day make enormous sacrifices in serving their country. They have committed their lives to public service and to upholding the high standards of the FBI. Since becoming Director over seven years ago, I have administered the FBI oath to each graduating class of Special Agents at the FBI Academy. Each time, I share the pride and sanctity of those words when new agents swear to "support and defend the Constitution of the United States against all enemies, foreign and domestic" and to "bear true faith and allegiance to the same."

Regrettably, I stand here today both saddened and outraged. An FBI Agent who raised his right hand and spoke those words over 25 years ago has been charged today with violating that oath in the most egregious and reprehensible manner imaginable. The FBI entrusted him with some of the most sensitive secrets of the United States Government and instead of being humbled by this honor, Hanssen has allegedly abused and betrayed that trust. The crimes alleged are an affront not only to his fellow FBI employees but to the American people, not to mention the pain and suffering he has brought upon his family. Our hearts go out to them. I take solace and satisfaction, however, that the FBI succeeded in this investigation. As an agency, we lived up to our responsibility, regardless of how painful it might be.

UN SECRETARY GENERAL
ON WAR IN THE CONGO
February 21, 2001

An international war centered in the Democratic Republic of the Congo (formerly Zaire) continued to flare during 2001, although at a much lower level than during the previous two-plus years of fighting. United Nations-sponsored efforts to end the fighting and bring relief to the nation's war-ravaged people had some success, but it was clear that years of international support would be needed to put the massive country back on its feet.

In a December 14 report on the war, the International Crisis Group— a global think tank that monitored conflict situations—said that despite some optimistic signs "the underlying causes of conflict remain to be resolved, and people are still dying every day from fighting, hunger and disease." By late 2001 most international observers agreed that some 2.5 million people had died as a consequence of fighting since 1998 in what former secretary of state Madeleine K. Albright had called "Africa's first world war." (Congo war, Historic Documents of 2000, p. 978; Historic Documents of 1999, p. 645)

Assassination of Kabila

At the outset of 2001, the Congo conflict had been in stalemate for nearly two years, in large part because of resistance to UN-sponsored peace moves by the Congo's self-declared president, Laurent Kabila.. A former guerrilla leader, Kabila had been the front-man for a coalition, backed by neighboring Rwanda, that swept into power in 1997 and ousted the country's long-term dictator, Mobutu Sese Seko. Kabila adopted a dictatorial ruling style himself, banning political parties and imprisoning opponents. His former allies in Rwanda and Uganda turned against him and in August 1998 launched an invasion in support of anti-Kabila guerrilla groups in eastern Congo. The governments of Angola, Namibia, and Zimbabwe rushed to Kabila's defense. Lacking an effective army of his own, Kabila also relied on a large militia of Hutu rebels whose leaders had been responsible for the 1994 genocide that killed hundreds of thousands of people in Rwanda. (Rwanda genocide, Historic Documents of 2000, p. 499; Mobutu ouster, Historic Documents of 1997, p. 877)

The resulting conflicts between and among these groups split the Congo in half, with part nominally controlled by Kabila's government and his allies, and the rest controlled by guerrilla groups and the armies of Rwanda and Uganda. One UN official said in February 2001 that nine separate but related conflicts were under way in the Congo, some strictly among Congolese factions and others involving the troops from other nations.

A bodyguard assassinated Kabila on January 16, 2001, possibly as part of a coup attempt by some aides. The next day, government officials turned to Kabila's twenty-nine-year-old son, Joseph Kabila, as his successor. Joseph Kabila had been a major general in the Congolese army, even though he had no formal military training. Joseph Kabila moved quickly to consolidate his own authority and to seek a peaceful solution to the country's war, firing government ministers who had opposed peace talks with opposition parties and rebel groups. Kabila also traveled in February to Paris and Washington, D.C., to appeal to French, UN, and U.S. officials for aid and political support; later in the year he met with the presidents of Rwanda and Uganda.

The assassination of Laurent Kabila and the peace overtures by his son led to a de facto cease-fire along the main lines of confrontation among the government, guerrilla groups, and other nations. Seizing on the first real signs of peace in two years, the UN Security Council on February 22 called on all sides to pull troops back from the front lines by mid-March, to be followed by a start toward the withdrawal of all foreign forces by mid-May. The council also approved plans for the full deployment of up to 5,537 UN peacekeepers that had been authorized for the Congo in 1999; with no peace to keep, only 200 of those troops had been stationed in the Congo.

In a February 12, 2001, report to the Security Council, UN Secretary General Kofi Annan gave the first published estimates of the presence of foreign troops in the Congo: siding with the government were 7,000 troops from Angola, 2,000 from Namibia, and 12,000 from Zimbabwe; opposing the government were 20,000 from Rwanda and 10,000 from Uganda. Annan did not attempt to estimate the number of guerrillas fighting on behalf of the numerous rebel groups in the Congo. Annan told the Security Council on February 21 that the parties to the conflict for the first time "have been talking to each other at the highest levels with a renewed determination to find a peaceful solution."

Rwanda was the first party to pull back some of its troops, starting on February 28. Later in the year Namibia withdrew all of its 2,000 troops, and Uganda withdrew or repositioned some of its forces beginning in mid-March. But most other fighting units remained in place or pulled back from the front lines only partly, despite the Security Council resolution mandating a full withdrawal from the Congo. Fighting flared periodically during the year, primarily in eastern regions where the Hutu militia backing the

Congo's government battled with a coalition of rebel groups and troops from Rwanda, Uganda, and (sometimes) Burundi.

The UN peacekeepers began arriving in late March. By October the force totaled 2,408 uniformed personnel, but it had been unable to reach several contested areas in the eastern part of the country. The UN troops came from nearly four dozen countries, but no U.S. personnel were assigned to the mission, which was called the UN Organization Mission in the Democratic Republic of the Congo (MONUC).

A delegation of ambassadors to the UN Security Council visited the Congo and other countries in the region in late May and reported that, for the first time since the war began, the "outlines of a solution appear to be taking shape." Citing progress, the council adopted a resolution on June 15 extending the mandate of the UN peacekeepers until June 2002 and demanding again that all parties to the Congo conflict withdraw their forces and participate in political dialogue.

Political Dialogue

Under a 1999 peace agreement that had never been implemented, the end to the war was to be accompanied by peace talks among all of the Congo's domestic political factions. Called the Inter-Congolese Dialogue, the talks were to be moderated by a neutral UN "facilitator," former Botswanan president Ketumile Masire. Masire made no headway in establishing peace talks while Laurent Kabila was alive. The elder Kabila refused to deal with Masire, ostensibly because the Botswanan spoke English but not French, the language most commonly used by the Congo's political leaders; most observers said Kabila's real objection was to negotiating with his opponents.

Joseph Kabila reversed his father's position and agreed to negotiations moderated by Masire. Preliminary talks were held in Lusaka, Zambia, in April and in Gaborene, Botswana, in August. Formal negotiations were convened starting October 16 in Addis Ababa, Ethiopia. But Kabila's representatives walked out after two days, arguing that the talks were pointless because several important groups were not present. That move brought a new round of recriminations among the parties, although all agreed to a new round of negotiations slated for January 2002 in South Africa.

Humanitarian Situation

With the winding down of the war, international aid workers gained increased access to regions of the country that had been off-limits because of the fighting. They found situations of incredible devastation and human misery. According to UN estimates, 2.3 million Congolese had been forced from their homes by the fighting; of these, about 2 million remained in the country (most in the eastern regions) and the rest had fled to neighboring countries. Of all the conflict scenes in the world in 2001, only Afghanistan had more refugees and displaced people than the Congo—about 4 million. (Afghanistan fighting, p. 686)

Estimates of how many people had died as a direct or indirect result

161

of the Congo war varied, from a low of 1 million to a high of 3 million. An epidemiological study conducted in eastern Congo by the U.S.-based International Rescue Committee produced a widely accepted estimate of 2.5 million, of whom some 200,000 were believed to have been fighters and the rest civilians who died from disease (especially malaria), starvation, or war-related injuries. The country had a total population of more than 50 million. If the 2.5 million estimate of deaths was correct, it meant that nearly 5 percent of the Congo's people had died because of the war; for the United States, a comparable figure would be 14 million.

Nationwide, the UN's Food and Agriculture Organization estimated that about two-thirds of the Congo's people were undernourished and about 15 million had "critical" nutritional needs (meaning that they were in danger of dying from lack of food). Less than one-third of the country's people had any access to health care, usually at the most rudimentary level.

Added to the Congo's internal problems during 2001 were two major influxes of refugees from other countries. In May approximately 26,000 civilians and guerrillas fled into the Congo from neighboring Central African Republic following an unsuccessful coup attempt there. Then, in August and October, renewed attacks against the government of Angola by the UNITA rebel force sent an estimated 12,000 refugees into the Congo, bringing the total number of Angolans there to about 190,000. In total, some 360,000 people from other countries had taken refuge in the Congo as of late 2001—about the same number as had fled from the Congo into other countries.

Its economy in ruins from years of war, the Congo had few resources to provide aid either to its own citizens displaced by the fighting or to refugees from other countries. Oxfam, the British relief agency, estimated that about half of the 2 million homeless Congolese had no access to aid, and most of the rest were receiving only minimal food, shelter, medicine, and other forms of relief. The United Nations appealed for $139.4 million in international relief aid to the Congo during 2001, but the United States and other major donors provided less than half that amount.

One humanitarian matter that drew significant international attention was the plight of thousands of young teenage boys who had been recruited as combatants by the Congolese government and rebel groups. Under pressure from the UN and aid agencies, the government in December turned over to UNICEF the first 235 of an estimated 6,000 "child soldiers" who had been serving with the army, many of them for several years. UNICEF planned to offer the children training in civilian occupations.

Looting Congo's Wealth

In theory, at least, the Congo should be one of Africa's wealthiest countries. Larger than western Europe and about one-fourth the size of the United States, the country has vast quantities of copper, diamonds, gold, timber, and other natural resources. But for more than a century those resources had been exploited for the narrow gain of the country's rulers: first, Belgian King Leopold II (who personally owned the Congo in the late

1800s), then the Belgian government, then Mobutu, and finally the combatants in the war.

By 2000 it had become clear that Laurent Kabila's government and the various factions aligned with or opposed to it were engaged in systematic looting of the Congo's natural resources. Most of the attention focused on Ugandan and Rwandan forces, which were mining diamonds and other minerals in the eastern part of the Congo. Troops from Zimbabwe had been given contracts by Kabila to extract natural resources in the southern part of the country to finance its military operations.

The UN Security Council appointed a panel of "eminent persons" to investigate the looting of the Congo's resources. That panel issued a preliminary report on April 16 that blamed Burundi, Rwanda, and Uganda for "wide-scale looting" of valuable resources. Uganda, according to the report, had illegally extracted an estimated $3 million worth of diamonds from the Congo, while Rwanda had taken at least $250 million worth of columbite-tantalite (also known as "col-tan"), a mineral used in the production of computer chips. Those countries complained that the report was "one-sided," and Uganda temporarily suspended its participation in the peace process to protest it.

The panel returned to the council with a follow-up report on November 24 that repeated the charges from the April report but added new information about Zimbabwe's activities. That country, the report said, demanded free access to the Congo's timber and diamond resources as the price for sending thousands of troops to support the Kabila government. "There is a clear link between the continuation of the conflict and the exploitation of natural resources," the panel said. "It would not be wrong to say that one drives the other." The panel suggested that the Security Council impose a temporary ban on international trade in natural resources extracted from the Congo, as a means of cutting off financial support for the war. The council did not follow that advice, however, and instead issued a statement demanding an end to the looting; it also extended the mandate of the investigating panel for another six months.

> *Following are excerpts from a statement made by UN Secretary General Kofi Annan on February 21, 2001, to the UN Security Council and the political committee that monitored compliance with the July 1999 cease-fire agreement, signed in Lusaka, Zambia, calling for an end to the regional war in the Democratic Republic of the Congo. Annan's statement is followed by excerpts from Resolution 1341, adopted by the council on February 22, calling on all parties to the Congo conflict to withdraw their forces from the front lines and for all foreign forces to be withdrawn from the country by May 15.*

> **The documents were obtained from the Internet at http://www.un.org/News/Press/docs/2001/sgsm7707.doc.htm; http://www.un.org/News/Press/docs/2001/sc7017.doc.htm.**

163

ANNAN STATEMENT

Last June, in this Chamber, the members of the Political Committee of the Lusaka Ceasefire Agreement met with the Security Council to discuss advancing the peace process in the Democratic Republic of the Congo.

Much has changed since last June, and in recent weeks some things, at least, have changed for the better. First, the parties have been talking to each other at the highest levels with a renewed determination to find a peaceful solution. Second, the way has been opened for the Congolese people to take part in the governance of their country, and to have a real say in determining their future. Third, a de facto cessation of hostilities prevails throughout much of the country.

As this Council—and all the parties—are aware, however, great challenges lie ahead which require the will to peace, and the ability to implement commitments made.

Today, the Democratic Republic of the Congo is divided by a line of confrontation between the forces of five foreign armies—a line that stretches from Lake Mweru on the Zambian border to the banks of the Ubangi River, the border with the Democratic Republic of the Congo. . . . For the last five weeks, calm has descended on that line.

In accordance with the plan devised by the Joint Military Commission and approved by the Political Committee, the opposing troops can soon begin to withdraw from their advance positions and step back from the line of confrontation. Such a move could be the first step towards an eventual withdrawal of all foreign forces from the territory of the Democratic Republic of the Congo. Since the Lusaka Agreement was signed in July and August 1999, this has been our common goal.

In spite of the obstacles, misunderstandings and delays that have prevented its implementation so far, all the parties can take a measure of credit for the recent progress. All the parties remain responsible for seeing this process to its logical, rightful and long-awaited conclusion.

The plan for the disengagement of forces was signed at Harare [Zimbabwe] on 6 December [2000].

I have since submitted to the Security Council a concept of operations, under which United Nations military personnel would be deployed to monitor and verify the actions to be taken by the parties in implementing the disengagement plan. The Council is now ready to endorse that concept, and the United Nations Organization Mission in the Democratic Republic of the Congo (MONUC) and the Secretariat have already begun to take the steps necessary to put it into practice.

Once you have finished your discussions here, a date will be set to begin the disengagement and redeployment exercise. The troops can then start drawing back, supervised and monitored by United Nations military observers. The implementation date should be chosen with care: not too late to lose the momentum already generated, but not before all the necessary preparations have been put in place to ensure an efficient and transparent operation.

These military movements will take place in a political environment which, however troubled and volatile, has also shown clear signs of improvement.

I welcome the decision of [Congo] President [Joseph] Kabila's Government to permit the neutral facilitator, Sir Ketumile Masire, to work with the various Congolese parties in conducting the national dialogue. Without broad political agreement among the Congolese people based on a dialogue leading to free and fair elections, no military solution can bring lasting peace and stability to the Democratic Republic of the Congo.

In view of the recent positive signs in the Democratic Republic of the Congo peace process, I urge all those donors who pledged to support the work of the neutral facilitator to move quickly to fulfil their promises. At the same time, I urge the members of the Security Council and the wider international community to provide financial and other support to President Masire's important work.

Before achieving the long-term political goals, however, we must address the humanitarian crisis that still affects large numbers of the Congolese people. At this point, in too many parts of the Democratic Republic of the Congo, humanitarian assistance workers are being prevented from reaching populations in dire need of aid.

At least 2 million people in the Democratic Republic of the Congo have been driven from their homes by the fighting. Fewer than half of them receive humanitarian assistance. There may be as many as 16 million people with not enough to eat. More than half the population lacks access to drinkable water, and almost two-thirds cannot obtain essential medicine. Finally, the security of neighboring countries not involved in the war has been placed at risk, not least through flows of refugees, as well as armed men, fleeing the fighting.

I wish to highlight the tragic fact that civilians—especially women and children—have been the principle victims of the fighting. Terrible crimes have been committed against women, including rape as a weapon of war. Children have been inducted into armies and sent to the front. They must be given a chance to build a better future.

The world has been waiting for the parties to this conflict—the parties that signed the Lusaka Ceasefire Agreement—to prove their determination to end the fighting and lay the foundations for peace and recovery.

Only as they do so can the international community and the United Nations materially assist them. We have heard complaints of the slowness of the United Nations to act, or the small size of the forces it plans to deploy. But governments that contribute troops to United Nations peacekeeping operations are not convinced that they should risk their soldiers' lives in circumstances where those most responsible are not themselves reliably committed. You may wish it were otherwise, but these are the facts.

That is why these meetings between the Security Council and the Political Committee are so important. Let us now build on the advances of the past few weeks: the agreements that have been signed, and the careful plans that have been made. Let the parties to the conflict show the world that they are willing and able to keep their promises, to end a shameful and disastrous conflict, and to work reliably with the international community in laying the foundations for recovery.

In this connection, I welcome the confirmation by President [Paul] Kagame [of Rwanda] to me in a telephone conversation on 19 February of his decision to withdraw his troops from Pweto [in eastern Congo], and pull back all his forces 200 kilometers, according to the Harare disengagement and redeployment plan. I have instructed my Special Representative, Mr. [Kamel] Morjane, and the Force Commander, General [Mountaga] Diallo, who are with us today, to prepare to assist in this withdrawal. I hope this move by Rwanda will help set the tone and lead the other parties to take similar steps towards the ultimate withdrawal of all foreign forces from the Democratic Republic of the Congo.

I am therefore pleased to note the statement issued yesterday by the Ugandan Government that it intends to withdraw two battalions from the Democratic Republic of the Congo. This is a further welcome development.

The parties should be given a clear message today: Let the disengagement of forces and the inter-Congolese dialogue begin. Draw up plans to bring all foreign forces home from Democratic Republic of the Congo territory. Work with your neighbors and with us to find innovative and creative ways to resolve the problems of armed groups and border security.

These are the outcomes expected from this meeting. I wish you every success in achieving them.

SECURITY COUNCIL
RESOLUTION 1341

The Security Council,

Reaffirming the sovereignty, territorial integrity and political independence of the Democratic Republic of the Congo and of all States in the region,

Reaffirming further the obligation of all States to refrain from the use of force against the territorial integrity and political independence of any State, or in any other manner inconsistent with the purposes of the United Nations,

Reaffirming also the sovereignty of the Democratic Republic of the Congo over its natural resources, and noting with concern reports of the illegal exploitation of the country's assets and the potential consequences of these actions for security conditions and the continuation of hostilities,

Expressing its alarm at the dire consequences of the prolonged conflict for the civilian population throughout the territory of the Democratic Republic of the Congo, in particular the increase in the number of refugees and displaced persons and stressing the urgent need for substantial humanitarian assistance to the Congolese population,

Expressing its deep concern at all violations of human rights and international humanitarian law, including atrocities against civilian populations, especially in the eastern provinces,

Deeply concerned at the increased rate of HIV/AIDS infection, in particular amongst women and girls as a result of the conflict,

Gravely concerned by the continued recruitment and use of child soldiers by armed forces and groups, including cross-border recruitment and abduction of children, . . .

Stressing the importance of giving new impetus to the peace process in order to secure the full and definitive withdrawal of all foreign troops from the Democratic Republic of the Congo,

Also stressing the importance of advancing the political process called for under the Lusaka Ceasefire Agreement and facilitating national reconciliation,

Recalling the responsibilities of all parties to cooperate in the full deployment of the United Nations Organization Mission in the Democratic Republic of the Congo (MONUC), and *noting* with satisfaction the recent statements by the President of the Democratic Republic of the Congo and his assurances of support for the deployment of MONUC, . . .

Taking note of the Secretary-General's report of 12 February 2001 and his conclusion that the conditions of respect for the ceasefire, a valid plan for disengagement and cooperation with MONUC are being met,

Determining that the situation in the Democratic Republic of the Congo continues to pose a threat to international peace and security in the region,

Acting under Chapter VII of the Charter of the United Nations,

1. *Notes* the recent progress made in achieving respect for the ceasefire, and *urgently calls* on all parties to the Lusaka Ceasefire Agreement not to resume hostilities and to implement this agreement, as well as the agreements reached in Kampala and Harare and the relevant Security Council resolutions;

2. *Demands once again* that Ugandan and Rwandan forces and all other foreign forces withdraw from the territory of the Democratic Republic of the Congo in compliance with paragraph 4 of its resolutions 1304 (2000) and the Lusaka Ceasefire Agreement, and urges these forces to take urgent steps to accelerate this withdrawal;

3. *Demands* that the parties implement fully the Kampala plan and the Harare sub-plans [agreements signed in 1999 and 2000] for disengagement and redeployment of forces without reservations within the 14-day period stipulated in the Harare Agreement, starting from 15 March 2001;

4. *Welcomes* the commitment by the Rwandan authorities in their letter of 18 February 2001 (S/2001/147), to withdraw their forces from Pweto in accordance with the Harare Agreement, *calls on* them to implement this commitment and *calls on* other parties to respect this withdrawal;

5. *Welcomes also* the commitment of the Ugandan authorities to reduce immediately by two battalions the strength of their forces in the territory of the Democratic Republic of the Congo, *calls on* the Ugandan authorities to implement this commitment and *calls on* MONUC to verify it;

6. *Urges* the parties to the Lusaka Ceasefire Agreement to prepare and adopt not later than 15 May 2001, in close liaison with MONUC, a precise plan and schedule which, in accordance with the Lusaka Ceasefire Agreement, would lead to the completion of the orderly withdrawal of all foreign troops from the territory of the Democratic Republic of the Congo, and *requests* the Secretary-General to report to it by 15 April 2001 on the progress of these efforts;

7. *Demands* all the parties to refrain from any offensive military action during the process of disengagement and withdrawal of foreign forces;

8. *Urges* all the parties to the conflict, in close liaison with MONUC, to prepare by 15 May 2001 for immediate implementation prioritized plans for the disarmament, demobilization, reintegration, repatriation or resettlement of all armed groups [as defined in the Lusaka Ceasefire Agreement], and demands that all parties cease all forms of assistance and cooperation with these groups and use their influence to urge such groups to cease their activities;

9. *Condemns* the massacres and atrocities committed in the territory of the Democratic Republic of the Congo, and *demands* once again that all the parties concerned put an immediate end to violations of human rights and international humanitarian law;

10. *Demands* that all armed forces and groups concerned bring an effective end to the recruitment, training and use of children into their armed forces, *calls upon* them to extend full cooperation to MONUC, the United Nations Children's Fund, and humanitarian organizations for speedy demobilization, return and rehabilitation of such children, and *requests* the Secretary-General to entrust the Special Representative of the Secretary-General for Children and Armed Conflict with pursuing these objectives on a priority basis;

11. *Calls on* all parties to ensure the safe and unhindered access of relief personnel to all those in need, and recalls that the parties must also provide guarantees for the safety, security and freedom of movement for United Nations and associated humanitarian relief personnel;

12. *Calls also on* all the parties to respect the principles of neutrality and impartiality in the delivery of humanitarian assistance;

13. *Calls on* the international community to increase its support to humanitarian relief activities within the Democratic Republic of the Congo and in neighboring countries affected by the crisis in the Democratic Republic of the Congo;

14. *Reminds* all parties of their obligations with respect of the security of civilian populations under the Fourth Geneva Convention relative to the Protection of Civilian Persons in Time of War of 12 August 1949 and *stresses* that occupying forces should be held responsible for human rights violations in the territory under their control;

15. *Welcomes* the expressed willingness of the authorities of the Democratic Republic of the Congo to proceed with the inter-Congolese Dialogue under the aegis of the neutral Facilitator, Sir Ketumile Masire, and in this regard *welcomes* the announcement by the President of the Democratic Republic of the Congo at the Summit in Lusaka on 15 February 2001 that the Facilitator has been invited to Kinshasa, and *calls on* all Congolese parties to take immediate concrete steps to take forward the inter-Congolese dialogue;

16. *Reiterates* that MONUC shall cooperate closely with the Facilitator of the Inter-Congolese Dialogue, provide support and technical assistance to him, and coordinate the activities of other United Nations agencies to this effect;

17. *Calls on* all the parties to the conflict to cooperate fully in the deployment and operations of MONUC including through full implementation of the

provisions and the principles of the Status of Forces Agreement throughout the territory of the Democratic Republic of the Congo, and *reaffirms* that it is the responsibility of all the parties to ensure the security of United Nations personnel, together with associated personnel;

18. *Requests* the parties, as a follow-up to the discussions on this matter at the Lusaka Summit on 15 February 2001, to relocate the Joint Military Commission (JMC) to Kinshasa, co-locating it at all levels with MONUC, and *calls on* the authorities of the Democratic Republic of the Congo to ensure the security of all the JMC members;

19. *Reaffirms* the authorization contained in resolution 1291 of 24 February 2000 and the mandate set out in its resolution for the expansion and deployment of MONUC, and *endorses* the updated concept of operations put forward by the Secretary-General in his report of 12 February 2001, with a view to the deployment of all the civilian and military personnel required to monitor and verify the implementation by the parties of the ceasefire and disengagement plans, stressing that this disengagement is a first step towards the full and definitive withdrawal of all foreign troops from the territory of the Democratic Republic of the Congo;

20. *Emphasizes* that it will be prepared to consider a further review of the concept of operations for MONUC, when appropriate and in the light of developments, in order to monitor and verify the withdrawal of foreign troops and the implementation of the plan mentioned in paragraph 8 above and, in coordination with existing mechanisms, to enhance security on the border of the Democratic Republic of the Congo with Rwanda, Uganda and Burundi, and *requests* the Secretary-General to make proposals when appropriate;

21. *Reaffirms* that it is ready to support the Secretary-General if and when he deems that it is necessary and that it determines conditions allow it to deploy troops in the border areas in the east of the Democratic Republic of the Congo, including possibly in Goma or Bukavu [two cities in eastern Congo];

22. *Welcomes* the dialogue initiated between the authorities of the Democratic Republic of the Congo and Burundi, *urges* them to continue their efforts, and *emphasizes* in this respect that the settlement of the crisis in Burundi would contribute positively to the settlement of the conflict in the Democratic Republic of the Congo;

23. *Welcomes also* the recent meetings of the parties, including the meeting of the Presidents of the Democratic Republic of the Congo and Rwanda, *encourages* them to intensify their dialogue with the goal of achieving regional security structures based on common interest and mutual respect for the territorial integrity, national sovereignty and security of both States, and *emphasizes* in this respect that disarmament, demobilization and cessation of any support to the ex-Rwandese Armed Forces and Interahamwe forces will facilitate the settlement of the conflict in the Democratic Republic of the Congo;

24. *Expresses* its full support for the work of the expert panel on the illegal exploitation of natural resources and other forms of wealth in the Democratic Republic of the Congo, and once again *urges* the parties to the conflict in the Democratic Republic of the Congo and the other parties concerned to cooperate fully with it;

25. *Reaffirms* that it attaches the highest importance to the cessation of the illegal exploitation of the natural resources of the Democratic Republic of the Congo, *affirms* that it is ready to consider the necessary actions to put an end to this exploitation, and *awaits with interest* in this respect the final conclusions of the expert panel, including the conclusions relating to the level of cooperation of States with the expert panel;

26. *Reaffirms also* that an international conference on peace, security, democracy and development in the Great Lakes region, with participation by all the Governments of the region and all the other parties concerned, should be organized at the appropriate time under the aegis of the United Nations and the Organization of African Unity with a view to strengthening stability in the region and working out conditions that will enable everyone to enjoy the right to live peacefully within national borders;

27. *Expresses* its intention to monitor closely progress by the parties in implementing the requirements of this resolution and to undertake a mission to the region, possibly in May 2001, to monitor progress and discuss the way forward;

28. *Expresses* its readiness to consider possible measures which could be imposed, in accordance with its responsibilities and obligations under the Charter of the United Nations, in case of failure by parties to comply fully with this resolution;

29. *Decides* to remain actively seized of the matter.

BUSH'S ADDRESS TO
CONGRESS AND THE NATION
February 27, 2001

*Five weeks after assuming the presidency, George W. Bush on Febru-
ary 27, 2001, presented an ambitious legislative program to Congress
headed by the most controversial of his campaign promises: a massive tax
cut benefiting primarily upper-income Americans. Bush also named education, increased military spending, and Social Security and Medicare reform as priorities, but he warned Congress against resuming what he called
the "unrestrained spending" of the last years of his predecessor, Bill Clinton.* (Bush inaugural, p. 94)

*Congress enacted the tax cut and elements of Bush's other priorities, but
two unanticipated events during the year upset his agenda and forced him
to revise his priorities and strategy. The first was the defection of a Republican senator, James Jeffords of Vermont, whose switch to independent status in late May gave the Democrats control of the Senate and derailed Bush's
hopes for smooth sailing of his legislative proposals. The second was the
September 11 terrorist attacks against the World Trade Center towers in
New York City and the Pentagon. The president immediately declared that
fighting terrorism was the number one goal of his administration, and for
the moment he put his domestic priorities on the back burner.* (Jeffords
switch, p. 377; Terrorist attacks, pp. 614, 624)

*In his first year as president, Bush was both sure-footed, as with his un-
relenting pursuit of the tax cut and his response to the September 11 terrorism, and hesitant, as with his responses to Jeffords's threats of a party
switch and to several early foreign policy challenges. Although he was the
son of a former president, Bush himself had little practical experience in
the rough-and-tumble world of Washington politics and was forced to rely
heavily on the advice of his advisers, many of whom had decades of such
experience.*

*During the transition period before the inauguration and for several
months afterward, it often seemed that Vice President Dick Cheney, a former House member and cabinet official under Bush's father, was a de facto*

prime minister. Cheney chaired a task force that examined the nation's energy needs, served as the chief White House lobbyist on Capitol Hill, and frequently represented the administration before the news media and special interest groups. Cheney's role underwent a sudden transformation after the September 11 terrorist attacks, when he effectively went into hiding so the nation could be assured of continued leadership in the event that the president was killed in any new terrorist strikes.

Setting a Tone

Strictly speaking, Bush's address to a joint session of Congress was not a State of the Union address—the annual presidential report to Congress required by the Constitution. Even so, the speech had all the trappings of such formal occasions, which presidents in recent decades had used to promote their legislative agendas and to bolster their overall political standings.

Inevitably, Bush's performance was judged against the eight State of the Union addresses by Clinton, whose personal charisma and oratorical powers were extraordinary even by presidential standards. Most observers agreed that Bush did well in the comparison. If he lacked Clinton's rhetorical abilities, he made up for it with a good-natured, self-effacing humor that came across as genuine, both to those present in the cavernous House of Representatives chamber and to those watching television at home. Bush opened his remarks with a sly reference to the virtually tied election that resulted in his occupying the presidency and in the narrow control of Congress by Republicans: "I know Congress had to formally invite me, and it could have been a close vote." Nodding to Vice President Dick Cheney, he added: "So, Mr. Vice President, I appreciate your being here to break the tie." The president slipped on his own tongue only once, when he said early in the speech that "education is not my top priority." He quickly recovered by saying that "education is my top priority."

Following through on his inaugural address, Bush emphasized civility and bipartisanship in Washington—hoping to strike a contrast with the bitter partisanship of the previous eight years. Bush asked members of Congress to "join me in setting a tone of civility and respect in Washington. I hope America is noticing the difference, because we're making progress." Members of Congress of both parties were especially touched by Bush's tribute to Representative Joe Moakley, a Massachusetts Democrat who recently had been diagnosed as having an incurable form of leukemia.

Legislative Priorities

Despite his halting designation of education as "my top priority," most of the political emphasis in the president's speech went to his tax cut proposal, an item with far less bipartisan support than increased funding for schools. The new president attempted to portray the tax cut in populist terms, telling members of Congress that supporting it would put them "firmly on the side of the people." Public opinion polls consistently had shown only tepid support for the tax cut, but Bush sought to use his new pulpit, the presidency, to generate momentum for it. "The people of America

have been overcharged, and on their behalf I am here asking for a refund,"
he said, to a rousing ovation from Republicans. Using a public relations
tactic from his election campaign, Bush noted the presence of a "tax
family"—Steven and Josefina Ramos of West Chester, Pennsylvania—who,
he said, would save $2,000 a year under his proposal. The Ramoses were
seated in the balcony next to First Lady Laura Bush.

Congress in May approved the bulk of Bush's proposal, but only after Sen-
ate moderates in both parties forced changes that reduced the overall size of
the tax cut and directed a larger share of the benefits than Bush had planned
toward low- and middle-income taxpayers. Bush said his plan would have
cut taxes by $1.64 trillion over the course of ten years. The congressional
Joint Committee on Taxation put the cost at $1.78 trillion, and Democratic
critics said the true cost would exceed $2 billion. The final package, cleared
May 26 (PL 107-16), set a $1.35 trillion limit for the tax cuts, which would
be phased in over the course of a decade. About two-thirds of the total was
for reduced income tax rates, and the rest was for specific tax breaks, such
as increasing the child tax credit, eliminating the federal estate tax, reduc-
ing the so-called marriage penalty in income tax rates, and offering credits
for retirement savings and education expenses. In an effort to stimulate
consumer spending—and thus moderate the effect of the economic recession
in 2001—the bill also provided immediate tax rebates of up to $300 for in-
dividuals, $500 for single parents, and $600 for married couples. A minor-
ity of Democrats in both chambers sided with Republicans in supporting the
tax cuts, giving Bush at least a modest claim of "bipartisan" support for his
chief legislative accomplishment of the year.

Bush devoted a substantial portion of his speech to his various proposals
for education programs, including increased federal aid for reading pro-
grams and for teacher recruitment and training. Along with the money,
Bush demanded annual testing to determine whether schools were meeting
the needs of their students. Responding to criticism among educators of his
emphasis on standardized testing, Bush said the federal government had
a right to "insist on results" when it provided money for local schools.
"Children should be tested on basic reading and math skills every year be-
tween grades three and eight," he said. "Measuring is the only way to know
whether all our children are learning."

Bush's education spending proposals had broad bipartisan support in
both chambers, but Congress spent months debating the details, especially
the bottom-line issues of how much money to add and how to structure the
testing program (called "accountability") to ensure that schools were using
the money effectively. Congress ultimately approved a new authorization
bill for federal aid to education (PL 107-110) on December 18, and in a
separate appropriations bill (PL 107-116) boosted funding for those pro-
grams by $3.5 billion in fiscal year 2002 beyond what had been provided the
previous year.

Stepping into an area always full of political hazards, Bush said he
would appoint a presidential commission "to reform Social Security." The
president offered three "principles" to guide the commission's work, two of

which were universally supported and the third of which was sure to generate controversy. The first two principles were that any reform "must preserve the benefits" of current retirees and of those "nearing retirement," and it "must return Social Security to sound financial footing." But Bush also said any proposed reform must also offer "personal savings accounts to young workers who want them." This proposal was controversial because it would require at least a partial privatization of the Social Security system. Bush's commission on December 11 issued its report calling for the private accounts the president had wanted. That panel's work seemed no more likely to resolve the volatile issues of how to "save" or "reform" Social Security than had numerous commissions and study groups before it. (Social Security reform panel, p. 913)

Bush offered a handful of other priority proposals, including some for increased spending. In total, they were enough to create the impression that he had a balanced legislative agenda but not so many that anyone could accuse him of returning to the "era of big government" that Clinton had declared ended. Among those priorities were $5.7 billion in increased spending in the current fiscal year (2001) for pay, health care, and other benefits for members of the armed forces; a boost of $4.9 billion over five years for upkeep of the national parks; and new programs to speed the redevelopment of environmentally contaminated industrial sites known as "brownfields." Congress generally approved those proposals during 2001.

One of Bush's top-priority programs outlined in the February 27 speech generated widespread controversy and failed to make it through Congress in 2001. This was a so-called faith-based initiative, intended to make federal money available to several new categories of social services run by religious organizations and to create new tax incentives for private donations to charities. "These groups are working in every neighborhood in America to fight homelessness and addiction and domestic violence; to provide a hot meal or a mentor or a safe haven for our children," Bush said. "Government should welcome these groups to apply for funds, not discriminate against them." Despite widespread support for the work of religious organizations, critics of Bush's proposals raised a host of objections to expanded funding for them, and a House-passed bill incorporating most of Bush's proposal stalled in the Senate. (Bush's faith initiative, p. 132)

Democratic Response

As of 2001, Democrats had been the minority party on Capitol Hill for six years, ever since the landmark 1994 elections that put Republicans in charge of both houses of Congress. But it had been nine years since Democrats had been in the position of delivering a rebuttal to a Republican president named Bush. Delivering that response, televised shortly after Bush's speech, were Richard Gephardt, of Missouri, the minority leader of the House, and Tom Daschle, of South Dakota, the minority leader of the Senate. Neither men knew at the time that within three months Senator Jeffords's defection from the Republican Party would make Daschle the Senate majority leader, and therefore the most senior elected Democrat in the nation.

In his part of the joint response, Daschle pledged to work with Bush on his proposals "that bring us closer" to a goal of a prosperity that will "work for all Americans." He specifically cited Bush's proposals for increased funding for literacy programs in schools and pay increases for members of the military. But both Daschle and Gephardt attacked the president's proposed tax cuts. "If what the president said tonight sounded too good to be true, it probably is," Gephardt said, charging that Bush's budget numbers "just don't add up." Daschle said the president's tax cut plan "is deeply unfair to middle-income Americans," citing statistics (disputed by the administration) that the wealthiest 1 percent of taxpayers would receive 43 percent of the benefits. "All Americans deserve a tax cut," Daschle said. "But surely, the wealthiest among us should not get it at the expense of working families."

Daschle and Gephardt offered no specific budget alternatives except for supporting prescription drug coverage for senior citizens and protecting the Social Security and Medicare systems.

Following is the text of an address to a joint session of Congress on February 27, 2001, by President George W. Bush, followed by the text of a response from Richard Gephardt, the minority leader of the House of Representatives, and Tom Daschle, the minority leader of the Senate.

The documents were obtained from the Internet at http:// www.whitehouse.gov/news/releases/2001/02/20010228 .html; http://www.democrats.org/gopwatch/sotu2001/ response.html.

PRESIDENT'S ADDRESS TO CONGRESS

Mr. Speaker, Mr. Vice President, members of Congress:

It's a great privilege to be here to outline a new budget and a new approach for governing our great country. I thank you for your invitation to speak here tonight. I know Congress had to formally invite me, and it could have been a close vote. (Laughter.) So, Mr. Vice President, I appreciate you being here to break the tie. (Laughter.)

I want to thank so many of you who have accepted my invitation to come to the White House to discuss important issues. We're off to a good start. I will continue to meet with you and ask for your input. You have been kind and candid, and I thank you for making a new President feel welcome.

The last time I visited the Capitol, I came to take an oath on the steps of this building. I pledged to honor our Constitution and laws. And I asked you to join me in setting a tone of civility and respect in Washington.

I hope America is noticing the difference, because we're making progress. Together, we are changing the tone in the Nation's Capital. And this spirit of respect and cooperation is vital, because, in the end, we will be judged not only by what we say or how we say it, we will be judged by what we're able to accomplish.

America today is a nation with great challenges, but greater resources. An artist using statistics as a brush could paint two very different pictures of our country. One would have warning signs: increasing layoffs, rising energy prices, too many failing schools, persistent poverty, the stubborn vestiges of racism. Another picture would be full of blessings: a balanced budget, big surpluses, a military that is second to none, a country at peace with its neighbors, technology that is revolutionizing the world, and our greatest strength—concerned citizens who care for our country and care for each other.

Neither picture is complete in and of itself. And tonight I challenge and invite Congress to work with me to use the resources of one picture to repaint the other; to direct the advantages of our time to solve the problems of our people. Some of these resources will come from government. Some, but not all.

Year after year in Washington, budget debates seem to come down to an old, tired argument: on one side, those who want more government, regardless of the cost; on the other, those who want less government, regardless of the need. We should leave those arguments to the last century, and chart a different course.

Government has a role, and an important role. Yet, too much government crowds out initiative and hard work, private charity and the private economy. Our new governing vision says government should be active, but limited; engaged, but not overbearing. And my budget is based on that philosophy.

It is reasonable, and it is responsible. It meets our obligations, and funds our growing needs. We increase spending next year for Social Security and Medicare, and other entitlement programs, by $81 billion. We've increased spending for discretionary programs by a very responsible 4 percent, above the rate of inflation. My plan pays down an unprecedented amount of our national debt. And then, when money is still left over, my plan returns it to the people who earned it in the first place.

A budget's impact is counted in dollars, but measured in lives. Excellent schools, quality health care, a secure retirement, a cleaner environment, a stronger defense—these are all important needs, and we fund them. The highest percentage increase in our budget should go to our children's education. Education is not my top priority—education is my top priority and, by supporting this budget, you'll make it yours, as well.

Reading is the foundation of all learning. So during the next five years, we triple spending, adding $5 billion to help every child in America learn to read. Values are important, so we've tripled funding for character education to teach our children not only reading and writing, but right from wrong.

We've increased funding to train and recruit teachers, because we know a good education starts with a good teacher. And I have a wonderful partner in this effort. I like teachers so much, I married one. Laura has begun a new effort to recruit Americans to the profession that will shape our future—teaching. She will travel across America to promote sound teaching practices and early reading skills in our schools and in programs such as Head Start.

When it comes to our schools, dollars alone do not always make the difference. Funding is important, and so is reform. So we must tie funding to higher standards and accountability for results.

I believe in local control of schools. We should not, and we will not, run public schools from Washington, D.C. Yet when the federal government spends tax dollars, we must insist on results. Children should be tested on basic reading and math skills every year between grades three and eight. Measuring is the only way to know whether all our children are learning. And I want to know, because I refuse to leave any child behind in America.

Critics of testing contend it distracts from learning. They talk about teaching to the test. But let's put that logic to the test. If you test a child on basic math and reading skills, and you're teaching to the test, you're teaching math and reading. And that's the whole idea. As standards rise, local schools will need more flexibility to meet them. So we must streamline the dozens of federal education programs into five, and let states spend money in those categories as they see fit.

Schools will be given a reasonable chance to improve and the support to do so. Yet, if they don't, if they continue to fail, we must give parents and students different options—a better public school, a private school, tutoring or a charter school. In the end, every child in a bad situation must be given a better choice because, when it comes to our children, failure is simply not an option.

Another priority in my budget is to keep the vital promises of Medicare and Social Security, and together we will do so. To meet the health care needs of all America's seniors, we double the Medicare budget over the next 10 years. My budget dedicates $238 billion to Medicare next year alone, enough to fund all current programs and to begin a new prescription drug benefit for low-income seniors. No senior in America should have to choose between buying food and buying prescriptions.

To make sure the retirement savings of America's seniors are not diverted in any other program, my budget protects all $2.6 trillion of the Social Security surplus for Social Security, and for Social Security alone.

My budget puts a priority on access to health care, without telling Americans what doctor they have to see or what coverage they must choose. Many working Americans do not have health care coverage, so we will help them buy their own insurance with refundable tax credits. And to provide quality care in low-income neighborhoods, over the next five years we will double the number of people served at community health care centers.

And we will address the concerns of those who have health coverage, yet worry their insurance company doesn't care and won't pay. Together this Congress and this President will find common ground to make sure doctors make medical decisions, and patients get the health care they deserve with a patients' bill of rights.

When it comes to their health, people want to get the medical care they need, not be forced to go to court because they didn't get it. We will ensure access to the courts for those with legitimate claims. But first, let's put in place a strong, independent review so we promote quality health care, not frivolous lawsuits.

My budget also increases funding for medical research, which gives hope to many who struggle with serious disease. Our prayers tonight are with one of your own who is engaged in his own fight against cancer—a fine representative, and a good man, Congressman Joe Moakley. I can think of no more appropriate tribute to Joe than to have the Congress finish the job of doubling the budget for the National Institutes of Health.

My new Freedom Initiative for Americans with Disabilities funds new technologies, expands opportunities to work, and makes our society more welcoming. For the more than 50 million Americans with disabilities, we need to break down barriers to equality.

The budget I propose to you also supports the people who keep our country strong and free, the men and women who serve in the United States military. I'm requesting $5.7 billion in increased military pay and benefits, and health care and housing. Our men and women in uniform give America their best and we owe them our support.

America's veterans honored their commitment to our country through their military service. I will honor our commitment to them with a million-dollar increase to ensure better access to quality care and faster decisions on benefit claims.

My budget will improve our environment by accelerating the cleanup of toxic brownfields. And I propose we make a major investment in conservation by fully funding the Land and Water Conservation Fund. Our national parks have a special place in our country's life. Our parks are places of great natural beauty and history. As good stewards, we must leave them better than we found them. So I propose providing $4.9 billion over five years for the upkeep of these national treasures.

And my budget adopts a hopeful new approach to help the poor and the disadvantaged. We must encourage and support the work of charities and faith-based and community groups that offer help and love one person at a time. These groups are working in every neighborhood in America to fight homelessness and addiction and domestic violence; to provide a hot meal or a mentor or a safe haven for our children. Government should welcome these groups to apply for funds, not discriminate against them.

Government cannot be replaced by charities or volunteers. Government should not fund religious activities. But our nation should support the good works of these good people who are helping their neighbors in need. So I propose allowing all taxpayers, whether they itemize or not, to deduct their charitable contributions. Estimates show this could encourage as much as $14 billion a year in new charitable giving, money that will save and change lives.

Our budget provides more than $700 million over the next 10 years for a federal compassion capital fund, with a focused and noble mission, to provide a mentor to the more than 100 million children with a parent in prison, and to support other local efforts to fight illiteracy, teen pregnancy, drug addiction and other difficult problems.

With us tonight is the Mayor of Philadelphia. Please help me welcome Mayor John Street. Mayor Street has encouraged faith-based and community organizations to make a significant difference in Philadelphia. He's invited me to his city this summer to see compassionate action. I'm personally aware of just how effective the Mayor is. Mayor Street's a Democrat. Let the record show, I lost his city, big time. But some things are bigger than politics. So I look forward to coming to your city, to see your faith-based programs in action.

As government promotes compassion, it also must promote justice. Too many of our citizens have cause to doubt our nation's justice, when the law points a finger of suspicion at groups, instead of individuals. All our citizens are created equal, and must be treated equally.

Earlier today, I asked John Ashcroft, the Attorney General, to develop specific recommendations to end racial profiling. It's wrong and we will end it in America. In so doing, we will not hinder the work of our nation's brave police officers. They protect us every day—often at great risk. But by stopping the abuses of a few, we will add to the public confidence our police officers earn and deserve.

My budget has funded a responsible increase in our ongoing operations. It has funded our nation's important priorities. It has protected Social Security and Medicare. And our surpluses are big enough that there is still money left over.

Many of you have talked about the need to pay down our national debt. I listened, and I agree. We owe it to our children and grandchildren to act now, and I hope you will join me to pay down $2 trillion in debt during the next 10 years. At the end of those 10 years, we will have paid down all the debt that is available to retire. That is more debt, repaid more quickly than has ever been repaid by any nation at any time in history.

We should also prepare for the unexpected, for the uncertainties of the future. We should approach our nation's budget as any prudent family would, with a contingency fund for emergencies or additional spending needs. For example, after a strategic review, we may need to increase defense spending. We may need to increase spending for our farmers or additional money to reform Medicare. And so, my budget sets aside almost a trillion dollars over 10 years for additional needs. That is one trillion additional reasons you can feel comfortable supporting this budget.

We have increased our budget at a responsible 4 percent. We have funded our priorities. We paid down all the available debt. We have prepared for contingencies. And we still have money left over.

Yogi Berra once said, "When you come to a fork in the road, take it." (Laughter.) Now, we come to a fork in the road; we have two choices. Even though we have already met our needs, we could spend the money on more and bigger government. That's the road our nation has traveled in recent years.

Last year, government spending shot up 8 percent. That's far more than our economy grew, far more than personal income grew, and far more than the rate of inflation. If you continue on that road, you will spend the surplus and have to dip into Social Security to pay other bills. Unrestrained government spending is a dangerous road to deficits, so we must take a different path. The other choice is to let the American people spend their own money to meet their own needs.

I hope you will join me in standing firmly on the side of the people. You see, the growing surplus exists because taxes are too high and government is charging more than it needs. The people of America have been overcharged and, on their behalf, I am here asking for a refund.

Some say my tax plan is too big. Others say it's too small. I respectfully disagree. (Laughter.) This plan is just right. I didn't throw darts at the board to come up with a number for tax relief. I didn't take a poll or develop an arbitrary formula that might sound good. I looked at problems in the Tax Code and calculated the cost to fix them.

A tax rate of 15 percent is too high for those who earn low wages, so we must lower the rate to 10 percent. No one should pay more than a third of the money they earn in federal income taxes, so we lowered the top rate to 33 percent.

This reform will be welcome relief for America's small businesses, which often pay taxes at the highest rate. And help for small business means jobs for Americans. We simplified the Tax Code by reducing the number of tax rates from the current five rates to four lower ones, 10 percent, 15, 25 and 33 percent. In my plan, no one is targeted in or targeted out. Everyone who pays income taxes will get relief.

Our government should not tax, and thereby discourage marriage, so we reduced the marriage penalty. I want to help families rear and support their children, so we doubled the child credit to $1,000 per child. It's not fair to tax the same earnings twice—once when you earn them, and again when you die—so we must repeal the death tax.

These changes add up to significant help. A typical family with two children will save $1,600 a year on their federal income taxes. Now, $1,600 may not sound like a lot to some, but it means a lot to many families: $1,600 buys gas for two cars for an entire year; it pays tuition for a year at a community college; it pays the average family grocery bill for three months. That's real money.

With us tonight representing many American families are Steven and Josefina Ramos. They are from Pennsylvania. But they could be from any one of your districts. Steven is the network administrator for a school district. Josefina is a Spanish teacher at a charter school. And they have a two-year-old daughter.

Steven and Josefina tell me they pay almost $8,000 a year in federal income taxes. My plan will save them more than $2,000. Let me tell you what Steven says: "Two thousand dollars a year means a lot to my family. If we had this money, it would help us reach our goal of paying off our personal debt in two years' time." After that, Steven and Josefina want to start saving for Lianna's college education.

My attitude is, government should never stand in the way of families achieving their dreams. And as we debate this issue, always remember, the surplus is not the government's money, the surplus is the people's money.

For lower-income families, my tax plan restores basic fairness. Right now, complicated tax rules punish hard work. A waitress supporting two children on $25,000 a year can lose nearly half of every additional dollar she earns above the $25,000. Her overtime, her hardest hours, are taxed at nearly 20 percent. This sends a terrible message: you'll never get ahead. But America's message must be different. We must honor hard work, never punish it. With tax relief, overtime will no longer be over-taxed time for the waitress. People with the smallest incomes will get the highest percentage of reductions. And millions of additional American families will be removed from the income tax rolls entirely.

Tax relief is right and tax relief is urgent. The long economic expansion that began almost 10 years ago is faltering. Lower interest rates will eventually help, but we cannot assume they will do the job all by themselves.

Forty years ago, and then 20 years ago, two Presidents, one Democrat, one Republican, John F. Kennedy and Ronald Reagan, advocated tax cuts to, in President Kennedy's words, get this country moving again. They knew then what we must do now. To create economic growth and opportunity, we must put money back into the hands of the people who buy goods and create jobs.

We must act quickly. The Chairman of the Federal Reserve has testified before Congress that tax cuts often come too late to stimulate economic recovery. So I want to work with you to give our economy an important jump-start by making tax relief retroactive.

We must act now because it is the right thing to do. We must also act now because we have other things to do. We must show courage to confront and resolve tough challenges, to restructure our nation's defenses, to meet our growing need for energy, and to reform Medicare and Social Security.

America has a window of opportunity to extend and secure our present peace by promoting a distinctly American internationalism. We will work with our allies and friends to be a force for good and a champion of freedom. We will work for free markets, free trade and freedom from oppression. Nations making progress toward freedom will find America is their friend. We will promote our values. We will promote the peace. And we need a strong military to keep the peace.

But our military was shaped to confront the challenges of the past. So I've asked the Secretary of Defense to review America's Armed Forces and prepare to transform them to meet emerging threats. My budget makes a down payment on the research and development that will be required. Yet, in our broader transformation effort, we must put strategy first, then spending. Our defense vision will drive our defense budget, not the other way around.

Our nation also needs a clear strategy to confront the threats of the 21st century—threats that are more widespread and less certain. They range from terrorists who threaten with bombs to tyrants in rogue nations intent upon developing weapons of mass destruction. To protect our own people, our allies and friends, we must develop and we must deploy effective missile defenses.

And as we transform our military, we can discard Cold War relics, and reduce our own nuclear forces to reflect today's needs. A strong America is the world's best hope for peace and freedom.

Yet the cause of freedom rests on more than our ability to defend ourselves and our allies. Freedom is exported every day, as we ship goods and products that improve the lives of millions of people. Free trade brings greater political and personal freedom. Each of the previous five Presidents has had the ability to negotiate far reaching trade agreements. Tonight I ask you to give me the strong hand of presidential trade promotion authority, and to do so quickly.

As we meet tonight, many citizens are struggling with the high cost of energy. We have a serious energy problem that demands a national energy policy. The West is confronting a major energy shortage that has resulted in high prices and uncertainty. I've asked federal agencies to work with California officials to help speed construction of new energy sources, and I have direct Vice President Cheney, Commerce Secretary Evans, Energy Secretary Abraham and other senior members in my administration to develop a national energy policy.

Our energy demand outstrips our supply. We can produce more energy at home while protecting our environment, and we must. We can produce more electricity to meet demand, and we must. We can promote alternative energy sources and conservation, and we must. America must become more energy-independent, and we will.

Perhaps the biggest test of our foresight and courage will be reforming Medicare and Social Security. Medicare's finances are strained and its coverage is outdated. Ninety-nine percent of employer-provided health plans offer some form of prescription drug coverage; Medicare does not. The framework for reform has been developed by Senators [Bill] Frist and [John] Breaux and Congressman [Bill] Thomas, and now is the time to act.

Medicare must be modernized, and we must make sure that every senior on Medicare can choose a health care plan that offers prescription drugs.

Seven years from now, the baby boom generation will begin to claim Social Security benefits. Every one in this chamber knows that Social Security is not prepared to fully fund their retirement. And we only have a couple of years to get prepared. Without reform, this country will one day awaken to a stark choice: either a drastic rise in payroll taxes or a radical cut in retirement benefits.

There is a better way. This spring I will form a presidential commission to reform Social Security. The commission will make its recommendations by next fall. Reform should be based on these principles: It must preserve the benefits of all current retirees and those nearing retirement. It must return Social Security to sound financial footing. And it must offer personal savings accounts to younger workers who want them.

Social Security now offers workers a return of less than 2 percent on the money they pay into the system. To save the system, we must increase that by allowing younger workers to make safe, sound investments that yield a higher rate of return. Ownership, access to wealth and independence should not be the privilege of the few. They are the hope of every American, and we must make them the foundation of Social Security.

By confronting the tough challenge of reform, by being responsible with our budget, we can earn the trust of the American people. And we can add to that trust by enacting fair and balanced election and campaign reforms.

The agenda I have set before you tonight is worthy of a great nation. America is a nation at peace, but not a nation at rest. Much has been given to us, and much is expected. Let us agree to bridge old divides. But let us also agree that our goodwill must be dedicated to great goals. Bipartisan is more than minding our matters. It is doing our duty.

No one can speak in this Capitol and not be awed by its history. As so many turning points, debates in these chambers have reflected the collected or divided conscience of our country. And when we walk through Statuary Hall and see those men and women of marble, we're reminded of their courage and achievement.

Yet America's purpose is never found only in statues or history. America's purpose always stands before us. Our generation must show courage in a time of blessing, as our nation has always shown in times of crisis. And our courage, issue by issue, can gather to greatness and serve our country. This is the privilege and responsibility we share. And if we work together, we can prove that public service is noble.

We all came here for a reason. We all have things we want to accomplish and promises to keep. *Juntos podemos*—together we can.

We can make Americans proud of their government. Together we can share in the credit of making our country more prosperous and generous and just, and earn from our conscience and from our fellow citizens the highest possible praise: Well done, good and faithful servants.

Thank you all. Good night and God bless.

DEMOCRATIC RESPONSE

House Minority Leader Dick Gephardt: Good evening. I'm Dick Gephardt from Missouri, Democratic Leader in the House of Representatives.

Senate Minority Leader Tom Daschle: I'm Tom Daschle, of South Dakota, the Democratic Leader in the Senate.

Tonight, our nation's Capitol was filled with hope as our new President spoke to Congress, for the first time, about his priorities for America. Now, we'd like to take a few minutes to speak to the American people: to those we are fortunate to represent in South Dakota and Missouri and across America, the hard-working Americans who deserve a booming and vibrant economy, the seniors who seek security in retirement after a lifetime of hard work. We want to speak to the teachers and students who are striving to master the ideas of the new century in crowded classrooms built in the last century and to all Americans who want to know that in the halls of our government, their voices are heard and their priorities matter. We believe—as they do—that America's prosperity must work for all Americans.

When President Bush proposes ideas that bring us closer to that goal—like his literacy initiative, or increases in military pay—we will work with him, and work hard, to turn those ideas into laws. When he makes proposals with which we disagree, we will work with him to find common ground. But when he insists on proposals that threaten the prosperity of all Americans—or that harm Social Security or Medicare—we will fight, and fight hard, to put the interests of working families first.

Tonight we begin a debate that will profoundly effect the strength of America's working families for years, perhaps generations, to come. The prosperity you have built these last eight years has given us all a chance to live better lives at every age. But this opportunity will be squandered if we repeat the mistakes of a generation ago.

In 1981, Dick and I sat in the House Chamber when another new President talked to the American people about stimulating our economy. The words spoken that evening were strikingly similar to the message we heard tonight. We were promised that if we gave huge tax cuts to the wealthiest Americans, the benefits would trickle down, deficits would disappear and the economy would flourish.

Congress supported that experiment. It was a huge mistake. As President Bush's own Treasury Secretary Paul O'Neill said recently, it put America "in a ditch that was horrendous" [Capitol Hill, Panel I of a Hearing of the House Ways and Means Committee February 13, 2001]. Deficits skyrocketed. The national debt quadrupled. High interest rates choked American industries. Unemployment soared Working families struggled to meet their mortgages, pay for health care, and save for college.

It took us 18 years, four acts of Congress, and a lot of hard work by the American people to get out of that ditch. But working together, we turned record deficits into record surpluses. Freed from the dead weight of deficits, you did what Americans do best. You worked hard, and you created the longest economic expansion in history.

Now America has a choice. What shall we do with the blessings of our new prosperity? Our first priority must be to continue paying down the trillions of dollars in federal debt Washington ran up in the 1980s. We can't just pass this debt onto our children—not when we have the ability to pay it off.

By paying down the debt, we'll also keep interest rates low—which will mean real savings for every American family. We agree with the President. We want a significant tax cut this year. But we want a different kind. A tax cut that is part of a responsible budget, that lets us pay off the debt, and invest in America's future. One that is fair to all Americans.

President Bush's plan doesn't do those things.

Think about your own family budget. Imagine you hadn't saved for your retirement, you owed money on your credit cards, and you couldn't afford health insurance. Then you're told you might get some extra money sometime down the road. What would you do? Under the President's approach, you would immediately spend that money—money you might never see—without taking care of your debts, your medical bills or your retirement. You wouldn't do that, and neither should we. But that's exactly what the President proposed tonight.

Let's take a closer look. First, the President's tax plan is far more expensive than the $1.6 trillion he claims. When you add interest on the debt and other hidden costs, the true cost of the President's tax cut is well over $2 trillion. It will consume nearly all of the available surplus—at the expense of prescription drug coverage, education, defense and other critical priorities.

Even worse, instead of strengthening Social Security and Medicare, the President's plan actually takes money from both programs. That is irresponsible, and it's wrong. Worse still, the President's plan depends far too heavily on a ten-year budget estimate, which is no more reliable than a ten-year weather forecast. And there's no room for error.

Nobody's crystal ball is that good. Just ask Texas. Two years ago, using rosy forecasts, then-Governor Bush signed a budget that cut taxes by $1.8 billion. But his budget projections were wrong. Today Texas faces a serious budget shortfall. If his budget predictions now are as faulty as they were then, his tax cut would bring back huge deficits, increase the national debt, and put our economy back in the ditch.

Finally, the President's plan is deeply unfair to middle-income Americans. The wealthiest 1 percent—people who make an average of over $900,000 a year—get 43 percent of the President's tax cut. The President also wants to eliminate the estate tax for the wealthiest of the wealthy. Democrats want to make it easier for you to pass family farms and small businesses onto the next generation, and our estate tax plan does that. But the President's proposal provides so much to America's wealthiest families that they themselves are calling it a mistake. Bill Gates Sr., Warren Buffett, members of the Rockefeller family have said it gives so much to so few that it will force tax increases, or cuts in Social Security, Medicare and other essential programs. They're right. And the President's estate tax cut is only part of the reason.

Let us be clear: All Americans deserve a tax cut. But surely, the wealthiest among us should not get it at the expense of working families. There's a better way.

Gephardt: Democrats have a different plan, a balanced plan that treats the national budget the way you treat your household budget. Our plan provides $900 billion in tax cuts for all Americans. Our plan protects every dollar of the Social Security and Medicare trust funds. It strengthens Medicare and adds an affordable prescription drug benefit, so seniors don't have to choose between food and medicine. It strengthens Social Security rather than subjecting it to a volatile stock market, so that it will be there, not only for the baby-boomers, but for their children and their grandchildren. Our plan enables us to keep paying down the national debt, the debt we ran up in the 80s, so we can keep interest rates low and keep our economy growing. And it invests in the future of our country, by making sure every child can get an excellent education at a first-rate public school.

The President touched on many of these goals tonight. But we can't accomplish any of them if we spend the entire surplus on the President's tax cut. If what the President said tonight sounded too good to be true, it probably is.

Education is one of our highest priorities, and we believe that strengthening public schools is one of our greatest challenges. The President has made education an important part of his agenda, and in this he has our support. We have our differences with his plan. Like most Americans, we do not support spending public money for private school vouchers, and we will never support a reduction in the federal commitment to under-served children and communities. We will work with the President to increase literacy, demand accountability, and improve every public school. But with tax cuts consuming almost all of the projected surplus, he cannot possibly keep his commitment to leave no child behind.

Millions of seniors depend on Social Security and Medicare, and we have a responsibility to preserve and protect them. We made promises. We need to keep them. The President said he is dedicated o preserving Social Security and Medicare. We take him at his word. But the President's plan threatens these critical programs. His plan fails to set aside the resources Social Security and Medicare will need in the future and uses them instead to pay for his tax cut.

All seniors need prescription drug coverage. Democrats believe we should use part of the surplus to provide a reliable, affordable Medicare prescription drug benefit for all seniors. The President has a different approach. His plan excludes millions of middle-income seniors who don't have prescription coverage and need it. We want to work with the President to solve the prescription drug problem the right way. But we can't add a Medicare prescription drug benefit, we can't improve public schools, we can't address any of our highest priorities if the President does not scale back the excesses of his tax plan.

President Bush's numbers just don't add up. Ours do. His plan leaves no money for anything except tax cuts. Ours does. Our plan is better. It invests in the greatest needs and highest priorities of our country.

The conversation we begin tonight is more than a struggle over this year's budget—it's really about our future. It is about the most important decisions this generation of Americans will make for a very long time to come. Our country is strong. But we can make it stronger. By fighting for stronger families with a higher minimum wage, a Patients' Bill of Rights, safer schools, safer streets, and a cleaner environment. By fighting for a stronger economy with a budget that extends the greatest economic expansion in American history. By fighting for a finance reform and a renewed commitment to fair and modern elections.

The challenge of writing a budget that is fair and responsible is considerable. But we face other challenges just as great.

All across America, too many people have lost faith in the fundamental principle of democracy—the principle of one person, one vote. We must act to restore their confidence. We should not leave this session of Congress without reforming our election process. Our democracy depends on it.

In addition, too many in Washington, and too many Americans, have lost faith in the possibility of principled compromise. With Congress so closely divided, some would say that finding common ground is simply impossible. We refuse to believe that. We are determined to steer our country on a more productive course.

We recognize that the President campaigned on an agenda. So did we. Where our agendas coincide, let us make quick progress for the people. Where our agendas differ, we ask the President to demonstrate his leadership by reaching out for the benefit of all Americans. If he extends his hand, we will grasp it. Tonight, we extend ours.

The things that are most meaningful in our lives often require real effort to meet others halfway. Business partnerships. Friendships. Marriages. It's the same with our democracy. We can do what the people sent us here to do if the President is willing to join us in the middle.

We believe that making America better is the greatest work of all. It is to that task that we pledge ourselves tonight.

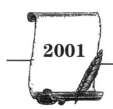

March

INSTITUTE OF MEDICINE ON THE QUALITY OF U.S. HEALTH CARE
March 1, 2001

In a report that minced few words, a panel of health experts condemned the nation's health care delivery system, saying that it had not kept pace with advancing technology or the changing health care needs of the American population. Too often, the panel said, treatment was inadequate, outdated, and even unsafe. "Health care today harms too frequently and routinely fails to deliver its potential benefits," the experts wrote. "Between the health care we have and the care we could have lies not just a gap but a chasm."

The report, released March 1, 2001, was prepared by the Committee on the Quality of Health Care in America, formed in 1998 by the Institute of Medicine, which advised Congress on scientific matters. The committee was charged with developing a strategy for improving the quality of the nation's health care over the next ten years. The same committee produced an equally hard-hitting report in 1999 on medical errors, finding that medical mistakes killed up to 98,000 hospital patients a year and that at least half of those deaths could be prevented if hospitals, clinics, and pharmacies redesigned their systems to make it harder for health care professionals to make mistakes. (Medical errors, Historic Documents of 1999, p. 779)

Although many health care facilities were making changes to prevent some of the most common mistakes, the Joint Commission on Accreditation of Healthcare Organizations warned that the number of surgeries on the wrong limb or body part was increasing. The commission, which monitored safety at about 5,000 hospitals and 12,000 other medical facilities, offered several recommendations for solving the problem, including urging patients to mark their own limbs to ensure surgeons operated on the correct one.

The quality of health care in the United States was also beginning to be affected by an acute shortage of health professionals, especially nurses. Hospitals, nursing homes, and home health care agencies were reporting difficulties in filling nursing vacancies, while several reports estimated that changing demographics would cause a significant nursing shortfall after 2010 when the aging baby-boom generation would begin to require more health care. Labor experts listed several reasons for the shortages, including the availability of better-paying, less-stressful jobs in other professions.

A "Quality Chasm"

As unsettling as its 1999 report on medical errors was, the committee said it reflected "only a small part" of the story about quality of health care delivery in the United States. In the past few decades, the committee said, medical science advanced rapidly, producing new technologies, new drugs, and new procedures for improving health, relieving pain, and extending life. But the health care delivery system "has floundered," frequently unable to "translate knowledge into practice, and to apply new technology safely and appropriately." Most disturbing, the panel said, was "the absence of real progress toward restructuring health care systems to address both quality and cost concerns" or to use new information technologies to improve administrative and clinical processes.

For example, the panel said, scientific knowledge about the best treatment practices was not applied systematically or quickly. An average of seventeen years was required for new knowledge about treatments and procedures to be incorporated into medical practice, and even then the application was "highly uneven."

One means for greater dissemination of best practices was the Internet, but the health care delivery system was "relatively untouched" by this and other advances in information technology, the panel said. The committee said automation of clinical, financial, and administrative transactions was "essential" to improve quality and efficiency and reduce medical errors. Without minimizing concerns about medical privacy, the panel said, patient information needed to be automated to provide better coordination of care among all the providers a patient might see, from general care physician to specialists, to therapists, to pharmacists. Simply computerizing medication records could produce "sizable benefits" by reducing the opportunity for misreading handwriting and by informing the physician and pharmacist of the other medications a patient was already taking.

The panel also said that better use of available and future information technology would assist the health care industry in providing patient-centered care. Patients, the committee said, should be able to receive care whenever they needed it, twenty-four hours a day, and through venues such as the Internet, e-mail, and the telephone as well as in hospitals or doctor's offices. They should also have access to their own medical records and to information about best practices and alternative treatments. Finally, the panel said, the insurance methods used to pay for health care services raised questions about both underuse and overuse of services, and too often worked against the efforts of health care providers to improve the quality of care. For example, more doctors would use electronic mail to communicate with their patients if insurance providers covered the service, the panel said, urging that payment methods be examined to determine how they could support innovation and quality care rather than discourage it. (Medical privacy, p., 485; health insurance, p. 710)

The panel recommended that the process of revamping the health care delivery system begin by focusing on fifteen common chronic conditions—including cancer, heart disease, diabetes, high cholesterol, stroke, hypertension, dementia, and depression—that affect thousands of people and account for the bulk of health care expenditures. The panel urged Congress to appropriate $1 billion over three to five years to help develop and disseminate evidence-based treatments for these conditions using the best available practices and to establish information, prevention, and payment strategies designed to achieve "substantial improvements in quality" within five years for each of the fifteen conditions.

Wrong-Site Surgery

The number of reports of surgeons operating on the wrong part of the body or even the wrong patient appeared to be increasing, the Joint Commission on Accreditation of Healthcare Organizations (JCAHO) reported December 5. In 1998 the commission issued a "sentinel event alert" after receiving 15 reports of wrong-site surgery; by December 2001 the commission had a total of 150 reports, including 11 in the last month. The commission said it suspected many more incidents had not been reported. Although the number of reports of wrong-site surgery was small compared with the 41 million surgical procedures performed in 1999, "the tolerance here is zero," said Dennis S. O'Leary, the president of the commission.

According to the report, 76 percent of the cases involved surgery on the wrong site, say, the right hip instead of the left. In 13 percent of the cases, the wrong person was operated on; in 11 percent, the wrong surgical procedure was used. About 40 percent of the cases involved orthopedic or foot surgery, while 20 percent occurred during general surgery. Nearly 60 percent of the mistakes occurred in ambulatory care facilities.

The commission said most cases involved a breakdown in communication between the patient and the surgeon. Other sources of error included similar sounding patient names, x-rays reversed in view boxes, and incomplete medical charts or failure to check them. The commission said surgical teams should take a "time-out" in the operating room to make sure they have the right patient, surgery site, and procedure. Patients should ask their doctors to mark the surgical site before going into the operating room, or they should mark it themselves. O'Leary also suggested that in cases where a doctor might confuse left and right, such as knees or eyes, the patient mark the body part that was not to be operated on. O'Leary said the commission had two reports of cases where the right limb was marked but not the wrong one "and, of course, the surgeon never went to the right one, so operated on the wrong one."

The commission said it planned to begin closer monitoring of hospitals and other health care facilities in 2002. Failure to comply with the commission's recommendations could lead to loss of accreditation.

The Nursing Shortage

The probability of a long-term nursing shortage was the result of demographics and had been apparent for some time. The aging of the baby-boom population meant that between 2000 and 2030 the number of people ages sixty-five and over would double, increasing the demand for health care. At the same time, the number of younger working women who traditionally made up the nursing workforce was expected to stay the same.

Current problems in the profession were likely to exacerbate the long-term situation, experts said. Already the profession was suffering spot shortages, with some hospitals, nursing homes, and home health care agencies experiencing high vacancy and high turnover rates. Health care facilities in rural areas and inner cities were especially vulnerable to shortages. A combination of factors appeared to account for these shortages. Traditionally, nursing had been one of the few professions women could enter, but as other professions opened to women in the last half of the twentieth century, fewer women chose to go into nursing. The National League of Nursing reported that the number of nursing school graduates had dropped 13 percent between 1995 and 1999.

Moreover, nurses were leaving the profession at a faster pace than usual, retiring not only for reasons of age but because they were dissatisfied with the low pay, high stress, and heavy workloads they faced. According to a survey by the Federation of Nurses and Health Professionals, 50 percent of the currently working registered nurses surveyed said they had considered leaving the patient-care field in the last two years for reasons other than retirement. Eighteen percent said they wanted higher wages; 56 percent said they wanted jobs that were less stressful and less physically demanding.

Growing numbers of nurses were joining unions and going on strike to seek better working conditions, arguing that the quality of patient care suffered when they were forced to pick up the slack caused by the high rate of vacancies. Many called for an end to the practice of mandatory overtime, which was required by many hospitals to cover the nursing shortfall. "The nursing shortage is one of the dominant issues in health care today," Peter Buerhaus, *associate dean at the Vanderbilt University School of Nursing told the* New York Times. *"In some cases the problem is so severe that hospitals have had to shut down nursing floors and cancel surgeries. This crisis has the potential to create a disaster scenario in terms of the quality of care."*

The House and Senate each passed bills in the final days of the 2001 session to help curb the shortage, but a conference to negotiate differences between the two bills was put off until 2002. Both bills would offer scholarships to attract people to go to nursing school and would authorize the Department of Health and Human Services to develop public service announcements promoting nursing as a career. The broader Senate bill also included programs to encourage nurses to advance in their careers or to obtain advanced nursing degrees that would allow them to teach in nursing schools.

Following are excerpts from the executive summary of "Crossing the Quality Chasm: A New Health System for the 21st Century," a report prepared by the Committee on the Quality of Health Care in America for the Institute of Medicine and released March 1, 2001.

The document was obtained from the Internet at http:// www.nap.edu/catalog/10027.html.

The American health care delivery system is in need of fundamental change. Many patients, doctors, nurses, and health care leaders are concerned that the care delivered is not, essentially, the care we should receive. The frustration levels of both patients and clinicians have probably never been higher. Yet the problems remain. Health care today harms too frequently and routinely fails to deliver its potential benefits.

Americans should be able to count on receiving care that meets their needs and is based on the best scientific knowledge. Yet there is strong evidence that this frequently is not the case. Crucial reports from disciplined review bodies document the scale and gravity of the problems. Quality problems are everywhere, affecting many patients. Between the health care we have and the care we could have lies not just a gap, but a chasm.

The Committee on the Quality of Health Care in America was formed in June 1998 and charged with developing a strategy that would result in a substantial improvement in the quality of health care over the next 10 years. In carrying out this charge, the committee commissioned a detailed review of the literature on the quality of care; convened a communications workshop to identify strategies for raising the awareness of the general public and key stakeholders of quality concerns; identified environmental forces that encourage or impede efforts to improve quality; developed strategies for fostering greater accountability for quality; and identified important areas of research that should be pursued to facilitate improvements in quality. The committee has focused on the personal health care delivery system, specifically, the provision of preventive, acute, chronic, and end-of-life health care for individuals. Although the committee recognizes the critical role of the public health system in protecting and improving the health of our communities, this issue lies beyond the purview of the present study.

The committee has already spoken to one urgent quality problem—patient safety. In our first report, *To Err Is Human: Building a Safer Health System*, we concluded that tens of thousands of Americans die each year from errors in their care, and hundreds of thousands suffer or barely escape from nonfatal injuries that a truly high-quality care system would largely prevent.

As disturbing as the committee's report on safety is, it reflects only a small part of the unfolding story of quality in American health care. Other defects are even more widespread and, taken together, detract still further from the health, functioning, dignity, comfort, satisfaction, and resources of Americans.

195

This report addresses these additional quality problems. As the patient safety report was a call for action to make care safer, this report is a call for action to improve the American health care delivery system as a whole, in all its quality dimensions, for all Americans.

Why Action Is Needed Now

At no time in the history of medicine has the growth in knowledge and technologies been so profound. Since the first contemporary randomized controlled trial was conducted more than 50 years ago, the number of trials conducted has grown to nearly 10,000 annually. Between 1993 and 1999, the budget of the National Institutes of Health increased from $10.9 to $15.6 billion, while investments by pharmaceutical firms in research and development increased from $12 to $24 billion. Genomics and other new technologies on the horizon offer the promise of further increasing longevity, improving health and functioning, and alleviating pain and suffering. Advances in rehabilitation, cell restoration, and prosthetic devices hold potential for improving the heath and functioning of many with disabilities. Americans are justifiably proud of the great strides that have been made in the health and medical sciences.

As medical science and technology have advanced at a rapid pace, however, the health care delivery system has floundered in its ability to provide consistently high-quality care to all Americans. Research on the quality of care reveals a health care system that frequently falls short in its ability to translate knowledge into practice, and to apply new technology safely and appropriately. During the last decade alone, more than 70 publications in leading peer-reviewed journals have documented serious quality shortcomings. The performance of the health care system varies considerably. It may be exemplary, but often is not, and millions of Americans fail to receive effective care. If the health care system cannot consistently deliver today's science and technology, we may conclude that it is even less prepared to respond to the extraordinary scientific advances that will surely emerge during the first half of the 21st century. And finally, more than 40 million Americans remain without health insurance, deprived of critically important access to basic care.

The health care system as currently structured does not, as a whole, make the best use of its resources. There is little doubt that the aging population and increased patient demand for new services, technologies, and drugs are contributing to the steady increase in health care expenditures, but so, too, is waste. Many types of medical errors result in the subsequent need for additional health care services to treat patients who have been harmed. A highly fragmented delivery system that largely lacks even rudimentary clinical information capabilities results in poorly designed care processes characterized by unnecessary duplication of services and long waiting times and delays. And there is substantial evidence documenting overuse of many services— services for which the potential risk of harm outweighs the potential benefits.

What is perhaps most disturbing is the absence of real progress toward restructuring health care systems to address both quality and cost concerns, or toward applying advances in information technology to improve administrative and clinical processes. Despite the efforts of many talented leaders acid dedicated professionals, the last quarter of the 20th century might best be described as the "era of Brownian motion in health care." Mergers, acquisitions, and affiliations have been commonplace within the health plan, hospital, and physician practice sectors. Yet all this organizational turmoil has resulted in little change in the way health care is delivered. Some of the new arrangements have failed following disappointing results. Leaders of health care institutions are under extraordinary pressure, trying on the one hand to strategically reposition their organizations for the future, and on the other to respond to today's challenges, such as reductions in third-party payments, shortfalls in nurse staffing, and growing numbers of uninsured patients seeking uncompensated care.

For several decades, the needs of the American public have been shifting from predominantly acute, episodic care to care for chronic conditions. Chronic conditions are now the leading cause of illness, disability, and death; they affect almost half of the U.S. population and account for the majority of health care expenditures. As the need for community-based acute and long-term care services has grown, the portion of health care resources devoted to hospital care has declined, while that expended on pharmaceuticals has risen dramatically. Yet there remains a dearth of clinical programs with the infrastructure required to provide the full complement of services needed by people with heart disease, diabetes, asthma, and other common chronic conditions. The fact that more than 40 percent of people with chronic conditions have more than one such condition argues strongly for more sophisticated mechanisms to communicate and coordinate care. Yet physician groups, hospitals, and other health care organizations operate as silos, often providing care without the benefit of complete information about the patient's condition, medical history, services provided in other settings, or medications prescribed by other clinicians. For those without insurance, care is often unobtainable except in emergencies. It is not surprising, then, that studies of patient experience document that the health system for some is a "nightmare to navigate."

Quality as a System Property

The committee is confident that Americans can have a health care system of the quality they need, want, and deserve. But we are also confident that this higher level of quality cannot be achieved by further stressing current systems of care. The current care systems cannot do the job. Trying harder will not work. Changing systems of care will.

The committee's report on patient safety offers a similar conclusion in its narrower realm. Safety flaws are unacceptably common, but the effective remedy is not to browbeat the health care workforce by asking them to try harder to give safe care. Members of the health care workforce are already trying hard to do their jobs well. In fact, the courage, hard work, and commitment of doctors, nurses, and others in health care are today the only real means we have of stemming the flood of errors that are latent in our health care systems.

Health care has safety and quality problems because it relies on outmoded systems of work. Poor designs set the workforce up to fail, regardless of how hard they try. If we want safer, higher-quality care, we will need to have redesigned systems of care, including the use of information technology to support clinical and administrative processes.

Throughout this report, the committee offers a strategy and action plan for building a stronger health system over the coming decade, one that is capable of delivering on the promise of state-of-the-art health care to all Americans. In some areas, achieving this ideal will require crossing a large chasm between today's system and the possibilities of tomorrow.

An Agenda for Crossing the Chasm

The need for leadership in health care has never been greater. Transforming the health care system will not be an easy process. But the potential benefits are large as well. Narrowing the quality chasm will make it possible to bring the benefits of medical science and technology to all Americans in every community, and this in turn will mean less pain and suffering, less disability, greater longevity, and a more productive workforce. To this end, the committee proposes the following agenda for redesigning the 21st-century health care system:

- **That all health care constituencies, including policymakers, purchasers, regulators, health professionals, health care trustees and management, and consumers, commit to a national statement of purpose for the health care system as a whole and to a shared agenda of six aims for improvement that can raise the quality of care to unprecedented levels.**
- **That clinicians and patients, and the health care organizations that support care delivery, adopt a new set of principles to guide the redesign of care processes.**
- **That the Department of Health and Human Services identify a set of priority conditions upon which to focus initial efforts, provide resources to stimulate innovation, and initiate the change process.**
- **That health care organizations design and implement more effective organizational support processes to make change in the delivery of care possible.**
- **That purchasers, regulators, health professions, educational institutions, and the Department of Health and Human Services create an environment that fosters and rewards improvement by (1) creating an infrastructure to support evidence-based practice, (2) facilitating the use of information technology, (3) aligning payment incentives, and (4) preparing the workforce to better serve patients in a world of expanding knowledge and rapid change.**

The committee recognizes that implementing this agenda will be a complex process and that it will be important to periodically evaluate progress and reassess strategies for overcoming barriers.

Establishing Aims for the
21st-Century Health Care System

The committee proposes six aims for improvement to address key dimensions in which today's health care system functions at far lower levels than it can and should. Health care should be:

- *Safe*—avoiding injuries to patients from the care that is intended to help them.
- *Effective*—providing services based on scientific knowledge to all who could benefit and refraining from providing services to those not likely to benefit (avoiding underuse and overuse, respectively).
- *Patient-centered*—providing care that is respectful of and responsive to individual patient preferences, needs, and values and ensuring that patient values guide all clinical decisions.
- *Timely*—reducing waits and sometimes harmful delays for both those who receive and those who give care.
- *Efficient*—avoiding waste, including waste of equipment, supplies, ideas, and energy.
- *Equitable*—providing care that does not vary in quality because of personal characteristics such as gender, ethnicity, geographic location, and socioeconomic status.

A health care system that achieved major gains in these six dimensions would be far better at meeting patient needs. Patients would experience care that was safer, more reliable, more responsive, more integrated, and more available. Patients could count on receiving the full array of preventive, acute, and chronic services from which they are likely to benefit. Such a system would also be better for clinicians and others who would experience the satisfaction of providing care that was more reliable, more responsive to patients, and more coordinated than is the case today.

The entire enterprise of care would ideally be united across these aims by a single, overarching purpose for the American health care system as a whole. For this crucial statement of purpose, the committee endorses and adopts the phrasing of the Advisory Commission on Consumer Protection and Quality in the Health Care Industry.

> **Recommendation 1: All health care organizations, professional groups, and private and public purchasers should adopt as their explicit purpose to continually reduce the burden of illness, injury, and disability, and to improve the health and functioning of the people of the United States.**

> **Recommendation 2: All health care organizations, professional groups, and private and public purchasers should pursue six major aims; specifically, health care should be safe, effective, patient-centered, timely, efficient, and equitable.**

Additionally, without ongoing tracking to assess progress in meeting the six aims, policy makers, leaders within the health professions and health organizations, purchasers, and consumers will be unable to determine progress or understand where improvement efforts have succeeded and where further work is most needed. The National Quality Report has the potential to play an important role in continuing to raise the awareness of the American public about the quality-of-care challenges facing the health care system. Public awareness of shortcomings in quality is critical to securing public support for the steps that must be taken to address these concerns.

> **Recommendation 3: Congress should continue to authorize and appropriate funds for, and the Department of Health and Human Services should move forward expeditiously with the establishment of, monitoring and tracking processes for use in evaluating the progress of the health system in pursuit of the above-cited aims of safety, effectiveness, patient-centeredness, timeliness, efficiency, and equity. The Secretary of the Department of Health and Human Services should report annually to Congress and the president on the quality of care provided to the American people.**

The committee applauds Congress and the Administration for their current efforts to establish a National Quality Report for tracking the quality of care. Ongoing input from the many public- and private-sector associations, professional groups, and others involved in quality measurement and improvement will contribute to the success of these efforts. The establishment of specific goals for each of the six aims could further enhance the usefulness of this monitoring and tracking system as a stimulus for performance improvement. Continued funding for this activity should be ensured, as well as regular reports that communicate progress to all concerned. It should be noted that although this report focuses only on health care for individuals, the above overarching statement of purpose and six aims for improvement are sufficiently robust that they can be applied equally to decisions and evaluations at the population-health level.

Formulating New Rules
to Redesign and Improve Care

As discussed earlier, improved performance will depend on new system designs. The committee believes it would be neither useful nor possible for us to specify in detail the design of 21st-century health care delivery systems. Imagination and valuable pluralism abound at the local level in the nation's health care enterprise. At the same time, we believe local efforts to implement innovation and achieve improvement can benefit from a set of simple rules to guide the redesign of the health care system.

In formulating these rules, the committee has been guided by the belief that care must be delivered by systems that are carefully and consciously designed to provide care that is safe, effective, patient-centered, timely, efficient, and equitable. Such systems must be designed to serve the needs of patients, and to ensure that they are fully informed, retain control and participate in care delivery whenever possible, and receive care that is respectful of their values and preferences. Such systems must facilitate the application of scientific knowledge to practice, and provide clinicians with the tools and supports necessary to deliver evidence-based care consistently and safely.

> **Recommendation 4: Private and public purchasers, health care organizations, clinicians, and patients should work together to redesign health care processes in accordance with the following rules:**
>
> 1. *Care based on continuous healing relationships.* Patients should receive care whenever they need it and in many forms, not just face-to-face visits. This rule implies that the health care system should be responsive at all times (24 hours a day, every day) and that access to care should be provided over the Internet, by telephone, and by other means in addition to face-to-face visits.
> 2. *Customization based on patient needs and values.* The system of care should be designed to meet the most common types of needs, but have the capability to respond to individual patient choices and preferences.
> 3. *The patient as the source of control.* Patients should be given the necessary information and the opportunity to exercise the degree of control they choose over health care decisions that affect them. The health system should be able to accommodate differences in patient preferences and encourage shared decision making.
> 4. *Shared knowledge and the free flow of information.* Patients should have unfettered access to their own medical information and to clinical knowledge. Clinicians and patients should communicate effectively and share information.
> 5. *Evidence-based decision making.* Patients should receive care based on the best available scientific knowledge. Care should not vary illogically from clinician to clinician or from place to place.
> 6. *Safety as a system property.* Patients should be safe from injury caused by the care system. Reducing risk and ensuring safety require greater attention to systems that help prevent and mitigate errors.
> 7. *The need for transparency.* The health care system should make information available to patients and their families that allows them to make informed decisions when selecting a health plan, hospital, or clinical practice, or choosing among alternative treatments. This should include information describing the system's performance on safety, evidence-based practice, and patient satisfaction.
> 8. *Anticipation of needs.* The health system should anticipate patient needs, rather than simply reacting to events.
> 9. *Continuous decrease in waste.* The health system should not waste resources or patient time.
> 10. *Cooperation among clinicians.* Clinicians and institutions should actively collaborate and communicate to ensure an appropriate exchange of information and coordination of care.

The above rules will lead the redesign effort in the right direction, guiding the innovation required to achieve the aims for improvement outlined earlier. Widespread application of these ten rules, each grounded in both logic and varying degrees of evidence, will represent a new paradigm for health care delivery. As the redesign effort moves forward, it will be important to assess not only progress toward meeting the aims, but also the specific effects attributable to the new rules and to adapt the rules as appropriate.

Design ideas are not enough, however. To initiate the process of change, both an action agenda and resources are needed.

Taking the First Steps

The committee recognizes the enormity of the change that will be required to achieve a substantial improvement in the nation's health care system. Although steps can be taken immediately to apply the ten rules set forth above to the redesign of health care, widespread application will require commitment to the provision of evidence-based care that is responsive to individual patients' needs and preferences. Well-designed and well-run systems of care will be required as well. These changes will occur most rapidly in an environment in which public policy and market forces are aligned and in which the change process is supported by an appropriate information technology infrastructure.

To initiate the process of change, the committee believes the health care system must focus greater attention on the development of care processes for the common conditions that afflict many people. A limited number of such conditions, about 15 to 25, account for the majority of health care services. Nearly all of these conditions are chronic. By focusing attention on a limited number of common conditions, the committee believes it will be possible to make sizable improvements in the quality of care received by many individuals within the coming decade.

Health care for chronic conditions is very different from care for acute episodic illnesses. Care for the chronically ill needs to be a collaborative, multidisciplinary process. Effective methods of communication, both among caregivers and between caregivers and patients, are critical to providing high-quality care. Personal health information must accompany patients as they transition from home to clinical office setting to hospital to nursing home and back.

Carefully designed, evidence-based care processes, supported by automated clinical information and decision support systems, offer the greatest promise of achieving the best outcomes from care for chronic conditions. Some efforts are now under way to synthesize the clinical evidence pertaining to common chronic conditions and to make this information available to consumers and clinicians on the Web and by other means. In addition, evidence-based practice guidelines have been developed for many chronic conditions. Yet studies of the quality of care document tremendous variability in practice for many such conditions. Given these variations and the prevalence of chronic conditions, these conditions represent an excellent starting point for efforts to better define optimum care or best practices, and to design care processes to meet patient needs. Moreover, such efforts to improve quality must be supported by payment methods that remove barriers to integrated care and provide strong incentives and rewards for improvement.

To facilitate this process, the Agency for Healthcare Research and Quality should identify a limited number of priority conditions that affect many people and account for a sizable portion of the national health burden and associated expenditures. In identifying these priority conditions, the agency should consider using the list of conditions identified through the Medical Expenditure Panel Survey. According to the most recent survey data, the top 15 priority conditions are cancer, diabetes, emphysema, high cholesterol, HIV/AIDS, hypertension, ischemic heart disease, stroke, arthritis, asthma, gall bladder disease, stomach ulcers, back problems, Alzheimer's disease and other dementias, and depression and anxiety disorders. Health care organizations, clinicians, purchasers, and other stakeholders should then work together to (1) organize evidence-based care processes consistent with best practices, (2) organize major prevention programs to target key health risk behaviors associated with the onset or progression of these conditions, (3) develop the information infrastructure needed to support the provision of care and the ongoing measurement of care processes and patient outcomes, and (4) align the incentives inherent in payment and accountability processes with the goal of quality improvement.

> **Recommendation 5: The Agency for Healthcare Research and Quality should identify not fewer than 15 priority conditions, taking into account frequency of occurrence, health burden, and resource use. In collaboration with the National Quality Forum, the agency should convene stakeholders, including purchasers, consumers, health care organizations, professional groups, and others, to develop strategies, goals, and action plans for achieving substantial improvements in quality in the next 5 years for each of the priority conditions.**

Redirecting the health care industry toward the implementation of well-designed care processes for priority conditions will require significant resources. Capital will be required to invest in enhancing organizational capacity, building an information infrastructure, and training multidisciplinary care teams, among other things. The committee believes it is appropriate for the public sector to take the lead in establishing an innovation fund to seed promising projects, but not to shoulder the full burden of the transition. Private-sector organizations, including foundations, purchasers, health care organizations, and others, should also make investments. High priority should be given to projects that are likely to result in making available in the public domain new programs, tools, and technologies that are broadly applicable throughout the health care sector.

> **Recommendation 6: Congress should establish a Health Care Quality Innovation Fund to support projects targeted at (1) achieving the six aims of safety, effectiveness, patient-centeredness, timeliness, efficiency, and equity; and/or (2) producing substantial improvements in quality for the priority conditions. The fund's resources should be invested in projects that will produce a public-domain portfolio of programs, tools, and technologies of widespread applicability.**

Americans now invest annually $1.1 trillion, or 13.5 percent, of the nation's gross domestic product (GDP) in the health care sector. This figure is expected to grow to more than $2 trillion, or 16 percent of GDP, by 2007. The committee believes a sizable commitment, on the order of $1 billion over 3 to 5 years, is needed to strongly communicate the need for rapid and significant change in the health care system and to help initiate the transition. Just as a vigorous public commitment has led to the mapping of human DNA, a similar commitment is needed to help the nation's health care system achieve the aims for improvement outlined above.

Building Organizational Supports for Change

Supporting front-line teams that deliver care are many types of health care organizations. Today, these are hospitals, physician practices, clinics, integrated delivery systems, and health plans, but new forms will unquestionably emerge. Whatever those forms, care that is responsive to patient needs and makes consistent use of the best evidence requires far more conscious and careful organization than we find today.

Organizations will need to negotiate successfully six major challenges. The first is to redesign care processes to serve more effectively the needs of the chronically ill for coordinated, seamless care across settings and clinicians and over time. The use of tools to organize and deliver care has lagged far behind biomedical and clinical knowledge. A number of well-understood design principles, drawn from other industries as well as some of today's health care organizations, could help greatly in improving the care that is provided to patients.

A second challenge is making effective use of information technologies to automate clinical information and make it readily accessible to patients and all members of the care team. An improved information infrastructure is needed to establish effective and timely communication among clinicians and between patients and clinicians.

A third challenge is to manage the growing knowledge base and ensure that all those in the health care workforce have the skills they need. Making use of new knowledge requires that health professionals develop new skills or assume new roles. It requires that they use new tools to access and apply the expanding knowledge base. It also requires that training and ongoing licensure and certification reflect the need for lifelong learning and evaluation of competencies.

A fourth challenge for organizations is coordination of care across patient conditions, services, and settings over time. Excellent information technologies and well-thought-out and -implemented modes of ongoing communication can reduce the need to craft laborious, case-by-case strategies for coordinating patient care.

A fifth challenge is to continually advance the effectiveness of teams. Team practice is common, but the training of health professionals is typically isolated by discipline. Making the necessary changes in roles to improve the work of teams is often slowed or stymied by institutional, labor, and financial structures, and by law and custom.

Finally, all organizations—whether or not health care related—can improve their performance only by incorporating care process and outcome measures into their daily work. Use of such measures makes it possible to understand the degree to which performance is consistent with best practices, and the extent to which patients are being helped.

Recommendation 7: The Agency for Healthcare Research and Quality and private foundations should convene a series of workshops involving representatives from health care and other industries and the research community to identify, adapt, and implement state-of-the-art approaches to addressing the following challenges:

- **Redesign of care processes based on best practices**
- **Use of information technologies to improve access to clinical information and support clinical decision making**
- **Knowledge and skills management**
- **Development of effective teams**
- **Coordination of care across patient conditions, services, and settings over time**
- **Incorporation of performance and outcome measurements for improvement and accountability**

Establishing a New Environment for Care

To enable the profound changes in health care recommended in this report, the *environment* of care must also change. The committee believes the current environment often inhibits the changes needed to achieve quality improvement. Two types of environmental change are needed:

- *Focus and align the environment toward the six aims for improvement.* To effect this set of changes, purchasers and health plans, for example, should eliminate or modify payment practices that fragment the care system, and should establish incentives designed to encourage and reward innovations aimed at improving quality. Purchasers and regulators should also create precise streams of accountability and measurement reflecting achievements in the six aims. Moreover, efforts should be made to help health care consumers understand the aims, why they are important, and how to interpret the levels of performance of various health care systems.
- *Provide, where possible, assets and encouragement for positive change.* For example, national funding agencies could promote research on new designs for the care of priority conditions, state and national activities could be undertaken to facilitate the exchange of best practices and shared learning among health care delivery systems, and a national system for monitoring progress toward the six aims for improvement could help improvement efforts remain on track.

Such environmental changes need to occur in four major areas: the infrastructure that supports the dissemination and application of new clinical knowledge and technologies, the information technology infrastructure, payment policies, and preparation of the health care workforce. . . .

Applying Evidence to Health Care Delivery

In the current health care system, scientific knowledge about best care is not applied systematically or expeditiously to clinical practice. An average of about 17 years is required for new knowledge generated by randomized controlled trials to be incorporated into practice, and even then application is highly uneven. The extreme variability in practice in clinical areas in which there is strong scientific evidence and a high degree of expert consensus about best practices indicates that current dissemination efforts fail to reach many clinicians and patients, and that there are insufficient tools and incentives to promote rapid adoption of best practices. The time has come to invest in the creation of a more effective infrastructure for the application of knowledge to health care delivery.

> **Recommendation 8: The Secretary of the Department of Health and Human Services should be given the responsibility and necessary resources to establish and maintain a comprehensive program aimed at making scientific evidence more useful and accessible to clinicians and patients. In developing this program, the Secretary should work with federal agencies and in collaboration with professional and health care associations, the academic and research communities, and the National Quality Forum and other organizations involved in quality measurement and accountability.**

It is critical that leadership from the private sector, both professional and other health care leaders and consumer representatives, be involved in all aspects of this effort to ensure its applicability and acceptability to clinicians and patients. The infrastructure developed through this public- and private-sector partnership should focus initially on priority conditions and include:

- Ongoing analysis and synthesis of the medical evidence
- Delineation of specific practice guidelines
- Identification of best practices in the design of care processes
- Enhanced dissemination efforts to communicate evidence and guidelines to the general public and professional communities
- Development of decision support tools to assist clinicians and patients in applying the evidence
- Establishment of goals for improvement in care processes and outcomes
- Development of quality measures for priority conditions

More systematic approaches are needed to analyze and synthesize medical evidence for both clinicians and patients. Far more sophisticated clinical decision support systems will be required to assist clinicians and patients in selecting the best treatment options and delivering safe and effective care. Many promising private- and public-sector activities now under way can serve as excellent models and building blocks for a more expanded effort. In particular, the Cochrane Collaboration and the Agency for Healthcare Research and Quality's Evidence-Based Practice Centers represent important efforts to synthesize medical evidence. The growth of the Internet has also opened up many new opportunities to make evidence more accessible to clinicians and consumers. The efforts of the National Library of Medicine to facilitate access to the medical literature by both consumers and health care professionals and to design Web sites that organize large amounts of information on particular health needs are particularly promising.

The development of a more effective infrastructure to synthesize and organize evidence around priority conditions would also offer new opportunities to enhance quality measurement and reporting. A stronger and more organized evidence base should facilitate the adoption of best practices, as well as the development of valid and reliable quality measures for priority conditions that could be used for both internal quality improvement and external accountability.

Using Information Technology

Health care delivery has been relatively untouched by the revolution in information technology that has been transforming nearly every other aspect of society. The majority of patient and clinician encounters take place for purposes of exchanging clinical information: patients share information with clinicians about their general health, symptoms, and concerns, and clinicians use their knowledge and skills to respond with pertinent medical information, and in many cases reassurance. Yet it is estimated that only a small fraction of physicians offer e-mail interaction, a simple and convenient tool for efficient communication, to their patients.

The meticulous collection of personal health information throughout a patient's life can be one of the most important inputs to the provision of proper care. Yet for most individuals, that health information is dispersed in a collection of paper records that are poorly organized and often illegible, and frequently cannot be retrieved in a timely fashion, making it nearly impossible to manage many forms of chronic illness that require frequent monitoring and ongoing patient support.

Although growth in clinical knowledge and technology has been profound, many health care settings lack basic computer systems to provide clinical information or support clinical decision making. The development and application of more sophisticated information systems is essential to enhance quality and improve efficiency.

The Internet has enormous potential to transform health care through information technology applications in such areas as consumer health, clinical care, administrative and financial transactions, public health, professional education, and biomedical and health services research. Many of these applications are currently within reach, including remote medical consultation with patients in their homes or offices; consumer and clinician access to the medical literature; creation of "communities" of patients and clinicians with shared interests; consumer access to information on health plans, participating providers, eligibility for procedures, and covered drugs in a formulary; and videoconferencing among public health officials during emergency situations. Other applications are more experimental, such as simulation of surgical procedures; consultation among providers involving manipulation of digital images; and control of experimental equipment, such as electron microscopes.

The Internet also supports rising interest among consumers in information and convenience in all areas of commerce, including health care. The number of Americans who use the Internet to retrieve health-related information is estimated to be about 70 million. Consumers access health-related Web sites to research an illness or disease; seek information on nutrition and fitness;

research drugs and their interactions; and search for doctors, hospitals, and online medical support groups.

The committee believes information technology must play a central role in the redesign of the health care system if a substantial improvement in quality is to be achieved over the coming decade. Automation of clinical, financial, and administrative transactions is essential to improving quality, preventing errors, enhancing consumer confidence in the health system, and improving efficiency.

Central to many information technology applications is the automation of patient-specific clinical information. A fully electronic medical record, including all types of patient information, is not needed to achieve many, if not most, of the benefits of automated clinical data. Sizable benefits can be derived in the near future from automating certain types of data, such as medication orders. Efforts to automate clinical information date back several decades, but progress has been slow, in part because of the barriers and risks involved. An important constraint is that consumers and policy makers share concerns about the privacy and confidentiality of these data. The United States also lacks national standards for the capture, storage, communication, processing, and presentation of health information.

The challenges of applying information technology to health care should not be underestimated. Health care is undoubtedly one of the most, if not the most, complex sector of the economy. The number of different types of transactions (i.e., patient needs, interactions, and services) is very large. Sizable capital investments and multiyear commitments to building systems will be required. Widespread adoption of many information technology applications will require behavioral adaptations on the part of large numbers of patients, clinicians, and organizations. Yet, the Internet is rapidly transforming many aspects of society, and many health-related processes stand to be reshaped as well.

In the absence of a national commitment and financial support to build a national health information infrastructure, the committee believes that progress on quality improvement will be painfully slow. The automation of clinical, financial, and administrative information and the electronic sharing of such information among clinicians, patients, and appropriate others within a secure environment are critical if the 21st-century health care system envisioned by the committee is to be realized.

> **Recommendation 9: Congress, the executive branch, leaders of health care organizations, public and private purchasers, and health informatics associations and vendors should make a renewed national commitment to building an information infrastructure to support health care delivery, consumer health, quality measurement and improvement, public accountability, clinical and health services research, and clinical education. This commitment should lead to the elimination of most handwritten clinical data by the end of the decade.**

Aligning Payment Policies with Quality Improvement

Current payment methods do not adequately encourage or support the provision of quality health care. Although payment is not the only factor that influences provider and patient behavior, it is an important one.

All payment methods affect behavior and quality. For example, fee-for-service payment methods for physicians and hospitals raise concerns about potential overuse of services—the provision of services that may not be necessary or may expose the patient to greater potential harm than benefit. On the other hand, capitation and per case payment methods for physicians and hospitals raise questions about potential underuse—the failure to provide services from which the patient would likely benefit. Indeed, no payment method perfectly aligns financial incentives with the goal of quality improvement for all health care decision makers, including clinicians, hospitals, and patients. This is one reason for the widespread interest in blended methods of payment designed to counter the disadvantages of one payment method with the advantages of another.

Too little attention has been paid to the careful analysis and alignment of payment incentives with quality improvement. The current health care environment is replete with examples of payment policies that work against the efforts of clinicians, health care administrators, and others to improve quality. The following example, presented at an Institute of Medicine workshop on payment and quality held on April 24, 2000, illustrates how payment policies can work against the efforts of clinicians, health care administrators, and others to improve quality:

> A physician group paid primarily on a fee-for-service basis instituted a new program to improve blood sugar control for diabetic patients. Specifically, pilot studies suggested that tighter diabetic management could decrease hemoglobin Alc levels by 2 percentage points for about 40 percent of all diabetic patients managed by the physician group. Data from two randomized controlled trials demonstrated that better sugar controls should translate into lower rates of retinopathy, nephropathy, peripheral neurological damage, and heart disease. The savings in direct health care costs (i.e., reduced visits and hospital episodes) from avoided complications have been estimated to generate a net savings of about $2,000 per patient per year, on average, over 15 years. Across the more than 13,000 diabetic patients managed by the physician group, the project had the potential to generate over $10 million in net savings each year. The project was costly to the medical group in two ways. First, expenses to conduct the project, including extra clinical time for tighter management, fell to the physician group. Second, over time, as diabetic complication rates fell, the project would reduce patient visits and, thus, revenues as well. But the savings from avoided complications would accrue to the insurer or a self-funded purchaser.

The committee believes that all purchasers, both public and private, should carefully reexamine their payment policies.

Recommendation 10: Private and public purchasers should examine their current payment methods to remove barriers that currently impede quality improvement, and to build in stronger incentives for quality enhancement.

Payment methods should:

- Provide fair payment for good clinical management of the types of patients seen. Clinicians should be adequately compensated for taking good care of all types of patients, neither gaining nor losing financially for caring for sicker patients or those with more complicated conditions. The risk of random incidence of disease in the population should reside with a larger risk pool, whether that be large groups of providers, health plans, or insurance companies.

- Provide an opportunity for providers to share in the benefits of quality improvement. Rewards should be located close to the level at which the reengineering and process redesign needed to improve quality are likely to take place.
- Provide the opportunity for consumers and purchasers to recognize quality differences in health care and direct their decisions accordingly. In particular, consumers need to have good information on quality and the ability to use that information as they see fit to meet their needs.
- Align financial incentives with the implementation of care processes based on best practices and the achievement of better patient outcomes. Substantial improvements in quality are most likely to be obtained when providers are highly motivated and rewarded for carefully designing and fine-tuning care processes to achieve increasingly higher levels of safety, effectiveness, patient-centeredness, timeliness, efficiency, and equity.
- Reduce fragmentation of care. Payment methods should not pose a barrier to providers' ability to coordinate care for patients across settings and over time.

To assist purchasers in the redesign of payment policy based on these fundamental principles, a vigorous program of pilot testing and evaluating alternative design options should be pursued.

> **Recommendation 11: The Health Care Financing Administration and the Agency for Healthcare Research and Quality, with input from private payers, health care organizations, and clinicians, should develop a research agenda to identify, pilot test, and evaluate various options for better aligning current payment methods with quality improvement goals.**

Examples of possible means of achieving this end include blended methods of payment for providers, multiyear contracts, payment modifications to encourage use of electronic interaction among clinicians and between clinicians and patients, risk adjustment, bundled payments for priority conditions, and alternative approaches for addressing the capital investments needed to improve quality.

Preparing the Workforce

A major challenge in transitioning to the health care system of the 21st century envisioned by the committee is preparing the workforce to acquire new skills and adopt new ways of relating to patients and each other. At least three approaches can be taken to support the workforce in this transition. One is to redesign the way health professionals are trained to emphasize the aims for improvement set forth earlier, including teaching evidence-based practice and using multidisciplinary approaches. Second is to modify the ways in which health professionals are regulated to facilitate the needed changes in care delivery. Scope-of-practice acts and other workforce regulations need to allow for innovation in the use of all types of clinicians to meet patient needs in the most effective and efficient way possible. Third is to examine how the liability system can constructively support changes in care delivery while remaining part of an overall approach to accountability for health care professionals and organizations. All three approaches are important and require additional study.

> **Recommendation 12: A multidisciplinary summit of leaders within the health professions should be held to discuss and develop strategies for (1) restructuring clinical education to be consistent with the principles of the 21st-century health system throughout the continuum of undergraduate, graduate, and continuing education for medical, nursing, and other professional training programs; and (2) assessing the implications of these changes for provider credentialing programs, funding, and sponsorship of education programs for health professionals.**

> **Recommendation 13: The Agency for Healthcare Research and Quality should fund research to evaluate how the current regulatory and legal systems (1) facilitate or inhibit the changes needed for the 21st-century health care delivery system, and (2) can be modified to support health care professionals and organizations that seek to accomplish the six aims set forth in Chapter 2.**

Summary

The changes needed to realize a substantial improvement in health care involve the health care system as a whole. The new rules set forth in this report will affect the role, self-image, and work of front-line doctors, nurses, and all other staff. The needed new infrastructures will challenge today's health care leaders—both clinical leaders and management. The necessary environmental changes will require the interest and commitment of payers, health plans, government officials, and regulatory and accrediting bodies. New skills will require new approaches by professional educators. The 21st-century health care system envisioned by the committee—providing care that is evidence-based, patientcentered, and systems-oriented—also implies new roles and responsibilities for patients and their families, who must become more aware, more participative, and more demanding in a care system that should be meeting their needs. And all involved must be united by the overarching purpose of reducing the burden of illness, injury, and disability in our nation.

American health care is beset by serious problems, but they are not intractable. Perfect care may be a long way off, but much better care is within our grasp. The committee envisions a system that uses the best knowledge, that is focused intensely on patients, and that works across health care providers and settings. Taking advantage of new information technologies will be an important catalyst to moving us beyond where we are today. The committee believes that achieving such a system is both possible and necessary.

EPA POLICY STATEMENTS
ON ARSENIC LEVELS IN WATER
March 20 and October 31, 2001

The new administration of President George W. Bush undertook a series of actions during 2001 to overturn environmental protection regulations that had been put in place by the administration of former president Bill Clinton—in some cases during the waning hours of Clinton's term. Most environmental organizations roundly condemned the new administration's steps as undermining environmental protections, but industry groups praised Bush for restoring what they called "balance" to federal policy.

In its apparent eagerness to distance itself from Clinton positions on the environment, the Bush administration committed at least one major political blunder when it reversed a Clinton policy reducing permissible levels of arsenic in the nation's drinking water. That move led to widespread protests that the administration was putting business interests ahead of public health. A chastened administration eventually reversed itself and stuck by the Clinton policy.

Changes in policy from one presidential administration to the next are common, but a combination of circumstances heightened the contrast between the Clinton and the Bush approaches to environmental issues. Largely because of the influence of Vice President Al Gore and key administration officials, Clinton had pursued an agenda that won broad praise from environmental organizations and condemnation from industry groups and many local politicians, especially in western states. During his second term Clinton set aside millions of acres of land from industrial and other types of development, created or expanded more than twenty national monuments, and implemented dozens of new government regulations to tighten enforcement of laws protecting air and water quality, wetlands, and other resources. Clinton took some of his most important actions at the very end of his presidency; some had been in the planning stages for years, but the impression was created that he waited until the last minute to solidify his own pro-environment legacy.

Bush, by contrast, was a conservative governor from a southwestern state who had close personal and political ties to the oil industry and had been avidly supported by a wide range of corporate executives. Bush had expressed an intense dislike of government regulations that limited the flexibility of business, preferring what he called voluntary and "market-based" solutions to environmental questions. The vast majority of Bush's appointees to top administration positions had expressed similar views; many had been lobbyists for timber, mining, and other industry organizations that had fought the Clinton administration's regulations. The close election that had resulted in Bush's entering the presidency also colored the year's political struggle over environmental issues—until the September 11 terrorist attacks against the United States gave Bush a new level of public support.

In nearly every case, Bush acted on his own authority—as had Clinton—revising federal regulations and issuing executive orders that did not require congressional approval. Many of Bush's actions came on obscure regulatory questions that received little public attention but had substantial public policy implications. Bush upheld several important decisions Clinton had made but reversed or undercut the effect of far more actions by his predecessor.

Many of Bush's actions on environmental issues were linked to the energy policy he announced May 17. That policy emphasized domestic production of oil, gas, and other energy supplies and called for reducing environmental restraints that hindered energy development. (Energy policy, p. 331)

Bush repeatedly defended his stance on environmental issues and rejected suggestions that he was not committed to safeguarding the nation's national parks and other treasures. After he was roundly criticized on the arsenic-in-water issue, Bush traveled to several natural beauty spots to pledge his support for environmental causes. Visiting the Florida Everglades on June 4, for example, Bush said the region's natural wonders "are here to be appreciated, not changed. Their beauty is beyond our power to improve. Our job is to be good stewards of the Everglades, to restore what has been damaged and to reduce the risk of harm."

Arsenic in Water

Until Bush came to office, the question of whether to toughen standards for arsenic levels in drinking water had not generated broad public interest. But the issue took on substantial political importance because it was relatively easy to understand; because it involved the word arsenic, *which had frightening implications; and because it was seen as an early test of Bush's environmental policies.*

Arsenic is a natural substance that commonly appears in the soil, water, and other parts of the environment, and is particularly prevalent in the southwestern states. Arsenic also is a byproduct of many industrial processes, most importantly mining and the use of chemicals to treat lumber; runoff from those industries often contaminated drinking water supplies. Numerous international studies had shown that long-term exposure to arsenic in drinking water could cause cancer. The federal government in 1943 had set a limit on arsenic in water of 50 parts per billion (ppb).

Under a congressional mandate from 1974 to eliminate all hazardous substances in the nation's drinking water supply, the Environmental Protection Agency (EPA) for years had studied whether and how to reduce arsenic levels below the 1943 standard. Congress in 1996 appropriated money for new studies but demanded action, requiring the Clinton administration to propose new regulations on arsenic by January 1, 2000, and to issue new regulations by January 1, 2001. Clinton issued the new regulations January 17, 2001; the rule lowered the maximum acceptable level of arsenic in drinking water to 10 ppb, equal to about 1 teaspoon in 1.3 million gallons of water. Water systems would not have to meet that new standard until 2006. The order would have affected the water systems in hundreds of cities (the largest of which was Albuquerque) and small towns; an estimated 11 million Americans drank water that contained higher levels of arsenic than Clinton's rule would allow.

On March 20 the EPA said it would withdraw Clinton's order and return to the old 50 ppb standard pending further studies. In its announcement, the agency said Clinton's order had not been supported by adequate scientific studies. EPA administrator Christine Whitman acknowledged that the standard should be less than 50 ppb, but said it was "unclear" what the level should be. Representatives of the National Mining Association and the chemical industry, both of which had opposed the Clinton rule, praised the EPA action, as did the National Rural Water Association, which represented water systems in about 22,000 small municipalities. Representatives of environmental groups expressed outrage and mounted a campaign to force a reversal of the decision.

Within days it became clear that the EPA action was a major public relations blunder for the new administration. Editorialists, members of Congress, and others denounced the move, likening it to an attack on the nation's public health. Bush's approval rating in public opinion surveys tumbled.

Less than a month later, on April 18, the EPA announced that it would issue new rules within nine months. Whitman asked the National Academy of Sciences to review recent scientific studies on the issue. Meanwhile, both houses of Congress called on the administration to set a standard lower than the existing one. The Republican-controlled House on July 27 narrowly approved a Democratic-sponsored proposal to require the administration to adopt Clinton's 10 ppb standard; the vote was 218–189, with nineteen Republicans siding with Democrats. The Senate on August 1 adopted vaguer language demanding a new standard but not specifying the level; the vote was 97–1, with Ted Stevens, an Alaska Republican, casting the lone "no" vote.

New pressure for action came with the release on September 11 of the study Whitman had requested from the National Academy of Sciences. Conducted by the academy's National Research Council, the study said that even the standard set by Clinton might pose a greater risk of cancer than longstanding EPA policy allowed. At 10 parts per billion, the study said, arsenic in drinking water could cause more than three cancer cases per 1,000 popu-

lation—three times the risk level decreed by the government as acceptable. EPA officials immediately announced that Whitman would set a standard at least as tight as the one Clinton had planned.

Whitman on October 31 announced that she had adopted the Clinton standard of 10 ppb and would allow water systems until January 2006 to comply. She said the new standard was "based on the best available science and ensures that the cost of the standard is achievable." The EPA also sought to make a virtue from its policy flip-flop, arguing that the new study had given it a firmer scientific basis for a decision than Clinton had used. Whitman said the EPA would budget $20 million for research and development into new technologies to help small communities meet the new standard.

As with the previous announcements on the issue, Whitman's decision generated opposite reactions. Environmental groups and most members of Congress praised the decision, although Democrats chided the administration for its policy reversals. A spokesman for the National Rural Water Association complained that the new standard would be costly for small communities.

Air Pollution Regulations

Even before the controversy over arsenic, the administration had generated wide criticism by backing away from a Bush campaign promise on air pollution. As a presidential candidate, Bush on September 29, 2000, had pledged to "require all power plants to meet clean air standards" by reducing emissions of carbon dioxide and other pollutants "within a reasonable period of time." Carbon dioxide was the most prevalent of the so-called greenhouse gases generally believed to be responsible for global warming, and Bush's pledge to curb carbon dioxide emissions was his most specific campaign promise on an environmental issue. Citing that promise, Whitman in February said the EPA would begin the process of writing rules to regulate the emissions.

On March 13 Bush told Whitman that he had decided to reverse his earlier position. According to press reports, Bush had come under intense pressure from congressional Republicans and representatives of the coal and oil industries. In a letter to four Republican senators who had opposed carbon dioxide controls, Bush said he would not impose "mandatory emissions reductions" on carbon dioxide. A White House spokesman said candidate Bush should never had made the promise in the first place. The four Republican senators and representatives of industry groups expressed relief at Bush's new stance, but Democrats and environmental groups cried foul.

The policy reversal was the first of two important steps Bush took during the year to distance himself from the positions on global warming issues that Clinton had taken. Bush in June halted U.S. participation in the 1997 Kyoto Protocol, which was intended to reduce greenhouse gas emissions by the industrialized countries. (Global warming, p. 109)

A report issued by the Energy Department on November 9 showed that U.S. emissions of carbon dioxide continued to climb, jumping 3.1 percent in 2000, the highest of any single year since the early 1990s. Emissions in 2000 were 14 percent higher than in 1990—the year set as a baseline for compliance with the Kyoto Protocol.

Roads in National Forests

Through regulatory and legal steps, the Bush administration in 2001 retreated from one of the centerpiece items of Clinton's environmental legacy: protecting tens of millions of acres of national forests. After a process that required three years of rule making and hundreds of public meetings and generated more than 1.6 million public comments, Clinton on January 5 issued regulations sharply curtailing or even banning the construction of roads in 58.5 million acres of national forests—about one-third of the total acreage in those forests. By keeping these lands "roadless," Clinton's action effectively would have halted logging, mining, oil and gas production, and other industrial activities in them. Environmentalists had praised the step as a far-sighted effort to preserve the nation's dwindling wilderness areas, but timber companies and local politicians, especially in western states, condemned it as federal "land-grab." (Roadless proposal; Historic Documents of 1999, p. 592)

Acknowledging that Clinton's regulation had broad public support in the nation as a whole—but not in many parts of the West—the Bush administration insisted it would not reverse it formally. The administration took several steps during the year, however, that undermined the most important elements of Clinton's plan.

On March 16 the Justice Department announced that it would not defend the regulation against a court challenge launched by business interests and the state of Idaho. Two months later, on May 10, a federal district court judge in Boise blocked enforcement of the regulation, citing "irreparable long term harm" to the economies of local communities. Environmental groups appealed the decision, but the Bush administration did not pursue an appeal, in effect leaving the roadless rule undefended by the government.

On May 4 Secretary of Agriculture Ann M. Veneman said the administration would "uphold" the Clinton regulation. But she also announced that local Forest Service officials would have authority to "opt out" of the roadless regulations on a case-by-case basis. That move was widely seen as giving western states, most of which opposed the rules, a near veto power over how they would be implemented. Veneman said the change was needed to address "reasonable concerns" that local officials had expressed about Clinton's rule.

The Forest Service issued additional regulations in July, August, and September that reduced many of the protections that Clinton's rule had given to roadless areas of the forests. Finally, on December 20, Dale Bosworth, director of the Forest Service, eliminated a key element of federal regulations that required detailed environmental impact reviews—complete with input from the public—before roads and other forms of development would be allowed in the national forests. That action appeared aimed at allowing expanded logging in several forests, notably Alaska's Tongass National

Forest—at 17 million acres the nation's largest remaining virgin forest wilderness.

Clinton's Monument Designations

During the last year of his presidency, Clinton used his executive powers under the 1906 Antiquities Act to create eighteen national monuments and to expand the boundaries of three others. Combined, those monuments— many in Western states—encompassed nearly 4 million acres. In addition, Clinton in 1996 had established the 1.7 million Grand Staircase-Escalante National Monument in Utah, a move that was bitterly opposed at the time by Utah politicians. Clinton's actions generally protected those areas from mining and other industrial activities that commercial interests were planning.

Bush at first sought to delay implementation of Clinton's monument designations, six of which had been made just four days before Clinton left office. After reviewing the legal hurdles to overturning Clinton's actions, Interior Secretary Gale Norton announced February 20 that the administration would allow the monument designations to stand. But she said she would consider proposals to alter the boundaries of the monuments and allow some of the commercial uses that Clinton had sought to prohibit. Norton on March 28 wrote to state and local officials asking them for suggested boundary changes. On October 11 the Interior Department's Bureau of Land Management issued new regulations allowing increased access to those properties by recreational vehicles (such as snowmobiles and all-terrain vehicles) and by industrial trucks. The regulation also allowed construction of power lines in areas that previously had been off-limits.

Other Environmental Issues

The Bush administration and environmental advocates, including Democrats and moderate Republicans in Congress, engaged in disputes on more than a dozen other significant policy issues during the year. Some of the most important were:

Mining permits. At the end of his presidency, Clinton had allowed the Interior Department to use potential environmental damage as a reason to block permits for the mining of copper, gold, lead, silver, zinc, and other minerals on federal public lands. That rule was hailed by environmental organizations and denounced by the mining industry. The Bush administration reversed Clinton's rule on October 25, eliminating environmental considerations from the final review of permits for "hard-rock mining" on public lands.

Water quality. The Clinton administration in 2000 issued rules that would have required states to develop plans to clean up an estimated 21,000 polluted lakes, ponds, rivers, and small streams. The rule had been developed primarily to curtail runoff of agricultural chemicals, one of the nation's major sources of water pollution. But farm groups and some states had opposed the rule and had persuaded Congress in 2000 to delay its implementation pending a report from the National Academy of Sciences on the problem. That report, issued June 15, 2001, confirmed the seriousness of water-quality problems in lakes and rivers but suggested a more cautious approach than Clinton had ordered. The EPA on July 16 said it would delay action on the Clinton plan at least until 2003 and would work on new rules in the meantime.

Environmental enforcement. *As part of Bush's broader plans to shift many government responsibilities from the federal to the state level, the administration in June and July announced that it wanted to give the states a greater role in enforcing federal environmental laws. In his fiscal 2002 budget Bush cut funding for the EPA's enforcement of regulations and argued that the states should pick up more of the burden. Two reports issued June 22 raised concerns about that approach: one, by the General Accounting Office, said the EPA enforcement department already was understaffed and ill-managed; another, by the EPA's own inspector general, said many states were doing a poor job of enforcing the Clean Water Act.*

Power plant pollution. *The Bush administration signaled in May and again in August that it would retreat from enforcing regulations, under the Clean Air Act, that required utilities to install new air pollution control equipment when they expanded existing coal-fired power plants. Many utilities had tried to avoid this requirement, called "new source review," but the Clinton administration and several northeastern states filed lawsuits to force compliance. The Bush administration settled four cases in 2001, but numerous news reports indicated that administration officials were divided over whether to pursue other pending cases or any new ones.*

Snowmobiles in national parks. *Citing noise and air pollution concerns, the Clinton administration had planned a gradual ban, beginning in the 2001–2002 winter season, on the use of recreational snowmobiles in national parks, especially in three parks: Voyaguers in Minnesota and Grand Teton and Yellowstone in Wyoming. Snowmobile organizations fought the regulation in court, and late in the year the Bush administration said it would indefinitely postpone the ban.*

The Bush administration supported some environmental enforcement measures from the Clinton and previous administrations, among them:

Dredging of the Hudson. *Rebuffing intense lobbying pressure by the GE Corporation, Whitman in August and again in December ordered the industrial giant to remove hundreds of tons of dangerous chemicals known as polychlorinated biphenyls (PCBs) from the upper Hudson River near Albany, New York. GE plants had dumped tons of PCBs into the river before the chemical was banned in 1977 as a cancer-causing agent. The Clinton administration had written an order requiring GE to remove the PCBs by dredging and other methods, at an estimated cost of about $500 million. Whitman upheld the order, thus forcing one of the largest environmental cleanups in U.S. history.*

Endangered species. *The administration and several environmental groups on August 29 announced agreement on a plan to protect twenty-nine plants and animals under the Endangered Species Act. Under the agree-*

ment, the environmental groups delayed lawsuits against the government in return for pledges by the Interior Department to speed up its review of legal protections for species that had declined because of pollution and habitat loss.

Wetlands. The administration on April 16 announced that it would retain a Clinton rule that prohibited developers from excavating in marshes and swamps without prior government approval. The rule would close a loophole in federal law that had enabled housing contractors and other developers to drain more than 20,000 acres of wetlands without submitting their plans to environmental reviews. Later in the year, however, the Bush administration overturned another Clinton-era regulation that had banned the Army Corps of Engineers from building dams and other projects that would cause a net loss of marshes and other wetlands.

Following are the texts of two statements by the Environmental Protection Agency: the first, on March 20, 2001, announced a decision to withdraw a regulation instituted in January by then-president Bill Clinton reducing the permitted levels of arsenic in the nation's drinking water supplies; the second, on October 31, 2001, announced that the Clinton regulation would be allowed to stand.

**The documents were obtained from the Internet at
http://yosemite.epa.gov/opa/admpress.nsf/
b1ab9f485b098972852562e7004dc686/
77e59dbb919fdf4785256a150063d6a0?OpenDocument;
http://yosemite.epa.gov/opa/admpress.nsf/
b1ab9f485b098972852562e7004dc686/
6d26c015b807156e85256af6007b9bed?OpenDocument.**

MARCH 20 STATEMENT

U.S. Environmental Protection Agency Administrator Christie Whitman announced today that EPA will propose to withdraw the pending arsenic standard for drinking water that was issued on January 22. The rule would have reduced the acceptable level of arsenic in water from 50 parts per billion [ppb] to 10 ppb.

EPA will seek independent reviews of both the science behind the standard and of the estimates of the costs to communities of implementing the rule. A final decision on withdrawal is expected after the public has an opportunity to comment.

"I am committed to safe and affordable drinking water for all Americans. I want to be sure that the conclusions about arsenic in the rule are supported by the best available science. When the federal government imposes costs on communities—especially small communities—we should be sure the facts support imposing the federal standard," said Whitman. "I am moving quickly to review the arsenic standard so communities that need to reduce arsenic in drinking water can proceed with confidence once the permanent standard is confirmed."

While scientists agree that the previous standard of 50 parts per billion should be lowered, there is no consensus on a particular safe level. Independent review of the science behind the final standard will help clear up uncertainties that have been raised about the health benefits of reducing arsenic to 10 parts per billion in drinking water.

"It is clear that arsenic, while naturally occurring, is something that needs to be regulated. Certainly the standard should be less than 50 ppb, but the scientific indicators are unclear as to whether the standard needs to go as low as 10 ppb," said Whitman.

"This decision will not lessen any existing protections for drinking water. The standards would remain the same, whether the rule went through or not, until it was time to enforce it under the compliance schedule five to nine years from now," said Whitman. "But, in the interim, EPA will examine what may have been a rushed decision."

Some cities and states that will have to comply with the arsenic rule have raised serious questions about whether the costs of the rule were fully understood when the rule was signed in early January. EPA estimates the cost to be about $200 million per year. Many small communities will be affected by the drinking water standard for arsenic, making it especially important to ensure that the Safe Drinking Water Act provision allowing balancing of costs is based on accurate information.

Arsenic is an element that occurs naturally in several parts of the country. The highest concentrations of arsenic occur mostly in the Western states, particularly in the Southwest. At unsafe levels, arsenic causes cancer and other diseases.

EPA today will ask for a 60-day extension of the effective date of the pending arsenic standard for drinking water, and expects to release a timetable for review within the next few weeks.

Whitman plans to attend the Western Governors Association meeting in Denver, Colorado on March 22 and March 23, where she plans to participate in round table discussions on arsenic with stakeholders.

OCTOBER 31 STATEMENT

U.S. Environmental Protection Agency Administrator Christie Whitman announced today that the arsenic standard in drinking water will be 10 parts per billion (ppb). "Throughout this process, I have made it clear that EPA intends to strengthen the standard for arsenic by substantially lowering the maximum acceptable level from 50 parts per billion (ppb), which has been the lawful limit for nearly half a century," Whitman wrote in a letter to the conferees on the Veterans Affairs, Housing and Urban Development and Independent Agencies appropriations measure.

"The Bush Administration is committed to protecting the environment and the health of all Americans," Whitman said. "This standard will improve the safety of drinking water for millions of Americans, and better protect against the risk of cancer, heart disease and diabetes."

When the Administrator initiated review of the standard for arsenic, there were indications that additional information was available that had not been considered previously. She asked for time to look at the new science and data that have come to light since the original (1999) study by the National Academy of Sciences on this matter. Whitman also asked that three expert panels review all the new and existing materials. The National Academy of Sciences looked at risk, the National Drinking Water Advisory Council examined costs to water systems throughout the nation and EPA's Science Advisory Board assessed benefits.

Whitman today reiterated that the additional study and consultation have not delayed the compliance date for implementing a new standard for arsenic in 2006. "Instead it has reinforced the basis for the decision," said Whitman. "I said in April that we would obtain the necessary scientific and cost review to ensure a standard that fully protects the health of all Americans, we did that, and we are reassured by all of the data that significant reductions are necessary. As required by the Safe Drinking Water Act, a standard of 10 ppb protects public health based on the best available science and ensures that the cost of the standard is achievable."

Nearly 97 percent of the water systems affected by this rule are small systems that serve less than 10,000 people each. EPA plans to provide $20 million over the next two years for the research and development of more cost-effective technologies. The Agency also will provide technical assistance and training to operators of small systems, which will reduce their compliance costs, Whitman told conferees.

EPA will work with small communities to maximize grants and loans under current State Revolving Fund and Rural Utilities Service programs of the Department of Agriculture. Last year EPA provided more than $600 million in grants and loans to water systems for drinking water compliance. "Our goal is to provide clean, safe, and affordable drinking water to all Americans," said Whitman.

SURGEON GENERAL ON
WOMEN AND SMOKING
March 27, 2001

The multifaceted campaign to reduce smoking both at home and abroad continued on several fronts in 2001. In the United States, Surgeon General David Satcher focused on smoking as a women's health issue. Reporting that smoking-related disease among women had become a "full-blown epidemic," he said that women should be "outraged" by tobacco company marketing campaigns that glamorized smoking.

Internationally, the European Union (EU) Parliament approved tough new health warning and disclosure labels on cigarette packs sold in its fifteen member nations. About one of every three Europeans was a regular smoker. Negotiations on an international treaty to control tobacco products worldwide continued, but some of the thorniest issues, such as a ban on cigarette advertising, were still unresolved at year's end. The World Health Organization (WHO), which was sponsoring the treaty, had estimated that, if current smoking trends continued, by 2030 as many as 10 million people a year would die from smoking-related illness.

Despite Satcher's calls for greater efforts to reduce the incidence of smoking, there were indications that the administration of George W. Bush was backing away from the tough antismoking campaign launched by the Clinton administration. In May Attorney General John Ashcroft announced that the Justice Department would try to settle its racketeering lawsuit against the tobacco companies. After settlement talks broke down during the summer, Ashcroft said the department would pursue its lawsuit. Antismoking advocates also accused the Bush administration of pushing positions more acceptable to the tobacco companies during the WHO treaty talks than the Clinton administration had.

The tobacco industry had been on the defensive in the United States since the early 1990s, when the disclosure of previously secret documents revealed that cigarette makers had long known about the health hazards of smoking, including the addictive properties of nicotine, despite their denials that tobacco products were directly linked to a host of serious diseases. Those revelations sparked two broad lines of attack on the tobacco industry, one aimed at forcing the tobacco companies to pay for smoking-related health care costs borne by public programs such as Medicaid and Medicare, and the other aimed at reducing the market for cigarette sales by curbing the advertising of tobacco products, particularly to teenagers.

In 1998 the big four tobacco companies agreed to pay the states $246 billion over twenty-five years in settlement of their lawsuits seeking to recoup the billions of dollars they had spent under Medicaid to treat sick smokers. But an effort by the Food and Drug Administration (FDA) to regulate cigarettes as an addictive drug and impose strict limits on advertising directed toward teens foundered in 2000, when the Supreme Court ruled that the agency could not regulate tobacco products unless it received authority to do so from Congress. (State tobacco settlement, Historic Documents of 1998, p. 842; Supreme Court on FDA regulation, Historic Documents of 2000, p. 556)

Meanwhile, WHO grew increasingly concerned by statistics estimating that more people throughout the world were dying of smoking-related diseases than of AIDS and tuberculosis combined and by evidence that tobacco companies were hoping to extend their markets for tobacco products into developing countries. In 1999 the health organization launched a drive for a treaty that would place worldwide regulations on tobacco products. The first round of negotiations took place in Geneva in October 2000. Two more took placed in May and November 2001. (Antismoking treaty, Historic Documents of 2000, p. 536)

Women and Smoking

Surgeon General Satcher opened his latest campaign in the war against smoking on March 27, releasing a report aimed at reducing smoking among women and girls. According to Satcher, women accounted for 39 percent of all smoking-related deaths in the United States in 2000—more than double the proportion in 1965. Although the percentage of women who smoked had declined somewhat from earlier peaks, it had remained fairly constant for several years at about 22 percent, while the percentage of teenage girls who started smoking rose steeply during the 1990s. "What starts out as a simple puff is turning into a death sentence," said Health and Human Services Secretary Tommy G. Thompson, who joined Satcher in releasing the first surgeon general's report on women and smoking to be issued since 1980.

Satcher said female smokers were at risk not only for the same diseases as male smokers, such as cancer, heart disease, stroke, and emphysema, but also for illnesses men did not share, including complications during pregnancy. The surgeon general's report did not offer new data but rather gathered together what had been learned in hundreds of studies about the health effects on women of smoking. Among the devastating facts:

- *Three million woman had died prematurely from smoking-related diseases since the last surgeon general's report on women and smoking was issued in 1980.*
- *Many more women died each year from lung cancer, about 90 percent of which is linked to smoking, than from breast cancer, which women*

often said was the disease they dreaded most. In 2000 approximately 68,000 women died of lung cancer; about 41,000 died from breast cancer. In 2000 lung cancer accounted for an estimated 25 percent of all cancer deaths among women. In 1950 it accounted for only 3 percent of cancer deaths.

- *Smoking contributed to infertility and to health complications during pregnancy. The risk of premature birth, low-birth-weight infants, stillbirth, and infant mortality was higher among women who smoked during pregnancy than among women who did not.*
- *Postmenopausal women who smoked had lower bone density than women who never smoked, and they were at greater risk of hip fractures.*
- *Exposure to secondary, or environmental, tobacco smoke was a cause of lung cancer and coronary heart disease among female nonsmokers.*
- *The link between smoking and depression was particularly important for women, the report said, because women were more likely than men to be diagnosed with depression.*

The good news, according to Satcher, was that women who stopped smoking greatly reduced their risk of premature death. The relative benefits were higher for women who quit at a younger age, the report said, "but smoking cessation is beneficial at all ages."

The report said that more research needed to be conducted to determine why smoking among women was not going down—and why smoking among young girls had gone up in the 1990s. But it said unequivocally that one reason was the extensive marketing campaigns the tobacco companies targeted specifically at women. "Tobacco advertisements suggest that women who smoke are liberated, sexually attractive, athletic, fun loving, and slim, whereas in reality women who smoke are often nicotine dependent, physically unhealthy, socioeconomically disadvantaged, or depressed," Satcher wrote in the report's preface. The report also said women should be "outraged" by the tobacco companies' attempts to silence their potential critics by supporting women's causes, such as curbing domestic violence.

The report also chastised women's magazines, the broadcasting media, and sponsors of sports, fashion, artistic, political, and other events that were dependent on tobacco advertising revenue. That dependence tended to stifle media coverage of the damaging health effects of smoking and "mute criticism" of the tobacco industry by female celebrities. The report called on women's and girl's organizations, women's magazines, female celebrities, and others to unite in a campaign to speak out against the tobacco companies and to raise awareness of the specific health risks of smoking to women.

The report urged the states to set up comprehensive stateside tobacco control efforts with the funds they received in their 1998 settlement with the tobacco companies. According to the Campaign for Tobacco-Free Kids, only six states were meeting the minimum standards recommended by the Centers for Disease Control and Prevention. The states that had adopted comprehensive tobacco control efforts were beginning to show dramatic reductions in smoking. For example, the report said, in California the rate of lung cancer among women had declined by 4.8 percent between 1988 and 1997, while increasing by 13.2 percent in other regions of the country. California had begun a statewide tobacco control effort in 1989, long before the tobacco settlement.

Two months later, on May 29, the World Health Organization released a report issuing similar warnings about the ill effects of smoking on women worldwide. Although about four times as many men as women smoked worldwide, the WHO said, rising incomes and weakening social and cultural constraints were contributing to a disturbing increase in smoking. Those trends, the report said, were being exploited by the tobacco industry, whose marketing campaigns "cleverly link the emancipation of women with smoking." Tobacco advertising depicted smoking as a way of "attaining maturity, gaining confidence, being sexually attractive and in control of one's destiny—effectively exploiting the struggle of women everywhere for equality and women's right."

Federal Lawsuit

Antismoking advocates raised questions about the Bush administration's commitment to efforts to reduce smoking after Attorney General Ashcroft announced in May that the Justice Department would attempt to settle the government's civil lawsuit charging the tobacco industry with violating federal laws against racketeering. The law suit, filed in 1999, charged the tobacco companies with conspiracy to commit fraud and sought the recovery of Medicare and other federal funds that had been spent on smoking-related health care costs for the elderly, veterans, and federal employees. In 2000 a federal district judge dismissed the government's claim for recovery but allowed the Justice Department to pursue the racketeering charges.

Some Republican legislators, including Ashcroft when he was in the Senate, had opposed the lawsuit from the beginning, trying unsuccessfully in 2000 to kill funding for it. During his election campaign, President Bush said he had reservations about the suit. After he was appointed attorney general, Ashcroft initiated a review of the case, and in June he told legislators that the department would try to settle the case with the tobacco companies. Saying that he was concerned that court rulings expected later in the year would weaken the government's case, Ashcroft reportedly said the department was then in a better position to negotiate a settlement than it might be later.

Antismoking advocates immediately criticized Ashcroft for undermining the government's case. "This looks like a plan to just cut and run," Senator Patrick J. Leahy, D-Vt., told the Washington Post. "They are throwing in the towel without breaking a sweat."

After settlement talks fell apart during the summer, Ashcroft issued a memo to all relevant cabinet departments, asking them to cooperate fully with the Justice Department in preparing for trial, which was scheduled for July 2003. The memo was construed as a positive development by Senator Richard J. Durbin, D-Ill., who had criticized the decision to seek a settlement. "This [memo] is the first thing from the attorney general in writing *pledging his commitment to the lawsuit," Durbin said. "I hope this will mean a more aggressive strategy in the future."*

International Developments

On May 15 the European Parliament approved new labeling rules for cigarettes in the fifteen member countries of the EU. The rules required that all cigarette packs sold or produced in the EU after September 2002 carry blunt warnings, such as "smoking kills" and "smoking seriously harms you and others around you." In addition, the rules authorized member countries to require that the packages display graphic color photographs depicting the adverse health effects of smoking, such as scarred lungs and rotted teeth. Cigarette companies would no longer be able to label their products as "mild" or "low-tar"—a practice that implied that the cigarettes were less harmful to one's health. Companies were also required to disclose all ingredients in cigarettes and to cut dramatically the levels of tar and nicotine in their cigarettes.

"These are badly needed, state-of-the-art rules based on solid science," said David Byrne, the EU's health commissioner, whose immediate goal was to cut the proportion of smokers in Europe from one-third of the population to one-fifth. The tobacco industry opposed the law, complaining that lower levels of tar would decimate exports of European cigarettes to Asia, Australia, and Africa, where smokers preferred stronger cigarettes, and would cost as many as 8,000 jobs. The industry also objected to the graphic photos on warning labels. "This kind of graphic description should not have a role in a sophisticated society," a spokesman for one European cigarette maker said. "It's a rather tasteless, worthless exercise."

During two rounds of talks, in May and November, on a draft treaty to control tobacco products worldwide, representatives from 191 countries were unable to come to agreement on a WHO proposal to ban advertising of tobacco products. The WHO insisted that any treaty contain such a ban, a position that was supported by the EU but opposed by the United States. U.S. representatives to the treaty talks under both Clinton and Bush said that an across-the-board advertising ban would violate free speech protections guaranteed under the U.S. Constitution.

Antismoking advocates charged, however, that the Bush administration was changing the stance taken by the U.S. delegation during the Clinton administration on several other key issues, including trying to water down restrictions on advertising aimed at teenagers. In a letter to Bush dated August 2, Rep. Henry A. Waxman, D-Calif., accused the Bush administration of engineering "a breath-taking reversal in U.S. policy—going from global leader on tobacco control to pulling back and advocating the tobacco's industry's position."

Following is the text of the executive summary of "Women and Smoking: A Report of the Surgeon General—2001," released March 27, 2001, at a news conference by Tommy G. Thompson, secretary of health and human services, and David Satcher, sur-geon general of the United States.

The document was obtained from the Internet at http://www.cdc.gov/tobacco/sgr_forwomen.htm.

This is the second report of the U.S. Surgeon General devoted to women and smoking. The first was published in 1980, 16 years after the initial land-mark report on smoking and health of the Advisory Committee to the Surgeon General appeared in 1964. The 1964 report summarized the accumulated evidence that demonstrated that smoking was a cause of human cancer and other diseases. Most of the early evidence was based on men. . . . By the time of the 1980 report, the evidence clearly showed that women were also experiencing devastating health consequences from smoking and that "the first signs of an epidemic of smoking-related disease among women are now appearing." . . . In the two decades since, numerous studies have expanded the breadth and depth of what is known about the health consequences of smoking among women, about historical and contemporary patterns of smoking in demographic subgroups of the female population, about factors that affect initiation and maintenance of smoking among women (including advertising and marketing of tobacco products), and about interventions to assist women to quit smoking. The present report reviews the now massive body of evidence on women and smoking—evidence that taken together compels the Nation to make reducing and preventing smoking one of the highest contemporary priorities for women's health.

A report focused on women is greatly needed. . . . Since 1980, hundreds of additional studies have expanded what is known about the health effects of smoking among women, and this report summarizes that knowledge. Today the Nation is in the midst of a full-blown epidemic. Lung cancer, once rare among women, has surpassed breast cancer as the leading cause of female cancer death in the United States, now accounting for 25 percent of all cancer deaths among women. Surveys have indicated that many women do not know this fact. And lung cancer is only one of myriad serious disease risks faced by women who smoke. Although women and men who smoke share excess risks for diseases such as cancer, heart disease, and emphysema, women also experience unique smoking-related disease risks related to pregnancy, oral contraceptive use, menstrual function, and cervical cancer. These risks deserve to be highlighted and broadly recognized. Moreover, much of what is known about the health effects of exposure to environmental tobacco smoke among nonsmokers comes from studies of women, because historically men were more likely than women to smoke and because many women who did not smoke were married to smokers.

In 1965, 51.9 percent of men were smokers, whereas 33.9 percent of women were smokers. By 1979, the percentage of women who smoked had declined somewhat, to 29.9 percent. However, the decline in smoking among men to 37.5 percent was much more dramatic. The gender gap in adult smoking prevalence continued to close after the 1980 report, but since the mid-1980s, the difference has been fairly stable at about 5 percentage points. In 1998, smoking prevalence was 22.0 percent among women and 26.4 percent among men. The gender difference in smoking prevalence among teens is smaller than that among adults. Smoking prevalence increased among both girls and boys in the 1990s. In 2000, 29.7 percent of high school senior girls and 32.8 percent of high school senior boys reported having smoked within the past 30 days.

In recent years, some research has suggested that the impact of a given amount of smoking on lung cancer risk might be even greater among women than among men, that exposure to environmental tobacco smoke might be associated with increased risk for breast cancer, and that women might be more susceptible than men to weight gain following smoking cessation. Other research indicated that persons with specific genetic polymorphisms may be especially susceptible to the effects of smoking and exposure to environmental tobacco smoke. These issues remain active areas of investigation, and no conclusions can be drawn about them at this time. Nonetheless, knowledge of the vast spectrum of smoking-related health effects continues to grow, as does knowledge that examination of gender-specific effects is important.

Smoking is one of the most studied of human behaviors and thousands of studies have documented its health consequences, yet certain questions and data needs exist with respect to women and smoking. For example, there is a need to better understand why smoking prevalence increased among teenage girls and young women in the 1990s despite the overwhelming data on adverse health effects; to identify interventions and policies that will prevent an epidemic of tobacco use among women whose smoking prevalence is currently low, including women in certain sociocultural groups within the United States and women in many developing countries throughout the world; to study the relationship of active smoking to diseases among women for which the evidence to date has been suggestive or inconsistent (e.g., risks for menstrual cycle irregularities, gallbladder disease, and systemic lupus erythematosus); to increase the data on the health effects of exposure to environmental tobacco smoke on diseases unique among women; to provide additional research on whether gender differences exist in susceptibility to nicotine addiction or in the magnitude of the effects of smoking on specific disease outcomes; and to determine whether gender differences exist in the modifying effects of genetic polymorphisms on disease risks associated with smoking. Many studies of smoking behavior and of the health consequences of smoking have included both females and males but have not reported results by gender. Investigators should be encouraged to report gender-specific results in the future. . . .

Major Conclusions

1. Despite all that is known of the devastating health consequences of smoking, 22.0 percent of women smoked cigarettes in 1998. Cigarette smoking became prevalent among men before women, and smoking

prevalence in the United States has always been lower among women than among men. However, the once-wide gender gap in smoking prevalence narrowed until the mid-1980s and has since remained fairly constant. Smoking prevalence today is nearly three times higher among women who have only 9 to 11 years of education (32.9 percent) than among women with 16 or more years of education (11.2 percent).

2. In 2000, 29.7 percent of high school senior girls reported having smoked within the past 30 days. Smoking prevalence among white girls declined from the mid-1970s to the early 1980s, followed by a decade of little change. Smoking prevalence then increased markedly in the early 1990s, and declined somewhat in the late 1990s. The increase dampened much of the earlier progress. Among black girls, smoking prevalence declined substantially from the mid-1970s to the early 1990s, followed by some increases until the mid-1990s. Data on long-term trends in smoking prevalence among high school seniors of other racial or ethnic groups are not available.

3. Since 1980, approximately 3 million U.S. women have died prematurely from smoking-related neoplastic, cardiovascular, respiratory, and pediatric diseases, as well as cigarette-caused burns. Each year during the 1990s, U.S. women lost an estimated 2.1 million years of life due to these smoking attributable premature deaths. Additionally, women who smoke experience gender-specific health consequences, including increased risk of various adverse reproductive outcomes.

4. Lung cancer is now the leading cause of cancer death among U.S. women; it surpassed breast cancer in 1987. About 90 percent of all lung cancer deaths among women who continue to smoke are attributable to smoking.

5. Exposure to environmental tobacco smoke is a cause of lung cancer and coronary heart disease among women who are lifetime nonsmokers. Infants born to women exposed to environmental tobacco smoke during pregnancy have a small decrement in birth weight and a slightly increased risk of intrauterine growth retardation compared to infants of nonexposed women.

6. Women who stop smoking greatly reduce their risk of dying prematurely, and quitting smoking is beneficial at all ages. Although some clinical intervention studies suggest that women may have more difficulty quitting smoking than men, national survey data show that women are quitting at rates similar to or even higher than those for men. Prevention and cessation interventions are generally of similar effectiveness for women and men and, to date, few gender differences in factors related to smoking initiation and successful quitting have been identified.

7. Smoking during pregnancy remains a major public health problem despite increased knowledge of the adverse health effects of smoking during pregnancy. Although the prevalence of smoking during pregnancy has declined steadily in recent years, substantial numbers of pregnant women continue to smoke, and only about one-third of women who stop smoking during pregnancy are still abstinent one year after the delivery.

8. Tobacco industry marketing is a factor influencing susceptibility to and initiation of smoking among girls, in the United States and overseas. Myriad examples of tobacco ads and promotions targeted to women indicate that such marketing is dominated by themes of social desirability and independence. These themes are conveyed through ads featuring slim, attractive, athletic models, images very much at odds with the serious health consequences experienced by so many women who smoke.

Chapter Conclusions

Conclusions from Chapters 2–5 are presented below. Separate conclusions are not included for Chapter 1 because it is a summary of the report. Chapter 6, which presents a vision for the future, is reproduced in its entirety following the conclusions for Chapters 2–5.

Chapter 2. Patterns of Tobacco Use Among Women and Girls

1. Cigarette smoking became prevalent among women after it did among men, and smoking prevalence has always been lower among women than among men. The gender-specific difference in smoking prevalence narrowed between 1965 and 1985. Since 1985, the decline in prevalence has been comparable among women and men.

2. The prevalence of current smoking among women increased from less than 6 percent in 1924 to 34 percent in 1965, then declined to 22 to 23 percent in the late 1990s. In 1997–1998, smoking prevalence was highest among American Indian or Alaska Native women (34.5 percent), intermediate among white women (23.5 percent) and black women (21.9 percent), and lowest among Hispanic women (13.8 percent) and Asian or Pacific Islander women (11.2 percent). By educational level, smoking prevalence is nearly three times higher among women with 9 to 11 years of education (30.9 percent) than among women with 16 or more years of education (10.6 percent).

3. Much of the progress in reducing smoking prevalence among girls in the 1970s and 1980s was lost with the increase in prevalence in the 1990s: current smoking among high school senior girls was the same in 2000 as in 1998. Although smoking prevalence was higher among high school senior girls than among high school senior boys in the 1970s and early 1980s, prevalence has been comparable since the mid-1980s.

4. Smoking declined substantially among black girls from the mid-1970s through the early 1990s; the decline among white girls for this same period was small. As adolescents age into young adulthood, these patterns are now being reflected in the racial and ethnic differences in smoking among young women. Data are not available on long-term trends in smoking prevalence among high school seniors of other racial and ethnic groups.

5. Smoking during pregnancy appears to have decreased from 1989 through 1998. Despite increased knowledge of the adverse health effects of smoking during pregnancy, estimates of women smoking dur-

ing pregnancy range from 12 percent based on birth certificate data to as high as 22 percent based on survey data.

6. Historically, women started to smoke at a later age than did men, but beginning with the 1960 cohort, the mean age at smoking initiation has not differed by gender.

7. Nicotine dependence is strongly associated with the number of cigarettes smoked per day. Girls and women who smoke appear to be equally dependent on nicotine when results are stratified by number of cigarettes smoked per day. Few gender-specific differences have been found in indicators of nicotine dependence among adolescents, young adults, or adults overall.

8. The percentage of persons who have ever smoked and who have quit smoking is somewhat lower among women (46.2 percent) than among men (50.1 percent). This finding is probably because men began to stop smoking earlier in the twentieth century than did women and because these data do not take into account that men are more likely than women to switch to or to continue to use other tobacco products when they stop smoking cigarettes. Since the late 1970s or early 1980s, the probability of attempting to quit smoking and to succeed has been equally high among women and men.

9. Prevalence of the use of cigars, pipes, and smokeless tobacco among women is generally low, but recent data suggest that cigar smoking among women and girls is increasing.

10. Smoking prevalence among women varies markedly across countries; the percentages range from an estimated 7 percent in developing countries to 24 percent in developed countries. Thwarting further increases in tobacco use among women is one of the greatest disease prevention opportunities in the world today.

Chapter 3. Health Consequences of Tobacco Use Among Women

Total Mortality

1. Cigarette smoking plays a major role in the mortality of U.S. women.

2. The excess risk for death from all causes among current smokers compared with persons who have never smoked increases with both the number of years of smoking and the number of cigarettes smoked per day.

3. Among women who smoke, the percentage of deaths attributable to smoking has increased over the past several decades, largely because of increases in the quantity of cigarettes smoked and the duration of smoking.

4. Cohort studies with follow-up data analyzed in the 1980s show that the annual risk for death from all causes is 80 to 90 percent greater among women who smoke cigarettes than among women who never smoked. A woman's annual risk for death more than doubles among continuing smokers compared with persons who have never smoked in every age group from 45 through 74 years.

5. In 1997, approximately 165,000 U.S. women died prematurely from a smoking-related disease. Since 1980, approximately three million U.S. women have died prematurely from a smoking-related disease.

6. U.S. females lost an estimated 2.1 million years of life each year during the 1990s as a result of smoking-related deaths due to neoplastic, cardiovascular, respiratory, and pediatric diseases, as well as from burns caused by cigarettes. For every smoking attributable death, an average of 14 years of life was lost.

7. Women who stop smoking greatly reduce their risk of dying prematurely. The relative benefits of smoking cessation are greater when women stop smoking at younger ages, but smoking cessation is beneficial at all ages.

Lung Cancer

8. Cigarette smoking is the major cause of lung cancer among women. About 90 percent of all lung cancer deaths among U.S. women smokers are attributable to smoking.

9. The risk for lung cancer increases with quantity, duration, and intensity of smoking. The risk for dying of lung cancer is 20 times higher among women who smoke two or more packs of cigarettes per day than among women who do not smoke.

10. Lung cancer mortality rates among U.S. women have increased about 600 percent since 1950. In 1987, lung cancer surpassed breast cancer to become the leading cause of cancer death among U.S. women. Overall age-adjusted incidence rates for lung cancer among women appear to have peaked in the mid-1990s.

11. In the past, men who smoked appeared to have a higher relative risk for lung cancer than did women who smoked, but recent data suggest that such differences have narrowed considerably. Earlier findings largely reflect past gender-specific differences in duration and amount of cigarette smoking.

12. Former smokers have a lower risk for lung cancer than do current smokers, and risk declines with the number of years of smoking cessation.

International Trends in Female Lung Cancer

13. International lung cancer death rates among women vary dramatically. This variation reflects historical differences in the adoption of cigarette smoking by women in different countries. In 1990, lung cancer accounted for about 10 percent of all cancer deaths among women worldwide and more than 20 percent of cancer deaths among women in some developed countries.

Female Cancers

14. The totality of the evidence does not support an association between smoking and risk for breast cancer.

15. Several studies suggest that exposure to environmental tobacco smoke is associated with an increased risk for breast cancer, but this association remains uncertain.

16. Current smoking is associated with a reduced risk for endometrial cancer, but the effect is probably limited to postmenopausal disease. The risk for this cancer among former smokers generally appears more similar to that of women who have never smoked.

17. Smoking does not appear to be associated with risk of ovarian cancer.

18. Smoking has been consistently associated with an increased risk for cervical cancer. The extent to which this association is independent of human papillomavirus infection is uncertain.

19. Smoking may be associated with an increased risk for vulvar cancer, but the extent to which the association is independent of human papillomavirus infection is uncertain.

Other Cancers

20. Smoking is a major cause of cancers of the oropharynx and bladder among women. Evidence is also strong that women who smoke have increased risks for cancers of the pancreas and kidney. For cancers of the larynx and esophagus, evidence among women is more limited but consistent with large increases in risk.

21. Women who smoke may have increased risks for liver cancer and colorectal cancer.

22. Data on smoking and cancer of the stomach among women are inconsistent.

23. Smoking may be associated with an increased risk for acute myeloid leukemia among women but does not appear to be associated with other lymphoproliferative or hematologic cancers.

24. Women who smoke may have a decreased risk for thyroid cancer.

25. Women who use smokeless tobacco have an increased risk for oral cancer.

Cardiovascular Disease

26. Smoking is a major cause of coronary heart disease among women. For women younger than 50 years, the majority of coronary heart disease is attributable to smoking. Risk increases with the number of cigarettes smoked and the duration of smoking.

27. The risk for coronary heart disease among women is substantially reduced within 1 or 2 years of smoking cessation. This immediate benefit is followed by a continuing but more gradual reduction in risk to that among non-smokers by 10 to 15 or more years after cessation.

28. Women who use oral contraceptives have a particularly elevated risk of coronary heart disease if they smoke. Currently, evidence is conflicting as to whether the effect of hormone replacement therapy on coronary heart disease risk differs between smokers and nonsmokers.

29. Women who smoke have an increased risk for ischemic stroke and sub-arachnoid hemorrhage. Evidence is inconsistent concerning the association between smoking and primary intracerebral hemorrhage.

30. In most studies that include women, the increased risk for stroke associated with smoking is reversible after smoking cessation; after 5 to 15 years of abstinence, the risk approaches that of women who have never smoked.

31. Conflicting evidence exists regarding the level of the risk for stroke among women who both smoke and use either the oral contraceptives commonly prescribed in the United States today or hormone replacement therapy.

32. Smoking is a strong predictor of the progression and severity of carotid atherosclerosis among women. Smoking cessation appears to slow the rate of progression of carotid atherosclerosis.

33. Women who are current smokers have an increased risk for peripheral vascular atherosclerosis. Smoking cessation is associated with improvements in symptoms, prognosis, and survival.

34. Women who smoke have an increased risk for death from ruptured abdominal aortic aneurysm.

Chronic Obstructive Pulmonary Disease (COPD) and Lung Function

35. Cigarette smoking is a primary cause of COPD among women, and the risk increases with the amount and duration of smoking. Approximately 90 percent of mortality from COPD among women in the United States can be attributed to cigarette smoking.

36. In utero exposure to maternal smoking is associated with reduced lung function among infants, and exposure to environmental tobacco smoke during childhood and adolescence may be associated with impaired lung function among girls.

37. Adolescent girls who smoke have reduced rates of lung growth, and adult women who smoke experience a premature decline of lung function.

38. The rate of decline in lung function is slower among women who stop smoking than among women who continue to smoke.

39. Mortality rates for COPD have increased among women over the past 20 to 30 years.

40. Although data for women are limited, former smokers appear to have a lower risk for dying from COPD than do current smokers.

Sex Hormones, Thyroid Disease, and Diabetes Mellitus

41. Women who smoke have an increased risk for estrogen-deficiency disorders and a decreased risk for estrogen-dependent disorders, but circulating levels of the major endogenous estrogens are not altered among women smokers.

42. Although consistent effects of smoking on thyroid hormone levels have not been noted, cigarette smokers may have an increased risk for Graves' ophthalmopathy, a thyroid-related disease.

43. Smoking appears to affect glucose regulation and related metabolic processes, but conflicting data exist on the relationship of smoking and the development of type 2 diabetes mellitus and gestational diabetes among women.

Menstrual Function, Menopause, and Benign Gynecologic Conditions

44. Some studies suggest that cigarette smoking may alter menstrual function by increasing the risks for dysmenorrhea (painful menstruation), secondary amenorrhea (lack of menses among women who ever had menstrual periods), and menstrual irregularity.

45. Women smokers have a younger age at natural menopause than do non-smokers and may experience more menopausal symptoms.

46. Women who smoke may have decreased risk for uterine fibroids.

Reproductive Outcomes

47. Women who smoke have increased risks for conception delay and for both primary and secondary infertility.

48. Women who smoke may have a modest increase in risks for ectopic pregnancy and spontaneous abortion.

49. Smoking during pregnancy is associated with increased risks for preterm premature rupture of membranes, abruptio placentae, and placenta previa, and with a modest increase in risk for preterm delivery.

50. Women who smoke during pregnancy have a decreased risk for preeclampsia.

51. The risk for perinatal mortality—both stillbirth and neonatal deaths—and the risk for sudden infant death syndrome (SIDS) are increased among the offspring of women who smoke during pregnancy.

52. Infants born to women who smoke during pregnancy have a lower average birth weight and are more likely to be small for gestational age than are infants born to women who do not smoke.

53. Smoking does not appear to affect the overall risk for congenital malformations.

54. Women smokers are less likely to breastfeed their infants than are women nonsmokers.

55. Women who quit smoking before or during pregnancy reduce the risk for adverse reproductive outcomes, including conception delay, infertility, preterm premature rupture of membranes, preterm delivery, and low birth weight.

Body Weight and Fat Distribution

56. Initiation of cigarette smoking does not appear to be associated with weight loss, but smoking does appear to attenuate weight gain over time.

57. The average weight of women who are current smokers is modestly lower than that of women who have never smoked or who are long-term former smokers.

58. Smoking cessation among women typically is associated with a weight gain of about 6 to 12 pounds in the year after they quit smoking.

59. Women smokers have a more masculine pattern of body fat distribution (i.e., a higher waist-to-hip ratio) than do women who have never smoked.

Bone Density and Fracture Risk

60. Postmenopausal women who currently smoke have lower bone density than do women who do not smoke.

61. Women who currently smoke have an increased risk for hip fracture compared with women who do not smoke.

62. The relationship among women between smoking and the risk for bone fracture at sites other than the hip is not clear.

Gastrointestinal Diseases

63. Some studies suggest that women who smoke have an increased risk for gallbladder disease (gallstones and cholecystitis), but the evidence is inconsistent.

64. Women who smoke have an increased risk for peptic ulcers.

65. Women who currently smoke have a decreased risk for ulcerative colitis, but former smokers have an increased risk—possibly because smoking suppresses symptoms of the disease.

66. Women who smoke appear to have an increased risk for Crohn's disease, and smokers with Crohn's disease have a worse prognosis than do nonsmokers.

Arthritis

67. Some but not all studies suggest that women who smoke may have a modestly elevated risk for rheumatoid arthritis.

68. Women who smoke have a modestly reduced risk for osteoarthritis of the knee; data regarding osteoarthritis of the hip are inconsistent.

69. The data on the risk of systemic lupus erythematosus among women who smoke are inconsistent.

Eye Disease

70. Women who smoke have an increased risk for cataract.

71. Women who smoke may have an increased risk for age related macular degeneration.

72. Studies show no consistent association between smoking and open-angle glaucoma.

Human Immunodeficiency Virus (HIV) Disease

73. Limited data suggest that women smokers may be at higher risk for HIV-1 infection than nonsmokers.

Facial Wrinkling

74. Limited but consistent data suggest that women smokers have more facial wrinkling than do nonsmokers.

Depression and Other Psychiatric Disorders

75. Smokers are more likely to be depressed than are nonsmokers, a finding that may reflect an effect of smoking on the risk for depression, the use of smoking for self-medication, or the influence of common genetic or other factors on both smoking and depression. The association of smoking and depression is particularly important among women because they are more likely to be diagnosed with depression than are men.

76. The prevalence of smoking generally has been found to be higher among patients with anxiety disorders, bulimia, attention deficit disorder, and alcoholism than among individuals without these conditions; the mechanisms underlying these associations are not yet understood.

77. The prevalence of smoking is very high among patients with schizophrenia, but the mechanisms underlying this association are not yet understood.

78. Smoking may be used by some persons who would otherwise manifest psychiatric symptoms to manage those symptoms; for such persons, cessation of smoking may lead to the emergence of depression or other dysphoric mood states.

Neurologic Diseases

79. Women who smoke have a decreased risk for Parkinson's disease.

80. Data regarding the association between smoking and Alzheimer's disease are inconsistent.

Nicotine Pharmacology and Addiction

81. Nicotine pharmacology and the behavioral processes that determine nicotine addiction appear generally similar among women and men; when standardized for the number of cigarettes smoked, the blood concentration of cotinine (the main metabolite of nicotine) is similar among women and men.

82. Women's regulation of nicotine intake may be less precise than men's. Factors other than nicotine (e.g., sensory cues) may play a greater role in determining smoking behavior among women.

Environmental Tobacco Smoke (ETS) and Lung Cancer

83. Exposure to ETS is a cause of lung cancer among women who have never smoked. ETS and Coronary Heart Disease.

84. Epidemiologic and other data support a causal relationship between ETS exposure from the spouse and coronary heart disease mortality among women nonsmokers.

ETS and Reproductive Outcomes

85. Infants born to women who are exposed to ETS during pregnancy may have a small decrement in birth weight and a slightly increased risk for intrauterine growth retardation compared with infants born to women who are not exposed; both effects are quite variable across studies.

86. Studies of ETS exposure and the risks for delay in conception, spontaneous abortion, and perinatal mortality are few, and the results are inconsistent.

Chapter 4. Factors Influencing Tobacco Use Among Women

1. Girls who initiate smoking are more likely than those who do not smoke to have parents or friends who smoke. They also tend to have weaker attachments to parents and family and stronger attachments to peers and friends. They perceive smoking prevalence to be higher than it actually is, are inclined to risk taking and rebelliousness, have a weaker commitment to school or religion, have less knowledge of the adverse consequences of smoking and the addictiveness of nicotine, believe that smoking can control weight and negative moods, and have a positive image of smokers. Although the strength of the association by gender differs across studies, most of these factors are associated with an increased risk for smoking among both girls and boys.

2. Girls appear to be more affected than boys by the desire to smoke for weight control and by the perception that smoking controls negative moods; girls may also be more influenced than boys to smoke by rebelliousness or a rejection of conventional values.

3. Women who continue to smoke and those who fail at attempts to stop smoking tend to have lower education and employment levels than do women who quit smoking. They also tend to be more addicted to cigarettes, as evidenced by the smoking of a higher number of cigarettes per day, to be cognitively less ready to stop smoking, to have less social support for stopping, and to be less confident in resisting temptations to smoke.

4. Women have been extensively targeted in tobacco marketing, and tobacco companies have produced brands specifically for women, both in the United States and overseas. Myriad examples of tobacco ads and promotions targeted to women indicated that such marketing is dominated by themes of both social desirability and independence, which are conveyed through ads featuring slim, attractive, athletic models. Between 1995 and 1998, expenditures for domestic cigarette advertising and promotion increased 37.3 percent, from $4.90 billion to $6.73 billion.

5. Tobacco industry marketing, including product design, advertising, and promotional activities, is a factor influencing susceptibility to and initiation of smoking.

6. The dependence of the media on revenues from tobacco advertising

oriented to women, coupled with tobacco company sponsorship of women's fashions and of artistic, athletic, political, and other events, has tended to stifle media coverage of the health consequences of smoking among women and to mute criticism of the tobacco industry by women public figures.

Chapter 5. Efforts to Reduce
Tobacco Use Among Women

1. Using evidence from studies that vary in design, sample characteristics, and intensity of the interventions studied, researchers to date have not found consistent gender-specific differences in the effectiveness of intervention programs for tobacco use. . . .

2. Among women, biopsychosocial factors, such as pregnancy, fear of weight gain, depression, and the need for social support, appear to be associated with smoking maintenance, cessation, or relapse.

3. A higher percentage of women stop smoking during pregnancy, both spontaneously and with assistance, than at other times in their lives. Using pregnancy-specific programs can increase smoking cessation rates, which benefits infant health and is cost effective. Only about one-third of women who stop smoking during pregnancy are still abstinent one year after the delivery.

4. Women fear weight gain during smoking cessation more than do men. However, few studies have found a relationship between weight concerns and smoking cessation for either women or men. Further, actual weight gain during cessation does not predict relapse to smoking.

5. Adolescent girls are more likely than adolescent boys to respond to smoking cessation programs that include social support from the family or their peer group.

6. Among persons who smoke heavily, women are more likely than men to report being dependent on cigarettes and to have lower expectations about stopping smoking, but it is not clear if such women are less likely to quit smoking.

7. Currently, no tobacco cessation method has proved to be any more or less successful among minority women than among white women in the same study, but research on smoking cessation among women of most racial and ethnic minorities has been scarce.

8. Women are more likely than men to affirm that they smoke less at work because of a worksite policy and are significantly more likely than men to attribute reduced amount of daily smoking to their worksite policy. Women also are more likely than men to support policies designed to prevent smoking initiation among adolescents, restrictions on youth access to tobacco products, and limits on tobacco advertising and promotion.

9. Successful interventions have been developed to prevent smoking among young people, but little systematic effort has been focused on developing and evaluating prevention interventions specifically for girls.

A Vision for the Future: What Is Needed to Reduce Smoking Among Women

This report summarizes what is known about smoking among women, including patterns and trends in smoking prevalence, factors associated with smoking initiation and maintenance, the consequences of smoking for women's health, and interventions for smoking cessation and prevention. The report also describes historical and contemporary tobacco marketing targeted to women. Evidence of the health consequences of smoking, which had emerged somewhat earlier among men because of their earlier uptake of smoking, is now overwhelming among women. Tragically, in the face of continually mounting evidence of the enormous consequences of smoking for women's health, the tobacco industry continues to heavily target women in its advertising and promotional campaigns and is now attempting to export the epidemic of smoking to women in areas of the world where the smoking prevalence among females has traditionally been low. The single overarching theme emerging from this report is that smoking is a women's issue. What is needed to curb the epidemic of smoking and smoking-related diseases among women in the United States and throughout the world?

Increase Awareness of the Impact of Smoking on Women's Health and Counter the Tobacco Industry's Targeting of Women

- *Increase awareness of the devastating impact of smoking on women's health. . . .* The media, including women's magazines and broadcast programming, can play an important role in raising women's awareness of the magnitude of the impact of smoking on their health and in prioritizing the importance of smoking relative to the myriad other health-related topics covered.
- *Expose and counter the tobacco industry's deliberate targeting of women and decry its efforts to link smoking, which is so harmful to women's health, with women's rights and progress in society.* Even in the face of amassing evidence that a large percentage of women who smoke will die early, the tobacco industry has exploited themes of liberation and success in its advertising—particularly in women's magazines—and promotions targeted to women. Through its sponsorship of women's sports, women's professional and leadership organizations, the arts, and so on, the industry has attempted to associate itself with things women most value (e.g., recent heavily advertised support from a major tobacco company for programs to curb domestic violence against women). Such associations should be decried for what they are: attempts by the tobacco industry to position itself as an ally of women's causes and thereby to silence potential critics. Women should be appropriately concerned by and speak out against tobacco marketing campaigns that coopt the language of women's empowerment, and they should recognize the irony of attempts by the tobacco industry to suggest that smoking— which leads to nicotine dependence and death among many women—is

a form of independence. Such efforts on the part of women would be unnecessary if the tobacco industry would voluntarily refrain from targeting women and associating tobacco use with women's freedom and progress.

Support Women's Anti-tobacco Advocacy Efforts and Publicize that Most Women Are Nonsmokers

- *Encourage a more vocal constituency on issues related to women and smoking.* Taking a lesson from the success of advocacy to reduce breast cancer, concerted efforts are needed to call public attention to the toll that lung cancer and other smoking-related diseases is exacting on women's health and to demand accountability on the part of the tobacco industry. Women affected by tobacco-related diseases and their families and friends can partner with women's and girls' organizations, women's magazines, female celebrities, and others—not only in an effort to raise awareness of tobacco-related disease as a women's issue, but also to call for policies and programs that deglamorize and discourage tobacco use. Some excellent but relatively small-scale efforts have already taken place in this area, but because of the magnitude of the problem, these efforts deserve much greater support.
- *Recognize that nonsmoking is by far the norm among women.* Although in recent years smoking prevalence has not declined as much as might be hoped, nearly four-fifths of U.S. women are nonsmokers. In some subgroups of the population, smoking is relatively rare (e.g., only 11.2 percent of adult women who have completed college are current smokers, and only 5.4 percent of black high school senior girls are daily smokers). Despite the positive images of women in tobacco advertisements, it is important to recognize that among adult women, those who are the most empowered, as measured by educational attainment, are the least likely to be smokers. Moreover, most women who do smoke say they would like to quit. The fact that almost all women have either rejected smoking for themselves or, if they do smoke now, wish to quit, should be promoted.

Continue to Build the Science Base on Gender-Specific Outcomes and on How to Reduce Disparities Among Women

- *Conduct further studies of the relationship between smoking and certain outcomes of importance to women's health. . . .*
- *Encourage the reporting of gender-specific results from studies of factors influencing smoking behavior, smoking prevention and cessation interventions, and the health effects of tobacco use, including use of new tobacco products. . . .*
- *Better understand how to reduce current disparities in smoking prevalence among women of different groups, as defined by socioeconomic status, race, ethnicity, and sexual orientation. . . .*

241

- *Determine why, during most of the 1990s, smoking prevalence declined so little among women and increased so markedly among teenage girls.* This lack of progress is a major concern and threatens to prolong the epidemic of smoking-related disease among women. What are the influences that have kept smoking prevalence relatively stagnant among women and have contributed to the sharp increases in prevalence among teenage girls? Tobacco control policies are known to be effective in reducing smoking, and smoking prevalence tends to decline most where these policies are strongest. However, efforts to curb tobacco use do not operate in a vacuum, and powerful pro tobacco influences (ranging from tobacco advertising to the use of tobacco in movies) have promoted the social acceptability of smoking and thereby have dampened the effects of tobacco control programs. Moreover, ongoing monitoring of tobacco industry attempts to target women in this country and abroad are necessary for a comprehensive understanding of the influences that encourage women to smoke and for designing effective countermarketing campaigns. If, for example, smoking in movies by female celebrities promotes smoking, then discouraging such practices as well as engaging well-known actresses to be spokespersons on the issue of women and smoking should be a high priority.
- *Develop a research and evaluation agenda related to women and smoking.* . . . Determining whether gender-tailored interventions increase the effectiveness of various smoking prevention and cessation methods is important, as is documenting whether any gender differences exist in the effectiveness of pharmacologic treatments for tobacco cessation. A need also exists to determine which tobacco prevention and cessation interventions are most effective for specific subgroups of girls and women, especially those at highest risk for tobacco use. . . .

Act Now: We Know More than Enough

- *Support efforts, at both individual and societal levels, to reduce smoking and exposure to environmental tobacco smoke among women.* Proven smoking cessation methods are available for individual smokers, including behavioral and pharmacologic approaches that benefit women and men alike. Tobacco use treatments are among the most cost-effective of preventive health interventions; they should be part of all women's health care programs, and health insurance plans should cover such services. Efforts to maximize smoking cessation and maintenance of smoking cessation among women before, during, and after pregnancy deserve high priority, because pregnancy is a time of high motivation to quit and occurs when women have many years of potential life left. With respect to prevention, the knowledge that girls who are more academically inclined or who are more physically active are less likely to smoke suggests that supporting positive outlets for mental and physical development will contribute to reducing the tobacco epidemic as well. Because regular cigarette smoking typically is initiated early in the teenage years, effective smoking cessation and prevention programs for adolescent girls and young women are greatly needed. Societal-level efforts to reduce tobacco use and exposure to environmental tobacco smoke include media counteradvertising, increased tobacco taxes, laws to reduce youth access to tobacco products, and bans on smoking in public places.

- *Enact comprehensive statewide tobacco control programs—because they work.* There are known strategies for reducing the burden of smoking-related diseases, but making the investment in these proven strategies remains a challenge. Results from states such as Arizona, California, Florida, Maine, Massachusetts, and Oregon have demonstrated that smoking rates among both girls and women can be dramatically reduced. California was the first state to establish a comprehensive statewide tobacco control program in 1990, and it is now starting to observe the benefits of its sustained efforts: between 1988 and 1997, the incidence rate of lung cancer among women declined by 4.8 percent in California but increased by 13.2 percent in other regions of the United States. Another recent study concluded that the California program was associated with 33,300 fewer deaths from heart disease between 1989 and 1997 among women and men combined than would have been predicted if trends like those observed in the rest of the country had continued. Enormous monetary settlement payments from state Medicaid lawsuits with the tobacco industry have provided the resources to fund major new comprehensive statewide tobacco control efforts. However, a recent report found that only six states were meeting the minimum funding recommendations from CDC's *Best Practices for Comprehensive Tobacco Control Programs.*

Stop the Epidemic of Smoking and Smoking-Related Diseases Among Women Globally

- *Do everything possible to thwart the emerging epidemic of smoking among women in developing countries.* Multinational policies that discourage spread of the epidemic of smoking and tobacco-related diseases among women in countries where smoking prevalence has traditionally been low should be strongly encouraged. Efforts to disassociate cigarette smoking from progress in achieving gender equity are particularly needed in the developing world. Because smoking prevalence among men is already high in many developing countries, even women who do not smoke themselves are already at risk because they are exposed to environmental tobacco smoke—and because they suffer the losses of male loved ones who are dying of tobacco-related diseases. It is urgent that what is already known about effective means of tobacco control at the societal level be disseminated as soon as possible throughout the world. A major measure of public health victory in the global war against smoking would be the arrest of smoking prevalence at its still generally low level among women in developing countries and a reversal of the now worrisome signs of increases in smoking among them. In November 1999, the World Health Organization sponsored an international conference on smoking among women and youth, which took place in Kobe,

Japan. The conference resulted in the Kobe Declaration, which states that, "The tobacco epidemic is an unrelenting public health disaster that spares no society. There are already over 200 million women smokers, and tobacco companies have launched aggressive campaigns to recruit women and girls worldwide. . . . It is urgent that we find comprehensive solutions to the danger of tobacco use and address the epidemic among women and girls."

- *All national governments should strongly support the World Health Organization's Framework Convention for Tobacco Control (FCTC).* The FCTC is an international legal instrument designed to curb the global spread of tobacco use through specific protocols, currently being negotiated, that cover tobacco pricing, smuggling, advertising and sponsorship, and other activities. In the words of Dr. Gro Harlem Brundtland, director-general of the WHO, "If we do not act decisively, a hundred years from now our grandchildren and their children will look back and seriously question how people claiming to be committed to public health and social justice allowed the tobacco epidemic to unfold unchecked."

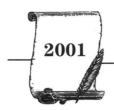

April

PRESIDENT BUSH, U.S. OFFICIALS ON SPY PLANE STANDOFF
April 2–11, 2001

The new administration of President George W. Bush successfully maneuvered through its first major foreign crisis in April—a crisis that for a brief period threatened to disrupt the always-fragile relations between the United States and China. During eleven days in early April, Washington and Beijing at first traded harsh rhetoric, then engaged in frantic diplomacy, over the fate of the crew of an American spy plane that collided with a Chinese jet fighter and crash-landed on an island just off the coast of China. China released the twenty-four crew members on April 11, 2001, after the Bush administration said it was "very sorry" about the incident. The outcome enabled leaders of both countries to save face and, more important, to avoid long-term damage to the U.S.-China relationship. Later in the year, China offered significant diplomatic support for the antiterrorism campaign the United States waged in the wake of the September 11 attacks against the World Trade Center towers in New York City and the Pentagon. (U.S.-China relations in antiterrorism, p. 738)

The spy plane incident was the most serious challenge to relations between the two countries since the inadvertent U.S. bombing of the Chinese embassy in Belgrade in 1999, during the NATO air war that forced Yugoslavia to withdraw from Kosovo. But the dispute over the spy plane was soon overshadowed by an even more serious issue involving Bush's announced determination to accelerate testing of a proposed missile defense system. Chinese officials viewed such a step as provocative because a U.S. missile defense system could undermine the strategic value of China's small arsenal of nuclear weapons. (Missile defense issues, pp. 281, 516; Belgrade embassy bombing, Historic Documents of 1999, p. 304)

Spy Plane Downed

The crisis began on April 1 when a U.S. Navy EP-3E "Aires" surveillance plane, operating in international airspace about eighty miles off the Chinese coast, was accosted by a Chinese jet fighter. According to U.S. officials, in previous months Chinese pilots had become increasingly aggressive in shadowing American surveillance planes, which had the task of monitoring radio, radar, and other electronic transmissions of the Chinese military.

Washington and Beijing gave diametrically opposing accounts of what happened in the skies over the South China Sea. U.S. officials said the Chinese jet flew next to, and then immediately under, the much larger and slower U.S. plane. Ultimately, they said, the tail of the Chinese jet hit one of the U.S. plane's four propellers; the impact caused the Chinese plane to break apart, and sections of it struck the U.S. plane, causing serious damage. Chinese spokesmen blamed the collision on the U.S. plane, which, they said, made a sudden turn toward the Chinese jet. Moreover, China insisted that the incident took place in Chinese airspace, not in international territory.

In any event, the Chinese jet, torn into pieces, crashed into the sea. The pilot of the one-man jet, Wang Wei, apparently bailed out but disappeared and was presumed dead. The American plane, severely crippled with only two engines running and many of its controls disabled, plunged about 8,000 feet before the pilot, Lt. Shane Osborne, could regain any control. Osborne headed for the nearest land, which was the large Chinese island of Hainan, just south of the Chinese mainland and east of Vietnam. The American plane repeatedly radioed a distress message to the island's Lingshui air base and then landed without receiving any response. No crew members were injured in the landing, which U.S. officials later described as a skillful maneuver by Osborne and the two other pilots on board.

As Chinese authorities surrounded the plane on the air base runway, the crew hurriedly destroyed much of the top-secret surveillance equipment and information on board. The Chinese then took the crew members into custody and carefully searched the plane. The twenty-one men and three women in the crew were moved to a military guesthouse and, according to reports, were treated well, but for two days they were not allowed to communicate with U.S. diplomatic or military officials in China.

The Letter of Two "Sorries"

The initial reactions to the incident from both Beijing and Washington were heated, leading many observers to worry about a dangerous downturn in U.S.-Chinese relations. Early on April 2 President Bush placed all the blame on China and demanded the "prompt and safe return" of both the crew and the plane, as required by international law and "standard diplomatic practice." The next day, April 3, Bush warned that the incident "has the potential of undermining our hopes for a fruitful and productive relationship" between the United States and China.

After a period of silence from Beijing, Chinese president Jiang Zemin on April 3 demanded that the United States "apologize to the Chinese and bear all responsibility." Chinese foreign minister Tang Jiaxuan told the U.S. ambassador, retired admiral Joseph W. Prueher, that Washington had "displayed an arrogant air, used lame arguments, confounded right and wrong, and made groundless accusations against China." But neither Bush nor Jiang made use of a "hot-line" system that had been installed for rapid communications between the two countries in emergency situations.

Significantly, the Bush administration did not describe the detained crew members as "hostages"—a word freighted with emotion for Americans, who in 1979 and 1980 had watched helplessly as Iranian militants held hostage fifty-two diplomats at the U.S. embassy in Tehran. Administration officials said use of that word would have complicated the delicate task of finding the right diplomatic language to end the crisis.

The two sides gradually turned to diplomacy to resolve what had become a standoff. The central issue involved what the United States would say formally to China to win release of the crew and the return of the damaged spy plane. In practical terms, the question was how close the United States would have to come to meeting China's demand for an apology, a demand Bush rejected. Over the course of a week, U.S. officials tried various wording formulations. Secretary of State Colin Powell started the bidding on April 4 with a statement of "regret" that the Chinese pilot had died, a sentiment that Bush echoed the next day. The "regret" formulation clearly did not satisfy leaders in Beijing, and so U.S. officials moved to the next level with the word "sorry." That word also failed to resolve the issue.

As the negotiations continued over wording, the Bush administration had to contend with less patient members of Congress, some of whom angrily denounced the Chinese for holding Americans "hostage" and called for strong measures against Beijing, including suspending normal trade relations between the two countries. The administration also rejected as too provocative a proposal by Admiral Dennis C. Blair, the commander of U.S. forces in the Pacific, to send the aircraft carrier Kitty Hawk *steaming close to Hainan Island as a signal of Washington's resolve. Moreover, the Pentagon quietly suspended U.S. surveillance flights near China. Progress toward a solution was eased by a Chinese decision to allow a senior U.S. military official to visit the crew members.*

After a series of attempts to find the right wording, administration officials hit upon the idea of saying the United States was "very sorry" about the incident, and that wording appeared to satisfy the Chinese. Bush approved the wording, and on April 11 Ambassador Prueher delivered a letter, which he signed, to Foreign Minister Tang. The letter said the United States was "very sorry" for the loss of the Chinese pilot and was "very sorry" that the U.S. plane entered Chinese airspace without receiving clearance. The letter also expressed the expectation that the crew members would be allowed to leave China "as soon as possible" and noted that U.S. and Chinese officials would meet on April 18 to discuss a plan for the "prompt return" of the spy plane.

The letter, which U.S. officials referred to as "the letter of two sorries," was in English only, enabling Beijing authorities to offer their own view of its content when translated into Chinese. The state-run Chinese news service, Xinhua, translated "very sorry" as shen biao qianyi, *which would mean "profound regret" or "deeply expressed regret" in English and is perceived by Chinese speakers as an apology.*

Early on April 12, local time, a Continental Airlines plane hired by the U.S. government arrived on Hainan Island and picked up the crew. They were taken first to Guam, then to the U.S. military complex at Honolulu, Hawaii, for a rousing welcome and several days of debriefings and check-ups. Crew members returned to their home base near Seattle on April 14.

With the crew members safely in U.S. hands, Bush returned to the some-what harsher language he had used in the early stages of the crisis. In a brief statement at the White House, Bush made no mention of being "sorry" about the loss of the Chinese pilot, and he insisted that the U.S. plane "did nothing to cause the accident."

Bush's handling of the spy plane crisis had popular support in the United States, according to public opinion polls, and was praised by most members of Congress and experts on U.S.-China relations. Some conservative Repub-licans, however, denounced Bush's willingness to negotiate with China and to express any sorrow for an incident they said was China's fault. The harshest criticism came in an editorial in the conservative magazine, The Weekly Standard, *by Robert Kagan, a conservative foreign policy expert, and William Kristol, who had been chief of staff for former vice president Dan Quayle. Bush had "revealed weakness" in the crisis, they said, bringing "profound national humiliation" to the United States.*

Follow-up Events

The release of the crew was followed by another series of negotiations over the status of the spy plane. U.S. technicians inspected the plane early in May and reportedly determined that it could be flown again if one or two engines were replaced. Chinese authorities vetoed a U.S. request to fly the plane out, but they did agree to allow the plane to be dismantled and shipped back to the United States. A team from Lockheed Martin, the plane's manufacturer, disassembled the plane in June, and it was shipped back to the United States in pieces early in July.

The Chinese government demanded $1 million in compensation from the United States, saying it had spent that much housing the crew and helping dismantle the spy plane. Moreover, China said it was entitled to compensa-tion for the unauthorized use of its airspace and the air base on Hainan Island. The Pentagon announced on August 9 that it would pay China $34,567—an amount officials described as a token to resolve any lingering disputes over the spy plane issue. The Chinese government angrily rejected that offer three days later, however.

During the spy plane crisis there was substantial speculation in Wash-ington about the potential effect on a decision that was pending at the time involving Taiwan's request to buy advanced naval systems from the United States. Taiwan wanted to buy destroyers equipped with the advanced Aegis combat system, submarines, and antisubmarine aircraft. The Beijing gov-ernment adamantly opposed any U.S. arms sales to Taiwan, which it con-sidered a "renegade" territory belonging to China.

Before the spy plane crisis, Bush reportedly had decided to reject Tai-wan's request for Aegis destroyers and to approve, instead, older destroyers of the Kidd class. During April administration officials reportedly consid-

ered authorizing the Aegis sale as a rebuke to China for its detention of the spy plane crew. Bush stuck with his earlier decision, however, and the administration on April 24 announced plans to sell Taiwan four Kidd destroyers, along with diesel-powered submarines and twelve P-3C Orion antisubmarine patrol planes. But Bush caused a brief flurry of excitement the following day when he said in a television interview that the United States would do "whatever it took" to help Taiwan defend itself against an attack by China. U.S. policy for decades had implied a defense of Taiwan if China attacked the island, but no president had ever made such a blunt statement of that policy.

The United States resumed reconnaissance flights near China early in May without encountering renewed challenges by Chinese aircraft. Then in early June news reports revealed that Defense Secretary Donald H. Rumsfeld had suspended routine contacts between U.S. and Chinese military officers. That move was criticized by some U.S. experts on China— including many former military officers who described the contacts as aiding U.S. understanding of Beijing's aims and military capabilities. Some conservatives supported the move, arguing that China had used the contacts to spy on the United States. Rumsfeld later allowed resumption of the U.S.-China military contacts on a case-by-case basis.

> *Following are four texts: a statement by President George W. Bush at the White House on April 2, 2001, demanding the "prompt and safe" release of twenty-four crew members of a U.S. surveillance plane being held in China; a statement by President Bush at the White House on April 3 warning that the spy plane incident could undermine U.S.-China relations; a letter dated April 11 from U.S. ambassador Joseph W. Prueher to Chinese foreign minister Tang Jiaxuan expressing U.S. sorrow over the incident; and a statement by President Bush at the White House on April 11 announcing that the American crew members would soon be released by China.*

> ***The documents were obtained from the Internet at http:// www.whitehouse.gov/news/releases/2001/04/20010402-2 .html; http://www.whitehouse.gov/news/releases/2001/04/ 20010403-3.html; http://www.whitehouse.gov/news/ releases/2001/04/20010411-1.html; http://www.whitehouse .gov/news/releases/2001/04/20010411-3.html.***

BUSH'S APRIL 2 STATEMENT

Late Saturday night in Washington, Sunday morning in China, a United States naval maritime patrol aircraft on a routine surveillance mission in international airspace over the South China Sea collided with one of two Chinese fighters that were shadowing our plane. Both our aircraft and a Chinese aircraft were damaged in the collision. Our aircraft made an emergency landing at an airfield on China's Hainan Island.

We have been in contact with the Chinese government about this incident since Saturday night. From our own information, we know that the United States naval plane landed safely. Our embassy in Beijing has been told by the Chinese government that all 24 crew members are safe.

Our priorities are the prompt and safe return of the crew, and the return of the aircraft without further damaging or tampering. The first step should be immediate access by our embassy personnel to our crew members. I am troubled by the lack of a timely Chinese response to our request for this access.

Our embassy officials are on the ground and prepared to visit the crew and aircraft as soon as the Chinese government allows them to do so. And I call on the Chinese government to grant this access promptly.

Failure of the Chinese government to react promptly to our request is inconsistent with standard diplomatic practice, and with the expressed desire of both our countries for better relations.

Finally, we have offered to provide search and rescue assistance to help the Chinese government locate its missing aircraft and pilot. Our military stands ready to help.

Thank you very much.

BUSH'S APRIL 3 STATEMENT

Good afternoon. I want to report to the American people, and especially to the families involved, that I've just talked with Brigadier General Sealock, who, earlier today, met with our 24 men and women in China.

The General tells me they are in good health, they suffered no injuries, and they have not been mistreated. I know this is a relief to their loved ones, and to all Americans.

Our crew members expressed their faith in America, and we have faith in them. They send their love to their families. They said they're looking forward to coming home, and we are looking forward to bringing them home.

This is an unusual situation, in which an American military aircraft had to make an emergency landing on Chinese soil. Our approach has been to keep this accident from becoming an international incident. We have allowed the Chinese government time to do the right thing. But now it is time for our servicemen and women to return home. And it is time for the Chinese government to return our plane.

This accident has the potential of undermining our hopes for a fruitful and productive relationship between our two countries. To keep that from happening, our servicemen and women need to come home.

Thank you very much.

AMBASSADOR'S LETTER TO CHINESE MINISTER

Dear Mr. Minister:

On behalf of the United States Government, I now outline steps to resolve this issue.

Both President Bush and Secretary of State Powell have expressed their sincere regret over your missing pilot and aircraft. Please convey to the Chinese people and to the family of pilot Wang Wei that we are very sorry for their loss.

Although the full picture of what transpired is still unclear, according to our information, our severely crippled aircraft made an emergency landing after following international emergency procedures. We are very sorry the entering of China's airspace and the landing did not have verbal clearance, but very pleased the crew landed safely. We appreciate China's efforts to see to the well-being of our crew.

In view of the tragic incident and based on my discussions with your representative, we have agreed to the following actions: Both sides agree to hold a meeting to discuss the incident. My government understands and expects that our aircrew will be permitted to depart China as soon as possible.

The meeting would start April 18, 2001.

The meeting agenda would include discussion of the causes of the incident, possible recommendations whereby such collisions could be avoided in the future, development of a plan for prompt return of the EP-3 aircraft, and other related issues. We acknowledge your government's intention to raise U.S. reconnaissance missions near China in the meeting.

Sincerely,
Joseph W. Prueher

BUSH'S APRIL 11 STATEMENT

Good morning. I'm pleased to be able to tell the American people that plans are underway to bring home our 24 American servicemen and women from Hainan Island.

his morning, the Chinese government assured our American Ambassador that the crew would leave promptly. We're working on arrangements to pick them up and to bring them home.

This has been a difficult situation for both our countries. I know the American people join me in expressing sorrow for the loss of life of a Chinese pilot. Our prayers are with his wife and his child.

I appreciate the hard work of our Ambassador to China, Joseph Prueher, and his entire embassy team, who worked tirelessly to solve this situation. The American people, their families, and I are proud of our crew, and we look forward to welcoming them home.

Thank you.

RUSSIAN PRESIDENT PUTIN
ON STATE OF THE NATION
April 3, 2001

A decade after the collapse of the Soviet Union, the Russian Federation in 2001 may have turned the corner in its turbulent path toward economic, political, and social stability. The Russian economy enjoyed its second straight year of strong expansion, the government took important steps to establish the rule of law and to curtail endemic corruption, and President Vladimir Putin firmly sided with the West following the September 11 terrorist attacks against the United States. (Russia and NATO, p. 892)

In a state-of-the-nation address delivered to a television audience April 3, 2001, Putin told Russians that during his first year in office he had been able to halt the "disintegration" of the federal government and make progress toward establishing Russia as a modern, functioning society. But the country still faced "serious risks, both economic and social ones," he said. Putin did not mention concerns expressed by some opposition leaders and Western observers that he was attempting to revive elements of the authoritarian Soviet system of government.

An Improved Economy

The Russian economy had been on a roller-coaster ride—almost all of it downhill—ever since the collapse of the Soviet state at the end of 1991. Russian president Boris Yeltsin, who took over the reins of government from the last Soviet leader, Mikhail Gorbachev, declared an end to communism and early in 1992 embarked on a crash course of privatization. Economic output plummeted and millions of Russians were put out of work as giant state-owned factories closed or were sold at bargain-basement prices to former Communist Party functionaries and "Wild West"-style entrepreneurs who came to be known as "oligarchs." Sagging world prices for oil and natural gas—Russia's chief exports—during most of the 1990s deprived the country of any significant foreign exchange earnings. Yeltsin's attempts to keep the economy running with large infusions of aid from the United States, the International Monetary Fund (IMF), and private lenders came to a sudden halt in 1998, when he was forced to devalue the ruble and de-

fault on billions of dollars in domestic loans. Yeltsin stepped aside at the end of 1999 and handed his government over to Putin, a former secret service official who had been prime minister for only five months. Putin won presidential elections in March 2000, becoming Russia's first elected president to succeed an elected president. (Russian economic collapse, Historic Documents of 1998, p. 601; Yeltsin resignation, Historic Documents of 1999, p. 917; Putin election, Historic Documents of 2000, p. 171)

Rising world oil prices, coupled with political stability following Putin's election, produced an economic revival for Russia starting in 2000. The country's gross domestic product grew by about 8 percent that year. Oil prices fell again in the last half of 2001, when the United States and many Western countries went into a recession; even so, the Russia economy grew by about 5 percent for the year, giving the country its best two-year economic performance in at least two decades. For the first time since the collapse of communism, Putin was able to report, the government was able to pay its employees and pensioners in full and on time. In previous years, millions of Russians had gone without pay for months or even years.

Putin and his government gradually chipped away at many of the obstacles to sustained economic growth in Russia, nearly all of which were holdovers from the Soviet era. Perhaps most important, Putin pushed laws through the national legislature guaranteeing private property rights, establishing a fair tax system, allowing independent labor unions and worker protections, creating a Western-style banking system, and cracking down on bribery and corruption. These laws, and the sometimes successful efforts to enforce them, helped build confidence in the economy among Russians and foreign businesses, some of which were returning to Russia after having fled in 1998. The government was able in 2001 to make early payments on more than $2.5 billion in foreign debt, most of which was owed to the IMF.

Despite the growth in 2000 and 2001, Russia's economy remained minuscule by Western standards. With a population of about 145 million (the sixth largest in the world), Russia in 2001 had a total gross domestic product of only $300 billion, about the same as Turkey (with 66 million people) or the state of Michigan (with just under 10 million people). Russia's per capita income was $2,000, about the same as in Colombia and Thailand (the U.S. per capita income in 2001 was $37,000).

Social and health conditions in Russia also were far below Western standards. Tens of millions of Russians lived in cramped, unsafe apartments with inadequate heating, plumbing, and electricity. Alcoholism, heavy smoking, and poor diets were prevalent in Russia, leading to rates of heart and circulatory diseases about three times greater than in the United States. The AIDS epidemic hit Russia, as well as the rest of Eastern Europe, during the late 1990s; by 2001 reported cases of HIV infection were increasing at a faster rate there than anywhere else in the world. (AIDS report, p. 438)

Reviving a Strong State

During his first year in office, Putin made it clear that restoring the power and influence of the national government was a priority on a par with reviving the economy. Critics, both domestically and internationally, worried that Putin was intending to revive elements of the Soviet state under the guise of democracy.

Putin in 2001 continued three aspects of this campaign. First, he kept pressure on the governors of eighty-nine regions who had accumulated political power during the 1990s at the expense of Yeltsin's government in Moscow. Putin had appointed seven administrators to help him exercise supervisory responsibility over the governors. That attempt to recentralize control had met with mixed success by 2001, but Putin declared in his April 3 speech that it had halted the "disintegration" of the Russian state.

Putin appeared to have more success in two other campaigns to curtail the influence of the news media and the wealthy "oligarchs." His government, and agencies aligned with it, succeeded during 2000 and 2001 in gaining control over the nation's only independent television stations, both headquartered in Moscow. One station, NTV, was owned by maverick millionaire Vladimir Gusinsky, who the government forced into exile in 2000 by pressing vague corruption charges. The government-controlled Gazprom natural gas monopoly then gained control of the station. Former employees of that station then turned another Moscow-based television network, TV-6, into an independent media voice, but the Kremlin in late 2001 launched a legal assault against it in an apparent attempt to gain control. Several newspapers remained independent of the government, but their circulation was limited to the big cities.

Gusinsky was just one of the oligarchs whose operations came under government pressure once Putin took control of the Kremlin. Putin's government pressed charges against another maverick millionaire, Boris A. Berezovsky, who had supported Putin in the 2000 elections; Berezovsky, like Gusinsky, went into exile to avoid prosecution. Putin also forced from office the heads of several government-related agencies, most notably the head of the notoriously corrupt railways ministry.

Putin's elimination of competing centers of power and influence coincided with a waning of political dialogue in Russia. Communists and other opposition parties in the legislature generally gave up trying to influence government-proposed legislation in 2001, and by year's end it was unclear who, if anyone, would be able to mount a serious reelection challenge to Putin in 2005. Lilia Shevtsova, a Moscow political analyst for the Washington-based Carnegie Endowment for International Peace, told the Washington Post *in November that Putin had succeeded in creating "a political desert."*

In his April 3 speech Putin staunchly defended his approach to governing, arguing that a strong hand—which he described as "consolidated and effective state power"—was necessary to end corruption, protect citizens from violence, and create the overall conditions for economic growth. Putin called in particular for judicial and legal reform, noting that the nation's court system could not guarantee prompt and fair justice and that the legislature had adopted too many laws that duplicated or contradicted one another. Other laws, he said, failed to achieve their stated ends because "they were adopted under the pressure of narrow groups or departmental [government] pressures."

War in Chechnya

Shortly after taking over as prime minister under Yeltsin in 1999, Putin sent the Russian army into the southern republic of Chechnya to suppress what he called "terrorism" against the government. Putin said Islamic guerrillas, who were fighting for the independence of Chechnya, were responsible for a series of bombings in Russia that killed several hundred people. The army destroyed the Chechen capital, Grozny, and by early 2000 succeeded in driving the guerrillas into the mountains, from which they staged hit-and-run attacks. International human rights groups and Western governments, including the United States, sharply criticized the army for serious human rights abuses during the war; Putin rejected these complaints and insisted that Moscow was simply trying to stamp out terrorism.

In his April 3 speech Putin said the army was withdrawing from Chechnya, but he acknowledged that the government would not be justified in "feeling euphoric from success." Terrorism remained a problem in Chechnya, he said, and rebuilding the province would be an expensive and time-consuming project. Despite Putin's statement, thousands of Russian troops remained in Chechnya at year's end.

Putin's endorsement of Washington's antiterrorism stance in the wake of the September 11 attacks in the United States bought him some relief from Western criticism of Russian actions in Chechnya. U.S. officials said late in 2001 that they now had a "better understanding" of the challenges Russia faced in Chechnya.

> *Following are excerpts from a speech delivered by Russian president Vladimir Putin on April 3, 2001, to the members of the State Duma and the Federation Council, the lower and upper chambers, respectively, of the national legislature. The speech was televised nationally. The translation from Russian to English was prepared by the Russian Ministry of Foreign Affairs.*
>
> ***The document was obtained from the Internet at http:// www.ln.mid.ru/website/bl.nsf/8bc3c105f5d1c44843256a14 004cad37/87213f1dd23eb1bd43256a25003d7908?Open Document.***

Esteemed deputies of the State Duma,
Esteemed members of the Federation Council,
Esteemed citizens of Russia,

As I present the Address for the year 2001 I would like first to say a few words about the past year.

The strategic task of the previous year was to strengthen the state. The state in the person of all institutes and all levels of government. It was obvious that without the solution of this key task we could not achieve successes either in the economy or in the social sphere. We set ourselves the aim to put in place a precisely functioning vertical of government, to achieve juridical discipline and an effective judiciary. And we should not retreat from this aim. It is precisely here that the mechanism of implementing state decisions is located, of effectively protecting the rights of our citizens.

A really strong state also means a strong federation. Today it can already be said that the period of the disintegration of statehood is already behind us. The disintegration of the state, that was mentioned in the previous Address, has been stopped.

We have done much last year to accomplish this, all of us. We drafted and adopted the federal package, the package of federal laws, reformed the Federation Council. The work of the plenipotentiary representatives in the federal districts has already produced the first results. The State Council has been formed and is actively working. Russia, at long last, has state symbols that are approved by law.

All this was achieved against the background of a favorable economic situation. In 2000 the Russian economy demonstrated growth rates that it had not known for almost 30 years. Growth remains in some sectors of industry. Investment activity has intensified. Tax payments have grown. People at long last are being paid their wages and pensions on time. For the first time after many years.

But these successes definitely cannot be qualified as sufficient. They can hardly satisfy us because the living standards of citizens remain extremely low. Russian entrepreneurs are still cautiously investing money in the economy of their own country, while officials, unfortunately, are continuing to stifle business, to restrain business initiative and activity.

We still have serious risks, both economic and social ones. This is evidenced by the Russian cities which found themselves without heat and electricity this winter, by numerous breakdowns in the worn-down utility services. This is evidenced by the big technical catastrophes that continued to hound us throughout the past year. In recent months we are worried by the worsening of a number of key economic indices. Especially against the background of the unstable development of the world economy.

So far we are only in a period of a relative economic stability. And it depends only on us if we are going to sustain the situation and ensure favorable conditions for our own development, for the growth of our people's prosperity, or if we are going to miss this unique chance. And this means that the necessary decisions will have to be taken after all, but already in different conditions, in conditions that will not be favorable ones for the country.

The situation compels us to return again to an analysis of the situation in the country and the tasks confronting us, including those that I spoke about in this very hall last summer. . . .

[Putin spoke next about the steps he had taken to exercise control from the Kremlin over Russia's eighty-nine regions, including the appointment of seven officials to supervise the regions, the redistribution of tax revenues among the regions, and Kremlin control over regional budgets.]

I will speak separately about the situation in the Chechen Republic. Today I call on representatives of all political forces, they are here in this room, all political forces in the country to show responsibility in settling the situation in the republic. We have been able to do it so far. We have been able not to speculate on blood and tragedy, not to gain political mileage and scores on this.

Only recently we heard that the army was falling into decay and that we should not expect any noticeable results in the military field, and that we allegedly could not expect anything positive in the political field because we would not be able to find even one Chechen who would support the federal center's efforts to fight terrorists and restore constitutional order.

But life itself has shown that both of these statements are wrong.

Having fulfilled their main tasks, the army is leaving the republic. This is a serious result. However, we paid a high price to achieve it. This is why I think we can break the tradition of annual messages today and remember, which will be quite appropriate, our servicemen, Dagestani [Dagestan is a region adjacent to Chechnya] militiamen, Chechen policemen, all those who have given their lives to stop the disintegration of the state.

The national television channels are broadcasting this meeting live to the entire country, and I am asking not only the people in this room but all those who are seeing and hearing us now to rise and observe a minute of silence in memory of our heroes.

(A minute of silence.)

Thank you.

I also want to point out that we have no right to speak of either marking time in Chechnya or feeling euphoric from success. We cannot generate unjustified optimism and give promises that cannot be kept or encourage expectations that we will not be able to live up to.

Yes, our tasks in the North Caucasus [the region including Chechnya] are changing now. In addition to the need to finish the destruction of sources of terrorism, the emphasis should be shifted toward the creation and strengthening of government bodies in the republic.

We must start ensuring citizens' rights, the social rehabilitation of the population and solving economic problems in Chechnya in a serious and responsible manner.

This will require professionalism and courage from all of us in order to both prevent acts of terrorism and to overcome the consequences of the crimes we failed to prevent. The threat of new crimes is still tremendous.

I must say this today.

But we will need as much persistence, patience and courage in the social and economic sphere. We will also need time, at least no less than the time during which the republic was brought to its current extreme condition.

We must understand this clearly. . . .

[Putin returned to the subject of the federal government's relations with the regions, explaining why regional laws and regulations needed to be in compliance with those of the nation.]

A key question of any government is people's confidence in the state. The degree of this confidence is directly determined by how the state protects its citizens from the lawlessness of racketeers, bandits and bribe-takers. Legislative and executive bodies, courts and law enforcement agencies have not done enough in this field. As a result, the rights and interests of citizens are violated, the authority of government as a whole is undermined. This is why this is a political problem.

We need judicial reform badly now. The Russian judicial system lags behind life and helps little in carrying out economic reforms. Neither for businessmen nor for many people who are trying to restore their rights in a lawful way, our judiciary has become prompt, just and fair. Not always, but unfortunately sometimes it is true. Our arbitration practice also has a controversial and unclear legislative basis. Departmental norm-setting is one of the main brakes in the development of entrepreneurship.

Government officials are used to acting according to instructions that often clash with laws that follow them. And yet, they are not canceled for years. This has been noted already hundreds of times but in practice there is no progress at all.

The government, the ministries and agencies should at long last take radical measures in respect of departmental law-making, up to and including the total abolition of the corps of departmental acts in those cases when direct action federal laws have already been adopted.

Today our legal framework . . . on the one hand, is excessive, on the other hand, is incomplete. Too many laws, in fact, have been adopted. Many of them duplicate one another. But in a whole number of instances they do not fulfill the set task because they were adopted under the pressure of narrow group or departmental interests.

In addition to this, it has been noted many times that any law must be backed organizationally and materially. But in practice we have a totally different picture. The Federal Assembly, unfortunately, continues to adopt laws the fulfillment of which requires a revision of the federal budget and the Pension Fund budget that were approved by the Federal Assembly itself. I regard such decisions, even if motivated by the best of intentions, as politically irresponsible ones. We ought to have systematized our legislation a long time ago. This will allow us not only to take into consideration new economic realities but also to preserve our traditional sectors that have been dangerously eroded in recent years. . . .

[Putin next described how judges had been making arbitrary decisions based on their own "norms" rather than the law, creating what he called a "shadow judiciary."]

The situation is no better with procedural legislation, both civil and criminal law procedure. A lot of complaints are coming in over unjustified coercion and arbitrary acts in launching criminal cases, in the course of investigation and litigation. Preliminary investigation drags on for years. More than a million people are kept in places of deprivation of freedom and pretrial detention centers. Ponder this figure. And a substantial part of these people are isolated from society under articles of the Criminal Code which envisage other forms of punishment than custodial punishment. And moreover, the state is unable to provide these people with normal conditions and subsequent social rehabilitation.

The result is the breakup of families, deteriorating health of the population and the moral climate in society. The problem has ceased to be a legal one and has emerged as a civil problem. Obviously, such application of law provides a lot of room for abuses in the sphere of ensuring the rights and freedoms of citizens. It creates a spawning ground for corruption among civil servants. And the roots of these problems lie both in ineffective law enforcement instruments and in the structure of our legislation.

Therefore, several tasks have to be addressed within a short period of time. They include issues connected with the status of judges and the procedure of their appointment. I think that the qualification colleges should include not only judges but also other authoritative members of the legal community.

Besides, the legal and civil processes should consistently implement the constitutional principles of adversarial and equal contest of the sides.

Much improvement is needed in the legislation that regulates the fulfillment of court rulings. At present by no means all the court rulings are fulfilled in practice.

It is high time we should put municipal legislation in order. It comes closest to the daily life of citizens and it is very inferior in quality, overloaded and often illogical. I think practicians and experts of local self-government, the public councils of cities and municipal entities should be brought into this because they have extensive theoretical and practical experience. We have enough such people.

And finally, I consider it to be an important task of the state to improve the work of the law-enforcement bodies, including the Prosecutor's Office.

Esteemed members of the State Duma and the Federation Council,

The previous Address pointed to the danger of increasing economic lag. That danger persists and lies in wait for us today.

Yes, from the results of the year 2000 we have impressive economic growth as I indicated in the beginning. Some increase of labor productivity, lower production costs. But a high rate of growth only over a period of one year is not enough. Indeed, at the end of last year growth slowed down. The conditions that ensure sustained growth, unfortunately, have not been created.

The country still has an unfavorable business climate. The flight of capital [overseas] exceeds 20 billion dollars a year. The total capitalization of the Russian stock market is about 50 billion dollars. Whereas the value of the major companies in Finland, our closest neighbor, is five times greater. Just compare the size of the two countries. Major Russian companies, the so-called blue chips cost many times less than similar foreign companies.

Obviously unless we start acting today, including on the issue of structural reform, tomorrow we may enter a prolonged period of economic stagnation.

We still live in an economy that depends on rent and not production. Our economic system has changed but little in essence. Most of the money is made by oil, gas and metals and other raw materials. The additional export revenue is either spent on current tasks or flow out of the country or at best is invested in the same extractive industries. Last year more than 60 percent of the total investments in industry went into the fuel and energy sector.

It happened, among other things, because export revenues could not be effectively used in other Russian industries. The transfer of capital is deterred by high risks of breach of contract, the underdeveloped financial market infrastructure, limited incentives and lack of confidence. As a result, the structure of economy is not being modernized and the tilt of our economy towards the extraction of raw materials is even increasing. This means our growing dependence on the market factors in the short term.

Another well-tried method of making money that still remains popular has been popular in Russia for ages. It is the assets of the state be it state property or the state budget. In other words, profits derived from distribution and in the process of distribution and redistribution of wealth are greater than the profits generated by the creation of wealth.

This explains the long-running battle over the reform of monopolies. It is not accidental that the government and the Federal Assembly only manifest enthusiasm when budgetary revenue is divided up and enthusiasm wanes when it comes to making decisions that contribute to the generation of revenue.

A kind of consensus has emerged. Many people are comfortable with the present point of equilibrium, or rather inaction, when some have got used to deriving financial incomes and others get political dividends out of this situation. That consensus is confused by many with stability. But nobody needs such stability. This is a way of perpetuating the flawed tradition based on waste of national resources. It is a way to economic and social stagnation.

It can be avoided if one does not end attempts at structural transformations with the writing of concepts and programs. And the government should at long last demonstrate that this will no longer be current practice.

I am convinced that the current state of affairs has arisen not only because of resistance to reform on the part of the bureaucratic apparatus although examples of this are many. But it has to do with the system of the work of the legislative and executive bodies. At present it is so organized as to impede and in many cases stop all transformations. The system is defending its rights to the so-called status rent. To put it in a more direct way, the right to bribes and kickbacks. This mode of existence of power poses a threat to society and the state. . . .

[Putin spoke next of his plans for administrative reform of the government, including what he called "de-bureaucratization and minimization" of state "interference" in private enterprise, and reforms in the government's budget process.]

Russia's integration in the world economy requires of us a civilized approach to the solution of the debt problem. We should draw lessons for the future from the present situation, we should borrow only then when we know exactly how to spend this money effectively and how to return it. We should not pass on the debt burden to our children and grandchildren. That is why the government should be very careful when taking decisions on new borrowing.

In this connection I would like to say a few words about the decision of the government not to sign an agreement with the International Monetary Fund. On clearing on the whole the program of budgetary, monetary, credit and structural policy the government undertook to fulfill it without concluding a formal agreement with the IMF. I think the government is capable of controlling what it is doing, however it will have to prove it. Without any control by international financial organizations but within the framework of the program that has been prepared.

Now about the business climate in the country. Unfortunately, ownership rights are still not protected properly. The quality of corporate management remains low. The property war continues even after court rulings. And these rulings are often based not on laws but on the pressure exerted by interested sides.

We must protect the rights of scrupulous buyers of both immovable property and securities, any property. We are talking, of course, not only and not so much of the property of major corporations. We must guarantee the rights of all people, including small-scale owners, major owners, domestic investors and foreign investors. I think the government and the Federal Assembly should draw up appropriate legislative acts already this year.

In addition it is necessary to step up the adoption of a new law on privatization, a law that will create clear and transparent rules for selling and buying state property and will allow us to stop political speculations about selling out Russia.

Unfortunately, these speculations continue. From time to time, we hear demands that property should be taken away, confiscated, etc., etc. We have already gone through a period when the state owned everything, absolutely everything. We all know the result.

I am convinced that the efficiency of the state is determined not so much by the amount of property it controls as by the effectiveness of political, legal and administrative mechanisms designed to ensure public interests in the country. I talked about this in the Tax Reform section. This also applies to such an important field as the defense and industrial complex. Already now private businesses meet almost half of its needs, including joint-stock companies in which the state has a share. I think the participation of non-state enterprises in defense research and production must be enhanced. Of course, this must be done in strict compliance with all existing requirements, through tenders for purchases for state needs. . . .

[Putin spoke next about the need for new legislation on private ownership of land, his opposition to state controls over the export of capital, his proposal for private medical insurance in conjunction with the existing system of state-guaranteed medical care, the need to reform the system of old-age pensions, the need for a reformed labor code, the need for education reform, and his analysis of the problems facing state-funded scientific research.]

Esteemed colleagues,

When fulfilling economic and social tasks we must take into consideration not only the domestic political situation but also the strength of our international positions. Foreign policy is both an indicator and a substantial factor of the state of affairs inside a country. Here we should have no illusions. Not only the prestige of our country in the international arena but also the political and economic situation inside Russia itself depend on the competence, skill and effectiveness with which we use our diplomatic resource.

I have said already more than once that Russia should base its foreign policy on the basis of a precise definition of national priorities, on the basis of pragmatism and economic effectiveness.

Today our country is increasingly integrating into the world economy and for this reason in the foreign policy sphere we must learn to protect the economic interests of the state as a whole, the interests of a Russian enterprise and a Russian citizen. We must really ensure, if you want, a servicing of the interests of the Russian economy. And this means resisting discrimination against Russian commodity producers, this means guaranteeing a preservation and optimum use of Russian property abroad, this means accelerating preparatory work to join the WTO [World Trade Organization]. Of course, on acceptable terms. To put it concretely, we must work for Russia's competitiveness in all the meanings of this word.

It is profitable to have a reliable reputation not only in the economy but also in politics. And that is why we must precisely fulfill our long-term obligations and accords, we must uphold the principles on which we are basing our ties with other countries. This is a balance of interests and this means mutually advantageous cooperation. Also respect and trust. Such approaches are much more productive than tough ideological dogmas. Those who subscribe to such approaches can be confident that in Russia they will always find an interested and predictable partner.

It is fundamental for us that our foreign partners take into account and respect Russia's national interests. All this fully applies to the discussion of the problem of preserving strategic stability, disarmament, the expansion of NATO, the forming of the fundamentals of world order in the 21st century.

It is not only historical closeness but also obvious practical considerations that dictate the need to step up our efforts in the CIS [Commonwealth of Independent States]. Russia remains the nucleus of integration processes in the Commonwealth. And at the time of economic growth new possibilities open up for Russia here. We will continue our painstaking work to create the union state with Byelorussia [Belarus]. . . .

We are duty-bound to inject new energy into our relations with European and other international structures while preserving and developing everything of a positive nature that has been accumulated in previous years. Dynamic processes are now taking place in Europe, the role of big European organizations, of regional forums is being transformed. In this respect the importance of further efforts to develop relations with the European Union definitely increases. The course of integration with Europe is becoming one of the key directions of our foreign policy.

We remain consistent also in our relations with NATO. These relations are regulated by the Founding Act on mutual relations, cooperation and security which was signed in 1997. We believe that the problem that we have is because this organization often ignores the opinion of the international community and the provisions of documents of international law when adopting its decisions. This is the cause of the main problem.

That is why the future of our relations with the Alliance directly depends on the precision with which the provisions of the Founding Act and international law are going to be observed. First of all in matters of the use of force and the threat to use force. Our position is clear. The only organization empowered to authorize the use of force in international relations is the United Nations Security Council. . . .

[Putin spoke next of the need to protect the rights of Russian citizens working abroad.]

Esteemed members of the Federation Council and deputies of the State Duma,

The past decade was a stormy one for Russia. It can be said without any whatsoever exaggeration that it was a revolutionary decade for Russia. The year 2000 and the beginning of 2001 appear to be relatively calm ones against this background. The absence of political upheavals has become a reason for many people who have grown used to constant crises to predict structural and personnel changes.

I would like to say clearly that we are not afraid of changes and should not be afraid of them. But any changes, political and administrative ones, should be justified by circumstances. Of course, public expectations and apprehensions do not grow out of thin air, they are based on the known logic that after a revolution there usually comes a counter-revolution, after a reform there comes a counter-reform and after that a search for those guilty of revolutionary excesses, and punishment. The more so that Russia's own historical experience abounds in such examples.

But it seems to me that it is time to say firmly that this cycle is over. There will be neither a revolution nor a counter-revolution. A firm and economically substantiated state stability is a boon for Russia and its people. And it is long time to learn to live according to this normal human logic. It is high time to understand that prolonged and hard work lies ahead. Our main problems are far too deep and they cannot be solved at one stroke, but only by daily qualified work.

But stability is not the same thing as stagnation under a bureaucracy. We will need bold and well-thought-out decisions, we will need skilled specialists among entrepreneurs and civil servants.

In conclusion I would like to stress that after a turbulent decade of reform we are entering a period when our will, our qualifications and stamina will determine the long-term success of the whole nation. Measures of a transitional character have been exhausted. But for present political stability to be translated into economic prosperity, it is necessary to exert a lot of effort and spend years. Power in Russia should work to make a renunciation of democratic freedoms impossible and to make the economic course that has been charted irreversible. The authorities should work to guarantee a policy that improves the life of all the social strata in Russia, legality and a consistent line for improving the business environment.

Addressing the Federal Assembly, the government, the regional and local authorities, I would like you to remember that we won't achieve tangible results if we do not remove the fears and the guarded attitude people have for the state. The root of many of our problems is the age-old mistrust of the state which has more than once deceived its citizens, the suspicion citizens feel for the state, a feature inherited from the past. In the absence of genuine civil equality and business partnership.

Today I deliberately concentrated on problem issues, on shortcomings. I thought that an objective analysis of our own shortcomings would be much more useful than comforting speeches. But one might, of course, have pursued that thesis too. The year 2000 has demonstrated that we can work together. Now we all should learn to work effectively. And I urge all those who are in the service of the state to take this as their main and chief task. I would like to repeat, as their main and chief task. Thank you.

CIA DEPUTY DIRECTOR ON
STATUS OF NORTH KOREA
April 17, 2001

Mutual distrust between the new Bush administration and North Korea's reclusive leadership brought at least a temporary halt during 2001 to what had appeared, just a year earlier, to be a promising opening of North Korea to the rest of the world. Harsher rhetoric in both Washington and North Korea's capital Pyongyang prevented a revival of high-level talks between the two cold war enemies and stalled peace negotiations between North and South Korea. The European Union attempted without success to break the stalemate, which deepened late in the year when Washington linked the North Korean regime to the broad threat of terrorism, as represented by the September 11 terrorist attacks against the United States.

U.S. concerns about North Korea were based on intelligence information indicating that Pyongyang was developing missiles for three reasons: as a source of income through the sale of missiles and missile technology to other countries; as a defense against a potential attack from South Korea and the United States; and as a bargaining chip to win concessions from Washington, including increased aid and a reduction of the U.S. military presence in South Korea (37,000 U.S. troops were stationed there). In unusually revealing remarks for a senior intelligence official, CIA deputy director John E. McLaughlin told a conference at Texas A&M University on April 17, 2001, that North Korea probably had built one or two nuclear weapons, had developed a sizable arsenal of chemical weapons, and might have succeeded in developing biological weapons. McLaughlin pictured North Korea as a danger to its neighbors and to the rest of the world because it was a nation deeply stressed by the collapse of its economic system, a humanitarian crisis resulting from years of famine and its secretive dictatorship.

Background

For more than a half century North Korea had suffered under one of the most repressive and insular governments in the world. Dictator Kim Il Sung built an enormous army while depriving his people of freedom and consumer goods. Kim Il Sung died in 1994 and was succeeded by his son,

Kim Jong Il, who kept the communist repression but gradually reached out to the noncommunist world that his father had spurned. Under U.S. pressure, North Korea in 1994 signed an accord, called the "Agreed Framework," promising to abandon its quest for nuclear weapons in exchange for American and Japanese help in building two civilian nuclear power plants. A series of famines caused by drought, floods, and crop failures starting in 1995 killed up to 2 million North Koreans and led the country to accept food aid from other countries, including the United States. (Nuclear agreement, Historic Documents of 1999, p. 568)

The year 2000 brought two historic developments for North Korea. First, in June, Kim Jong Il hosted South Korean president Kim Dae Jung for three days in Pyongyang; the two leaders talked optimistically of improved relations and signed an agreement calling for eventual reunification of the Korean peninsula. Kim Dae Jung later was awarded the Nobel Peace Prize for his "Sunshine Policy" of luring the North out of its isolation. In the closing months of 2000, the administration of President Bill Clinton held high-level talks with North Korea, culminating in a visit to Pyongyang by Secretary of State Madeleine K. Albright that was intended to pave the way for a visit by Clinton before he left office. But Clinton devoted his final months in office to a failed attempt to negotiate a peace agreement between Israel and the Palestinians, leaving it to the incoming Bush administration to pursue further talks with North Korea. (Middle East peace, p. 360; Korea developments, Historic Documents of 2000, p. 359)

Administration Policy Review

The new Bush administration appeared to have a much more skeptical view of North Korea's intentions than had the Clinton administration. Shortly after taking office senior officials in the Bush White House and Defense Department suggested that Clinton had been too eager to bargain with North Korea and had failed to press Pyongyang for proof that it had stopped trying to develop nuclear weapons and had suspended a program to build a long-range ballistic missile capable of reaching the United States. Kim Jong Il had said North Korea had suspended its missile program after conducting a test flight in 1998. Even so, Bush administration officials cited North Korea's missile program as a major justification for the United States to develop a missile defense system. (Missile defense, p. 281)

South Korea's leader, Kim Dae Jung, was scheduled to be one of the first overseas leaders to meet with Bush in Washington early in 2001. One day before the scheduled March 7 visit, Secretary of State Colin Powell told reporters that the administration was ready to "pick up where President Clinton and his administration left off" in their talks with North Korea. But in his meeting with Kim at the White House, Bush said he was not prepared for further contacts with North Korea and instead would undertake a "review" of U.S. policy on the matter. Later, with Kim seated next to him in the Oval Office, Bush told reporters his concern about North Korea was that "we're not certain as to whether or not they're keeping all terms of all agreements." Administration officials later acknowledged that Pyongyang ap-

peared to be complying with its past agreements, including the 1994 Agreed Framework. The president had simply misspoken, the aides said, and had intended to raise doubts about North Korea's willingness to carry out future agreements.

Although administration officials denied it, Bush's posture amounted to a serious rebuff to South Korea's Kim, who had hoped the new administration would follow through on Clinton's diplomatic moves, thereby giving him a U.S. go-ahead to pursue further peace talks with the North. The next day, March 8, Kim gave a speech in Washington appealing to the United States to "seize this opportunity we have for peace." Even so, Kim effectively acknowledged that his Sunshine Policy had been undercut. Kim took a somewhat harder line than in the past, demanding that North Korea abandon its missile program and take other steps toward peace before getting any new aid from the United States and the South.

Kim then turned for help to the European Union, which in late March agreed to step into the diplomatic void. Three senior EU diplomats—Swedish prime minister Goran Persson, EU external relations commissioner Chris Patten, and foreign policy director Javier Solana—met with Kim Jong Il in Pyongyang on May 2–3, then in Seoul with Kim Dae Jung. The Europeans said Kim Jong Il had promised to observe the moratorium on his nation's ballistic missile program at least until 2003 and was committed to a second summit meeting with Kim Dae Jung. Both statements were welcomed in Washington and Seoul. But the Europeans said Kim Jong Il refused another U.S. demand, to stop exporting ballistic missiles and missile technology to other countries, including Iran and Pakistan, because it needed the money it got from the sales. Washington had long accused North Korea of aiding the missile programs of both countries.

The European Commission—the executive branch of the European Union—announced on May 14 that it would establish diplomatic relations with North Korea. As part of its opening to the outside world, North Korea had established relations with about a dozen nations.

The European diplomatic offensive was just one of several moves by parties outside the administration calling for renewed contacts between the United States and North Korea. On March 26 a group of thirty senior U.S. foreign policy experts wrote to Bush suggesting that continued negotiation was part of a comprehensive policy to persuade North Korea "that it has no better options than diplomacy." That panel was headed by Morton I. Abromowitz, a former diplomat and senior official in the state and defense departments, and James T. Laney, a former U.S. ambassador to South Korea. Even more influential, according to news reports, was a similar suggestion from President Bush's father, former president George Bush.

Bush announced on June 6 that his administration had completed its policy review toward North Korea and was ready for "serious discussions" with that country on a "broad agenda." The agenda Bush outlined was somewhat broader than the list of items Clinton's aides had pursued with North Korea. In one new item, Bush said he wanted to discuss an "improved implementation" of the 1994 Framework Agreement halting the North's nuclear weapons program. Aides said that meant the United States wanted the International Atomic Energy Agency to inspect all of North Korea's nuclear facilities to determine if the country had hidden any weapons-grade plutonium before it signed the 1994 agreement and handed over several canisters of the material. Also, Bush demanded a "less threatening conventional military posture" by North Korea; that was a reference, aides said, to recent military maneuvers by North Korean forces near the demilitarized zone that had separated the two Koreas since the end of the Korean War in 1953.

Mid-level U.S. and North Korean diplomats met in New York City on July 13—the first official contact between the two countries since the end of the Clinton administration. The meeting was intended to set the stage for further discussions on an agenda for more formal negotiations, but it turned out to be the last such meeting of the year. The North Korean Foreign Ministry on June 18 objected to what it called a "unilateral" attempt by the United States to set the agenda for talks between the two countries. In particular, the statement objected to Bush's call for discussions about North Korea's conventional military forces, saying such a move was "hostile in its intention."

The prospects for renewed talks between Washington and Pyongyang did not improve after the September 11 terrorist attacks against the United States—even though North Korea officially expressed condolences to the United States for the loss of life in the attacks and pledged to sign several United Nations antiterrorism treaties. A Bush complaint in October about North Korea's "secrecy" brought forth a torrent of invective from Pyongyang, as did the president's warning on November 12 that North Korea "will be held accountable" if it developed weapons of mass destruction (biological, chemical, or nuclear weapons). North Korea's response to that vague warning was an equally vague pledge to "take proper countermeasures."

North-South Talks

South Korean president Kim's hopes of continuing his Sunshine Policy talks with Kim Jong Il faded into oblivion following the Bush administration's decision to put its own contacts with North Korea on ice. At their meeting in June 2000, the two Kims had agreed to meet again in South Korea during 2001. But the northern Kim made no move toward setting a date for such a meeting, and the hostile rhetoric directed by his government at the United States seemed to indicate that he was having second thoughts on the subject.

Senior diplomats from the two Koreas held several meetings during the year but appeared to reach no agreements on matters of substance. In frustration, Kim Dae Jung on August 15 appealed again to the United States for help, saying that "South-North talks are inextricably related to North Korea-United States relations." But the Bush administration stood by its broader agenda that North Korea had rejected, and so both sets of negotiations—between North and South Korea, and between North Korea and the United States—made no headway.

*In the meantime, Kim Dae Jung found himself in an increasingly diffi-
cult position. A former opposition leader who had courageously fought
South Korea's dictatorial regimes before the advent of democracy in the late
1980s, Kim had been elected in 1997 with a mandate to seek better relations
with the North. In 2001 he had less than two years left in his presidency but
little to show for his Sunshine Policy except his meeting with Kim Jong Il,
his Nobel Prize, and several emotional reunions among elderly North and
South Koreans who had been separated since the peninsula was divided following World War II. Kim was under increasing attack from his more conservative domestic opponents, who had reluctantly endorsed the Sunshine
Policy when it was succeeding but were anxious to use its more recent failures to score political points. Kim's government also endured a series of
scandals that hastened his lame duck status.*

Deteriorating Situation in the North

*The diplomatic maneuvering between and among the United States and
the two Koreas took place in the context of a continuing collapse of the North
Korean economy. Building on the country's relatively strong industrial base
after World War II, the communist regime in Pyongyang had developed the
economy during the 1950s and 1960s and managed to provide education
and health care services for the population—but not political freedom or
consumer goods. The communist-inspired economic growth stopped in the
1970s, even as the capitalist economy of South Korea boomed.*

*Then an annual series of droughts and floods beginning in 1995 devas-
tated North Korea's agricultural output, which had already begun to falter
because of inefficient farming practices and the government's inability to
pay for imported fertilizer, machinery, and other farming supplies. International relief agencies and major donor countries, including the United
States, poured food supplies into North Korea in an effort to head off famine. Those efforts saved millions of lives, but as of 2001 experts estimated
that somewhere between 200,000 and 2 million North Koreans (out of a estimated population of 23 million) died in the late 1990s because of lack of
food. Even worse for the country's long-term future, an estimated 40 percent
of the country's 6 million children were malnourished, with dangerous consequences for their physical and mental development.*

*The United Nation's Food and Agricultural Organization reported in No-
vember that many Koreans had reached the end of their "coping mechanisms"—their ability to deal with a lack of food and other necessities that
had continued for years on end. The FAO estimated that 6–8 million North
Koreans were routinely short of food. Most of them lived in urban areas in
the north of the country, where most large-scale industries had closed because antiquated machinery had broken down and the government could
not afford to buy raw materials and spare parts.*

*Aid agencies and foreign governments pressed the Pyongyang govern-
ment to abandon its strict communist policies and adopt at least some of the
market-based economic reforms that had stimulated growth in neighboring*

China. Kim Jong Il had visited China and reportedly expressed admiration for its economic success, and he sent a delegation of senior officials to Europe to learn about free-market economies.

In the meantime, international aid kept North Korea afloat. UN agencies in November 2001 issued a joint appeal for $258 million in aid for the country in 2002; of that $216 million was for food for an estimated 6.4 million people, primarily children and pregnant and nursing women. The major aid donors were the United States, South Korea, Japan, and China, in that order.

Following are excerpts from a speech delivered April 17, 2001, by CIA deputy director John E. McLaughlin to a conference at Texas A & M University on "North Korea: Engagement or Confrontation."

The document was obtained from the Internet at http://www.cia.gov/cia/public_affairs/speeches/ddci_speech_041 72001.html.

The title of your Conference centers on a question: engagement or confrontation? We all know the second very well. Confrontation has been a virtual constant in US relations with North Korea for more than half a century. The far newer phenomenon is engagement—cautious, tentative, guarded, halting—apply the adjective of your choice. . . .

When it comes to North Korea, conditions there clearly hold the potential for both engagement and confrontation. For a state like the North—often reflexively hostile to the outside world, yet in need of it as never before—engagement and the potential for confrontation can coexist—and are likely to co-exist—even in the best of scenarios.

The Nature of the Challenge

What are the elements of the problem? For the United States, North Korea is—first and foremost—a challenge. It was throughout the Cold War, and it is so now. In fact, it could be said that North Korea was a metaphor for some of the most extreme aspects of the Cold War and is today a metaphor for the most challenging aspects of the new world that has come in its wake.

Let's look back for a moment and then talk about how the picture has changed. As you all know, the armistice of July 1953 created on the Korean peninsula a long pattern of tense standoff, punctuated by occasional crisis. For US Intelligence, North Korea became—as much as anything—an order-of-battle problem. Count the troops. Count the tanks. Count the guns. Add up the capabilities. Estimate their intentions. I know I'm making this sound easier and simpler than it was, but my point is that we were dealing with a much less fluid picture back then.

Like everyone else, we knew the regime was brutal within its borders and a menace beyond. Its commando raids into South Korea and its assassination attempts against successive South Korean presidents—including the 1983 bombing in Rangoon that killed 21 people—were clear windows into the minds and morals of North Korean leaders.

And yet, North Korea's status as a client of the Soviet Union and China—a prickly client, to be sure—did impose constraints on its behavior. With the end of the Cold War and the scaling back of the subsidies that went with it, those constraints began to erode. Today, it may be a fragile regime, but it is one that operates with fewer constraints on its behavior and often outside international norms. And, as I implied earlier, it operates in a world where the reference points—technological, geopolitical, economic, military—are themselves in flux.

In short order, the challenge that North Korea poses to us and our allies has grown in complexity and peril. Its traditional feature—the conventional threat we examined this afternoon—remains in place. And—as we saw in September, 1996 and June, 1999—the North has found it hard to abandon tactics like commando incursions and naval confrontations—even when they fail miserably.

But added into this mix is an increased threat from weapons of mass destruction and the humanitarian challenge we could face, given the increased stress that poverty and economic decline must be creating in the North.

The Conventional Threat . . .

Let's talk for a minute about the conventional military picture. I reveal no secret when I say that on the battlefield North Korea cannot defeat the South and the United States. But it could inflict tremendous damage in a losing cause.

The North Korean military, like all but the most elite of North Korean society, has suffered the effects of the country's economic implosion. It does not exercise often or well. Its equipment is aging. Its military production is scant. But it is large, and most of it is forward deployed.

Its artillery could rain havoc down on Seoul, a mere 30 miles from the DMZ [demilitarized zone separating North and South Korea]. It has the biggest pool of special forces in the world—not the best, as we have seen, but with enough punch to sow panic and destruction.

These are capabilities. The intention to use them is a very different matter, and this has been debated thoroughly for years. The case can be made that it would be foolish for the North to use these capabilities. And the case can be made that it would be foolish to make that assumption. But, the bottom line is that like any military commander, we in the intelligence profession can ill-afford to ignore capabilities.

In fact, I can tell you that we tend to make our mistakes not when we convince ourselves that a foreign group or leader might do something, but when we convince ourselves that they will *not*.

Here is a short passage from one of our intelligence assessments: ". . . an invasion of South Korea is unlikely unless North Korean forces can develop a clear-cut superiority over the increasingly efficient South Korean army." That judgment came out on the 13th of January—1950. It had a fairly short shelf life [North Korea invaded the South in June 1950].

No matter what we think the North Korean leadership might do with its military, it is a linchpin of their state. They take it very seriously. And so must we—as the ally of South Korea and its democracy, and as a nation with 37,000 of its own troops serving, working, and living among forty-five million friends in what could one day be harm's way.

That holds true whether we believe the North sees its armed forces as a mark of prestige, a constituency to be satisfied, a tool that might bring respect, or even one that might bring conquest. The military has priority on whatever resources the North has. This is stated policy, the so-called "military first" policy. But it is hardly the whole story.

. . . and the Unconventional Ones

Were Kim Jong Il and his lieutenants simply sitting atop a large collection of conventional forces, they would still be a grave concern. But it would be one whose destructive power and geographic reach the United States and South Korea have together understood and managed for decades.

As real as the conventional threat may be, North Korea's challenge to regional and global security is magnified by two other factors I've already mentioned.

First, the North's pursuit of weapons of mass destruction and long-range missiles, and its readiness—even eagerness—to become missile salesman to the world. And second, the economic and humanitarian disaster that has afflicted the people of the North—a catastrophe whose effects will endure for generations, no matter how the Korean situation finally plays out.

Weapons of Terror

Looking first at those advanced weapons: as we all know, it was not a brigade of tanks or division of infantry that riveted our attention and concern on the Korean peninsula early in the last decade. It was the nuclear plant at Yongbyon [which produced weapons-grade plutonium].

The [1994] Agreed Framework has frozen activity there. But we still cannot account for all of North Korea's plutonium. And—with an opaque regime in which the practice of denial and deception is embedded in national strategy— we still cannot say for sure that nuclear weapons-related work is not going on somewhere else.

Indeed, the North probably has one or two nuclear bombs—and it may also have biological weapons alongside its chemical ones.

Regarding missiles, the outlines of the North's program are far less mysterious, for the leadership sees the No Dong and Taepo Dong [missiles] as tools of public diplomacy as well as national defense.

It has so far held to its missile launch moratorium and it has signaled its interest in negotiating a missile deal with us. At the same time, the North's proliferation activities remain robust—for a profit and for a purpose: To keep our attention, to underline their greatest source of leverage, and to remind us of what it is they are willing to haggle over.

North Korea continues to aggressively market its ballistic missiles, equipment, and technology. We find the No Dong [medium range ballistic missile] and its variants in places like Iran and Pakistan, where they have the potential to alter geopolitical and military calculations in important ways throughout the Middle East and South Asia.

In short, the North has accelerated the pace at which other countries acquire and refine potential delivery systems for weapons of mass destruction.

The flight of a Taepo Dong [medium-to-long range ballistic missile] over Japan more than two years ago added a new and worrisome dimension to the North's own definitions of deterrence and power projection. And it is busy at work on new models that could reach the United States itself with nuclear-sized payloads.

The Humanitarian Challenge

Turning to the second factor I mentioned: even as the North challenges the world in one small but lethal field of modern technology, it presents another challenge as old as life itself: malnutrition and starvation.

A combination of natural calamity and human mismanagement may have claimed up to a million lives in the 1990s. Even today, the North's sputtering economy remains unable to provide remotely sufficient food or work for its people.

Even with the charity of other nations, malnutrition is widespread. Without this charity, famine would be epidemic. Many North Koreans must simply fend for themselves, seemingly forgotten by a system that nonetheless demands their obedience. Some just flee.

As for the others, their dire poverty is captured in a single picture—one that I am sure many of you in this room have seen. It is a satellite photo of the Korean peninsula at night. North China and South Korea are a blaze of lights. North Korea is totally dark outside the single dot that is Pyongyang. The fishing fleets in the Sea of Japan give off far more light than does all of North Korea.

No one who looks at that photograph should forget that there are some 23 million human beings struggling in that darkness.

North Korea's Leadership: Tactical Flexibility . . .

And what of the small group in that dot of light, the small group that commands North Korea. It was rich ground for analysis this morning.

And we, too, see changes—some encouraging, some not.

No matter what you make of Kim John Il's diplomatic opening, it does at least reflect a tactical flexibility. His words and actions are well worth weighing and watching. We have all seen the signposts.

His behavior at the North-South summit. His dispatch of Vice Marshal Jo [North Korea's number-two leader, Jo Myon Rok] to Washington and his reception of American diplomats in Pyongyang. His acceptance of foreign aid and foreign aid workers. His efforts to attract foreign money to his investment enclaves. His small adjustments to the domestic economy.

But the key is whether any of these steps signal the start of a process. For in and of themselves, they have yet to bring real improvement to the North. Yet they do suggest the leadership there knows it must do something to better conditions in the country—for its own survival, if nothing else.

Kim's trips to China in January of this year and May of last year are also significant. But so is the fact that China's economic reform was made possible in large part by the passing of Mao [Chinese leader Mao Zedong] and the de-emphasis of major portions of his legacy. In North Korea, we have yet to see any comparable movement away from the legacy of Kim Il-song and all that it represents. Real change will not come until that happens.

. . . Risky Strategy

So far in Pyongyang, the son has held fast to the father's legacy, including the goal of Northern preeminence in a reunified Korea.

It is easy to caricature Kim Jong Il—either as a simple tyrant blind to his dilemma or as a technocratic champion of sweeping change. But the extreme views of him tend to be the product of bias, ignorance, or wishful thinking. The reality is more complex.

At home, he has shown his hard side—through his purges of the elite, his light regard for the suffering of ordinary Koreans, and the swift destruction of any expression of popular discontent. Abroad, he has shown his pragmatic side—through his willingness to engage old enemies and his skilled brink-manship as he does so.

Like his father, he has been shrewd enough to make bad behavior the key-stone of his foreign policy. He knows that proliferation is something we want to stop. Thus, Kim Jong Il has tried to drum up outside assistance by trading off international concerns about his missile programs and sales. He has—more subtly, of course—done much the same thing with foreign fears of re-newed famine and the chaos that could accompany any unraveling of his regime.

These are the wild cards he adds to strengthen what would otherwise be a deuce-high hand. This is his leverage with the world. Along the way, he will seek to exploit any daylight he can find between the United States, South Korea, Japan, the European Union, or anyone else who might be inclined to offer him economic help. And from his perspective, it makes good sense.

Decisive to the success of this strategy is the projection of a credible threat. And here—as we know—the North has its bases covered. But, like any pol-icy founded on threats, it comes with the built-in possibility of accident or mis-calculation—by those who conduct it, or by those who react to it.

The Nature of the Regime

Before I can say anything about the future of the North Korean regime—and its challenge—a few words are in order about what makes it tick today.

It is a peculiar creation. The leaden, bureaucratic Marxism we saw falter in the late 20th Century—with its gray Central Committees and half-forgotten Central European ideology—is an imperfect guide to North Korea and offers few reliable analogies for how the North Korean regime might some day ex-perience transformation.

The transformation of the Central European countries at the beginning of the last decade was eased by at least three things not present in the North Korean equation: extensive exposure to and penetration by the outside world (East Germany is the best example); economies already on the road to privatization (Hungary was the extreme case); and the presence of dissident movements powerful enough in a country like Poland to represent an effective parallel society.

Instead of these cushioning factors, in North Korea, the command economy, central planning, and other familiar features introduced there long ago by the Soviets exist alongside something else. A single story makes the point. A foreign visitor asked a North Korean what he thought of Kim Il Song. "He is God," came the answer. Then a tougher one. "What do you think of Kim Jong Il?" The Korean thought a moment, looked around, and replied: "He is 70 percent God."

Those answers might be very different were the North Korean outside the country. But they do say something about the tone and tenor of the regime on the inside.

Now I'm sure there are subtleties and complexities about the regime that we can neither discern nor appreciate. But that aside, the key is that power continues to reside with Kim Jong Il and the cluster of relatives and allies who run the military, the security forces, and the rest of the state and party apparatus.

No matter how you view them, it is evident they rule a state that is simultaneously impoverished and addicted to living beyond its means. They preach the values of self-reliance, but they rely on foreign aid. The priorities they set and enforce have delivered a huge army, a broken economy, widespread hunger, and a challenge for all of us.

. . . and Its Future

Because totalitarian elites tend to mask their own policy deliberations and drive opposition underground, the health and stability of their regimes are notoriously difficult for outsiders to gauge. North Korea is no exception. Predictions of its collapse have come and gone, and I will not venture one here now.

But I will say the North faces tough choices. Kim Jong Il probably recognizes the obvious truth that the economic competition with the South is lost. And he has seen for himself the economic gains brought by reform in China.

Yet he also knows the security risks involved and he knows the fates of other leaders who fell victim to change they could not control. He may have seen images of Gorbachev [former Soviet leader Mikhail Gorbachev] in retirement. Of Honecker [former East German leader Erich Honecker] in exile. Of a startled Ceausescu [former Romanian leader Nicolae Ceausescu] on his palace balcony the day the crowd stopped cheering.

At this point, Kim Jong Il may have a toe in the river of change. And he is moving just as we would expect him to: Slowly, carefully, with plenty of room to bargain, maneuver, or pull back.

After a decade of deprivation, the real story may be the durability of the North—a grim testament to the power of a people's ability to endure hardship.

Clearly, the North is under serious stress and it is likely to remain so. But frankly, no one can be confident about when, how, or even whether that stress might achieve critical mass and lead to fracture.

That formulation may not be intellectually satisfying. But I hope you will agree that it is intellectually honest.

The Regional Context

As the situation in the North unfolds, there is a final element of change we must consider: The regional context, which—like so many other things we have talked about today—was reshaped by the close of the Cold War.

Russia and China are each redefining their power, their influence, and their reach, and their relationship with each other. Japan is focused on ending its long economic recession and has heightened security concerns in the aftermath of Pyongyang's missile tests. And South Korea has emerged as a vibrant society with a strong democracy and the world's twelfth largest economy—a stark contrast to the stagnation in North Korea, whose economy barely registers on the charts.

And East Asia as a whole is looking anew at the United States, now the only global superpower. In that capacity, we are still often called on to be partner, protector, or honest broker. But we are also seen as a nation whose interests and priorities do not always coincide with the other major actors in the region.

It is in this fluid environment that the United States must work the problem of North Korea. We find in the immediate neighborhood friends and allies like South Korea and Japan, and others, like Russia and China, whose interests may converge less frequently with ours but who nonetheless share with us a common, significant stake in the ultimate destiny of North Korea. No one will benefit from prolonged instability. There and the cost of reconstruction—whenever the time comes to tally it up—will demand the resources of more than one country.

If we ever face a crisis in the North, its solution will fall to the nations of East Asia and the United States. We will together have the chance to resolve it in concert, not conflict. It is a chance none of us can afford to miss.

Conclusion

Intelligence officers like to say that change typically brings uncertainty, and that uncertainty raises the odds of surprise. With so much change in and around the Korean peninsula, that old truth certainly applies. But none of us should be surprised by the prominence of North Korea as a challenge for policymakers and intelligence analysts.

In a very real sense, it is one of the inevitable issues of American foreign policy. Inevitable because—no matter what level of engagement we may want—the North seems sure to engage us. It could be across a table. It could be with the consequences of its negative behavior or its own instability. Or it could be some combination of them all.

What is clear—as this conference demonstrates—is the complexity, gravity, and importance of the North Korean issue and its very certain role as a signpost for the future of East Asia.

May

PRESIDENT BUSH ON PLANS FOR A MISSILE DEFENSE
May 1, 2001

President George W. Bush on May 1, 2001, committed the United States to the development of a complex system of defenses to protect the country against a limited attack of long-range ballistic missiles, such as a possible threat from North Korea or Iran. Bush's pursuit of a missile defense led inevitably seven months later to his decision to withdraw from the 1972 Antiballistic Missile (ABM) treaty, negotiated by the United States and the Soviet Union during the cold war to block such a defense system. (ABM treaty, p. 927)

Congress later in 2001 approved nearly all of the $8.3 billion that Bush had requested for work on missile defenses in fiscal year 2002, which began October 1, 2001. That figure represented a $3.5 billion increase over what former president Bill Clinton originally had suggested. Opposition to that funding on the part of congressional Democrats evaporated after the September 11 terrorist attacks against the United States. The missile defense Bush proposed could have done nothing to stop such an attack using civilian airliners, but patriotic fervor in the wake of the attack made resistance to military spending politically impossible on Capitol Hill. (Terrorist attacks, p. 614)

During the late 1990s the Clinton administration had tested elements of a limited ground-based missile defense system. The testing turned up numerous technical problems, however, and in September 2000 Clinton announced that he was suspending plans to proceed with deployment of the system and leaving a decision to his successor. (Clinton delay, Historic Documents of 2000, p. 677)

A "Vastly Different World"

Bush sought to place his proposal for missile defense in the context of the dramatic changes in the world since the collapse of the Soviet Union a decade earlier. During the cold war, he said, the United States and the Soviet Union were "locked in a hostile rivalry," each with thousands of nuclear-armed missiles and bombs pointed at the other. With the landmark ABM treaty, the two superpowers acknowledged that a nuclear war between them would be less likely if each side was "open and vulnerable" to a nuclear attack, Bush said.

"Today, the sun comes up on a vastly different world," Bush told his audience at the National Defense University in Washington. The communist regime of the Soviet Union had vanished and was replaced by Russia, "a country in transition with an opportunity to emerge as a great nation, democratic, at peace with itself and its neighbors," he said.

Even though Washington and Moscow no longer were enemies, the world remained a dangerous place, Bush said, "a less certain, a less predictable one." Bush said the greatest danger to the United States came from the "world's least responsible states" for whom "terror and blackmail are a way of life." Some of those states were attempting to acquire nuclear, chemical, and biological weapons, along with the ballistic missiles that would enable them to deliver those weapons to targets, such as the United States, thousands of miles away. Bush named only one such state—Iraq, and its leader Saddam Hussein—but aides made it clear that he had Iran and North Korea in mind as well. The president made no direct reference in his speech to terrorist groups, such as the al Qaeda network of Osama bin Laden. While such groups were known to be trying to develop chemical and nuclear weapons, none were considered close to acquiring ballistic missiles, as of 2001.

In that context, Bush called for "a new framework that allows us to build missile defenses to counter the different threats of today's world." The president did not explain what he meant by a "framework"—whether it would be a new treaty or a less formal set of written or verbal agreements—but he made it clear that he intended to "move beyond the constraints" of the ABM treaty, which he said "enshrines the past." Later in the year, Bush and his aides failed to convince Russian president Vladimir Putin to embrace any plan for post-ABM agreements. The failure of those talks led to Bush's notice on December 13 that the United States would withdraw from the ABM treaty in six months, as the treaty allowed.

Missile Defense Proposal

The heart of Bush's May 1 speech was his plan for a missile defense system, one he said should provide a "credible deterrent." Bush offered no specifics for such a system. Instead, he described in general terms a variety of options suggested by Secretary of Defense Donald H. Rumsfeld, long an avid proponent of missile defense. Rumsfeld had chaired a commission that in 1998 warned that North Korea might be able within five years to develop a ballistic missile capable of attacking the United States. (Rumsfeld commission, Historic Documents of 1998, p. 481)

Bush said Rumsfeld had developed "near-term options that could allow us to deploy an initial capability against limited threats." Some of the options would use "already established technologies," Bush said, involving the use of missiles based on land and on seaborne ships or submarines to intercept ballistic missiles that were in mid-course or as they reentered the atmosphere. The president also spoke of the "substantial advantages" of intercepting missiles shortly after they take off—in what is called the "boost phase."

In the days after Bush's speech, administration officials offered a limited elaboration on the options the president had described in vague terms. A key component, they said, would be an expanded version of the army's system that had been tested, with only limited success, by the Clinton administration. That system was to use a few dozen interceptor rockets, based in Alaska, to attack ballistic missiles as they headed toward the United States. Defense Department officials said such a system could be in place as early as 2004. Several preliminary tests of components of that system conducted later in 2001 were declared successful by the army, although one key test failed in December.

Bush administration officials said the president's proposed system would go beyond what Clinton had planned, adding components based at sea, in the air, and possibly even in space (Bush did not mention a space-based defense in his speech, but his aides specifically included it as one option). As examples, officials said some of the navy's Aegis cruisers could be equipped with interceptor rockets capable of hunting down and striking incoming ballistic missiles, and high-powered lasers mounted on air force planes could strike missiles, as well. In addition, sensors attached to satellites could determine when a ballistic missile is launched and then send a warning back to Earth. Added together, these various components would create what the Pentagon called a "layered" approach to missile defense—if one layer failed to detect and stop an incoming missile, another layer might succeed.

The navy's hopes for a sea-based missile defense suffered a major setback in December when the Pentagon canceled work on a multibillion dollar system originally intended to protect ships from attacks by ballistic missiles or aircraft. The navy had hoped such a system, called Area Missile Defense, could be expanded to help block missile attacks against the U.S. mainland. But the Pentagon halted work on the system, citing "poor performance" and a 65 percent cost increase.

In describing their plans, Bush and Rumsfeld specifically avoided promising an air-tight "missile shield" such as President Ronald Reagan had suggested in the early 1980s with his Strategic Defense Initiative, derided by opponents as "Star Wars." Reagan spent billions of dollars pursuing his dream of a perfect defense against ballistic missiles but at the end of his term in 1989 had little to show for it.

Rumsfeld told reporters May 2 that the administration intended to "explore a variety of ways that missile defense can conceivably evolve without prejudging exactly which ones will be the most fruitful." Land, sea, air, and space-based defenses "are all things that need to be considered," he said.

That open-ended approach offered Bush considerable flexibility to pursue what he called "promising options" as they were developed and tested, with-

out committing him to specific approaches that might prove unworkable or too expensive. This approach also gave Bush an enormous short-term political benefit in selling missile defense to members of Congress and the public because it enabled him to avoid setting a total price tag on his plan. The Congressional Budget Office had estimated that Clinton's much more limited ground-based defense system would have cost $60 billion to develop and operate over fifteen years. Most experts suggested that the more complex "layered" system described by Bush would cost several times that amount. A large cost estimate in the range of $200 billion to $500 billion would have offered an inviting target for missile defense critics.

Criticism of the Proposal

Congressional Democrats, arms control experts who opposed Bush's missile defense proposals, and many world leaders offered numerous criticisms. Perhaps the foremost objection was that an aggressive pursuit of the defenses Bush envisioned ultimately would require a major change to, or abandonment of, the ABM treaty, which for nearly three decades had been considered the cornerstone of international efforts to curb the nuclear arms race. While acknowledging Bush's point that the world had changed since the treaty was negotiated in 1972, ABM supporters insisted that the treaty remained a valid and necessary means of maintaining a balance among the major nuclear powers, primarily the United States, Russia, and China. "The ABM treaty worked well," German foreign minister Joschka Fischer said during a visit to Washington on May 2. "We don't want a new arms race."

That prospect—that Russia and China would rush to build new weapons to overcome U.S. defenses, and that nations such as Iran and North Korea would not be deterred from their projects to build such weapons—became the major theme of domestic critics of Bush's plan. Tom Daschle of South Dakota, at the time the Senate minority leader, argued on May 2 that a major U.S. push toward missile defenses would spark an arms race similar to the enormous nuclear buildup by the United States and the Soviet Union from the 1950s to the 1980s. Such a development would prove to be destabilizing and ultimately counterproductive, he said. "A missile defense system that undermines our nation politically, economically, and strategically, without providing any real security, is no defense at all."

Critics also suggested that Bush was proposing to spend huge sums of money on vague plans for a security system that had yet to be tested, much less deployed and proven effective. Carl Levin of Michigan, the senior Democrat on the Senate Armed Services Committee, suggested that Bush instead should proceed cautiously with a limited testing program such as the one Clinton had pursued until late 2000.

During the summer of 2001 Democrats in both the House and Senate attempted to defer a portion of Bush's budget request for missile defense. In the House, Democrats on the Republican-controlled Armed Services Committee tried and failed to shift $985 million from missile defense to other military programs that were popular in members' districts, such as buying *cargo planes and repairing navy ships. After Democrats took control of the Senate in late May, prospects for missile defense critics brightened somewhat. Under Levin's leadership, the Senate Armed Services Committee voted along party lines to cut $1.3 billion from Bush's $8.3 billion request and would have required congressional approval for any missile defense tests that would violate the ABM treaty.*

The September 11 terrorist attacks against the World Trade Center towers and the Pentagon dramatically changed the political situation in the United States and gave Bush a powerful argument for improving defenses—even for plans such as a missile defense that would not have stopped the September 11 attack in which terrorists hijacked civilian airliners and flew them into buildings. In the new political atmosphere, Levin withdrew the amendment on the ABM treaty and agreed to language giving the president discretion to spend all of his $8.3 billion request on missile defense. However, in December conferees on the fiscal 2002 Defense appropriations bill (PL 107-117) pared $500 million from Bush's request. The cut reflected congressional unhappiness with the Pentagon's plans for a satellite system to detect incoming missiles, and it also reflected the Pentagon's cancellation of the navy antimissile program.

> *Following is the text of a speech delivered by President George W. Bush on May 2, 2001, to the students and faculty at the National Defense University at Fort McNair in Washington, D.C., in which he described his general plans for a missile defense system.*
>
> **The document was obtained from the Internet at http:// www.whitehouse.gov/news/releases/2001/05/20010501-10 .html.**

For almost 100 years, this campus has served as one of our country's premier centers for learning and thinking about America's national security. Some of America's finest soldiers have studied here: Dwight Eisenhower and Colin Powell. Some of America's finest statesmen have taught here; George Kennan. Today, you're carrying on this proud tradition forward, continuing to train tomorrow's generals, admirals and other national security thinkers, and continuing to provide the intellectual capital for our nation's strategic vision.

This afternoon, I want us to thank back some 30 years to a far different time in a far different world. The United States and the Soviet Union were locked in a hostile rivalry. The Soviet Union was our unquestioned enemy; a highly-armed threat to freedom and democracy. Far more than that wall in Berlin divided us.

Our highest ideal was—and remains—individual liberty. Theirs was the construction of a vast communist empire. Their totalitarian regime held much of Europe captive behind an iron curtain.

We didn't trust them, and for good reason. Our deep differences were expressed in a dangerous military confrontation that resulted in thousands of nuclear weapons pointed at each other on hair-trigger alert. Security of both the United States and the Soviet Union was based on a grim premise: that neither side would fire nuclear weapons at each other, because doing so would mean the end of both nations.

We even went so far as to codify this relationship in a 1972 ABM Treaty, based on the doctrine that our very survival would best be insured by leaving both sides completely open and vulnerable to nuclear attack. The threat was real and vivid. The Strategic Air Command had an airborne command post called the Looking Glass, aloft 24 hours a day, ready in case the President ordered our strategic forces to move toward their targets and release their nuclear ordnance.

The Soviet Union had almost 1.5 million troops deep in the heart of Europe, in Poland and Czechoslovakia, Hungary and East Germany. We used our nuclear weapons not just to prevent the Soviet Union from using their nuclear weapons, but also to contain their conventional military forces, to prevent them from extending the Iron Curtain into parts of Europe and Asia that were still free.

In that world, few other nations had nuclear weapons and most of those who did were responsible allies, such as Britain and France. We worried about the proliferation of nuclear weapons to other countries, but it was mostly a distant threat, not yet a reality.

Today, the sun comes up on a vastly different world. The [Berlin] Wall is gone, and so is the Soviet Union. Today's Russia is not yesterday's Soviet Union. Its government is no longer Communist. Its president is elected. Today's Russia is not our enemy, but a country in transition with an opportunity to emerge as a great nation, democratic, at peace with itself and its neighbors. The Iron Curtain no longer exists. Poland, Hungary and the Czech Republic are free nations, and they are now our allies in NATO, together with a reunited Germany.

Yet, this is still a dangerous world, a less certain, a less predictable one. More nations have nuclear weapons and still more have nuclear aspirations. Many have chemical and biological weapons. Some already have developed the ballistic missile technology that would allow them to deliver weapons of mass destruction at long distances and at incredible speeds. And a number of these countries are spreading these technologies around the world.

Most troubling of all, the list of these countries includes some of the world's least-responsible states. Unlike the Cold War, today's most urgent threat stems not from thousands of ballistic missiles in the Soviet hands, but from a small number of missiles in the hands of these states, states for whom terror and blackmail are a way of life. They seek weapons of mass destruction to intimidate their neighbors, and to keep the United States and other responsible nations from helping allies and friends in strategic parts of the world.

When Saddam Hussein invaded Kuwait in 1990, the world joined forces to turn him back. But the international community would have faced a very different situation had Hussein been able to blackmail with nuclear weapons.

Like Saddam Hussein, some of today's tyrants are gripped by an implacable hatred of the United States of America. They hate our friends, they hate our values, they hate democracy and freedom and individual liberty. Many care little for the lives of their own people. In such a world, Cold War deterrence is no longer enough.

To maintain peace, to protect our own citizens and our own allies and friends, we must seek security based on more than the grim premise that we can destroy those who seek to destroy us. This is an important opportunity for the world to re-think the unthinkable, and to find new ways to keep the peace.

Today's world requires a new policy, a broad strategy of active nonproliferation, counterproliferation and defenses. We must work together with other like-minded nations to deny weapons of terror from those seeking to acquire them. We must work with allies and friends who wish to join with us to defend against the harm they can inflict. And together we must deter anyone who would contemplate their use.

We need new concepts of deterrence that rely on both offensive and defensive forces. Deterrence can no longer be based solely on the threat of nuclear retaliation. Defenses can strengthen deterrence by reducing the incentive for proliferation.

We need a new framework that allows us to build missile defenses to counter the different threats of today's world. To do so, we must move beyond the constraints of the 30 year old ABM Treaty. This treaty does not recognize the present, or point us to the future. It enshrines the past. No treaty that prevents us from addressing today's threats, that prohibits us from pursuing promising technology to defend ourselves, our friends and our allies is in our interests or in the interests of world peace.

This new framework must encourage still further cuts in nuclear weapons. Nuclear weapons still have a vital role to play in our security and that of our allies. We can, and will, change the size, the composition, the character of our nuclear forces in a way that reflects the reality that the Cold War is over.

I am committed to achieving a credible deterrent with the lowest-possible number of nuclear weapons consistent with our national security needs, including our obligations to our allies. My goal is to move quickly to reduce nuclear forces. The United States will lead by example to achieve our interests and the interests for peace in the world.

Several months ago, I asked Secretary of Defense Rumsfeld to examine all available technologies and basing modes for effective missile defenses that could protect the United States, our deployed forces, our friends and our allies. The Secretary has explored a number of complementary and innovative approaches.

The Secretary has identified near-term options that could allow us to deploy an initial capability against limited threats. In some cases, we can draw on already established technologies that might involve land-based and sea-based capabilities to intercept missiles in mid-course or after they re-enter the atmosphere. We also recognize the substantial advantages of intercepting missiles early in their flight, especially in the boost phase.

The preliminary work has produced some promising options for advanced sensors and interceptors that may provide this capability. If based at sea or on aircraft, such approaches could provide limited, but effective, defenses.

We have more work to do to determine the final form the defenses might take. We will explore all these options further. We recognize the technological difficulties we face and we look forward to the challenge. Our nation will assign the best people to this critical task.

We will evaluate what works and what does not. We know that some approaches will not work. We also know that we will be able to build on our successes. When ready, and working with Congress, we will deploy missile defenses to strengthen global security and stability.

I've made it clear from the very beginning that I would consult closely on the important subject with our friends and allies who are also threatened by missiles and weapons of mass destruction.

Today, I'm announcing the dispatch of high-level representatives to Allied capitals in Europe, Asia, Australia and Canada to discuss our common responsibility to create a new framework for security and stability that reflects the world of today. They will begin leaving next week.

The delegations will be headed by three men on this stage: Rich Armitage, Paul Wolfowitz, and Steve Hadley; Deputies of the State Department, the Defense Department and the National Security staff. Their trips will be part of an ongoing process of consultation, involving many people and many levels of government, including my Cabinet Secretaries.

These will be real consultations. We are not presenting our friends and allies with unilateral decisions already made. We look forward to hearing their views, the views of our friends, and to take them into account.

We will seek their input on all the issues surrounding the new strategic environment. We'll also need to reach out to other interested states, including China and Russia. Russia and the United States should work together to develop a new foundation for world peace and security in the 21st century. We should leave behind the constraints of an ABM Treaty that perpetuates a relationship based on distrust and mutual vulnerability. This Treaty ignores the fundamental breakthroughs in technology during the last 30 years. It prohibits us from exploring all options for defending against the threats that face us, our allies and other countries.

That's why we should work together to replace this Treaty with a new framework that reflects a clear and clean break from the past, and especially from the adversarial legacy of the Cold War. This new cooperative relationship should look to the future, not to the past. It should be reassuring, rather than threatening. It should be premised on openness, mutual confidence and real opportunities for cooperation, including the area of missile defense. It should allow us to share information so that each nation can improve its early warning capability, and its capability to defend its people and territory. And perhaps one day, we can even cooperate in a joint defense.

I want to complete the work of changing our relationship from one based on a nuclear balance of terror, to one based on common responsibilities and common interests. We may have areas of difference with Russia, but we are not and must not be strategic adversaries. Russia and America both face new threats to security. Together, we can address today's threats and pursue today's opportunities. We can explore technologies that have the potential to make us all safer.

This is a time for vision; a time for a new way of thinking; a time for bold leadership. The Looking Glass no longer stands its 24-hour-day vigil. We must all look at the world in a new, realistic way, to preserve peace for generations to come.

SURGEON GENERAL ON
SUICIDE PREVENTION
May 2, 2001

The federal government on May 2, 2001, issued a national strategy to prevent suicide, the eighth leading cause of death in the United States and third leading cause of death among young people ages fifteen through twenty-four. The strategy envisioned a broad range of community-based programs aimed at transforming attitudes about suicide and the mental illness and substance abuse that so often accompanied it. "Only recently have the knowledge and tools become available to approach suicide as a preventable problem with realistic opportunities to save many lives," said Surgeon General David Satcher.

About 30,000 Americans a year take their own lives, and an estimated 500,000 attempt suicide. According to a national survey conducted for the National Mental Health Association and released May 2, about 4 percent of American adults—8.6 million people—had considered killing themselves.

"Suicide has stolen lives and contributed to the disability and suffering of hundreds of thousands of Americans each year," Satcher said. "There are few who escape being touched by the tragedy of suicide in their lifetimes."

The national strategy was the second step in a concerted campaign to combat suicide that was begun in 1999, when Satcher issued a "call to action" identifying suicide as a serious public health problem. The prevention campaign was also a major part of a broader program mounted by the surgeon general to focus national attention on mental health. (Surgeon general on mental health, p. 575; Suicide prevention, Historic Documents of 1999, p. 436)

In one state, Oregon, public debate on suicide prevention focused on efforts to overturn the state's assisted suicide law. In November Attorney General John Ashcroft announced that physicians in Oregon who deliberately prescribed federally controlled drugs to help a terminally ill patient commit suicide were risking revocation of their license to prescribe drugs. The announcement was a reversal of federal policy during the Clinton administration and drew widespread applause from right-to-life groups even as many in Oregon, including several elected officials, protested the ruling as a federal trampling of states' rights. A federal district judge in Portland issued a temporary restraining order, and a trial on the merits of the case was expected early in 2002.

National Suicide Prevention Strategy

The national strategy for preventing suicide was a blueprint for integrating suicide prevention into activities in a wide range of settings, including schools, workplaces, clinics, medical offices, correctional and detention centers, eldercare facilities, faith-based institutions, and community centers. The strategy was aimed not only at making the general public more aware of the complex nature of suicide but at reaching populations that were specifically at risk. The strategy offered eleven goals and sixty-eight objectives to achieve the overall aims of preventing suicides, reducing the rates of other suicidal behaviors, and creating an environment of resiliency, resourcefulness, and interconnectedness among individuals, their families, and communities.

One major goal was to eliminate the social stigma attached to suicide, mental illness, and substance abuse. Between 60 and 90 percent of all suicides were linked to some form of mental illness or substance abuse, or both, and too often people suffering these conditions were reluctant to seek treatment for fear of being shunned or belittled. To help build understanding of these conditions as illnesses rather than character flaws, the report suggested developing at least three specific sets of public service announcements. In one set well-known individuals would portray the effectiveness of treatment for mental illness and substance abuse. In another individuals who sought help for their conditions would be portrayed as exhibiting responsible behavior. The third set would describe the role of lithium in treating persons with bipolar disease, one of the mood disorder illnesses that had a high risk of suicide associated with it.

Other objectives included:

- *Increasing the number of schools that had effective programs for addressing severe distress among children and adolescents at the earliest stages. Such programs would teach children techniques for solving problems and building positive relations with schoolmates.*
- *Encouraging employers to insist that their employee health insurance plans provide mental health and substance abuse coverage on a par with coverage for traditional physical illnesses.*
- *Mounting public information campaigns about safe storage of firearms, medicines, poisons, and other means suicides commonly used to inflict self-harm.*
- *Teaching primary care physicians to routinely screen patients for risk factors for suicide and to remind parents about the potential dangers of lethal means of self-harm in the home.*
- *Increasing the proportion of divorce and family law attorneys who have been trained in identifying and responding to persons at risk for suicide.*

- *Making patient screening for depression, substance abuse, and suicide risk a routine part of all federally supported health care programs, such as Medicare and Medicaid.*
- *Monitoring the way the media portrays suicide, mental health, and substance abuse, with a view to promoting accurate and responsible depiction of these conditions. The report also urged news outlets to monitor the way they report suicides, suggesting that such reports should be concise and factual, avoiding sensationalism and "how-to" descriptions.*

To accomplish these aims, the report sought to develop integrated health care, environmental, and sociocultural interventions tailored to the community, specific groups at risk for suicide, and individuals who have been identified as being at risk. For example, a universal environmental intervention would promote the safe storage of guns, ammunition, and medication; a "selective" intervention would aim to reduce the means for self-harm in jails and prisons; and an "indicated" intervention would teach caregivers to remove guns and old medicines from the home before hospitalized suicide patients were discharged. A universal sociocultural intervention might teach conflict resolution skills to elementary school children; a selective intervention would develop programs to reduce despair and provide opportunities for high risk populations, such as Native American youths; and an indicated intervention would develop programs and promote ways for law enforcement officers to receive treatment for mental and substance use disorders and return to full duty without prejudice.

The national strategy, entitled "Goals and Objectives for Action," was developed by four federal agencies: the Centers for Disease Control and Prevention, the Health Resources and Services Administration, the National Institutes of Health, and the Substance Abuse and Mental Health Services Administration. These agencies worked with the Indian Health Service and the Public Health Service and a broad range of health researchers and clinicians, community activists, and people with direct experience with suicide. The next step was to develop a detailed action plan including specific activities corresponding to each objective. The report acknowledged that the national strategy was "highly ambitious," but stressed that "the devastation wrought by suicide demands the strongest possible response."

Penalizing Physicians Assisting Suicides

Ashcroft's November 6 announcement came in a memorandum to the Drug Enforcement Administration (DEA) specifically authorizing federal agents to identify Oregon doctors who wrote prescriptions for federally controlled drugs to help terminally patients commit suicide and to seek to have their drug licenses revoked. Oregon was the only state to permit physician-assisted suicide. Since the law went into effect in 1997, at least seventy people had deliberately committed suicide using federally controlled drugs, usually barbiturates, they had obtained from their physicians. In his memo Ashcroft said dispensing controlled substances for the purpose of assisting suicide was not a "legitimate medical purpose" within the meaning of the 1970 Controlled Substances Act and was therefore illegal under federal law.

Oregon voters first approved physician-assisted suicide in a state ballot initiative in 1994 and in 1997 rejected a move to repeal it. Immediately after the repeal attempt failed, the DEA said it would consider any doctor who prescribed a lethal dose of narcotics with the intent of assisting a suicide to be in violation of federal law. But in June 1998, Janet Reno, the attorney general during the Clinton administration, ruled that the penalties under the Controlled Substances Act did not reach physicians who were acting in accordance with the state's assisted-suicide law. It was Reno's ruling that Ashcroft reversed. (Reno ruling, Historic Documents of 1999, p. 441)

Ashcroft personally believed that assisted suicide, like abortion, was immoral. As a U.S. senator from Missouri, he objected to Reno's ruling when it was issued. His memo reversing the Reno ruling was widely applauded by right-to-life and other conservative groups, as well as some religious groups, such as the United States Conference of Catholic Bishops, and the American Medical Association, which held that assisted suicide was in "severe conflict" with the physician's duty to heal. In Oregon Ashcroft's staunchest supporter was U.S. senator Gordon H. Smith, a Republican up for reelection in 2002, who said the matter was "an issue of principle upon which I'm prepared to stake my political future."

Other Oregon politicians were outraged by the decision. "This attorney general is supposed to be figuring out who's responsible for the anthrax," said Oregon governor John Kitzhaber, a Democrat and a former physician, referring to the anthrax spores mailed to news organizations and the U.S. Capitol that resulted in several deaths among those who handled the tainted letters. "To introduce this divisive issue at this point in time is just, to me, unthinkable." Oregon's Democratic senator, Ron Wyden, said Ashcroft's ruling trampled the rights of Oregon's voters. "I guess the Bush administration is frustrated by the inconvenience of the democratic process," Wyden said. "They have administratively tossed the ballots of Oregon's voters in the trash." Wyden personally opposed assisted suicide but led a successful effort to block Congress from overturning it. (Anthrax scare, p. 672)

Oregon attorney general Hardy Myers and several terminally ill people sought a temporary restraining order to prevent DEA agents from acting on the Ashcroft memo. Federal District Court Judge Robert E. Jones granted the order on November 8, and on November 21 he extended it for several months and ordered the case to move directly to trial based on the merits. The Justice Department was expected to buttress its position by relying in part on a Supreme Court ruling, issued in May, holding that there was no exception to the federal Controlled Substances Act for the medical use of marijuana even though several states had passed laws legalizing such uses. (Supreme Court on medical marijuana, p. 325)

> *Following is the text of the summary from the "National Strategy for Suicide Prevention: Goals and Objectives for Action," prepared by the Centers for Mental Health Services for the Substance*

*Abuse and Mental Health Services Administration, U.S. Depart-
ment of Health and Human Services, and released May 2, 2001.*

**The document was obtained from the Internet at http://
www.mentalhealth.org/suicideprevention/strategy.asp.**

*The suffering of the suicidal is private and inexpressible, leaving family mem-
bers, friends, and colleagues to deal with an almost unfathomable kind of loss,
as well as guilt. Suicide carries in its aftermath a level of confusion and devastation that is, for the most part, beyond description.*

Kay Redfield Jamison

Suicide has stolen lives around the world and across the centuries. Meanings attributed to suicide and notions of what to do about it have varied with
time and place, but suicide has continued to exact a relentless toll. In the
United States, suicide is the eighth leading cause of death and contributes—
through suicide attempts—to disability and suffering for hundreds of thousands of Americans each year. There are few who escape being touched by the
tragedy of suicide in their lifetimes; those who lose someone close as a result
of suicide experience an emotional trauma that may take leave, but never
departs.

Suicide: Cost to the Nation

- Every 17 minutes another life is lost to suicide. Every day 86 Americans
  take their own life and over 1500 attempt suicide.
- Suicide is now the eighth leading cause of death in Americans.
- For every two victims of homicide in the U.S. there are three deaths from
  suicide.
- There are now twice as many deaths due to suicide than due to HIV/AIDS.
- Between 1952 and 1995, the incidence of suicide among adolescents and
  young adults nearly tripled.
- In the month prior to their suicide, 75% of elderly persons had visited a
  physician.
- Over half of all suicides occur in adult men, aged 25–65.
- Many who make suicide attempts never seek professional care immedi-
  ately after the attempt.
- Males are four times more likely to die from suicide than are females.
- More teenagers and young adults die from suicide than from cancer,
  heart disease, AIDS, birth defects, stroke, pneumonia and influenza, and
  chronic lung disease, combined.
- Suicide takes the lives of more than 30,000 Americans every year.

Only recently have the knowledge and tools become available to approach
suicide as a preventable problem with realistic opportunities to save many
lives. The *National Strategy for Suicide Prevention: Goals and Objectives for
Action* (NSSP or *National Strategy*) is designed to be a catalyst for social

change, with the power to transform attitudes, policies, and services. It reflects a comprehensive and integrated approach to reducing the loss and suffering from suicide and suicidal behaviors in the United States. The effective implementation of the *National Strategy* will play a critical role in reaching the suicide prevention goals outlined in the Nation's public health agenda, Healthy People 2010. Representing the combined work of advocates, clinicians, researchers and survivors, the *National Strategy* lays out a framework for action and guides development of an array of services and programs yet to be set in motion. It strives to promote and provide direction to efforts to modify the social infrastructure in ways that will affect the most basic attitudes about suicide and that will also change judicial, educational, social service, and health care systems. The NSSP is highly ambitious because the devastation wrought by suicide demands the strongest possible response.

Because suicide is such a serious public health problem, the *National Strategy* proposes public health methods to address it. The public health approach to suicide prevention represents a rational and organized way to marshal prevention efforts and ensure that they are effective. Only within the last few decades has a public health approach to suicide prevention emerged with good understanding of the biological and psychosocial factors that contribute to suicidal behaviors. Its five basic steps are to clearly define the problem; identify risk and protective factors; develop and test interventions; implement interventions; and evaluate effectiveness.

As conceived, the *National Strategy* requires a variety of organizations and individuals to become involved in suicide prevention and emphasizes coordination of resources and culturally appropriate services at all levels of government—Federal, State, tribal and community—and with the private sector. The NSSP represents the first attempt in the United States to prevent suicide through such a coordinated approach.

Goals and Objectives for Action articulates a set of 11 goals and 68 objectives, and provides a blueprint for action. The next step for the *National Strategy* will be to prepare a detailed plan that includes specific activities corresponding to each of the 68 objectives.

Aims of the National Strategy

- Prevent premature deaths due to suicide across the life span
- Reduce the rates of other suicidal behaviors
- Reduce the harmful after-effects associated with suicidal behaviors and the traumatic impact of suicide on family and friends
- Promote opportunities and settings to enhance resiliency, resourcefulness, respect, and interconnectedness for individuals, families, and communities

Goal 1: Promote Awareness that Suicide is a Public Health Problem that is Preventable

In a democratic society, the stronger and broader the support for a public health initiative, the greater its chance for success. If the general public understands that suicide and suicidal behaviors can be prevented, and people are made aware of the roles individuals and groups can play in prevention, the suicide rate can be reduced.

The objectives established for this goal are focused on increasing the degree of cooperation and collaboration between and among public and private entities that have made a commitment to public awareness of suicide and suicide prevention. They include:

- Developing public education campaigns
- Sponsoring national conferences on suicide and suicide prevention
- Organizing special-issue forums, and
- Disseminating information through the Internet.

Goal 2: Develop Broad-based Support for Suicide Prevention

Because there are many paths to suicide, prevention must address psychological, biological, and social factors if it is to be effective. Collaboration across a broad spectrum of agencies, institutions, and groups—from schools to faith-based organizations to health care associations—is a way to ensure that prevention efforts are comprehensive. Such collaboration can also generate greater and more effective attention to suicide prevention than can these groups working alone. Public/private partnerships that evolve from collaboration are able to blend resources and build upon each group's strengths. Broad-based support for suicide prevention may also lead to additional funding, through governmental programs as well as private philanthropy, and to the incorporation of suicide prevention activities into the mission of organizations that have not previously addressed it.

The objectives established for this goal are focused on developing collective leadership and on increasing the number of groups working to prevent suicide. They will help ensure that suicide prevention is better understood and that organizational support exists for implementing prevention activities. The objectives include:

- Organizing a Federal interagency committee to improve coordination and to ensure implementation of the National Strategy
- Establishing public/private partnerships dedicated to implementing the National Strategy
- Increasing the number of professional, volunteer, and other groups that integrate suicide prevention activities into their ongoing activities, and
- Increasing the number of faith communities that adopt policies designed to prevent suicide.

Goal 3: Develop and Implement Strategies to Reduce the Stigma Associated with Being a Consumer of Mental Health, Substance Abuse, and Suicide Prevention Services

Suicide is closely linked to mental illness and to substance abuse, and effective treatments exist for both. However, the stigma of mental illness and substance abuse prevents many persons from seeking assistance; they fear prejudice and discrimination. The stigma of suicide itself—the view that suicide is shameful and/or sinful—is also a barrier to treatment for persons who have suicidal thoughts or who have attempted suicide. Family members of suicide attempters often hide the behavior from friends and relatives, and those who have survived the suicide of a loved one suffer not only the grief of loss but often the added pain stemming from stigma.

Historically, the stigma associated with mental illness, substance abuse, and suicide has contributed to inadequate funding for preventive services and to low insurance reimbursements for treatments. It has also resulted in the establishment of separate systems for physical health and mental health care. One consequence is that preventive services and treatment for mental illness and substance abuse are much less available than for other health problems. Moreover, this separation has led to bureaucratic and institutional barriers between the two systems that complicate the provision of services and further impede access to care. Destigmatizing mental illness and substance use disorders could increase access to treatment by reducing financial barriers, integrating care, and increasing the willingness of individuals to seek treatment.

The objectives established for this goal are designed to create the conditions that enable persons in need of mental health and substance abuse services to receive them. They include:

- Increasing the number of suicidal persons with underlying mental disorders who receive appropriate mental health treatment, and
- Transforming public attitudes to view mental and substance use disorders as real illnesses, equal to physical illness, that respond to specific treatments and to view persons who obtain treatment as pursuing basic health care.

Goal 4: Develop and Implement Suicide Prevention Programs

Research has shown that many suicides are preventable; however, effective suicide prevention programs require commitment and resources. The public health approach provides a framework for developing preventive interventions. Programs may be specific to one particular organization, such as a university or a community health center, or they may encompass an entire State. While other goals in the NSSP address interventions to prevent suicide, a special emphasis of this goal is that of ensuring a range of interventions that in concert represent a comprehensive and coordinated program.

The objectives established for this goal are designed to foster planning and program development work and to ensure the integration of suicide prevention into organizations and agencies that have access to groups of individuals for other purposes. The objectives also address the need for systematic planning at both the State and local levels, the need for technical assistance in the development of suicide prevention programs, and the need for ongoing evaluation. Objectives include:

- Increasing the proportion of States with comprehensive suicide prevention plans

- Increasing the number of evidence-based suicide prevention programs in schools, colleges and universities, work sites, correctional institutions, aging programs, and family, youth, and community service programs, and
- Developing technical support centers to build the capacity across the States to implement and evaluate suicide prevention programs.

Goal 5: Promote Efforts to Reduce Access to Lethal Means and Methods of Self-Harm

Evidence from many countries and cultures shows that limiting access to lethal means of self-harm may be an effective strategy to prevent self-destructive behaviors. Often referred to as "means restriction," this approach is based on the belief that a small but significant minority of suicidal acts are, in fact, impulsive and of the moment; they result from a combination of psychological pain or despair coupled with the easy availability of the means by which to inflict self-injury. Thus, a self-destructive act may be prevented by limiting the individual's access to the means of self-harm. Evidence suggests that there may be a limited time effect for decreasing self-destructive behaviors in susceptible and impulsive individuals when access to the means for self-harm is restricted. Controversy exists about how to accomplish this goal because restricting means can take many forms and signifies different things to different people. For some, means restriction may connote redesigning or altering the existing lethal means of self-harm currently available, while to others it means eliminating or limiting their availability.

The objectives established for this goal are designed to separate in time and space the suicidal impulse from access to lethal means of self-harm. They include:

- Educating health care providers and health and safety officials on the assessment of lethal means in the home and actions to reduce suicide risk
- Implementing a public information campaign designed to reduce accessibility of lethal means
- Improving firearm safety design, establishing safer methods for dispensing potentially lethal quantities of medications and seeking methods for reducing carbon monoxide poisoning from automobile exhaust systems, and
- Supporting the discovery of new technologies to prevent suicide.

Goal 6: Implement Training For Recognition of At-Risk Behavior and Delivery of Effective Treatment

Studies indicate that many health professionals are not adequately trained to provide proper assessment, treatment, and management of suicidal patients, nor do they know how to refer clients properly for specialized assessment and treatment. Despite the increased awareness of suicide as a major public health problem, gaps remain in training programs for health professionals and others who often come into contact with patients in need of these specialized assessment techniques and treatment approaches. In addition, many health professionals lack training in the recognition of risk factors often found in grieving family members of loved ones who have died by suicide (suicide survivors).

Key gatekeepers—people who regularly come into contact with individuals or families in distress—need training in order to be able to recognize factors that place individuals at risk for suicide, and to learn appropriate interventions. Key gatekeepers include teachers and school personnel, clergy, police officers, primary health care providers, mental health care providers, correctional personnel, and emergency health care personnel.

The objectives established for this goal are designed to ensure that health professionals and key community gatekeepers obtain the training that will help them prevent suicide. They include:

- Improving education for nurses, physician assistants, physicians, social workers, psychologists, and other counselors
- Providing training for clergy, teachers and other educational staff, correctional workers, and attorneys on how to identify and respond to persons at risk for suicide, and
- Providing educational programs for family members of persons at elevated risk.

Goal 7: Develop and Promote Effective Clinical and Professional Practices

One way to prevent suicide is to identify individuals at risk and to engage them in treatments that are effective in reducing the personal and situational factors associated with suicidal behaviors (e.g., depressed mood, hopelessness, helplessness, alcohol and other drug abuse, among others). Another way to prevent suicide is to promote and support the presence of protective factors, such as learning skills in problem solving, conflict resolution, and nonviolent handling of disputes. By improving clinical practices in the assessment, management, and treatment for individuals at risk for suicide, the chances for preventing those individuals from acting on their despair and distress in self-destructive ways are greatly improved. Moreover, promoting the presence of protective factors for these individuals can contribute importantly to reducing their risk.

The objectives established for this goal are designed to heighten awareness of the presence or absence of risk and protective conditions associated with suicide, leading to better triage systems and better allocation of resources for those in need of specialized treatment. They include:

- Changing procedures and/or policies in certain settings, including hospital emergency departments, substance abuse treatment centers, specialty mental health treatment centers, and various institutional treatment settings, designed to assess suicide risk
- Incorporating suicide-risk screening in primary care
- Ensuring that individuals who typically provide services to suicide survivors have been trained to understand and respond appropriately to

their unique needs (e.g., emergency medical technicians, firefighters, police, funeral directors)

- Increasing the numbers of persons with mood disorders who receive and maintain treatment
- Ensuring that persons treated for trauma, sexual assault, or physical abuse in emergency departments receive mental health services
- Fostering the education of family members and significant others of persons receiving care for the treatment of mental health and substance abuse disorders with risk of suicide.

Goal 8: Improve Access to and Community Linkages with Mental Health and Substance Abuse Services

The elimination of health disparities and the improvement of the quality of life for all Americans are central goals of Healthy People 2010. Some of these health disparities are attributable to differences of gender, race or ethnicity, education, income, disability, stigma, geographic location, or sexual orientation. Many of these factors place individuals at increased risk for suicidal behaviors.

Barriers to equal access and affordability of health care may be influenced by financial, structural, and personal factors. Financial barriers include not having enough health insurance or not having the financial capacity to pay for services outside a health plan or insurance program. Structural barriers include the lack of primary care providers, medical specialists or other health care professionals to meet special needs or the lack of health care facilities. Personal barriers include cultural or spiritual differences, language, not knowing when or how to seek care, or concerns about confidentiality or discrimination. Reducing disparities is a necessary step in ensuring that all Americans receive appropriate physical health, mental health, and substance abuse services. One aspect of improving access is to better coordinate the services of a variety of community institutions. This will help ensure that at-risk populations receive the services they need, and that all community members receive regular preventive health services.

The objectives established for this goal are designed to enhance interorganizational communication to facilitate the provision of health services to those in need of them. They include:

- Increasing the number of States that require health insurance plans to cover mental health and substance abuse care on par with coverage for physical health care
- Implementing utilization management guidelines for suicidal risk in managed care and insurance plans
- Integrating mental health and suicide prevention into health and social services outreach programs for at-risk populations
- Defining and implementing screening guidelines for schools, colleges, and correctional institutions, along with guidelines on linkages with service providers, and
- Implementing support programs for persons who have survived the suicide of someone close.

Goal 9: Improve Reporting and Portrayals of Suicidal Behavior, Mental Illness, and Substance Abuse in the Entertainment and News Media

The media—movies, television, radio, newspapers, and magazines—have a powerful impact on perceptions of reality and on behavior. Research over many years has found that media representations of suicide may increase suicide rates, especially among youth. "Cluster suicides" and "suicide contagion" have been documented, and studies have shown that both news reports and fictional accounts of suicide in movies and on television can lead to increases in suicide. It appears that imitation plays a role in certain individuals engaging in suicidal behavior.

On the other hand, it is widely acknowledged that the media can play a positive role in suicide prevention, even as they report on suicide or depict it and related issues in movies and on television. The way suicide is presented is particularly important. Changing media representation of suicidal behaviors is one of several strategies needed to reduce the suicide rate.

Media portrayals of mental illness and substance abuse may also affect the suicide rate. Negative views of these problems may lead individuals to deny they have a problem or be reluctant to seek treatment—and untreated mental illness and substance abuse are strongly correlated with suicide.

The objectives established for this goal are designed to foster consideration among media leaders of the impact of different styles of describing or otherwise depicting suicide and suicidal behavior, mental illness, and substance abuse, and to encourage media representations of suicide that can help prevent rather than increase suicide. They include:

- Establishing a public/private group designed to promote the responsible representation of suicidal behaviors and mental illness on television and in movies
- Increasing the number of television programs, movies, and news reports that observe recommended guidelines in the depiction of suicide and mental illness, and
- Increasing the number of journalism schools that adequately address reporting of mental illness and suicide in their curricula.

Goal 10: Promote and Support Research on Suicide and Suicide Prevention

All suicides are highly complex. The volume of research on suicide and its risk factors has increased considerably in the past decade and has generated new questions about why individuals become suicidal or remain suicidal. The important contributions of underlying mental illness, substance use, and biological factors, as well as potential risk that comes from certain environmental influences are becoming clearer. Increasing the understanding of how individual and environmental risk and protective factors interact with each other to affect an individual's risk for suicidal behavior is the next challenge. This understanding can contribute to the limited but growing information about how modifying risk and protective factors change outcomes pertaining to suicidal behavior.

The objectives established for this goal are designed to support a wide range of research endeavors focused on the etiology, expression, and maintenance of suicidal behaviors across the lifespan. The enhanced understanding to be derived from this research will lead to better assessment tools, treatments, and preventive interventions. The objectives include:

- Developing a national suicide research agenda
- Increasing funds for suicide prevention research
- Evaluating preventive interventions, and
- Establishing a registry of interventions with demonstrated effectiveness for prevention of suicide or suicidal behavior.

Goal 11: Improve and Expand Surveillance Systems

Surveillance has been defined as the systematic and ongoing collection of data. Surveillance systems are key to health planning. They are used to track trends in rates, to identify new problems, to provide evidence to support activities and initiatives, to identify risk and protective factors, to target high risk populations for interventions, and to assess the impact of prevention efforts.

Data on suicide and suicidal behavior are needed at national, State and local levels. National data can be used to draw attention to the magnitude of the suicide problem and to examine differences in rates among groups (e.g., ethnic groups), locales (e.g., rural vs. urban) and whether suicidal individuals were cared for in certain settings (e.g., primary care, emergency departments). State and local data help establish local program priorities and are necessary for evaluating the impact of suicide prevention strategies.

The objectives established for this goal are designed to enhance the quality and quantity of data available on suicide and suicidal behaviors and ensure that the data are useful for prevention purposes. They include:

- Developing and implementing standardized protocols for death scene investigations
- Increasing the number of follow-back studies of suicides
- Increasing the number of hospitals that code for external cause of injuries
- Increasing the number of nationally representative surveys with questions on suicidal behavior
- Implementing a national violent death reporting system that includes suicide
- Increasing the number of States that produce annual reports on suicide, and
- Supporting pilot projects to link and analyze information on self-destructive behavior from various, distinct data systems.

Looking Ahead

The *National Strategy for Suicide Prevention* creates a framework for suicide prevention for the Nation. It is designed to encourage and empower groups and individuals to work together. The stronger and broader the support and collaboration on suicide prevention, the greater the chance for the success of this public health initiative. Suicide and suicidal behaviors can be reduced as the general public gains more understanding about the extent to which suicide is a problem, about the ways in which it can be prevented, and about the roles individuals and groups can play in prevention efforts.

The *National Strategy* is comprehensive and sufficiently broad so that individuals and groups can select those objectives and activities that best correspond to their responsibilities and resources. The plan's objectives suggest a number of roles for different groups. Individuals from a variety of occupations need to be involved in implementing the plan, such as health care professionals, police, attorneys, educators, and clergy. Institutions such as community groups, faith-based organizations, and schools all have a necessary part to play. Sites for suicide prevention work include jails, emergency departments and the workplace. Survivors, consumers and the media need to be partners as well, and governments at the Federal, State, and local levels are key in providing funding for public health and safety issues.

Ideally, the *National Strategy* will motivate and illuminate. It can serve as a model and be adopted or modified by States, communities, and tribes as they develop their own, local suicide prevention plans. The NSSP articulates the framework for national efforts and provides legitimacy for local groups to make suicide prevention a high priority for action.

The *National Strategy* encompasses the development, promotion and support of programs that will be implemented in communities across the country designed to achieve significant, measurable, and sustainable reductions in suicide and suicidal behaviors. This requires a major investment in public health action.

Now is the time for making great strides in suicide prevention. Implementing the *National Strategy for Suicide Prevention* provides the means to realize success in reducing the toll from this important public health problem. Sustaining action on behalf of all Americans will depend on effective public and private collaboration—because suicide prevention is truly everyone's business.

JAPANESE PRIME MINISTER ON HIS REFORM PLANS
May 7, 2001

Japan in 2001 turned to an eccentric politician, whose motto was "no pain, no gain," in hopes of arresting a decade-long economic decline. Junichiro Koizumi, elected prime minister in late April after staging an unprecedented revolt within the long-ruling Liberal Democratic Party, promised painful reforms to stimulate an economy weighted down by a half-century of mismanagement, corruption, and failed policies. In his first seven months in office, Koizumi shot to the top of Japan's popularity charts, but he made only modest progress in carrying out reforms opposed by the country's entrenched business interests and government bureaucracy. At year's end Japan's economy was in recession, and the most optimistic predictions were that growth would not resume until 2003 at the earliest.

For four decades, from the 1950s through the 1980s, Japan's economy was one of the marvels of the world, converting a country devastated by World War II into an industrial and financial powerhouse second only to the United States. But an overheated economic surge in the 1980s—a "bubble economy" based on inflated real estate values and unrestrained consumer spending—came to a crashing halt in 1991 and ushered in a decade of economic stagnation.

At the time of Koizumi's election, the litany of economic bad news in Japan was enough to discourage any politician, economist, or ordinary citizen. Since the 1991 crash, the economy had periodically been in recession, even while most of the rest of the world boomed, and it had grown at an average annual rate of just over 1 percent. Prices had fallen so persistently that Japan had become the first major industrial country in recent years to suffer serious deflation, which has just as negative an effect on any economy as does inflation. The government's debt had soared to about 130 percent of Japan's gross domestic product, by far the highest level of any industrialized country. Banks held hundreds of billions of dollars worth of bad loans (the government estimated $100 billion, but most economists put the actual figure at several times that level), and additional bad loans were mounting up faster than old ones could be cleared from bank ledger sheets. Japan's

304

currency, the yen, had fallen to an historic low against the dollar (about 122 yen to the dollar in August, then even lower to 130 at year's end), making Japanese export products cheaper overseas but also making imports more expensive. Bankruptcies and business closings continued at a record rate during 2001. Unemployment, which historically had been nearly nonexistent in Japan, had held steady at more than 4 percent for three years. (Japanese economic problems, Historic Documents of 1998, p. 532)

Koizumi's Election

Koizumi owed his political rise to the weakness of his immediate predecessor—Yoshiro Mori—who for many Japanese symbolized the failings of the country's political establishment. Mori had taken office in 2000 as the latest in a long line of prime ministers from the Liberal Democratic Party, which, despite its name, was a conservative party that had governed Japan for all but ten months (in 1993–1994) since its founding in 1955. Mori represented one of three factions within the party that rotated in and out of government leadership, in effect creating a multiparty system within one large party. Mori's inability to do anything about the sluggish economy had sent his approval rating in public opinion polls below the 10 percent mark by early 2001 and created irresistible pressure for him to resign.

When Mori finally succumbed to that pressure in April, the first indications were that the new prime minister would be selected in the time-honored fashion of backroom deals among the leaders of factions of the Liberal Democratic Party, which had a solid majority in the Diet, the lower house of parliament. But polls showed that the voters were fed up with old-fashioned politics and opposed all the party's traditional leaders, some of whom had served earlier as prime minister. In that context, the fifty-nine-year-old Koizumi emerged as a fresh face, despite his nearly thirty years in parliament. Koizumi had developed a reputation as a political maverick who avoided association with his party's barons and was not afraid to take unconventional positions. With his long, curly hair and movie star good looks, Koizumi did not resemble a typical Japanese politician—clearly an asset with a frustrated citizenry.

Koizumi easily won support from a majority of the party's 2 million members in local primaries, and then on April 24 won the party presidency (and thus the post of prime minister) by a vote of 298–155 among party leaders. His closest rival was former prime minister Ryutaro Hashimoto, who had been the favorite among party bosses until opinion polls demonstrated Koizumi's overwhelming popularity.

Koizumi took office April 26 and named a cabinet with many unconventional faces, including five women (a record) and three nonpoliticians from the private sector. As he took office, analysts said his great strength was the popular support that gave him a mandate no recent prime minister had enjoyed. Koizumi quickly achieved rock-star celebrity status. Posters of him sold by the millions, teenagers and even many adults adopted his hair style, and his approval ratings zoomed above 80 percent—an unheard of level for a Japanese prime minister. Even so, his atypical route to office was

*considered a handicap in winning over legislators and government bu-
reaucrats who were accustomed to old ways of doing business.*

Koizumi's Reforms

*In the universal style of politicians, Koizumi's predecessors had tended
to sugarcoat their budgets and economic proposals and to promise that better times were just around the corner. Koizumi chose a different path, acknowledging on May 7 in his first speech to parliament as prime minister
that Japanese society "has been enveloped in a spirit of disillusionment."
The economy had suffered from "long-term stagnation," he said, and the voters had lost faith in politics and their government.*

*Koizumi outlined, in general terms, a sweeping series of reforms involv-
ing both the government and the private sector, starting with the country's
troubled banking system. Koizumi set a goal of clearing all bad loans from
the banks within two to three years, a monumental task given the hundreds
of billions of dollars at risk and the past unwillingness of banking officials
and the government to confront the problem head-on. Acknowledging that it
would produce "some pains in our society," Koizumi also pledged to "scrap"
the government's previous method of dealing with economic downturns:
mounting huge public works projects, such as highways and ports, that employed millions of construction workers and enriched government-owned
contracting companies but that pushed the government budget deep into
deficit. As an alternative, he proposed spending money on education and
telecommunications infrastructure to make Japan "the most advanced IT
[information technology] state in the world within five years." To build
public confidence in the nation's political system, Koizumi said he was
creating a commission to draft proposals for direct election of the prime
minister.*

*Koizumi's proposals won broad support from the public and from inde-
pendent political and economic analysts. Jesper Koll, chief economist for the
Japanese branch of Merrill Lynch & Co., told the* Washington Post *that
the prime minister had set out "a good balance between providing a long-
term vision and leaving short-term flexibility. You have to remember that
the most important challenge for him is to get time. None of these problems
can be fixed overnight."*

*Many skeptics, however, suggested that Koizumi's reform plans would
die a thousand deaths when the time came to implement them with legislation and with actions in government ministries, all of which were managed
on a day-to-day basis by career bureaucrats seeking to protect their own jobs
and turf. Most economists also noted that Koizumi's proposals, such as cutting back on road-building projects, would have the collective short-term effect of worsening the economy before any longer-term improvements could
take place. Coupled with a recession then getting under way in the United
States, a deepening economic decline in Japan could lead to an economic
downturn in the rest of Asia and possibly worldwide, these economists said.*

*Despite his sweeping statements about needed reforms, Koizumi delayed
offering specifics until after July 29 elections for 121 of the 247 seats in the*

upper house of parliament. That election was widely seen as a strong endorsement for Koizumi and his policies; candidates aligned with his party and two coalition partners won 78 of the contested seats.

Claiming a new mandate for reform, Koizumi on August 10 presented a budget proposal (for the fiscal year beginning April 1, 2002) calling for cutbacks in spending on public works, defense, social security, and other areas. But in a bow to political realities, Koizumi trimmed his earlier proposals to revamp the 163 quasi-public corporations, called tokusu jojin, *that accounted for a large share of the Japanese economy and had acquired substantial independence from the government that funded them. Koizumi's cabinet voted to "study" only 77 of the corporations.*

As Koizumi had warned, the Japanese people kept experiencing the pain of economic retraction through the rest of 2001. Overall unemployment topped 5 percent in August and reached 5.5 percent by the end of the year, a record high since the post-World War II period of economic reconstruction. The Japanese stock market fell steadily, as did Japan's once-vaunted trade balance with other countries (due largely to surging low-cost imports from China). The government acknowledged in November that the economy was about to fall into recession and would contract by nearly 1 percent in the fiscal year ending March 31, 2002. At year's end the Bank of Japan predicted that the economy would be flat, at best, for the following fiscal year.

As the bad news continued, Koizumi followed through on some of his reforms, including his proposal to trim the tokusu jojin *corporations. His cabinet on December 19 approved a plan to abolish seventeen of the corporations and to sell forty-five others to private buyers. This plan fell far short of Koizumi's original sweeping proposal to close or sell all the corporations, and it did not touch some of the biggest and most controversial of them— but it represented a bigger change in this key area of government than previous prime ministers had enacted.*

Perhaps Koizumi's major failure, as of the end of 2001, was his inability to do much about the bad loans held by Japan's banks. Many analysts gave him credit for talking about the need for banks to clear such loans from their books, but little action was evident. The Japanese parliament in December passed a law giving a government agency, the Resolution and Collection Corporation, increased authority to buy bad loans from the banks; even so, most estimates were that bad loans were continuing to mount.

Amid the continuing economic gloom, Koizumi managed to hold onto his personal popularity, which hovered around 80 percent in the polls, and most Japanese expressed confidence in his ability to turn the country around. "I think he's smarter than everybody thought," Ikuo Kabashima, a professor of Japanese politics at the University of Tokyo, told the Far Eastern Economic Review *in late December. "You never know what's going to happen in Japanese politics. But at this moment he's won" the battle with the antireformers in his party.*

Following are excerpts from a speech delivered May 7, 2001, by Japanese prime minister Junichiro Koizumi to the Diet, the lower house of the Japanese parliament, describing his plans for economic and political reforms.

The document was obtained from the Internet at http:// www.kantei.go.jp/foreign/koizumispeech/2001/0507policy speech_e.html.

Aiming for Restoration in a New Century

Humbly accepting your support, I have taken office as Prime Minister of our nation. The pressure and tension of this office are greater than I could have imagined, but I am resolved to devote myself entirely to managing the affairs of state and to measuring up to the great level of support and expectations that the people of our nation and the distinguished members of the Diet have given me with this noble task.

After the Second World War Japan achieved dynamic economic development, resulting in a tremendous increase in the standard of living enjoyed by our people. Indeed, today more than 127 million people enjoy a high standard of living in this small nation with scarce natural resources. We should be proud of what we have accomplished in such a short period of time.

Since the outset of the decade of the 1990s, however, the Japanese economy has been unable to break free of long-term stagnation as trust in our political leadership has been eroded and our society has become enveloped in a spirit of disillusionment. It is now apparent that the structures that hitherto served us so well may not be appropriate for our society in the 21st century.

Given this context, the top priority that I must address is to rebuild our economy and reconstruct our society as one in full of pride and confidence. Moreover, Japan must fulfill a constructive role as a member of the global community. In the belief that "without structural reform there can be no rebirth for Japan," I am resolved to ceaselessly advance structural reforms, including economic reforms, fiscal reforms, administrative reforms, social reforms and political reforms, in the spirit of an era dedicated to reforms worthy of being called "Restoration in a New Century." We must embrace difficulties ahead, overcome barriers of fixed interests and free ourselves of past limitations as we create an economic social structure befitting the 21st century in the spirit of "No fear, no hesitation, and no constraint."

I formed my Ceaseless Reform Cabinet in order to achieve Restoration in a New Century based on the strong relations of trust among the Liberal Democratic Party, New Komeito and the New Conservative Party as we cooperate in tackling structural reforms, leaving no sacred areas exempt from these reforms. I further promise to strengthen various forms of dialogues with the people as we move forward with sweeping reforms. Through greater dialogues, my Cabinet will ensure transparency in policy deliberation processes in order to gain wide understanding among the people and share the perception of issues with the people, thereby achieving my goal of bringing back "politics of trust."

The series of unfortunate scandals that our nation has suffered have greatly reduced the faith that is placed in the government by the people. Each and every one of us involved in politics and administration must sincerely and solemnly hear the criticism from the people and as we earnestly strive to carry our missions of public service, we must work to restore people's faith in politics.

Moreover, it is essential that we expand avenues for participation in politics by the people. Towards this end, an advisory council will be promptly established to draft concrete proposals on modalities for the direct election of the Prime Minister.

Aiming for Economic Revitalization

The top priority for our nation is to achieve an economic rebirth. The first task for the Koizumi Cabinet will be to implement promptly the Emergency Economic Package compiled under the administration of former Prime Minister Yoshiro Mori. These economic measures will steer our nation along the path from traditional demand-driven policies to active policies focusing on the disposal of non-performing loans and structural reforms of our capital markets.

Various discussions and proposals have been offered as the right prescription needed to achieve a rebirth of the Japanese economy. Crafted with a view to meeting the needs of this age of global competition and creating a self-sustaining economy, these proposals have met with the approval of many and are in line with my long-held position that "without structural reforms there can be no economic recovery."

The prescription has been written and awaits dispensing. My duty in order for us to truly realize a rebirth of the Japanese economy is to move forward decisively and perform my tasks.

Economic and Fiscal Structural Reforms—Without Structural Reforms There Can Be No Economic Recovery

Since the outset of the 1990s the Japanese economy has been suffering from a complex illness resulting from the confluence of various factors. Comprehensive structural reforms are imperative in order to solve these problems. The Koizumi Cabinet will ceaselessly implement the following three key economic and fiscal structural reforms.

First of all, we will aim for final disposal of non-performing loans within the coming two to three years. That will be achieved by creating a framework for promoting a final disposal of non-performing loans in which the Government will compile guidelines to sort out discussions by banks and other concerned parties aiming for rebuilding corporations.

Furthermore, concrete measures will be drawn up to create limitations on shareholdings of banks and to lead the way toward the creation of the Bank Equity Purchasing Corporation (BEPC). These measures will be premised on ensuring harmony between stabilization of our financial systems and the market mechanism.

Secondly, we must create a competitive economic system that is appropriate for the environment of the 21st century. Such structural reforms will enhance the great potential for development inherent in the Japanese economy. In order to usher in a competitive industrial society we will promote the creation of new industries and employment opportunities and ensure the effective functioning of the Council for Comprehensive Regulatory Reform and advance thorough regulatory reforms spanning all of our economic and social structures. Furthermore, we will strengthen the structure of the Fair Trade Commission, which should serve as the guardian of the market, thereby establishing competition policies appropriate for the 21st century.

In order to activate the securities market we must promptly implement wide-ranging systemic reforms, including tax measures that will stimulate more active market participation by individual investors.

In terms of promoting the information technology revolution (IT Revolution), you are all aware of the ambitious goal of making our nation the most advanced IT state in the world within five years. In order to ensure we achieve this goal, I will steadily implement the "e-Japan Priority Policy Program." As a mid-term goal I also intend to formulate the "IT 2002 Program."

Moreover, focusing on the Council for Science and Technology Policy, which I chair, I intend for Japan to be a "nation built by the promotion of science and technology." In this context I will promote strategic investments in research and development in the science and technology areas that form the foundation of industrial competitiveness and ensure a high-quality standard of living for our people. I will also strive to reform our research and development systems.

By revitalizing our cities and creating greater liquidity in real estate transactions we will make our cities more attractive and enhance their international competitiveness. With that in mind, I intend to establish promptly the "Urban Rejuvenation Headquarters," which I will chair myself.

Fiscal structural reforms are the third key area. During recent years the Government has taken demand-driven measures such as increasing public works spending and reducing taxes in order to respond to the ongoing economic stagnation. However, we have been forced to maintain these policies for a long time, and this has left Japan with a tremendous fiscal deficit. The goal of our fiscal structural reform will be to improve this situation and establish a simple and efficient government structure that will meet the needs of this 21st century.

I will implement these structural reforms through a two-phased approach. First of all, as an initial step toward fiscal soundness, new government bond issues will be targeted to less than 30 trillion yen in the [fiscal year] FY2002 budget. At the same time, vigorous efforts will be made to review government expenditures. Subsequently we will seek a sustainable fiscal balance by comprehensively rebuilding our fiscal structures, through steps such as setting the goal of not relying on new borrowing for expenditures other than interest payments on past loans.

In the process of implementing such structural reforms we will need to scrap and build inefficient sectors in order to achieve rejuvenation in certain sectors, and this process may result in some pains in our society. I intend to enhance policies to relieve anxieties in the employment sector, such as measures to assist the unemployed to re-enter the work force and to take financial measures to assist small- and medium- enterprises and to help companies to innovate their management practices.

The economic society that we aim to achieve is one in which each and every individual, as well as our corporations and local regions, can freely realize their great latent potential, and even expand their potential. It is in just such a nation that I envision our economy as one that is truly abundant, proud and independent. In the Council on Economic and Fiscal Policy (CEFP), which I chair, we are aiming to draft basic guidelines on future economic and fiscal management and further economic and social structural reforms by June of this year.

Administrative Structural Reforms—All That Can Be Accomplished by the Private Sector Should be Left in its Hands, and All That Can be Delegated to Local Governments Should Be Delegated to Them

The reorganization of central government that was conducted at the beginning of this year was merely the beginning of administrative reforms. I believe that we must start from scratch in ceaselessly reforming the very modalities under which we organize our administration. As I move forward with administrative structural reforms I will conduct a thorough review of the rationality and necessity of all operations carried out by the national government under the principle that "all that can be accomplished by the private sector should be left in its hands, and all that can be delegated to local governments, should be delegated to them.

A thorough review of all special public institutions will be made without exception, with a view to greatly reducing government funding. Furthermore, sweeping reforms will be made of public service corporations. The three postal businesses will be reorganized as public corporations in the year 2003 as planned, with future modalities for those operations to be considered by an advisory council that will be promptly established to consider all options, including privatization, and to present concrete proposals to the people. . . .

[Koizumi then described proposals for decentralizing the federal government, revising the civil service and judicial systems, promoting education and other social programs, and protecting the environment.]

21st Century Diplomacy and National Security

In order for Japan to continue to enjoy prosperity in peace, it is essential that we steadfastly devote ourselves to international cooperation. Japan must never again isolate itself from the international community and must never again wage war. Indeed, the prosperity that Japan enjoys is based upon the Japan-US relationship that has functioned effectively. Based on the foundation of the Japan-US alliance, we must maintain and enhance Japan's friendly relations with its neighbors, including the People's Republic of China, the Republic of Korea and the Russian Federation. As one of the leading nations shouldering responsibilities of the international community, Japan will demonstrate its leadership in enhancing the international system appropriate for the 21st century. In that context, Japan will take initiative in seeking to reform the United Nations, strengthen the multilateral free trading system centered on the World Trade Organization (WTO) and in addressing challenges of a global scale, including environmental issues.

In our bilateral relations with the United States, I will work to ensure that the Japan-US Security Arrangements function even more effectively. Furthermore, I will seek new ways to enhance bilateral dialogue on economic and trade issues and strengthen dialogue and cooperation on matters pertaining to political and national security issues. Moreover, while earnestly striving to promote growth and development in Okinawa [the site of major U.S. military installations], I intend to concentrate my fullest efforts on the steady implementation of the Final Report of the Special Action Committee on Okinawa (SACO), including the relocation and return of Futenma Air Station and to make efforts to alleviate the burden borne by the people of Okinawa Prefecture.

Our relations with the People's Republic of China are one of the most important bilateral relationships for Japan. I hope that China will fulfill an even more constructive role in the international community, through such opportunities as the Asia-Pacific Economic Cooperation (APEC) Leaders Meeting scheduled for this autumn in Shanghai, and I intend to continue to deepen our cooperative relations with China.

Japan shares the values of democracy with its closest geographic neighbor, the Republic of Korea, and the importance of this relationship cannot be overstated. I intend to work hand-in-hand with the Republic of Korea to maintain and strengthen this relationship and to ensure the success of next year's joint hosting of the World Cup Soccer tournament and The Year of Japan-Republic of Korea National Exchange, also to be held in 2002.

Last year there were many noteworthy developments on the Korean Peninsula, including the North-South Summit. While maintaining close cooperation among Japan, the United States and the Republic of Korea, I intend to continue to persevere in the normalization talks between Japan and North Korea in a manner that contributes to the peace and stability of Northeast Asia. Moreover, I intend to devote my fullest efforts toward resolving through dialogue the humanitarian issues and security issues with North Korea.

As for Japan's relations with the Russian Federation, I intend to firmly carry forward the results that have been achieved up to the recent Japan-Russia Summit Meeting in Irkutsk. Based on the consistent position that we should conclude a peace treaty by resolving the issue of the attribution of the four islands [Kurile Islands disputed between Russia and Japan], I intend to earnestly carry forward the negotiations, while simultaneously making progress on cooperation in economic fields and cooperation in the international arena, in order to advance our relations across a broad spectrum.

We must not allow ourselves to be complacent with peace and become oblivious to the possibility of disturbances. Indeed, it is the fundamental responsibility of politics to plan for all eventualities and be ready to respond to any situation. I believe that it is the duty of the political leadership to consider what kind of structure can be created in the event that the state or the people are exposed to crises and I intend to move forward with consideration on Emergency Legislation, bearing fully in mind the views expressed by the ruling party last year.

Conclusion

Through active and honest dialogues with the public, with the cooperation and support of the people, I intend to take steady steps needed to give rise to a new society and lead to the creation of a new future for our nation. During the next six months we will hold town meetings attended by relevant Cabinet members and others in all prefectures and will launch a "Koizumi Cabinet Mail Magazine." These, and other efforts, will foster momentum among the people to participate in policy formulation.

Let us remember that at the beginning of the Meiji era [in the mid-nineteenth century] the Nagaoka Clan was in a state of severe poverty. As a gesture of assistance an offering of 100 sacks of rice was sent to the clan. Consumed immediately this would have been enough to fill the hungry stomachs of the Clan members for a few days. However, the wise leader of the Clan chose to forgo the immediate satisfaction of feeding his people in favor of selling the food and investing the proceeds in the establishment of a school to educate his people, thereby ensuring a future harvest of thousands and even tens of thousands of sacks of rice for his people. In fact, the school that was established went on to train many of the leaders who made Japan the nation that she has become. More than anything else what is needed in Japan today is to strive forward steadfastly with the implementation of reforms in a spirit of persevering through the difficulties of the present in order to build a better tomorrow. Whether or not we will greet this new century emboldened with the courage to build a future full of hope for our nation depends on the determination of each and every one of our people to carry out the reforms that are needed.

I am resolved that my Cabinet will ceaselessly advance structural reforms, while leaving no areas exempt from reforms in Japan's social and economic structures. I stand here before you today in a spirit of absolute discipline, fully ready to devote my entire being to fulfilling my duty as Prime Minister of Japan.

I call upon each and every member of the Diet to rise to challenges at hand and, billowed by the winds of change in an era of reform, to join with me in undertaking trustworthy political action.

Here I humbly ask for the support and cooperation of the people of Japan and the members of the Diet.

U.S. CENSUS REPORT ON
THE HISPANIC POPULATION
May 10, 2001

The United States at the start of the new century was a much more diverse and older nation than ever before, according to data from the 2000 census released during 2001. That trend was likely to continue well into the twenty-first century, when non-Hispanic whites might become a minority for the first time since the early days of European colonization of North America, and a higher proportion of Americans would be of retirement age. The 2000 census confirmed several other important trends in the U.S. population, including the continued rapid growth in many urban areas of the South and West, and the declining prominence of "nuclear families" of married couples with children. In short, the census demonstrated that the U.S. population remained the most dynamic in the world, changing constantly in response to social trends and immigration, both past and present.

Several reports by the United Nations and private research organizations pointed to disturbing demographic trends elsewhere in the world, including declining populations in most industrialized countries and lagging food production and worsening environmental conditions in many developing countries (especially in Africa). The United Nations Population Fund said the world population stood at 6.1 billion in mid-2000 and probably would reach 9.3 by mid-century. World population stood at 1 billion at the start of the twentieth century. (Previous world population projections, Historic Documents of 1999, p. 584)

Overall U.S. Population

The 2000 census put the total U.S. population at 281.4 million as of April 1, 2001. This figure included all residents of the fifty states and the District of Columbia but did not include those in Puerto Rico (a commonwealth) and the island territories of the U.S. Virgin Islands, Guam, American Samoa, and the Northern Mariana Islands. The U.S. population increased 13.1 percent since the 1990 census, when the comparable total figure had been 248.7 million. Much of the increase during the 1990s was due to immigration and births in families of those who had immigrated in recent decades—especially Hispanics and Asians.

Another result of immigration was that the United States continued to be one of the most racially and ethnically diverse countries on the planet. More than two-thirds of Americans (194.5 million) described themselves as "white" but not Hispanic; 12.5 percent (35.3 million) described themselves as "Hispanic" or "Latino"; 12.1 percent (33.9 million) described themselves as "black" or "African American" (but not Hispanic); 3.5 percent (10.1 million) described themselves as "Asian"; and 0.7 percent (2.5 million) as "America Indian" or "Alaskan Native."

About 15.4 million people—nearly all of them Hispanics—checked a category labeled "some other race" when asked about their race. In addition, 6.8 million Americans identified themselves with two or more racial categories. The 2000 census was the first in which respondents were able to identify themselves with more than one race or to use the "some other race" category. Some critics said these changes made it impossible to compare the results of the 2000 census directly with previous censuses. One source of confusion was that under federal regulations, Hispanics were considered an ethnic group but not a race; in 2000 respondents were asked first whether they were Hispanic and then to identify with one or more racial categories. Despite the regulations, Census Bureau officials said many Hispanics, especially young adults, told census takers that they considered themselves to be a separate racial group, accounting for the large number choosing the "some other race" category.

The proportion of Americans describing themselves solely as "white" (but not Hispanic) continued to decline during the 1990s, as it had in recent decades. Three-fourths of Americans in the 1990 census were classified as non-Hispanic whites, but ten years later the proportion had dropped to 69 percent. Looked at another way, the percentage of blacks and Hispanics went from 20.4 percent of Americans in 1990 to 24.5 percent in 2000. Yet another perspective could be gained from the growth rates for each of the major groups. From 1990 to 2000 the non-Hispanic white population grew by 3.4 percent, the Hispanic population grew by 57.9 percent, the black population grew by 15.6 percent, and the Asian population grew by 52.4 percent. If similar rates continued, non-Hispanic whites could become a minority in the United States by the middle of the twenty-first century.

In many ways, California continued to represent the leading edge of changes in American demographics. Once again, California was by far the most populous state, with 33.9 million people—one in eight Americans. But for the first time non-Hispanic whites represented a minority in the state, just 46.7 percent of the total. During the 1990s, Hispanic and Asian populations grew rapidly, while the number of whites and blacks in California held steady. In 2000 nearly 11 million Californians listed themselves as Hispanic, just shy of one-third of the total state population. As in the past, California remained one of the nation's principal points of entry for immigrants, especially for Asians. California was home to just less than one-third of all Americans who said they were born in another country.

Growth of the Hispanic Population

One key finding of the 2000 census was that Hispanics had matched blacks as the country's second-largest minority group. A total of 35.3 million people, or 12.5 percent of the total, described themselves as "Hispanic" or "Latino" (the Census Bureau used those terms interchangeably). A majority of those also included themselves in the "white" racial category, but millions of Hispanics also chose the "some other race" category.

As in the past, a majority, 58.5 percent, of those calling themselves Hispanic said they were of Mexican descent. Americans of Puerto Rican descent were second, at 9.6 percent, followed by those from Central America at 4.8 percent, South America at 3.8 percent, Cuba at 3.5 percent, and the Dominican Republic at 2.2 percent. About 6 million Hispanics chose the "other Hispanic" category.

As could be expected, about 75 percent of Hispanics were in western and southern states, with just four states in those regions accounting for a majority of the national total: California (about 11 million), Texas (about 6.7 million), Florida (about 2.7 million), and Arizona (about 1.3 million). Three northern states also had Hispanic populations of more than 1 million: New York (about 2.9 million), Illinois (about 1.5 million), and New Jersey (about 1.1 million). In terms of statewide representation, New Mexico had the nation's highest proportion of Hispanic residents (42.1 percent), followed by California (32.4 percent), Texas (32 percent), and Arizona (25.3 percent). At the other end of the scale, less than 1 percent of the residents of Maine, Vermont, and West Virginia called themselves Hispanic.

One intriguing finding of the census was the penetration of Hispanics into areas of the country not traditionally associated with such populations, including the South (outside Florida) and the Midwest. North Carolina, Arkansas, and Georgia (in that order) had the highest percentage growth rates in Hispanic populations during the 1990s. Hispanic populations more than doubled in seven midwestern states: Minnesota, Nebraska, Iowa, Indiana, Wisconsin, South Dakota, and Kansas, in descending order of increase. Tens of thousands of Hispanics were lured to these states, including to small towns, by the prospect of jobs and a better quality of life, according to Linda Barros, an official with the National Council of La Raza, a Latino civil rights organization.

The future of America's Hispanic population could be seen with one census finding: Hispanics tended to be the youngest of the three major groups in the United States. Nearly half (47.6 percent) of Hispanics were age 24 or less, compared with 42.4 percent of blacks and 32 percent of all non-Hispanic whites. Among Hispanics, Mexicans tended to be the youngest, with a median age of 24.2 years, compared with a median age of 25.9 years for all Hispanics and 35.3 years for all Americans. Cuban Americans, many of whom had come to the United States shortly after the communist regime of Fidel Castro took power in 1959, tended to be the nation's oldest Hispanics, with a median age of 40.7 years.

Other Demographic Trends

Changes in ethnic and racial composition were paralleled by other demographic shifts made evident by the 2000 census and related surveys. Most of the trends followed those that had been under way in the United States throughout the last half of the twentieth century.

So-called nuclear families (married couples with children under the age of 18) continued to decline as a percentage of all households. The Census Bureau defined a "household" as one or more persons living in a housing unit. In the 1960 census nuclear families made up nearly half of all households (45 percent); by 2000 the percentage had dropped to 25 percent. Despite this decline, the percentage of all children living with their married biological parents remained at about 60 percent, similar to historical trends. Although they might appear contradictory, most experts said these two sets of findings simply reflected the fact that the makeup of American households became more diverse during the late twentieth century. For example, experts said an increasing number of households featured such arrangements as grandparents living with a family with children, or adult children continuing to live with their parents while saving money for a marriage or their own housing.

The 1990s saw a growth in the number and percentage of Americans living alone (26 percent of all households), married couples without children (nearly 28 percent), unmarried couples (9 percent), and households headed by single mothers (7 percent). One explanation was that American were getting married much later than ever before: the median age of the first marriage for men stood at 27 in 2000, up from age 22 in 1960, and for women at 25, up from 20 in 1960.

The median age of Americans in 2000 was 35.3 years, the highest in history. This was largely the result of the aging of the so-called baby boom generation, born between 1946 and 1964. The median age would have been even higher without the arrival of immigrants, who tended to be younger than the overall population.

Some areas of the country, especially in the South and West, continued to experience explosive growth, while some cities and rural areas in the North lost population. The Las Vegas, Nevada, metropolitan area led the nation in growth, nearly doubling to about 1.6 million people during the 1900s. Naples, Florida; Yuma, Arizona; Austin, Texas; and Phoenix, Arizona, were among the other metropolitan areas that grew by more than 40 percent during the decade. Meanwhile, a study of census data by the Brookings Institution, a Washington think tank, showed that white flight from the nation's big cities continued during the 1990s. By 2000 whites were still the majority in only 52 of the 100 largest cities, down from 70 cities a decade earlier. Among the 18 cities losing their white majorities were Boston, Milwaukee, Philadelphia, Rochester, San Diego, and St. Louis. Dozens of small communities in the Midwest also suffered dramatic population losses as sons and daughters of farming families left for urban areas.

A survey of 700,000 households conducted in conjunction with the census turned up many interesting findings about the social and economic status of Americans at the turn of the century. Among the findings: 17.6 percent of people age 5 or older spoke a language other than English at home, and 4.1 percent of Americans (or more than 10 million) spoke little or no English; 11 percent of Americans said they were foreign-born, statistically a very large increase from the 8 percent who said they were foreign-born in 1990; only a tiny portion of Americans lived in housing conditions prevalent in most of the developing world, including 4.2 percent living in what the Census Bureau defined as "crowded housing," 0.5 percent living in homes without plumbing, and 3 percent living in homes without telephones.

The Census and Redistricting

The U.S. Constitution requires the government to take a census every ten years for a practical purpose: Current population figures are needed to determine how many seats each state will get in the U.S. House of Representatives. That chamber's 435 seats are determined strictly by population, with each seat representing about 647,000 people as a result of the 2000 census. During the late twentieth century, population shifts meant that large states in the Midwest and Northeast had lost seats in the House, while the rapidly growing states in the South and West had gained seats.

The Census Bureau in December 2000 had announced the reapportionment of districts among the states, starting with elections in 2002 for the 108th Congress. Under that plan, Arizona, Florida, Georgia, and Texas would each gain two House seats, while California, Colorado, Nevada, and North Carolina would each gain one seat. Offsetting those gains, New York and Pennsylvania were each to lose two seats, while Connecticut, Illinois, Indiana, Michigan, Mississippi, Ohio, Oklahoma, and Wisconsin were each to lose one seat. Each state was responsible for drawing the lines of its congressional districts—a highly political process known as "redistricting."

The federal and state governments also used census figures to allocate funds for education, health, social welfare, and other programs among local governing bodies. For that reason, mayors and city councils often were anxious to ensure that all their citizens were counted, but undercounting of inner-city minorities had been a persistent problem with previous censuses. During the presidency of Bill Clinton, a Democrat, the Census Bureau had proposed using statistical sampling in an attempt to ensure that the census fully counted groups that traditionally had been undercounted, especially inner-city blacks. Congressional Republicans objected to that procedure and attempted to use legislation to block the Census Bureau from using sampling. Ultimately, the question was decided in 2001 by the new administration of George W. Bush, a Republican, which rejected the sampling technique.

World Population Reports

The United Nations Population Fund and other organizations issued numerous reports during 2001 that attempted to describe the status of the world's population as of the turn of the century. Perhaps the single most striking conclusion from those reports was that the populations of most in-

dustrialized countries had stopped growing, while most poor, developing countries were continuing to grow rapidly. As of mid-2000 the total world population was estimated at 6.1 billion. By 2050, the UN agency said on February 28, total world population would reach an estimated 9.3 billion, based on an estimated range of 7.9 billion to 10.9 billion. The vast majority of the population at mid-century, about 8.2 billion, would be living in countries now classified as "developing," the UN said; only about 1.2 billion would be living in countries now considered "developed" or "industrialized."

According to UN figures, the United States was the only industrialized country in the world where the "fertility rate" (births per women of child-bearing age) was greater than the "replacement rate" (the number of births needed to keep to keep the population stable, not counting immigration). The U.S. fertility rate in 2000 was just above the replacement rate.

Total populations were declining at the turn of the century in most of Europe (especially Italy and Germany) and in Japan. However, Bangladesh, China, India, Indonesia, Nigeria, Pakistan, and many other developing countries were growing rapidly. By mid-century, India was expected to catch up with China as the world's most populous country; both countries would then have about 1.5 billion people.

Unfortunately, according to UN reports, the population growth in many developing countries will not be accompanied by improved living or environmental standards. Food production lagged behind population growth in nearly two-thirds of the 105 developing countries, the UN said, as did access to drinking water. In 2000, according to agency figures, 508 million people lived in thirty-one countries considered to be "water-stressed" or "water-scarce." By 2025 the comparable figures were expected to be 3 billion people in 48 such countries. This did not mean that all 3 billion people would lack access to water, but it did portend increasing competition for water—possibly even resulting in wars over water access, the UN said.

The AIDS crisis also was expected to continue unabated in many countries, especially in sub-Saharan Africa, through the early part of the twenty-first century. The UN agency estimated that AIDS would kill about 15 million people in the forty-five most affected countries during the first five years of the century. (AIDS, p. 438)

> *Following are excerpts from "The Hispanic Population: Census 2000 Brief," issued May 10, 2001, by the U.S. Census Bureau. This was one of numerous summaries of results of the 2000 census issued by the bureau during 2001.*
>
> **The document was obtained from the Internet at http://www.census.gov/prod/2001pubs/c2kbr01-3.pdf.**

In Census 2000, 281.4 million residents were counted in the United States (excluding the Commonwealth of Puerto Rico and the U.S. Island Areas), of which 35.3 million (or 12.5 percent) were Hispanic. Mexicans represented 7.3 percent, Puerto Ricans 1.2 percent, Cubans 0.4 percent, and other Hispanics 3.6 percent of the total population. An additional 3.8 million Hispanics were enumerated in the Commonwealth of Puerto Rico. This report, part of a series that analyzes population and housing data collected by Census 2000, provides a profile of the Hispanic population in the United States.

The concept and measurement of Hispanic origin have evolved across several censuses.

In Census 2000, people of Spanish/Hispanic/Latino origin could identify as Mexican, Puerto Rican, Cuban, or other Spanish/Hispanic/Latino. The term "Latino" appeared on the census form for the first time in 2000. People who marked "other Spanish/Hispanic/Latino" had additional space to write Hispanic origins, such as Salvadoran or Dominican, a practice started in the 1990 census. The 1990 and 1980 censuses asked people if they were of Spanish/Hispanic origin or descent and if so, to choose Mexican, Puerto Rican, Cuban, or other Spanish/Hispanic.

The census in 1970 was the first to include a separate question specifically on Hispanic origin, although it was only asked of 5 percent sample of households. In 1970, respondents were asked to choose whether their origin or descent was Mexican, Puerto Rican, Cuban, Central or South American, or other Spanish. Prior to 1970, Hispanic origin was determined only indirectly; for example, the 1960 and 1950 censuses collected and published data for "persons of Spanish surname" in five southwestern states, whereas the 1940 census identified people who reported Spanish as their mother tongue. Mexican was included as a category within the race question only in the 1930 census.

The Hispanic population increased by more than 50 percent since 1990.

The Hispanic population increased by 57.9 percent, from 22.4 million in 1990 to 35.3 million in 2000, compared with an increase of 13.2 percent for the total U.S. population. Population growth varied by group. Mexicans increased by 52.9 percent, from 13.5 million to 20.6 million. Puerto Ricans increased by 24.9 percent, from 2.7 million to 3.4 million. Cubans increased by 18.9 percent, from 1.0 million to 1.2 million. Hispanics who reported other origins increased by 96.9 percent, from 5.1 million to 10.0 million.

As a result of these different growth rates, the proportionate distribution of Hispanics by type changed between 1990 and 2000. In 2000, Mexicans were 58.5 percent of all Hispanics (down from 60.4 percent in 1990), Puerto Ricans were 9.6 percent (down from 12.2 percent), Cubans were 3.5 percent (down from 4.7 percent), and the remaining 28.4 percent were of other Hispanic origins (up from 22.8 percent).

Other Hispanic origins refer to a variety of identifications.

Among the 10.0 million other Hispanics in 2000, 1.7 million were Central American, 1.4 million were South American, and 765,000 were Dominican.

Most other Hispanics did not specify a detailed Hispanic origin, but either checked the Spanish/Hispanic/Latino box without providing any additional information or wrote in answers such as "Hispanic" or "Latino" or "Spanish." At 17.3 percent (6.1 million) of the total Hispanic population, Hispanic respondents who did not give a detailed origin answer were second in size only to the Mexican origin group.

Salvadorans were the largest Central American group.

Central Americans represented 4.8 percent of the total Hispanic population. There were 655,000 Salvadorans (1.9 percent of the total Hispanic population), 372,000 Guatemalans (1.1 percent), and 218,000 Hondurans (0.6 percent).

South Americans represented 3.8 percent of the total Hispanic population. There were 471,000 Colombians (1.3 percent of the total Hispanic population), 261,000 Ecuadorians (0.7 percent), and 234,000 Peruvians (0.7 percent).

More than three-quarters of Hispanics lived in the West or South.

In 2000, 43.5 percent of Hispanics lived in the West and 32.8 percent lived in the South. The Northeast and Midwest accounted for 14.9 percent and 8.9 percent, respectively, of the Hispanic population.

Hispanics accounted for 24.3 percent of the population in the West, the only region in which Hispanics exceeded the national level of 12.5 percent. Hispanics accounted for 11.6 percent of the population in the South, 9.8 percent in the Northeast, and 4.9 percent in the Midwest.

Mexicans, Puerto Ricans, and Cubans were concentrated in different regions. Among Mexicans, 55.3 percent lived in the West, 31.7 percent in the South, 10.7 percent in the Midwest, and 2.3 percent in the Northeast. Among Puerto Ricans, 60.9 percent lived in the Northeast, 22.3 percent in the South, 9.6 percent in the Midwest, and 7.2 percent in the West. Among Cubans, 74.2 percent lived in the South, 13.6 percent in the Northeast, 8.5 percent in the West, and 3.6 percent in the Midwest.

Half of all Hispanics lived in just two states: California and Texas.

In 2000, 27.1 million, or 76.8 percent, of Hispanics lived in the seven states with Hispanic populations of 1.0 million or more (California, Texas, New York, Florida, Illinois, Arizona, and New Jersey). Hispanics in California accounted for 11.0 million (31.1 percent) of the total Hispanic population, while the Hispanic population in Texas accounted for 6.7 million (18.9 percent). Hispanics numbered between 500,000 and 999,999 in only two states (Colorado and New Mexico). Hispanics in 22 states were between 100,000 and 499,999. Hispanics were less than 100,000 in 19 states and the District of Columbia.

Hispanics in New Mexico were 42.1 percent of the total state population, the highest proportion for any state. Hispanics were 12.5 percent (the national level) or more of the state population in eight other states (California, Texas,

Arizona, Nevada, Colorado, Florida, New York, and New Jersey). Mexicans were the largest Hispanic group in five of these states (California, Texas, Arizona, Nevada, and Colorado), while Hispanics of other Hispanic origins were the largest group in the remaining states (New Mexico, Florida, New York, and New Jersey). Hispanics accounted for less than 12.5 percent of the population in 41 states and the District of Columbia.

Hispanic origin groups were concentrated in different states. The largest Mexican populations (more than million) were in California, Texas, Illinois and Arizona, mostly southwestern states. The largest Puerto Rican populations (more than 250,000) were in New York, Florida, New Jersey, and Pennsylvania, mostly northeastern states. About two-thirds of all Cubans were in Florida.

Counties with the highest proportions of Hispanics were along the southwestern border of the United States.

In 2000, the proportion of Hispanics within a county exceeded the national level (12.5 percent) most often in the counties of the South and West, especially in counties along the border with Mexico.

Hispanics were the majority of the population in 50 counties, accounting for 13.5 percent of the total Hispanic population. Of these counties, 35 are in the South and 15 are in the West. In the South, Hispanics were the majority in 34 counties in Texas and one in Florida. In the West, Hispanics were the majority in nine counties in New Mexico, and two counties in each of the following states: Arizona, California, and Colorado.

Hispanics also were concentrated in groupings of counties outside of the four states bordering Mexico. In particular, Hispanic concentrations occurred in counties within central Washington, in counties within the mountain states of Idaho, Wyoming, Utah, and Colorado, in counties around Chicago, New York, and the District of Colombia, and in counties within southern Florida.

Hispanics represented more than one-quarter but less than half of the county population in 152 counties. The percent Hispanic exceeded the national level of 12.5 percent but was less than 25.0 percent of the population in 181 counties. The percent Hispanic ranged from 6.0 percent to just under the national level in 311 counties. Hispanics represented less than 6.0 percent of the county's population in 2,447 counties. Furthermore, Hispanics represented less than 1.0 percent of a county s population in 899 counties.

Hispanics were also present in some counties within nontraditional states.

While most Hispanics lived in the South or West, some counties in nontraditional Hispanic states such as Georgia and North Carolina had sizable proportions of Hispanic populations. Hispanics within some counties in North Carolina, Georgia, Iowa, Arkansas, Minnesota, and Nebraska represented between 6.0 percent and 24.9 percent of the county's total population. The percent Hispanic within these counties exceeded the percent Hispanic (less than 6.0 percent) for these states.

More than 4 million Hispanics lived in Los Angeles County, California.

In 2000, Hispanics in four counties accounted for 21.9 percent of the total Hispanic population. There were 4.2 million Hispanics in Los Angeles County, California, 1.3 million in Miami-Dade County, Florida, 1.1 million in Harris County, Texas, and 1.1 million in Cook County, Illinois.

Hispanic origin groups were concentrated in different counties. The largest Mexican populations lived in counties that had large Hispanic populations, including Los Angeles County, California (3.0 million), Harris County, Texas (815,000), and Cook County, Illinois (786,000). The two largest Puerto Rican populations lived in two New York counties: Bronx County (319,000), and Kings County (213,000). More than half (651,000 or 52.4 percent) of all Cubans lived in Miami-Dade County, Florida.

The Commonwealth of Puerto Rico was 98.8 percent Hispanic.

Of all Hispanics in Puerto Rico, 96.3 percent were of Puerto Rican origin. The second largest Hispanic population in Puerto Rico was Dominican, accounting for 1.5 percent of all Hispanics there.

The proportion Hispanic ranges from 97 percent to 99 percent in the four places in Puerto Rico with 100,000 or more population (Ponce, Bayomón, Carolina, and San Juan).

In 2000, more than a million Hispanics lived in New York and in Los Angeles.

More than 500,000 Hispanics resided in Chicago, Houston, and San Antonio. Among the ten places with the largest Hispanic populations, Puerto Ricans represented the largest share (36.5 percent) of all Hispanics in New York, while Mexicans represented the largest share (varying from 63.5 percent in Los Angeles to 83.4 percent in San Diego) of all Hispanics in the nine other places.

Additional Findings on the Hispanic Population

Was the Hispanic population younger than the U.S. population?

The relative youthfulness of the Hispanic population is reflected in its population under age 18 and in its median age. While 25.7 percent of the U.S. population was under 18 years of age in 2000, 35.0 percent of Hispanics were less than age 18. The median age for Hispanics was 25.9 years while the median age for the entire U.S. population was 35.3 years. Mexicans had a median age of 24.2 years, Puerto Ricans 27.3 years, Central Americans 29.2 years, Dominicans 29.5 years, South Americans 33.1 years, Spaniards 36.4 years, Cubans 40.7 years, and all other Hispanics had a median age of 24.7 years.

In what places were Hispanics the majority?

Hispanics in East Los Angeles were 96.8 percent (120,000) of the population, the highest for any place outside the Commonwealth of Puerto Rico with

100,000 or more total population. Hispanics were the majority of the population in eighteen other places. Two of the top ten places in terms of numbers of Hispanics, El Paso and San Antonio, also had majority who were Hispanic (76.6 percent and 58.7 percent, respectively).

What were the top places for different Hispanic groups, by size?

Most, but not all, of the places with the largest specific Hispanic group populations were among the ten places with the largest Hispanic populations. The largest Mexican populations lived in Los Angeles, Chicago, Houston, San Antonio, and Phoenix. The largest Puerto Rican populations lived in New York, Chicago, and Philadelphia. The largest Cuban populations lived in Hialeah, Miami, New York, Tampa, and Los Angeles.

The largest Central American populations lived in the following places: Los Angeles, New York, Houston, Miami, and San Francisco, while the largest South American populations lived in New York, Los Angeles, Chicago, and Miami.

SUPREME COURT ON
MEDICAL USE OF MARIJUANA
May 14, 2001

In a unanimous ruling issued May 14, 2001, the Supreme Court held that federal law prohibiting the cultivation, distribution, and use of marijuana did not permit any exceptions for medical purposes. Some doctors and their patients said that the drug was effective, when legal alternatives were not, in relieving pain and nausea and stimulating appetite for patients with cancer, AIDS, and other serious illnesses. The federal government and others in the medical community said those claims had not been proven and that legalization of the drug for medical purposes would undermine the federal government's war on illegal drugs and send a confusing message to the nation's teenagers.

Since California first passed a ballot initiative in 1996 legalizing marijuana for medical use, seven more states—Alaska, Colorado, Hawaii, Maine, Nevada, Oregon, and Washington—had enacted similar laws, and several more were considering them. The Supreme Court ruling did not invalidate the state laws. Patients who met the states' guidelines could use the drug without fear of state prosecution. But they were still liable to federal prosecution, even though the federal government rarely enforced the law against individuals. All but Hawaii's law were approved by ballot initiative; Hawaii's law was passed by the state legislature and signed by the governor in June 2000. The District of Columbia also approved a medical marijuana law, but Congress prevented it from taking effect.

The Supreme Court ruling appeared to threaten the continued existence of the "cannabis clubs" that had sprung up to grow and distribute the drug to registered patients. Some supporters of medical marijuana had speculated that the Bush administration, which espoused the philosophy of "compassionate conservatism," might seek to avoid negative publicity by deciding not to move against the groups that were easing the suffering of the terminally ill. In October, however, federal Drug Enforcement Administration (DEA) agents moved to close down several major medical marijuana distributors in California, and Justice Department officials said more enforcement actions were likely.

In November Attorney General John Ashcroft used the ruling in the marijuana case to justify his decision to move against physicians in Oregon who prescribed federally controlled narcotics, in accordance with Oregon law, to assist the terminally ill to commit suicide. Ashcroft said assisted suicide was not a "legitimate medical purpose" for prescribing or dispensing such drugs. Later in November a federal district court in Portland issued a restraining order against Ashcroft's ruling until the matter could be taken to trial.

Broad Ruling on a Narrow Issue

The case before the Supreme Court, U.S. v. Oakland Cannabis Buyers' Cooperative, had its beginnings in 1996, when California's voters approved Proposition 215 by a solid majority. Proposition 215 allowed persons in the state to grow, possess, and use marijuana when it had been recommended by a physician for a medical purpose. The use of the drug would be permitted for treatment of cancer, anorexia, AIDS, chronic pain, spasticity, glaucoma, arthritis, migraine, or "any other illness for which marijuana provides relief." Caregivers could grow and possess marijuana for a person for whom the drug was recommended, and doctors could not be prosecuted under state law for recommending its use. (Proposition 215, 1996 Historic Documents, p. 755)

Passage of Proposition 215 (and a broader initiative in Arizona, which never took effect) caught the administration of Bill Clinton by surprise. After some deliberation, it denounced the initiatives and said it would continue to enforce federal laws banning the possession or use of marijuana and other narcotic drugs. Noting that state and local law enforcement agencies always had handled most of the cases involving small amounts of marijuana, Attorney General Janet Reno said that would continue to be the case. The federal government would take over prosecutions involving large amounts of drugs or cases that local officials could not handle because of the new conflict between federal and state law.

In 1998 the Clinton administration sought an injunction against the Oakland cannabis club and five others, arguing that these clubs, which acted somewhat like informal pharmacies, broke federal law by distributing and in some cases growing marijuana for medical use. Federal District Court Judge Charles Breyer, younger brother of Justice Steven Breyer, granted the injunction. The five other clubs eventually closed down, but the Oakland club appealed the ruling, arguing that an exception from the federal law prohibiting distribution should be made for it on grounds that it was supplying a "medical necessity." In 2000 the federal appeals court for the ninth circuit upheld the medical necessity defense, and Judge Breyer then issued strict guidelines that anyone making that claim was to follow.

The Clinton administration appealed to the Supreme Court, arguing that marijuana had not been proven to be a medical necessity and that Congress had been very clear when it put the drug on schedule 1 under the 1970 Controlled Substances Act, which was reserved for drugs deemed to have no ac-

cepted medical use. A lower court "may not override those determinations by reweighing the scientific and medical data and social policies considered by Congress, the attorney general, and the secretary of health and human services, and concluding that the public interest supports the illegal distribution of marijuana," then solicitor general Seth Waxman wrote in the government's brief. Waxman also asked the Supreme Court to keep the cooperative closed while it made its decision, a request the court granted.

Although California was not a party to the case, state attorney general Bill Lockyer filed a brief in behalf of the cooperative, arguing that the federal government's intervention threatened a state's "traditional right to regulate for the health and welfare of their citizens." The California Medical Association also supported the use of medical marijuana when other treatments had failed.

In an 8–0 decision, the Supreme Court upheld the federal government's authority to seek an injunction to stop the cooperative from distributing marijuana for medical purposes. (Justice Breyer recused himself from the case because of his brother's involvement.) Federal law "reflects a determination that marijuana has no medical benefits worthy of an exception," wrote Justice Clarence Thomas for the Court. Justices John Paul Stevens, David H. Souter, and Ruth Bader Ginsburg concurred with the ruling, but said Thomas's opinion might have been too far-reaching. "Most notably, whether the [medical necessity] defense might be available to a seriously ill patient for whom there is no other means of avoiding starvation or extraordinary suffering is a difficult issue that is not presented here," Stevens wrote for the three.

Stevens also said that "the overbroad language of the Court's opinion is especially unfortunate given the importance of showing respect for sovereign states that comprise our federal union." Thomas said the Court shared Stevens's concern but reminded him that the job of the federal courts was to interpret the federal criminal code, not to rewrite it.

Enforcing an Unpopular Ruling

Although the Justice Department said it would enforce the law, it was unclear immediately after the ruling how vigorous the government would be in shutting down distributors, especially in states where a majority of the population had voted for legalizing medical marijuana, and where the distribution centers had been supported by politicians, attorneys, physicians, and even law enforcement officials. Asa Hutchinson, a former Republican U.S. House member from Arkansas, who was sworn in as DEA director in August, said the administration would enforce the federal laws on marijuana, adding that there were "many different aspects" that would have to be considered in developing enforcement policy.

Despite those warnings, medical marijuana advocates expressed surprise when DEA agents began to move against California's cannabis clubs in October, just weeks after the terrorist attacks on the World Trade Center in New York and the Pentagon outside Washington, D.C. "This was a

serious effort to provide relief for people who were ill," said a city council-
man in West Hollywood, the site of one cannabis club raided by DEA agents.
"The Bush administration is forcing sick people to become criminals." A
spokeswoman for the Justice Department reiterated that all marijuana was
illegal and said that the raids in California were "indicative that we have
not lost our priorities in other areas since September 11."

The federal government also put in motion the process to approve experi-
ments into the medical efficacy of marijuana. In late November the DEA
gave final approval to two research projects designed to test whether mari-
juana could help patients with multiple sclerosis or with limb pain associ-
ated with AIDS. They would be the first approved experiments testing the
medical benefits of the drug since the early 1980s. Eight other experiments
were expected to win approval in the near future.

The United States could also keep tabs on an even larger experiment
undertaken by its northern neighbor. As of July 30, Canada allowed the use
of marijuana for patients with terminal illness and severe disabilities who
could show that legal medications did not provide the same relief. The rules
required patients to obtain a physician's recommendation, allowed third
parties to grow marijuana for those patients who could not grow it for them-
selves, and legalized possession and transportation of the drug for medical
purposes.

Following are excerpts from the opinion in the case of U.S. v. Oakland Cannabis Buyers' Cooperative, *in which the Supreme Court*
ruled, 8–0, on May 14, 2001, that the distribution of marijuana
for medical purposes was illegal under federal law.

The document was obtained from the Internet at http://
www.supremecourtus.gov/opinions/00pdf/00-151.pdf.

No. 00–151

United States, Petitioner	On writ of certiorari to the
v.	United States Court of Appeals
Oakland Cannabis Buyers'	for the Ninth Circuit
Cooperative and Jeffrey Jones	

[May 14, 2001]

JUSTICE THOMAS delivered the opinion of the Court.

The Controlled Substances Act prohibits the manufacture and distribution
of various drugs, including marijuana. In this case, we must decide whether
there is a medical necessity exception to these prohibitions. We hold that
there is not.

I [omitted]

II

The Controlled Substances Act provides that, "[e]xcept as authorized by this subchapter, it shall be unlawful for any person knowingly or intentionally . . . to manufacture, distribute, or dispense, or possess with intent to manufacture, distribute, or dispense, a controlled substance." The subchapter, in turn, establishes exceptions. For marijuana (and other drugs that have been classified as "schedule I" controlled substances), there is but one express exception, and it is available only for Government-approved research projects. Not conducting such a project, the [Oakland Cannabis Buyers'] Cooperative cannot, and indeed does not, claim this statutory exemption.

The Cooperative contends, however, that notwithstanding the apparently absolute language of [the Controlled Substances Act], the statute is subject to additional, implied exceptions, one of which is medical necessity. According to the Cooperative, because necessity was a defense at common law, medical necessity should be read into the Controlled Substances Act. We disagree.

As an initial matter, we note that it is an open question whether federal courts ever have authority to recognize a necessity defense not provided by statute. A necessity defense "traditionally covered the situation where physical forces beyond the actor's control rendered illegal conduct the lesser of two evils." Even at common law, the defense of necessity was somewhat controversial. And under our constitutional system, in which federal crimes are defined by statute rather than by common law, it is especially so. . . . Nonetheless, we recognize that this Court has discussed the possibility of a necessity defense without altogether rejecting it.

We need not decide, however, whether necessity can ever be a defense when the federal statute does not expressly provide for it. In this case, to resolve the question presented, we need only recognize that a medical necessity exception for marijuana is at odds with the terms of the Controlled Substances Act. The statute, to be sure, does not explicitly abrogate the defense. But its provisions leave no doubt that the defense is unavailable.

Under any conception of legal necessity, one principle is clear: The defense cannot succeed when the legislature itself has made a "determination of values." In the case of the Controlled Substances Act, the statute reflects a determination that marijuana has no medical benefits worthy of an exception (outside the confines of a Government-approved research project). Whereas some other drugs can be dispensed and prescribed for medical use, the same is not true for marijuana. Indeed, for purposes of the Controlled Substances Act, marijuana has "no currently accepted medical use" at all. . . .

The Cooperative points out, however, that the Attorney General did not place marijuana into schedule I. Congress put it there, and Congress was not required to find that a drug lacks an accepted medical use before including the drug in schedule I. We are not persuaded that this distinction has any significance to our inquiry. Under the Cooperative's logic, drugs that Congress places in schedule I could be distributed when medically necessary whereas drugs that the Attorney General places in schedule I could not. Nothing in the statute, however, suggests that there are two tiers of schedule I narcotics, with drugs in one tier more readily available than drugs in the other. On the contrary, the statute consistently treats all schedule I drugs alike. . . . Moreover, the Cooperative offers no convincing explanation for why drugs that Congress placed on schedule I should be subject to fewer controls than the drugs that the Attorney General placed on the schedule. Indeed, the Cooperative argues that, in placing marijuana and other drugs on schedule I, Congress "wishe[d] to assert the most restrictive level of controls created by the [Controlled Substances Act]." If marijuana should be subject to the most restrictive level of controls, it should not be treated any less restrictively than other schedule I drugs.

The Cooperative further argues that use of schedule I drugs generally— whether placed in schedule I by Congress or the Attorney General—can be medically necessary, notwithstanding that they have "no currently accepted medical use." According to the Cooperative, a drug may not yet have achieved general acceptance as a medical treatment but may nonetheless have medical benefits to a particular patient or class of patients. We decline to parse the statute in this manner. It is clear from the text of the Act that Congress has made a determination that marijuana has no medical benefits worthy of an exception. The statute expressly contemplates that many drugs "have a useful and legitimate medical purpose and are necessary to maintain the health and general welfare of the American people," but it includes no exception at all for any medical use of marijuana. Unwilling to view this omission as an accident, and unable in any event to override a legislative determination manifest in a statute, we reject the Cooperative's argument. . . .

For these reasons, we hold that medical necessity is not a defense to manufacturing and distributing marijuana. The Court of Appeals erred when it held that medical necessity is a "legally cognizable defense." 190 F.3d, at 1114. It further erred when it instructed the District Court on remand to consider "the criteria for a medical necessity exemption, and, should it modify the injunction, to set forth those criteria in the modification order." *Id.*, at 1115.

III [omitted]

***

The judgment of the Court of Appeals is reversed, and the case is remanded for further proceedings consistent with this opinion.

It is so ordered.

JUSTICE BREYER took no part in the consideration or decision of this case.

BUSH TASK FORCE PLANS FOR A NATIONAL ENERGY POLICY
May 17, 2001

A deep but temporary energy crisis in California gave initial impetus to a broad plan by President George W. Bush to use federal policies to promote the energy industries. The plan, drafted by a task force headed by Vice President Dick Cheney, was made public on May 17, 2001, and it set off a storm of debate because of its heavy emphasis on energy production and its call for reducing environmental regulations that hindered energy companies. The plan's most controversial element was a proposal, long advocated by Bush, to open the Arctic National Wildlife Refuge in Alaska to oil drilling.

Bush said the energy plan struck a balance between meeting energy needs and protecting the environment. "Too often Americans are asked to take sides between energy production and environmental protection," he said. "As if people who revere the Alaskan wilderness do not also care about America's energy future. As if the people who produce America's energy do not care about the planet their children will inherit." It was time for those on both sides of that equation to "listen to each other," Bush added.

The nation had been nervous about energy supplies ever since late 2000, when an increase in world petroleum prices sent gasoline and home heating oil prices to near-record levels for the United States—although still far below those in most other countries. Then, early in 2001, skyrocketing electricity prices and periodic power outages in California created the impression that the nation was experiencing its most serious energy crisis since Middle East countries sent oil prices surging in the 1970s. These factors lent a sense of urgency to Bush's demand for Congress to act speedily on his energy proposals. The Republican-controlled House complied, giving approval on August 1 to most of what Bush requested. But the sense of urgency faded when energy prices unexpectedly declined during the summer months and California's problems eased considerably. Coupled with a controversy over Bush's demand for oil drilling in the Alaskan wilderness, those factors blocked action in the Senate for the rest of the year.

The California "Crisis"

The energy crisis in California resulted from a combination of factors, including a failure by the state government and the private sector to foresee and plan for the consequences of a deregulation of the energy industry proposed by Republican governor Pete Wilson and enacted by the state legislature in 1996. Under deregulation, wholesale power prices were allowed to float to whatever level the market set, but retail prices charged residential and business consumers were subject to limits set by the state's Public Utilities Commission. California utilities were ordered to sell their power-generating plants and then were barred from locking in wholesale prices through long-term contracts—forcing them to buy much of their electricity on the short-term market, where rates are much higher. In late 2000 and early 2001, according to news reports, several private energy companies that had bought many of the state's power plants under deregulation held back power in what appeared to be a deliberate move to drive up wholesale prices. As a result, the utilities that bought power from these firms piled up enormous debts.

Meanwhile, electricity production in California lagged behind demand. Utilities had not built any new power plants in nearly a decade, despite the state's continued population growth. An exceptionally large number of existing plants were idled in 2000 and 2001 for maintenance. In addition, the 2000–2001 winter was one of the driest on record in the West, reducing the amount of water available for the hydroelectric plants that generated much of the region's power, especially in the Pacific Northwest, which shared California's power grid. Finally, prices for natural gas—the energy source for most California power plants—rose dramatically nationwide in 2000, even as natural gas supplies in the state were curtailed by transportation problems, including a major pipeline explosion in August 2000.

If the causes of the crisis were complex and often obscured in political rhetoric, the results were easy for all to see. Wholesale prices for electricity shot up dramatically—from an average of about $30 per megawatt hour in 1999 to more than $100 in mid-2000 and then to $400 or more early in 2001.

Caught in the crunch, California utilities appealed to the state for authority to pass these increases on to consumers. Before the crisis began, average residential electricity prices in California were slightly higher than the national average but well below those charged in some other states, particularly in the Northeast. The state's public utility commission approved a 10 percent rate increase in January and then added further increases in March that boosted prices by as much as 36 percent more. Governor Gray Davis, a Democrat who succeeded Wilson in 1999, declared an emergency, launched a crash course of speeding construction of new power plants, and mandated a state takeover of the private agency that determined where electricity was distributed. The state's Department of Water Resources also took over responsibility for buying electricity for the utilities; ultimately it signed long-term contracts to buy about $43 billion worth of power.

Beginning in mid-January the state was forced to carry out limited blackouts on six days to curb demand. Only a small portion of state residents and businesses were affected, but the rolling blackouts symbolized the extent of the state's energy problem. More damaging to the economy were the rate increases, which heightened the effects of the national recession then getting under way and forced hundreds of California manufacturing and service companies to curtail production.

Caught in the rate crunch, the state's giant utility, Pacific Gas and Electric, filed for bankruptcy in April, although its national parent company, PG&E Corporation, remained profitable—in part because of $4.6 billion in cash transfers from the utility during the previous three years. The state's number two utility, Southern California Edison, avoided bankruptcy only with the help of a state plan that kept its rates high in exchange for shareholders foregoing dividends for two years..

As could be expected, political and business leaders traded blame for the crisis, and much of the finger pointing was directed between Sacramento and Washington. Davis demanded that the federal government step in to control wholesale energy prices, offering at least temporary relief to consumers. The Federal Energy Regulatory Commission, an independent agency, had that power, but its Republican chairman, Curt Hebert, and Bush both objected on grounds that price caps would interfere in the marketplace and would do nothing to increase energy supplies.

As the crisis worsened, political pressure mounted for action at the federal level. The commission took limited actions beginning in March, imposing price caps on emergency power supplies in California. When it appeared that power wholesalers were shipping electricity out of California to avoid the caps, the commission on June 18 broadened its rule, applying price caps to all hours of the day and to ten other western states. The commission made its price caps effective until September 2002.

Davis and other political leaders also sought to blame the private energy-trading companies that had bought much of California's power system after deregulation and then jacked up wholesale energy prices. One of the chief culprits, according to this view, was the Houston-based Enron Corporation, which owned much of the state's natural gas grid. Troubled by financial mismanagement unrelated to the California crisis, Enron filed for bankruptcy in December; it was the largest corporate failure in American history. (Enron collapse, p. 857)

Early in 2001 it appeared that California's energy problems would only worsen later in the year, especially with the onset of high demand for air conditioning in the summer. But just as a combination of circumstances led to the crisis, a new set of circumstances eased the crisis by June. For the rest of the year wholesale energy prices fell sharply and power demand and supply came into a closer match. Among the reasons for the easing of the crisis were state-mandated and voluntary conservation measures, which pared demand by up to 10 percent; California's summer weather turned out to be milder than usual; power plants that had been off-line for maintenance returned to service by the spring and the first of nine new plants began operating; lower natural gas prices reduced energy costs; and the federal government's caps on wholesale prices effectively forced energy suppliers to retreat from their pricing strategy. Davis's decision to sign long-term contracts to buy electricity also helped stabilize prices, although critics said the contracts locked the state into excessively high rates.

Compiling an Industry "Wish List"

Bush took office as president just three days after the first blackouts in California. The growing energy crisis in the nation's biggest state offered a substantial boost to Bush's plans, which he advocated during his election campaign, to seek new domestic energy supplies. Bush grew up in the oil business—his father, former president George Bush, had headed a Texas oil company before going into politics—and had run his own oil business before winning election as governor of Texas in 1994. Cheney had been chairman of the board of Haliburton Inc., an oil service company, for several years before becoming vice president.

Newsweek *magazine reported in its May 14 issue that many of the recommendations of Cheney's task force originated with a meeting in mid-January of industry executives and lobbyists hosted by the American Petroleum Institute—the trade group of the U.S. oil industry. Attendees were asked to present their proposals for an oil industry "wish list,"* Newsweek *said; the resulting suggestions were then sent to the Interior Department and then to Cheney's task force, which included many of them in its final report. Several of the industry executives who had attended the January meeting later were appointed to senior positions within the Bush administration, giving them a chance to promote their proposals from within the government. "Not since the rise of the railroads more than a century ago has a single industry placed so many foot soldiers at the top of a new administration,"* Newsweek *reported.*

During the course of their work on the report, staffers and members of Cheney's task force said they sought ideas from "hundreds" of individuals, most of whom were associated with various components of the energy industry. The task force staff held only one brief session with representatives of the environmental movement. Later in 2001 the administration repeatedly denied requests from the news media and Congress for a list of those whose views had been solicited during work on the report. At year's end the General Accounting Office, the congressional watchdog agency, was threatening to sue the administration to force it to release such a list.

Task Force Recommendations

The task force made 105 recommendations, many of them general policy suggestions not backed by any specific proposals. Even some of the specific items contained only vague language about how the new policies should be implemented. Only twenty of the recommendations required congressional action, such as revising current law or approving new funding. Bush was able to undertake all other recommendations on his own authority, either by issuing executive orders or by sending directives to federal agencies, including those whose chiefs sat on the task force. Bush issued the first such order just a week after the Cheney report was released; it directed that federal agencies expedite the issuance of permits for new electric power plants. The task force report had called for 1,300 to 1,900 new plants over the next two decades—a figure in line with current construction plans.

On energy production, the underlying thrust of the report was to shift the central focus of federal policy. Since the emergence of the environmental movement in the early 1970s, the government had forced energy companies to prove that their production plans would not needlessly spoil the environment. While acknowledging that regulations sometimes were necessary, the report said that many rules had become "overly burdensome" and had contributed to the nation's energy shortage.

Under Bush's new vision, the government would assign the first priority to energy production and reduce the prospect for denying permits to the energy industry on environmental grounds. The clearest statement of this policy shift was the requirement for an "energy impact statement" justifying government regulations that would "significantly and adversely" affect energy supplies, distribution, or use.

The report offered some of the best news in years for the coal mining and nuclear power industries, both of which had long been in decline because of environmental concerns. Bush called for $2 billion in government subsidies for "clean coal" technology to reduce pollution from the majority of the nation's power plants that ran on coal. The report also touted increased safety and environmental protection standards at nuclear power plants, which provided about 20 percent of the nation's electricity. The report offered two specifics for the industry: a promise of speedy renewal of permits for existing plants and a cut in taxes that the industry said had stymied needed mergers among nuclear power producers. In addition, the report suggested a revival of the reprocessing of spent nuclear fuel to create plutonium that could fuel nuclear reactors; the United States had abandoned reprocessing in the 1980s because of high costs and fears that the resulting plutonium could fall into the hands of terrorists or others trying to make nuclear weapons.

Drilling in the Arctic

The report listed only one specific location for new or expanded oil and gas exploration: the Arctic National Wildlife Refuge, an area the report called "the single most promising prospect in the United States" for new energy supplies. Other areas reportedly high on the administration's priority list included the Gulf of Mexico and the Rocky Mountains, but neither was mentioned specifically in the report.

The administration called for opening approximately 1.5 million acres—about 8 percent of the total land in the refuge—to exploration and production. Cheney's report said the refuge had reserves that would allow production of 600,000 barrels of oil daily for forty-seven years. As one selling point, Bush said that amount "happens to be exactly the amount the

United States now imports from Iraq," the country that had been a chief nemesis of the United States in the Middle East for a decade.

The Arctic refuge was on the eastern side of Prudhoe Bay, a petroleum-rich area where oil production had been under way for more than two decades. Congress had made the wildlife refugee off-limits for energy exploration and other industrial uses because it was one of the last unspoiled areas in the United States for caribou and other northern wildlife. Protecting the refuge was a top priority for environmental groups, just as seeking access to its petroleum reserves was a major goal of oil companies. The issue was one of the most clearly drawn disagreements between Bush and his election opponent in 2000, then vice president Al Gore. Bush advocated oil production in the Arctic refuge; Gore vigorously opposed it.

In an attempt to ease potential opposition to the proposal, the report called for using the federal government's oil royalties from the new fields to fund land and energy conservation programs. But most environmental groups were not impressed. William H. Meadows, president of the Wilderness Society, called the proposal a "cruel joke" and likened it to "burning your furniture to heat your house."

Conservation and Alternative Energy

As the task force was working on its report, Cheney made it clear that promoting energy conservation and alternative energy sources would not be the main thrust of its recommendations. "Conservation may be a sign of personal virtue, but it is not a sufficient basis for a sound, comprehensive energy policy," he told a meeting of the Associated Press on April 30. Critics seized on that remark as evidence of the administration's eagerness to do the bidding of the oil industry. Buffeted by the criticism, Cheney ordered the task force to give more emphasis to conservation measures. The final report listed more than forty such recommendations. Conservation and efficiency, the report said, "are important elements of a sound energy policy." Likewise, it said, renewable and alternative energy sources (such as solar and wind power) "not only help diversify our energy portfolio, they do so with few adverse environmental impacts."

Key recommendations in these areas included several kinds of tax credits for the development and use of alternative energy sources (for example, a 15 percent tax credit for homeowners who install solar panels) and tax credits and other benefits for conservation measures such as the purchase of "hybrid" cars powered by both electricity and gas and for the development of "co-generation" power plants that produce both electricity and heat. Bush sought to emphasize his commitment to alternative sources by appearing May 17 at a power plant near St. Paul, Minnesota, that burned wood chips in addition to oil.

The report made no commitment on what was widely considered the single most important conservation issue: boosting fuel efficiency standards for automobiles and trucks. Fuel standards were introduced in 1975 but had not been updated since 1985; in the meantime, the growing popularity of vans and sport utility vehicles had reduced the average fuel *efficiency of vehicles on the nation's roads to its lowest point in twenty years. The report called for studies on the question of whether and how to mandate higher standards but said that doing so should be done "without negatively impacting the automobile industry."*

Critics in the environmental movement noted that the proposals were vague and contained only modest funds. They noted, for example, that Bush's highly touted pledge of spending $10 billion over the next ten years on alternative energy sources was less than Clinton had budgeted just a few months earlier—and far below the $3 billion annual budget for such programs at the end of the Carter administration two decades earlier. Environmental groups also charged that the report virtually guaranteed no action on improving automobile fuel efficiency even though, they said, doing so would save more energy than most of Bush's oil production plans would generate.

Congressional Action

The energy report won expected support from Republican congressional leaders, who pledged rapid action on the legislative portions of the plan. "I believe it meets the goals most important to the American people by increasing our energy supplies, providing price stability, and protecting our previous environment," House Speaker J. Dennis Hastert, R-Ill., said. Even though the report did not contain all their recommendations, representatives of the oil and other energy industries were enthusiastic, saying the plan brought "balance" to federal policy that they considered tilted too far toward environmental concerns. "It's balanced, I think it has something for everybody, and it addresses the problems that should be addressed," Thomas E. Capps, chairman of Dominion Energy Resources, an electricity supplier in Virginia, told the Washington Post.

Just as predictably, most Democrats on Capitol Hill and all major environmental groups attacked the plan, especially the proposals for oil drilling in the Arctic refuge and weakening environmental regulations. "The language throughout the report conveys the idea that environmental protections equal impediments and we have to find a way to surmount them," David Alberswerth, a former Clinton administration official who had joined the Wilderness Society, told the New York Times. *"But we view these protections as necessary to protecting the wildlife, water quality, and scenic quality of public lands."*

Environmentalists and Democrats were not the only critics. John Taylor, an analyst for the libertarian Cato Institute, based in Washington, said the administration had developed "a smorgasbord of handouts and subsidies for virtually every energy lobby in Washington."

The Republican-controlled House got to work quickly on Bush's plan, and three of its committees produced bills in July that largely mirrored the president's requests. The full House combined those bills into an omnibus measure (HR 4), which it passed August 1. The administration prevailed in two major fights on the House floor: by a narrow margin of 206–223 the House rejected an effort by Democrats and moderate Republicans to remove language allowing oil exploration in the Arctic reserve, and by a wider margin of 160–269 the House rejected another effort to mandate improved fuel efficiency standards for automobiles. The administration's victory on the Arctic refuge vote was made possible, in large part, by the lobbying of the Teamsters union, which claimed that oil exploration there would create 750,000 jobs—a figure that environmental groups said was vastly inflated.

Democrats took over leadership of the Senate a few weeks after Bush issued his energy plan and so were in a better position than their Democratic colleagues in the House to shape energy legislation. Senate Democrats took a go-slow approach to the issue for the rest of the year and issued their own alternative energy proposal on December 5; it gave greater emphasis than did the Bush plan to energy conservation and the use of alternative energy sources, and it did not allow oil drilling in the Arctic reserve. Majority Leader Tom Daschle, a South Dakota Democrat, said the Senate would take up energy legislation in 2002.

Administration plans to open new exploration for oil and gas in the eastern Gulf of Mexico and on federal lands in the Rocky Mountain region encountered strong opposition during the year. The president's own brother, Florida governor Jeb Bush, had raised objections to a plan for energy exploration in nearly 6 million acres of coastal waters off Florida. Responding to the governor's objections and to a vote in the House opposing the drilling, the Interior Department on July 2 announced plans to reduce the proposed size of the oil and gas fields to 1.5 million acres. Similarly, Congress in October adopted legislation that blocked new oil and gas exploration in national monuments—a move that would thwart many of the administration's plans for expanded energy production in the Rocky Mountain region.

> *Following is the text of the "overview" of the report on "National Energy Policy" made public May 17, 2001, by President George W. Bush. The report was drafted by the National Energy Policy Development Group, a cabinet-level task force chaired by Vice President Dick Cheney.*
>
> ***The document was obtained from the Internet at http:// www.whitehouse.gov/energy.***

In his second week in office, President George W. Bush established the National Energy Policy Development Group, directing it to develop a national energy policy designed to help the private sector, and, as necessary and appropriate, State and local governments, promote dependable, affordable, and environmentally sound production and distribution of energy for the future. This Overview sets forth the National Energy Policy Development (NEPD) Group's findings and key recommendations for a National Energy Policy.

America in the year 2001 faces the most serious energy shortage since the oil embargoes of the 1970s. The effects are already being felt nationwide. Many families face energy bills two to three times higher than they were a year ago. Millions of Americans find themselves dealing with rolling blackouts or brownouts; some employers must lay off workers or curtail production to absorb the rising cost of energy. Drivers across America are paying higher and higher gasoline prices.

Californians have felt these problems most acutely. California actually began the 1990s with a surplus of electricity generating capacity. Yet despite an economic boom, a rapidly growing population, and a corresponding increase in energy needs, California did not add a single new major electric power plant during the 1990s. The result is a demand for electricity that greatly succeeds the amount available.

A fundamental imbalance between supply and demand defines our nation's energy crisis. . . . [I]f energy production increases at the same rate as during the last decade our projected energy needs will far outstrip expected levels of production.

This imbalance, if allowed to continue, will inevitably undermine our economy, our standard of living, and our national security. But it is not beyond our power to correct. America leads the world in scientific achievement, technical skill, and entrepreneurial drive. Within our country are abundant natural resources, unrivaled technology, and unlimited human creativity. With forward-looking leadership and sensible policies, we can meet our future energy demands and promote energy conservation, and do so in environmentally responsible ways that set a standard for the world.

The Challenge

America's energy challenge begins with our expanding economy, growing population, and rising standard of living. Our prosperity and way of life are sustained by energy use. America has the technological know-how and environmentally sound 21st century technologies needed to meet the principal energy challenges we face: promoting energy conservation, repairing and modernizing our energy infrastructure, and increasing our energy supplies in ways that protect and improve the environment. Meeting each of these challenges is critical to expanding our economy, meeting the needs of a growing population, and raising the American standard of living.

We are already working to meet the first challenge: using energy more wisely. Dramatic technological advances in energy efficiency have enabled us to make great strides in conservation, from the operation of farms and factories to the construction of buildings and automobiles. New technology allows us to go about our lives and work with less cost, less effort, and less burden on the natural environment. While such advances cannot alone solve America's energy problems, they can and will continue to play an important role in our energy future.

The second challenge is to repair and expand our energy infrastructure. Our current, outdated network of electric generators, transmission lines, pipelines, and refineries that convert raw materials into usable fuel has been allowed to deteriorate. Oil pipelines and refining capacity are in need of repair and expansion. Not a single major oil refinery has been built in the United States in nearly a generation, causing the kind of bottlenecks that lead to sudden spikes in the price of gasoline. Natural gas distribution, likewise, is hindered by an aging and inadequate network of pipelines. To match supply and demand will require some 38,000 miles of new gas pipelines, along with 255,000 miles of distribution lines. Similarly, an antiquated and inadequate transmission grid prevents us from routing electricity over long distances and thereby avoiding regional blackouts, such as California's.

Increasing energy supplies while protecting the environment is the third challenge. Even with successful conservation efforts, America will need more energy.

Renewable and alternative fuels offer hope for America's energy future. But they supply only a small fraction of present energy needs. The day they fulfill the bulk of our needs is still years away. Until that day comes, we must continue meeting the nation's energy requirements by the means available to us.

Estimates indicate that over the next 20 years, U.S. oil consumption will increase by 33 percent, natural gas consumption by well over 50 percent, and demand for electricity will rise by 45 percent. If America's energy production grows at the same rate as it did in the 1990s we will face an ever-increasing gap.

Increases on this scale will require preparation and action today. Yet America has not been bringing on line the necessary supplies and infrastructure.

Extraordinary advances in technology have transformed energy exploration and production. Yet we produce 39 percent less oil today than we did in 1970, leaving us ever more reliant on foreign suppliers. On our present course, America 20 years from now will import nearly two of every three barrels of oil—a condition of increased dependency on foreign powers that do not always have America's interests at heart. Our increasing demand for natural gas—one of the cleanest forms of energy—far exceeds the current rate of production. We should reconsider any regulatory restrictions that do not take technological advances into account.

We have a similar opportunity to in crease our supplies of electricity. To meet projected demand over the next two decades, America must have in place between 1,300 and 1,900 new electric plants. Much of this new generation will be fueled by natural gas. However, existing and new technologies offer us the opportunity to expand nuclear generation as well. Nuclear power today accounts for 20 percent of our country's electricity. This power source, which causes no greenhouse gas emissions, can play an expanding part in our energy future.

The recommendations of this report address the energy challenges facing America. Taken together, they offer the thorough and responsible energy plan our nation has long needed. . . .

Modernize Conservation

Americans share the goal of energy conservation. The best way of meeting this goal is to increase energy efficiency by applying new technology—raising productivity, reducing waste, and trimming costs. In addition, it holds out great hope for improving the quality of the environment. American families, communities, and businesses all depend upon reliable and affordable energy services for their well being and safety. From transportation to communication, from air conditioning to lighting, energy is critical to nearly everything we do in life and work. Public policy can and should encourage energy conservation.

Over the past three decades, America has made impressive gains in energy efficiency. Today's automobiles, for example, use about 60 percent of the gasoline they did in 1972, while new refrigerators require just one-third the electricity they did 30 years ago. As a result, since 1973, the U.S. economy has grown by 126 percent, while energy use has increased by only 30 percent. In the 1990s alone, manufacturing output expanded by 41 percent, while industrial electricity consumption grew by only 11 percent. We must build on this progress and strengthen America's commitment to energy efficiency and conservation.

The National Energy Policy builds on our nation's successful track record and will promote further improvements in the productive and efficient use of energy. This report includes recommendations to:

- Direct federal agencies to take appropriate actions to responsibly conserve energy use at their facilities, especially during periods of peak demand in regions where electricity shortages are possible, and to report to the President on actions taken.
- Increase funding for renewable energy and energy efficiency research and development programs that are performance-based and cost-shared.
- Create an income tax credit for the purchase of hybrid and fuel cell vehicles to promote fuel-efficient vehicles.
- Extend the Department of Energy's "Energy Star" efficiency program to include schools, retail buildings, health care facilities, and homes and extend the "Energy Star" labeling program to additional products and appliances.
- Fund the federal government's Intelligent Transportation Systems program, the fuel cell powered transit bus program, and the Clean Buses program.
- Provide a tax incentive and streamline permitting to accelerate the development of clean Combined Heat and Power technology.
- Direct the secretary of Transportation to review and provide recommendations on establishing Corporate Average Fuel Economy (CAFE) standards with due consideration to the National Academy of sciences study of CAFE standards to be released in July, 2001.

Modernize Our Energy Infrastructure

The energy we use passes through a vast nationwide network of generating facilities, transmission lines, pipelines, and refineries that converts raw resources into us able fuel and power. That system is deteriorating, and is now strained to capacity.

One reason for this is government regulation, often excessive and redundant. Regulation is needed in such a complex field, but it has become overly burdensome. Regulatory hurdles, delays in issuing permits, and economic uncertainty are limiting investment in new facilities, making our energy markets more vulnerable to transmission bottlenecks, price spikes, and supply disruptions. America needs more environmentally-sound energy projects to connect supply sources to growing markets and to deliver energy to homes and business.

To reduce the incidence of electricity blackouts, we must greatly enhance our ability to transmit electric power between geographic regions, that is, sending power to where it is needed from where it is produced. Most of America's transmission lines, substations, and transformers were built when utilities were tightly regulated and provided service only within their as signed regions. The system is simply unequipped for large-scale swapping of power in the highly competitive market of the 21st century.

The National Energy Policy will modernize and expand our energy infrastructure in order to ensure that energy supplies can be safely, reliably, and affordably transported to homes and businesses. This report includes recommendations to:

- Direct agencies to improve pipeline safety and expedite pipeline permitting.
- Issue an Executive Order directing federal agencies to expedite permits and coordinate federal, state, and local actions necessary for energy-related project approvals on a national basis in an environmentally sound manner, and establish an interagency task force chaired by the Council on Environmental Quality. The task force will ensure that federal agencies set up appropriate mechanisms to coordinate federal, state, and local permitting activity in particular regions where increased activity is expected.
- Grant authority to obtain rights-of-way for electricity transmission lines with the goal of creating a reliable national transmission grid. Similar authority already exists for natural gas pipelines and highways.
- Enact comprehensive electricity legislation that promotes competition, encourages new generation, protects consumers, enhances reliability, and promotes renewable energy.
- Implement administrative and regulatory changes to improve the reliability of the interstate transmission system and enact legislation to provide for enforcement of electricity reliability standards.
- Expand the Energy Department's research and development on transmission reliability and superconductivity.

Increase Energy Supplies

A primary goal of the National Energy Policy is to add supply from diverse sources. This means domestic oil, gas, and coal. It also means hydropower and nuclear power. And it means making greater use of non-hydro renewable sources now available.

One aspect of the present crisis is an increased dependence, not only on foreign oil, but on a narrow range of energy options. For example, about 90 percent of all new electricity plants currently under construction will be fueled by natural gas. While natural gas has many advantages, an over-reliance on any one fuel source leaves consumers vulnerable to price spikes and supply disruptions. There are several other fuel sources available that can help meet our needs.

Currently, the U.S. has enough coal to last for another 250 years. Yet very few coal-powered electric plants are now under construction. Research into clean coal technologies may increase the attractiveness of coal as a source for new generation plants.

Nuclear power plants serve millions of American homes and businesses, have a dependable record for safety and efficiency, and discharge no greenhouse gases into the atmosphere. As noted earlier, these facilities currently generate 20 percent of all electricity in America, and more than 40 percent of electricity generated in 10 states in the Northeast, South, and Midwest. Other nations, such as Japan and France, generate a much higher percentage of their electricity from nuclear power. Yet the number of nuclear plants in America is actually projected to decline in coming years, as old plants close and none are built to replace them.

Enormous advances in technology have made oil and natural gas exploration and production both more efficient and more environmentally sound. Better technology means fewer rigs, more accurate drilling, greater resource recovery and environmentally friendly exploration. Drilling pads are 80 percent smaller than a generation ago. High-tech drilling allows us to access supplies five to six miles away from a single compact drilling site, leaving sensitive wetlands and wildlife habitats undisturbed. Yet the current regulatory structure fails to take sufficient account of these extraordinary advances, excessively restricting the environmentally safe production of energy from many known sources.

Our policy will increase and diversify our nation's sources of traditional and alternative fuels in order to furnish families and businesses with reliable and affordable energy, to enhance national security, and to improve the environment. This report includes recommendations to:

- Issue an Executive Order directing all federal agencies to include in any regulatory action that could significantly and adversely affect energy supplies a detailed statement on the energy impact of the proposed action.
- Open a small fraction of the Arctic National Wildlife Refuge to environmentally regulated exploration and production using leading-edge technology. Examine the potential for the regulated increase in oil and natural gas development on other federal lands.
- Earmark $1.2 billion of bid bonuses from the environmentally responsible leasing of ANWR to fund research into alternative and renewable energy resources—including wind, solar, biomass, and geothermal.

- Enact legislation to expand existing alternative fuels tax incentives to include landfills that capture methane gas emissions for electricity generation and to electricity produced from wind and biomass. Extend the number of eligible biomass sources to include forest-related sources, agricultural sources, and certain urban sources.
- Provide $2 billion over 10 years to fund clean coal technology research and a new credit for electricity produced from biomass co-fired with coal.
- Direct federal agencies to streamline the hydropower relicensing process with proper regard given to environmental factors.
- Provide for the safe expansion of nuclear energy by establishing a national repository for nuclear waste, and by streamlining the licensing of nuclear power plants.

Accelerate Protection and Improvement of the Environment

America's commitment to environmental protection runs deep. We are all aware of past excesses in our use of the natural world and its resources. No one wishes to see them repeated. In the 21st century, the ethic of good stewardship is well established in American life and law.

We do not accept the false choice between environmental protection and energy production. An integrated approach to policy can yield a cleaner environment, a stronger economy, and a sufficient supply of energy for our future. The primary reason for that has been steady advances in the technology of locating, producing, and using energy. Since 1970, emissions of key air emissions are down 31 percent. Cars today emit 85 percent less carbon monoxide than 30 years ago. Lead emissions are down 90 percent. Lead levels in ambient air today are 98 percent lower than they were in 1970. America is using more, and polluting less.

One of the factors harming the environment today is the very lack of a comprehensive, long-term national energy policy. States confronting blackouts must take desperate measures, often at the expense of environmental standards, requesting waivers of environmental rules, and delaying the implementation of anti-pollution efforts. Shortfalls in electricity generating capacity and shortsighted policies have blocked construction of new, cleaner plants, leaving no choice but to rely on older, inefficient plants to meet demand. The increased use of emergency power sources, such as diesel generators, results in greater air pollution.

New anti-pollution technologies hold great promise for the environment. The same can be said of 21st century power generators that must soon replace older models; significant new resources for land conservation efforts; and continued research into renewable energy sources. All have a place in the National Energy Policy.

The National Energy Policy will build upon our nation's successful track record and will promote further improvements in the productive and efficient use of energy. This report includes recommendations to:

- Enact "multi-pollutant" legislation to establish a flexible, market-based program to significantly reduce and cap emissions of sulfur dioxide, nitrogen oxides, and mercury from electric power generators.
- Increase exports of environmentally friendly, market-ready U.S. technologies that generate a clean environment and increase energy efficiency.
- Establish a new "Royalties Conservation Fund" and earmark royalties from new, clean oil and gas exploration in ANWR to fund land conservation efforts.
- Implement new guidelines to reduce truck idling emissions at truck stops.

Increase Energy Security

The National Energy Policy seeks to lessen the impact on Americans of energy price volatility and supply uncertainty. Such uncertainty increases as we reduce America's dependence on foreign sources of energy. At the same time, however, we recognize that a significant percentage of our resources will come from overseas. Energy security must be a priority of U.S. trade and foreign policy.

We must look beyond our borders and restore America's credibility with overseas suppliers. In addition, we must build strong relationships with energy-producing nations in our own hemisphere, improving the outlook for trade, investment, and reliable supplies.

Energy security also requires preparing our nation for supply emergencies, and assisting low-income Americans who are most vulnerable in times of supply disruption, price spikes, and extreme weather.

To ensure energy security for our nation and its families, our report includes these recommendations:

- Dedicate new funds to the Low Income Home Energy Assistance Program [LIHEAP] by funneling a portion of oil and gas royalty payments to LIHEAP when oil and natural gas prices exceed a certain amount.
- Double funding for the Department of Energy's Weatherization Assistance Program, increasing funding by $1.4 billion over 10 years.
- Direct the Federal Emergency Management Agency to prepare for potential energy-related emergencies.
- Support a North American Energy Framework to expand and accelerate cross-border energy investment, oil and gas pipelines, and electricity grid connections by streamlining and expediting permitting procedures with Mexico and Canada. Direct federal agencies to expedite necessary permits for a gas pipeline route from Alaska to the lower 48 states.

Looking Toward the Future

The President's goal of reliable, affordable, and environmentally sound energy supplies will not be reached overnight. It will call forth innovations in science, research, and engineering. It will require time and the best efforts of leaders in both political parties. It will require also that we deal with the facts as they are, meeting serious problems in a serious way. The complacency of the past decade must now give way to swift but well-considered action.

Present trends are not encouraging, but they are not immutable. They are among today's most urgent challenges, and well within our power to overcome. Our country has met many great tests. Some have imposed extreme hardship and sacrifice. Others have demanded only resolve, ingenuity, and clarity of purpose. Such is the case with energy today.

We submit these recommendations with optimism. We believe that the tasks ahead, while great, are achievable. The energy crisis is a call to put to good use the resources around us, and the talents within us. It summons the best of America, and offers the best of rewards—in new jobs, a healthier environment, a stronger economy, and a brighter future for our people.

GOVERNOR'S COMMISSION ON COLUMBINE SHOOTINGS
May 17, 2001

An independent commission reported May 17, 2001, that the shootings of thirteen people at Columbine High School in Littleton, Colorado, could have been averted if authorities had paid attention to several warning signals. The tragedy occurred on April 20, 1999, when two disaffected teenagers, Dylan Klebold and Eric Harris, went on a rampage at the school, killing twelve students and one teacher and wounding twenty-three others before killing themselves. The commission also found that poor coordination among the many police and emergency units that came to help contributed to the death of the teacher, who might have been saved if emergency care had reached him sooner. (Columbine disaster, Historic Documents of 1999, p. 179)

The commission was set up by Colorado governor Bill Owens in September 1999 to review the events surrounding the shootings, including the backgrounds of the shooters and the response by police, emergency rescue squads, and school authorities. The commission made numerous and broad-ranging recommendations designed to prevent such attacks from happening in the future and, if they did, to respond more effectively.

Meanwhile a federal report on school crime found that although the percentage of students who said they were victims of a crime at school was decreasing, the percentage of high schools students who said they were threatened or injured with a weapon while at school did not change. A second federal report found that the number of violent deaths at school was decreasing, but that when shootings did happen, they often claimed more than one life.

The statistics, however, were overwhelmed in the media by continual reports of violence in the nation's schools, particularly in March when a wave of shootings rippled across the country. On March 5 a high school freshman in the San Diego suburb of Santee killed two students and injured thirteen before being disarmed. Two days later, an eighth-grade girl shot and wounded a classmate during the lunch break at a Williamsport, Pennsylvania, school. On March 22 a high school student shot several students and teachers at a suburban San Diego high school, which was located within a few miles of the Santee school. No one was killed in that incident. But on March 31 a tenth-grade boy was shot and killed in a Gary, Indiana, school parking lot by a former student. In addition, schools and police across the country reported a high number of arrests of students who had either threatened fellow students or brought guns to school.

The Santee shooting reinforced warnings about taking threats seriously. Acquaintances of the shooter, including an adult, apparently heard the student making threats during the previous weekend, but they thought he was joking and did nothing about it. "Basically, one thing that comes out over and over, not just in school shooting cases but in nearly all homicides by teenagers, is that kids talk about it before they do it," Paul Mones, a Portland, Oregon, lawyer and author of a book on child killers, told the New York Times *after the incident in Santee. "Kids want to vent their anger, their worries, their frustrations, their fantasies. They will talk about wanting to get a gun or wanting to kill somebody prior to it happening." Even though a teenager or child might make such statements with no intention of following through on them, Mones and others said all such threats should be taken seriously and reported to authorities.*

The Commission's Findings

The twenty-member Columbine Review Commission, which formally began its work on January 28, 2000, was headed by William H. Erickson, a retired chief justice of the state supreme court. Other members were current and former law enforcement officials, school administrators, and attorneys, including attorney Gale Norton, who resigned from the panel after she was named secretary of the interior in the Bush administration. The panel conducted fifteen public hearings, heard testimony from scores of people involved in the crisis, and reviewed thousands of documents related to the killings.

The picture the commission painted of the scene at the high school was one of horror, shock, and overwhelming confusion that lasted long—too long, the commission said—after Klebold and Harris died. Hundreds of police and rescue squads from surrounding jurisdictions rushed to the school, but once there, lack of coordinated command, poor communications, inadequate equipment, and little training for dealing with this sort of emergency hampered efforts to evacuate and secure the school and rescue the wounded. Fleeing students and the first law enforcement officers on the scene gave conflicting reports about whether the shooters were still alive, how many there were, and whether the school had been salted with bombs set to explode. Radio communications between different units did not work because they were on different frequencies, and police and rescue workers were unfamiliar with the layout of the school.

As a result SWAT teams were instructed to move slowly from the outside in, securing each area of the building before moving on to the next. That cautious approach meant that emergency medical personnel did not reach some of the wounded for nearly four hours after they had been shot—even though some of the wounded and other trapped students used their cell phones to report on their locations. For one, science teacher Dave Sanders, the response was too slow. Despite the efforts of several students to inform the police that Sanders was bleeding to death (including putting a sign in a window that was seen by SWAT officers at 1:45 P.M.), rescue workers did not reach the science room until 2:30 P.M. Sanders had died only moments before. "There was very poor coordination of the facts in this case, and the response in not getting to Dave Sanders before they did resulted in his death," Erickson said at a May 17 news conference. "As it was, they didn't know where the science room was. The students tied a rag around the door knob on the science room to try to lead the people to it."

The commission, however, seemed most disturbed by the fact that authorities missed several opportunities to stop the massacre while it was still in the planning stages. "There was a long planning period, a period where it should have been discovered but wasn't," Erickson said. Although he said school authorities and the boys' parents must share some of the responsibility for failing to heed several red flags, Erickson reserved most of his blame for Jefferson County Sheriff John P. Stone and his office. Erickson said authorities had prepared a search warrant for Harris's house early in 1998 after finding a pipe bomb near the suburban Denver home and viewing a Web site where Harris described how he intended to kill people and stated that he was making pipebombs. For some reason, the warrant was never executed. Erickson said if the police had executed the warrant and searched the house, they would have found videotapes made by Harris and Klebold that outlined "their entire plan and demonstrated their weaponry."

Stone, whose office was being sued by the families of several students killed or wounded at Columbine, had refused the panel's invitation to testify. In a statement issued May 25, Stone said he felt "compelled to clarify several critical points . . . and to emphatically disagree with direct criticisms made of actions of sheriff's officers." Stone, however, endorsed the commission's recommendations for preventing future Columbine-like incidents and said his office had already adopted some of them.

Among the key recommendations made by the commission were the following:

- *The highest priority for law enforcement officers arriving on a scene with active shooters should be to stop the ongoing assault. "First responders" among law enforcement and school resource officers should be trained in rapid emergency deployment and be equipped with the appropriate weapons and protective gear.*
- *Law enforcement command personnel should be trained to take command at the beginning of a crisis, to control the actions of the personnel under them, and to communicate clearly orders and objectives to their subordinates.*
- *Local police agencies, emergency rescue agencies, and any other agency likely to be involved in a crisis situation like Columbine should coordinate their radios and other communications gear.*

349

- *Local county authorities should prepare an emergency response plan for handling emergencies, and each school should develop crisis plans tailored to meet its specific circumstances. School emergency kits should include a diagram of the school with exits clearly marked, a current list of students, and information about how to shut off alarms, sprinkler systems, and utilities.*
- *School officials should work to break the "code of silence" among students that prevents them from telling authorities about threats of violence. "Students and their parents should be brought to understand that threats of violence are never appropriate even as jokes, and may well have consequences for students who utter them," the commission wrote. The commission also said that every school should adopt at least one of the bullying prevention programs that have been shown to be effective.*
- *Any agency with specific information about a juvenile who has threatened or shown the potential for violent behavior or who has engaged in other delinquent acts should share that information with all other agencies dealing with that juvenile, to the extent permitted by law. The commission specifically mentioned police, courts, probation offices, schools, social services, and mental health agencies.*

School Violence Reports

The "Indicators of School Crime and Safety," a report published annually by the Departments of Education and Justice, found that serious crimes committed at schools continued on a generally downward trend in the 1998–1999 school year, the last year for which data were available. Between 1995 and 1999, for example, the percentage of students aged twelve through eighteen who reported being victims of crime at school decreased from 10 percent to 8 percent. Despite the Columbine shootings, students also reported feeling more secure in their own schools. Only 5 percent said they avoided one or more places at school for their own safety in 1999, compared with 9 percent in 1995. The percentage of students reporting the presence of street gangs at their school fell from 29 percent in 1995 to 17 percent in 1999. (Youth violence, p. 73; Previous "indicators" reports, Historic Documents of 1998, p. 735; Historic Documents of 2000, p. 873)

The report acknowledged that serious crime was a problem in the nation's schools, but it stressed that many more students were victims of crimes that occurred away from school. Of the 2,407 homicides of children ages five through nineteen between July 1, 1998, and June 30, 1999, only 38 (including the 12 at Columbine) took place on school grounds. Four of the 1,854 suicides among the same age group (including the two at Columbine) occurred on school grounds. Similarly, the report said, about 186,000 students were victims of serious nonfatal attacks—rape, sexual assault, robbery, and aggravated assault—at school, compared with 476,000 such attacks away from school.

Although the incidence of violent death at school was relatively uncommon, another federal report found that the incidents were more likely to involve multiple victims. In 1992–1993 there were no multiple victims of school slayings, but 42 percent of the slayings in 1998–1999 occurred in incidents where more than one student was killed. Still, the report stressed that the risk that a child would be killed in school was less than one in a million.

The study said the incidence of multiple victims was increasing because more children were somehow obtaining guns and because the shootings usually happened before or after school or during lunch, when students tended to be gathered together in bunches, making it easier for a shooter to hit multiple targets. The report said almost 70 percent of all school homicides were committed with guns, usually handguns. Another 14 percent were committed with knives, about 6 percent were beatings, and the remainder were strangulation or some other method. The study also found that, in more than 30 percent of the deadly attacks, the perpetrator had made direct threats beforehand. The study was prepared by the Centers for Disease Control and the Departments of Education and Justice. The results were reported in the December 5 issue of the Journal of the American Medical Association.

At least one group questioned the accuracy of school crime statistics. In October the National Association of School Resource Officers reported that 84 percent of its members said crimes were underreported to police. School administrators often downgraded assaults to "fights" and thefts to "missing property" in order to minimize the seriousness of the problem, the executive director for the organization said.

Following are excerpts from the executive summary of the "Report of Governor Bill Owens' Columbine Review Commission," released May 17, 2001, reviewing the handling of the shootings at Columbine High School on April 20, 1999, and setting out recommendations to prevent similar tragedies in the future.

The document was obtained from the Internet at http://www .state.co.us/columbine/Columbine_20Report_WEB.pdf.

On January 28, 2000, Governor Bill Owens created by executive order a Columbine Review Commission to inquire into the Columbine High School tragedy on April 20, 1999, and to submit recommendations on several matters: (1) law enforcement handling of the crisis; (2) the sufficiency of safety protocols as used at Columbine High School; (3) an evaluation of emergency medical response and evacuation techniques employed at Columbine; (4) the appropriateness of victim assistance efforts at the scene; (5) identification of key factors that might have contributed to the tragedy and of methods that might prevent similar future occurrences; and (6) an examination of other relevant issues relating to the tragedy.

The Columbine High School tragedy was the work of two disgruntled seniors at the school, Dylan Klebold and Eric Harris, who determined to kill as many teachers and fellow students as possible, first, by planting and detonating two 20-pound propane bombs in the school cafeteria and then by shooting survivors fleeing the inferno they hoped to create. When their explosive devices failed to ignite, the two approached the school and killed one student and seriously wounded a second as they ate their lunches on the grass. They then entered the school building and began firing at students leaving the school cafeteria, wounding five students and deliberately executing one of them.

Klebold entered the school cafeteria briefly but did not fire his weapon inside; he returned outside the building and fired at students near the school parking lot, wounding one of them seriously. Meanwhile, a number of students, two school custodians, and at least one teacher fled to the cafeteria from which, in turn, many either fled from the building or climbed stairs to the second-story library; one teacher and a student were wounded when Harris fired a rifle at them through the school's double glass doors. Emergency calls were made to the 911 number, and teachers urged students in the library to take cover under the tables. Klebold and Harris reentered the building and fired at students in the main hallway and hallway outside the library, wounding one. They also detonated or left for later detonation a number of pipe bombs. Encountering a teacher, Dave Sanders, they seriously wounded him with a shotgun blast. Sanders bled to death from his wounds before medical assistance was provided more than three hours afterwards.

About 15 minutes into their onslaught, the two entered the library where 56 students, two teachers and two library employees had sought concealment. Within seven-and-a-half minutes, Klebold and Harris killed 10 students and seriously wounded a number of other persons by rifle and shotgun fire; they detonated pipe bombs, although without inflicting severe wounds. Several students were deliberately killed execution-style.

Klebold and Harris fired at police from library windows and received return fire. They left the library and moved to the science wing, where they shot at fleeing students. After returning briefly to the cafeteria, the two perpetrators tried again to explode by gunfire the two propane bombs they had carried earlier into the cafeteria, without success, but managed to detonate smaller bombs, one of which was attached to a container of flammable liquid. The resulting firebomb activated the cafeteria sprinkler system, and soon thereafter the sprinkler and fire alarm systems were activated throughout the school building.

The final moments of the perpetrators' lives have not been clearly tracked. Apparently they moved into the office area on the second floor, and then returned to the cafeteria. A surveillance video camera captured their movements there: they seemed to survey the damage to the cafeteria and police activities in the school parking area. From there they went back to the library and exchanged gunfire from the library windows with police who were protecting paramedics rescuing students wounded outside the school building. At about 12:08 P.M., or 47 minutes after the two had commenced their assault, the two turned their weapons on themselves and committed suicide, having left behind them a trail of 13 dead (12 students and one teacher) and many wounded persons. Because the response teams outside the school building were unaware of their deaths, it required several more hours before officers could secure the building, obtain medical attention for the wounded, and collect the dead.

Since the Columbine High School event left so many important questions to be answered, questions that would not be answered if the Columbine tragedy were simply relegated to the archives of history, Governor Owens entrusted the Commission with the responsibility to identify the lessons that Columbine taught. It could not bring back to life or physical wholeness any of the victims of Klebold's and Harris's depredations. But the Commission's efforts and the disbursement of state funds would be well expended if even one life could be saved by effective law enforcement and rescue responses to a future emergency like Columbine. . . .

The Commission conducted 15 meetings open to members of the public. Only one meeting, lasting not more than one-and-a-half hours, was closed to the public at the specific request of Jefferson County Sheriff John Stone, who was apprehensive of the possible adverse impact of a public meeting on an ongoing criminal investigation into the Columbine incident; Undersheriff John A. Dunaway and Division Commander John Kiekbusch of the Jefferson County Sheriff's Office presented only a brief overview of the events at Columbine. In the course of its public hearings, the Commission questioned experts from the Federal Bureau of Investigation, the Colorado Bureau of Investigation, the Arapahoe County Sheriff's Office, the Arvada Police Department, the Lakewood Police Department, the Littleton Fire Department as well as many criminal justice experts. However, it was denied the privilege of interviewing Sheriff Stone and his deputies, even though Sheriff Stone had agreed to appear before the Commission on three separate occasions.

Emergency medical relief personnel and staff members from the six hospitals providing treatment for victims of the Columbine assault testified before the Commission and provided it with valuable information on proper procedures for responding to critical emergencies like that at Columbine High School. Testimony was also received from Littleton Fire Department personnel who provided emergency medical services at the scene. The training and crisis management engaged in by the medical technicians and hospital personnel were exemplary. Experts also testified concerning the victims assistance programs employed in the aftermath of Columbine; their performance was likewise outstanding.

The Commission's assigned duties were to review the events occurring on April 20, 1999 at Columbine High School and to submit recommendations for preventing or handling similar emergencies should they arise in the future. The Commission anticipated, and in most instances found, that subpoenas were not necessary to the completion of its assignment. With the notable exception of the conduct of Sheriff John Stone and a very few others, which foreclosed the Commission from completing its investigation in depth of the law enforcement response at Columbine High School, law enforcement and response agencies were quite helpful in providing most of the information Sheriff Stone had refused to produce for the Commission.

In sum, the Commission received statements from an extensive list of state and local officials and private persons who had experience with or information concerning the Columbine High School event; its staff reviewed thousands of pages of official and nonofficial documents, reports and studies. Its findings, set out at length below, support a number of recommendations for remedial and preventive measures at all levels of Colorado's governmental structure, and by the executive and legislative branches of state and local government:

A. Recommendations Relating to Crisis Response Actions.

- Law enforcement policy and training should emphasize that the highest priority law enforcement officers, after arriving at the scene of a crisis, is to stop any ongoing assault. All law enforcement officers who may be first responders at a crisis, and all school resource officers (SROs) should be trained in concepts and skills of rapid emergency deployment, whether or not assigned as members of standing or reserve special weapons and tactics (SWAT) teams, and should have immediately available all weapons and protective equipment that might be required in a pursuit of active armed perpetrators.
- Because the establishment of an incident command system is an essential component of successful planning for emergencies, implemented by well-conceived and frequent intra- and interagency training programs, the Commission recommends a much-increased emphasis on training in preparation for large-scale emergencies. Designated law enforcement command personnel should be trained to take command at the beginning of a crisis, to control assembled personnel, and to communicate incident objectives clearly to their subordinates.

B. Recommendations for Improved Communications for Critical Emergencies.

- Law enforcement agencies should plan their communications systems to facilitate crisis communication with other agencies with whom they might reasonably be expected to interface in emergencies. Because effective radio communications are indispensable to rapid deployment to meet critical incidents, school districts where local police and rescue agencies utilize digital bandwidths for communications should consider the installation of transmission repeaters in larger school buildings to facilitate communications from within those buildings to outside receivers.
- To promote interoperability of communications among agencies responding to a critical emergency, the Commission recommends that Colorado continue to develop a single statewide digital trunked communications system. The Commission also recommends that agencies in

parts of the state not yet within the statewide system should receive state funds for the purchase of TRP 1000 or similar systems, enabling at least one of them to be available in the event of a serious catastrophe in any part of the state.

C. Recommendations for Advance Planning for Critical Emergencies.

- Appropriate officials in each Colorado County should prepare and keep current a major critical emergency response plan addressing large-scale crises, including those arising at local schools; the appropriate contents of such a plan should include assessments of public and community response resources, the location and availability of needed resources, and the operational requirements to cope with such emergencies (for example, designation of officers to be in charge of a command post and crime-scene processing, procedures to be followed in evacuating injured persons and in designating medical facilities to which they are to be transported, and assignment of responsibility for extinguishing fires and disposing of incendiary and explosive devices).

- Regular planning sessions should be held, participated in by representatives from federal, county and local law enforcement entities, fire and rescue agencies and local school administrators, to focus on preparations for a range of foreseeable emergencies (including worst-case scenarios), based on the county's critical emergency response plan. Participating officials and agencies should base interagency training and disaster-response rehearsals on the current plan.

- Every school in Colorado should develop an emergency crisis plan tailored to meet the particular safety concerns at that school. In drawing up such a plan, school administrators at each school should solicit advice from local law enforcement and rescue agency personnel. School safety planning likewise should take into account the needs and expected responses to emergencies not only of students, administrators and faculty, but also of custodial staff, clerical personnel, cafeteria workers, nurses, bus drivers and other school employees.

- School district officials should consider requiring local school administrators to assemble an appropriate number of emergency kits, depending on the size of the school, to include such things as school diagrams with exit routes clearly indicated; information about procedures to shut off alarms, sprinkler systems and utilities within the building; important telephone numbers; and a current school roster. District school officials should review the safety plan for each school in the district to ensure that it is appropriate for that school.

- Because school-based training and preparedness rehearsals are critical components of an effective emergency plan, preparedness requires that key members of each emergency response team know the roles they will be required to play in the event of a crisis and that they practice or rehearse those roles. Each school should schedule crisis drills at least once a year, and preferably once each school term. It is desirable to include police and rescue agency personnel in preparing for scenarios in which those agencies would likely be involved.

D. Recommendations Bearing on Interaction with Media Representatives.

- Because substantial media coverage of major critical emergencies is to be expected, each major response agency should designate a public information officer of command rank, experienced and trained for the role, who will respond promptly to notice that a major critical incident is in progress at which personnel of his or her response agency are present. The official in charge at an incident command center should designate a principal public information officer if two or more such officers arrive together at the center; otherwise, the first-arriving public information officer should serve as the official liaison with media personnel at the scene.
- Police, fire and rescue agencies, hospitals and victim support agencies, as part of their planning for serious future crises, should prepare themselves to cope with a spate of media attention that probably will become manifest well before a crisis has ended. It would be well to include media representatives in that planning process.

E. Recommendations Concerning Tasks of School Resource Officers (SROs).

- The primary tasks of SROs are to enforce the law and to protect the public safety. SROs and school authorities alike must understand clearly that SROs are law enforcement officers and, as such, should normally be in uniform whenever assigned to a school. SROs should be trained like other first-responders in rapid deployment tactics in case of a school emergency. If SROs are to ensure the safety of persons within a school, school administrators should provide them with all relevant information about students at the school, unless the information is privileged by law. Police command officials should transmit to SROs all information relevant to school safety, including reported criminal conduct on the part of students at the school.

F. Recommendations Concerning Detection by School Administrators of Potential Perpetrators of School-Based Violence and Administrative Countermeasures.

- School officials should continue to work to change the "code of silence" dimension of the prevailing student culture, by emphasizing to students that loyalty to fellow students has its limits, one of which is that statements or conduct carrying with it a possible threat of violence, even an indirect threat, must be reported to school authorities. Students, teachers, administrators and parents also must be reminded that many perpetrators of school violence are quite young. Therefore, threats of violence must not be discounted because a student issuing a threat is young.

School authorities should make it quite clear to students and their parents that all threats of violence, whether of violence to others or to the person making the threat, and whether direct or indirect, will be taken seriously and evaluated. Students and their parents should be brought to understand that threats of violence are never appropriate even as jokes, and may well have consequences for students who utter them. If a threat relates to a specific person, it should not matter that the person toward whom the threat was directed does not wish the matter pursued; it should be evaluated like any other threat.

- Each school district should establish a mechanism like an anonymous telephone line, through which students and others may anonymously report statements or conduct that worries them. The Commission endorses the efforts of the Colorado Attorney General and others to develop a statewide hotline number that students and others can use to report threats and other forms of behavior that concern them. Whatever the mechanism for anonymous reporting eventually established in a school district, it is important that students learn of it and be advised of its importance to their safety and the security of school premises.

- All schools in the state should adopt one or more of the bullying-prevention programs that have already been tested and proven effective. Every school administration should adopt a code of behavior that sets forth clearly the rights and responsibilities of both students and adults within the school community, and should ensure that its code is enforced equably against all violators. Because it is difficult for administrators in large schools to create a supportive atmosphere for students, if fiscal and other concerns do not allow for the continuation of smaller schools, communities should explore the use of alternative approaches in larger facilities like schools-within-a-school.

- A state task force should be created to develop model threat-assessment plans, standards and training programs.

- A threat assessment team should be established at every Colorado high school and middle school, responsible for evaluating threats of violence reported by students, teachers, school staff or law enforcement personnel. All reports of verbal and written threats, "hit lists," or other indicia of future violence should be taken seriously by a team. Each team should include a school staff member like a counselor or a vice-principal who knows the students and the student culture at the school, and who is able to gather information at the school useful in assessing each threat. It is desirable, if feasible, to appoint to each threat assessment team a trained mental health professional, for example, a school psychologist, and someone with a background in law enforcement. Members of each threat assessment team should receive training on such matters as threat assessment, suicide prevention and the law relating to student confidentiality. To ensure that a threat assessment team acquires all information needed to evaluate threats, each school should be expected to maintain accurate records about earlier threats and crime incidents there. Every school should adopt an effective violence prevention program that meet the needs of that school, including both in-school programs and community-based programs, to which students and their families can be referred.

- All agencies that possess specific information regarding threatening behavior of a juvenile, the potential for violent behavior by a juvenile or other delinquent acts of a juvenile, should share that information with other agencies dealing with that juvenile, to the extent allowed by law. Agencies that deal with juveniles, including law enforcement, courts, probation, schools, social services, and mental health agencies, should familiarize themselves with the Colorado juvenile information exchange laws in order to understand what is required under the law. Those agencies should then work to implement protocols to ensure a full and timely exchange of appropriate information regarding juveniles.

- Although security devices can effectively deter certain forms of school crimes, including theft, graffiti, and gang violence, they have not yet been proven to be cost-effective in preventing major school violence like that experienced at Columbine High School. Therefore, the Commission does not recommend the universal installation of metal detectors, video surveillance cameras and other security equipment as a means of forestalling school violence generally; for the present, such security devices can serve only to offer transient solutions to specific problems at individual schools.

G. Recommendations Concerning Medical Treatment for Attack Victims.

- Medical facilities in a given area should consider the advisability and feasibility of instituting an intranet system among hospital emergency and critical care units, not only to assist trauma centers in the course of major emergencies, but to promote efficiencies in the routine diversion of patients from one hospital trauma center to another.

- One technique for resolving time gaps between a SWAT team entry and the arrival of EMTs is to include one or more EMTs in SWAT teams so that emergency medical help arrives as a component of each SWAT team. An alternative solution is for one or more members of each SWAT team to be trained in emergency medical procedures and to carry emergency medical equipment with them. Therefore, SWAT teams should include one or more members with emergency medical training to reduce or minimize the time interval between a SWAT team's arrival and primary treatment of injured victims.

H. Recommendations Concerning Reuniting Attack Victims and Their Families.

- Command centers at the sites of large-scale emergencies with many victims should include a victim advocate at the command center so that accurate information can be provided more directly to the families and friends of victims. Adequate provision for staff support and stress debriefing should be a part of each responding agency's planning for a major crisis.

- Families of victims of major emergencies should be assigned to victim advocates whose offices or residences are nearby where they live.

I. Recommendations Concerning Identification of Victims' Bodies and Family Access to Bodies.

- In acknowledgment of the human anguish created by occurrences like that at Columbine High School, the procedures for victim identification appropriate to most emergencies perhaps ought to be relaxed to accommodate the immediate emotional needs of victims and their families.

J. Recommendations Concerning Suicide Prevention in the Aftermath of Incidents Like Columbine.

- Because suicide constitutes a very serious public health problem in Colorado, and is an observable phenomenon in the aftermath of incidents like Columbine, programs should be developed and implemented to enable teachers and school administrators to discuss with students the subject of suicide before it occurs and not exclusively afterwards. In particular, faculty and staff at Colorado's schools need to be conversant with the common warning signs for suicide and the appropriate responses and nonresponses to them when observed.

In conclusion, April 20, 1999 memorializes a tragic and lethal school assault that resulted in the deaths of 12 students and a teacher and the wounding of 24 other students who encountered Dylan Klebold and Eric Harris before they turned their own weapons on themselves and took their own lives. The sole purpose motivating the assailants' acts was to kill as many students and teachers as they could before ending their own lives.

The Commission hopes that the recommendations embodied in its report will provide methods of avoiding another Columbine and of more effective responses to such assaults should they occur in the future.

"MITCHELL COMMISSION" REPORT ON THE MIDDLE EAST
May 21, 2001

Extreme violence became a way of life for Israel and the Palestinians during 2001. More than 800 people died and thousands were wounded in a cycle of attacks and counterattacks that had begun in 2000 and continued throughout 2001 despite repeated international efforts to halt the bloodshed. The vast majority of those killed were Palestinian Arabs, but repeated suicide bombings by Palestinian militants struck fear into the hearts of Israelis. Hardened positions on both sides seemed to make ending the violence in the short term almost as elusive as the longer-term dream of a permanent accommodation between two peoples who had fought over the same land.

The year began with a last-minute, but ultimately unsuccessful, effort by lame duck president Bill Clinton to broker the peace deal that had escaped him at a summit meeting in July 2000 between then-Israeli prime minister Ehud Barak and Palestinian leader Yasir Arafat. International diplomacy continued sporadically during the rest of the year but—like Clinton's desperate effort—failed in an atmosphere of escalating violence and a victory of revenge over conciliation. (Middle East peace background, Historic Documents of 2000, pp. 494, 930)

An eloquent warning of the long-term dangers faced by both Israelis and Palestinians came from an international commission, the Sharm el-Sheikh Fact-Finding Committee, which Clinton had appointed to investigate the reasons behind the outbreak of violence in September 2000. "Fear, hate, anger, and frustration have risen on both sides," the committee, headed by former U.S. senator George Mitchell, D-Maine, said in report released May 21, 2001. "The greatest danger of all is that the culture of peace, nurtured over the previous decade, is being shattered. In its place there is a growing sense of futility and despair, and a growing resort to violence." Mitchell's panel offered suggestions for restarting the peace process that became the basis for U.S. policy. But neither the Palestinians nor the Israelis seemed ready to follow that path to peace.

Clinton Peace Effort

Even as the movers were packing boxes at the White House, Clinton pressed Israeli and Palestinian leaders for the last bits of compromise that might secure a final peace agreement. Clinton argued that he had come close to a deal during high-stakes negotiations at Camp David in July 2000. At that time, Arafat backed away from an offer by Barak that would have led to creation of a Palestinian state in the Gaza Strip and about 95 percent of the West Bank of the Jordan River. The stumbling blocks were control of East Jerusalem, which was contested by both sides, and the status of hundreds of thousands of Palestinian refugees.

Those issues remained on the table in January as Barak and Arafat considered a compromise proposal Clinton had offered on December 23, 2000. Under that plan, Israel and the Palestinians would each have control of the holy sites in Jerusalem that were important to them, and the city would become the capital of both Israel and a new Palestinian state. Other aspects of the plan also gave each side some, but not all, of what it wanted.

Barak, who had lost much of his domestic political backing because of perceptions in Israel that he had been too willing to make concessions to Arafat, accepted Clinton's proposal on the condition that Arafat accept it as well. But Arafat balked, as he had at Camp David, and sought numerous "clarifications" that put prospects for an agreement out of reach by the time Clinton left office January 20.

The failure of Clinton's last attempt to negotiate a peace deal also doomed the political prospects for Barak, who had resigned in December to force new elections. Barak's election opponent was Ariel Sharon, the far-right politician who had opposed all peace negotiations by Israel since the original Camp David peace agreement between Israel and Egypt in 1978–1979. Promising a tougher line against the Palestinians and declaring the peace process "dead," Sharon easily defeated Barak in the February 6 elections with 62 percent of the vote. Sharon on March 7 took office as prime minister at the head of a fragile coalition government.

Mitchell Commission

Clinton's appointment of a commission to investigate the violence was the key element of a short-lived cease-fire that he and other international leaders negotiated during a summit meeting in Sharm el-Sheikh, Egypt, in mid-October 2000. Clinton selected Mitchell, who had won world praise for his mediation efforts that led to a landmark peace agreement in Northern Ireland in 1998, as chairman. Other members were Mitchell's former Senate colleague, Warren Rudman, R-N.H.; former president of Turkey Suleyman Demirel; Norwegian foreign minister Thorbjoern Jagland; and Javier Solana, the European Union's high representative for the Common Foreign and Security Policy.

Clinton had asked the commission for a report on why the violence erupted in late September immediately following a visit by Sharon to a holy place in Jerusalem known to Jews as Temple Mount and to Muslims as Haram al-Sharif ("Noble Sanctuary"). Sharon, accompanied by 1,000 armed police, said he visited Temple Mount to demonstrate that Israelis had the right to go anywhere they pleased in Jerusalem. Palestinians saw the visit as a deliberately provocative act by a man who had based his political career on thwarting Palestinian aspirations.

In its report, the Mitchell commission concluded that the Sharon visit was provocative and should have been prevented by the Israeli government. Even so, Sharon's visit was not the direct cause of the violence that raged afterwards, the panel said. Instead, it blamed both sides for acting irresponsibly: the Palestinian leadership by not containing the protests, and the Israeli security forces by responding with lethal force against demonstrators. "Amid rising anger, fear, and mistrust, each side assumed the worst about the other and acted accordingly," the panel said.

Assessing the longer-term causes of the violence, the commission determined that both Israelis and Palestinians had been frustrated by failures of the peace process, which started at an international conference in Madrid in 1991 and continued with the signing of a landmark peace accord negotiated at Oslo, Norway, in 1993. Each side accused the other of abusing the peace process, the panel said. Israelis accused the Palestinians of being too willing to resort to violent protests, while the Palestinians accused the Israelis of failing to turn land over to Palestinians as promised. "Each side views the other as having acted in bad faith; as having turned the optimism of Oslo into the suffering and grief of victims and their loved ones," the panel said. "In their statements and actions, each side demonstrates a perspective that fails to recognize any truth in the perspective of the other."

The only way for the cycle of violence to be broken was for each side to take steps that would restore the other side's confidence in its genuine desire for peace, the panel said. For the Palestinian authority, the panel said, that meant "by making clear to both communities that terrorism is reprehensible and unacceptable, and by taking all measures to prevent terrorist operations and to punish perpetrators." Likewise, Israel could restore Palestinian confidence only by freezing all construction of Jewish settlements in the Israeli-occupied portions of the Gaza Strip and the West Bank. The panel noted that U.S. policy had opposed expansion of the settlements for more than a quarter-century, but Israel had continued to build more housing for Jews on land that once belonged to Palestinians. The panel endorsed a statement by President Ronald Reagan in 1982: "The immediate adoption of a settlements freeze by Israel, more than any other action, could create the confidence needed for wider participation in these [peace] talks."

The panel also offered specific steps that each side could take to reduce the risk of violence. For example, it called on Israel to station senior officers at "friction points" to supervise young soldiers when they were called upon to respond to Palestinian rock-throwing and demonstrations. Similarly, the panel demanded that the Palestinian Authority "establish a clear and unchallenged chain of command" for its armed forces, some of which had appeared to operate independently of any central control.

As political leaders themselves, the members of the Mitchell panel acknowledged that the Israeli and Palestinian political leaders faced constraints on their actions and faced domestic opponents ready to denounce any concessions. Even so, the panel said neither side could afford to give "extremists, common criminals and revenge seekers the final say in defining their joint future."

The Mitchell commission report won broad praise internationally. Perhaps most important, the Bush administration adopted its recommendations as the basis for U.S. policy. But illustrating the very difficulties the commission had described, Israeli and Palestinian leaders both found something to complain about in the report. Sharon announced a unilateral cease-fire on May 22, the day after the report was published, but he adamantly refused to accept the central recommendation for a freeze on settlements, saying such an action would "reward" Palestinian terrorism. Palestinian officials generally endorsed the report, but some aides to Arafat charged that it failed to pinpoint Israel's occupation of Palestinian territories as the underlying cause of the conflict.

Escalating Violence

The violence between Israelis and Palestinians intensified during 2001 because of escalating actions by both sides. On the Palestinian side, Arafat and his fellow secular leaders in the Palestine Liberation Organization ceded the initiative to two more radical groups that used the Islamic religion to appeal to young, disaffected Palestinians: Hamas (the acronym for the Islamic Resistance Movement) and Islamic Jihad. Those groups had initiated much of the violence against Israel during the first Palestinian uprising (or intifada) from 1987 to 1991, and both were successful in recruiting suicide bombers willing to destroy themselves, and as many Israelis as possible, for the rewards of heaven as promised by the Koran. With their aggressive rhetoric and actions against Israel, these groups attracted substantial support from Palestinians frustrated by Arafat's inability to secure the independent state he had long sought.

Hamas and Islamic Jihad did not hesitate to attack Israelis in their cities, especially Jerusalem and Tel Aviv—not just in the Jewish settlements that had been vulnerable targets in Gaza and the West Bank. The Hamas bombings came in a bloody succession that terrorized Israelis. Among them, on June 1 a Hamas bomber killed twenty-one Israelis in Tel Aviv, and on August 8 a Hamas terrorist set off a bomb at a pizzeria in Jerusalem, killing fifteen and wounding more than one hundred.

Bombs were not the only instruments of terror used by the Palestinians. Palestinian gunmen fired on Israeli civilians in the West Bank during the first week of October, killing a half-dozen people. On November 4 a gunman affiliated with Islamic Jihad fired on a school bus in Jerusalem, killing two girls and injuring dozens of others.

Israel became increasingly aggressive in its retaliation. Since late 2000 Israel had used helicopter-launched missiles and other high-tech military *weapons to assassinate senior Palestinian figures who, the government said, were responsible for planning the violence. The most spectacular action along this line was the August 27 assassination of Abu Ali Mustafa, head of the Popular Front for the Liberation of Palestine, a secular organization nominally aligned with Arafat. In a technically stunning achievement, an Israeli helicopter fired a missile through a window into Mustafa's office, killing him as he sat at his desk.*

Israel also used its overwhelming military force to attack Palestinian civilian areas in retaliation for terrorist bombings and other killings of Israeli civilians. Israeli tanks moved into several Palestinian towns on the West Bank on a continuous basis for the first time since the government had given up control of them to the Palestine Authority during the peace talks of the 1990s. According to a UN report, the military bulldozed more than 300 Palestinian homes and uprooted nearly 400,000 fruit and olive trees owned by Palestinians, justifying the actions as a retaliation against terrorism. Palestinians and international human rights groups accused Israel of engaging in "collective punishment"—a term the government rejected. Israel stepped up its military presence in the West Bank on October 19, two days after Palestinian gunmen killed Israeli tourism minister Rehavam Zeevi in retaliation for the killing of Mustafa. Sharon withdrew some of the tanks under U.S. pressure, but he had made the point that Israel stood ready to seize land back from the Palestinians.

Symbolism was another important tactic used by Sharon and his military, which humiliated Arafat and other Palestinian leaders to demonstrate to them that Israel had the upper hand. Israel on August 10 seized Orient House, a Palestinian headquarters in East Jerusalem that was an important symbol of Arafat's intention to make Jerusalem the capital of a Palestinian state. In December Israeli troops surrounded the Palestine Authority buildings in Ramallah that served as Arafat's headquarters in the West Bank. The military also destroyed Arafat's helicopters. Arafat was in Ramallah at the time, and the Israeli move effectively made him a captive of the government.

Arafat thus joined tens of thousands of Palestinians who could no longer travel from their homes to places of work—which in many cases had been inside Israel proper. The military banned nearly all Palestinians from entering Israel; even when travel was permitted, Palestinians were forced to undergo repeated searches that turned even short journeys into daylong tribulations.

Arafat at several points during the year attempted to distance himself from these terrorist bombings, but he and the Palestine Authority hesitated to act decisively to stop the attacks. The Israeli government said Arafat was simply unwilling to act because he supported the use of terrorism, no matter what he said to the contrary. Many outside observers said Arafat was in a bind, perhaps of his own making: He had lost much of his ability to control the actions of Hamas and Islamic Jihad, which drew new support among Palestinians with each successful attack against Israel, further undermining Arafat's authority. Whatever the explanation—willful support of terrorism, loss of control to more radical elements, or both—Arafat's lack of action seemed to make him increasingly irrelevant to the conflict.

In addition to killing hundreds of people, the violence and the government's restrictions on Palestinians severely undermined the economies of both communities, which had become closely linked because of Israel's need for Palestinian labor. In a report issued September 6, Terje Larsen, the United Nations special coordinator for the Middle East, estimated that the Palestinian economy had lost $1.8 billion to $2.5 billion since the violence began the previous September. Larsen said the official unemployment figure for Palestinians was 38 percent, but actual unemployment probably was higher. Israel's economy suffered, as well, in part because of the lack of Palestinian labor and in part because the violence disrupted normal transportation systems; the government estimated monthly economic losses at more than $150 million.

U.S. Hesitations

From its first days in office, the Bush administration made clear that it did not intend to follow Clinton's example of cajoling Israeli and Palestinian leaders into a peace agreement. News reports early in the year quoted senior administration officials as criticizing Clinton's hands-on negotiating approach, and they appeared anxious to avoid getting bogged down in a similar haggling process. Secretary of State Colin L. Powell on March 19 outlined a strategy of limited support for the peace process: "The United States stands ready to assist, not insist." Bush repeated that theme two days later during his first meeting at the White House with the newly installed Prime Minister Sharon: "I told him that our nation will not try to force peace, that we will facilitate peace and that we will work with those responsible for peace." More powerful than words were the administration's actions. In late March, for example, the administration ended mediation by the CIA of talks between the Israeli and Palestinian security services; Clinton had authorized the CIA role in 1998 as a means of promoting cooperation between the two sides.

Throughout the year, administration officials called on both Israelis and Palestinians to halt the violence. The administration condemned Palestinian "terrorism" against Israeli civilians, but it also appealed for "restraint" by Israel in its use of military force. As had previous administrations, the Bush administration walked a fine line in the use of leverage over the Israeli government, which enjoyed powerful political support in Washington and was heavily dependent on U.S. financial and military aid. The administration made no overt attempt to restrict Israel's use of U.S.-supplied jets, helicopters, or missiles against Palestinian targets, but it repeatedly objected to Israeli invasions of Palestinian territories. On April 17, for example, Powell criticized Israel for using "excessive and disproportionate" force when it entered the Gaza strip.

The formal release of the Mitchell commission report on May 21 offered the administration a new opportunity to step up its involvement in efforts to end the conflict. Despite earlier hesitations among some administration officials about embracing the report, Powell strongly endorsed it as a "constructive and positive approach" and suggested that Washington would help to get its recommendations implemented.

The administration's first active diplomacy of the year came with a visit to Israel and the Palestinian territories in late May by William J. Burns, the newly confirmed assistant secretary of state for Near Eastern Affairs who was given additional duties as the U.S. "special envoy" for the Israeli-Palestinian conflict. A week later, Bush sent CIA director George Tenet to the region for talks with Israeli and Palestinian security officials; the move reversed his decision in March to pull the CIA out of its mediating role. Tenet succeeded in negotiating a cease-fire agreement on June 13, but both Arafat and Sharon expressed objections even as they grudgingly endorsed it. The cease-fire quieted the violence for a few days but never went into effect, despite an urgent visit to Israel by Powell in late June to shore up support for it. The level of violence gradually escalated during July and continued through August and September before exploding into a series of murderous Palestinian attacks and Israeli retaliations in October. During this period the Bush administration denounced Israel's policy of assassinating Palestinian leaders but also demanded that Arafat take serious steps against Palestinian terrorism.

In the immediate aftermath of the September 11 terrorist attacks against the United States, the Bush administration focused on that crisis and dropped any pretense of involvement in the Israeli-Palestinian dispute. Then on October 1 administration officials leaked word that, before September 11, Bush had been planning to launch a new diplomatic initiative that included formal support for creation of a Palestinian state. Bush confirmed that report on October 2, saying that "the idea of a Palestinian state has always been part of a vision, so long as the right of Israel to exist is respected." While breaking no new ground, this statement was the Bush administration's most authoritative comment on the question of a Palestinian state. More important, the administration's sudden revelation of this position appeared to be part of an effort to bolster the U.S. standing in the Arab world as Washington sought international support for its retaliation against the Islamic extremist group said to be responsible for the September 11 attacks. Reassuring as they might have been to some Arabs, the administration's statements came as a shock to Sharon, who compared them with the actions of European leaders who tried to appease Nazi Germany before the outbreak of World War II. Sharon retracted that remark after the White House called it "unacceptable."

On November 19, six months after the release of the Mitchell commission report, the Bush administration took its most assertive step so far to press for an end to Israel-Palestinian violence. Speaking to a forum in Louisville, Kentucky, Powell said he would send a senior envoy to the Middle East with an assignment to arrange a permanent cease-fire and begin new negotiations toward a long-term peace settlement. "We will do all we can to help the process along," Powell said. "We will push and prod. We will present ideas. . . . But notwithstanding everything we do, at the end of the day, it is the people in the region taking the risks and making the hard choices who must find the way ahead. The only lasting peace will be the peace the parties make themselves."

The new U.S. negotiator, retired marine general Anthony C. Zinni, arrived in Israel on November 26 and was greeted by a new outburst of violence. The next day, Palestinian gunmen killed two people and wounded ten others during a rampage in the northern Israeli city of Afula. A series of suicide bombings over the next week killed twenty-five Israelis and wounded dozens others. Israeli warplanes and helicopters launched retaliatory attacks on Palestinian targets, including office buildings near Arafat's office in Ramallah. As the violence escalated into a new round of the by-now-familiar cycle of Palestinian attacks and Israeli retaliations, Zinni continued his meetings, but to no avail. Administration officials announced on December 15 that Zinni would return to the United States for "consultations" and for the holidays. He had not returned to the region by year's end.

The new violence in December convinced the Bush administration to put more pressure on Arafat, who increasingly seemed unable to influence the actions of Hamas and other more radical Palestinian groups. The tougher line from Washington also followed an announcement by the Israeli cabinet that it was severing all official ties to Arafat and his Palestinian government.

Arafat responded on December 17 with a televised address renewing his previous calls for an end to violent attacks against Israel. Arafat also demanded that Sharon's government halt its "war" against the Palestinian Authority. Over the next several days Palestinian police loyal to Arafat swept through Palestinian neighborhoods arresting Hamas members and closing the offices of organizations connected to Hamas and other radical groups. Hamas announced on December 21 that it had ordered a suspension of attacks against Israel "until further notice." The level of violence dropped sharply during the last ten days of the year, but it seemed highly unlikely that any turning point toward peace had been reached.

> *Following are excerpts from the report of the Sharm el-Sheikh Fact-Finding Committee, appointed in October 2000 by President Bill Clinton to investigate the causes of violence between Israelis and Palestinians and to make recommendations for stopping the violence. The report was made public May 21, 2001. In the report, quotations attributed to the government of Israel (GOI), the Palestine Liberation Organization (PLO), and the Palestinian Authority (PA) refer to written submissions that those agencies gave the committee.*

> **The document was obtained from the Internet at http:// usinfo.state.gov/regional/nea/mitchell.htm.**

Introduction

... After our first meeting, held before we visited the region, we urged an end to all violence. Our meetings and our observations during our subsequent visits to the region have intensified our convictions in this regard. Whatever the source, violence will not solve the problems of the region. It will only make them worse. Death and destruction will not bring peace, but will deepen the hatred and harden the resolve on both sides. There is only one way to peace, justice, and security in the Middle East, and that is through negotiation.

Despite their long history and close proximity, some Israelis and Palestinians seem not to fully appreciate each other's problems and concerns. Some Israelis appear not to comprehend the humiliation and frustration that Palestinians must endure every day as a result of living with the continuing effects of occupation, sustained by the presence of Israeli military forces and settlements in their midst, or the determination of the Palestinians to achieve independence and genuine self-determination. Some Palestinians appear not to comprehend the extent to which terrorism creates fear among the Israeli people and undermines their belief in the possibility of co-existence, or the determination of the GOI [Government of Israel] to do whatever is necessary to protect its people.

Fear, hate, anger, and frustration have risen on both sides. The greatest danger of all is that the culture of peace, nurtured over the previous decade, is being shattered. In its place there is a growing sense of futility and despair, and a growing resort to violence.

Political leaders on both sides must act and speak decisively to reverse these dangerous trends; they must rekindle the desire and the drive for peace. That will be difficult. But it can be done and it must be done, for the alternative is unacceptable and should be unthinkable.

Two proud peoples share a land and a destiny. Their competing claims and religious differences have led to a grinding, demoralizing, dehumanizing conflict. They can continue in conflict or they can negotiate to find a way to live side-by-side in peace.

There is a record of achievement. In 1991 the first peace conference with Israelis and Palestinians took place in Madrid to achieve peace based on UN Security Council Resolutions 242 and 338. In 1993, the Palestine Liberation Organization (PLO) and Israel met in Oslo for the first face-to-face negotiations; they led to mutual recognition and the Declaration of Principles (signed by the parties in Washington, D.C. on September 13, 1993), which provided a road map to reach the destination agreed in Madrid. Since then, important steps have been taken in Cairo, in Washington, and elsewhere. Last year the parties came very close to a permanent settlement.

So much has been achieved. So much is at risk. If the parties are to succeed in completing their journey to their common destination, agreed commitments must be implemented, international law respected, and human rights protected. We encourage them to return to negotiations, however difficult. It is the only path to peace, justice and security.

Discussion

It is clear from their statements that the participants in the summit of last October hoped and intended that the outbreak of violence, then less than a month old, would soon end. The U.S. President's letters to us, asking that we make recommendations on how to prevent a recurrence of violence, reflect that intention.

Yet the violence has not ended. It has worsened. Thus the overriding concern of those in the region with whom we spoke is to end the violence and to return to the process of shaping a sustainable peace. That is what we were told, and were asked to address, by Israelis and Palestinians alike. It was the message conveyed to us as well by President [Hosni] Mubarak of Egypt, King Abdullah of Jordan, and UN Secretary General [Kofi] Annan.

Their concern must be ours. If our report is to have effect, it must deal with the situation that exists, which is different from that envisaged by the summit participants. In this report, we will try to answer the questions assigned to us by the Sharm el-Sheikh summit: What happened? Why did it happen? . . .

What Happened?

We are not a tribunal. We complied with the request that we not determine the guilt or innocence of individuals or of the parties. We did not have the power to compel the testimony of witnesses or the production of documents. Most of the information we received came from the parties and, understandably, it largely tended to support their arguments.

In this part of our report, we do not attempt to chronicle all of the events from late September 2000 onward. Rather, we discuss only those that shed light on the underlying causes of violence.

In late September 2000, Israeli, Palestinian, and other officials received reports that Member of the Knesset (now Prime Minister) Ariel Sharon was planning a visit to the Haram al-Sharif/Temple Mount in Jerusalem. Palestinian and U.S. officials urged then Prime Minister Ehud Barak to prohibit the visit. Mr. Barak told us that he believed the visit was intended to be an internal political act directed against him by a political opponent, and he declined to prohibit it.

Mr. Sharon made the visit on September 28 accompanied by over 1,000 Israeli police officers. Although Israelis viewed the visit in an internal political context, Palestinians saw it as highly provocative to them. On the following day, in the same place, a large number of unarmed Palestinian demonstrators and a large Israeli police contingent confronted each other. According to the U.S. Department of State, "Palestinians held large demonstrations and threw stones at police in the vicinity of the Western Wall. Police used rubber-coated metal bullets and live ammunition to disperse the demonstrators, killing 4 persons and injuring about 200." According to the GOI, 14 Israeli policemen were injured.

Similar demonstrations took place over the following several days. Thus began what has become known as the "Al-Aqsa Intifada" (Al-Aqsa being a mosque at the Haram al-Sharif/Temple Mount).

The GOI asserts that the immediate catalyst for the violence was the break-down of the Camp David negotiations on July 25, 2000 and the "widespread appreciation in the international community of Palestinian responsibility for the impasse." In this view, Palestinian violence was planned by the PA leadership, and was aimed at "provoking and incurring Palestinian casualties as a means of regaining the diplomatic initiative."

The Palestine Liberation Organization (PLO) denies the allegation that the intifada was planned. It claims, however, that "Camp David represented nothing less than an attempt by Israel to extend the force it exercises on the ground to negotiations," and that "the failure of the summit, and the attempts to allocate blame on the Palestinian side only added to the tension on the ground. . . ."

From the perspective of the PLO, Israel responded to the disturbances with excessive and illegal use of deadly force against demonstrators; behavior which, in the PLO's view, reflected Israel's contempt for the lives and safety of Palestinians. For Palestinians, the widely seen images of the killing of 12-year-old Muhammad al Durra in Gaza on September 30, shot as he huddled behind his father, reinforced that perception.

From the perspective of the GOI, the demonstrations were organized and directed by the Palestinian leadership to create sympathy for their cause around the world by provoking Israeli security forces to fire upon demonstrators, especially young people. For Israelis, the lynching of two military reservists, First Sgt. Vadim Novesche and First Cpl. Yosef Avrahami, in Ramallah on October 12, reflected a deep-seated Palestinian hatred of Israel and Jews.

What began as a series of confrontations between Palestinian demonstrators and Israeli security forces, which resulted in the GOI's initial restrictions on the movement of people and goods in the West Bank and Gaza Strip (closures), has since evolved into a wider array of violent actions and responses. There have been exchanges of fire between built-up areas, sniping incidents and clashes between Israeli settlers and Palestinians. There have also been terrorist acts and Israeli reactions thereto (characterized by the GOI as counter-terrorism), including killings, further destruction of property and economic measures. Most recently, there have been mortar attacks on Israeli locations and IDF ground incursions into Palestinian areas.

From the Palestinian perspective, the decision of Israel to characterize the current crisis as "an armed conflict short of war" is simply a means "to justify its assassination policy, its collective punishment policy, and its use of lethal force." From the Israeli perspective, "The Palestinian leadership have instigated, orchestrated and directed the violence. It has used, and continues to use, terror and attrition as strategic tools."

In their submissions, the parties traded allegations about the motivation and degree of control exercised by the other. However, we were provided with no persuasive evidence that the Sharon visit was anything other than an internal political act; neither were we provided with persuasive evidence that the PA planned the uprising.

Accordingly, we have no basis on which to conclude that there was a deliberate plan by the PA [Palestinian Authority] to initiate a campaign of violence at the first opportunity; or to conclude that there was a deliberate plan by the GOI to respond with lethal force.

However, there is also no evidence on which to conclude that the PA made a consistent effort to contain the demonstrations and control the violence once it began; or that the GOI made a consistent effort to use non-lethal means to control demonstrations of unarmed Palestinians. Amid rising anger, fear, and mistrust, each side assumed the worst about the other and acted accordingly.

The Sharon visit did not cause the "Al-Aqsa Intifada." But it was poorly timed and the provocative effect should have been foreseen; indeed it was foreseen by those who urged that the visit be prohibited. More significant were the events that followed: the decision of the Israeli police on September 29 to use lethal means against the Palestinian demonstrators; and the subsequent failure, as noted above, of either party to exercise restraint.

Why Did It Happen?

The roots of the current violence extend much deeper than an inconclusive summit conference. Both sides have made clear a profound disillusionment with the behavior of the other in failing to meet the expectations arising from the peace process launched in Madrid in 1991 and then in Oslo in 1993. Each side has accused the other of violating specific undertakings and undermining the spirit of their commitment to resolving their political differences peacefully.

Divergent Expectations

We are struck by the divergent expectations expressed by the parties relating to the implementation of the Oslo process. Results achieved from this process were unthinkable less than 10 years ago. During the latest round of negotiations, the parties were closer to a permanent settlement than ever before.

Nonetheless, Palestinians and Israelis alike told us that the premise on which the Oslo process is based—that tackling the hard "permanent status" issues be deferred to the end of the process—has gradually come under serious pressure. The step-by-step process agreed to by the parties was based on the assumption that each step in the negotiating process would lead to enhanced trust and confidence. To achieve this, each party would have to implement agreed upon commitments and abstain from actions that would be seen by the other as attempts to abuse the process in order to predetermine the shape of the final outcome. If this requirement is not met, the Oslo road map cannot successfully lead to its agreed destination. Today, each side blames the other for having ignored this fundamental aspect, resulting in a crisis in confidence. This problem became even more pressing with the opening of permanent status talks.

The GOI has placed primacy on moving toward a Permanent Status Agreement in a nonviolent atmosphere, consistent with commitments contained in the agreements between the parties. "Even if slower than was initially envisaged, there has, since the start of the peace process in Madrid in 1991, been steady progress towards the goal of a Permanent Status Agreement without the resort to violence on a scale that has characterized recent weeks." The "goal" is the Permanent Status Agreement, the terms of which must be negotiated by the parties.

The PLO view is that delays in the process have been the result of an Israeli attempt to prolong and solidify the occupation. Palestinians "believed that the Oslo process would yield an end to Israeli occupation in five years," the timeframe for the transitional period specified in the Declaration of Principles. Instead there have been, in the PLO's view, repeated Israeli delays culminating in the Camp David summit, where, "Israel proposed to annex about 11.2% of the West Bank (excluding Jerusalem) . . ." and offered unacceptable proposals concerning Jerusalem, security and refugees. "In sum, Israel's proposals at Camp David provided for Israel's annexation of the best Palestinian lands, the perpetuation of Israeli control over East Jerusalem, a continued Israeli military presence on Palestinian territory, Israeli control over Palestinian natural resources, airspace and borders, and the return of fewer than 1 per cent of refugees to their homes."

Both sides see the lack of full compliance with agreements reached since the opening of the peace process as evidence of a lack of good faith. This conclusion led to an erosion of trust even before the permanent status negotiations began.

Divergent Perspectives

During the last seven months, these views have hardened into divergent realities. Each side views the other as having acted in bad faith; as having turned the optimism of Oslo into the suffering and grief of victims and their loved ones. In their statements and actions, each side demonstrates a perspective that fails to recognize any truth in the perspective of the other.

The Palestinian Perspective

For the Palestinian side, "Madrid" and "Oslo" heralded the prospect of a State, and guaranteed an end to the occupation and a resolution of outstanding matters within an agreed time frame. Palestinians are genuinely angry at the continued growth of settlements and at their daily experiences of humiliation and disruption as a result of Israel's presence in the Palestinian territories. Palestinians see settlers and settlements in their midst not only as violating the spirit of the Oslo process, but also as an application of force in the form of Israel's overwhelming military superiority, which sustains and protects the settlements. . . .

The PLO alleges that Israeli political leaders "have made no secret of the fact that the Israeli interpretation of Oslo was designed to segregate the Palestinians in non-contiguous enclaves, surrounded by Israeli military-controlled borders, with settlements and settlement roads violating the territories' integrity." According to the PLO, "In the seven years since the [Declaration of Principles], the settler population in the West Bank, excluding East Jerusalem and the Gaza Strip, has doubled to 200,000, and the settler population in East Jerusalem has risen to 170,000. Israel has constructed approximately 30 new settlements, and expanded a number of existing ones to house these new settlers."

The PLO also claims that the GOI has failed to comply with other commitments such as the further withdrawal from the West Bank and the release of Palestinian prisoners. In addition, Palestinians expressed frustration with the impasse over refugees and the deteriorating economic circumstances in the West Bank and Gaza Strip.

The Israeli Perspective

From the GOI perspective, the expansion of settlement activity and the taking of measures to facilitate the convenience and safety of settlers do not prejudice the outcome of permanent status negotiations. . . .

Indeed, Israelis point out that at the Camp David summit and during subsequent talks the GOI offered to make significant concessions with respect to settlements in the context of an overall agreement.

Security, however, is the key GOI concern. The GOI maintains that the PLO has breached its solemn commitments by continuing the use of violence in the pursuit of political objectives. "Israel's principal concern in the peace process has been security. This issue is of overriding importance. . . . [S]ecurity is not something on which Israel will bargain or compromise. The failure of the Palestinian side to comply with both the letter and spirit of the security provisions in the various agreements has long been a source of disturbance in Israel."

According to the GOI, the Palestinian failure takes several forms: institutionalized anti-Israel, anti-Jewish incitement; the release from detention of terrorists; the failure to control illegal weapons; and the actual conduct of violent operations, ranging from the insertion of riflemen into demonstrations to terrorist attacks on Israeli civilians. The GOI maintains that the PLO has explicitly violated its renunciation of terrorism and other acts of violence, thereby significantly eroding trust between the parties. The GOI perceives "a thread, implied but nonetheless clear, that runs throughout the Palestinian submissions. It is that Palestinian violence against Israel and Israelis is somehow explicable, understandable, legitimate." . . .

Recommendations

The GOI and the PA must act swiftly and decisively to halt the violence. Their immediate objectives then should be to rebuild confidence and resume negotiations. What we are asking is not easy. Palestinians and Israelis—not just their leaders, but two publics at large—have lost confidence in one another. We are asking political leaders to do, for the sake of their people, the politically difficult: to lead without knowing how many will follow.

During this mission our aim has been to fulfill the mandate agreed at Sharm el-Sheikh. We value the support given our work by the participants at the summit, and we commend the parties for their cooperation. Our principal recommendation is that they recommit themselves to the Sharm el-Sheikh spirit, and that they implement the decisions made there in 1999 and 2000. We believe that the summit participants will support bold action by the parties to achieve these objectives.

End the Violence

- The GOI and the PA should reaffirm their commitment to existing agreements and undertakings and should immediately implement an unconditional cessation of violence.

  Anything less than a complete effort by both parties to end the violence will render the effort itself ineffective, and will likely be interpreted by the other side as evidence of hostile intent.
- The GOI and PA should immediately resume security cooperation.

  Effective bilateral cooperation aimed at preventing violence will encourage the resumption of negotiations. We are particularly concerned that, absent effective, transparent security cooperation, terrorism and other acts of violence will continue and may be seen as officially sanctioned whether they are or not. The parties should consider widening the scope of security cooperation to reflect the priorities of both communities and to seek acceptance for these efforts from those communities.

We acknowledge the PA's position that security cooperation presents a political difficulty absent a suitable political context, i.e., the relaxation of stringent Israeli security measures combined with ongoing, fruitful negotiations. We also acknowledge the PA's fear that, with security cooperation in hand, the GOI may not be disposed to deal forthrightly with Palestinian political concerns. We believe that security cooperation cannot long be sustained if meaningful negotiations are unreasonably deferred, if security measures "on the ground" are seen as hostile, or if steps are taken that are perceived as provocative or as prejudicing the outcome of negotiations.

Rebuild Confidence

- The PA and GOI should work together to establish a meaningful "cooling off period" and implement additional confidence building measures, some of which were proposed in the October 2000 Sharm el-Sheikh Statement and some of which were offered by the U.S. on January 7, 2001 in Cairo.
- The PA and GOI should resume their efforts to identify, condemn and discourage incitement in all its forms.
- The PA should make clear through concrete action to Palestinians and Israelis alike that terrorism is reprehensible and unacceptable, and that the PA will make a 100 percent effort to prevent terrorist operations and to punish perpetrators. This effort should include immediate steps to apprehend and incarcerate terrorists operating within the PA's jurisdiction.
- The GOI should freeze all settlement activity, including the "natural growth" of existing settlements.

  The kind of security cooperation desired by the GOI cannot for long co-exist with settlement activity described very recently by the European Union as causing "great concern" and by the U.S. as "provocative."
  - ◇ The GOI should give careful consideration to whether settlements which are focal points for substantial friction are valuable bargain-

ing chips for future negotiations or provocations likely to preclude the onset of productive talks.

◇ The GOI may wish to make it clear to the PA that a future peace would pose no threat to the territorial contiguity of a Palestinian State to be established in the West Bank and the Gaza Strip.

- The IDF should consider withdrawing to positions held before September 28, 2000 which will reduce the number of friction points and the potential for violent confrontations.
- The GOI should ensure that the IDF adopt and enforce policies and procedures encouraging non-lethal responses to unarmed demonstrators, with a view to minimizing casualties and friction between the two communities. The IDF [Israeli Defense Force] should:

  ◇ Re-institute, as a matter of course, military police investigations into Palestinian deaths resulting from IDF actions in the Palestinian territories in incidents not involving terrorism. The IDF should abandon the blanket characterization of the current uprising as "an armed conflict short of war," which fails to discriminate between terrorism and protest.

  ◇ Adopt tactics of crowd-control that minimize the potential for deaths and casualties, including the withdrawal of metal-cored rubber rounds from general use.

  ◇ Ensure that experienced, seasoned personnel are present for duty at all times at known friction points.

  ◇ Ensure that the stated values and standard operating procedures of the IDF effectively instill the duty of caring for Palestinians in the West Bank and Gaza Strip as well as Israelis living there, consistent with *The Ethical Code of The IDF.*

- The GOI should lift closures, transfer to the PA all tax revenues owed, and permit Palestinians who had been employed in Israel to return to their jobs; and should ensure that security forces and settlers refrain from the destruction of homes and roads, as well as trees and other agricultural property in Palestinian areas. We acknowledge the GOI's position that actions of this nature have been taken for security reasons. Nevertheless, their economic effects will persist for years.

- The PA should renew cooperation with Israeli security agencies to ensure, to the maximum extent possible, that Palestinian workers employed within Israel are fully vetted and free of connections to organizations and individuals engaged in terrorism.

- The PA should prevent gunmen from using Palestinian populated areas to fire upon Israeli populated areas and IDF positions. This tactic places civilians on both sides at unnecessary risk.

- The GOI and IDF should adopt and enforce policies and procedures designed to ensure that the response to any gunfire emanating from Palestinian populated areas minimizes the danger to the lives and property of Palestinian civilians, bearing in mind that it is probably the objective of gunmen to elicit an excessive IDF response.

- The GOI should take all necessary steps to prevent acts of violence by settlers.
- The parties should abide by the provisions of the Wye River Agreement prohibiting illegal weapons.
- The PA should take all necessary steps to establish a clear and unchallenged chain of command for armed personnel operating under its authority.
- The PA should institute and enforce effective standards of conduct and accountability, both within the uniformed ranks and between the police and the civilian political leadership to which it reports.
- The PA and GOI should consider a joint undertaking to preserve and protect holy places sacred to the traditions of Muslims, Jews, and Christians. An initiative of this nature might help to reverse a disturbing trend: the increasing use of religious themes to encourage and justify violence.
- The GOI and PA should jointly endorse and support the work of Palestinian and Israeli non-governmental organizations (NGOs) involved in cross-community initiatives linking the two peoples. It is important that these activities, including the provision of humanitarian aid to Palestinian villages by Israeli NGOs, receive the full backing of both parties.

Resume Negotiations

- We reiterate our belief that a 100 percent effort to stop the violence, an immediate resumption of security cooperation and an exchange of confidence building measures are all important for the resumption of negotiations. Yet none of these steps will long be sustained absent a return to serious negotiations.

  It is not within our mandate to prescribe the venue, the basis or the agenda of negotiations. However, in order to provide an effective political context for practical cooperation between the parties, negotiations must not be unreasonably deferred and they must, in our view, manifest a spirit of compromise, reconciliation and partnership, notwithstanding the events of the past seven months.
- In the spirit of the Sharm el-Sheikh agreements and understandings of 1999 and 2000, we recommend that the parties meet to reaffirm their commitment to signed agreements and mutual understandings, and take corresponding action. This should be the basis for resuming full and meaningful negotiations.

The parties are at a crossroads. If they do not return to the negotiating table, they face the prospect of fighting it out for years on end, with many of their citizens leaving for distant shores to live their lives and raise their children. We pray they make the right choice. That means stopping the violence now. Israelis and Palestinians have to live, work, and prosper together. History and geography have destined them to be neighbors. That cannot be changed. Only when their actions are guided by this awareness will they be able to develop the vision and reality of peace and shared prosperity.

SENATOR JAMES JEFFORDS ON LEAVING THE REPUBLICAN PARTY
May 24, 2001

The partisan gridlock that afflicted Congress for much of the last two decades of the twentieth century left many on Capitol Hill wondering whether a single member could make a difference. Dozens of members, still in the prime of their careers, had retired out of frustration with their inability to accomplish much of anything. But on May 24, 2001, Senator James M. Jeffords of Vermont demonstrated that a single member could have an enormous impact on Capitol Hill. He announced that he was leaving the Republican Party, becoming an independent, and siding with Democrats in the Senate. Jeffords's defection cost Republicans control of what had been an evenly divided Senate and put Democrats in charge for the first time in six years. Just four months after George W. Bush was sworn in as president, Republicans found their control of both the presidency and the Congress surprisingly diminished. (Bush inauguration, p. 94)

Jeffords made it crystal clear that his departure from the Republican Party was a result of disagreements with policy positions by Bush and key members of his administration. Long considered one of the most liberal Republicans in Congress, Jeffords disagreed with Bush's conservative positions on the environment, education, and social programs. His defection put the Democrats in an improved position to affect the outcome of legislation on those matters during the 107th Congress and temporarily weakened Bush's political clout in Washington. After the September 11 terrorist attacks in New York and Washington, however, Bush regained a strong position by winning broad public support for his war against terrorism. (Terrorist attacks, pp. 614, 624)

Jeffords was the latest in a long line of members of Congress who had switched parties, but he was the first whose switch had an immediate effect on the control of either chamber. Four Republicans who served with Jeffords had originally been elected to Congress as Democrats: Ben Nighthorse Campbell of Colorado, Phil Gramm of Texas, Richard Shelby of Alabama, and Strom Thurmond of South Carolina. Robert Smith, a Republican from New Hampshire, had left the party for a failed shot at the presidency in 2000 but then returned. Party switches were more common in state legislatures, and defections from the Democratic Party had given Republicans control of at least one chamber in Kentucky, Pennsylvania, and South Carolina during the 1990s. Jeffords's action made Vermont the only state with two independents serving in the 107th Congress: Representative Bernard Sanders also was an independent, and he generally caucused with the Democrats.

Jeffords as Independent

In some ways, Jeffords's defection from the Republican Party was the formal severing of ties that had been frayed for many years. A lifelong Republican, Jeffords was first elected to the House of Representatives in 1974 and then to the Senate in 1988 after the retirement of another moderate Republican, Robert Stafford. In both the House and Senate, Jeffords routinely took positions, especially on social policy issues, that were substantially more liberal than those of the majority of his fellow Republicans. Jeffords said he was responding to his personal convictions and to the general feelings of Vermonters, who in recent decades had tended to support moderate and liberal political leaders.

By 2001 only a handful of Senate Republicans, including Jeffords, could be described as moderate or even liberal on a broad range of practical and philosophical matters. Most of the others also were from New England and the Northeast: Susan Collins and Olympia Snowe from Maine, Lincoln Chafee from Rhode Island, and Arlen Specter from Pennsylvania. John McCain of Arizona was a conservative who occasionally sided with these moderates. In general, however, the Republican Party in both the Senate and House was under the tight control of conservatives who disdained compromising with more moderate colleagues in their party, much less Democrats.

Republicans controlled the Senate by virtue of a situation rare in American history. The 2000 elections left the Senate evenly split, with fifty Republicans and fifty Democrats. Republicans gained the upper hand through the tie-breaking power of the new vice president, Dick Cheney, who under the Constitution served as president of the Senate. The two parties worked out an unusual power-sharing arrangement that put Republicans in charge of committees but gave Democrats equality in staffing and other privileges.

During his general election campaign in 2000, Bush had described himself as a "compassionate conservative" and had played down his positions on social issues such as abortion that appealed to hard-line conservatives. Once he was declared the winner of the protracted postelection struggle, however, Bush moved to shore up his support among conservatives by appointing leading figures of the Republican Party's right wing to his administration, most notably defeated senator John Ashcroft as attorney general. Jeffords described Ashcroft as a "friend," but the two men had almost nothing in common politically aside from their membership in the Republican Party.

In private conversations with friends and colleagues during the early months of 2001, Jeffords began expressing unease about the direction of the Bush presidency. Jeffords was upset in particular about the size and makeup of Bush's proposed tax cut and what he saw as a decision by the White House to back away from promises for increased spending on education. The two top Democrats in the Senate, Minority Leader Tom Daschle of South Dakota and Minority Whip Harry Reid of Nevada, discretely lobbied Jeffords about the prospect of switching parties.

Rumors about a possible switch by Jeffords emerged on the Sunday morning television talk shows on May 20, sparking an uproar in Washington. On May 22, Jeffords met at the Capitol with Cheney and then at the White House with Bush. If the president hoped to persuade Jeffords to remain a Republican, he failed. According to accounts from both sides, Bush asked Jeffords if administration officials had treated him poorly, and Jeffords responded that his differences with the administration were over policy matters, not political niceties. Jeffords later told reporters that he had warned Bush that he would be "a one-term president if he doesn't listen to his moderates."

Reportedly caught by surprise, Senate Republicans made a frantic last-ditch effort to persuade Jeffords not to switch parties, and Democratic leaders kept a smug silence. Jeffords then flew to Burlington, Vermont's largest city, where on May 24 he announced that his differences with the president and leaders of the Republican Party were insurmountable.

"It is only natural to expect that people like myself, who have been honored with positions of leadership, will largely support the president's agenda. And yet, more and more, I find I cannot," he said. "Looking ahead, I can see more and more instances where I'll disagree with the president on very fundamental issues—the issues of choice [abortion], the direction of the judiciary, tax and spending decisions, missile defense, energy, and the environment, and a host of other issues, large and small." Jeffords added that the "largest" issue had been education, specifically Bush's reluctance to seek a level of education funding that the senator considered adequate.

Acknowledging that his decision would cause "anguish" among fellow Republicans, Jeffords said he would become an independent and would meet with the Democratic caucus and would side with the Democrats for the purpose of reorganizing the Senate. He said his switch would become official after Congress returned from the then-pending Memorial Day recess early in June. Among other things, this delay enabled the Republican leaders in Congress to push through the final compromise agreement on tax cut legislation (Bush's chief priority at the time) and nineteen nominations that were pending.

Reaction

As could be expected, reaction to Jeffords's announcement broke along party lines in Washington, with Republicans expressing dismay and Democrats quietly jubilant. Among Republicans, attention focused first on party leaders who had failed to grasp the depth of Jeffords's unhappiness and had done little, if anything, to counter it. Some Republicans talked briefly about a challenge to Majority Leader Trent Lott, of Mississippi, but nothing came of that talk. McCain, ever the maverick within the Republican caucus, issued a statement saying Jeffords had been "unfairly targeted for abuse, usu-

ally anonymously, by short-sighted party operatives . . . and by some Re-publican members of Congress and their staff." McCain did not name names, but he added: "Tolerance of dissent is a hallmark of a mature party, and it is well past time for the Republican Party to grow up."

Republican moderates moved quickly to gain some leverage within the party caucus, demanding and getting a leadership post for one of their own, Specter. "This should never have happened," Snowe told reporters. "We had all three branches of government, and now we've lost it. Hopefully, we're go-ing to learn something from that." Whether intended or not, Snowe's com-ment appeared to be a tacit acknowledgment that the Supreme Court was widely considered to be in Republican hands, despite its official nonparti-san status.

Ironically, some of the harshest criticism of Jeffords came from Gramm, one of the Republicans who years before had bolted from the Democratic Party. Gramm said Jeffords left the party because "he wanted things that we could not give him."

Bush insisted that Jeffords had been wrong to leave the Republican Party, which, the president said, remained committed to the principles of "moder-ation, tolerance, fiscal responsibility." Speaking in Cleveland two hours af-ter Jeffords made his announcement, Bush said: "I respect Senator Jeffords, but respectfully, I couldn't disagree more. I was elected to get things done on behalf of the American people, and to work with both Republicans and Democrats, and we're doing just that."

A brief flurry of excitement erupted over rumors that Republicans might be able to cancel the impact of the Jeffords move by persuading Georgia's Zell Miller, one of several conservative Democrats, to cross the aisle. Miller quashed rumors that he might defect but said in a statement: "A word of warning to my fellow Democrats: What is sorely needed around here is much more getting along and much less getting even."

A New Senate

When the Senate returned from its recess June 6, Daschle took over as majority leader and Democrats became chairmen of all committees and subcommittees except one. The exception was the Environment and Public Works Committee, whose new chairman was named Jeffords. An ardent en-vironmentalist and critic of many of Bush's policies on environmental is-sue, Jeffords received the chairmanship in part as a reward for his party switch. Reid was the panel's senior Democrat and was in line for the chair, but he said he gave up that opportunity so he could focus his attention on his position as majority whip, the number-two leadership position.

Although the Jeffords defection gave Democrats custody of the levers of power, it did not give Democrats absolute control of what happened in the Senate. There were two reasons for this. The first was an institutional one: under Senate rules, sixty votes were needed to break a filibuster (extended debate), and so neither party could guarantee passage of any of its priori-ties unless it could assemble a cross-party coalition of at least sixty votes. Jeffords's own independent stance reinforced the second reason: leaders of neither party could absolutely count on the votes of all party members. Several conservative Democrats—notably Miller and John Breaux of Louisiana—were just as willing to bolt from their party on specific issues as had been Jeffords and other moderate Republicans. Even if they could prevail in the Senate on a priority item, Democrats still faced the fact that Republicans had close to absolute control of the House, and a Republican in the White House had the power of the veto.

Reflecting on his new responsibilities, but also on the realities of modern-day legislating, Daschle called for a "spirit of bipartisanship" when the newly reorganized Senate met. "Polarized positions are an indulgence, an indulgence the Senate cannot afford and our nation will not tolerate," he said. Daschle promised to give Republicans a greater opportunity to offer amendments on the floor than Republicans had afforded Democrats in previous years. "I think it would be hypocrisy at its worse if we were to take the same tactics, so we're not going to do that."

Democrats during the rest of 2001 were able to shape some pieces of legislation more to their liking than they might have been able to without Jeffords's party switch. Important examples were a sweeping revision of federal aid to local school districts and a bill forcing the government to take over from private security agencies the task of screening passengers at the nation's airports. Democrats also succeeded in blocking, at least for 2001, a controversial Bush plan to open the Arctic National Wildlife Refuge in Alaska to oil drilling, and a House Republican plan for massive corporate tax cuts. But Democrats were unable to win full approval of many of their own priority items, including an increase in the minimum wage, a "patients' bill of rights" for managed health care, and a reform of campaign finance laws banning unregulated contributions known as "soft money."

For most of the session, Republicans gave Daschle and Democratic committee chairmen generally high marks for acting in the bipartisan spirit they had promised. There were exceptions, however, most notably Daschle's refusal in December to take up an "economic stimulus" bill Republicans wanted. Daschle argued that Bush and Republicans had refused to compromise on the measure, but Republicans bitterly accused him of delaying a measure they insisted was needed to revive the economy, which had gone into recession.

Late in the congressional session, Jeffords told reporters that he was more certain than ever that his party switch had been correct. "We have seen compromises that would not have happened" if the Republicans still controlled the Senate, he told the Associated Press. "The moderates are back in a significant position to make a difference."

> *Following is the text of a statement by Senator James M. Jeffords to friends and supporters in Burlington, Vermont, on May 24, 2001, announcing that he was leaving the Republican Party, becoming an independent, and siding with Democrats for purposes of organizing the Senate.*

The document was obtained from the Internet at http://
www.senate.gov/~jeffords/524statement.html.

Anyone who knows me, knows I love the State of Vermont.

It has always been known for its independence and social conscience. It was the first state to outlaw slavery in its constitution. It proudly elected Matthew Lyon to Congress despite his flouting of the Act. It sacrificed a higher share of its sons to the Civil War than perhaps any other state in the Union.

I recall Vermont Senator Ralph Flanders' dramatic statement almost 50 years ago, helping to bring to a close the McCarthy hearings, a sorry chapter in our history.

Today's chapter is of much smaller consequence, but I think it appropriate that I share my thoughts with my fellow Vermonters.

For the past several weeks, I have been struggling with a very difficult decision. It is difficult on a personal level, but it is even more difficult because of its larger impact on the Senate and the nation.

I've been talking with my family, and a few close advisors, about whether or not I should remain a Republican. I do not approach this question lightly. I have spent a lifetime in the Republican Party, and served for 12 years in what I believe is the longest continuously held Republican seat in the U.S. Senate. I ran for re-election as a Republican just last fall, and had no thoughts whatsoever then about changing parties.

The party I grew up in was the party of George Aiken, Ernest Gibson, Ralph Flanders, and Bob Stafford. These names may not mean much today outside Vermont. But each served Vermont as a Republican Senator in the 20th century.

I became a Republican not because I was born into the party but because of the kind of fundamental principles that these and many other Republicans stood for moderation, tolerance, and fiscal responsibility. Their party, our party, was the party of Lincoln.

To be sure, we had our differences in the Vermont Republican Party. But even our more conservative leaders were in many ways progressive. Our former governor, Deane Davis, championed Act 250, which preserved our environmental heritage. And Vermont's Calvin Coolidge, our nation's 30th president, could point with pride to our state's willingness to sacrifice in the service of others.

Aiken and Gibson and Flanders and Stafford were all Republicans. But they were Vermonters first. They spoke their minds—often to the dismay of their party leaders—and did their best to guide the party in the direction of our fundamental principles.

For 26 years in Washington, first in the House of Representatives and now in the Senate, I have tried to do the same. But I can no longer do so.

Increasingly, I find myself in disagreement with my party. I understand that many people are more conservative than I am, and they form the Republican

Party. Given the changing nature of the national party, it has become a struggle for our leaders to deal with me, and for me to deal with them.

Indeed, the party's electoral success has underscored the dilemma I face within my party.

In the past, without the presidency, the various wings of the Republican Party in Congress have had some freedom to argue and ultimately to shape the party's agenda. The election of President Bush changed that dramatically. We don't live in a parliamentary system, but it is only natural to expect that people such as myself, who have been honored with positions of leadership, will largely support the president's agenda.

And yet, more and more, I find I cannot. Those who don't know me may have thought I took pleasure in resisting the president's budget, or that I enjoyed the limelight. Nothing could be further from the truth. I had serious, substantive reservations about that budget, and the decisions it sets in place for today and the future.

Looking ahead, I can see more and more instances where I will disagree with the President on very fundamental issues: the issues of choice, the direction of the judiciary, tax and spending decisions, missile defense, energy and the environment, and a host of other issues, large and small.

The largest for me is education. I come from the state of Justin Smith Morrill, a U.S. Senator who gave America the land grant college system. His Republican Party stood for opportunity for all, for opening the doors of public school education to every American child. Now, for some, success seems to be measured by the number of students moved out of public schools.

In order to best represent my state of Vermont, my own conscience, and the principles I have stood for my whole life, I will leave the Republican Party and become an Independent. Control of the Senate will soon be changed by my decision. I will make this change and will caucus with the Democrats for organizational purposes, once the conference report on the tax bill is sent to the President.

My colleagues, many of them my friends for years, may find it difficult in their hearts to befriend me any longer. Many of my supporters will be disappointed, and some of my staffers will see their lives upended. I regret this very much. Having made my decision, the weight that has been lifted from my shoulders now hangs on my heart.

But I was not elected to this office to be something that I am not. This comes as no surprise to Vermonters, because independence is the Vermont way. My friends back home have supported and encouraged my independence even when they did not agree with my decisions. I appreciate the support they have shown when they have agreed with me, and their patience when they have not. I will ask for that support and patience again, which I understand will be difficult for a number of my friends.

I have informed President Bush, Vice President Cheney, and Senator Lott of my decision. They are good people with whom I disagree. They have been fair and decent to me. I have also informed Senator Daschle of my decision. Three of these four men disagreed with my decision, but I hope each understood my reasons. And it is entirely possible that the fourth may well have second thoughts down the road.

I have changed my party label, but I have not changed my beliefs. Indeed, my decision is about affirming the principles that have shaped my career. I hope the people of Vermont will understand it. I hope, in time, that my colleagues will as well. I am confident that it is the right decision.

June

SUPREME COURT ON FAIRNESS
OF THE DEATH PENALTY
June 4, 2001

Opponents of the death penalty made significant inroads in their quest to outlaw the practice as questions intensified in 2001 about the fairness with which the death penalty is imposed in the United States. Five states adopted laws barring the execution of the mentally retarded, and the Supreme Court agreed to hear a case in its 2001–2002 term asking whether such executions amounted to "cruel and unusual punishment." Two Supreme Court justices appeared to support calls for setting minimum standards to ensure that poor persons charged with capital crimes were adequately defended and to prevent innocent people from being convicted and sentenced to death. Ten states had completed reviews of the process followed in death penalty cases, from arrests to trial to appeals, to ensure that the penalty was administered fairly.

Meanwhile the first two federal executions since the death penalty was reinstated in 1976 took place within eight days of each other. Timothy McVeigh, who was convicted of killing 168 people in the 1995 Oklahoma City bombing of a federal office building, was put to death by lethal injection at a federal prison in Terre Haute, Indiana, on June 11, 2001. On June 19, Juan Raul Garza, the head of a drug ring who was convicted of murder in 1993, died in the same prison, after President George W. Bush refused to grant his plea to reduce his sentence from death to life in prison without the possibility of parole. Garza's attorneys had claimed that the Mexican American was a victim of racial bias because the federal death penalty as currently administered discriminated against minorities and was applied unevenly across the states. A report issued by the Justice Department earlier in June said there was no evidence of racial or ethnic bias in the federal application of the death penalty. (McVeigh execution, p. 433)

A total of sixty-six people were executed in 2001, according to the Death Penalty Information Center, an organization opposing capital punishment. That number was down from eighty-five in 2000 and ninety-eight in 1999. About two-thirds of Americans supported the death penalty, according to public opinion polls, down from roughly 80 percent in the early 1990s, when violent crime was reaching a peak.

Executions for the Mentally Retarded?

The Supreme Court announced on March 26 that in its 2001–2002 term it would reconsider whether execution of mentally retarded murderers was cruel and unusual punishment, barred by the Eighth Amendment to the Constitution. In 1989, the last time the court ruled on the issue, it held, 5–4, that there was "insufficient evidence of a national consensus against executing mentally retarded people . . . for us to conclude that it is categorically prohibited by the Eighth Amendment." The Court has applied a similar "evolving standards of decency" test to bar as unconstitutional executions of the insane, of rapists who were not also convicted of murder, and of murderers under age sixteen.

At the time of its 1989 ruling in Penry v. Lynaugh, *only two states, Maryland and Georgia, prohibited such executions. By mid-2001 the federal government and eighteen of the thirty-eight states that allowed the death penalty had stopped executing the mentally retarded, and several others were considering doing so. "It is time for this Court to assess whether American society has changed significantly over the past decade so that the execution of the mentally retarded now violates American standards of decency," said the attorney for Ernest P. McCarver, a North Carolina inmate then on death row. McCarver, who was convicted of robbing and killing a fellow worker in 1987, had an IQ of sixty-seven. Most experts considered a person with an IQ below seventy to be mentally retarded. Human Rights Watch estimated that between 200 and 300 of the 3,600 inmates on death row were mentally retarded, while the Death Penalty Information Center said that thirty-five mentally retarded inmates had been put to death since executions resumed in 1976.*

In July North Carolina passed a law barring execution of the mentally retarded. As a result the Supreme Court dropped McGarver's case and agreed instead to hear a similar case brought by a Virginia death row inmate, Daryl "James" Atkins, who was convicted in the 1996 robbing-abduction-shooting of a U.S. airman. Atkins's attorneys said he had an IQ of fifty-nine.

Supporters of a ban on executing the mentally retarded argued that the death penalty was neither a deterrent nor a reasonable punishment for the mentally retarded, who were unable to weigh the consequences of their actions rationally. Law enforcement agencies, prosecutors, and families of victims opposed to the ban said many people who were retarded could still tell right from wrong. Warning that if such executions were banned, more criminals would claim to be mentally retarded, opponents of a ban argued that each case should be tried on its individual merits.

A Second Reprieve for Penry

In the 1989 case of Penry v. Lynaugh, *the Court upheld the constitutionality of executing the mentally retarded, but it nonetheless overturned the death sentence of Texas inmate Johnny Paul Penry because the jury was given flawed instructions that prevented them from adequately taking into account Penry's retardation. Penry, whose IQ had variously been measured at sixty-three or lower, had been convicted of rape and murder. Penry was retried in 1990 and again convicted and sentenced to death. Again he appealed on grounds that the jury instructions were flawed, and again the Supreme Court agreed, in a 6–3 decision handed down June 4. The jury instructions in the sentencing phase were "internally contradictory" and did not permit the jurors "to make a reasoned moral response" to the mitigating circumstances in Penry's case, Justice Sandra Day O'Connor wrote for the majority. Chief Justice William H. Rehnquist and Justices Antonin Scalia and Clarence Thomas dissented.*

Two weeks after Penry's case was returned to Texas for further consideration and possibly a third trial, Governor Rick Perry vetoed a law passed by the state legislature barring executions of the mentally retarded. Penry's fate was unclear at year's end.

Shifting Momentum

Declining support for the death penalty among the American public was traceable to evidence that more than ninety people in twenty-two states had been released from death row since 1973 because they had been wrongfully convicted of the crime that put them there. The governor of Illinois, George Ryan, imposed a moratorium on executions in 2000 after the Chicago Tribune *and journalism students at Northwestern University separately published reports showing that thirteen people in the state had been wrongly convicted in capital crimes; all were released from death row. In Oklahoma a police chemist was fired for providing false information in numerous cases, and a federal grand jury there was investigating the role the false information might have played in the convictions of at least nine people who had already been executed.*

Still other reports detailed sloppy and inept work by attorneys appointed to represent poor defendants. A federal court in Texas, for example, overturned the conviction of a man whose lawyer had slept through parts of the trial. In November the Supreme Court heard arguments in a case, Mickens v. Director, Virginia Department of Corrections, *where the defendant's lawyer had previously represented the man the defendant was charged with killing and thus had a conflict of interest.*

At least two Supreme Court justices indicated during the year that they were concerned about these and similar incidents. "After twenty years on [the] High Court, I have to acknowledge that serious questions are being raised about whether the death penalty is being fairly administered in this country," O'Connor told a meeting of Minnesota Woman Lawyers in early July. "The system may well be allowing some innocent defendants to be executed," she added. A swing voter on the Court, O'Connor had supported the death penalty in the past, but she also said that it might be time "to look at minimum standards for appointed counsel in death cases and adequate compensation for appointed counsel when they are used." In an April speech Justice Ruth Bader Ginsburg, a liberal, sounded similar sentiments. "I have yet to see a death case among the dozens coming to the Supreme Court on eve-of-execution [reprieve] applications in which the defendant was well represented at trial," she said.

On June 27 the Committee to Prevent Wrongful Executions, a bipartisan panel of judges, former prosecutors, and victims' advocates, released a report outlining eighteen proposals designed to make the administration of the death penalty more reliable and even-handed. Among other things, the panel recommended that mandatory minimum standards be set for court-appointed defense lawyers and that they be paid adequately; that the death penalty be limited to people who intended to kill their victims; that juries be given an option to sentence a person to life without parole, instead of death, if they have any doubt about his or her guilt; that DNA be preserved and tested after convictions that carry a death sentence; and that new trials on the basis of newly discovered evidence be made easier to obtain.

The report represented "a practical recognition that the death penalty is going to be part of our judicial system [so] where can we find a middle ground where we can make some improvements? The idea is, how to make the system work," said Beth Wilkinson, a panel cochairman and former federal prosecutor who sought the death penalty for McVeigh. The panel was sponsored by the Constitution Project, a nonprofit organization seeking to build a national consensus on controversial legal issues. Members of the committee included both supporters and opponents of capital punishment.

Several states that allowed the death penalty took action in 2001 to try to prevent it from being applied wrongfully or unfairly. Seventeen states passed laws requiring DNA testing of all convicts sentenced to death row, while at least nine states took steps to ensure that indigent defendants were better represented.

Race and the Death Penalty

Attorney General John Ashcroft issued a Justice Department report June 6 that concluded that the disproportionate number of blacks and Hispanics represented in federal capital cases was caused not by intentional racial bias but by "normal factors," such as the violent nature of the offenses that were subject to federal jurisdiction, the demographics of crime in areas were federal jurisdiction was exercised, and decisions made by state prosecutors. "In areas where large-scale, organized drug trafficking is largely carried out by gangs whose membership is drawn from minority groups, the active federal role in investigating and prosecuting these crimes results in a high proportion of minority defendants in the federal cases, including a high proportion of minority defendants in potential capital cases arising from the lethal violence associated with the drug trade," the report said.

Ashcroft's predecessor in the Clinton administration, Janet Reno, had ordered the study in September 2000 after the Justice Department reported that roughly four of every five defendants facing federal charges involving the death penalty were minorities. President Bill Clinton cited the pending study on December 6, 2000, when he ordered a six-month reprieve for Juan Raul Garza, who was scheduled to be the first person executed in a federal prison since 1963. (Reno order, Historic Documents of 2000, p. 990)

While denying any intentional racial bias in application of the death penalty in federal cases, Ashcroft said that administrative changes would be made "to promote public confidence in the process's fairness and to improve its efficiency." Current practice required that U.S. prosecuting attorneys supply information, including racial and ethnic data, only for defendants charged with capital crimes and not for those who could have been charged with a capital crime but were instead charged with a noncapital offense. In the future, Ashcroft said, racial and ethnic data would be collected for all actual and potential federal capital crime cases.

Following are excerpts from the majority opinion in the case of Penry v. Johnson, Texas Department of Criminal Justice, Institutional Division, *in which the Supreme Court, by a 6–3 vote on June 4, 2001, overturned the death sentence of a mentally retarded convicted rapist and murderer because of flawed jury instructions.*

The document was obtained from the Internet at http:// www.supremecourtus.gov/opinions/00pdf/00-6677.pdf.

No. 00–6677

Johnny Paul Penry, Petitioner v. Gary L. Johnson, Director, Texas Department of Criminal Justice, Institutional Division	On writ of certiorari to the United States Court of Appeals for the Fifth Circuit

[June 4, 2001]

JUSTICE O'CONNOR delivered the opinion of the Court.

In 1989, we held that Johnny Paul Penry had been sentenced to death in violation of the Eighth Amendment because his jury had not been adequately instructed with respect to mitigating evidence. See *Penry v. Lynaugh* (1989) (*Penry I*). The State of Texas retried Penry in 1990, and that jury also found him guilty of capital murder and sentenced him to death. We now consider whether the jury instructions at Penry's resentencing complied with our mandate in *Penry I*. . . .

I, II, and III, A [omitted]

B

Penry also contends that the jury instructions given at his second sentencing hearing did not comport with our holding in *Penry I* because they did not provide the jury with a vehicle for expressing its reasoned moral response to the mitigating evidence of Penry's mental retardation and childhood abuse. The Texas Court of Criminal Appeals disagreed. The court summarized *Penry I* as holding that when a defendant proffers "mitigating evidence that is not relevant to the special issues or that has relevance to the defendant's moral culpability beyond the scope of the special issues . . . the jury must be given a special instruction in order to allow it to consider and give effect to such evidence." The court then stated that the supplemental jury instruction given at Penry's second sentencing hearing satisfied that mandate.

The Texas court did not make the rationale of its holding entirely clear. On one hand, it might have believed that *Penry I* was satisfied merely by virtue of the fact that a supplemental instruction had been given. On the other hand, it might have believed that it was the substance of that instruction which satisfied *Penry I*.

While the latter seems to be more likely, to the extent it was the former, the Texas court clearly misapprehended our prior decision. *Penry I* did not hold that the mere mention of "mitigating circumstances" to a capital sentencing jury satisfies the Eighth Amendment. Nor does it stand for the proposition that it is constitutionally sufficient to inform the jury that it may "consider" mitigating circumstances in deciding the appropriate sentence. Rather, the key under *Penry I* is that the jury be able to "consider and *give effect to* [a defendants mitigating] evidence in imposing sentence." . . .

The State contends that the substance of the supplemental instruction satisfied *Penry I* because it provided the jury with the requisite vehicle for expressing its reasoned moral response to Penry's particular mitigating evidence. Specifically, the State points to the admittedly "less than artful" portion of the supplemental instruction which says:

> "If you find that there are any mitigating circumstances in this case, you must decide how much weight they deserve, if any, and therefore, give effect and consideration to them in assessing the defendant's personal culpability *at the time you answer the special issue*. If you determine, when giving effect to the mitigating evidence, if any, that a life sentence, *as reflected by a negative finding to the issue under consideration*, rather than a death sentence, is an appropriate response to the personal culpability of the defendant, *a negative finding should be given to one of the special issues.*" . . .

We see two possible ways to interpret this confusing instruction. First . . . it can be understood as telling the jurors to take Penry's mitigating evidence into account in determining their truthful answers to each special issue. Viewed in this light, however, the supplemental instruction placed the jury in no better position than was the jury in *Penry I*. As we made clear in *Penry I*, none of the special issues is broad enough to provide a vehicle for the jury to give mitigating effect to the evidence of Penry's mental retardation and childhood abuse. . . . Thus, because the supplemental instruction had no practical effect, the jury instructions at Penry's second sentencing were not meaningfully different from the ones we found constitutionally inadequate in *Penry I*.

Alternatively, the State urges, it is possible to understand the supplemental instruction as informing the jury that it could "simply answer one of the special issues no if it believed that mitigating circumstances made a life sentence . . . appropriate . . . regardless of its initial answers to the questions.". . . The Texas Court of Criminal Appeals appeared to understand the instruction in this sense, when it termed the supplemental instruction a "nullification instruction." Even assuming the jurors could have understood the instruction to operate in this way, the instruction was not as simple to implement as the State contends. Rather, it made the jury charge as a whole internally contradictory, and placed law-abiding jurors in an impossible situation.

The jury was clearly instructed that a "yes" answer to a special issue was appropriate only when supported "by the evidence beyond a reasonable doubt." A "no" answer was appropriate only when there was a reasonable doubt as to whether the answer to a Special Issue should be . . . Yes. The verdict form listed the three special issues and, with no mention of mitigating circumstances, confirmed and clarified the jury's two choices with respect to each special issue. The jury could swear that it had unanimously determined "beyond a reasonable doubt that the answer to this Special Issue is Yes." Or it could swear that at least 10 jurors had "a reasonable doubt *as to the matter inquired about in this Special Issue* and that the jury thus had "determin[ed] that the answer to this Special Issue is No."

In the State's view, however, the jury was also told that it could ignore these clear guidelines and—even if there was in fact no reasonable doubt as to the matter inquired About—answer any special issue in the negative if the mitigating circumstances warranted a life sentence. In other words, the jury could change one or more truthful yes answers to an untruthful no answer in order to avoid a death sentence for Penry.

We generally presume that jurors follow their instructions. Here, however, it would have been both logically and ethically impossible for a juror to follow both sets of instructions. Because Penry's mitigating evidence did not fit within the scope of the special issues, answering those issues in the manner prescribed on the verdict form necessarily meant ignoring the command of the supplemental instruction. And answering the special issues in the mode prescribed by the supplemental instruction necessarily meant ignoring the verdict form instructions. Indeed, jurors who wanted to answer one of the special issues falsely to give effect to the mitigating evidence would have had to violate their oath to render a "true verdict."

The mechanism created by the supplemental instruction thus inserted "an element of capriciousness" into the sentencing decision, making the jurors power to avoid the death penalty dependent on their willingncss to elevate the supplemental instruction over the verdict form instructions. There is, at the very least, "a reasonable likelihood that the jury . . . applied the challenged instruction in a way that prevent[ed] the consideration" of Penry's mental retardation and childhood abuse. The supplemental instruction therefore provided an inadequate vehicle for the jury to make a reasoned moral response to Penry's mitigating evidence. . . .

Thus, to the extent the Texas Court of Criminal Appeals concluded that the substance of the jury instructions given at Penry's second sentencing hearing satisfied our mandate in *Penry I*, that determination was objectively unreasonable. . . . The three special issues submitted to the jury were identical to the ones we found constitutionally inadequate as applied in *Penry I.* Although the supplemental instruction made mention of mitigating evidence, the mechanism it purported to create for the jurors to give effect to that evidence was ineffective and illogical. The comments of the court and counsel accomplished little by way of clarification. Any realistic assessment of the manner in which the supplemental instruction operated would therefore lead to the same conclusion we reached in*Penry I*: "[A] reasonable juror could well have believed that there was no vehicle for expressing the view that Penry did not deserve to be sentenced to death based upon his mitigating evidence."

The judgment of the United States Court of Appeals for the Fifth Circuit is therefore affirmed in part and reversed in part, and the case is remanded for further proceedings consistent with this opinion.

It is so ordered.

OAS GENERAL ASSEMBLY
ON THE SITUATION IN HAITI
June 5, 2001

Haiti, one of the poorest and most troubled countries in the Western Hemisphere, fell into the grip of a political stalemate during 2001. The inability of the country's political leaders to resolve their deeply held differences led to sporadic violence, including an apparent coup attempt in December against President Jean-Bertrand Aristide. More important for the lives of Haiti's 8 million long-suffering people, the political standoff prevented the renewal of international aid to the country; the United States and other donors withheld about $500 million in hopes of pressuring Aristide and his opponents to come to terms with one another.

Haiti's crisis was a prime demonstration of the obstacles international diplomats faced in trying to overcome ingrained differences in the world's poorest countries. Unlike conflicts between ethnic or racial groups in many other countries, Haiti's problems stemmed more from disagreements between economic and social classes, combined with regional and personal hatreds that had persisted for generations. Moreover, Haiti was so poor that many of its people seemed to feel they had nothing to lose, and possibly something to gain, through political violence. (Background, Historic Documents of 2000, p. 952)

Disputes over Elections

Ruled for much of the latter part of the twentieth century by a dictatorship of the Duvalier family, Haiti held its first democratic elections in 1990. The winner was Aristide, a former priest who was an unrelenting advocate for the poor. The army ousted Aristide from power just seven months later, and he fled into exile. President Bill Clinton in 1994 sent 20,000 U.S. troops into Haiti to oust the military coup leaders, restore Aristide to power, and dismantle the army. The return of Aristide did not signal the return of pure democracy, however. Aristide and his hand-picked successor, Renee Preval, ruled autocratically and blocked opposition forces from playing any serious role in government. Clinton withdrew the last remaining U.S. troops from Haiti in 1999. (U.S. intervention, Historic Documents of 1994, p. 436)

As disputes between the government and opposition forces hardened in late 1999 and early 2000, the United States, France, and other international donors withheld about $500 million in pending aid until legislative elections were held. Preval called elections for the two-chamber legislature in May 2000, and the voting went well, considering Haiti's lack of experience with free elections. But the government then changed the rules for determining the winners of Senate races—a step that gave victories to ten candidates of the ruling Lavalas Party under highly questionable circumstances. The legitimacy of those elections became the focal point of disputes plaguing Haiti's politics. The government then held elections for president in November 2000. With most opposition parties boycotting the election, Aristide won an overwhelming victory.

In his last weeks in office, President Clinton in December 2000 extracted a written promise from Aristide to settle Haiti's political problems peacefully and to call new elections for the disputed Senate seats. The new administration of President George W. Bush decided early in 2001 to stand by Clinton's policy of pressuring Aristide to carry out reforms, with most of the actual diplomatic work being handled by the Organization of American States (OAS). That approach received an important endorsement from the leaders of nearly all Western Hemisphere countries, at a mid-April 2001 summit meeting in Quebec City.

In the meantime, Aristide was inaugurated as president on February 7, 2001. The ceremony was shunned by opposition politicians and the leaders of nearly all other countries in the region. Perhaps an even more important signal of Haiti's isolation was the final withdrawal on February 6 of the last elements of what once was a large United Nations mission that tried to promote security and good governance in Haiti. Frustrated by the lack of progress and the rise of political violence—including attacks on UN workers—Secretary General Kofi Annan had ordered the mission closed.

Negotiations During 2001

Senior OAS officials, including Secretary General Cesar Gaviria (a former president of Colombia) and Deputy Secretary General Luigi Einaudi (a U.S. diplomat), traveled to Haiti repeatedly during 2001 for extensive meetings with government officials and representatives of the two main political factions: Aristide's Lavalas Party and a coalition of fifteen opposition parties known as the Democratic Convergence. The OAS's main bargaining chip was the $500 million in aid that had been withheld. Once the regional body certified that a workable political agreement was at hand, Washington and other donors would allow the aid to flow, bringing at least some relief to Haiti's impoverished people.

Negotiations in May, June, and July 2001 made some progress on the central issue of calling new elections for the legislature in November 2002. As those talks got under way, the OAS General Assembly on June 5 passed a resolution urging both sides in Haiti to demonstrate new flexibility. But Aristide's party and opposition leaders bogged down in a bitter dispute over how and when to hold elections for local officials, who had substantial power in Haiti, especially over security forces. An incident on July 28 hardened positions on both sides, as armed men attacked several police stations—killing five police officers and wounding fourteen others. Eleven men said to have been members of the disbanded Haitian army were later arrested in the neighboring Dominican Republic in connection with the attacks, which the government blamed on the opposition.

OAS mediators brought both sides back to the bargaining table in October and offered a compromise proposal. That effort failed to break the stalemate, however, as did a follow-up visit to Haiti by Secretary General Gaviria in late November.

Violence once again poisoned the atmosphere. On December 3 a local journalist, Brignol Lindor, was killed by a mob said by many observers to be associated with Aristide's Lavalas Party. Killing journalists had become a form of political protest in Haiti; the April 2000 slaying of the country's best-known radio journalist, Jean Dominique, had led to a major outburst of violence.

Two weeks after the killing of Lindor, a group of twenty to thirty armed men invaded the presidential palace in Port-au-Prince and engaged in a prolonged gun battle with police, several of whom were killed, along with at least one of the attackers. Aristide was not in the palace at the time, but his spokesman called the attack an attempted coup d'état. Aristide appealed for calm, but large crowds of his supporters mounted violent protests and attacked and burned the homes and offices of several opposition politicians. Government officials accused Guy Philippe, a former Haitian police chief who had been living in exile in the Dominican Republic, of planning the attack. Amid the violence and charges back and forth, the only certainty at year's end was that violence once again had trumped political dialogue in Haiti.

Following are excerpts from a resolution adopted on June 5, 2001, by the General Assembly of the Organization of American States, calling on political leaders in Haiti to "commit themselves fully" to democracy and respect for human rights.

The document was obtained from the Internet at http:// www.oas.org/Assembly2001/documentsE/AG264.htm.

THE GENERAL ASSEMBLY,
 BEARING IN MIND:
 That the preamble of the OAS Charter establishes that representative democracy is an indispensable condition for the stability, peace, and development of the region;
 That, according to the Charter, one of the essential purposes of the Organization is to promote and consolidate representative democracy, with due respect for the principle of nonintervention;

That another purpose is to promote, by cooperative action, economic, social, and cultural development;

The Santiago Commitment to Democracy and the Renewal of the Inter-American System (1991), the Declaration of Managua (1993), and the declarations and plans of action of the Summits of the Americas (Miami, 1994; Santiago, 1998);

That the Heads of State and Government at the Third Summit of the Americas, emphasized their commitment to defend and strengthen democracy across the Hemisphere; and

The commitment of the OAS and of the Caribbean Community (CARICOM) to continue their contributions to the strengthening of democracy in Haiti;

RECALLING the conclusions of the OAS Electoral Observation Mission to Haiti on the elections of May 21, 2000, presented in the report to the Permanent Council;

RECALLING ALSO [a] resolution of August 4, 2000, in which the Permanent Council, at the request of the Government of Haiti, authorized the Secretary General to lead a Mission to Haiti to "identify, together with the Government of Haiti and other sectors of the political community and civil society, options and recommendations for resolving, as expeditiously as possible, difficulties such as those that have arisen from differing interpretations of the Electoral Law, and for further strengthening democracy in that country"; . . .

CONCERNED that the political crisis is still unresolved and that persistent mistrust among political actors continues to hinder the possibility of wide-ranging talks that would bring about a sustainable solution to the problems arising from the May 21, 2000, elections, based on a general agreement among the government of Haiti, political parties, and civil society and other relevant institutions of Haitian society, with a view to resolving the political crisis and strengthening democracy and respect for human rights in that country;

RECOGNIZING the need for financial and technical assistance with a view to contributing to the promotion of Haiti's social and economic development; . . .

RESOLVES:

1. To reiterate its deep concern at the continuing political crisis in Haiti, arising from the elections of May 21, 2000.

2. To take note of the initiative, consisting of five elements, contained in [a] letter from the President of Haiti with regard to the process toward a definitive resolution to the current political crisis.

3. To acknowledge the concerns expressed in said letter regarding the urgency of normalizing relations between Haiti and the international financial institutions.

4. To urge the Government of Haiti to follow the resignations of seven senators with the expeditious constitution, by June 25, 2001, of a credible, independent, and neutral Provisional Electoral Council (CEP), composed of nine members nominated by the Executive, the Judiciary, political parties—including the Convergence démocratique, Fanmi Lavalas, and other political parties and churches, both Catholic and

Protestant. This is a necessary step to create a climate of confidence conducive to a broad-based agreement among the Government of Haiti, political parties, and civil society, and other relevant institutions of Haitian society, with a view to resolving the political crisis and strengthening democracy and respect for human rights in Haiti.

5. To call upon the Government of Haiti, political parties, and civil society, and other relevant institutions of Haitian society to commit themselves fully to this end.

6. To instruct the Secretary General to monitor and report to the Permanent Council on implementation of the commitments [made during negotiations among the parties in May];

7. To instruct the Secretary General to increase his efforts, in consultation with CARICOM and with other interested countries, to contribute further to the resolution of the existing political crisis in Haiti, to its social and economic development, to the strengthening of democracy, and to respect for human rights in that country.

8. To invite the Secretary General to establish a Group of Friends of Haiti from interested OAS member states and permanent observers to assist him in these efforts.

9. To request the Permanent Council to examine, as a matter of urgency, the mandate, modalities, budget, financing, and other arrangements concerning the establishment of a possible mission to Haiti.

10. To instruct the Secretary General to work jointly with member states toward normalizing relations between Haiti and the international community, including the international financial institutions, as progress is achieved in reaching a sustainable solution to the crisis arising from the May 21, 2000, elections.

11. To instruct the Secretary General to report to the Permanent Council or the General Assembly, as appropriate, on the implementation of this resolution.

BUSH ON SIGNING
THE TAX RELIEF BILL
June 7, 2001

A little less than five months after taking office, President George W. Bush delivered on the centerpiece of his campaign platform, proudly signing into law June 7, 2001, a ten-year, $1.35 trillion tax relief bill. The biggest tax cut since 1981, the major features of the measure (PL 107-16) gradually reduced income tax rates across the board, eased the so-called marriage penalty, phased out the estate tax, and expanded the child tax credit. At a formal signing ceremony in the White House East Room, Bush hailed the law as "the first major achievement of a new era."

Perhaps just as pleased by the signing ceremony as Bush were most congressional Republicans, who had been repeatedly frustrated in their attempts to enact major tax relief legislation since the federal government began running a budget surplus in 1998. President Bill Clinton consistently vetoed their bills, arguing that the surplus should be used to restore Social Security and pay down the national debt, not for tax relief that primarily benefited the wealthy. In some ways the tax cut also represented a vindication of Bush's father, George H. W. Bush, who, when facing an unprecedented budget deficit, was forced to raise taxes in 1990 after promising voters "no new taxes."

Enactment of the tax cut was an undeniable political victory for the new president, who had entered the White House under the cloud of a disputed election and questions about his ability to lead. Even after making concessions to win the crucial support of a handful of moderate Democrats in the Senate, which was split 50–50, Bush got most of what he asked for. The celebration was dampened only by the May 24 announcement that Senator James Jeffords of Vermont was leaving the Republican Party to become an independent and would caucus with the Democrats, giving them control of the Senate. A week after the tax bill passed, the reins of leadership in the Senate passed from the Republicans to Democrats. (Jeffords announcement, p. 377)

Supporters and opponents of the tax cut agreed that it had the potential for enormous impacts on the economy and the shape of the federal govern-

ment for many years to come. They disagreed about what those results would be. Bush and other supporters argued that, by keeping more money in the hands of taxpayers rather than the government, the tax cut would spur consumer spending, personal savings, and private investment—and thus stimulate the economy. A side benefit of more than incidental importance for Republican proponents was that a tax cut would reduce revenue available to the government and thus force cuts in domestic programs they did not like. Opponents argued just the opposite. They said the tax cut, which was heavily weighted toward future years, would do almost nothing to stimulate the currently faltering economy and would, instead, have a long-term negative effect by forcing the government back into deficit spending, which in turn would ratchet up interest rates and weaken the economy.

Genesis of a Tax Cut

Republicans had been pushing for an across-the-board tax cut ever since the federal government began to run a budget surplus in 1998. In 1999 the Republican-led Congress passed a measure cutting taxes by $792 billion over ten years, but Clinton promptly vetoed it, saying that it gave too much relief to high-income taxpayers and soaked up money that should be left for debt reduction and spending on high-priority federal programs. In 2000 the Republicans again pressed unsuccessfully for tax-relief legislation, but this time their effort was intended to bolster the presidential efforts of Texas governor George W. Bush, who was pushing a substantial cut in income tax rates on the campaign trail.

Bush had adopted the tax cut as a focal point of his campaign in large part to siphon off support from a Republican primary opponent, Malcolm S. "Steve" Forbes Jr. A billionaire media magnate, Forbes was a single-issue candidate whose issue was tax reform, and he used his personal wealth to promote his candidacy and his issue in a quest for the Republican presidential nomination. Bush had a natural base among middle-of-the-road conservatives but needed to attract more support from the more conservative elements of the Republican Party to whom Forbes was appealing with his plan for a flat tax of 17 percent for all but the lowest-income taxpayers. Adopting his own tax cut proposal helped gain Bush that support in primaries where he faced a more formidable opponent than Forbes, Arizona senator John McCain.

Once he gained the nomination in 2000, Bush continued to promote the tax cut as a core issue against the Democratic candidate, Vice President Al Gore, despite repeated polls that showed voters placed tax relief well behind other issues, such as promoting education, saving Social Security, and providing prescription drug coverage for the elderly. Gore attacked Bush's plan as favoring the wealthy, noting that most of the benefits would go to Americans in the top 1 percent income bracket. But during the campaign Bush doggedly promoted his plan as a needed reform to put money back into the hands of the taxpayers. (2000 Republican presidential campaign, Historic Documents of 2000, pp. 519, 797)

After the protracted post election battle in Florida was resolved, the victorious Bush and his allies, including Vice President-elect Dick Cheney, shifted the primary rationale for the tax cut. The economy had begun to weaken after a decade of sustained growth, they said, and a major tax cut would help stimulate the spending and investment that would prevent a recession or make it a short and relatively mild one. On February 27, in his first speech to a joint session of Congress, Bush expressed a sense of urgency about adopting a tax cut as an economic stimulus, saying: "To create economic growth and opportunity, we must put money back into the hands of the people who buy goods and create jobs." (Bush speech to Congress, p. 171)

Bush had received an important—and possibly vital—endorsement for his tax cut plan from Federal Reserve Board Chairman Alan Greenspan, whose opinion carried great weight among members of Congress. Testifying before the Senate Budget Committee on January 25, Greenspan suggested that taxes needed to be cut primarily to reduce federal budget surpluses in future years. Enormous surpluses, which were projected at that point, would tempt Congress to spend too much money, he said. Greenspan offered only a lukewarm endorsement of Bush's tax cut as an economic stimulus measure, however. His nominee for Treasury secretary, Paul O'Neill, also undercut the president's argument on that score. At his confirmation hearing on January 17, O'Neill said he would not "make a huge case" that the tax cut proposal was "the instrument to ensure that we don't go into recession."

Congress Tackles the Tax Cut

The new president had little trouble getting the Republican-controlled House to adopt his tax cut plan. Republican leaders at first made no effort to gather Democratic support, which they did not need anyway. The House Ways and Means Committee put Bush's plan into four separate bills: a reduction in income tax rates (HR 3), which passed the House on March 8; a reduction in tax rates for married couples and people with children (HR 6), which passed the House on March 29; a phase-out of the federal estate tax (HR 8), which passed the House on April 4; and, finally, a package of tax incentives for retirement savings (HR 10), which passed the House on May 2. Of the four, only the vote on the rate reduction bill was close, with 10 Democrats joining all 219 Republicans to pass it. The retirement savings bill commanded a majority of support from both Republicans and Democrats; the other two passed with overwhelming support from Republicans and a few dozen conservative Democrats. After Congress finished work on a fiscal year 2002 budget resolution, the House on May 16 again passed the income tax cut as part of a budget reconciliation bill (HR 1836), which freed it from some procedural hurdles in the Senate.

The momentum slowed in the Senate, which was evenly divided between Republicans and Democrats, but with Republicans holding the chairmanship of committees by virtue of Cheney's tie-breaking power as president of the Senate. Because of that split, the balance of power in the Senate was held by a small group of moderate Republicans and Democrats. Most of the moderates favored Bush's tax cut proposal, but several were concerned about specific elements. One of those features was the size of the proposed cuts. On

*the campaign trail Bush had put the price tag for his proposal at $1.3 tril-
lion, a figure Gore challenged as not representing the true cost, which he said
would be much higher. When Bush presented his tax cut plan to Congress,
his aides said the plan would cost $1.64 trillion through the rest of the de-
cade. The congressional Joint Committee on Taxation estimated the actual
cost at $1.78 trillion, and some private experts put the figure even higher, at
$2 trillion or more.*

*In Senate negotiations, the overall size of the tax cut became a central
issue, with moderate Democrats determined to reduce the total number so
Bush could not claim an unalloyed victory. The moderates in both parties
settled on a ceiling of $1.35 trillion over ten years; that figure ultimately be-
came the core of the bill that passed the Senate on May 23 by a 62–38 vote,
with all the "no" votes cast by Democrats.*

*A new dynamic lent a sense of urgency to House-Senate negotiations over
the bill when James Jeffords of Vermont announced on May 24 that he was
leaving the Republican Party, becoming an independent, and siding with
the Democrats for purposes of organizing the Senate—thus putting Democrats in a narrow majority. But Jeffords agreed to delay his party switch
until the tax cut bill cleared Congress. Under that time pressure, House-
Senate negotiators quickly crafted a final compromise, which cleared both
chambers just before the Memorial Day recess.*

*"Across-the-board tax relief does not happen often in Washington, D.C.,"
Bush said, signing the tax cut into law June 7. "In fact, since World War II,
it has happened only twice: President Kennedy's tax cut in the 1960s and
President Reagan's tax cut in the 1980s. And now it's happening for the
third time, and it's about time."*

*Democratic opponents predicted that the tax cut would prove counterpro-
ductive. "This bill ignores the true cost of the tax cut and damages the priorities of our country," House Minority Leader Richard A. Gephardt, D-Mo.,
said after the signing ceremony. At his first news conference as the new Senate majority leader, Tom Daschle, D-S.D., was asked if the Democrats would
try to rescind some of the tax breaks before they took effect. "I know we're going to revisit it. I just know that at some point that reality is going to come
crashing down on all of us, and we're going to have to deal with it."*

Major Provisions

*The earliest effective tax breaks in the package, added late in the process
in hopes of stimulating the economy, were rebate checks of up to $300 for in-
dividuals, $500 for single parents, and $600 for married couples. The rebates were criticized on two grounds—that the total cost, $39 billion, was
not enough to give the $10 trillion U.S. economy much of a jolt; and that low-
income taxpayers would get no rebate because their earnings were so low
they paid little or nothing in income tax (although most of them paid payroll taxes for Social Security and Medicare).*

*Among its other key provisions, the law replaced five existing tax brack-
ets (15 percent, 28 percent, 31 percent, 36 percent, and 39.6 percent) with
six brackets (10 percent, 15 percent, 25 percent, 28 percent, 33 percent, and*

35 percent) by 2006. By 2010 the child tax credit would double to $1,000. By 2005 the standard deduction for married couples, and the amount of income subject to the 15 percent bracket, would rise to be double that of single taxpayers. Taxes on estates would be phased out gradually and eliminated entirely by 2010. Tax benefits for contributions to individual retirement accounts and pension plans would be increased starting in 2002, and various tax breaks for education would be instituted or expanded.

Unless Congress took action to make the tax breaks permanent, all the law's provisions would automatically lapse on December 31, 2010. This "sunset" provision was required to keep the cost of the tax cut under the limit permitted in the congressional budget resolution.

The Aftermath

The president's optimistic assumptions about his tax cut fell victim later in the year to real-world developments, some of which had been predicted by tax-cut opponents and others that were totally unforeseen. The economic slowdown, which had become obvious by the spring, began cutting into tax revenue by the summer. In late August the White House Office of Management and Budget lowered its surplus projections for fiscal 2001 from $281 billion to $158 billion, with all but $1 billion coming from surpluses in the Social Security trusts fund, which both parties had promised not to touch.

Then came the September 11 terrorist attack against the World Trade Center towers and the Pentagon—an event that sent the stock markets into a nosedive, led to a depression in the travel industry, and deepened the recession, if only temporarily. Congress approved $40 billion in emergency spending to deal with several aspects of the war against terrorism. But a prolonged political battle over which party was responsible for the recession killed a bill to stimulate the economy through additional tax cuts for individuals and business and extended unemployment compensation for laid-off workers. (U.S. and world economies after September 11, p. 663)

Following is the text of remarks made June 7, 2001, by President George W. Bush at a White House ceremony at which he signed a bill cutting taxes by $1.35 trillion over ten years.

The document was obtained from the Internet at http://www.whitehouse.gov/news/releases/2001/06.

Thank you. . . .

Laura, thank you very much for being here on this historic moment. Mr. Vice President [Dick Cheney], Secretary [of the Treasury Paul] O'Neill, [Office of Management and Budget] Director [Mitchell] Daniels, Secretary [of Commerce Don] Evans and [Secretary of Labor Elaine] Chao are here, as well. Secretary [of Energy Spencer] Abraham, [EPA] Administrator Christine Todd

Whitman, members of the United States Senate, members of the House of Representatives, fellow Americans. Welcome.

Some months ago, in my speech to the Joint Session of Congress, I had the honor of introducing Steven Ramos to the nation. Steven is the network administrator for a school district. His wife, Josefina, teaches at a charter school. They have a little girl named Lianna. And they're trying to save for Lianna's college education.

High taxes made saving difficult. Last year, they paid nearly $8,000 in federal income taxes. Well, today, we're beginning to make life for the Ramos' a lot easier. Today, we start to return some of the Ramos' money—and not only their money, but the money of everybody who paid taxes in the United States of America.

Across the board tax relief does not happen often in Washington, D.C. In fact, since World War II, it has happened only twice: President Kennedy's tax cut in the '60s and President Reagan's tax cuts in the 1980s. And now it's happening for the third time, and it's about time.

A year ago, tax relief was said to be a political impossibility. Six months ago, it was supposed to be a political liability. Today, it becomes reality. It becomes reality because of the bipartisan leadership of the members of the United States Congress. Members like Bill Thomas, of California; Ralph Hall, of Texas; Charles Grassley, of Iowa; Max Baucus of Montana; Zell Miller, of Georgia; John Breaux, of Louisiana; Trent Lott, of Mississippi; and the entire leadership team in the Senate; and Denny Hastert of Illinois and the leadership team in the House of Representatives. Some Democrats, many Republicans, who worked tirelessly and effectively to produce this important result.

I also want to pay tribute to the members of my administration who worked with Congress to bring about this day: Vice President Cheney, Secretary O'Neill, Director Daniels and the team inside the White House of Andy Card and Larry Lindsey, Nick Calio and their staffs.

With us today are 15 of the many families I met as I toured our country making the case for tax relief, hard-working Americans. I was able to talk about their stories and their struggles and their hopes, which made the case for tax relief much stronger than my words could possible convey. And I want to thank you all for coming.

And here at the White House today are representatives of millions of Americans, including labor union members, small business owners and family farmers. Your persistence and determination helped bring us to this day. The American people should be proud of your efforts on their behalf, and I personally thank you all for coming.

Tax relief is a great achievement for the American people. Tax relief is the first achievement produced by the new tone in Washington, and it was produced in record time. Tax relief is an achievement for families struggling to enter the middle class. For hard working lower income families, we have cut the bottom rate of federal income tax from 15 percent to 10 percent. We doubled the per-child tax credit to $1,000, and made it refundable. Tax relief is compassionate and it is now on the way.

Tax relief is an achievement for middle class families squeezed by high energy prices and credit card debt. Most families can look forward to a $600 tax rebate, before they have to pay the September back-to-school bills. And in the years ahead, taxpayers can look forward to steadily declining income tax rates.

Tax relief is an achievement for families that want the government tax policy to be fair and not penalize them for making good choices, good choices such as marriage and raising a family. So we cut the marriage penalty.

Tax relief makes the code more fair for small businesses and farmers and individuals by eliminating the death tax. Over the long haul, tax relief will encourage work and innovation. It will allow American workers to save more on their pension plan or individual retirement accounts. Tax relief expands individual freedom. The money we return, or don't take in the first place, can be saved for a child's education, spent on family needs, invested in a home or in a business or a mutual fund or used to reduce personal debt.

The message we send today, it's up to the American people; it's the American people's choice. We recognize loud and clear the surplus is not the government's money. The surplus is the people's money and we ought to trust them with their own money.

This tax relief plan is principled. We cut taxes for every income taxpayer. We target nobody in, we target nobody out. And tax relief is now on the way.

Today is a great day for America. It is the first major achievement of a new era, an era of steady cooperation. And more achievements are ahead. I thank the members of Congress in both parties who made today possible. Together, we will lead our country to new progress and new possibilities. It is now my honor to sign the first broad tax relief in a generation.

SUPREME COURT ON UNREASONABLE SEARCHES
June 11, 2001

In two important decisions the Supreme Court elaborated on the circumstances under which law enforcement agents must procure a search warrant or run afoul of the Fourth Amendment protections against unreasonable searches and seizures. In the first case, Kyllo v. United States, *the Court ruled that police needed a search warrant before they could use a thermal imaging device outside a private home to detect whether high-intensity lights were being used inside to grow marijuana. The majority used this case to set out a new test for determining when the use of high-tech snooping equipment was an unconstitutional invasion of privacy.*

In the second case, Ferguson v. City of Charleston, *the Court held that police could not test pregnant women for cocaine use without their consent and then turn the evidence over to police. The sponsors of the program said its purpose was to protect unborn babies by forcing their mothers into treatment programs. But the Court majority said that the program was directly related to law enforcement and the hospital thus needed permission from the women or a search warrant before conducting the tests.*

In a third ruling broadening the protections of the Fourth Amendment, the Court ruled that police could not set up roadblocks specifically to look for drugs. The majority in this case, City of Indianapolis v. Edmond, *said that unlike roadblocks to check for drunken drivers, this check was primarily intended to enforce criminal law and thus violated the Fourth Amendment.*

In two other rulings, however, the Court sided with law enforcement officers. In one case, Illinois v. McArthur, *the Court ruled that police could detain someone outside his or her home while obtaining a warrant to go inside and search for drugs. And in a case that got national coverage, the Court ruled 5–4 that the Fourth Amendment's protections against unreasonable seizure did not prevent police from taking someone into custody for a minor traffic violation or other minor offenses. The case,* Atwater v. City of Lago Vista, *involved a woman in Lago Vista, Texas, who was jailed for failing to buckle her children into their seat belts before she drove them home from soccer practice. Writing for the majority, Justice David H. Souter said that while the arresting officer may have used "extremely poor judgment," his actions "satisfied constitutional requirements." The arrest may have been "inconvenient and embarrassing" for the mother, "but not so extraordinary as to violate the Fourth Amendment." In dissent Justice Sandra Day O'Connor said the ruling "ran counter" to the principles of the Fourth Amendment and could lead to greater racial and ethnic profiling. Minor traffic violations "may often serve as an excuse for stopping and harassing an individual," she wrote. "After today, the arsenal available to any officer extends to a full arrest and the searches permissible concomitant to that arrest."*

High-Tech Searches

In 1992 federal narcotics agents, working from utility bills and a tip from an informant, trained a heat-seeking device on a house in Florence, Oregon, where they suspected the resident was growing marijuana indoors under high-intensity lights. When the thermal imaging device indicated that part of the house was emitting more heat than the rest of the house and neighboring houses, they requested a search warrant. During the subsequent search the agents found more than one hundred marijuana plants growing under halide lights, and they arrested the resident, Danny Kyllo.

Although he pleaded guilty, Kyllo reserved the right to challenge the use of the heat sensor as an unconstitutional search. "The public justifiably expects that the walls of our homes sanctify a zone of privacy against the government and represent physical barriers that assure our privacy," Kyllo's attorney, Kenneth Lerner, wrote in his brief to the Supreme Court. "Since we don't permit police to break into people's homes, should we permit them to use technology to accomplish the same thing?"

In a 5–4 decision handed down June 11, 2001, in the case of Kyllo v. United States, *the Supreme Court said the answer was no. Writing for the majority, Justice Antonin Scalia laid out a new rule for determining whether a search using high-tech surveillance equipment was unreasonable: "Where, as here, the government uses a device that is not in general public use, to explore details of a home that would previously have been unknowable without physical intrusion, the surveillance is a 'search' and is presumptively unreasonable without a warrant." To rule otherwise, Scalia said, "would leave the homeowner at the mercy of advancing technology— including imaging technology that could discern all human activity in the home."*

Scalia denied the government's argument that the detection of heat loss from a house did not violate reasonable expectations of privacy because it did not reveal the cause of the heat loss. In the home, Scalia wrote, "all details are intimate details, because the entire area is held safe from prying government eyes."

Writing for the four dissenting justices, Justice John Paul Stevens distinguished between " 'through-the-wall surveillance' that gives the observer or listener direct access to information in a private area" and "off-the-wall surveillance," or observations of the exterior of the home from which the agents made inferences about activities inside. Such technology would not "invade any constitutionally protected interest in privacy," Stevens said, "unless it provides its user with the functional equivalent of actual presence in the area being searched." Stevens also said the majority's new rule went too far in suggesting that all future developments in technological snooping would be off limits without a warrant. Such a rule, Stevens said, was "unnecessary, unwise, and inconsistent with the Fourth Amendment."

The opinion was notable for its unusual voting pattern. Scalia, widely regarded as one of the most conservative members of the Court, was joined in the majority by another conservative, Justice Clarence Thomas, and three liberal justices, Stephen G. Breyer, Ruth Bader Ginsburg, and Souter. Stevens, usually considered the most liberal of the current justices, was joined in his dissent by Chief Justice William H. Rehnquist, a conservative, and the Court's two swing voters, O'Connor and Anthony M. Kennedy.

Steven R. Shapiro, national legal director of the American Civil Liberties Union, which backed Kyllo's appeal, was pleased with the ruling. "It means that the Fourth Amendment is going to apply to all the high-tech technology that is rapidly being developed. Big Brother must now pay attention to constitutional principles." But several law enforcement officials indicated they were not troubled by the requirement to get a warrant. "Now we just add one more step in our investigations," one said.

Legal experts cautioned that technology might outstrip the rule enunciated by Scalia, who stressed that he was talking about technology that was not generally available to the public. "Twenty years from now," Harvard Law School professor Bill Stuntz told the Washington Post, *"you may be able to buy thermal imaging technology at a Wal-Mart. Then either we get less privacy or the Court has to draw another line. Kyllo is not the last word on this."*

Drug Tests for Pregnant Women

In the drug-testing case, the Court ruled 6–3 on March 21 that maternity patients could not be tested for illegal drugs without their consent if the results of the tests were to be used to enforce drug laws. The case involved a public hospital in Charleston, South Carolina, which in 1989 set up a program in accordance with city policy to test pregnant women for cocaine. The idea was to reduce the use of crack cocaine, which was harmful to the fetus as well as the mother. Under the initial program women whose urine tested positive for cocaine were arrested for violating the state's child endangerment law. Some women who tested positive for cocaine during labor were taken to jail in handcuffs shortly after delivering their babies. In 1990 the program was altered to give the women a choice of being jailed or obtaining drug treatment. By the time the program was abandoned in 1994, thirty women had been arrested. Several of them sued, arguing that the testing, without their consent and without a warrant, violated the Fourth Amendment's protection against unreasonable searches.

The city argued that the warrantless searches were justified under the "special needs" exception to the Fourth Amendment for searches deemed necessary to protect health and safety. In the past the Supreme Court had approved special needs exceptions for drug testing for school athletes, customs agents, and railroad workers involved in train accidents. In this case, however, the majority said the exception did not apply. In previous cases, the health and safety justifications were "divorced from the state's general interest in law enforcement," Justice John Paul Stevens wrote for the majority in Ferguson v. Charleston. *Here the health justifications were directly connected to law enforcement.*

"While the ultimate goal of the program may well have been to get the women in question into substance abuse treatment and off drugs, the immediate objective was to generate evidence for law enforcement purposes in order to reach the goal," Stevens wrote. The Charleston testing program "was designed to obtain evidence of criminal conduct by the tested patients that would be turned over to the police and that could be admissible in subsequent criminal prosecutions." In such cases hospitals had a "special obligation to make sure that the patients are fully informed about their constitutional rights." Joining Stevens in the opinion were Justices O'Connor, Souter, Ginsburg, and Breyer. Kennedy wrote a separate concurring opinion.

Chief Justice Rehnquist and Justices Scalia and Thomas dissented. In a dissent signed by all three, Scalia said doctors were supposed to have the welfare of their patients in mind and "that they have in mind in addition the provision of evidence to the police should make no difference."

An attorney who represented the women hailed the decision as "a victory for all patients who are entitled to expect that when they go to the doctor they will receive medical care and not a search for police purposes." South Carolina attorney general Charles Condon, who was instrumental in starting the program when he was a prosecutor in Charleston, said the program would continue if police got a search warrant or the woman's consent. "There is no right of a mother to jeopardize the health and safety of an unborn child through her own drug abuse," Condon said after the decision was announced. Many medical professionals suggested that the program could raise the dangers to unborn children. In briefs filed in support of the women, the American Medical Association, the American Public Health Association, and similar organizations said the most likely direct effect of the testing program would be to prevent pregnant women from seeking prenatal care altogether.

Following are excerpts from the majority and dissenting opinions in the case of Kyllo v. United States, *in which the Supreme Court ruled, 5–4, on June 11, 2001, that the use, without a search warrant, of a thermal imaging device to scan the outside of a house in search of illegal drugs was a violation of the Fourth Amendment.*

*The document was obtained from the Internet at http://
www.supremecourtus.gov/opinions/00pdf/99-8508.pdf.*

No. 99–8508

Danny Lee Kyllo, Petitioner,	}	On writ of certiorari to the
v.		United States Court of Appeals
United States		for the Ninth Circuit

[June 11, 2001]

JUSTICE SCALIA delivered the opinion of the Court.

This case presents the question whether the use of a thermal-imaging device aimed at a private home from a public street to detect relative amounts of heat within the home constitutes a "search" within the meaning of the Fourth Amendment.

I

In 1991 Agent William Elliott of the United States Department of the Interior came to suspect that marijuana was being grown in the home belonging to petitioner Danny Kyllo, part of a triplex on Rhododendron Drive in Florence, Oregon. Indoor marijuana growth typically requires high-intensity lamps. In order to determine whether an amount of heat was emanating from petitioner's home consistent with the use of such lamps, at 3:20 A.M. on January 16, 1992, Agent Elliott and Dan Haas used an Agema Thermovision 210 thermal imager to scan the triplex. Thermal imagers detect infrared radiation, which virtually all objects emit but which is not visible to the naked eye. The imager converts radiation into images based on relative warmth—black is cool, white is hot, shades of gray connote relative differences; in that respect, it operates somewhat like a video camera showing heat images. The scan of Kyllo's home took only a few minutes and was performed from the passenger seat of Agent Elliott's vehicle across the street from the front of the house and also from the street in back of the house. The scan showed that the roof over the garage and a side wall of petitioner's home were relatively hot compared to the rest of the home and substantially warmer than neighboring homes in the triplex. Agent Elliott concluded that petitioner was using halide lights to grow marijuana in his house, which indeed he was. Based on tips from informants, utility bills, and the thermal imaging, a Federal Magistrate Judge issued a warrant authorizing a search of petitioner's home, and the agents found an indoor growing operation involving more than 100 plants. Petitioner was indicted on one count of manufacturing marijuana, in violation of 21 U.S.C. 841(a)(1). He unsuccessfully moved to suppress the evidence seized from his home and then entered a conditional guilty plea.

The Court of Appeals for the Ninth Circuit remanded the case for an evidentiary hearing regarding the intrusiveness of thermal imaging. On re-mand the District Court found that the Agema 210 "is a non-intrusive device which emits no rays or beams and shows a crude visual image of the heat be-ing radiated from the outside of the house"; it "did not show any people or ac-tivity within the walls of the structure"; "[t]he device used cannot penetrate walls or windows to reveal conversations or human activities"; and "[n]o inti-mate details of the home were observed." Based on these findings, the District Court upheld the validity of the warrant that relied in part upon the thermal imaging, and reaffirmed its denial of the motion to suppress. A divided Court of Appeals initially reversed (1998), but that opinion was withdrawn and the panel (after a change in composition) affirmed (1999), with Judge Noonan dis-senting. The court held that petitioner had shown no subjective expectation of privacy because he had made no attempt to conceal the heat escaping from his home, and even if he had, there was no objectively reasonable expectation of privacy because the imager "did not expose any intimate details of Kyllo's life, only amorphous hot spots on the roof and exterior wall." We granted cer-tiorari (2000).

II

The Fourth Amendment provides that "[t]he right of the people to be secure in their persons, houses, papers, and effects, against unreasonable searches and seizures, shall not be violated." "At the very core" of the Fourth Amend-ment "stands the right of a man to retreat into his own home and there be free from unreasonable governmental intrusion." [Citation omitted.] With few ex-ceptions, the question whether a warrantless search of a home is reasonable and hence constitutional must be answered no.

On the other hand, the antecedent question of whether or not a Fourth Amendment "search" has occurred is not so simple under our precedent. The permissibility of ordinary visual surveillance of a home used to be clear be-cause, well into the 20th century, our Fourth Amendment jurisprudence was tied to common-law trespass. . . . Visual surveillance was unquestionably law-ful. . . . We have since decoupled violation of a person's Fourth Amendment rights from trespassory violation of his property, but the lawfulness of war-rantless visual surveillance of a home has still been preserved.

One might think that the new validating rationale would be that examin-ing the portion of a house that is in plain public view, while it is a "search" de-spite the absence of trespass, is not an unreasonable one under the Fourth Amendment. But in fact we have held that visual observation is no search at all—perhaps in order to preserve somewhat more intact our doctrine that warrantless searches are presumptively unconstitutional. In assessing when a search is not a search, we have applied somewhat in reverse the principle first enunciated in *Katz v. United States* (1967). *Katz* involved eavesdropping by means of an electronic listening device placed on the outside of a telephone booth—a location not within the catalog ("persons, houses, papers, and ef-fects") that the Fourth Amendment protects against unreasonable searches. We held that the Fourth Amendment nonetheless protected *Katz* from the warrantless eavesdropping because he "justifiably relied" upon the privacy of the telephone booth. As Justice Harlan's oft-quoted concurrence described it, a Fourth Amendment search occurs when the government violates a subjective expectation of privacy that society recognizes as reasonable. We have subsequently applied this principle to hold that a Fourth Amendment search does *not* occur—even when the explicitly protected location of a *house* is concerned—unless "the individual manifested a subjective expectation of privacy in the object of the challenged search, and society [is] willing to recognize that expectation as reasonable." [*California v.*] *Ciraolo* [(1986)]. We have applied this test in holding that it is not a search for the police to use a pen register at the phone company to determine what numbers were dialed in a private home, *Smith v. Maryland* (1979), and we have applied the test on two different occasions in holding that aerial surveillance of private homes and surrounding areas does not constitute a search, *Ciraolo; Florida v. Riley* (1989).

The present case involves officers on a public street engaged in more than naked-eye surveillance of a home. We have previously reserved judgment as to how much technological enhancement of ordinary perception from such a vantage point, if any, is too much. While we upheld enhanced aerial photography of an industrial complex in *Dow Chemical* [*v. United States* (1986)], we noted that we found "it important that this is *not* an area immediately adjacent to a private home, where privacy expectations are most heightened" (emphasis in original).

III

It would be foolish to contend that the degree of privacy secured to citizens by the Fourth Amendment has been entirely unaffected by the advance of technology. For example, ... the technology enabling human flight has exposed to public view (and hence, we have said, to official observation) uncovered portions of the house and its curtilage that once were private. The question we confront today is what limits there are upon this power of technology to shrink the realm of guaranteed privacy.

The *Katz* test—whether the individual has an expectation of privacy that society is prepared to recognize as reasonable—has often been criticized as circular, and hence subjective and unpredictable. [Citations omitted.] While it may be difficult to refine *Katz* when the search of areas such as telephone booths, automobiles, or even the curtilage and uncovered portions of residences are at issue, in the case of the search of the interior of homes—the prototypical and hence most commonly litigated area of protected privacy—there is a ready criterion, with roots deep in the common law, of the minimal expectation of privacy that *exists*, and that is acknowledged to be *reasonable*. To withdraw protection of this minimum expectation would be to permit police technology to erode the privacy guaranteed by the Fourth Amendment. We think that obtaining by sense-enhancing technology any information regarding the interior of the home that could not otherwise have been obtained without physical "intrusion into a constitutionally protected area" [quoting prior case] constitutes a search—at least where (as here) the technology in question is not in general public use. This assures preservation of that degree of privacy against government that existed when the Fourth Amendment was adopted. On the basis of this criterion, the information obtained by the thermal imager in this case was the product of a search.

The Government maintains, however, that the thermal imaging must be upheld because it detected only heat radiating from the external surface of the house. The dissent makes this its leading point, contending that there is a fundamental difference between what it calls "off-the-wall observations" and "through-the-wall surveillance." But just as a thermal imager captures only heat emanating from a house, so also a powerful directional microphone picks up only sound emanating from a house—and a satellite capable of scanning from many miles away would pick up only visible light emanating from a house. We rejected such a mechanical interpretation of the Fourth Amendment in *Katz*, where the eavesdropping device picked up only sound waves that reached the exterior of the phone booth. Reversing that approach would leave the homeowner at the mercy of advancing technology—including imaging technology that could discern all human activity in the home. While the technology used in the present case was relatively crude, the rule we adopt must take account of more sophisticated systems that are already in use or in development. The dissent's reliance on the distinction between "off-the-wall" and "through-the-wall" observation is entirely incompatible with the dissent's belief . . . that thermal-imaging observations of the intimate details of a home are impermissible. The most sophisticated thermal imaging devices continue to measure heat off-the-wall rather than through-the-wall; the dissent's disapproval of those more sophisticated thermal-imaging devices is an acknowledgement that there is no substance to this distinction. As for the dissent's extraordinary assertion that anything learned through "an inference" cannot be a search, that would validate even the "through-the-wall" technologies that the dissent purports to disapprove. Surely the dissent does not believe that the through-the-wall radar or ultrasound technology produces an 8-by-10 Kodak glossy that needs no analysis (*i.e.*, the making of inferences). And, of course, the novel proposition that inference insulates a search is blatantly contrary to *United States v. Karo* (1984), where the police "inferred" from the activation of a beeper that a certain can of ether was in the home. The police activity was held to be a search, and the search was held unlawful.

The Government also contends that the thermal imaging was constitutional because it did not "detect private activities occurring in private areas." It points out that in *Dow Chemical* we observed that the enhanced aerial photography did not reveal any "intimate details." *Dow Chemical*, however, involved enhanced aerial photography of an industrial complex, which does not share the Fourth Amendment sanctity of the home. The Fourth Amendment's protection of the home has never been tied to measurement of the quality or quantity of information obtained.

Limiting the prohibition of thermal imaging to "intimate details" would not only be wrong in principle; it would be impractical in application. . . . To begin with, there is no necessary connection between the sophistication of the surveillance equipment and the "intimacy" of the details that it observes—which means that one cannot say (and the police cannot be assured) that use of the relatively crude equipment at issue here will always be lawful. The Agema Thermovision 210 might disclose, for example, at what hour each night the lady of the house takes her daily sauna and bath—a detail that many would consider "intimate"; and a much more sophisticated system might detect nothing more intimate than the fact that someone left a closet light on. We . . . would have to develop a jurisprudence specifying which home activities are intimate and which are not. And even when (if ever) that jurisprudence were fully developed, no police officer would be able to know in advance whether his through-the-wall surveillance picks up "intimate" details—and thus would be unable to know in advance whether it is constitutional.

The dissent's proposed standard—whether the technology offers the "functional equivalent of actual presence in the area being searched"—would seem quite similar to our own at first blush. The dissent concludes that *Katz* was such a case, but then inexplicably asserts that if the same listening device only revealed the volume of the conversation, the surveillance would be permissible. Yet if, without technology, the police could not discern volume without being actually present in the phone booth, JUSTICE STEVENS should conclude a search has occurred. Cf. *Karo* (STEVENS, J., concurring in part and dissenting in part) ("I find little comfort in the Court's notion that no invasion of privacy occurs until a listener obtains some significant information by use of the device. . . . A bathtub is a less private area when the plumber is present even if his back is turned"). The same should hold for the interior heat of the home if only a person present in the home could discern the heat. Thus the driving force of the dissent, despite its recitation of the above standard, appears to be a distinction among different types of information—whether the homeowner would even care if anybody noticed. The dissent offers no practical guidance for the application of this standard, and for reasons already discussed, we believe there can be none. The people in their houses, as well as the police, deserve more precision.

We have said that the Fourth Amendment draws a firm line at the entrance to the house. That line, we think, must be not only firm but also bright—which requires clear specification of those methods of surveillance that require a warrant. While it is certainly possible to conclude from the videotape of the thermal imaging that occurred in this case that no "significant" compromise of the homeowner's privacy has occurred, we must take the long view, from the original meaning of the Fourth Amendment forward.

> The Fourth Amendment is to be construed in the light of what was deemed an unreasonable search and seizure when it was adopted, and in a manner which will conserve public interests as well as the interests and rights of individual citizens. *Carroll v. United States* (1925).

Where, as here, the Government uses a device that is not in general public use, to explore details of the home that would previously have been unknowable without physical intrusion, the surveillance is a search and is presumptively unreasonable without a warrant.

Since we hold the Thermovision imaging to have been an unlawful search, it will remain for the District Court to determine whether, without the evidence it provided, the search warrant issued in this case was supported by probable cause—and if not, whether there is any other basis for supporting admission of the evidence that the search pursuant to the warrant produced.

* * *

The judgment of the Court of Appeals is reversed; the case is remanded for further proceedings consistent with this opinion.

It is so ordered.

JUSTICE STEVENS, with whom THE CHIEF JUSTICE, JUSTICE O'CONNOR, and JUSTICE KENNEDY join, dissenting.

There is, in my judgment, a distinction of constitutional magnitude between "through-the-wall surveillance" that gives the observer or listener direct access to information in a private area, on the one hand, and the thought processes used to draw inferences from information in the public domain, on the other hand. The Court has crafted a rule that purports to deal with direct observations of the inside of the home, but the case before us merely involves indirect deductions from "off-the-wall" surveillance, that is, observations of the exterior of the home. Those observations were made with a fairly primitive thermal imager that gathered data exposed on the outside of petitioners home but did not invade any constitutionally protected interest in privacy. Moreover, I believe that the supposedly "bright-line" rule the Court has created in response to its concerns about future technological developments is unnecessary, unwise, and inconsistent with the Fourth Amendment.

I

There is no need for the Court to craft a new rule to decide this case, as it is controlled by established principles from our Fourth Amendment jurisprudence. One of those core principles, of course, is that "searches and seizures *inside a home* without a warrant are presumptively unreasonable." *Payton v. New York* (1980) (emphasis added). But it is equally well settled that searches and seizures of property in plain view are presumptively reasonable. Whether that property is residential or commercial, the basic principle is the same: " 'What a person knowingly exposes to the public, even in his own home or office, is not a subject of Fourth Amendment protection.' " *California v. Ciraolo* (1986) (quoting *Katz v. United States* (1967)). [Other citations omitted.] That is the principle implicated here.

. . . [T]his case involves nothing more than off-the-wall surveillance by law enforcement officers to gather information exposed to the general public from the outside of petitioners home. All that the infrared camera did in this case was passively measure heat emitted from the exterior surfaces of petitioner's home; all that those measurements showed were relative differences in emission levels, vaguely indicating that some areas of the roof and outside walls were warmer than others. As still images from the infrared scans show [shown in Appendix, omitted], no details regarding the interior of petitioner's home were revealed. Unlike an x-ray scan, or other possible "through-the-wall" techniques, the detection of infrared radiation emanating from the home did not accomplish "an unauthorized physical penetration into the premises," *Silverman v. United States* (1961), nor did it "obtain information that it could not have obtained by observation from outside the curtilage of the house," *United States v. Karo* (1984).

Indeed, the ordinary use of the senses might enable a neighbor or passerby to notice the heat emanating from a building, particularly if it is vented, as was the case here. Additionally, any member of the public might notice that one part of a house is warmer than another part or a nearby building if, for example, rainwater evaporates or snow melts at different rates across its surfaces. Such use of the senses would not convert into an unreasonable search if, instead, an adjoining neighbor allowed an officer onto her property to verify her perceptions with a sensitive thermometer. Nor, in my view, does such observation become an unreasonable search if made from a distance with the aid of a device that merely discloses that the exterior of one house, or one area of the house, is much warmer than another. Nothing more occurred in this case.

Thus, the notion that heat emissions from the outside of a dwelling is a private matter implicating the protections of the Fourth Amendment (the text of which guarantees the right of people "to be secure *in* their . . . houses" against unreasonable searches and seizures (emphasis added)) is not only unprecedented but also quite difficult to take seriously. Heat waves, like aromas that are generated in a kitchen, or in a laboratory or opium den, enter the public domain if and when they leave a building. A subjective expectation that they would remain private is not only implausible but also surely not "one that society is prepared to recognize as reasonable." *Katz* (Harlan, J., concurring).

To be sure, the homeowner has a reasonable expectation of privacy concerning what takes place within the home, and the Fourth Amendment's protection against physical invasions of the home should apply to their functional equivalent. But the equipment in this case did not penetrate the walls of petitioner's home, and while it did pick up "details of the home" that were exposed to the public, it did not obtain "any information regarding the *interior* of the home" (emphasis added). In the Court's own words, based on what the thermal imager "showed" regarding the outside of petitioner's home, the officers "concluded" that petitioner was engaging in illegal activity inside the home. It would be quite absurd to characterize their thought processes as "searches," regardless of whether they inferred (rightly) that petitioner was growing marijuana in his house, or (wrongly) that "the lady of the house [was taking] her daily sauna and bath." In either case, the only conclusions the officers reached concerning the interior of the home were at least as indirect as those that might have been inferred from the contents of discarded garbage, see *California v. Greenwood* (1988), or pen register data, see *Smith v. Maryland* (1979), or, as in this case, subpoenaed utility records [citing Ninth Circuit's decision]. For the first time in its history, the Court assumes that an inference can amount to a Fourth Amendment violation.

Notwithstanding the implications of today's decision, there is a strong public interest in avoiding constitutional litigation over the monitoring of emissions from homes, and over the inferences drawn from such monitoring. Just as the police cannot reasonably be expected to avert their eyes from evidence of criminal activity that could have been observed by any member of the public, so too public officials should not have to avert their senses or their equipment from detecting emissions in the public domain such as excessive heat, traces of smoke, suspicious odors, odorless gases, airborne particulates, or radioactive emissions, any of which could identify hazards to the community. In my judgment, monitoring such emissions with sense-enhancing technology, and drawing useful conclusions from such monitoring, is an entirely reasonable public service.

On the other hand, the countervailing privacy interest is at best trivial. After all, homes generally are insulated to keep heat in, rather than to prevent the detection of heat going out, and it does not seem to me that society will suffer from a rule requiring the rare homeowner who both intends to engage in uncommon activities that produce extraordinary amounts of heat, and wishes to conceal that production from outsiders, to make sure that the surrounding area is well insulated. . . . The interest in concealing the heat escaping from one's house pales in significance to "the chief evil against which the wording of the Fourth Amendment is directed, the physical entry of the home" [citation omitted], and it is hard to believe that it is an interest the Framers sought to protect in our Constitution.

Since what was involved in this case was nothing more than drawing inferences from off-the-wall surveillance, rather than any "through-the-wall" surveillance, the officers' conduct did not amount to a search and was perfectly reasonable.

II

Instead of trying to answer the question whether the use of the thermal imager in this case was even arguably unreasonable, the Court has fashioned a rule that is intended to provide essential guidance for the day when more sophisticated systems gain the ability to see through walls and other opaque barriers. The newly minted rule encompasses "obtaining [1] by sense-enhancing technology [2] any information regarding the interior of the home [3] that could not otherwise have been obtained without physical intrusion into a constitutionally protected area . . . [4] at least where (as here) the technology in question is not in general public use." In my judgment, the Court's new rule is at once too broad and too narrow, and is not justified by the Court's explanation for its adoption. As I have suggested, I would not erect a constitutional impediment to the use of sense-enhancing technology unless it provides its user with the functional equivalent of actual presence in the area being searched. [Remainder of section omitted.]

III

Although the Court is properly and commendably concerned about the threats to privacy that may flow from advances in the technology available to the law enforcement profession, it has unfortunately failed to heed the tried and true counsel of judicial restraint. Instead of concentrating on the rather mundane issue that is actually presented by the case before it, the Court has endeavored to craft an all-encompassing rule for the future. It would be far wiser to give legislators an unimpeded opportunity to grapple with these emerging issues rather than to shackle them with prematurely devised constitutional constraints.

I respectfully dissent.

SUPREME COURT ON RELIGIOUS CLUBS IN PUBLIC SCHOOLS
June 11, 2001

Religious organizations won an important victory on June 11, 2001, when the Supreme Court ruled, 6–3, that public schools could not prohibit religious groups from meeting there after school, even if the meetings involved young school children and contained what some might construe as religious instruction. To deny access to such groups while opening the schools to other nonreligious groups amounted to discrimination on the basis of religious viewpoint, in violation of the First Amendment's guarantee of free speech, the majority said.

The case involved the Good News Club of Milford, N.Y., one of more than 4,000 Good News Clubs scattered throughout the United States. According to Court documents, the clubs' mission was to evangelize children ages six through twelve "with the Gospel of the Lord Jesus Christ." At the meetings children prayed, sang songs, and played games designed to teach them about the Bible, and they were given treats when they recited Bible verses.

The ruling was expected to make it easier for the Good News Clubs and other similar groups to meet in public elementary schools. "It's no secret that it helps [such clubs] attract children when they meet in a more convenient location," said a spokesman for Religious Liberty Advocates, which supported the Good News Club. Before this ruling, he added, "a lot of school districts were nervous about letting them in. Now, I can say, 'Read the Supreme Court case.'"

Opponents of the ruling, including the dissenting justices, said the majority ignored reality when it rejected arguments that permitting such meetings might leave children with the impression that the school was endorsing religion. They questioned whether young children would be able to distinguish between regular instruction during the school day and religious instruction that took place in the same location immediately after the school day ended.

Some observers also suggested that the decision could have implications for the constitutionality of President George W. Bush's controversial "faith-based initiative," which was intended to allow religious and other faith-based groups to compete for federal funds for operating social service programs on the same basis as nonreligious groups. (Faith-based initiative, p. 132)

In other action on church-state issues, the Court let stand a lower court ruling ordering the removal of a monument inscribed with the Ten Commandments from the lawn of the Elkhart, Indiana, town hall. It also refused to take a case questioning the constitutionality of allowing student-led prayer at high school graduations. In 2000 the Court barred student-led prayer at public high school football games.

Good News for the Good News Club

Almost since the moment the Supreme Court ruled against organized prayer and Bible reading in public schools in the 1960s, Christian activists had been seeking to introduce religion into the public schools through extra-curricular Christian clubs. Those efforts were boosted in 1984 when Congress passed the Equal Access Act, which required schools to allow religious clubs the use of school facilities on the same terms as any other approved student extracurricular club. The Supreme Court upheld that act in 1990 and in subsequent cases involving high schools and colleges reiterated that speech expressing a religious viewpoint was protected under the Constitution and entitled to the same access to public facilities as other protected speech.

Writing for the majority, Justice Clarence Thomas said the school district had erred when it argued that the club's meetings were the equivalent of religious worship, which the school district's community-use policy did not permit. It also did not permit use of the school for commercial or political purposes. Thomas characterized the religious content of the Good News Club not as religious instruction, but as the teaching of morals and character development from a religious viewpoint. From that perspective, Thomas said, the case was a straightforward application of the Court's ruling in the case of Lamb's Chapel v. Center Moriches Union Free School District *(1993), which held that a school district's decision to forbid its high school facilities to show a Christian film series on child rearing was a violation of free speech. "Like the church in* Lamb's Chapel," *the Good News Club wanted to address a permissible subject—"the teaching of morals and character—from a religious viewpoint," Thomas said. The only difference—the church's use of a film opposed to the club's use of storytelling and prayer—was "inconsequential."*

Thomas also rejected the notion that children would perceive the club's meetings on school property as the school's endorsement of religion, a violation of the First Amendment's Establishment Clause. Thomas said the children had to have permission from their parents to attend the club meetings, and the parents would understand that the school was not supporting religion. Moreover, the club met in a room used during the day by older students; the club's instructors were not school teachers; and, unlike students in a regular classroom, club members spanned a range of ages. "We cannot say the danger that children would misperceive the endorsement of religion is any greater than the danger that they would perceive a hostility toward a religious viewpoint if the club were excluded from the public forum," Thomas concluded.

Chief Justice William H. Rehnquist and Justices Antonin Scalia, Sandra Day O'Connor, and Anthony M. Kennedy joined all of Thomas's opinion. Scalia also wrote a separate concurring opinion. Justice Stephen G. Breyer concurred that the school had discriminated against the club but said that the issue of whether children participating in the club's activities could perceive a governmental endorsement of religion was not yet fully resolved.

Justices John Paul Stevens, David H. Souter, and Ruth Bader Ginsburg dissented. Souter, joined by Ginsburg, said the school district was justified in deciding that the club's activities amounted to religious worship. "It is beyond question," Souter wrote, "that Good News intends to use the public school premises not for the mere discussion of a subject from a particular Christian point of view, but for an evangelical service of worship calling children to commit themselves in an act of Christian conversion." Souter also said the majority should not have considered the Establishment Clause issue because it had not been addressed in the lower courts. Stevens said it was permissible for the school to bar "proselytizing religious speech" for fear that such speech could "introduce divisiveness and tend to separate young children into cliques that undermine the school's educational mission."

The Ten Commandments and Student-Led Prayer

Whether monuments inscribed with the Ten Commandments and displayed on government property represented government endorsement of religion and thus were a violation of the Establishment Clause was a question of long standing. Monuments like the one in Elkhart had been donated by the Fraternal Order of Eagles to dozens of small towns in the 1950s, and occasionally someone challenged their constitutionality. In the Elkhart case, the Seventh U.S. Circuit Court of Appeals had ruled that the display amounted to government endorsement of a particular religious belief and was thus a violation of separation of church and state. In a similar case the Tenth Circuit Court of Appeals ruled the opposite way, allowing an Eagles monument to remain standing.

In refusing to hear the appeal in the Elkhart case, the Supreme Court followed its usual procedure, revealing neither its reasons for declining to take the case nor the vote by which it made its decision. (Four votes are needed to grant review.) In this case, however, the three justices who wanted the Court to take the case—Chief Justice Rehnquist and Justices Scalia and Thomas—took the unusual step of making their views publicly known. In a statement issued May 29 the three said the monument did not express the city's preference for a particular religion, but rather the role the Ten Commandments played in the development of the American legal system. In response Justice John Paul Stevens noted that the words "I AM THE LORD

THY GOD" were carved in large letters at the top of the monument. These words, Stevens wrote, were "rather hard to square with the proposition that the monument expresses no particular religious preference."

The suit was supported by the American Center for Law and Justice, the legal arm of the Christian Coalition, which was fighting similar battles in other cities. A spokesman for the center said that the Court, in turning down Elkhart's appeal, had "missed an opportunity to clarify an issue that has become the center of a national debate." But the Rev. Barry Lynn, executive director of Americans United for Separation of Church and State, said the Court's refusal to hear the appeal "should help bring the religious right's Ten Commandments crusade to a screeching halt."

On December 10 the Supreme Court declined to review an appeals court decision upholding a school policy in Duval County, Florida, that allowed high school seniors to decide whether to choose a fellow student to give a brief opening or closing message at the graduation ceremony. The student would decide on the content of the message, which could include prayer; the message was not subject to review by school authorities.

The policy had been in place since 1993 and had been challenged as a violation of the separation of church and state. The case was awaiting Supreme Court review in 2000 when the Court ruled in Santa Fe Independent School District v. Doe *that a Texas school district's policy allowing an elected student representative to deliver a prayer at home football games coerced those present to participate in a religious exercise. The Court subsequently sent the Florida case back to the Eleventh Circuit Court of Appeals for review in light of its* Santa Fe *decision. The appeals court again upheld the Duval County policy on the grounds that the students, not the school, made the choice about what to hear at graduation and that prayer was only one of several possible messages a student could give. (*Santa Fe *decision, Historic Documents of 2000, p. 365)*

Lawyers on both sides of the issue said that the Supreme Court's decision to let the appeals court ruling stand sent a clear signal that similar policies allowing student-led prayer at high school graduations would likely pass constitutional muster. "The fact that the Supreme Court refused to review the case sends a green light to other school districts that they can produce a neutral policy," said a spokesman for Liberty Counsel, a religious civil liberties and legal defense organization.

Following are excerpts from the majority and dissenting opinions in the case of Good News Club v. Milford Central School, *in which the Supreme Court held, 6–3, on June 11, 2001, that a public school district violated the free speech rights of a Christian club for elementary school students by denying it access to school facilities for after-school meetings.*

The document was obtained from the Internet at http://www.supremecourtus.gov/opinions/00pdf/99-2036.pdf.

No. 99–2036

Good News Club, et al.,
Petitioners
v.
Milford Central School

On writ of certiorari to the
United States Court of Appeals
for the Second Circuit

[June 11, 2001]

JUSTICE THOMAS delivered the opinion of the Court.

This case presents two questions. The first question is whether Milford
Central School violated the free speech rights of the Good News Club when
it excluded the Club from meeting after hours at the school. The second
question is whether any such violation is justified by Milford's concern that
permitting the Club's activities would violate the Establishment Clause. We
conclude that Milford's restriction violates the Club's free speech rights and
that no Establishment Clause concern justifies that violation.

I

. . . In 1992, respondent Milford Central School (Milford) enacted a community use policy adopting seven . . . purposes for which its building could be
used after school. Two of the stated purposes are relevant here. First, district
residents may use the school for "instruction in any branch of education,
learning or the arts." Second, the school is available for "social, civic and
recreational meetings and entertainment events, and other uses pertaining to
the welfare of the community, provided that such uses shall be nonexclusive
and shall be opened to the general public."

Stephen and Darleen Fournier . . . are sponsors of the local Good News
Club, a private Christian organization for children ages 6 to 12. Pursuant
to Milford's policy, in September 1996 the Fourniers submitted a request to
Dr. Robert McGruder, interim superintendent of the district, in which they
sought permission to hold the Club's weekly afterschool meetings in the
school cafeteria. The next month, McGruder formally denied the Fourniers'
request on the ground that the proposed use—to have "a fun time of singing
songs, hearing a Bible lesson and memorizing scripture"—was "the equivalent
of religious worship." According to McGruder, the community use policy,
which prohibits use "by any individual or organization for religious purposes,"
foreclosed the Club's activities.

In response to a letter submitted by the Club's counsel, Milford's attorney
requested information to clarify the nature of the Clubs activities. The Club
sent a set of materials used or distributed at the meetings and the following
description of its meeting:

> "The Club opens its session with Ms. Fournier taking attendance. As she calls
> a Child's name, if the child recites a Bible verse the child receives a treat. Af-
> ter attendance, the Club sings songs. Next Club members engage in games
> that involve, *inter alia*, learning Bible verses. Ms. Fournier then relates a Bible
> story and explains how it applies to Club members lives. The Club closes

with prayer. Finally, Ms. Fournier distributes treats and the Bible verses for memorization."

McGruder and Milford's attorney reviewed the materials and concluded that "the kinds of activities proposed to be engaged in by the Good News Club were not a discussion of secular subjects such as child rearing, development of character and development of morals from a religious perspective, but were in fact the equivalent of religious instruction itself." In February 1997, the Milford Board of Education adopted a resolution rejecting the Club's request to use Milford's facilities "for the purpose of conducting religious instruction and Bible study."

In March 1997, petitioners, the Good News Club, Ms. Fournier, and her daughter Andrea Fournier (collectively, the Club), filed an action . . . against Milford in the United States District Court for the Northern District of New York. The Club alleged that Milford's denial of its application violated its free speech rights under the First and Fourteenth Amendments, its right to equal protection under the Fourteenth Amendment, and its right to religious freedom under the Religious Freedom Restoration Act of 1993.

[Thomas explained that the federal district court on April 14, 1997, granted a preliminary injunction preventing the school from enforcing its policy. "The Club held weekly afterschool meetings from April 1997 until June 1998 in a high school resource and middle school special education room," he continued. In August 1998, however, the district court granted Milford's motion for summary judgment, holding that denying access to the club did not amount to unconstitutional viewpoint discrimination.]

The Club appealed, and a divided panel of the United States Court of Appeals for the Second Circuit affirmed (2000). First, the court rejected the Club's contention that Milford's restriction against allowing religious instruction in its facilities is unreasonable. Second, it held that, because the subject matter of the Club's activities is "quintessentially religious," and the activities "fall outside the bounds of pure 'moral and character development,'" Milford's policy of excluding the Club's meetings was constitutional subject discrimination, not unconstitutional viewpoint discrimination. Judge Jacobs filed a dissenting opinion in which he concluded that the schools restriction did constitute viewpoint discrimination under *Lamb's Chapel v. Center Moriches Union Free School Dist.* (1993).

There is a conflict among the Courts of Appeals on the question whether speech can be excluded from a limited public forum on the basis of the religious nature of the speech. [Citing conflicting decisions.] We granted certiorari to resolve this conflict (2000).

II

[Thomas explained that Milford had created a "limited public forum" by opening school facilities to outside groups. Under the Court's prior cases, he said, the government may limit use of facilities to certain groups or for the discussion of certain topics. But, Thomas concluded, any restriction "must not discriminate against speech on the basis of viewpoint. . . ."]

III

Applying this test, we first address whether the exclusion constituted viewpoint discrimination. We are guided in our analysis by two of our prior opinions, *Lamb's Chapel* and *Rosenberger* [*v. Rectors of the Univ. of Va.* (1995)]. In *Lamb's Chapel*, we held that a school district violated the Free Speech Clause of the First Amendment when it excluded a private group from presenting films at the school based solely on the films discussions of family values from a religious perspective. Likewise, in *Rosenberger*, we held that a university's refusal to fund a student publication because the publication addressed issues from a religious perspective violated the Free Speech Clause. Concluding that Milford's exclusion of the Good News Club based on its religious nature is indistinguishable from the exclusions in these cases, we hold that the exclusion constitutes viewpoint discrimination. . . .

Just as there is no question that teaching morals and character development to children is a permissible purpose under Milford's policy, it is clear that the Club teaches morals and character development to children. For example, no one disputes that the Club instructs children to overcome feelings of jealousy, to treat others well regardless of how they treat the children, and to be obedient, even if it does so in a nonsecular way. Nonetheless, because Milford found the Club's activities to be religious in nature—"the equivalent of religious instruction itself:"—it excluded the Club from use of its facilities.

Like the church in *Lamb's Chapel*, the Club seeks to address a subject otherwise permitted under the rule, the teaching of morals and character, from a religious standpoint. . . . The only apparent difference between the activity of Lambs Chapel and the activities of the Good News Club is that the Club chooses to teach moral lessons from a Christian perspective through live storytelling and prayer, whereas Lamb's Chapel taught lessons through films. This distinction is inconsequential. Both modes of speech use a religious viewpoint. Thus, the exclusion of the Good News Club' activities, like the exclusion of Lamb's Chapel's films, constitutes unconstitutional viewpoint discrimination.

Despite our holdings in *Lamb's Chapel* and *Rosenberger*, the Court of Appeals, like Milford, believed that its characterization of the Club' activities as religious in nature warranted treating the Club's activities as different in kind from the other activities permitted by the school. . . . The "Christian viewpoint" is unique, according to the court, because it contains an "additional layer" that other kinds of viewpoints do not. That is, the Club "is focused on teaching children how to cultivate their relationship with God through Jesus Christ," which it characterized as "quintessentially religious." With these observations, the court concluded that, because the Club's activities "fall outside the bounds of pure 'moral and character development,'" the exclusion did not constitute viewpoint discrimination.

We disagree that something that is "quintessentially religious" or "decidedly religious in nature" cannot also be characterized properly as the teaching of morals and character development from a particular viewpoint. . . . What matters for purposes of the Free Speech Clause is that we can see no logical difference in kind between the invocation of Christianity by the Club and the invocation of teamwork, loyalty, or patriotism by other associations to provide a foundation for their lessons. It is apparent that the unstated principle of the Court of Appeals reasoning is its conclusion that any time religious instruction and prayer are used to discuss morals and character, the discussion is simply not a "pure" discussion of those issues. According to the Court of Appeals, reliance on Christian principles taints moral and character instruction in a way that other foundations for thought or viewpoints do not. We, however, have never reached such a conclusion. Instead, we reaffirm our holdings in *Lamb's Chapel* and *Rosenberger* that speech discussing otherwise permissible subjects cannot be excluded from a limited public forum on the ground that the subject is discussed from a religious viewpoint. Thus, we conclude that Milford's exclusion of the Club from use of the school, pursuant to its community use policy, constitutes impermissible viewpoint discrimination.

IV

Milford argues that, even if its restriction constitutes viewpoint discrimination, its interest in not violating the Establishment Clause outweighs the Club's interest in gaining equal access to the schools facilities. In other words, according to Milford, its restriction was required to avoid violating the Establishment Clause. We disagree.

. . . We rejected Establishment Clause defenses similar to Milford's in two previous free speech cases, *Lamb's Chapel* and *Widmar* [*v. Vincent* (1981)]. In particular, in *Lamb's Chapel*, we explained that "[t]he showing of th[e] film series would not have been during school hours, would not have been sponsored by the school, and would have been open to the public, not just to church members." Accordingly, we found that "there would have been no realistic danger that the community would think that the District was endorsing religion or any particular creed." Likewise, in *Widmar*, where the university's forum was already available to other groups, this Court concluded that there was no Establishment Clause problem.

The Establishment Clause defense fares no better in this case. As in *Lamb's Chapel*, the Club's meetings were held after school hours, not sponsored by the school, and open to any student who obtained parental consent, not just to Club members. As in *Widmar*, Milford made its forum available to other organizations. The Club's activities are materially indistinguishable from those in *Lamb's Chapel* and *Widmar*. Thus, Milford's reliance on the Establishment Clause is unavailing.

Milford attempts to distinguish *Lamb's Chapel* and *Widmar* by emphasizing that Milford's policy involves elementary school children. According to Milford, children will perceive that the school is endorsing the Club and will feel coercive pressure to participate, because the Club's activities take place on school grounds, even though they occur during nonschool hours. This argument is unpersuasive.

First, we have held that "a significant factor in upholding governmental programs in the face of Establishment Clause attack is their *neutrality* towards religion." [Citing *Rosenberger*, emphasis added.] . . . Milford's implication that granting access to the Club would do damage to the neutrality principle defies logic. . . . The Good News Club seeks nothing more than to be treated neutrally and given access to speak about the same topics as are other groups. Because allowing the Club to speak on school grounds would ensure neutrality, not threaten it, Milford faces an uphill battle in arguing that the Establishment Clause compels it to exclude the Good News Club.

Second, to the extent we consider whether the community would feel coercive pressure to engage in the Club's activities, the relevant community would be the parents, not the elementary school children. It is the parents who choose whether their children will attend the Good News Club meetings. Because the children cannot attend without their parents' permission, they cannot be coerced into engaging in the Good News Club's religious activities. Milford does not suggest that the parents of elementary school children would be confused about whether the school was endorsing religion. Nor do we believe that such an argument could be reasonably advanced.

Third, whatever significance we may have assigned in the Establishment Clause context to the suggestion that elementary school children are more impressionable than adults . . . , we have never extended our Establishment Clause jurisprudence to foreclose private religious conduct during nonschool hours merely because it takes place on school premises where elementary school children may be present. . . .

Fourth, even if we were to consider the possible misperceptions by schoolchildren in deciding whether Milfords permitting the Club's activities would violate the Establishment Clause, the facts of this case simply do not support Milford's conclusion. There is no evidence that young children are permitted to loiter outside classrooms after the schoolday has ended. Surely even young children are aware of events for which their parents must sign permission forms. The meetings were held in a combined high school resource room and middle school special education room, not in an elementary school classroom. The instructors are not schoolteachers. And the children in the group are not all the same age as in the normal classroom setting; their ages range from 6 to 12. In sum, these circumstances simply do not support the theory that small children would perceive endorsement here.

Finally, even if we were to inquire into the minds of schoolchildren in this case, we cannot say the danger that children would misperceive the endorsement of religion is any greater than the danger that they would perceive a hostility toward the religious viewpoint if the Club were excluded from the public forum. This concern is particularly acute given the reality that Milford's building is not used only for elementary school children. Students, from kindergarten through the 12th grade, all attend school in the same building. There may be as many, if not more, upperclassmen than elementary school children who occupy the school after hours. For that matter, members of the public writ large are permitted in the school after hours pursuant to the community use policy. Any bystander could conceivably be aware of the school's use policy and its exclusion of the Good News Club, and could suffer as much from viewpoint discrimination as elementary school children could suffer from perceived endorsement. . . .

We cannot operate, as Milford would have us do, under the assumption that any risk that small children would perceive endorsement should counsel in favor of excluding the Club's religious activity. We decline to employ Establishment Clause jurisprudence using a modified hecklers veto, in which a group's religious activity can be proscribed on the basis of what the youngest members of the audience might misperceive. . . . There are countervailing constitutional concerns related to rights of other individuals in the community. In this case, those countervailing concerns are the free speech rights of the Club and its members. . . . And, we have already found that those rights have been violated, not merely perceived to have been violated, by the school's actions toward the Club.

We are not convinced that there is any significance in this case to the possibility that elementary school children may witness the Good News Club's activities on school premises, and therefore we can find no reason to depart from our holdings in *Lamb's Chapel* and *Widmar*. Accordingly, we conclude that permitting the Club to meet on the schools premises would not have violated the Establishment Clause.

V

When Milford denied the Good News Club access to the schools limited public forum on the ground that the Club was religious in nature, it discriminated against the Club because of its religious viewpoint in violation of the Free Speech Clause of the First Amendment. Because Milford has not raised a valid Establishment Clause claim, we do not address the question whether such a claim could excuse Milford's viewpoint discrimination.

* * *

The judgment of the Court of Appeals is reversed, and the case is remanded for further proceedings consistent with this opinion.

It is so ordered.

JUSTICE STEVENS, dissenting.

The Milford Central School has invited the public to use its facilities for educational and recreational purposes, but not for religious purposes. Speech for religious purposes may reasonably be understood to encompass three different categories. First, there is religious speech that is simply speech about a particular topic from a religious point of view. [Citing "the film in *Lamb's Chapel v. Center Moriches Union Free School Dist.* (1993).] Second, there is religious speech that amounts to worship, or its equivalent. [Citing *Widmar v. Vincent* (1981).] Third, there is an intermediate category that is aimed principally at proselytizing or inculcating belief in a particular religious faith.

. . . Distinguishing speech from a religious viewpoint, on the one hand, from religious proselytizing, on the other, is comparable to distinguishing meetings to discuss political issues from meetings whose principal purpose is to recruit new members to join a political organization. If a school decides to authorize after school discussions of current events in its classrooms, it may not exclude people from expressing their views simply because it dislikes their particular political opinions. But must it therefore allow organized political groups—for example, the Democratic Party, the Libertarian Party, or the Ku Klux Klan— to hold meetings, the principal purpose of which is not to discuss the current-events topic from their own unique point of view but rather to recruit others to join their respective groups? I think not. Such recruiting meetings may introduce divisiveness and tend to separate young children into cliques that undermine the school's educational mission. . . .

School officials may reasonably believe that evangelical meetings designed to convert children to a particular religious faith pose the same risk. And, just as a school may allow meetings to discuss current events from a political perspective without also allowing organized political recruitment, so too can a school allow discussion of topics such as moral development from a religious (or nonreligious) perspective without thereby opening its forum to religious proselytizing or worship. . . . Moreover, any doubt on a question such as this should be resolved in a way that minimizes intrusion by the Federal Government into the operation of our public schools. . . .

This case is undoubtedly close. Nonetheless, . . . I am persuaded that the school district could (and did) permissibly exclude from its limited public forum proselytizing religious speech that does not rise to the level of actual worship. I would therefore affirm the judgment of the Court of Appeals.

Even if I agreed with Part II of the majority opinion, however, I would not reach out, as it does in Part IV, to decide a constitutional question that was not addressed by either the District Court or the Court of Appeals.

Accordingly, I respectfully dissent.

JUSTICE SOUTER, with whom JUSTICE GINSBURG joins, dissenting.

The majority rules on two issues. First, it decides that the Court of Appeals failed to apply the rule in *Lamb's Chapel v. Center Moriches Union Free School Dist.* (1993), which held that the government may not discriminate on the basis of viewpoint in operating a limited public forum. The majority applies that rule and concludes that Milford violated *Lamb's Chapel* in denying Good News the use of the school. The majority then goes on to determine that it would not violate the Establishment Clause of the First Amendment for the Milford School District to allow the Good News Club to hold its intended gatherings of public school children in Milford's elementary school. The majority is mistaken on both points. The Court of Appeals unmistakably distinguished this case from *Lamb's Chapel*, though not by name, and accordingly affirmed the application of a policy, unchallenged in the District Court, that Milford's public schools may not be used for religious purposes. As for the applicability of the Establishment Clause to the Good News Clubs intended use of Milford's school, the majority commits error even in reaching the issue, which was addressed neither by the Court of Appeals nor by the District Court. I respectfully dissent.

I

[Souter began by stressing that the Good News Club had not objected to the school district's policy of prohibiting the use of school facilities for "religious purposes."]

The sole question before the District Court was, therefore, whether, in refusing to allow Good News's intended use, Milford was misapplying its unchallenged restriction in a way that amounted to imposing a viewpoint-based restriction on what could be said or done by a group entitled to use the forum for an educational, civic, or other permitted purpose. The question was whether Good News was being disqualified when it merely sought to use the school property the same way that the Milford Boy and Girl Scouts and the 4-H Club did. . . .

[Souter said that both the district and appeals courts had concluded—"on the basis of undisputed facts"—that the club's activities were "unlike the presentation of views on secular issues from a religious standpoint held to be protected in *Lamb's Chapel.*" "A sampling of those facts," he said, "shows why both courts were correct."]

[Souter continued with detailed excerpts from a "sample lesson considered by the District Court." ". . . [T]he heart of the meeting is the 'challenge' and 'invitation,' which are repeated at various times throughout the lesson," Souter wrote. "During the challenge, 'saved' children who 'already believe in the Lord Jesus as their Savior' are challenged to 'stop and ask God for the strength and the "want" . . . to obey Him.' . . . During the 'invitation,' the teacher 'invites' the 'unsaved' children to 'trust the Lord Jesus to be your Savior from sin,' and 'receiv[e] [him] as your Savior from sin.'"]

It is beyond question that Good News intends to use the public school premises not for the mere discussion of a subject from a particular, Christian point of view, but for an evangelical service of worship calling children to commit themselves in an act of Christian conversion. The majority avoids this reality only by resorting to the bland and general characterization of Good News's activity as "teaching of morals and character, from a religious standpoint." If the majority's statement ignores reality, as it surely does, then today's holding may be understood only in equally generic terms. Otherwise, indeed, this case would stand for the remarkable proposition that any public school opened for civic meetings must be opened for use as a church, synagogue, or mosque.

II

I also respectfully dissent from the majority's refusal to remand on all other issues, insisting instead on acting as a court of first instance in reviewing Milford's claim that it would violate the Establishment Clause to grant Good News's application. . . . Whereas the District Court and Court of Appeals resolved this case entirely on the ground that Milford's actions did not offend the First Amendments Speech Clause, the majority now sees fit to rule on the application of the Establishment Clause. . . .

. . . I am in no better position than the majority to perform an Establishment

Clause analysis in the first instance. . . . I can, however, speak to the doubtful underpinnings of the majority's conclusion.

This Court has accepted the independent obligation to obey the Establishment Clause as sufficiently compelling to satisfy strict scrutiny under the First Amendment. [Citations omitted.] Milford's actions would offend the Establishment Clause if they carried the message of endorsing religion under the circumstances, as viewed by a reasonable observer. The majority concludes that such an endorsement effect is out of the question in Milford's case, because the context here is materially indistinguishable from the facts in *Lamb's Chapel* and *Widmar*. In fact, . . . the principal grounds on which we based our Establishment Clause holdings in those cases are clearly absent here.

In *Widmar*, we held that the Establishment Clause did not bar a religious student group from using a public university's meeting space for worship as well as discussion. . . .

Lamb's Chapel involved an evening film series on child-rearing open to the general public (and, given the subject matter, directed at an adult audience). . . .

What we know about this case looks very little like *Widmar* or *Lamb's Chapel*. The cohort addressed by Good News is not university students with relative maturity, or even high school pupils, but elementary school children as young as six. . . .

Nor is Milford's limited forum anything like the sites for wide-ranging intellectual exchange that were home to the challenged activities in *Widmar* and *Lamb's Chapel*. . . .

The timing and format of Good News's gatherings, on the other hand, may well affirmatively suggest the *imprimatur* of officialdom in the minds of the young children. The club is open solely to elementary students. . . , only four outside groups have been identified as meeting in the school, and Good News is, seemingly, the only one whose instruction follows immediately on the conclusion of the official school day. Although school is out at 2:56 P.M., Good News apparently requested use of the school beginning at 2:30 on Tuesdays "during the school year," so that instruction could begin promptly at 3:00, at which time children who are compelled by law to attend school surely remain in the building. . . . In fact, the temporal and physical continuity of Good News's meetings with the regular school routine seems to be the whole point of using the school. When meetings were held in a community church, 8 or 10 children attended; after the school became the site, the number went up three-fold.

Even on the summary judgment record, then, . . . we can say this: there is a good case that Good News's exercises blur the line between public classroom instruction and private religious indoctrination, leaving a reasonable elementary school pupil unable to appreciate that the former instruction is the business of the school while the latter evangelism is not. Thus, the facts we know (or think we know) point away from the majority's conclusion, and while the consolation may be that nothing really gets resolved when the judicial process is so truncated, that is not much to recommend today's result.

WARDEN'S STATEMENT ON TIMOTHY MCVEIGH'S EXECUTION
June 11, 2001

Timothy McVeigh, the man convicted of bombing a federal building in Oklahoma City in which 168 people died, was executed on June 11, 2001. He was pronounced dead from lethal injection at 7:14 A.M. in the federal prison at Terre Haute, Indiana. "This morning, the United States of America carried out the severest sentence for the gravest of crimes. The victims of the Oklahoma City bombing have been given not vengeance, but justice. And one young man met the fate he chose for himself," President George W. Bush said in a statement following the execution.

The 1995 Oklahoma City bombing was the worst act of domestic terrorism to that point, and it rocked Americans' sense of security as few other events had done—until the attacks by foreign terrorists on the World Trade Center and Pentagon in September 2001. McVeigh was motivated by a profound hatred of the U.S. government and what he considered to be its authoritarian tactics. He said the bombing was in retaliation for a government raid on a cult compound near Waco, Texas, and a shootout between federal agents and a white supremacist in Ruby Ridge, Idaho, in which the man's wife and child were killed.

McVeigh made no final statement, but he asked prison officials to give reporters a poem that he had copied onto notebook paper. The poem, "Invictus," written by William Ernest Henley in 1875, contains the well-known lines:

> *I am the master of my fate.*
> *I am the captain of my soul.*

Originally scheduled for May 16, the execution was postponed for a month after it was revealed that the FBI had not delivered thousands of pages of evidence to McVeigh's trial attorneys, as it had agreed to do. McVeigh's attorneys asked for an even longer stay of execution so that they could review the documents in detail, but a federal district judge denied the request. The episode, however, gave McVeigh another opportunity to raise questions about the tactics of the FBI, which had carried out the actions at Waco and Ruby Ridge.

McVeigh's execution intensified debate about the use of the death penalty in the United States. Although nearly two-thirds of all Americans supported it as appropriate punishment for certain crimes, the number had been declining in recent years—in part due to findings that dozens of people had been wrongfully convicted of capital crimes. That was not the case with McVeigh, who had admitted that he was responsible for the bombing. (Death penalty, p. 387)

The execution also intensified questions about the media's handling of the execution. Although only ten representatives of the press and ten representatives of victims' families were allowed to view the execution, an estimated 1,400 reporters and broadcast crews were outside the prison in Indiana and in Oklahoma City to get reaction from the three hundred survivors and victims' relatives who watched the execution on closed-circuit television. The execution was the subject of television talk and news shows for days beforehand, making the event itself almost anticlimactic. Many critics lamented the national spectacle that resulted, accusing the media of doing just what McVeigh had hoped for—turning him into a celebrity and giving his views yet one more airing.

McVeigh's Views on his Crime

On April 19, 1995, the second anniversary of the FBI raid on the Waco compound, McVeigh drove a rented Ryder truck to the Alfred P. Murrah Federal Building in Oklahoma City, parked it outside the building, and walked away. A minute or so later, a 7,000-pound fertilizer bomb exploded, collapsing most of the building, killing 168 people—including 19 children in the building's day care center, and injuring hundreds more.

McVeigh, driving a getaway car he had left near the building, was stopped about ninety minutes later in Perry, Oklahoma, for a traffic violation and then arrested when a loaded semiautomatic handgun was found in the car. He was about to be released two days later when his jailers realized that he was one of the men the FBI was looking for in connection with the bombing.

On June 2, 1997, a federal court jury sitting in Denver, Colorado, convicted McVeigh of eleven counts of conspiracy and murder, and on August 14, 1997, he was sentenced to death. A second jury convicted McVeigh's friend Terry L. Nichols of conspiracy and manslaughter, but not murder. Nichols was sentenced to life in prison without parole. (Oklahoma bombing, Historic Documents of 1995, p. 176; bombing trial, Historic Documents of 1997, p. 623)

During the next three years, McVeigh's attorneys filed appeals, all of which were rejected. After the federal district court in Denver refused a request for a new trial in October 2000, McVeigh asked his lawyers to drop any further appeals and began to prepare for his execution, which was scheduled for May 16, 2001. On February 16 McVeigh let pass a deadline for seeking a pardon from the president. Attorneys speaking for McVeigh said he did not believe he had much chance of receiving clemency and in any event did not believe he would be better off. "Having nothing to look forward to but solitary confinement in a federal penitentiary does not appeal to him," the attorneys said.

In interviews with two reporters for the Buffalo News *that became the basis of the book* American Terrorist, *published on April 3, 2001, McVeigh explained what motivated him to bomb the federal building. A former soldier who won a Bronze Star during the Persian Gulf War, McVeigh said he could not stand to think of himself as an ally "of the biggest bully in the world, the U.S. government." He spoke of crying as he heard reports of the FBI assault on the Branch Davidian compound in Waco, where about eighty members of an armed religious cult led by David Koresh died in a fire that swept through the compound during the siege. (Waco disaster, Historic Documents of 1993, p. 293)*

McVeigh told the Buffalo News *reporters that he chose the Murrah building because some of the FBI agents who had been at Waco were stationed there and because it had a glass front, which made it vulnerable. He also thought the building would make a good shot on television. "Bombing the Murrah Federal Building was morally and strategically equivalent to the U.S. hitting a government building in Serbia, Iraq, or other nations," McVeigh said in a letter to Fox News made public on April 27. "Based on the observations of the policies of my own government, I viewed this action as an acceptable option."*

Asked by the Buffalo News *reporters if he was aware the building housed a day care center, McVeigh said that he "recognized beforehand that someone might be . . . bringing their kid to work. However, if I had known there was an entire day care center, it might have given me pause to switch targets. That's a large amount of collateral damage." He also said he understood "what they felt in Oklahoma City. I have no sympathy." After meeting with McVeigh on June 10, his attorneys said McVeigh "wishes to make it known that he does feel for people; he is sorry for the suffering. But again, this is not to say that he thinks he was wrong. . . . In his mind, it was a military action."*

Temporary Postponement

On May 11 Attorney General John Ashcroft postponed McVeigh's execution until June 11 after the FBI revealed that it found 3,135 pages of documents that had never been turned over to McVeigh's defense attorneys. FBI director Louis J. Freeh said it was highly unlikely that any information contained in the documents would change the verdict in the McVeigh case. The revelations were highly embarrassing for the FBI, which had already come under heavy criticism for its mishandling of several high-profile cases, including those of Wen Ho Lee and Robert Hanssen. Lee, a scientist at the Los Alamos National Laboratory, had been charged with giving China nuclear weapons secrets. In 2000 all but one count was dropped, and the judge gave federal prosecutors a dressing down for the way the Justice Department and FBI had handled the case. In February 2001 the FBI arrested Hanssen, a senior FBI counterintelligence agent, for spying for the former

Soviet Union and Russia since 1979. Hanssen pleaded guilty to avoid the death penalty. (Hanssen case, p. 150; Lee case, Historic Documents of 2000, p. 740)

At congressional hearings on May 16, the day McVeigh was to have been executed, Freeh took full responsibility for the missing documents. He said the agency had "committed a serious error" in failing to turn over all the evidence required under an agreement with McVeigh's attorneys. Although the agency had sent out sixteen requests for material to its branch offices around the country, most FBI offices either "failed to locate the documents, misinterpreted their instructions, and likely produced only those that would be disclosed under normal discovery or sent documents only to have them unaccounted for on the other end." Earlier in the month Freeh had announced that he was resigning as director.

On May 31 McVeigh's defense team asked Federal District Judge Richard P. Matsch for a stay of execution, reporting that McVeigh wanted to "promote integrity in the criminal justice system" and that he believed the "Department of Justice and the FBI will not otherwise be held to account unless he takes this action." Ashcroft repeated that nothing in the documents indicated that McVeigh's conviction should be overturned. "The Department of Justice is prepared to oppose vigorously any attempts by Timothy McVeigh to overturn his conviction and sentence or to force a new trial. No document in this case creates any doubt about McVeigh's guilt or establishes his innocence. To overturn the jury's verdict or to force a new trial, McVeigh must prove that the documents establish his innocence."

At a June 6 hearing in Denver, Matsch, who had also been the judge at McVeigh's trial, refused the stay request. The newly discovered evidence does "not change the fact that Timothy McVeigh was the instrument of death and destruction," Matsch said, adding that he found "no good cause" to delay the execution any longer. Matsch admitted that he was shocked by the FBI's discovery of the documents only days before McVeigh's execution. "It's a good thing I was in quiet chambers because my judicial temperament escaped me," he said. But, he said, he found nothing in the "pattern of what was not disclosed" to indicate that the FBI deliberately withheld the documents in question.

The following day the U.S. federal court of appeals for the Tenth Circuit rejected McVeigh's appeal of Matsch's ruling, and McVeigh, through his lawyers, said he would not proceed with any further legal action.

McVeigh was the first federal prisoner to be executed since 1963, when Victor Feguer, convicted of kidnapping and murder, was hung in Madison, Iowa. On June 19, 2001, just eight days after McVeigh's death, Juan Raul Garza was executed at the Terre Haute facility. Garza, a drug smuggler, had been convicted of ordering the slaying of three people. President Bush denied his plea for clemency. (Garza case, p. 387; Historic Documents of 2000, p. 990)

On September 5 the district attorney in Oklahoma City announced that he would charge Terry Nichols with 160 counts of murder in state court and seek the death penalty. Nichols was already serving a life sentence in fed-

eral prison for conspiracy and manslaughter in the deaths of eight federal agents.

Following are excerpts from remarks to the press made by Harley Lappin, warden of the U.S. Penitentiary in Terre Haute, Indiana, following the execution June 11, 2001, of Timothy J. McVeigh, who was convicted of bombing a federal building in Oklahoma City in which 168 people lost their lives.

The document was not available on the Internet at the time of publication.

Following are excerpts from remarks to the press made by Harley Lappin, warden of the U.S. Penitentiary in Terre Haute, Indiana, following the execution of Timothy J. McVeigh, convicted of bombing a federal building in Oklahoma City, on April 19, 1995, in which 168 people lost their lives:

I am Harley Lappin, the warden here at the United States Penitentiary, Terre Haute. The U.S. marshal is still on the execution facility completing his protocol responsibilities.

The court order to execute inmate Timothy James McVeigh has been fulfilled. Pursuant to the sentence of the United States District Court in the District of Colorado, Timothy James McVeigh has been executed by lethal injection. He was pronounced dead at 7:14 a.m., Central Daylight Time. McVeigh's body will be released to a representative of his family. . . .

Inmate McVeigh did not make a final statement. I have provided to the press a written statement he provided to me and I've asked them to share that with you. . . .

Inmate McVeigh was calm throughout the entire process. He cooperated entirely during the time he was restrained in the execution holding cell to the time he walked into the execution room. He stepped up on to a small step and sat down on the table where . . . he then positioned himself for us to apply the restraints. He cooperated throughout this entire process.

As you've heard me say before, I anticipated this to be a very difficult thing to do and it was. But I think today my thoughts and prayers are with the many victims of this tragedy in Oklahoma City.

UN GENERAL ASSEMBLY DECLARATION ON AIDS
June 27, 2001

Twenty years after a U.S. health agency first recognized the existence of a killing disease that came to be known as acquired immunodeficiency syndrome, AIDS had spread around the globe to become the fourth leading cause of death worldwide and the "most devastating disease humankind has ever faced," according to a key United Nations agency. By the end of 2001 an estimated 22 million people had already died of AIDS, for which there was as yet no vaccine and no cure. Forty million more were thought to be living with AIDS or infected with the human immunodeficiency virus (HIV), the virus that causes AIDS. The disease had already decimated sub-Saharan Africa, wiping out entire generations in some towns and villages, turning hundreds of thousands of children into orphans, and shortening overall life expectancies in several countries. Now AIDS appeared to be on the verge of breaking out in some of the most populous areas on earth, including China, India, and Russia.

As in other years, the world made some progress in combating the disease. In an unprecedented special session, the UN General Assembly on June 27, 2001, approved an ambitious set of measurable goals for slowing the spread of HIV/AIDS. In the "Declaration of Commitment on HIV/AIDS," each nation pledged to develop, by 2003, a strategy for addressing the factors that made individuals vulnerable to HIV infection, including poverty, underdevelopment, illiteracy and lack of education, social exclusion and discrimination, lack of information about AIDS/HIV, and lack of self-protective materials, such as condoms. Several of the world's major pharmaceutical companies succumbed to public pressure and agreed to make their anti-AIDS drugs available to hard-hit African countries at deep discounts. Several African leaders, notably President Olusegun Obasanjo of Nigeria, were showing new willingness to confront the AIDS epidemic directly. Bowing to signs of an emerging AIDS epidemic within its borders, the government of China broke its long silence on the subject and called publicly for educating of sex workers, making condom-dispensing machines available, and having a more open discussion if HIV/AIDS in schools.

438

At the same time, relatively few countries, corporations, and individuals pledged contributions to a global fund proposed by UN Secretary General Kofi Annan to help developing countries combat AIDS, malaria, and tuberculosis. By year's end about $1.5 billion had been committed to the Global AIDS and Health Fund, far short of the $7 billion to $10 billion a year that Annan hoped would eventually be forthcoming. (President George W. Bush pledged $200 million on behalf of the United States.) This problem was heightened after the terrorist attacks on the United States in September diverted attention and funding from the AIDS/HIV crisis. The terrorist attacks also tipped the world into a recession, further slowing efforts to deal with poverty, education levels, and health care in developing countries. (U.S. and world economies after September 11, p. 663)

The AIDS Epidemic at Twenty

According to the annual survey published by the Joint United Nations Programme on HIV/AIDS (UNAIDS) and the World Health Organization (WHO), sub-Saharan Africa remained the region most affected by the disease. More than 28 million people in the region had HIV, many of them without knowing it. Most were not expected to survive the decade without adequate treatment and care. At least 10 percent of the population ages fifteen to forty-nine were infected with HIV/AIDS in sixteen African countries, and the prevalence rate was between 5 and 10 percent in at least five other countries, including Nigeria, the most populous country in Africa, with more than 120 million people. The Caribbean was the second most affected region in world, with 2 percent HIV prevalence among the adult population.

The fastest growing epidemic was in Eastern Europe and central Asia, especially in Russia, where the disease was spreading primarily through intravenous drug use among the young. In the Russian Federation alone, the number of reported cases of HIV rose from 10,993 at the end of 1998 to more than 129,000 in June 2001. In Moscow on November 28 UNAIDS executive director Peter Piot said the actual figures in Eastern Europe and Central Asia were probably four to five times higher than official figures were stating because of poor reporting systems. The UNAIDS/WHO report warned that the high probability of infection from needle-sharing among injecting drug users who were also sexually active meant that a "huge epidemic may be imminent."

HIV/AIDS was spreading slowly in the Middle East and North Africa, but surveys were beginning to detect an increase in some countries, including Djibouti, Sudan, and Somalia, which were all in political turmoil, and in Iran, Libya, and Pakistan. While prevalence rates were still low in much of Asia, in populous countries such as China and India low rates still translated into millions of infected people. For example, the report said the national adult prevalence rate in India at the end of 2000 was under 1 percent, but that still amounted to nearly 3.9 million people living with HIV/AIDS. The only country with more infected people was South Africa. Despite pockets of infections in some subregions of Asia, the report said there was still a chance of heading off a generalized epidemic in Asia if governments moved quickly and firmly.

China took several significant steps toward dealing with its burgeoning AIDS epidemic. For the first time the government admitted in August that it was facing a "very serious epidemic" of HIV/AIDS that it had not "effectively stemmed." At an August 23 press conference the country's vice minister for health reported that the rate of new infections had jumped 67 percent in the first six months of 2001, compared with the same period in 2000. About 5 percent of intravenous drug users in China carried the infection in 2001, compared with 0.5 percent in 1995. The minister also discussed an AIDS epidemic in Henan province, which had been caused when tens of thousands of farmers contracted HIV by selling their blood to collectors who used unsanitary collection practices. China banned the sale of blood in the 1990s. In November China held its first international conference on AIDS, bringing more than 2,700 medical, social, and education experts from twenty nations to help it formulate a strategy for dealing with the epidemic. The official Xinhua News Agency said the conference was intended "to spur vigilance against the disease in all corners of Chinese society." UNAIDS director Piot called the convention "historic."

The UNAIDS/WHO survey said it feared a resurgence of the epidemic in the United States and other industrial countries, propelled by unsafe sex, rising rates of sexually transmitted diseases and injecting drug use, and a shift of the epidemic into "deprived communities," where vulnerable populations had less access to information and health care. Death rates from AIDS and rates of new HIV infection had leveled off in the United States in the late 1990s after declining sharply earlier in the decade. Since 1998 approximately 40,000 new infections and 16,000 deaths were reported annually, down from a peak in the mid-1990s of 60,000 new infections and 40,000 deaths. However, it appeared that high-risk sexual activity among gay men was increasing, and HIV infections were fast increasing among African-American women, particularly in the South where a new crack cocaine epidemic and sex-for-drugs trade was spreading the virus. Blacks comprised only 13 percent of the U.S. population but accounted for more than half of all new infections, and AIDS was the leading cause of death among African Americans ages twenty-five through forty-four.

General Assembly Session on AIDS

Stopping the AIDS/HIV epidemic was vastly complicated by the fact that it was spread primarily through unprotected and unsafe sex practices, subjects that were not only difficult to discuss but involved cultural and social mores that differed from country to country and that changed very slowly. Poverty, lack of education, war and migration, inequality of women, prostitution, injected drug use, and sexually transmitted diseases all fueled the spread of disease. In a special session of the UN General Assembly held June 25–27 in New York, representatives from some 180 countries pledged themselves to developing national strategies for dealing with these underlying problems of the AIDS epidemic. The targets included:

- *reducing HIV infections among fifteen- to twenty-four-year-olds in the most affected countries by 25 percent by 2003 and globally by 2010*
- *reducing the proportion of infants infected with HIV by 20 percent by 2005 and by 50 percent in 2010*
- *developing national strategies and financing plans by 2003 that address the epidemic in forthright terms; confront stigma, silence and denial; address gender and "age-based dimensions" of the problem; and "eliminate discrimination and marginalization"*
- *having in place strategies to protect groups at greatest risk and most vulnerable to new infection "as indicated by such factors as the local history of the epidemic, poverty, sexual practices, drug-using behaviour, livelihood, institutional location, disrupted social structures and population movements forced or otherwise"*

This last target was the focus of one of the few major disagreements that erupted during the session. In listing vulnerable populations, the original draft referred explicitly to gay men, prostitutes, and intravenous drug users, but, after a number of representatives from Islamic countries objected on the grounds that specific acknowledgement of homosexuality violated the teachings of the Koran, the compromise language was found.

Another divisive argument flared over the appropriate balance between prevention and treatment. For months a coalition of nongovernmental organizations and AIDS activists had complained that not enough was being done to provide AIDS victims in poor countries with affordable antiretroviral drugs that lengthened lives and improved the quality of life of AIDS sufferers in the developed world. Others contended that the issue of affordable drugs was almost irrelevant for countries that did not have the health care facilities to support patients on the complicated drug regimen and were hard pressed to provide basic needs such as adequate food, clean water, and inexpensive drugs to fight the opportunistic infections that killed so many AIDS victims. The declaration, adopted without a vote on June 27, said that prevention was the mainstay in the effort to stop the AIDS epidemic, but acknowledged that prevention, care, support, and treatment for those infected were mutually reinforcing and should be integrated in a comprehensive approach.

Discounted AIDS Drugs

The treatment-versus-prevention debate had intensified earlier in 2001 when major drug manufacturers bowed to pressure and began to drop the prices of some of their anti-AIDS drugs sold in Africa. Much of the focus was on a three-year-old law in South Africa that threatened to break the patent protection on AIDS drugs by allowing the health minister to produce or import cheaper copies of patented drugs. Thirty-nine drug manufacturers filed suit in South Africa, claiming that the law violated intellectual property rights protections under the World Trade Organization (WTO). Initially the administration of President Bill Clinton backed the drug companies, threatening trade sanctions against South Africa if it used its law to produce or import generic drugs. But in 1999 the Clinton administration agreed to drop its threat as long as South Africa abided by WTO rules, and the Bush administration continued that policy.

In 2000 several of the major drug manufacturers had agreed to negotiate discounted prices with African countries severely affected by HIV/AIDS, but those agreements were moving slowly and the prices were still out of reach of all but a comparative handful of well-off AIDS patients. Public pressure on the drug companies by AIDS activists and other groups picked up in early 2001 as the suit headed for trial in March. At the same time, generic drug manufacturers, such as the Indian company Cipla, began to put pressure on the drug companies by offering their drugs at deep discounts to nongovernmental organizations working with AIDS patients in Africa. Cipla, for example, said it would make its antiretroviral drug "cocktail" available to Doctors without Borders for $350 for a year's supply. The branded version of the same drugs cost $10,0000 to $15,000 in the United States.

Starting the same week as the trial in South Africa, several multinational companies, including Merck and Bristol-Myers-Squibb, switched tactics, offering their AIDS drugs to African countries at greatly reduced prices in the hopes of persuading them not to turn to the generic market. The prices, which varied depending on the drug and the manufacturer, were still generally higher than the generic versions of the same drug, however, and higher than most Africans could afford. Several countries, including Botswana, the country with the highest rate of HIV in the world, were working with the drug companies. With subsidies from major donors, such as Microsoft chief Bill Gates, Botswana hoped to implement a plan for distributing the reduced-cost, branded antiretrovirals to all of its HIV-infected citizens.

By year's end a new controversy seemed likely to erupt. In December Nigeria became the first African country to announce that it would begin to import huge quantities of generic drugs from Cipla. The government hoped to distribute the drugs to 10,000 people at 100 clinics as a pilot program that would eventually be expanded to Nigeria's 3.5 million HIV/AIDS sufferers.

Meanwhile, another controversy was brewing in South African where President Thabo Mbeki had already raised international eyebrows with his statements questioning whether HIV was really the cause of AIDS and raising doubts about the safety of some of the AIDS drugs. One of the drugs he questioned was nevirapine, which had been shown to reduce dramatically the transmission of HIV from infected women to their infants. In 2000 the drug's German manufacturer, Boehringer-Ingelheim, said it would donate the drug for five years to developing countries. The South African government began distributing the free drug in small pilot programs, saying that thorough research was needed to determine the long-term safety of nevirapine. (Mbeki controversy, Historic Documents of 2000, p. 410)

In August an organization called the Treatment Action Campaign said South Africa's government programs covered too few women and were moving too slowly, and it filed suit asking for broader and faster distribution. According to court documents, about one-fourth of all pregnant South Afri-

can women were infected with HIV, and about 70,000 infants were infected through mother-to-child transmission each year. In mid-December the court ruled that HIV-infected women in the care of the state were entitled to the drug and ordered the government to come up with a plan for widespread distribution. The South African government said it would appeal the decision.

Following are excerpts from the "Declaration of Commitment on HIV/AIDS," a resolution adopted by the United Nations General Assembly while meeting in special session June 27, 2001.

The document was obtained from the Internet at http:// www.un.org/ga/aids/coverage/FinalDeclarationHIVAIDS .html.

"Global Crisis—Global Action"

1. We, Heads of State and Government and Representatives of States and Governments, assembled at the United Nations, from 25 to 27 June 2001, for the twenty-sixth special session of the General Assembly convened in accordance with resolution 55/13, as a matter of urgency, to review and address the problem of HIV/AIDS in all its aspects as well as to secure a global commitment to enhancing coordination and intensification of national, regional and international efforts to combat it in a comprehensive manner;

2. Deeply concerned that the global HIV/AIDS epidemic, through its devastating scale and impact, constitutes a global emergency and one of the most formidable challenges to human life and dignity, as well as to the effective enjoyment of human rights, which undermines social and economic development throughout the world and affects all levels of society—national, community, family and individual;

3. Noting with profound concern, that by the end of the year 2000, 36.1 million people worldwide were living with HIV/AIDS, 90 per cent in developing countries and 75 per cent in sub-Saharan Africa;

4. Noting with grave concern that all people, rich and poor, without distinction of age, gender or race are affected by the HIV/AIDS epidemic, further noting that people in developing countries are the most affected and that women, young adults and children, in particular girls, are the most vulnerable;

5. Concerned also that the continuing spread of HIV/AIDS will constitute a serious obstacle to the realization of the global development goals we adopted at the Millennium Summit;

6. Recalling and reaffirming our previous commitments on HIV/AIDS. . . ;

7. Convinced of the need to have an urgent, coordinated and sustained response to the HIV/AIDS epidemic, which will build on the experience and lessons learned over the past 20 years; . . .

11. Recognizing that poverty, underdevelopment and illiteracy are among

the principal contributing factors to the spread of HIV/AIDS and noting with grave concern that HIV/AIDS is compounding poverty and is now reversing or impeding development in many countries and should therefore be addressed in an integrated manner;

12. Noting that armed conflicts and natural disasters also exacerbate the spread of the epidemic;

13. Noting further that stigma, silence, discrimination, and denial, as well as lack of confidentiality, undermine prevention, care and treatment efforts and increase the impact of the epidemic on individuals, families, communities and nations and must also be addressed;

14. Stressing that gender equality and the empowerment of women are fundamental elements in the reduction of the vulnerability of women and girls to HIV/AIDS; . . .

16. Recognizing that the full realization of human rights and fundamental freedoms for all is an essential element in a global response to the HIV/AIDS pandemic, including in the areas of prevention, care, support and treatment, and that it reduces vulnerability to HIV/AIDS and prevents stigma and related discrimination against people living with or at risk of HIV/AIDS;

17. Acknowledging that prevention of HIV infection must be the mainstay of the national, regional and international response to the epidemic; and that prevention, care, support and treatment for those infected and affected by HIV/AIDS are mutually reinforcing elements of an effective response and must be integrated in a comprehensive approach to combat the epidemic; . . .

21. Noting with concern that some negative economic, social, cultural, political, financial and legal factors are hampering awareness, education, prevention, care, treatment and support efforts; . . .

23. Recognizing that effective prevention, care and treatment strategies will require behavioural changes and increased availability of and non-discriminatory access to, inter alia, vaccines, condoms, microbicides, lubricants, sterile injecting equipment, drugs including anti-retroviral therapy, diagnostics and related technologies as well as increased research and development;

24. Recognizing also that the cost availability and affordability of drugs and related technology are significant factors to be reviewed and addressed in all aspects and that there is a need to reduce the cost of these drugs and technologies in close collaboration with the private sector and pharmaceutical companies;

25. Acknowledging that the lack of affordable pharmaceuticals and of feasible supply structures and health systems continue to hinder an effective response to HIV/AIDS in many countries, especially for the poorest people and recalling efforts to make drugs available at low prices for those in need; . . .

28. Acknowledging that resources devoted to combating the epidemic both at the national and international levels are not commensurate with the magnitude of the problem;

29. Recognizing the fundamental importance of strengthening national, regional and subregional capacities to address and effectively combat HIV/AIDS and that this will require increased and sustained human, financial and tech-

nical resources through strengthened national action and cooperation and increased regional, subregional and international cooperation;

30. Recognizing that external debt and debt-servicing problems have substantially constrained the capacity of many developing countries, as well as countries with economies in transition, to finance the fight against HIV/AIDS;

31. Affirming the key role played by the family in prevention, care, support and treatment of persons affected and infected by HIV/AIDS, bearing in mind that in different cultural, social and political systems various forms of the family exist; . . .

36. Solemnly declare our commitment to address the HIV/AIDS crisis by taking action as follows, taking into account the diverse situations and circumstances in different regions and countries throughout the world;

Leadership

Strong leadership at all levels of society is essential for an effective response to the epidemic

Leadership by Governments in combating HIV/AIDS is essential and their efforts should be complemented by the full and active participation of civil society, the business community and the private sector

Leadership involves personal commitment and concrete actions

At the national level

37. By 2003, ensure the development and implementation of multisectoral national strategies and financing plans for combating HIV/AIDS that: address the epidemic in forthright terms; confront stigma, silence and denial; address gender and age-based dimensions of the epidemic; eliminate discrimination and marginalization; involve partnerships with civil society and the business sector and the full participation of people living with HIV/AIDS, those in vulnerable groups and people mostly at risk, particularly women and young people; are resourced to the extent possible from national budgets without excluding other sources, inter alia international cooperation; fully promote and protect all human rights and fundamental freedoms, including the right to the highest attainable standard of physical and mental health; integrate a gender perspective; and address risk, vulnerability, prevention, care, treatment and support and reduction of the impact of the epidemic; and strengthen health, education and legal system capacity;

38. By 2003, integrate HIV/AIDS prevention, care, treatment and support and impact mitigation priorities into the mainstream of development planning, including in poverty eradication strategies, national budget allocations and sectoral development plans;

At the regional and subregional level

39. Urge and support regional organizations and partners to: be actively involved in addressing the crisis; intensify regional, subregional and interregional cooperation and coordination; and develop regional strategies and responses in support of expanded country level efforts;

40. Support all regional and subregional initiatives on HIV/AIDS. . . ;

41. Encourage the development of regional approaches and plans to address HIV/AIDS;

42. Encourage and support local and national organizations to expand and strengthen regional partnerships, coalitions and networks;

43. Encourage the United Nations Economic and Social Council to request the regional commissions within their respective mandates and resources to support national efforts in their respective regions in combating HIV/AIDS;

At the global level

44. Support greater action and coordination by all relevant United Nations system organizations, including their full participation in the development and implementation of a regularly updated United Nations strategic plan for HIV/AIDS, guided by the principles contained in the present Declaration;

45. Support greater cooperation between relevant United Nations system organizations and international organizations combating HIV/AIDS;

46. Foster stronger collaboration and the development of innovative partnerships between the public and private sectors and by 2003, establish and strengthen mechanisms that involve the private sector and civil society partners and people living with HIV/AIDS and vulnerable groups in the fight against HIV/AIDS;

Prevention

Prevention must be the mainstay of our response

47. By 2003, establish time-bound national targets to achieve the internationally agreed global prevention goal to reduce by 2005 HIV prevalence among young men and women aged 15 to 24 in the most affected countries by 25 per cent and by 25 per cent globally by 2010, and to intensify efforts to achieve these targets as well as to challenge gender stereotypes and attitudes, and gender inequalities in relation to HIV/AIDS, encouraging the active involvement of men and boys;

48. By 2003, establish national prevention targets, recognizing and addressing factors leading to the spread of the epidemic and increasing people's vulnerability, to reduce HIV incidence for those identifiable groups, within particular local contexts, which currently have high or increasing rates of HIV infection, or which available public health information indicates are at the highest risk for new infection;

49. By 2005, strengthen the response to HIV/AIDS in the world of work by establishing and implementing prevention and care programmes in public, private and informal work sectors and take measures to provide a supportive workplace environment for people living with HIV/AIDS;

50. By 2005, develop and begin to implement national, regional and international strategies that facilitate access to HIV/AIDS prevention programmes for migrants and mobile workers, including the provision of information on health and social services;

51. By 2003, implement universal precautions in health-care settings to prevent transmission of HIV infection;

52. By 2005, ensure: that a wide range of prevention programmes which take account of local circumstances, ethics and cultural values, is available in all countries, particularly the most affected countries, including information, education and communication, in languages most understood by communities and respectful of cultures, aimed at reducing risk-taking behaviour and encouraging responsible sexual behaviour, including abstinence and fidelity; expanded access to essential commodities, including male and female condoms and sterile injecting equipment; harm reduction efforts related to drug use; expanded access to voluntary and confidential counselling and testing; safe blood supplies; and early and effective treatment of sexually transmittable infections;

53. By 2005, ensure that at least 90 per cent, and by 2010 at least 95 per cent of young men and women aged 15 to 24 have access to the information, education, including peer education and youth-specific HIV education, and services necessary to develop the life skills required to reduce their vulnerability to HIV infection; in full partnership with youth, parents, families, educators and health-care providers;

54. By 2005, reduce the proportion of infants infected with HIV by 20 per cent, and by 50 per cent by 2010, by: ensuring that 80 per cent of pregnant women accessing antenatal care have information, counselling and other HIV prevention services available to them, increasing the availability of and by providing access for HIV-infected women and babies to effective treatment to reduce mother-to-child transmission of HIV, as well as through effective interventions for HIV-infected women, including voluntary and confidential counselling and testing, access to treatment, especially anti-retroviral therapy and, where appropriate, breast milk substitutes and the provision of a continuum of care;

Care, support and treatment

Care, support and treatment are fundamental elements of an effective response

55. By 2003, ensure that national strategies, supported by regional and international strategies, are developed in close collaboration with the international community, including Governments and relevant intergovernmental organizations as well as with civil society and the business sector, to strengthen health care systems and address factors affecting the provision of HIV-related drugs, including anti-retroviral drugs, inter alia affordability and pricing, including differential pricing, and technical and health care systems capacity. Also, in an urgent manner make every effort to: provide progressively and in a sustainable manner, the highest attainable standard of treatment for HIV/AIDS, including the prevention and treatment of opportunistic infections, and effective use of quality-controlled anti-retroviral therapy in a careful and monitored manner to improve adherence and effectiveness and reduce the risk of developing resistance; to cooperate constructively in strengthening pharmaceutical policies and practices, including those applicable to generic drugs and intellectual property regimes, in order further to promote innovation and the development of domestic industries consistent with international law;

56. By 2005, develop and make significant progress in implementing comprehensive care strategies to: strengthen family and community-based care including that provided by the informal sector, and health care systems to provide and monitor treatment to people living with HIV/AIDS, including infected children, and to support individuals, households, families and communities affected by HIV/ AIDS; improve the capacity and working conditions of health care personnel, and the effectiveness of supply systems, financing plans and referral mechanisms required to provide access to affordable medicines, including anti-retroviral drugs, diagnostics and related technologies, as well as quality medical, palliative and psycho-social care;

57. By 2003, ensure that national strategies are developed in order to provide psycho-social care for individuals, families, and communities affected by HIV/AIDS;

HIV/AIDS and human rights

Realization of human rights and fundamental freedoms for all is essential to reduce vulnerability to HIV/AIDS

Respect for the rights of people living with HIV/AIDS drives an effective response

58. By 2003, enact, strengthen or enforce as appropriate legislation, regulations and other measures to eliminate all forms of discrimination against, and to ensure the full enjoyment of all human rights and fundamental freedoms by people living with HIV/AIDS and members of vulnerable groups; in particular to ensure their access to, inter alia education, inheritance, employment, health care, social and health services, prevention, support, treatment, information and legal protection, while respecting their privacy and confidentiality; and develop strategies to combat stigma and social exclusion connected with the epidemic;

59. By 2005, bearing in mind the context and character of the epidemic and that globally women and girls are disproportionately affected by HIV/AIDS, develop and accelerate the implementation of national strategies that: promote the advancement of women and women's full enjoyment of all human rights; promote shared responsibility of men and women to ensure safe sex; empower women to have control over and decide freely and responsibly on matters related to their sexuality to increase their ability to protect themselves from HIV infection;

60. By 2005, implement measures to increase capacities of women and adolescent girls to protect themselves from the risk of HIV infection, principally through the provision of health care and health services, including sexual and reproductive health, and through prevention education that promotes gender equality within a culturally and gender sensitive framework;

61. By 2005, ensure development and accelerated implementation of national strategies for women's empowerment, promotion and protection of women's full enjoyment of all human rights and reduction of their vulnerability to HIV/AIDS through the elimination of all forms of discrimination, as well as all forms of violence against women and girls, including harmful traditional

and customary practices, abuse, rape and other forms of sexual violence, battering and trafficking in women and girls;

Reducing vulnerability

The vulnerable must be given priority in the response
Empowering women is essential for reducing vulnerability

62. By 2003, in order to complement prevention programmes that address activities which place individuals at risk of HIV infection, such as risky and unsafe sexual behaviour and injecting drug use, have in place in all countries strategies, policies and programmes that identify and begin to address those factors that make individuals particularly vulnerable to HIV infection, including underdevelopment, economic insecurity, poverty, lack of empowerment of women, lack of education, social exclusion, illiteracy, discrimination, lack of information and/or commodities for self-protection, all types of sexual exploitation of women, girls and boys, including for commercial reasons; such strategies, policies and programmes should address the gender dimension of the epidemic, specify the action that will be taken to address vulnerability and set targets for achievement;

63. By 2003, develop and/or strengthen strategies, policies and programmes, which recognize the importance of the family in reducing vulnerability, inter alia, in educating and guiding children and take account of cultural, religious and ethical factors, to reduce the vulnerability of children and young people by: ensuring access of both girls and boys to primary and secondary education, including on HIV/AIDS in curricula for adolescents; ensuring safe and secure environments, especially for young girls; expanding good quality youth-friendly information and sexual health education and counselling service; strengthening reproductive and sexual health programmes; and involving families and young people in planning, implementing and evaluating IIIV/AIDS prevention and care programmes, to the extent possible;

64. By 2003, develop and/or strengthen national strategies, policies and programmes, supported by regional and international initiatives, as appropriate, through a participatory approach, to promote and protect the health of those identifiable groups which currently have high or increasing rates of HIV infection or which public health information indicates are at greatest risk of and most vulnerable to new infection as indicated by such factors as the local history of the epidemic, poverty, sexual practices, drug using behaviour, livelihood, institutional location, disrupted social structures and population movements forced or otherwise;

Children orphaned and made vulnerable by HIV/AIDS

Children orphaned and affected by HIV/AIDS need special assistance

65. By 2003, develop and by 2005 implement national policies and strategies to: build and strengthen governmental, family and community capacities to provide a supportive environment for orphans and girls and boys infected and affected by HIV/AIDS including by providing appropriate counselling and psycho-social support; ensuring their enrolment in school and access to

449

shelter, good nutrition, health and social services on an equal basis with other children; to protect orphans and vulnerable children from all forms of abuse, violence, exploitation, discrimination, trafficking and loss of inheritance;

66. Ensure non-discrimination and full and equal enjoyment of all human rights through the promotion of an active and visible policy of de-stigmatization of children orphaned and made vulnerable by HIV/AIDS;

67. Urge the international community, particularly donor countries, civil society, as well as the private sector to complement effectively national programmes to support programmes for children orphaned or made vulnerable by HIV/AIDS in affected regions, in countries at high risk and to direct special assistance to sub-Saharan Africa;

Alleviating social and economic impact

To address HIV/AIDS is to invest in sustainable development

68. By 2003, evaluate the economic and social impact of the HIV/AIDS epidemic and develop multisectoral strategies to: address the impact at the individual, family, community and national levels; develop and accelerate the implementation of national poverty eradication strategies to address the impact of HIV/AIDS on household income, livelihoods, and access to basic social services, with special focus on individuals, families and communities severely affected by the epidemic; review the social and economic impact of HIV/AIDS at all levels of society especially on women and the elderly, particularly in their role as caregivers and in families affected by HIV/AIDS and address their special needs; adjust and adapt economic and social development policies, including social protection policies, to address the impact of HIV/AIDS on economic growth, provision of essential economic services, labour productivity, government revenues, and deficit-creating pressures on public resources;

69. By 2003, develop a national legal and policy framework that protects in the workplace the rights and dignity of persons living with and affected by HIV/AIDS and those at the greatest risk of HIV/AIDS in consultation with representatives of employers and workers, taking account of established international guidelines on HIV/AIDS in the workplace;

Research and development

With no cure for HIV/AIDS yet found, further research and development is crucial

70. Increase investment and accelerate research on the development of HIV vaccines, while building national research capacity especially in developing countries, and especially for viral strains prevalent in highly affected regions; in addition, support and encourage increased national and international investment in HIV/AIDS-related research and development including biomedical, operations, social, cultural and behavioural research and in traditional medicine to: improve prevention and therapeutic approaches; accelerate access to prevention, care and treatment and care technologies for HIV/AIDS (and its associated opportunistic infections and malignancies and sexually transmitted diseases), including female controlled methods and microbicides,

and in particular, appropriate, safe and affordable HIV vaccines and their delivery, and to diagnostics, tests, methods to prevent mother-to-child transmission; and improve our understanding of factors which influence the epidemic and actions which address it, inter alia, through increased funding and public/private partnerships; create a conducive environment for research and ensure that it is based on highest ethical standards;

71. Support and encourage the development of national and international research infrastructure, laboratory capacity, improved surveillance systems, data collection, processing and dissemination, and training of basic and clinical researchers, social scientists, health-care providers and technicians, with a focus on the countries most affected by HIV/AIDS, particularly developing countries and those countries experiencing or at risk of rapid expansion of the epidemic;

72. Develop and evaluate suitable approaches for monitoring treatment efficacy, toxicity, side effects, drug interactions, and drug resistance, develop methodologies to monitor the impact of treatment on HIV transmission and risk behaviours;

73. Strengthen international and regional cooperation in particular North/South, South/South and triangular cooperation, related to transfer of relevant technologies, suitable to the environment in prevention and care of HIV/AIDS, the exchange of experiences and best practices, researchers and research findings and strengthen the role of UNAIDS in this process. In this context, encourage that the end results of these cooperative research findings and technologies be owned by all parties to the research, reflecting their relevant contribution and dependent upon their providing legal protection to such findings; and affirm that all such research should be free from bias;

74. By 2003, ensure that all research protocols for the investigation of HIV-related treatment including anti-retroviral therapies and vaccines based on international guidelines and best practices are evaluated by independent committees of ethics, in which persons living with HIV/AIDS and caregivers for anti-retroviral therapy participate;

HIV/AIDS in conflict and disaster affected regions

Conflicts and disasters contribute to the spread of HIV/AIDS

75. By 2003, develop and begin to implement national strategies that incorporate HIV/AIDS awareness, prevention, care and treatment elements into programmes or actions that respond to emergency situations, recognizing that populations destabilized by armed conflict, humanitarian emergencies and natural disasters, including refugees, internally displaced persons and in particular, women and children, are at increased risk of exposure to HIV infection; and, where appropriate, factor HIV/AIDS components into international assistance programmes;

76. Call on all United Nations agencies, regional and international organizations, as well as non-governmental organizations involved with the provision and delivery of international assistance to countries and regions affected by conflicts, humanitarian crises or natural disasters, to incorporate as a

matter of urgency HIV/AIDS prevention, care and awareness elements into their plans and programmes and provide HIV/AIDS awareness and training to their personnel;

77. By 2003, have in place national strategies to address the spread of HIV among national uniformed services, where this is required, including armed forces and civil defence force and consider ways of using personnel from these services who are educated and trained in HIV/AIDS awareness and prevention to assist with HIV/ AIDS awareness and prevention activities including participation in emergency, humanitarian, disaster relief and rehabilitation assistance;

78. By 2003, ensure the inclusion of HIV/AIDS awareness and training, including a gender component, into guidelines designed for use by defence personnel and other personnel involved in international peacekeeping operations while also continuing with ongoing education and prevention efforts, including pre-deployment orientation, for these personnel;

Resources

The HIV/AIDS challenge cannot be met without new, additional and sustained resources

79. Ensure that the resources provided for the global response to address HIV/AIDS are substantial, sustained and geared towards achieving results;

80. By 2005, through a series of incremental steps, reach an overall target of annual expenditure on the epidemic of between US$ 7 billion and US$ 10 billion in low and middle-income countries and those countries experiencing or at risk of experiencing rapid expansion for prevention, care, treatment, support and mitigation of the impact of HIV/AIDS, and take measures to ensure that needed resources are made available, particularly from donor countries and also from national budgets, bearing in mind that resources of the most affected countries are seriously limited;

81. Call on the international community, where possible, to provide assistance for HIV/AIDS prevention, care and treatment in developing countries on a grant basis;

82. Increase and prioritize national budgetary allocations for HIV/AIDS programmes as required and ensure that adequate allocations are made by all ministries and other relevant stakeholders;

83. Urge the developed countries that have not done so to strive to meet the targets of 0.7 per cent of their gross national product for overall official development assistance and the targets of earmarking of 0.15 per cent to 0.20 per cent of gross national product as official development assistance for least developed countries as agreed, as soon as possible, taking into account the urgency and gravity of the HIV/AIDS epidemic;

84. Urge the international community to complement and supplement efforts of developing countries that commit increased national funds to fight the HIV/AIDS epidemic through increased international development assistance, particularly those countries most affected by HIV/AIDS, particularly in Africa, especially in sub-Saharan Africa, the Caribbean, countries at high risk of ex-

pansion of the HIV/AIDS epidemic and other affected regions whose resources to deal with the epidemic are seriously limited;

85. Integrate HIV/AIDS actions in development assistance programmes and poverty eradication strategies as appropriate and encourage the most effective and transparent use of all resources allocated;

86. Call on the international community and invite civil society and the private sector to take appropriate measures to help alleviate the social and economic impact of HIV/AIDS in the most affected developing countries;

87. Without further delay implement the enhanced Heavily Indebted Poor Country (HIPC) Initiative and agree to cancel all bilateral official debts of HIPC countries as soon as possible, especially those most affected by HIV/AIDS, in return for their making demonstrable commitments to poverty eradication and urge the use of debt service savings to finance poverty eradication programmes, particularly for HIV/AIDS prevention, treatment, care and support and other infections;

88. Call for speedy and concerted action to address effectively the debt problems of least developed countries, low-income developing countries, and middle-income developing countries, particularly those affected by HIV/AIDS, in a comprehensive, equitable, development-oriented and durable way through various national and international measures designed to make their debt sustainable in the long term and thereby to improve their capacity to deal with the HIV/AIDS epidemic, including, as appropriate, existing orderly mechanisms for debt reduction, such as debt swaps for projects aimed at the prevention, care and treatment of HIV/AIDS;

89. Encourage increased investment in HIV/AIDS-related research, nationally, regionally and internationally, in particular for the development of sustainable and affordable prevention technologies, such as vaccines and microbicides, and encourage the proactive preparation of financial and logistic plans to facilitate rapid access to vaccines when they become available;

90. Support the establishment, on an urgent basis, of a global HIV/AIDS and health fund to finance an urgent and expanded response to the epidemic based on an integrated approach to prevention, care, support and treatment and to assist Governments inter alia in their efforts to combat HIV/AIDS with due priority to the most affected countries, notably in sub-Saharan Africa and the Caribbean and to those countries at high risk, mobilize contributions to the fund from public and private sources with a special appeal to donor countries, foundations, the business community including pharmaceutical companies, the private sector, philanthropists and wealthy individuals;

91. By 2002, launch a worldwide fund-raising campaign aimed at the general public as well as the private sector, conducted by UNAIDS with the support and collaboration of interested partners at all levels, to contribute to the global HIV/ AIDS and health fund;

92. Direct increased funding to national, regional and subregional commissions and organizations to enable them to assist Governments at the national, subregional and regional level in their efforts to respond to the crisis;

93. Provide the UNAIDS co-sponsoring agencies and the UNAIDS secretariat

with the resources needed to work with countries in support of the goals of this Declaration;

Follow-up

Maintaining the momentum and monitoring progress are essential

At the national level

94. Conduct national periodic reviews involving the participation of civil society, particularly people living with HIV/AIDS, vulnerable groups and care-givers, of progress achieved in realizing these commitments and identify problems and obstacles to achieving progress and ensure wide dissemination of the results of these reviews;

95. Develop appropriate monitoring and evaluation mechanisms to assist with follow-up in measuring and assessing progress, develop appropriate monitoring and evaluation instruments, with adequate epidemiological data;

96. By 2003, establish or strengthen effective monitoring systems, where appropriate, for the promotion and protection of human rights of people living with HIV/AIDS;

At the regional level

97. Include HIV/AIDS and related public health concerns as appropriate on the agenda of regional meetings at the ministerial and Head of State and Government level;

98. Support data collection and processing to facilitate periodic reviews by regional commissions and/or regional organizations of progress in implementing regional strategies and addressing regional priorities and ensure wide dissemination of the results of these reviews;

99. Encourage the exchange between countries of information and experiences in implementing the measures and commitments contained in this Declaration, and in particular facilitate intensified South-South and triangular cooperation;

At the global level

100. Devote sufficient time and at least one full day of the annual General Assembly session to review and debate a report of the Secretary-General on progress achieved in realizing the commitments set out in this Declaration, with a view to identifying problems and constraints and making recommendations on action needed to make further progress;

101. Ensure that HIV/AIDS issues are included on the agenda of all appropriate United Nations conferences and meetings;

102. Support initiatives to convene conferences, seminars, workshops, training programmes and courses to follow up issues raised in this Declaration. . . ;

103. Explore, with a view to improving equity in access to essential drugs, the feasibility of developing and implementing, in collaboration with non-governmental organizations and other concerned partners, systems for voluntary monitoring and reporting of global drug prices;

We recognize and express our appreciation to those who have led the effort to raise awareness of the HIV/AIDS epidemic and to deal with its complex challenges;

We look forward to strong leadership by Governments, and concerted efforts with full and active participation of the United Nations, the entire multilateral system, civil society, the business community and private sector;

And finally, we call on all countries to take the necessary steps to implement this Declaration, in strengthened partnership and cooperation with other multilateral and bilateral partners and with civil society.

SURGEON GENERAL ON PROMOTING SEXUAL HEALTH
June 28, 2001

Citing "significant public health challenges" including "alarmingly high levels" of sexually transmitted diseases, abortion, and sexual violence, Surgeon General David Satcher said June 28, 2001, that it was time for Americans to engage in a "mature and thoughtful" discussion about the most effective ways to solve those problems and to promote sexual health in the United States. In a thirty-page report based on a review of hundreds of studies and research projects, Satcher gave broad definitions of sexual health and responsible sexual behavior, and he outlined a set of strategies that had been shown to be effective in reaching those goals. Satcher suggested that parents, teachers, and communities use the report as an aid to discussion. "Given the diversity of attitudes, beliefs, values and opinions, finding common ground might not be easy, but it is attainable," he said.

The difficulty of reaching consensus became immediately apparent, as religious and conservative groups lambasted the report and Satcher for advocating teaching teenagers about human sexuality and methods of contraception and for advocating tolerance of homosexuality. One outraged director of a church-based conservative organization called the report "ideology disguised as science from the beginning to the end." The Bush administration, which strongly supported "abstinence-only" programs, also distanced itself from the report.

A Comprehensive Approach

Satcher approached what he called the "most controversial and sensitive" issue he had dealt with as surgeon general from a public health perspective, detailing the dangers to public health from sex-related diseases and problems. The main threats included:

- *Some 12 million people in the United States were infected with sexually transmitted diseases (STDs) every year, causing a wide range of problems from incurable AIDS, to infertility, to an increased risk of cancer.*

- *An estimated 800,000 to 900,000 people were living with HIV, the virus that caused AIDS, and about 40,000 new infections occurred each year. (AIDS, p. 438)*
- *Nearly half of all pregnancies were unintended, due largely to lack of information about contraception or failure to use it properly. The highest rates of unintended pregnancy occurred among adolescents, poor women, and African American women.*
- *About 1.4 million induced abortions were performed annually. Although adolescents accounted for only 20 percent of all abortions, nearly three of every ten adolescent pregnancies ended in abortion.*
- *More than 100,000 children were sexually abused each year. According to one study, 22 percent of all women and 2 percent of all men had been the victims of a forced sexual act. Nearly 80 percent of all gays and lesbians had been subjected to some form of harassment.*

To counter these threats, Satcher said, sexuality education must begin early, be available throughout life, and be comprehensive. The best place for children to begin to learn about sexual health was through parenting that promoted healthy social and emotional development and protected against abuse. But schools were also an appropriate place for sexuality education, Satcher said, noting that opinion polls showed repeatedly that a majority of Americans favored some form of sex education, including providing information about contraception, in the public schools.

Satcher said that "sexual abstinence until engaged in a committed and mutually monogamous relationship" was "an important component" of any sex education program and the only sure way to avoid unwanted pregnancy or a sexually transmitted disease. But he noted that there was insufficient evidence to show that abstinence-only programs delayed the initiation of sexual activity among adolescents, as many of its promoters argued. At the same time, he said, evidence did show that providing teenagers with information about contraception did not hasten the onset of sexual activity and sometimes delayed it. Some studies found that such programs also increased contraceptive use more generally among already sexually active adolescents. "Given that one-half of adolescents in the United States are already sexually active—and at risk of unintended pregnancy and STD/HIV infection—it also seems clear that adolescents need accurate information about contraceptive methods so that they can reduce those risks," Satcher said.

Calling on Americans to respect diversity in sexual orientation, Satcher said there was no valid evidence showing that sexual orientation, usually determined by adolescence, could be changed. In remarks made when he released the report, Satcher said society had "a responsibility to be more supportive and proactive than judgmental" toward gays and lesbians. "We're certainly not trying to get anyone in any religious group to change their views," he said. "We're just saying these are people, these are human beings."

Satcher also called for a variety of other interventions, including strengthening the American family, improving access to both information and health care services, providing adequate training in sexual health to all professionals who deal with those issues, and targeting interventions to the most vulnerable populations.

Conflict with the White House

Satcher's report on sexual health was originally scheduled to be issued in fall 2000 in the midst of the presidential election campaign, but it was reportedly delayed to avoid raising a sensitive issue for the Democrats, who had already been embarrassed by President Bill Clinton's sex scandal. (Clinton scandal and impeachment, Historic Documents of 1998, p. 564; Historic Documents of 1999, p. 15)

According to some news accounts, officials within the new Bush administration also wanted to delay its release. President George W. Bush was a strong supporter of abstinence-only sex education programs in the public schools and had pledged to increase federal funding for them during his election campaign. Instead, the administration allowed Satcher to release the report but took immediate steps to disassociate itself both from Satcher and the report. Health and Human Services Secretary Tommy G. Thompson, who had appeared with Satcher when he released earlier reports on public health issues, was noticeably absent for the release of this one. White House press secretary Ari Fleischer said that President Bush "understands the report was issued by a surgeon general that he did not appoint, a surgeon general who was appointed by the previous administration. The president continues to believe that abstinence and abstinence education is the most effective way to prevent AIDS, to prevent unwanted pregnancy."

Conservative groups, which were the core of Bush's political support, demanded that the president ask for Satcher's resignation. White House officials later said that Bush would likely wait and appoint his own surgeon general when Satcher's term expired in February 2002. Satcher himself ended any further speculation when he announced in November 2001 that he planned to leave at the end of his term. The target of conservatives since he was nominated by President Bill Clinton in 1998, Satcher became surgeon general after surviving a filibuster against his nomination led by then-senator John Ashcroft, R-Mo., later Bush's attorney general.

Satcher said he was not taking sides in the political debate over sex education programs. "We try to make very clear what's needed to improve sexual health and what's supported by the science," he said.

Following are excerpts from the report "The Surgeon General's Call to Action to Promote Sexual Health and Responsible Sexual Behavior," released June 28, 2001, by Surgeon General David Satcher.

The document was obtained from the Internet at http:// www.surgeongeneral.gov/library/sexualhealth/default .htm.

A Letter from the Surgeon General U.S. Department of Health and Human Service

I am introducing the *Surgeon General's Call to Action to Promote Sexual Health and Responsible Sexual Behavior* because we, as a nation, must address the significant public health challenges regarding the sexual health of our citizens. In recognition of these challenges, promoting responsible sexual behavior is included among the Surgeon General's Public Health Priorities and is also one of the Healthy People 2010 Ten Leading Health Indicators for the Nation. While it is important to acknowledge the many positive aspects of sexuality, we also need to understand that there are undesirable consequences as well-alarmingly high levels of sexually transmitted disease (STD) and HIV/AIDS infection, unintended pregnancy, abortion, sexual dysfunction, and sexual violence. In the United States:

- STDs infect approximately 12 million persons each year;
- 774,467 AIDS cases, nearly two-thirds of which were sexually transmitted, have been reported since 1981;
- an estimated 800,000 to 900,000 persons are living with HIV;
- an estimated one-third of those living with HIV are aware of their status and are in treatment, one-third are aware but not in treatment, and one-third have not been tested and are not aware;
- an estimated 40,000 new HIV infections occur each year;
- an estimated 1,366,000 induced abortions occurred in 1996;
- nearly one-half of pregnancies are unintended;
- an estimated 22 percent of women and two percent of men have been victims of a forced sexual act; and
- an estimated 104,000 children are victims of sexual abuse each year.

Each of these problems carries with it the potential for lifelong consequences-for individuals, families, communities, and the nation as a whole. As is the case with so many public health problems, there are serious disparities among the populations affected. The economically disadvantaged, racial and ethnic minorities, persons with different sexual identities, disabled persons, and adolescents often bear the heaviest burden. Yet it is important to recognize that persons of all ages and backgrounds are at risk and should have access to the knowledge and services necessary for optimal sexual health.

These challenges can be met but first we must find common ground and reach consensus on some important problems and their possible solutions. It is necessary to appreciate what sexual health is, that it is connected with both physical and mental health, and that it is important throughout the entire lifespan, not just the reproductive years. It is also important to recognize the responsibilities that individuals and communities have in protecting sexual health. The responsibility of well-informed adults as educators and role models for their children cannot be overstated. Issues around sexuality can be difficult to discuss-because they are personal and because there is great diversity in how they are perceived and approached. Yet, they greatly impact public health and, thus, it is time to begin that discussion and, to that end, this *Surgeon General's Call to Action* is offered as a framework.

It is, however, only a first step—a call to begin a mature and thoughtful discussion about sexuality. We must understand that sexuality encompasses more than sexual behavior, that the many aspects of sexuality include not only the physical, but the mental and spiritual as well, and that sexuality is a core component of personality. Sexuality is a fundamental part of human life. While the problems usually associated with sexual behavior are real and need to be addressed, human sexuality also has significant meaning and value in each individual's life. This call, and the discussion it is meant to generate, is not just intended for health care professionals or policy makers. It is intended for parents, teachers, clergy, social service professionals—all of us.

I would like to add a few words for the many thousands of persons living with HIV/AIDS in this country. We realize that you are not the enemy; that the enemy in this epidemic is the virus, not those who are infected with it. You need our support and encouragement. At the same time, it is also important that you realize you have an opportunity to partner with us in stemming the spread of this illness; to be responsible in your own behavior and to help others become aware of the need for responsible behavior in their sexual lives. Working together, we can make a difference.

This *Call to Action* has been developed through a collaborative process. It is based on a series of scientific review papers contributed by experts in relevant fields, on recommendations developed at two national conferences, and on extensive review and comment as the document was being prepared-all of which sought the broadest possible input and brought together a wide range of experience, expertise and perspective with representation from the academic, medical and religious communities, policy makers, advocates, teachers, parents and youth. The strategies presented here provide a point of reference for advancing a national dialogue on issues of sexuality, sexual health, and responsible sexual behavior. It can begin among individuals, but must also involve communities, the media, government and non-government agencies, institutions, and foundations.

In developing this Call to Action, we have received a wide range of input, and have identified several areas of common ground. A major responsibility of the Surgeon General is to provide the best available science based information to the American people to assist in protecting and advancing the health and safety of our Nation. This report represents another effort to meet that responsibility.

Finding common ground might not be easy, but it is possible. The process leading to this *Call to Action* has already shown that persons with very different views can come together and discuss difficult issues and find broad areas of agreement. Approaches and solutions might be complex, but we do have evidence of success. We need to appreciate the diversity of our culture, engage in mature, thoughtful and respectful discussion, be informed by the science that is available to us, and invest in continued research. This is a call to action. We cannot remain complacent. Doing nothing is unacceptable. Our efforts not only will have an impact on the current health status of our citizens, but will lay a foundation for a healthier society in the future.

David Satcher, M.D., Ph.D.
Surgeon General

I. Introduction

Sexuality is an integral part of human life. It carries the awesome potential to create new life. It can foster intimacy and bonding as well as shared pleasure in our relationships. It fulfills a number of personal and social needs, and we value the sexual part of our being for the pleasures and benefits it affords us. Yet when exercised irresponsibly it can also have negative aspects such as sexually transmitted diseases—including HIV/AIDS—unintended pregnancy, and coercive or violent behavior. To enjoy the important benefits of sexuality, while avoiding negative consequences, some of which may have long term or even life time implications, it is necessary for individuals to be sexually healthy, to behave responsibly, and to have a supportive environment—to protect their own sexual health, as well as that of others.

Sexual health is inextricably bound to both physical and mental health. Just as physical and mental health problems can contribute to sexual dysfunction and diseases, those dysfunctions and diseases can contribute to physical and mental health problems. Sexual health is not limited to the absence of disease or dysfunction, nor is its importance confined to just the reproductive years. It includes the ability to understand and weigh the risks, responsibilities, outcomes and impacts of sexual actions and to practice abstinence when appropriate. It includes freedom from sexual abuse and discrimination and the ability of individuals to integrate their sexuality into their lives, derive pleasure from it, and to reproduce if they so choose.

Sexual responsibility should be understood in its broadest sense. While personal responsibility is crucial to any individual's health status, communities also have important responsibilities. Individual responsibility includes: understanding and awareness of one's sexuality and sexual development; respect for oneself and one's partner; avoidance of physical or emotional harm to either oneself or one's partner; ensuring that pregnancy occurs only when welcomed; and recognition and tolerance of the diversity of sexual values within any community. Community responsibility includes assurance that its members have: access to developmentally and culturally appropriate sexuality education, as well as sexual and reproductive health care and counseling; the latitude to make appropriate sexual and reproductive choices; respect for diversity; and freedom from stigmatization and violence on the basis of gender, race, ethnicity, religion, or sexual orientation. . . .

This *Call to Action* focuses on the need to promote sexual health and responsible sexual behavior throughout the lifespan. Its primary goal is to stimulate respectful, thoughtful, and mature discussion in our communities and in our homes. While sexuality may be difficult to discuss for some, and there are certainly many different views and beliefs regarding it, we cannot afford the consequences of continued or selective silence. It is necessary to find common ground—balancing diversity of opinion with the best available scientific evidence and best practice models—to improve the health of our nation. This *Call to Action* is also the first step toward the development of guidelines to assist parents, clergy, teachers, and others in their work of improving sexual health and responsible sexual behavior.

II. The Public Health Approach

Use of a public health approach is requisite to promoting sexual health and responsible sexual behavior. This approach has four central components: 1) identifying the problem; 2) identifying risk and protective factors; 3) developing and testing interventions; and 4) implementing, and further evaluating, those interventions that have demonstrated effectiveness. In the present case, public health responds to the problem-sexually transmitted diseases, unintended pregnancies, and sexual violence-by asking what is known about its distribution and rates, what factors can be modified, if those modifications are acceptable to the community, and if they are likely to address the problem. Such approaches can range from provision of information about responsible sexuality and interventions designed to promote healthy behavior—such as sexuality education that starts from within the family, where educated and informed adults can also serve as positive role models—to developing vaccines against sexually transmitted diseases (STDs) and AIDS, and to making sexual health care more available and accessible. Additionally, public health focuses on involving communities in their own health and tailoring health promotion programs to the needs and cultures of the communities involved. Because sexuality is one of the human attributes most endowed with meaning and symbolism, it is of particular importance that addressing sexual health issues involve community wide discussion, consultation, and implementation.

This *Call to Action* provides an evidence based foundation for developing a public health approach to sexual health and responsible sexual behavior. It identifies the problems and then discusses risk and protective factors. Numerous intervention models that have been evaluated and shown to be effective, as well as some that are promising but not yet adequately evaluated, are also presented. The last step, implementation of effective interventions, will depend heavily on individual communities and their members.

III. The Public Health Problem

The United States faces a significant challenge related to the sexual health of its citizens. Concerns include: STDs; infertility and cancer resulting from STDs; HIV/AIDS; sexual abuse, coercion and prejudice; unintended pregnancy; and abortion.

Five of the ten most commonly reported infectious diseases in the U.S. are STDs; and, in 1995, STDs accounted for 87 percent of cases reported among those ten. Nevertheless, public awareness regarding STDs is not widespread, nor is their disproportionate impact on women, adolescents, and racial and ethnic minorities well known:

- Chlamydia infection is the most commonly reported STD. While reported rates of infection in women greatly exceed those in men, largely because screening programs have been primarily directed toward women, the rates for both women and men are probably similar. Chlamydia rates for women are highest among those aged 15–19 years and rates for Black and Hispanic women are also considerably higher than those for White women.
- Rates for gonorrhea are highest among women aged 15–19 years and Blacks.
- It is estimated that 45 million persons in the U.S. are infected with genital herpes and that one million new cases occur per year.
- Sexually transmitted infections in both women and men contribute to infertility, which affects approximately 14 percent of all couples in the United States at some time. For example, chlamydia and gonorrhea infections account for 15 percent of cases of infertility in women.
- Human Papillomavirus (HPV) is a sexually transmissible virus that causes genital warts. An estimated 5.5 million persons become infected with HPV each year in the U.S. and an estimated 20 million are currently infected. There are many different types of HPV. While most women who have HPV do not develop cervical cancer, four HPV subtypes are responsible for an estimated 80 percent of cervical cancer cases, with approximately 14,000 new cervical cancer cases occurring per year.

Currently, there are an estimated 800,000 to 900,000 persons living with HIV in the United States, with approximately 40,000 new HIV infections occurring every year. Among those who are currently positive for HIV, an estimated one-third are aware of their status and in treatment, one-third are aware of their status but not in treatment, and one-third have not been tested and are unaware of their status.

Since 1981, a total of more than 774,467 AIDS cases had been reported to the U.S. Centers for Disease Control and Prevention (CDC). The disease has disproportionately affected men who have sex with men—47 percent of reported cases—and minority men who have sex with men have now emerged as the population most affected. A recently released seven city survey indicates that new HIV infection was substantially higher for young Black gay and bisexual men than for their White or Hispanic counterparts. During the 1990s, the epidemic also shifted toward women. While women account for 28 percent of HIV cases reported since 1981, they accounted for 32 percent of those reported between July 1999 and June 2000. Similarly, women account for 17 percent of AIDS cases reported since 1981, but 24 percent of those reported between July 1999 and June 2000.

Sexual abuse contributes to sexual dysfunction and other public health problems such as substance abuse and mental health problems. There are an estimated 104,000 child victims of sexual abuse per year, and the proportion of women in current relationships who are subject to sexual violence is estimated at eight percent. While it is estimated that only a relatively small proportion of rapes are reported, a major national study found that 22 percent of women and approximately two percent of men had been victims of a forced sexual act.

Sexual orientation is usually determined by adolescence, if not earlier, and there is no valid scientific evidence that sexual orientation can be changed. Nonetheless, our culture often stigmatizes homosexual behavior, identity and relationships. These anti-homosexual attitudes are associated with psychological distress for homosexual persons and may have a negative impact on mental health, including a greater incidence of depression and suicide, lower self-acceptance and a greater likelihood of hiding sexual orientation. Although the research is limited, transgendered persons are reported to experience similar problems. In their extreme form, these negative attitudes lead to antigay violence. Averaged over two dozen studies, 80 percent of gay men and lesbians had experienced verbal or physical harassment on the basis of their orientation, 45 percent had been threatened with violence, and 17 percent had experienced a physical attack.

There are also persons who are challenged with developmental, physical or mental disabilities whose sexuality and sexual needs have often been ignored, or at worst, exploited and abused. Although appropriate assistance has been developed for these vulnerable populations, it is seriously underutilized. Additional materials and programs, as well as further research, are needed.

It is estimated that nearly one-half of all pregnancies in the U.S. are unintended. While women in all age, income, race and ethnicity categories experience unintended pregnancies, the highest rates occur among adolescents, lower-income women and Black women. Unintended pregnancy is medically costly in terms of the precluded opportunity for preconception care and counseling, as well as increased likelihood of late or no prenatal care, increased risk for low birthweight, and increased risk for infant mortality. It is also socially costly in terms of out-of-wedlock births, reduced educational attainment and employment opportunity, increased welfare dependency, and later child abuse and neglect—and economically in terms of health care costs.

An estimated 1,366,000 induced abortions occurred in the U.S. in 1996, a slight increase from the 1,364,000 in 1995, but a 15 percent decrease from the 1,609,000 in 1990. A similar pattern of decrease has been observed in abortion rates with 22.9 abortions per 1000 women aged 15-44 years in 1996 compared to 27.4 in 1990. Moreover, surveillance data indicate that for those States that report previous induced abortions, nearly 45 percent of abortions reported in 1996 were obtained by women who had already had at least one abortion.

The belief that adolescents obtain the majority of abortions in the U.S. is inaccurate. Abortion rates are substantially higher for women in their twenties than for adolescents. Rates in 1996 were 50.7 abortions per 1000 for women aged 20-24 years and 33.6 per 1000 for women aged 25-29 years, compared with a rate of 29.2 abortions per 1000 women aged 15–19 years. Moreover, women over 20 years of age account for 80 percent of total induced abortions. Nonetheless, a higher proportion of adolescent pregnancies end in abortion (29 percent) than do pregnancies for women over 20 years of age (21 percent).

Significant differences of opinion exist regarding the morality of abortion. In general, U.S. courts have ruled that the procedure is legal and health care technology has made abortion relatively safe. However, there is broad accord that abortion should be a rare procedure and that improvements in sexual health and an emphasis on a reduction in the number of unintended pregnancies will clearly move this objective forward. The underpinning of the public health approach to this issue is to apply a variety of interventions at key points to prevent unintended pregnancy from occurring, and thus, ensure that all pregnancies are welcomed.

IV. Risk and Protective Factors for Sexual Health

Human beings are sexual beings throughout their lives and human sexual development involves many other aspects of development—physical, behavioral, intellectual, emotional, and interpersonal. Human sexual development follows a progression that, within certain ranges, applies to most persons. The challenge of achieving sexual health begins early in life and continues throughout the lifespan. The actions communities and health care professionals must take to support healthy sexual development vary from one stage of development to the next. Children need stable environments, parenting that promotes healthy social and emotional development, and protection from abuse. Adolescents need education, skills training, self-esteem promoting experiences, and appropriate services related to sexuality, along with positive expectations and sound preparation for their future roles as partners in committed relationships and as parents. Adults need continuing education as they achieve sexual maturity—to learn to communicate effectively with their children and partners and to accept continued responsibility for their sexuality, as well as necessary sexual and reproductive health care services.

There are also a number of more variable risk and protective factors that shape human sexual behavior and can have an impact on sexual health and the practice of responsible sexual behavior. These include biological factors, parents and other family members, schools, friends, the community, the media, religion, health care professionals, the law, and the availability of reproductive and sexual health services. . . .

V. Evidence-based Intervention Models

Substantial work has been done in the areas of sexual health and responsible sexual behavior, through public-private partnerships at the national as well as community level, by many researchers and organizations throughout the country. Many of these approaches and programs to improve sexual health have been evaluated and shown to be effective. They include: community based programs, school based programs, clinic based programs, and religion based programs.

Community Based Programs

Youth development programs, although they typically do not specifically address sexuality, have been shown to have a significant impact on sexual health and behavior. Programs that improve education and life options for adolescents have been demonstrated to reduce their pregnancy and birth rates. These programs may increase attachment to school, improve opportunities for careers, increase belief in the future, increase interaction with adults, and structure young people's time.

The CDC has identified a number of effective STD and HIV prevention programs that are curriculum based and presented by peer and health educators in various community settings. Other community interventions have involved changing community norms and the distribution of condoms to reduce unwanted pregnancies and STDs, including HIV. Such interventions have the advantages of reaching large numbers of people at a relatively low cost and engaging the active involvement of community members, including local opinion leaders. They have had considerable success in changing community norms about sexual behavior as evidenced by substantial increases in condom use. It is important to point out that although the correct and consistent use of condoms has been shown to be effective in reducing the risk of pregnancy, HIV infection, and some STDs, more research is needed on the level of effectiveness.

School Based Programs

A majority of Americans favor some form of sexuality education in the public schools and also believe that some sort of birth control information should be available to adolescents. School based sexuality education programs are generally of two types: abstinence-only programs that emphasize sexual abstinence as the most appropriate choice for young people; and sexuality and STD/HIV education programs that also cover abstinence but, in addition, include condoms and other methods of contraception to provide protection against STDs or pregnancy.

To date, there are only a few published evaluations of abstinence-only programs. Due to this limited number of studies it is too early to draw definite conclusions about this approach. Similarly, the value of these programs for adolescents who have initiated sexual activity is not yet understood. More research is clearly needed.

Programs that typically emphasize abstinence, but also cover condoms and other methods of contraception, have a larger body of evaluation evidence that indicates either no effect on initiation of sexual activity or, in some cases, a delay in the initiation of sexual activity. This evidence gives strong support to the conclusion that providing information about contraception does not increase adolescent sexual activity, either by hastening the onset of sexual intercourse, increasing the frequency of sexual intercourse, or increasing the number of sexual partners. In addition, some of these evaluated programs increased condom use or contraceptive use more generally for adolescents who were sexually active.

Despite the available evidence regarding the effectiveness of school-based sexuality education, it remains a controversial issue for many—in terms of whether schools are the most appropriate venue for such education, as well as curriculum content. Few would disagree that parents should be the primary sexuality educators of their children or that sexual abstinence until engaged in a committed and mutually monogamous relationship is an important component in any sexuality education program. It does seem clear, however, that providing sexuality education in the schools is a useful mechanism to ensure that this Nation's youth have a basic understanding of sexuality. Traditionally, schools have had a role in ensuring equity of access to information that is perhaps greater than most other institutions. In addition, given that one-half of adolescents in the United States are already sexually active—and at risk of unintended pregnancy and STD/HIV infection—it also seems clear that adolescents need accurate information about contraceptive methods so that they can reduce those risks.

Clinic Based Programs

Prevention programs based in health clinics that have an impact on sexual health and behavior are of three types: counseling and education; condom or contraceptive distribution; and STD/HIV screening. Successful counseling and education programs have several elements in common: they have a clear scientific basis for their design; they require a commitment of staff time and effort, as well as additional time from clients; they are tailored to the individual; and they include building clients' skills through, for example, exercises in negotiation. Even brief risk-reduction messages have been shown, in some studies, to lead to substantial increases in condom use; although other studies have shown little effect. More extensive counseling, either individual or small group, can produce additional increases in consistent condom use.

Most school clinic based condom and contraceptive availability programs include some form of abstinence or risk-reduction counseling to address the concern that increased condom availability could lead to increased sexual behavior. The evidence indicates these programs, while still controversial in some communities, do not increase sexual behavior and that they are generally accepted by adolescents, parents, and school staff.

Because many STDs have no clear symptoms, STD/HIV screening promotes sexual health and responsible sexual behavior by detecting these diseases and preventing their unintentional spread. Routine screening in clinics has also been shown to reduce the incidence of some STDs, particularly chlamydia infection.

Religion Based Programs

Religion based sexuality education programs have been developed and cover a wide spectrum of different belief systems. Taken as a whole, they cover all age ranges, from early elementary school to adults, as well as youth with different sexual orientations and identities. Although it is reasonable to expect that religion based programs would have an impact on sexual behavior, the absence of scientific evaluations precludes arriving at a definitive conclusion on the effectiveness of these programs. More research is needed.

VI. Vision for the Future

Strategies that cover three fundamental areas—increasing awareness, implementing and strengthening interventions, and expanding the research base-could help provide a foundation for promoting sexual health and responsible sexual behavior in a manner that is consistent with the best available science.

1. Increasing Public Awareness of Issues Relating to Sexual Health and Responsible Sexual Behavior

- Begin a national dialogue on sexual health and responsible sexual behavior that is honest, mature and respectful, and has the ultimate goal of developing a national strategy that recognizes the need for common ground.
- Encourage opinion leaders to address issues related to sexual health and responsible sexual behavior in ways that are informed by the best available science and that respect diversity.
- Provide access to education about sexual health and responsible sexual behavior that is thorough, wide-ranging, begins early, and continues throughout the lifespan. Such education should:
  - recognize the special place that sexuality has in our lives;
  - stress the value and benefits of remaining abstinent until involved in a committed, enduring, and mutually monogamous relationship; but
  - assure awareness of optimal protection from sexually transmitted diseases and unintended pregnancy, for those who are sexually active, while also stressing that there are no infallible methods of protection, except abstinence, and that condoms cannot protect against some forms of STDs.
- Recognize that sexuality education can be provided in a number of venues—homes, schools, churches, other community settings—but must always be developmentally and culturally appropriate.
- Recognize that parents are the child's first educators and should help guide other sexuality education efforts so that they are consistent with their values and beliefs.
- Recognize, also, that families differ in their level of knowledge, as well as their emotional capability to discuss sexuality issues. In moving toward equity of access to information for promoting sexual health and responsible sexual behavior, school sexuality education is a vital component of community responsibility.

2. Providing the Health and Social Interventions Necessary to Promote and Enhance Sexual Health and Responsible Sexual Behavior

- Eliminate disparities in sexual health status that arise from social and economic disadvantage, diminished access to information and health care services, and stereotyping and discrimination.
- Target interventions to the most socioeconomically vulnerable communities where community members have less access to health education and services and are, thus, likely to suffer most from sexual health problems.
- Improve access to sexual health and reproductive health care services for all persons in all communities.
- Provide adequate training in sexual health to all professionals who deal with sexual issues in their work, encourage them to use this training, and ensure that they are reflective of the populations they serve.

- Encourage the implementation of health and social interventions to improve sexual health that have been adequately evaluated and shown to be effective.
- Ensure the availability of programs that promote both awareness and prevention of sexual abuse and coercion.
- Strengthen families, whatever their structure, by encouraging stable, committed, and enduring adult relationships, particularly marriage. Recognize, though, that there are times when the health interests of adults and children can be hurt within relationships with sexual health problems, and that sexual health problems within a family can be a concern in and of themselves.

3. Investing in Research Related to Sexual Health and Disseminating Findings Widely

- Promote basic research in human sexual development, sexual health, and reproductive health, as well as social and behavioral research on risk and protective factors for sexual health.
- Expand the research base to cover the entire human life span-children, adolescents, young adults, middle age adults, and the elderly.
- Research, develop, disseminate, and evaluate educational materials and guidelines for sexuality education, covering the full continuum of human sexual development, for use by parents, clergy, teachers, and other community leaders.
- Expand evaluation efforts for community, school and clinic based interventions that address sexual health and responsibility.

VII. Advancing a National Dialogue

The primary purpose of this *Surgeon General's Call to Action* is to initiate a mature national dialogue on issues of sexuality, sexual health, and responsible sexual behavior. As stated so eloquently in the Institute of Medicine report, *No Time to Lose:*

> "Society's reluctance to openly confront issues regarding sexuality results in a number of untoward effects. This social inhibition impedes the development and implementation of effective sexual health and HIV/STD education programs, and it stands in the way of communication between parents and children and between sex partners. It perpetuates misperceptions about individual risk and ignorance about the consequences of sexual activities and may encourage high-risk sexual practices. It also impacts the level of counseling training given to health care providers to assess sexual histories, as well as providers' comfort levels in conducting risk-behavior discussions with clients. In addition, the "code of silence" has resulted in missed opportunities to use the mass media (e.g., television, radio, printed media, and the Internet) to encourage healthy sexual behaviors."

The strategies set out above provide a point of reference for a national dialogue. How it will be implemented will be determined by individuals and families, communities, the media, and by government and non-government agencies, institutions, and foundations. We must all share in the responsibility for initiating this dialogue, working at every level of society to promote sexual health and responsible sexual behavior.

Individuals can begin the dialogue—adult with adult, adult with child—by developing their own personal knowledge, attitudes, and skills with respect to sexual health and responsible sexual behavior. Adults can communicate with other adults about their views on responsible sexual behavior, what it is, and how to promote it. Parents can educate their children about sexuality and responsibility, most importantly by being healthy and positive role models.

Communities must necessarily approach a dialogue on sexual health and responsible sexual behavior in different ways, according to their diverse composition and norms. But all must participate so that all voices are heard. This dialogue can be sponsored by local governments, businesses, churches, schools, youth-serving organizations and other community based organizations and should, at a minimum, include: emphasis on respect for diversity of perspective, opinion and values; assessment of community resources available for educating community members and delivering necessary services; attention to policies and programs that support and strengthen families; and assurance that systems are in place to promote equitable access and respect for all cultural, gender, age, and sexual orientation groups.

Media in all its forms can be engaged, by both public and private entities, in a national dialogue to promote sexual health and responsible sexual behavior. This dialogue should be a long-term effort and should treat sexuality issues responsibly, accurately, and positively. With respect to media programming, the portrayal of sexual relationships should be mature and honest, and responsible sexual behavior should be stressed. Finally, it is also important that young people, as well as adults, be educated to critically examine media messages.

Government, in partnership with foundations and other private organizations, can target support for the research, education, and services necessary to sustain a meaningful campaign to promote sexual health and responsible sexual behavior. Government should continue to develop objective and measurable indicators to monitor progress over time. It can also review policies and laws to ensure that they facilitate—rather than impede—the promotion of sexual health and responsible sexual behavior.

Conclusion

Based on the scientific evidence, we face a serious public health challenge regarding the sexual health of our nation. Doing nothing is unacceptable. More than anyone, it is our children who will suffer the consequences of our failure to meet these responsibilities.

Solutions are complex but we do have evidence that we can promote sexual health and responsible sexual behavior. Given the diversity of attitudes, beliefs, values and opinions, finding common ground might not be easy but it is attainable. We are more likely to find this common ground through a national dialogue with honest and respectful communication. We need to appreciate and respect the diversity of our culture and be informed by the science that is available to us.

This is a call to all of society to respond to this challenge. These efforts will not only have an impact on the current health status of our nation, but lay the groundwork for a healthier society for future generations.

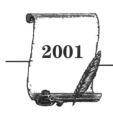

July

SURGICAL TEAM ON FIRST ARTIFICIAL HEART IMPLANT
July 4, 2001

Several important advances were made in 2001 in the effort to prevent and treat heart disease, the leading cause of death in the United States. About 500,000 Americans die each year from heart disease, and some 61 million Americans—nearly one out of every five—suffer from some sort of heart disease. Doctors fear that the rising incidence of diabetes and obesity, two of the main risk factors for heart problems, will push the number afflicted with heart disease even higher. (Report on obesity, p. 935)

Perhaps the development that drew the most public attention was the July 4, 2001, announcement that doctors had implanted a wholly internal artificial heart in a man whose rapidly failing heart had left him with only days to live. Although the recipient died at the end of November, he lived several months longer than his doctors had expected, and he recovered enough energy and mobility to be able to enjoy occasional outings from his hospital room in Louisville, Kentucky. The experimental artificial hearts were subsequently implanted in five more patients, three of whom were still alive at the end of the year, and the makers of the artificial heart hoped that at a minimum it might eventually be used to reduce the backlog of patients waiting to receive heart transplants.

Perhaps the development that should have drawn the most public attention was a new set of guidelines from the National Institutes of Health (NIH) recommending that doctors and their patients take an aggressive approach to lowering blood cholesterol and thus reduce the incidence of heart attacks. About 1 million Americans suffered heart attacks every year. The NIH recommendations would sharply increase not only the number of Americans who should follow a low-fat diet and get more exercise, but also the number of Americans who should be prescribed cholesterol-reducing drugs.

One of those drugs, cerivastatin, or Baycol, was voluntarily removed from the market by its maker, the German company Bayer AG, after thirty-one people died from complications related to severe muscle breakdown, a rare side-effect of the statin class of drugs. About 700,000 people took cerivastatin in the United States; about 12 million Americans took one of several statins on the market. Despite the side-effect, several studies were beginning to show that statins might have benefits that reached well beyond their cholesterol-lowering properties, including helping to prevent stroke and the development of diabetes and Alzheimer's. Some early laboratory studies also showed that statins might play a useful role in treating cancer.

Internal Artificial Heart

On July 2 a surgical team operating at Jewish Hospital in Louisville, Kentucky, removed the diseased portion of the patient's heart and attached an internal artificial pump, powered by electricity from an external battery flowing through the skin to electrodes also implanted in the patient. The AbioCor heart was grapefruit size, weighed a little more than a pound, and was made of titanium and plastic. Abiomed, Inc., in Danvers, Mass., had been working on the device for twenty years. The July 2 operation was the first of five that that the federal Food and Drug Administration had approved; the FDA subsequently gave Abiomed permission to implant ten more.

The patient, Robert Tools (whose identity was not revealed until August 21, when he first spoke with reporters), was on the verge of death when he asked to be considered for the experimental procedure. A diabetic and former heart attack patient, he met Abiomed's criteria for the operation: he was deemed to have less than thirty days to live, he was not eligible to receive a heart transplant, and he no longer responded to standard treatments for heart failure. His doctors said he could barely lift his head or talk to them when he entered the hospital.

Abiomed said its goals for the experiment were to double the patient's expected life span—from thirty to sixty days—and to make those final days reasonably comfortable. By that measure the device far exceeded expectations. Tools lived nearly five months before dying on November 30 of abdominal bleeding that the doctors said did not result from the artificial device, or from a stroke he had three weeks earlier, but from his body's inability to tolerate the anticoagulating drugs given to heart patients to help prevent blood clots. In the months before he died, Tools regained some of the weight and energy he had lost and was able to leave the hospital occasionally to go bass fishing or to a restaurant.

With Tools responding so much better than anticipated, Abiomed proceeded with five more implants before the end of the year. One patient, in Houston, died during surgery. A second, a seventy-four-year-old man in Los Angeles, died fifty-six days after receiving his implant. The three other patients were still alive at year's end.

The AbioCor artificial heart was much different than the first artificial heart, known as the Jarvik-7, which was implanted in a Seattle dentist, Barney Clark, in 1982. That artificial device received its power through a large external console attached to the patient by wires and tubes. Clark and the few other recipients of the artificial heart lived for varying lengths of time—the longest was 620 days—but the patients suffered from kidney failure, stroke, and other medical conditions that did little to improve their quality of life. The project was abandoned in the mid-1980s, and the AbioCor experiments were the first to be approved since then. The NIH funded much of the work on artificial hearts.

Abiomed officials said that the potential market for its AbioCor device might be as large as 100,000 patients, although others disputed that figure. Of the thousands of patients waiting for donor hearts, only 2,000 to 2,300 currently receive heart transplants each year.

Possibly Permanent Partial Pumps

Meanwhile, a team of doctors found that a mechanical pump that did not replace a failing heart, but simply helped it to pump, did a better job of prolonging life in heart failure patients than did the most potent drugs used to treat heart failure. The pumps, known as ventricular assist devices, or VADs, were often used to help stabilize people with advanced heart failure or other severe cardiac problems while they awaited heart transplants. When some patients, unable to get heart transplants, remained on the pumps for as many as four years, doctors began to look at the devices as possible permanent implants. The study, released at a meeting of the American Heart Association on November 12, indicated that such permanent installations of the pump might have significant beneficial results.

According to Dr. Eric A. Rose, the head of the team and chairman of the department of surgery at Columbia University College of Physicians and Surgeons, the risk of death was 48 percent lower for patients who received a VAD than for those taking drug therapies. The survival rate for patients with the pumps was 52 percent after one year and 23 percent after two years, compared with 25 percent and 8 percent, respectively, for patients on drugs. Moreover, the people using pumps were more likely to feel better, be more active, and feel less depressed than patients receiving drugs. On the negative side, complications from the pumps, such as infection, bleeding, and mechanical malfunction, were more than twice as likely to occur as complications from the drug therapy. Rose said the complication rate was expected to fall as modifications were made to the pumps.

If approved for permanent use, VADs could help ease the serious shortage of hearts available for transplant and perhaps even eliminate the need for transplants in some cases. The pumps also might eventually be useful in sustaining damaged hearts while they regenerated new cells to replace the damaged ones—something scientists had thought was impossible until recently. Two separate experiments reported in March showed that bone marrow cells injected into rodents that had suffered heart attacks showed clear signs of rejuvenating damaged tissue. In one experiment, human bone marrow cells injected into rats spurred the growth of new blood vessels in the heart and suppressed the growth of scar tissue caused by the heart attack. In the other experiment, mouse bone marrow cells were injected into the hearts of mice, where they appeared to turn into heart muscle cells.

The findings were spurring cautious hope that medical science was on the verge of a major breakthrough in treating heart attack victims. The reports were also likely to feed the controversial debate on stem cell research. The primitive cells found in embryos and fetuses that develop into many different types of cells have been looked upon as a potential source of replacement tissues and organs for the human body. While adults produce some stem cells, but until these and other recent studies, these cells were thought to be less versatile than those derived from embryos. (Stem cell debate, p. 539)

New Cholesterol Guidelines

In a new effort to prevent heart disease, the NIH issued revised guidelines May 15 recommending aggressive treatments to reduce cholesterol to safe levels, including nearly tripling the number of people taking cholesterol-reducing drugs. High levels of cholesterol could result in fat-clogged arteries, leading to increased risk of heart attacks and other forms of heart disease. The last guidelines, issued in 1993, were much more cautious in recommending drug treatment for high cholesterol levels.

Under the new guidelines, the desirable levels of total blood cholesterol remained at 200 milligrams, while the safe level for low-density lipoprotein (LDL)—or "bad" cholesterol—remained at 130 milligrams or less. The desirable level of high-density lipoprotein (HDL)—or "good" cholesterol—was raised to 40 milligrams, and the guidelines offered a new formula for determining a person's risk of having a heart attack within the next ten years. Risk factors included age, smoking status, and blood pressure, as well as a person's cholesterol levels.

The guidelines recommended that people with a 20 percent or greater chance of having a heart attack be treated as if they had already had a heart attack and be given cholesterol-lowering drugs. For the first time, diabetics were considered to be at the same risk for heart disease as people who had already had a heart attack. The expert panel that drafted the new guidelines said that, under its recommendations, about 36 million Americans were candidates for the cholesterol-reducing drugs, compared with 13 percent under the old guidelines. About 65 million Americans who did not fall into the high-risk category, but still had elevated cholesterol, would benefit from a low-fat diet and greater exercise, the report said, and some of them might also be candidates for the cholesterol-lowering drugs.

"We can now say with certainty that lowering a high blood cholesterol level, specifically high LDL, or bad cholesterol, dramatically reduces a person's risk for coronary heart disease," said Claude Lenfant, director of the National Heart, Lung, and Blood Institute, the unit at NIH that oversaw the development of the guidelines. If Americans and their doctors would take the guidelines seriously, Lenfant said, heart disease would "no longer be the No.1 killer."

> *Following are excerpts from a news briefing given at Jewish Hospital of Louisville, Kentucky, on July 4, 2001, by the surgical team that implanted the first wholly internal artificial heart in a human patient.*

The document was not available on the Internet at the time of publication.

Linda McGinity Jackson: Good morning. I am Linda McGinity Jackson, Vice President of Jewish Hospital, Louisville, Kentucky and welcome to the Rudd Heart and Lung Center. We are pleased you are here today. Those of you who are in the audience and those that are tuning in via satellite, we are broadcasting around the world. . . .

Today is the 4th of July, a celebration of history for our country, and it is a day of celebration for medical science. As people around the world recognize our country's history, we are here to recognize history as well in the medical field. . . .

Now I am going to introduce two people that . . . have made medical history. Dr. Laman Gray is Professor of Surgery and Director of the Division of Thoracic and Cardiovascular Surgery at the University of Louisville School of Medicine and he is Co-Principal Investigator for the Jewish Hospital University of Louisville Abiocor Research Team. Dr. Robert Dowling is an Associate Professor of Surgery at the University of Louisville and also Co-Principal Investigator for the Jewish Hospital University of Louisville Abiocor Research Team. . . .

Dr. Laman Gray: . . . I will start with a little background. . . . Our experience started about 3½ years ago with Abiomed, and actually we had been working with them 10 or 15 years earlier on other devices. But we began working in the animal lab with the device and helping them as they modified the device and changed it and perfected it, and that has taken almost two years, and then actually the last year of this has been really the perfected device where we have been working through and helping them test all of the components and the completed system.

So the animal studies were done in detail and the information obtained from the animal studies was then submitted to the FDA along with what we call Reliability Studies . . . that looked at the durability of the device and having both of these put together plus extensive protocols and everything, the FDA then gave us permission to go ahead now with five initial implants and then after that, it will be reviewed. It is actually reviewed on a case-by-case basis, but we will then plan to expand the study to more centers and also more patients in the future.

Now, we did do the implant on Monday, as everybody is aware. I will tell you a little about the conditions and who we are looking for. The patients that are eligible to go into the study have to have end-stage heart disease. They have to have basically no other options. They cannot be transplant candidates and they have to basically have a life expectancy of less than 30 days with any conventional therapy. So the group we are using for this . . . obviously are the sickest of the sick patients and their chances of survival with conventional therapy is very limited. We have some very sophisticated algorithms that we use to help determine this and we can statistically, through parameters, help determine what their probability is of survival or non-survival, before we put it in.

So the patient has to meet this criteria, if they have an 80 percent chance of dying within 30 days with conventional therapy. The second thing that we look at is the setting of the device and we take . . . a CAT scan of the chest or chest x-ray, and basically put it into a type of CAD program and then by computer we extract the negative heart and then put in the Abiocor and are able to turn it around and look at all angles to make sure it will fit properly. So, once those two things meet the criteria, then obviously we discuss this with the patient and the family. We try to do this very honestly. We give them all options and go over everything in detail with them.

I mentioned that we are very concerned about the ethics and the morality of doing this, so every patient that will be entered into this study has a patient advocate. A patient advocate is somebody who is unrelated to Abiomed, unrelated to the University of Louisville, Jewish Hospital and is a totally independent person who is available to advise the patient and the family of anything they want. It is their helper. It is a person that will help if the family wants it, to guide them through the process in what needs to be done. Following that, and the decision is made to do this, which was done sort of over the weekend, we then are able to proceed.

The patient and family have asked not to release information on them and we will honor that and I hope that everybody will respect their wishes. What we can say about them, as I think most people understand, it is a gentleman at this time, he is in his late to mid-50s. He was turned down at a transplant center—not in this area—and had no other option. When he came to see us and we evaluated him, he was extremely sick; what we call a Class IV patient. We admitted him to the hospital and actually it wound up that he had, at the time he came in, he was so sick, we had to put an intra-aortic balloon pump in to help support his pressure and in addition, he was on three drugs to help him maintain his pressure, so he was in as dire shape as you could ever have anybody in.

In addition, he had chronic pre-existing renal failure with an acute exacerbation because he had gotten sicker recently, the week or so before he had come in and his creatinine level when he came in was in the three range, which means he had moderately severe end stage, not end stage, but renal problems.

For the technical people, with all of the therapy and maximum support, we get his creatinine down some but we never got it under about 2.2. In addition, he has diabetes and he had severe, severe bi-ventricular failure. By that, I mean, consider the heart as two hearts, it is a right and a left side, both the right and the left side were severely failing and the feeling was that he would not be a very good candidate because of the right ventricular failure and some high blood pressure in the lung circuit for a left ventricular assist device.

The operation was then performed on Monday morning. Oh, I want to mention one other thing, I forgot, he had previous coronary bypass surgery and the reason for the cardiomyopathy was he had multiple heart attacks in the past and he had bypass surgery in 1992 or something around there. So it was an ischemic cardiomyopathy. We then began the implant. Rob, why don't you would go through the technical aspects of the implant.

Dr. Robert Dowling: . . . So, the first thing we had to do was, for those medically oriented, because he had previous surgery, we had to prepare to go on cardiopulmonary bypass in an emergency situation so we did that, exposing the arteries in the groin and the vein in the groin. That is routine for a lot of patients who have had previous surgery. And, before we even opened the breast bone, we have to make plans not only for putting in a thoracic unit, which is the heart per se, but also the other units that are needed to power this device.

So the first thing we did was we implanted a TED coil, and that is a coil that receives energy from the outside world and powers the device. So we put that in for a lot of technical reasons that you can ask about later if you are interested. We then went and just did a standard, just like we would do for any open heart surgery procedure and because of the previous surgery there was a lot of scar tissue and it was a very difficult operation that was made much more difficult by the previous surgery and the extent of the scar tissue in this particular patient.

But, once we opened up and took down all of the adhesions, which is our name for the scar tissue, we put the patient on the heart/lung machine and our first really big step is to excise the heart, I shouldn't say excise the heart, we don't excise the heart entirely, we excise the right and left ventricles. We have to leave enough of the heart in place so that the old heart, the native heart, for us to sew the new heart to. So we left intact the entire native right atrium and native left atrium and also the blood vessels that go to those bodies, the aorta and the blood vessels that go along the pulmonary artery, we have to leave those intact to hook up to the new heart. . . .

Now, once we have that and that probably took us a couple three hours to get to that point, we have to sew what is called atrial cuffs to the native right atrial remnant and an atrial cuff to the native left atrial remnant and once we do that, we put a plastic model of the artificial heart in so we know how to design, tailor and bevel these grafts that go the aorta and pulmonary artery. Once we have the anatomy figured out for the particular person, we cut those grafts to the appropriate length and then sew them to the aorta and pulmonary artery as is depicted here. So, we do the left atrium followed by the right atrium, followed by the pulmonary artery and followed by the aorta.

So, that is a lot of sewing and a fair amount of operative time. Everything has to be perfectly precise. We place hundreds and hundreds of stitches, any one of which could bleed, so they all have to be perfect if we want to have a good outcome. Once we have all of those in place and we are as sure as we can be that there is not going to be bleeding from any of these anastomoses, where the native tissue is sewn to this part of the artificial heart, we put the artificial heart in place, and these are just "quick connects" and snap on very quickly, thus the name "quick connects," so it is just a matter of minutes and once we have all of this set up we bring the artificial heart up into the field, hook it into the "quick connects" and proceed.

Our next big step is to get all of the, from a technical kind of surgical/ medical point of view, is to get all of the air out of the device and this was one of the things that we were impressed about for this particular operation, it went very smoothly and very quickly. It was significantly easier than had been in the research lab to de-air the device. Once we had the device de-aired— I should stop and say that before we put the artificial heart in we put the other components. . . . One of them is a battery, one is a controller.

Now probably all of you, if you don't remember, at least you have seen pictures of the old artificial heart where the controllers were bigger than the podium and so forth. The controller, like all other electronics, has recently been miniaturized and can literally fit in the palm of your hand. So before we implanted the total artificial heart itself, the thoracic unit, we implanted a battery and a controller then we implanted the total heart, made sure it was working well and took the patient from the heart/lung machine onto the total artificial heart in probably a matter of less than two minutes.

So, the rest of the operation was just ensuring that we positioned it correctly in the chest. There was not a single flaw in terms of the mechanics and the transmission of information from the heart to the controller or the controller to the heart or another, probably the most sophisticated engineering, or at least one of the most sophisticated engineering aspects of the device, is that our right and left heart never beat the same at the same time, so this device has been exquisitely designed to accommodate for changes between the right and left side of the heart that occur when you breathe, when you strain, when you move and that is an extremely sophisticated part of this device and that worked also flawlessly. . . .

Dr. Gray: I will give you some facts and I may reminisce a little if I can. Since the surgery, the patient has done I would say well. As a matter [of] fact, I will say that he has done much better than Rob or I would have ever anticipated or expected considering how sick he was preoperatively, and he continues to do so.

Now, I say this with some caveats. Currently, to give you some ideas, he is totally neurologically normal. His blood pressure, etc., is normal. His kidney function this morning is, his creatinine was at 2.6 or 2.8, anyhow, remember he came in with creatinine of 3. So his kidney function has not gotten any worse and we are in the process today of weaning him off the ventilator and hopefully will get him extubated this afternoon, the tube out of his windpipe. So, we are extremely pleased with his progress.

Now, once I say that, let's get reality in here. This is an experimental procedure and everybody realizes it is and there are lots of problems and complications that can occur. And, this is a beginning. This is the first step in a long group of steps that we have to do to develop this device. I can't even predict what the complications could be in the future that we have to deal with and I am sure we will have them. It sort of goes back to the heart transplants. When we do a heart transplant, everybody is happy and elated because everything usually goes very well but then in about a week, they start to reject and when they start to reject, you know, the families get a little upset about it, the patient gets upset about it and this is sort of reality.

So what I am saying is that although everything has gone, to date, absolutely perfectly, I think that we can expect that we will have some complications. Now what they are I don't know. What I can tell you is that as of today, we are doing so well it is just unbelievable, to be honest. But again, this is an experimental procedure and we have to be very careful about how we project out what can happen from just a couple of days.

I think that it is extremely encouraging what we have seen so far and I think it has tremendous potential for huge success and I personally anticipate that we will do very well, but I put the caution sign up that we don't know yet. There are a lot of unknowns, there are a lot of hurdles to pass in the future. I will sort of reminisce for a second. The most thrilling thing that happened to me, and everybody has sort of moments that you think about, but when we put the device in and we were just in the process of closing, we switched over to the internal battery power to test everything and I must admit that at that time it was pretty awesome to think that we had a patient living on a device totally internally powered with no external energy or anything going into it and it is amazing. It truly is.

Since I am reminiscing, I want to talk a little bit about my philosophies about the ethics of this. Rob and I and the entire Abiomed staff and Jewish Hospital and the University have all been very concerned about the ethics about what we are doing and we want to make sure we are doing it right and make sure we are doing it honestly and I am sure that we can be and will be criticized in the future for some problems that will occur. But we are trying to do it right and I guess that is the reason we have taken such extreme efforts to have a patient advocate. Not only are we going through the IRB, but we have gone through ethics committees to make sure we are trying to do it right.

I'll mention one thing, a problem that can come up and I put it right out. Rob and I have no financial contact or anything with Abiomed. Neither one of us own one piece of stock, they have never paid either one of us one penny since we have been involved in the project. We have received nothing from them nor any promises or anything and I think that is important. I have no connection with Abiomed other than I think it is a good project and I am committed to the project. I guess I would be willing to answer any questions.

Dr. Dowling: One thing when we were deciding whether to give this information or wait for someone to ask, because it is a frequently asked question, and the question is who can potentially benefit from this device. Maybe not all of you know, but congestive heart failure has a very high incidence, very prevalent in our society. There are over 5 million Americans with congestive heart failure and there are anywhere from one half to three quarters of a million cases of heart failure new each year. That is a very large number. On average, there are one quarter of a million deaths from chronic congestive heart failure annually.

We have discussed this back and forth about how many hundreds of thousands of people that this could potentially benefit and the arguments are whether we are talking about benefiting 100,000 per year or 150,000 per year. So we are talking about a very large number of patients. If you look at patients that are candidates for transplantation, the number of transplants performed in this country has peaked at 2,500, so 2,500 patients get a heart transplant per year. At any one time, there are approximately twice that many people on the waiting list. . . .

And if you are looking at the numbers of people that die from congestive heart failure that could benefit from a heart but, for some reason or another, are not a transplant candidate, the number is clearly a very large number. So, probably in this country alone, potentially 100,000 people or more could benefit from some type of cardiac replacement therapy. . . .

REGULATIONS TO PROTECT MEDICAL RECORD PRIVACY
July 6, 2001

*President George W. Bush surprised privacy advocates when he an-
nounced April 12, 2001, that federal privacy standards governing patient
medical records written by the Clinton administration would take affect on
April 14, as scheduled. The announcement was considered a defeat for the
health care industry, which had lobbied heavily against the standards when
they were being drawn up and had hoped to convince the new Republican
administration to overturn them. Bush softened the blow by promising to
"clarify" some of the standards that the industry found most egregious. In
guidelines issued July 6, the Bush administration set forth an initial interpretation of the standards and what the health care industry did and
did not have to do to come into compliance. Hospitals would not have to
soundproof walls to ensure patient confidentiality, for example, and a relative or friend could pick up a prescription that a doctor had phoned into a
pharmacy.*

*The decision to go ahead with the standards while holding open the door
for later revisions averted criticism of the sort the Bush administration had
already encountered when it announced that it was reversing or watering
down several other Clinton policies. Among these were ergonomics rules to
reduce repetitive-motion injuries in the workplace, arsenic levels in drinking water, and reductions in carbon dioxide emissions that contributed to
global warming.* (Global warming, p. 109; Arsenic levels, p. 212)

*The first comprehensive federal standard covering medical privacy ever
promulgated, the medical privacy rules required health care providers to obtain advance written consent from patients before disclosing information
in their medical records to other parties, on paper, electronically, or orally.
The rule applied to doctors, hospitals, health insurers, pharmacies, and most
other institutions that had access to patient medical records. Patients would
have to give specific authorization, on a case-by-case basis, for "nonroutine"
disclosures, such as the release of medical information to employers, banks,
or companies that sold medical products and services. Most health care*

organizations were required to be in compliance with the rules as of April 14, 2003.

Advocates of medical privacy had pushed for the regulations on two grounds. In general, they said, the need for privacy had grown with the widespread computerization of medical records, which allowed records to be shared almost instantly without a patient's consent. Privacy advocates also said that some unknown number of people were forgoing treatment or withholding information from their doctors because they feared that employers, banks, insurers, and others would discover their medical problems, such as alcohol or drug abuse. (Privacy regulations, Historic Documents of 2000, p. 1063)

Representatives of the health care industry said they agreed with the need to protect patient privacy, but they complained that the federal regulations would be administratively burdensome and costly to implement. One insurer estimated that the regulations would cost the industry $40 billion over five years. The Clinton administration had estimated the cost at about $18 billion over ten years.

The Clinton Administration Regulations

The public debate over medical record privacy went into high gear in 1996 when Congress passed the Health Insurance Portability and Accountability Act (PL 194–191), which made it easier for Americans to keep their health insurance when they changed jobs. Little noticed by the public at the time were two provisions dealing with medical records. One required the health care industry to maintain medical records in a uniform electronic format to ease the sharing of information among doctors, hospitals, and insurers. To protect the confidentiality of the records, the law stipulated that if Congress did not develop privacy standards within three years, by August 21, 1999, the task would be turned over to the executive branch.

The Republican-controlled Congress missed its three-year deadline, and in November 1999 the Clinton administration used its authority under the 1996 law to propose regulations preventing the unauthorized disclosure of most, but not all, medical records. During the next year, the Department of Health and Human Services (HHS) said it received more than 50,000 comments on the proposed regulations.

The final version of the regulations, issued December 20, 2000, just a month before President Bill Clinton was scheduled to leave the White House, was substantially stronger than had been proposed just a year earlier. The original version had applied only to records in electronic format, but the final rules covered all types of medical records, including paper files and oral communications. The original rule had applied only to nonroutine disclosures, but the final rule required advance written consent for routine disclosures as well.

The health care industry immediately said the final rules went too far and began lobbying the incoming Bush administration to drop them or at the least delay their implementation. The industry complained that the tougher rules were unrealistic and unworkable. "It does not make sense to apply these prohibitions to oral communications," Melinda R. Hatton, vice president of the American Hospital Association told the New York Times. *"That goes way overboard. There will be many unintended consequences. Doctors could be inhibited from talking to one another, to nurses and even to patients in places where other people might be present." Others were concerned about the requirement that only the minimum amount of information necessary be disclosed to achieve a specific outcome, saying such a restriction would compromise quality of care by stifling a free flow of information among health care professionals.*

Pharmacy chains warned that the new rules would create chaos for customers. "Under the rules, a pharmacy could not even begin filling a prescription unless it had a signed, written consent from the patient," said Carlos Ortiz, director of governmental affairs for the CVS Corporation. "That requirement would increase waiting times and inconvenience patients." Pharmacists also said the new rules might prohibit them from allowing a friend or relative to pick up a prescription for a sick person and even prevent them from giving advice to customers about over-the-counter medications.

On February 26 HHS secretary Tommy G. Thompson announced that he was delaying implementation of the rules until April 14. The delay ostensibly was to give Congress sixty days to review the final rules, as required under the 1996 laws. In what a former Clinton official said was an "unintended oversight," the Clinton administration had failed to submit the rules to Congress. During the sixty days, Thompson said, HHS would invite public comment on the final rules with an eye to revising some of them. Thompson said the Bush administration was "absolutely committed" to protecting medical privacy, but he wanted to ensure that "they will work as intended throughout the complex field of health care, without creating unanticipated consequences that might harm patients, access to care or the quality of care."

Privacy advocates regarded the delay as a "bad sign," in the words of Janlori Goldman, director of the Health Privacy Project at Georgetown University. "The reopening of the comment period is unjustified and appears to signal an attempt to weaken and roll back privacy protections. . . . People have been waiting years for these rules." The American Civil Liberties Union and the American Psychoanalytic Association threatened to sue the government if it delayed the rules past April 14, saying that the administration could not ignore Congress's mandate that privacy rules be promulgated.

Common Sense Guidelines

Many consumer groups were thus surprised by Bush's April 12 announcement to proceed with the new privacy rules. But they warned that the devil was in the details and that the administration might still undercut the privacy protections when it issued its clarification of the rules. In an interview with the Washington Post, *HHS secretary Thompson indicated that he was not expecting to make "wholesale changes" in the rules. The clarification, he said was "more a way to simplify and reduce some of the onerous financial burden and include a degree of common sense."*

Issued July 6, the clarification went through the privacy rules section by section, posing questions and then answering them. For example: "Can a patient have a friend or family member pick up a prescription for her? Yes. A pharmacist may use professional judgment and experience with common practice to make reasonable inferences of the patient's best interest in allowing a person, other than a patient, to pick up a prescription." On other frequent complaints, the clarification said the rules did not prohibit common practices, such as maintaining medical charts at patients' bedsides or calling out patients" names in doctors' offices, or preclude doctors, nurses, and others from sharing information necessary to treat a patient.

The guidance made clear that doctors, hospitals, and other providers were allowed to market their own products and services to patients but were not allowed to sell or otherwise disclose medical information to third parties, such as pharmaceutical companies for marketing purposes. An obstetrician, for example, could not sell the names of pregnant women to makers of baby formula. But providers could recommend specific brand-name drugs to patients and give them free product samples.

The clarifications all had to be formally modified through a process that allowed public comment. The administration made clear that nothing in its July 6 statement precluded it from proposing modifications at a future time. One controversial revision the administration said it was considering was whether to guarantee parents access to the medical records of their minor children, as many conservative groups had requested. Child advocates and many health professionals supported confidentiality laws for minors, however, arguing that teenagers would not seek treatment for mental health disorders, substance abuse, or contraception, including abortion, if they knew their parents would be notified. Thompson had indicated earlier that the administration supported changing the privacy rules to give parents access, but the July 6 guidance said only that Thompson was "reassessing these provisions of the regulation."

Privacy advocates as well as many health care organizations praised the clarifications. "We're pleased with the guidance issued today," said Joy L. Pitts of the Health Privacy Project. "It addresses misstatements and hyperbole that some in the health care industry were spreading in recent weeks." Hatton of the American Hospital Association said her group was "very encouraged" that the Bush administration had taken steps to address some of their "most pressing concerns." But some in the health care industry said the clarification had not gone far enough. "This is a first step," said Mary R. Grealy, president of the Health Care Leadership Council, a group of about fifty large health care companies. "Further changes are necessary."

> *Following are excerpts from "Standards for Privacy of Individually Identifiable Health Information," issued by the Department of Health and Human Services on July 6, 2001, clarifying and*

interpreting the new regulations on protecting medical record privacy that went into effect April 14, 2001.

The document was obtained from the Internet at http:// www.hhs.gov/ocr/hipaa/finalmaster.html.

General Overview

The following is an overview that provides answers to general questions regarding the regulation entitled, *Standards for Privacy of Individually Identifiable Health Information* (the Privacy Rule), promulgated by the Department of Health and Human Services (HHS), and process for modifications to that rule. Detailed guidance on specific requirements in the regulation is presented in subsequent sections, each of which addresses a different standard.

The Privacy Rule provides the first comprehensive federal protection for the privacy of health information. All segments of the health care industry have expressed their support for the objective of enhanced patient privacy in the health care system. At the same time, HHS and most parties agree that privacy protections must not interfere with a patient's access to or the quality of health care delivery.

The guidance provided in this section and those that follow is meant to communicate as clearly as possible the privacy policies contained in the rule. Each section has a short summary of a particular standard in the Privacy Rule, followed by "Frequently Asked Questions" about that provision. In some cases, the guidance identifies areas of the Privacy Rule where a modification or change to the rule is necessary. These areas are summarized below in response to the question "What changes might you make to the final rule?" and discussed in more detail in the subsequent sections of this guidance. We emphasize that this guidance document is only the first of several technical assistance materials that we will issue to provide clarification and help covered entities implement the rule. We anticipate that there will be many questions that will arise on an ongoing basis which we will need to answer in future guidance. In addition, the Department will issue proposed modifications as necessary in one or more rulemakings to ensure that patients' privacy needs are appropriately met. The Department plans to work expeditiously to address these additional questions and propose modifications as necessary. . . .

Frequently Asked Questions . . .

Q: Do you expect to make any changes to this rule before the compliance date?

A: We can and will issue proposed modifications to correct any unintended negative effects of the Privacy Rule on health care quality or on access to such care.

In February 2001, Secretary [of Health and Human Services Tommy G.]

Thompson requested public comments on the final rule to help HHS assess the rule's real-world impact in health care delivery. During the 30-day comment period, we received more than 11,000 letters or comments—including some petitions with thousands of names. These comments are helping to guide the Department's efforts to clarify areas of the rule to eliminate uncertainties and to help covered entities begin their implementation efforts.

Q: What changes might you make in the final rule?

A: We continue to review the input received during the recent public comment period to determine what changes are appropriate to ensure that the rule protects patient privacy as intended without harming consumers' access to care or the quality of that care.

Examples of standards in the Privacy Rule for which we will propose changes are:

- *Phoned-in Prescriptions*—A change will permit pharmacists to fill prescriptions phoned in by a patient's doctor before obtaining the patient's written consent (see the "Consent" section of this guidance for more discussion).
- *Referral Appointments*—A change will permit direct treatment providers receiving a first time patient referral to schedule appointments, surgery, or other procedures before obtaining the patient's signed consent (see the "Consent" section of this guidance for more discussion).
- *Allowable Communications*—A change will increase the confidence of covered entities that they are free to engage in whatever communications are required for quick, effective, high quality health care, including routine oral communications with family members, treatment discussions with staff involved in coordination of patient care, and using patient names to locate them in waiting areas (see the "Oral Communications" section of this guidance for more discussion).
- *Minimum Necessary Scope*—A change will increase covered entities' confidence that certain common practices, such as use of sign-up sheets and X-ray lightboards, and maintenance of patient medical charts at bedside, are not prohibited under the rule (see the "Minimum Necessary" section of this guidance for more discussion).

In addition, HHS may reevaluate the Privacy Rule to ensure that parents have appropriate access to information about the health and well-being of their children. This issue is discussed further in the "Parents and Minors" section of this guidance.

Other changes to the Privacy Rule also may be considered as appropriate.

Q: How will you make any changes?

A: Any changes to the final rule must be made in accordance with the Administrative Procedures Act (APA). HHS intends to comply with the APA by publishing its rule changes in the *Federal Register* through a Notice of Proposed Rulemaking and will invite comment from the public. After reviewing and addressing those comments, HHS will issue a final rule to implement appropriate modifications.

Congress specifically authorized HHS to make appropriate modifications in the first year after the final rule took effect in order to ensure the rule could be properly implemented in the real world. We are working as quickly as we can to identify where modifications are needed and what corrections need to be made so as to give covered entities as much time as possible to implement the rule. Covered entities can and should begin the process of implementing the privacy standards in order to meet their compliance dates.

CONSENT

Background

The Privacy Rule establishes a federal requirement that most doctors, hospitals, or other health care providers obtain a patient's written consent before using or disclosing the patient's personal health information to carry out treatment, payment, or health care operations (TPO). Today, many health care providers, for professional or ethical reasons, routinely obtain a patient's consent for disclosure of information to insurance companies or for other purposes. The Privacy Rule builds on these practices by establishing a uniform standard for certain health care providers to obtain their patients' consent for uses and disclosures of health information about the patient to carry out TPO.

General Provisions

- Patient consent is required before a covered health care provider that has a direct treatment relationship with the patient may use or disclose protected health information (PHI) for purposes of TPO. Exceptions to this standard are shown in the next bullet.
- Uses and disclosures for TPO may be permitted without prior consent in an emergency, when a provider is required by law to treat the individual, or when there are substantial communication barriers.
- Health care providers that have indirect treatment relationships with patients (such as laboratories that only interact with physicians and not patients), health plans, and health care clearinghouses may use and disclose PHI for purposes of TPO without obtaining a patient's consent. The rule permits such entities to obtain consent, if they choose.
- If a patient refuses to consent to the use or disclosure of their PHI to carry out TPO, the health care provider may refuse to treat the patient.
- A patient's written consent need only be obtained by a provider one time.
- The consent document may be brief and may be written in general terms. It must be written in plain language, inform the individual that information may be used and disclosed for TPO, state the patient's rights to review the provider's privacy notice, to request restrictions and to revoke consent, and be dated and signed by the individual (or his or her representative).

Individual Rights

- An individual may revoke consent in writing, except to the extent that the covered entity has taken action in reliance on the consent.
- An individual may request restrictions on uses or disclosures of health information for TPO. The covered entity need not agree to the restriction requested, but is bound by any restriction to which it agrees.
- An individual must be given a notice of the covered entity's privacy practices and may review that notice prior to signing a consent.

Administrative Issues

- A covered entity must retain the signed consent for 6 years from the date it was last in effect. The Privacy Rule does not dictate the form in which these consents are to be retained by the covered entity.
- Certain integrated covered entities may obtain one joint consent for multiple entities.
- If a covered entity obtains consent and also receives an authorization to disclose PHI for TPO, the covered entity may disclose information only in accordance with the more restrictive document, unless the covered entity resolves the conflict with the individual.
- Transition provisions allow providers to rely on consents received prior to April 14, 2003 (the compliance date of the Privacy Rule for most covered entities), for uses and disclosures of health information obtained prior to that date.

Frequently Asked Questions

Q. Are health plans or clearinghouses required to obtain an individual's consent to use or disclose PHI to carry out TPO?

A: No. Health plans and clearinghouses may use and disclose PHI for these purposes without obtaining consent. These entities are permitted to obtain consent. If they choose to seek individual consent for these uses and disclosures, the consent must meet the standards, requirements, and implementation specifications for consents set forth under the rule.

Q: Can a pharmacist use PHI to fill a prescription that was telephoned in by a patient's physician if the patient is a new patient to the pharmacy and has not yet provided written consent to the pharmacy?

A: The Privacy Rule, as written, does not permit this activity without prior patient consent. It poses a problem for first-time users of a particular pharmacy or pharmacy chain. The Department of Health and Human Services did not intend the rule to interfere with a pharmacist's normal activities in this way. The Secretary is aware of this problem, and will propose modifications to fix it to ensure ready patient access to high quality health care.

Q: Can direct treatment providers, such as a specialist or hospital, to whom a patient is referred for the first time, use PHI to set up appointments or schedule surgery or other procedures before obtaining the patient's written consent?

A: As in the pharmacist example above, the Privacy Rule, as written, does not permit uses of PHI prior to obtaining the patient's written consent for TPO. This unintended problem potentially exists in any circumstance when a patient's first contact with a direct treatment provider is not in person. As noted above, the Secretary is aware of this problem and will propose modifications to fix it.

Q: Will the consent requirement restrict the ability of providers to consult with other providers about a patient's condition?

A: No. A provider with a direct treatment relationship with a patient would have to have initially obtained consent to use that patient's health information for treatment purposes. Consulting with another health care provider about the patient's case falls within the definition of "treatment" and, therefore, is permissible. If the provider being consulted does not otherwise have a direct treatment relationship with the patient, that provider does not need to obtain the patient's consent to engage in the consultation.

Q: Does a pharmacist have to obtain a consent under the Privacy Rule in order to provide advice about over-the-counter medicines to customers?

A: No. A pharmacist may provide advice about over-the-counter medicines without obtaining the customers' prior consent, provided that the pharmacist does not create or keep a record of any PHI. In this case, the only interaction or disclosure of information is a conversation between the pharmacist and the customer. The pharmacist may disclose PHI about the customer to the customer without obtaining his or her consent (§ 164.502(a)(1)(i)), but may not otherwise use or disclose that information.

Q: Can a patient have a friend or family member pick up a prescription for her?

A: Yes. A pharmacist may use professional judgment and experience with common practice to make reasonable inferences of the patient's best interest in allowing a person, other than the patient, to pick up a prescription (see § 164.510(b)). For example, the fact that a relative or friend arrives at a pharmacy and asks to pick up a specific prescription for an individual effectively verifies that he or she is involved in the individual's care, and the rule allows the pharmacist to give the filled prescription to the relative or friend. The individual does not need to provide the pharmacist with the names of such persons in advance. . .

MINIMUM NECESSARY

General Requirement

The Privacy Rule generally requires covered entities to take reasonable steps to limit the use or disclosure of, and requests for protected health information (PHI) to the minimum necessary to accomplish the intended purpose. . .

Treatment Settings

We understand that medical information must be conveyed freely and quickly in treatment settings, and thus understand the heightened concern that covered entities have about how the minimum necessary standard applies in such settings. Therefore, we are taking the following steps to clarify the application of the minimum necessary standard in treatment settings. First, we clarify some of the issues here, including the application of minimum necessary to specific practices, so that covered entities may begin implementation of the Privacy Rule. Second, we will propose corresponding changes to the regulation text, to increase the confidence of covered entities that they are free to engage in whatever communications are required for quick, effective, high quality health care. We understand that issues of this importance need to be addressed directly and clearly to eliminate any ambiguities.

Frequently Asked Questions

Q: How are covered entities expected to determine what is the minimum necessary information that can be used, disclosed, or requested for a particular purpose?

A: The Privacy Rule requires a covered entity to make reasonable efforts to limit use, disclosure of, and requests for PHI to the minimum necessary to accomplish the intended purpose. To allow covered entities the flexibility to address their unique circumstances, the rule requires covered entities to make their own assessment of what PHI is reasonably necessary for a particular purpose, given the characteristics of their business and workforce, and to implement policies and procedures accordingly. This is not a strict standard and covered entities need not limit information uses or disclosures to those that are absolutely needed to serve the purpose. Rather, this is a reasonableness standard that calls for an approach consistent with the best practices and guidelines already used by many providers today to limit the unnecessary sharing of medical information.

The minimum necessary standard is intended to make covered entities evaluate their practices and enhance protections as needed to prevent unnecessary or inappropriate access to PHI. It is intended to reflect and be consistent with, not override, professional judgment and standards. Therefore, we expect that covered entities will utilize the input of prudent professionals involved in health care activities when developing policies and procedures that appropriately will limit access to personal health information without sacrificing the quality of health care.

Q: Won't the minimum necessary restrictions impede the delivery of quality health care by preventing or hindering necessary exchanges of patient medical information among health care providers involved in treatment?

A: No. Disclosures for treatment purposes (including requests for disclosures) between health care providers are explicitly exempted from the minimum necessary requirements.

The Privacy Rule provides the covered entity with substantial discretion as to how to implement the minimum necessary standard, and appropriately and reasonably limit access to the use of identifiable health information within the covered entity. The rule recognizes that the covered entity is in the best position to know and determine who in its workforce needs access to personal health information to perform their jobs. Therefore, the covered entity can develop role-based access policies that allow its health care providers and other employees, as appropriate, access to patient information, including entire medical records, for treatment purposes. . . .

Q: In limiting access, are covered entities required to completely restructure existing workflow systems, including redesigns of office space and upgrades of computer systems, in order to comply with the minimum necessary requirements?

A: No. The basic standard for minimum necessary uses requires that covered entities make reasonable efforts to limit access to PHI to those in the workforce that need access based on their roles in the covered entity.

The Department generally does not consider facility redesigns as necessary to meet the reasonableness standard for minimum necessary uses. However, covered entities may need to make certain adjustments to their facilities to minimize access, such as isolating and locking file cabinets or records rooms, or providing additional security, such as passwords, on computers maintaining personal information.

Covered entities should also take into account their ability to configure their record systems to allow access to only certain fields, and the practicality of organizing systems to allow this capacity. For example, it may not be reasonable for a small, solo practitioner who has largely a paper-based records system to limit access of employees with certain functions to only limited fields in a patient record, while other employees have access to the complete record. Alternatively, a hospital with an electronic patient record system may reasonably implement such controls, and therefore, may choose to limit access in this manner to comply with the rule.

Q: Do the minimum necessary requirements prohibit covered entities from maintaining patient medical charts at bedside, require that covered entities shred empty prescription vials, or require that X-ray light boards be isolated?

A: No. The minimum necessary standards do not require that covered entities take any of these specific measures. Covered entities must, in accordance with other provisions of the Privacy Rule, take reasonable precautions to prevent inadvertent or unnecessary disclosures. For example, while the Privacy Rule does not require that X-ray boards be totally isolated from all other functions, it does require covered entities to take reasonable precautions to protect X-rays from being accessible to the public. We understand that these and similar matters are of special concern to many covered entities, and we will propose modifications to the rule to increase covered entities' confidence that these practices are not prohibited.

Q: Will doctors' and physicians' offices be allowed to continue using sign-in sheets in waiting rooms?

A: We did not intend to prohibit the use of sign-in sheets, but understand that the Privacy Rule is ambiguous about this common practice. We, therefore, intend to propose modifications to the rule to clarify that this and similar practices are permissible.

Q: What happens when a covered entity believes that a request is seeking more than the minimum necessary PHI?

A: In such a situation, the Privacy Rule requires a covered entity to limit the disclosure to the minimum necessary as determined by the disclosing entity. Where the rule permits covered entities to rely on the judgment of the person requesting the information, and if such reliance is reasonable despite the covered entity's concerns, the covered entity may make the disclosure as requested.

Nothing in the Privacy Rule prevents a covered entity from discussing its concerns with the person making the request, and negotiating an information exchange that meets the needs of both parties. Such discussions occur today and may continue after the compliance date of the Privacy Rule.

ORAL COMMUNICATIONS

Background

The Privacy Rule applies to individually identifiable health information in all forms, electronic, written, oral, and any other. Coverage of oral (spoken) information ensures that information retains protections when discussed or read aloud from a computer screen or a written document. If oral communications were not covered, any health information could be disclosed to any person, so long as the disclosure was spoken.

Providers and health plans understand the sensitivity of oral information. For example, many hospitals already have confidentiality policies and concrete procedures for addressing privacy, such as posting signs in elevators that remind employees to protect patient confidentiality.

We also understand that oral communications must occur freely and quickly in treatment settings, and thus understand the heightened concern that covered entities have about how the rule applies. Therefore, we are taking a two-step approach to clarifying the regulation with respect to these communications. First, we provide some clarification of these issues here, so that covered entities may begin implementing the rule by the compliance date. Second, we will propose appropriate changes to the regulation text to clarify the regulatory basis for the policies discussed below in order to minimize confusion and to increase the confidence of covered entities that they are free to engage in communications as required for quick, effective, and high quality health care. We understand that issues of this importance need to be addressed directly and clearly in the Privacy Rule and that any ambiguities need to be eliminated. . . .

Frequently Asked Questions

Q: If health care providers engage in confidential conversations with other providers or with patients, have they violated the rule if there is a possibility that they could be overheard?

A: The Privacy Rule is not intended to prohibit providers from talking to each other and to their patients. Provisions of this rule requiring covered entities to implement reasonable safeguards that reflect their particular circumstances and exempting treatment disclosures from certain requirements are intended to ensure that providers' primary consideration is the appropriate treatment of their patients. We also understand that overheard communications are unavoidable. For example, in a busy emergency room, it may be necessary for providers to speak loudly in order to ensure appropriate treatment. The Privacy Rule is not intended to prevent this appropriate behavior. We would consider the following practices to be permissible, if reasonable precautions are taken to minimize the chance of inadvertent disclosures to others who may be nearby (such as using lowered voices, talking apart):

- Health care staff may orally coordinate services at hospital nursing stations.
- Nurses or other health care professionals may discuss a patient's condition over the phone with the patient, a provider, or a family member.
- A health care professional may discuss lab test results with a patient or other provider in a joint treatment area.
- Health care professionals may discuss a patient's condition during training rounds in an academic or training institution.

We will propose regulatory language to reinforce and clarify that these and similar oral communications (such as calling out patient names in a waiting room) are permissible.

Q: Does the Privacy Rule require hospitals and doctors' offices to be retrofitted, to provide private rooms, and soundproof walls to avoid any possibility that a conversation is overheard?

A: No, the Privacy Rule does not require these types of structural changes be made to facilities.

Covered entities must have in place appropriate administrative, technical, and physical safeguards to protect the privacy of PHI. "Reasonable safeguards" mean that covered entities must make reasonable efforts to prevent uses and disclosures not permitted by the rule. The Department does not consider facility restructuring to be a requirement under this standard. In determining what is reasonable, the Department will take into account the concerns of covered entities regarding potential effects on patient care and financial burden.

For example, the Privacy Rule does not require the following types of structural or systems changes:

- Private rooms.
- Soundproofing of rooms.

- Encryption of wireless or other emergency medical radio communications which can be intercepted by scanners.
- Encryption of telephone systems.

Covered entities must provide reasonable safeguards to avoid prohibited disclosures. The rule does not require that all risk be eliminated to satisfy this standard. Covered entities must review their own practices and determine what steps are reasonable to safeguard their patient information.

Examples of the types of adjustments or modifications to facilities or systems that may constitute reasonable safeguards are:

- Pharmacies could ask waiting customers to stand a few feet back from a counter used for patient counseling.
- Providers could add curtains or screens to areas where oral communications often occur between doctors and patients or among professionals treating the patient.
- In an area where multiple patient-staff communications routinely occur, use of cubicles, dividers, shields, or similar barriers may constitute a reasonable safeguard. For example, a large clinic intake area may reasonably use cubicles or shield-type dividers, rather than separate rooms.
- In assessing what is "reasonable," covered entities may consider the viewpoint of prudent professionals. . . .

PARENTS AND MINORS

General Requirements

. . . Because a parent usually has authority to make health care decisions about his or her minor child, a parent is generally a "personal representative" of his or her minor child under the Privacy Rule and has the right to obtain access to health information about his or her minor child. This would also be true in the case of a guardian or other person acting in loco parentis of a minor.

There are exceptions in which a parent might not be the "personal representative" with respect to certain health information about a minor child. In the following situations, the Privacy Rule defers to determinations under other law that the parent does not control the minor's health care decisions and, thus, does not control the PHI related to that care.

- When state or other law does not require consent of a parent or other person before a minor can obtain a particular health care service, and the minor consents to the health care service, the parent is not the minor's personal representative under the Privacy Rule. For example, when a state law provides an adolescent the right to consent to mental health treatment without the consent of his or her parent, and the adolescent obtains such treatment without the consent of the parent, the parent is not the personal representative under the Privacy Rule for that treatment. The minor may choose to involve a parent in these health care decisions without giving up his or her right to control the related health information. Of course, the minor may always have the parent continue to be his or her personal representative even in these situations.

- When a court determines or other law authorizes someone other than the parent to make treatment decisions for a minor, the parent is not the personal representative of the minor for the relevant services. For example, courts may grant authority to make health care decisions for the minor to an adult other than the parent, to the minor, or the court may make the decision(s) itself. In order to not undermine these court decisions, the parent is not the personal representative under the Privacy Rule in these circumstances.

In the following situations, the Privacy Rule reflects current professional practice in determining that the parent is not the minor's personal representative with respect to the relevant PHI:

- When a parent agrees to a confidential relationship between the minor and the physician, the parent does not have access to the health information related to that conversation or relationship. For example, if a physician asks the parent of a 16-year old if the physician can talk with the child confidentially about a medical condition and the parent agrees, the parent would not control the PHI that was discussed during that confidential conference.
- When a physician (or other covered entity) reasonably believes in his or her professional judgment that the child has been or may be subjected to abuse or neglect, or that treating the parent as the child's personal representative could endanger the child, the physician may choose not to treat the parent as the personal representative of the child.

Relation to State Law

In addition to the provisions (described above) tying the right to control information to the right to control treatment, the Privacy Rule also states that it does not preempt state laws that specifically address disclosure of health information about a minor to a parent (§ 160.202). This is true whether the state law authorizes or prohibits such disclosure. Thus, if a physician believes that disclosure of information about a minor would endanger that minor, but a state law requires disclosure to a parent, the physician may comply with the state law without violating the Privacy Rule. Similarly, a provider may comply with a state law that requires disclosure to a parent and would not have to accommodate a request for confidential communications that would be contrary to state law.

Frequently Asked Questions

Q: Does the Privacy Rule allow parents the right to see their children's medical records?

A: The Privacy Rule generally allows parents, as their minor children's personal representatives, to have access to information about the health and well-being of their children when state or other underlying law allows parents to make treatment decisions for the child. There are two exceptions: (1) when the parent agrees that the minor and the health care provider may have a confidential relationship, the provider is allowed to withhold information from the parent to the extent of that agreement; and (2) when the provider reasonably believes in his or her professional judgment that the child has been or may be subjected to abuse or neglect, or that treating the parent as the child's personal representative could endanger the child, the provider is permitted not to treat the parent as the child's personal representative with respect to health information.

Secretary Thompson has stated that he is reassessing these provisions of the regulation.

Q: Does the Privacy Rule provide rights for children to be treated without parental consent?

A: No. The Privacy Rule does not address consent to treatment, nor does it preempt or change state or other laws that address consent to treatment. The Rule addresses access to health information, not the underlying treatment. . . .

HEALTH-RELATED COMMUNICATIONS AND MARKETING . . .

What Is Marketing

The Privacy Rule defines "marketing" as "a communication about a product or service a purpose of which is to encourage recipients of the communication to purchase or use the product or service." To make this definition easier for covered entities to understand and comply with, we specified what "marketing" is not, as well as generally defined what it is. As questions arise about what activities are "marketing" under the Privacy Rule, we will provide additional clarification regarding such activities.

Communications That Are Not Marketing

The Privacy Rule carves out activities that are not considered marketing under this definition. In recommending treatments or describing available services, health care providers and health plans are advising us to purchase goods and services. To prevent any interference with essential treatment or similar health-related communications with a patient, the rule identifies the following activities as not subject to the marketing provision, even if the activity otherwise meets the definition of marketing. (Written communications for which the covered entity is compensated by a third party are not carved out of the marketing definition.)

Thus, a covered entity is not "marketing" when it:

- Describes the participating providers or plans in a network. For example, a health plan is not marketing when it tells its enrollees about which doctors and hospitals are preferred providers, which are included in its network, or which providers offer a particular service. Similarly, a health insurer notifying enrollees of a new pharmacy that has begun to accept its drug coverage is not engaging in marketing.

- Describes the services offered by a provider or the benefits covered by a health plan. For example, informing a plan enrollee about drug formulary coverage is not marketing.

Furthermore, it is not marketing for a covered entity to use an individual's PHI to tailor a health-related communication to that individual, when the communication is:

- Part of a provider's treatment of the patient and for the purpose of furthering that treatment. For example, recommendations of specific brand-name or over-the-counter pharmaceuticals or referrals of patients to other providers are not marketing.
- Made in the course of managing the individual's treatment or recommending alternative treatment. For example, reminder notices for appointments, annual exams, or prescription refills are not marketing. Similarly, informing an individual who is a smoker about an effective smoking-cessation program is not marketing, even if that program is offered by someone other than the provider or plan making the recommendation.

Limitations on Marketing Communications

If a communication is marketing, a covered entity may use or disclose PHI to create or make the communication, pursuant to any applicable consent . . . only in the following circumstances:

- It is a face-to-face communication with the individual. For example, sample products may be provided to a patient during an office visit.
- It involves products or services of nominal value. For example, a provider can distribute pens, toothbrushes, or key chains with the name of the covered entity or a health care product manufacturer on it.
- It concerns the health-related products and services of the covered entity or a third party, and only if the communication:
  —Identifies the covered entity that is making the communication. Thus, consumers will know the source of these marketing calls or materials.
  —States that the covered entity is being compensated for making the communication, when that is so.
  —Tells individuals how to opt out of further marketing communications, with some exceptions as provided in the rule. The covered entity must make reasonable efforts to honor requests to opt-out.
  —Explains why individuals with specific conditions or characteristics (e.g., diabetics, smokers) have been targeted, if that is so, and how the product or service relates to the health of the individual. The covered entity must also have made a determination that the product or service may be of benefit to individuals with that condition or characteristic.

For all other communications that are "marketing" under the Privacy Rule, the covered entity must obtain the individual's authorization to use or disclose PHI to create or make the marketing communication.

Business Associates

Disclosure of PHI for marketing purposes is limited to disclosure to business associates that undertake marketing activities on behalf of the covered entity. No other disclosure for marketing is permitted. Covered entities may not give away or sell lists of patients or enrollees without obtaining authorization from each person on the list. As with any disclosure to a business associate, the covered entity must obtain the business associate's agreement to use the PHI only for the covered entity's marketing activities. A covered entity may not give PHI to a business associate for the business associate's own purposes.

Frequently Asked Questions

Q: Does this rule expand the ability of providers, plans, marketers and others to use my PHI to market goods and services to me? Does the Privacy Rule make it easier for health care businesses to engage in door-to-door sales and marketing efforts?

A: No. The provisions described above impose limits on the use or disclosure of PHI for marketing that do not exist in most states today. For example, the rule requires patients' authorization for the following types of uses or disclosures of PHI for marketing:

- Selling PHI to third parties for their use and re-use. Under the rule, a hospital or other provider may not sell names of pregnant women to baby formula manufacturers or magazines.
- Disclosing PHI to outsiders for the outsiders' independent marketing use. Under the rule, doctors may not provide patient lists to pharmaceutical companies for those companies' drug promotions.

These activities can occur today with no authorization from the individual. In addition, for the marketing activities that are allowed by the rule without authorization from the individual, the Privacy Rule requires covered entities to offer individuals the ability to opt-out of further marketing communications.

Similarly, under the business associate provisions of the rule, a covered entity may not give PHI to a telemarketer, door-to-door salesperson, or other marketer it has hired unless that marketer has agreed by contract to use the information only for marketing on behalf of the covered entity. Today, there may be no restrictions on how marketers re-use information they obtain from health plans and providers.

Q: Can telemarketers gain access to PHI and call individuals to sell goods and services?

A: Under the rule, unless the covered entity obtains the individual's authorization, it may only give health information to a telemarketer that it has hired to undertake marketing on its behalf. The telemarketer must be a business associate under the rule, which means that it must agree by contract to use the information only for marketing on behalf of the covered entity, and not to market its own goods or services (or those of another third party). The caller must identify the covered entity that is sponsoring the marketing call. The caller must provide individuals the opportunity to opt-out of further marketing.

Q: When is an authorization required from the patient before a provider or health plan engages in marketing to that individual?

A: An authorization for use or disclosure of PHI for marketing is always required, unless one of the following three exceptions apply:

- The marketing occurs during an in-person meeting with the patient (e.g., during a medical appointment).
- The marketing concerns products or services of nominal value.
- The covered entity is marketing health-related products and services (of either the covered entity or a third party), the marketing identifies the covered entity that is responsible for the marketing, and the individual is offered an opportunity to opt-out of further marketing. In addition, the marketing must tell people if they have been targeted based on their health status, and must also tell people when the covered entity is compensated (directly or indirectly) for making the communication. . . .

PROPOSAL FOR ECONOMIC DEVELOPMENT IN AFRICA
July 11, 2001

African leaders adopted ambitious plans during 2001 to transform their troubled continent by ending wars, adopting democracy, and promoting economic development with limited—but important—financial help from the industrialized world. The leaders started by scrapping the Organization of African Unity (OAU), a regional debating society often derided as a "trade union for dictators," and replacing it with an African Union modeled after the European Union (EU).

As the cornerstone of their plan to lift Africa out of poverty, the leaders on July 11, 2001, endorsed a plan called the "New African Initiative," which linked economic development to the necessity of ending the continent's numerous civil and cross-border wars. In essence, the plan called for a deal between African leaders and the industrialized world: African leaders promised to stop fighting and to establish responsible governments in exchange for increased economic backing from wealthy nations in the form of debt relief, free trade, private investment, and development aid.

The plan received at least rhetorical support from the leaders of the industrialized countries whose financial backing would be needed to make it a success. U.S. president George W. Bush, British prime minister Tony Blair, leaders of the Group of Seven industrialized countries, and the EU all endorsed the plan. Belgian prime minister Guy Verhofstadt, who held the EU presidency in 2001, praised the plan as being "based on ideas from Africa itself," rather than on prescriptions imposed by the industrialized world. It was far from clear, however, whether wealthy nations were ready to back their words of praise with financial resources.

The obstacles that African leaders faced in carrying out the plan were illustrated in two of the countries where they held summit meetings during the year. When the leaders first endorsed the plan in July, they met in Lusaka, the capital of Zambia, where political turmoil arose early in the year over a failed attempt by democratically elected president Joseph Chiluba to amend the constitution so that he could run for another term. In October the leaders met in Abuja, Nigeria, where democratically elected President

Olusegun Obasanjo was battling independence movements and civil conflicts stemming from disputes between Muslims and non-Muslims and among various ethnic groups. Moreover, Zimbabwe's rapid descent into civil strife was posing a major test of the new commitment by African leaders to demand adherence to democratic values in each of their countries.

Assessing the OAU

The Organization of African Unity was founded in 1963, just after most of the continent gained its independence in a rush of decolonialization by Britain, France, and other European powers. Headquartered in Addis Ababa, Ethiopia, the OAU was seen by Africa's new leaders as a mutual support group to help them meet the challenges of running their own countries after a century of domination by outsiders interested more in exploiting the continent's natural resources than in promoting the welfare of its people.

After nearly four decades in existence, however, the OAU could point to few significant accomplishments aside from maintaining a small staff that conducted studies on economic development and other issues. The OAU was often seen as a club of African leaders that issued promising declarations but rarely carried them out. According to most observers, the OAU had little connection with or meaning for ordinary people. One of its central tenets was "noninterference" in the internal affairs of member countries, which in practice meant turning a blind eye to the deeds of dictators, many of whom sat in the councils of the OAU leadership. For many critics, the OAU's low point came in the late 1970s when the chairmanship went to Ugandan dictator Idi Amin, whose brutal suppression of opponents was the continent's worst postindependence abuse of human rights until the 1994 genocide in Rwanda.

Although not citing the OAU directly, United Nations Secretary General Kofi Annan (himself a Ghanian) in 1998 lambasted Africa's leaders for neglecting the needs of their own people while blaming all the continent's woes on the legacy of colonialism. Annan returned to that theme July 9 in an address to the opening session of the final OAU summit in Lusaka. Annan congratulated African leaders on the vision of the new union but warned that they faced "immense" obstacles, some dating from the colonial era and others created by the "political and economic mismanagement" of Africans themselves. "This historic effort will require leadership, courage, and a willingness to depart from the ways of the past, if it is to do for Africa what the European Union has done for Europe," Annan told the leaders. Most important among the "ways of the past" that needed to be discarded, Annan said, was the resort to war to settle disputes over borders, ethnic and tribal claims, and access to natural resources. Unless the region's conflicts ended, he said, "no amount of aid or trade, assistance or advice, will make the difference" that leaders sought. Noting that some conflicts were winding down in 2001, but that others still raged in Africa, Annan bluntly told the leaders: "Bringing these conflicts to an end requires that we acknowledge two central truths: that they imperil the peace of all of Africa, and that they are in great measure the result of misguided leadership which is unwilling or unable to put the people's interest first." (Annan report on Africa's problems, Historic Documents of 1998, p. 220)

African Union Proposal

The idea of a union of African nations was nearly a half-century old, dating from the independence movements of the 1950s. The leading exponent at that time was Kwame Nkrumah, who led Ghana to independence in 1957 and promoted "pan-Africanism" as an alternative to colonialism. Nkrumah's dreams of a united Africa went nowhere, however, as the continent's new leaders focused on the problems of their individual countries.

In the 1990s a new pan-Africa visionary emerged in the form of Libyan leader Muammar al-Qaddafi, who called on his fellow leaders to emulate the European Union, which was then putting in place key elements of a continentwide economic and political system, including a common currency, the euro. Qaddafi used his own country's oil wealth to finance the meetings, studies, and reports that led to a treaty creating the African Union out of the shell of the old OAU. Qaddafi's central role in creating the African Union was a major source of controversy, both within Africa and internationally, and fostered concerns that he saw the African Union as a platform for his own ambitions of regional leadership. His radical anti-Western stance had long alienated the United States and its key allies; as an Arab, his promotion of Islam was not always popular among sub-Saharan leaders whose countries were increasingly torn by disputes between Islamic and non-Islamic populations.

By the time the treaty went into effect May 25, forty of the fifty-three African nations had ratified it. All but three had ratified it by the time of the summit meeting in Abuja, Nigeria, in October. Leaders selected Amara Essy, the foreign minister of the Ivory Coast, as the first secretary general of the African Union. He succeeded Salim Ahmed Salim, who had been secretary general of the OAU.

May 25 initiated a year-long transition period during which the OAU was to give way to the African Union. But even as that period began, many of the specifics of what the union would do and how it would operate remained unclear. In addition to an administrative staff inherited from the OAU, the union was to have at least two institutions: an assembly of heads of state and an executive council composed of government ministers. Other institutions that were planned—but far from reality as of 2001—included a central bank, a common currency, and a court of justice. The African Union treaty also suggested a popularly elected African parliament, but no action toward that goal was taken during the rest of the year. Overall, leaders described the union as a democratic institution, but Ahmed Rajab, editor of the London-based Africa Analysis *journal wrote that "it is difficult to see how the union could be democratic if its constituent member-states are not."*

Along with the African Union, the region's leaders on July 11 adopted the "New African Initiative," a compromise between separate proposals made by South African president Thabo Mbeki and Senegal's president, Abdoulaye Wade. The initiative was a complex document loaded with proposals for economic development, political reform, and conflict resolution.

At the core of the initiative was a call by African leaders for each of their countries to adopt democracy and free markets and to eliminate the causes of ethnic, racial, and religious conflict. These central propositions stood in sharp contrast to the theories embraced by many of the region's leaders during the independence era, when democracy was deemed a luxury reserved for wealthy countries and when socialist economic policies promised a ready cure for the continent's poverty. In contrast to many previous reports and proposals offered by African leaders, the initiative acknowledged that colonialism was not the sole cause of the continent's problems and that misguided economic policies and "poor governance" had contributed to "Africa's peripheral and diminishing role in the world economy."

The initiative offered dozens of proposals for specific actions by African nations and by donor nations and organizations, including the United States and the World Bank. Some ideas had a narrow focus, such as reducing the waiting time at shipping ports, while others called for broad reforms and major programs, such as promoting exports and establishing reliable health services. The initiative called on the industrialized nations to provide increased development aid to Africa, but it also placed the burden on African countries to ensure that additional aid was used to benefit broad populations, not just the elites of society.

Mbeki and Wade suggested four priorities: programs to combat communicable diseases such as HIV/AIDS, malaria, and tuberculosis; development of information and communications technology industries and capabilities; "debt reduction," which meant the increased forgiveness of development loans from international banks and industrialized countries during the previous four decades; and access to the markets of industrialized countries. The question of market access prompted one of the few harsh criticisms of Western countries in the document. Noting the "crucial" need for African nations to be able to export agricultural and manufactured products to the industrialized countries, the document said: "The most flagrant cause of injustice lies in the fact that Europe and the United States amply subsidize their agriculture but they do not allow Africa to do likewise to protect its own commodities and its own markets or to impose a compensatory tariff. If an African county is protected by either mechanism, it is threatened with suspension for all aid programs."

In addition to economic development, a key element of the African Initiative endorsed by the leaders on July 11 was a call for an Africa-based peacekeeping force to stabilize conflict situations. In the past, Africa's wars were ended with the help either of regional peacekeeping forces or by international forces assembled by the United Nations. An example of the former was the West African peacekeeping force, led by Nigeria, that halted fighting among political factions in Liberia during the early 1990s. The UN had mounted numerous peacekeeping missions in Africa since the 1960s, some successful (such as one in Namibia) and others failures (such as one in Angola).

Recognizing that the United States and other wealthy countries were increasingly reluctant to send troops to end Africa's wars, the region's leaders agreed that Africa should assume the principal peacekeeping responsibility. Some critics suggested that this proposal was beyond reach, however. "When conflict erupts, it is only the international community and the developed world that has the capacity to respond," said Jakkie Childers, director of the Institute for Security Studies in South Africa.

Growing Crisis in Zimbabwe

Even as the African leaders proclaimed the lofty goals of democracy, economic development, and peace, a mounting political crisis in Zimbabwe demonstrated the continent's difficulty in confronting the "ways of the past" that Annan warned against. Two developments in Zimbabwe raised international concerns. The first was an apparent decision by President Robert Mugabe to allow army veterans and other groups to attack white-owned businesses in an attempt to eliminate all vestiges of what had once been the country's ruling power structure. As a British colony and later as an independent country, Zimbabwe (then known as Rhodesia) was controlled by a tiny minority of whites; even after the black majority took over the government in 1980, whites continued to own most of the country's farmland and many of its businesses. During 2001 black squatters (many of them claiming to be veterans) invaded dozens of white farms, and Mugabe's government responded by legalizing the takeovers without compensation to the owners. This brought Zimbabwe into direct confrontation with the British government, which had promised to subsidize land reform but objected to Mugabe's use of squatters and violence to drive white farmers from their lands. A related issue was Mugabe's evident determination to use whatever tactics were necessary to win a presidential election scheduled for March 2002. Despite government intimidation, opposition parties had nearly won a majority in legislative elections in 2000, signaling broad public dissatisfaction with Mugabe's increasingly autocratic rule. Mugabe made it clear in 2001 that he was determined to thwart the opposition again in the presidential election, by curtailing what remained of an independent news media in the country, limiting news coverage by the foreign media, and using violence against opposition forces if necessary.

Mugabe's fellow African leaders gave a mixed response to the developments in Zimbabwe. Prior to the July summit in Lusaka, the continent's foreign ministers drafted a resolution essentially supporting Mugabe and denouncing outside "interference"—a reference to British pressure against the forced takeover of white farms. But in their July 11 session, the heads of state took a milder stance, calling instead on Zimbabwe and Britain to seek a joint solution to the conflict over white farms. Later in the year, Mbeki and other leaders in southern Africa took a tougher stance, telling Mugabe both privately and publicly that rising turmoil in his country could threaten stability in the entire region.

Following are excerpts from the "New African Initiative," a proposal for economic development, political reform, and conflict resolution, adopted by African heads of state at a summit meeting in Lusaka, Zambia, on July 11, 2001.

The document was obtained from the Internet at http:// www.dfa.gov.za/events/afrinit.htm.

I. Introduction

1. This new African initiative is a pledge by African leaders, based on a common vision and a firm and shared conviction, that they have a pressing duty to eradicate poverty and to place their countries, both individually and collectively, on a path of sustainable growth and development, and at the same time to participate actively in the world economy and body politic. The Program is anchored on the determination of Africans to extricate themselves and the continent from the malaise of underdevelopment and exclusion in a globalizing world.

2. The poverty and backwardness of Africa stand in stark contrast to the prosperity of the developed world. The continued marginalization of Africa from the globalization process and the social exclusion of the vast majority of its peoples constitute a serious threat to global stability.

3. Since the 1970s, and their accession to the institutions of the international community, the credit and aid binomial has underlined the logic of African development. Credit has led to the debt deadlock, which, from instalments to rescheduling, still exists and hinders the growth of African countries. The limits of this option have been reached. Concerning the other element of the binomial—aid—we can also note the reduction of private 1970s objectives.

4. In Africa, 340 million people, or half the population, live on less than US $1 per day. The mortality rate of children under 5 years of age is 140 per 1000, and life expectancy at birth is only 54 years. Only 58 per cent of the population have access to safe water. The rate of illiteracy for people over 15 is 41 per cent. There are only 18 mainline telephones per 1000 people in Africa, compared with 146 for the world as a whole and 567 for high-income countries.

5. The initiative calls for the reversal of this abnormal situation by changing the relationship that underpins it. Africans are appealing neither for the further entrenchment of dependency through aid, nor for marginal concessions.

6. We are convinced that an historic opportunity presents itself to end the scourge of underdevelopment that afflicts Africa. The resources, including capital, technology and human skills, that are required to launch a global war on poverty and underdevelopment exist in abundance, and are within our grasp. What is required to mobilize these resources and to use them properly, is bold and imaginative leadership that is genuinely committed to a sustained

effort of human upliftment and poverty eradication, as well as a new global partnership based on shared responsibility and mutual interest.

7. Across the continent, Africans declare that we will no longer allow ourselves to be conditioned by circumstance. We will determine our own destiny and call on the rest of the world to complement our efforts. There are already signs of progress and hope. Democratic regimes that are committed to the protection of human rights, people-centred development and market-oriented economies are on the increase. African peoples have begun to demonstrate their refusal to accept poor economic and political leadership. These developments are, however, uneven and inadequate and need to be further expedited.

8. The African initiative is about consolidating and accelerating these gains. It is a call for a new relationship of partnership between Africa and the international community, especially the highly industrialized countries, to overcome the development chasm that has widened over centuries of unequal relations. . . .

[II omitted]

III. The New Political Will of African Leaders

42. The African initiative recognizes that there have been attempts in the past to set out continent-wide development programs. For a variety of reasons, both internal and external, including questionable leadership and ownership by Africans themselves, these have been less than successful. However, there is today a new set of circumstances, which lend themselves to integrated practical implementation.

43. The new phase of globalization coincided with the reshaping of international relations in the aftermath of the Cold War. This is associated with the emergence of new concepts of security and self-interest, which encompass the right to development and the eradication of poverty. Democracy and state legitimacy have been redefined to include accountable government, a culture of human rights and popular participation as central elements.

44. Significantly, the numbers of democratically elected leaders are on the increase. Through their actions, they have declared that the hopes of Africa's peoples for a better life can no longer rest on the magnanimity of others.

45. Across the continent, democracy is spreading, backed by the African Union (AU), which has shown a new resolve to deal with conflicts and censure deviation from the norm. These efforts are reinforced by voices in civil society, including associations of women, youth and the independent media. In addition, African governments are much more resolute about regional and continental goals of economic cooperation and integration. This serves both to consolidate the economic turnaround and to reinforce the advantages of mutual interdependence. . . .

47. The African initiative centers around African ownership and management.

Through this program, African leaders are setting an agenda for the renewal of the continent. The agenda is based on national and regional priorities and development plans that must be prepared through participative processes involving the people. We believe that while our African leaders derive their mandates from these plans, it is their role to articulate them as well as lead the processes of implementation on behalf of the people.

The program is a new framework of interaction with the rest of the world, including the industrialized countries and multilateral organisations. It is based on the agenda set by African peoples through their own initiatives and of their own volition, to shape their own destiny.

To achieve these objectives, African leaders will take joint responsibility for the following:

- To strengthen mechanisms for conflict prevention, management and resolution at the regional and continental levels, and to ensure that these mechanisms are used to restore and maintain peace;
- To promote and protect democracy and human rights in their respective countries and regions, by developing clear standards of accountability, transparency and participative governance at the national and subnational levels;
- To restore and maintain macroeconomic stability, especially by developing appropriate standards and targets for fiscal and monetary policies, and introducing appropriate institutional frameworks to achieve these standards;
- To institute transparent legal and regulatory frameworks for financial markets and auditing of private companies and the public sector;
- To revitalize and extend the provision of education, technical training and health services, with high priority given to tackling HIV/AIDS, malaria and other communicable diseases;
- To promote the role of women in social and economic development by reinforcing their capacity in the domains of education and training; by the development of revenue-generating activities through facilitating access to credit; and by assuring their participation in the political and economic life of African countries;
- To build the capacity of the states in Africa to set and enforce the legal framework, as well as maintain law and order;
- To promote the development of infrastructure, agriculture and its diversification into agro-industries and manufacturing to serve both domestic and export markets. . . .

IV. The Strategy for Achieving Sustainable Development in the 21st Century . . .

53. Key Themes

A. Preconditions for Development

53.1 Promotion of peace, democracy, human rights and sound economic management.

African leaders have learnt from their own experiences that peace, security, democracy, good governance, human rights and sound economic management are conditions for sustainable development. They are making a pledge to work, both individually and collectively, to promote these principles in their countries, regions and the continent. . . .

V. Programme of Action

54. The action plan is presented under eight themes, structured in the same way as the strategy outlined. It covers what needs to be done immediately and what has to be done to initiate medium- and long-term interventions.

A. Preconditions for Development

54.1 The Peace, Security and Political Governance Initiatives
(i) Peace and Security Initiative
The Peace and Security Initiative consists of three elements:

- Promoting long-term conditions for development and security;
- Building the capacity of African institutions for early warning, as well as enhancing African institutions' capacity to prevent, manage and resolve conflict;
- Institutionalizing commitment to the core values of the African initiative through the leadership. . . .

Efforts to build Africa's capacity to manage all aspects of conflict focus on the means necessary to strengthen existing continental and regional institutions, especially in four key areas:

- Prevention, management and resolution of conflict;
- Peacemaking, peacekeeping and peace enforcement;
- Post-conflict reconciliation, rehabilitation and reconstruction;
- Combating the illicit proliferation of small arms, light weapons and landmines.

The African initiative leadership will consider, within six months of its establishment, setting out detailed and costed measures required in each of the four areas above. The exercise will also include actions required of partners, and the nature and sources of financing such activities.

The envisaged Heads of State Forum will serve as a platform for the African initiative leadership to seek to enhance the capacity of African mechanisms to promote peace and security on the continent, to share experience and to mobilize collective action. The Forum will ensure that the principles and commitments implicit in the initiative are abided by. . . .

VI. A New Global Partnership

55. Africa recognizes the centuries-old historical injustice and the need to correct it. The central injunction of the new partnership is, however, for combined efforts to improve the quality of life of Africa's people as rapidly as possible. In this, there are shared responsibilities and mutual benefits between Africa and her partners.

56. The global technological revolution needs an expanding base of resources, a widening sphere of markets, new frontiers of scientific endeavour,

the collective capacity of human wisdom, and a well-managed ecological system. We are aware that much of Africa's mineral and other material resources are critical inputs into production processes in developed countries.

57. In addition to its indispensable resource base, Africa offers a vast and growing market for producers across the world. A developing Africa, with increased numbers of employed and skilled workers and a burgeoning middle class, would constitute an expanding market for world manufactured products, intermediate goods and services.

58. At the same time, Africa provides a great opportunity for investment. The African initiative creates opportunities for joint international efforts in the development of infrastructure, especially in ICT [information and communications technology] and transportation.

59. Africa also provides prospects for creative partnerships between the public and private sectors in beneficiation, agro-industries, tourism, human resource development and in tackling the challenges of urban renewal and rural development.

60. Furthermore, Africa's biodiversity—including its rich flora and fauna and the rain forests—is an important global resource combating the environmental degradation posed by the depletion of the ozone layer and climate change, as well as the pollution of air and water by industrial emissions and toxic effluents. . . .

64. The African initiative has, as one of its foundations, the expansion of democratic frontiers and the deepening of the culture of human rights. A democratic Africa will become one of the pillars of world democracy, human rights and tolerance. The resources of the world currently dedicated to resolving civil and interstate conflict could therefore be freed for more rewarding endeavours.

65. The converse of such an initiative, the collapse of more African states, poses a threat not only to Africans, but also to global peace and security. For industrialized countries, development in Africa will reduce the levels of global social exclusion and mitigate a major potential source of global social instability.

66. Africa is committed to the development and strengthening of South-South partnerships.

Establishing a new relationship with industrialized countries and multilateral organizations

67. A critical dimension of Africans taking responsibility for the continent's destiny is the need to negotiate a new relationship with the development partners. The manner in which development assistance is delivered in itself creates serious problems for developing countries. The need to negotiate and account separately to donors supporting the same sector or program is both cumbersome and inefficient. Also, the tying of development assistance generates further inefficiencies. The appeal is for a new relationship that takes the country program as a point of departure. The new relationship should set out mutually agreed performance targets and standards for both donor and

recipient. There are many cases that clearly show that the failure of projects is not caused only by the poor performance of recipients, but also by bad advice given by donors.

69. The African leaders envisage the following responsibilities and obligations of the developed countries and multilateral institutions:

- To support materially mechanisms for and processes of conflict prevention, management and resolution in Africa, as well as peacekeeping initiatives;
- To accelerate debt reduction for heavily indebted African countries, in conjunction with more effective poverty reduction programs, of which the Strategic Partnership with Africa and the PRSP {poverty reduction strategy paper] initiatives are an important starting point;
- To improve debt relief strategies for middle-income countries;
- To reverse the decline in ODA [official development assistance] flows to Africa and to meet the target level of ODA flows equivalent to 0.7 per cent of each developed country's gross national product (GNP) within an agreed short-term period. Increased aid flows will be used to complement funds released by debt reduction for accelerating the fight against poverty;
- To translate into concrete commitments the international strategies adopted in the fields of education and health;
- To facilitate the development of a partnership between countries, international pharmaceutical corporations and civil society organisations to urgently secure access to existing drugs for Africans suffering from infectious diseases;
- To admit goods into markets of the developed countries through bilateral initiatives, and to negotiate more equitable terms for African countries in the WTO multilateral framework;
- To work with African leaders to encourage investment in Africa by the private sector in developed countries, including the establishment of insurance mechanisms and financial instruments that will help lower risk premiums in Africa;
- To raise consumer protection standards for exports from developed countries to developing countries to the same levels applied in developed countries' domestic markets;
- To ensure that the World Bank and other multilateral development finance institutions participate as investors in the key economic infrastructure projects, in order to facilitate and support the securing of private sector participation;
- To provide technical support to accelerate the implementation of the program of action, including strengthening Africa's capacity in planning and development management, financial and infrastructure regulation, accounting and auditing, and development, construction and management of infrastructure;
- To support governance reforms of multilateral financial institutions to better cater for the needs and concerns of countries in Africa;

- To set up coordinated mechanisms to combat corruption effectively, as well as commit themselves to the return of monies (proceeds) of such practices to Africa. . . .

VII. Implementation of the African Initiative

70. Immediate priorities

Recognising the need to sequence and prioritise, the initiating Presidents propose that the following programmes be fast-tracked, in collaboration with development partners.

70.1 Programmes: (a) Communicable diseases—HIV/AIDS, malaria and tuberculosis; (b) Information and Communications Technology; (c) Debt reduction; (d) Market access. . . .

VIII. Conclusion

73. The African initiative's objective is to consolidate democracy and sound economic management on the continent. Through the program, African leaders are making a commitment to the African people and the world to work together in rebuilding the continent. It is a pledge to promote peace and stability, democracy, sound economic management and people-centered development and to hold each other accountable in terms of the agreements outlined in the program.

In proposing the partnership, Africa recognizes that it holds the key to its own development. We affirm that the African initiative offers an historical opportunity for the developed countries of the world to enter into a genuine partnership with Africa, based on mutual interest, shared commitments and binding agreements.

UN CONFERENCE ON ILLICIT TRADE IN SMALL ARMS
July 21, 2001

A first-ever attempt by the United Nations to limit the international trade in small arms, such as automatic rifles and grenades, fell victim in 2001 to global dissension on whether and how to accomplish the task. UN officials, notably Secretary General Kofi Annan, had argued that millions of people had been killed in civil conflicts and regional wars that were fueled in part by the availability of small arms. But the United States, with help from China, Russia, and other arms suppliers, blocked a proposal to mandate reductions in the arms trade. Instead, the United Nations Conference on the Illicit Trade in Small Arms and Light Weapons in All Its Aspects on July 21, 2001, adopted a watered-down measure calling for voluntary measures to curb such sales.

The international dispute pitted the new administration of President George W. Bush against many key U.S. allies, especially in Europe, who had supported tough measures to control the small arms trade. The Bush administration's rejection of that approach was one of a series of actions during 2001 that raised questions about its interest in global treaties and agreements. Among other things, the administration withdrew the United States from negotiations to strengthen the 1997 Kyoto Protocol on global warming, opposed attempts to enforce a 1972 UN treaty banning biological weapons, and announced its intention to withdraw from the 1972 Anti-Ballistic Missile (ABM) treaty, generally considered the cornerstone of nuclear weapons control. In each case, Bush and his aides said they were acting to protect U.S. national interests. (Global warming, p. 109; ABM treaty, p. 927)

Small Arms Trade

Ever since taking over as secretary general in 1997, Annan had prodded UN agencies and world leaders to take seriously the dangers posed by the unrestricted world trade in small arms and light weapons—generally defined as weapons that could be used by a single person. In a landmark speech to the Security Council in September 1999, Annan called limiting arms sales "one of the key challenges to preventing conflict in the next century." Annan cited estimates that more than 500 million automatic rifles, grenades, and other small arms were in circulation around the world, many of them traded illegally. These were the "weapons of choice" in forty-six of the forty-nine armed conflicts in the world during the 1990s, he said. Most of the conflicts took place in poor countries, especially Africa and Asia, while many of the weapons used in those conflicts came from the United States and other industrialized nations.

At Annan's instigation, the UN called the conference in 2001 to develop an international plan to curb the trade in such weapons. Committees held preparatory sessions during 2000 and the first half of 2001. Annan's efforts were rewarded in December when he and the United Nations were jointly awarded the Nobel Peace Prize. (Annan's Nobel Prize, p. 899)

The question of how to control the small arms trade brought to the fore a host of difficult issues that had plagued nearly every arms control effort launched by the UN in previous decades. Countries that manufactured and sold small arms were reluctant to cut off a small but important source of commerce. Many countries opposed what they saw as international interference in their domestic affairs. Countries that were battling domestic insurgencies were anxious to ban weapons sales to rebel groups, while the United States wanted to maintain the option of aiding some of those groups for foreign policy reasons. And even when there was general agreement on a desirable goal—such as preventing international conflicts—getting dozens of nations to agree on practical actions toward that goal required patient diplomacy.

By May 2001 diplomats at the UN had reached agreement on a proposed "program of action" to be presented at the small arms conference, scheduled for July 9–20 at UN headquarters in New York. The proposal included tough measures to encourage nations to reduce international trafficking in small arms, such as a ban on private ownership of assault rifles, grenade launchers, and similar weapons intended for military purposes. The proposal was not phrased as a legally enforceable treaty—as were most UN arms control agreements—but advocates described it as the first step toward such a treaty.

The UN conference of about 170 nations had just begun on July 9 when the Bush administration signaled that it opposed key sections of the proposed agreement and would walk away from the conference if its views were not adopted. John R. Bolton, undersecretary of state for arms control and international security affairs, told the conference that the administration rejected any measure that could be interpreted as interfering with private ownership of weapons. "The United States will not join consensus on a final document that contains measures contrary to our constitutional right to keep and bear arms," he told fellow delegates. Bolton also said the administration opposed the proposed definition of small arms and light weapons, arguing that it could be read to include "firearms such as hunting rifles and pistols, which are commonly owned and used by citizens in many countries."

Delegates from other countries said they had been prepared for the Bush administration to take a different position on some issues than had the *previous Clinton administration, which had helped draft the proposed agreement. President Bush, Attorney General John Ashcroft, and other senior figures in the new administration had long opposed many gun controls laws in the United States and could be expected to carry such views into the international arena. But the vehemence of Bolton's arguments surprised many delegates, especially European diplomats who had been staunch proponents of the arms control plan. "The content of the speech was what we expected, but the tone was quite negative—and surprising, because it wasn't necessary," one anonymous European diplomat told the* Washington Post. *That newspaper editorially attacked the Bush administration for using the UN conference "as a way to pander to the National Rifle Association, anti-UN zealots, and far-right conspiracy theorists."*

Behind the scenes, diplomats from China and Russia joined the United States in criticizing parts of the proposed agreement. Along with the United States, which for years has been the world's largest arms exporter, those countries were major sources of the small arms and other weapons used in local and regional conflicts. U.S. and African diplomats also were at loggerheads over the issue of aid to rebel groups. Bolton had said that Washington wanted to be able to provide weapons to "an oppressed non-state group defending itself from a genocidal government." But African governments, many of them battling insurgencies, wanted an international ban on arms sales to such groups.

Nearly two weeks of speeches and negotiations resulted in a stalemate in the conference, broken only during a late-night session after the conference was supposed to conclude on July 20. In the end, the Bush administration prevailed. The conference on July 21 adopted a "program of action" that included calls for nations to curb arms sales but no firm requirements for them to do so. In deference to the U.S. position, the final agreement did not propose any limits on private ownership of small arms but simply called on governments to take steps to regulate the sales of such weapons. The agreement also dropped the proposed ban on sales of weapons to rebel groups.

Lincoln Bloomfield, the U.S. assistant secretary of state for political-military affairs, praised the final agreement as setting "the basis for cooperative action to try to address some very serious problems caused by flows of illicit small arms and light weapons in areas of instability." But Sally Joss of the International Action Network on Small Arms—a coalition of 320 nongovernmental groups worldwide—said the UN conference had "squandered a golden opportunity to commit itself to pro-active measures needed to tackle gun violence around the world."

At an August 2 UN Security Council debate, several delegates called the conference a "first step" and expressed hope that a follow-up conference to be held no later than 2006 would take stronger action to curb arms sales. But others called the conference disappointing. Among them was Bernd Niehaus, Costa Rica's ambassador to the UN, who said the outcome resulted from "inflexibility on the part of a few delegations around the table today, who professed to want to maintain peace and security."

Report on Global Arms Sales

Less than a month after the UN conference, the Congressional Research Service—a branch of the Library of Congress—published the latest install-ment in a series of reports indicating that the United States continued to be the world's biggest arms salesman. The report, "Conventional Arms Trans-fers to Developing Nations: 1993–2000," was written by Richard F. Grim-mett, a respected expert in the field who used unclassified data from the United States and other governments. The report covered sales of all types of weapons, including major systems such as naval ships and warplanes as well as small arms.

Grimmett reported that from 1993 to 2000 developing nations accounted for two-thirds of all arms purchases worldwide. In 2000, he said, develop-ing countries signed contracts to buy $25.4 billion worth of weapons (many of which would not be delivered for several years) and took actual delivery on $19.4 billion worth. Saudi Arabia, the United Arab Emirates, China, Egypt, India, Israel, and South Korea (in descending order) were the biggest weapons purchasers during the 1990s.

Throughout the 1990s the United States sold far more weapons to devel-oping countries than any other country. In 2000, Grimmett reported, the United States agreed to sell $12.6 billion in weapons, just shy of one-half of all sales in the world. Russia was the second biggest arms supplier in 2000, followed by France, Germany, and China.

> *Following are excerpts from a news release issued July 21, 2001, by the United Nations Department for Disarmament Affairs de-scribing the "Programme of Action" adopted at the United Na-tions Conference on the Illicit Trade in Small Arms and Light Weapons in All Its Aspects.*
>
> **The document was obtained from the Internet at http://www.un.org/News/Press/docs/2001/DC2795.doc.htm.**

In preventing, combating and eradicating the illicit trade in small arms and light weapons in all its aspects, States undertook, at the national level, to:

- put in place adequate laws, regulations and administrative procedures to exercise effective control over the production of small arms and light weapons within their areas of jurisdiction, and over the export, import, transit or retransfer of such weapons, in order to prevent illegal manu-facture of and illicit trafficking in these weapons, or their diversion to unauthorized recipients;

- establish national coordination agencies responsible for policy guid-ance, research and monitoring of efforts to prevent, combat and eradi-cate the illicit trade, including aspects of the illicit manufacture, control, trafficking, circulation, brokering, trade, as well as tracing, finance, collection and destruction of small arms and light weapons;

- identify groups and individuals engaged in the illegal manufacture, trade, stockpiling, transfer, possession, as well as financing for acquisition, of illicit small arms and light weapons, and take action under appropriate national law against such groups and individuals;
- ensure responsibility for all small arms and light weapons held and issued by the State and effective measures for tracing such weapons;
- put in place and implement adequate laws, regulations and administrative procedures to ensure the effective control over the export and transit of small arms and light weapons, including the use of authenticated end-user certificates;
- make every effort, without prejudice to the right of States to re-export small arms and light weapons that they have previously imported, to notify the original exporting State in accordance with their bilateral agreements before the retransfer of those weapons;
- and develop and implement, where possible, effective disarmament, demobilization and reintegration programmes, including effective collection, control, storage and destruction of small arms and light weapons, particularly in post-conflict zones, as well as address the special needs of children affected by armed conflict.

At the regional level, States undertook to:

- encourage regional negotiations with the aim of concluding relevant legally binding instruments aimed at preventing, combating and eradicating the illicit trade, and where they do exist to ratify and fully implement them;
- encourage the strengthening and establishing of moratoria or similar initiatives in affected regions or subregions on the transfer and manufacture of small arms and light weapons and/or regional action programmes to prevent, combat and eradicate the illicit trade, and to respect such moratoria, similar initiatives and/or action programmes;
- and establish, where appropriate, subregional or regional mechanisms, in particular trans-border customs cooperation and networks for information-sharing among law-enforcement, border and customs control agencies.

Among measures at the global level, States and the World Customs Organization would be encouraged to enhance cooperation with the International Criminal Police Organization (Interpol) to identify those groups and individuals engaged in the illicit trade in small arms and light weapons in all its aspects, in order to allow national authorities to proceed against them in accordance with their national laws.

With regard to implementation, international cooperation and assistance, States undertook to encourage the establishment and strengthening of cooperation and partnerships at all levels among international and intergovernmental organizations and civil society, including non-governmental organizations (NGOs) and international financial institutions.

States and appropriate international and regional organizations in a position to do so should, upon request of the relevant authorities, seriously consider rendering assistance, including technical and financial support where needed, such as small arms funds.

In addition, States undertook to cooperate with each other, including on the basis of the relevant existing regional and global legally binding instruments, in tracing illicit small arms and light weapons, particularly by strengthening mechanisms based on the exchange of relevant information. They are encouraged to exchange information on a voluntary basis on their national marking systems on small arms and light weapons.

Annexed to the Programme of Action is a list of initiatives undertaken at the regional and subregional levels to address the illicit trade in small arms and light weapons. . . .

BIPARTISAN COMMISSION ON ELECTION SYSTEM REFORM
July 31, 2001

Congress, state legislatures, and a host of commissions and special task forces devoted extensive effort during 2001 to analyzing the botched 2000 presidential election vote counting in Florida and its implications for American democracy. Despite numerous agreements over specific steps, a surprising degree of consensus emerged in the country in favor of national action to prevent the recurrence of Florida-type problems, which had caused deep uncertainty about the true winner of the 2000 presidential election. Congress considered, but did not enact, legislation urging the states to improve election procedures and providing money to help them do it. Some states, including Florida, took steps to upgrade voting equipment and procedures. But many states appeared to be waiting for action at the federal level—which they generally opposed—before spending large sums of money to reform how they conducted elections.

Many of the studies issued during 2001 indicated that failures in the 2000 election were much broader than the high-profile Florida case. A study conducted by scientists from the California Institute of Technology and the Massachusetts Institute of Technology estimated that from 4 million to 6 million Americans who went to the polls either failed to vote because of long lines and questions about their registrations or had their votes thrown out because of technical problems with voting machines and other failures at polling places. Slightly more than 100 million Americans did have their votes for president counted.

By year's end, most Americans apparently had put aside the thirty-six days of partisan bickering and legal maneuvering that followed the disputed result of the November 2000 voting in Florida. Republican George W. Bush, the declared winner of Florida's contested electoral votes, and thus the presi-

dency, took the oath of office in January. His defeated foe, Democrat Al Gore, who had won 500,000 more popular votes than Bush nationwide, was seated nearby as an observer. Eight months later, terrorist attacks against the United States spawned a new patriotic fervor in the country that buried any lingering questions about the legitimacy of Bush's hold on the White House. In November, extensive newspaper investigations of the Florida election demonstrated that a majority of Florida's voters probably went to the polls intending to vote for Gore, but a combination of circumstances led to an outcome that essentially was tied. (Bush inauguration, p. 94; Terrorist attacks, p. 614; Florida election controversy, Historic Documents of 2000, pp. 999, 1025)

Civil Rights Commission Findings

During the wrangling over Florida's vote, many Americans probably were surprised to discover that how one's vote was counted—or even if one's vote was counted—depended heavily on where one lived. In 2000 there were no national standards for determining how votes were to be counted, and many states lacked uniform election standards. Florida was typical in this regard: some localities used up-to-date voting equipment and had good records of ensuring that all valid votes were counted, while others had faulty equipment and routinely had high rates of votes that were disqualified.

Several studies issued during 2001 indicated that the disparities in election procedures often had the greatest impact on the poor and minorities. Polling places in affluent localities, especially suburbs, tended to be equipped with modern voting equipment and were staffed by trained workers and volunteers, these studies said. By contrast, polling places in the inner cities and in many rural areas tended to be understaffed and to have outdated or ill-maintained voting equipment. Extensive news coverage during the Florida recount process focused national attention on these issues for the first time in many years.

The harshest condemnation of Florida's record on voting disparities came from the U.S. Commission on Civil Rights, which conducted hearings and an investigation into the November 2000 election there. The commission's investigation had been prompted by reports that an unusually high number of blacks were prevented from voting on election day.

In a report issued June 8, 2001, the commission said it had found "a strong basis for concluding" that actions by some officials in Florida had violated the 1965 Voting Rights Act, which was intended to bar discrimination against minority voters. Florida election officials did not conspire to deprive voters of their rights, the commission said, but they "failed to fulfill their responsibilities" to ensure fairness in the conduct of the election. The commission issued its report on a split vote of 6–2; the six members in favor were all appointed by Democrats and the two members opposed were appointed by Republicans.

The commission cited statistical and anecdotal evidence to back its claim that blacks were more likely than nonblacks to have been turned away at the polls and to have their ballots rejected as invalid. Voters and poll workers in majority-black precincts testified to the commission that hundreds of people who believed they were registered to vote were turned away at the polls because their registration records could not be found or had been purged from computer systems. Frustrated poll workers in Miami-Dade County, Broward County, and other areas told the commission they had been unable to get through to the county election offices on election day to determine if the people who showed up at the polls actually were registered. Few similar problems were reported in nonblack precincts.

Votes cast by blacks also were much more likely to be rejected than those cast by other voters, the commission said. Statewide, the panel estimated that 14.4 percent of black voters cast ballots that later were rejected, nearly ten times the estimated rate of 1.6 percent invalidated votes for nonblack voters. One Republican member of the commission, Abigail Thernstrom, argued that this difference probably resulted from lower literacy levels and higher rates of first-time voters among blacks—a position rejected by the commission majority.

The commission sent its report to the Justice Department and asked for an investigation of possible violations of the Voting Rights Act. By year's end the department had brought no charges against anyone in connection with the Florida election.

In a follow-up report issued November 9, the Civil Rights Commission called on Congress to enact legislation mandating election standards nationwide. Among its specific recommendations, the commission called for requiring states to allow "provisional ballots" enabling voters whose eligibility is questioned to cast a vote, with the eligibility to be determined later; require that states provide adequate resources so that all registered voters have an equal opportunity to vote and have their votes counted; and require improved training of poll workers and better voter education materials.

Newspaper Investigations

For nearly a year after the 2000 election was officially declared over, major American news organizations carried out exhaustive examinations of the disputed ballots in Florida in hopes of determining whether Bush or Gore actually "won" the state. One investigation was conducted by USA Today, the Miami Herald, *and several other Florida newspapers, which hired an accounting firm to examine the state's disputed votes; the results of that study were published in June. A second major vote-counting effort was mounted by a consortium that included the Associated Press, the* New York Times, *the* Washington Post, *Cable News Network, the* Los Angeles Times, *the* Wall Street Journal, *the* St. Petersburg Times, *and the* Palm Beach Post. *That consortium used the National Opinion Research Center at the University of Chicago to examine the votes; the newspapers published results of the study on November 12. Both investigations were made possible by Florida's strict "sunshine law," under which the actual ballots were considered public documents open to public scrutiny.*

Both studies came to the same general conclusions: even if the U.S. Supreme Court had not stopped the partial recounts that Gore requested in four Florida counties after the election, Bush probably would have won a narrow victory, comparable to the 537-vote margin that put him in the White House. But Gore probably would have won a narrow victory if all of Florida's 175,000 disputed votes had been counted, the studies said.

"It's too close to call," was the overall assessment of Kirk Wolter, a senior vice president of the National Opinion Research Center. "One could never know from this study alone who won the election."

In effect, the studies showed that Gore and his legal team mistakenly pursued a strategy after the election of challenging the votes only in four heavily Democratic counties. In retrospect, many analysts said, Gore should have demanded an immediate recount of all votes in Florida—a move that might have put him in the White House.

The studies also offered a degree of political vindication to both sides: Bush could claim that the Supreme Court did not "give" him the presidency when it stopped the vote counting, and Gore could claim that he really did carry Florida. Neither side chose to make such claims, however. Speaking for Bush, White House press secretary Ari Fleischer said: "This is one more inconclusive study that doesn't change anything." And Gore issued this statement: "We are a nation of laws, and the presidential election of 2000 is over."

Both studies confirmed that Gore probably would have won a convincing victory in Florida had it not been for the notorious "butterfly ballot" in Palm Beach County. That ballot, which listed presidential candidates on opposing pages, confused thousands of voters and led many to vote for two candidates (called an "overvote"), thereby invalidating their ballots. The newspaper consortium report published in November determined that the vast majority of invalidated ballots likely were cast by those wanting to vote for Gore: 11,140 of the overvotes listed Gore and one other candidate, while 2,298 listed Bush and another candidate. The ballot was so confusing that thousands of Democratic voters said they mistakenly cast their votes for Patrick Buchanan, the conservative Reform Party candidate.

A statistical analysis of the Florida returns by the New York Times tended to confirm the report by the civil rights commission and other observers that ballots cast by blacks and Hispanics were rejected in far greater numbers than those by whites. Even after accounting for education, income, and other socioeconomic differences, the Times said, voters in black- majority and Hispanic-majority precincts were about three times as likely as voters in white-majority precincts to have had their ballots thrown out. This trend was the case no matter what kind of voting machines were used, the newspaper said.

Carter-Ford Commission Report

More than a dozen national bodies conducted studies and issued reports making recommendations for correcting problems with the U.S. elections system. Several national organizations representing state elections officials issued their own reports calling for reforms, but most opposed mandates by the federal government.

The issue of federal mandates turned out to be the principal dividing point among members of the most prominent panel to study the matter: the National Commission on Federal Election Reform. Former presidents Jimmy Carter and Gerald R. Ford were the honorary cochairs of the commission; its cochairs were Robert H. Michel, former Republican leader of the House of Representatives, and Lloyd Cutler, a Washington attorney who had served as Carter's White House counsel. The commission issued its report, "To Assure Pride and Confidence in the Electoral Process," on July 31 and presented it the following day to Bush, who endorsed most of its recommendations.

The commission called for numerous reforms in election procedures, most importantly the adoption by each state of uniform standards for how votes are cast and counted. The commission noted that Florida was just one of many states that allowed each county—or in some cases each local jurisdiction—to set its own standards for elections. However, the commission took no position on a single nationwide set of election rules mandated by Congress. The panel's vote on that question was divided, with six of the nineteen members (all Democrats) favoring federal mandates.

In other areas, the commission suggested that Congress appropriate up to $200 million each year to help the states upgrade voting equipment and make improvements, that election day be declared a national holiday, that television networks refrain from broadcasting presidential election results until all states in the Pacific time zone had closed their polls, that procedures for absentee voting by armed service personnel be simplified, and that the states allow former convicts to vote once they complete their prison sentences and any probationary periods.

GAO Studies on U.S. Election Procedures

A series of studies by the General Accounting Office (GAO), the congressional watchdog agency, indicated that many of the problems evident with Florida's election procedures were common around the country. A GAO report issued October 15, "Perspectives on Activities and Challenges Across the Nation," was based on results from a survey of state and local election officials. That survey found that about 57 percent of the nation's voting jurisdictions experienced "major problems" in the November 2000 election. The most common problems were a lack of poll workers (51 percent of jurisdictions reported this problem) and dealing with voters who showed up at the polls but were not on voter registration lists (30 percent reported this problem). Combined, these problems created long lines, frustration among voters and poll workers alike, and poor communication between polling places and election headquarters, the GAO said. On the controversial question of counting votes, about one-third of the jurisdictions surveyed by the GAO said they had no written instructions from state or local authorities on how to interpret voter intent.

The GAO appeared to reject the arguments, advanced by many observers during and after the Florida dispute, that outdated equipment was principally at fault and that replacing old equipment would ensure more accurate counting. Noting that local jurisdictions successfully used a variety of methods to record and count votes, the agency said its work "showed that any voting method can produce complete and accurate counts as long as the technology used is properly maintained and effectively integrated with the associated people (workers and election volunteers) and processes." The GAO gave cost estimates for upgrading all voting equipment nationwide: installing optical scanning devices in all 186,000 precincts would cost about $191 million, and installing computer touch-screen equipment would cost about $3 billion. The GAO was one of several organizations warning states and Congress against a rush to allow voting over the Internet, primarily because of concerns about security.

In a summary report issued October 15, the GAO suggested that Congress and local jurisdictions proceed cautiously when considering changing voting equipment. "Introducing new technology alone may not necessarily reduce voter error," the agency said. "In fact, switching equipment may actually introduce new opportunities for voter error unless the jurisdiction deals with the people aspects of successfully fielding new voting technology and offers voter education on how to use the new equipment effectively."

Reform Efforts at Federal and State Levels

The recommendations of the Carter-Ford commission became the basis for much of the legislation considered by Congress during the year. In both the House and Senate, the principal issue became whether the federal government should require the states to adopt uniform standards. Generally, Democrats favored national standards and Republicans wanted the states to retain individual control over the election process.

Despite those fundamental differences, lengthy negotiations led to compromises in both chambers that produced broad agreement on strong federal requirements, backed by money, for the states to improve election standards. The House on December 12 approved a measure (HR 3295) that authorized $2.65 billion to help states reform election procedures, including $400 million to help replace punch card machines and other outdated equipment. The bill would establish a four-member commission to oversee the states' compliance with general election standards, such as having a uniform system for what constitutes a vote. Also late in the year, key Senate leaders reached agreement on an even stricter bill setting explicit federal mandates, including requiring each state to use voting machines that notify voters when they improperly select more than one candidate for an office. The Senate was scheduled to consider that measure in 2002.

Florida was among the few states taking any specific action. The legislature passed, and Governor Jeb Bush signed, legislation intended to replace punch card voting equipment with optical scanning devices in time for the 2002 elections. Neighboring Georgia adopted legislation requiring every precinct to have computer touch-screen voting machines in place for the

2004 elections—but the legislature then failed to approve any funding to implement the requirement.

Following is the summary of recommendations from the report "To Assure Pride and Confidence in the Electoral Process," released July 31, 2001, by the National Commission on Federal Election Reform.

The document was obtained from the Internet at http:// www.reformelections.org/data/reports/99_full_report.pdf.

The Goals of Federal Election Reform

When they choose the president, the vice president, and members of Congress, the American people should expect all levels of government to provide a democratic process that:

- Maintains an accurate list of citizens who are qualified to vote;
- Encourages every eligible voter to participate effectively;
- Uses equipment that reliably clarifies and registers the voter's choices;
- Handles close elections in a foreseeable and fair way;
- Operates with equal effectiveness for every citizen and every community; and
- Reflects limited but responsible federal participation.

For Americans, democracy is a precious birthright. But each generation must nourish and improve the processes of democracy for its successors. In the near-term, the next three to five years for instance, we envision a country where each state maintains accurate, computerized lists of who can vote, networked with local administrators.

Using that system, qualified voters in our mobile society would be able to vote throughout their state without being turned away because of the vagaries of local administration. Using the system we recommend here, millions of military and other overseas voters would find it easier to get and return their ballots. Election Day would be held on a national holiday, freeing up more people to serve as poll workers and making polling places more accessible. Voting machines would meet a common standard of excellent performance. Each state would have its uniform, objective definitions of what constitutes a vote. News organizations would exert necessary restraint in predicting election outcomes. Every jurisdiction and every official would obey the Voting Rights Act and other statutes that secure the franchise and prohibit discrimination. In all of this there would be a delicate balance of shared responsibilities between levels of government, and between officials and the voters they serve.

This report sets forth our recommendations for the next, immediate steps on the road to attainment of these goals.

Policy Recommendation 1

Every state should adopt a system of statewide voter registration.

1. The statewide computerized voter file should be networked with and accessible to every election jurisdiction in the state so that any level can initiate registrations and updates with prompt notification to the others. It should include provisions for sharing data with other states.
2. When a citizen either applies for a driver's license or registers to vote, each state should obtain residential address and other information, such as a digitized signature, in a form that is equally usable for both the motor vehicle and voter databases. The address information can then be linked to a statewide street index.
3. Each state's driver's license and voter registration applications should require applicants to provide at least the last four digits of their Social Security number. States should also ask applicants if they are registered in another state, so that that state can be notified of the new registration.
4. Each state's voter registration applications should require a separate and specific affirmation that the applicant is a U.S. citizen.

Policy Recommendation 2

Every state should permit provisional voting by any voter who claims to be qualified to vote in that state.

1. Provisional voting authorizes any person whose name does not appear on the list of registered voters, but who wishes to vote, to be issued a ballot. The ballot shall be counted only upon verification by election officials that the provisional voter is eligible and qualified to vote within the state and only for the offices for which the voter is qualified to vote.
2. Another option, for states with statewide computerized voting lists, would be to let a voter who is not on the list submit proof of identification and swear to or affirm an appropriate affidavit of eligibility to vote in that jurisdiction. This information could then be used as an application for voter registration and the voter list would be amended accordingly. If qualified, the voter could either be issued a regular ballot or, if the state preferred, be allowed to vote provisionally pending confirmation of the voter's eligibility.

Policy Recommendation 3

Congress should enact legislation to hold presidential and congressional elections on a national holiday.

1. Holding national elections on a national holiday will increase availability of poll workers and suitable polling places and might make voting easier for some workers.
2. One approach, which this Commission favors, would be to specify that in even-numbered years the Veterans Day national holiday be held on the Tuesday next after the first Monday in November and serve also as our Election Day.

Policy Recommendation 4

Congress should adopt legislation that simplifies and facilitates absentee voting by uniformed and overseas citizens.

1. Each state should designate a responsible official for absentee voting by uniformed and overseas citizens who are residents of that state. That official should become the single point of contact for the citizens of that state who are served by the Federal Voting Assistance Program, which helps such uniformed and overseas citizens.

2. In 1986 Congress passed the Uniformed and Overseas Citizens Absentee Voting Act (UOCAVA) to help eligible members of the armed services and their families, and other citizens overseas, to vote. Utilizing standardized forms for voter registration and absentee ballot requests, all UOCAVA-covered residents from a home state should be authorized to mail these applications to the designated official for their state If that state uses a statewide voter registration system networked to local jurisdictions, as we have recommended, the state official should be authorized to act directly on these applications or to forward them for action by the appropriate local jurisdiction. States should accept one absentee ballot application as a valid application for all subsequent elections being held by that state in that year.

3. The designated state official should be authorized to accept either a voted ballot being returned for any jurisdiction of that state or a standardized Federal Write-In Absentee Ballot that is an option for a UOCAVA-covered citizen. States should be obliged to accept and tally a Federal Write-In Absentee Ballot for those contests in which they determine the voter was eligible to vote.

4. Properly filed absentee ballots should be accepted if they have been received by the time the polls of that state have closed on Election Day. States and the Federal Voting Assistance Program should develop common standards for validation of ballots that have been voted and mailed on or before Election Day, even if they are received after that date.

Policy Recommendation 5

Each state should allow for restoration of voting rights to otherwise eligible citizens who have been convicted of a felony once they have fully served their sentence, including any term of probation or parole.

Policy Recommendation 6

The state and federal governments should take additional steps to assure the voting rights of all citizens and to enforce the principle of one person, one vote.

1. Federal and state governments should intensify efforts to enforce compliance with the several statutes guaranteeing the right to vote and prohibiting various forms of discrimination in voting and registration.

2. The methods for funding and administering elections—from invest-

ments in equipment through voter education to procedures at the polling place—should seek to ensure that every qualified citizen has an equal opportunity to vote and that every individual's vote is equally effective. No individual, group, or community should be left with a justified belief that the electoral process works less well for some than for others.

3. Federal and state governments should consider uses of technology, for example when developing voting equipment system standards, that will make it feasible to provide greater assistance to language minorities.

Policy Recommendation 7

Each state should set a benchmark for voting system performance, uniform in each local jurisdiction that conducts elections. The benchmark should be expressed as a percentage of residual vote (the combination of overvotes, spoiled votes, and undervotes) in the contest at the top of the ballot and should take account of deliberate decisions of voters not to make a choice.

1. Benchmarks should consider the results obtained by best practices within that state, taking local circumstances into account. In general, we suggest that the benchmarks in the next election cycle should be set no higher than 2%, with the goal of further reductions in succeeding cycles.
2. Each state should require its election jurisdictions to issue a public report on the number of residual votes after every statewide election, including the probable causes of error, if any.
3. Each state should determine for itself how to hold its election jurisdictions accountable for achieving the benchmarks.

Policy Recommendation 8

The federal government should develop a comprehensive set of voting equipment system standards for the benefit of state and local election administration.

1. Congress should grant statutory authority to an appropriate federal agency to develop such standards in consultation with state and local election officials.
2. The scope of the voting system standards should include security (including a documentary audit for non-ballot systems), procedures for decertification as well as certification of both software and hardware, assessment of human usability, and operational guidelines for proper use and maintenance of the equipment. The agency should maintain a clearinghouse of information about experience in practice.
3. Voters should have the opportunity to correct errors at the precinct or other polling place, either within the voting equipment itself or in the operational guidelines to administrators for using the equipment.
4. Each voting tally system certified for use should include, as part of the certification, a proposed statement of what constitutes a proper vote in the design and operation of the system.

5. New voting equipment systems certified either by the federal government or by any state should provide a practical and effective means for voters with physical disabilities to cast a secret ballot.

6. In addition to developing the voting system standards, the federal agency should provide its own certification and decertification of hardware and software, including components in voter registration systems. These federal certifications and decertifications, like the remainder of the standards, will be recommendations to states which they can adopt or not.

7. This federal service should include selection and oversight of a federally supervised set of independent testing authorities who will apply the standards in assessing equipment. After the federal agency develops and approves the relevant voluntary voting system standards in consultation with state and local administrators, this further, technical task should be delegated to the highly regarded and relatively independent National Institute of Standards and Technology (NIST) of the Department of Commerce.

Policy Recommendation 9

Each state should adopt uniform statewide standards for defining what will constitute a vote on each category of voting equipment certified for use in that state. Statewide recount, election certification, and contest procedures should take account of the timelines for selection of presidential electors.

1. Statewide standards for defining a vote in advance of an election should be uniform and as objective as possible.

2. Each state should reevaluate its election code to consider adopting a predictable sequence of: a) vote tabulation and retabulation; b) machine or manual recounts to encompass the entire jurisdiction of the office being recounted, triggered by whatever threshold the state may choose; c) certification of a final count; followed then by, d) contests of the certification limited to allegations of fraud or other misconduct.

3. In such a sequence, each state should allow at least 21 days before requiring certification of the final count. But we recommend retention of a federal deadline under which the "safe harbor" for conclusive state determination of presidential electors will expire.

4. Each state should also develop a uniform design for the federal portion of the state ballot, for use in each of that state's certified voting equipment systems.

Policy Recommendation 10

News organizations should not project any presidential election results in any state so long as polls remain open elsewhere in the 48 contiguous states. If necessary, Congress and the states should consider legislation, within First Amendment limits, to protect the integrity of the electoral process.

1. In practice, this would mean that news organizations would voluntarily refrain from projecting the outcomes of the presidential elections in any state until 11:00 P.M. Eastern Standard Time (8:00 P.M. Pacific Standard Time).Voluntary restraint is preferable to government action.
2. If news organizations refuse to exercise voluntary restraint, Congress and the states should consider prohibiting any public disclosure by government entities of official tallies in the race for president and vice-president at the precinct level and above until 11:00 P.M. EST (8:00 P.M. PST), where such regulations are consistent with existing provisions for public observation of the vote tabulation process.
3. If news organizations refuse to exercise voluntary restraint and other measures cannot protect the integrity of the electoral process, Congress should impose a plan for uniform poll closing hours in the continental United States for presidential elections.
4. National television broadcasters should provide, during the last thirty days of the presidential campaign, at least five minutes each night of free prime television time to each presidential candidate who has qualified for federal matching funds. They or their local affiliates should further make free time available for state and local election officials to provide necessary voter education.

Policy Recommendation 11

The federal government, on a matching basis with the governments of the 50 states, should provide funds that will add another $300–400 million to the level of annual spending on election administration in the United States. The federal share will require a federal contribution totaling $1–2 billion spread out over two or three years to help capitalize state revolving funds that will provide long-term assistance.

1. These responsibilities should be apportioned about 50–50 between the federal government and the states, so that the federal contribution has the effect of raising the annual federal and state level of spending on election administration by an added $150–200 million. This is a modest sum, lower than some other current estimates about what is needed.
2. The federal expenditures should be made in the form of matching grants to the states, and the states should directly administer the disbursement of funds for administration at the state, county, and local level.
3. Instead of planning on permanent expenditures of federal funds, Congress should instead consider leveraging temporary funding over a two- or three-year period in an amount, totaling perhaps $1–2 billion, that will be sufficient to capitalize the federal share of state revolving funds. These funds can leverage the initial federal contribution, after it has been matched by the states, to create a long-term source of federal and state support to election administration. The capitalization should be sufficient to sustain our proposed federal increment of $150–200 million of continued additional spending on election administration that, when

matched by state contributions to the funds, will reach the $300–400 million annual nationwide target.

4. Such state revolving funds would be used to carry out flexible state programs, allowing the states to support a variety of election administration activities undertaken by state, county, and local governments and do so with a variety of financing options that can include grants, loans at or below market rates, loan guarantees, and other arrangements. States would assess relative needs among their election jurisdictions and be accountable for maintaining the fund.

5. Federal funds should be allocated among the states in proportion to the electoral votes that each state will cast in the presidential election of 2004. This reflects a slight per capita weighting toward rural states. Such a modest weighting is appropriate, given the greater average per capita cost of election administration in rural counties.

Policy Recommendation 12

The federal responsibilities envisioned in this report should be assigned to a new agency, an Election Administration Commission (EAC).

1. The number of governing commissioners in this agency should be small; the members should be distinguished citizens with a reputation for integrity.

2. The commission should: a) develop federal voting system standards in consultation with state and local election administrators; b) oversee the implementation of these standards in conjunction with the National Institute of Standards and Technology; c) maintain a national clearinghouse of information on best practices in election administration; and d) administer the limited federal assistance program to the states.

3. Enforcement of other federal election laws should remain a separate function, centered in the Civil Rights and Criminal Divisions of the Department of Justice.

4. States that do not have them should also consider establishing nonpartisan election commissions.

Policy Recommendation 13

Congress should enact legislation that includes federal assistance for election administration, setting forth policy objectives for the states while leaving the choice of strategies to the discretion of the states. The Commission as a whole takes no position on whether Congress should use the powerful incentive of conditional grants or instead establish requirements or mandates wholly independent of funding. A majority of the Commission members suggests the approach described below. However, a minority suggests a more direct federal role as detailed in an additional statement of views appended to this report.

1. Congress should enact legislation to create a new federal election administration agency, to facilitate military and overseas citizen voting,

to address a national election holiday, to constrain—if necessary—premature official disclosure of presidential election results, and to appropriate federal assistance in election administration.

2. To be eligible for federal assistance, states shall:
   a. match the federal assistance with an added contribution of their own in the proportion fixed by Congress;
   b. adopt legislation that will establish a statewide voter registration system networked to every local jurisdiction in that state, with provisions for sharing data with other states;
   c. permit on-site provisional voting by every voter who claims to be qualified to vote in that state, or adopt an alternative that achieves the same objective;
   d. set a uniform statewide benchmark for voting system performance in each local jurisdiction administering elections expressed as a percentage of residual vote in the contest at the top of the ballot, and require local jurisdictions to report data relevant to this benchmark;
   e. either agree to comply with the federal voting system standards and certification processes or develop their own state voting system standards and processes that, at a minimum:
      i. give voters the opportunity to correct errors, either within the voting equipment itself or in the operational guidelines to administrators for using the equipment at a precinct or other polling place and
      ii. require that new voting systems should provide a practical and effective means for voters with physical disabilities to cast a secret ballot; and
   f. adopt uniform statewide standards that define what will constitute a vote on each category of voting equipment certified for use in that state;
   g. certify that they are in compliance with existing federal voting rights statutes.
3. Specific choices on how to comply with these conditions should be left to the discretion of the states.
4. States that qualify for federal assistance should have broad discretion in how they disburse this money, so long as the money is expended on: a) establishing and maintaining accurate lists of eligible voters; b) encouraging eligible voters to vote; c) improving verification of voter identification at the polling place; d) improving equipment and methods for casting and counting votes; e) recruiting and training election officials and poll workers; f) improving the quantity and quality of available polling places; and g) educating voters about their rights and responsibilities.

August

PRESIDENT BUSH ON
STEM CELL RESEARCH
August 9, 2001

Announcing that "we must proceed with great care," President George W. Bush said August 9, 2001, that he would permit limited federal funding of scientific research on human embryonic stem cells. Bush's decision represented a marked shift in his position. During his election campaign, he said that he was flatly opposed to any federal funding for this type of research, which involved destroying an embryo to extract the stem cells. But the decision also represented far less than full federal support for a line of promising research that scientists hoped would lead to new cures and treatments for many debilitating conditions such as diabetes, Parkinson's disease, and spinal cord injuries.

Bush approved federal funding for research on stem cells that had already been extracted from human embryos. The president said private researchers had already produced about sixty stem cell cultures, or lines, that were genetically diverse and capable of reproducing themselves indefinitely. By permitting federal funding only on these stem cell lines, "where the life and death decision had already been made," Bush said, the potential of embryonic stem cells could be explored "without crossing a fundamental moral line by providing taxpayer funding that would sanction or encourage further destruction of human embryos that have at least the potential for human life."

Reflecting the seriousness of the issue as well as the public interest in it, the president made his announcement in a formal, televised address to the nation—the first since his inaugural address in January. By all accounts, Bush struggled with the ethical and moral complexities of embryonic stem cell research and sought input from a diverse group of bioethicists, scientists, health officials, religious leaders, White House advisers, and personal friends before making his decision. Politically, Bush's decision may not have been as costly as some commentators anticipated. The decision appeared to have split the Christian right and other social conservatives who formed the core of Bush's political support. Abortion opponents who equated the destruction of an embryo to obtain the stem cells with the taking of life

accused the president of abandoning his principles. But many other abor-
tion foes favored the research, pointing out that the stem cells were extracted
from unused embryos created in vitro at fertility clinics that eventually
would have been discarded. Still, the White House sought to quell some of the
uproar by having Bush deliver his speech from his ranch in Crawford,
Texas, in early August when Congress was on vacation.

Prelude to a Decision

Embryonic stem cells are primordial master cells capable of transform-
ing themselves into most of the specialized tissues that make up the human
body, such as blood, bone, muscle, and nerve. They begin to form about four
days after a human egg was fertilized and quickly differentiate into special-
ized cells. For some time, scientists had postulated that these cells, which
were capable of endless division in the laboratory, might be used to grow re-
placement tissues and organs for the human body and thus allow scientists
to develop treatments for numerous diseases and conditions.

Scientists had also derived stem cells from adults and found that some of
them, such as bone marrow stem cells that make red and white blood cells,
might be forced under laboratory conditions to make muscle or nerve
cells. Early research on adult stem cells, however, raised numerous questions
about whether these cells were as versatile as those extracted from embryos.

The first embryonic stem cells were isolated in 1998 by a team of scien-
tists from the University of Wisconsin. The research was privately funded
so that it would not be in violation of a federal ban on embryo research, first
enacted in 1995. But the discovery put pressure on the government to be-
come involved in the research, if only to be able to set ethical standards for
the research. In January 1999 the National Institutes of Health (NIH) im-
posed a moratorium on human stem cell research while it wrote guidelines
addressing the scientific and ethical questions involved in the research.

Those guidelines were released August 23, 2000. They got around the ban
on funding of embryonic research by allowing federal funding of stem cell
research so long as the researchers did not directly destroy embryos to ob-
tain the stem cells. The guidelines also set out several rules to prevent any-
one from donating embryos for profit or for the medical benefit of relatives
and to prohibit researchers from creating embryos specifically to harvest
stem cells.

Among those protesting the guidelines was Republican presidential nom-
inee George W. Bush, who said that he was opposed to federal funding for
research "that involves destroying a living human embryo." Bush and oth-
ers also scorned as meaningless the provision requiring federally funded
researchers to obtain stem cells indirectly. Whether they obtained them di-
rectly or indirectly, these opponents said, the result was the same—the em-
bryo was destroyed.

After Bush was elected president, it was widely anticipated that he would
overturn the NIH guidelines drawn up under his Democratic predecessor
Bill Clinton. In his first months in office, he acted quickly to reverse or wa-

*ter down several other Clinton administration policies with which he dis-
agreed, including arsenic levels in drinking water and reductions in carbon
dioxide emissions that contributed to global warming. In April NIH said it
was postponing making any grants for federal funding until after the new
administration completed a policy review.* (Global warming, p. 109; Arsenic
levels, p. 212)

*Bush's decision took on new urgency during the summer when two
research organizations, Advanced Cell Technology in Worcester, Massachusetts, and the Jones Institute for Reproductive Medicine in Norfolk, Virginia, separately announced plans to clone human embryos specifically to
harvest stem cells. (The House on July 31 easily passed legislation making
it a crime to clone human embryos and banning the importation either of
cloned human embryos or stem cells derived from them. Companion legislation in the Senate was not acted upon in 2001.)*

Explaining a Decision

*In his August 9 speech, Bush said the cloning of the human embryos was
"deeply troubling and a warning sign that should prompt all of us to think
through these issues very carefully." Bush said he was a "strong supporter"
of science and technology and the potential they had for curing disease
and ending suffering. He said Ronald Reagan's wife, Nancy, had written to
him about the former president's struggle with Alzheimer's disease, and he
obliquely mentioned the death of his sister at age three from leukemia. But,
he said, he also believed that human life was sacred, and he said he worried
about "a culture that devalues life." Bush said he had been assured that research on the sixty already existing stem cell lines "could lead to breakthrough therapies and cures." As a result, he said, the federal government
could fund research on those lines without destroying additional human
embryos. Bush also said he would seek increased federal funding available
for research on adult and animal stem cells, which did "not involve the same
moral dilemma."*

*Bush created a panel to monitor stem cell research and to draw up ap-
propriate guidelines and regulations governing federal funding. The panel
was to be headed by University of Chicago bioethicist Leon Kass, who advised Bush during his deliberations. Bush's announcement had the effect
of negating the NIH guidelines adopted in 1999.*

Reaction to Bush's Compromise

*As expected, antiabortion groups and other conservative groups were di-
vided in their reaction to Bush's announcement. For example, Pat Robertson, founder of the Christian Coalition, said the president found "an elegant
solution to the thorny issue of stem research by firmly protecting the rights
of the unborn." But others argued that Bush's decision was morally and
ethically wrong and would set the nation on an inevitable path toward
the killing of more embryos for research. "The president has introduced the
camel's nose into the tent, and inevitably we'll soon have the whole beast in*

*there," said Kenneth Cooper of the Family Research Council. "Moral prin-
ciples are not divisible. [The decision is] going to encourage members of
Congress to advocate additional research and to kill additional embryos."*

*Scientists also offered a mixed assessment, with some expressing dis-
appointment that federal funding would be so limited and others pleased
that there would be any federal funding at all. Researchers and others
warned that the United States could lose researchers and patents to other
countries that supported stem cell research. Several noted that before Bush's
announcement, one leading researcher had already decided to move his laboratory from California to Great Britain for "the possibility of carrying out
my research with human embryonic stem cells with public support."*

*Many scientists were skeptical whether the sixty lines Bush discussed in
his speech actually existed. On September 5 Health and Human Services
Secretary Tommy G. Thompson told a Senate committee that in fact only
about two dozen stem cell colonies were fully established and ready for use.
Researchers also questioned whether a limited number of stem cell lines
would be sufficient to provide the genetic diversity necessary to create effective therapies, and whether therapies using the existing lines, which were
nourished with mice cells, would be safe for human use. There was some
concern that the mouse cells could transmit viruses to humans when the
stem cells were implanted in people.*

*In a report issued in September the influential National Academy of Sci-
ences called for the development of new lines. "While there is much that can
be learned using existing stem cell lines if they are made widely available
for research, concerns about changing genetic and biological properties of
these stem cell lines necessitate continued monitoring as well as the development of new stem cell lines in the future," the report said. The panel of
experts also backed federal funding, saying that it "offers the most efficient
and responsible means of fulfilling the promise of stem cells to meet the need
for regenerative medical therapies."*

*These differing viewpoints were all mirrored during brief debate in the
Senate later in the year over language in the annual spending bill for the National Institutes of Health that would ease the restrictions on the embryos
that could be used by researchers. The language was dropped after opponents threatened to offer an amendment banning human cloning. Many
senators who supported the use of discarded human embryos for research
leading to medical therapies opposed the cloning of human embryos for the
specific purpose of creating stem cells to use in medical research. The final
version of the fiscal 2002 spending bill continued the 1995 ban on funding
for embryo research. But in the nonbinding report accompanying the final
bill, Congress declared that Bush's proposal to fund research on stem cells already extracted from embryos did not violate this ban.*

*Following is the text of a speech delivered by President George W.
Bush on August 10, 2001, announcing his support for federal
funding of research on stem cells already extracted from human
embryos.*

The document was obtained from the Internet at http://www.whitehouse.gov/news/releases/2001/08/20010809-2.html.

Good evening. I appreciate you giving me a few minutes of your time tonight so I can discuss with you a complex and difficult issue, an issue that is one of the most profound of our time.

The issue of research involving stem cells derived from human embryos is increasingly the subject of a national debate and dinner table discussions. The issue is confronted every day in laboratories as scientists ponder the ethical ramifications of their work. It is agonized over by parents and many couples as they try to have children, or to save children already born.

The issue is debated within the church, with people of different faiths, even many of the same faith coming to different conclusions. Many people are finding that the more they know about stem cell research, the less certain they are about the right ethical and moral conclusions.

My administration must decide whether to allow federal funds, your tax dollars, to be used for scientific research on stem cells derived from human embryos. A large number of these embryos already exist. They are the product of a process called in vitro fertilization, which helps so many couples conceive children. When doctors match sperm and egg to create life outside the womb, they usually produce more embryos than are planted in the mother. Once a couple successfully has children, or if they are unsuccessful, the additional embryos remain frozen in laboratories.

Some will not survive during long storage; others are destroyed. A number have been donated to science and used to create privately funded stem cell lines. And a few have been implanted in an adoptive mother and born, and are today healthy children.

Based on preliminary work that has been privately funded, scientists believe further research using stem cells offers great promise that could help improve the lives of those who suffer from many terrible diseases—from juvenile diabetes to Alzheimer's, from Parkinson's to spinal cord injuries. And while scientists admit they are not yet certain, they believe stem cells derived from embryos have unique potential.

You should also know that stem cells can be derived from sources other than embryos—from adult cells, from umbilical cords that are discarded after babies are born, from human placenta. And many scientists feel research on these type of stem cells is also promising. Many patients suffering from a range of diseases are already being helped with treatments developed from adult stem cells.

However, most scientists, at least today, believe that research on embryonic stem cells offers the most promise because these cells have the potential to develop in all of the tissues in the body.

Scientists further believe that rapid progress in this research will come only with federal funds. Federal dollars help attract the best and brightest scientists. They ensure new discoveries are widely shared at the largest number of research facilities and that the research is directed toward the greatest public good.

The United States has a long and proud record of leading the world toward advances in science and medicine that improve human life. And the United States has a long and proud record of upholding the highest standards of ethics as we expand the limits of science and knowledge. Research on embryonic stem cells raises profound ethical questions, because extracting the stem cell destroys the embryo, and thus destroys its potential for life. Like a snowflake, each of these embryos is unique, with the unique genetic potential of an individual human being.

As I thought through this issue, I kept returning to two fundamental questions: First, are these frozen embryos human life, and therefore, something precious to be protected? And second, if they're going to be destroyed anyway, shouldn't they be used for a greater good, for research that has the potential to save and improve other lives?

I've asked those questions and others of scientists, scholars, bioethicists, religious leaders, doctors, researchers, members of Congress, my Cabinet, and my friends. I have read heartfelt letters from many Americans. I have given this issue a great deal of thought, prayer and considerable reflection. And I have found widespread disagreement.

On the first issue, are these embryos human life—well, one researcher told me he believes this five-day-old cluster of cells is not an embryo, not yet an individual, but a pre-embryo. He argued that it has the potential for life, but it is not a life because it cannot develop on its own.

An ethicist dismissed that as a callous attempt at rationalization. Make no mistake, he told me, that cluster of cells is the same way you and I, and all the rest of us, started our lives. One goes with a heavy heart if we use these, he said, because we are dealing with the seeds of the next generation.

And to the other crucial question, if these are going to be destroyed anyway, why not use them for good purpose—I also found different answers. Many argue these embryos are byproducts of a process that helps create life, and we should allow couples to donate them to science so they can be used for good purpose instead of wasting their potential. Others will argue there's no such thing as excess life, and the fact that a living being is going to die does not justify experimenting on it or exploiting it as a natural resource.

At its core, this issue forces us to confront fundamental questions about the beginnings of life and the ends of science. It lies at a difficult moral intersection, juxtaposing the need to protect life in all its phases with the prospect of saving and improving life in all its stages.

As the discoveries of modern science create tremendous hope, they also lay vast ethical mine fields. As the genius of science extends the horizons of what we can do, we increasingly confront complex questions about what we should do. We have arrived at that brave new world that seemed so distant in 1932, when Aldous Huxley wrote about human beings created in test tubes in what he called a "hatchery."

In recent weeks, we learned that scientists have created human embryos in test tubes solely to experiment on them. This is deeply troubling, and a warning sign that should prompt all of us to think through these issues very carefully.

Embryonic stem cell research is at the leading edge of a series of moral hazards. The initial stem cell researcher was at first reluctant to begin his research, fearing it might be used for human cloning. Scientists have already cloned a sheep. Researchers are telling us the next step could be to clone human beings to create individual designer stem cells, essentially to grow another you, to be available in case you need another heart or lung or liver.

I strongly oppose human cloning, as do most Americans. We recoil at the idea of growing human beings for spare body parts, or creating life for our convenience. And while we must devote enormous energy to conquering disease, it is equally important that we pay attention to the moral concerns raised by the new frontier of human embryo stem cell research. Even the most noble ends do not justify any means.

My position on these issues is shaped by deeply held beliefs. I'm a strong supporter of science and technology, and believe they have the potential for incredible good—to improve lives, to save life, to conquer disease. Research offers hope that millions of our loved ones may be cured of a disease and rid of their suffering. I have friends whose children suffer from juvenile diabetes. Nancy Reagan has written me about President Reagan's struggle with Alzheimer's. My own family has confronted the tragedy of childhood leukemia. And, like all Americans, I have great hope for cures.

I also believe human life is a sacred gift from our Creator. I worry about a culture that devalues life, and believe as your President I have an important obligation to foster and encourage respect for life in America and throughout the world. And while we're all hopeful about the potential of this research, no one can be certain that the science will live up to the hope it has generated.

Eight years ago, scientists believed fetal tissue research offered great hope for cures and treatments—yet, the progress to date has not lived up to its initial expectations. Embryonic stem cell research offers both great promise and great peril. So I have decided we must proceed with great care.

As a result of private research, more than 60 genetically diverse stem cell lines already exist. They were created from embryos that have already been destroyed, and they have the ability to regenerate themselves indefinitely, creating ongoing opportunities for research. I have concluded that we should allow federal funds to be used for research on these existing stem cell lines, where the life and death decision has already been made.

Leading scientists tell me research on these 60 lines has great promise that could lead to breakthrough therapies and cures. This allows us to explore the promise and potential of stem cell research without crossing a fundamental moral line, by providing taxpayer funding that would sanction or encourage further destruction of human embryos that have at least the potential for life.

I also believe that great scientific progress can be made through aggressive federal funding of research on umbilical cord placenta, adult and animal stem cells, which do not involve the same moral dilemma. This year, your government will spend $250 million on this important research.

I will also name a President's council to monitor stem cell research, to recommend appropriate guidelines and regulations, and to consider all of the medical and ethical ramifications of biomedical innovation. This council will consist of leading scientists, doctors, ethicists, lawyers, theologians and others, and will be chaired by Dr. Leon Kass, a leading biomedical ethicist from the University of Chicago.

This council will keep us apprised of new developments and give our nation a forum to continue to discuss and evaluate these important issues. As we go forward, I hope we will always be guided by both intellect and heart, by both our capabilities and our conscience.

I have made this decision with great care, and I pray it is the right one.

Thank you for listening. Good night, and God bless America.

LABOR DEPARTMENT REPORT ON WOMEN'S EARNINGS
August 10, 2001

Women were steadily, if unevenly, closing the gender pay gap with men, according to a Labor Department report issued August 10, 2001. Overall, women's median weekly paychecks were about 75 percent those of men. But the ratio differed considerably by age, profession, and other demographic characteristics. Young women in many professions had similar earnings to young men, for example, while earnings for older women were much lower than those for older men.

Women were also entering more professions that once were considered male strongholds. Forty-three percent of all veterinarians were women in 2001, up from just 2 percent in 1989. There were also more female public administrators, dentists, car salespeople, and members of the clergy. Women made up nearly 50 percent of all law school and medical school admissions. Twenty-five percent of all companies were owned by women.

But these advances sometimes masked other, less positive trends. One reason, for example, for the increasing number of female veterinarians was an overall drop in earnings in the profession that prompted many men to seek other, more lucrative professions. Overall, women were still predominantly employed as secretaries, school teachers, nurses, and retail sales clerks, where salaries traditionally were low. "Let's acknowledge the occupations where women are doing well, but let's not use the jobs where women are making up ground to minimize what's happening" to other working women, said a spokesperson for the AFL-CIO.

Demographics of the Gender Gap

According to the Labor Department report "Highlights of Women's Earnings in 2000," median weekly earnings for women working full-time in 2000 were $491—76 percent of the $646 median for men, and a 13-point increase in earnings since 1979, when the department began to track the gender pay gap. The pay gap was narrower for younger workers, with women ages twenty to twenty-four earning 91.9 percent as much as men of the same age, and women ages twenty-five to thirty-four earning 81.9 percent as *much as men in that category. Women ages fifty-five to sixty-four had the widest pay gap, earning just 68.5 percent of the median earned by men in the age group.*

Although both white men and women earned more than black or Hispanic workers, the gender gap was greater for white women (whose median pay was 74.7 percent of that of white men) than for either black (85.2 percent) or Hispanic (87.7 percent) women. Working mothers, whether of preschoolers or school-age children, earned less than 70 percent of what working fathers earned.

Women's share of jobs in the high-paying managerial and professional occupations grew significantly between 1983, when such data were first collected, and 2000. But the report noted that although women earned the most in these occupations, they were much less likely than men to be employed in some of the highest paying occupations, such as engineers and computer scientists. Within individual professions, women were still clustered on the lower rungs or in less prestigious positions. Female lawyers, for example, "remain underrepresented in positions of greatest status, influence, and economic reward," according to the American Bar Association. "They account for only about 15 percent of federal judges and law firm partners, 10 percent of law school deans and general counsels, and 5 percent of managing partners of large firms."

While some unions and women's rights organizations claimed that the gender gap was rooted in discrimination and traditional views of the role of women, which placed less value on their work outside the home, other groups argued that much of the existing gender gap resulted from choices women made to take less demanding jobs while they were raising their children.

The Census Bureau reported in October that the percentage of working women with infants under a year old fell in 2000 to 55 percent, down from 59 percent in 1998. It was the first statistically significant decline in that measure since the Census Bureau began collecting such statistics in 1976. The Census Bureau said the decline was among women who could most afford to leave work—older mothers, white women, married women living with their husbands, and women with at least one year of college. Experts said the decline did not signal that women were likely to leave the labor force, but that they felt well enough off financially to decide to stay at home longer with their infant children. Some suggested that women might also feel able to take time off and then resume their working careers without losing too much ground professionally.

A study of attitudes about working women, issued by the David and Lucile Packard Foundation in September, found that even though more than two-thirds of all women with preschool children worked, the vast majority of Americans still thought it was best for mothers to stay home to care for their young children. "There's a wealth of polls showing that the younger the child, the more the public feels the parents should be responsible for their care, and even though the public feels women should be able to work, they also believe the mother should be the parent who stays home," Kathleen

Sylvester, director of the Social Policy Action Network and an author of the report, told the New York Times.

The report also found that many employers were implementing family-friendly policies in the workplace, such as flextime, childcare, and other benefits. But often these benefits went disproportionately to better-paid employees. One survey of families with children under six found that flextime was available to 62 percent of those whose family incomes were above $71,600 but only to 31 percent of those with family incomes under $28,000.

Landmarks and Lawsuits

Meanwhile, two female politicians were added to the list of "first woman to have. . . ." In October Nancy Pelosi, a California Democrat, became the first woman elected minority whip in the House of Representatives, making her the highest ranking woman in congressional history. Pelosi, who was in her eighth term in the House, defeated Maryland Democrat Steny Hoyer, 118–95, for the right to replace Democratic whip David E. Bonior, who was retiring from the House to run for governor in his home state of Michigan.

In May Massachusetts acting governor Jane Swift became the first governor to give birth, to twins, while in office. In 1998 Swift gave birth to her first child in the middle of her successful race for lieutenant governor. She later ran into controversy, and an ethics fine, for using aides as babysitters. Her decision to take a short working maternity leave after the birth of the twins also generated controversy, much of it politically inspired, over whether she could successfully mother three children and govern the state.

Two major sex discrimination suits were winding their way through the court system as 2001 drew to a close. In September the federal Equal Employment Opportunity Commission (EEOC) filed suit against Morgan Stanley Dean Witter & Co., alleging that the securities firm paid its female employees less than its male employees for the same work and denied the women promotions. One of the women, a bond saleswoman who made more than $500,000 a year, also alleged that she had been fired after she filed a discrimination suit against Morgan Stanley. The size of the woman's salary was not an issue, according to an EEOC attorney. "What's important here is that no woman, no matter how much she earns, should be subjected to discrimination and be compensated less than a comparable-performing man, simply because she's a woman," the lawyer said.

Late in the year, a federal district court judge in Illinois ruled that a class action suit alleging sex discrimination against Rent-A-Center Inc., the nation's largest rent-to-own appliance and home furnishings company. More than 4,800 women joined the suit, alleging that company had a policy of blatant employment discrimination against women. In letting the class action suit go forward, the judge wrote: "Witnesses testified independently to statements made by the company's Chairman and CEO J. Ernest Talley articulating Rent-A-Center's anti-female policy: 'A woman's place is not in my stores'; 'Women don't belong in rent-to-own'; and 'Get rid of women in any way you can.' Mr. Talley's expressions of the company's policy are echoed in statements made by officers, vice president, regional directors, market managers and store managers across the country." The company denied the allegations.

Following are excerpts from "Highlights of Women's Earnings in 2000," a report issued August 10, 2001, by the Department of Labor.

The document was obtained from the Internet at http:// www.bls.gov/cps/cpswom2000.pdf.

Introduction

In 2000, median weekly earnings for female full-time wage and salary workers were $491, or 76 percent of the $646 median for their male counterparts. In 1979, when comparable earnings data were first available, women earned about 63 percent as much as men did.

The women's-to-men's earnings ratio varies considerably by demographic group. Among blacks and Hispanics, for example, the ratios were about 85 and 88 percent, respectively; for whites, the ratio was about 75 percent. Young women and men (those 16 to 24 years old) had fairly similar earnings; however, in the older age groups, women's earnings were much lower than men's.

This report presents earnings data from the Current Population Survey (CPS). The CPS is a national monthly survey of approximately 50,000 households conducted by the U.S. Census Bureau for the Bureau of Labor Statistics. The earnings data are collected from one-fourth of the CPS monthly sample. Users should note that the comparisons by sex in this report are on a broad level and do not control for many factors that can be significant in explaining earnings differences. . . .

Highlights

Following are some highlights of women's and men's earnings in 2000:

Full-time workers

- Among women, 45- to 54-year-olds had the highest earnings ($565), followed by 35- to 44-year-olds ($520). Men's earnings also peaked among 45- to 54-year-olds ($777). The difference between women's and men's earnings is larger among middle-aged and older workers than it is among younger ones. For example, among workers aged 45 to 54, women earned 72.7 percent as much as men did and, among those 55 to 64 years old, the women's-to-men's earnings ratio was just 68.5 percent. In contrast, among those 25 to 34 years old, women's earnings were 81.9 percent of those of men, and 20- to 24-year-old women earned 91.9 percent as much as did men.
- Between 1979 and 2000, the earnings gap between women and men narrowed for most major age groups. The women's-to-men's earnings ratio

among 35- to 44-year-olds, for example, increased from 58.3 percent in 1979 to 71.1 percent in 2000, and that for 45- to 54-year-olds rose from 56.9 percent to 72.7 percent. The earnings ratios for teenagers and for workers aged 65 and over, however, showed no clear trend over the period.

- White workers of either gender earned more than their black or Hispanic counterparts. The differences among women were much smaller than those among men. White women's earnings ($500) were 16.6 percent higher than black women's ($429), and 37.4 percent higher than those of Hispanic women ($364). In contrast, white men's earnings ($669) were 33 percent higher than the earnings of their black counterparts ($503) and 61.6 percent greater than those of Hispanic men ($414).

- The earnings difference between women and men was widest for whites. White women earned 74.7 percent as much as white men did. Black women's earnings were 85.2 percent of black men's, and Hispanic women made 87.7 percent as much as did Hispanic men.

- Between 1979 and 2000, inflation-adjusted earnings for white women grew fairly steadily, rising by 22.9 percent. Over the same period, earnings growth among black women, at 14.7 percent, was much smaller, and Hispanic women's earnings rose just 4.6 percent. In contrast, real earnings for both white and black men showed little or no net change from 1979 to 2000, while those for Hispanic men fell.

- Median weekly earnings of full-time workers aged 25 and over without a high school diploma were considerably below those of persons with college degrees. Among women, those without a high school diploma earned $303 per week, compared with $760 for those with college degrees. Among men, school dropouts had earnings of $409 a week, compared with $1,022 for college graduates.

- At all levels of education, women have fared better over time with respect to earnings growth than have men. Although both women and men without a high school diploma have experienced a decline in inflation-adjusted earnings since 1979, women's earnings have fallen significantly less—9.8 percent, compared with a 26.7-percent drop for men. Earnings for women with college degrees have increased by 30.4 percent since 1979 on an inflation-adjusted basis, while those of male college graduates rose by only 16.7 percent.

- Women working full time in professional specialty occupations earned $725, more than did women in any other occupational category. Within the professional specialty occupations, women working as engineers, computer scientists, pharmacists, and lawyers had the highest median earnings.

- Women's share of employment in occupations typified by high earnings has grown. In 2000, 47 percent of full-time wage and salary workers in executive, administrative, and managerial occupations were women, up from 34.2 percent in 1983 (the first year for which comparable data are available). Over the same period, women's share of employment in professional specialty occupations rose from 46.8 percent to 51.9 percent.

- Despite increased representation in the higher paying managerial and professional occupations, women remained a relatively small proportion of other high paying occupations, such as protective service and precision production, craft, and repair. Men were about 8 times as likely as women to be employed in precision production, craft, and repair occupations and about 4 times as likely to be in protective service occupations. The proportions of women and men in these occupations were very similar in 1983.
- In both the managerial and professional occupational categories, women and men tend to work in different specific occupations. In the professional specialty occupations, where women earned the most, they were much less likely than men to be employed in some of the highest paying occupations, such as engineers and mathematical and computer scientists. Women were more likely to work in relatively lower paying professional occupations, such as teachers (except college and university) and registered nurses.
- The earnings gap among parents was wider than that among workers overall. Mothers earned just two-thirds of what fathers earned; this ratio held whether their children were preschoolers or of school age.
- The ratio of female-to-male earnings varied by State, from a high of 89.3 percent in the District of Columbia to a low of 66.8 percent in Wyoming. The differences among the States reflect in part variations in the occupation, industry, and age composition of State labor forces. In addition, sampling error in the State estimates is considerably larger than it is for the national data.

Part-time workers

- Women who worked part time—that is, less than 35 hours per week—represented 24.5 percent of all female wage and salary workers in 2000. In contrast, 10 percent of men in wage and salary jobs worked part time.
- Median weekly earnings of female part-time workers were $177, or 36 percent of the median for women who worked full time. The earnings of male part-time workers ($156) were somewhat lower than those of female part-timers. This is largely because male part-time workers, unlike their female counterparts, are highly concentrated in the youngest age groups, which typically have low earnings. About 56 percent of male part-time workers were 16 to 24 years old, compared with 32 percent of female part-timers.

Workers paid by the hour

- About 63 percent of women and 58 percent of men employed in wage and salary jobs were paid by the hour. Women who worked at such jobs had median hourly earnings of $9.03 in 2000. This was 83.2 percent of the hourly median for men ($10.85).
- About 5 percent of women who were paid hourly rates in 2000 reported hourly earnings at or below the prevailing Federal minimum wage of

$5.15. This compares with approximately 3 percent of men in jobs paid by the hour. . . .

- As would be expected, 16- to 19-year-old women and men who were hourly paid workers were the most likely to have earnings at or below the minimum wage. Women 45 to 54 years old and men 35 to 44 years old were the least likely to earn the minimum wage or less.

PEACE AGREEMENT BETWEEN MACEDONIA AND REBELS
August 13, 2001

Aggressive diplomacy by the European Union (EU), with help from the United States, headed off a potentially dangerous conflict during 2001 in Macedonia—one of the ethnic tinder boxes of the Balkans. Ethnic Albanian Muslim guerrillas launched attacks against the Macedonian government early in the year, creating the risk of a repeat of the ethnic warfare that had consumed much of the former Yugoslavia since the disintegration of that nation in 1991. As with the previous conflicts in Bosnia, Croatia, and Kosovo, world leaders feared that an ethnic battle in Macedonia could spill over into other parts of the region, including Albania, Greece, and Turkey. But international diplomacy and political pressure, primarily from Europe, led to a peace agreement in August that addressed many of the underlying issues and stopped the fighting in Macedonia.

As with other conflicts in the Balkans, the year's events in Macedonia were closely linked to developments outside the country—in this case, in neighboring Serbia and its province of Kosovo. Kosovo, which had an overwhelming majority ethnic Albanian population, was the scene of bloody fighting in 1998 and early 1999 between Albanian guerrillas and Serbian-Yugoslav security forces. NATO settled that conflict with an overpowering air war in the spring of 1999 that forced Yugoslavia to pull all its security forces out of Kosovo. Since then, Kosovo technically remained a part of Serbia (and thus of Yugoslavia), but it was governed under a United Nations protectorate. The peace was enforced by NATO troops. (Kosovo, p. 819; other events in the Balkans, Historic Documents of 2000, p. 141)

The end of the war in Kosovo did not end ethnic conflict in the region, however. Since late 2000, Albanian Muslim guerrillas in Serbia's Presevo valley (southeast of Kosovo) had been staging hit-and-run attacks against Serbian security forces and even NATO peacekeepers stationed in Kosovo. Under the 1999 Kosovo peace agreement, the Presevo valley was a demilitarized buffer zone. That status had the unintended effect of creating a security void in the valley, giving the Albanian Muslim guerrillas a base of operations. The guerrillas, many of whom were former fighters with the

Kosovo Liberation Army, hoped to force NATO into allowing the de facto annexation of the Presevo valley to Kosovo. Ultimately, however, some of the guerrillas wanted to make Kosovo officially independent of Serbia, and some hoped to establish a "greater Albania" consisting of Albania, Kosovo, and parts of Serbia and Macedonia where Albanians were in the majority.

Outbreak of Fighting in Macedonia

NATO peacekeepers and diplomats had reacted cautiously to the fighting in the Presevo valley, fearing that a strong military response might inflame the situation unnecessarily. But when the fighting spilled over into Macedonia, NATO responded quickly. The reason was simple: Macedonia had many of the same characteristics that had led to full-scale war during the 1990s in other parts of the former Yugoslavia, and NATO leaders had learned from painful experience that ending such conflicts was time-consuming and expensive.

Along with Bosnia, Croatia, and Slovenia, Macedonia had broken away from Yugoslavia in 1991, just as communism was collapsing in eastern Europe. Macedonia elected a noncommunist government and during the 1990s managed to escape most of the ravages of conflict that beset the other breakaway Yugoslav republics. That changed in 1999, when the Serbian military expelled nearly a million ethnic Albanians from Kosovo; about one-fourth of them ended up in Macedonia, an impoverished country that needed massive amounts of international assistance to cope with the situation. Macedonia already had a delicate balance of ethnic groups. About 60 percent of its 2 million people were ethnic Macedonians, a Slavic people who spoke a language similar to Bulgarian and observed the Eastern Orthodox religion. About 30 percent were ethnic Albanian Muslims, and the rest were Turks, Gypsies (also known as Roma), and others. The country's ethnic Macedonian majority and ethnic Albanian minority had lived in relative peace for many years, first under the strong hand of the Yugoslav government, and since 1991 under a compromise arrangement that gave the Albanians a small voice in national government.

Macedonia's peace was broken on January 22, 2001, when a policeman was killed in a grenade attack on a police station in the predominantly ethnic Albanian village of Tearce, near the border with Serbia. Government forces and a newly emerged Albanian guerrilla force calling itself the National Liberation Army fought for the first time in mid-February. Fighting stepped up early in March when the guerrillas systematically attacked government and police outposts, coming within a dozen miles of Skopje, the national capital.

The rebel force was small, numbering fewer than 200 in its early stages, according to most observers. But the fighting attracted new recruits to the guerrilla cause and, more important, threatened to destabilize the country's delicate political and social balance. For several years moderate Albanian politicians had served in a coalition government with the ethnic Macedonian majority and had won significant concessions, including improved schools and other social services. Clashes between the guerrillas and

Macedonian security forces put severe pressure on those moderates and led to a deterioration of relations between the two ethnic groups—replaying a scenario from Bosnia, Croatia, and Kosovo. Friends, neighbors, and even relatives on opposite sides of the ethnic divide suddenly turned against one another.

As the fighting escalated, NATO at first sought to stem the supply of weapons and fighters coming into Macedonia from Kosovo and Serbia. The Western nations gradually stepped up their diplomatic intervention as well, with senior officials from the EU visiting Skopje to plead for restraint. However, the United States and other NATO nations refused to send armed troops into Macedonia, arguing that such a step would worsen the conflict. The Macedonian government appealed in March for aggressive action by the West against the guerrillas, and on March 19 the chief UN envoy for the Balkans, Carl Bildt, raised an alarm that drew attention in Western capitals. The fighting in Macedonia amounted to a "civil war," he said, that was "eating up the fabric of a fragile state. We are uncomfortably close to the precipice."

In March the EU's chief diplomat, Javier Solana, began a regular series of visits to Skopje intended to begin a political dialogue among the various Macedonian and Albanian factions. Solana's visits invariably calmed the situation for a few days, but then fighting renewed shortly after he left. An important step away from the brink of all-out war came on May 11, when the country's four main political parties representing both Macedonians and Albanians agreed to a new coalition government committed to resolving ethnic disputes. Even so, fighting continued as the new government tried to deal with emotionally explosive issues and as foreign diplomats dropped in with advice and warnings.

Another turning point came in mid-June when NATO diplomats began talking seriously about mounting a peacekeeping force to guarantee any long-term political agreement. The Bush administration at first made it clear that no U.S. troops would be assigned to such a mission. On June 25 the United States found itself smack in the middle of the Macedonia crisis, anyway: U.S. troops stationed in the country as part of a NATO mission supporting the peacekeeping operation in Kosovo were given the assignment of escorting several hundred Albanian rebels out of a conflict zone just six miles from Skopje. The move headed off what could have been a disastrous confrontation between the guerrillas and government forces, but it infuriated ethnic Macedonians, who saw it as an intervention on behalf of the rebels. Lingering resentment against the United States led one month later to violent protests against the U.S. embassy in Skopje.

Several cease-fires calmed the fighting temporarily during the late spring and early summer and provided an incentive for political leaders to begin talking to each other about compromise solutions. Those talks got down to serious business in late July, under the mediation of Solana and other EU diplomats and U.S. special envoy James Pardew. The negotiations produced a tentative agreement on August 8—amid some of the most serious guerrilla attacks yet—and then a final agreement signed by the four major po-

litical parties on August 13. Lord George Robertson, secretary general of NATO, attended the signing ceremony and warned that "both sides have got to mean it, and they've got to deliver it."

Putting the Agreement into Effect

The August 13 agreement called for a series of legal and constitutional changes to give the Albanian minority more rights, including allowing the use of Albanian as an "official" language and removing from the constitution most references to Macedonians being the nation's primary ethnic group. Albanians also were to be given 1,000 slots in the 6,000-man national police force, which in the past had been almost exclusively Macedonian. The national parliament was given forty-five days to ratify these changes. During that period a NATO peacekeeping force of 3,500 troops would arrive on the scene to disarm the Albanian guerrillas, who were to be given amnesty.

The first British troops assigned to the NATO force arrived in Skopje on August 17, and four days later NATO foreign ministers gave formal approval for the full 3,500-troop force to be sent into Macedonia; the force was to include 300 Americans, most of whom were already in Macedonia as part of the support group for NATO's mission in Kosovo.

NATO troops began disarming the Albanian guerrillas on August 27, with an initial thirty-day deadline, after which the peacekeepers were to be withdrawn. The disarmament went smoothly, and by September 24 the Albanian guerrillas had given up more than 3,300 weapons and tens of thousands of mines, grenades, other explosives, and rounds of ammunition. But even as that mission proceeded, European and U.S. diplomats began discussing the need to keep peacekeeping forces in Macedonia past the original thirty-day assignment. Ultimately, NATO agreed to keep 1,000 troops in Macedonia into early 2002, with a further extension possible.

Meanwhile, the Macedonian parliament took up fifteen constitutional changes required by the peace agreement. The parliament quickly gave tentative approval to most of the changes but then bogged down in weeks of argument over the specific wording of key provisions. The most controversial item turned out to be the preamble to the constitution, which defined who the people of Macedonia were. EU and NATO officials repeatedly warned the parliament that it risked losing the entire peace agreement if it did not act. On October 19 Lord Robertson and Solana flew to Skopje to deliver the demand for action in person. "We have done our part of the bargain," Lord Robertson said. "It is up to the others to deliver on their side of the bargain, too." Finally, on November 16—more than three months after the peace agreement was signed—the parliament adopted the preamble and the last of the necessary constitutional changes. Under the preamble, the citizens of Macedonia were defined as "the Macedonian people, as well as citizens living within its borders who are part of the Albanian people" and other ethnic minorities.

The government began pardoning Albanian guerrillas in December, but news organizations reported that dozens of armed guerrillas remained hidden in rural areas, ready to renew the fight. In one ominous sign, a key moderate ethnic Macedonian political party pulled out of the governing coalition in late November, leaving hard-line politicians in charge of most government ministries.

> *Following are excerpts from the "Framework Agreement," signed August 13, 2001, by representatives of the majority-Macedonian and minority-Albanian communities in the former Yugoslav Republic of Macedonia. The agreement was intended to end a civil conflict that began the previous January.*
>
> **The document was obtained from the Internet at http:// www.president.gov.mk/eng/info/dogovor.htm.**

The following points comprise an agreed framework for securing the future of Macedonia's democracy and permitting the development of closer and more integrated relations between the Republic of Macedonia and the Euro-Atlantic community. This Framework will promote the peaceful and harmonious development of civil society while respecting the ethnic identity and the interests of all Macedonian citizens.

1. Basic Principles

1.1. The use of violence in pursuit of political aims is rejected completely and unconditionally. Only peaceful political solutions can assure a stable and democratic future for Macedonia.

1.2. Macedonia's sovereignty and territorial integrity, and the unitary character of the State are inviolable and must be preserved. There are no territorial solutions to ethnic issues.

1.3. The multi-ethnic character of Macedonia's society must be preserved and reflected in public life.

1.4. A modern democratic state in its natural course of development and maturation must continually ensure that its Constitution fully meets the needs of all its citizens and comports with the highest international standards, which themselves continue to evolve.

1.5. The development of local self-government is essential for encouraging the participation of citizens in democratic life, and for promoting respect for the identity of communities.

2. Cessation of Hostilities

2.1. The parties underline the importance of the commitments of July 5, 2001 [when a temporary cease-fire was signed]. There shall be a complete cessation of hostilities, complete voluntary disarmament of the ethnic Albanian armed groups and their complete voluntary disbandment. They acknowledge that a decision by NATO to assist in this context will require the establishment of a general, unconditional and open-ended cease-fire, agreement on a political solution to the problems of this country, a clear commitment by the armed groups to voluntarily disarm, and acceptance by all the parties of the conditions and limitations under which the NATO forces will operate.

3. Development of Decentralized Government

3.1. A revised Law on Local Self-Government will be adopted that reinforces the powers of elected local officials and enlarges substantially their competencies in conformity with the Constitution (as amended in accordance with Annex A [listing constitutional amendments]) and the European Charter on Local Self-Government, and reflecting the principle of subsidiarity in effect in the European Union. Enhanced competencies will relate principally to the areas of public services, urban and rural planning, environmental protection, local economic development, culture, local finances, education, social welfare, and health care. A law on financing of local self-government will be adopted to ensure an adequate system of financing to enable local governments to fulfill all of their responsibilities.

3.2. Boundaries of municipalities will be revised within one year of the completion of a new census, which will be conducted under international supervision by the end of 2001. The revision of the municipal boundaries will be effectuated by the local and national authorities with international participation.

3.3. In order to ensure that police are aware of and responsive to the needs and interests of the local population, local heads of police will be selected by municipal councils from lists of candidates proposed by the Ministry of Interior, and will communicate regularly with the councils. The Ministry of Interior will retain the authority to remove local heads of police in accordance with the law.

4. Non-Discrimination and Equitable Representation

4.1. The principle of non-discrimination and equal treatment of all under the law will be respected completely. This principle will be applied in particular with respect to employment in public administration and public enterprises, and access to public financing for business development.

4.2. Laws regulating employment in public administration will include measures to assure equitable representation of communities in all central and local public bodies and at all levels of employment within such bodies, while respecting the rules concerning competence and integrity that govern public administration. The authorities will take action to correct present imbalances in the composition of the public administration, in particular communities. Particular attention will be given to ensuring as rapidly as possible that the police services will generally reflect the composition and distribution of the population of Macedonia, as specified in Annex C [which deals with "confidence building measures" among the ethnic communities].

4.3. For the Constitutional Court, one-third of the judges will be chosen by the Assembly by a majority of the total number of Representatives that includes a majority of the total number of Representatives claiming to belong to the communities not in the majority in the population of Macedonia. This procedure also will apply to the election of the Ombudsman (Public Attorney) and the election of three of the members of the Judicial Council.

5. Special Parliamentary Procedures

5.1. On the central level, certain Constitutional amendments in accordance with Annex A and the Law on Local Self-Government cannot be approved without a qualified majority of two-thirds of votes, within which there must be a majority of the votes of Representatives claiming to belong to the communities not in the majority in the population of Macedonia.

5.2. Laws that directly affect culture, use of language, education, personal documentation, and use of symbols, as well as laws on local finances, local elections, the city of Skopje, and boundaries of municipalities must receive a majority of votes, within which there must be a majority of the votes of the Representatives claiming to belong to the communities not in the majority in the population of Macedonia.

6. Education and Use of Languages

6.1. With respect to primary and secondary education, instruction will be provided in the students' native languages, while at the same time uniform standards for academic programs will be applied throughout Macedonia.

6.2. State funding will be provided for university level education in languages spoken by at least 20 percent of the population of Macedonia, on the basis of specific agreements.

6.3. The principle of positive discrimination will be applied in the enrolment in State universities of candidates belonging to communities not in the majority in the population of Macedonia until the enrolment reflects equitably the composition of the population of Macedonia.

6.4. The official language throughout Macedonia and in the international relations of Macedonia is the Macedonian language.

6.5. Any other language spoken by at least 20 percent of the population is also an official language, as set forth herein. In the organs of the Republic of Macedonia, any official language other than Macedonian may be used in accordance with the law, as further elaborated in Annex B [a list of laws to be revised in accordance with this agreement]. Any person living in a unit of local self-government in which at least 20 percent of the population speaks an official language other than Macedonian may use any official language to communicate with the regional office of the central government with responsibility for that municipality; such an office will reply in that language in addition to Macedonian. Any person may use any official language to communicate with a main office of the central government, which will reply in that language in addition to Macedonian.

6.6. With respect to local self-government, in municipalities where a community comprises at least 20 percent of the population of the municipality, the language of that community will be used as an official language in addition to Macedonian. With respect to languages spoken by less than 20 percent of the population of the municipality, the local authorities will decide democratically on their use in public bodies.

6.7. In criminal and civil judicial proceedings at any level, an accused person or any party will have the right to translation at State expense of all proceedings as well as documents in accordance with relevant Council of Europe documents.

6.8. Any official personal documents of citizens speaking an official language other than Macedonian will also be issued in that language, in addition to the Macedonian language, in accordance with the law.

7. Expression of Identity

7.1. With respect to emblems, next to the emblem of the Republic of Macedonia, local authorities will be free to place on front of local public buildings emblems marking the identity of the community in the majority in the municipality, respecting international rules and usages.

8. Implementation

8.1. The Constitutional amendments attached at Annex A will be presented to the Assembly immediately. The parties will take all measures to assure adoption of these amendments within 45 days of signature of this Framework Agreement.

8.2. The legislative modifications identified in Annex B will be adopted in accordance with the timetables specified therein.

8.3. The parties invite the international community to convene at the earliest possible time a meeting of international donors that would address in particular macro-financial assistance; support for the financing of measures to be undertaken for the purpose of implementing this Framework Agreement, including measures to strengthen local self-government; and rehabilitation and reconstruction in areas affected by the fighting. . . .

PRESIDENT SUKARNOPUTRI
ON CHALLENGES IN INDONESIA
August 16, 2001

Indonesia in mid-2001 got its third new president since longtime dictator Suharto fell from power in 1998. The new leader, Megawati Sukarnoputri, was the first female president of the world's most populous Muslim country. Megawati faced enormous challenges in the huge island nation of 225 million people. The economy was still reeling from the effects of the Asian financial crisis of 1997–1998; political turmoil that led to the ouster of Suharto had devolved into long-running feuds among numerous factions despite relatively successful elections in 1999; independence movements in several remote provinces threatened the territorial integrity of a nation consisting of more than 13,000 islands; the army was an independent power not always responsive to the central government; and violent disputes raged among ethnic and religious groups in several provinces, some resulting in thousands of deaths. Moreover, after the September 11 terrorist attacks against the United States, fundamentalist Islamist groups protested Megawati's support for Washington's war in Afghanistan and other antiterrorism moves. (Terrorist attacks, pp. 614, 624; Asian financial crisis, Historic Documents of 1997, p. 832; Suharto ouster, Historic Documents of 1998, p. 284)

Megawati readily acknowledged these and other challenges in her first major speech after taking office. Addressing the parliament, Megawati said on August 16: "The so many crises cannot be possibly resolved all at once. In the short-term, we need to restore the living condition of the people, nation and state, bringing a breath of fresh air, secured feelings and a better living environment for all of our people. This is closely related to normalizing the situation, which among other things is needed for the functioning of democracy and the upholding of law. We are aware that there is not much we can do unless these minimum conditions are met."

Removal of Wahid

Indonesia's current round of turmoil began in 1998, when a financial crisis throughout East Asia swamped the country's economy and created a surge of public protest against Suharto's increasingly dictatorial and cor-

rupt regime. The protests, led by college students and workers on the island of Java, quickly demonstrated that Suharto had little support beyond the military and the leaders of business conglomerates associated with his regime. Suharto abruptly left office in May 1998 and was succeeded by his vice president, B.J. Habibie, who proved to be a hapless leader but managed to oversee successful parliamentary elections in 1999. The Indonesian Democratic Party of Struggle, led by Megawati, won the largest bloc of seats in parliament, but Megawati was outmaneuvered in parliamentary voting for president by Abdurrahman Wahid, a cleric who headed a moderate Islamic organization called Nahdatul Ulama. As consolation, Megawati was given the vice presidency. (Wahid presidency, Historic Documents of 1999, p. 718)

Wahid quickly matched Habibie in political and governmental incompetence. Nearly blind and in frail health, he did not project the commanding image that the deeply troubled country sorely needed. Although he was able to oust the controversial army chief, General Wiranto, it was clear that he had little effective control over the country's powerful military or the cabinet agencies that technically reported to him. Wahid failed to address longstanding battles with independence movements in Aceh and other provinces. His government also was foiled in attempts to prosecute Suharto and members of his family on corruption charges. Finally, the government could not locate any of those responsible for more than two dozen bombings in 1999 and 2000; many of the bombings reportedly were carried out by guerrillas from Aceh and by various radical Islamist groups.

With parliamentary criticism of his performance rising, Wahid agreed in mid-2000 to turn over much of the day-to-day tasks of governing to cabinet members. Parliamentary critics then lodged charges that Wahid had knowingly allowed associates to engage in corrupt behavior. In one case, known as "Buloggate," a man who was Wahid's personal masseur and former business partner was accused of embezzling $3.7 million from the national food agency, Bulog. Another case came to be known as "Bruneigate" because it involved a $2 million donation from the Sultan of Brunei—the tiny oil-rich country on the island of Borneo. Wahid said the money was for aid projects in Aceh, but opponents alleged that he took it for himself.

Parliament in September 2000 established a fifty-member committee to investigate the corruption charges. Wahid refused to cooperate with the investigation, which he termed illegal. As the investigation neared its conclusion, violent street protests against Wahid erupted in Jakarta in late January, 2001. Led by students, the protests were reminiscent of those that pushed Suharto from power nearly two years earlier.

The parliament on February 1 voted overwhelmingly to accept the investigating inquiry's vague, but still damning, finding that Wahid had abused his office and lied about his role in the two scandals. With relations between Wahid and the parliament becoming increasingly hostile, the parliament voted on April 30 to censure the president. That move generally was seen as one step short of impeachment, and it created enormous pressure on Wahid to step aside and hand power to Megawati—something he angrily refused to do. A month later, the attorney general, who had been appointed by Wahid, concluded that there was no evidence that Wahid had been directly involved in either of the two scandals.

The final stage of Wahid's presidency began on May 30, when the parliament voted to convene a special session of the People's Consultative Assembly, the superparliamentary body that had the responsibility of choosing a president. The vote was generally seen as the initiation of impeachment proceedings, which were not clearly spelled out in the national constitution. In subsequent weeks Wahid tried numerous tactics to head off impeachment, such as repeatedly shuffling his cabinet and threatening to declare a state of emergency, which would shut down the parliament. But those moves failed, especially after military leaders announced in mid-July that they would not enforce a state of emergency and Wahid's security minister refused to carry out Wahid's firing of the national police chief.

Meeting on July 23, the People's Consultative Assembly voted 591–0 to dismiss Wahid and to replace him with Megawati, the vice president. Nearly 100 members of Wahid's minority party boycotted the vote. The action came several hours after Wahid made one final attempt to declare a state of emergency, but security officials refused to follow the order. In a brief inaugural address, Megawati called on "all parties to accept this democratic process with sincerity." Wahid at first refused to heed that call, however, and remained in the presidential palace, acting as if he were still in charge. Finally, on July 26, Wahid left the palace and flew to the United States, where he sought medical treatment.

Megawati in Office

Megawati took over the presidential palace on August 6, two weeks after assuming office, and slowly began carrying out the official duties of the presidency. She had one enormous asset: great popularity, stemming in large part from her status as the daughter of Indonesia's first postindependence leader, Sukarno, who was ousted from power in 1965 by the military under Suharto's leadership. She had carefully preserved that popularity by avoiding public stands on controversial issues, including Wahid's struggle to remain in power; even close associates insisted they did not know her views on many of the major questions facing the country. It was widely assumed, however, that she would allow the military to resume its traditional role as a dominant force in Indonesian politics.

Signs of potential trouble came almost immediately after Megawati took the oath of office. The People's Consultative Assembly chose as her vice president a conservative Muslim leader, Hamzah Haz, who in 1999 opposed naming Megawati as president because she was a female; his action helped Wahid gain the presidency at that time. Megawati also came under strong pressure to stack her cabinet with representatives of all the leading parties represented in parliament, including the Golkar Party of former president Suharto. When her thirty-two-member cabinet was announced August 9, it appeared that she had resisted most of the political pressure and had instead chosen nonpartisan technocrats, especially for key economic posts. Most analysts said the appointments demonstrated a surprising degree of independence from Indonesia's political and military establishments. But human rights advocates sharply criticized the appointments of A.M. Hendropriyono, a retired army general accused of human rights abuses during the Suharto era, as head of the intelligence service, and of M.A. Rahman, a career prosecutor said to have obstructed investigations in human rights cases, as attorney general.

Megawati again demonstrated independence—at least of a rhetorical nature—when she made her first major address as president August 16, the eve of the national independence day. In a direct challenge to the military, which had brutally fought independence movements in Aceh and Irian Jaya provinces and in East Timor, Megawati said: "We convey our deep apologies to our brothers who have long suffered as a result of inappropriate national policies. We need to pay more attention to human rights. We need a security force which is effective, highly disciplined, and under the control of the government." Even while apologizing for past abuses, Megawati stood firm in opposing independence for Aceh and Irian Jaya, and she asked rebel groups there to lay down their arms and "help build a new Indonesia." However, she explicitly acknowledged that East Timor had won full independence from Indonesia in a 1999 referendum. (East Timor, p. 593)

Megawati also promised to combat corruption, saying she had even instructed family members not to "allow any opportunity for corruption, collusion, and nepotism"—a clear reference to the profiteering of Suharto's family during his long tenure. She appealed to the international financial community to give Indonesia "breathing space" by not pressing too hard for payments on the nation's estimated $140 billion in private and public foreign debt.

Officials in the United States and other countries praised Megawati's first actions and promised renewed support for the Indonesian economy. The first practical help came early in September when the International Monetary Fund released a $400 million loan that had been delayed for months because of the Wahid government's inability to keep promises of economic reforms. Later in the year, however, Megawati's government—matching a pattern of previous governments—fell behind on some of its economic reform promises and faced new demands from international lenders to privatize numerous government-run industrial enterprises, to reform the chaotic banking system, and to eliminate deeply embedded corruption

Reaction to September 11

Less than a month after Megawati took office, Indonesia faced a new crisis in the wake of the September 11 terrorist attacks against the United States. Indonesia was home to more Muslims than any other nation—an estimated 175 million of its 225 million people—and fundamentalist Islamist groups had been at the center of much of the nation's strife during the past two decades. Officials in both Washington and Jakarta worried that new instability could arise in Indonesia once the United States retaliated against the al Qaeda terrorist network, based in Afghanistan, that President George W. Bush said was responsible for the September 11 attacks. These concerns were heightened when Indonesian vice president Hamzah Haz suggested that the United States deserved to be attacked. "Hopefully, this tragedy will cleanse the sins of the United States," he said.

In a previously scheduled visit to Washington, Megawati met with Bush on September 19 and expressed support for the U.S. position. Bush, in turn, offered Megawati a $400 million package of aid and trade benefits, along with a relaxation of restrictions on U.S. training and nonlethal supplies for the Indonesian military.

Megawati's attitude of cooperation with the United States was predictably unpopular with radical Islamist groups, which mounted numerous demonstrations both before and after the U.S. military campaign began in Afghanistan on October 7. Some groups threatened to conduct what they called a "sweep" of all foreigners, especially Americans, to force them out of the country. The anti-U.S. demonstrations gradually faded in Indonesia, as in other Islamic countries. To protect her standing among Islamic groups, Megawati on November 1 called on the United States to keep the war in Afghanistan as limited as possible, warning that a lengthy war, with many civilian casualties, "will not only be counterproductive, but will also weaken the global coalition to wage war on terrorism."

Over the long term, a greater concern for Indonesian and international officials was the continuing violence among the country's numerous ethnic and religious conflicts. Most observers said the violence was fueled by the country's deteriorating economic situation, which threw millions of Indonesians even deeper into poverty and made for easy recruiting by fundamentalist Islamic groups. In a speech October 28, Megawati voiced concern that Indonesia could become "the Balkans of the East" by splitting "into lots of small races, into lots of small countries, all of which will be weak in the face of outside forces."

The country's most serious violence continued to be in Aceh, an oil-rich province at the extreme northwest end of Sumatra. There, a separatist Islamist guerrilla force, the Aceh Freedom Movement (known as GAM) had battled since 1975 to gain independence; an estimated 6,000 people had died in fighting between the government and the rebels. More than 1,000 people were killed during 2001, and an increasingly large proportion of the casualties were civilians killed by the guerrillas and by government security forces, according to Human Rights Watch. Megawati on August 11 signed a law giving Aceh a measure of autonomy, but few observers believed the measure would end the guerrillas' struggle for full independence.

Other independence movements were fighting the government in Irian Jaya (the western half of the island of New Guinea), in the Moluccan islands, and on the large island of Sulawesi in central Indonesia. On both the Moluccan islands and Sulawesi, an Islamic guerrilla force known as Laskar Jihad repeatedly attacked Christians in an evident attempt to force them to flee. According to the International Crisis Group, which monitored such conflicts, about 5,000 people had died in the Moluccan island fighting since 1999. Government officials and independent observers said Laskar Jihad had thousands of fighters on the islands, most of them imported from Java since 2000. One senior Indonesian military official said in December that Laskar Jihad was linked to the al Qaeda terrorist network—a link that captured the attention of U.S. officials determined to eliminate al Qaeda wherever it operated. The exact nature of the link was not clear, however, and some news reports said it was just as possible that Laskar Jihad operated with at least tacit support from elements of the Indonesian military.

Following are excerpts from an address to the Indonesian parliament on August 16, 2001, by Megawati Sukarnoputri, three weeks after her election as the country's first female president.

The document was obtained from the Internet at http:// www.indonesianembassy.org.uk/nnv_2001_08_17.html.

. . . First, tomorrow morning our beloved Republic will celebrate its 56th Anniversary. During the last year we together could also show to ourselves and to the outside world, that this complex multi-ethnic nation at a glance, although seemingly prone to conflict, in fact has an endurance beyond the expectations of many people. We must be indeed very thankful for that.

Secondly, after going through tense months, laden with political conflict, even constitutional one, we all, from whatever group, finally succeeded to prove that we are capable of settling our differences of opinion peacefully. With all the criticisms, we also witness that the Constitution of Proclamation still in fact serves us well.

Previously, many observers and our friendly nations were truly worried that we would slide into an even deeper anarchy. Thanks to God the Almighty, all this did not happen. The spirit of togetherness which we built with perseverance and determination since the beginning of the 20th Century, turned out to be far stronger than all short-term challenges that we faced. Now, God willing, we are ready again to roll up our sleeves to handle many difficult problems long awaiting for us to solve. In my observation, it is one of the indications that we are becoming more mature as a nation.

Yet, above all, there is really something more important. Since the beginning, when this nation was formed, we agreed that to form and maintain our beloved nation was only made possible by the blessings of the Almighty Allah. I am sure that this is not only the declaration of faith from our very religious people, but also the explanation that cannot be denied by anybody. Seemingly, there is no other explanation which can be given as to why we were able to overcome the so many throbbing problems.

Once again, indeed we are obliged to be thankful, without slipping into complacency. During the last four years our whole nation lived under a constant fear, because we were stricken by the monetary, economic, security, political crises, coming just one after the other and, worse still, we felt that there had been institutional crisis and conflict. This was not only felt at the central level, but also in the villages. It is then understandable that many were worried, even very worried, of whether or not the Republic painstakingly established by our founding fathers, would be able to survive or otherwise disintegrate.

Ladies and Gentlemen,

With such a condition, it is not surprising if then many questions arise whether we are able to resolve the multi-faceted problems quickly and holistically. Certainly, it is not the case. Like a disease, a crisis can erupt very suddenly, however, its recovery is obviously a time-consuming process. Many problems and arrangement which we have to correct are not only technical and small in nature, but also there are instances when we have to correct the functions, structures and working methods of our national and state institutions, both at the supra-structure as well as infra-structure levels.

Beyond our expectations, the weakness of the political supra-structure and infrastructure in fact instigates also a chance for various conflicts among people to emerge in an unprecedented form and intensity. There have been already many losses, both in human casualties and material losses. There are many things we have to correct before we can enter the normal life as a society, nation and state, at least in accordance with common standards generally recognized in modern nations. The question is what we should do to implement the correction.

We need to make corrections based on our own vision and strength notwithstanding the many shortcomings and weaknesses we have. Clearly, we have the ability to do so. We have so far succeeded in developing adequately our human resources at all levels and professions, which can be utilized to the maximum possible extent in managing the national resources for the prosperity of the people.

Only a few countries in the world are as blessed as Indonesia which is laden with abundance of natural resources. If only would those natural resources be well managed, our people would have been living in a much prosperous environment. Now, we should find out the root of the problem as to why it did not so happen. Would it be possible that there could be a mistake in the vision and strategy of development, which we applied in the past? Or is it due to the mechanism and working procedure we now use? Or is it because there are many deviations in the implementation?

We can only accomplish this gradually, starting from the most urgent needs, which cannot be delayed. Indeed the so many crises cannot be possibly resolved all at once. In the short-term, we need to restore the living condition of the people, nation and state, bringing a breath of fresh air, secured feelings and a better living environment for all of our people. This is closely related to normalizing the situation, which among other things is needed for the functioning of democracy and the upholding of law. We are aware that there is not much we can do unless these minimum conditions are met.

More or less, we have started to achieve these minimum requirements. In the environment which is already becoming better, we are witnessing that our people are able to develop and make use of their endurance, perseverance and creativity to survive and improve their prosperity. We ought to admire the tough endurance and creativity of our people. During the four years of mone-tary and economic crises, their creativity did not only succeed in supporting their lives, even perhaps rescuing the Republic. . . .

The development of a new Indonesia also requires restructuring the rela-tions between the central and local governments. We are aware of the fact that not only have the overly centralistic infrastructures been inefficient so far, but they also have not been able to provide an opportunity for the emergence and development of initiatives and creativities of our citizens. In the framework of relations between the central and regional governments, much of the authori-ties and state budget supports should be allotted to the districts and mayoral-ties. Whereas the central government's tasks and authorities will only be focused on a number of strategic fields that are really needed by the nation.

In a more operational mode, which would directly or indirectly influence the policy of law and the policy of law enforcement, there is also a need to draw a clearer line on the essence, character, method and materialization of the reforms movement as well as the democratization process that we have embarked upon since 1998. I observe and carefully listen to complaints lodged by some members of the society indicating that under the banner of reforms and democratization there have been many flaws committed forcing us to question whether or not they are still considered to be legitimate reform drives or have instead exceeded their proportion. In several instances, we wit-nessed the outbreak of various mass riots, some of which have been con-ducted in the name of reforms and democratization. These series of actions have arisen concerns over the possibility of the emergence of anarchy in the midst of our society be it in soft, mild, or harsh forms. These have forced us to ponder on the need to gradually carry out genuine reforms and democratiza-tion drives with a clear agenda and conducted in the framework of our indi-rect and representative democratic system namely through the Houses of Representatives. These Houses of Representatives consisted of people's rep-resentatives who are chosen by us through general elections organized di-rectly, generally, freely, confidentially, fairly, and justly, hence command our trust.

We do not indeed need to address these problems from the scratch. Apart from self-crystallizing the many experiences of our national and state liveli-hood, we can also benefit from various ideas, especially those related to the promotion and fulfillment of civil rights and political rights as well as social, economic and cultural rights in our concerted respect for human rights within the framework of the United Nations' system.

We have to admit that our understanding on human rights in the context of today's modern life is indeed insufficient and hollow. We need to observe this important point, for human rights are progressively advancing and becoming one of those basic cornerstones or, better still, they have become widely ac-knowledged parameters to judge whether or not a given nation-state has man-aged to reach a modern stage.

Another important point that we need to ponder upon in drafting and im-plementing the modernization of the 1945 Constitution is the decrease of our social discipline. There have been cases in which we are not consistent in implementing what we have so far agreed upon as manifested in our disrespect of the laws and the rules of the game normally found in a modern nation-state. All of these create an impression that there has been a missing link between what we think, see, and do in real life.

Our difficulty in eradicating the *KKN* (*Korupsi, Kolusi dan Nepotisme*— Corruption, Collision and Nepotism) practices, directly or indirectly, has put us into crisis sweeping the nation since 1997. In contrast to the feudalistic society's framework that seemingly fails to see these *KKN* practices as a major issue, in the democratic framework it will be instead considered to be a formidable problem. The *KKN* practices regardless of how trivial they are, will transgress the public's trust and at the same time violate the official oath.

In this context, allow me to humbly report to this august gathering that I have privately gathered all members of my extended family, requesting them to solemnly pledge not to open a slightest window of opportunity to allow the recurrence of these *KKN* practices entrapping them. They have given me their solemn pledge, and I hope that they would be able to also resist any temptation arising from their environment.

I am sure that we will be able to undertake a major breakthrough to stop and overcome these *KKN* practices if we in this Nusantara Room promise— at least in our heart—not to redo them.

I have also requested all my cabinet members to report their wealth and as soon as possible submit it to the State Officials' Wealth Audit Commission.

Although it looks simple, perhaps this small step will become a starting point of a much bigger social change that we have to carry out promptly. We need to start from our respective family and ourselves. God willing, gradually, but in the not-so-distant future, we will be able to become one of those highly rated governments that are well managed. More importantly, with this step we will be able to utilize effectively and efficiently our national resources chiefly for the welfare of the nation. . . .

Distinguished Ladies and Gentlemen,

To operate a modern economic system without the support of a reliable national banking system is apparently impossible. We need to learn a lot from the past bitter experience in managing the banking sector, especially after the economic liberalization in 1983. We have violated so many conservative norms of managing the banking sectors traditionally cultivated by the world. We need indeed to derive lessons from it, so that we would not lose track for the second time.

Like it or not, to date we have been part of a new world characterized by the globalization in the field of politics, economics, and socio-cultural. What happens in another country influences also our nation, and vice versa. In pursuing economic interests, we have even ventured into formal commitments with other countries both bilaterally and multilaterally.

Generally these commitments are purposely designed with the spirit of mutual benefit. It has to be admitted that some of them have been recently burdensome. Therefore, it is not absolutely wrong if amidst us there emerges a thought to demand to adjust these burdensome commitments. Notwithstanding the reasons, and without attempting to prejudge the goodwill behind this thinking: commitments are commitments. Agreement is agreement, be it national or international in nature.

We have to do our utmost in order to honor the obligations contained in each of this commitment. Nonetheless, it is more than apparent that we will be more than thankful if our friendly countries as well as other donors are ready to provide us with enough room to maneuver and also give us ample time to respite, enabling us thereby to restructure our national live in this difficult transitional period.

We are also facing a short-term challenge to be seriously dealt with through an uphill struggle, which is our participation in the AFTA [Asian Free Trade Agreement] and the WTO [World Trade Organization]. Indeed, I believe it is not easy a task to maintain the national competitiveness in an open and highly competitive international trade when our economy is entrapped in a meager bargaining position.

Ladies and gentlemen,

Allow me now to touch upon the issues of recovery and the efforts to maintain the stability of our national security and defense. Not much we can do should there be no guaranty of security, or should there be no prevention or resistance on our part while our territorial integrity is being threatened. We do need an effective, highly discipline system as well as security apparatus, which are under the control of the government but remain inspired by the people's aspiration.

In tandem with the process of national reforms aimed at creating a more democratic Indonesian society, the *TNI* (*Tentara Nasional Indonesia*—The Indonesian National Military) has pledged its commitment to continue carrying out its internal reforms by way of taking concrete measures to position itself professionally and functionally as the instrument of state defense and to uphold the enforcement of democracy as well as to abide by the law and to respect human rights.

We also are consistently able to set apart the National Police from the *TNI*, notwithstanding the fact that there are cases where the military should provide assistance to the police. Yet, it is lucid that the *TNI* must focus its tasks on defending the territorial integrity, while the police would concentrate more on creating and maintaining security and feeling of secure among the people at large.

In this regard, together with the mounting need to complement and improve the professional capacity of the *TNI* and the National Police, it is incumbent upon the state to ensure the availability of the equipments and the minimum backups aimed at supporting the conduct of the maintenance of defense and security as mandated. It would be simply unfair if we give an uphill task to the *TNI* but fall short of providing them with proper equipments and logistical supports in an appropriate quantity and high quality.

As a result, there is a compelling need of an agenda and clear schedule to follow up the national policy on the *TNI* and the National Police. There are a lot of regulations to be amended, basic and implementing doctrines to be revised, and education and training programs to be conducted.

I am aware of the fact that there are issues we are inheriting from the past with regard to the reposition of the *TNI* and the National Police that need to be dealt with carefully, in particular those relating to the alleged human rights violations in the conflict-hit regions. We learned some of the violations from the international media right after they took place, but some come to the fore only recently.

It has to be admitted that some contents of the news have pinned us down. Nevertheless, we also have a clear stance in this regard. Should there be any convincing proofs that human rights are violated outside the battleground, those who are found guilty should be held responsible according to the prevailing rules and regulations. We will not entertain any impression that we turn a blind eye to serious violations of human rights. For, it is clear that Indonesia is a state based on law. There are no single person is beyond the reach of law, even a president.

Ladies and gentlemen,

In preparing ourselves to embark upon a better future, allow me to dwell on the three questions from the past that need a comprehensive solution. They are the questions of East Timor, Aceh and Irian Jaya.

Right from the outset, the issue of East Timor has an international dimension, especially in the framework of de-colonization. There was no specific design of the Republic of Indonesia on that region. Our involvement in the region should have been inadvertent, for it was the stance adopted by the state founding fathers that the territory of the Republic of Indonesia was the ex-territory of the Dutch Indies. No more, no less.

Leaving behind any intention to find out the background of this bitter experience, we have disentangled the question of East Timor in 1999 and honestly respected the choice of our brothers and sisters in the region to have their own state. Yet, some lingering issues remain to be solved, such as the solution for a considerable amount of the refugees and displaced persons in the province of East Nusa Tenggara, [West Timor] and the assistance for our East Timorese who feel more comfortable to remain living in our soil or to become the citizens of the Republic of Indonesia.

On the other hand, the context of the questions of Aceh and Irian Jaya is far different with that of the East Timor's. These questions are strictly the internal matter of Indonesia, especially in the context of nation- and state-building. We have to honestly admit that the crux of the issues is the various policies of the past, which are considered compromising the interests of the people of those regions. It is therefore normal that we as a nation offer a sincere apology to our fellow citizens who have long been suffering from those inappropriate policies.

It is indeed true that an apology does not suffice. It has to be accompanied by a series of rearrangement aimed at ensuring the recovery of the condition in a soonest possible fashion. Therefore, we are now doing basic corrections on the condition of the two regions, not only by way of paying respect to cultural identities and specific characteristics of the people in those regions, but also by means of granting the regional administrations more authorities to manage their respective regions in the framework of special autonomy. Yet, one thing is clear, all these should remain within the context of preserving the territorial integrity of the Unitary State of the Republic of Indonesia.

Allow me now to take this opportunity to ponder upon the urgency of maintaining the territorial integrity of the country. Territorial integrity is not only of high importance to the attribute of a nation-state, but also serves as an integral part of a stable world order, which has permanent boundaries. In this context, any movements carrying an intention to secede from the Unitary State of the Republic of Indonesia would not only face our strong rejection, but also would never win the support from the international communities.

This very fact has to be taken into due consideration by those advocating such movements, especially those taking on violent actions that claim many lives of innocent people. From this august forum I call on my brothers and sisters who, due to many reasons, have involved in the armed conflict, to return to their society and together develop a new Indonesia, the one better than what we have now. As I said earlier, now we have at our disposal the instruments of special autonomy, which I believe could serve as a proper vehicle to bring the wish and aspiration as well as legitimate interests of all of you.

Honorable Speaker and Vice-Speakers, Members of the House, Ladies and Gentlemen,

It was based on my comprehension on all of those conditions that I formed the Gotong Royong Cabinet in order to carry out the mandate you have entrusted to me until the end of my tenure in 2004.

I do apologize for being late in announcing the line up of the new cabinet. The reasons was simply because it was not easy to pick up the most accurate ministers among the many nominees who are all of excellent quality and respected personage. It was due to the limited posts that I could not accommodate more candidates to take up the posts of coordinating ministers, ministers, or state ministers. I wish they would have the chance to assume their turn in the future.

In an attempt to withstand the questions I have stated earlier, allow me to recap the six programs of the *Gotong Royong* Cabinet.

- Maintaining the unity of the nation in the framework of the Unitary State of the Republic of Indonesia;
- Continuing the process of reforms and democratization in all aspects of national life through clearer framework, direction and agenda, while improving the respect for human rights;
- Normalizing economic life and strengthening the basis for people's economy;
- Implementing law enforcement consistently, creating feeling of safe and secure in people's life, eradicating corruption, collusion and nepotism;

- Conducting the free and active foreign policy, recovering state's and nation's dignity and returning the trust of foreign countries, including international donor institutions and investors, to the government; and
- Preparing safe, orderly, secret and direct general elections of 2004.

I am fully aware that this cabinet would be unable to perform without understanding, cooperation and support from every quarters of the society. From this majestic forum, I, again, ask for those understanding, cooperation and support. Only through this approach will we be able to slowly but surely come out of this painful crisis.

May God the Almighty shower us with His blessings. Amen.

SURGEON GENERAL ON
MINORITY MENTAL HEALTH
August 26, 2001

Mental health received widespread attention both in the United States and internationally in 2001 as health care officials tried to raise awareness about mental illnesses and improve the availability and quality of care for the millions worldwide suffering from depression, dementia, and other debilitating disorders. In the United States, Surgeon General David Satcher released two reports, one pointing out large disparities in access, quality, and availability of mental health services for the nation's minorities, and the other presenting a "national action plan" for improving mental health treatment and services for children. A third report, by the Administration on Aging, focused on mental health problems of the aging.

Internationally, the World Health Organization (WHO) made mental health the focus of World Health Day on April 7. In October the United Nations agency released a report detailing the extent of mental disorders around the world and urging governments to take steps to improve health services for the mentally ill.

Spotlight on Minorities

Satcher initially focused national attention on mental illness in 1999 with a landmark report declaring a crisis in mental health care in the United States. Satcher reported then that approximately one-fifth of all Americans suffered from a mental disorder in any given year but that only one third of them ever sought treatment. Although effective treatments were available for many mental illnesses, the report said, most Americans suffering from mental illness stayed out of treatment, largely because they could not afford it or were too ashamed or embarrassed to make their condition publicly known. (Mental health report, Historic Documents of 1999, p. 836)

A 200-page supplemental study, released on August 26, 2001, looked at the particular problems and barriers faced by four minority groups in the United States—African Americans, Hispanic Americans, Asian Americans, and American Indians and Native Alaskans. Without exception the report found that minorities bore "a disproportionate burden" of mental health disability, compared with white Americans, because they had less access to mental health services and because they were less likely to receive the necessary services or, if they did, to receive the same quality services. Moreover, minorities were overrepresented among vulnerable populations, such as the homeless and the incarcerated, who were at greater risk for mental illness and less likely to receive appropriate treatment.

As with the overall population, the cost of care, the social stigma attached to mental illness, and the fragmented nature of health care services were all substantial obstacles preventing minorities from seeking or receiving adequate treatment for mental disorders. But cultural differences were also a critical factor, influencing how patients display, communicate, and cope with their symptoms, and their willingness to seek treatment. Clinicians' ability, or lack of it, to recognize these cultural variations further influenced diagnosis and treatment as well as the degree of trust and confidence that a patient had in the health care system.

For example, the report said, about 40 percent of Hispanic Americans did not speak English very well, but very few mental health care providers spoke Spanish. Communications difficulties were not the only problem. Bias, stereotyping, and lack of knowledge about various cultures also led to misdiagnoses and misunderstanding. For example, the report said, in some cultures hearings voices or seeing visions might be part of a normal religious experience, but an unaware clinician could easily misinterpret the situation and misdiagnose the patient. African Americans, for example, were more often misdiagnosed as being schizophrenic or having mood disorders than were whites. African Americans, Hispanic Americans, and Asian Americans were all more likely than whites to manifest mental disorders through physical symptoms, such as chest pain, stomach ache, or dizziness. Among Asian Americans, an exceptionally high degree of stigma and shame attached to mental illness prevented many from seeking treatment until their conditions were severe and thus more difficult to treat.

The report expressed particular concern about the lack of research that had been done on the causes and treatments of mental disorders that were particularly prevalent in some racial and ethnic groups. For example, the suicide rate among Native Americans was 50 percent higher than the national rate, yet little research had been done to tailor specific interventions to Indians. (Surgeon general on suicide, p. 290)

The report suggested several steps for improving access to and quality of care for minorities, including integrating mental health care and primary care, putting more health care clinics in areas where minorities lived, encouraging more minorities to enter the mental health care profession, funding more research on the effect of specific mental disorders and treatments on specific cultures, increasing the number of bilingual health care workers, and working cooperatively with practitioners of alternative and traditional medicine.

Satcher also called for greater health insurance coverage for minorities and again endorsed health insurance "parity"—equal treatment under health insurance plans for mental and physical illness. Late in the year the Senate approved a provision requiring parity, but House negotiators dropped it from the final bill on a straight party-line vote. The House Republicans who voted against the Senate proposal said they did not want to increase insurance costs to employers during a recession when many of them were already cutting back on their health insurance benefits.

Mental Health Care for the Young and the Old

In a second supplemental to the 1999 report released on January 3, Satcher outlined a "national action agenda" to improve mental health services for children and adolescents. According to the report, one in every ten children suffered from a mental illness severe enough to cause some level of impairment, but only one in five of these afflicted children ever received treatment. Anxiety disorders affected the most children, followed by attention deficit hyperactivity disorder (ADHD), and depression. Acknowledging allegations that rambunctious children were sometimes misdiagnosed as having ADHD and given unnecessary medication to calm them, Satcher said that many children nonetheless could benefit from medication as well as behavioral treatment.

The report outlined eight steps to improve mental health services for children, including promoting public awareness of children's mental health issues and reducing the stigma associated with mental illness, improving the infrastructure for mental health services targeted on children, and increasing access to quality mental health care services. "We need to help families understand that these problems are real, that they often can be prevented, and that effective treatments are available," Satcher said. "We also need to better educate frontline providers—teachers, health care workers, school counselors and coaches, faith-based workers, and clinicians of all disciplines—to recognize mental health issues. Finally, we need to train health care providers in scientifically-proven, state-of-the-art approaches of assessment, treatment, and prevention."

A report issued in January by the federal Administration on Aging found that nearly one-fifth of Americans over age fifty-five experienced mental disorders that were not part of the normal aging process. The most common illnesses were anxiety disorders such as phobias; severe cognitive impairments such as Alzheimer's disease, and depression. Yet, like other segments of the population, most older Americans suffering mental illness were not treated for it. "It is estimated that only half of older adults who acknowledge mental health problems receive treatment from any health care provider, and only a fraction of those receive specialty mental health services," the report said.

Failure to recognize or treat mental illness, particularly depression, in older adults was thought to be the major factor explaining the suicide rate among older Americans, which was the highest of any age group in the nation. Studies showed that about 20 percent of the elderly who committed suicide had seen their primary care physician on the day that they died and

*that about 70 percent had seen a physician within a month before the sui-
cide. The report was entitled "Older Adults and Mental Health: Issues and
Opportunities."*

The WHO Report

*The United States was not alone in its inadequate care for the mentally
ill. A report issued by the World Health Organization (WHO) on October 4
said that an estimated 450 million people worldwide suffered from mental
disorders, but only a "small minority" received even basic treatment. About
two-thirds of the nations spent less than 1 percent of their health budgets on
the mentally ill, while two-fifths lacked a national mental health policy.*

*"The global toll of mental illness and neurological disorders is stagger-
ing," WHO director general Gro Harlem Bruntland told a news conference.
"Neuropsychiatric disorders account for 31 percent of the disability in the
world." An estimated 121 million people suffered from depression. Depressive disorders were already the fourth leading cause of death and disability
and were expected to move up to second place by 2020, right behind heart
disease.*

*Many of the same factors that prevented adequate treatment of mental ill-
nesses in the United States were prevalent throughout the world. "In both developed and developing countries," Bruntland said, "less than 25 percent of
those affected receive treatment for a variety of reasons, including stigma,
discrimination, scarce resources, lack of skills in primary health care and
deficient public health policies." Bruntland urged governments to adopt
treatments for mental health that were already available and affordable. The
WHO report, entitled "Mental Health: New Understanding, New Hope," represented the first time in forty-two years that the world health agency had
targeted attention on mental health.*

> *Following are excerpts from the executive summary of "Culture,
> Race, and Ethnicity," a supplement to "Mental Health: A Report
> of the Surgeon General," released August 26, 2001, by the U.S.
> Public Health Service, detailing the disparities in mental health
> care services for four minority groups in the United States.*
>
> ***The document was obtained from the Internet at http://
> www.ment.alhealth.org/cre.***

America is home to a boundless array of cultures, races, and ethnicities.
With this diversity comes incalculable energy and optimism. Diversity has enriched our Nation by bringing global ideas, perspectives, and productive contributions to all areas of contemporary life. The enduring contributions of
minorities, like those of all Americans, rest on a foundation of mental health.

Mental health is fundamental to overall health and productivity. It is the
basis for successful contributions to family, community, and society. Through-

out the lifespan, mental health is the wellspring of thinking and communication skills, learning, resilience, and self-esteem. It is all too easy to dismiss the value of mental health until problems appear. Mental health problems and illnesses are *real and disabling* conditions that are experienced by one in five Americans. Left untreated, mental illnesses can result in disability and despair for families, schools, communities, and the workplace. This toll is more than any society can afford.

This report is a Supplement to the first ever Surgeon General's Report on Mental Health, *Mental Health: A Report of the Surgeon General.* That report provided extensive documentation of the scientific advances illuminating our understanding of mental illness and its treatment. It found a range of effective treatments for most mental disorders. The efficacy of mental health treatment is so well documented that the Surgeon General made this single, explicit recommendation for all people: *Seek help if you have a mental health problem or think you have symptoms of a mental disorder.*

The recommendation to seek help is particularly vital, considering the *majority of people with diagnosable disorders, regardless of race or ethnicity, do not receive treatment.* The stigma surrounding mental illness is a powerful barrier to reaching treatment. People with mental illness feel shame and fear of discrimination about a condition that is as real and disabling as any other serious health condition.

Overall, the earlier Surgeon General's report provided hope for people with mental disorders by laying out the evidence for what can be done to prevent and treat them. It strove to dispel the myths and stigma that surround mental illness. It underscored several overarching points about mental health and mental illness. Above all, it furnished hope for recovery from mental illness.

But in the Preface to the earlier report, the Surgeon General pointed out that all Americans do not share equally in the hope for recovery from mental illness:

> *Even more than other areas of health and medicine, the mental health field is plagued by disparities in the availability of and access to its services. These disparities are viewed readily through the lenses of racial and cultural diversity, age, and gender. . . .*

This Supplement covers the four most recognized racial and ethnic minority groups in the United States. According to Federal classifications, African Americans (blacks), American Indians and Alaska Natives, Asian Americans and Pacific Islanders and white Americans (whites) are races. Hispanic American (Latino) is an ethnicity and may apply to a person of any race. For example, many people from the Dominican Republic identify their ethnicity as Hispanic or Latino and their race as black.

The Federal Government created these broad racial and ethnic categories in the 1970s for collecting census and other types of demographic information. Within each of the broad categories, including white Americans, are many distinct ethnic subgroups. Asian Americans and Pacific Islanders, for example, include 43 ethnic groups speaking over 100 languages and dialects. For American Indians and Alaska Natives, the Bureau of Indian Affairs currently recognizes 561 tribes. African Americans are also becoming more diverse, especially with the influx of refugees and immigrants from many countries of Africa and the Caribbean. White Americans, too, are a profoundly diverse group, covering the span of immigration from the 1400's to the 21st century, and including innumerable cultural, ethnic, and social subgroups.

Each ethnic subgroup, by definition, has a common heritage, values, rituals, and traditions, but there is no such thing as a homogeneous racial or ethnic group (white or nonwhite). Though the data presented in this Supplement are often in the form of group averages, or sample means (standard scientific practice for illustrating group differences and health disparities), it should be well noted that each racial or ethnic group contains the full range of variation on almost every social, psychological, and biological dimension presented. One of the goals of the Surgeon General is that no one will come away from reading this Supplement without an appreciation for the intrinsic diversity within each of the recognized racial or ethnic groups and the implications of that diversity for mental health.

Clearly, the four racial and ethnic minority groups that are the focus of this supplement are by no means the only populations that encounter disparities in mental health services. However, assessing disparities for groups such as people who are gay, lesbian, bisexual, and transgender or people with co-occurring physical and mental illnesses is beyond the scope of this Supplement. Nevertheless, many of the conclusions of this Supplement could apply to these and other groups currently experiencing mental health disparities.

Main Findings

Mental Illnesses are Real, Disabling Conditions Affecting All Populations, Regardless of Race or Ethnicity

Major mental disorders like schizophrenia, bipolar disorder, depression, and panic disorder are found world-wide, across all racial and ethnic groups. They have been found across the globe, wherever researchers have surveyed. In the United States, the overall annual prevalence of mental disorders is about 21 percent of adults and children. This Supplement finds that, based on the available evidence, the prevalence of mental disorders for racial and ethnic minorities in the United States is similar to that for whites.

This general finding about similarities in overall prevalence applies to minorities living in the community. It does not apply to those individuals in vulnerable, high-need subgroups such as persons who are homeless, incarcerated, or institutionalized. People in these groups have higher rates of mental disorders. Further, the rates of mental disorders are not sufficiently studied in many smaller racial and ethnic groups—most notably American Indians, Alaska Natives, Asian Americans, and Pacific Islander groups—to permit firm conclusions about overall prevalence within those populations.

This Supplement pays special attention to vulnerable, high-need populations in which minorities are over-represented. Although individuals in these groups are known to have a high-need for mental health care, they often do not receive adequate services. This represents a critical public health concern, and this Supplement identifies as a course of action the need for earlier identification and care for these individuals within a coordinated and comprehensive service delivery system.

Striking Disparities in Mental Health Care Are Found for Racial and Ethnic Minorities

This Supplement documents the existence of several disparities affecting mental health care of racial and ethnic minorities compared with whites:

- Minorities have less access to, and availability of, mental health services.
- Minorities are less likely to receive needed mental health services.
- Minorities in treatment often receive a poorer quality of mental health care.
- Minorities are underrepresented in mental health research.

The recognition of these disparities brings hope that they can be seriously addressed and remedied. This Supplement offers guidance on future courses of action to eliminate these disparities and to ensure equality in access, utilization, and outcomes of mental health care.

More is known about the disparities than the reasons behind them. A constellation of barriers deters minorities from reaching treatment. Many of these barriers operate for all Americans: cost, fragmentation of services, lack of availability of services, and societal stigma toward mental illness. But additional barriers deter racial and ethnic minorities; mistrust and fear of treatment, racism and discrimination, and differences in language and communication. The ability for consumers and providers to communicate with one another is essential for all aspects of health care, yet it carries special significance in the area of mental health because mental disorders affect thoughts, moods, and the highest integrative aspects of behavior. The diagnosis and treatment of mental disorders greatly depend on verbal communication and trust between patient and clinician. More broadly, mental health care disparities may also stem from minorities' historical and present day struggles with racism and discrimination, which affect their mental health and contribute to their lower economic, social, and political status. The cumulative weight and interplay of all barriers to care, not any single one alone, is likely responsible for mental health disparities.

Disparities Impose a Greater Disability Burden on Minorities

This Supplement finds that racial and ethnic minorities collectively experience a greater disability burden from mental illness than do whites. This higher level of burden stems from minorities receiving less care and poorer quality of care, rather than from their illnesses being inherently more severe or prevalent in the community.

This finding draws on several lines of evidence. First, mental disorders are highly disabling for all the world's populations. Second, minorities are less likely than whites to receive needed services and more likely to receive poor quality of care. By not receiving effective treatment, they have greater levels of disability in terms of lost workdays and limitations in daily activities. Further, minorities are overrepresented among the Nation's most vulnerable populations, which have higher rates of mental disorders and more barriers to care. Taken together, these disparate lines of evidence support the finding that minorities suffer a disproportionately high disability burden from unmet mental health needs.

The greater disability burden is of grave concern to public health, and it has very real consequences. Ethnic and racial minorities do not yet completely share in the hope afforded by remarkable scientific advances in understanding and treating mental disorders. Because of disparities in mental health services, a disproportionate number of minorities with mental illnesses do not fully benefit from, or contribute to, the opportunities and prosperity of our society. This preventable disability from mental illness exacts a high societal toll and affects all Americans. Most troubling of all, the burden for minorities is growing. They are becoming more populous, all the while experiencing continuing inequality of income and economic opportunity. Racial and ethnic minorities in the United States face a social and economic environment of inequality that includes greater exposure to racism and discrimination, violence, and poverty, all of which take a toll on mental health.

Main Message: Culture Counts

Culture and society play pivotal roles in mental health, mental illness, and mental health services. Understanding the wide-ranging roles of culture and society enables the mental health field to design and deliver services that are more responsive to the needs of racial and ethnic minorities.

Culture is broadly defined as a common heritage or set of beliefs, norms, and values. It refers to the shared attributes of one group. Anthropologists often describe culture as a system of shared meanings. The term "culture" is as applicable to whites as it is to racial and ethnic minorities. The dominant culture for much of United States history focused on the beliefs, norms, and values of European Americans. But today's America is unmistakably multicultural. And because there are a variety of ways to define a cultural group (e.g., by ethnicity, religion, geographic region, age group, sexual orientation, or profession), many people consider themselves as having multiple cultural identities.

With a seemingly endless range of cultural sub-groups and individual variations, culture is important because it bears upon what all people bring to the clinical setting. It can account for variations in how consumers communicate their symptoms and which ones they report. Some aspects of culture may also underlie *culture-bound syndromes*—sets of symptoms much more common in some societies than in others. More often, culture bears upon whether people even seek help in the first place, what types of help they seek, what coping styles and social supports they have, and how much stigma they attach to mental illness. All cultures also feature strengths, such as resilience and adaptive ways of coping, which may buffer some people from developing certain disorders. Consumers of mental health services naturally carry this cultural diversity directly into the treatment setting.

Culture is a concept not limited to patients. It also applies to the professionals who treat them. Every group of professionals embodies a "culture" in the sense that they too have a shared set of beliefs, norms, and values. This is as true for health professionals as it is for other professional groups such as engineers and teachers. Any professional group's culture can be gleaned from the jargon they use, the orientation and emphasis in their textbooks, and from their mindset or way of looking at the world.

Health professionals in the United States and the institutions in which they train and practice are rooted in Western medicine which emphasizes the primacy of the human body in disease and the acquisition of knowledge through scientific and empirical methods. Through objective methods, Western medicine strives to uncover universal truths about disease: its causation, diagnosis, and treatment. Its achievements have become the cornerstone of medicine worldwide.

To say that physicians or mental health professionals have their own culture does not detract from the universal truths discovered by their fields. Rather, it means that most clinicians share a worldview about the interrelationship between body, mind, and environment informed by knowledge acquired through the scientific method. It also means that clinicians view symptoms, diagnoses, and treatments in ways that sometimes diverge from their clients' views, especially when the cultural backgrounds of the consumer and provider are dissimilar. This divergence of viewpoints can create barriers to effective care.

The culture of the clinician and the larger health care system govern the societal response to a patient with mental illness. They influence many aspects of the delivery of care, including diagnosis, treatments, and the organization and reimbursement of services. Clinicians and service systems, naturally immersed in their own cultures, have been ill-equipped to meet the needs of patients from different backgrounds and, in some cases, have displayed bias in the delivery of care.

The main message of this Supplement is that "culture counts." The cultures that patients come from shape their mental health and affect the types of mental health services they use. Likewise, the cultures of the clinician and the service system affect diagnosis, treatment, and the organization and financing of services. Cultural and social influences are not the only influences on mental health and service delivery, but they have been historically underestimated—*and they do count*. Cultural differences must be *accounted for* to ensure that minorities, like all Americans, receive mental health care tailored to their needs. . . .

Chapter Summaries & Conclusions

Chapter 2: Culture Counts

The cultures of racial and ethnic minorities influence many aspects of mental illness, including how patients from a given culture communicate and manifest their symptoms, their style of coping, their family and community supports, and their willingness to seek treatment. Likewise, the cultures of the clinician and the service system influence diagnosis, treatment, and service delivery. Cultural and social influences are not the only determinants of mental illness and patterns of service use, but they do play important roles.

- Cultural and social factors contribute to the causation of mental illness, yet that contribution varies by disorder. Mental illness is considered the product of a complex interaction among biological, psychological, social, and cultural factors. The role of any of these major factors can be stronger or weaker depending on the specific disorder.
- Ethnic and racial minorities in the United States face a social and economic environment of inequality that includes greater exposure to racism, discrimination, violence, and poverty. Living in poverty has the most measurable effect on the rates of mental illness. People in the lowest strata of income, education, and occupation (known as socioeconomic status) are about two to three times more likely than those in the highest strata to have a mental disorder.
- Racism and discrimination are stressful events that adversely affect health and mental health. They place minorities at risk for mental disorders such as depression and anxiety. Whether racism and discrimination can by themselves cause these disorders is less clear, yet deserves research attention.
- Mistrust of mental health services is an important reason deterring minorities from seeking treatment. Their concerns are reinforced by evidence, both direct and indirect, of clinician bias and stereotyping.
- The cultures of racial and ethnic minorities alter the types of mental health services they need. Clinical environments that do not respect, or are incompatible with, the cultures of the people they serve may deter minorities from using services and receiving appropriate care.

Chapter 3: African Americans

The overwhelming majority of today's African American population traces its ancestry to the slave trade from Africa. The legacy of slavery, racism, and discrimination continues to influence the social and economic standing of this group. Almost one-quarter of African Americans are poor, and their per capita income is much lower than that of whites. They bear a disproportionate burden of health problems and higher mortality rates from disease. Nevertheless, African Americans are a diverse group, experiencing a range of challenges as well as successes in measures of education, income, and other indices of social well-being. Their steady improvement in social standing is significant and serves as testimony to the resilience and adaptive traditions of the African American community.

- **Need for Services:** For African Americans who live in the community, rates of mental illness appear to be similar to those for whites. In one study, this similarity was found before, and in another study, **after** controlling for differences in income, education, and marital status. But African Americans are overrepresented in vulnerable, high-need populations because of homelessness, incarceration, and, for children, placement in foster care. The rates of mental illness in high-need populations are much higher.

- **Availability of Services:** "Safety net" providers furnish a disproportionate share of mental health care to African Americans. The financial viability of such providers is threatened as a result of the national transformation in financing of health care over the past two decades. A jeopardized safety net reduces availability of care to African Americans. Further, there are very few African American mental health specialists for those who prefer specialists of their own race or ethnicity.

- **Access to Services:** African Americans have less access to mental health services than do whites. Less access results, in part, from lack of health insurance, especially for working poor who do not qualify for public coverage and who work in jobs that do not provide private health coverage. About 25 percent of African Americans are uninsured. Yet better insurance coverage by itself is not sufficient to eliminate disparities in access because many African Americans with adequate private coverage still are less inclined to use services.

- **Utilization of Services:** African Americans with mental health needs are less likely than whites to receive treatment. If treated, they are likely to have sought help in primary care, as opposed to mental health specialty care. They frequently receive mental health care in emergency rooms and in psychiatric hospitals. They are overrepresented in these settings partly because they delay seeking treatment until their symptoms are more severe.

- **Appropriateness and Outcomes of Services:** For certain disorders (e.g., schizophrenia and mood disorders), errors in diagnosis are made more often for African Americans than for whites. The limited body of research suggests that, when receiving care for appropriate diagnoses, African Americans respond as favorably as do whites. Increasing evidence suggests that, in clinical settings, African Americans are less likely than whites to receive evidence-based care in accordance with professional treatment guidelines.

Chapter 4: American Indians and Alaska Natives

American Indians and Alaska Natives (AI/ANs) flourished in North America for thousands of years before Europeans colonized the continent. As Europeans migrated westward through the 19th century, the conquest of Indian lands reduced the population to 5 percent of its original size. Movement to reservations and other Federal policies have had enduring social and economic effects, as AI/ANs are the most impoverished of today's minority groups. Over one quarter live in poverty, compared to 8 percent of whites. A heterogeneous grouping of more than 500 Federally recognized tribes, the AI/AN population experiences a range of health and mental health outcomes. While AI/ANs are, on average, five times more likely to die of alcohol-related causes than are whites, they are less likely to die from cancer and heart disease. The Indian Health Service, established in 1955, is the Federal agency with primary responsibility for delivering health and mental health care to AI/ANs.

Traditional healing practices and spirituality figure prominently in the lives of AI/ANs—yet they complement, rather than compete with Western medicine.

- **Need for Services:** Research on AI/ANs is limited by the small size of this population and by its heterogeneity. Nevertheless, existing studies suggest that youth and adults suffer a disproportionate burden of mental health problems and disorders. As one indication of distress, the suicide rate is 50 percent higher than the national rate. The groups within the AI/AN population with the greatest need for services are people who are homeless, incarcerated, or victims of trauma.

- **Availability of Services:** The availability of mental health services is severely limited by the rural, isolated location of many AI/AN communities. Clinics and hospitals of the Indian Health Service are located on reservations, yet the majority of American Indians no longer live on them. Moreover, there are fewer mental health providers, especially child and adolescent specialists, in rural communities than elsewhere.

- **Access to Services:** About 20 percent of AI/ANs do not have health insurance, compared to 14 percent of whites.

- **Utilization of Services:** An understanding of the nature and the extent to which AI/ANs use mental health services is limited by the lack of research. Traditional healing is used by a majority of AI/ANs.

- **Appropriateness and Outcomes of Services:** The appropriateness and outcomes of mental health care for AI/ANs have yet to be examined, but are critical for planning treatment and prevention programs.

Chapter 5: Asian Americans and Pacific Islanders

Asian Americans and Pacific Islanders (AA/PIs) are highly diverse, consisting of at least 43 separate ethnic groups. The AA/PI population in the United States is increasing rapidly; in 2001, about 60 percent were born overseas. Most Pacific Islanders are not immigrants; their ancestors were original inhabitants of land taken over by the United States a century ago. While the per capita income of AA/PIs is almost as high as that for whites, there is great variability both between and within subgroups. For example, there are many successful Southeast Asian and Pacific Islander Americans; however, overall poverty rates for these two groups are much higher than the national average. AA/PIs collectively exhibit a wide range of strengths—family cohesion, educational achievements, and motivation for upward mobility—and risk factors for mental illness such as pre-immigration trauma from harsh social conditions.

Diversity within this population and other hurdles make research on AA/PIs difficult to carry out.

- **Need for Services:** Available research, while limited, suggests that the overall prevalence of mental health problems and disorders among AA/PIs does not significantly differ from prevalence rates for other Americans. Thus, contrary to popular stereotypes, AA/PIs are not, as a group, "mentally healthier" than other groups. Refugees from Southeast Asian countries are at risk for post-traumatic stress disorder as a result of the trauma and terror preceding their immigration.

- **Availability of Services:** Nearly half of AA/PIs have problems with availability of mental health services because of limited English proficiency and lack of providers who have appropriate language skills.
- **Access to Services:** About 21 percent of AA/PIs lack health insurance, but again there is much variability. The rate of public health insurance for AA/PIs with low income, who are likely to qualify for Medicaid, is well below that of whites from the same income bracket.
- **Utilization of Services:** AA/PIs have lower rates of utilization compared to whites. This underrepresentation in care is characteristic of most AAPI groups, regardless of gender, age, and geographic location. Among those who use services, the severity of their condition is high, suggesting that they delay using services until problems become very serious. Stigma and shame are major deterrents to their utilization of services.
- **Appropriateness and Outcomes of Services:** There is very limited evidence regarding treatment outcomes for AA/PIs. Because of differences in their rates of drug metabolism, some AA/PIs may require lower doses of certain drugs than those prescribed for whites. Ethnic matching of therapists with AAPI clients, especially those who are less acculturated, has increased their use of mental health services.

Chapter 6: Hispanic Americans

The Spanish language and culture forge common bonds for many Hispanic Americans, regardless of whether they trace their ancestry to Africa, Asia, Europe or the Americas. Hispanic Americans are now the largest and fastest growing minority group in the United States.

Their per capita income is among the lowest of the minority groups covered by this Supplement. Yet there is great diversity among individuals and groups, depending on factors such as level of education, generation, and country of origin. For example, 27 percent of Mexican Americans live in poverty, compared to 14 percent of Cuban Americans. Despite their lower average economic and social standing, which place many at risk for mental health problems and illness, Hispanic Americans display resilience and coping styles that promote mental health.

- **Need for Services:** Hispanic Americans have overall rates of mental illness similar to those for whites, yet there is wide variation. Rates are lowest for Hispanic immigrants born in Mexico or living in Puerto Rico, compared to Hispanic Americans born in the United States. Hispanic American youth are at significantly higher risk for poor mental health than white youth are by virtue of higher rates of depressive and anxiety symptoms, as well as higher rates of suicidal ideation and suicide attempts.
- **Availability of Services:** About 40 percent of Hispanic Americans in the 1990 census reported that they did not speak English very well. Very few

providers identify themselves as Hispanic or Spanish-speaking. The result is that most Hispanic Americans have limited access to ethnically or linguistically similar providers.

- **Access to Services:** Of all ethnic groups in the United States, Hispanic Americans are the least likely to have health insurance (public or private). Their rate of uninsurance, at 37 percent, is twice that for whites.
- **Utilization of Services:** Hispanic Americans, both adults and children, are less likely than whites to receive needed mental health care. Those who seek care are more likely to go to primary health providers than to mental health specialists.
- **Appropriateness and Outcomes of Services:** The degree to which Hispanic Americans receive appropriate diagnoses is not known because of limited research. Research on outcomes, while similarly sparse, indicates that Hispanic Americans can benefit from mental health treatment. Increasing evidence suggests that Hispanic Americans are less likely in clinical settings to receive evidence-based care in accordance with professional treatment guidelines.

Chapter 7: A Vision for the Future

This Supplement has identified striking disparities in knowledge, access, utilization, and quality of mental health care for racial and ethnic minorities. Reducing or eliminating these disparities requires a steadfast commitment by all sectors of American society. Changing systems of mental health care must bring together the public and private sectors, health service providers, universities and researchers, foundations, mental health advocates, consumers, families, and communities. Overcoming mental health disparities and promoting mental health for all Americans underscores the Nation's commitment to public health and to equality. This chapter highlights promising courses of action for reducing barriers and promoting equal access to quality mental health services for all people who need them.

1. Continue to expand the science base.

Good science is an essential underpinning of the public health approach to mental health and mental illness. The science base regarding racial and ethnic minority mental health is limited but growing. Since 1994, the National Institutes of Health (NIH) has required inclusion of ethnic minorities in all NIH-funded research. Several large epidemiological studies that include significant samples of racial and ethnic minorities have recently been initiated or completed. These surveys, when combined with smaller, ethnic-specific epidemiological surveys, may help resolve some of the uncertainties about the extent of mental illness among racial and ethnic groups.

These studies also will facilitate a better understanding of how factors such as acculturation, help-seeking behaviors, stigma, ethnic identity, racism, and spirituality provide protection from, or risk for, mental illness in racial and ethnic minority populations. The researchers have collaborated on a set of core questions that will enable them to compare how factors such as socioeconomic status, wealth, education, neighborhood context, social support, religiosity, and spirituality relate to mental illness. Similarly, it will be possible to assess how acculturation, ethnic identity, and perceived discrimination affect mental health outcomes for these groups. With these groundbreaking studies, the mental health field will gain crucial insight into how social and cultural factors operate across race and ethnicity to affect mental illness in diverse communities.

A major aspect of the vision for an adequate knowledge base includes research that confirms the efficacy of guideline- or other evidence-based treatments for racial and ethnic minorities. A special analysis performed for this Supplement reveals that the researchers who conducted the clinical trials used to generate treatment guidelines for several major mental disorders did not conduct specific analyses for any minority group. While the lack of ethnic-specific analyses does not mean that current treatment guidelines are ineffective for racial or ethnic minorities, it does highlight a gap in knowledge. Nevertheless, these guidelines, extrapolated from largely majority populations, are clearly the best available treatments for major mental disorders affecting all Americans. As a matter of public health prudence, existing treatment guidelines should continue to be used as research proceeds to identify ways in which service delivery systems can better serve the needs of racial and ethnic minorities.

The science base of the future will also determine the efficacy of ethnic- or culture-specific interventions for minority populations and their effectiveness in clinical practice settings. In the area of psychopharmacology, research is needed to determine the extent to which the variability in peoples' response to medications is accounted for by factors related to race, ethnicity, age, gender, family history, and/or lifestyle.

This Supplement documents the fact that minorities tend to receive less accurate diagnoses than whites. While further study is needed on how to address issues such as clinician bias and diagnostic accuracy, the fifth edition of the Diagnostic and Statistical Manual of Mental Disorders, now under development, will extend and elaborate the "Glossary of Culture-Bound Syndromes," the "Outline for Cultural Formulation," and other concepts introduced in DSM–IV regarding the role and importance of culture and ethnicity in the diagnostic process.

In terms of the promotion of mental health and the prevention of mental and behavioral disorders, important opportunities exist for researchers to study cultural differences in stress, coping, and resilience as part of the complex of factors that influence mental health. Such work will lay the groundwork for developing new prevention and treatment strategies—building upon community strengths to foster mental health and ameliorate negative health outcomes.

2. Improve access to treatment.

Simply put, the Nation's health systems must work to bring mental health services to where the people are.

Many racial and ethnic minorities live in areas where general health care and specialty mental health care are in short supply. One major course of action is to *improve geographic availability of mental health services.* Innovative strategies for training providers, delivering services, creating incentives for providers to work in underserved areas, and strengthening the public health safety net promise to provide greater geographic access to mental health services for those in need.

Another step towards better access to care is to *integrate mental health care and primary care.* Primary care is where many minority individuals prefer to receive mental health care and where most people who need treatment are first recognized and diagnosed. A variety of research and demonstration programs have been or will be created to strengthen the capacity of these providers to meet the demand for mental health services and to encourage the delivery of integrated primary health and mental health services that match the needs of the diverse communities they serve.

Another major step in improving access to mental health services is to *improve language access.* Improving communication between clinicians and patients is essential to mental health care. Service providers receiving Federal financial assistance have an obligation under the 1964 Civil Rights Act to ensure that people with limited English proficiency have meaningful and equal access to services.

Finally, a major way to improve access to mental health services is to *coordinate care to vulnerable, high-need groups.* People from all backgrounds may experience disparities in prevalence of illness, access to services, and quality of services if they are in under-served or vulnerable populations such as people who are incarcerated or homeless and children living in out of home placements. As noted earlier, racial and ethnic minorities are overrepresented in these groups. To prevent individuals from entering these vulnerable groups, early intervention is an important component to systems of care, though research is needed to determine which interventions work best at prevention. For individuals already in underserved or high-need groups, mental health services, delivered in a comprehensive and coordinated manner, are essential. It is not enough to deliver effective mental health treatments: Mental health and substance abuse treatments must be incorporated into effective service delivery systems, which include supported housing, supported employment, and other social services.

3. Reduce barriers to mental health care.

The foremost barriers that deter racial and ethnic minorities from reaching treatment are the cost of services, the fragmented organization of these services, and societal stigma toward mental illness. These obstacles are intimidating for all Americans, yet they may be even more formidable for racial and ethnic minorities. The Nation must strive to dismantle these barriers to care.

Mental Health: A Report of the Surgeon General spotlighted the importance of overcoming stigma, facilitating entry into treatment, and reducing financial barriers to treatment. This Supplement brings urgency to these goals. It aims to make services more accessible and appropriate to racial and ethnic minorities, it encourages mental health coverage for the millions of Americans who are uninsured, and it maintains that parity, or equivalence, between mental health coverage and other health coverage is an affordable and effective strategy for reducing racial and ethnic disparities.

4. Improve quality of mental health services.

Above all, improving the quality of mental health care is a vital goal for the Nation. Persons with mental illness who receive quality care are more likely to stay in treatment and to have better outcomes. This result is critical, as many treatments require at least four to six weeks to show a clear benefit to the patient. Through relief of distress and disability, consumers can begin to recover from mental illness. They can become more productive and make more fulfilling contributions to family and community.

Quality care conforms to professional guidelines that carry the highest standards of scientific rigor. *To improve the quality of care for minorities, this Supplement encourages providers to deliver effective treatments based on evidence-based professional guidelines.* Treatments with the strongest evidence of efficacy have been incorporated into treatment guidelines issued by organizations of mental health professionals and by government agencies.

A major priority for the Nation is to transform mental health services by tailoring them to meet the needs of all Americans, including racial and ethnic minorities. To be most effective, *treatments always need to be individualized in the clinical setting according to each patient's age, gender, race, ethnicity, and culture.* No simple blueprint exists for how to accomplish this transformation, but there are many promising courses of action for the Nation to pursue.

At the same time, research is needed on several fronts, such as how to adapt evidence-based treatments to maximize their appeal and effectiveness for racial and ethnic minorities. While "ethnic-specific" and "culturally competent" service models take into account the cultures of racial and ethnic groups, including their languages, histories, traditions, beliefs, and values, these approaches to service delivery have thus far been promoted on the basis of humanistic values rather than rigorous empirical evidence. Further study may reveal how these models build an important, yet intangible, aspect of treatment: trust and rapport between patients and service providers.

5. Support capacity development.

This Supplement encourages all mental health professionals to develop their skills in tailoring treatment to age, gender, race, ethnicity, and culture. In addition, because minorities are dramatically underrepresented among mental health providers, researchers, administrators, policy makers, and consumer and family organizations, racial and ethnic minorities are encouraged to enter the mental health field. Training programs and funding sources also need to work toward equitable racial and ethnic minority representation in all these groups.

Another way to support capacity development and maximize systems of care is to promote leadership from within the community in which a mental health system is located. Issues of race, culture, and ethnicity may be addressed while engaging consumers, families, and communities in the design, planning, and implementation of their own mental health service systems. To reduce disparities in knowledge, and the availability, utilization, and quality of mental health services for racial and ethnic minority consumers, mental health educational, research, and service programs must develop a climate that conveys an appreciation of diverse cultures and an understanding of the impact of these cultures on mental health and mental illness. Doing so will help systems better meet the needs of all consumers and families, including racial and ethnic minorities.

6. Promote mental health.

Mental health promotion and mental illness prevention can improve the health of a community and the Nation. Because mental health is adversely affected by chronic social conditions such as poverty, community violence, racism, and discrimination, the reduction of these adverse conditions is quite likely to be vital to improving the mental health of racial and ethnic minorities.

Efforts to prevent mental illness and promote mental health should build on intrinsic community strengths such as spirituality, positive ethnic identity, traditional values, educational attainment, and local leadership. Programs founded on individual, family, and community strengths have the potential to both ameliorate risk and foster resilience.

Families are the primary source of care and support for the majority of adults and children with mental problems or disorders. Efforts to promote mental health for racial and ethnic minorities must include strategies to strengthen families to function at their fullest potential and to mitigate the stressful effects of caring for a relative with a mental illness or a serious emotional disturbance.

UN SECRETARY GENERAL ON INDEPENDENCE IN EAST TIMOR
August 30 and October 22, 2001

East Timor, the beleaguered former province of Indonesia that had been a ward of the United Nations since 1999, took a big step in August toward full independence, scheduled for May 2002. Timorese citizens went to the polls on August 30, 2001, and elected an assembly that was empowered to draft a constitution for the country when it became independent. This election and its aftermath were entirely peaceful—a marked contrast to a 1999 referendum on independence that was followed by a deadly rampage.

UN Secretary General Kofi Annan hailed the "spirit of peace, maturity, and tolerance" that he said Timorese demonstrated in the election. But in reports to the UN Security Council, Annan repeatedly warned the international community that it needed to "stay engaged" in East Timor with financial aid and administrative support. After the disastrous events of 1999, East Timor appeared to be emerging as a success story for the United Nations, and Annan clearly was anxious to protect the world body's investment there.

East Timor is the eastern half of a 5,700-square-mile island located between the Indonesian island of Java and Australia. After Portugal, the colonial power, withdrew from East Timor in 1974, the province became engulfed in a civil war between pro- and anticommunist factions, and Indonesia invaded in 1975. Indonesia annexed the province a year later—an action never recognized by the United Nations—and carried out a brutal campaign against Communists and others who opposed Indonesian authority. According to reliable independent estimates, the military killed at least 200,000 people, out of a population of less than 1 million, during the next quarter-century.

After the overthrow of Indonesian dictator Suharto in 1998, the UN arranged for East Timorese to vote on whether they wanted independence or to remain part of Indonesia. More than 78 percent voted for independence in the September 1999 referendum. Immediately afterward, militias organized and armed by the Indonesian military attacked anyone they suspected of supporting independence. During more than two weeks of violence, the militias killed more than 1,000 people and destroyed much of the province's limited infrastructure. More than 200,000 people fled their homes across the border into Indonesian-controlled West Timor. The killings stopped only when the United States and other countries forced Indonesia to allow an Australian-led international peacekeeping force into East Timor. The United Nations then established an administration to run the province until stability could be restored and arrangements made for full independence. The head of the UN mission, Brazilian diplomat Vieira de Mello, acknowledged to Timorese that the world body had failed to take adequate steps prevent the violence. (East Timor background, Historic Documents of 1999, p. 511)

Rebuilding a Society

By most accounts, the UN compensated for its disastrous handling of the 1999 referendum by helping the people of East Timor build a solid foundation for the new nation when it became independent. In effect, the UN task force had to build from the ground up because neither Portugal nor Indonesia had supplied much in the way of public services such as roads, schools, and health clinics for the impoverished province. Most of the services that did exist were destroyed during Indonesia's anticommunist suppression and then during the postreferendum violence of 1999.

With financial help from the World Bank and other international financial institutions, as well as the United States, Japan, Australia, and other donor nations, the United Nations repaired much of East Timor's damaged infrastructure and built new facilities in places where they had been lacking. The UN budget for East Timor was $563 million in the 2000–2001 fiscal year. Annan told the Security Council in October 2001 that De Mello's UN agency (called the UN Transitional Administration in East Timor) recruited and trained nearly 10,000 civil servants, more than 1,000 police officers, and nearly 600 soldiers. More than 185,000 refugees had returned to East Timor, leaving an estimated 60,000 to 80,000 still living in squalid camps in West Timor. The Indonesian government, meanwhile, was threatening to cut off humanitarian aid to those camps at the end of 2001, Annan said.

The security situation in East Timor had markedly improved from the violent days after the 1999 referendum—so much so that de Mello was able to tell the Security Council on October 31 that there was "little cause for concern" at that time. Even so, Annan and de Mello said armed militias were still present in neighboring West Timor. One such group had attacked a UN compound in West Timor on September 6, 2000, killing three employees of the UN High Commissioner for Refugees. An Indonesian court in 2001 found six men guilty of the murders but imposed minimal sentences, prompting an outraged denunciation from Annan.

One of the UN's main tasks in East Timor in 2001 was overseeing the election of an eighty-eight-member Constituent Assembly, which would draft a constitution. The voting took place on August 30, with 91.3 percent of the eligible voters participating. As expected, a majority of seats (fifty-five) were won by representatives of the East Timor National Liberation Front (Fretilin), the former leftist guerrilla group that had fought for independence from Indonesia and then transformed itself into a moderate political party. Fretilin polled about 57 percent of the vote, and with a minority party had the needed two-thirds majority in the assembly to draft the constitution. The assembly began work on the constitution in October. De Mello on September 20 appointed a "transitional government" headed by Mari Alkatiri, a Fretilin leader. It was the first government for East Timor ever to be controlled by Timorese. The transitional government and the UN planned to hold a presidential election early in 2002, which was widely expected to be won by Jose Alexandre Gusmao, the chief Fretilin leader during the independence struggle.

Concerns About the Future

Throughout 2001 UN officials and Timorese leaders suggested that the progress made since 1999 was fragile and that continued international support would be necessary to help East Timor confront the many challenges of a newly independent nation. Annan and de Mello proposed, and the Security Council approved, plans for a staged withdrawal of UN peacekeepers and administrative support staff after East Timor achieved independence in 2002. "We cannot simply walk away" after independence, de Mello told the Security Council on July 30. That view was endorsed by Jose Ramos Horta, the Timorese cabinet minister for foreign affairs, who said the province's people looked forward to the day when UN workers were no longer needed, but he also warned against a "hasty withdrawal" by the UN after independence.

Annan and de Mello pointed to several major problems facing the new government of East Timor, starting with its reliance on international aid. Subsistence agriculture remained the primary source of employment for Timorese, so the new government would have little tax revenue to provide basic services for its people or promote economic development. East Timor had a potential source of wealth in offshore oil fields in the Timor Sea that it shared with Australia. An interim agreement completed in July 2001 provided for East Timor to receive an increased portion of the oil proceeds—possibly more than $200 million a year by 2005, according to Horta. But in the meantime, the new government would have to get almost all its operating funds from international aid agencies. UN and other international officials warned that once the oil money started flowing, the government would have to be careful that it was not squandered on unnecessary projects or siphoned off by corrupt officials.

One of East Timor's greatest obstacles, de Mello said, was the lack of trained teachers, policemen, health workers, lawyers, and other technicians who were necessary to develop the country into a modern society. De Mello said his agency was working as quickly as possible to recruit and train those workers, but hundreds more would be needed to replace the UN staffers when they began leaving in 2002.

Although East Timor itself remained calm, the province still faced a threat of violence from "a core of hard-line militia" in Indonesian West Timor, Annan said in his October 22 report to the Security Council. For that reason, Annan said the United Nations should maintain a peacekeeping force of about 5,000 troops in East Timor through independence, down from about 8,000 in October 2001. The force would be gradually pulled out after independence, according to a schedule yet to be determined. Plans called for East Timor to have its own defense force of 1,500 soldiers; as of October 594 had graduated from basic training. UN staff had trained nearly 1,000 local police officers, but the police force was in desperate need of all types of equipment, Annan said.

One significant advance during the latter part of 2001 was an improvement in relations between the new leaders of East Timor and the Indonesian government. Three top Timorese officials met on September 12 with Indonesia's new president, Megawati Sukarnoputri, who pledged cooperation, including restraining the pro-Indonesian militias in West Timor. On August 16, in her first major speech after taking over as president, Megawati said Indonesia "honestly respected the choice of our brothers and sisters in the region to have their own state." She had opposed independence for East Timor in 1999. (Indonesian politics, p. 562)

It was far from clear that Megawati's pledge of cooperation extended to prosecuting militia members and Indonesian army officials responsible for the 1999 violence in East Timor. The Indonesian government promised to establish a tribunal to handle cases stemming from the violence, but by the end of 2001 had not done so. Human Rights Watch and other organizations charged that bureaucratic delays and limitations on the tribunal's mandate raised questions about whether Indonesia would ever hold any of its citizens to account.

Meanwhile, in East Timor a panel of UN judges on December 12 found ten militia members guilty of murder, torture, and other crimes against humanity committed in the district of Los Palos after the 1999 referendum. Among the thirteen people killed by the militiamen were two nuns, three priests, and an Indonesian journalist. The men were given prison terms of up to thirty-three years. The convictions were the first for what the UN called "crimes against humanity" during the postreferendum violence. At year's end the UN panel was continuing to work on a list of more than 700 murder cases.

Following is the text of a statement by UN Secretary General Kofi Annan on August 30, 2001, praising elections held that day for the Constituent Assembly in East Timor. The statement is followed by excerpts from a report given October 22 by Annan to the UN Security Council on the situation in East Timor.

The documents were obtained from the Internet at http://www.un.org/News/Press/docs/2001/sgsm7927.doc.htm; http://www.un.org/Docs/sc/reports/2001/983e.pdf.

ANNAN ON EAST TIMOR ELECTIONS

I congratulate you on the success of today's Constituent Assembly elections.

The level of popular participation in the vote proved exceptionally high, an estimated 93 per cent, which is far greater, in fact, than that of most democratic nations. I commend the spirit of peace, maturity and tolerance shown by each and every one of you and by all political parties—both throughout the campaign period and at the polls. It provides a glowing example to the world community.

Over the past two years, your unique determination has been the catalyst for all the support that the United Nations, its agencies, non-governmental organizations and the international community have given East Timor in reviving lives and livelihoods and in re-establishing the institutions of government. The conviction which you have shown in embracing democracy only strengthens our commitment to your cause, as you now set about drafting your first Constitution that will soon lead to independence.

The United Nations stands with you in the challenging months that follow as you embark upon the complex second phase in the establishment of government institutions and an economic structure that are sustainable well into the future.

ANNAN REPORT TO THE UN

. . . 4. Since my report of 24 July, three crucial steps have been taken in continuing the progress towards independence for East Timor: the election of a Constituent Assembly; the start of the 90-day Constitution-drafting process; and the formation of an all-East Timorese Council of Ministers.

5. After the peaceful elections for the Constituent Assembly on 30 August, in which 91.3 per cent of eligible voters participated, the Independent Electoral Commission announced the final certified results on 10 September, and assessed that the criteria for a free and fair election had been met. On 15 September, my Special Representative, Sergio Vieira de Mello, swore in the 88 members of the Constituent Assembly.

6. Following the drafting and adoption of its rules and procedures on 8 October, the Assembly established a Committee to make recommendations on the Constitution and to oversee its drafting. They have before them the reports of the 13 Constitutional Commissions, which summarize the views expressed by over 36,000 Timorese. The topics addressed include national and territorial sovereignty; the country name and flag; systems of government, including presidential and semi-presidential, centralized and decentralized systems; economy, taxation and investment; language and citizenship. Members of the Assembly completed a three-day training course with the Inter-Parliamentary Union, the first in a series of training sessions on procedural issues, legislative work practices and comparative international constitutional experience.

7. On 20 September, my Special Representative appointed the "Second Transitional Government". The appointment of its 20 ministers, vice-ministers and secretaries of state, all Timorese, broadly reflects the outcome of the elections of 30 August, as well as sectoral expertise, with an emphasis on youth and geographical representation. A Council of Ministers, led by a Chief Minister, Mari Alkatiri, presides over the Transitional Government and supervises the East Timor Public Administration. This is the first time that executive government in East Timor is controlled by East Timorese, albeit under the overall authority of my Special Representative.

8. Strong regional relationships will clearly play a key role in ensuring the long-term stability and development of East Timor. In a welcome development, the President of Indonesia, Megawati Soekarnoputri, invited my Special Representative, accompanied by Mari Alkatiri, Chief Minister, and José Ramos-Horta, Senior Minister for Foreign Affairs, together with Xanana Gusmão, to Jakarta for meetings on 12 September. The discussions focused on the need to resolve outstanding matters, including border issues, pensions, land transit between the Oecussi enclave and East Timor, cultural cooperation and scholarships. . . .

VI. Observations and recommendations

83. In considering the requirements of the successor mission to UNTAET [United Nations Transitional Administration in East Timor], it bears repeating that UNTAET began its mandate two years ago in the aftermath of a thorough destruction of East Timor's infrastructure and all institutions of government. The human resource base available in East Timor was limited by a history of scant opportunity and training and further depleted by the flight of many civil servants. Against this background, the mandate given by the Security Council in resolution 1272 (1999) to establish a national civil administration, assist in the development of civil and social services and support capacity-building for self-government was unprecedented in scope.

84. In a recent report to the Security Council entitled "No exit without strategy: Security Council decision-making and the closure or transition of United Nations peacekeeping operations", while noting the importance of bringing to fruition the achievements of a peacekeeping operation, I made the following specific reflection regarding East Timor:

> The essential requirement in the case of East Timor is to ensure that the enormous sacrifices of the East Timorese, the substantial investments of the international community, and the cooperation of the parties required to bring about a successful transition to independence are not squandered for lack of international attention and support for the new State. At the same time, it is important to move towards a normal development assistance framework as quickly as is responsibly possible.

In a note prepared in response to my report, the President of the Security Council agreed that a major criterion for the Council's decision on the scaling down or withdrawal of a peacekeeping operation is the successful completion of its mandate. The members of the Council undertook to give consideration to the related questions or concerns identified in my report.

85. It is in this context that I submit to the Security Council for its consideration and approval the proposals contained in Section IV above. [These proposals called for a phasing out of the UN mission, with East Timor assuming full responsibility for defense by mid-2004. Elements of the UN police force and UN civil administrators would remain in East Timor until the local government was able to assume all those functions.] Mindful of the desirability of relying upon a "normal development assistance framework" wherever feasible, the plan for the successor mission contains core tasks that are crucial to protecting the progress made to date. It will be essential, however, that this contribution be supplemented by multilateral and bilateral arrangements.

86. [T]these core tasks will be performed by international staff for a period of two years or less after independence, as responsibilities are transferred progressively to the East Timorese within that period. In this connection, it is my intention, in the near future, to write to the President of the Security Council recommending a date for East Timor's independence, following consultations with my Special Representative and the Constituent Assembly, which is currently seized of this matter. [Subsequently a date of May 20, 2002, was chosen for independence]. The successor mission would be established on that date, and the mandate of UNTAET would therefore need to be extended accordingly.

87. Ultimately, the responsibility to establish a viable state in East Timor clearly belongs to its people. The East Timorese have amply demonstrated the depth of their commitment to this task through sacrifice, imagination and determination. I urge the Security Council to ensure that these foundations are not undermined and to consolidate the remarkable contribution it has already made to this historic undertaking.

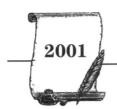

September

UNITED NATIONS ON WORLD CONFERENCE AGAINST RACISM
September 8, 2001

A United Nations conference that intended to focus world attention on the evils of racism became bogged down in a contentious dispute over Israel's treatment of Palestinians. The United States and Israel walked out of the conference after just three days and played no role in the final declaration issued September 8, 2001. Subsequent pressure from European diplomats resulted in elimination of the denunciations of Israel that had led to the U.S. and Israeli walk out. Even so, a full week of international arguing over such issues provided new evidence, if any was needed, that the world was not yet ready to put away bigotry and intolerance.

The conference, formally known as the World Conference Against Racism, Racial Discrimination, Xenophobia, and Related Intolerance, was the UN's third attempt to reach international agreement on a plan of action to combat these human failings. It was held in Durban, South Africa, from August 31 to September 8. The two previous meetings, in 1978 and 1983, also had resulted in flare-ups over ethnic and racial disputes in the Middle East and other regions. The disputes among diplomats mirrored the harsh realities of the real world, where genocidal killings and regional wars in such places as the Balkans and central Africa continued throughout the late twentieth century and killed hundreds of thousands of people.

The U.S. Walkout

The UN conference had been in the planning stages for several years, with various committees meeting to draw up agendas and proposed statements. By early 2001 it became clear that the most contentious issues would be similar to those in the past: an effort by Arab and Muslim nations to denounce Israel for its treatment of Palestinians in occupied territories, and an effort by some African nations to force European nations to acknowledge, and possibly pay reparations for, the lingering consequences of slavery.

Just four days before the conference was to begin, the U.S. State Department announced that Secretary of State Colin Powell would not lead the U.S. delegation, as he had long planned. Powell was the first black to be secretary of state, and supporters of the conference had argued that his presence would send a powerful signal to the world about America's progress in resolving its deeply embedded racial problems. But Powell decided to boycott the conference because Arab and Muslim nations had succeeded in forcing the inclusion of language in the draft declaration denouncing "the racist practices of Zionism" and Israel's treatment of Palestinians.

Less senior State Department officials did register at the conference, but during the opening days they played no active role in the deliberations. On September 3, with the anti-Israel language still intact despite behind-the-scenes efforts to remove it, U.S. and Israeli delegates walked out of the meeting. "You do not combat racism by conferences that produce declarations containing hateful language," Powell said in a statement from Washington announcing the walk-out. Representatives of several human rights and civil rights organizations expressed regret at the walk-out, arguing that U.S. diplomats should have tried harder to develop a compromise on the issue.

In the days after the U.S. and Israeli departure, European diplomats launched an intense effort to convince delegates from Arab and Muslim nations to modify the language about Israel. That effort succeeded late on September 7, but then on September 8, the last day of the meeting, delegates from Pakistan and Syria raised the issue again, insisting that some language denouncing the "racist" practices of Israel be included in the final conference document. Once again, diplomatic maneuvering headed off a conflict, as Israel's foes reluctantly agreed to drop their proposed language. The final document called for an end to violence in the Middle East and for the resumption of negotiations so that both Israel and the Palestinians could "develop and prosper in security and freedom."

The outcome left none of the parties satisfied. Arab and Muslim diplomats expressed frustration at their inability to hold Israel to account, Israeli officials expressed anger at having been subjected to such rhetorical attacks, and diplomats from other countries worried that the dispute overshadowed other important issues. In a broader sense, the outcome may also have been a reflection of the fact that nearly a decade of diplomatic work to resolve the Israeli-Palestinian dispute was hanging by a slender thread in September 2001, just one year after the outbreak of a new cycle of violence in which hundreds of people had been killed. (Middle East violence, p. 360)

Other Issues at the Conference

The dispute over the anti-Israel language was the most attention-getting of numerous conflicts during the conference over what should be said about the world's many racial and ethnic problems. A close second, in terms of attention and heated rhetoric, was a move by some African nations to include language calling for European nations, and possibly the United States as well, to apologize for and pay reparations for the slave trade, which sent millions of black Africans into slavery between the 1500s and the mid-1800s. In particular, the Africans called for the major industrialized countries to promise substantial increases in foreign aid to this region, including cancellation of all remaining debts from development loans made since the colonial era ended in the 1950s and 1960s. European diplomats rejected the demands for an apology and specific promises but ultimately did accept language declaring that slavery was "a crime against humanity and should always have been so" and recommending that former slave-trading nations offer apologies or expressions of regret when "appropriate."

Representatives of numerous minority groups around the world fought, with mixed success, for language recognizing their suffering at the hands majorities. Among them were the Gypsies (or Roma) of central and eastern Europe, the Kurdish minority in Iraq and Turkey, indigenous groups such as Native Americans from Canada and the United States, and the Dalit (formerly known as the "Untouchables") from India. Even when representatives of such groups failed to win adoption of the language they wanted in conference documents, the very fact of getting attention for their causes could be considered a success. "Everywhere people are talking about Dalits," Jyothi Raj, a representative of that group told the New York Times. *"We are feeling connected. We are not alone. We are battling together."*

The final conference document consisted of 122 "general issues" covering the broad spectrum of racism and 219 points in a "program of action" that urged governments, nongovernmental organizations, and individuals to become more respectful and tolerant of those who came from different backgrounds. Among the latter points were such proposals as the banning of "racial profiling" by law enforcement agencies and the trafficking in women and children.

U.S. Record on Racism Issues

In preparation for the conference many countries submitted reports to the UN explaining how they had complied with the International Convention on the Elimination of All Forms of Racial Discrimination. The General Assembly approved that convention in 1965, and the United States ratified it in 1994. The administration of President Bill Clinton submitted the first report on U.S. compliance with the convention in 1997. As of 2001, 157 countries had agreed to abide by the convention's provisions, which called on countries to take all necessary legal and other steps to banish discrimination.

Ralph F. Boyd Jr., the assistant attorney general for civil rights, presented the Bush administration's first report under the convention to the UN at Geneva, Switzerland, on August 3. In his statement, Boyd, an African American, recalled Martin Luther King Jr.'s famous "I Have a Dream" speech of August 1963 and said that King's dream of racial justice in America "is becoming a concrete reality." Boyd cited numerous statistics to show that black Americans had joined the ranks of professionals (such as engineers, doctors, and teachers); had gained political influence at the state, local, and national levels; and had made strides toward legal, social, and economic equality with whites. "There is considerable good news emanating from the century-old struggle of the United States against racism and bigotry," Boyd said. "Of course our nation can do better," he added, noting that the Bush administration had promised to enforce all existing laws banning discrimination.

The UN's Committee on the Elimination of Racial Discrimination, which received Boyd's report, agreed in an assessment released August 14 that the United States had made progress by passing and enforcing important civil rights legislation in the last half of the twentieth century. But the panel also expressed concern about such continuing problems as police brutality against minority groups and foreigners and what it called a "disturbing correlation" between race and the imposition of the death penalty in some states. The committee also suggested that the United States needed to make more extensive use of "affirmative action" programs to ensure improved access to education and employment by members of minority groups.

Perhaps it was understandable that the Bush administration and the UN committee would have different perceptions about the status of race relations in the United States. A public opinion survey conducted by the Washington Post, *the Henry J. Kaiser Family Foundation, and Harvard University indicated that Americans had sharply differing views on the subject, as well. According to results published June 11 by the* Post, *a majority of whites expressed the beliefs that racial discrimination against blacks was no longer a serious problem in the country and that blacks had the same, or even better, opportunities in life than did whites. The findings were the reverse among blacks, who tended to believe that racial discrimination remained a problem and that blacks did not have the same opportunities as whites.*

One consultant on the survey project, Swarthmore College political science associate professor Keith Reeves, told the Post *that the survey results suggested an "overwhelming sense among most whites that this is 2001— we could not possibly be saddled with segregation and discrimination and therefore things can't possibly be as bad as black Americans say they are."*

Following are excerpts from the United Nations news release issued September 8, 2001, summarizing the results of the World Conference Against Racism, Discrimination, Xenophobia and Related Intolerance held in Durban, South Africa, from August 31 to September 8, 2001.

The document was obtained from the Internet at http:// www.unhchr.ch/html/racism/02-documents-cnt.html.

The World Conference Against Racism, Racial Discrimination, Xenophobia and Related Intolerance ended in Durban, South Africa, today with a condemnation of those scourges and a call for action by the international community to eradicate them wherever they may be found.

After intensive and often difficult deliberations on a number of issues, the Conference adopted a Declaration and Programme of Action that commits Member States to undertake a wide range of measures to combat racism and discrimination at the international, regional and national levels. However, a number of delegations made known their reservations or disassociations on certain issues, including those relating to the Middle East and to the legacy of the past.

On the Middle East, the Conference called for the end of violence and the swift resumption of peace negotiations; respect for international human rights and humanitarian law; and respect for the principle of self-determination and the end of all suffering, thus allowing Israel and the Palestinians to resume the peace process, and to develop and prosper in security and freedom.

Expressing concern about the plight of the Palestinian people under foreign occupation, the Conference, in its Declaration, recognized the inalienable right of the Palestinian people to self-determination and to the establishment of an independent state. It also recognized the right to security for all States in the region, including Israel, and called upon all States to support the peace process and bring it to an early conclusion.

On the question of slavery, the Conference agreed on text that acknowledges and profoundly regrets the massive human sufferings and the tragic plight of millions of men, women and children as a result of slavery, slave trade, transatlantic slave trade, apartheid, colonialism and genocide. Acknowledging that these were appalling tragedies in the history of humanity, the Conference further acknowledged that slavery and the slave trade are a crime against humanity and should always have been so, especially the transatlantic slave trade.

Inviting the international community to honour the memory of the victims of these tragedies, the Conference also noted that some States have taken the initiative of regretting or expressing remorse or presenting apologies, and called on all those who have not yet contributed to restoring the dignity of the victims to find appropriate ways to do so.

Concerning compensation and reparations by so-called "concerned States" for slavery, the slave trade and other historical injustices, the Conference recognizes that those historical injustices have undeniably contributed to poverty, underdevelopment, marginalization, social exclusion, economic disparities, instability and insecurity that affect many people in different parts of the world, particularly in developing countries. The Conference recognized the need to develop programmes for the social and economic development of those societies and the diaspora within the framework of a new partnership based on the spirit of solidarity and mutual respect in the following areas: debt relief, poverty eradication, building or strengthening democratic institutions, promotion of foreign direct investment and market access.

The Conference, recognizing the efforts of African leaders to address the challenges of poverty, calls on developed countries, as well as the United Nations system, to support the New African Initiative and other innovative mechanisms, such as the World Solidarity Fund for the Eradication of Poverty.

On the question of victims of racism, another issue that had been difficult to resolve, the Conference agreed on a generic text which stated that "the victims of racism, racial discrimination, xenophobia and related intolerance are individuals or groups of individuals who are or who have been affected by or subjected to or targets of those scourges".

Regarding the grounds for discrimination, the Conference recognized that racism, racial discrimination, xenophobia and related intolerance occur on the grounds of race, colour, descent or national or ethnic origins, and that the victims can suffer multiple or aggravated forms of discrimination based on other or related grounds, including language, sex, religion, political or other opinion, social origin, property, birth or other status. . . .

In her closing remarks, the President of the Conference, Nkosazana Dlamini Zuma, said that Durban had agreed a fresh start and a new road-map for the fight against racism. Endorsing the point that the Conference had set explicit goals and action for combating discrimination, the United Nations High Commissioner for Human Rights, Mary Robinson, who acted as Secretary-General of the Conference, said that the main message she would like to leave the delegates with was that Durban must be a beginning and not an end. "There must be follow-up", she said.

Participating in the World Conference were 2,300 representatives from 163 countries, including 16 heads of State, 58 foreign ministers and 44 ministers. Nearly 4,000 representatives of NGOs and over 1,100 media representatives were accredited.

Programme of Action Highlights

The Conference Programme of Action discusses the sources and causes of racism, racial discrimination, xenophobia and related intolerance and calls for concrete action to eradicate them. A large part of the document is devoted to prevention, education and protection measures at the national level. It also recommends a number of measures at the international level, including the establishment of a follow-up observatory composed of five eminent persons from the various regions to work with the High Commissioner for Human Rights and United Nations bodies to help in implementation of the Declaration and Programme of Action and other tasks.

Calling on States to accede to the International Convention on the Elimination of Racial Discrimination, with a view to universal ratification by 2005, the programme urges them to promote the use of public and private investment to eradicate poverty in areas predominantly inhabited by victims of discrimination.

The Programme further urges States to implement policies and measures designed to prevent and eliminate discrimination on the basis of religion or belief that many people of African descent experience. The document further calls on States to ensure full and effective access to the justice system for all individuals, particularly those of African descent.

States are also urged to adopt or continue to apply all necessary measures to promote, protect and ensure the enjoyment by indigenous people of their rights; to facilitate family reunification, which has a positive effect on integration of migrants; and to take all possible measures to promote the full enjoyment by all migrants of all human rights. The document further encourages States to develop strategies to address discrimination against refugees; and to end impunity and prosecute those responsible for crimes against humanity and war crimes, including crimes related to sexual and other gender-based violence against women and girls.

Among other things, States are encouraged to develop or implement effective legislation and other measures to protect migrant workers, with special attention to people engaged in domestic work and trafficked persons; to ensure accountability for misconduct by law enforcement personnel motivated by racism; to eliminate racial profiling; and to protect the privacy of genetic information.

The Programme of Action further urges States to prohibit discriminatory treatment against foreigners and migrant workers; to enact laws against trafficking in persons, especially women and children; and to compile and publish reliable statistical data to assess the situation of individuals and groups who are victims of discrimination.

Under the Programme of Action, States are also urged to enhance measures to fulfil the right of everyone to the enjoyment of the highest attainable standard of physical and mental health, with a view to eliminating disparities in health status that might have resulted from racial discrimination.

The Programme further urges States, where appropriate, to commit financial resources to anti-racism education and media campaigns promoting tolerance and to take or strengthen measures to address root causes, such as poverty, underdevelopment and lack of equal opportunity, that make persons vulnerable to trafficking.

It calls on States taking all necessary measures to guarantee the right to freedom of expression, to encourage Internet service providers to establish and disseminate specific voluntary codes of conduct and self-regulatory measures against the dissemination of racist messages. The document also calls on States to encourage access to and use by all people of the Internet.

The document calls on States to ensure that education and training, especially teacher training, promote respect for human rights and the fight against racism; to intensify efforts in the field of education efforts to promote awareness of the causes of racism; and urges States to encourage the media to avoid stereotyping based on racism, racial discrimination, xenophobia and related intolerance.

Declaration Highlights

The Declaration expresses solidarity with the peoples of Africa in their continuing struggle against racism, racial discrimination, xenophobia and related intolerance. It also affirms the great importance of solidarity, respect, tolerance and multiculturalism, which constitute the moral ground and inspiration for the worldwide struggle against the inhuman tragedies that have affected people throughout the world, especially in Africa, for too long.

Noting the importance of paying special attention to new manifestations of racism, discrimination, xenophobia and related intolerance to which youth and other vulnerable groups might be exposed, the Declaration recognizes that those evils are among the root causes of armed conflict and very often among its consequences. It expresses deep concern that socio-economic development is being hampered by widespread internal conflicts, including those arising from racism, discrimination, xenophobia and related intolerance, and from lack of democratic, inclusive and participatory governance.

It also expresses concern that in some States, political and legal structures or institutions, many of them inherited and persisting today, do not correspond to the multi-ethnic, multicultural and multi-lingual characteristics of the population, in many cases constituting an important factor of discrimination in the exclusion of indigenous peoples.

The Declaration states that the use of the term "indigenous peoples" is in the context of, and without prejudice to the outcome of, ongoing international negotiations on texts dealing specifically with that issue and cannot be construed as having any implications as to rights under international law.

Welcoming the decision to create the Permanent Forum for Indigenous Issues and the appointment by the United Nations of a Special Rapporteur on the human rights and fundamental freedoms of indigenous peoples, the Declaration recognizes with deep concern the ongoing manifestations of racism, discrimination, xenophobia and intolerance, including violence against the Roma/Gypsies/Sinti/Travellers. It recognizes the need to develop effective policies and implementation mechanisms for their full achievement of equality.

The Declaration describes victims of racism, racial discrimination, xenophobia and related intolerance as individuals or groups of individuals who are or have been negatively affected by, subjected to or targets of those scourges. It recognizes that people of African descent have for centuries been victims of racism, discrimination and enslavement and of history's denial of their rights. It also recognizes that they, as well as Asians and people of Asian descent, face barriers as a result of social biases and discrimination.

Strongly condemning racism and discrimination against migrants and the stereotypes often applied to them, the Declaration reaffirms the responsibility of States to protect their human rights and that of governments to safeguard and protect them against illegal or violent acts perpetrated with racist or xenophobic motivation.

Noting that racism, discrimination and xenophobia contribute to forced displacement and movement of people as refugees and asylum seekers, the Declaration recognizes with concern that despite efforts to combat them, intolerance against refugees, asylum seekers and internally displaced persons continue. It underlines the urgency of addressing the root causes of displacement, and of finding durable solutions, particularly voluntary return to countries of origin and resettlement in third countries.

It recognizes with deep concern the existence of religious intolerance against religious communities, particularly limitation of their right to practise their beliefs freely, as well as the emergence of increased negative stereotyping, hostile acts and violence against such communities because of their religious beliefs and their ethnic or so-called racial origins.

The Declaration strongly reaffirms as a pressing requirement of justice that victims of human rights violations resulting from racism, discrimination, xenophobia and intolerance should be assured of access to justice, including legal assistance where appropriate, effective and appropriate protection and remedies, including the right to seek just and adequate reparation or satisfaction for any damage suffered.

It condemns the persistence and resurgence of neo-nazism, neo-fascism and violent nationalist ideologies based on racial or national prejudice. It also condemns political platforms and organizations based on racism; xenophobia or doctrines of racial superiority and related discrimination; legislation and practices based on racism, discrimination, xenophobia and intolerance as incompatible with democracy and with transparent and accountable governance.

The Declaration recognizes that media should represent the diversity of a multicultural society by fighting racism, discrimination, xenophobia and intolerance. It recognizes that quality education, the elimination of illiteracy and access to free primary education for all can contribute to more inclusive societies, equity, stable and harmonious relations and friendships among nations, peoples, groups and individuals, as well as a culture of peace, fostering mutual understanding, solidarity, social justice and respect for all human rights for all.

It reiterates that the international response and policy, including financial assistance, towards refugees and displaced persons should not be based on the grounds of race, colour, descent, national or ethnic origin of the refugees and displaced persons concerned. . . .

Slavery and Reparations

One of the dominant themes throughout the week-long plenary debate was the insistence by most African countries that countries that participated in and benefited from the slave trade and the colonization of other nations acknowledge the misdeeds of the past and make reparations for them. A number of African heads of State, in addressing the issues of racism and continued discrimination, raised the need to recognize the legacy of slavery and colonialism, and pointed to the links with the poverty and economic imbalances that exist in the world today.

Many speakers blamed slavery, the slave trade and colonialism for the current underdevelopment in Africa and elsewhere, and others pointed out that precedent for compensation had been set in a number of instances, including by Germany after the First World War, to the Japanese Americans interned during the Second World War and to the victims of the Nazi Holocaust. A number of speakers suggested that the reparations did not necessarily have to come in the form of payments to individuals. Many African representatives referred to the New African Initiative, which envisions a united Africa with the assistance of targeted foreign aid. Additionally, others spoke about compensation for African descendants who were also victimized by the scourge of slavery. Cancellation of the crippling debts owed by Africa and the developing world to the industrialized nations and other measures such as support to education funds were also proposed.

Speakers stressed that the issue was not simply about money. One said basic truths were best expressed in simple words—the transatlantic slave trade was a horrible and depraved action and was, quite clearly, a crime against humanity. A number of speakers insisted upon an apology for the suffering the colonial Powers had caused, maintaining that it was impossible to move towards a peaceful future without an acknowledgment of the past. Several European countries, notably the United Kingdom and the Netherlands, acknowledging the slave trade as an abhorrence, expressed regret.

Contemporary Forms of Intolerance

Although speakers noted progress in eradicating racism and racial discrimination, they warned that contemporary forms of racism, racial discrimination, xenophobia and related intolerance, although sometimes more subtle, afflicted every country in the world.

Many speakers emphasized that the growing gap between rich and poor in the era of globalization was a legacy from the era of slavery, the slave trade and colonialism. Countries that had been victim of those practices had been robbed of their natural resources and their society had been deeply affected. As poverty was a breeding ground for intolerance, speakers said, bridging the gap between rich and poor would contribute to combating those phenomena.

Another form of contemporary intolerance, as a by-product of globalization and technological innovation, was the incitement to hatred and dissemination of racist ideas on the Internet. Speakers stressed that such incitement should be prohibited.

Another issue of concern to many speakers was the unique plight of vulnerable groups and people in distress, particularly migrants, asylum seekers, refugees and internally displaced persons. Most agreed there was a need to make a special commitment to ensure the protection of the rights of those groups. With globalization virtually removing all borders and boundaries, international migration had been rendered not only feasible but inevitable. Poverty, as a cause of ethnic conflict, also caused waves of refugees and displaced persons.

Other vulnerable groups also suffered multiple forms of intolerance—women in particular. They were discriminated against because of their gender, origin, economic, social and cultural circumstances and colour. The multiple forms of discrimination faced by AIDS victims was also emphasized by speakers.

Human Rights Education

During the debate, many speakers stressed the need for enhanced education programmes and initiatives aimed at combating prejudice and intolerance, particularly the promotion of human rights in schools. One representative said that the power of education should be harnessed as early as possible in order to instil respect for diversity and compassion in young minds. Education remained the key to the promotion of respect for the racial, ethnic, cultural and linguistic diversity of societies, and for the promotion and protection of values, which were essential to prevent the spread of racism, racial discrimination, xenophobia and related intolerance. It was necessary to foster a culture of respect, starting with formal education systems.

Indigenous Peoples

Another common theme of the past week was indigenous peoples. It was pointed out that the United Nations investment in the world's indigenous peoples made up one tenth of 1 per cent of its operational budget—or roughly one cent for every indigenous family. At the same time, indigenous populations were losing their lands faster than ever because of increased development resulting from growing foreign direct investment in certain parts of the world. They regarded that as discriminatory, since they received little or no assistance from most of the countries in which they lived.

Rigoberta Menchu, a Guatemalan Nobel Prize for Peace winner, speaking in her own personal capacity, told the plenary session that indigenous people expected the Conference to be critical to the recognition of their rights, which have been denied for centuries. Other speakers noted that proposals made at the Conference to allow them the right of self-determination had been disregarded. Instead, there was language that directed them to negotiate their territorial integrity with the States in which they lay, prompting one speaker to say that only the human rights of indigenous peoples were subject to that restriction.

Middle East Situation

Many speakers, most from Arab countries, argued that the problem in the Middle East was one of racism and colonialism, denying the Palestinian people their human rights and fundamental freedoms, including their right to an independent State. Yasser Arafat, the President of the Palestinian Authority, said Palestinians were suffering under the most severe policies of oppression and racial discrimination resulting from the Israeli occupation of their land and holy places. The Secretary-General of the Organization of the Islamic Conference said Israel—based on cynicism, so-called racial superiority, the idea of chosen people and its cavalier attitude towards international legitimacy—felt it could use brute force against unarmed civilians, assassinate Palestinian politicians, close or seal their sanctuaries and Judaize their cities.

The representative of Israel said that those who could not bring themselves to say the word "Holocaust", would call for the condemnation of "racist practices of Zionism". Anti-Zionism was nothing but anti-Semitism, "pure and simple". Speaking on behalf of the European Union and associated States, the Deputy Prime Minister and Minister for Foreign Affairs of Belgium said that the long-running tragedy was primarily a territorial dispute which should not be discussed at this Conference. . . .

BUSH ON TERRORIST ATTACKS AGAINST THE UNITED STATES
September 11 and 14, 2001

The number 911, once recalled nationwide as the emergency response telephone number, also became a date in 2001, representing the day America was subjected to terrorism on a massive scale. On the morning of September 11, four groups of terrorists hijacked jetliners on the East Coast and deliberately flew three of them into buildings that represented American financial and military might: the two World Trade Center towers in New York City and the Pentagon, just outside Washington, D.C. The fourth jet crashed in rural Pennsylvania after failing to reach whatever destination was intended for it by the terrorists. The attacks killed approximately 3,000 people and collapsed the 110-story Trade Center towers into a fiery mass of rubble. For days afterwards, American waited apprehensively for even more terrorist attacks, which did not come.

The audacity of the terrorists and the carnage they caused outraged Americans as had no single act since the Japanese attack on Pearl Harbor nearly sixty years earlier. President George W. Bush, facing his first overwhelming crisis, quickly laid the blame on a radical Islamist network headed by Saudi Arabian exile Osama bin Laden. "These acts of mass murder were intended to frighten our nation into chaos and retreat, but they have failed," the president told a stunned nation and world less than a dozen hours after the attacks began in New York. Nine days later, Bush went before a special joint session of Congress and pledged to eliminate all terrorist groups "with a global reach." And on October 7 U.S. and British forces launched an enormous military campaign in Afghanistan that, within weeks, appeared to decimate bin Laden's network and led to the overthrow of the Taliban regime that had given bin Laden a base of operation in that country. (War in Afghanistan, p. 686)

As terrifying as the attacks were for the immediate victims, their families, their communities, and the world at large, the broader implications of the events of September 11 were certain to be felt for many years to come. World financial markets tumbled, and the U.S. economy—already troubled by a recession that began six months earlier—went into a steep, but brief, decline. The demonstrated vulnerability of the U.S. civil aviation system to infiltration by terrorists finally persuaded Congress to enact some aspects of aviation security legislation that experts had been advocating for years. The Bush administration also persuaded Congress to give it sweeping legal powers to act against presumed terrorists; within weeks law enforcement officials had arrested more than 1,000 Middle Eastern men and held hundreds of them indefinitely. (Aviation security, p. 650; Economic impact, p. 663)

Capitalizing on world sympathy for the United States, Bush and his aides assembled an international coalition providing broad diplomatic and limited military support for a broad war against terrorism, starting with a war of revenge in Afghanistan. One of the most important roles was played by the military leader of Pakistan, who reversed his backing of the Afghanistan government, jailed Islamic extremists, and provided vital logistical support to the U.S. military and intelligence services. World reaction to the terrorist attack also offered the possibility for improved relations between Washington and Moscow. Russian president Vladimir Putin moved to align his country with the United States, both rhetorically and with concrete steps such as allowing U.S. planes to pass through Russian air space on their way to Afghanistan and agreeing to U.S. use of former Soviet bases in Central Asia. Widespread concerns that U.S. retaliation against bin Laden's network and the Afghanistan regime would provoke violent unrest in Pakistan and other Islamic countries proved unfounded. (Pakistan role, p. 624)

Americans had barely begun to absorb the implications of September 11 when the country was hit with a new, and in some ways more mysterious, attack: the arrival of envelopes laden with deadly anthrax bacteria at various offices along the East Coast. Five people died after being exposed to the bacteria, and an intense federal investigation was under way to locate whoever was responsible. (Anthrax attack, p. 672)

By the end of the year, Americans, along with their leaders, were still grappling with the meaning and consequences of the events of September 11. If they remained uncertain why suicidal terrorists would fly airplanes into buildings, they had received a rude education about the grievances that many groups in foreign lands held against the United States. Americans suddenly discovered that the country with the world's largest economy and the mightiest military force could be shaken to the foundations by a handful of men armed only with knives and fanatical ideas.

Sudden Chaos

September 11 began as a beautiful, warm, late-summer day in most of the United States, seemingly a perfect day for an airplane trip across the country. Within a fifteen-minute period around 8:00 A.M., 266 people boarded four planes headed from the East to the West coasts: American Airlines Flight 11, with ninety-two people on board, left Logan Airport in Boston at 7:59 A.M. headed to Los Angeles; United Airlines Flight 93, with forty-five people on board, left Newark Airport at 8:01 A.M. headed to San Francisco;

American Flight 77, with sixty-four people on board, left Washington Dulles Airport at 8:10 A.M. headed to Los Angeles; and United Flight 175 with 65 people on board left Boston Logan Airport at 8:14 A.M. headed to Los Angeles.

The four planes shared at least two important characteristics: they were loaded with the aviation fuel necessary for cross-country flights of about 3,000 miles, and among the passengers on each plane were terrorists recruited for a special assignment by bin Laden's network, known as al Qaeda. Terrorist crews of five men were on three of the planes, and a four-man crew was aboard the fourth plane (United Flight 93). Within minutes of the departures, the terrorists went to work with the box-cutter knives they had carried on board (passengers at the time were allowed to carry such knives). According to accounts reconstructed from a few in-flight telephone calls that passengers were able to make, the terrorists overwhelmed flight attendants and pilots, took over the controls, and proceeded to steer the planes away from their normal flight paths and toward unsuspecting targets. The unusual movements of the planes soon attracted the attention of air traffic controllers, but an alert to military authorities arrived too late to enable air force jets to intervene.

At 8:48 A.M., not quite an hour after it left Boston, American Flight 11 slammed into the upper floors of the north tower of the World Trade Center, causing an enormous fireball explosion and sending glass and metal flying hundreds of feet away. Eighteen minutes later, at 9:06 A.M., United Flight 175 slammed into the south tower, creating a duplicate explosion. Millions of people around the world watched as the second plane hit and then as terrified occupants of the towers fled, or tried to flee. An undetermined number of people jumped from the upper stories in desperate and fatal attempts to escape the flames that were consuming the buildings. Firemen, policemen, emergency medical crews, and other rescue personnel rushed into the towers in heroic efforts to save as many people as possible; hundreds of them became victims themselves, as did countless office workers who tried to save colleagues and strangers.

Authorities acted to prevent more attacks, shutting down New York City-area airports (and later all airports nationwide) and closing all bridges and tunnels into Manhattan. President Bush, meeting with school children in Sarasota, Florida, was told of the crashes and at 9:31 A.M. and called them an "apparent terrorist attack on our country." Thirteen minutes later, at 9:43 A.M., American Flight 77 crashed into the Pentagon, just across the Potomac River from Washington, nearly demolishing one of the building's famous five sides.

The south tower of the World Trade Center shuddered at 9:55 A.M. and collapsed, with a deafening roar, into a cloud of dust and debris. The north tower collapsed at 10:29 A.M., doubling the debris and the terror. New York mayor Rudolph Giuliani ordered all of lower Manhattan evacuated. Experts later said the tremendous heat generated by the explosions literally melted the buildings' steel girders. Seven hours after the north tower fell, the forty-seven-story building known as Seven World Trade Center also collapsed from the stress of the explosions and fires.

Hospitals and morgues prepared for an expected influx of thousands of victims, but few showed up. Early estimates of how many people could have been killed or injured in the World Trade Center buildings ran as high as 20,000 to 30,000, based on an assumption that some 30,000 people worked in the buildings on a normal business day. At the Pentagon, Secretary of Defense Donald H. Rumsfeld was among those who rushed to the part of the building where the plane had hit, helping to rescue injured civilian and uniformed workers.

Even as buildings were aflame in New York and Washington, United Flight 93, which had been in the air for more than two hours, crashed into a field in western Pennsylvania near Pittsburgh, at 10:10 A.M. Authorities said that plane also had been hijacked, but its intended role in the events of September 11 appeared to be lost with the hijackers who died in the crash.

An All-Out Attack?

Whether they were at the scenes of the attacks or monitoring the horrible events on television or radio, Americans were terrified not only by the spectacle of airplanes plunging into buildings but also by uncertainty about what was happening. Was this a general attack on the United States? Were other planes headed toward other buildings? Were terrorists preparing to explode nuclear or chemical weapons in public buildings, subways, and other places with large numbers of civilians? As these and similar questions raced through people's minds, and as rumors emerged that more hijacked planes were headed toward the White House and other targets, President Bush jetted across the country in Air Force One. From Sarasota he went first to Barksdale Air Force base in Louisiana, where he announced that he had put the U.S. military on a worldwide high alert, then to the Strategic Air Command at Offutt Air Force Base in Nebraska, then back to Washington, where he arrived at 7 P.M. Vice President Dick Cheney and the administration's top national security officials remained closeted in the underground Situation Room at the White House—the only occupants after it, the Capitol building, and other federal buildings were ordered evacuated. Washington became a capital under military control.

No one claimed responsibility for the attacks—either on September 11 or afterward—but speculation quickly focused on bin Laden, the one known terrorist leader with a demonstrated capacity to orchestrate complex, simultaneous attacks. U.S. officials had developed compelling evidence that bin Laden's al Qaeda network was responsible for the August 1998 bombings of U.S. embassies in Nairobi, Kenya, and Dar es Salaam, Tanzania, which killed 224 people and injured thousands of others. (African embassy bombings and bin Laden background, Historic Documents of 1998, p. 555)

Addressing the nation from the White House at 8:30 P.M., Bush did not attempt to identify the perpetrators but said he had directed "the full resource of our intelligence and law enforcement communities to find those responsible and bring them to justice. We will make no distinction between the terrorists who committed these acts and those who harbor them." The president also sought to reassure a shaken nation that the military was on alert,

*the government would "continue without interruption," and the economy
would be "open for business." The next day, Bush and his key aides began
saying the nation was at "war" against the "enemies of freedom," and they
insisted the United States would win the war whatever the cost.*

*Despite the president's assurances, much of the country was on hold for
days after September 11. The Federal Aviation Administration closed airports and prohibited air travel immediately after the attacks, and air service resumed slowly during the following week, with few passengers willing
to test their luck. New York's financial markets—their computers and telephone lines crippled by the damage in lower Manhattan—were closed for
the rest of the week, and stock prices plunged once the markets reopened September 16. The nation's travel industry fell into a depression, as Americans
and foreigners by the millions canceled plans to fly to Disney World, Las Vegas, and other destinations.*

*Three days after the attacks, on September 14, Bush addressed the nation
again at a ceremony in Washington National Cathedral marking what he
had declared as a National Day of Prayer and Remembrance. Using more
eloquent language than he had managed to summon at any point on September 11, the president recalled previous challenges the nation had faced
and overcome: "In every generation, the world has produced enemies of human freedom. They have attacked America because we are freedom's home
and defender. And the commitment of our fathers is now the calling of our
time." As he spoke the last words, the president looked at his own father
seated nearby, former president George Bush, who had fought in World
War II and had led the nation in the Persian Gulf war against Iraq in 1991.*

*Over the next few weeks, life in the United States slowly returned to nor-
mal as Americans went about their daily lives, perhaps casting an anxious
glance skyward when airplanes passed overhead. The major exception was
lower Manhattan, where the risky and grisly task of sorting through the
rubble of the Trade Center towers continued twenty-four hours a day, seven
days a week. The fires that brought down the buildings raged for weeks afterwards, severely limiting the rescue work. One-by-one, and sometimes
two-at-a-time, more than 700 bodies emerged from the debris, each attended
by chaplains on duty around the clock.*

*Gradually it became clear that the initial predictions of tens of thousands
of casualties had been mercifully wrong. The estimated death toll at the
World Trade Center fell to about 6,000, then to 5,000, then to 4,000, and
finally to below 3,000. At year's end, the city's official estimate was that
nearly 2,900 people had died in the towers, not counting the 147 passengers
and crew and 10 hijackers aboard the two airplanes. Another 184 civilian
and military personnel died at the Pentagon, plus the 64 people (including 5 hijackers) aboard Flight 77. Most of the day's victims were business
people, professionals, emergency workers, and vacationers—a cross-section
of the working and traveling public in the United States. Nationals of more
than sixty foreign countries were among the dead, most of them workers at
the World Trade Center. Ironically, one of those who died in the World Trade
Center was John O'Neill, a former senior FBI official who had helped over-*

see investigations into bin Laden's previous terrorist activities. O'Neill had taken a job several months earlier as security director for the New York-New Jersey Port Authority, which owned the trade center buildings.

Naming the Suspects

Four days after the attacks, the FBI named nineteen men as the hijackers of the four planes. Fifteen of the men were citizens of Saudi Arabia, two were from the United Arab Emirates, one was from Egypt, and one was from Lebanon. At least sixteen had entered the United States legally with business, tourist, or other types of visas. Six had taken courses at flight schools, either in the United States or overseas, apparently in preparation for the suicidal task of piloting planes into buildings.

FBI officials said the apparent leader of the hijacking crews was Mohamed Atta, an Egyptian who had first entered the United States in June 2000 on a tourist visa and later took pilot lessons in Venice, Florida. Atta's activities never aroused suspicions because his name did not appear in any data bases of criminal and terrorist organizations. In fact, according to subsequent investigations, Atta and at least three other hijackers had been part of a terrorist cell financed by bin Laden's organization that had started in Hamburg, Germany, in 1999.

Many of the hijackers fit the standard police theory that terrorists tended to emerge from the impoverished masses in Third World countries. These hijackers, who came from rural villages in Saudi Arabia, had little formal education and almost no command of English. On September 11 they were the strongmen who used knives and muscle to overpower the crews and passengers on board the planes, while Atta and other "pilots" among the hijackers flew the planes to their intended targets. These latter hijackers were educated men of middle-class backgrounds who had studied in Germany and other European countries before arriving in the United States. As they prepared for their assigned tasks while living in New Jersey and Florida, according to news reports, some of the hijackers engaged in activities strictly forbidden by the Islamic laws that bin Laden's organization supposedly was dedicated to enforcing: smoking cigarettes and consuming large quantities of beer and hard liquor at bars. The hijackers' living expenses, flight school tuition, and numerous airplane flights around the country reportedly were financed by wire transfers of cash totaling several hundred thousand dollars from a bank in the United Arab Emirates.

In the weeks after September 11, law enforcement officials arrested more than 1,000 individuals in a dragnet of suspicious Middle Eastern noncitizens. Nearly all were held on immigration violations or for other minor offenses. Dozens were released after being held for days or weeks, but at year's end several hundred remained in detention.

The government charged only one detainee with a crime in connection with the terrorist attacks: Zacarias Moussaoui, a French citizen of Moroccan descent. In mid-August Moussaoui had worried a flight instructor in Minnesota when he said he wanted to learn how to fly large jets but not how to land them. According to later reports, the flight instructor warned the FBI that Moussaoui appeared to be planning a terrorist attack. Those warnings led federal agents to detain Moussaoui for visa violations on August 16, but the FBI was unable at that time to determine that Moussaoui's activities were part of a broader conspiracy. Moussaoui was indicted on December 11 on six charges relating to the September 11 attacks. Others named in a comprehensive indictment approved by a grand jury in Virginia were bin Laden and three key associates: Ayman al-Zawahiri, head of the Egyptian Islamic Jihad; Moustaffa Ahmed al-Hawasawi, who allegedly funneled money to the hijackers from the United Arab Emirates; and Ramzi Binalshibh, an alleged member of al Qaeda's Hamburg cell who was alleged to have sent money to Moussaoui. The nineteen hijackers were named as unindicted coconspirators.

Following are the texts of two statements by President George W. Bush in the wake of terrorist attacks against the United States on September 11, 2001. The first is a televised address delivered from the White House on the evening of September 11; the second is an address delivered at a ceremony in Washington's National Cathedral marking a National Day of Prayer and Remembrance on September 14, 2001.

The documents were obtained from the Internet at http:// www.whitehouse.gov/news/releases/2001/09/20010911-16 .html; http://www.whitehouse.gov/news/releases/2001/09/ 20010914-2.html.

BUSH STATEMENT, SEPTEMBER 11

Good evening. Today, our fellow citizens, our way of life, our very freedom came under attack in a series of deliberate and deadly terrorist acts. The victims were in airplanes, or in their offices; secretaries, businessmen and women, military and federal workers; moms and dads, friends and neighbors. Thousands of lives were suddenly ended by evil, despicable acts of terror.

The pictures of airplanes flying into buildings, fires burning, huge structures collapsing, have filled us with disbelief, terrible sadness, and a quiet, unyielding anger. These acts of mass murder were intended to frighten our nation into chaos and retreat. But they have failed; our country is strong.

A great people has been moved to defend a great nation. Terrorist attacks can shake the foundations of our biggest buildings, but they cannot touch the foundation of America. These acts shattered steel, but they cannot dent the steel of American resolve.

America was targeted for attack because we're the brightest beacon for freedom and opportunity in the world. And no one will keep that light from shining.

Today, our nation saw evil, the very worst of human nature. And we responded with the best of America—with the daring of our rescue workers, with the caring for strangers and neighbors who came to give blood and help in any way they could.

Immediately following the first attack, I implemented our government's emergency response plans. Our military is powerful, and it's prepared. Our emergency teams are working in New York City and Washington, D.C. to help with local rescue efforts.

Our first priority is to get help to those who have been injured, and to take every precaution to protect our citizens at home and around the world from further attacks.

The functions of our government continue without interruption. Federal agencies in Washington which had to be evacuated today are reopening for essential personnel tonight, and will be open for business tomorrow. Our financial institutions remain strong, and the American economy will be open for business, as well.

The search is underway for those who are behind these evil acts. I've directed the full resources of our intelligence and law enforcement communities to find those responsible and to bring them to justice. We will make no distinction between the terrorists who committed these acts and those who harbor them.

I appreciate so very much the members of Congress who have joined me in strongly condemning these attacks. And on behalf of the American people, I thank the many world leaders who have called to offer their condolences and assistance.

America and our friends and allies join with all those who want peace and security in the world, and we stand together to win the war against terrorism. Tonight, I ask for your prayers for all those who grieve, for the children whose worlds have been shattered, for all whose sense of safety and security has been threatened. And I pray they will be comforted by a power greater than any of us, spoken through the ages in Psalm 23: "Even though I walk through the valley of the shadow of death, I fear no evil, for You are with me."

This is a day when all Americans from every walk of life unite in our resolve for justice and peace. America has stood down enemies before, and we will do so this time. None of us will ever forget this day. Yet, we go forward to defend freedom and all that is good and just in our world.

Thank you. Good night, and God bless America.

BUSH STATEMENT, SEPTEMBER 14

We are here in the middle hour of our grief. So many have suffered so great a loss, and today we express our nation's sorrow. We come before God to pray for the missing and the dead, and for those who love them.

On Tuesday, our country was attacked with deliberate and massive cruelty. We have seen the images of fire and ashes, and bent steel.

Now come the names, the list of casualties we are only beginning to read. They are the names of men and women who began their day at a desk or in an airport, busy with life. They are the names of people who faced death, and in their last moments called home to say, be brave, and I love you.

They are the names of passengers who defied their murderers, and prevented the murder of others on the ground. They are the names of men and women who wore the uniform of the United States, and died at their posts.

They are the names of rescuers, the ones whom death found running up the stairs and into the fires to help others. We will read all these names. We will linger over them, and learn their stories, and many Americans will weep.

To the children and parents and spouses and families and friends of the lost, we offer the deepest sympathy of the nation. And I assure you, you are not alone.

Just three days removed from these events, Americans do not yet have the distance of history. But our responsibility to history is already clear: to answer these attacks and rid the world of evil.

War has been waged against us by stealth and deceit and murder. This nation is peaceful, but fierce when stirred to anger. This conflict was begun on the timing and terms of others. It will end in a way, and at an hour, of our choosing.

Our purpose as a nation is firm. Yet our wounds as a people are recent and unhealed, and lead us to pray. In many of our prayers this week, there is a searching, and an honesty. At St. Patrick's Cathedral in New York on Tuesday, a woman said, "I prayed to God to give us a sign that He is still here." Others have prayed for the same, searching hospital to hospital, carrying pictures of those still missing.

God's signs are not always the ones we look for. We learn in tragedy that his purposes are not always our own. Yet the prayers of private suffering, whether in our homes or in this great cathedral, are known and heard, and understood.

There are prayers that help us last through the day, or endure the night. There are prayers of friends and strangers, that give us strength for the journey. And there are prayers that yield our will to a will greater than our own.

This world He created is of moral design. Grief and tragedy and hatred are only for a time. Goodness, remembrance, and love have no end. And the Lord of life holds all who die, and all who mourn.

It is said that adversity introduces us to ourselves. This is true of a nation as well. In this trial, we have been reminded, and the world has seen, that our fellow Americans are generous and kind, resourceful and brave. We see our national character in rescuers working past exhaustion; in long lines of blood donors; in thousands of citizens who have asked to work and serve in any way possible.

And we have seen our national character in eloquent acts of sacrifice. Inside the World Trade Center, one man who could have saved himself stayed until the end at the side of his quadriplegic friend. A beloved priest died giving the last rites to a firefighter. Two office workers, finding a disabled stranger, carried her down sixty-eight floors to safety. A group of men drove through the night from Dallas to Washington to bring skin grafts for burn victims.

In these acts, and in many others, Americans showed a deep commitment to one another, and an abiding love for our country. Today, we feel what Franklin Roosevelt called the warm courage of national unity. This is a unity of every faith, and every background.

It has joined together political parties in both houses of Congress. It is evident in services of prayer and candlelight vigils, and American flags, which are displayed in pride, and wave in defiance.

Our unity is a kinship of grief, and a steadfast resolve to prevail against our enemies. And this unity against terror is now extending across the world.

America is a nation full of good fortune, with so much to be grateful for. But we are not spared from suffering. In every generation, the world has produced enemies of human freedom. They have attacked America, because we are freedom's home and defender. And the commitment of our fathers is now the calling of our time.

On this national day of prayer and remembrance, we ask almighty God to watch over our nation, and grant us patience and resolve in all that is to come. We pray that He will comfort and console those who now walk in sorrow. We thank Him for each life we now must mourn, and the promise of a life to come.

As we have been assured, neither death nor life, nor angels nor principalities nor powers, nor things present nor things to come, nor height nor depth, can separate us from God's love. May He bless the souls of the departed. May He comfort our own. And may He always guide our country.

God bless America.

INTERNATIONAL REACTION TO
THE TERRORIST ATTACKS
September 11, 12, and 19, 2001

The September 11 terrorist attacks against the United States prompted worldwide outrage and gave the United States a degree of international sympathy and support that had been lacking for many years. World leaders, both traditional allies and adversaries of the United States, quickly offered rhetorical backing for a U.S. campaign to root out the terrorists responsible for the attacks. Dozens of countries also provided direct support, including British warplanes and missiles, the use of Russian air space and Central Asian military bases, and cooperation by Pakistan in combating the Afghanistan government that it had helped sustain in power.

President George W. Bush and his aides were given wide credit for carefully assembling an international coalition that made possible a successful military campaign against Afghanistan's Taliban regime and the al Qaeda terrorist network, based in Afghanistan, that Bush accused of sponsoring the September 11 attacks. By the end of the year, however, cracks were beginning to appear in Bush's antiterrorism alliance. Even Washington's closest allies were distancing themselves from administration talk of carrying the antiterror war into Iraq and possibly other countries. The administration's impulses toward unilateral actions also worried many foreign leaders, who in private and public statements encouraged Washington to act more like a leader and less like an angry loner. (September 11 attacks, p. 614; war in Afghanistan, p. 686; Iraq issue, p. 849).

A Surge of Sympathy and Support

Except for a few seemingly isolated instances, the United States long had appeared to be immune to the kinds of terrorist attacks that much of the world had taken for granted during the twentieth century. Suddenly, the televised images of airplanes flying into the World Trade Center towers and the Pentagon put the United States in uncomfortable company with much of Europe, the Middle East, Asia, and Latin America, where terrorist gangs had used bombings, kidnappings, shootings, and other tactics to score points or influence public policy. The scale of the September 11 attacks—far exceeding any other terrorist incidents in modern times—shocked and terrified millions of people around the world.

Almost immediately, world leaders went before television cameras and issued statements condemning the attacks, expressing condolences, and offering unspecified help for a U.S. response. Some of the statements came from close friends and allies of the United States, such as British prime minister Tony Blair, who pledged on the evening of September 11 that the people of Britain "stand shoulder to shoulder with our American friends in this hour of tragedy, and we, like them, will not rest until this evil is driven from our world." The next day, the United Nations Security Council unanimously condemned the attacks and pledged to "take all necessary steps" to combat "all forms of terrorism." Other statements of support came from quarters usually less friendly to the United States, among them North Korea, which condemned all terrorism; Syria's President Bashar al-Assad, who called for "global mutual help" to eliminate terrorism; and Iran's supreme leader, Ayatollah Ali Khameni, who said on September 17 that "mass killings of human beings are catastrophic acts which are condemned wherever they may happen and whoever the perpetrators and the victims may be."

There were exceptions, of course. Iraqi leader Saddam Hussein said the United States was paying for its "evil policy" in the Middle East; Arabs in some Middle Eastern countries (including some Palestinians) celebrated the attacks or suggested that the culprits were Jews trying to shift blame onto Muslims; and state-controlled newspapers in Cuba at first ignored the big news story and instead heralded an official visit to Havana by the president of Mali.

As the initial shock wore off, world leaders began focusing on the consequences of the events of September 11, starting with the reality that the United States would soon retaliate against whoever was responsible. Just one day after the attacks, Bush and his aides started talking about a "war" against terrorism, and the president made it clear that he saw "no distinction between the terrorists who committed these acts and those who harbor them."

The first concrete action of support for Bush's position came from the U.S.-led NATO alliance, which on September 12 declared that the attacks represented an attack on the entire alliance. In making that declaration, NATO ministers invoked—for the first time in its five-decade history—Article 5 of the North Atlantic treaty mandating a collective response by all nineteen alliance members to an attack against one member.

Two weeks later, on September 28, the UN Security Council unanimously adopted Resolution 1368, a U.S.-sponsored resolution requiring all member nations to end financial, military, and political support for terrorist groups. The council insisted that member nations report every ninety days to a special compliance committee on steps they had taken to meet the resolution, including such actions as freezing terrorist group bank accounts and other assets.

Assembling a Coalition

In both public and private diplomacy, the Bush administration mounted an aggressive campaign to win broad support for retaliation against those responsible for the September 11 attacks. The most important public component of the campaign was Bush's speech on September 20 to a special joint session of Congress. The president identified the al Qaeda terrorist network, headed by Saudi Arabian exile Osama bin Laden, as the sponsor of the attacks, and he pledged an unrelenting battle "until every terrorist group of global reach has been found, stopped, and defeated." Bush also appealed to "every nation" to support that campaign, saying: "We will ask, and we will need, the help of police forces, intelligence services, and banking systems around the world." (Bush speech, p. 637)

Applauding Bush from the gallery of the chamber of the House of Representatives was Tony Blair, who was in the midst of several journeys around the world to shore up support for the U.S. campaign. Essentially acting as an ambassador extraordinaire on behalf of the United States, Blair argued that Washington had "convincing" evidence of bin Laden's sponsorship of the September 11 attacks, and he made the case for an aggressive response. In some instances, Blair simply reinforced the U.S. message. In others, he was able to deliver that message to leaders who might have been less receptive to a direct approach from Washington; an example was Iran, which had diplomatic relations with Britain but not the United States. (Blair report on bin Laden, p. 802)

Among those receiving a personal appeal from Blair was Pakistan's military president, General Pervez Musharraf. Pakistan for more than five years had been the principal outside source of support for the radical Islamist Taliban regime in neighboring Afghanistan; the Taliban, in turn, provided a safe haven for, and received financial backing from, bin Laden's al Qaeda network. Under intense pressure from the United States, Musharraf decided that Pakistan had more to gain by siding with the United States than by standing by the Taliban. In a landmark speech to his nation on September 19, Musharraf said Pakistan had to make a "critical choice," and he made it clear that his decision was to support the United States by honoring its request for intelligence information, logistical support, and use of Pakistani air space and bases for the war against al Qaeda and the Taliban.

In the coming days, the United States asked for and received promises of help from other nations that had not always been allies of Washington. On September 21 Chinese foreign minister Tang Jiaxuan promised to share intelligence information about Afghanistan. On September 23 the foreign ministers of the Gulf Cooperation Council (which included Saudi Arabia and its neighbors in the Persian Gulf region) pledged "total support and cooperation" with the United States in its war against terrorism. And on September 24 President Vladimir Putin announced that he had allowed the use of Russian air space for U.S. "humanitarian" aid flights to anti-Taliban groups in Afghanistan. Putin's stance was widely seen as giving the go-ahead for the Central Asian republics that bordered Afghanistan—most im-

portantly Uzbekistan—to allow the United States to use their air space and military bases for at least some operations in Afghanistan. Secretary of Defense Donald H. Rumsfeld completed arrangements for U.S. use of facilities in Uzbekistan and other countries in the region during an October 2–5 visit to the Middle East and Central Asia. By that point it was clear that the United States would be able to use NATO air bases in Western Europe and Turkey and air and naval bases in Oman, Saudi Arabia, and the Indian Ocean for its planned campaign to rout the Taliban and al Qaeda in Afghanistan.

In a speech on October 1 to employees of the Federal Emergency Management Agency, Bush said the United States had secured air space and land rights for its military forces in twenty-seven countries and that 29,000 military personnel had been deployed overseas for the war against terrorism. Nineteen countries had agreed to freeze the assets of terrorist groups, he said, and so far $6 million had been frozen in fifty bank accounts.

Bush did not mention it in his speech, but some U.S. allies had offered troops and other military support to the United States, only to have the offers rebuffed, at least for the moment. Several NATO allies, reportedly including Belgium and Spain, sought active roles in the Afghanistan war but were told by Washington that their help was not needed. A major reason, it soon became clear, was that the Bush administration feared that having too many active participants might dilute U.S. control over the Afghanistan operation. Several Arab nations, on the other hand, offered use of their military facilities—but on the condition that nothing be said formally about it. Saudi Arabia, for example, reportedly agreed that the U.S. Air Force could use a major base at Dhahran to direct air operations in Afghanistan.

Among the countries that agreed to provide military support were Germany and Japan, both of which had foresworn combat operations, except in self-defense, following their defeat in World War II. Japan offered "logistical support" and assumed some of the U.S. responsibility for protecting U.S. and Japanese military bases in the Pacific while the Afghanistan war was under way; Germany provided nearly 4,000 troops for noncombat support duty. The Japanese parliament voted overwhelmingly to approve that country's role, but the German parliament gave its approval by a narrow two-vote margin on November 16.

Some countries clearly expected that the United States would reward them for supporting the antiterrorism campaign, and the Bush administration took numerous steps to do so. Pakistani leader Musharraf, who perhaps took the biggest risk of any leader in supporting Washington, got the biggest rewards from the United States: $1 billion in new economic aid and debt forgiveness for his country, plus a lifting of sanctions that the United States had imposed after Pakistan tested nuclear weapons in 1998 and Musharraf had ousted a civilian prime minister in 1999. The administration also lifted sanctions that had been imposed against India because of its 1998 nuclear weapons tests. Similarly, the Senate hurriedly approved a free-trade agreement with Jordan that had previously been stalled; Congress *lifted restrictions on financial aid to Azerbaijan that had been imposed in response to that country's embargo against its historic enemy, Armenia; and Bush on October 25 designated Bahrain a "a major non-NATO ally," a step just short of committing the United States to defend the country if it was attacked.* (India-Pakistan dispute, p. 963)

Support for War, then Concerns

When U.S. and British forces launched the first attacks against Afghanistan on October 7, international support was solid for a campaign to eliminate the al Qaeda network and the Taliban regime. That support survived modest antiwar marches in some Western cities and a brief outbreak of violent anti-U.S. demonstrations in many Islamic countries. In Europe, for example, German chancellor Gerhard Schroeder announced his country's "unconditional solidarity" with the United States despite calls by leaders of the Green Party, his coalition partner, for a "pause" in the fighting after just one week. Leaders of some Islamic countries allowed anti-U.S. demonstrators to vent their sentiments for several weeks, but some—including Pakistan's Musharraf—quickly placed radical Islamic leaders in jail and suppressed the demonstrations.

As almost always is the case during wars, the allied solidarity soon began to weaken. First, the inevitable civilian casualties of the massive U.S. and British bombing raids in Afghanistan angered public sentiment in Western Europe and in many Islamic countries. The Pentagon had imposed extraordinarily tight restrictions on news coverage of the war, in part to reduce the questioning of its tactics. Even so, provocative reports of Afghani villagers being killed by high-tech bombs and missiles undermined public support in many countries for what had been seen as legitimate retaliation for the deaths of American civilians. By mid-November, public opinion polls in most Western European countries showed increasing edginess about the war.

More fundamental, and potentially more significant, concerns emerged shortly after the beginning of the war when it became increasingly clear that Bush viewed Afghanistan as just the beginning of a long-term, international campaign against terrorism. Bush had hinted at such a strategy in his September 20 speech to Congress with his pledge to wipe out all terrorist groups "of global reach"—but that remark offered no specifics on where the United States might be headed after Afghanistan. A further indication came on October 8, when John Negroponte, the U.S. ambassador to the United Nations, sent a letter to the Security Council explaining Washington's goals in Afghanistan and adding: "We may find that our self-defense requires further action with respect to other organizations and other states." The open-ended nature of that statement brought expressions of concern in many capitals, including a suggestion by British foreign minister Jack Straw that the United States and Great Britain had agreed to limit the war to Afghanistan.

Bush raised the international stakes on November 10 when he appeared before the UN General Assembly and bluntly told leaders of other countries that the obligation to fight terrorism was "binding on every nation with a place in this chamber." The United States no longer wanted mere condolences for its losses on September 11 but action as well, he said. "Every nation has a stake in this cause," he said. "As we meet, the terrorists are planning more murder, perhaps in my country, or perhaps in yours."

The president's vision of a world consumed by the threat of terrorism did not sit well with many foreign leaders who said he was overlooking other problems, such as poverty, environmental degradation, and AIDS, that were more urgent concerns in much of the world. Inadvertently, three days after the UN speech Bush heightened foreign fears about his intentions when he issued a directive authorizing the creation of military tribunals to conduct secret trials of foreign terrorist suspects and those who aided them. Officials in France, Germany, Spain, and several other countries expressed reluctance to extradite terrorism suspects to the United States if they would be tried by secret military tribunals and would face the death penalty, which had been outlawed in most of Europe.

The question of a continuing campaign after Afghanistan increasingly became a point of possible friction between the United States and some of its allies. In November and December news reports in Washington indicated that the Bush administration was giving serious consideration to attacking terrorists in other countries. The administration took direct action in two cases, offering to send troops or military aid to Indonesia and the Philippines for their battles against Islamic guerrilla groups said to have links to bin Laden's al Qaeda organization.

More controversial was the suggestion, offered with increasing frequency in Washington, that Bush was entertaining plans to try to topple Iraqi leader Saddam Hussein. The talk in Washington about taking the war to Iraq worried many administration allies in Europe and the Middle East, however. (Iraq war threat, p. 849)

On a broader scale, U.S. allies expressed concern that the Bush administration was reverting to the go-it-alone, unilateralist impulses that it had exhibited earlier in the year when the United States had abruptly pulled out of negotiations on several international treaties, including the Kyoto Protocol on global warming and an enforcement protocol for the 1972 Biological Weapons Convention. Few world leaders challenged Bush directly, but comments by senior officials and diplomats indicated an increasing anxiety that he might be headed in a direction that others did not want to follow. On October 16, for example, the Washington Post *quoted a senior European diplomat as saying that a unilateral decision by the United States to intervene in Iraq would "tend to have rather damaging effects on the cohesion of the grand coalition that you have put together on the anti-terrorist front."* (Global warming, p. 109)

In a December 18 meeting with his NATO counterparts, Defense Secretary Rumsfeld appeared to be laying the groundwork to broaden the antiterror campaign beyond Afghanistan. "The only way to deal with a terrorist network that is global is to go after it where it is," Rumsfeld said, adding that NATO needed to "prepare now for the next war." NATO defense ministers did not respond directly to Rumsfeld's suggestion. That cautious response, diplomats said, indicated that U.S. allies were waiting for more specifics on what the Bush administration had in mind.

Following are a televised statement on the evening of September 11, 2001, by British prime minister Tony Blair expressing support for the United States in the wake of terrorist attacks earlier that day; the text of Resolution 1368, condemning the terrorist attacks, which was adopted September 12, 2001, by the United Nations Security Council; and excerpts from a speech delivered September 19 to the people of Pakistan by President Pervez Musharraf, in which he indicated that Pakistan would be aiding the United States in its forthcoming war against terrorism.

The documents were obtained from the Internet at http:// www.pm.gov.uk/news.asp?NewsId=2544&SectionId=32; http://www.un.org/Docs/scres/2001/res1368e.pdf; http:// www.pak.gov.pk/public/president-address-19-09-01.htm.

STATEMENT BY BRITISH PRIME MINISTER

The full horror of what has happened in the United States earlier today is now becoming clearer. It is hard even to contemplate the utter carnage and terror which has engulfed so many innocent people. We've offered President Bush and the American people our solidarity, our profound sympathy, and our prayers. But it is plain that citizens of many countries round the world, including Britain, will have been caught up in this terror.

I have just chaired an emergency meeting of the British government Civil Contingencies Committee, and I would like to explain some of the measures that we have agreed to take here. There are a range of precautionary measures. We have stepped up security at airports to the highest levels. No flights will take off from the United Kingdom for which we cannot apply the highest standards of security for air crew and passengers. Private flights have been stopped except where specifically authorised. Flight paths into London have been changed, so there will be no civil over-flights of central London.

Security has been increased across the full range of government buildings and military premises. The police across the whole of the UK are on full alert. All our defence facilities round the world have been moved to high alert to ensure the protection of British service personnel. Advice is being given to major financial and business institutions about appropriate security measures. A number of other security measures have been taken, and of course we are in close touch with US, European, and other allies, and are co-operating with them on issues of security. All relevant ministers remain in communication, and the committee—the Civil Contingencies Committee—will meet again tomorrow at 8 A.M.

Obviously some of these measures, not least the effect upon airports, will lead to some disruption, and I hope people understand that. But other than the specific measures we have taken, or that we have advised others to take, business and everyday life can continue as normal. As for those that carried out these attacks, there are no adequate words of condemnation. Their barbarism will stand as their shame for all eternity.

As I said earlier, this mass terrorism is the new evil in our world. The people who perpetrate it have no regard whatever for the sanctity or value of human life, and we, the democracies of the world, must come together to defeat it and eradicate it. This is not a battle between the United States of America and terrorism, but between the free and democratic world and terrorism. We, therefore, here in Britain stand shoulder to shoulder with our American friends in this hour of tragedy, and we, like them, will not rest until this evil is driven from our world.

UN RESOLUTION 1368

The Security Council,

Reaffirming the principles and purposes of the Charter of the United Nations,

Determined to combat by all means threats to international peace and security caused by terrorist acts,

Recognizing the inherent right of individual or collective self-defence in accordance with the Charter,

1. *Unequivocally condemns* in the strongest terms the horrifying terrorist attacks which took place on 11 September 2001 in New York, Washington, D.C., and Pennsylvania and *regards* such acts, like any act of international terrorism, as a threat to international peace and security;

2. *Expresses* its deepest sympathy and condolences to the victims and their families and to the people and Government of the United States of America;

3. *Calls* on all States to work together urgently to bring to justice the perpetrators, organizers and sponsors of these terrorist attacks and *stresses* that those responsible for aiding, supporting or harbouring the perpetrators, organizers and sponsors of these acts will be held accountable;

4. *Calls also* on the international community to redouble their efforts to prevent and suppress terrorist acts including by increased cooperation and full implementation of the relevant international anti-terrorist conventions and Security Council resolutions, in particular resolution 1269 (1999) of 19 October 1999;

5. *Expresses* its readiness to take all necessary steps to respond to the terrorist attacks of 11 September 2001, and to combat all forms of terrorism, in accordance with its responsibilities under the Charter of the United Nations;

6. *Decides* to remain seized of the matter.

STATEMENT BY PRESIDENT OF PAKISTAN

My dear countrymen, Asslam-o-Alaikum:

The situation confronting the nation today and the international crisis have impelled me to take the nation into confidence. First of all, I would like to express heartfelt sympathies to the United States for the thousands of valuable lives lost in the United States due to horrendous acts of terrorism. We are all the more grieved because in this incident people from about 45 countries from all over the world lost their lives. People of all ages old, children, women and people from all and every religion lost their lives. Many Pakistanis also lost their lives. These people were capable Pakistanis who had gone to improve their lives.

On this loss of lives I express my sympathies with those families. I pray to Allah to rest their souls in peace. This act of terrorism has raised a wave of deep grief, anger and retaliation in the United States. Their first target from day one is Osama bin Laden's movement Al-Qaida, about which they say that it is their first target. The second target are Taliban and that is because Taliban have given refuge to Osama and his network. This has been their demand for many years. They have been demanding their extradition and presentation before the international court of justice. Taliban have been rejecting this.

The third target is a long war against terrorism at the international level. The thing to ponder is that in these three targets nobody is talking about war against Islam or the people of Afghanistan. Pakistan is being asked to support this campaign. What is this support? Generally speaking, these are three important things in which America is asking for our help. First is intelligence and information exchange, second support is the use of our airspace and the third is that they are asking for logistic support from us.

I would like to tell you now that they do not have any operational plan right now. Therefore we do not have any details on this count but we know that whatever are the United States' intentions they have the support of the UN Security Council and the General Assembly in the form of a resolution. This is a resolution for war against terrorism and this is a resolution for punishing those people who support terrorism. Islamic countries have supported this resolution. This is the situation as it prevailed in the outside world.

Now I would like to inform you about the internal situation. Pakistan is facing a very critical situation and I believe that after 1971, this is the most critical period. The decision we take today can have far-reaching and wide-ranging consequences. The crisis is formidable and unprecedented. If we take wrong decisions in this crisis, it can lead to worst consequences. On the other hand, if we take right decisions, its results will be good. The negative consequences can endanger Pakistan's integrity and solidarity. Our critical concerns, our important concerns can come under threat. When I say critical concerns, I mean our strategic assets and the cause of Kashmir. If these come under threat it would be a worse situation for us.

On the other hand, we can re-emerge politically as a responsible and dignified nation and all our difficulties can be minimized. I have considered all these factors and held consultations with those who hold different opinions. I met the corps commanders, National Security Council and the Federal Cabinet. I interacted with the media. I invited the religious scholars and held discussions with them. I met politicians. I also invited intellectuals. I will be meeting with the tribal chiefs and Kashmiri leaders tomorrow. This is the same process of consultation that I held earlier. I noted that there was difference of opinion but an overwhelming majority favours patience, prudence and wisdom. Some of them, I think about ten percent, favoured sentimental approach.

Let us now take a look at the designs of our neighbouring country [India]. They offered all their military facilities to the United States. They have offered, without hesitation, all their facilities, all their bases and full logistic support. They want to enter into any alliance with the Unites States and get Pakistan declared a terrorist state. They want to harm our strategic assets and the Kashmir cause. Not only this, recently certain countries met in Dushanbe. India was one of them. Indian representative was there. What do the Indians want? They do not have common borders with Afghanistan anywhere. It is totally isolated from Afghanistan. In my view, it would not be surprising that the Indians want to ensure that if and when the government in Afghanistan changes, it shall be an anti-Pakistan government.

It is very important that while the entire world is talking about this horrible terrorist attack, our neighbouring country, instead of talking peace and cooperation, was trying hard to harm Pakistan and defame Islam. If you watch their television, you will find them dishing out propaganda against Pakistan, day in and day out. I would like to tell India "Lay Off."

Pakistan's armed forces and every Pakistani citizen is ready to offer any sacrifice in order to defend Pakistan and secure its strategic assets. Make no mistake and entertain no misunderstanding. At this very moment our Air Force is at high alert; and they are ready for "Do or die" Missions My countrymen! In such a situation, a wrong decision can lead to unbearable losses. What are our critical concerns and priorities? These are four:

1. First of all is the security of the country and external threat.
2. Second is our economy and its revival.
3. Third are our strategic nuclear and missile assets.
4. And Kashmir cause.

The four are our critical concerns. Any wrong judgement on our part can damage all our interests. While taking a decision, we have to keep in mind all these factors. The decision should reflect supremacy of righteousness and it should be in conformity with Islam. Whatever we are doing, it is according to Islam and it upholds the principle of righteousness.

I would like to say that decisions about the national interests should be made with wisdom and rational judgement. At this moment, it is not the question of bravery or cowardice. We are all very brave. My own response in such situations is usually of daring. But bravery without rational judgement tantamounts to stupidity. There is no clash between bravery and sound judgement. Allah Almighty says in the holy Quran, "The one bestowed with sagacity is the one who get a big favour from Allah."

We have to take recourse to sanity. We have to save our nation from damage. We have to build up our national respect. "Pakistan comes first, everything else comes later." Some scholars and religious leaders are inclined towards taking emotional decisions. I would like to remind them the events of the first six years of the history of Islam.

The Islamic calendar started from migration. The significance of migration is manifested from the fact that the Holy Prophet [Mohammed] went from Mecca to Medina. He migrated to safeguard Islam. What was migration? God forbid, was it an act of cowardice? The Holy Prophet signed the charter of Medina (Meesaq-e-Medinah) with the Jewish tribes. It was an act of sagacity. This treaty remained effective for six years. Three battles were fought with non-believers of Mecca during this period—the battle of Badr, Uhad and Khandaq. The Muslims emerged victorious in these battles with the non-believers of Mecca because the Jews had signed a treaty with the Muslims.

After six years, the Jews were visibly disturbed with the progress of Islam, which was getting stronger and stronger. They conspired to forge covert relations with the non-believers of Mecca. Realizing the danger, the Holy Prophet signed the treaty of Hudaibiya with the Meccans who had been imposing wars on Islam. This was a no war pact. I would like to draw your attention to one significant point of this pact. The last portion of the pact was required to be signed by the Holy Prophet as Muhammad Rasool Allah.

The non-believers contested that they did not recognize Muhammad as the Prophet of Allah. They demanded to erase these words from the text of the treaty. The Holy Prophet agreed but Hazrat Umar (R.A) protested against it. He got emotional and asked the Holy Prophet if he was not the messenger of God (God forbid) and whether the Muslims were not on the right path while signing the treaty.

The Holy Prophet advised Hazrat Umar (R.A) not to be led by emotions as the dictates of national thinking demanded signing of the treaty at that time. He (PBUH) said, this was advantageous to Islam and as years would pass by you would come to know of its benefits. This is exactly what happened. Six months later in the battle of Khyber, Muslims, by the grace of Allah, again became victorious. It should be remembered that this became possible because Meccans could not attack because of the treaty. On 8 Hijra by the grace of Allah glory of Islam spread to Mecca.

What is the lesson for us in this? The lesson is that when there is a crisis situation, the path of wisdom is better than the path of emotions. Therefore, we have to make a strategic decision. There is no question of weakness of faith or cowardice.

For Pakistan, life can be sacrificed and I am sure every Pakistani will give his life for Pakistan. I have fought two wars. I have seen dangers. I faced them and by the grace of Allah never committed a cowardly act. But at this time one should not bring harm to the country. We cannot make the future of a hundred and forty million people bleak. Even otherwise it is said in Shariah that if there are two difficulties at a time and a selection has to be made it is better to opt for the lesser one.

Some of our friends seem to be much worried about Afghanistan. I must tell them that I and my government are much more worried about Afghanistan and Taliban. I have done everything for Afghanistan and Taliban when the entire world is against them. I have met about twenty to twenty five world leaders and talked to each of them in favour of the Taliban. I have told them that sanctions should not be imposed on Afghanistan and that we should engage them. I have been repeating this stance before all leaders but I am sorry to say that none of our friends accepted this.

Even in this situation, we are trying our best to cooperate with them. I sent Director General ISI [Pakistani intelligence service] with my personal letter to Mullah Omar [head of the Taliban]. He returned after spending two days there. I have informed Mullah Omar about the gravity of the situation. We are trying our best to come out of this critical situation without any damage to Afghanistan and Taliban. This is my earnest endeavor and with the blessings of Allah I will continue to seek such a way out.

We are telling the Americans too that they should be patient. Whatever their plans, they should be cautious and balanced. We are asking them to come up with whatever evidence they have against Osama bin Laden. What I would like to know is how do we save Afghanistan and Taliban. And how do we ensure that they suffer minimum losses. I am sure that you will favour that we do so and bring some improvement by working with the nations of the world. At this juncture, I am worried about Pakistan only. I am the Supreme Commander of Pakistan and I give top priority to the defence of Pakistan. Defence of any other country comes later.

We want to take decisions in the interest of Pakistan. I know that the majority of the people favour our decisions. I also know that some elements are trying to take unfair advantage of the situation and promote their personal agenda and advance the interests of their parties. They are poised to create dissensions and damage the country. There is no reason why this minority should be allowed to hold the sane majority as a hostage.

I appeal to all Pakistanis to display unity and solidarity and foil the nefarious designs of such elements who intend to harm the interests of the country. At this critical juncture, we have to frustrate the evil designs of our enemies and safeguard national interests. Pakistan is considered a fortress of Islam. God forbid, if this fortress is harmed in any way it would cause damage to the cause of Islam. My dear countrymen, have trust in me the way you reposed trust in me before going to Agra. I did not disappoint the nation there.

We have not compromised on national honor and integrity and I shall not disappoint you on this occasion either. This is firm pledge to you. In the end before I take your leave, I would like to end with the prayer of Hazrat Musa (A.S)(Prophet Moses) as given in Sura-e-Taha: "May Allah open my chest, make my task easier, untie my tongue so that they may comprehend my intent."

May Allah be with us in our endeavours.

Pakistan Paindabad.

PRESIDENT BUSH ON PLANS TO LAUNCH A "WAR ON TERRORISM"
September 20, 2001

Nine days after terrorist hijackers flew airliners into the World Trade Center towers and the Pentagon, killing about 3,000 people, President George W. Bush told Americans to be prepared for a years-long campaign to wipe out all terrorist groups "of global reach." To rousing applause from members of Congress assembled for a special joint session September 20, 2001, Bush pledged: "I will not yield, I will not rest, I will not relent in waging this struggle for the freedom and security of the American people."

The most visible element of the president's new war against terrorism began just seventeen days later, when U.S. and British ships and planes began firing missiles and dropping bombs against targets in Afghanistan, the home base of the al Qaeda terrorist network that Bush said was responsible for the September 11 attacks. That military campaign quickly achieved its goal of decimating al Qaeda operations in Afghanistan and driving from power the Taliban regime that had given al Qaeda safe haven. But thousands of al Qaeda and Taliban fighters were thought to have escaped, including al Qaeda's leader, Saudi Arabian exile Osama bin Laden. Bush warned that al Qaeda and other international terrorist groups continued to operate in many other countries, and he insisted the United States would use all necessary means to eliminate them.

Bush and his administration also took steps to combat terrorism at home. With the public and political leaders outraged by the September 11 attacks, the administration had little trouble getting Congress to approve sweeping new legal authorities to be used against suspected terrorists in the United States. Congress also approved billions of dollars for programs to help protect the country against terrorist attacks and to respond to them when they occurred. The federal government's handling of these programs was to be supervised by a new Office of Homeland Security in the White House, headed by former Pennsylvania governor Tom Ridge. An early challenge was improving the government handling of crises, starting with an anthrax scare that began early in October. (Terrorist attacks, p. 614; Bioterrorism, p. 672; War in Afghanistan, p. 686)

Bush Speech

In his speech to a Congress and nation aroused by the September 11 attacks, Bush outlined an ambitious agenda of combating terrorism both at home and abroad. The president, who had struggled during his first eight months in office to define an agenda that could win broad public support, suddenly found himself with a mission that commanded instant backing and brought at least a temporary end to the incessant partisan bickering in the nation's capital. Bush was greeted with ovations that would have been unimaginable just a couple weeks earlier, when he and his Democratic critics on Capitol Hill had been preparing for serious struggles over spending priorities on domestic issues.

The heart of Bush's September 20 speech was his pledge to root out terrorists, whom he compared to the Fascists, Nazis, and other totalitarians who had been the scourge of the twentieth century. In one sentence, Bush offered a general description of his wide-ranging plan: "We will direct every resource at our command—every means of diplomacy, every tool of intelligence, every instrument of law enforcement, every financial influence, and every necessary weapon of war—to the disruption and to the defeat of the global terrorism network."

Bush called his plan a "war" but insisted it would be unlike any previous war and would involve the use of financial instruments as much as bombs to attack the terrorists. The president set no geographical limits on the war, saying he would pursue terrorists no matter where they might be. In some of the bluntest and most sweeping rhetoric used by any president in many years, the president outlined what his aides called the "Bush Doctrine": "Every nation, in every region, now has a decision to make. Either you are with us, or you are with the terrorists. From this day forward, any nation that continues to harbor or support terrorism will be regarded by the United States as a hostile regime." Bush mentioned only one nation directly, Afghanistan, but in numerous remarks later in the year he and his aides listed several others as potential targets in one form or another, including Iraq, Iran, Somalia, Syria, and Sudan.

The president said he was also committed to defending the United States against future terrorist attacks—as the country had so clearly been unable to do on September 11, when nineteen men armed with knives commandeered four planes and flew three of them into major buildings. Bush announced the appointment of Ridge to a cabinet-level position to "oversee and coordinate a comprehensive national strategy to safeguard our country against terrorism, and respond to any attacks that may come."

Bush won nearly universal praise from American political leaders and commentators. Senate Majority Leader Tom Daschle, D-S.D., who before September 11 had proven increasingly adept at battling many of the president's priorities, made it clear that Bush would get what he wanted for the war. "We want President Bush to know, we want the world to know, that he can depend on us," Daschle said, referring to Congress. Congress had already passed a resolution (PL 107–40) authorizing the president to use "all necessary means" to respond to the terrorist attacks, and it later gave the president added funding for the war. Opinion polls quickly registered broad public support for Bush's ambitious—if only vaguely defined—plan to combat terrorism. Most foreign leaders also applauded the president's approach and pledged their cooperation. (Foreign reaction, p. 624)

Homeland Security Office

The September 11 attacks forced the nation's leaders to confront issues of protecting domestic security that had been debated for years but had received little concerted action. Some issues were bureaucratic in nature, such as how to coordinate the actions of dozens of federal agencies and thousands of state and local agencies that had responsibilities to protect Americans and to care for them once an attack came. Other questions involved money, most notably the question of who should pay for domestic security. More fundamentally, there were questions about what types of protections were needed and how they would be implemented.

Government commissions, private think tanks, and other groups had offered numerous proposals on these "homeland security" questions. Two major reports on the matter reached the president's desk, or at least the White House, early in 2001, both calling for a high-level federal office to coordinate security programs within the United States. One, sponsored by the Center for Strategic and International Studies in Washington, called for a cabinet-level office to coordinate the nation's homeland defenses. Another government-sponsored commission, headed by former senators Warren B. Rudman and Gary Hart, on January 31 released the last in a series of reports on national security matters. Titled "Road Map for National Security: Imperative for Change," the panel's report called for sweeping reforms in the nation's defense structures, including establishment of a new cabinet-level National Homeland Security Agency assigned to prevent and respond to terrorist attacks and other threats to domestic security. "If we have a disaster, and we think it is quite probable in the next twenty to twenty-five years, we are not prepared to deal with it," Rudman said. (First Hart-Rudman report, Historic Documents of 1999, p. 499)

Although these and similar reports came from prominent panels whose members were highly respected and influential in Washington politics, few of their recommendations were adopted by Congress or the executive branch as federal policy. That changed after September 11, when the type of disaster that Rudman and others had warned about happened. The old reports were dusted off, and the Bush administration quickly embraced some of the proposals that it had previously put on the back burner.

When he announced his appointment of Ridge on September 20, Bush offered no specifics on what responsibilities the new office would have. Some details were forthcoming in an executive order Bush signed on October 8, the day Ridge formally took office after finishing his duties as governor of Pennsylvania. The order used the words coordinate *and* facilitate *to describe Ridge's duties in dealing with more than forty federal agencies that had responsibility for preventing and responding to terrorism and other attacks on U.S. domestic security.*

Bush's order did not give Ridge the ultimate power that many commissions and members of Congress had said would be necessary for such a coordinator to have any real influence: control over the budgets of the departments he was supposed to coordinate. Instead, Bush said the Homeland Security office would review budgets and inform the president whether proposed spending levels were "necessary and appropriate." On Capitol Hill, supporters of greater power for Ridge's office introduced numerous legislative proposals to establish the office as a formal cabinet department with its own budget and legal power. The administration opposed these proposals, which Ridge said were unnecessary, and none made much progress in Congress by the end of 2001.

One disagreement between Bush and Congress was certain to cause problems later on: Bush named Ridge as a White House staff member, meaning that he would not have to testify before congressional committees. Many on Capitol Hill said that Ridge, to be more influential within the administration and more accountable to Congress, should be an agency head subject to Senate confirmation.

Continued Alerts

In addition to dealing with the anthrax scare, one of Ridge's early duties was to supervise warnings to Americans that additional terrorist attacks were possible. In the weeks after September 11 officials had said the country should be prepared for more attacks—but the administration offered no specifics on when or where. On October 11 the FBI put out its most specific alert to date: that new terrorist attacks against U.S. interests at home or abroad were possible "over the next several days." Officials told reporters that the alert resulted from information given the CIA by a source who had been reliable in the past. Nothing happened in the days after the alert was issued; it was not clear whether any terrorist acts had actually been planned or if the alert had foiled such plans.

The administration issued two other nationwide alerts, on October 29 and December 3, justifying both as necessary precautions based on information deemed to be credible. The alerts heightened nervousness and caused considerable confusion among Americans already distraught by the September 11 attacks. The level of anxiety was increased even further by the anthrax scare.

Security versus Civil Liberties

The September 11 attacks were carried out by young Middle Eastern men, most of whom entered the United States legally and were able to avoid arousing the suspicion of legal authorities. In the wake of the attacks, the Bush administration moved aggressively to determine if any potential terrorists remained in the United States and to strengthen the government's ability to ferret out terrorist plots. Bush demanded that other governments do the same, and many complied by cracking down on terrorist cells. The admin-

istration argued that bin Laden's al Qaeda network operated in sixty-eight countries but provided no public information to back up the claim. Opinion polls indicated that a strong majority of the public supported a crackdown on possible terrorists—even if it meant curtailing civil liberties. (Immigration issues, p. 764)

The centerpiece of the administration domestic crackdown against terrorism was a request that Congress give law enforcement agencies sweeping new powers to use in investigating and prosecuting those suspected of aiding terrorist organizations. Bush asked Congress to repeal or loosen restrictions on the ability of the FBI and other federal, state, and local law enforcement agencies to eavesdrop on the telephone calls of suspects, to conduct secret "sneak-and-peak" searches of property without notifying suspects, to track Internet communications, and to track financial transactions of noncitizens and foreign financial institutions operating in the United States.

Bush's request generated concerns, on both the right and left of the ideological spectrum, about possible violations of civil liberties protections against unreasonable government intrusion into the private lives of Americans. But such concerns stood little chance against the political imperative for Congress to take action against those perceived as responsible for the September 11 attacks. One indication of the political heft of the legislation was the formal name give by its House sponsors: the USA Patriot Act (PL 107–56)—an obvious effort to undermine opposition to the new police powers contained in it. Congress cleared the bill on October 25 over the "no" votes of one senator (Russell Feingold, a Wisconsin Democrat) and sixty-six House members, only three of whom were Republicans. Potential opposition to the bill was overcome in large measure by "sunset" provisions that ended the new legal powers in 2005 unless extended by Congress.

Even without the powers contained in the USA Patriot Act, the administration was able to launch a broad attack on possible terrorists in the United States. Immediately after the September 11 attacks, FBI and other law enforcement agents began detaining suspicious individuals—nearly all of them young men from the Middle East—and holding them indefinitely in secret, most for minor legal infractions and visa violations. By the end of the year more than 1,200 people had been detained under these arrangements. Most of the detainees ultimately were released, and some told harrowing stories to the news media of being arrested by FBI agents who charged into their homes with guns drawn, and then sitting in jail for weeks without any explanation. The Justice Department offered little information to the public about those who were being held, or why. On November 27 the department released the names of ninety-three people who had been charged with crimes; another 548 remained in detention at that time, but the department did not reveal their identities. Only one man was charged with a crime related to the September 11 attacks: Zacarias Moussaoui, a French national of Moroccan heritage who was indicted as conspirator in the plot to hijack the airplanes used in those attacks. (Moussaoui arrest, p. 619)

In a related move, the Justice Department on October 31 published a rule, which had taken effect the previous day, allowing investigators to listen in on some lawyer-client conversations. Officials said the intent was to obtain information that might help stop future terrorist attacks, not to gather evidence for use against terrorism suspects. But civil liberties advocates sharply criticized the plan, in part because it applied to all federal prisoners, not just those held in terrorism cases. By early December the Justice Department said the new authority had not yet been used.

The administration accelerated its action against possible terrorists on November 9, when the Justice Department announced plans to interview 5,146 men ages eighteen to thirty-three who entered the United States after January 1, 2000, from countries in the Middle East and other regions that supported terrorism. Critics, including Islamic and Arab-American groups, said the administration was simply targeting Middle Eastern foreigners in the United States without any basis for suspecting them of criminal behavior—a blanket approach that had come to be known as "racial profiling." Police authorities in some jurisdictions refused to cooperate with the federal government's request that they participate in these interviews. The Justice Department said on December 21 that law enforcement agencies had nearly completed the interviews, but no results were announced.

Criticism of the administration's dragnet tactics grew during the latter part of the year as the news media began to report more extensively on the activities of law enforcement agencies. Referring to Bush's use of executive orders, without advance consultation with Congress, Senate Judiciary Committee Chairman Patrick J. Leahy, D-Vt., on November 28 complained about a "lengthening list of unilateral actions." Such complaints brought a sharp retort from Attorney General John Ashcroft, Bush's point man on the legal attack against terrorism. Testifying to Leahy's committee on December 6, Ashcroft brushed aside questions about possible violations of civil liberties. "To those who scare peace-loving people with phantoms of lost liberty, my message is this: Your tactics only aid terrorists," he told the committee. When editorialists and others angrily denounced Ashcroft for attempting to silence criticism, his chief spokesman said that the attorney general was merely complaining about "misstatements of fact," not about criticisms of administration policy.

Military Tribunals Created

By far the most controversial legal action the Bush administration took in its war against terrorism was a plan to establish secret military tribunals to try foreigners accused of terrorism against the United States. Bush on November 13 signed an executive order authorizing the defense secretary to draft regulations for such tribunals, which would be the first used by the United States since World War II. Under Bush's order, any foreigners accused of participating in or supporting "international terrorism" directed against the United States could be held indefinitely and subject to trial in military tribunals. The trials, including the evidence used in them and the sentences handed down, could be kept secret indefinitely. A two-thirds vote of sitting military judges would be required for conviction, not the unanimous verdict typically required in civilian jury trials.

Bush's order appeared to be popular with the public, according to opinion polls, but civil libertarians and some members of Congress objected to the broad and somewhat vague language of the order. Critics said the order also would weaken the U.S. argument against possible mistreatment of Americans arrested by foreign governments unfriendly to the United States. Administration officials said the tribunals would be used only to try members of al Qaeda and other terrorist groups. Critics, however, noted that the vague language of Bush's order would allow use of the tribunals against any foreigners held on terrorism charges, without any public accountability or review by civilian courts. More than 300 law professors sent a letter to Senator Leahy on December 7 arguing that the administration's plans for the tribunal were "legally deficient, unnecessary, and unwise." The professors and some members of Congress of both parties questioned whether Bush had the legal authority to establish military tribunals on his own, without authorization from Congress.

Apparently in response to the criticisms, Defense Department lawyers drafted proposed regulations modifying some aspects of Bush's original order; the new rules would give defendants the right to hire civilian lawyers and require a unanimous verdict for imposition of the death penalty (but only a two-thirds vote of judges for other penalties). Bush on December 28 said the regulations were still under review. Defense Secretary Donald H. Rumsfeld had said that al Qaeda and Taliban members captured in Afghanistan—the people most likely to be subject to military tribunals—would be transferred to the U.S. naval base at Guantanamo Bay, in Cuba. But the tribunals would not be conducted at the base, Rumsfeld said.

Following is the text of a speech by President George W. Bush to a joint session of Congress on September 20, 2001, in which he announced his plans to attack and defeat all terrorist networks "of global reach."

The document was obtained from the Internet at http:// www.whitehouse.gov/news/releases/2001/09/20010920-8 .html.

Mr. Speaker, Mr. President Pro Tempore, members of Congress, and fellow Americans:

In the normal course of events, Presidents come to this chamber to report on the state of the Union. Tonight, no such report is needed. It has already been delivered by the American people.

We have seen it in the courage of passengers, who rushed terrorists to save others on the ground—passengers like an exceptional man named Todd

Beamer. And would you please help me to welcome his wife, Lisa Beamer, here tonight.

We have seen the state of our Union in the endurance of rescuers, working past exhaustion. We have seen the unfurling of flags, the lighting of candles, the giving of blood, the saying of prayers—in English, Hebrew, and Arabic. We have seen the decency of a loving and giving people who have made the grief of strangers their own.

My fellow citizens, for the last nine days, the entire world has seen for itself the state of our Union—and it is strong.

Tonight we are a country awakened to danger and called to defend freedom. Our grief has turned to anger, and anger to resolution. Whether we bring our enemies to justice, or bring justice to our enemies, justice will be done.

I thank the Congress for its leadership at such an important time. All of America was touched on the evening of the tragedy to see Republicans and Democrats joined together on the steps of this Capitol, singing "God Bless America." And you did more than sing; you acted, by delivering $40 billion to rebuild our communities and meet the needs of our military.

Speaker [Dennis]Hastert, Minority Leader [Richard] Gephardt, Majority Leader [Tom] Daschle and Senator [Trent] Lott, I thank you for your friendship, for your leadership and for your service to our country.

And on behalf of the American people, I thank the world for its outpouring of support. America will never forget the sounds of our National Anthem playing at Buckingham Palace, on the streets of Paris, and at Berlin's Brandenburg Gate.

We will not forget South Korean children gathering to pray outside our embassy in Seoul, or the prayers of sympathy offered at a mosque in Cairo. We will not forget moments of silence and days of mourning in Australia and Africa and Latin America.

Nor will we forget the citizens of 80 other nations who died with our own: dozens of Pakistanis; more than 130 Israelis; more than 250 citizens of India; men and women from El Salvador, Iran, Mexico, and Japan; and hundreds of British citizens. America has no truer friend than Great Britain. Once again, we are joined together in a great cause—so honored the British Prime Minister has crossed an ocean to show his unity of purpose with America. Thank you for coming, friend.

On September the 11th, enemies of freedom committed an act of war against our country. Americans have known wars—but for the past 136 years, they have been wars on foreign soil, except for one Sunday in 1941. Americans have known the casualties of war—but not at the center of a great city on a peaceful morning. Americans have known surprise attacks—but never before on thousands of civilians. All of this was brought upon us in a single day—and night fell on a different world, a world where freedom itself is under attack.

Americans have many questions tonight. Americans are asking: Who attacked our country? The evidence we have gathered all points to a collection of loosely affiliated terrorist organizations known as al Qaeda. They are the same murderers indicted for bombing American embassies in Tanzania and Kenya, and responsible for bombing the USS *Cole*.

Al Qaeda is to terror what the mafia is to crime. But its goal is not making money; its goal is remaking the world—and imposing its radical beliefs on people everywhere.

The terrorists practice a fringe form of Islamic extremism that has been rejected by Muslim scholars and the vast majority of Muslim clerics—a fringe movement that perverts the peaceful teachings of Islam. The terrorists' directive commands them to kill Christians and Jews, to kill all Americans, and make no distinction among military and civilians, including women and children.

This group and its leader—a person named Osama bin Laden—are linked to many other organizations in different countries, including the Egyptian Islamic Jihad and the Islamic Movement of Uzbekistan. There are thousands of these terrorists in more than 60 countries. They are recruited from their own nations and neighborhoods and brought to camps in places like Afghanistan, where they are trained in the tactics of terror. They are sent back to their homes or sent to hide in countries around the world to plot evil and destruction.

The leadership of al Qaeda has great influence in Afghanistan and supports the Taliban regime in controlling most of that country. In Afghanistan, we see al Qaeda's vision for the world.

Afghanistan's people have been brutalized—many are starving and many have fled. Women are not allowed to attend school. You can be jailed for owning a television. Religion can be practiced only as their leaders dictate. A man can be jailed in Afghanistan if his beard is not long enough.

The United States respects the people of Afghanistan—after all, we are currently its largest source of humanitarian aid—but we condemn the Taliban regime. It is not only repressing its own people, it is threatening people everywhere by sponsoring and sheltering and supplying terrorists. By aiding and abetting murder, the Taliban regime is committing murder.

And tonight, the United States of America makes the following demands on the Taliban: Deliver to United States authorities all the leaders of al Qaeda who hide in your land. Release all foreign nationals, including American citizens, you have unjustly imprisoned. Protect foreign journalists, diplomats, and aid workers in your country. Close immediately and permanently every terrorist training camp in Afghanistan, and hand over every terrorist, and every person in their support structure, to appropriate authorities. Give the United States full access to terrorist training camps, so we can make sure they are no longer operating.

These demands are not open to negotiation or discussion. The Taliban must act, and act immediately. They will hand over the terrorists, or they will share in their fate.

I also want to speak tonight directly to Muslims throughout the world. We respect your faith. It's practiced freely by many millions of Americans, and by millions more in countries that America counts as friends. Its teachings are good and peaceful, and those who commit evil in the name of Allah blaspheme the name of Allah. The terrorists are traitors to their own faith, trying, in effect, to hijack Islam itself. The enemy of America is not our many Muslim friends; it is not our many Arab friends. Our enemy is a radical network of terrorists, and every government that supports them.

Our war on terror begins with al Qaeda, but it does not end there. It will not end until every terrorist group of global reach has been found, stopped, and defeated.

Americans are asking, why do they hate us? They hate what we see right here in this chamber—a democratically elected government. Their leaders are self-appointed. They hate our freedoms—our freedom of religion, our freedom of speech, our freedom to vote and assemble and disagree with each other.

They want to overthrow existing governments in many Muslim countries, such as Egypt, Saudi Arabia, and Jordan. They want to drive Israel out of the Middle East. They want to drive Christians and Jews out of vast regions of Asia and Africa.

These terrorists kill not merely to end lives, but to disrupt and end a way of life. With every atrocity, they hope that America grows fearful, retreating from the world and forsaking our friends. They stand against us, because we stand in their way.

We are not deceived by their pretenses to piety. We have seen their kind before. They are the heirs of all the murderous ideologies of the 20th century. By sacrificing human life to serve their radical visions—by abandoning every value except the will to power—they follow in the path of fascism, and Nazism, and totalitarianism. And they will follow that path all the way, to where it ends: in history's unmarked grave of discarded lies.

Americans are asking: How will we fight and win this war? We will direct every resource at our command—every means of diplomacy, every tool of intelligence, every instrument of law enforcement, every financial influence, and every necessary weapon of war—to the disruption and to the defeat of the global terror network.

This war will not be like the war against Iraq a decade ago, with a decisive liberation of territory and a swift conclusion. It will not look like the air war above Kosovo two years ago, where no ground troops were used and not a single American was lost in combat.

Our response involves far more than instant retaliation and isolated strikes. Americans should not expect one battle, but a lengthy campaign, unlike any other we have ever seen. It may include dramatic strikes, visible on TV, and covert operations, secret even in success. We will starve terrorists of funding, turn them one against another, drive them from place to place, until there is no refuge or no rest. And we will pursue nations that provide aid or safe haven to terrorism. Every nation, in every region, now has a decision to make. Either you are with us, or you are with the terrorists. From this day forward, any nation that continues to harbor or support terrorism will be regarded by the United States as a hostile regime.

Our nation has been put on notice: We are not immune from attack. We will take defensive measures against terrorism to protect Americans. Today, dozens of federal departments and agencies, as well as state and local governments, have responsibilities affecting homeland security. These efforts must be coordinated at the highest level. So tonight I announce the creation of a Cabinet-level position reporting directly to me—the Office of Homeland Security.

And tonight I also announce a distinguished American to lead this effort, to strengthen American security: a military veteran, an effective governor, a true patriot, a trusted friend—Pennsylvania's Tom Ridge. He will lead, oversee, and coordinate a comprehensive national strategy to safeguard our country against terrorism, and respond to any attacks that may come.

These measures are essential. But the only way to defeat terrorism as a threat to our way of life is to stop it, eliminate it, and destroy it where it grows.

Many will be involved in this effort, from FBI agents to intelligence operatives to the reservists we have called to active duty. All deserve our thanks, and all have our prayers. And tonight, a few miles from the damaged Pentagon, I have a message for our military: Be ready. I've called the Armed Forces to alert, and there is a reason. The hour is coming when America will act, and you will make us proud.

This is not, however, just America's fight. And what is at stake is not just America's freedom. This is the world's fight. This is civilization's fight. This is the fight of all who believe in progress and pluralism, tolerance and freedom.

We ask every nation to join us. We will ask, and we will need, the help of police forces, intelligence services, and banking systems around the world. The United States is grateful that many nations and many international organizations have already responded—with sympathy and with support. Nations from Latin America, to Asia, to Africa, to Europe, to the Islamic world. Perhaps the NATO Charter reflects best the attitude of the world: An attack on one is an attack on all.

The civilized world is rallying to America's side. They understand that if this terror goes unpunished, their own cities, their own citizens may be next. Terror, unanswered, can not only bring down buildings, it can threaten the stability of legitimate governments. And you know what—we're not going to allow it.

Americans are asking: What is expected of us? I ask you to live your lives, and hug your children. I know many citizens have fears tonight, and I ask you to be calm and resolute, even in the face of a continuing threat.

I ask you to uphold the values of America, and remember why so many have come here. We are in a fight for our principles, and our first responsibility is to live by them. No one should be singled out for unfair treatment or unkind words because of their ethnic background or religious faith.

I ask you to continue to support the victims of this tragedy with your contributions. Those who want to give can go to a central source of information, libertyunites.org, to find the names of groups providing direct help in New York, Pennsylvania, and Virginia.

The thousands of FBI agents who are now at work in this investigation may need your cooperation, and I ask you to give it.

I ask for your patience, with the delays and inconveniences that may accompany tighter security; and for your patience in what will be a long struggle.

I ask your continued participation and confidence in the American economy.

Terrorists attacked a symbol of American prosperity. They did not touch its source. America is successful because of the hard work, and creativity, and enterprise of our people. These were the true strengths of our economy before September 11th, and they are our strengths today.

And, finally, please continue praying for the victims of terror and their families, for those in uniform, and for our great country. Prayer has comforted us in sorrow, and will help strengthen us for the journey ahead.

Tonight I thank my fellow Americans for what you have already done and for what you will do. And ladies and gentlemen of the Congress, I thank you, their representatives, for what you have already done and for what we will do together.

Tonight, we face new and sudden national challenges. We will come together to improve air safety, to dramatically expand the number of air marshals on domestic flights, and take new measures to prevent hijacking. We will come together to promote stability and keep our airlines flying, with direct assistance during this emergency.

We will come together to give law enforcement the additional tools it needs to track down terror here at home. We will come together to strengthen our intelligence capabilities to know the plans of terrorists before they act, and find them before they strike.

We will come together to take active steps that strengthen America's economy, and put our people back to work.

Tonight we welcome two leaders who embody the extraordinary spirit of all New Yorkers: Governor George Pataki, and Mayor Rudolph Giuliani. As a symbol of America's resolve, my administration will work with Congress, and these two leaders, to show the world that we will rebuild New York City.

After all that has just passed—all the lives taken, and all the possibilities and hopes that died with them—it is natural to wonder if America's future is one of fear. Some speak of an age of terror. I know there are struggles ahead, and dangers to face. But this country will define our times, not be defined by them. As long as the United States of America is determined and strong, this will not be an age of terror; this will be an age of liberty, here and across the world.

Great harm has been done to us. We have suffered great loss. And in our grief and anger we have found our mission and our moment. Freedom and fear are at war. The advance of human freedom—the great achievement of our time, and the great hope of every time—now depends on us. Our nation—this generation—will lift a dark threat of violence from our people and our future. We will rally the world to this cause by our efforts, by our courage. We will not tire, we will not falter, and we will not fail.

It is my hope that in the months and years ahead, life will return almost to normal. We'll go back to our lives and routines, and that is good. Even grief recedes with time and grace. But our resolve must not pass. Each of us will remember what happened that day, and to whom it happened. We'll remember the moment the news came—where we were and what we were doing. Some will remember an image of a fire, or a story of rescue. Some will carry memories of a face and a voice gone forever.

And I will carry this: It is the police shield of a man named George Howard, who died at the World Trade Center trying to save others. It was given to me by his mom, Arlene, as a proud memorial to her son. This is my reminder of lives that ended, and a task that does not end.

I will not forget this wound to our country or those who inflicted it. I will not yield; I will not rest; I will not relent in waging this struggle for freedom and security for the American people.

The course of this conflict is not known, yet its outcome is certain. Freedom and fear, justice and cruelty, have always been at war, and we know that God is not neutral between them.

Fellow citizens, we'll meet violence with patient justice—assured of the rightness of our cause, and confident of the victories to come. In all that lies before us, may God grant us wisdom, and may He watch over the United States of America.

Thank you.

GENERAL ACCOUNTING OFFICE
ON AVIATION SECURITY
September 20, 2001

The nineteen terrorists who on September 11 used knives and muscle power to hijack four airliners, and then flew three of them into the Pentagon and the World Trade Center towers, suddenly awoke Americans and their political leaders to serious lapses in the nation's aviation security system. Many of the security faults had been identified in numerous reports issued over the years by government agencies and independent commissions. But it took the deadliest terrorist attack in the nation's history to force action correcting many of those problems. Congress in November passed, and President George W. Bush signed, legislation putting the federal government in charge of key aviation security procedures.

By year's end the aviation industry was slowly returning to normal after the intense shocks caused by the September 11 attacks. The nation's airlines, which lost hundreds of millions of dollars worth of business after September 11, began the process of recovery with the help of a multi-billion-dollar bailout voted by Congress. The public cautiously returned to air travel despite continuing fears about possible terrorist attacks and new inconveniences resulting from tightened security measures. In the weeks before Congress acted on long-term security legislation, public confidence was helped by temporary measures taken by the government, including stationing armed National Guard troops in most major airports and armed, but anonymous, marshals aboard selected flights. (Terrorist attacks, p. 614)

At the end of the year, public confidence in aviation security was shaken again when a man identified as Richard C. Reid attempted to ignite explosives packed in his shoes while on board an American Airlines flight from Paris to Miami. Alert crew members and passengers on the December 22 flight subdued Reid, who was charged with assaulting a flight attendant. A subsequent investigation turned up links between Reid and the al Qaeda terrorist network, which the United States said was responsible for the September 11 attacks.

September 11 Events and Aftermath

The September 11 attacks represented the biggest and best coordinated terrorist action in U.S. history. Nineteen Middle Eastern men, allegedly organized by al Qaeda, boarded four civilian airliners on the East Coast early in the morning of September 11, hijacked the planes after they reached cruising altitude, and flew two of them into the World Trade Center towers and a third into the Pentagon. The fourth plane crashed in rural western Pennsylvania—its intended target unknown. The men reportedly were armed with box-cutting knives they had carried when boarding the planes in Boston, Newark, and Washington; at the time, passengers were allowed to carry such knives. Their plans had gone undetected, even though an alleged accomplice was detained by federal authorities in mid-August when a flight instructor became suspicious about his desire to learn how to fly a jetliner—except for the crucial steps of taking off and landing.

The attacks brought an immediate halt to all air travel in the United States. The Federal Aviation Administration (FAA) ordered all airports closed and all planes grounded after those then in the air reached their destinations. By late in the day on September 11, the only planes flying over the United States were military jets and Air Force One, which delivered President Bush back to Washington after a day of travel to avoid another potential terrorist attack.

The FAA allowed service to resume gradually starting on September 14, after airports filed plans indicating they had met tighter security procedures. Within two weeks, most airports and most airlines were back in business—but at sharply reduced levels because customer demand for flights had plummeted. Many planes flew with only a handful of passengers. Travelers and airline crew members were equally nervous, and even veteran travelers suddenly started paying attention to routine safety announcements. Reagan National Airport in Washington was the last major airport to reopen for business; authorities had seriously considered closing permanently the recently rebuilt facility because flight paths to it were uncomfortably close to the Pentagon, the Capitol building, and the White House.

Even with airports open and airplanes in the skies, the nation's aviation industry was suffering. The Air Transport Association reported in November that the number of domestic flights in the weeks after September 11 was down by nearly 20 percent compared with the same period in 2000, and passenger boardings were off by 25 percent. In response to lower demand, the major airlines and other aviation companies cut hundreds of flights and laid off more than 100,000 people after September 11. Few of the laid-off employees had been rehired by the end of the year.

Congress on September 21 approved a $15 billion aid package for the airlines, many of which had been in financial trouble even before the September 11 attacks. That measure (PL 107–42) provided $10 billion in loan guarantees and $5 billion in cash grants to be allocated according to each airline's passenger count and mileage. The bill also established a $100 million liability for U.S. airlines affected by terrorist attacks before March 31,

2002; the federal government would pay for liability judgments in excess of that amount.

GAO Report

For years one of the most persistent critics of aviation security in the United States had been the General Accounting Office (GAO), the congressional watchdog agency. The GAO had filed dozens of reports pointing out flaws, both large and small, in nearly every aspect of systems intended to make air travel safe and secure. Many of the GAO's findings had been echoed in 1996 and 1997 by a commission headed by then-Vice President Al Gore. That panel made numerous recommendations for improving aviation security, including giving airline ticket agents and other employees "profiles" of likely terrorists. (Gore commission, Historic Documents of 1997, p. 113)

Testifying before an unusual joint meeting of House and Senate Appropriations subcommittees on September 20, Gerald L. Dillingham, director of physical infrastructure issues for the GAO, reported that many of the most important aviation security recommendations of the GAO, the Gore panel, and other bodies had still not been implemented by the FAA, by other government agencies, or by airlines and other private companies. Among the major problems that remain uncorrected, Dillingham said, were:

- *The FAA's computerized air traffic control system was "susceptible to intrusion and malicious attacks." The FAA had started to carry out some of the twenty-two recommendations that the GAO had made to improve security of the system, but most improvements had not been made.*
- *Airports and airlines were not doing a good job of controlling access to supposedly secure areas. For example, he said, unauthorized individuals posing as law enforcement agents could, in many cases, bypass security checks and gain access to boarding areas and aircraft.*
- *Security personnel responsible for screening passengers and their luggage tended to be poorly paid and poorly trained; the turnover rate of screeners at most large airports exceeded 100 percent annually. More than two years after it decided to certify the private companies that most airlines had hired to do the screening, the FAA still had not issued the necessary regulations for a certification program.*

The GAO told Congress that several other countries appeared to have better aviation security procedures, in part because they had adopted tougher regulations and had improved the pay and training of airport screeners. Noting that the United States had developed many plans for improved security but often failed to follow through, Dillingham said: "The future of aviation security hinges in large part on overcoming this cycle of limited action that has too often characterized the response to aviation security concerns."

Congress Acts

Congress did act in the following weeks, but some of the problems that had stymied past reform efforts emerged again to create delays and political controversy. Because the September 11 terrorists had carried knives onto the planes they hijacked, most of the attention focused on improving the procedures for screening passengers and their baggage. That introduced the delicate issues of who should be responsible for that job and who should pay for it. Almost unavoidably, those questions became ensnared in partisan politics.

The Senate was the first to act, unanimously approving a bill on October 11 to require the federal government to take over passenger screening at the nation's 142 largest airports. President Bush and the Republican leaders of the House adamantly opposed that approach, however, arguing that private companies should continue to run airport security checkpoints, but with stricter federal guidelines than in the past. In large part, the question became one of whether the government would take on 20,000 airport personnel as employees who would be protected by civil service rules and able to join government employee unions. Private airport security firms, and the union that represented many of their employees, sided with the administration and House Republicans; most Democrats and the American Federation of Government Employees (the union representing most government workers) favored federalizing the airport security work force.

The House on November 1 approved Republican-sponsored legislation more to the administration's liking; it kept the airport workers as private employees but offered incentives for private firms to upgrade the work force and security procedures. The House measure also proposed giving the Transportation Department continued supervisory power over airport security, whereas the Senate bill would have shifted those functions to the Justice Department.

The diametrically opposing approaches of the House and Senate bills led to a political standoff that lasted until the November 12 crash of an American Airlines flight shortly after takeoff from Kennedy Airport in New York. The crash, which killed all 260 passengers and crew on board, appeared to be the result of an accident, not terrorism. But coming almost exactly two months after the September 11 attacks, the crash renewed public fears about air travel and forced serious rethinking of positions on Capitol Hill. Two days after the crash, Senate Minority Leader Trent Lott, R-Miss., crafted a compromise proposal that became the basis for a deal among the House, the Senate, and the administration.

As approved by Congress on November 16, and signed by President Bush on November 19, the new law (PL 107-71) required the federal government to take over the screening of all passengers and bags at airports within one year. Five airports, approved by the Transportation Department, could use private screeners, and other airports could revert to private screeners after three years—a prospect that most experts called unlikely. The bill also established uniform security standards that all airports would be required to meet and training standards for all screeners. Within sixty days of enactment of the bill all checked baggage would have to be screened by one of several methods. The bill paid for these improvements with a passenger fee of $2.50 per leg of a flight, up to a maximum of $5 per one-way trip; the fee *was expected to generate about $1.6 billion annually. A new Transportation Security Agency within the Transportation Department would oversee security for all modes of transportation; that provision took responsibility away from the FAA, which had repeatedly been criticized for failing to police the aviation industry.*

Following are excerpts from testimony given September 20, 2001, by Gerald L. Dillingham, director of physical infrastructure issues at the General Accounting Office, to the transportation subcommittees of the House and Senate Appropriations committees on aviation security matters and the government's failure to implement the suggested improvements.

The document was obtained from the Internet at http:// www.gao.gov/new.items/d011166t.pdf.

Background

Some context for my remarks is appropriate. The threat of terrorism was significant throughout the 1990s; a plot to destroy 12 U.S. airliners was discovered and thwarted in 1995, for instance. Yet the task of providing security to the nation's aviation system is unquestionably daunting, and we must reluctantly acknowledge that any form of travel can never be made totally secure. The enormous size of U.S. airspace alone defies easy protection. Furthermore, given this country's hundreds of airports, thousands of planes, tens of thousands of daily flights, and the seemingly limitless ways terrorists or criminals can devise to attack the system, aviation security must be enforced on several fronts. Safeguarding airplanes and passengers requires, at the least, ensuring that perpetrators are kept from breaching security checkpoints and gaining access to secure airport areas or to aircraft. Additionally, vigilance is required to prevent attacks against the extensive computer networks that FAA uses to guide thousands of flights safely through U.S. airspace. FAA has developed several mechanisms to prevent criminal acts against aircraft, such as adopting technology to detect explosives and establishing procedures to ensure that passengers are positively identified before boarding a flight. Still, in recent years, we and others have often demonstrated that significant weaknesses continue to plague the nation's aviation security.

Potential for Unauthorized Access to Aviation Computer Systems

Our work has identified numerous problems with aspects of aviation security in recent years. One such problems is FAA's computer-based air traffic control (ATC) system. The ATC system is an enormous, complex collection of interrelated systems, including navigation, surveillance, weather, and automated information processing and display systems that link hundreds of ATC facilities and provide information to air traffic controllers and pilots. Failure to adequately protect these systems could increase the risk of regional or nationwide disruption of air traffic—or even collisions.

In five reports issued from 1998 through 2000, we pointed out numerous weaknesses in FAA's computer security. FAA had not (1) completed background checks on thousands of contractor employees, (2) assessed and accredited as secure many of its ATC facilities, (3) performed appropriate risk assessments to determine the vulnerability of the majority of its ATC systems, (4) established a comprehensive security program, (5) developed service continuity controls to ensure that critical operations continue without undue interruption when unexpected events occur, and (6) fully implemented an intrusion detection capability to detect and respond to malicious intrusions. Some of these weaknesses could have led to serious problems. For example, as part of its Year 2000 readiness efforts, FAA allowed 36 mainland Chinese nationals who had not undergone required background checks to review the computer source code for eight mission-critical systems.

To date, we have made nearly 22 recommendations to improve FAA's computer security. FAA has worked to address these recommendations, but most of them have yet to be completed. For example, it is making progress in obtaining background checks on contractors and accrediting facilities and systems as secure. However, it will take time to complete these efforts.

Weaknesses in Airport Access Controls

Control of access to aircraft, airfields, and certain airport facilities is another component of aviation security. Among the access controls in place are requirements intended to prevent unauthorized individuals from using forged, stolen, or outdated identification or their familiarity with airport procedures to gain access to secured areas. In May 2000, we reported that our special agents, in an undercover capacity, obtained access to secure areas of two airports by using counterfeit law enforcement credentials and badges. At these airports, our agents declared themselves as armed law enforcement officers, displayed simulated badges and credentials created from commercially available software packages or downloaded from the Internet, and were issued "law enforcement" boarding passes. They were then waved around the screening checkpoints without being screened. Our agents could thus have carried weapons, explosives, chemical/biological agents, or other dangerous objects onto aircraft. In response to our findings, FAA now requires that each airport's law enforcement officers examine the badges and credentials of any individual seeking to bypass passenger screening. FAA is also working on a "smart card" computer system that would verify law enforcement officers' identity and authorization for bypassing passenger screening.

The Department of Transportation's Inspector General has also uncovered problems with access controls at airports. The Inspector General's staff conducted testing in 1998 and 1999 of the access controls at eight major airports and succeeded in gaining access to secure areas in 68 percent of the tests; they were able to board aircraft 117 times. After the release of its report describing its successes in breaching security, the Inspector General conducted additional testing between December 1999 and March 2000 and found that, although improvements had been made, access to secure areas was still gained more than 30 percent of the time.

Inadequate Detection of Dangerous Objects by Screeners

Screening checkpoints and the screeners who operate them are a key line of defense against the introduction of dangerous objects into the aviation system. Over 2 million passengers and their baggage must be checked each day for articles that could pose threats to the safety of an aircraft and those aboard it. The air carriers are responsible for screening passengers and their baggage before they are permitted into the secure areas of an airport or onto an aircraft. Air carriers can use their own employees to conduct screening activities, but mostly air carriers hire security companies to do the screening. Currently, multiple carriers and screening companies are responsible for screening at some of the nation's larger airports.

Concerns have long existed over screeners' ability to detect and prevent dangerous objects from entering secure areas. Each year, weapons were discovered to have passed through one checkpoint and have later been found during screening for a subsequent flight. FAA monitors the performance of screeners by periodically testing their ability to detect potentially dangerous objects carried by FAA special agents posing as passengers. In 1978, screeners failed to detect 13 percent of the objects during FAA tests. In 1987, screeners missed 20 percent of the objects during the same type of test. Test data for the 1991 to 1999 period show that the declining trend in detection rates continues. [Information on FAA tests results is now designated as sensitive security information and cannot be publicly released. Consequently, we cannot discuss the actual detection rates for the 1991–1999 period.] Furthermore, the recent tests show that as tests become more realistic and more closely approximate how a terrorist might attempt to penetrate a checkpoint, screeners' ability to detect dangerous objects declines even further.

As we reported last year, there is no single reason why screeners fail to identify dangerous objects. Two conditions—rapid screener turnover and inadequate attention to human factors—are believed to be important causes. Rapid turnover among screeners has been a long-standing problem, having been identified as a concern by FAA and by us in reports dating back to at least 1979. We reported in 1987 that turnover among screeners was about 100 percent a year at some airports, and according to our more recent work, the turnover is considerably higher. From May 1998 through April 1999, screener turnover averaged 126 percent at the nation's 19 largest airports; 5 of these airports reported turnover of 200 percent or more, and one reported turnover of 416 percent. At one airport we visited, of the 993 screeners trained at that airport over about a 1-year period, only 142, or 14 percent, were still employed at the end of that year. Such rapid turnover can seriously limit the level of experience among screeners operating a checkpoint.

Both FAA and the aviation industry attribute the rapid turnover to the low wages and minimal benefits screeners receive, along with the daily stress of the job. Generally, screeners are paid at or near the minimum wage. We reported last year that some of the screening companies at 14 of the nation's 19 largest airports paid screeners a starting salary of $6.00 an hour or less and, at 5 of these airports, the starting salary was the then-minimum wage—$ 5.15 an hour. It is common for the starting wages at airport fast-food restaurants to be higher than the wages screeners receive. For instance, at one airport we visited, screeners' wages started as low as $6.25 an hour, whereas the starting wage at one of the airport's fast-food restaurants was $7 an hour.

The demands of the job also affect performance. Screening duties require repetitive tasks as well as intense monitoring for the very rare event when a dangerous object might be observed. Too little attention has been given to factors such as (1) improving individuals' aptitudes for effectively performing screener duties, (2) the sufficiency of the training provided to screeners and how well they comprehend it, and (3) the monotony of the job and the distractions that reduce screeners' vigilance. As a result, screeners are being placed on the job who do not have the necessary aptitudes, nor the adequate knowledge to effectively perform the work, and who then find the duties tedious and dull.

We reported in June 2000 that FAA was implementing a number of actions to improve screeners' performance. However, FAA did not have an integrated management plan for these efforts that would identify and prioritize checkpoint and human factors problems that needed to be resolved, and identify measures—and related milestone and funding information—for addressing the performance problems. Additionally, FAA did not have adequate goals by which to measure and report its progress in improving screeners' performance.

FAA is implementing our recommendations. However, two key actions to improving screeners' performance are still not complete. These actions are the deployment of threat image projection systems—which place images of dangerous objects on the monitors of X-ray machines to keep screeners alert and monitor their performance—and a certification program to make screening companies accountable for the training and performance of the screeners they employ. Threat image projection systems are expected to keep screeners alert by periodically imposing the image of a dangerous object on the X-ray screen. They also are used to measure how well screeners perform in detecting these objects. Additionally, the systems serve as a device to train screeners to become more adept at identifying harder-to-spot objects. FAA is currently deploying the threat image projections systems and expects to have them deployed at all airports by 2003.

The screening company certification program, required by the Federal Aviation Reauthorization Act of 1996, will establish performance, training, and equipment standards that screening companies will have to meet to earn and retain certification. However, FAA has still not issued its final regulation establishing the certification program. This regulation is particularly significant because it is to include requirements mandated by the Airport Security Improvement Act of 2000 to increase screener training—from 12 hours to 40 hours—as well as expand background check requirements. FAA had been expecting to issue the final regulation this month, 2½ years later than it originally planned.

Differences in the Screening Practices
of Five Other Countries and the United States

We visited five countries—Belgium, Canada, France, the Netherlands, and the United Kingdom—viewed by FAA and the civil aviation industry as having effective screening operations to identify screening practices that differ from those in the United States. We found that some significant differences exist in four areas: screening operations, screener qualifications, screener pay and benefits, and institutional responsibility for screening.

First, screening operations in some of the countries we visited are more stringent. For example, Belgium, the Netherlands, and the United Kingdom routinely touch or "pat down" passengers in response to metal detector alarms. Additionally, all five countries allow only ticketed passengers through the screening checkpoints, thereby allowing the screeners to more thoroughly check fewer people. Some countries also have a greater police or military presence near checkpoints. In the United Kingdom, for example, security forces—often armed with automatic weapons—patrol at or near checkpoints. At Belgium's main airport in Brussels, a constant police presence is maintained at one of two glass-enclosed rooms directly behind the checkpoints.

Second, screeners' qualifications are usually more extensive. In contrast to the United States, Belgium requires screeners to be citizens; France requires screeners to be citizens of a European Union country. In the Netherlands, screeners do not have to be citizens, but they must have been residents of the country for 5 years. Training requirements for screeners were also greater in four of the countries we visited than in the United States. While FAA requires that screeners in this country have 12 hours of classroom training before they can begin work, Belgium, Canada, France, and the Netherlands require more. For example, France requires 60 hours of training and Belgium requires at least 40 hours of training with an additional 16 to 24 hours for each activity, such as X-ray machine operations, that the screener will conduct.

Third, screeners receive relatively better pay and benefits in most of these countries. Whereas screeners in the United States receive wages that are at or slightly above minimum wage, screeners in some countries receive wages that are viewed as being at the "middle income" level in those countries. In the Netherlands, for example, screeners received at least the equivalent of about $7.50 per hour. This wage was about 30 percent higher than the wages at fast-food restaurants in that country. In Belgium, screeners received the equivalent of about $14 per hour. Not only is pay higher, but the screeners in some countries receive benefits, such as health care or vacations—in large part because these benefits are required under the laws of these countries. These countries also have significantly lower screener turnover than the United States: turnover rates were about 50 percent or lower in these countries.

Finally, the responsibility for screening in most of these countries is placed with the airport authority or with the government, not with the air carriers as it is in the United States. In Belgium, France, and the United Kingdom, the responsibility for screening has been placed with the airports, which either hire screening companies to conduct the screening operations or, as at some airports in the United Kingdom, hire screeners and manage the checkpoints themselves. In the Netherlands, the government is responsible for passenger screening and hires a screening company to conduct checkpoint operations, which are overseen by a Dutch police force. We note that, worldwide, of 102 other countries with international airports, 100 have placed screening responsibility with the airports or the government; only 2 other countries—Canada and Bermuda—place screening responsibility with air carriers.

Because each country follows its own unique set of screening practices, and because data on screeners' performance in each country were not available to us, it is difficult to measure the impact of these different practices on improving screeners' performance. Nevertheless, there are indications that for least one country, practices may help to improve screeners' performance. This country conducted a screener testing program jointly with FAA that showed that its screeners detected over twice as many test objects as did screeners in the United States. . . .

October

WORLD BANK ON ECONOMIC AFTERMATH OF SEPTEMBER 11
October 1, 2001

Yet another victim of the September 11 terrorist attacks on the World Trade Center towers and the Pentagon was the economy. In the United States, which was already flirting with recession before the attacks, stock markets plunged, business investment fell, and unemployment rose. Less than three weeks after the attacks, the federal government reported negative growth in the third quarter (July–September) for the first time since 1993, and in late November it was announced that the country was now in a recession. In Washington, President George W. Bush and Congress began to consider an economic stimulus package to get the country moving again.

But the U.S. economy proved more resilient than many had expected. Although unemployment continued to rise, the pace had slowed by November. Retail sales remained surprisingly strong, and business inventories began to decline, indicating that firms might soon be ordering new goods to replenish their shelves. By the end of the year, it looked to many analysts as if the recession might be one of the mildest on record and that the economy would begin to start growing again, albeit slowly, in the spring or summer of 2002. With the urgency to act diminishing, Democrats and Republicans in Washington, who had come together to support Bush's war on terrorism, fell back into their old habits and wrangled to a standstill over the details of the stimulus package.

Economies elsewhere in the world did not appear to be faring as well. As in the United States, most of the world's industrial economies had been declining before September 11, and the economic shock waves from the attacks in the United States pushed their growth rates even lower. Growth was eventually expected to pick up in Europe and elsewhere, but the pace was expected to be slower than in the United States. With international trade and investment off markedly from their highs in 2000, the real economic victims of the September attacks were likely to be the developing countries. The World Bank on October 1, 2001, predicted that 40,000 more children would die and 10 million more people would be living below the poverty line of $1 a day as a direct result of the terrorist attacks.

U.S. Economy after the Attacks

Confusion and fear of yet more attacks brought vast portions of the U.S. economy to a momentary standstill in the hours immediately after terrorists hijacked commercial airliners and flew them into the World Trade Center towers and the Pentagon. Although most economic activity was soon up and running again, the loss of life and destruction at the financial hub of the free world was physically and emotionally devastating. More than thirty brokerage firms were headquartered in the World Trade Center; dozens of others were in the surrounding area. Both the nearby American Stock Exchange and the New York Stock Exchange were having problems with their computers and phone connections as a result of the attacks. (Terrorist attacks, p. 614)

The U.S. stock markets, which never opened on September 11, remained closed until September 17 as financial firms and policymakers struggled to calm the world's fears and maintain confidence in the economy. Major central banks around the world pumped nearly $120 billion into their financial systems in the days immediately after the attacks to ensure a normal flow of credit through world markets, and member banks were allowed to borrow liberally to prop themselves up against financial crisis. "We are committed to ensuring that this tragedy will not be compounded by disruption to the global economy," the finance ministers and heads of central banks of the Group of Seven major industrial nations said in a joint statement on September 13.

While those actions did much to stabilize commercial dealings around the world, they did not prevent a loss of investor confidence. The reopening of U.S. stock markets on September 17 ushered in the worst week on Wall Street since the Great Depression. Fifty companies posted profit warnings in a single day, September 19. By the closing bell on Friday, September 21, about $1.4 trillion in stock value had been wiped out. The Dow-Jones industrial average fell 14.3 percent to 8235.81, the biggest weekly percentage drop since July 1933. All told, the Dow-Jones index was off 30 percent from its peak in January 2000. The NASDAQ composite index lost 16 percent for the week and was down a total of 72 percent from its peak in March 2000. Standard & Poor's 500 stock index was down 12 percent.

The tourism and travel industries also suffered immediate and direct losses as a result of the attacks. The federal government allowed only military flights for several days after the attacks; airports and airlines reopened for business only after they were able to put stepped-up security procedures into place. In the first ten days following the attacks, the airline and aviation industries laid off more than 100,000 workers. Several airlines warned that they were nearly bankrupt, although no American carrier actually filed for bankruptcy by the end of the year. Tourism destinations like Las Vegas and Disney World were like ghost towns, and hotels, restaurants, theaters, and night spots across the country reported slow times. Retail sales were also down as people, fearing more attacks, stayed close to home.

Not surprisingly, New York City was especially hurt by the attacks. A pre-

liminary estimate by the city's comptroller put the cost of the attacks at as much as $105 billion. That included property losses, loss of tax revenue, and loss of economic activity that would have occurred had it not been for the attacks, as well as the cost of the clean-up. Insurance was expected to cover $37–39 billion, including $21 billion for loss of life and property. Congress pledged to provide $20 billion to help New York in its recovery efforts, but by the end of the year less than half that amount had been appropriated.

Uncertainty about the future of the economy continued unabated in October as the United States entered a war against terrorism in Afghanistan and faced what appeared to be a new terrorist threat at home: anthrax contamination of the U.S. mails. Some 400,000 jobs were lost in October, the biggest monthly jump in unemployment since 1980. More than one-quarter of the lost jobs were in the service sector, which had been the engine of job creation throughout most of the 1990s. Hotels laid off 46,000 people in October, while retailers, including restaurants and car dealerships, lost 81,000 jobs. Many car companies began to offer zero financing on the new 2002 models to lure customers back into the showrooms. Companies large and small blamed the September 11 attacks for their poor showing in the third quarter, although many were already performing poorly before the attacks. September 11 "is becoming the excuse du jour," said one observer. (Afghan war, p. 686)

Preliminary figures released by the Commerce Department on October 31 showed that the economy had contracted by 0.4 percent in the quarter ending September 30—the first contraction since the spring of 1993. That figure was subsequently revised upward to 1.1 percent. On November 26 the Business Cycle Dating Committee of the National Bureau of Economic Research, which dated the beginning and end of recessions, said that the U.S. economy had entered its tenth recession since World War II in March. Had it not been for the terrorist attacks, however, the decline in the economy might have been "too mild to qualify as a recession," according to the committee. The recession brought to a close an economic expansion that had begun exactly ten years earlier and was thus the longest expansion on record. The previous record had been held by the expansion in the 1960s, which lasted eight years and two months.

More bad news followed two days later, when the Bush administration acknowledged that it expected the federal budget to run a deficit for at least the next three years. Mitchell E. Daniels Jr., the director of the White House Office of Management and Budget, blamed the deficit on the recession, less optimistic projections about the growth of tax revenue, and increased spending required by the terrorist attacks. Democrats said they were not surprised by the return to deficit spending, but said the primary cause was the president's $1.3 trillion tax cut, enacted in June.

There was good news, as well. The jobless rate continued to go up in November, but at a slower pace, and the number of new filings for unemployment claims began to decline. Perhaps the best news was that retail sales, which were expected to be way down in October, actually rose 7.1 percent.

Most of that increase was attributable to sales of new cars, which increased a whopping 26.4 percent, largely as a result of the zero financing and other incentives dealers offered buyers. Low mortgage rates and a mild winter pushed sales of new homes up 6.4 percent in November, and consumer confidence, as measured by the private Conference Board, jumped from 84.9 percent in November to 93.7 percent in December. By year's end, analysts and policymakers were cautiously optimistic that the country was already emerging from its downturn.

Stimulus Package Piques Partisanship

In Washington, Congress adjourned without enacting the economic stimulus package that both parties had originally said was necessary to get the economy moving again. Signs that the economy was improving on its own dimmed some of the urgency for passing a stimulus measure, but it was partisan political bickering over who was to blame for causing the recession and how best to stimulate the economy that ground the debate to a standstill. The two political parties were replaying their debate on the massive tax cut bill enacted earlier in the year and on the basic philosophical issue that separated them—the size and scope of the federal government. (Tax cut, p. 400)

The party differences obscured general agreement on a host of provisions designed to stimulate the economy. Legislators in both parties supported some business tax breaks, including extension of a package of narrow, expiring tax provisions. They also agreed that a stimulus bill should extend unemployment compensation and include $300 rebate checks for the working poor who did not receive rebate checks earlier in the year (rebates under the president's tax cut measure went only to those individuals who had paid income taxes and not to the working poor who paid only payroll taxes).

The difficulty between the parties came in the details. Republicans wanted to speed up at least some of the marginal individual tax rate reductions included in the earlier bill and to give businesses relief from the corporate alternative minimum tax. Democrats demanded that a stimulus package expand eligibility for jobless benefits and subsidize 75 percent of the cost of temporarily continuing health insurance coverage for those who had lost their jobs. Republicans argued that tax cuts would increase consumer spending and business investment and thus would ensure a faster and more long-lasting economic recovery. Senator Don Nickles of Oklahoma said Republicans were "not just interested in just paying more people not to work. We want to create jobs and put people back to work." Senate Majority Leader Thomas A. Daschle dismissed that argument. Republicans "believe there has to be a tax cut for the common cold," he said.

In late October the House passed by the barest of margins, 216–214, a Republican-backed bill that devoted about $96 billion to corporate and individual tax cuts and about $3 billion for jobless and health insurance aid for laid-off workers. In the Senate Republicans killed a Democratic stimulus bill that earmarked about half of its $66 billion price tag for aid to the jobless. The same Senate moderates whose support had made enactment of the Bush tax cut possible drew up a stimulus plan in late December that offered a *middle ground on health insurance coverage for the unemployed. The House passed that version, 224–193, but Senate Democrats, who said the bill offered no guarantees to the poorest of the poor, kept the bill from reaching the floor. Congress adjourned having stimulated only partisan rancor. One victim of the dispute was a package of tax breaks for reinvestment in New York City. It was widely expected that those tax breaks as well as provisions extending several expiring tax provisions would be approved early in 2002.*

Effects on the World Economy

An overall decline in international trade and investment, combined with circumstances unique to each country and region, had slowed growth worldwide before the September 11 attacks. Afterwards, major international financial organizations warned that the world might have fallen into a recession, as business and consumer confidence slipped even further. (Definitions of a worldwide recession varied, but generally held that annual growth below 2 or 2.5 percent indicated that the world was losing economic ground rather than gaining it.)

Travel and tourism were down worldwide, insurance and security measures increased shipping costs, and commodity prices fell. According to the World Bank, agricultural prices fell by about 5 percent globally in the weeks immediately after the attacks. While those trends affected all countries, they were hardest on developing countries that relied on commodity exports and tourism for much of their income. "The 300 million poor in sub-Saharan Africa are particularly vulnerable because most countries have little or no safety nets, and poor households have minimal savings to cushion bad times," the bank said in a statement released October 1.

Japan, the world's second largest economy, was in recession at year's end and was expected to stay there at least through 2002. Most of the industrialized countries of Europe as well as emerging markets in Asia and Latin America were also experiencing economic strains. The Organization for Economic Cooperation and Development, a group of thirty industrialized countries, primarily in Europe, in November lopped more than a point off its projected growth for Europe in 2002, predicting a growth rate of 1.5 percent, down from 2.7 percent. In December the International Monetary Fund lowered its projections for global growth from those it had made just prior to the terrorist attacks. The IMF said it now expected global growth of 2.4 percent in both 2001 and 2002. "While there are good reasons to expect a recovery to get under way in 2002, the outlook remains highly uncertain," the IMF report said, "and there is a significant possibility of a worse outcome."

The IMF said a "particularly disturbing feature" of the current world slowdown was its synchronicity, which was the most marked in at least two decades. The IMF said economic shocks experienced in common by the world's economies, including increased oil prices and the bursting of the information technology bubble, were main factors in the synchronized slowdown, along with greater global integration of corporations and financial markets. With the world's major economies all slowing at roughly the same time, analysts said no single economy was likely to have a strong enough

667

recovery to pull the rest of the world along with it. Virtually no analyst, public or private, was expecting a rapid return to the booming worldwide economy of the 1990s.

Following is the text of a statement issued October 1, 2001, by the World Bank warning that poverty would increase in developing countries as a result of the September 11 terrorist attacks on the United States.

The document was obtained from the Internet at http://www .worldbank.org.cn/english/content/156e6285177.shtml.

The September 11 terrorist attacks in the US will hurt economic growth in developing countries worldwide in 2001 and 2002, condemning as many as 10 million more people to live in poverty next year, and hampering the fight against childhood diseases and malnutrition, the World Bank says in a preliminary economic assessment released today.

Before September 11, the Bank expected developing country growth to fall from 5.5 percent in 2000 to 2.9 percent in 2001 as a result of slowdowns in the US, Japan and Europe, and then rebound to 4.3 percent in 2002. But because the attacks will delay the rich countries' recovery into 2002, the Bank now warns that developing countries' growth could be lower by 0.5–0.75 percentage points in 2002.

"We have seen the human toll the recent attacks wrought in the US, with citizens from some 80 nations perishing in New York, Washington and Pennsylvania," says World Bank President James D. Wolfensohn. "But there is another human toll that is largely unseen and one that will be felt in all parts of the developing world, especially Africa. We estimate that tens of thousands more children will die worldwide and some 10 million more people are likely to be living below the poverty line of $1 a day because of the terrorist attacks. This is simply from loss of income. Many, many more people will be thrown into poverty if development strategies are disrupted."

Ripples Felt Throughout World

Prior to the crisis, the Bank estimated that the US and other OECD countries would grow by 1.1 percent in 2001 and recover to 2.2 percent in 2002. But now, GDP growth rates in the OECD could be lower by 0.75–1.25 percentage points in 2002. This assumes that business returns to normal by mid-2002, that consumers eventually respond to lower interest rates as they have in the past recession, and that no new events shock the global economy.

Already, there are signs that higher costs and reduced economic activity are putting a damper on global trade. Insurance and security costs and delays at customs clearance are among the main factors pushing up the costs of trade. Major shipping lines, for example, have increased freight rates to India by 10 to 15 percent.

Tourism related trade flows are being hit exceptionally hard. The immediate impact in the Caribbean is such that 65 percent of the holidays booked for the Caribbean have been cancelled . The Middle East is also likely to suffer a sharp decline in tourism revenues during the coming winter.

The fallout from the September 11 attacks will affect different groups of developing countries in different ways, reflecting their particular vulnerabilities. For the poorest countries that stall or fall into recession as a result of a decline in exports, tourism, commodity prices, or foreign investment, the number of people living below $1 a day will rise. In countries that experience positive but slower growth, fewer people will be able to climb out of poverty than otherwise would have been the case.

The slower growth and recessions will hit the most vulnerable people in developing countries the hardest. The Bank estimates that an additional 20,000–40,000 children under five years old could die from the economic consequences of the September 11 attack as poverty worsens.

As investors flee to safer havens, the already weak flow of capital to developing countries will decline further and be increasingly concentrated in countries that are considered to be relatively immune from the crisis. The pattern established in the 1990s of private capital flows accounting for a much greater share of developing countries' financing needs is expected to be reversed in the near term as both equity and lending activities contract in lower risk countries. This will require greater support from bilateral and multilateral official sources if the financing needs of a growing number of developing countries are to be met.

Outside of the US and OECD [Organization for Economic Cooperation and Development] countries, the ripples from the September 11 attacks will be felt across all of the world's regions, particularly in countries dependent on tourism, remittances from populations living overseas, and foreign investment.

The worst hit area will be Africa, where in addition to the possible increases in poverty of 2–3 million people as a result of lower growth and incomes, a further 2 million people may be condemned to living below $1 a day due to the effects of falling commodity prices. Commodity prices were forecast to fall 7:4 percent on average this year, and are likely to fall even more as a result of the events of September 11. Farmers, rural laborers, and others tied to agriculture will bear a major portion of the burden. Travel and tourism represent almost 10 percent of merchandise exports for the region and are also likely to be disrupted. The 300 million poor in Sub-Saharan Africa are particularly vulnerable because most countries have little or no safety nets, and poor households have minimal savings to cushion bad times. About half the additional child deaths worldwide are likely to be in Africa.

Oil prices are now at $22/bbl, $5/bbl lower than just before September 11, after a brief upward spike following the attacks. Prices of non-oil commodities have also declined. Many agricultural futures have declined by 5 percent since the attacks. These declines are likely to set the stage for lower commodity prices, that are lower by 3 percent for agriculture and 5 percent for metals next year. These prices have never recovered the levels seen prior to the East Asia crisis of 1997–98, and now find themselves buffeted by yet another global downturn. For economies that are dependent on commodity exports, particularly for cotton and beverage exporters, this portends a potentially large terms of trade shock over and above the impacts of slower growth in GDP.

Aid, Trade and Policies Key to Sustaining Poverty Fight

The Bank's assessment is subject to revision in coming weeks and depends on how events unfold. But World Bank Chief Economist Nicholas Stern stresses that both rich and developing countries must be vigorous and vigilant to ensure that the global rebound occurs next year and continues strongly into 2003.

"Policy responses have to be swift and somewhat bolder in rich and poor countries because of the heightened level of risk to the global economy—and they have to be vigilant because the uncertainties associated with future political and military events are unusually large," says Stern. "Maintaining world trade is more important than ever, especially in the face of an economic slowdown which is often accompanied by pressures for increased protectionism."

Several steps are crucial in sustaining the global fight against poverty in the wake of September 11:

- **Boost Foreign Aid**—Private capital flows to developing countries are going down sharply, reversing the trend of the last decade. They are estimated to fall from $240 billion last year to an estimated $160 billion this year. This makes it even more imperative that governments increase official assistance to fill the financing gap. Currently, aid claims only 0.22 percent of GNP of the OECD countries, far short of the 0.7 percent goal agreed to by the international community. The evidence from the Bank's work on aid effectiveness demonstrates that well-directed aid, combined with strong reform efforts, can greatly reduce poverty, and can also mitigate particular effects of crises, such as terms of trade shocks.
- **Reduce Trade Barriers**—Now more than ever, the WTO summit must go ahead, and it must be a development round, one that is motivated primarily by a desire to use trade as a tool for poverty reduction and development. Substantial trade liberalization such as this would provide an additional cumulative income in developing countries of some $1.5 trillion over a decade.
- **More Coordination**—The major industrial countries are likely to have a greater positive impact if their policies move in the same direction as they did immediately after the attacks. Building additional coordination into the conduct of economic policy, particularly monetary policy, could help counteract large shocks in the global financial system. Beyond reliance on all-important automatic stabilizers, fiscal policy may have to be better targeted in the coming months, particularly in providing assistance to low income groups and to affected regions, which are most likely to feel the immediate brunt of a slowdown and disruption.
- **Building Social Consensus for Continued Reforms**—Only a limited number of developing countries can adopt counter-cyclical macro-

economic policies. Most countries are too small to counteract imported shocks, and many face limited financing capabilities. For these countries, accelerating reforms to improve the investment climate may help encourage foreign and domestic investment during this time of heightened uncertainty. Additional financing from the international financial institutions may help implement pro-poor programs and leverage directly or indirectly more private investment.

World Bank Group Support

The World Bank stands ready to do its part. Managers and staff—many of whom are stationed in the field—have been in contact with high-level officials in all client countries to assure them of the Bank's continued commitment to deliver on previously agreed programs, and to offer help in minimizing and mitigating adverse impacts from the heightened uncertainty, risk, and volatility in the current global economic environment.

Work is currently underway to assess needs on a country-by-country basis. Particular attention is being paid to Africa, given the extreme poverty and vulnerability to declining commodity prices of so many countries there. The IDA [International Development Association] program, including possible additional debt relief under the HIPC [Heavily Indebted Poor Countries] Initiative, is being reviewed, and IFC [International Finance Corporation] is paying particular attention to its programs there. Countries in other parts of the world—especially those directly affected by an increased influx of refugees or a downturn in tourist receipts—also are getting special attention.

At the same time, the Bank is reviewing its lending instruments and financial resources to see how they might be best deployed in current circumstances. The menu of responses is likely to include quick disbursing policy-based adjustment lending, emergency recovery loans/credits, and supplements to existing loans/credits designed to protect essential programs. New investment lending and portfolio restructurings designed to target assistance to newly emerging priorities and to protect pro-poor programs also are being considered.

GENERAL ACCOUNTING OFFICE ON BIOTERRORISM PREPARATION
October 5, 2001

Bioterrorism—the use of biological weapons to spread terror among civilian populations—moved from a theoretical to a real danger in the United States in late 2001. Just one week after the September 11 attacks by terrorists using hijacked airplanes, envelopes containing deadly anthrax spores began turning up in the nation's mail. A first wave of anthrax mailings in September targeted news media offices, and a second wave in October was aimed at Capitol Hill. Five people, two of them postal workers, died after inhaling the anthrax spores; at least eighteen other people became ill, and thousands were given preventative treatment with antibiotics. By year's end law enforcement agencies had not been able to find who was responsible for the anthrax mailings, but officials suggested that the culprit was more likely to be a disgruntled American than a foreign terrorist.

Whatever the ultimate outcome of the investigation, the anthrax mailings had the effect of terrifying, at least temporarily, an American public still reeling from the horror of the September 11 attacks, which killed approximately 3,000 people and ended the country's complacency about terrorism. The uncertainty about who was responsible led millions of people to wonder whether the country was under a concerted attack by determined terrorists using a range of tactics. Moreover, the federal government's response to the anthrax mailings often seemed hesitant, and leading medical officials offered advice that many critics said was more confusing than helpful. Public anxiety waned later in the year when no further anthrax mailings occurred. But the double scare of the September 11 attacks and then the anthrax-laced mail forced public officials, from President George W. Bush on down, to make new plans for dealing with such threats in the future. (Terrorist attacks, pp. 614, 624)

A Multitude of Warnings

For years government commissions and academic experts had warned that terrorist or extremist groups, or possibly even an individual nursing a grudge against society, some day would use biological or chemical weapons against the American public. Numerous reports had shown that the local, state, and federal governments were ill prepared to deal with a large-scale attack using such weapons. Hospitals, emergency personnel, and law enforcement agencies across the country were said to lack the resources to deal with the thousands of deaths and injuries that could result from a well-placed bomb or other weapon containing dangerous agents such as anthrax, nerve gas, or smallpox.

Congress responded to these warnings in 1996 with legislation (PL 104–201) providing federal aid for equipment and training for local and state agencies to deal with catastrophic events such as terrorist attacks. By 2001 the federal government was providing about $10 billion annually for crisis training and preparedness in the nation.

Despite this infusion of money, critics argued that federal programs were unwieldy and inordinately expensive and had failed to reach most of the nation's "first responders"—local health and emergency personnel who would be on the front lines of dealing with crisis situations. Two major reports issued in 2000 were especially damning. One, by the Henry L. Stimson Center in Washington, D.C., reported that most local agencies were still incapable of dealing adequately with a major terrorist attack or public health emergency. Another, by a national terrorism advisory panel chaired by Virginia governor James S. Gilmore, repeated earlier criticisms of lack of coordination among government agencies and said a "disproportionately small" share of the federal antiterrorism budget reached state and local agencies. (Terrorism issues, Historic Documents of 2000, p. 277)

Yet another alarm came in testimony to a House subcommittee by a senior official of the Government Accounting Office (GAO) on October 5, 2001, just as the anthrax threat was starting. Janet Heinrich, director of public health issues for the GAO, painted a broad picture of government agencies at all levels poorly prepared to deal with a serious bioterrorism attack. Heinrich said the federal government still had not coordinated its approach to crisis situations despite numerous proposals over the years for better coordination. More than forty federal agencies had a role in combating terrorism, she said, and more than twenty had a role in responding to public health and medical consequences of a bioterrorism attack.

Congress responded to the anthrax scare by including $2.5 billion in a fiscal 2002 supplemental appropriations bill (PL 107–117) for programs "countering potential biological, disease, and chemical threats to civilian populations." The biggest share of this—$1.1 billion—was for the purchase of stockpiled pharmaceuticals, including smallpox vaccines. The Centers for Disease Control and Prevention received $865 million to help state and local governments respond to biological and chemical warfare threats and $100 million for its own research programs.

One of Bush's responses to the September 11 attacks had been to establish a new Office of Homeland Security in the White House. Headed by former Pennsylvania governor Tom Ridge, this office was responsible for coordinating the federal government's planning for and response to domestic crises. Ridge began work on October 8 and immediately found himself at the center of the anthrax scare. (Ridge appointment, p. 637)

Anthrax Mailings

The numerous predictions that the nation's health system and government agencies would have difficulty coping with a bioterrorism attack were played out in real life starting in October, when it became clear that someone had mailed deadly anthrax spores to news organizations and to Capitol Hill. Doctors unfamiliar with anthrax misdiagnosed some of the anthrax victims who came to them, public health officials gave out conflicting and confusing information, basic medicines needed to treat anthrax were found to be in short supply, and law enforcement and public health agencies were pushed to the limit of their resources as they sought to track down the source of the anthrax and help the victims deal with the disease.

The first public indication that an anthrax attack might be under way came on October 4, when medical authorities confirmed reports that Bob Stevens, a photo editor for The Sun, a supermarket tabloid based in Boca Raton, Florida, was suffering from a form of anthrax that is inhaled. Stevens died the next day; he was the first person in the United States to die from anthrax (an animal disease) since 1976, and he was considered the first person ever to die as the result of a bioterrorism attack in the United States.

On October 12 authorities announced that Erin O'Connor, assistant to NBC News anchor Tom Brokaw, had developed skin anthrax after opening a letter. Employees at CBS and the New York Post also developed skin anthrax, as did the infant son of an ABC employee. Investigations showed that at least some of those infected had opened letters posted at Trenton, New Jersey, on September 18.

An aide to Senate Majority Leader Tom Daschle, D-S.D., opened a letter on October 14 containing millions of anthrax spores. Daschle's office was quarantined, and within three days more than two dozen Capitol Hill staff members tested positive for exposure to anthrax. The House of Representatives closed its offices on October 17 to allow for testing, and the Senate followed suit two days later. The FBI announced on November 16 that another anthrax-laced letter had been delivered to the office of Senator Patrick J. Leahy, D-Vt., prompting the longer-term closing of the Hart Senate Office Building, where both Daschle and Leahy had their offices. Both letters were postmarked from Trenton, and both implied a link to the September 11 terrorist attacks.

By late October the entire country was in an uproar over anthrax. The news media was filled with frightening reports that dozens of Capitol Hill staff members and postal workers in New Jersey and the Washington, D.C. area had been exposed to the deadly disease. Washington postal worker Thomas L. Morris Jr. became the second fatality on October 21. Another postal worker, Joseph P. Curseen, went to a hospital that same day complaining of flu-like symptoms but was sent home; he returned to the hospital by ambulance early the next morning and died six hours later. When *traces of anthrax were found on equipment at a military base where mail for the White House was sorted, President Bush went before reporters to announce: "I don't have anthrax." The president's statement was intended to reassure a worried public, but, as with many other statements by government officials, it did little to reduce public confusion and anxiety.*

Two more anthrax deaths mystified authorities because they appeared to have no connection to the other cases. The first was the death on October 31 of Kathy T. Nguyen, a stockroom clerk at a New York City hospital; an intense investigation turned up no evidence of anthrax at any place she was known to have visited. Even more puzzling was the November 21 death of Ottilie Lundgren, a ninety-four-year-old widow in Oxford, Connecticut. Again, there was no evidence that she had come in contact with anthrax, except for the fact that she died from an inhaled form of the disease. At year's end authorities were working on the hypothesis that Lundgren had received a letter that had come in contact with anthrax-laced letters or postal machinery in New Jersey. Small traces of anthrax also were discovered at more than a dozen other locations around the country, but it was unclear whether those traces reached their destinations through the mail or by some other route.

Throughout the anthrax scare, the government's response was marked by uncertainty and confusion. Some agencies told news organizations that the anthrax was "weapons grade," indicating that it originated from sophisticated laboratories either in the United States or overseas. Officials in other agencies were quoted as disputing that assessment. Officials at first said that only those people who opened an envelope containing anthrax spores would get the disease. That was proven wrong when postal workers operating mail-sorting equipment—and possibly even people who received letters that went through that equipment—came down with anthrax. With Americans already concerned about the safety of the mails, U.S. Postmaster General John Potter said on October 24 that people should be careful about opening suspicious envelopes and packages, and possibly even wash their hands after handling mail, because "there are no guarantees that mail is safe." That statement heightened public anxieties even further, prompting a White House spokesman to offer reassurance that "people should feel safe opening their mail."

In addition, medical advice offered by top government doctors was not always consistent or clear. For example, Capitol Hill staff members were given prescriptions for ciprofloxacin (generally known as Cipro), an expensive antibiotic that suddenly was in short supply, while postal workers just a few miles away were given a less expensive (but reportedly just as effective) alternative. The postal workers, most of whom were black, suspected they were given less favorable treatment than the Capitol Hill employees, most of whom were white and obviously had greater political clout. Postal workers were further annoyed in December when the Department of Health and Human Services offered to provide them, and others exposed to anthrax, with a vaccine on an experimental basis, but refused to offer a recommendation on whether the workers should take it. "First it was Cipro, then it was the other pill, now it's this," Willard Tucker, a postal employee in Maryland told the Washington Post. "Why do we have to be guinea pigs for them? They don't even know what's going on."

For many people, perhaps the most worrisome feature of the government's response was the apparent inability of investigators to locate the source of the anthrax. By late October officials said they had concluded that the anthrax probably originated at a government, university, or other research laboratory in the United States. But officials from the FBI and other agencies told Congress in November—a month after the anthrax scare started—that they did not know how many U.S. laboratories handled the bacteria or how many people might have access to it.

Ridge struggled to improve coordination among government agencies dealing with the anthrax scare, but it was unclear to the public how much success he had. Some members of Congress, newspaper editorialists, and other critics lambasted the government for a fumbling response. The criticism brought a frank admission on October 24 from Surgeon General David Satcher that "we were wrong" not to have responded more aggressively to the cases of mail contaminated with anthrax.

Key government agencies responded to the criticism by announcing reorganization plans. Early in November, Health and Human Services Secretary Tommy G. Thompson and Attorney General John Ashcroft said their agencies would put new officials in charge of dealing with terrorist attacks and other calamities. The FBI, widely criticized for its lack of progress in the investigation, took the unusual step of hiring specialists from outside the government to offer advice on tracking down the source of the anthrax.

At year's end many experts were saying the government had improved its response to the anthrax scare but still needed to find a better way to manage major health crises. Experts noted that the anthrax outbreak killed or sickened only a small number of people but still frightened the public and threw the government into confusion. A more widespread terrorist attack with biological or chemical weapons could kill thousands of people and cause even more panic and confusion, they said. Among other things, many observers said government officials needed to provide a more consistent and believable message to the public in such cases. "The one thing you can't lose is trust," Beverly Sauer, a specialist in crisis communications at Carnegie-Mellon University told the Washington Post. "That's the one thing you can't recover in a crisis."

Biological Weapons Convention

By coincidence, negotiators from the United States and 143 other nations met in Geneva, Switzerland, in late November and early December to discuss ways of enforcing the 1972 Biological Weapons Convention. That United Nations treaty banned the possession of biological weapons but included no means for enforcing the ban. Negotiations on an enforcement procedure had been held at various points since 1994, and by 2001 most other nations had agreed on proposal calling for strict enforcement, including unannounced inspections of weapons laboratories in countries adhering to the treaty. *The Bush administration had rejected that proposal when it was raised at a conference in July, prompting a negotiating recess until November.*

The September 11 attacks and the anthrax scare forced the administration to reassess its total opposition to an enforcement mechanism for the treaty. On November 1 the White House publicly outlined a proposal to be presented to other nations later that month in Geneva. The core of that proposal was a requirement that nations adhering to the biological weapons treaty enact laws barring research on those weapons and agree to extradite persons accused by other countries of violating the treaty. But the White House rejected the underlying premise of the agreement that had been accepted by most other nations: that the United Nations should have new powers to enforce compliance with the treaty. Most important, the administration plan would not have allowed so-called challenge inspections of a country's suspected biological weapons facilities. Administration officials said private U.S. companies could be subjected to UN inspections that might endanger trade secrets simply because another country wanted to investigate them.

When other countries represented at the Geneva conference rejected Bush's new proposal, U.S. diplomats demanded that the negotiations be ended. The U.S. demand prompted widespread complaints that Washington was insisting on having its way or no way at all. Rather than allow a total collapse of the talks, diplomats agreed to postpone further negotiations at least until November 2002.

The dispute over the biological weapons treaty was one of several during the year in which the Bush administration refused to accept agreements negotiated among most other countries, including key U.S. allies. By far the most important of those disagreements concerned the Kyoto Protocol on global warming, which the administration flatly rejected. (Global warming, p. 109)

Following are excerpts from a report given October 5, 2001, by Janet Heinrich, director of health care-public health issues at the General Accounting Office, to the Subcommittee on Governmental Efficiency, Financial Management and Intergovernmental Relations of the House Committee on Government Reform.

The document was obtained from the Internet at http://www.gao.gov/new.items/d02129t.pdf.

Background

A domestic bioterrorist attack is considered to be a low-probability event, in part because of the various difficulties involved in successfully delivering biological agents to achieve large-scale casualties. However, a number of cases involving biological agents, including at least one completed bioterrorist act and numerous threats and hoaxes, have occurred domestically. In 1984, a group intentionally contaminated salad bars in restaurants in Oregon with salmonella bacteria. Although no one died, 751 people were diagnosed with food-borne illness. Some experts predict that more domestic bioterrorist attacks are likely to occur.

The burden of responding to such an attack would fall initially on personnel in state and local emergency response agencies. These "first responders" include firefighters, emergency medical service personnel, law enforcement officers, public health officials, health care workers (including doctors, nurses, and other medical professionals), and public works personnel. If the emergency required federal disaster assistance, federal departments and agencies would respond according to responsibilities outlined in the Federal Response Plan. [The plan outlines the planning assumptions, policies, concept of operations, organizational structures, and specific assignment of responsibilities to lead departments and agencies in providing federal assistance once the President has declared an emergency requiring federal assistance.]. Several groups, including the Advisory Panel to Assess Domestic Response Capabilities for Terrorism Involving Weapons of Mass Destruction (known as the Gilmore Panel), have assessed the capabilities at the federal, state, and local levels to respond to a domestic terrorist incident involving a weapon of mass destruction (WMD), that is, a chemical, biological, radiological, or nuclear agent or weapon.

While many aspects of an effective response to a bioterrorism are the same as those for any disaster, there are some unique features. For example, if a biological agent is released covertly, it may not be recognized for a week or more because symptoms may not appear for several days after the initial exposure and may be misdiagnosed at first. In addition, some biological agents, such as smallpox, are communicable and can spread to others who were not initially exposed. These differences require a type of response that is unique to bioterrorism, including infectious disease surveillance, epidemiologic investigation, laboratory identification of biological agents, and distribution of antibiotics to large segments of the population to prevent the spread of an infectious disease. However, some aspects of an effective response to bioterrorism are also important in responding to any type of large-scale disaster, such as providing emergency medical services, continuing health care services delivery, and managing mass fatalities.

Federal Departments and Agencies Reported a Variety of Research and Preparedness Activities

Federal spending on domestic preparedness for terrorist attacks involving WMDs has risen 310 percent since fiscal year 1998, to approximately $1.7 billion in fiscal year 2001, and may increase significantly after the events of September 11, 2001. However, only a portion of these funds were used to conduct a variety of activities related to research on and preparedness for the public health and medical consequences of a bioterrorist attack. We cannot measure the total investment in such activities because departments and agencies provided funding information in various forms—as appropriations, obligations, or expenditures. . . .

Research Activities Focus on Detection, Treatment, Vaccination, and Equipment

Research is currently being done to enable the rapid identification of biological agents in a variety of settings; develop new or improved vaccines, antibiotics, and antivirals to improve treatment and vaccination for infectious diseases caused by biological agents; and develop and test emergency response equipment such as respiratory and other personal protective equipment. . . .

The Department of Agriculture (USDA), Department of Defense (DOD), Department of Energy, Department of Health and Human Services (HHS), Department of Justice (DOJ), Department of the Treasury, and the Environmental Protection Agency (EPA) have all sponsored or conducted projects to improve the detection and characterization of biological agents in a variety of different settings, from water to clinical samples (such as blood). For example, EPA is sponsoring research to improve its ability to detect biological agents in the water supply. Some of these projects, such as those conducted or sponsored by the DOD and DOJ, are not primarily for the public health and medical consequences of a bioterrorist attack against the civilian population, but could eventually benefit research for those purposes.

Departments and agencies are also conducting or sponsoring studies to improve treatment and vaccination for diseases caused by biological agents. For example, HHS' projects include basic research sponsored by the National Institutes of Health to develop drugs and diagnostics and applied research sponsored by the Agency for Healthcare Research and Quality to improve health care delivery systems by studying the use of information systems and decision support systems to enhance preparedness for the delivery of medical care in an emergency.

In addition, several agencies, including the Department of Commerce's National Institute of Standards and Technology and the DOJ's National Institute of Justice are conducting research that focuses on developing performance standards and methods for testing the performance of emergency response equipment, such as respirators and personal protective equipment.

Preparedness Efforts Include Multiple Actions

Federal departments' and agencies' preparedness efforts have included efforts to increase federal, state, and local response capabilities, develop response teams of medical professionals, increase availability of medical treatments, participate in and sponsor terrorism response exercises, plan to aid victims, and provide support during special events such as presidential inaugurations, major political party conventions, and the Superbowl. . . .

Several federal departments and agencies, such as the Federal Emergency Management Agency (FEMA) and the Centers for Disease Control and Prevention (CDC), have programs to increase the ability of state and local authorities to successfully respond to an emergency, including a bioterrorist attack. These departments and agencies contribute to state and local jurisdictions by helping them pay for equipment and develop emergency response plans, providing technical assistance, increasing communications capabilities, and conducting training courses.

Federal departments and agencies have also been increasing their own capacity to identify and deal with a bioterrorist incident. For example, CDC, USDA, and the Food and Drug Administration (FDA) are improving surveillance methods for detecting disease outbreaks in humans and animals. They have also established laboratory response networks to maintain state-of-the-art capabilities for biological agent identification and characterization of human clinical samples.

Some federal departments and agencies have developed teams to directly respond to terrorist events and other emergencies. For example, HHS' Office of Emergency Preparedness (OEP) created Disaster Medical Assistance Teams to provide medical treatment and assistance in the event of an emergency. Four of these teams, known as National Medical Response Teams, are specially trained and equipped to provide medical care to victims of WMD events, such as bioterrorist attacks.

Several agencies are involved in increasing the availability of medical supplies that could be used in an emergency, including a bioterrorist attack. CDC's National Pharmaceutical Stockpile contains pharmaceuticals, antidotes, and medical supplies that can be delivered anywhere in the United States within 12 hours of the decision to deploy. The stockpile was deployed for the first time on September 11, 2001, in response to the terrorist attacks on New York City.

Federally initiated bioterrorism response exercises have been conducted across the country. For example, in May 2000, many departments and agencies took part in the Top Officials 2000 exercise (TOPOFF 2000) in Denver, Colorado, which featured the simulated release of a biological agent. . . .

Several agencies also provide assistance to victims of terrorism. FEMA can provide supplemental funds to state and local mental health agencies for crisis counseling to eligible survivors of presidentially declared emergencies. In the aftermath of the recent terrorist attacks, HHS released $1 million in funding to New York State to support mental health services and strategic planning for comprehensive and long-term support to address the mental health needs of the community. DOJ's Office of Justice Programs (OJP) also manages a program that provides funds for victims of terrorist attacks that can be used to provide a variety of services, including mental health treatment and financial assistance to attend related criminal proceedings.

Federal departments and agencies also provide support at special events to improve response in case of an emergency. For example, CDC has deployed a system to provide increased surveillance and epidemiological capacity before, during, and after special events. Besides improving emergency response at the events, participation by departments and agencies gives them valuable experience working together to develop and practice plans to combat terrorism.

Fragmentation Remains Despite Efforts to Coordinate Federal Programs

Federal departments and agencies are using a variety of interagency plans, work groups, and agreements to coordinate their activities to combat terrorism. However, we found evidence that coordination remains fragmented. For example, several different agencies are responsible for various coordination functions, which limits accountability and hinders unity of effort; several key agencies have not been included in bioterrorism-related policy and response planning; and the programs that agencies have developed to provide assistance to state and local governments are similar and potentially duplicative. The President recently took steps to improve oversight and coordination, including the creation of the Office of Homeland Security.

Departments and Agencies Use a Variety of Methods to Coordinate Activities

Over 40 federal departments and agencies have some role in combating terrorism, and coordinating their activities is a significant challenge. We identified over 20 departments and agencies as having a role in preparing for or responding to the public health and medical consequences of a bioterrorist attack. . . .

Departments and agencies use several approaches to coordinate their activities on terrorism, including interagency response plans, work groups, and formal agreements. Interagency plans for responding to a terrorist incident help outline agency responsibilities and identify resources that could be used during a response. For example, the Federal Response Plan provides a broad framework for coordinating the delivery of federal disaster assistance to state and local governments when an emergency overwhelms their ability to respond effectively. The Federal Response Plan also designates primary and supporting federal agencies for a variety of emergency support operations. For example, HHS is the primary agency for coordinating federal assistance in response to public health and medical care needs in an emergency. HHS could receive support from other agencies and organizations, such as DOD, USDA, and FEMA, to assist state and local jurisdictions.

Interagency work groups are being used to minimize duplication of funding and effort in federal activities to combat terrorism. For example, the Technical Support Working Group is chartered to coordinate interagency research and development requirements across the federal government in order to prevent duplication of effort between agencies. The Technical Support Working Group, among other projects, helped to identify research needs and fund a project to detect biological agents in food that can be used by both DOD and USDA.

Formal agreements between departments and agencies are being used to share resources and knowledge. For example, CDC contracts with the Department of Veterans Affairs (VA) to purchase drugs and medical supplies for the National Pharmaceutical Stockpile because of VA's purchasing power and ability to negotiate large discounts.

Coordination Remains Fragmented
Within the Federal Government

Overall coordination of federal programs to combat terrorism is fragmented. For example, several agencies have coordination functions, including DOJ, the FBI, FEMA, and the Office of Management and Budget. Officials from a number of the agencies that combat terrorism told us that the coordination roles of these various agencies are not always clear and sometimes overlap, leading to a fragmented approach. We have found that the overall coordination of federal research and development efforts to combat terrorism is still limited by a number of factors, including the compartmentalization or security classification of some research efforts. The Gilmore Panel also concluded that the current coordination structure does not provide for the requisite authority or accountability to impose the discipline necessary among the federal agencies involved.

The multiplicity of federal assistance programs requires focus and attention to minimize redundancy of effort. . . .

We have also recommended that the federal government conduct multidisciplinary and analytically sound threat and risk assessments to define and prioritize requirements and properly focus programs and investments in combating terrorism. Such assessments would be useful in addressing the fragmentation that is evident in the different threat lists of biological agents developed by federal departments and agencies. Understanding which biological agents are considered most likely to be used in an act of domestic terrorism is necessary to focus the investment in new technologies, equipment, training, and planning. Several different agencies have or are in the process of developing biological agent threat lists, which differ based on the agencies' focus. For example, CDC collaborated with law enforcement, intelligence, and defense agencies to develop a critical agent list that focuses on the biological agents that would have the greatest impact on public health. The FBI, the National Institute of Justice, and the Technical Support Working Group are completing a report that lists biological agents that may be more likely to be used by a terrorist group working in the United States that is not sponsored by a foreign government. In addition, an official at USDA's Animal and Plant Health Inspection Service told us that it uses two lists of agents of concern for a potential bioterrorist attack developed through an international process (although only some of these agents are capable of making both animals and humans sick). According to agency officials, separate threat lists are appropriate because of the different focuses of these agencies. In our view, the existence of competing lists makes the assignment of priorities difficult for state and local officials.

Fragmentation has also hindered unity of effort. Officials at the Department of Transportation (DOT) told us that the department has been overlooked in bioterrorism-related planning and policy. DOT officials noted that even though the nation's transportation centers account for a significant percentage of the nation's potential terrorist targets, DOT was not part of the founding group of agencies that worked on bioterrorism issues and has not been included in bioterrorism response plans. DOT officials also told us that the department is supposed to deliver supplies for FEMA under the Federal Response Plan, but it was not brought into the planning early enough to understand the extent of its responsibilities in the transportation process. The department learned what its responsibilities would be during TOPOFF 2000.

Recent Actions Seek to Improve Coordination Across Federal Departments and Agencies

In May 2001, the President asked the Vice President to oversee the development of a coordinated national effort dealing with WMDs. At the same time, the President asked the Director of FEMA to establish an Office of National Preparedness to implement the results of the Vice President's effort that relate to programs within federal agencies that address consequence management resulting from the use of WMDs. The purpose of this effort is to better focus policies and ensure that programs and activities are fully coordinated in support of building the needed preparedness and response capabilities. In addition, on September 20, 2001, the President announced the creation of the Office of Homeland Security to lead, oversee, and coordinate a comprehensive national strategy to protect the country from terrorism and respond to any attacks that may occur. These actions represent potentially significant steps toward improved coordination of federal activities. In a recent report, we listed a number of important characteristics and responsibilities necessary for a single focal point, such as the proposed Office of Homeland Security, to improve coordination and accountability.

Despite Federal Efforts, Concerns Exist Regarding Preparedness at State and Local Levels

Nonprofit research organizations, congressionally chartered advisory panels, government documents, and articles in peer-reviewed literature have identified concerns about the preparedness of states and local areas to respond to a bioterrorist attack. These concerns include insufficient state and local planning for response to terrorist events, inadequacies in the public health infrastructure, a lack of hospital participation in training on terrorism and emergency response planning, insufficient capacity for treating mass casualties from a terrorist act, and questions regarding the timely availability of medical teams and resources in an emergency.

Questions exist regarding how effectively federal programs have prepared state and local governments to respond to terrorism. All 50 states and approximately 255 local jurisdictions have received or are scheduled to receive at least some federal assistance, including training and equipment grants, to help them prepare for a terrorist WMD incident. In 1997, FEMA identified planning and equipment for response to nuclear, biological, and chemical incidents as an area in need of significant improvement at the state level. However, an October 2000 report concluded that even those cities receiving federal aid are still not adequately prepared to respond to a bioterrorist attack.

Components of the nation's infectious disease surveillance system are also not well prepared to detect or respond to a bioterrorist attack. Reductions in public health laboratory staffing and training have affected the ability of state and local authorities to identify biological agents. Even the initial West Nile virus outbreak in 1999, which was relatively small and occurred in an area with one of the nation's largest local public health agencies, taxed the federal, state, and local laboratory resources. Both the New York State and the CDC laboratories were inundated with requests for tests, and the CDC laboratory handled the bulk of the testing because of the limited capacity at the New York laboratories. Officials indicated that the CDC laboratory would have been unable to respond to another outbreak, had one occurred at the same time. In fiscal year 2000, CDC awarded approximately $11 million to 48 states and four major urban health departments to improve and upgrade their surveillance and epidemiological capabilities.

Inadequate training and planning for bioterrorism response by hospitals is a major problem. The Gilmore Panel concluded that the level of expertise in recognizing and dealing with a terrorist attack involving a biological or chemical agent is problematic in many hospitals. A recent research report concluded that hospitals need to improve their preparedness for mass casualty incidents. Local officials told us that it has been difficult to get hospitals and medical personnel to participate in local training, planning, and exercises to improve their preparedness.

Several federal and local officials reported that there is little excess capacity in the health care system for treating mass casualty patients. Studies have reported that emergency rooms in some areas are routinely filled and unable to accept patients in need of urgent care. According to one local official, the health care system might not be able to handle the aftermath of a disaster because of the problems caused by overcrowding and the lack of excess capacity.

Local officials are also concerned about whether the federal government could quickly deliver enough medical teams and resources to help after a biological attack. Agency officials say that federal response teams, such as Disaster Medical Assistance Teams, could be on site within 12 to 24 hours. However, local officials who have deployed with such teams say that the federal assistance probably would not arrive for 24 to 72 hours. Local officials also told us that they were concerned about the time and resources required to prepare and distribute drugs from the National Pharmaceutical Stockpile during an emergency. Partially in response to these concerns, CDC has developed training for state and local officials on using the stockpile and will deploy a small staff with the supplies to assist the local jurisdiction with distribution.

Concluding Observations

We found that federal departments and agencies are participating in a variety of research and preparedness activities that are important steps in improving our readiness. Although federal departments and agencies have engaged in a number of efforts to coordinate these activities on a formal and informal basis, we found that coordination between departments and agencies is fragmented, as illustrated by the many and complex relationships between federal departments and agencies ... In addition, we found concerns about the preparedness of state and local jurisdictions, including the level of state and local planning for response to terrorist events, inadequacies in the public health infrastructure, a lack of hospital participation in training on terrorism and emergency response planning, capabilities for treating mass casualties, and the timely availability of medical teams and resources in an emergency. . . .

BUSH AND BLAIR ON THE START OF THE WAR IN AFGHANISTAN
October 7, 2001

The United States and Great Britain on October 7, 2001, launched a large-scale war against the Taliban regime of Afghanistan and the al Qaeda terrorist network that was based in that country. The war came less than one month after the September 11 terrorist attacks that destroyed the World Trade Center towers in New York, damaged the Pentagon, and killed approximately 3,000 people. President George W. Bush accused the al Qaeda network and its leader, Saudi Arabian exile Osama bin Laden, of sponsoring the attacks against the United States. Announcing the start of the war in Afghanistan, Bush and British prime minister Tony Blair both insisted that the war would continue until the terrorists in Afghanistan had been defeated.

The U.S. and British allies—with substantial logistical, intelligence, and other forms of help from about two dozen countries—quickly achieved their initial goals. The Taliban, who had imposed their extreme interpretation of Islamic law on Afghanistan, fell from power two months after the war began. At about the same time, thousands of fighters associated with the Taliban and the al Qaeda network dispersed into the general population or fled the country (most of them into neighboring Pakistan). In any event, the Taliban and al Qaeda ceased to exist in Afghanistan as tightly controlled organizations. Under United Nations sponsorship, Afghan leaders in December created an interim government that replaced the Taliban until a traditional assembly convened in 2002 to establish a permanent government for that troubled land.

Despite those successes, Bush and his allies were frustrated by a failure to capture or kill bin Laden, his senior associates, and the Taliban leader Mullah Mohammad Omar. Pockets of Taliban and al Qaeda resistance also remained at year's end.

The president said the war in Afghanistan was just the beginning of what likely would be a years-long, worldwide, and multifaceted conflict to defeat terrorists and those who supported them. To this end, the United States and many other countries froze or seized bank accounts and other physical as-

sets of al Qaeda and other terrorist organizations. Washington began providing military supplies, and planned to send military advisors, to help the government of the Philippines battle a small guerrilla group that was thought to be aligned with al Qaeda. Governments in Western Europe, the Middle East, and South Asia arrested dozens of suspects on charges directly or indirectly related to terrorist activities. The Bush administration put Iraq on notice that it might be the next target of a U.S. antiterrorism strike, despite the lack of evidence of any direct link between al Qaeda and the despotic regime in Baghdad.

As of January 8, 2002, the war in Afghanistan had cost the United States $6.4 billion, according to Pentagon figures. Slightly more than half of the total, $3.8 billion, was spent to deploy U.S. forces in and around Afghanistan; the rest was spent to mobilize and pay national guard and reserve forces, and on logistical support, humanitarian aid missions to Afghanistan, replacement of lost equipment and munitions, and other costs. The United States also pledged $300 million to a multibillion dollar UN program to rebuild Afghanistan after more than two decades of war.

The United States lost twenty-two servicemen and one CIA agent during the first three months of fighting. Eighteen died in accidents, three were killed by the mistaken "friendly fire" of U.S. bombing, one was killed by hostile fire from Taliban fighters, and a CIA agent was killed during an uprising of Taliban prisoners. The Pentagon made no attempt to determine how many Taliban and al Qaeda fighters died in the conflict. (Terrorist attacks, p. 614; Foreign reaction, p. 624; Rebuilding Afghanistan, p. 880).

Setting out Objectives

In back-to-back announcements shortly after their nations' forces began attacking targets in Afghanistan on October 7, Bush and Blair laid out objectives that, in one sense, appeared to be limited. Bush said the "carefully targeted actions are designed to disrupt the use of Afghanistan as a terrorist base of operations, and to attack the military capability of the Taliban regime." Blair said the objective was "to eradicate Osama bin Laden's network of terror and to take action against the Taliban regime that is sponsoring it." Although couched in narrow and somewhat vague terms, those objectives provided room for broad implementation. For example, neither man discussed a goal of ousting the Taliban from power, although U.S. and British officials said doing so would be a prerequisite to ending the use of Afghan territory as a terrorist base.

Bush—but not Blair—also put the war against Afghanistan into the context of a much wider struggle against terrorism globally. "Today we focus on Afghanistan, but the battle is broader," Bush said in his address from the White House. "Every nation has a choice to make. In this conflict, there is no neutral ground. If any government sponsors the outlaws and killers of innocents, they have become outlaws and murderers themselves. And they will take that lonely path at their own peril." The president at that point did not spell out what specific governments he had in mind, but in later weeks he cited Iraq as a sponsor of terrorism, and some officials of his administration *worked to generate support within the government and among the public for an unspecified type of attack against the regime of Iraqi leader Saddam Hussein. (Iraq, p. 849)*

Both leaders said the war was not directed against Islam. "It angers me, as it angers the vast majority of Muslims, to hear bin Laden and his associates described as Islamic terrorists," Blair said. "They are terrorists pure and simple."

Bush and Blair also said the allies would carry out humanitarian operations in Afghanistan, along with the war. More than 3.5 million Afghan citizens had taken refugee in neighboring Pakistan and Iran, and at least one million were homeless in Afghanistan, because of continued fighting and a famine caused by drought.

High-Tech War in a Low-Tech Country

By late 2001 Afghanistan had been at war almost nonstop for twenty-two years, ever since the Soviet Union invaded at the end of 1979 to prop up a communist regime. The United States, Saudi Arabia, Iran, Pakistan, China, and other countries had backed numerous Afghan guerrilla groups that fought the Soviet occupation throughout the 1980s. Osama bin Laden had been among thousands of Arabs who went to Afghanistan to help the Afghan rebels. The Soviet forces withdrew in 1989, but the Moscow-based government held onto power for three more years in the face of continued resistance by the guerillas. The regime fell in 1992, ushering in a violent free-for-all among the guerrillas that lasted for three years and devastated what little remained of the country's limited infrastructure.

The Taliban—a faction that adhered to a radical version of an India-based Islamic school of thought known as Deobondism—*emerged in 1995 as the victors, in part because they had support from the government of Pakistan, which hoped to be able to control them. The Taliban imposed their strict Islamic views on the country and quickly gained notoriety around the world for such steps as banning all entertainment and prohibiting women from working or getting an education. The ascendancy of the Taliban did not end Afghanistan's wars, however. Some of the guerrillas that had fought the Soviets, and then fought amongst themselves, formed a loose affiliation called the Northern Alliance; with limited support from Iran and Russia, the Northern Alliance fought the Taliban during the late 1990s from the remote territories of northeastern Afghanistan.*

A crucial step on the road toward the events of 2001 occurred in 1996, when the United States pressured the government of Sudan to expel bin Laden, who had used that country as a base for building his al Qaeda terrorist network. Bin Laden headed again to Afghanistan, where the Taliban provided a safe haven. He used money from a personal fortune to build camps to train anti-Western terrorists. In 1998, after members of his network bombed U.S. embassies in Kenya and Tanzania, the United States fired missiles and bombs on one of bin Laden's bases in Afghanistan, but the attack failed to kill him or cause lasting damage to his operations.

In planning for a new assault on bin Laden and his associates in 2001, Bush administration officials said they were determined to carry out a sustained campaign, not just the one-day strike that former president Bill Clinton had ordered three years earlier. President Bush had one important advantage Clinton lacked: the September 11 terrorist attacks against the United States had aroused Americans, and indeed much of the world, to a far greater extent than had the embassy bombings in Africa. Riding a crest of public outrage, Bush ordered his aides to develop a multinational effort that would destroy the al Qaeda network and drive the Taliban from power.

The military campaign began shortly after noon on October 7 with a display of high-tech weaponry that had become familiar in numerous military campaigns since the Persian Gulf war of 1991. "Tomahawk" cruise missiles were launched from British submarines and U.S. surface ships in the Arabian Sea. Conventional and precision-guided bombs were dropped by U.S. bombers that made round-trips from bases in Missouri and the Middle East. Dozens of jet fighters and other planes controlled the air space around Afghanistan and monitored all telecommunications in that country. The initial targets of these attacks were military bases, airfields, electrical grids around cities, ammunition dumps, and concentrations of Taliban tanks and other heavy weaponry.

By the third day of fighting U.S. Secretary of Defense Donald H. Rumsfeld was able to say that the allies had total air superiority over Afghanistan and could strike Taliban targets at will. Bush on October 11 offered the Taliban what he called a "second chance." If they would "cough up" bin Laden and his followers, he said, "we'll reconsider what we're doing to your country." As Bush almost certainly expected, Taliban spokesmen rejected that offer, and air strikes resumed after a one-day suspension out of respect for an Islamic holy day on October 13.

The air attacks had barely gotten under way when, on October 8, U.S. bombs caused their first proven civilian casualties: four UN aid workers in Kabul. American bombers also mistakenly struck International Red Cross warehouses in Kabul twice, on October 16 and 20, and at least another half-dozen air strikes resulted in civilian deaths through the rest of the year. Taliban spokesmen claimed that some of the strikes killed hundreds of people, and those claims were echoed by inflammatory news media reports throughout the Islamic world. Reports of civilian casualties were impossible to verify, but by the end of the year the Associated Press estimated that 500 to 600 civilians had died because of U.S. and allied air strikes.

On October 17 the Pentagon verified reports that the United States was using a "revolutionary" new weapon in the war: unarmed, propeller-driven aircraft that used live video cameras to locate troops and other mobile targets and then fired missiles at the targets by remote control. One type of this aircraft, called the "Predator," was used by the Central Intelligence Agency. Another high-tech aspect of the conflict was the Pentagon's heavy reliance on so-called smart bombs and missiles that were guided to their targets by munitions experts aboard planes or by radio contact with satellites. Of some

18,000 munitions dropped on Afghanistan by early 2002, about 56 percent were precision-guided; this compared with about 35 percent of the munitions used by NATO during the 1999 war against Serbian forces in Kosovo and about 10 percent of the munitions used by the U.S.-led alliance against Iraq in the 1991 Persian Gulf war. (Persian Gulf war, Historic Documents of 1991, p. 97; Kosovo conflict, Historic Documents of 1999, p. 134)

A new phase in the war began October 19 when 100 U.S. Army Rangers attacked an airfield and a Taliban compound outside the southern city of Kandahar. This was the first major ground operation of the war, and it signaled growing confidence by the allies in their ability to control the fighting. Special Forces troops from the United States, Britain, Germany, and other countries continued to operate in Afghanistan throughout the rest of 2001. Their assignments included locating bombing targets, attacking Taliban and al Qaeda troops and equipment that could not be reached by bombs or missiles, training and coordinating the operations of anti-Taliban guerrillas in the country, interviewing Taliban and al Qaeda prisoners, and setting up bases for later ground operations.

In the third week of the war allied warplanes began hitting Taliban forces that were entrenched in northern Afghanistan opposite the positions of the Northern Alliance rebel forces. The allies had at first resisted such strikes, fearing that weakening the Taliban in that area would enable the Northern Alliance to drive south into Kabul and establish itself in power before all anti-Taliban Afghan factions had been able to work out a broad political settlement. Such an outcome would have alienated the alliance's long-time enemies, including ethnic groups in southern Afghanistan and the government of Pakistan. Two developments in late October led to a shift in tactics: political representatives of most major Afghan groups began meeting in Pakistan to plan for a post-Taliban government, and the allies—concluding that they had nearly run out of Taliban military targets in and near Afghan cities—turned their attention to the masses of Taliban troops positioned against the Northern Alliance.

The first major break in the war came on November 9 when the Northern Alliance drove the Taliban out of the north Afghanistan city of Mazar e-Sharif, which had passed back and forth between the two sides during the previous five years of fighting. The capture of that city by the Northern Alliance led to a surprisingly rapid collapse of Taliban resistance in the northern part of the country. On November 13 the Taliban abandoned Kabul, the capital, and fled south toward Kandahar. Throngs of cheering people greeted Northern Alliance forces as they took over the capital; within hours Kabul residents were playing radios (one of many entertainment activities strictly banned by the Taliban), and a few hesitant women were emerging from behind their Taliban-mandated veils.

About 100 British Marines landed in Afghanistan on November 15 as the advance units of a multinational peacekeeping force approved the previous day by the UN Security Council. Known as the International Security and Assistance Force, the peacekeeping force was to have up to 4,500 troops from more than a dozen countries; the major exception was the United States, which refused to contribute troops to the UN force. The force had a limited mandate—to protect Kabul and the environs—and was not authorized to operate elsewhere in Afghanistan.

Kunduz, the last Taliban stronghold in northern Afghanistan, fell to the Northern Alliance on November 25–26. At the same time, several hundred Taliban soldiers who had been imprisoned at an ancient fortress near Kunduz revolted. Dozens were killed before the revolt was suppressed, among them CIA officer Johnny Michael Spann, who had been questioning the Taliban. Spann was the first American to die in combat during the war.

On December 9, just two months after the first allied bombs fell on Afghanistan, the Taliban lost control of Kandahar, the city where the Taliban movement had emerged in the early 1990s. That step effectively ended the Taliban's five-year rule of the country. Taliban forces fled the city by the thousands—many into the surrounding countryside and an undetermined number across the border into Pakistan—after their leaders negotiated a surrender agreement with Hamid Karzai, a leader of the country's largest ethnic group, the Pashtun. Four days earlier Karzai had been designated interim prime minister of Afghanistan by political representatives from various Afghan factions meeting at a UN-sponsored conference in Bonn, Germany.

The collapse of the Taliban occurred much more rapidly than U.S. officials and most experts outside the government had expected. At the outset of the war some analysts had predicted that the Taliban regime, backed by bin Laden's al Qaeda fighters, might be able to resist the bombing campaign and the ground attacks of the poorly equipped Northern Alliance for many months. Once the Taliban fell from power, the general consensus among most analysts was that several factors combined to cause the unexpectedly rapid deterioration of the regime. The Taliban turned out to be so unpopular that they were unable to rouse widespread resistance against the Northern Alliance and other anti-Taliban factions. The ferocity and accuracy of the U.S. and British bombing overwhelmed Taliban military positions and terrified Taliban fighters. Many of the Taliban and al Qaeda fighters were young men from urban areas (in Afghanistan and elsewhere in Central Asia and the Middle East) who had no serious combat experience, especially in guerrilla warfare. And the Northern Alliance, while poorly equipped and often disorganized, was composed of thousands of dedicated fighters who had years of guerrilla warfare experience during Afghanistan's previous two decades of war. Another significant factor was that the country's warlords did not hesitate to switch sides when it became clear who was winning; once the Taliban were on the run, many of their allies abandoned them.

Searching for Taliban and al Qaeda Leaders

Although they were gone from power in Kabul and Kandahar, the Taliban and al Qaeda were not totally gone from Afghanistan. Thousands of fighters simply disappeared into the countryside or trimmed their beards and merged into the general population. Among those disappearing was Taliban leader Mullah Omar, whose location was a mystery after the fall of Kandahar in early December. Al Qaeda leaders, including bin Laden, were thought to have taken refuge in an enormous complex of caves in the rugged Tora Bora mountains of eastern Afghanistan, south of the city of Jalalabad. U.S. bombers dropped heavy "bunker-buster" bombs on the caves during much of November, and by the middle of December anti-Taliban forces claimed to have effective control over much of the region. But searches of the caves by anti-Taliban troops and U.S. Special Forces units failed to turn up any sign of bin Laden or his senior associates. Senior Pentagon officials expressed confidence that bin Laden had not escaped into Pakistan—as many of his fighters apparently had—but the high-tech U.S. satellites and other surveillance gear proved unable to locate one man, or even a small group of men, in one of the most rugged environments on Earth. On December 27 Defense Secretary Rumsfeld, obviously frustrated by the failure to capture bin Laden, told reporters he had "stopped chasing" conflicting reports on the terrorist leader's whereabouts.

The Pentagon did claim during the war that several high-ranking al Qaeda officials had been killed or captured. Among those reportedly killed were Muhammad Atef, an Egyptian described by the United States as bin Laden's security chief, who was wanted by the United States because of his alleged involvement in the 1998 bombing of U.S. embassies in Kenya and Tanzania. The highest-ranking al Qaeda official to fall into U.S. hands during the first months of the war reportedly was Abdul Aziz, the head of a Saudi Arabian group, the Wafa Humanitarian Organization, that U.S. officials said raised money for al Qaeda.

At year's end some analysts criticized the United States for relying too much on Afghan warlords for the labor-intensive work of searching the Tora Bora caves and patrolling the border regions to prevent Taliban and al Qaeda fighters from escaping into Pakistan. This dependence on proxy forces, the critics said, meant that the United States was in danger of allowing bin Laden to survive and regroup his al Qaeda network somewhere else, perhaps in Somalia, Sudan, or another country without much of a central government. Rumsfeld and other administration officials defended their approach against such criticism, saying that the United States had no practical alternative to relying on local men who supposedly knew the terrain and might be motivated by a $25 million reward that Washington had placed on bin Laden's head.

> *Following are the texts of statements made October 7, 2001, by U.S. president George W. Bush and British prime minister Tony Blair announcing the start of military operations against the Taliban regime and the al Qaeda terrorist network in Afghanistan.*

> ***The document was obtained from the Internet at http:// www.whitehouse.gov/news/releases/2001/10/20011007-8 .html;   http://www.pm.gov.uk/news.asp?NewsId=2712& SectionId=32.***

BUSH ON START OF MILITARY STRIKES

Good afternoon. On my orders, the United States military has begun strikes against al Qaeda terrorist training camps and military installations of the Taliban regime in Afghanistan. These carefully targeted actions are designed to disrupt the use of Afghanistan as a terrorist base of operations, and to attack the military capability of the Taliban regime.

We are joined in this operation by our staunch friend, Great Britain. Other close friends, including Canada, Australia, Germany and France, have pledged forces as the operation unfolds. More than 40 countries in the Middle East, Africa, Europe and across Asia have granted air transit or landing rights. Many more have shared intelligence. We are supported by the collective will of the world.

More than two weeks ago, I gave Taliban leaders a series of clear and specific demands: Close terrorist training camps; hand over leaders of the al Qaeda network; and return all foreign nationals, including American citizens, unjustly detained in your country. None of these demands were met. And now the Taliban will pay a price. By destroying camps and disrupting communications, we will make it more difficult for the terror network to train new recruits and coordinate their evil plans.

Initially, the terrorists may burrow deeper into caves and other entrenched hiding places. Our military action is also designed to clear the way for sustained, comprehensive and relentless operations to drive them out and bring them to justice.

At the same time, the oppressed people of Afghanistan will know the generosity of America and our allies. As we strike military targets, we'll also drop food, medicine and supplies to the starving and suffering men and women and children of Afghanistan.

The United States of America is a friend to the Afghan people, and we are the friends of almost a billion worldwide who practice the Islamic faith. The United States of America is an enemy of those who aid terrorists and of the barbaric criminals who profane a great religion by committing murder in its name.

This military action is a part of our campaign against terrorism, another front in a war that has already been joined through diplomacy, intelligence, the freezing of financial assets and the arrests of known terrorists by law enforcement agents in 38 countries. Given the nature and reach of our enemies, we will win this conflict by the patient accumulation of successes, by meeting a series of challenges with determination and will and purpose.

Today we focus on Afghanistan, but the battle is broader. Every nation has a choice to make. In this conflict, there is no neutral ground. If any government sponsors the outlaws and killers of innocents, they have become outlaws and murderers, themselves. And they will take that lonely path at their own peril.

I'm speaking to you today from the Treaty Room of the White House, a place where American Presidents have worked for peace. We're a peaceful nation. Yet, as we have learned, so suddenly and so tragically, there can be no peace in a world of sudden terror. In the face of today's new threat, the only way to pursue peace is to pursue those who threaten it.

We did not ask for this mission, but we will fulfill it. The name of today's military operation is Enduring Freedom. We defend not only our precious freedoms, but also the freedom of people everywhere to live and raise their children free from fear.

I know many Americans feel fear today. And our government is taking strong precautions. All law enforcement and intelligence agencies are working aggressively around America, around the world and around the clock. At my request, many governors have activated the National Guard to strengthen airport security. We have called up Reserves to reinforce our military capability and strengthen the protection of our homeland.

In the months ahead, our patience will be one of our strengths—patience with the long waits that will result from tighter security; patience and understanding that it will take time to achieve our goals; patience in all the sacrifices that may come.

Today, those sacrifices are being made by members of our Armed Forces who now defend us so far from home, and by their proud and worried families. A Commander-in-Chief sends America's sons and daughters into a battle in a foreign land only after the greatest care and a lot of prayer. We ask a lot of those who wear our uniform. We ask them to leave their loved ones, to travel great distances, to risk injury, even to be prepared to make the ultimate sacrifice of their lives. They are dedicated, they are honorable; they represent the best of our country. And we are grateful.

To all the men and women in our military—every sailor, every soldier, every airman, every coastguardsman, every Marine—I say this: Your mission is defined; your objectives are clear; your goal is just. You have my full confidence, and you will have every tool you need to carry out your duty.

I recently received a touching letter that says a lot about the state of America in these difficult times—a letter from a 4th-grade girl, with a father in the military: "As much as I don't want my Dad to fight," she wrote, "I'm willing to give him to you."

This is a precious gift, the greatest she could give. This young girl knows what America is all about. Since September 11, an entire generation of young Americans has gained new understanding of the value of freedom, and its cost in duty and in sacrifice.

The battle is now joined on many fronts. We will not waver; we will not tire; we will not falter; and we will not fail. Peace and freedom will prevail.

Thank you. May God continue to bless America.

BLAIR'S SUPPORT OF MILITARY ACTION

As you will know from the announcement by President Bush military action against targets inside Afghanistan has begun. I can confirm that UK forces are engaged in this action. I want to pay tribute if I might right at the outset to

Britain's armed forces. There is no greater strength for a British Prime Minister and the British nation at a time like this than to know that the forces we are calling upon are amongst the very best in the world.

They and their families are, of course, carrying an immense burden at this moment and will be feeling deep anxiety as will the British people. But we can take pride in their courage, their sense of duty and the esteem with which they're held throughout the world.

No country lightly commits forces to military action and the inevitable risks involved but we made it clear following the attacks upon the United States on September 11th that we would take part in action once it was clear who was responsible.

There is no doubt in my mind, nor in the mind of anyone who has been through all the available evidence, including intelligence material, that these attacks were carried out by the al Qaeda network masterminded by Osama bin Laden. Equally it is clear that his network is harbored and supported by the Taliban regime inside Afghanistan.

It is now almost a month since the atrocity occurred, it is more than two weeks since an ultimatum was delivered to the Taliban to yield up the terrorists or face the consequences. It is clear beyond doubt that they will not do this. They were given the choice of siding with justice or siding with terror and they chose to side with terror.

There are three parts all equally important to the operation of which we're engaged: military, diplomatic and humanitarian. The military action we are taking will be targeted against places we know to be involved in the operation of terror or against the military apparatus of the Taliban. This military plan has been put together mindful of our determination to do all we humanly can to avoid civilian casualties.

I cannot disclose, obviously, how long this action will last but we will act with reason and resolve. We have set the objectives to eradicate Osama bin Laden's network of terror and to take action against the Taliban regime that is sponsoring it. As to the precise British involvement I can confirm that last Wednesday the U.S. Government made a specific request that a number of UK military assets be used in the operation which has now begun. And I gave authority for these assets to be deployed. They include the base at Diego Garcia, reconnaissance and flight support aircraft and missile firing submarines. Missile firing submarines are in use tonight. The air assets will be available for use in the coming days.

The United States are obviously providing the bulk of the force required in leading this operation. But this is an international effort as well as UK, France, Germany, Australia and Canada have also committed themselves to take part in the operation.

On the diplomatic and political front in the time I've been Prime Minister I cannot recall a situation that has commanded so quickly such a powerful coalition of support and not just from those countries directly involved in military action but from many others in all parts of the world. The coalition has, I believe, strengthened not weakened in the twenty six days since the atrocity occurred. And this is in no small measure due to the statesmanship of President Bush to whom I pay tribute tonight.

The world understands that whilst, of course, there are dangers in acting the dangers of inaction are far, far greater. The threat of further such outrages, the threat to our economies, the threat to the stability of the world.

On the humanitarian front we are assembling a coalition of support for refugees in and outside Afghanistan which is as vital as the military coalition. Even before September 11th four million Afghans were on the move. There are two million refugees in Pakistan and one and a half million in Iran. We have to act for humanitarian reasons to alleviate the appalling suffering of the Afghan people and deliver stability so that people from that region stay in that region. Britain, of course, is heavily involved in this effort.

So we are taking action therefore on all those three fronts: military, diplomatic and humanitarian. I also want to say very directly to the British people why this matters so much directly to Britain. First let us not forget that the attacks of the September 11th represented the worst terrorist outrage against British citizens in our history. The murder of British citizens, whether it happens overseas or not, is an attack upon Britain. But even if no British citizen had died it would be right to act.

This atrocity was an attack on us all, on people of all faiths and people of none. We know the al Qaeda network threaten Europe, including Britain, and, indeed, any nation throughout the world that does not share their fanatical views. So we have a direct interest in acting in our own self defence to protect British lives. It was also an attack not just on lives but on livelihoods. We can see since the 11th of September how economic confidence has suffered with all that means for British jobs and British industry. Our prosperity and standard of living, therefore, require us to deal with this terrorist threat.

We act also because the al Qaeda network and the Taliban regime are funded in large part on the drugs trade. Ninety per cent of all the heroin sold on British streets originates from Afghanistan. Stopping that trade is, again, directly in our interests.

I wish to say finally, as I've said many times before, that this is not a war with Islam. It angers me, as it angers the vast majority of Muslims, to hear bin Laden and his associates described as Islamic terrorists. They are terrorists pure and simple. Islam is a peaceful and tolerant religion and the acts of these people are wholly contrary to the teachings of the Koran.

These are difficult and testing times therefore for all of us. People are bound to be concerned about what the terrorists may seek to do in response. I should say there is at present no specific credible threat to the UK that we know of and that we have in place tried and tested contingency plans which are the best possible response to any further attempts at terror.

This, of course, is a moment of the utmost gravity for the world. None of the leaders involved in this action want war. None of our nations want it. We are a peaceful people. But we know that sometimes to safeguard peace we have to fight. Britain has learnt that lesson many times in our history. We only do it if the cause is just but this cause is just. The murder of almost seven thousand innocent people in America was an attack on our freedom, our way of life, an attack on civilized values the world over. We waited so that those responsible could be yielded up by those shielding them. That offer was refused, we have now no choice so we will act. And our determination in acting is total. We will not let up or rest until our objectives are met in full.

Thank you.

GENERAL ACCOUNTING OFFICE ON THREATS TO FOOD SUPPLY
October 10, 2001

The terrorist attacks of September 11 heightened concerns about the safety of the nation's food supply and renewed calls from consumer advocates to consolidate responsibility for monitoring food safety in a single agency, instead of the fragmented system that currently existed. Advocates of a single agency said there were too few inspectors, distributed unevenly through the system, with too little authority to ensure the safety of both domestic and imported food. "We believe there is reason to doubt our ability to detect and fully respond to an organized bioterrorist attack," Robert A. Robinson of the General Accounting Office (GAO) told a Senate subcommittee hearing on the matter.

As part of its homeland security measures, the Bush administration requested additional funding for more inspections, especially of imported food. But with little support from top government officials and opposition within the food industry, calls for more comprehensive reforms to tighten safety and inspection procedures did not advance very far by the end of the year. Moreover, a federal court ruling in December appeared to strip the Agriculture Department of its authority to close down meat processing plants that repeatedly failed tests for salmonella *contamination. The* salmonella *bacterium was a leading cause of food-borne illness and could cause death.*

Earlier in the year the processed food industry voluntarily agreed to expand its nutrition labels to include information on even small amounts of ingredients, such as milk, eggs, and nuts, that could cause life-threatening allergic reactions in some people. By adopting the guidelines voluntarily, the industry hoped to ward off the imposition of even tighter federal regulations.

Calls for Food Safety Reforms

The United States prided itself on having the safest food production system in the world. Thanks to relatively strong regulations regarding the components of animal feed, mad cow disease (bovine spongiform encephalopathy, or BSE), which had caused widespread consumer panic in Europe and Japan in 2000 and led to the slaughter of thousands of cattle, was not a problem in the United States, and experts did not expect it to become one. But food tainted with more ordinary pathogens, such as E. coli *and* salmonella *still caused 76 million illnesses, 325,000 hospitalizations, and 5,000 deaths every year in the United States and cost the nation nearly $7 billion annually in medical costs and lost productivity.* (Mad cow disease, Historic Documents of 2000, p. 880)

Only one major incident of deliberate contamination of food had been known to occur in the United States. That was in 1984, when a religious sect in Oregon intentionally contaminated salad bars in local restaurants with salmonella *bacteria to prevent people from voting in a local election. A total of 751 people were diagnosed with foodborne illness as a result of the incident, but no one died.*

Still, consumer advocates and others warned that the patchwork system of laws and agencies regulating food safety would make it relatively easy for terrorists to deliberately taint the food supply. Particular concern was raised about imported food, especially produce, that was not subject to the same level of scrutiny as food produced in the United States. "Should a crisis arise—real or manufactured as a hoax—the deficiencies of the current system would become glaringly obvious," Tom Hammonds, chief executive of the Food Marketing Institute, told a Senate Government Affairs subcommittee October 10. "Since it is rare that a single agency has complete jurisdiction over the entire scope of a major food safety problem, it has been our experience that none of the agencies step forward in time of crisis." The institute represented food retailers and wholesalers.

Twelve different federal agencies administered thirty-five laws protecting food in the United States. The main agencies were the Food Safety and Inspection Service (FSIS) within the Department of Agriculture, which was responsible for the safety of meat, poultry, and processed eggs, and the Food and Drug Administration (FDA), which was responsible for monitoring the safety of most other foods.

In his testimony before the Senate subcommittee, GAO's Robinson pointed out some of the inconsistencies of the fragmented federal food safety monitoring system. For one thing, he said, the system was based on legal requirements rather than on the relative risks posed by the various categories of foods. The FDA, he said, had a smaller budget and one-tenth as many inspectors as the FSIS but was responsible for monitoring the safety of about 80 percent of all regulated foods. Moreover, the foods under FDA jurisdiction accounted for about 85 percent of all foodborne illness. FDA had about 750 inspectors and a budget of about $283 million to oversee some 57,000 food establishments and about 3.7 million imported food entries. The FSIS spent about $712 million and employed about 7,500 inspectors, who made inspections at more than 6,000 meat and poultry processing plants.

The two agencies also had very different enforcement powers. FSIS could require meat and poultry producers to register for inspection, prohibit the use of processing equipment that could potentially contaminate food products, and temporarily impound any suspect foods. FDA had none of those authorities. Moreover, a country could not export meat or poultry to the United States unless the FSIS determined that the country's system for ensuring the safety of the meat and poultry was equivalent to the U.S. system. FDA had to rely primarily on inspections of imported food at its point of entry. In 2000 FDA inspections covered about 1 percent of all the food imports under its jurisdiction.

Robinson called for the creation of a single food safety agency to administer a comprehensive, uniform, and risk-based inspection system, a position that was endorsed by the subcommittee chairman, Senator Richard Durbin, D-Ill. Another proposal, by senators Edward M. Kennedy, D-Mass., and Bill Frist, R-Tenn., sought to increase the safety of imported food by giving the FDA the authority to inspect records of food manufacturers, detain food suspected of being contaminated, and ban imports from any company with a record of trying to bring in suspect food.

Lobbyists for much of the food industry said the proposed regulations and reorganization would add unnecessarily to their compliance costs and could cause delays in moving perishable goods to market. "I think we've already got a system in place to deal with terrorism. We just need more information from the government to make sure we can address any potential threat," said Kelly Johnston, executive vice president for the National Food Processors Association. The Agriculture Department and the FDA also resisted a reorganization of the federal food safety system, asking instead for more money for more inspectors.

Without support from the affected agencies, it seemed unlikely that reorganization legislation would be enacted. Congress was more likely to expand FDA's authority to deal with imported food, although several consumer groups predicted the legislation would lack teeth. ". . . Congress is willing to protect us but only to the extent that the new law doesn't offend the food processing and marketing bureaucracy or cost too much money," Carol Tucker Foreman, of the Consumer Federation of America, told the Washington Post *in December. "In the end, Congress will do a lot of talking and flapping and then bring forth a very small egg."*

Salmonella Testing

At the same time Congress was considering increasing the FDA's authority to enforce food safety, the Fifth Circuit Court of Appeals appeared to take away some of the Agriculture Department's authority to keep contaminated meat and poultry out of the marketplace. The case involved the Hazard Analysis Critical Control Points (HACCP) system, which the department had implemented in 1996 to modernize its procedures for determining whether meat and poultry were free of salmonella *and other foodborne pathogens. Under the HACCP system, meat and poultry producers were required to identify potential points in the slaughtering and processing process that made the meat and poultry susceptible to foodborne pathogens and then to take steps to reduce the possibility of contamination. To make sure that the controls were working, federal inspectors conducted limited testing for* salmonella *bacteria and other microbes.*

It was unclear, however, whether the HACCP system would survive its first major legal challenge. In May 2000 a federal district court in Texas ruled that the Agriculture Department could not shut down a Dallas hamburger processing plant after it failed to meet the performance standard for salmonella *three times. The processing plant, Supreme Beef, was a major supplier of the ground beef used in the school lunch program; it subsequently declared bankruptcy.*

In December 2001 the Fifth Circuit Court of Appeals upheld that ruling, holding that the performance standard was invalid because the salmonella *was already in the meat when it came from the slaughterhouse. In essence the appeals court agreed with the argument of the National Meat Association, which had intervened in behalf of Supreme Beef. The Agriculture Department was "trying to enforce a standard on plants that had nothing to do with the sanitation of those plants," a spokesman for the association told the* Washington Post. *"The* salmonella *was coming in from the slaughterhouses, and there is nothing a grinder could do to remove it." The appeals court further ruled that* salmonella *was not an adulterant under the Federal Meat Inspection Act because it was destroyed under normal cooking practices and therefore was not "injurious to health."*

The ruling drew the ire of consumer advocates. The Agriculture Department "can close down a plant for having too many cockroaches, but cannot if there is too much salmonella *in the meat the plant is processing," said Caroline Smith DeWaal of the Center for Science in the Public Interest. "This clearly shows that we need a new, modern meat inspection statute." In an editorial, the* New York Times *called the ruling "misguided," saying that it overlooked "the serious danger, unresolved by proper cooking, that arises when contaminated raw meat and poultry come in contact with cutting boards, utensils and other foods, such as fruits and vegetables."*

The Agriculture Department said it would continue to test for salmonella. *If the plant failed two sample sets of tests, inspectors would conduct an immediate in-depth review of the entire food safety process at the plant and could close down the plant if it failed to address any deficiencies. Foreman of the Consumer Federation of America said the department was trying to play down the impact of the appeals court ruling. "It is disingenuous to say that this is a minor change," she said. "The court has blown a huge hole in consumer protection and the [department] wants to fix it with a tiny Band-Aid."*

The Consumer Federation of America and the Center for Science in the Public Interest were among several consumer advocacy groups that asked Congress to enforce standards for harmful pathogens in meat and poultry. Until such a provision was enacted, the groups said the Agriculture Department should publish the names of meat processors that did not pass the tests.

Following are excerpts from testimony on threats to a safe food supply, delivered October 10, 2001, by Robert A. Robinson, managing director of the division of natural resources and environment

*at the General Accounting Office, before the Senate Governmental
Affairs Subcommittee on Oversight of Government Management.*

**The document was obtained from the Internet at http://
www.gao.gov/new.items/d0247t.pdf.**

Mr. Chairman and Members of the Subcommittee:

We are pleased to be here today to discuss the federal food safety system
and whether the system's current design can meet the food safety challenges
of today. While the food supply is generally safe, each year tens of millions of
Americans become ill and thousands die from eating unsafe foods, according
to the Centers for Disease Control and Prevention (CDC).

As we have stated in previous reports and testimonies, fundamental
changes are needed to ensure a safer food supply. My testimony today provides an overview of the nation's fragmented food safety system, the problems
that it causes, and the changes necessary to create lasting improvements. In
addition, I want to bring to your attention some work GAO has done addressing deliberate food contamination and federal research on and preparedness
for bioterrorism in light of the tragic events of September 11, 2001.

In summary, the current food safety system is a patchwork structure that
hampers efforts to adequately address existing and emerging food safety
risks, whether those risks involve inadvertent or deliberate contamination.
The current system is not the product of a comprehensive planning process;
rather, it was cobbled together over many years to address specific health
threats from particular food products. The resulting fragmented organizational and legal structure causes inefficient use of resources, inconsistent
oversight and enforcement, and ineffective coordination, which together hamper federal efforts to comprehensively address food safety concerns. Many
states modeled their organizational structure for food safety on the federal
system and thus face the same issues.

It is now widely recognized that food safety issues must be addressed comprehensively—that is, by preventing contamination through the entire food
production cycle, from farm to table. A single, food safety agency responsible
for administering a uniform set of laws is needed to resolve the long-standing
problems with the current system; deal with emerging food safety issues, such
as the safety of genetically modified foods or deliberate acts of contamination;
and ensure a safe food supply. While we believe that an independent agency
could offer the most effective approach, we recognize that there are short-
term costs and other considerations associated with setting up a new government agency. A second option would be to consolidate food safety activities
in an existing department, such as the U.S. Department of Agriculture (USDA)
or the Department of Health and Human Service (HHS). Regardless, however,
choosing an organizational structure only represents half the job. For any
single food safety agency to be ultimately successful, it will also be necessary

to rationalize the current patchwork of food safety legislation to make it uniform and risk-based.

Background

Despite spending more than $1 billion annually on the federal food safety system, food safety remains a concern. For example, between May and November 2000, sliced and packaged turkey meat contaminated with *Listeria monocytogenes* caused 29 individuals in 10 states to become ill. In April and May of this year, imported cantaloupes contaminated with a pathogenic strain of *Salmonella* were linked to 54 illnesses and 2 deaths in 16 states, and in June six people in California were sickened, two of whom died, from eating oysters contaminated with *Vibrio vulnificus*. CDC estimates that foodborne diseases cause approximately 76 million illnesses, 325, 000 hospitalizations, and 5,000 deaths each year. In medical costs and productivity losses, foodborne illnesses related to five principal pathogens cost the nation about $6.9 billion annually, USDA estimates.

Twelve different agencies administer as many as 35 laws that make up the federal food safety system. Two agencies account for most federal food safety spending and regulatory responsibilities: the Food Safety and Inspection Service (FSIS), in USDA, is responsible for the safety of meat, poultry, and processed eggs, while the Food and Drug Administration (FDA), in HHS, is responsible for the safety of most other foods. Other agencies with food safety responsibilities and/ or programs include HHS' Centers for Disease Control and Prevention; USDA's Agricultural Marketing Service (AMS), Animal and Plant Health Inspection Service (APHIS), Agricultural Research Service (ARS), and Grain Inspection, Packers and Stockyards Administration (GIPSA); the Department of Commerce's National Marine Fisheries Service; the Department of the Treasury's U.S. Customs Service and Bureau of Alcohol, Tobacco, and Firearms; the Environmental Protection Agency (EPA); and the Federal Trade Commission. . . .

State and local governments also conduct inspection and regulation activities that help ensure the safety of foods produced, processed, or sold within their borders. State and local governments would generally be the first to identify and respond to deliberate acts of food contamination.

Fragmented System Hampers the Effectiveness of Food Safety Efforts

During the past 25 years, we and other organizations, such as the National Academy of Sciences, have issued reports detailing problems with the federal food safety system and have made numerous recommendations for change. While many of these recommendations have been acted upon, food safety problems persist, largely because food safety responsibilities are still divided among several agencies that continue to operate under different regulatory approaches.

The federal regulatory system for food safety did not emerge from a comprehensive design but rather evolved piecemeal, typically in response to particular health threats or economic crises. Addressing one new worry after another, legislators amended old laws and enacted new ones. The resulting organizational and legal patchwork has given responsibility for specific food commodities to different agencies and provided them with significantly different regulatory authorities and responsibilities.

The number of agencies involved in regulating a sandwich illustrates the fragmented nature of the current food safety system. . . . The responsible regulatory agency as well as the frequency with which inspections occur depends on how the sandwich is presented. FSIS inspects manufacturers of packaged open-face meat or poultry sandwiches (e.g., those with one slice of bread), but FDA inspects manufacturers of packaged closed-face meat or poultry sandwiches (e.g., those with two slices of bread). According to FSIS officials, the agency lacked the resources to inspect all meat and poultry sandwich manufacturers, so it was decided that FSIS would inspect manufacturers of the less common open-face sandwich, leaving inspection of other sandwich manufacturers to FDA. Although there are no differences in the risks posed by these products, wholesale manufacturers of open-face sandwiches sold in interstate commerce are inspected by FSIS daily, while wholesale manufacturers of closed-face sandwiches sold in interstate commerce are generally inspected by FDA on average once every 5 years. . . .

Because the nation's food safety system evolved piecemeal over time, the nation has essentially two very different approaches to food safety—one at USDA and the other at FDA—that have led to inefficient use of resources and inconsistencies in oversight and enforcement. These problems, along with ineffective coordination between the agencies, have hampered and continue to impede efforts to address public health concerns associated with existing and emerging food safety risks. The following examples represent some of the problems we identified during our reviews of the nation's food safety system.

Federal food safety expenditures are based on legal requirements, not on risk. . . . [F]unding for ensuring the safety of products is disproportionate to the level of consumption of those products because the frequency of inspection is based not on risk but on the agencies' legal authority and regulatory approach. Likewise, funding for ensuring the safety of products is disproportionate to the percentage of foodborne illnesses linked to those products. For example, to ensure the safety of meat, poultry, and processed egg products in fiscal year 1999, FSIS spent about $712 million to, among other things, inspect more than 6,000 meat, poultry, and egg product establishments and conduct product inspections at 130 import establishments. FSIS' expenditures reflect its interpretation of federal law as requiring daily inspection of meat and poultry processing plants and its traditional implementation of its statutory inspection mandate through continuous government inspection of every egg products plant and every meat and poultry slaughter plant, including the examination of every carcass slaughtered. These plants account for about 20 percent of federally regulated foods and 15 percent of reported foodborne illnesses. In comparison, FDA, which has responsibility for all foods except meat, poultry, and processed egg products and has no mandated inspection frequencies, spent about $283 million to, among other things, oversee some 57,000 food establishments and 3.7 million imported food entries. These establishments and entries account for about 80 percent of federally regulated foods and 85 percent of reported foodborne illnesses.

Federal agencies' authorities to enforce food safety requirements differ. USDA agencies have the authority to (1) require food firms to register so that they can be inspected, (2) prohibit the use of processing equipment that may potentially contaminate food products, and (3) temporarily detain any suspect foods. Conversely, FDA lacks such authority and is often hindered in its food oversight efforts. For example, both USDA and FDA oversee recalls when foods they regulate are found to be contaminated or adulterated. However, if a USDA-regulated company does not voluntarily conduct the recall, USDA can detain the product for up to 20 days while it seeks a court order to seize the food. Because FDA does not have detention authority, it cannot ensure that tainted food is kept out of commerce while it seeks a court-ordered seizure. As another example, while FDA is responsible for overseeing all seafood-processing firms operating in interstate commerce, the agency does not have an effective system to identify the firms subject to regulation because there is no registration requirement for seafood firms. As a result, some firms may not be subjected to FDA oversight, thus increasing the risk of consumers' contracting a foodborne illness from unsafe seafood.

USDA and FDA implementation of the new food safety approach is inconsistent. Since December 1997, both USDA and FDA have implemented a new science-based regulatory approach—the Hazard Analysis and Critical Control Point (HACCP) system—for ensuring the safety of meat, poultry, and seafood. The HACCP system places the primary responsibility on industry, not government inspectors, for identifying and controlling hazards in the production process. However, . . . FDA and USDA implemented the HACCP system differently. While USDA reported that in 1999, 96 percent of federally regulated plants were in compliance with the basic HACCP requirements for meat and poultry, FDA reported that less than half of federally regulated seafood firms were in compliance with HACCP requirements. In addition, while USDA collects data on *Salmonella* contamination to assess the effectiveness of its HACCP system for meat and poultry, FDA does not have similar data for seafood. Without more effective compliance programs and adequate performance data, the benefits of HACCP will not be fully realized.

Oversight of imported food is inconsistent and unreliable. As we reported in 1998, the meat and poultry acts require that, before a country can export meat and poultry to the United States, FSIS must make a determination that the exporting country's food safety system provides a level of safety equivalent to the U.S. system. Under the equivalency requirement, FSIS has shifted most of the responsibility for ensuring product safety to the exporting country. The exporting country performs the primary inspection, allowing FSIS to leverage its resources by focusing its reviews on verifying the efficacy of the exporting countries' systems. In addition, until FSIS approves release of imported meat and poultry products into U.S. commerce, they generally must be kept in an FSIS-registered warehouse. In contrast, FDA lacks the legal authority to require that countries exporting foods to the United States have food safety systems that provide a level of safety equivalent to ours. Without such authority, FDA must rely primarily on its port-of-entry inspections to detect and bar the entry of unsafe imported foods. Such an approach has been widely discredited as resource-intensive and ineffective. In fiscal year 2000, FDA inspections covered about 1 percent of the imported food entries under its jurisdiction. In addition, FDA does not control imported foods or require that they be kept in a registered warehouse prior to FDA approval for release into U.S. commerce. As a result, some adulterated imports that were ultimately refused entry by FDA had already been released into U.S. commerce. For example, in 1998 we reported that in a U.S. Customs Service operation called "Bad Apple," about 40 percent of the imported foods FDA checked and found in violation of U.S. standards were never redelivered to Customs for disposition. These foods were not destroyed or reexported as required and presumably were released into U.S. commerce. . . .

Effective enforcement of limits on certain drugs in food-producing animals is hindered by the regulatory system's fragmented organizational structure. FDA has regulatory responsibility for enforcing animal-drug residue levels in food producing animals. However, FDA in conjunction with the states have only investigated between 43 and 50 percent of each year's USDA animal-drug residue referrals made between fiscal year 1996 and 2000. According to FDA officials, the agency lacks the resources to conduct prompt follow-up investigations and does not have an adequate referral assignment and tracking system to ensure that investigations are made in a timely manner. FDA has relied on the states, through contracts and cooperative agreements, to conduct the bulk of the investigations. FDA only has resources to investigate repeat violators. As a result, animal producers not investigated may continue to use animal drugs improperly putting consumer health at greater risk. . . .

Fundamental Changes Needed to the
Federal Food Safety System

We continue to believe . . . that a single, Independent food safety agency administering a unified, risk-based food safety system is the most effective solution to the current fragmentation of the federal food safety system. While there are difficulties involved in establishing a new government agency and opinions differ about the best organizational model for food safety, there is widespread national and international recognition of the need for uniform laws and consolidation of food safety activities under a single organization. Both the National Academy of Sciences and the President's Council on Food Safety have joined us in calling for fundamental changes to the federal food safety system, including a reevaluation of the system's organizational structure. Likewise, several former senior-level government officials that were responsible for federal food safety activities have called for major organizational and legal changes. Internationally, four countries—Canada, Denmark, Great Britain, and Ireland—have each recently consolidated their food safety responsibilities under a single agency. Several other countries or government organizations may be considering this option as well, including Argentina, Chile, Hong Kong, the Netherlands, and the European Union.

In an August 1998 report, the National Academy of Sciences concluded that the current fragmented federal food safety system is not well equipped to meet emerging challenges. The academy found that "there are inconsistent, uneven, and at times archaic food statutes that inhibit use of science-based decision-making in activities related to food safety, and these statutes can be inconsistently interpreted and enforced among agencies." As such, the academy concluded that to create a science-based food safety system current laws must be revised. Accordingly, it recommended that the Congress change federal statutes so that food safety inspection and enforcement are based on scientific assessments of public health risks. The academy also recommended that food safety programs be administered by a single official in charge of all federal food safety resources and activities, including outbreak management, standard-setting, inspection, monitoring, surveillance, risk assessment, enforcement, research, and education.

According to the academy's report, many members of the committee tasked to conduct the study believed that a single agency headed by one administrator was the best way to provide the central, unified framework critical to improving the food safety system. However, assessing alternative organizational approaches was not possible in the time available or part of the committee's charge. Therefore, the committee did not recommend a specific organizational structure but instead provided several possible configurations for illustrative purposes. These were

- forming a Food Safety Council of representatives from the agencies, with a central chair appointed by the President, reporting to the Congress and having control of resources;
- designating one current agency as the lead agency and making the head of that agency the responsible individual;
- establishing a single agency reporting to one current cabinet-level secretary; and
- establishing an independent single agency at the cabinet level.

The committee also proposed that a detailed examination of specific organizational changes be conducted as a part of a future study. Such a study would be in keeping with the Congress' intent, as expressed in the fiscal year 1998 conference report on food safety appropriations. This conference report directed that if the academy's study recommended an independent food safety agency, a second study be conducted to determine the agency's responsibilities to ensure that the food safety system protects the public health.

In response to the academy's report, the President established a Council on Food Safety and charged it to develop a comprehensive strategic plan for federal food safety activities, among other things. The Council's Food Safety Strategic Plan, released on January 19, 2001, recognized the need for a comprehensive food safety statute and concluded that "the current organizational structure makes it more difficult to achieve future improvements in efficiency, efficacy, and allocation of resources based on risk." The council analyzed several organizational reform options. Two of the options involved enhanced coordination within the existing structure, and the other two involved consolidation of responsibilities, either within an existing organization or a stand-alone food safety agency. The council's analysis of the options found that coordination may lead to marginal improvements but do little to address the fragmentation, duplication, and conflict inherent in the current system. The council concluded that consolidation could eliminate duplication and fragmentation, create a single voice for food safety, facilitate priority setting and resource allocation based on risk, and provide greater accountability. The council recommended the development of comprehensive, unifying food safety legislation to provide a risk-based, prevention-oriented system for all food, followed by the development of a corresponding organizational reform plan.

Former key government food safety officials at USDA and FDA have acknowledged the limitations of the current regulatory system. . . . [M]any former government officials recognize the need for and support the transition to a single food safety agency. Some of these officials believe the single agency could be consolidated within an existing department, and others favor an independent agency. Regardless, they all recognize the need for legislative overhaul to provide a uniform, risk-based approach to food safety. . . .

Bioterrorism and Deliberate Acts of Food Contamination

Recent events have raised the specter of bioterrorism as an emerging risk factor for our food safety system. Bioterrorism is the threatened or intentional release of biological agents (viruses, bacteria, or their toxins) for the purpose of influencing the conduct of government or of intimidating or coercing a civilian population. These agents can be released through food as well as the air, water, or insects. To respond to potential bioterrorism, federal food safety regulatory agencies need to be prepared to efficiently coordinate their activities and respond quickly to protect the public health. Under the current structure, we believe that there are very real doubts about the system's ability to detect and quickly respond to any such event.

To date, the only known bioterrorist act in the United States involved deliberate contamination of food with a biological agent. In 1984, a religious cult intentionally contaminated salad bars in local restaurants in Oregon to prevent people from voting in a local election. Although no one died, 751 people were diagnosed with foodborne illnesses. Since then federal officials identified only one other act of deliberate food contamination with a biological agent that affected 13 individuals in 1996, but numerous threats and hoaxes have been reported. Both FDA and FSIS have plans and procedures for responding to deliberate food contamination incidents, but the effectiveness of these procedures is largely untested for contamination involving biological agents. Therefore, we recommended in 1999 that FDA and FSIS test their plans and procedures using simulated exercises that evaluate the effectiveness of federal, state, and local agencies' and industry's responses to various types of deliberate food contamination with a biological agent.

Moreover, in September 2001 we reported that coordination of federal terrorism research, preparedness, and response programs is fragmented. Separately, we reported that several relevant agencies have not been included in bioterrorism-related policy and response planning. For example, USDA officials told us that their department was not involved, even though it would have key responsibilities if terrorists targeted the food supply.

Conclusions

To conclude, Mr. Chairman, we believe that creating a single food safety agency to administer a uniform, risk-based inspection system is the most effective way for the federal government to resolve long-standing problems; address emerging food safety issues, including acts of deliberate contamination involving biological agents; and ensure the safety of the nation's food supply. In addition, the National Academy of Sciences and the President's Council on Food Safety have reported that comprehensive, uniform, and risk-based food safety legislation is needed to provide the foundation for a consolidated food safety system. While we believe the case for a single food safety agency has been compelling for some time, recent events make this action more imperative. Numerous details, of course, remain to be worked out but it is essential that the fundamental decision to create such an agency be made and the process for resolving outstanding technical issues be started. . . .

INSTITUTE OF MEDICINE ON
HEALTH INSURANCE COVERAGE
October 11, 2001

The number of Americans without health insurance fell in 2000, for the second year in a row. According to the U.S. Census Bureau, an estimated 14 percent of the population was without health insurance coverage in 2000, compared with 14.3 percent in 1999. As in 1999, the improvement in coverage appeared to be attributable to employers who were using health insurance benefits to attract workers in a tight labor market.

With the economy dipping into recession in 2001 and the number of unemployed rising, many analysts expected the number of uninsured to begin rising as well. Those fears were exacerbated by increasing costs both of health care and health insurance premiums, which forced some employers to raise the share of the premiums paid by their employees or to drop coverage altogether. The chief factors in rising health care costs were higher costs for prescription drugs and higher payments to both doctors and hospitals. (Health insurance coverage, Historic Documents of 2000, p. 787)

Meanwhile, an expert panel for the Institute of Medicine issued the first in a planned series of reports on the consequences of being without health insurance not only for the uninsured and their families, but also for their communities and society as a whole. The series was expected to examine the consequences for the health of the uninsured, the economic well-being of the family and surrounding community, and the cost to society and to offer strategies and recommendations for expanding health insurance coverage. The Institute of Medicine was a unit of the National Academy of Sciences, a private research organization chartered by Congress to provide advice to the government.

The Census Bureau Report

The annual Census Bureau report found that the number of people without health insurance in 2000 was down 0.6 million, from 39.3 million to

38.7 million. The proportion of uninsured children also declined, from 12.6 percent in 1999 to 11.6 percent in 2000. One group that experienced a significant increase was the near poor (those with a family income above the poverty line but not more than 125 percent of the poverty line). The percentage of uninsured in that category rose from 24.7 percent in 1999 to 26.9 percent in 2000. Analysts said that many of the near poor held jobs, but many of their employers did not offer health benefits and the near poor could not typically afford to buy health insurance on their own.

The Census Bureau said it revised the way it made its estimates for its report, adding some survey questions to help verify whether the respondents were actually uninsured. The revision, which lowered the number of people reported as uninsured, meant that the data for 1999 and 2000 in its 2000 report were not directly comparable to those in its earlier reports, including the one released in 1999. The unrevised figures for 2000 were 42.3 million uninsured, or 15.3 percent of the population, compared with 42.6 million uninsured in 1999, or 15.5 percent of the population.

Myths and Realities

Whether the number of uninsured was 42 million, 39 million, or even 32 million, as other surveys had estimated, the number was still substantial. That was the conclusion of an expert panel convened by the Institute of Medicine that said it found the variations in the estimates "less critical" than the order of magnitude found by all the surveys. "As a society, we have tolerated substantial populations of uninsured persons," the panel wrote, adding that "the consequences . . . are becoming more apparent and cannot be ignored."

In the first of six planned reports, the Committee on the Consequences of Uninsurance tried to dispel many of the myths that the American public held about who was uninsured and why. "Much of what Americans think they know about the uninsured is wrong," said Arthur Kellerman, a public health professor at Emory University School of Medicine, who was one of the authors of the report "Coverage Matters: Insurance and Health Care."

In addition to underestimating the numbers of people uninsured, the report said, the American public mistakenly assumed that people without health insurance still received medical care. In reality, the committee said, the uninsured were much more likely to go without needed care, to receive fewer preventive services, and to receive less regular care for chronic conditions. More than 30 percent of uninsured adults and 15 percent of uninsured children had no regular doctor, the committee said

Another mistaken assumption, the committee said, was that most uninsured people did not work. In fact, the committee said, more than 80 percent of all uninsured children and adults under age sixty-five lived in working families. Most private health insurance was offered through one's employer, but only 75 percent of all workers received health benefits through their jobs. The options for workers without coverage through their employer were to purchase coverage on their own or participate, if eligible, in public programs, such as Medicaid or the Children's Health Insurance Program

(CHIP). Not all employees offered health benefits by their employers took them, primarily because of the expense. According to the committee, wage-earners typically paid from 25 percent to more than 30 percent of the total cost of the premium, as well as deductibles, copayments, and the cost of health services that were not fully covered under the plan.

The report also looked at the demographics of the uninsured and found that the risk of being uninsured was higher among low-income individuals, people who had not graduated from high school, and young adults. Hispanics were more than three times as likely to be uninsured as non-Hispanic whites, while African Americans were twice as likely to be uninsured. Although more men were uninsured than women, women were more likely to obtain coverage through individual policies and public insurance programs. Their insurance status was thus more unstable, the committee said, "with more opportunities for gaps in coverage."

Continuing Rise in Health Care Costs

Health care costs continued to rise. A report by the nonpartisan Center for Studying Health System Change reported that health care spending in 2000 rose 7.2 percent, the largest increase in a decade. Several factors contributed to the increase. Spending on prescription drugs rose nearly 19 percent, in part because drugs cost more and in part because doctors were prescribing more of them. An aging population was also seeking more hospital services. Hospitals, their numbers reduced as a result of mergers and acquisitions, wielded more clout with insurance companies and were demanding—and getting—higher reimbursements for their services. In many areas doctors had organized and were asking for and receiving higher fees from insurers. Dissatisfaction with the restrictive coverage under health maintenance organizations (HMOs) was driving many patients into preferred provider plans, which were a less restrictive but more expensive form of managed care. Meanwhile HMOs were trying to regain lost patients by loosening some of their restrictions, which also raised costs.

One consequence of the increased health care costs was increasing insurance premiums, which rose 10 percent or more in 2001 and were expected to rise at least that much in 2002. Employers of all sizes were passing some of those costs through to their employees, many of whom saw an increase in the size of their contribution to the premium payment as well as increases in copayments and deductibles. Some employers said they hoped that by having to share more of the costs of their health care, employees would become "more judicious buyers," as one executive said. But health care experts said that higher costs were likely to make people forgo needed treatment or even give up insurance altogether.

Policy Standoff

Neither Congress nor the president were able to provide much relief to the uninsured or anyone else grappling with the high cost of health care in

2001. A proposal to provide federal subsidies so that laid-off workers could retain their health insurance was added to an economic stimulus package in Congress late in the year, but the stimulus package died in the Senate after becoming snarled in a political battle over which party was to blame for the recession. (Postattack economy, p. 663)

During the 2000 election campaign, both political parties promised to enact prescription drug coverage for the elderly. Medicare, the federal health insurance program for the elderly that covered nearly every American over age sixty-five, did not provide drug coverage. Congress in 2001 set aside money in principle to cover prescriptions as part of a Medicare overhaul, but there was little action on Medicare reform during the year. By the end of the year, recession, the tax cuts enacted earlier in the year, and the war on terrorism had dried up the federal budget surplus, making action on a prescription drug benefit unlikely at least in the near future.

In July President George W. Bush unveiled a voluntary plan to help Medicare recipients obtain discounts on prescription drugs. Under the plan, Medicare recipients would pay a one-time enrollment fee of no more than $25 to sign up with a company, known as a pharmacy benefit manager. These companies, which already managed drug benefits for millions of Americans with private health insurance, would pool the purchasing power of the Medicare recipients to negotiate drug discounts from drug manufacturers and pharmacies. Secretary Health and Human Services Tommy G. Thompson said he hoped the plan would cut drug prices for the elderly by 15 to 25 percent or more. Five major pharmacy benefit managers had already agreed to participate in the plan when it was announced at the White House on July 12, and several more were expected to sign on.

The plan was criticized by Democrats, who said the discount would not do enough to defray the costs of drugs for the elderly, and by drug stores, who said the plan would undercut their businesses. On September 6 a federal district judge in the District of Columbia issued an injunction barring the plan from taking effect, while a suit brought by the National Association of Chain Drug Stores and the National Community Pharmacy Association was being played out in the courts. The judge said he thought the two trade organizations had a "substantial likelihood" of winning their case on the grounds that the administration lacked the legal authority to enact the program without specific authorization from Congress and that it had not followed the regular procedure for issuing regulations.

Following are excerpts from the executive summary of "Coverage Matters: Insurance and Health Care," a report issued October 11, 2001, by the Institute of Medicine Committee on the Consequences of Uninsurance.

The document was obtained from the Internet at http:// www.nap.edu/catalog/10188.html.

Health care increasingly affects our personal lives and the national economy as its benefits to our health, longevity and quality of life grow. Over the past quarter of a century, clinical medicine has become more sophisticated, technological advances have become more commonplace, and the range of health care interventions has been much expanded. Yet over the same period, the numbers of persons without health insurance to help them purchase health services has increased by about one million per year—faster than the rate of overall population growth. The total number of uninsured Americans grew even during years of economic prosperity.

This report and the five reports that will follow endeavor to present a wide-angle view of health insurance and examine the consequences of being without insurance, not only for persons who are uninsured and their families, but also for the communities in which they live and for society. Health insurance is one of the best-known and most common means used to obtain access to health care. What are the consequences for all of us of having tens of millions of people uninsured?

Over the next two years, the Institute of Medicine Committee on the Consequences of Uninsurance will evaluate and report what is known about the impacts of being uninsured and how being uninsured affects individuals, families, communities, and society. The Committee will focus on uninsured people, defined as persons with no health insurance and no assistance in paying for health care beyond what is available through charity and safety-net institutions. It recognizes, however, that many people have insurance that offers incomplete coverage and that being underinsured poses problems as well, though these are generally less severe. While the implications and potentially harmful consequences are greater for those who are uninsured for longer periods, in this report we consider persons who lack insurance for any period of time to be uninsured and at risk for some adverse effects as a result. . . .

In this first report, the Committee provides an overview of health insurance in America, looking specifically at how coverage is gained and lost, why so many people have none, and who lacks insurance, as individuals and as members of groups within the general population. In addition, this report introduces the Committee's analytic plan for the entire series of reports and presents the conceptual framework that will guide the Committee's evaluations of specific impacts of uninsurance in its subsequent reports.

Myths and Realities

This report begins by examining pervasive popular ideas about the scope and nature of the problem of uninsurance that frustrate attempts to address this complex issue constructively. Americans persistently underestimate the numbers of uninsured people and hold many misperceptions about their identity, about how one becomes uninsured, and about the economic and health consequences of being uninsured.

Myth: People without health insurance get the medical care they need.

Reality: **The uninsured are much more likely than persons with insurance coverage to go without needed care. They also receive fewer**

preventive services and less regular care for chronic conditions than people with insurance.

Myth: The number of uninsured Americans is not particularly large and has not been increasing in recent years.

Reality: **The number of uninsured people is greater than the combined populations of Texas, Florida, and Connecticut. During 1999, the Census Bureau estimated that approximately 42 million people in the United States lacked health insurance coverage. This number represents about 15 percent of a total population of 274 million persons and 17 percent of the population under 65 years of age.** An estimated ten million of the uninsured are children under the age of 18 (about 14 percent of all children), and about 32 million are adults between ages 18 and 65 (about 19 percent of all adults in this group). The estimate of uninsured people is even larger when coverage is measured over several years. **Almost three out of every ten Americans, more than 70 million people, lacked health insurance for at least a month over a 36-month period.**

Estimates of the number of persons who lack insurance vary depending on the survey and range from 32 million to 42 million for those without coverage throughout the year. Surveys differ in their size and sampling methods, the ways in which questions are asked about insurance coverage, and the period over which insurance coverage or uninsurance is measured. The Current Population Survey (CPS), conducted annually by the Census Bureau, is the most widely cited source of estimates of the number of uninsured persons and is used throughout this report as the primary data source. The CPS is particularly useful because it produces yearly estimates in a timely fashion, reporting the previous year's insurance coverage rates each September, and because information about insurance coverage has been gathered since the mid-1970s, allowing for analysis of coverage trends over time. Although the CPS nominally reports persons uninsured throughout the entire calendar year, some analysts believe that its estimates actually reflect shorter periods of uninsurance, and thus that its estimates of the number uninsured throughout the year are too high.

Whether one uses the estimate of 42 million uninsured, as reported by the CPS, or the lower estimates generated on the basis of other governmentally and privately sponsored surveys, the number of uninsured Americans is substantial. In light of the CPS's usefulness and its limitations, this report relies on estimates based on CPS data, with caveats. The Committee finds the variation in estimates among surveys less critical than the order of magnitude of the entire range of estimates that different surveys yield.

Myth: Most people who lack health insurance are in families where no one works.

Reality: **More than 80 percent of uninsured children and adults under the age of 65 live in working families.** Although working does improve the chances that one and one's family will have insurance, even members of families with two full-time wage earners have almost a one-in-ten chance of being uninsured.

Myth: Growth in the numbers of recent immigrants has been a major source of the increase in the number of uninsured persons.

Reality: **Although immigrants who have arrived within 4 years have higher-than-average uninsurance rates, they comprise a relatively small proportion of the general population.** In fact, between 1994 and 1998, there has been a net decrease in the number of recently arrived immigrants. Overall, noncitizens account for fewer than one in five uninsured persons.

Through its work, the Committee hopes to replace misperceptions with facts and in doing so, to lay the groundwork for a more informed public debate about health insurance coverage.

Relating Health Insurance to Access to Health Services

Health insurance serves multiple constituencies and distinct purposes. For individuals and families, insurance coverage is one means to promote health and access to care and to protect against exceptional health care costs. Insurance pools the risks and resources of a group of people so that each is protected from financially disruptive medical expenses and each may plan ahead or budget for health care. In contrast with many other insurance products, such as automobile or homeowner's insurance, health insurance has evolved as a mechanism for financing routine health care expenses and encouraging the use of preventive services, in addition to protecting against uncommon events and expenses. As the scope and effectiveness of health care interventions have grown, so have consumers' expectations for coverage and benefits through health insurance.

Other constituencies also have a stake in our mechanisms for financing health care. Providers of health care benefit from insurance as a reliable source of payment. Employers offer health benefits to attract and retain workers and to maintain a productive workforce. Governments provide health insurance to special populations as a means to secure health care for them.

Health insurance is neither necessary nor sufficient to obtain health care, yet coverage remains one of the most important ways to obtain access to health services. The level of out-of-pocket costs for care has been demonstrated to have substantial effects on the use of health services. Uninsured persons may be charged more than patients with coverage, who benefit from discounts negotiated by their insurer. In addition, uninsured people face 100 percent cost sharing, although some providers are willing to absorb part of the cost for some of their patients some of the time by negotiating a reduced rate. Even though many publicly supported institutions offer free care or reduced fees and many other providers offer some charity care, people without insurance generally have reduced access to care.

Evidence accumulated over the past several decades of health services research has consistently found that persons without insurance are less likely to have any physician visit within a year, have fewer visits annually, and are less likely to have a regular source of care. Children without insurance are three times as likely as children with Medicaid coverage to have no regular source of care (15 percent of uninsured children do not have a regular provider compared with just 5 percent of children with Medicaid), and uninsured adults are more than three times as likely as either privately or publicly insured adults to lack a regular source of care (35 percent compared with 11 percent). The likelihood that those without health insurance lack a regular source of care has increased substantially since 1977.

Uninsured adults are less likely to receive health services, even for certain serious conditions. One nationally representative survey that took into account age, sex, income, and health status found that uninsured people were less than half as likely as those with insurance to receive needed care, as judged by physicians, for a serious medical condition. People without insurance are also less likely to receive preventive services and appropriate routine care for chronic conditions than those with insurance, even as the importance of preventive care and the prevalence of chronic disease become more prominent elements within health care.

To guide its assessment of the relationship between the lack of health insurance, access to care, and the consequences of no coverage, the Committee has based its conceptual framework on a widely used behavioral model of access to health services. In this framework the major determinants of insurance coverage are heavily, but not exclusively, economic. The model links these determinants to features of the process of obtaining health services and to morbidity, mortality, and health status. Insurance coverage is thus linked in this model to an array of outcomes through the mediating effect of health care services. The model allows us to track the effects from lack of coverage on individuals and families, in a sizable uninsured population, to the viability of health care providers and institutions at a community level and the implications for the nation's economy.

How Coverage Is Gained and Lost

In the United States, health insurance is a voluntary matter, yet many people are involuntarily without coverage. There is no guarantee for most people under the age of 65 years that they will be eligible for, or able to afford to purchase or retain, health insurance. The historical tension rooted in American social values, between considering health care as a market commodity and as a social good, has fostered the development of variegated and complex arrangements for financing the delivery of health care.

Within the private sector, insurance coverage depends on an employer's decision to offer a health benefit plan and an employee's decision to enroll or take up this offer. When workers are not offered the chance to purchase employment-based insurance for themselves and their dependent family members (spouses and minor children), or when they decline to enroll, individual policies and public insurance (Medicaid or the State Children's Health Insurance Program [SCHIP]) offer limited opportunities for coverage. Poor health status or low income may preclude the purchase of an affordable (or any) individual policy from an insurance company. The combination of strict eligibility requirements and complex enrollment procedures often makes public coverage difficult to obtain and even more difficult to maintain over time.

Opportunities to Purchase Coverage

Almost seven out of every ten Americans under age 65 years (66 percent) are covered by employment-based health insurance, from either their job or that of their parent or spouse. Among workers 76 percent are offered health insurance by their employers, and 83 percent of those offered insurance decide to purchase or take up the offer of coverage. The 17 percent of workers that decline an employer's offer include about 13 percent who are covered through a spouse or elsewhere and 4 percent who remain uninsured. The expense and competing demands on family income are the main reasons given for declining the offer of employment-based insurance.

Individually purchased policies and public insurance (primarily Medicaid) both fill some of the coverage gaps created by the employment-based system. Together they account for 21 percent of coverage. Self-employed people (about 10 percent of workers) and their families must often rely on individually purchased health insurance. Individual coverage also serves as a stop-gap measure, however, for adult children who lose their coverage as dependents before they can obtain job-based coverage and for retirees under the age of 65 before they become eligible for Medicare. Medicaid coverage also tends to be transitory, with two-thirds of new enrollees losing coverage within the first year.

Gaining and Losing Coverage

Many normal social and economic transitions can trigger a loss of health insurance coverage for a person or family because income, health status, marital status, and terms of employment affect eligibility for and participation in health insurance. Conversely, many of these transitional events can result in becoming eligible for coverage. Because so many different common events are associated with a change in health insurance status, the chance of being uninsured over the course of a lifetime may be substantial. For example, a young adult (18–24) has a greater-than-even chance of being uninsured for at least one month over a 36-month period.

For some people, lack of insurance is a temporary or one-time interruption of coverage, while for others, being uninsured is an experience that recurs periodically or may last for several years. Lower income persons tend to remain uninsured for longer than do those with incomes above the federal poverty level. Educational attainment and employment sector are factors that also are related to the length of uninsured periods. Short periods without health insurance are less likely than longer periods to adversely affect access to health services. Yet even short periods without insurance carry with them the financial risk of extraordinarily high health expenses.

Limited Coverage Options

Insurance industry underwriting practices, the costs of health services, and the patchwork of public policies regarding insurance coverage all contribute to the economic pressures on employers, insurers, and government programs offering health insurance. Small employers frequently face higher group health insurance premium rates than large employers do. Larger firms can cushion themselves from the financial impact of insurance company medical underwriting and restrictions by choosing to self-insure their employees' health benefits. Small employers may receive poorer benefits for premiums comparable to those of large firms, because of both a higher risk premium and higher administrative costs per person, and inadequate resources to evaluate and negotiate good coverage. As a result, some small employers may decline to offer coverage altogether. Among a group of 955 small businesses (fewer than 50 employees) surveyed, the most common and the highest-ranking reason for not offering insurance benefits was the expense of coverage.

The expense and competing demands on family income are the main reasons given by individuals for declining an offer of employment-based coverage. Wage-earners who accept or take up an employer's offer of a subsidized health benefit typically pay between one-quarter and one-third of the total cost of their insurance premium, in addition to deductibles, copayments, and the costs of health services that are not covered or are covered only in part. For families earning less than 200 percent of the federal poverty level (FPL), $33,400 for a family of four in 1999, the cost of an unsubsidized insurance premium may exceed 10 percent of annual income.

Coverage Trends over Time

Since the mid-1970s, growth in the cost of health insurance has outpaced the rise in real income, creating a gap in purchasing ability that has added roughly one million persons to the ranks of the uninsured each year. These cost increases result in part from advances in medical and pharmaceutical technology, an aging population, and reduced consumer sensitivity to prices through expanded insurance coverage. Despite the economic prosperity of recent years, between 1998 and 1999 there was only a slight drop in the number and proportion of uninsured Americans. Through the early 1990s the rising uninsurance rate reflected a decline in employment-based coverage. Since the mid-1990s increases in employment-based coverage have been offset by steady or declining rates of public and individually purchased coverage.

A Portrait of the Uninsured

People lack coverage regardless of education, age, or state of residence. Employment and geographic factors are central because private insurance is closely tied to employment, and eligibility for public programs is partly determined by work and income criteria.

Social and Economic Factors Affect Coverage

Full-time, full-year employment offers families the best chance of having health insurance, as does an annual income of at least a moderate level (greater than 200 percent of FPL). Wage earners in smaller firms, lower-waged firms, nonunionized firms, and nonmanufacturing employment sectors are more likely than average to go without coverage. Members of families without wage earners are more likely to be uninsured than are members of families with wage earners. Two-thirds of all uninsured persons are members of lower-income families (earning less than 200 percent of FPL), and nearly one-third of all members of lower-income families are uninsured. More than one-quarter of all uninsured adults have not earned a high school diploma, and almost four out of every ten adults who have not graduated from high school are uninsured.

Coverage Varies over the Life Cycle

The average individual's chances of being uninsured trace a curve across the life span, from a lower-than-average likelihood for minor children and a higher-than-average likelihood for young adults to a gradual decline in probability with advancing age and increasing connection to the labor force. People 65 and older have a minimal likelihood of being uninsured because Medicare provides virtually universal coverage to that age group. Marriage and the rearing of infants and young children both decrease the chances, on average, that an adult will be uninsured. Sources of coverage and health status, as well as participation in the work force, also affect one's chances of lacking coverage.

Demographic Disparities in Coverage

Higher uninsured rates among members of racial and ethnic minority groups and among recent immigrants reflect their lower rates of employment-based coverage and lower family incomes, on average, compared to non-Hispanic whites and U.S.-born residents. African Americans are twice as likely as non-Hispanic whites to be uninsured, and Hispanics are three times as likely to be uninsured, although more than half of all uninsured persons are non-Hispanic whites. Foreign-born residents are almost three times as likely to be uninsured as are those born in the United States, and among the foreign born, noncitizens are more than twice as likely as citizens to be uninsured.

In addition, there are gender disparities in coverage, reflecting the different experiences of adult men and women in the workplace and with public policies. Although men are more likely than women to be uninsured, women have a lower rate of employment-based coverage. Because women are more likely to obtain coverage through individual policies and public programs, their insurance status tends to be less stable, with more opportunities for gaps in coverage.

Geographic Differences Affect Coverage

The decentralized labor and health services markets of the United States and the distinctive public policies of each state and locality together create unique contexts for the patterns of insurance coverage for individuals, families, and population groups. Differences among the states with respect to population characteristics, industrial economic base, eligibility for public insurance, and relative purchasing power of family income shape the geographic disparities in insurance coverage rates. Residents of the South and West are more likely than average to be uninsured. Reflecting the predominantly urban location of the general population, most uninsured persons live in urban areas, although rural and urban residents are about equally uninsured. . . .

Summary

Most Americans expect and receive health services when they and their families need care, but for the approximately 40 million people who have no health insurance, this is not always the reality. Health insurance is a key factor affecting whether an individual or family obtains health care. Uninsured Americans are not able to realize the benefits of American health care because they cannot obtain certain services or the services they do receive are not timely, appropriate, or well coordinated.

The most apparent deficits in care experienced by those without insurance are for chronic conditions and in preventive and screening services. Far too often, key aspects of quality health care, regular care and communication with a provider to prevent and manage chronic health conditions, are beyond the reach of uninsured persons.

As a society, we have tolerated substantial populations of uninsured persons as a residual of employment-based and public coverage since the introduction of Medicare and Medicaid more than three and a half decades ago. Regardless of whether this result is by design or default, the consequences of our policy choices are becoming more apparent and cannot be ignored. Current public policies and insurance practices will sustain a large uninsured population under a range of projected scenarios for the national economy. The decline in the number of uninsured people between 1997 and 1999 is not expected to continue if the economy remains slow and health care costs and insurance premiums continue to rise rapidly. By clarifying the dynamics of health insurance coverage and identifying underlying factors that contribute to uninsurance, this report and those that follow should help inform ongoing discussions about how to remedy this long-standing social problem.

FEDERAL APPEALS COURT ON THE RIGHT TO BEAR ARMS
October 16, 2001

George W. Bush, an ardent opponent of gun control who benefited from active campaigning on his behalf by the National Rifle Association (NRA) during the 2000 presidential election campaign, moved quickly in his first year in office to roll back some of the more controversial federal restrictions on guns and gun ownership enacted during Bill Clinton's presidency. In quick succession, the Justice Department moved to reduce, from ninety days to one day, the amount of time the Federal Bureau of Investigation had to keep records on gun purchasers; the Department of Housing and Urban Development canceled a gun buyback program that it said was ineffective; and the State Department opposed a United Nations plan to mandate reductions in international trafficking of small arms, such as automatic rifles, saying that the United States would not support measures that interfered with the legal right to trade weapons or bear arms. (Small arms trade, p. 516)

Perhaps the most provocative actions, however, came from Bush's attorney general, John Ashcroft, himself a long-time member of the NRA. In May Ashcroft appeared to reverse decades of settled judicial policy when he told the pro-gun lobby that he "unequivocally" believed that the Second Amendment to the Constitution protected the right of individuals to keep and bear arms. Ashcroft's position was directly counter to the ensconced legal interpretation of the amendment, which held that the right was a collective one, applying to state and federal militias, but not to individual gun owners. At the end of the year, Ashcroft provoked further criticism when the Justice Department refused to let the FBI check its records to see if any of the 1,200 foreigners detained after the terrorist attacks on September 11 had purchased firearms. (Terrorist attacks, p. 614)

The NRA, long one of the most influential lobbying groups in Washington, expressed pleasure with these changes, although it said some did not go far enough. For example, the group said it was opposed to any record keeping on legal gun purchases. Opponents of the NRA said they were disappointed by the administration's actions on some issues and outraged by others, but not surprised by any of them. "It's clear that they [the Bush administration] are beholden to the NRA and they feel obligated to them, and so they'll do whatever the NRA wants," said Brendan Daly of the Brady Center to Prevent Gun Violence.

Gun sales surged in the days following the September 11 terrorist attacks on the World Trade Center and the Pentagon. The FBI said that in the twenty-five states where it performed the instant background checks on gun purchasers, applications were up by 15 percent between September 11 and September 13. Gun shop owners reported that many of the new customers had never owned a gun before. A Gallup Poll conducted in mid-October found that the number of Americans supporting strict gun control measures had dropped to 53 percent, after hovering at 60 percent or higher for almost a decade.

In April the federal Centers for Disease Control and Prevention (CDC) reported that there were 30,708 gun-related deaths in 1998, the last year for which statistics were available. That number was down 26 percent from its peak in 1993. The number of gun-related injuries fell to 64,484 in 1998. The drop in gun-related deaths coincided with a significant decline in violent crime, but accidental and self-inflicted gun-related deaths and injuries also declined. The CDC said it was particularly concerned by the high number of gun suicides among elderly men, one of the most vulnerable groups to suicide by any means. (Suicide, p. 290; crime report, p. 746)

NRA Back on Top

Long considered one of the most powerful lobbying forces in Washington, D.C., the National Rifle Association lost some of its clout during Clinton's tenure in the White House. In 1993 and 1994, Clinton's first two years in office, Congress passed the Brady Bill, which mandated a waiting period for purchasing handguns and a ban on certain types of assault weapons. Although the Supreme Court in 1997 struck down parts of the Brady Bill as unconstitutional, the waiting period for handgun purchases remained in effect, and in 1998 an instant background check on gun purchasers also was implemented.

Although it had backing from Republicans and several moderate and conservative Democrats, NRA efforts to overturn these and other gun restrictions were largely unsuccessful during Clinton's term. The NRA lost some measure of public support when it referred loudly and publicly to federal agents as "armed terrorists" who used "Gestapo tactics" to intimidate and harass innocent citizens. One person who objected to these characterizations was former president George Bush, who resigned his membership in the NRA in the wake of the Oklahoma City bombing in which 168 people including several federal agents were killed. Bush said he was "outraged" by an NRA fundraising letter that referred to federal agents as "jack-booted thugs." (Bush NRA resignation, Historic Documents of 1995, p. 208)

A series of school shootings across the nation in the late 1990s renewed calls for tighter gun controls. The NRA succeeded in stopping new gun control legislation in Congress, but it was unable to get any legislation relaxing federal gun controls past Senate Democrats and a Democratic president willing to use his veto power. (Columbine High School shootings, p. 347, Historic Documents of 1999, p. 179)

To regain lost ground, the NRA mounted an all-out campaign to put a Republican in the White House and keep the House and Senate in GOP control. The lobby claimed that gun control was the key issue that allowed Bush to carry three swing states—Arkansas, Tennessee, and West Virginia— without which he would not have won the electoral college vote that gave him the presidency. Many Democrats, including Clinton, agreed that the NRA's support had been crucial not only to Bush's victory but to helping the GOP hang onto control of the House. The NRA "probably had more to do than anyone else in the fact that we didn't win the House this time, and they hurt Al Gore," Clinton said after the election. One Democratic pollster found that 48 percent of the people who voted in the 2000 presidential election owned a gun, up from 37 percent in 1996. "That eleven-point rise in the gun-owning electorate was not produced by massive gun sales; it was produced by the increased engagement and mobilization of pro-gun voters," said pollster Stan Greenburg.

New Support for an Old Argument

At least in the initial skirmishes between proponents and opponents of gun control, Attorney General Ashcroft was clearly the lightening rod. Ashcroft, a long-time member of the NRA, offered his opinion on the Second Amendment in a May 17 letter to NRA executive director James Jay Baker, who made it public at the organization's annual convention on May 21. "Let me state unequivocally my view that the text and the original intent of the Second Amendment clearly protect the right of individuals to keep and bear firearms," Ashcroft wrote. "While some have argued that the Second Amendment guarantees only a 'collective right' of the states to maintain militias, I believe the amendment's plain meaning and original intent provide otherwise."

Ashcroft promised during his confirmation hearings to uphold federal gun laws, including those he disagreed with. His letter contained a footnote saying that the Second Amendment "does not prohibit Congress from enacting laws restricting firearms ownership for compelling state interests, such as prohibiting firearms ownership by convicted felons." But both proponents and opponents of gun controls said that, as attorney general, Ashcroft's opinion on the Second Amendment made it much more likely that gun control laws could be successfully challenged both politically and legally. "The practical effect of what he's done with this letter is to produce a 180-degree shift in policy on the Second Amendment," Kirsten Rand of the Violence Policy Center, a gun control lobby, told the Washington Post. *"If Ashcroft's view prevails, the NRA will go back and challenge every gun law on the books. It would be a massive shift in how federal gun laws might be implemented and enforced."*

The "collective right" interpretation had been the version held by most courts and attorneys general since 1939 when the Supreme Court ruled in

United States v. Miller *that there was no individual right to own a sawed-off shotgun because the weapon had no "reasonable relationship to the preservation or efficiency of a well-regulated militia." In recent years, however, some constitutional lawyers and legal scholars have begun to argue that the Founding Fathers intended the right to be an individual one.*

A test of Ashcroft's view was already working its way through the federal courts. In 1999 Judge Sam R. Cummings of the Federal District Court in Lubbock, Texas, dismissed charges against a doctor, Timothy Joe Emerson, who was in possession of a handgun while under a restraining order taken out by his estranged wife. The federal Violence Against Women Act of 1994 forbids anyone under a restraining order from possessing a gun, but Cummings ruled that the federal law violated Emerson's right to own a gun. In his opinion Cumming said that "a textual analysis of the Second Amendment supports an individual right to bear arms." The Clinton Justice Department appealed the case.

On October 15, 2001, the Court of Appeals for the Fifth Circuit agreed, 2–1, that "the Second Amendment does protect individual rights." But it also said that the right was subject to "limited, narrowly tailored specific exceptions" such as the federal law intended to protect someone from being threatened with a gun. The appeals court sent the case back to the district court for trial on the gun possession charge. In a concurring opinion, the third judge on the appeals court panel, Robert M. Parker, agreed that Emerson should be tried on the gun possession charges, but said that the case could have been decided without invoking the Second Amendment. "By overreaching in the area of the Second Amendment law, the majority stirs this controversy without necessity" and "may have done more harm than good for those who embrace a right to gun ownership," Parker said.

FBI Gun Checks

In early December it was reported that the Justice Department in October had refused to let the FBI search through its records that had been created during background checks on gun purchasers to see if any of the 1,200 foreign men detained after the September 11 terrorist bombings had purchased guns. According to a spokeswoman for the Justice Department, the law creating the National Instant Criminal Background Check System did not permit use of the background records to investigate individuals. Top officials in the Justice Department reportedly said that such checks would violate the privacy of the detainees.

The decision was in keeping with the department's move earlier in the year toward reducing the length of time such records were kept on file to one day. As a senator, Ashcroft had supported legislative language that would have required the background checks to be destroyed immediately; that language did not pass.

Some law enforcement officers and politicians were appalled at the decision, suggesting that concern for the gun rights of detainees suspected of terrorist activities appeared contradictory at the least. "This is absurd and unconscionable," a spokesman for the International Association of Chiefs of Police told the New York Times. *"The decision has no rational basis in public safety."*

> *Following are excerpts from the majority and concurring opinions in the case of* United States v. Emerson, *in which a three-judge panel of the U.S. Court of Appeals for the Fifth Circuit rule that the Second Amendment guaranteed the right of an individual to own a gun subject to limited, narrowly tailored exceptions.*
>
> **The document was obtained from the Internet at http:// www.ca5.uscourts.gov/opinions/pub/99/99-10331-cr0.htm.**

GARWOOD, Circuit Judge:

The United States appeals the district court's dismissal of the indictment of Defendant-Appellee Dr. Timothy Joe Emerson (Emerson) for violating 18 U.S.C. § 922(g)(8)(C)(ii). The district court held that section 922(g)(8)(C)(ii) was unconstitutional on its face under the Second Amendment and as applied to Emerson under the Due Process Clause of the Fifth Amendment. We reverse and remand.

Facts and Proceedings Below

On August 28, 1998, Sacha Emerson, Emerson's wife, filed a petition for divorce in the 119th District Court of Tom Green County, Texas. The petition also requested, inter alia, a temporary injunction enjoining Emerson from engaging in any of twenty-nine enumerated acts. . . .

On September 14, 1998, Judge Sutton issued a temporary order that included a "Temporary Injunction" which stated that Emerson "is enjoined from" engaging in any of twenty-two enumerated acts, including the following:

"2. Threatening Petitioner in person, by telephone, or in writing to take unlawful action against any person."

"4. Intentionally, knowingly, or recklessly causing bodily injury to Petitioner or to a child of either party."

"5. Threatening Petitioner or a child of either party with imminent bodily injury."

The order provides that it "shall continue in force until the signing of the final decree of divorce or until further order of this court." The September 14, 1998 order did not include any express finding that Emerson posed a future danger to Sacha or to his daughter Logan. There is nothing to indicate that Emerson ever sought to modify or challenge any of the provisions of the September 14, 1998 order.

On December 8, 1998, the grand jury for the Northern District of Texas, San Angelo division, returned a five-count indictment against Emerson. The government moved to dismiss counts 2 through 5, which motion the district court subsequently granted Count 1, the only remaining count and the count here at issue, alleged that Emerson on November 16, 1998, unlawfully possessed "in and affecting interstate commerce" a firearm, a Beretta pistol, while subject to the above mentioned September 14, 1998 order, in violation of 18 U.S.C. § 922(g)(8) [the Violence Against Women Act of 1994]. It appears that Emerson had purchased the pistol on October 10, 1997, in San Angelo, Texas, from a licensed firearms dealer. Emerson does not claim that the pistol had not previously traveled in interstate or foreign commerce. It is not disputed that the September 14, 1998 order was in effect at least through November 16, 1998.

Emerson moved pretrial to dismiss the indictment, asserting that section 922(g)(8), facially and as applied to him, violates the Second Amendment and the Due Process Clause of the Fifth Amendment. He also moved to dismiss on the basis that section 922(g)(8) was an improper exertion of federal power under the Commerce Clause and that, in any case, the law unconstitutionally usurps powers reserved to the states by the Tenth Amendment. An evidentiary hearing was held on Emerson's motion to dismiss.

The district court granted Emerson's motions to dismiss. Subsequently, the district court issued an amended memorandum opinion reported at 46 F.Supp.2d 598 (N.D. Tex. 1999). The district court held that dismissal of the indictment was proper on Second or Fifth Amendment grounds, but rejected Emerson's Tenth Amendment and Commerce Clause arguments.

The government appealed. Emerson filed a notice of cross-appeal, which was dismissed by this Court. The government challenges the district court's dismissal on Second and Fifth Amendment grounds. Emerson defends the district court's dismissal on those grounds and also urges that dismissal was in any event proper under the Commerce Clause and on statutory grounds.

Discussion

[Sections I, II, III, IV, discussing the Fifth and Tenth amendments, the Commerce Clause, and construction of the statute, are omitted.]

V. Second Amendment

The Second Amendment provides:

"A well regulated Militia, being necessary to the security of a free State, the right of the people to keep and bear arms, shall not be infringed."

A. Introduction and Overview of Second Amendment Models

The district court held that the Second Amendment recognizes the right of individual citizens to own and possess firearms, and declared that section 922(g)(8) was unconstitutional on its face because it requires that a citizen be disarmed merely because of being subject to a "boilerplate [domestic relations injunction] order with no particularized findings." *Emerson*, 46 F.Supp.2d at 611. The government opines that *stare decisis* requires us to reverse the district court's embrace of the individual rights model. Amici for the government argue that even if binding precedent does not require reversal, the flaws in the district court's Second Amendment analysis do.

In the last few decades, courts and commentators have offered what may fairly be characterized as three different basic interpretations of the Second Amendment. The first is that the Second Amendment does not apply to individuals; rather, it merely recognizes the right of a state to arm its militia. This "states' rights" or "collective rights" interpretation of the Second Amendment has been embraced by several of our sister circuits. The government commended the states' rights view of the Second Amendment to the district court, urging that the Second Amendment does not apply to individual citizens.

Proponents of the next model admit that the Second Amendment recognizes some limited species of individual right. However, this supposedly "individual" right to *bear* arms can only be exercised by members of a functioning, organized state militia who bear the arms while and as a part of actively participating in the organized militia's activities. The "individual" right to keep arms only applies to members of such a militia, and then only if the federal and state governments fail to provide the firearms necessary for such militia service. At present, virtually the only such organized and actively functioning militia is the National Guard, and this has been the case for many years. Currently, the federal government provides the necessary implements of warfare, including firearms, to the National Guard, and this likewise has long been the case. Thus, under this model, the Second Amendment poses no obstacle to the wholesale disarmament of the American people. A number of our sister circuits have accepted this model, sometimes referred to by commentators as the sophisticated collective rights model. On appeal the government has abandoned the states' rights model and now advocates the sophisticated collective rights model.

The third model is simply that the Second Amendment recognizes the right of individuals to keep and bear arms. This is the view advanced by Emerson and adopted by the district court. None of our sister circuits has subscribed to this model, known by commentators as the individual rights model or the standard model. The individual rights view has enjoyed considerable academic endorsement, especially in the last two decades.

We now turn to the question of whether the district court erred in adopting an individual rights or standard model as the basis of its construction of the Second Amendment.

B. *Stare Decisis* and *United States v. Miller*

The government steadfastly maintains that the Supreme Court's decision in *United States v. Miller* (1939), mandated acceptance of the collective rights or sophisticated collective rights model, and rejection of the individual rights or standard model, as a basis for construction of the Second Amendment. We disagree.

Only in *United States v. Miller* has the Supreme Court rendered any holding respecting the Second Amendment as applied to the federal government. There, the indictment charged the defendants with transporting in interstate commerce, from Oklahoma to Arkansas, an unregistered "Stevens shotgun having a barrel less than 18 inches in length" without having the required stamped written order, contrary to the National Firearms Act.(14) The defendants filed a demurrer challenging the facial validity of the indictment on the ground that "[t]he National Firearms Act . . . offends the inhibition of the Second Amendment," and "[t]he District Court held that section 11 of the Act [proscribing interstate transportation of a firearm, as therein defined, that lacked registration or a stamped order] violates the Second Amendment. It accordingly sustained the demurrer and quashed the indictment." Id. at 817-18. The government appealed, and we have examined a copy of its brief. (15) The *Miller* defendants neither filed any brief nor made any appearance in the Supreme Court.

The government's Supreme Court brief "[p]reliminarily" points out that:

> ". . . the National Firearms Act does not apply to all firearms but only to a limited class of firearms. The term 'firearm' is defined in Section 1 of the Act . . . to refer only to 'a shotgun or rifle having a barrel of less than 18 inches in length, or any other weapon, except a pistol or revolver, from which a shot is discharged by an explosive if such weapon is capable of being concealed on the person, or a machine gun, and includes a muffler or silencer for any firearm whether or not such firearm is included within the foregoing definition.'" (id. at 6).

In this connection the brief goes on to assert that it is "indisputable that Congress was striking not at weapons intended for legitimate use but at weapons which form the arsenal of the gangster and the desperado" (id. at 7) and that the National Firearms Act restricts interstate transportation "of only those weapons which are the tools of the criminal" (id. at 8).

The government's brief thereafter makes essentially two legal arguments.

First, it contends that the right secured by the Second Amendment is "only one which exists where the arms are borne in the militia or some other military organization provided for by law and intended for the protection of the state." Id. at 15. This, in essence, is the sophisticated collective rights model.

The second of the government's two arguments in *Miller* is reflected by the following passage from its brief:

> "While some courts have said that the right to bear arms includes the right of the individual to have them for the protection of his person and property as well as the right of the people to bear them collectively (*People v. Brown*, 253 Mich. 537; *State v. Duke*, 42 Tex. 455), the cases are unanimous in holding that the term "arms" as used in constitutional provisions refers only to those weapons which are ordinarily used for military or public defense purposes and does not relate to those weapons which are commonly used by criminals. . . .

Miller reversed the decision of the district court and "remanded for further proceedings." We believe it is entirely clear that the Supreme Court decided *Miller* on the basis of the government's second argument-that a "shotgun having a barrel of less than eighteen inches in length" as stated in the National Firearms Act is not (or cannot merely be assumed to be) one of the "Arms" which the Second Amendment prohibits infringement of the right of the people to keep and bear-and not on the basis of the government's first argument (that the Second Amendment protects the right of the people to keep and bear no character of "arms" when not borne in actual, active service in the militia or some other military organization provided for by law"). *Miller* expresses its holding as follows:

> "In the absence of any evidence tending to show that possession or use of a 'shotgun having a barrel of less than eighteen inches in length' at this time has some reasonable relationship to the preservation or efficiency of a well regulated militia, we cannot say that the Second Amendment guarantees the right to keep and bear such an instrument. Certainly it is not within judicial notice that this weapon is any part of the ordinary military equipment or that its use could contribute to the common defense. . . .

Nor do we believe that any other portion of the *Miller* opinion supports the sophisticated collective rights model. . . .

We conclude that *Miller* does not support the government's collective rights or sophisticated collective rights approach to the Second Amendment. Indeed, to the extent that *Miller* sheds light on the matter it cuts against the government's position. Nor does the government cite any other authority binding on this panel which mandates acceptance of its position in this respect. However, we do not proceed on the assumption that *Miller* actually accepted an individual rights, as opposed to a collective or sophisticated collective rights, interpretation of the Second Amendment. Thus, *Miller* itself does not resolve that issue. We turn, therefore, to an analysis of history and wording of the Second Amendment for guidance. In undertaking this analysis, we are mindful that almost all of our sister circuits have rejected any individual rights view of the Second Amendment. However, it respectfully appears to us that all or almost all of these opinions seem to have done so either on the erroneous assumption that *Miller* resolved that issue or without sufficient articulated examination of the history and text of the Second Amendment.

C. Text

We begin construing the Second Amendment by examining its text: "[a] well regulated Militia, being necessary to the security of a free State, the right of the people to keep and bear Arms, shall not be infringed." U.S. Const. amend. II.

1. Substantive Guarantee

a. "People"

The states rights model requires the word "people" to be read as though it were "States" or "States respectively." This would also require a corresponding change in the balance of the text to something like "to provide for the militia to keep and bear arms." That is not only far removed from the actual wording of the Second Amendment, but also would be in substantial tension with Art. 1, § 8, Cl. 16 (Congress has the power "To provide for . . . arming . . . the militia. . . ."). For the sophisticated collective rights model to be viable, the word "people" must be read as the words "members of a select militia". The individual rights model, of course, does not require that any special or unique meaning be attributed to the word "people." It gives the same meaning to the words "the people" as used in the Second Amendment phrase "the right of the people" as when used in the exact same phrase in the contemporaneously submitted and ratified First and Fourth Amendments.

There is no evidence in the text of the Second Amendment, or any other part of the Constitution, that the words "the people" have a different connotation within the Second Amendment than when employed elsewhere in the Constitution. In fact, the text of the Constitution, as a whole, strongly suggests that the words "the people" have precisely the same meaning within the Second Amendment as without. . . .

It appears clear that "the people," as used in the Constitution, including the Second Amendment, refers to individual Americans.

b. "Bear Arms"

Proponents of the states' rights and sophisticated collective rights models argue that the phrase "bear arms" only applies to a member of the militia carrying weapons during actual militia service. Champions of the individual rights model opine that "bear arms" refers to any carrying of weapons, whether by a soldier or a civilian. There is no question that the phrase "bear arms" may be used to refer to the carrying of arms by a soldier or militiaman. The issue is whether "bear arms" was also commonly used to refer to the carrying of arms by a civilian.

[Discussion of early interpretations of the meaning of the phrase "bear arms" omitted.]

We conclude that the phrase "bear arms" refers generally to the carrying or wearing of arms. It is certainly proper to use the phrase in reference to the carrying or wearing of arms by a soldier or militiaman; thus, the context in which "bear arms" appears may indicate that it refers to a military situation, e.g. the conscientious objector clauses cited by amici supporting the government. However, amici's argument that "bear arms" was exclusively, or even usually, used to *only* refer to the carrying or wearing of arms by a soldier or militiaman must be rejected. The appearance of "bear Arms" in the Second Amendment accords fully with the plain meaning of the subject of the substantive guarantee, "the people," and offers no support for the proposition that the Second Amendment applies only during periods of actual military service or only to those who are members of a select militia. Finally, our view of "bear arms" as used in the Second Amendment appears to be the same as that expressed in the dissenting opinion of Justice [Ruth Bader]Ginsburg (joined by the Chief Justice [William H. Rehnquist] and Justices [Antonin] Scalia and [David H. Souter) in *Muscarello v. United States* (1998); viz:

> "Surely a most familiar meaning [of carrying a firearm] is, as the Constitution's Second Amendment ("keep and bear Arms") (emphasis added) and Black's Law Dictionary, at 214, indicate: "wear, bear, or carry . . . upon the person or in the clothing or in a pocket, for the purpose . . . of being armed and ready for offensive or defensive action in a case of conflict with another person."

c. "Keep . . . Arms"

Neither the government nor amici argue that "keep . . . Arms" commands a military connotation. The plain meaning of the right of the people to keep arms is that it is an individual, rather than a collective, right and is not limited to keeping arms while engaged in active military service or as a member of a select militia such as the National Guard.

d. Substantive Guarantee as a Whole

Taken as a whole, the text of the Second Amendment's substantive guarantee is not suggestive of a collective rights or sophisticated collective rights interpretation, and the implausibility of either such interpretation is enhanced by consideration of the guarantee's placement within the Bill of Rights and the wording of the other articles thereof and of the original Constitution as a whole.

2. Effect of Preamble

We turn now to the Second Amendment's preamble: "A well-regulated Militia, being necessary to the security of a free State." And, we ask ourselves whether this preamble suffices to mandate what would be an otherwise implausible collective rights or sophisticated collective rights interpretation of the amendment. We conclude that it does not.

Certainly, the preamble implies that the substantive guarantee is one which tends to enable, promote or further the existence, continuation or effectiveness of that "well-regulated Militia" which is "necessary to the security of a free State." As the Court said in *Miller*, immediately after quoting the militia clauses of Article I, § 8 (cl. 15 and 16), "[w]ith obvious purpose to assure the continuation and render possible the effectiveness of such forces the declaration and guarantee of the Second Amendment were made." Id., 59 S.Ct. at 818. We conclude that the Second Amendment's substantive guarantee, read as guaranteeing individual rights, may as so read reasonably be understood as being a guarantee which tends to enable, promote or further the existence, continuation or effectiveness of that "well-regulated Militia" which is "necessary to the security of a free State." Accordingly, the preamble does not support an interpretation of the amendment's substantive guarantee in accordance with the collective rights or sophisticated collective rights model, as such an interpretation is contrary to the plain meaning of the text of the guarantee, its placement within the Bill of Rights and the wording of the other articles thereof and of the original Constitution as a whole. . . .

D. History

[1–6 omitted.]

7. Analysis

The history we have recounted largely speaks for itself. We briefly summarize. The Anti-Federalists desired a bill of rights, express provision for increased state power over the militia, and a meaningful express limitation of the power of the federal government to maintain a standing army. These issues were somewhat interrelated. The prospect of federal power to render the militia useless and to maintain a large standing army combined with the absence of any specific guarantees of individual liberty frightened Anti-Federalists. But the Anti-Federalist complaint that resonated best with the people at large was the lack of a bill of rights.

In mid-1788 the Constitution was ratified unchanged and in the spring of 1789 the Federalists gained control of both houses of the First Congress. Hard-core Anti-Federalists persisted in all three demands, but more moderate Anti-Federalists and the people at large were primarily focused on securing a bill of rights. Most Federalists were not really averse to a bill of rights, but, like James Madison himself, had been forced to oppose any modifications to the Constitution since it could only be ratified unchanged. The Federalists wanted to please the Anti-Federalists as much as possible without fundamentally altering the balance of federal-state power. James Madison plainly stated this goal when he submitted his proposed amendments to the House.

Given the political dynamic of the day, the wording of the Second Amendment is exactly what would have been expected. The Federalists had no qualms with recognizing the individual right of all Americans to keep and bear arms. In fact, as we have documented, one of the Federalists' favorite 1787-88 talking points on the standing army and federal power over the militia issues was to remind the Anti-Federalists that the American people were armed and hence could not possibly be placed in danger by a federal standing army or federal control over the militia. The Second Amendment's preamble represents a successful attempt, by the Federalists, to further pacify moderate Anti-Federalists without actually conceding any additional ground, i.e. without limiting the power of the federal government to maintain a standing army or increasing the power of the states over the militia.

This is not to say that the Second Amendment's preamble was not appropriate or is in any way marginal or lacking in true significance. Quite the contrary. Absent a citizenry generally keeping and bearing their own private arms, a militia as it was then thought of could not meaningfully exist. As pointed out by Thomas Cooley, the right of individual Americans to keep, carry, and acquaint themselves with firearms does indeed promote a well-regulated militia by fostering the development of a pool of firearms-familiar citizens that could be called upon to serve in the militia. While standing armies are not mentioned in the preamble, history shows that the reason a well-regulated militia was declared necessary to the security of a *free* state was because such a militia would greatly reduce the need for a standing army. Thus, the Second Amendment dealt directly with one of the Anti-Federalists' concerns and indirectly addressed the other two. While the hard-core Anti-Federalists recognized that the Second Amendment did not assure a well-regulated militia or curtail the federal government's power to maintain a large standing army, they did not control either branch of Congress (or the presidency) and had to be content with the right of individuals to keep and bear arms.

Finally, the many newspaper articles and personal letters cited indicate that, at the time, Americans viewed the Second Amendment as applying to individuals. This is confirmed by the First Congress's rejection of amendments that would have directly and explicitly addressed the Anti-Federalists' standing army and power over the militia concerns.

We have found no historical evidence that the Second Amendment was intended to convey militia power to the states, limit the federal government's power to maintain a standing army, or applies only to members of a select militia while on active duty. All of the evidence indicates that the Second Amendment, like other parts of the Bill of Rights, applies to and protects individual Americans.

We find that the history of the Second Amendment reinforces the plain meaning of its text, namely that it protects individual Americans in their right to keep and bear arms whether or not they are a member of a select militia or performing active military service or training.

E. Second Amendment protects individual rights

We reject the collective rights and sophisticated collective rights models for interpreting the Second Amendment. We hold, consistent with *Miller*, that it protects the right of individuals, including those not then actually a member of any militia or engaged in active military service or training, to privately possess and bear their own firearms, such as the pistol involved here, that are suitable as personal, individual weapons and are not of the general kind or type excluded by *Miller*. However, because of our holding that section 922(g)(8), as applied to Emerson, does not infringe his individual rights under the Second Amendment we will not now further elaborate as to the exact scope of all Second Amendment rights.

VI. Application to Emerson

The district court held that section 922(g)(8) was unconstitutionally overbroad because it allows second amendment rights to be infringed absent any express judicial finding that the person subject to the order posed a future danger. In other words, the section 922(g)(8) threshold for deprivation of the fundamental right to keep and bear arms is too low.

Although, as we have held, the Second Amendment does protect individual rights, that does not mean that those rights may never be made subject to any limited, narrowly tailored specific exceptions or restrictions for particular cases that are reasonable and not inconsistent with the right of Americans generally to individually keep and bear their private arms as historically understood in this country. Indeed, Emerson does not contend, and the district court did not hold, otherwise. As we have previously noted, it is clear that felons, infants and those of unsound mind may be prohibited from possessing firearms. . . . Emerson's argument that his Second Amendment rights have been violated is grounded on the propositions that the September 14, 1998 order contains no express finding that he represents a credible threat to the physical safety of his wife (or child), that the evidence before the court issuing the order would not sustain such a finding and that the provisions of the order bringing it within clause (C)(ii) of section 922(g)(8) were no more than uncontested boiler-plate. In essence, Emerson, and the district court, concede that had the order contained an express finding, on the basis of adequate evidence, that Emerson actually posed a credible threat to the physical safety of his wife, and had that been a genuinely contested matter at the hearing, with the parties and the court aware of section 922(g)(8), then Emerson could, consistent with the Second Amendment, be precluded from possessing a firearm while he remained subject to the order.

Though we are concerned with the lack of express findings in the order, and with the absence of any requirement for same in clause (C)(ii) of section 922(g)(8), we are ultimately unpersuaded by Emerson's argument. . . .

In light of the foregoing, we cannot say that section 922(g)(8)(C)(ii)'s lack of a requirement for an explicit, express credible threat finding by the court issuing the order—of itself or together with appellate court review being available (prior to final judgment) only by mandamus—renders that section infirm under the Second Amendment. The presence of such an explicit finding would likely furnish some additional indication that the issuing court properly considered the matter, but such findings can be as much "boilerplate" or in error as any other part of such an order. . . .

VII. Conclusion

Error has not been demonstrated in the district court's refusal to dismiss the indictment on commerce clause grounds.

For the reasons stated, we reverse the district court's order granting the motion to dismiss the indictment under the Fifth Amendment.

We agree with the district court that the Second Amendment protects the right of individuals to privately keep and bear their own firearms that are suitable as individual, personal weapons and are not of the general kind or type excluded by *Miller*, regardless of whether the particular individual is then actually a member of a militia. However, for the reasons stated, we also conclude that the predicate order in question here is sufficient, albeit likely minimally so, to support the deprivation, while it remains in effect, of the defendant's Second Amendment rights. Accordingly, we reverse the district court's dismissal of the indictment on Second Amendment grounds.

We remand the cause for further proceedings not inconsistent herewith.

Reversed and *Remanded.*

[Appendix omitted.]

ROBERT M. PARKER, Circuit Judge, specially concurring:

I concur in the opinion except for Section V. I choose not to join Section V, which concludes that the right to keep and bear arms under the Second Amendment is an individual right, because it is dicta and is therefore not binding on us or on any other court. The determination whether the rights bestowed by the Second Amendment are collective or individual is entirely unnecessary to resolve this case and has no bearing on the judgment we dictate by this opinion. The fact that the 84 pages of dicta contained in Section V are interesting, scholarly, and well written does not change the fact that they are dicta and amount to at best an advisory treatise on this long-running debate.

As federal judges it is our special charge to avoid constitutional questions when the outcome of the case does not turn on how we answer. . . .

Furthermore, the fact that a trial court passed on a novel question of constitutional law does not require us to do likewise. Appellate courts are supposed to review judgments, not opinions. . . . Here, whether "the district court erred in adopting an individual rights or standard model as the basis for its construction of the Second Amendment" . . . is not a question that affects the outcome of this case no matter how it is answered. In holding that § 922(g)(8) is not infirm as to Emerson, and at the same time finding an individual right to gunownership, the majority today departs from these sound precepts of judicial restraint.

No doubt the special interests and academics on both sides of this debate will take great interest in the fact that at long last some court has determined (albeit in dicta) that the Second Amendment bestows an individual right. The real issue, however, is the fact that whatever the nature or parameters of the Second Amendment right, be it collective or individual, it is a right subject to reasonable regulation. The debate, therefore, over the nature of the right is misplaced. In the final analysis, whether the right to keep and bear arms is collective or individual is of no legal consequence. It is, as duly noted by the majority opinion, a right subject to reasonable regulation. If determining that Emerson had an individual Second Amendment right that could have been successfully asserted as a defense against the charge of violating § 922(g)(8), then the issue would be cloaked with legal significance. As it stands, it makes no difference. Section 922(g)(8) is simply another example of a reasonable restriction on whatever right is contained in the Second Amendment.

And whatever the scope of the claimed Second Amendment right, no responsible individual or organization would suggest that it would protect Emerson's possession of the other guns found in his military-style arsenal the day the federal indictment was handed down. In addition to the Beretta nine millimeter pistol at issue here, Emerson had a second Beretta like the first, a semi-automatic M-1 carbine, an SKS assault rifle with bayonet, and a semi-automatic M-14 assault rifle. Nor would anyone suggest that Emerson's claimed right to keep and bear arms supercedes that of his wife, their daughter, and of others to be free from bodily harm or threats of harm. Though I see no mention of it in the majority's opinion, the evidence shows that Emerson pointed the Beretta at his wife and daughter when the two went to his office to retrieve an insurance payment. When his wife moved to retrieve her shoes, Emerson cocked the hammer and made ready to fire. Emerson's instability and threatening conduct also manifested itself in comments to his office staff and the police. Emerson told an employee that he had an AK-47 and in the same breath that he planned to pay a visit to his wife's boyfriend. To a police officer he said that if any of his wife's friends were to set foot on his property they would "be found dead in the parking lot."

If the majority was only filling the *Federal Reporter* with page after page of non-binding dicta there would be no need for me to write separately. As I have said, nothing in this case turns on the original meaning of the Second Amendment, so no court need follow what the majority has said in that regard. Unfortunately, however, the majority's exposition pertains to one of the most hotly-contested issues of the day. By overreaching in the area of Second Amendment law, the majority stirs this controversy without necessity when prudence and respect for *stare decisis* calls for it to say nothing at all. . . . Indeed, in the end, the majority today may have done more harm than good for those who embrace a right to gunownership.

PRESIDENTS BUSH AND JIANG
ON U.S.-CHINESE RELATIONS
October 19, 2001

Relations between the United States, the world's most powerful nation, and China, the world's most populous nation, swung from frosty cold to lukewarm during 2001. The seesaw in relations took place in a year of transition for both countries. For the United States, it was the first year of George W. Bush's presidency and the year of the worst terrorist attack in the nation's history. For China, the year marked the beginning of a drawn-out political process as President Jiang Zemin prepared to retire and give way to a younger generation of leaders that was expected to accelerate the country's transition from a communist to a capitalist economy, but with an authoritarian government. It was also the year when China finally gained admission to the World Trade Organization, bringing the world's fastest-growing major economy fully into the mainstream of global commerce. In recognition of that event, Bush on December 27 granted China permanent normal trade status, a landmark in U.S.-China relations that had been in the works for years. (China trade status, Historic Documents of 2000, p. 213)

Following the September 11 terrorist attacks against the United States, Bush and Jiang found common cause in opposing global terrorism. Both leaders suddenly saw new opportunities for cooperation on a range of issues, and they set aside, at least for the moment, contentious matters that had arisen earlier in the year. Chief among the latter were lingering suspicions on both sides stemming from the crash-landing in April of a U.S. spy plane on a Chinese island. Each country had blamed the other for the incident, in which China held the American crew for eleven days before accepting a statement that the U.S. government was "sorry" the plane landed on the island. (Spy plane incident, p. 247)

A Troubled Relationship

George W. Bush entered the White House in January 2001 expressing a skeptical view of the Chinese leadership. Bush's father, George Bush, had been the first U.S. representative to communist China in 1974–1975 and had been president in 1989 when the Chinese government brutally sup-

pressed thousands of prodemocracy protesters gathered at Tiananmen Square in Beijing. During the 1992 election campaign, the first President Bush came under strong criticism from his Democratic opponent, Bill Clinton, for not speaking forcefully enough against Chinese repression and human rights abuses.

In his presidential election campaign eight years later, in 2000, the younger Bush turned that rhetoric against then-president Clinton, who in the meantime had developed closer relations with Chinese leaders and had even described China as a "strategic partner" for the United States. Bush called China a "strategic competitor" and suggested that he would take a more realistic view toward that country than had Clinton or his vice president, Al Gore, who was Bush's election opponent.

Some Chinese leaders, and even many U.S. foreign policy experts, expressed puzzlement about Bush's intentions. But President Jiang told the Washington Post, *in an interview published March 23, 2001, that what counted was the substance of the relationship. "I believe that no matter what the formulations are, the U.S. cannot escape the strategic significance and the strategic dimension of U.S.-China relations, which is a fundamental fact," Jiang said. "No matter who administers the government in the United States, and no matter what kind of slightly different language he might use, one thing is very certain: The United States has to look at U.S.-China cooperation from a strategic standpoint, looking at strategic interests." The two countries might have "ups and downs" in dealing with each other, he said, but "the relationship between us has been, on the whole, moving forward."*

That interview came a little more than a week before the U.S. spy plane crash-landed in China, plunging the relationship temporarily into one of the "downs" Jiang had mentioned. A regular contributor to the down cycle was the issue of Taiwan, the large island southeast of China that was taken over in 1949 by the Nationalist Chinese leaders after they were defeated by the communists in China's great civil war. Beijing claimed Taiwan as part of China, but ever since 1949 the United States had been Taiwan's chief benefactor and protector. Just two weeks after the spy plane incident was resolved, Bush had to approve or deny Taiwan's request for a large weapons package, including an advanced naval system that China perceived as a threat. Bush took a compromise approach, agreeing to sell Taiwan most of what it wanted, but not the naval system. But Bush also warned that the United States would defend Taiwan against an attack from China—a blunt statement of a policy that had long been understood but never discussed.

Then in May Bush announced plans to build a system to defend the United States against a possible ballistic attack. Bush cited North Korea as the country most likely to threaten the United States with missiles. The proposed missile defense system also would diminish the importance of China's small nuclear weapons arsenal, which had been one of Beijing's principal claims to great power status. Although they had long known that Bush intended to proceed with a missile defense system, Chinese leaders reacted angrily to the president's announcement. The state-run Xinhua News

Agency said Bush's plan "will spark a new arms race and create a prolifera-
tion of weapons of mass destruction." (Missile defense, p. 927)

Wary of the sudden downturn in its ties with the United States, China
stepped up moves already under way to improve its cooperation with Rus-
sia, another country with which it had long had a rocky relationship. In
the late 1950s China and the former Soviet Union, then the two world's big
communist powers, had fallen out because of a variety of disagreements
and had even fought a border war in 1969. Diplomats from Moscow and Bei-
jing had begun working in 2000 on a formal agreement to restore closer
ties on political and economic issues. With both countries suddenly con-
cerned in 2001 about the course of U.S. policy, such an agreement took on
greater political significance when Jiang and Russian president Vladimir
Putin met in Moscow on July 16 and signed the "Treaty of Good Neighborly
and Friendly Cooperation." The two leaders expressed warm words about
the improving relationship between their countries, but most analysts
said the United States remained a more important partner for both China
and Russia.

Post-September 11 Events

The September 11 terrorist attacks changed many things in world poli-
tics, and one of them was the sagging relationship between Washington and
Beijing. As they looked for ways to retaliate against the Afghanistan-based
terrorists said to be responsible for the attacks, U.S. policymakers realized
that China could play an important role. A major Asian power with influ-
ence over many countries in the region (notably Pakistan), China was a
veto-wielding member of the United Nations Security Council and a coun-
try with intelligence information and other resources that might prove use-
ful in what was expected to be a prolonged war against terrorism.

China's leaders also saw reasons for cooperating with a U.S. antiterror-
ism campaign, according to experts. For years China had been plagued by
small-scale terrorist attacks that officials said were committed by radical
groups in Xinjiang, the northwestern province peopled primarily by the
Uygars, the largest Muslim minority in China. Largely in reaction to those
attacks, China in 2000 had taken the lead in forming the Shanghai Coopera-
tive Organization, an antiterrorism alliance that included Russia and four
Central Asian nations: Kazakhstan, Kyrgyzstan, Tajikistan, and Uzbeki-
stan. Many analysts viewed the establishment of that group as China's most
important foreign policy initiative in years—one that demonstrated Bei-
jing's fear of Islamist terrorism and a determination to destroy it.

Some of the Xinjiang terrorists were believed to be based in Afghanistan,
or at least to receive support from the Taliban regime that also offered safe
haven for the al Qaeda terrorists whom Bush accused of carrying out the
September 11 attacks. Chinese leaders almost certainly believed that joining
the U.S.-led campaign against the Afghan-based terrorists might help Bei-
jing eliminate its own terrorist foes. Moreover, it was widely assumed that
officials in Beijing hoped that cooperating with Washington might give

them leverage at some future time on sensitive China-U.S. issues, such as the fate of Taiwan or Washington's repeated denunciation of Chinese human rights abuses and its repression of Tibet.

Whatever the motivations, China responded quickly to the events of September. Jiang immediately sent Bush a message condemning the attacks and offering condolences to the families of the victims. Jiang followed that message with a telephone call on September 12, in which he offered to cooperate with a U.S. campaign against terrorism. The government also suppressed anti-American reactions within China to the September 11 attacks, including censoring statements supporting the terrorists that had been posted on Chinese Web sites. On September 20, the day Bush formally proclaimed war against all terrorist groups "of global reach," Jiang publicly expressed his "unconditional support" for the U.S. effort. China voted for two UN Security Council resolutions pledging steps against terrorism, and the government in late September sent a delegation of intelligence and counterterrorism experts to Washington to confer with U.S. officials. Demonstrating its role as an Asian power, China also pledged $150 million to a United Nations fund for postwar reconstruction in Afghanistan. (Rebuilding Afghanistan, p. 880)

Jiang's talk of unconditional support did not mean that China was ready to endorse everything the United States did in its war against terrorism. When dozens of Afghan civilians died in U.S. bombing raids, Chinese spokesmen and government-controlled news media demanded an end to any raids that might result in civilian casualties.

Bush-Jiang Meeting

After months of trading hostile, then friendly, words across the Pacific, Bush and Jiang met for the first time in Shanghai on October 19, during the annual Asia-Pacific Economic Cooperation Forum. Bush's visit marked his first venture into China since his father was the U.S. representative there a quarter-century earlier.

In an hour-long meeting, the two leaders exchanged pleasantries and discussed the need for cooperation in the war against terrorism. Bush said afterward that "President Jiang and the [Chinese] government stand side by side with the American people as we fight this evil force."

But Bush came up empty-handed in his quest for Chinese help on an important related topic: sales of missile technology to countries that were trying to develop biological, chemical, and nuclear weapons. Washington for years had been pressing China to stop selling missile technology to Iran, Libya, Pakistan, and North Korea. China had made vague pledges of cooperation in response to such urgings but kept selling the technology. Its most recent promise was in November 2000, when China told the Clinton administration that it would publish a long-delayed list of missile technology items that it would no longer export. But that list did not materialize during 2001, and in September the Bush administration imposed trade sanctions on a Chinese company said to have been involved in the missile sales.

In preparation for the Bush-Jiang meeting, U.S. officials reportedly pressed their Chinese counterparts to produce the list of banned items, but they were not successful.

Following are excerpts from a news conference held by Chinese president Jiang Zemin and U.S. president George W. Bush following their meeting October 19, 2001, in Shanghai.

The document was obtained from the Internet at http://www .whitehouse.gov/news/releases/2001/10/print/20011019-4 .html.

President Jiang: Mr. President, ladies and gentlemen, I've just had a very good talk with President Bush. This is our first meeting, and we have had an in-depth exchange of views and reached a series of consensus with respect to such major issues as Sino-U.S. relations, counterterrorism, and maintenance of world peace and stability.

China and the United States are two countries with significant influence in the world. As such, we share common responsibility and interest in maintaining peace and security in the Asia Pacific and the world at large, promoting regional and global economic growth and prosperity, and working together with the rest of the international community to combat terrorism.

China attaches importance to its relations with the United States and stands ready to make joint efforts with the U.S. side to develop a constructive and cooperative relationship.

We live in a world of diversity. Given the differences in national conditions, it is not surprising that there are certain disagreements between China and the United States. I believe that different civilizations and social systems ought to have long-term coexistence and achieve common development in the spirit of seeking common ground while shelving differences.

The Sino-U.S. relations are currently faced with the important opportunities of development. We will conduct high-level strategic dialogue, advance exchanges in cooperation in economic, trade, energy, and other fields, and strengthen consultation and coordination on major international and regional issues.

I'm confident that so long as the two sides keep a firm hold of the common interests of the two countries, properly handled, bilateral ties, especially the question of Taiwan, in accordance with the three Sino-U.S. joint communiqués, the relations between China and the United States will continuously move forward.

President Bush: Mr. President, thank you very much. I, too, felt like we had a very good meeting. I've come to Shanghai because China and other Asia Pacific nations are important partners in the global coalition against terror.

I've also come because the economic future of my nation and this region are inseparable. The nations of APEC share the same threat, and we share the same hope for greater trade and prosperity.

Thank you so much for hosting this meeting. You and the city of Shanghai have done an outstanding job. Mr. President, I visited this city 25 years ago— a little over 25 years ago. Then I could not have imagined the dynamic and impressive Shanghai of 2001. It's an impressive place, and I know you're proud. It's a tribute to the leadership of the current officials of Shanghai, as well as to your leadership as a former mayor, Mr. President.

We have a common understanding of the magnitude of the threat posed by international terrorism. All civilized nations must join together to defeat this threat. And I believe that the United States and China can accomplish a lot when we work together to fight terrorism.

The President and the government of China responded immediately to the attacks of September 11th. There was no hesitation, there was no doubt that they would stand with the United States and our people during this terrible time. There is a firm commitment by this government to cooperate in intelligence matters, to help interdict financing of terrorist organizations. It is— President Jiang and the government stand side by side with the American people as we fight this evil force.

China is a great power. And America wants a constructive relationship with China. We welcome a China that is a full member of world community, that is at peace with its neighbors. We welcome and support China's accession into the World Trade Organization. We believe it's a very important development that will benefit our two peoples and the world.

In the long run, the advance of Chinese prosperity depends on China's full integration into the rules and norms of international institutions. And in the long run, economic freedom and political freedom will go hand in hand.

We've had a very broad discussion, including the fact that the war on terrorism must never be an excuse to persecute minorities. I explained my views on Taiwan and preserving regional stability in East Asia. I stressed the need to combat the proliferation of weapons of mass destruction and missile technology.

Today's meetings convinced me that we can build on our common interests. Two great nations will rarely agree on everything; I understand that. But I assured the President that we'll always deal with our differences in a spirit of mutual respect. We seek a relationship that is candid, constructive and cooperative.

I leave my country at a very difficult time. But this meeting is important because of the campaign against terror, because of the ties between two great nations, because the opportunity and hope that trade provides for both our people.

I regret, Mr. President, I couldn't accept your invitation to visit Beijing, but it will happen at a different time.

Jiang: Next time.

Bush: That's right. Thank you for your hospitality.

Question: I'm a correspondent from China Central Television. Recently, there has been improvement in Sino-U.S. relations. Just now you've had your first meeting with President Bush. How would you envisage the future growth of the bilateral ties?

Jiang: The developments of international situation has, time and again, shown that, despite our disagreements of this type or that, the two countries share extensive common responsibility and interest on major issues that bare on the survival and development of mankind.

I'm pleased to note that, recently, there has been improvement in our bilateral ties. The two sides have maintained close consultation and cooperation on major issue of counterterrorism. We've also made new headway in our economic and trade fields in such exchanges and cooperation.

China and the United States are different in their national conditions, so it's normal that there are certain disagreements between us. So long as both sides respect each other, treat each other with sincerity, enhance trust through frequent exchange of views, than the disagreements can get addressed properly.

Just now, in my meeting with President Bush, we once again had an extensive and in-depth exchange of views on bilateral relations. We also reached important consensus. We stand ready to work together with the U.S. side to increase our exchanges and cooperation, enhance understanding and trust, and develop a constructive and cooperative relations between us.

I'm convinced that so long as the three signed U.S. joint communiqués and fundamental norms governing international relations are adhered to, and so long as the problems between us, especially the problem of Taiwan—the question of Taiwan is properly addressed, then there will be a bright future of our relationship.

Question: Thank you, Mr. President. Thank you, sir, for having us here. Mr. President, do you know yet whether there is a definite link between the anthrax attacks and any foreign interests, particularly al Qaeda or Iraq? And separately, there's a report that we have special forces in southern Afghanistan now. Can you confirm that the ground war has begun?

And a quick question to our host, sir. Do you support the U.S. military action in Afghanistan, which President Bush says could last one or two years?

Bush: First, I spent some time explaining to the President of my determination to bring people to justice that murdered our citizens. And I told the President that our nation will do what it takes to bring them to justice, no matter how long it takes. And, Ron, I don't know the time, but I do know the desire.

And secondly, I explained to the President that we will hold people accountable who harbor terrorists. And that's exactly what we're doing.

I will not comment upon military operations. I made it very clear from the outset of this campaign that I will not respond to rumors and information that seeps into the public consciousness, for fear of disrupting the operations that are taking place. But let me reiterate what I've told the American people and the world. We will use whatever means are necessary to achieve our objective.

Thirdly, I do not have a direct—I don't have knowledge of a direct link of the anthrax incidents to the enemy. But I wouldn't put it past them. These are evil people and the deeds that have been conducted on the American people are evil deeds. And anybody who would mail anthrax letters, trying to affect the lives of innocent people, is evil. And I want to say this as clearly as I can, that anybody in America who will use this opportunity to threaten our citizens, will think it's funny as a hoax to put out some kind of threat, will be held accountable and will be prosecuted.

Now is the time in America—now is the time—for us to stand up against terror, and for American citizens to unite against terror. And we're looking, we're on the search to find out who's conducting these evil acts.

I'm also pleased that the government is responding very quickly, that people who have been exposed to anthrax are getting the necessary treatments. I think it's very important for people of all the world to understand that if anthrax—if people are exposed to anthrax, there is a treatment for it. And it's very important for all our governments to react and respond as quickly as possible to make sure the citizens who get exposed receive the necessary antibiotics. And we're doing that in America.

And the American people also have got to understand that we will make sure that there is ample supplies, as we deal with this evil act, that we'll make sure there's ample supplies available for the American people. . . .

Jiang: In my discussion with President Bush this morning, I've made clear that we are opposed to terrorism of all forms. And what we have done in the past has shown this attitude of ours very clearly. We hope that anti-terrorism efforts can have clearly defined targets. And efforts should hit accurately, and also avoid innocent casualties. And what is more, the role of the United Nations should be brought into full play. . . .

FBI REPORT ON CRIME IN THE UNITED STATES
October 22, 2001

The level of serious crime in the United States and the growth of the prison population both appeared to stabilize in 2000. Serious crime— including murder, rape, and robbery—remained about the same in 2000 as it was in 1999, indicating to many observers that the end to the decline in crime they had been expecting may have arrived. Although the Federal Bureau of Investigation's "Crime Index" showed a drop of just 0.2 percent from 1999 to 2000, serious crime had dropped 22 percent since 1991. "Compared to the marked drops noted in recent years, the current slight decline . . . is certain to be viewed by many as no change at all from the previous year's" figures, the FBI said in its annual report, Crime in the United States, *issued October 22, 2001. "Only after publication of the next few issues . . . will we know whether the figures for 2000 signaled an end to the current downward trend or were merely a bump in the road." James Alan Fox, a professor of criminal justice at Northeastern University, was more succinct: "The great 1990s crime drop is over."* (Previous reports, Historic Documents of 2000, p. 852)

Slowing rates of incarceration reflected the drop in crime during the 1990s. In 2000 the rate of growth in the nation's prison population was 1.3 percent, the smallest annual growth rate since 1972 and well below its peak of 8.7 percent in 1994. Experts said the slowing pace of incarceration also represented an effort by many states to find alternatives to imprisonment for offenders, such as putting drug offenders into treatment programs.

Stabilizing Crime Rates

The FBI report, which was compiled from reports filed by law enforcement agencies representing 94 percent of the nation's population, looked at both the volume of serious crime and the rate of serious crime per 100,000 people. Serious crimes included murder, forcible rape, robbery, aggravated assault, burglary, larceny-theft, and vehicle theft. In 2000, 1.6 million offenses were reported, for an average of 4,124 crimes for every 100,000 people. That rate was 3.3 percent below the 1999 rate and 30.1 percent lower than the rate recorded in 1991.

Overall violent crime dropped 0.1 percent in 2000, the lowest volume since 1985. Murder, aggravated assault, and robbery all showed small declines; rape, which had been declining since 1992, showed a 0.9 percent increase. Overall property crime dropped 0.3 percent, compared with 1999, with small increases in larceny-theft and vehicle theft being offset by a decline in burglary.

Regionally, the southern states remained the most crime ridden, accounting for 41 percent of crime in the United States in 2000, followed by the West (23 percent), the Midwest (22 percent), and the Northeast (14 percent). But crime declined marginally in the South as well as in the Northeast and Midwest. Crime was up marginally in the West.

Firearms were used in more than 60 percent of all murders committed in 2000 and in 25 percent of all violent crimes. Slightly more than 50 percent of the 15,517 murders in 2000 were committed with a handgun. (Gun control, p. 722)

Experts cited many factors for the decline in crime during the 1990s, including the waning of the crack cocaine epidemic and the violence that accompanied it, the economic expansion that lasted through the 1990s, better policing efforts, and a decline in the teenage and young adult population that was responsible for much of the crime. Criminologists warned that the teenage population was about to grow again and could bring with it another crime wave.

Contradictory Statistics

Although some observers thought the 2000 FBI statistics indicated that the decline in crime had reached its low point and was likely to stay about the same or start climbing again, others were not as sure. They cited a survey released by the Justice Department in June that showed violent crime falling by 15 percent in 2000. According to the National Crime Victimization Survey, about 1 million fewer violent crimes occurred in 2000 than in 1999. The survey also found that property crime was down 10 percent in 2000.

Much of the discrepancy between the two reports could be explained by differences in what was measured. The FBI crime report counted only serious crimes reported to it by law enforcement agencies. The victimization report was based on a survey of 160,000 victims of crime of all sorts. Since it was a survey of victims, it did not include homicide, but it did include simple assault, which was the most common violent crime, but which was not considered "serious" and so was not included in the FBI statistics. According to the victimization survey, more than 60 percent of all violent crimes were simple assaults in 2000. That was a drop of 14.4 percent from 1999, which accounted for much of the difference between the victimization survey and the FBI report. Another source of the discrepancy between the two reports was that many of the crimes counted in the victimization survey were not reported to police and so were not included in the FBI report. The survey report said that 48 percent of the violent victimizations and 36 percent of the property crimes were not reported to police.

Slowing Incarceration Rates

The number of people in prison or jail in the United States continued to grow in 2000, but at a far slower pace than in the past. During the last six months of the year, the number of people held in state prisons actually declined slightly—the first decline in that population since 1972. The decline was all the more notable in that state prison rates had gone up by 75 percent between 1990 and 2000. State prison rates decreased in thirteen states in 2000, led by Massachusetts with a 5.6 percent decline, and followed by New Jersey, New York, and Texas. They went up by more than 10 percent in five states—Idaho, North Dakota, Mississippi, Vermont, and Idaho. The number of federal prisoners continued to grow.

Several factors helped explain why growth in the prison population was just beginning to show signs of slowing even though the crime rate had been in decline for some time. One factor had to do with state sentencing laws. To combat the crime wave of the late 1980s and early 1990s, many states toughened their sentencing laws. As a result criminals who would have been out of prison much earlier under the old laws were just now finishing their sentences. States were also relaxing some of their mandatory sentencing laws, making some criminals eligible for parole sooner, and monitoring parolees more carefully so that fewer returned to prison. States were also experimenting with alternative sentencing for some crimes, such as putting drug users into treatment programs rather than putting them behind bars.

Altogether 2.1 million people were incarcerated at the end of 2000. Of those, 1.3 million were in federal or state prison, 621,000 were in local jails, and the rest were in other facilities, such as juvenile or military facilities. Nearly 10 percent of black males ages twenty-five to twenty-nine were in prison, compared with 3 percent of Hispanic males and 1 percent of white males in the same age group. The number of women in prison had more than doubled since 1990; by 2000 nearly 7 percent of all prisoners were women.

Following is the text of a news release issued October 19, 2001, by the Federal Bureau of Investigation summarizing the findings of its annual report, Crime in the United States, 2000.

The document was obtained from the Internet at http:// www.fbi.gov/pressrel/pressrel01/cius2000.htm.

The Federal Bureau of Investigation announced today that there was virtually no change in the Crime Index in 2000 compared to the 1999 figures. The

Crime Index (composed of murder, forcible rape, robbery, aggravated assault, burglary, larceny-theft, and motor vehicle theft) decreased 0.2 percent in 2000, the smallest year-to-year decrease in volume since 1991. Final 2000 data released by the Uniform Crime Reporting (UCR) Program in the annual publication *Crime in the United States, 2000*, show that serious crime was 14.0 percent lower than in 1996 and 22.0 percent less than in 1991.

Both violent and property crime experienced marginal declines in volume when compared to the 1999 volume.

Collectively, violent crime (murder, forcible rape, robbery, and aggravated assault) decreased 0.1 percent from 1999 to 2000. Decreases in violent crime occurred for robbery, 0.4 percent, and for aggravated assault, 0.1 percent. Murder declined by less than one-tenth of 1 percent. Forcible rape increased 0.9 percent, the first volume increase for that offense since 1992.

Overall, property crime in 2000 (burglary, larceny-theft, and motor vehicle theft) decreased 0.3 percent when compared to the 1999 data. Increases in larceny-theft, 0.2 percent, and motor vehicle theft, 1.2 percent, were offset by a 2.4-percent decline in volume for burglary.

By community type, Index crime decreased 1.8 percent in the Nation's suburban counties and 0.1 percent in the Nation's cities collectively. Rural counties experienced a 0.5-percent increase in Index crime, which can be attributed to increases in robbery, larceny-thefts, and motor vehicle thefts from 1999 to 2000.

An estimated 11.6 million offenses were reported to law enforcement agencies across the Nation in 2000, an average of 4,124.0 crimes for every 100,000 inhabitants. This rate is 3.3 percent less than the 1999 rate, 18.9 percent less than the 1996 rate, and 30.1 percent less than the crime rate recorded in 1991.

Crime in the United States, 2000 is compiled from data provided to the FBI's UCR Program by approximately 17,000 law enforcement agencies representing nearly 254 million United States inhabitants, 94 percent of the Nation's population as established by the Bureau of the Census. Estimates are included for nonreporting areas.

Crime Volume

- The Crime Index total, the measure of serious crime volume, decreased 0.2 percent from reported 1999 data.
- From 1999 to 2000, violent crime declined 0.1 percent. The following decreases in volume were recorded: robbery, 0.4 percent; aggravated assault, 0.1 percent; and murder, less than one-tenth of 1 percent. Forcible rape, which had been in decline since 1992, increased 0.9 percent. Among the Nation's counties, forcible rape volumes decreased 0.9 percent in suburban counties and 0.1 percent in rural counties from 1999 to 2000; however, during this 2-year period, the Nation's cities collectively experienced a 1.5-percent increase in volume for forcible rape.
- Three of the Nation's 4 geographic regions experienced decreases in estimated crime volumes. With 35.6 percent of the country's population, the Southern region accounted for 41.0 percent of the estimated crime

for 2000. Crime in the South declined 0.1 percent from 1999 to 2000. The Midwestern region, with 22.9 percent of the U.S. population and 21.9 percent of the Nation's estimated crime, had a decline of 0.6 percent in Index crime. The Northeastern region, comprising 19.0 percent of the country's population and 14.2 percent of the country's crime, experienced a 2.0-percent decline in Index crime. The Western region, which makes up 22.5 percent of the Nation's population, accounted for 23.0 percent of the total estimated crime and had the only regional increase in the number of offenses, 1.0 percent. Collectively, the states which make up the Western region experienced increases in crime volume for motor vehicle theft, 7.1 percent; forcible rape, 3.5 percent; robbery and aggravated assault, both increasing 0.9 percent; and larceny-theft, which increased 0.2 percent in volume.

Crime Index Rate

- The 2000 Crime Index rate, which measures the average number of the 7 Index offenses per 100,000 inhabitants in the United States, decreased 3.3 percent from the 1999 rate. The Crime Index rate for 2000 was 4,124.0 Index offenses per 100,000 population, 18.9 percent lower than in 1996 and 30.1 percent less than in 1991.
- In 2000, the Nation's cities collectively had a crime rate of 5,071.0 Index offenses for every 100,000 inhabitants. The country's largest cities, those with populations of 250,000 or more inhabitants, were measured at 6,382.1 Crime Index offenses per 100,000 population. The Nation's smallest cities, those having populations of less than 25,000 inhabitants, collectively experienced a Crime Index rate of 3,923.1 Index offenses per 100,000 inhabitants. In 2000, suburban counties had a rate of 3,043.7 Index offenses per 100,000 population and rural counties, a rate of 1,928.1.
- By region, the Southern States had a Crime Index rate of 4,743.4 Index offenses per 100,000 population for 2000, a decrease of 3.9 percent from the 1999 rate. The Western States recorded 4,222.4 Index crimes per 100,000 inhabitants, a decline of 2.3 percent from the previous year's rate. The Midwestern States experienced a Crime Index rate of 3,945.0 Index offenses per 100,000 inhabitants, down 2.4 percent from the 1999 rate. The Northeastern States, with a rate of 3,064.3 Index offenses per 100,000 population, showed a 5.2-percent decrease from 1999 to 2000.

Violent Crime

- The year 2000 marked the lowest volume of violent crimes (murder, forcible rape, robbery, and aggravated assault) since 1985. Violent crime decreased 0.1 percent from the 1999 volume. The estimated 1.4 million violent crimes in 2000 were also down 15.6 percent from the 1996 estimate and 25.5 percent from the 1991 estimate.
- The violent crime rate for 2000 was computed at 506.1 offenses for every 100,000 in population. The 2000 violent crime rate decreased 3.2 percent from the 1999 rate, 20.5 percent from the 1996 rate, and 33.2 percent from the 1991 rate.

- Aggravated assault accounted for 63.9 percent of the total violent crimes in 2000. Robbery made up 28.6 percent of the total violent crime, forcible rape comprised 6.3 percent, and murder 1.1 percent.
- The robbery volume in 2000 declined 0.4 percent from the 1999 volume. And when compared to the 1999 volume, the volume of aggravated assaults decreased by 0.1 percent in 2000. The murder volume between 1999 and 2000 showed virtually no change, decreasing by less than one-tenth of 1 percent. Forcible rape was the only violent crime that had an increase in volume over the 2-year period, showing a 0.9-percent rise.
- Firearms were used in 25.6 percent of the total murders, robberies, and aggravated assaults collectively during 2000. Personal weapons (hands, fists, feet, etc.) were involved in 31.5 percent of these crimes, and knives or cutting instruments were employed in another 15.0 percent. Other dangerous weapons were used in 27.9 percent of the offenses.

Property Crime

- Property crimes (burglary, larceny-theft, and motor vehicle theft) were collectively estimated at 10.2 million offenses for 2000, a decrease of 0.3 percent from the 1999 estimate. The 2000 property crime offense total was 13.8 percent less than in 1996 and 21.4 percent lower than in 1991.
- In 2000, the estimated number of motor vehicle theft offenses and larceny-theft offenses increased 1.2 and 0.2 percent, respectively. These volume increases for motor vehicle theft and larceny-theft were offset by a 2.4-percent decline in the number of burglaries reported to law enforcement for 2000 and allowed for a cumulative decrease of 0.3 percent for property crimes in 2000.
- The Nation's property crime rate for 2000 was 3,617.9 offenses for every 100,000 inhabitants. The property crime rate was 3.4 percent less than the 1999 rate, 18.7 percent below the 1996 rate, and 29.6 percent less than the 1991 rate.
- Total dollar losses for property crime are estimated to be more than $15.9 billion. The average dollar loss connected with property crime offenses was $1,562.
- Limited arson data showed an average of $11,042 in property losses per incident reported.

Hate Crime

- There was a total of 8,152 hate crime incidents reported to law enforcement in 2000. These incidents involved 9,524 distinct offenses.
- Among the 8,144 single-bias incidents in 2000, racially motivated bias made up the largest number of offenses reported, 5,206. Religious bias was the motivation for 1,568 of the single-bias offenses. Offenses committed with a bias against a sexual orientation accounted for 1,517 offenses, bias against ethnicity or national origin led to 1,180 offenses, and disability was the bias motivation for 36 offenses. There were an additional 17 offenses that occurred during 8 incidents involving multiple biases.

- In 2000, for the 8,152 bias incidents reported, the identity of 7,642 offenders are known.
- The most common hate crime offense in 2000 was intimidation with 3,294 bias-motivated offenses. The destruction/damage/vandalism of property accounted for 2,766 offenses; simple assault, 1,616 offenses; and aggravated assault, 1,274 offenses.
- Hate crime data for 2000 was provided by 11,691 law enforcement agencies representing nearly 237 million or 84.2 percent of the Nation's population.

Index Crime Clearances

- Law enforcement agencies nationwide reported a 20.5-percent Crime Index offense clearance rate for 2000. The clearance rate for violent crimes was 47.5 percent; property crimes had a clearance rate of 16.7 percent.
- Among violent crimes, the offense of murder had a clearance rate of 63.1 percent and was the most frequently cleared offense in 2000. The aggravated assault clearance rate was 56.9 percent; 46.9 percent of forcible rapes and 25.7 percent of robberies were also cleared.
- For property crimes, 18.2 percent of larceny-thefts were cleared in 2000. Motor vehicle theft was cleared at a rate of 14.1 percent; burglary, the offense least often cleared, had a clearance rate of 13.4 percent.
- Arson had a clearance rate of 16.0 percent in 2000.
- In 2000, Index offenses involving only juvenile offenders (under 18 years of age) accounted for 19.3 percent of the overall Crime Index offenses cleared. Additionally, juveniles were held accountable for 12.2 percent of all violent crimes cleared and 22.1 percent of the total property crimes cleared. Murder had the least juvenile involvement with 5.3 percent of the offenses cleared. Juveniles, however, were most often involved in the crime of arson, representing 45.9 percent of the total arson offenses cleared.

Arrests

- In 2000, law enforcement agencies made an estimated 14 million arrests for all criminal infractions (excluding traffic violations). Drug abuse violations, with an estimated 1.6 million arrests, were the most frequent cause for arrest, continuing a 6-year trend. Among specific crime classifications, some of the highest arrest counts in 2000 were for driving under the influence, accounting for an estimated 1.5 million arrests; simple assaults, 1.3 million arrests; and larceny-thefts, 1.2 million arrests.
- Relating the number of arrests in 2000 to the Nation's population, there were 5,010.4 arrests for every 100,000 inhabitants. Collectively, the country's cities had a rate of 5,418.1 arrests for every 100,000 city inhabitants. Cities with populations of under 10,000 inhabitants had the highest arrest rate, 6,460.1 per 100,000 population. The arrest rate for rural county law enforcement agencies was 4,027.1 and for suburban county law enforcement, 4,021.5 arrests per 100,000 county inhabitants.

- The number of total arrests for the Nation decreased 2.2 percent from 1999 to 2000. Arrests for the Crime Index offenses declined 3.7 percent as violent crime arrests decreased 1.4 percent and property crime arrests decreased 4.6 percent.
- Total juvenile arrests declined 4.8 percent from 1999 to 2000, and adult arrests fell by 1.7 percent. For the Crime Index offenses, juvenile arrests decreased by 5.1 percent. The number of adult arrests for Index crimes was also down, showing a 3.1-percent decrease. Juvenile arrests for violent and property crimes declined 4.4 and 5.3 percent, respectively. Adult arrests also showed a downward trend, declining 0.8 percent for violent crimes and 4.2 percent for property crimes.
- Among persons arrested for Index offenses in 2000, 55.1 percent were under the age of 25. This age group accounted for 44.4 percent of the violent crime arrests and 59.2 percent of the property crime arrests. Juveniles made up 27.5 percent of those arrested for Index crime, 15.9 percent of those arrested for violent crime, and 32.0 percent of those arrested for property crime.
- Males comprised 77.8 percent of the total arrestees in 2000. Males also accounted for 82.6 percent of the violent crime arrestees and 70.1 percent of property crime arrestees.
- In 2000, whites accounted for 69.7 percent of the total arrestees, 59.9 percent of the violent crime arrestees, and 66.2 percent of the property crime arrestees.

Murder

- There were an estimated 15,517 murders in 2000, virtually no change from the 1999 murder estimate of 15,522. The number of murders was 21 percent less than in 1996 and 37.2 percent less than in 1991.
- Murder trends for the Nation's cities collectively indicated murder increased by 0.7 percent from 1999 to 2000. Murder declined 3.8 percent in the suburban counties and 3.5 percent in rural counties.
- Based on supplemental murder data provided for 12,943 of the estimated 15,517 murders in 2000, males comprised 76.2 percent of the murder victims. By race, 49.0 percent of the victims were white, 48.5 percent were black, and other races accounted for 2.5 percent of the victims. Adults, persons aged 18 or older, made up 89.7 percent of the murder victims.
- Supplemental data for 14,697 murder offenders indicate that 90.2 percent of the offenders were male and 91.3 percent of the murder offenders were aged 18 or older. By race, 51.4 percent were black, 46.1 percent were white, and 2.6 percent of the offenders were of other races.
- Data continue to indicate that murder is most often intraracial. In 2000, 93.7 percent of black murder victims were slain by black offenders and 86.2 percent of white murder victims were slain by white offenders.
- In 2000, relationship data between victims and their offenders indicated that 44.3 percent of the victims were acquainted with or related to their assailants. Familial relationships existed between 13.4 percent of the

victims and their murderers; acquaintances murdered 30.9 percent of the victims.

- Husbands or boyfriends murdered 33.0 percent of the female victims, and wives or girlfriends killed 3.2 percent of male victims during 2000.
- During 2000, arguments were the predominant circumstance leading to murder. According to supplemental data, 29.4 percent of murders resulted from an argument. Felonious activities such as forcible rape, robbery, arson, etc., precipitated 16.7 percent of the murders, and 0.5 percent of the murders were suspected of having felonious intent.
- Firearms were used in 65.6 percent of the murders in 2000. By firearm type, handguns accounted for 51.7 percent of the murder total; shotguns, 3.6 percent; rifles, 3.1 percent; and other or unknown types of firearms another 7.3 percent.

Forcible Rape

- An estimated 90,186 forcible rapes of females were reported by law enforcement agencies during 2000, an increase of 0.9 percent from the 1999 rate, and the first increase for female forcible rape since 1992. By volume, forcible rape in 2000 was 6.3 percent less than in 1996 and 15.4 percent lower than in 1991.
- Collectively, the Nation's cities experienced a 1.5-percent increase in forcible rape volumes; suburban counties had a decrease of 0.9 percent, and rural counties a 0.1 percent decrease.
- In 2000, an estimated 62.7 of every 100,000 females in the country were victims of forcible rape. By community type, cities outside of metropolitan areas had the highest rate of female forcible rape, 69.0 for every 100,000 females. Metropolitan Statistical Areas had a rate of 65.0 female rapes per 100,000 females, and rural counties recorded a rate of 43.4 forcible rapes for every 100,000 females.
- Law enforcement cleared 46.9 percent of reported female forcible rapes during 2000. Juveniles were involved in 12.1 percent of the total law enforcement clearances for forcible rape nationwide.

Robbery

- The estimated number of robberies decreased 0.4 percent from 1999 to 2000. Additionally, robbery offenses declined 23.9 percent from the 1996 estimate and 40.7 percent from the 1991 estimate.
- In 2000, the monetary value attributed to property stolen during robbery was estimated at over $477 million. The average dollar loss per robbery offense was $1,170.
- Robberies on streets and highways comprised 46.0 percent of all robberies. Robberies of financial establishments and commercial businesses accounted for 25.3 percent of robberies, and residential robberies made up 12.2 percent of all robberies.
- Firearms were used in 40.9 percent of robberies during 2000. Strong-arm tactics were used in 40.4 percent of robberies, knives or cutting instru-

ments were the weapon used in 8.4 percent of robberies, and other types of weapons were used in 10.3 percent of robberies.

Aggravated Assault

- The estimated 910,744 aggravated assault offenses in 2000 represented a slight decline, 0.1 percent, from the 1999 figure. This is the lowest estimated volume since 1989. The estimated number of aggravated assaults was 12.2 percent lower than the 1996 figure and 16.7 percent lower than the 1991 number.
- By community type, the number of aggravated assaults declined 3.7 percent in rural counties and increased 0.2 percent in the Nation's cities collectively and 0.2 percent in suburban counties.
- Aggravated assault accounted for 63.9 percent of the violent crimes in 2000.
- Nationally, there was an average offense rate of 323.6 aggravated assaults for every 100,000 inhabitants during 2000, a decrease of 3.2 percent from the 1999 rate. The country's cities, collectively, had a rate of 395.2 per 100,000 inhabitants, suburban counties averaged 262.1 aggravated assaults per 100,000, and rural counties, a rate of 171.1 offenses per 100,000 populace.
- In 2000, 35.9 percent of aggravated assaults were committed with blunt objects or other dangerous weapons. Personal weapons (hands, fists, feet, etc.) were used in 28.0 percent of the assaults; firearms, in 18.1 percent; and knives or cutting instruments, in 18.0 percent.

Burglary

- The estimated number of burglary offenses in 2000 declined 2.4 percent from the previous year's figure. The estimated 2,049,946 offenses are the lowest measure since 1969. National 5- and 10-year trends indicated that burglary declined 18.2 percent from the 1996 figure and decreased 35.1 percent from the 1991 estimate.
- In 2000, an estimated dollar value of nearly $3 billion was attributed to property losses from burglary. The average dollar loss per burglary was $1,462. For residential offenses, the average loss was $1,381 and for nonresidential burglaries, $1,615.
- In 2000, 65.1 percent of burglaries were residential in nature. Burglaries of residences occurred most frequently during daytime hours, 60.7 percent, and burglaries of nonresidences occurred most often at night, 57.7 percent.

Larceny-theft

- Nearly 7 million larceny-theft offenses are estimated to have been reported to law enforcement agencies during 2000, an increase of 0.2 percent from the 1999 estimate. Larceny-theft comprised 68.4 percent of all the property crimes.
- Thefts of motor vehicle parts, accessories, and contents accounted for

the largest segment of larceny-thefts, 34.9 percent. Shoplifting made up 13.8 percent of the larceny-thefts and thefts from buildings, 13.1 percent. The remainder of larceny-thefts was attributable to other types of larceny-theft (pocket-picking, purse-snatching, bicycle thefts, etc.)

- In 2000, the average value of property stolen as a result of larceny-theft was $735. The estimated collective value of all property stolen during larceny-thefts was over $5.1 billion. Losses over $200 accounted for 38.9 percent of reported larceny-thefts, losses under $50 comprised 37.7 percent, and those between $50 and $200, made up 23.4 percent of the offenses.

Motor Vehicle Theft

- Nearly 1.2 million motor vehicle thefts are estimated to have occurred in 2000, a 1.2-percent increase from the 1999 estimate and the first such increase since 1990. Collectively, the Nation's cities had a 1.4-percent increase in motor vehicle thefts. Motor vehicle theft also increased 2.9 percent in the country's suburban counties and 1.6 percent in the rural counties.
- During 2000, the value of stolen vehicles was estimated at close to $7.8 billion. The average value of a stolen motor vehicle was $6,682. The recovery rate of stolen motor vehicles, 62.2 percent, was higher than for any other property type.
- Automobiles comprised 74.5 percent of all motor vehicle theft offenses, trucks and buses accounted for 18.7 percent of the vehicle thefts, and the remainder included other type vehicles.

Arson

- More than 78,280 arson offenses were reported by law enforcement in 2000, an increase of 0.4 percent from the 1999 figure.
- Among community types, the Nation's cities, collectively, experienced a 0.2-percent decline in reported arson offenses. Cities with populations of 1 million or more inhabitants had the greatest decrease in arson, 7.1 percent. In contrast, cities with populations of 10,000 to 24,999 saw an increase of 6.6 percent for arson offenses and cities of 25,000 to 49,999 inhabitants, an increase of 5.6 percent. The number of arson offenses increased 2.7 percent in the suburban counties. The rural counties had a 0.5-percent decrease in reported offenses.
- Supplemental arson data provided for 68,756 of the 78,280 reported arson offenses in 2000 indicated that 43.8 percent of all arson were structural in nature. Mobile properties were targeted in 31.2 percent of the arson offenses, and other types of property (crops, timber, etc.) accounted for 25.0 percent.
- Among the 30,116 structural arson offenses, residential property comprised 60.3 percent, with 42.2 percent of the structural arson directed at single-family dwellings. Uninhabited or abandoned structural property was targeted in 18.2 percent of the offenses.

- Supplemental arson data indicate that the average monetary value of property damaged due to reported arson in 2000 was $11,042 per incident. The dollar value for damaged structural property averaged $19,479. Mobile property loss averaged $5,803 per incident, and for other property types, the average was $2,706.
- Juveniles were involved in 45.0 percent of arson incidents cleared by law enforcement in 2000.

Law Enforcement Employees

- Law enforcement agencies in the United States employed an average of 2.5 full-time sworn officers for every 1,000 inhabitants during 2000. When full-time civilian employees are included, the rate was 3.5 employees per 1,000 inhabitants.
- The 13,535 city, county, and state police agencies that voluntarily reported personnel data in 2000 collectively employed 654,601 officers and 271,982 civilians and provided law enforcement services to nearly 265 million of the Nation's approximately 281 million inhabitants.
- By community type, the rate of sworn officers in the Nation's cities collectively was 2.4 officers per 1,000 inhabitants. Both the suburban and rural counties had a rate of 2.6 sworn officers for every 1,000 population.
- In 2000, 70.6 percent of the Nation's law enforcement personnel were sworn officers. Males made up 89.0 percent of the total number of sworn officers.
- Civilians comprised 29.4 percent of the total law enforcement employee force in the United States during 2000. Females accounted for 62.7 percent of all civilian law enforcement personnel.

WEAPONS DESTRUCTION BY THE IRISH REPUBLICAN ARMY
October 23, 2001

Northern Ireland's peace process emerged again from the land of the near-dead late in 2001, offering yet more hope that three decades of sectarian conflict might finally be nearing an end. The Irish Republican Army (IRA), the Catholic paramilitary group, did what it long had said it would never do: destroy some of its weapons. The British government responded by withdrawing some of its military presence from the province. A Northern Ireland government, consisting of Catholic and Protestant representatives, convened again after one of several periodic shutdowns.

The 2001 edition of Northern Ireland's on-and-off peace process was typical of others since a landmark agreement was signed in April 1998. Violence in the streets, political maneuvers, and threats by diehard extremists on both sides repeatedly put the peace process in jeopardy, only to be rescued by last-minute concessions enabling those who wanted peace to continue pursuing it. (Northern Ireland agreement, Historic Documents of 1998, p. 203; Historic Documents of 1999, p. 753)

Northern Ireland consisted of the six northernmost counties on the island of Ireland. After the southern part of the island gained independence from Great Britain in 1921–1922 and became the Republic of Ireland, the northern section stayed under British control. More than 90 percent of the republic's citizens were Roman Catholic, while about 60 percent of Northern Ireland's inhabitants were Protestant and the rest were Catholic. The IRA launched bombing and other terrorist attacks against the British government in the late 1960s, seeking to force unification of Northern Ireland with the republic. Those attacks, the British military response, and counterattacks by Protestant militias killed more than 3,000 people in subsequent decades.

The IRA Switches Tactics

The 1998 agreement had established a two-track approach toward ending the fighting. One track was a political process in which mainstream Catho-

lic and Protestant leaders would form a provincial government that would replace the direct rule that Britain had exercised from London since the outbreak of violence. The second track was persuading paramilitary groups on both sides to give up their weapons and allow politics to replace violent struggle. That process was called "decommissioning," or voluntary disarmament.

The political process was surprisingly successful at first, but it was knocked askew on a distressingly regular basis by obstructionist tactics from hard-line Protestants and by the IRA's reluctance to give up its weapons. The IRA insisted it had never been defeated by the British and should not have to disarm. This stance put two groups of politicians in Northern Ireland in a difficult position: Sinn Fein, the IRA's political wing, whose leaders had given up the military fight and had committed themselves to the peace process; and moderate Protestant leaders, notably David Trimble, leader of the Ulster Unionist Party, who also had staked their political careers on the peace process. Trimble had been chosen "first minister" in a unity government appointed by the new Northern Ireland Assembly; Sinn Fein leaders Gerry Adams and Martin McGuinness were among the Catholic representatives in the assembly.

The IRA in 2000 had begun negotiating with the Independent International Commission on Decommissioning, a body established by the 1998 peace accord. Its chairman was John de Chastelain, a retired Canadian general. That step preserved the peace process for a while, but it did not fully satisfy either the British government or Northern Ireland's Protestant leaders, both of whom insisted that the IRA destroy its weapons as a sign that it would actually abide by the peace agreement.

All through 2000 and into 2001, Trimble was under severe pressure from hard-line elements of his party who argued that the peace process was a sham so long as the IRA remained armed. Trimble progressively lost support within his party and was forced to set a series of deadlines for the IRA to follow through on disarmament. Trimble set his latest deadline for June 30, saying that he would resign as head of the Northern Ireland Assembly unless the IRA had begun disarming by then. As the deadline approached, rioting broke out in Belfast, and British prime minister Tony Blair and Republic of Ireland prime minister Bertie Ahern joined negotiations to find a political solution. Those talks failed, and London once again assumed control of the Northern Ireland government while further compromise efforts continued.

Although they were frustrating and inconclusive, the repeated political crises ultimately heightened pressure on the IRA to begin disarming. By the middle of 2001 it was clear to all sides that the IRA held the key to continuing the peace process. The IRA budged, if only slightly, on August 6, when it announced that it would put some of its weapons "beyond use." But Trimble rejected that offer as insufficient, and the peace process went back onto life-support systems.

Further pressure on the IRA came later in August, when three IRA representatives were arrested in Colombia, where they reportedly were training members of a leftist guerrilla group that was fighting the government, which was backed by the United States. That incident proved to be particularly embarrassing for Sinn Fein because one of the arrested men was the party's representative in Cuba.

Then came the September 11 terrorist attacks against the United States, which set in motion political changes in much of the world, including Northern Ireland. According to news reports, the September 11 attacks brought about a change of heart on the part of influential, but anonymous, Irish Americans who had long supplied the money that helped the IRA buy weapons and enabled Sinn Fein to launch itself as a political party. With the United States having been attacked by terrorists, these Irish Americans reportedly told the IRA and Sinn Fein that they could no longer support any form of paramilitary action in Northern Ireland. At the same time, U.S. diplomats bluntly told Sinn Fein representatives that the IRA had to choose between peace or terror, and that the Bush administration would not intervene to help save the peace process, as the previous Clinton administration had done repeatedly. (Terrorist attacks, pp. 614, 624)

As a new political crisis approached in Northern Ireland in October, Sinn Fein leader Gerry Adams stepped up public pressure on his IRA colleagues to compromise on the disarmament issue. The exact sequence of steps was not disclosed publicly—the IRA remained a secretive organization that did not explain how it made decisions—but by mid-October the IRA apparently had decided to begin disarming. Adams said on October 22 that he had appealed to the IRA to make a "ground-breaking" move on the issue, a signal that a major development was afoot.

The IRA Acts

The long-awaited announcement came October 23. De Chastelain's international commission said that it had witnessed an event, "which we regard as significant, in which the IRA has put a quantity of arms completely beyond use. The material in question includes arms, ammunition, and explosives." The commission refused to disclose further details, but British and Irish officials said the IRA had, in fact, destroyed a large quantity of weapons. In its own announcement, the IRA did not mention directly the destruction of weapons but merely stated that it had "implemented the scheme agreed" with de Chastelain's commission. The IRA acknowledged that the step caused the organization and its supporters unspecified "difficulties," but it justified the move as necessary because the political process "is now on the point of collapse" and such a collapse would put the entire peace process "in jeopardy."

Trimble, after hearing details of the IRA action from de Chastelain's commission, said he was satisfied. "This is the day we were told would never happen," he said. "We have always said that actions speak louder than words, and what we are seeing now is action."

The British government also said it accepted the legitimacy of the IRA's move, and it pledged to respond by moving ahead with several aspects of the 1998 peace agreement. Among the steps would be a "progressive rolling program" of reducing British troop levels and military installations in Northern Ireland.

Not surprisingly, hard-line Protestant groups, including the leaders of paramilitary organizations, were not satisfied by the IRA move. Billy Hutchinson, leader of the Progressive Unionist Party, said the party's Ulster Volunteer Force would retain its weapons. "For loyalists to reciprocate in terms of giving up weapons, they would be doing something just to satisfy Irish America, who they don't agree with in the first place," he said. The term "loyalists" referred to those who said they remained loyal to British control over Northern Ireland but also were affiliated with a paramilitary organization. By "Irish America," Hutchinson was referring to Irish American Catholics who supported the IRA.

Protestant militias were not the only paramilitary forces holding on to their weapons after the IRA move. A group that called itself the "'Real IRA" said it would not give up weapons or the struggle against British control of Northern Ireland. After the IRA declared a cease-fire in 1996, the Real IRA had emerged as the main anti-British militia. That group claimed responsibility for a bomb that exploded in the town of Omagh in August 1998, killing 29 people and injuring more than 200. That bombing was the single most deadly incident in the three decades of violence in the province.

Britain quickly moved to reduce its military presence in Northern Ireland, starting with the dismantling of watchtowers along the border between the province and the Republic of Ireland. The towers, equipped with sophisticated surveillance devices to monitor arms smuggling, had been a symbol of the British role in the province—hated by most Catholics and grudgingly accepted by most Protestants.

Despite the positive steps, Northern Ireland's political climate remained as unsettled as always. Just nine days after the IRA destroyed weapons, Trimble lost an election as the provincial unity government when a slight majority of Protestant representatives voted against him. That embarrassing outcome once again threatened the peace process, but only momentarily. A small party composed of moderate Catholics and Protestants, which had remained neutral, threw its support to Trimble, who then won back his old post as head of the Northern Ireland government on November 6. Referring to the tenuous grip the government had on its political life, Trimble said: "We need time for people to get accustomed to it working and see that it can work, because I believe it can."

> Following are the texts of statements issued October 23, 2002, by the Independent International Commission on Decommissioning, announcing that the Irish Republican Army (IRA) had destroyed some of its weapons, and a statement from the IRA explaining its action.

*The documents were obtained from the Internet at http://
www.nio.gov.uk/pdf/iicd1001.pdf.*

COMMISSION STATEMENT

1. On 6th August 2001 the [Independent International] Commission [on Decommissioning] reported that agreement had been reached with the IRA on a method to put IRA arms completely and verifiably beyond use. This would be done in such a way as to involve no risk to the public and avoid the possibility of misappropriation by others.

2. We have now witnessed an event—which we regard as significant—in which the IRA has put a quantity of arms completely beyond use. The materiel in question includes arms, ammunition and explosives.

3. We are satisfied that the arms in question have been dealt with in accordance with the scheme and regulations. We are also satisfied that it would not further the process of putting all arms beyond use were we to provide further details of this event.

4. We will continue our contact with the IRA representative in the pursuit of our mandate.

IRA STATEMENT

The IRA is committed to our republican objectives and to the establishment of a united Ireland based on justice, equality and freedom.

In August 1994, against a background of lengthy and intensive discussions involving the two governments and others, the leadership of the IRA called a complete cessation of military operations in order to create the dynamic for a peace process.

Decommissioning was no part of that. There was no ambiguity about this. Unfortunately, there are those within the British establishment and the leadership of Unionism who are fundamentally opposed to change. At every opportunity they have used the issue of arms as an excuse to undermine and frustrate progress.

It is for this reason that decommissioning was introduced to the process by the British Government. It has been used since to prevent the changes that a lasting peace requires.

In order to overcome this and to encourage the changes necessary for a lasting peace, the leadership of Oglaigh na hEireann (IRA) has taken a number of substantial initiatives. These include our engagement with the IICD (Independent International Commission on Decommissioning) and the inspection of a number of arms dumps by the two international inspectors, Cyril Ramaphosa and Martti Ahtisaari.

No one should doubt the difficulties these initiatives cause for us, our volunteers and our supporters.

The political process is now on the point of collapse. Such a collapse would certainly, and eventually, put the overall peace process in jeopardy. There is a responsibility upon everyone seriously committed to a just peace to do our best to avoid this.

Therefore, in order to save the peace process, we have implemented the scheme agreed with the IICD in August.

Our motivation is clear. This unprecedented move is to save the peace process and to persuade others of our genuine intentions.

EXECUTIVE ORDER TIGHTENING IMMIGRATION POLICIES
October 29, 2001

The reform of U.S. immigration law to make it easier for foreigners to enter the United States legally fell victim to the September 11 terrorist attacks. Before the attacks, President George W. Bush, and many members of Congress, had supported efforts to make it easier for foreigners—especially citizens of Mexico—to work in the United States. But after nineteen Middle Eastern men, most of whom were in the country legally, hijacked four airplanes and flew three of them into buildings, killing about 3,000 people, the political mood swung dramatically against immigration reform.

Following the terrorist attacks, the Bush administration took several significant steps to increase the scrutiny of foreigners trying to enter the United States, as well as noncitizens already in the country. Federal and local law enforcement agents detained more than 1,200 foreigners and questioned them about possible connections to the September 11 attacks; only one was charged with conspiring to participate in the attacks. Law enforcement agents also questioned some 5,000 young men from Middle Eastern countries. (Terrorist attacks, p. 614)

President Bush on October 29 issued new regulations tightening procedures for student visas, such as the one obtained by one of the alleged hijackers, who never attended the school listed on his visa application. On November 14, Attorney General John Ashcroft issued an order splitting the much-criticized Immigration and Naturalization Service (INS) into two bureaus, one charged with dealing with foreigners at border crossings, and the other charged with enforcing U.S. immigration laws.

The shifting winds in the United States on immigration policy constituted a major setback for Mexico's new president, Vicente Fox, who had taken office in December 2000. Fox had lobbied intently for a loosening of U.S. immigration standards so millions of Mexicans could work legally north of the border, thus relieving the pressure for job creation in Mexico. Fox and Bush had established a close working relationship when Bush was governor of Texas. Largely because of that relationship, Fox was the first for-

764

eign head of state treated by Bush to an official state dinner at the White House, on September 5. Fox used his visit to call for an agreement on immigration issues before the end of the year. But the terrorist attacks came less than a week after Fox left Washington, creating political imperatives in the United States that trumped improvements in U.S.-Mexican relations— at least for the time being. (Fox election, Historic Documents of 2000, p. 963)

The U.S. Census Bureau on October 24 released estimates showing that 7 to 8 million illegal immigrants were in the United States at the time of the 2000 Census. That range was about twice as high as the 1990 census estimate of 3.5 million illegal immigrants. Most of those immigrants—known officially as "undocumented" immigrants because they lacked visas and working papers—had arrived from Mexico and Central America.

Bush Immigration Order

At the first meeting of his new Homeland Security Council—itself an outgrowth of the September 11 attacks—Bush on October 29 announced several initiatives to increase the scrutiny on immigrants. None of the initiatives created direct action; all were in the form of directives to administration officials to study specific problems and come up with solutions.

As a politician who had long advocated making it easier for immigrants to work and live in the United States, Bush was clearly troubled by the issue and was careful to say that he did not oppose immigration in general—just some of the immigrants. "We welcome legal immigration and we welcome people coming to America," he said. "What we don't welcome are people who come to hurt the American people, and so therefore we're going to try to be diligent with our visas and observant with the behavior of people who come to this country."

The president's most specific step announced October 29 was to demand a crackdown on the abuse of student visas. In particular, the president's order said that "certain international students" should be prohibited from receiving education and training "in sensitive areas," including those with "direct application to the development and use of weapons of mass destruction." Bush also ordered a ban on "the education and training of foreign nationals who would use such training to harm the United States or its allies." Key federal agencies were to develop specific guidelines to enforce these general prohibitions, including listing "sensitive" courses, identifying "problematic applicants," and tracking the status of foreign students. This last provision appeared to echo what had been a controversial recommendation made in June 2000 by the National Commission on Terrorism. That panel called for expanding nationwide a test program used by some colleges in southern states to report to the government when foreign students switched into certain lines of study (for example, from English literature to nuclear physics). As an enforcement mechanism, Bush ordered the INS to conduct "periodic reviews" of record keeping on foreign students by academic institutions. (Terrorism commission, Historic Documents of 2000, p. 277)

The president also directed Ashcroft to appoint a Foreign Terrorist

Tracking Task Force to take specific steps against foreigners suspected of in-volvement with terrorist activity. The task force was to be composed of rep-resentatives from the State Department, the FBI, the INS, and other agencies, including intelligence agencies. Ashcroft on October 31 an-nounced the appointment of Steven C. McCraw, a FBI intelligence officer, as chairman of the task force.

Finally, the president directed the White House Office of Science and Technology Policy to work with other agencies to develop recommendations on the use of "advanced technology" to help enforce immigration laws. As with other aspects of his order, Bush offered little in the way of specifics, but he did mention the so-called data mining of government and commercial databases as one possibility.

The State Department on November 13 announced plans to subject men from twenty-five Arabic and Islamic countries to more rigorous screening when they applied for U.S. visas. Under new procedures, the names of men ages sixteen to forty-five from those countries would be sent to the FBI for background checks when they applied for visas at U.S. consular offices. Offi-cials said that step could add up to four weeks to the regular time required to process those visa applications. In the past, the State Department had re-quired FBI background checks only for residents of countries on the depart-ment's list of governments that supported terrorism, such as Iran, Libya, and Syria.

In one of many other consequences of the terrorist attacks, the INS an-nounced in December that it was asking law enforcement agencies to help it track down an estimated 314,000 foreigners who had remained in the United States illegally after they were ordered deported. The INS entered the names of those people into the FBI's national crime data base, hoping that some of them might be caught by state and local law enforcement agen-cies. Because of the large numbers involved, the INS in the past had made little effort to go after aliens who had been ordered deported.

Splitting the INS

The Immigration and Naturalization Service had long been one of the most unpopular and beleaguered federal agencies. Immigrants and groups that advocated on their behalf regularly criticized the INS for onerous regu-lations, lengthy delays, and bureaucratic incompetence. Those who sought to crack down on immigration complained that the agency was incapable of keeping illegal immigrants out of the country and enforcing immigration laws. Even though most of the hijackers had entered the country legally and had generally kept low profiles, criticism of the INS mounted after the Sep-tember 11 attacks, but it was unclear what the agency could have done to thwart their actions.

INS critics in Congress had offered numerous proposals to revamp the agency, including several types of suggestions for splitting its two main, somewhat conflicting, functions: providing services to immigrants and en-forcing U.S. immigration law. Preempting congressional action, Ashcroft on November 14 ordered the INS split into two divisions. One, the Bureau of Immigration Enforcement, was to be responsible for enforcing immigration laws and regulations, especially the tracking down of illegal immigrants and those who might be planning acts of terrorism. The other half of the INS, the Bureau of Immigration Services, was given the responsibility of helping immigrants deal with the government's bewildering laws and regulations.

The INS "has struggled to perform two often competing missions," Ashcroft said, and the new plan would give the agency "clear lines of authority." While creating two bureaus, Ashcroft's order kept the INS under the overall supervision of one top official, the INS commissioner. The current commissioner, James W. Ziglar, noted that some functions and laws affecting the two bureaus overlapped.

Ashcroft's order received a mixed reception on Capitol Hill. Some members of Congress praised it as a long overdue reform. But Rep. F. James Sensenbrenner Jr., R-Wis., chairman of the House Judiciary Committee, criticized the move as inadequate.

"The INS is dysfunctional," he said. Sensenbrenner had proposed legislation splitting the INS into two entirely separate agencies, a step he said would do a better job than Ashcroft's order in producing the necessary changes.

> *Following is the text of the "Homeland Security Presidential Directive 2," an executive order signed by President George W. Bush on October 29, 2001, ordering federal agencies to develop stricter procedures for preventing suspected terrorists from entering the United States and detaining those already in the country.*
>
> ***The document was obtained from the Internet at http:// www.whitehouse.gov/news/releases/2001/10/20011030-2 .html.***

SUBJECT: Combating Terrorism Through Immigration Policies

A. National Policy

The United States has a long and valued tradition of welcoming immigrants and visitors. But the attacks of September 11, 2001, showed that some come to the United States to commit terrorist acts, to raise funds for illegal terrorist activities, or to provide other support for terrorist operations, here and abroad. It is the policy of the United States to work aggressively to prevent aliens who engage in or support terrorist activity from entering the United States and to detain, prosecute, or deport any such aliens who are within the United States.

1. Foreign Terrorist Tracking Task Force

By November 1, 2001, the Attorney General shall create the Foreign Terrorist Tracking Task Force (Task Force), with assistance from the Secretary of State, the Director of Central Intelligence and other officers of the government, as appropriate. The Task Force shall ensure that, to the maximum extent permitted by law, Federal agencies coordinate programs to accomplish the following: 1) deny entry into the United States of aliens associated with, suspected of being engaged in, or supporting terrorist activity; and 2) locate, detain, prosecute, or deport any such aliens already present in the United States.

The Attorney General shall appoint a senior official as the full-time Director of the Task Force. The Director shall report to the Deputy Attorney General, serve as a Senior Advisor to the Assistant to the President for Homeland Security, and maintain direct liaison with the Commissioner of the Immigration and Naturalization Service (INS) on issues related to immigration and the foreign terrorist presence in the United States. The Director shall also consult with the Assistant Secretary of State for Consular Affairs on issues related to visa matters.

The Task Force shall be staffed by expert personnel from the Department of State, the INS, the Federal Bureau of Investigation, the Secret Service, the Customs Service, the Intelligence Community, military support components, and other Federal agencies as appropriate to accomplish the Task Force's mission.

The Attorney General and the Director of Central Intelligence shall ensure, to the maximum extent permitted by law, that the Task Force has access to all available information necessary to perform its mission, and they shall request information from State and local governments, where appropriate.

With the concurrence of the Attorney General and the Director of Central Intelligence, foreign liaison officers from cooperating countries shall be invited to serve as liaisons to the Task Force, where appropriate, to expedite investigation and data sharing.

Other Federal entities, such as the Migrant Smuggling and Trafficking in Persons Coordination Center and the Foreign Leads Development Activity, shall provide the Task Force with any relevant information they possess concerning aliens suspected of engaging in or supporting terrorist activity.

2. Enhanced INS and Customs Enforcement Capability

The Attorney General and the Secretary of the Treasury, assisted by the Director of Central Intelligence, shall immediately develop and implement multiyear plans to enhance the investigative and intelligence analysis capabilities of the INS and the Customs Service. The goal of this enhancement is to increase significantly efforts to identify, locate, detain, prosecute or deport aliens associated with, suspected of being engaged in, or supporting terrorist activity within the United States.

The new multi-year plans should significantly increase the number of Customs and INS special agents assigned to Joint Terrorism Task Forces, as deemed appropriate by the Attorney General and the Secretary of the Treasury. These officers shall constitute new positions over and above the existing on-duty special agent forces of the two agencies.

3. Abuse of International Student Status

The United States benefits greatly from international students who study in our country. The United States Government shall continue to foster and support international students.

The Government shall implement measures to end the abuse of student visas and prohibit certain international students from receiving education and training in sensitive areas, including areas of study with direct application to the development and use of weapons of mass destruction. The Government shall also prohibit the education and training of foreign nationals who would use such training to harm the United States or its Allies.

The Secretary of State and the Attorney General, working in conjunction with the Secretary of Education, the Director of the Office of Science and Technology Policy, the Secretary of Defense, the Secretary of Energy, and any other departments or entities they deem necessary, shall develop a program to accomplish this goal. The program shall identify sensitive courses of study, and shall include measures whereby the Department of State, the Department of Justice, and United States academic institutions, working together, can identify problematic applicants for student visas and deny their applications. The program shall provide for tracking the status of a foreign student who receives a visa (to include the proposed major course of study, the status of the individual as a full-time student, the classes in which the student enrolls, and the source of the funds supporting the student's education).

The program shall develop guidelines that may include control mechanisms, such as limited duration student immigration status, and may implement strict criteria for renewing such student immigration status. The program shall include guidelines for exempting students from countries or groups of countries from this set of requirements.

In developing this new program of control, the Secretary of State, the Attorney General, and the Secretary of Education shall consult with the academic community and other interested parties. This new program shall be presented through the Homeland Security Council to the President within 60 days.

The INS, in consultation with the Department of Education, shall conduct periodic reviews of all institutions certified to receive nonimmigrant students and exchange visitor program students. These reviews shall include checks for compliance with record keeping and reporting requirements. Failure of institutions to comply may result in the termination of the institution's approval to receive such students.

4. North American Complementary Immigration Policies

The Secretary of State, in coordination with the Secretary of the Treasury and the Attorney General, shall promptly initiate negotiations with Canada and Mexico to assure maximum possible compatibility of immigration, customs, and visa policies. The goal of the negotiations shall be to provide all involved countries the highest possible level of assurance that only individuals seeking entry for legitimate purposes enter any of the countries, while at the same time minimizing border restrictions that hinder legitimate trans-border commerce.

As part of this effort, the Secretaries of State and the Treasury and the Attorney General shall seek to substantially increase sharing of immigration and customs information. They shall also seek to establish a shared immigration and customs control data-base with both countries. The Secretary of State, the Secretary of the Treasury, and the Attorney General shall explore existing mechanisms to accomplish this goal and, to the maximum extent possible, develop new methods to achieve optimal effectiveness and relative transparency. To the extent statutory provisions prevent such information sharing, the Attorney General and the Secretaries of State and the Treasury shall submit to the Director of the Office of Management and Budget proposed remedial legislation.

5. Use of Advanced Technologies for Data Sharing and Enforcement Efforts

The Director of the OSTP [Office of Science and Technology Policy], in conjunction with the Attorney General and the Director of Central Intelligence, shall make recommendations about the use of advanced technology to help enforce United States immigration laws, to implement United States immigration programs, to facilitate the rapid identification of aliens who are suspected of engaging in or supporting terrorist activity, to deny them access to the United States, and to recommend ways in which existing government databases can be best utilized to maximize the ability of the government to detect, identify, locate, and apprehend potential terrorists in the United States. Databases from all appropriate Federal agencies, state and local governments, and commercial databases should be included in this review. The utility of advanced data mining software should also be addressed. To the extent that there may be legal barriers to such data sharing, the Director of the OSTP shall submit to the Director of the Office of Management and Budget proposed legislative remedies. The study also should make recommendations, propose timelines, and project budgetary requirements.

The Director of the OSTP shall make these recommendations to the President through the Homeland Security Council within 60 days.

6. Budgetary Support

The Office of Management and Budget shall work closely with the Attorney General, the Secretaries of State and of the Treasury, the Assistant to the President for Homeland Security, and all other appropriate agencies to review the budgetary support and identify changes in legislation necessary for the implementation of this directive and recommend appropriate support for a multi-year program to provide the United States a robust capability to prevent aliens who engage in or support terrorist activity from entering or remaining in the United States or the smuggling of implements of terrorism into the United States. The Director of the Office of Management and Budget shall make an interim report through the Homeland Security Council to the President on the recommended program within 30 days, and shall make a final report through the Homeland Security Council to the President on the recommended program within 60 days.

GEORGE W. BUSH

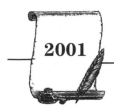
November

SETTLEMENT OF THE MICROSOFT ANTITRUST CASE
November 6, 2001

The Microsoft Corporation, the world's dominant computer software company, lost a major legal step in the government's long-running antitrust case against it—but then won a more important victory when the Bush administration decided to settle for a compromise. At year's end the company was still facing court proceedings in the United States and a potential antitrust challenge from the European Union (EU). The threat of a court-ordered breakup of the company had disappeared, however, and Microsoft was able to issue a new personal computer operating system that was designed to ensure its monopoly control of the market for years to come.

The case against Microsoft dated to 1994, when the administration of President Bill Clinton opened an investigation into the company's alleged anticompetitive practices that discouraged computer manufacturers and consumers from using non-Microsoft products. Microsoft agreed to end those practices, but in 1998 the Justice Department and attorneys general from nineteen states and the District of Columbia filed an antitrust suit against the company, alleging that it had illegally suppressed competition to maintain its monopoly. Federal District Court Judge Thomas Penfield Jackson, in Washington, D.C., ruled in 1999 that Microsoft was, indeed, a monopoly. After attempts to negotiate a settlement in the case fell apart, Jackson ruled in April 2000 that the company had violated the Sherman Antitrust Act by using its monopoly to stifle competition. Another round of settlement talks failed, and in June 2000 Jackson ordered Microsoft broken into two companies—one to produce computer operating systems and the other to produce software applications. (Microsoft case rulings, Historic Documents of 1999, p. 654; Historic Documents of 2000, pp. 105, 308)

Microsoft immediately appealed Jackson's rulings to the Supreme Court, which in September 2000 refused to hear the case and sent it to the Court of Appeals for the District of Columbia—a panel that had sparred with Jackson in the past and had proven receptive to Microsoft's point of view on antitrust matters. The appeals court heard oral arguments in the case on February 26 and 27, 2001, and it quickly became apparent that the seven-judge panel would take Jackson to task for comments he had made to reporters outside the courtroom. Among other things, Jackson had told reporters for the New York Times, New Yorker *magazine, and other publications that Microsoft founder William H. Gates had a "Napoleonic concept of himself and his company," was arrogant, and had given testimony in the case that was "inherently without credibility." Jackson also said some actions by Microsoft executives reminded him of drug traffickers and a notorious street gang in Washington.*

At the February 27 hearing, Appeals Court Chief Judge Harry T. Edwards referred to those statements and said judges were not supposed to "run off our mouths in a pejorative way." Edwards and other judges also criticized specific aspects of Jackson's rulings, including his "findings of fact" that had declared Microsoft a monopoly. Jackson had told journalist Ken Auletta, who was writing a book about the case, that he had structured his rulings in such a way as to make it difficult for the appeals court to challenge his factual findings. He did so, he said, because at a previous stage in the Microsoft case the appeals court had "made up about 90 percent of the facts on their own."

Appeals Court Decision

In their decision handed down June 28, the seven judges of the appeals court took three major actions in the Microsoft case: they accepted the underlying premise of Jackson's findings that Microsoft was a monopoly that had engaged in illegal, anticompetitive behavior intended to maintain its monopoly; they rejected Jackson's proposed "remedy" of breaking Microsoft into two companies; and they blistered Jackson for his comments to the news media, took him off the case, and sent it back to district court so a different judge could come up with another remedy. The court's decision was unsigned but unanimous. Three other appeals court judges had removed themselves from the case because of personal conflicts.

The heart of the appellate court decision was its confirmation of Jackson's fundamental ruling that Microsoft's monopolistic actions had illegally stifled competition in the software industry, which during the 1990s was one of the fastest growing segments of the U.S. economy. Microsoft had maintained its monopoly, the court ruled, with restrictive licensing agreements that had the effect of preventing computer manufacturers, other software vendors, and Internet service providers from using operating systems other than Microsoft's "Windows," which had a market share exceeding 90 percent. The appeals court wrote: "Suffice it to say that it would be inimical to the purposes of the Sherman [Antitrust] Act to allow monopolists free rein to squash nascent, albeit unproven, competitors at will—particularly in industries marked by rapid technological advance and frequent paradigm shifts."

However, the appeals court panel rejected Jackson's findings in other areas. First, it ruled that the government had not proved that Microsoft had used its dominance of the markets in personal computer operating systems to establish a new monopoly over browsers for the Internet. Jackson had accepted the government's claim, but the appeals court did not agree that Microsoft's actions had the effect of stifling competition in the browser market. The appeals court also rejected the legal reasoning behind Jackson's ruling that Microsoft had illegally combined, or "bundled," its Internet Explorer browser with its Windows operating systems. In effect, Jackson had accepted the government's contention that Microsoft bundled its products with the aim of harming competitors, especially the Netscape Corporation, which had dominated the Internet browser market until Microsoft offered its Internet Explorer as a free component of Windows. The appellate court, in effect, said Microsoft should have another opportunity to argue its case that it had bundled its products for acceptable business reasons, not just to establish a new monopoly.

Having agreed with Jackson that Microsoft was a monopoly that had engaged in illegal behavior, the appeals court overturned Jackson's acceptance of the government's proposal to break Microsoft into two companies. The panel rebuked Jackson for not allowing Microsoft an opportunity to propose an alternative remedy, and it said he had failed to provide an adequate legal justification for breaking the company in two, as opposed to some less drastic remedy.

Finally, the appeals court issued a scathing attack on Jackson, saying that he had violated the federal code of judicial conduct by commenting publicly on a pending case. Jackson's remarks about Microsoft and its executives were "deliberate, repeated, egregious, and flagrant" violations of the code, the judges said. "Public confidence in judicial impartiality cannot survive if judges, in disregard of their ethical obligations, pander to the press," they wrote. The judges ordered Jackson removed from further consideration of the case, but they rejected Microsoft's contentions that all of Jackson's findings should be vacated because of his behavior. The appeals court ordered the case returned to the district court level for another judge to examine the Internet browser "bundling" question and a proposed remedy for Microsoft's illegal behavior.

The appeals court decision led to a round of disputes over who had "won"—the federal government and the states that had filed the antitrust suit, or Microsoft. Microsoft gained an immediate public relations advantage by claiming victory and arguing that the time had come for the government to abandon the case. A grinning Gates, claiming vindication, said: "The ruling lifts the cloud of breakup over the company." The company's chief lawyer, William Neukom, said that "any fair characterization of today's decision is that Microsoft very substantially prevailed." Many news organizations accepted Microsoft's characterization of the ruling. Some critics of the company, however, said that those who took that viewpoint overlooked the court's unanimous ruling that Microsoft had engaged in illegal, anticompetitive behavior. "Microsoft lost on every hard question; they won on every easy question," Stanford University law professor Lawrence

Lessig told the Washington Post. *"The court has found them liable for monopoly maintenance—that's the essence of the government's case."*

Compromising with Microsoft

At least in the short term, the issue of who "won" at the appeals court level turned out to be less important than the question of what the Bush administration would do with the court's ruling. During his election campaign George W. Bush had criticized the Clinton administration's case against Microsoft, but his administration had not given a clear indication of how it would deal with the matter.

The government's first major step after the appeals court decision was to announce, on July 13, that it would not appeal those aspects that reversed Judge Jackson's rulings. On September 6 the government said it would no longer try to have Microsoft broken in two and was abandoning its attempt to show that Microsoft had illegally bundled Internet Explorer with the Windows operating system. The government said it would, instead, enter into new talks with the company in hopes of reaching a settlement. Negotiations for a settlement received a firm push three weeks later from the new district court judge assigned, in a random drawing, to take Jackson's place, Colleen Kollar-Kotelly. She told the government and Microsoft to negotiate around the clock, if necessary, to come up with a settlement by November 2. The judge also named a professional mediator to help speed the talks. Shortly after Kollar-Kotelly gave her marching orders, the Supreme Court rejected another request by Microsoft to take up the case.

One important development during that time period seemingly had no direct legal bearing on the Microsoft case, but as a practical matter had enormous significance: the September 11 terrorist attacks in New York and Washington. The attacks sent the stock markets plunging and threatened a sharp economic downturn. According to news accounts, some administration officials argued that, under those circumstances, the country could not afford continued uncertainty about the future of Microsoft, one of its biggest and most important companies. (Terrorist attacks, p. 614)

It soon became clear that some of the states that had joined the federal government's suit against Microsoft were prepared to take a harder line toward Microsoft than the Bush administration appeared to be adopting. Several of the attorneys general involved in the case said on September 7 that they would insist that any settlement impose restrictions on Microsoft's new operating system, Windows XP, which was then been readied for public release. That system went much further than any previous Windows system in linking, or bundling, applications for Internet browsing, music, photography, and instant messaging. Microsoft critics said that if the company were able to force computer manufacturers to install Windows XP, without any restrictions, competitors would have little chance of gaining market acceptance of their products. The Bush administration took no action to restrain Microsoft, however, and the company released its XP system on October 25. That same day some of the states hired their own lawyer to pursue the case: Brendan Sullivan, best known nationally for his aggressive defense of former White House aide Oliver North in the 1987 Iran-contra affair. (Iran-legal outcomes, Historic Documents of 1989, p. 391; Historic Documents of 1994, p. 12)

Negotiations between the Justice Department and Microsoft bore fruit with an agreement reached on October 31 and offered to the court November 2. That agreement imposed several limited restrictions on Microsoft's conduct. Microsoft agreed, as it had in previous phases of the case, to stop using use licensing agreements to force computer manufacturers to use Microsoft's "middleware" (software applications such as Internet browsers and word processors); Microsoft agreed to allow computer manufacturers to modify the Windows operating system to make it easier for users to adopt non-Microsoft applications; and Microsoft agreed to give other software developers limited access to the basic text, or "source code," of Windows to make it easier for them to develop products compatible with that system. The agreement also provided for a three-person panel of experts to supervise Microsoft's compliance with the agreement, in part by acting as a mediator between the company and its software competitors. The settlement would run for five years and could be extended for two more years if the court found that Microsoft repeatedly violated it.

The announcement of the settlement set off another argument over who "won" this latest round in the antitrust case. The difference this time, however, was that nearly everyone except for the Bush Justice Department agreed that Microsoft was the clear victor. Attorney General John Ashcroft hailed the settlement as a victory for everyone because it produced "the right result for consumers and for business, the right result for the economy, and the right result for government." Ashcroft rejected as "totally false" assertions by critics that Microsoft's strong political connections to the Republican Party had played a role in the administration's eagerness to settle the case. Microsoft officials praised the agreement, and the stock markets agreed that the company had won a major victory: Microsoft stock soared in the days after it was announced.

Microsoft critics denounced the settlement on several grounds. They noted that it contained fewer restrictions on Microsoft's behavior than Microsoft had been prepared to accept during a previous round of negotiations early in 2000. Critics said numerous loopholes would enable Microsoft to undermine the spirit of the agreement; for example, Microsoft could program Windows in such a way as to encourage users to adopt Microsoft products rather than competing products installed by computer manufacturers. Most important, critics said the settlement placed no serious restrictions on Microsoft's new XP system, which was then being shipped to computer manufacturers and consumers.

"This is a total capitulation" to Microsoft by the government, said Ed Black, president of the Computer and Communications Industry Association, which represented Microsoft competitors. Black argued that the government settled "for something less than what they could have had a year

and a half ago," a reference to concessions Microsoft reportedly was willing to make before Jackson issued his rulings in 2000.

The Justice Department had negotiated its accord with Microsoft without any participation by the states that were party to the antitrust suit. As a result, the states were put in the difficult position of having to decide whether to accept what the Justice Department had agreed to or to press ahead with the case without the federal government's backing. Some states attempted to negotiate a better deal, and during a late-night session on November 5 won several modest changes that increased the amount of information about Windows that Microsoft would have to disclose to competing software producers. With those changes, nine states agreed on November 6 to support the Justice Department's settlement with Microsoft: Illinois, Kentucky, Louisiana, Maryland, Michigan, New York, North Carolina, Ohio, and Wisconsin.

Nine states and the District of Columbia were then left as the holdouts. In a court filing on December 7, those states asked Judge Kollar-Kotelly to impose tougher requirements on Microsoft than the Justice Department had accepted. Among their proposals, the states demanded that Microsoft be required to offer computer manufacturers and users a basic version of Windows without Microsoft's other applications (such as Internet Explorer and Word) and to offer its Office suite of applications to the makers of competing operating systems (such as Macintosh and Linux). The states also asked the judge to eliminate numerous "loopholes" in the Justice Department settlement that, they said, would enable Microsoft to continue practices that the appeals court found to be illegal. In addition to the District of Columbia, the states joining this argument were California, Connecticut, Florida, Iowa, Kansas, Massachusetts, Minnesota, Utah, and West Virginia.

Judge Kollar-Kotelly gave the public sixty days to comment on the proposed Justice Department settlement. According to news reports, thousands of comments were filed by the end of the year, the overwhelming majority opposed to the settlement. Judge Kollar-Kotelly scheduled hearings for March 2002 on the question of whether the settlement was in the public interest and on the objections filed by the dissenting states.

Microsoft faced one other serious legal challenge, from the European Union, which in 2001 opened an investigation into the company's domination of the world market for computer operating systems. The EU lodged objections to Microsoft's behavior that were similar to the charges that led to Judge Jackson's rulings. Among the European complaints were the company's practices of "bundling" applications with Windows, strong-arming computer manufacturers into using only Microsoft products, and making it difficult for competitors to develop products compatible with Windows.

> *Following are excerpts from the revised proposed settlement of the antitrust case,* United States v. Microsoft, *submitted November 6, 2001, to the federal district court in Washington, D.C., by the Justice Department and nine states that had been party to the case. This proposal made several changes to a proposed settle-*

ment that had been submitted to the court by the Justice Department on November 2, 2001.

The document was obtained from the Internet at http:// www.usdoj.gov/opa/pr/2001/November/01_at_569.htm.

Revised Proposed Final Judgment

WHEREAS, plaintiffs United States of America ("United States") and the States of New York, Ohio, Illinois, Kentucky, Louisiana, Maryland, Michigan, North Carolina and Wisconsin and defendant Microsoft Corporation ("Microsoft"), by their respective attorneys, have consented to the entry of this Final Judgment;

AND WHEREAS, this Final Judgment does not constitute any admission by any party regarding any issue of fact or law;

AND WHEREAS, Microsoft agrees to be bound by the provisions of this Final Judgment pending its approval by the Court;

NOW THEREFORE, upon remand from the United States Court of Appeals for the District of Columbia Circuit, and upon the consent of the aforementioned parties, it is hereby ORDERED, ADJUDGED, AND DECREED:

I. Jurisdiction

This Court has jurisdiction of the subject matter of this action and of the person of Microsoft.

II. Applicability

This Final Judgment applies to Microsoft and to each of its officers, directors, agents, employees, subsidiaries, successors and assigns; and to all other persons in active concert or participation with any of them who shall have received actual notice of this Final Judgment by personal service or otherwise.

III. Prohibited Conduct

A. Microsoft shall not retaliate against an OEM [Original Equipment Manufacturer—a computer maker] by altering Microsoft's commercial relations with that OEM, or by withholding newly introduced forms of non-monetary Consideration (including but not limited to new versions of existing forms of non-monetary Consideration) from that OEM, because it is known to Microsoft that the OEM is or is contemplating:

1. developing, distributing, promoting, using, selling, or licensing any software that competes with Microsoft Platform Software or any product or service that distributes or promotes any Non-Microsoft Middleware;

2. shipping a Personal Computer that (a) includes both a Windows Operating System Product and a non-Microsoft Operating System, or (b) will boot with more than one Operating System; or

3. exercising any of the options or alternatives provided for under this Final Judgment.

Nothing in this provision shall prohibit Microsoft from enforcing any provision of any license with any OEM or any intellectual property right that is not inconsistent with this Final Judgment. Microsoft shall not terminate a Covered OEM's license for a Windows Operating System Product without having first given the Covered OEM written notice of the reasons for the proposed termination and not less than thirty days' opportunity to cure. Notwithstanding the foregoing, Microsoft shall have no obligation to provide such a termination notice and opportunity to cure to any Covered OEM that has received two or more such notices during the term of its Windows Operating System Product license.

Nothing in this provision shall prohibit Microsoft from providing Consideration to any OEM with respect to any Microsoft product or service where that Consideration is commensurate with the absolute level or amount of that OEM's development, distribution, promotion, or licensing of that Microsoft product or service.

B. Microsoft's provision of Windows Operating System Products to Covered OEMs shall be pursuant to uniform license agreements with uniform terms and conditions. Without limiting the foregoing, Microsoft shall charge each Covered OEM the applicable royalty for Windows Operating System Products as set forth on a schedule, to be established by Microsoft and published on a web site accessible to the Plaintiffs and all Covered OEMs, that provides for uniform royalties for Windows Operating System Products, except that:

1. the schedule may specify different royalties for different language versions;
2. the schedule may specify reasonable volume discounts based upon the actual volume of licenses of any Windows Operating System Product or any group of such products; and
3. the schedule may include market development allowances, programs, or other discounts in connection with Windows Operating System Products, provided that:
   a. such discounts are offered and available uniformly to all Covered OEMs, except that Microsoft may establish one uniform discount schedule for the ten largest Covered OEMs and a second uniform discount schedule for the eleventh through twentieth largest Covered OEMs, where the size of the OEM is measured by volume of licenses;
   b. such discounts are based on objective, verifiable criteria that shall be applied and enforced on a uniform basis for all Covered OEMs; and
   c. such discounts or their award shall not be based on or impose any criterion or requirement that is otherwise inconsistent with any portion of this Final Judgment.

C. Microsoft shall not restrict by agreement any OEM licensee from exercising any of the following options or alternatives:

1. Installing, and displaying icons, shortcuts, or menu entries for, any Non-Microsoft Middleware or any product or service (including but not limited to IAP [Internet Access Provider] products or services) that distributes, uses, promotes, or supports any Non-Microsoft Middleware, on the desktop or Start menu, or anywhere else in a Windows Operating System Product where a list of icons, shortcuts, or menu entries for applications are generally displayed, except that Microsoft may restrict an OEM from displaying icons, shortcuts and menu entries for any product in any list of such icons, shortcuts, or menu entries specified in the Windows documentation as being limited to products that provide particular types of functionality, provided that the restrictions are non-discriminatory with respect to non-Microsoft and Microsoft products.

2. Distributing or promoting Non-Microsoft Middleware by installing and displaying on the desktop shortcuts of any size or shape so long as such shortcuts do not impair the functionality of the user interface.

3. Launching automatically, at the conclusion of the initial boot sequence or subsequent boot sequences, or upon connections to or disconnections from the Internet, any Non-Microsoft Middleware if a Microsoft Middleware Product that provides similar functionality would otherwise be launched automatically at that time, provided that any such Non-Microsoft Middleware displays on the desktop no user interface or a user interface of similar size and shape to the user interface displayed by the corresponding Microsoft Middleware Product.

4. Offering users the option of launching other Operating Systems from the Basic Input/Output System or a non-Microsoft boot-loader or similar program that launches prior to the start of the Windows Operating System Product.

5. Presenting in the initial boot sequence its own IAP offer provided that the OEM complies with reasonable technical specifications established by Microsoft, including a requirement that the end user be returned to the initial boot sequence upon the conclusion of any such offer.

6. Exercising any of the options provided in Section III.H of this Final Judgment.

D. Starting at the earlier of the release of Service Pack 1 for Windows XP or 12 months after the submission of this Final Judgment to the Court, Microsoft shall disclose to ISVs [Independent Software Vendors], IHVs [Independent Hardware Vendor], IAPs, ICPs [Internet Content Provider], and OEMs, for the sole purpose of interoperating with a Windows Operating System Product, via the Microsoft Developer Network ("MSDN") or similar mechanisms, the APIs [Application Programming Interfaces] and related Documentation that are used by Microsoft Middleware to interoperate with a Windows Operating System Product. In the case of a new major version of Microsoft Middleware, the disclosures required by this Section III.D shall occur no later than the last major beta test release of that Microsoft Middleware. In the case of a new version of a Windows Operating System Product, the obligations imposed by this Section III.D shall occur in a Timely Manner.

E. Starting nine months after the submission of this proposed Final Judgment to the Court, Microsoft shall make available for use by third parties, for the sole purpose of interoperating with a Windows Operating System Product, on reasonable and non-discriminatory terms (consistent with Section III.I), any Communications Protocol that is, on or after the date this Final Judgment is submitted to the Court, (i) implemented in a Windows Operating System Product installed on a client computer, and (ii) used to interoperate natively (i.e., without the addition of software code to the client operating system product) with a Microsoft server operating system product.

F.

1. Microsoft shall not retaliate against any ISV or IHV because of that ISV's or IHV's:
   a. developing, using, distributing, promoting or supporting any software that competes with Microsoft Platform Software or any software that runs on any software that competes with Microsoft Platform Software, or
   b. exercising any of the options or alternatives provided for under this Final Judgment.
2. Microsoft shall not enter into any agreement relating to a Windows Operating System Product that conditions the grant of any Consideration on an ISV's refraining from developing, using, distributing, or promoting any software that competes with Microsoft Platform Software or any software that runs on any software that competes with Microsoft Platform Software, except that Microsoft may enter into agreements that place limitations on an ISV's development, use, distribution or promotion of any such software if those limitations are reasonably necessary to and of reasonable scope and duration in relation to a bona fide contractual obligation of the ISV to use, distribute or promote any Microsoft software or to develop software for, or in conjunction with, Microsoft.
3. Nothing in this section shall prohibit Microsoft from enforcing any provision of any agreement with any ISV or IHV, or any intellectual property right, that is not inconsistent with this Final Judgment.

G. Microsoft shall not enter into any agreement with:

1. any IAP, ICP, ISV, IHV or OEM that grants Consideration on the condition that such entity distributes, promotes, uses, or supports, exclusively or in a fixed percentage, any Microsoft Platform Software, except that Microsoft may enter into agreements in which such an entity agrees to distribute, promote, use or support Microsoft Platform Software in a fixed percentage whenever Microsoft in good faith obtains a representation that it is commercially practicable for the entity to provide equal or greater distribution, promotion, use or support for software that competes with Microsoft Platform Software, or
2. any IAP or ICP that grants placement on the desktop or elsewhere in any Windows Operating System Product to that IAP or ICP on the condition

that the IAP or ICP refrain from distributing, promoting or using any software that competes with Microsoft Middleware.

Nothing in this section shall prohibit Microsoft from entering into (a) any bona fide joint venture or (b) any joint development or joint services arrangement with any ISV, IHV, IAP, ICP, or OEM for a new product, technology or service, or any material value-add to an existing product, technology or service, in which both Microsoft and the ISV, IHV, IAP, ICP, or OEM contribute significant developer or other resources, that prohibits such entity from competing with the object of the joint venture or other arrangement for a reasonable period of time.

This Section does not apply to any agreements in which Microsoft licenses intellectual property in from a third party.

H. Starting at the earlier of the release of Service Pack 1 for Windows XP or 12 months after the submission of this Final Judgment to the Court, Microsoft shall:

1. Allow end users (via a mechanism readily accessible from the desktop or Start menu such as an Add/Remove icon) and OEMs (via standard pre-installation kits) to enable or remove access to each Microsoft Middleware Product or Non-Microsoft Middleware Product by (a) displaying or removing icons, shortcuts, or menu entries on the desktop or Start menu, or anywhere else in a Windows Operating System Product where a list of icons, shortcuts, or menu entries for applications are generally displayed, except that Microsoft may restrict the display of icons, shortcuts, or menu entries for any product in any list of such icons, shortcuts, or menu entries specified in the Windows documentation as being limited to products that provide particular types of functionality, provided that the restrictions are non-discriminatory with respect to non-Microsoft and Microsoft products; and (b) enabling or disabling automatic invocations pursuant to Section III.C.3 of this Final Judgment that are used to launch Non-Microsoft Middleware Products or Microsoft Middleware Products. The mechanism shall offer the end user a separate and unbiased choice with respect to enabling or removing access (as described in this subsection III.H.1) and altering default invocations (as described in the following subsection III.H.2) with regard to each such Microsoft Middleware Product or Non-Microsoft Middleware Product and may offer the end-user a separate and unbiased choice of enabling or removing access and altering default configurations as to all Microsoft Middleware Products as a group or all Non-Microsoft Middleware Products as a group.

2. Allow end users (via a mechanism readily available from the desktop or Start menu), OEMs (via standard OEM preinstallation kits), and Non-Microsoft Middleware Products (via a mechanism which may, at Microsoft's option, require confirmation from the end user) to designate a Non-Microsoft Middleware Product to be invoked in place of that Microsoft Middleware Product (or vice versa) in any case where the Windows Operating System Product would otherwise launch the Microsoft Middleware Product in a separate Top-Level Window and display either

(i) all of the user interface elements or (ii) the Trademark of the Microsoft Middleware Product.

3. Ensure that a Windows Operating System Product does not (a) automatically alter an OEM's configuration of icons, shortcuts or menu entries installed or displayed by the OEM pursuant to Section III.C of this Final Judgment without first seeking confirmation from the user and (b) seek such confirmation from the end user for an automatic (as opposed to user-initiated) alteration of the OEM's configuration until 14 days after the initial boot up of a new Personal Computer. Microsoft shall not alter the manner in which a Windows Operating System Product automatically alters an OEM's configuration of icons, shortcuts or menu entries other than in a new version of a Windows Operating System Product.

Notwithstanding the foregoing Section III.H.2, the Windows Operating System Product may invoke a Microsoft Middleware Product in any instance in which:

1. that Microsoft Middleware Product would be invoked solely for use in interoperating with a server maintained by Microsoft (outside the context of general Web browsing), or

2. that designated Non-Microsoft Middleware Product fails to implement a reasonable technical requirement (e.g., a requirement to be able to host a particular ActiveX control) that is necessary for valid technical reasons to supply the end user with functionality consistent with a Windows Operating System Product, provided that the technical reasons are described in a reasonably prompt manner to any ISV that requests them.

Microsoft's obligations under this Section III.H as to any new Windows Operating System Product shall be determined based on the Microsoft Middleware Products which exist seven months prior to the last beta test version (i.e., the one immediately preceding the first release candidate) of that Windows Operating System Product.

I. Microsoft shall offer to license to ISVs, IHVs, IAPs, ICPs, and OEMs any intellectual property rights owned or licensable by Microsoft that are required to exercise any of the options or alternatives expressly provided to them under this Final Judgment, provided that

1. all terms, including royalties or other payment of monetary consideration, are reasonable and non-discriminatory;

2. the scope of any such license (and the intellectual property rights licensed thereunder) need be no broader than is necessary to ensure that an ISV, IHV, IAP, ICP or OEM is able to exercise the options or alternatives expressly provided under this Final Judgment (e.g., an ISV's, IHV's, IAP's, ICP's and OEM's option to promote Non-Microsoft Middleware shall not confer any rights to any Microsoft intellectual property rights infringed by that Non-Microsoft Middleware);

3. an ISV's, IHV's, IAP's, ICP's, or OEM's rights may be conditioned on its not assigning, transferring or sublicensing its rights under any license granted under this provision;

4. the terms of any license granted under this section are in all respects consistent with the express terms of this Final Judgment; and

5. an ISV, IHV, IAP, ICP, or OEM may be required to grant to Microsoft on reasonable and nondiscriminatory terms a license to any intellectual property rights it may have relating to the exercise of their options or alternatives provided by this Final Judgment; the scope of such license shall be no broader than is necessary to insure that Microsoft can provide such options or alternatives.

Beyond the express terms of any license granted by Microsoft pursuant to this section, this Final Judgment does not, directly or by implication, estoppel or otherwise, confer any rights, licenses, covenants or immunities with regard to any Microsoft intellectual property to anyone.

J. No provision of this Final Judgment shall:

1. Require Microsoft to document, disclose or license to third parties: (a) portions of APIs or Documentation or portions or layers of Communications Protocols the disclosure of which would compromise the security of a particular installation or group of installations of anti-piracy, anti-virus, software licensing, digital rights management, encryption or authentication systems, including without limitation, keys, authorization tokens or enforcement criteria; or (b) any API, interface or other information related to any Microsoft product if lawfully directed not to do so by a governmental agency of competent jurisdiction.

2. Prevent Microsoft from conditioning any license of any API, Documentation or Communications Protocol related to anti-piracy systems, anti-virus technologies, license enforcement mechanisms, authentication/ authorization security, or third party intellectual property protection mechanisms of any Microsoft product to any person or entity on the requirement that the licensee: (a) has no history of software counterfeiting or piracy or willful violation of intellectual property rights, (b) has a reasonable business need for the API, Documentation or Communications Protocol for a planned or shipping product, (c) meets reasonable, objective standards established by Microsoft for certifying the authenticity and viability of its business, (d) agrees to submit, at its own expense, any computer program using such APIs, Documentation or Communication Protocols to third-party verification, approved by Microsoft, to test for and ensure verification and compliance with Microsoft specifications for use of the API or interface, which specifications shall be related to proper operation and integrity of the systems and mechanisms identified in this paragraph.

IV. Compliance and Enforcement Procedures

A. Enforcement Authority

1. The Plaintiffs shall have exclusive responsibility for enforcing this Final Judgment. Without in any way limiting the sovereign enforcement authority of each of the plaintiff States, the plaintiff States shall form

a committee to coordinate their enforcement of this Final Judgment. A plaintiff State shall take no action to enforce this Final Judgment without first consulting with the United States and with the plaintiff States' enforcement committee.

2. To determine and enforce compliance with this Final Judgment, duly authorized representatives of the United States and the plaintiff States, on reasonable notice to Microsoft and subject to any lawful privilege, shall be permitted the following:

    a. Access during normal office hours to inspect any and all source code, books, ledgers, accounts, correspondence, memoranda and other documents and records in the possession, custody, or control of Microsoft, which may have counsel present, regarding any matters contained in this Final Judgment.

    b. Subject to the reasonable convenience of Microsoft and without restraint or interference from it, to interview, informally or on the record, officers, employees, or agents of Microsoft, who may have counsel present, regarding any matters contained in this Final Judgment.

    c. Upon written request of the United States or a duly designated representative of a plaintiff State, on reasonable notice given to Microsoft, Microsoft shall submit such written reports under oath as requested regarding any matters contained in this Final Judgment.

    Individual plaintiff States will consult with the plaintiff States' enforcement committee to minimize the duplication and burden of the exercise of the foregoing powers, where practicable.

3. The Plaintiffs shall not disclose any information or documents obtained from Microsoft under this Final Judgment except for the purpose of securing compliance with this Final Judgment, in a legal proceeding to which one or more of the Plaintiffs is a party, or as otherwise required by law; provided that the relevant Plaintiff(s) must provide ten days' advance notice to Microsoft before disclosing in any legal proceeding (other than a grand jury proceeding) to which Microsoft is not a party any information or documents provided by Microsoft pursuant to this Final Judgment which Microsoft has identified in writing as material as to which a claim of protection may be asserted under Rule 26(c)(7) of the Federal Rules of Civil Procedure.

4. The Plaintiffs shall have the authority to seek such orders as are necessary from the Court to enforce this Final Judgment, provided, however, that the Plaintiffs shall afford Microsoft a reasonable opportunity to cure alleged violations of Sections III.C, III.D, III.E and III.H, provided further that any action by Microsoft to cure any such violation shall not be a defense to enforcement with respect to any knowing, willful or systematic violations.

B. **Appointment of a Technical Committee**

1. Within 30 days of entry of this Final Judgment, the parties shall create and recommend to the Court for its appointment a three-person Techni-

cal Committee ("TC") to assist in enforcement of and compliance with this Final Judgment.

2. The TC members shall be experts in software design and programming. No TC member shall have a conflict of interest that could prevent him or her from performing his or her duties under this Final Judgment in a fair and unbiased manner. Without limitation to the foregoing, no TC member (absent the agreement of both parties):

a. shall have been employed in any capacity by Microsoft or any competitor to Microsoft within the past year, nor shall she or he be so employed during his or her term on the TC;

b. shall have been retained as a consulting or testifying expert by any person in this action or in any other action adverse to or on behalf of Microsoft; or

c. shall perform any other work for Microsoft or any competitor of Microsoft for two years after the expiration of the term of his or her service on the TC.

3. Within 7 days of entry of this Final Judgment, the Plaintiffs as a group and Microsoft shall each select one member of the TC, and those two members shall then select the third member. The selection and approval process shall proceed as follows.

a. As soon as practicable after submission of this Final Judgment to the Court, the Plaintiffs as a group and Microsoft shall each identify to the other the individual it proposes to select as its designee to the TC. The Plaintiffs and Microsoft shall not object to each other's selection on any ground other than failure to satisfy the requirements of Section IV.B.2 above. Any such objection shall be made within ten business days of the receipt of notification of selection.

b. The Plaintiffs shall apply to the Court for appointment of the persons selected by the Plaintiffs and Microsoft pursuant to Section IV.B.3.a above. Any objections to the eligibility of a selected person that the parties have failed to resolve between themselves shall be decided by the Court based solely on the requirements stated in Section IV.B.2 above.

c. As soon as practical after their appointment by the Court, the two members of the TC selected by the Plaintiffs and Microsoft (the "Standing Committee Members") shall identify to the Plaintiffs and Microsoft the person that they in turn propose to select as the third member of the TC. The Plaintiffs and Microsoft shall not object to this selection on any grounds other than failure to satisfy the requirements of Section IV.B.2 above. Any such objection shall be made within ten business days of the receipt of notification of the selection and shall be served on the other party as well as on the Standing Committee Members.

d. The Plaintiffs shall apply to the Court for appointment of the person selected by the Standing Committee Members. If the Standing Committee Members cannot agree on a third member of the TC, the third member shall be appointed by the Court. Any objection by Microsoft or the Plaintiffs to the eligibility of the person selected by the Standing Committee Members which the parties have failed to resolve among themselves shall also be decided by the Court based on the requirements stated in Section IV.B.2 above.

4. Each TC member shall serve for an initial term of 30 months. At the end of a TC member's initial 30-month term, the party that originally selected him or her may, in its sole discretion, either request re-appointment by the Court to a second 30-month term or replace the TC member in the same manner as provided for in Section IV.B.3.a above. In the case of the third member of the TC, that member shall be re-appointed or replaced in the manner provided in Section IV.B.3.c above.

5. If the United States determines that a member of the TC has failed to act diligently and consistently with the purposes of this Final Judgment, or if a member of the TC resigns, or for any other reason ceases to serve in his or her capacity as a member of the TC, the person or persons that originally selected the TC member shall select a replacement member in the same manner as provided for in Section IV.B.3.

6. Promptly after appointment of the TC by the Court, the United States shall enter into a Technical Committee services agreement ("TC Services Agreement") with each TC member that grants the rights, powers and authorities necessary to permit the TC to perform its duties under this Final Judgment. Microsoft shall indemnify each TC member and hold him or her harmless against any losses, claims, damages, liabilities or expenses arising out of, or in connection with, the performance of the TC's duties, except to the extent that such liabilities, losses, damages, claims, or expenses result from misfeasance, gross negligence, willful or wanton acts, or bad faith by the TC member. The TC Services Agreements shall include the following.

   a. The TC members shall serve, without bond or other security, at the cost and expense of Microsoft on such terms and conditions as the Plaintiffs approve, including the payment of reasonable fees and expenses.

   b. The TC Services Agreement shall provide that each member of the TC shall comply with the limitations provided for in Section IV.B.2 above.

7. Microsoft shall provide the TC with a permanent office, telephone, and other office support facilities at Microsoft's corporate campus in Redmond, Washington. Microsoft shall also, upon reasonable advance notice from the TC, provide the TC with reasonable access to available office space, telephone, and other office support facilities at any other Microsoft facility identified by the TC.

8. The TC shall have the following powers and duties:

   a. The TC shall have the power and authority to monitor Microsoft's compliance with its obligations under this final judgment.

   b. The TC may, on reasonable notice to Microsoft:

    i. interview, either informally or on the record, any Microsoft personnel, who may have counsel present; any such interview to be subject to the reasonable convenience of such personnel and without restraint or interference by Microsoft;

    ii. inspect and copy any document in the possession, custody or control of Microsoft personnel;

    iii. obtain reasonable access to any systems or equipment to which Microsoft personnel have access;

    iv. obtain access to, and inspect, any physical facility, building or other premises to which Microsoft personnel have access; and

    v. require Microsoft personnel to provide compilations of documents, data and other information, and to submit reports to the TC containing such material, in such form as the TC may reasonably direct.

c. The TC shall have access to Microsoft's source code, subject to the terms of Microsoft's standard source code Confidentiality Agreement, as approved by the Plaintiffs and to be agreed to by the TC members pursuant to Section IV.B.9 below, and by any staff or consultants who may have access to the source code. The TC may study, interrogate and interact with the source code in order to perform its functions and duties, including the handling of complaints and other inquiries from non-parties.

d. The TC shall receive complaints from the Compliance Officer, third parties or the Plaintiffs and handle them in the manner specified in Section IV.D below.

e. The TC shall report in writing to the Plaintiffs every six months until expiration of this Final Judgment the actions it has undertaken in performing its duties pursuant to this Final Judgment, including the identification of each business practice reviewed and any recommendations made by the TC.

f. Regardless of when reports are due, when the TC has reason to believe that there may have been a failure by Microsoft to comply with any term of this Final Judgment, the TC shall immediately notify the Plaintiffs in writing setting forth the relevant details.

g. TC members may communicate with non-parties about how their complaints or inquiries might be resolved with Microsoft, so long as the confidentiality of information obtained from Microsoft is maintained.

h. The TC may hire at the cost and expense of Microsoft, with prior notice to Microsoft and subject to approval by the Plaintiffs, such staff or consultants (all of whom must meet the qualifications of Section IV.B.2) as are reasonably necessary for the TC to carry out its duties and responsibilities under this Final Judgment. The compensation of any person retained by the TC shall be based on reasonable and customary terms commensurate with the individual's experience and responsibilities.

     i. The TC shall account for all reasonable expenses incurred, including agreed upon fees for the TC members' services, subject to the approval of the Plaintiffs. Microsoft may, on application to the Court, object to the reasonableness of any such fees or other expenses. On any such application: (a) the burden shall be on Microsoft to demonstrate unreasonableness; and (b) the TC member(s) shall be entitled to recover all costs incurred on such application (including reasonable attorneys' fees and costs), regardless of the Court's disposition of such application, unless the Court shall expressly find that the TC's opposition to the application was without substantial justification.

9. Each TC member, and any consultants or staff hired by the TC, shall sign a confidentiality agreement prohibiting disclosure of any information obtained in the course of performing his or her duties as a member of the TC or as a person assisting the TC to anyone other than Microsoft, the Plaintiffs, or the Court. All information gathered by the TC in connection with this Final Judgment and any report and recommendations prepared by the TC shall be treated as Highly Confidential under the Protective Order in this case, and shall not be disclosed to any person other than Microsoft and the Plaintiffs except as allowed by the Protective Order entered in the Action or by further order of this Court.

10. No member of the TC shall make any public statements relating to the TC's activities.

C. **Appointment of a Microsoft Internal Compliance Officer.** . . .

[The following section detailed the duties of an officer to be appointed by Microsoft to oversee the company's compliance with the agreement.]

D. **Voluntary Dispute Resolution.** . . .

[The following section detailed various procedures for third parties to take complaints about Microsoft's compliance with the agreement to the Plaintiffs, to the Technical Committee, or to Microsoft's compliance officer.]

V. Termination

A. Unless this Court grants an extension, this Final Judgment will expire on the fifth anniversary of the date it is entered by the Court.

B. In any enforcement proceeding in which the Court has found that Microsoft has engaged in a pattern of willful and systematic violations, the Plaintiffs may apply to the Court for a one-time extension of this Final Judgment of up to two years, together with such other relief as the Court may deem appropriate. . . .

IRANIAN PRESIDENT ON A DIALOGUE AMONG CIVILIZATIONS
November 9, 2001

Iran continued on its uncertain path away from Islamist extremism in 2001. Voters reelected a reform-minded president and majority in the parliament, and the country's religious and political leaders condemned the September 11 terrorist attacks against the United States. But the religious leaders who held real power in Iran continued to suppress dissent, an indication of their fear about the steady loss of popular support for the 1979 revolution. Some officials in Tehran took hesitant steps to patch up the two-way antagonism between Iran and the United States, but the administration of President George W. Bush did not seem inclined to respond in kind.

Khatami Reelected

The 1979 revolution, which overthrew the U.S.-backed shah, brought to power senior religious figures who imposed a fundamentalist form of Islam on all aspects of Iranian society. The religious leaders' tight grip began to weaken after the 1980–1988 Iran-Iraq war, which severely weakened the country's economy. With unemployment and public dissatisfaction soaring, especially among young people, the leadership allowed a free presidential election in 1997, won overwhelmingly by a moderate, mid-level cleric, Mohammad Khatami, who positioned himself as the leader of a reform movement. (Iran-Iraq war, Historic Documents of 1988, p. 529; Khatami election, Historic Documents of 1997, p. 284)

Despite his obvious public support, Khatami had only limited ability to bring about changes. The real power under the 1979 constitution was retained by more senior religious figures headed by Ayatollah Ali Khamenei, who held the title of Iran's "Supreme Leader." Khatami moved cautiously during his first four years in office, offering support for those who sought to reduce the influence of the religious leaders but taking no direct actions that would have caused an outright split among the country's leadership. A report issued at the end 2001 by Human Rights Watch said: "Increasingly, through his statements, he appeared to represent more of a safety valve for public frustration than an agent of tangible change."

Khatami's greatest success may have been the passage of legislation by parliament that enabled the publication of numerous independent newspapers and magazines for the first time since the revolution. Aided by a newly free press, reform candidates swept parliamentary races in February 2000. But that success prompted a backlash. The conservative Council of Guardians—assigned by the constitution to uphold the standards of the 1979 religious revolution—prevented some of the reformers from taking their seats. The council also closed several pro-reform newspapers and jailed dozens of intellectuals, journalists, and government officials who had advocated reform.

In the meantime, the Iranian economy stubbornly refused to improve from its sorry state after the war with Iraq. U.S. economic sanctions, which had been in effect for two decades, discouraged international lending and investment, as did Iranian religious rules severely limiting most forms of foreign involvement in the country's economy. At the turn of the century about two-thirds of Iran's 66 million people were under thirty years of age; the young also made up the vast majority of the estimated 20 percent of the population that was unemployed.

Many of Khatami's most ardent supporters, especially the young, had become disillusioned by his inability to improve the economy or reform religious rules that severely restricted social behavior and intellectual discourse. By late 2000 Khatami had adopted an almost defeatist posture, saying he had done his best to pursue reforms but had been blocked by religious leaders. As the end of his four-year term approached, however, Khatami returned to the offense, making a televised speech on March 11 in which he said that "no pressure can make me give up this path." Khatami waged a vigorous campaign for reelection and won the balloting on June 9 with about 77 percent of the vote against nine other candidates. Reform candidates aligned with Khatami also won a majority of seats in the parliament.

The election results did not deter the conservative hard-liners. Khatami's inauguration in August was delayed for three days because of a dispute over the membership of the Council of Guardians. Ayatollah Khamenei and his followers also stepped up a campaign of repressing the news media and reformers linked to Khatami. Typical of the repression was the imprisonment in December of Abdullah Ramazanadeh, Khatami's cabinet secretary, who had made critical remarks about the Council of Guardians and suggested that Khatami meet with President Bush for negotiations about Afghanistan.

U.S.-Iranian Relations

The United States severed diplomatic relations with Iran after militant students and others seized the U.S. embassy in Tehran in November 1979 and held more than four dozen Americans hostage for more than a year. The two countries had been implacable enemies ever since, as Iran's religious leaders referred to the United States as "the Great Satan" and successive ad-

ministrations in Washington accused the Iranian government of repressing human and political rights and sponsoring terrorism in the region.

Attitudes on both sides began to shift slightly after Khatami's election in 1997. President Bill Clinton welcomed the emergence of democracy in Iran, and Khatami voiced hopes for an eventual improvement in relations between the two countries. The Clinton administration took two modest steps in that direction in 2000: Secretary of State Madeleine K. Albright expressed regret for Washington's involvement in a 1953 coup that overthrew a popular, leftist prime minister in Tehran, and the United States allowed limited imports of Iranian caviar, pistachio nuts, and rugs.

Early in 2001, with Khatami poised to run yet again, influential voices within the U.S. foreign policy establishment argued that the Bush administration should go further than the Clinton administration in reaching out to the people of Iran and moderate leaders there. Among them was Brent Scowcroft, who was national security advisor to Bush's father, George H. Bush, when he was president from 1989 to 1993. He argued in a column in the Washington Post *on May 11 that "an active struggle is underway to determine the future course of Iran" and that a U.S. signal of a desire for improved relations "might provide encouragement and impetus to reformers and the people who so eagerly seek change." As a possible signal, Scowcroft suggested that Congress allow a 1996 law requiring U.S. economic sanctions against Iran and Libya to lapse when it expired later in 2001. Khatami might be a "weak reed," Scowcroft acknowledged, but "he is the symbol of reform and the only such symbol available."*

The Bush administration took a modest step toward Scowcroft's suggestion, urging Congress during the summer to extend the 1996 Iran-Libya sanctions law for just two years, rather than for another five years. Congress refused that request, which was adamantly opposed by the influential pro-Israel lobby on Capitol Hill. However, Congress did continue a provision that allowed the president to waive the sanctions if he determined that doing so was in the U.S. "national interest." Bush had said that he did not plan to lift sanctions "any time soon."

Attitudes began to shift slightly after September 11, but both sides found it difficult to move much beyond the confrontational postures of the previous two decades. The first move came from Iran when officials there expressed condolences for the thousands who had died and strongly condemned the terrorist attacks. Ayatollah Khamenei denounced "the killing of innocent people" but repeated standard Iranian rhetoric against U.S. support for Israel and other forms of "interference" in the Middle East. The Bush administration reportedly thanked Iran for the condolences and asked if the government would be willing to join in the U.S.-led war against terrorism that Bush announced on September 20. Such a step proved to be too much for Khamenei, who responded on September 26 that "Iran will not participate in any move under U.S. leadership."

Khamenei returned to the hard-line rhetoric in November, issuing a blunt attack on those in Iran who might advocate improving relations with the

United States; anyone holding such views was "unfit for office," he said. This was seen as a direct warning to Khatami, who was about to travel to New York for the opening session of the UN General Assembly. Even so, Khatami made numerous statements while in New York that clearly were intended to improve Iran's image among Americans, including sharp denunciations of bin Laden and others who took an "extremist, narrow-minded approach to religion." In an address to the General Assembly on November 9, Khatami referred repeatedly to the September 11 terrorist attacks, which he said were carried out by a "cult of fanatics who had self-mutilated their ears and tongues, and could only communicate with perceived opponents through carnage and destruction." Khatami's speech was the keynote address of a special meeting called the "Dialogue of Civilizations," which he had proposed as a means of getting world leaders to listen to one another.

Other steps by Khatami's government appeared to be intended to send a positive signal to the United States and probably had at least tacit approval from Khamenei, according to many analysts. One such step was a dinner meeting in November between Iran's ambassador to the United Nations, Hadi Nejad Hosseinian, and several members of Congress. Another was the attendance by Iranian foreign minister Khamal Kharrzi at a UN-sponsored meeting on November 12 of six countries, including the United States, that for several years had held periodic, but fruitless, talks about peace in Afghanistan. Yet another step was a speech delivered by Hosseinian on December 17 to a conference in New York of the American Iranian Council, a group that had promoted improved relations between the two countries. While couched in delicate diplomatic language, Hosseinian's speech was an unmistakable call for the United States to respond positively to the Iranian condemnation of the September 11 terrorist attacks. Hosseinian said the Clinton administration's had made a "good start" toward improving relations between the two countries in 2000 "and we need to build upon what we achieved then."

Iran and Terrorism

From Washington's perspective the main obstacle to improved relations between the United States and Iran was Iran's long history of supporting and encouraging terrorist movements that targeted Israel and U.S. interests in the Middle East. In particular, administrations since the presidency of Ronald Reagan had accused Iran of providing money and weapons to Hezbollah, the radical Shiite group in Lebanon said to be responsible for bombings in 1983 that killed several hundred American, British, and French servicemen and diplomats. Hezbollah had since become a major political force in Lebanon, while at the same time mounting frequent attacks against Israel. In 1996 Secretary of State Warren Christopher cited U.S. intelligence information indicating that Iran subsidized Hezbollah with about $100 million annually.

The 1996 bombing of the Khobar towers apartment complex housing U.S. servicemen in Saudi Arabia created another source of friction. Nine-

teen servicemen died and five hundred people were wounded in that attack, which senior officials in the Clinton administration attributed to Hezbollah. After an investigation lasting nearly five years, a federal grand jury in June indicted thirteen Saudi Arabian citizens and one Lebanese on charges of organizing and carrying out the bombing. The indictment referred to Iranian government involvement, but no Iranians were indicted. Attorney General John Ashcroft said elements within the Iranian government had "inspired, supported, and supervised" those who carried out the bombing. (Khobar towers bombing, Historic Documents of 1996, p. 672)

Condoleezza Rice, Bush's national security advisor, repeated that charge in a December 20, 2001, interview with the Arabic newspaper al-Hayat. *"When we questioned those who carried out the explosion in the Khobar complex, they clearly mentioned training and finance provided by Iran," she said. For that and other reasons, she added, Washington had a "major problem" with Iran's support for terrorist activities "against the United States and in the Middle East."*

Although the United States repeatedly charged that Iran was continuing to foment radical Palestinian resistance to Israel through Hezbollah, Washington had not accused Iran of sponsoring any subsequent terrorist acts against the United States since Khatami's election in 1997. Moreover, annual reports on terrorism issued by the State Department attributed Tehran's support for Hezbollah to the Iranian Revolutionary Guard and the Ministry of Intelligence and Security—both of which were controlled by Khamenei's hard-line religious factions, not by Khatami's government.

U.S. officials in late 2001 suggested that Iran was not involved in the September 11 attacks against the United States or with the al Qaeda terrorist network that Bush said was responsible. The New York Times *reported on December 31 that U.S. intelligence information showed that aides to bin Laden during the mid-1990s had solicited help from Iran but apparently had been rebuffed. The* Times *quoted an unidentified U.S. official as saying that there was "no credible evidence" of any cooperation between Iran and bin Laden's al Qaeda network. At least on the surface, there were significant differences between the Iranian government, dominated by Shiite Muslims, and al Qaeda, which represented a movement among radical Sunni Muslims. Moreover, Iran had strongly opposed the Taliban regime in neighboring Afghanistan, which had harbored bin Laden and his al Qaeda network since 1996.*

> *Following are excerpts from a speech delivered to the United Nations General Assembly on November 9, 2001, by Mohammad Khatami, the president of Iran. Khatami spoke as part of a special General Assembly program called "Dialogue Among Civilizations," which he had proposed.*
>
> **The document was obtained from the Internet at http://www.un.int/Iran/dialogue/2001/articles/2.html.**

In the circle of those who cherished rational thinking, twenty five hundred years before this, Socrates would employ the method of dialogue to discuss philosophical questions. Those who, unlike the philosophers, felt less love for wisdom and yet showed more passion to grab it in their possession, i.e. the sophists, did all they could to defeat Socrates, and when his life was found to contradict their interests and credibility, they eventually had him put to death. The call to dialogue, however, did not die with Socrates. Inside places of learning, places of worship, as well as in forums on world politics and culture, we can still hear Socrates inviting us to dialogue. That appeal transcends realms of formal learning and philosophy, for Socrates was more than a philosopher. He was indeed a great mentor of morality and a master of culture and politics.

It is precisely for this reason that dialogue presupposes and embodies a principled moral discipline of culture and politics. Today, as in ancient centuries, engagement in dialogue requires wisdom, discipline and good will. Today, as then, any exclusive claim to absolute truth needs to be relinquished. Truth, as absolute as it essentially is, should drive us in light of its true unity not only to recognize plurality in human culture, religion, language and color, but also to embrace this variety as a unique opportunity for establishing peace, freedom and justice in our world. For this we would need to put an end to playing deaf. Devastating wars have always erupted when some party has refused to listen to what others have had to say.

When Iran proposed the idea of Dialogue among Civilization in the General Assembly of the United Nations, few foresaw how soon this proposal could prove so instrumental in saving the world from an imminent war of carnage and devastation. The horrific terrorist attacks of September 11th, 2001 in the United States were perpetrated by a cult of fanatics who had self-mutilated their ears and tongues, and could only communicate with perceived opponents through carnage and devastation.

The perception of a need for revenge coupled with a misplaced sense of might could lead to failure to hear the calls of people of good will or the cries of children, women and the elderly in Afghanistan: a people whose share in life has been no more than to suffer a prolonged death in the shadow of perpetual horror, hunger and disease.

In the opening years of the twentieth century, some prominent political thinkers had rightly prophesied the imminence of a century of war and revolution. This was later attributed to the escalation of violence in the twentieth century: and violence was seen as the common characteristic shared by both wars and revolutions. War of course is always concomitant with violence. But it would be incorrect to identify all revolutions with violence. One could cite examples of revolutions based on the very renunciation of violence. Apt consideration of the liberation movement in India should suffice to patently rebut the universality of the mentioned claim. The Islamic Revolution in Iran, which in a sense re-breathed the soul of morality into the body of politics, was also a revolution that faced fired bullets with flower stems, and did not exclusively combat its opponents with retaliation and revenge. Eventually, it was our revolution and the government emerging from it which in the closing years of the twentieth century proposed the idea of Dialogue among Civilizations to the United Nations. . . .

Regrettably, the dawn of this new millennium has turned out bloody and filled with gloom. The apparatus of terror and violence never seized [ceased] a moment. A most brutal and appalling crime has been perpetrated against American civilians. In the name of the people and the government of the Islamic Republic of Iran, I have firmly and unequivocally condemned that inhuman and anti-Islamic act of terror. I have already asked the Secretary General of the United Nations to bring together heads of states to set an agenda for combating terrorism, and to unify international political will in uprooting this evil phenomenon. This juncture in time provides the most opportune time to reflect upon the causes and means of this catastrophe.

In our world today, the issue of political seclusion, transgresses the boundaries of morality, and falls into the realm of impossibility. All cultures, civilizations and faiths are now bound to co-habit the same world by the inviolable verdict of technology. It is therefore the best of times to bring harmony and foster empathy amidst this variety. A rare opportunity has now presented itself, which could either lead to interminable war, or to enduring peace and compassion among human societies.

Terrorism is begotten through the ominous combination of blind fanaticism with brute force, and it always serves a systematized illusion. In spite of the propaganda it utilizes and the nomenclature it employs, terrorism is nothing more than a projection of destructive forces of the human unconscious.

Should human beings be deprived of compassion, and be divested of morality, religious spirituality, sense of aesthetics, and the ability to engage in poetic visualization, and should they be incapable of experiencing death and destruction through artistic creativity, then horrendous hidden forces of the unconscious should wreak havoc, death and devastation upon the world of humanity.

Whoever chooses to reduce religion, art or science into destructive weapons, bears no other than an inimical relationship to them.

In the intellectual world of Iran and Islam, magnificent achievements attained in the realm of literature are all deeply rooted in the rich resources of divine revelation and Islamic tradition. For instance such an understanding of tradition would be expressed by a Muslim mystic saying, "From the East to the West, should any one man be hurt by a thorn in his finger or by a stone in his way, I shall feel the pain. Any heart encumbered with chagrin, my heart would share the burden." In the same way, the essence of religious spiritually is expressed by a poet writing in tradition of Zen: "Should I have a black cloak as befitting as it should be, I would have covered all the needy of the world." Human beings are capable of unbounded love, as the Gospels present love of human neighbors on par with the love of God. The Upanishads [ancient Hindu texts] teach that the human soul, the lily of the heart, grows from the soil out of which all humans have been created. Precisely for the homogeneity of this common soil, which refuses to be molded by politics and geography, empathic dialogue among human beings is possible.

A Manichean [a school of thought deriving from the ancient Persian philosopher Manes, who divided the world into "good" and "evil"] perspective on world geopolitics which dualistically assumes one region to be the source of light and the other to be the source of darkness would lead to appalling political and security consequences. The long-known device of "making enemies" is a product of paranoid illusion, but its products are real and do not remain illusory.

Another question still remains to be elaborated, and that is to inquire in what soil would the seed of enmity and making of enemies grow and produce such unpalatable fruit. It is evident that the seed of infinite enmity grows well wherever infinite injustice is entrenched and begets utter despair and frustration.

Politicians and military generals could simply attribute the recent catastrophe in the United States as well as all terrorist atrocities and casualties in various regions to the evil deeds of a certain state, group or religion. Yet this would simply amount to evading the question, not answering it. The correct answer to this question like that of many other correct answers in philosophy and politics, has a long history. Having a long history in and of itself, however, does not provide a remedy. We can only hope to learn a new lesson from an old answer if we should prepare ourselves to accept the verdict of fairness and justice.

Injustice is neither unprecedented nor confined to particular communities. However, when injustice accumulates so much as it engenders despair and frustration, it turns into an explosive brew. Only when people are deprived of a right to life—merely life in the sense of survival and not even a good life of quality—they could become capable of perpetrating crimes to which they are the first victims. People should not be led into utter despair. I do not mean this merely as a humanitarian advice, but as a precondition for social and political coexistence in a world in which our fates are inevitably intertwined. Even for those of us who have lost the capacity to have compassion for "others," and their motivation drives from self-love and an urge to survive, it remains imperative not to push others into the dark realm of frustration. A frustrated person may choose death as the only remedy of his predicament: death of himself and death of others. At least part of our minds and hearts need to be set free from the clench of instrumental and utilitarian reason and be opened up to moral rationality and altruistic reason. Thereby having compassion for others should become attainable. Let us have compassion not only for ourselves but also for the others. Let us have compassion for the others within their own idiosyncratic realms. Having compassion for others should not coerce them to assimilate within us, or to succumb to our values. Compassion should come unconditionally. The only condition is a mutual agreement to refrain from atrocity and violence.

Let us welcome any plea to refrain from violence and to embrace compassion. Let us welcome any call that prefers the voice of humanity over and above the noise of explosions. Let us welcome any party that invites us not to racism but to respecting the human race. Let us respect the fundamental right of all parties to existence.

Moral rationality, heartfelt compassion for others, and the ability to share in both the sufferings as well as the happiness of other peoples, have so far managed to sustain our world. Let us breathe into the solemn and dry body of politics the soul of morality and ethics, thereby making it humane. When it comes to enmity and revenge, let us be as inclined to remember as a mirror. A tall clean truthful mirror can reflect to infinity the beauties of our own and of the others. It is unwise to shatter the mirror.

BRITISH GOVERNMENT ON OSAMA BIN LADEN
November 14, 2001

Osama bin Laden, a soft-spoken Saudi Arabian exile said to be the leader of the world's largest terrorist network, in 2001 became the man most hated by Americans since Adolph Hitler. President George W. Bush accused bin Laden and his network known as al Qaeda ("the Base" in Arabic) of sponsoring the September 11 terrorist attacks that killed approximately 3,000 people in New York and Washington. Bush launched a large-scale military campaign in Afghanistan to destroy al Qaeda and the Taliban government that gave it safe haven. That military effort, backed directly or indirectly by Great Britain and about two dozen other countries, quickly disrupted al Qaeda and drove the Taliban from power. But as of the end of the year bin Laden and most of his senior associates remained at large. (Terrorist attacks, p. 614; war in Afghanistan, p. 686)

While feared and reviled in the United States and much of the West, bin Laden was widely considered a hero in much of the Islamic world. Bin Laden used his personal wealth and apparent organizational skills to oppose U.S. influence in the Middle East, in particular the large U.S. military presence in Saudi Arabia (the birthplace of Islam) and Washington's backing for the Jewish state of Israel. In several videotapes broadcast around the world before and after the September 11 attacks, bin Laden called for an Islamic uprising against the United States, which he said had brought "humiliation and disgrace" to the Islamic world. Such urgings failed to produce the widespread anti-U.S. tumult bin Laden sought, but they did find a receptive audience among millions of Arabs and other Muslims, many of whom refused to believe U.S. accusations that bin Laden was behind the September 11 attacks.

Attempting to persuade world opinion on the question of bin Laden's guilt, the British government issued two reports detailing some of the evidence against him. One of the reports included comments attributed to bin Laden in an October 20 videotape claiming responsibility for the attacks and bragging about their success.

For its part, the Bush administration switched tactics in its treatment of bin Laden three times during the year. In the spring, shortly after taking office, administration officials reportedly decided that the prior Clinton administration had made a mistake in focusing on bin Laden personally as a terrorist mastermind; that approach was said to have helped make bin Laden a hero among millions of Muslims disenchanted with U.S. policies in the Middle East. But after the September 11 attacks, officials from Bush on down returned to a policy of demonizing bin Laden, calling him "evil" and making it clear that the United States would not relent until it had destroyed him and his terrorist network. Bush himself used Wild West rhetoric to say that he wanted bin Laden "dead or alive." Late in the year, when the United States was frustrated in its attempt to capture or kill bin Laden during the war in Afghanistan, the administration once again played down his personal significance and argued that the important goal was eliminating his network's ability to conduct terrorism.

Born in 1957, bin Laden was the seventeenth of twenty-four sons of Mohammed bin Oud bin Laden, a Yemeni who emigrated to Saudi Arabia in 1932 and built the country's largest construction firm. As a young man, Osama bin Laden fought with rebels opposed to the Soviet Union's occupation of Afghanistan. In 1988 he and a group of Egyptians founded al Qaeda, with the dedicated mission of waging holy war against those who opposed Islam. Saudi Arabia revoked bin Laden's citizenship in 1994, when he was living in Sudan and using his inherited wealth to run several companies and to develop the al Qaeda network. The United States pressured Sudan into expelling bin Laden in 1996, and he moved his al Qaeda operations to Afghanistan. There he provided financial support for the Taliban regime and, in return, was given free rein to establish terrorist training camps.

Embassy Bombing Convictions

An important window into the world of al Qaeda had been opened during a lengthy trial in New York of four men accused of plotting the 1998 bombings of U.S. embassies in Nairobi, Kenya, and Dar es Salaam, Tanzania. The bombings killed 224 people and injured nearly 5,000 others; the vast majority of the victims were Africans. (Bombings, Historic Documents of 1998, p. 555)

A federal jury convicted all four defendants on a total of 302 counts related to the bombings. Two of the men—Mohamed Rashed Daoud al 'Owali, a Saudi Arabian, and Khalfan Khamis Mohamed, a Tanzanian—were found guilty of murder and could have faced the death penalty. But the jury deadlocked on the question of whether to impose that penalty, and so they were sentenced to life in prison without the possibility of parole. Two other men found guilty of lesser crimes in connection with the embassy bombings also were sentenced to life in prison without parole: Mohamed Sadeek Odeh, a Jordanian, and Wadih El-Hage, a naturalized U.S. citizen born in Lebanon. Both were convicted of conspiring to kill Americans and related charges.

Three other men indicted in the case—two Egyptians and one Saudi

Arabian—had been arrested in Great Britain in 1998 and had fought extradition to the United States. A court composed of five members of the House of Lords voted on December 17 to order them sent to the United States to stand trial. Thirteen other men, including bin Laden, also had been indicted on charges related to the embassy bombings but remained at large. The Clinton administration had offered a $5 million reward for information leading to bin Laden's capture and conviction in the case.

Much of the evidence in the New York trial came from the testimony of two men who said they had been part of al Qaeda for years but had defected before the embassy bombings. Jamal Ahmed Fadl, from Sudan, and L'Houssaine Kherchtou, from Morocco, described al Qaeda training camps and other operations in Afghanistan, Pakistan, Sudan, and other countries. Neither man worked closely with bin Laden, but both claimed to have had some direct dealings with him and his top aides. Among other things, the two men described how senior al Qaeda members frequently carried large sums of cash—in some cases $100,000 or more—to finance weapons purchases and other operations. Fadl described numerous al Qaeda attempts to buy components for chemical or nuclear weapons, but he offered no direct evidence that the group had succeeded in that quest. Experts said testimony and evidence used in the trial indicated that al Qaeda was a organization with cells in many countries but little central direction.

The convictions marked the fourth time that the U.S. government had successfully prosecuted defendants in cases involving actual or planned foreign terrorist attacks against U.S. targets during the 1990s. In 1997 a federal jury in New York found five men guilty on charges related to the 1993 bombing of the World Trade Center. In that case a truck bomb was exploded in a parking garage beneath the trade center; six people died and more than 1,000 were wounded. U.S. officials did not link bin Laden and al Qaeda directly to the 1993 bombing, although one of those convicted was said to have possessed an al Qaeda training manual. The key figure convicted in that case was Ramzi Yousef. In 1996 prosecutors secured the conviction of Sheik Omar Abdul Rahman, an Egyptian living in the United States, on charges of plotting to blow up New York's Lincoln Tunnel and other landmarks.

In April 2001 a jury in New York convicted Ahmed Ressam, an Algerian, of conspiring to bomb Los Angeles International Airport during the height of millennium celebrations in December 1999. Ressam had been arrested as he crossed into the United States at Port Angeles, Washington, carrying explosives. Prosecutors in the case insisted that Ressam's actions were part of a broader plot, orchestrated by bin Laden's organization, to attack high-profile targets in the United States during the millennium celebrations. Two other Algerians were convicted of helping Ressam, and a third was indicted on charges of serving as a link between bin Laden and Ressam. (Ressam arrest, Historic Documents of 1999, p. 499)

British Report on bin Laden

Shortly after the September 11 attacks, Secretary of State Colin Powell said the United States intended to publish information supporting its case that bin Laden and al Qaeda were responsible. But such a report was not forthcoming; officials later said they did not want to disclose sensitive intelligence information and sources. Instead, British prime minister Tony Blair, who played a leading role in rounding up international support for the U.S. war in Afghanistan, published two extensive reports on bin Laden's role in the September 11 attacks.

In his first report, issued October 4, Blair said there was "absolutely no doubt that bin Laden and his network are responsible" for the September 11 attacks. Citing intelligence information—but without detailing where it came from—the report said a senior aide to bin Laden was in charge of planning the attacks. Further, the report said that three of the nineteen hijackers "have already been positively identified as associates of al Qaeda." The report also provided general information about al Qaeda's alleged involvement in other terrorist attacks, including the Africa embassy bombings and the October 2000 bombing of the USS Cole in Yemen. (Cole attack, p. 3)

Blair's report, along with secret information supplied by the United States, appeared to convince the government of Pakistan, which issued a statement saying the evidence was "sufficient for an indictment" of bin Laden. That statement was considered an important part of the U.S. campaign to convince Islamic nations of bin Laden's guilt. Millions of Muslims reportedly had believed televised rumors that American Jews, possibly in collaboration with the Israeli government, had plotted the attacks and then sought to place the blame on the Islamic world. One common element of these rumors was that several thousand Jews had been warned not to show up for work at the World Trade Center towers on September 11.

Blair issued a second report on November 14, asserting that he had additional evidence linking bin Laden and al Qaeda to the September 11 attacks. Blair said the evidence showed that "the majority" of the hijackers were linked to al Qaeda, and he has insisted that his government had "evidence of a very specific nature relating to the guilt of bin Laden and his associates that is too sensitive to release." Blair's report also included quotations attributed to bin Laden from a videotape reportedly made on October 20. On that tape, according to the report, bin Laden appeared to take credit for the September 11 attacks, saying that "the battle has been moved inside America, and we shall continue until we win the battle, or die in the cause and meet our maker."

Bin Laden Videotapes

The October 20 videotape cited by Blair was just one of several tapes that gave the world a chance to see the planet's most-wanted terrorist explain his cause. In previous years bin Laden had given a handful of interviews to Western and Arabic news organizations, but none had nearly as much impact as did his taped appearances after U.S. and British bombs and missiles started falling on Afghanistan on October 7.

The first tape, aired internationally the day the war began, obviously had been filmed beforehand. It featured bin Laden and three aides at a rocky, remote location. Bin Laden repeatedly taunted the United States, which he said led "the camp of disbelief" against Islam. "Here is America struck by Almighty God in one of its vital organs, so that the greatest buildings are destroyed," he said. "Grace and gratitude to God."

Speaking directly to fellow Muslims, bin Laden offered this case against the United States: "America has been filled with horror from north to south and east to west, and thanks be to God. What America is tasting now is only a copy of what we have tasted. Our Islamic nation has been tasting the same for more than eighty years, of humiliation and disgrace, its sons killed and their blood spilled, its sanctities desecrated." The last sentence referred to Britain's attempts after World War I to establish de facto control over much of the Middle East, including the Arabian peninsula, the home of the most holy sites in the Islamic world.

In another videotape broadcast November 3, bin Laden again sought to convince fellow Muslims that they were the targets of the U.S. war. "This is a matter of religion and creed, it is not what Bush and Blair maintain, that it is a war against terrorism," he said.

Two more videotapes aroused widespread controversy. The first, released by the United States on December 13, was said to show bin Laden boasting about the success of the September 11 attacks. Seated on the floor of a house, possibly in the southern Afghan city of Kandahar, bin Laden described the planning of the attacks on the World Trade Center towers. "We calculated in advance the number of casualties from the enemy, who would be killed based on the position of the tower," bin Laden said, according to a U.S. translation of the tape. Pentagon officials said the tape was found in a house in Jalalabad, Afghanistan. The murky origins of the tape led some critics, especially in Islamic countries, to question its authenticity.

A fourth videotape, aired worldwide on December 27, raised many questions about bin Laden's health. Apparently filmed earlier in December, the tape showed a pale and gaunt bin Laden who kept his entire left side hidden from view—prompting some observers to speculate that he had been wounded in the U.S. bombing of Afghanistan. Bin Laden also seemed more fatalistic than in previous videotapes, mentioning repeatedly that his own fate was unimportant. "Regardless if Osama is killed or survives, the great awakening has started, praise be to God," he said. Bin Laden also praised, with a poem, the nineteen hijackers who carried out the September 11 attacks.

U.S. Attempts to Target bin Laden

Numerous news reports after September 11 offered the public a glimpse into U.S. efforts since the mid-1990s to attack bin Laden's network and even to kill the terrorist leader. After the August 1998 embassy bombings in Africa, Clinton ordered highly publicized air strikes against bin Laden's camps, which caused physical damage but failed to strike bin Laden. But at the same time, according to reports by the New York Times, the Washington Post, and other news organizations, Clinton signed secret directives directing the CIA to attempt to assassinate bin Laden and disrupt his network in any way possible.

According to reports in the Post *on December 19 and 20, 2001, Clinton on three occasions after August 1998 authorized specific CIA attacks on bin Laden, but each mission was aborted because of doubts about the available intelligence information. The* Post *also reported that the CIA recruited forces from Afghanistan and neighboring countries to attack bin Laden but without success.*

Khobar Towers Indictment

Attorney General John Ashcroft announced June 21 that a federal grand jury had indicted fourteen men on charges related to the 1996 bombing of the Khobar Towers apartment building in Saudi Arabia, which housed U.S. servicemen working at the large Dhahran air base. The bombing killed nineteen American servicemen; about 500 people were wounded, including 327 Americans. (Khobar Tower bombings, Historic Documents of 1996, p. 672)

The indictments charged thirteen Saudi Arabians and one Lebanese, all of whom were said to be members of the Iranian-backed group Hezbollah. No Iranians were named in the indictment, which referred vaguely to "Iranian officials" having participated in the bombing plot. U.S. officials had long said that the Iranian government was involved in the bombing, a charge that Iranian representatives adamantly denied. According to the indictments, planning for the bombing began in 1993 and was organized by Ahmed al-Mughassil, said to be a leader of the Saudi branch of Hezbollah. Bin Laden was not named in the indictments because U.S. officials said they had no direct evidence that he or al Qaeda were involved in the Khobar Towers bombing.

Saudi Arabia refused a U.S. request to extradite the thirteen Saudi citizens named in the indictments. On June 30 the Saudi interior minister, Prince Nayef bin Abdel Aziz, said eleven of the men were in custody and would be tried in Saudi Arabian courts but would "never" be handed over to the United States.

> *Following is the text of "Responsibility for the Terrorist Atrocities in the United States, 11 September 2001: An Updated Account," a report released November 14, 2001, by the office of British prime minister Tony Blair.*

> **The document was obtained from the Internet at http:// www.number-10.gov.uk/news.asp?newsID=3025.**

Introduction

1. The clear conclusions reached by the government are:

- Osama Bin Laden and Al Qaeda, the terrorist network which he heads, planned and carried out the atrocities on 11 September 2001;

- Osama Bin Laden and Al Qaeda retain the will and resources to carry out further atrocities;
- the United Kingdom, and United Kingdom nationals are potential targets; and
- Osama Bin Laden and Al Qaeda were able to commit these atrocities because of their close alliance with the Taliban régime, which allowed them to operate with impunity in pursuing their terrorist activity.

2. The material in respect of 1998 and the USS *Cole* comes from indictments and intelligence sources. The material in respect of 11 September comes from intelligence and the criminal investigation to date. The details of some aspects cannot be given, but the facts are clear from the intelligence.

3. The document does not contain the totality of the material known to HMG, given the continuing and absolute need to protect intelligence sources.

Summary

4. The relevant facts show:

Background

- Al Qaeda is a terrorist organisation with ties to a global network, which has been in existence for over 10 years. It was founded, and has been led at all times, by Osama Bin Laden.
- Osama Bin Laden and Al Qaeda have been engaged in a jihad against the United States, and its allies. One of their stated aims is the murder of US citizens, and attacks on America's allies.
- Osama Bin Laden and Al Qaeda have been based in Afghanistan since 1996, but have a network of operations throughout the world. The network includes training camps, warehouses, communication facilities and commercial operations able to raise significant sums of money to support its activity. That activity includes substantial exploitation of the illegal drugs trade from Afghanistan.
- Osama Bin Laden's Al Qaeda and the Taliban régime have a close and mutually dependent alliance. Osama Bin Laden and Al Qaeda provide the Taliban régime with material, financial and military support. They jointly exploit the drugs trade. The Taliban régime allows Bin Laden to operate his terrorist training camps and activities from Afghanistan, protects him from attacks from outside, and protects the drugs stockpiles. Osama Bin Laden could not operate his terrorist activities without the alliance and support of the Taliban régime. The Taliban's strength would be seriously weakened without Osama Bin Laden's military and financial support.
- Osama Bin Laden and Al Qaeda have the capability to execute major terrorist attacks.
- Osama Bin Laden has claimed credit for the attack on US soldiers in Somalia in October 1993, which killed 18; for the attack on the US Embassies in Kenya and Tanzania in August 1998 which killed 224 and injured nearly 5000; and was linked to the attack on the USS Cole on

12 October 2000, in which 17 crew members were killed and 40 others injured.

- They have sought to acquire nuclear and chemical materials for use as terrorist weapons.

In relation to the terrorist attacks on 11 September

5. After 11 September we learned that, not long before, Bin Laden had indicated he was about to launch a major attack on America. The detailed planning for the terrorist attacks of 11 September was carried out by one of OBL's [Osama bin Laden's] close associates. Of the 19 hijackers involved in 11 September 2001, it has been established that the majority had links with Al Qaeda. A senior Bin Laden associate claimed to have trained some of the hijackers in Afghanistan. The attacks on 11 September 2001 were similar in both their ambition and intended impact to previous attacks undertaken by Osama Bin laden and Al Qaeda, and also had features in common. In particular:

- Suicide attackers
- Co-ordinated attacks on the same day
- The aim to cause maximum American casualties
- Total disregard for other casualties, including Muslim
- Meticulous long-term planning
- Absence of warning.

6. Al Qaeda retains the capability and the will to make further attacks on the US and its allies, including the United Kingdom.

7. Al Qaeda gives no warning of terrorist attack.

The Facts

Osama Bin Laden and Al Qaeda

8. In 1989 Osama Bin Laden, and others, founded an international terrorist group known as "Al Qaeda" (the Base). At all times he has been the leader of Al Qaeda.

9. From 1989 until 1991 Osama Bin Laden was based in Afghanistan and Peshawar, Pakistan. In 1991 he moved to Sudan, where he stayed until 1996. In that year he returned to Afghanistan, where he remains.

The Taliban Régime

10. The Taliban emerged from the Afghan refugee camps in Pakistan in the early 1990s. By 1996 they had captured Kabul. They are still engaged in a bloody civil war to control the whole of Afghanistan. They are led by Mullah Omar.

11. In 1996 Osama Bin Laden moved back to Afghanistan. He established a close relationship with Mullah Omar, and threw his support behind the Taliban. Osama Bin Laden and the Taliban régime have a close alliance on which both depend for their continued existence. They also share the same religious values and vision.

12. Osama Bin Laden has provided the Taliban régime with troops, arms

and money to fight the Northern Alliance. He is closely involved with Taliban military training, planning and operations. He has representatives in the Taliban military command structure. He has also given infrastructure assistance and humanitarian aid. Forces under the control of Osama Bin Laden have fought alongside the Taliban in the civil war in Afghanistan.

13. Omar has provided Bin Laden with a safe haven in which to operate, and has allowed him to establish terrorist training camps in Afghanistan. They jointly exploit the Afghan drugs trade. In return for active Al Qaeda support, the Taliban allow Al Qaeda to operate freely, including planning, training and preparing for terrorist activity. In addition the Taliban provide security for the stockpiles of drugs.

14. Since 1996, when the Taliban captured Kabul, the United States government has consistently raised with them a whole range of issues, including humanitarian aid and terrorism. Well before 11 September 2001 they had provided evidence to the Taliban of the responsibility of Al Qaeda for the terrorist attacks in East Africa. This evidence had been provided to senior leaders of the Taliban at their request.

15. The United States government had made it clear to the Taliban régime that Al Qaeda had murdered US citizens, and planned to murder more. The US offered to work with the Taliban to expel the terrorists from Afghanistan. These talks, which have been continuing since 1996, have failed to produce any results.

16. In June 2001, in the face of mounting evidence of the Al Qaeda threat, the United States warned the Taliban that it had the right to defend itself and that it would hold the régime responsible for attacks against US citizens by terrorists sheltered in Afghanistan.

17. In this, the United States had the support of the United Nations. The Security Council, in Resolution 1267, condemned Osama Bin Laden for sponsoring international terrorism and operating a network of terrorist camps, and demanded that the Taliban surrender Osama Bin Laden without further delay so that he could be brought to justice.

18. Despite the evidence provided by the US of the responsibility of Osama Bin Laden and Al Qaeda for the 1998 East Africa bombings, despite the accurately perceived threats of further atrocities, and despite the demands of the United Nations, the Taliban régime responded by saying no evidence existed against Osama Bin Laden, and that neither he nor his network would be expelled.

19. A former Government official in Afghanistan has described the Taliban and Osama Bin Laden as "two sides of the same coin: Osama cannot exist in Afghanistan without the Taliban and the Taliban cannot exist without Osama."

Al Qaeda

20. Al Qaeda is dedicated to opposing "un-Islamic" governments in Muslim countries with force and violence.

21. Al Qaeda virulently opposes the United States. Osama Bin Laden has urged and incited his followers to kill American citizens, in the most unequivocal terms.

22. On 12 October 1996 he issued a declaration of jihad as follows:

"The people of Islam have suffered from aggression, iniquity and injustice imposed by the Zionist-Crusader alliance and their collaborators. . . .

It is the duty now on every tribe in the Arabian peninsula to fight jihad and cleanse the land from these Crusader occupiers. Their wealth is booty to those who kill them.

My Muslim brothers: your brothers in Palestine and in the land of the two Holy Places [Saudi Arabia] are calling upon your help and asking you to take part in fighting against the enemy—the Americans and the Israelis. They are asking you to do whatever you can to expel the enemies out of the sanctities of Islam."

Later in the same year he said that

"terrorising the American occupiers [of Islamic Holy Places] is a religious and logical obligation."

In February 1998 he issued and signed a "fatwa" which included a decree to all Muslims:

". . . the killing of Americans and their civilian and military allies is a religious duty for each and every Muslim to be carried out in whichever country they are until Al Aqsa mosque has been liberated from their grasp and until their armies have left Muslim lands."

In the same "fatwa" he called on Muslim scholars and their leaders and their youths to

"launch an attack on the American soldiers of Satan"

and concluded:

"We—with God's help—call on every Muslim who believes in God and wishes to be rewarded to comply with God's order to kill Americans and plunder their money whenever and wherever they find it. We also call on Muslims . . . to launch the raid on Satan's US troops and the devil's supporters allying with them, and to displace those who are behind them."

When asked, in 1998, about obtaining chemical or nuclear weapons he said "acquiring such weapons for the defence of Muslims [is] a religious duty", and made the following claim in an interview printed in the Pakistan newspaper *Dawn* in November 2001:

"I wish to declare that if America used chemical or nuclear weapons against us, then we may retort with chemical and nuclear weapons. We have the weapons as deterrent."

In an interview aired on Al Jazira (Doha, Qatar) television he stated:

"Our enemy is every American male, whether he is directly fighting us or paying taxes."

In two interviews broadcast on US television in 1997 and 1998 he referred to the terrorists who carried out the earlier attack on the World Trade Center in 1993 as "role models." He went on to exhort his followers "to take the fighting to America."

23. From the early 1990s Osama Bin Laden has sought to obtain nuclear and chemical materials for use as weapons of terror.

24. Although US targets are Al Qaeda's priority, it also explicitly threatens the United States' allies. References to "Zionist-Crusader alliance and their collaborators", and to "Satan's US troops and the devil's supporters allying with them" are references which unquestionably include the United Kingdom. This is confirmed by more specific references in a broadcast of 13 October, during which Bin Laden's spokesman said:

> *"Al Qaeda declares that Bush Sr, Bush Jr, Clinton, Blair and Sharon are the arch-criminals from among the Zionists and Crusaders. . . . Al Qaeda stresses that the blood of those killed will not go to waste, God willing, until we punish these criminals. . . . We also say and advise the Muslims in the United States and Britain . . . not to travel by plane. We also advise them not to live in high-rise buildings and towers."*

25. There is a continuing threat. Based on our experience of the way the network has operated in the past, other cells, like those that carried out the terrorist attacks on 11 September, must be assumed to exist.

26. Al Qaeda functions both on its own and through a network of other terrorist organisations. These include Egyptian Islamic Jihad and other north African Islamic extremist terrorist groups, and a number of other jihadi groups in other countries including the Sudan, Yemen, Somalia, Pakistan and India. Al Qaeda also maintains cells and personnel in a number of other countries to facilitate its activities.

27. Osama Bin Laden heads the Al Qaeda network. Below him is a body known as the Shura, which includes representatives of other terrorist groups, such as Egyptian Islamic Jihad leader Ayman Zawahiri and prominent lieutenants of Bin Laden such as Mohamed Atef (also known as Abu Hafs Al-Masri). Egyptian Islamic Jihad has, in effect, merged with Al Qaeda.

28. In addition to the Shura, Al Qaeda has several groups dealing with military, media, financial and Islamic issues.

29. Mohamed Atef is a member of the group that deals with military and terrorist operations. His duties include principal responsibility for training Al Qaeda members.

30. Members of Al Qaeda must make a pledge of allegiance to follow the orders of Osama Bin Laden.

31. A great deal of evidence about Osama Bin Laden and Al Qaeda has been made available in the US indictment for earlier crimes.

32. Since 1989, Osama Bin Laden has conducted substantial financial and business transactions on behalf of Al Qaeda and in pursuit of its goals. These include purchasing land for training camps, purchasing warehouses for the storage of items, including explosives, purchasing communications and electronics equipment, and transporting currency and weapons to members of Al Qaeda and associated terrorist groups in countries throughout the world.

33. Since 1989 Osama Bin Laden has provided training camps and guest

houses in Afghanistan, Pakistan, the Sudan, Somalia and Kenya for the use of Al Qaeda and associated terrorist groups. We know from intelligence that there are currently at least a dozen camps across Afghanistan, of which at least four are used for training terrorists.

34. Since 1989, Osama Bin Laden has established a series of businesses to provide income for Al Qaeda, and to provide cover for the procurement of explosives, weapons and chemicals, and for the travel of Al Qaeda operatives. The businesses have included a holding company known as "Wadi Al Aqiq," a construction business known as "Al Hijra," an agricultural business known as "Al Themar Al Mubaraka," and investment companies known as "Ladin International" and "Taba Investments."

Osama Bin Laden and previous attacks

35. In 1992 and 1993 Mohamed Atef travelled to Somalia on several occasions for the purpose of organising violence against United States and United Nations troops then stationed in Somalia. On each occasion he reported back to Osama Bin Laden, at his base in the Riyadh district of Khartoum.

36. In the spring of 1993 Atef, Saif al Adel, another senior member of Al Qaeda, and other members began to provide military training to Somali tribes for the purpose of fighting the United Nations forces.

37. On 3 and 4 October 1993 operatives of Al Qaeda participated in the attack on US military personnel serving in Somalia as part of the operation "Restore Hope." Eighteen US military personnel were killed in the attack.

38. From 1993 members of Al Qaeda began to live in Nairobi and set up businesses there, including Asma Ltd, and Tanzanite King. They were regularly visited there by senior members of Al Qaeda, in particular by Atef and Abu Ubadiah al Banshiri.

39. Beginning in the latter part of 1993, members of Al Qaeda in Kenya began to discuss the possibility of attacking the US Embassy in Nairobi in retaliation for US participation in Operation Restore Hope in Somalia. Ali Mohamed, a US citizen and admitted member of Al Qaeda, surveyed the US Embassy as a possible target for a terrorist attack. He took photographs and made sketches, which he presented to Osama Bin Laden while Bin Laden was in Sudan. He also admitted that he had trained terrorists for Al Qaeda in Afghanistan in the early 1990s, and that those whom he trained included many involved in the East African bombings in August 1998.

40. In June or July 1998, two Al Qaeda operatives, Fahid Mohammed Ali Msalam and Sheik Ahmed Salim Swedan, purchased a Toyota truck and made various alterations to the back of the truck.

41. In early August 1998, operatives of Al Qaeda gathered in 43, New Runda Estates, Nairobi to execute the bombing of the US Embassy in Nairobi.

42. On 7 August 1998, Assam, a Saudi national and Al Qaeda operative, drove the Toyota truck to the US Embassy. There was a large bomb in the back of the truck.

43. Also in the truck was Mohamed Rashed Daoud Al 'Owali, another Saudi. He, by his own confession, was an Al Qaeda operative, who from about 1996 had been trained in Al Qaeda camps in Afghanistan in explosives, hijacking,

kidnapping, assassination and intelligence techniques. With Osama Bin Laden's express permission, he fought alongside the Taliban in Afghanistan. He had met Osama Bin Laden personally in 1996 and asked for another "mission." Osama Bin Laden sent him to East Africa after extensive specialised training at camps in Afghanistan.

44. As the truck approached the Embassy, Al 'Owali got out and threw a stun grenade at a security guard. Assam drove the truck up to the rear of the Embassy. He got out and then detonated the bomb, which demolished a multi-storey secretarial college and severely damaged the US Embassy, and the Co-operative bank building. The bomb killed 213 people and injured 4500. Assam was killed in the explosion.

45. Al 'Owali expected the mission to end in his death. He had been willing to die for Al Qaeda. But at the last minute he ran away from the bomb truck and survived. He had no money, passport or plan to escape after the mission, because he had expected to die.

46. After a few days, he called a telephone number in Yemen to have money transferred to him in Kenya. The number he rang in Yemen was contacted by Osama Bin Laden's phone on the same day as Al 'Owali was arranging to get the money.

47. Another person arrested in connection with the Nairobi bombing was Mohamed Sadeek Odeh. He admitted to his involvement. He identified the principal participants in the bombing. He named three other persons, all of whom were Al Qaeda or Egyptian Islamic Jihad members.

48. In Dar es Salaam the same day, at about the same time, operatives of Al Qaeda detonated a bomb at the US Embassy, killing 11 people. The Al Qaeda operatives involved included Mustafa Mohamed Fadhil and Khaflan Khamis Mohamed. The bomb was carried in a Nissan Atlas truck, which Ahmed Khfaklan Ghailani and Sheikh Ahmed Salim Swedan, two Al Qaeda operatives, had purchased in July 1998, in Dar es Salaam.

49. Khaflan Khamis Mohamed was arrested for the bombing. He admitted membership of Al Qaeda, and implicated other members of Al Qaeda in the bombing.

50. On 7 and 8 August 1998, two other members of Al Qaeda disseminated claims of responsibility for the two bombings by sending faxes to media organisations in Paris, Doha in Qatar, and Dubai in the United Arab Emirates.

51. Additional evidence of the involvement of Al Qaeda in the East African bombings came from a search conducted in London of several residences and businesses belonging to Al Qaeda and Egyptian Islamic Jihad members. In those searches a number of documents were found including claims of responsibility for the East African bombings in the name of a fictitious group, "the Islamic Army for the liberation of the Holy Places."

52. Al 'Owali, the would-be suicide bomber, admitted he was told to make a videotape of himself using the name of the same fictitious group.

53. The faxed claims of responsibility were traced to a telephone number, which had been in contact with Osama Bin Laden's cell phone. The claims disseminated to the press were clearly written by someone familiar with the con-

spiracy. They stated that the bombings had been carried out by two Saudis in Kenya, and one Egyptian in Dar es Salaam. They were probably sent before the bombings had even taken place. They referred to two Saudis dying in the Nairobi attack. In fact, because Al 'Owali fled at the last minute, only one Saudi died.

54. On 22 December 1998 Osama Bin Laden was asked by Time magazine whether he was responsible for the August 1998 attacks. He replied:

> *"The International Islamic Jihad Front for the jihad against the US and Israel has, by the grace of God, issued a crystal clear fatwa calling on the Islamic nation to carry on Jihad aimed at liberating the holy sites. The nation of Mohammed has responded to this appeal. If instigation for jihad against the Jews and the Americans . . . is considered to be a crime, then let history be a witness that I am a criminal. Our job is to instigate and, by the grace of God, we did that, and certain people responded to this instigation."*

He was asked if he knew the attackers:

> *". . . those who risked their lives to earn the pleasure of God are real men. They managed to rid the Islamic nation of disgrace. We hold them in the highest esteem."*

And what the US could expect of him:

> *". . . any thief or criminal who enters another country to steal should expect to be exposed to murder at any time. . . . The US knows that I have attacked it, by the grace of God, for more than ten years now. . . . God knows that we have been pleased by the killing of American soldiers [in Somalia in 1993]. This was achieved by the grace of God and the efforts of the mujahideen. . . . Hostility towards America is a religious duty and we hope to be rewarded for it by God. I am confident that Muslims will be able to end the legend of the so-called superpower that is America."*

55. In December 1999 a terrorist cell linked to Al Qaeda was discovered trying to carry out attacks inside the United States. An Algerian, Ahmed Ressam, was stopped at the US-Canadian border, and over 100 lbs [pounds] of bomb-making material was found in his car. Ressam admitted he was planning to set off a large bomb at Los Angeles International airport on New Year's Day. He said that he had received terrorist training at Al Qaeda camps in Afghanistan and then been instructed to go abroad and kill US civilians and military personnel.

56. On 3 January 2000, a group of Al Qaeda members, and other terrorists who had trained in Al Qaeda camps in Afghanistan, attempted to attack a US destroyer with a small boat loaded with explosives. Their boat sank, aborting the attack.

57. On 12 October 2000, however, the USS *Cole* was struck by an explosive-laden boat while refuelling in Aden harbour. Seventeen crew were killed, and 40 injured.

58. Several of the perpetrators of the *Cole* attack (mostly Yemenis and Saudis) were trained at Osama Bin Laden's camps in Afghanistan. Al 'Owali

has identified the two commanders of the attack on the USS *Cole* as having participated in the planning and preparation for the East African Embassy bombings.

59. In the months before the September 11 attacks, propaganda videos were distributed throughout the Middle East and Muslim world by Al Qaeda, in which Osama Bin Laden and others were shown encouraging Muslims to attack American and Jewish targets.

60. Similar videos, extolling violence against the United States and other targets, were distributed before the East African Embassy attacks in August 1998.

Osama Bin Laden and the 11 September attacks

61. Nineteen men have been identified as the hijackers from the passenger lists of the four planes hijacked on 11 September 2001. Many of them had previous links with Al Qaeda or have so far been positively identified as associates of Al Qaeda. An associate of some of the hijackers has been identified as playing key roles in both the East African Embassy attacks and the USS *Cole* attack. Investigations continue into the backgrounds of all the hijackers.

62. From intelligence sources, the following facts have been established subsequent to 11 September; for intelligence reasons, the names of associates, though known, are not given.

- In the run-up to 11 September, Bin Laden was mounting a concerted propaganda campaign amongst like-minded groups of people—including videos and documentation—justifying attacks on Jewish and American targets; and claiming that those who died in the course of them were carrying out God's work.
- We have learned, subsequent to 11 September, that Bin Laden himself asserted shortly before 11 September that he was preparing a major attack on America.
- In August and early September close associates of Bin Laden were warned to return to Afghanistan from other parts of the world by 10 September.
- Immediately prior to 11 September some known associates of Bin Laden were naming the date for action as on or around 11 September.
- A senior associate claimed to have trained some of the hijackers in Afghanistan.
- Since 11 September we have learned that one of Bin Laden's closest and most senior associates was responsible for the detailed planning of the attacks.
- There is evidence of a very specific nature relating to the guilt of Bin Laden and his associates that is too sensitive to release.

63. In addition, Osama Bin Laden has issued a number of public statements since the US strikes on Afghanistan began. The language used in these, while not an open admission of guilt, is self-incriminating.

64. For example, on 7 October he said:

"Here is America struck by God Almighty in one of its vital organs, so that its greatest buildings are destroyed. Grace and gratitude to God. . . . I swear to God that America will not live in peace before peace reigns in Palestine, and before all the army of infidels depart the land of Mohammed, peace by upon him."

65. On 9 October his spokesman praised the "good deed" of the hijackers, who *"transferred the battle into the US heartland."* He warned that the *"storm of plane attacks will not abate."*

66. On 20 October Bin Laden gave an inflammatory interview which has been circulating, in the form of a video, among supporters in the Al Qaeda network. In the transcript, when referring to the US buildings that were attacked, he says:

"It is what we instigated for a while, in self-defence. And it was in revenge for our people killed in Palestine and Iraq. So if avenging the killing of our people is terrorism, let history be a witness that we are terrorists."

Later in the interview he said:

"Bush and Blair . . . don't understand any language but the language of force. Every time they kill us, we will kill them, so the balance of terror can be achieved."

He went on:

"The battle has been moved inside America, and we shall continue until we win this battle, or die in the cause and meet our maker."

He also said:

"The bad terror is what America and Israel are practising against our people, and what we are practising is the good terror that will stop them doing what they are doing."

67. Osama Bin Laden remains in charge, and the mastermind, of Al Qaeda. In Al Qaeda, an operation on the scale of the 11 September attacks would have been approved by Osama Bin Laden himself.

68. The modus operandi of 11 September was entirely consistent with previous attacks. Al Qaeda's record of atrocities is characterised by meticulous long-term planning, a desire to inflict mass casualties, suicide bombers, and multiple simultaneous attacks.

69. The attacks of 11 September 2001 are entirely consistent with the scale and sophistication of the planning which went into the attacks on the East African Embassies and the USS *Cole*. No warnings were given for these three attacks, just as there was none on 11 September.

70. Al Qaeda operatives, in evidence given in the East African Embassy bomb trials, have described how the group spends years preparing for an attack. They conduct repeated surveillance, patiently gather materials, and identify and vet operatives, who have the skills to participate in the attack and the willingness to die for their cause.

71. The operatives involved in the 11 September atrocities attended flight schools, used flight simulators to study the controls of larger aircraft and placed potential airports and routes under surveillance.

72. Al Qaeda's attacks are characterised by total disregard for innocent lives, including Muslims. In an interview after the East African bombings, Osama Bin Laden insisted that the need to attack the United States excused the killing of other innocent civilians, Muslim and non-Muslim alike.

73. No other organisation has both the motivation and the capability to carry out attacks like those of the 11 September—only the Al Qaeda network under Osama Bin Laden.

Conclusion

74. The attacks of the 11 September 2001 were planned and carried out by Al Qaeda, an organisation whose head is Osama Bin Laden. That organisation has the will, and the resources, to execute further attacks of similar scale. Both the United States and its close allies are targets for such attacks. The attack could not have occurred without the alliance between the Taliban and Osama Bin Laden, which allowed Bin Laden to operate freely in Afghanistan, promoting, planning and executing terrorist activity.

COUNCIL OF EUROPE ON ELECTIONS IN KOSOVO
November 18, 2001

Kosovo, the troubled province of Serbia, spent its second full year of being neither a true part of Serbia nor independent of it. As a ward of the United Nations and NATO, Kosovo in 2001 continued in the uncertain status to which it had been relegated following NATO's 1999 air war that freed it from Serbian control. Nearly all of the province's ethnic Albanian Muslim majority clearly wanted official independence from Serbia. But the greater powers that controlled Kosovo's fate—most important being Western Europe and the United States—remained reluctant to allow yet another ministate in the already balkanized Balkans.

Kosovo reached a major landmark on November 18, 2001, when UN-sponsored legislative elections were conducted peacefully and produced a strong, if less than overwhelming, showing by a moderate party. Kosovo's first-ever freely elected, multiethnic assembly took office on December 10. UN Secretary General Kofi Annan, who on that same day received the Nobel Peace Prize, called it a "day of hope" but also noted that Kosovo's new political leaders faced "particularly difficult challenges." The extent of the difficulty was displayed just three days later, when the assembly deadlocked on the choice of a president, forcing a postponement until early in 2002. (Annan peace prize, p. 880; Kosovo war, Historic Documents of 1999, pp. 134, 285, 802; peace-building, Historic Documents of 2000, p. 143)

Confronting Albanian Extremists

NATO had intervened in Kosovo to protect the Albanian majority there from the oppressive military might of Serbia's army and security forces. But by 2000 it was clear that NATO's long-term role would be protecting the small Serbian minority in Kosovo from revenge-seeking Albanian militants. About 90 percent of Kosovo's 1 million people were ethnic Albanian Muslims; most of the rest were ethnic Serbs, who had traditionally controlled the province because it was part of Serbia, which in turn was the dominant partner in the federation of Yugoslavia. A United Nations mission served

*as a political buffer between the two communities, exercising overall control
over management and directing postwar reconstruction of the province.*

*After the NATO war drove Serbian security forces from Kosovo in 1999,
the Albanian guerrilla force that had rebelled against Serbian control—the
Kosovo Liberation Army—officially disbanded, turned its weapons over to
NATO, and was reconstituted under NATO supervision as the provincial police force. But hundreds, and possibly thousands, of former guerrillas had
illegally held on to their weapons and remained a potent threat to stability
in the province. Some of the former guerrillas formed gangs that engaged in
widespread criminal activity for profit; others intimidated Serbs in hopes
of forcing them out of the province. Still others launched attacks, starting
in late 2000, on NATO forces from bases in the supposedly demilitarized
Presevo valley in an adjacent area of Serbia southeast of Kosovo. Then, early
in 2001, some of the Kosovo Albanian guerrillas joined fellow Albanians in
neighboring Macedonia to attack the government there. The outbreak of
guerrilla warfare in Macedonia threatened to plunge the entire region into
ethnic conflict once again; that fighting was headed off, at least for the moment, by the aggressive diplomacy of the European Union, with help from
the United States. (Macedonia, p. 554)*

*In Kosovo both the UN mission and the NATO peacekeeping force often
had been reluctant to confront the former guerrillas directly, apparently
fearing a backlash that could renew the warfare. The northern Kosovo town
of Mitrovica provided the clearest demonstration of the dangers. That
town since late 1999 had effectively been partitioned into Serbian and Albanian sectors, and French peacekeeping forces there had struggled to control repeated instances of violence between the two communities. The worst
violence since the war occurred on February 16, 2001, when a bomb destroyed a bus full of Serbs who were being escorted into the province by
Swedish peacekeepers for a religious observance. Eleven Serbs died in that
incident, which UN and NATO officials attributed to renegade Albanian
guerrillas.*

*In his final day in office, Bernard Kouchner, who had headed the UN mis-
sion since July 1999, pleaded with Albanian leaders to "stop the violence"
against the Serb minority. In a message broadcast throughout the province
on January 13, Kouchner said: "As one friend to another, I want to warn
you that you are in danger. In the eyes of the outside world, the victims, in
a way, have become the oppressors." Kouchner was succeeded by Hans
Haekkerup, a former defense minister of Denmark.*

The U.S. Role

*Hanging over the developments inside Kosovo was the role of the United
States. The new president, George W. Bush, had campaigned in 2000 on a
platform that included withdrawing the United States from international
peacekeeping missions, especially those run by the United Nations but even
NATO missions over which Washington had substantial control. Bush had
also sneered at what he called "nation-building"—the internationally*

funded and managed process of reconstituting places such as Bosnia and Kosovo that had been torn by ethnic, racial, or religious conflict.

As of early 2001 about 5,000 of the 36,000 NATO troops in Kosovo were from the United States. In keeping with Bush's campaign statements, his aides talked about reducing the U.S. troop level in Kosovo (as well as Bosnia), but they took no action to do so. One major reason was that ethnic conflict surfaced early in the year in Macedonia, next door to Kosovo; even those in the Bush administration most opposed to U.S. involvement in peacekeeping missions recognized that a perceived U.S. withdrawal from the region would embolden extremists there. Bush himself visited a large U.S. base in southern Kosovo on July 24 and told cheering American troops that he would not withdraw American forces unilaterally. The NATO peacekeepers "came in together, and we will leave together," Bush said. "Our goal is to hasten the day when peace is self-sustaining, when local democratically elected authorities can assume full responsibility, and when NATO forces can go home."

Elections

For much of the last half of the twentieth century, Kosovo enjoyed a substantial measure of political autonomy, even though it was part of Serbia, and therefore of Yugoslavia. But in 1989 Slobodan Milosevic, a Serbian nationalist who at that time was Serbia's leader, stripped Kosovo of its autonomy and imposed direct rule from Belgrade. Milosevic later became president of Yugoslavia, and he maintained a tight grip on Kosovo through the heavy-handed presence of the police and military.

The UN's plan for elections in 2001 essentially called for a return to autonomy for Kosovo—but with the province still remaining, if only technically, a part of Serbia. The issue put forward insistently by Kosovo's Albanian political leaders, however, was independence, and which faction could claim the best chance of producing it. The UN election plan made no mention of independence, and as of late 2001 there was no evidence that the Security Council, which had the final say, was even close to considering the matter.

The UN had sponsored one successful election in Kosovo, in October 2000, when voters selected municipal leaders. That election had generally been viewed as a victory for the party of moderate Albanian leader Ibrahim Rugova, who during the 1990s had been the mainstream politician leading the charge for independence from Serbia. Representatives of his party, the Democratic League of Kosovo, won about 58 percent of the vote and a majority of council seats in twenty of the twenty-seven cities and towns were voting was held.

The elections in 2001 were for a 120-member assembly, which would in turn elect a president. Under plans drawn up by the United Nations, 20 of the 120 seats in the new assembly were set aside for minorities: 10 for Serbs and 10 for the Roma (Gypsy), Turkish, Bosnian, and other minorities. Most, if not all, of the remaining 100 seats were expected to be won by Albanians.

The voting on November 17, as reported by the Council of Europe, went remarkably smoothly for a province with a recent history of terrible, inter-communal violence. Most encouraging, for the UN mission, was that turn-out was higher than expected among the 100,000 or so Serbs who remained in Kosovo. The 47 percent Serb turnout was below the provincewide level of 65 percent, but it was remarkably high considering that many Serbs feared to go out in public and that the Serbian government in Belgrade had only re-cently encouraged Kosovo Serbs to go to the polls.

Rugova's party won 47 seats, by far the strongest showing of the three main Albanian parties, but not nearly enough to ensure a working major-ity of the assembly. The Democratic Party of Kosovo, headed by former guer-rilla leader Hashim Thaci and generally considered to represent the guerrilla movement, finished second with 26 seats. A coalition of Serbian parties won 22 seats, and other parties took the remaining seats.

The first session of the new assembly was marred when Thaci and his col-leagues walked out to protest a ruling that prevented him from making a speech. More serious was the assembly's failure to elect a president three days later. Rugova could not assemble a majority, in large part because the various factions had not yet learned the difficult work of putting together po-litical compromises. Further negotiations were expected in 2002.

Elections in Bosnia

Bosnia, the deadliest flashpoint in the Balkans during the 1990s, also made some progress during 2001. A key step came on February 22, when a coalition of moderate parties, the Alliance for Change, managed to assemble a government that excluded the hard-line nationalist representatives of the country's three main ethnic communities: the Croats, the Muslims, and the Serbs. (Bosnia background, Historic Documents of 2000, p. 141; Historic Documents of 1995, p. 717)

Bosnia, like Kosovo, had been under the general supervision of a UN mis-sion and a NATO peacekeeping force since a U.S.-brokered peace agreement in 1995 ended three years of brutal ethnic warfare in which tens of thou-sands died. The agreement kept Bosnia as a unified country but with eth-nic-based provinces, a federation headed by Croats and Muslims, and a republic dominated by Serbs. A national government exercised nominal control (under strong UN supervision), but nationalists from each of the three communities had generally dominated the government. Since the late 1990s the single most obstructionist force had been the Croat nationalist party, the Croatian Democratic Union (know as the HDZ).

Elections in November 2000 for Bosnia's parliament had produced mixed results. On the one hand, the various hard-line nationalist parties failed to win a majority of the votes or the seats up for election. But the HDZ was able for months to block the formation of a new government by preventing the election of a moderate Croat as prime minister. That stalemate finally was broken in February, when the parliament elected moderate Croat represen-tatives to that post and other high-level positions. Despite that setback, or perhaps because of it, the Croat nationalists continued to threaten a split of the Croat-majority areas from the rest of Bosnia.

NATO decided in May to reduce its peacekeeping force in Bosnia to 18,000, down from the previous level of 21,000 and from its initial size, in 1995–1996, of 60,000. The U.S. component was set at 3,100, a cut of 500; initially, the United States had 20,000 troops in the NATO force. The Pentagon had been pushing for even deeper reductions in the U.S. role. NATO commander General Joseph Ralston argued successfully, however, that a sizable peacekeeping presence was still needed in Bosnia because of potential instability and that the United States, as the author of the 1995 peace agreement, had an obligation to continue doing its part.

Following are excerpts from statements issued November 18, 2001, by the Council of Europe and the International Election Observation Mission on the successful conduct of parliamentary elections the previous day in Kosovo.

The document was obtained from the Internet at http://www .reliefweb.int/w/rwb.nsf/f303799b16d207428525683000fb3 3f/5230c7908cbda394c1256b0c003f17a7?OpenDocument.

Yesterday's Assembly elections in Kosovo society based on human rights and the rule of law in the aftermath of the 1999 conflict, concluded the International Election Observation Mission in a statement issued in Pristina today.

The joint statement welcomed the peaceful atmosphere of the election period and Election Day itself. It was issued by Roman Jakic MP (Slovenia), on behalf of the Council of Europe Parliamentary Assembly delegation; Doris Pack MEP (Germany), on behalf of the European Parliament delegation; Bruce George MP (UK), on behalf of the OSCE [Organization for Security and Cooperation in Europe] Parliamentary Assembly delegation; and Owen Masters, Head of the Council of Europe Election Observation Mission (CEEOM).

"The people of Kosovo are ready to take a larger part in managing their own affairs. The election opens the way for a better-balanced partnership with the international community," said Doris Pack, head of the European Parliament delegation.

"We understand the difficulties of ethnic Serbs and other communities in Kosovo. It is vital that the new Assembly, as provided for in the Constitutional Framework, should work from the start on a multi-ethnic basis," said Roman Jakic, head of the Council of Europe Parliamentary Assembly delegation.

"Democracy based on the integration of all ethnic communities is the key to stability and economic improvement in South East Europe. The test of this election will be the functioning of the new Kosovo Assembly," said Bruce George, head of the OSCE Parliamentary Assembly delegation.

The Mission leaders said that the elections were well organised and that yesterday's voting was orderly. The turnout of around 65% is markedly lower than last year's municipal elections and this is a cause of some concern. However, indications are that all communities participated in these elections. Although they were late to enter into the election campaign, well over 40% of the Serbs cast their vote. The Mission also welcomed the very high number of domestic observers.

The International Observation Mission

The International Observation Mission was one of the biggest of its kind ever organised, with a strong parliamentary component—a 12-strong delegation from the Council of Europe Parliamentary Assembly, 9 Members of the European Parliament and a 50-strong delegation of the OSCE Parliamentary Assembly.

The three parliamentary delegations were also joined by the Congress of Local and Regional Authorities of Europe (CLRAE) and by international observers from Europe, North America and Japan, bringing the total to over 200.

The observation was led and organised by the Council of Europe Election Observation Mission (CEEOM), which has worked with 21 long-term observers in the field and a core team in Pristina since July. . . .

International Election Observation Mission— Preliminary Statement

These first Kosovo-wide elections—held in the aftermath of the 1999 conflict—were a significant step in the challenging process of constructing a democratic society based on the respect of human rights and the rule of law.

The International Observation Mission welcomes the fact that the elections took place in a more peaceful atmosphere than the local elections of 28th October 2000.

It recognises the unique nature of the elections that follow United Nations Security Council Resolution 1244 which calls for the development of provisional democratic self-governing institutions to ensure conditions for a peaceful and normal life for all inhabitants of Kosovo. The people of Kosovo were given an opportunity to elect their Assembly, with political and technical support by the international community.

The Mission congratulates the people of Kosovo for actively participating in the elections. It was encouraging that voters from all communities participated, giving hope for reconciliation between them. Serb participation in the elections was essential for building confidence in the future administration of Kosovo. It was also positive to see so many domestic observers active on Election Day.

The Mission concluded:

- The Electoral Code provided conditions for free and fair elections.
- Registration was carried out successfully. Enough time and resources were given to this vital process. Even more importantly, the people of Kosovo made a decision to fully participate. It was significant that a large number of the Serb population of Kosovo registered.

- The campaign was not as high profile as last year, but party rallies were often well attended and the political leaders made themselves available to the voters in each region. A number of incidents and disturbances did take place, but the level of violence was much lower than last year, which is to be welcomed. Sadly the Serbs delayed the decision to participate, leaving a short time for their campaign.
- In general, the media gave good coverage to rallies and other political events. However, 70% of coverage went to the three main Albanian parties, giving scant visibility to the smaller parties and to representatives of the minority population.
- Mail-In voting was organised worldwide from 33 countries. The International Organisation for Migration in Vienna was in charge of processing these postal votes. The mail-in process was efficient and transparent, with enough security guarantees to ensure that ballots were not mislaid or lost.
- Based on the debriefing at 12h00 today (Sunday 18th November) of over 200 short-term observers, the elections were conducted in an efficient manner. Polling stations opened and closed on time. Last year's queues were not repeated and this is proof that lessons learned have led to improvement.
- Overall turnout was markedly lower than last year.
- Questions remain about the participation late in the day of some none Albanian communities.
- The flying of community flags in and around polling stations was a cause of concern as in last year's elections, and should be the subject of future consultation and eventually a clear policy.
- The organising authorities performed their duties in a constructive and professional manner.

The Mission expects all parties and political leaders to respect the result of these elections. The significance of the 2001 Kosovo Assembly election will depend on the work of the elected Assembly. The International Election Observation Mission stresses the responsible role that must be played by the political leaders and all Assembly members in promoting reconciliation and the construction of democratic institutions in Kosovo. Their main task will be to develop a civil society based on the respect of European standards of human rights and the rule of law. Immediate issues include ensuring free movement, finding solutions on both sides to the question of missing people and releasing remaining political prisoners.

The Council of Europe Parliamentary Assembly, The OSCE Parliamentary Assembly and the European Parliament pledge their continued support and solidarity to the people of Kosovo in this historic task. . . .

UN WAR CRIMES INDICTMENT
OF SLOBODAN MILOSEVIC
November 22, 2001

Former Yugoslav president Slobodan Milosevic, whose drive for a "greater Serbia" led to bloody wars in the Balkans during the 1990s, finally faced prosecution in 2001. Extradited to a United Nations war crimes tribunal by some of the leaders who had supplanted him in power, Milosevic faced three indictments charging him with orchestrating the murder, expulsion, and suppression of tens of thousands of non-Serbs in Bosnia, Croatia, and Kosovo. The brutal war in Bosnia introduced the world to the term "ethnic cleansing," a euphemism for the Serbian campaign to drive Muslims and Croats from areas of Bosnia and Croatia that Serbs wanted to occupy. For his role in sponsoring the war in Bosnia, Milosevic became the first head of state ever charged with the most terrible of all crimes, genocide.

The extradition of Milosevic to the UN tribunal, seated at The Hague, Netherlands, left about three dozen persons accused of war crimes in the Balkans still at large. The two most important were Radovan Karadzic, the political leader of Bosnian Serbs, and his military chief, former general Ratko Mladic. Both had been charged with numerous crimes against humanity in Bosnia, the most important of which was the slaughter of some 7,000 Muslims in the town of Srebrenica in July 1995. Karadzic and Mladic were both presumed to be living in the Serbian sector of Bosnia, but NATO peacekeeping forces, which had ultimate control over Bosnia's security, had never made a serious attempt to arrest them. (Bosnia war, Historic Documents of 1995, p. 717; Srebrenica massacre, Historic Documents of 1999, p. 737)

One of Karadzic's aides, Biljana Plavsic, voluntarily surrendered to the UN tribunal in January and pleaded not guilty to genocide and other war crimes. After breaking with Karadzic, Plavsic in 1996 succeeded him as president of the Serbian republic in Bosnia, but he was ousted two years later by hard-liners because of his increasingly moderate stance.

The UN tribunal on August 2, 2001, convicted a key aide to General Mladic of genocide for his role in the Srebrenica killings. Former general Radislav Krstic was sentenced to forty-six years in prison after he was

*found guilty of supervising the Srebrenica killings, which Mladic allegedly
had ordered. In another landmark development, the UN tribunal on February 22 convicted three Bosnian Serbs on charges of raping, torturing, and
enslaving Muslim women during the war. The conviction marked the first
time that rape had been determined to be a "crime against humanity" in
time of war.*

Bringing Milosevic to Justice

*Milosevic lost power in late 2000 after he tried to rig the results of a presi-
dential election. An outpouring of public condemnation, coupled with the
loss of support among the military, forced him to hand over the Yugoslav
presidency to Voislav Kostunica, who clearly had beaten Milosevic in the
election. The question of what to do with Milosevic then became one of
the principal torments for Yugoslavia. The former leader had been indicted
in 1999 by the UN tribunal for war crimes in Kosovo, and he faced likely indictments for fomenting the wars in Bosnia and Croatia. Moreover, leaders
in Western Europe and the United States were becoming increasingly adamant that Milosevic be held to account for his sponsorship of those wars.*
(Milosevic ouster, Historic Documents of 2000, p. 833)

*The first major act of the 2001 drama came on March 31, when the Yugo-
slav government sent a representative to talk to Milosevic about giving himself up. Early the next day, after the former president resisted the demand,
police stormed his government-owned house in a suburb of Belgrade and
were greeted with gunfire. After the police gained entry to the house and demanded his surrender, Milosevic reportedly waved a gun and threatened to
kill himself and other family members present, but he ultimately yielded
and allowed himself to be bundled into a waiting police car. As the car was
pulling away, his enraged daughter, Marija, fired several shots, but no one
was hurt.*

*The arrest came just as the Bush administration was nearing an April 1
deadline for certifying to Congress whether Yugoslavia was cooperating
with the Hague tribunal. After Kostunica's election in late 2000, Congress
had approved $100 million in economic aid for Yugoslavia, conditioned on
the country's willingness to aid the tribunal's investigations. By late March,
nearly half of that money had been disbursed, but release of the remaining
$50 million depended on a willingness by President George W. Bush to re-
port to Congress that Yugoslavia was continuing to help the tribunal. Even
more important than the $50 million was Washington's support for loans to
Yugoslavia, which were expected to total several hundred million dollars,
from the International Monetary Fund and the World Bank.*

*Authorities in Belgrade charged Milosevic with corruption, including
embezzling state funds, and held him in prison while they debated whether
to comply with the UN demand that he be extradited to The Hague. Yugoslav
president Kostunica opposed the extradition and said Milosevic should
stand trial at home for his crimes during the Balkan wars. The day after Milosevic was arrested, Kostunica said the extradition "should never*

happen." *The Hague tribunal was biased against Serbs and practiced selective justice by failing to prosecute Bosnians, Croats, and even NATO for their killing of Serbs, he told the* New York Times *in an interview. But Kostunica's political rival, Serbian prime minister Zoran Djindjic, who at first shared a reluctance to send Milosevic to The Hague, later changed his mind under international pressure. Serbia was one of two republics (the other was Montenegro) in the Yugoslav federation. Serbia had its own government which, under Djindjic's leadership, increasingly distanced itself from Kostunica's federal government. Among other things, the Serbian government tried to prepare public opinion for the extradition of Milosevic by announcing the discovery of mass graves where his regime had buried victims of the Kosovo war.*

Belgrade was not the only capital where disagreements emerged about the fate of Milosevic. In Washington the Bush administration took the position that the Yugoslav government should send Milosevic to The Hague "ultimately," but at first it did not press for immediate action. Key congressional leaders were less patient, however, saying throughout the spring that they would accept no excuses for further delay. The administration gradually toughened its position, and in June demanded that Milosevic be surrendered to the tribunal without delay.

Another deadline approached in late June: the opening of an international "donors' conference" at which Western nations would consider Serbia's request for an additional $1.3 billion in aid. On June 23, a few days ahead of that conference, the Yugoslav government adopted a decree committing the country to cooperating with The Hague; aides to Serbian leader Djindjic then suggested that Milosevic might be extradited in a matter of a few weeks. On June 28, as it seemed likely that the government was about to act, four judges of the federal Yugoslavia's Constitutional Court issued an order to block the extradition. All four judges had been appointed by Milosevic.

In defiance of the court order, the twenty-one cabinet members of the Serbian government signed an order authorizing the Justice Ministry to extradite Milosevic immediately. Police then took the former president from his Belgrade prison cell and hustled him aboard a helicopter, which flew him to a base at Tuzla, Bosnia, used by U.S. elements of the NATO peacekeeping mission there. Milosevic was then transferred to a British jet and flown, with a NATO escort, to an air base in the Netherlands, where he was transferred to another helicopter and flown to the UN tribunal's prison at The Hague. NATO's role in the extradition had to be infuriating for Milosevic, who for years had excoriated the alliance as the ultimate suppressor of Serbs.

As Milosevic was on his way, a smiling Djindjic appeared before reporters to announce that Serbia was ready to take its place "in the international community." Speaking directly to his countrymen, Djindjic said: "I beg for your understanding of this hard but correct decision at this moment."

*Among those unwilling to offer understanding—at least for the moment—
was Kostunica, who said he had not been told of the Serbian decision to extradite Milosevic in defiance of the court order. He issued a statement
saying the extradition "cannot be considered legal or constitutional." A
couple thousand diehard Milosevic supporters gathered on the streets of Belgrade to protest, but most opinion surveys showed strong public support for
ridding the country of the disgraced leader.*

*Western leaders heaped praise on Serbia's decision to extradite Milosevic.
Bush said the country was moving toward "a brighter future as a full
member of the community of European democracies," and he pledged continued U.S. support. At the international donors' conference in Brussels on
June 29, the United States pledged $181 million in additional aid to help re-
build Yugoslavia. The European Union pledged $450 million, and pledges
by Japan, the World Bank, the International Monetary Fund, and other
donors brought the total to $1.28 billion—the amount requested by Belgrade
as the price for handing over Milosevic.*

*Perhaps fittingly, Milosevic's extradition to face war crimes charges
came exactly twelve years to the day after his famous 1989 speech in Kosovo
that stoked the fires of Serbian nationalism and led to the conflicts in the
Balkans during the 1990s. Standing on the battlefield where Serbs had been
defeated by the Ottoman empire in 1389, Milosevic had pledged to unite into
a "greater Serbia" all the lands where Serbs lived and had historic claims.
Less than three years later, as communism collapsed all through Eastern
Europe, Yugoslavia began to disintegrate. To fulfill his pledge, Milosevic
launched a series of wars—all of which he lost—that killed tens of thousands and produced an impoverished, demoralized, and weakened, not a
greater, Serbia.*

Milosevic at The Hague

*Milosevic had been under indictment for war crimes since May 24, 1999,
during the latter stages of NATO's air war that forced the Yugoslav leader to
pull his country's security forces out of Kosovo. That indictment by the UN
prosecutor dealt strictly with war crimes in Kosovo; it accused Milosevic
of ordering the repression of the 900,000 or so Albanian Muslims who were
the majority in the southern province of Serbia. During 1998 and early
1999 Serbian and Yugoslav security forces burned houses and entire villages, raped and murdered thousands of civilians, and finally drove at least
800,000 people from their homes into neighboring countries, including Albania, Bosnia, Macedonia, and Montenegro. The indictment specifically accused Milosevic of complicity in the murders of 340 Kosovar Albanians,
most of them young men.* (Kosovo war, Historic Documents of 1999, pp. 134,
285, 802)

*On June 29, hours after he arrived at the tribunal's detention center,
prosecutors handed Milosevic an expanded version of the Kosovo indictment. It included details of additional atrocities and the names of additional victims. "We are today only at the start of the case against Slobodan*

Milosevic, not at the end," the tribunal's chief prosecutor, Carla Del Ponte told reporters.

For his part, Milosevic lost no time in showing the world how he viewed the situation. Appearing at his arraignment before the UN tribunal on July 3, Milosevic refused to cooperate in any manner. Asked how he pleaded to the charges against him, Milosevic said in English: "This trial's aim is to produce false justification for the war crimes of NATO"—a reference to the alliance's bombing of Yugoslavia in 1999. At another point, he said: "I consider this tribunal false tribunal and indictments false indictments." The tribunal's chief judge, Richard May of Britain, entered a plea of "not guilty" on Milosevic's behalf.

While it accused Milosevic of war crimes and crimes against humanity, the Kosovo indictment did not charge him with the gravest crime of all— genocide. Declared a crime by the UN's 1948 Genocide Convention, genocide was defined as the attempt to eliminate an entire race, ethnic group, or other class of people through violent means. Del Ponte long had made it clear that she intended to charge Milosevic for genocide and other war crimes during the brutal wars in Croatia from 1991 to 1995, and in Bosnia from 1992 to 1995. But her team of prosecutors took their time assembling a case documenting Milosevic's actions in those wars, which were much bloodier, longer, and more complex than the one in Kosovo.

On October 9 the tribunal released a new indictment charging Milosevic with war crimes and crimes against humanity, but not genocide, during the Croatia war. Covering the first year of the war, from August 1991 to June 1992, the indictment said Yugoslav and Serb forces under Milosevic's control killed hundreds of Croats and other non-Serbs and drove at least 170,000 Croats from their homes as part of a campaign to take over about one-third of Croatia as a Serbian homeland. The indictment also named fifteen other Serbian officials, all of whom were said to have reported to Milosevic. Milosevic was forced to sit through a reading of the indictment on October 29, but he again refused to enter a plea.

The last—and possibly the most important—of three indictments against Milosevic was issued at the UN tribunal on November 22. The indictment listed twenty-nine counts against Milosevic, saying that he led "a joint criminal enterprise, the purpose of which was the forcible and permanent removal of the majority of non-Serbs from the Republic of Bosnia-Herzegovina." Among the crimes was that of genocide. In all, the indictment said Milosevic bore ultimate responsibility for the expulsion of more than 250,000 people from their homes, the deaths of at least 8,000 people (most of them Bosnian Muslims), and the destruction of numerous towns and villages.

Once again, Milosevic refused to enter a plea when the indictment was read to him on December 11. "I would like to say to you that what we have just heard, this tragic text, is a supreme absurdity," he told the court. "I should be given credit for peace in Bosnia, not war."

At year's end it was unclear whether Milosevic would face one or two trials on the three indictments. Del Ponte said she expected the proceedings could last as long as two-and-a-half years.

Deteriorating Political Situation in Yugoslavia

The dispute in June over the extradition of Milosevic deepened a political falling out between the former allies who had helped topple him from power in 2000. Kostunica, who had defeated Milosevic for the presidency of the Yugoslav federation, headed a faction that appeared to want only limited reforms of the system that Milosevic had crafted during his years in power. Kostunica espoused some of the same Serbian nationalist ideas that got Milosevic into trouble, but in much more moderate and diplomatic language. Serbian prime minister Djindjic, on the other hand, seemed eager to press for the more sweeping political and economic reforms that the European Union and the United States insisted were necessary. By appealing to Serbian pride and criticizing outside "interference," Kostunica remained the single most popular political figure in the country. But Djindjic, as head of the coalition that governed Serbia—the dominant partner in the Yugoslav federation that also included Montenegro—also had important influence, as well as the confidence of Western lenders.

An open break between the two leaders came in August, when the killing of a police officer led to charges of corruption and bad faith. Kostunica withdrew his party from the coalition that governed Serbia and in December demanded new elections for the Serbian government. At year's end the political feud appeared to be jeopardizing prospects that the country would be able to overcome the tragedies that Milosevic had initiated.

Following are excerpts from the indictment of Slobodan Milosevic, former president of Yugoslavia, for crimes committed during the war in Bosnia from 1992 to 1995. The indictment, unsealed November 22, 2001, was issued by the prosecutor for the United Nations International Criminal Tribunal for the Former Yugoslavia, based at The Hague, Netherlands.

The document was obtained from the Internet at http://www.un.org/icty/indictment/english/mil-ii011122e.htm.

The Prosecutor of the International Criminal Tribunal for the former Yugoslavia, pursuant to her authority under Article 18 of the Statute of the International Criminal Tribunal for the former Yugoslavia ("the Statute of the Tribunal"), charges:

SLOBODAN MILOSEVIC

with GENOCIDE, CRIMES AGAINST HUMANITY, GRAVE BREACHES OF THE GENEVA CONVENTIONS and VIOLATIONS OF THE LAWS OR CUSTOMS OF WAR as set forth below:

The Accused

[Sections 1 through 4 detailed Milosevic's career, including his rise to the head of the Communist Party in Serbia in 1986, his election as president of Serbia in 1989, his election as president of Yugoslavia in 1997, and his resignation for the latter post in 2000 after losing an election.]

Individual Criminal Responsibility

Article 7(1) of the Statute of the Tribunal

5. **Slobodan Milosevic** is individually criminally responsible for the crimes referred to in Articles 2, 3, 4 and 5 of the Statute of the Tribunal as described in this indictment, which he planned, instigated, ordered, committed, or in whose planning, preparation, or execution he otherwise aided and abetted. By using the word "committed" in this indictment, the Prosecutor does not intend to suggest that the accused physically committed any of the crimes charged personally. "Committed" in this indictment refers to participation in a joint criminal enterprise as a co-perpetrator.

6. **Slobodan Milosevic** participated in the joint criminal enterprise as set out below. The purpose of this joint criminal enterprise was the forcible and permanent removal of the majority of non-Serbs, principally Bosnian Muslims and Bosnian Croats, from large areas of the Republic of Bosnia and Herzegovina (hereinafter referred to as "Bosnia and Herzegovina"), through the commission of crimes which are in violation of Articles 2, 3, 4 and 5 of the Statute of the Tribunal.

7. The joint criminal enterprise was in existence by 1 August 1991 and continued until at least 31 December 1995. The individuals participating in this joint criminal enterprise included **Slobodan Milosevic,** Radovan Karadzic, Momcilo Krajisnik, Biljana Plavsic, General Ratko Mladic, Borisav Jovic, Branko Kostic, Veljko Kadijevic, Blagoje Adzic, Milan Martic, Jovica Stanisic, Franko Simatovic, also known as "Frenki," Radovan Stojicic, also known as "Badza," Vojislav Seselj, Zeljko Raznatovic, also known as "Arkan," and other known and unknown participants.

8. The crimes enumerated in Counts 1 to 29 of this indictment were within the object of the joint criminal enterprise. Alternatively, the crimes enumerated in Counts 1 to 15 and 19 to 29 were natural and foreseeable consequences of the execution of the object of the joint criminal enterprise and the accused was aware that such crimes were the possible outcome of the execution of the joint criminal enterprise.

9. In order for the joint criminal enterprise to succeed in its objective, **Slobodan Milosevic** worked in concert with or through other individuals in the joint criminal enterprise. Each participant or co-perpetrator within the joint criminal enterprise, sharing the intent to contribute to the enterprise, played his or her own role or roles that significantly contributed to achieving the objective of the enterprise. The roles of the participants or co-perpetrators include, but are not limited to, the following:

10. Radovan Karadzic was President of the Serbian Democratic Party of

Bosnia and Herzegovina (*Srpska demokratska stranka Bosne i Hercegovine* or "SDS") throughout the period of the indictment. On 27 March 1992, Karadzic became the President of the Bosnian Serb "National Security Council." On 12 May 1992, he was elected President of the three-member Presidency of the self-proclaimed Serbian Republic of Bosnia and Herzegovina (hereinafter referred to as "Republika Srpska") and remained in this position after the Presidency was expanded to five members on 2 June 1992. On 17 December 1992, Karadzic was elected President of Republika Srpska and remained in that position throughout the period of this indictment. In his capacity as a member of the Bosnian Serb National Security Council, member of the Presidency, as President of Republika Srpska, and in his position of leadership within the SDS party and organs of the Republika Srpska government, Radovan Karadzic, together with others, commanded, directed, or otherwise exercised effective control over the Territorial Defence ("TO"), the Bosnian Serb army ("VRS") and the police forces of Republika Srpska who participated in the crimes specified in this indictment.

11. Momcilo Krajisnik, a close associate of Radovan Karadzic, was a member of the SDS Main Board from 12 July 1991. On 24 October 1991, the day of the founding of the "Assembly of the Serbian People of Bosnia and Herzegovina," (hereinafter referred to as the "Bosnian Serb Assembly") Krajisnik was elected its President. From 27 March 1992, Krajisnik was a member of the Bosnian Serb National Security Council. He became a member of the five-member Presidency on 2 June 1992. When the Bosnian Serb Assembly elected Radovan Karadzic President of Republika Srpska on 17 December 1992, Krajisnik ceased to be a member of the Presidency, but continued to be one of the most important political leaders in Republika Srpska and remained the President of its National Assembly until 19 October 1996. In his capacity as a member of the Bosnian Serb National Security Council as a member of the Presidency of Republika Srpska, and in his position of leadership within the SDS party and organs of the Republika Srpska government, Momcilo Krajisnik, together with others, commanded, directed, or otherwise exercised effective control over the TO, the VRS and the police forces of Republika Srpska who participated in the crimes specified in this indictment.

12. Biljana Plavsic, a high-ranking SDS politician, on 28 February 1992, became one of two Acting Presidents of the Serbian Republic of Bosnia and Herzegovina, together with Nikola Koljevic. As an Acting President, Biljana Plavsic became an *ex officio* member of the Bosnian Serb National Security Council. On 12 May 1992, she was elected as a member of the three-member Presidency and remained in this position after it was expanded to five members. When the Bosnian Serb Assembly elected Radovan Karadzic President of Republika Srpska on 17 December 1992, it also elected Biljana Plavsic one of two Vice-Presidents, a position she held until 19 July 1996. In her capacity as Vice-President, member of the Bosnian Serb National Security Council as a member of the Presidency of Republika Srpska, and in her position of leadership within the SDS party and organs of the Republika Srpska government, Biljana Plavsic, together with others, commanded, directed, or otherwise

exercised effective control over the TO, the VRS and the police forces of Republika Srpska who participated in the crimes specified in this indictment.

13. General Ratko Mladic, a military career officer previously stationed in Macedonia and Kosovo, became the commander of the 9th Corps (Knin Corps) of the Yugoslav People's Army ("JNA") in June 1991 and participated in the fighting in Croatia. On 4 October 1991, the SFRY Presidency promoted him to Major General. Subsequently, in May 1992, he assumed command of the forces of the Second Military District of the JNA in Sarajevo. From 12 May 1992 until November 1996, he was the Commander of the Main Staff of the VRS and in this capacity, together with others, commanded, directed, or otherwise exercised effective control over the VRS and other units acting in co-ordination with the VRS who participated in the crimes specified in this indictment.

14. Borisav Jovic was successively the Vice-President, President and then a member of the SFRY Presidency from 15 May 1989 until April 1992, as well as the President of the SPS from May 1991 until October 1992, and a high ranking official of the SPS until November 1995. Borisav Jovic and Branko Kostic, the Vice-President and then Acting President of the Presidency of the SFRY, together with others during the relevant period, commanded, directed, or otherwise exercised effective control over the JNA and members of the TO and paramilitary units acting in co-ordination with, and under supervision of, the JNA.

15. General Veljko Kadijevic, as Federal Secretary for National Defence from 15 May 1988 until 6 January 1992, commanded, directed, or otherwise exercised effective control over the JNA and other units acting in co-ordination with the JNA.

16. General Blagoje Adzic, in his capacity as JNA Chief of Staff from 1990 to 28 February 1992 and Acting Federal Secretary for National Defence from mid-1991 to 28 February 1992, Federal Secretary for National Defence from 28 February 1992 to 27 April 1992 and JNA Chief of Staff from 27 April 1992 to 8 May 1992, together with others, commanded, directed, or otherwise exercised effective control over the JNA and other units acting in co-ordination with the JNA.

17. Jovica Stanisic, in his capacity as chief of the State Security (*Drzavna bezbednost* or "DB") of the Republic of Serbia from March 1991 to October 1998, commanded, directed, or otherwise exercised effective control over members of the DB, who participated in the perpetration of the crimes specified in this indictment. In addition, he provided arms, funds, training, or other substantial assistance or support to Serb paramilitary units and police units that were subsequently involved in the crimes specified in this indictment.

18. Franko Simatovic, also known as "Frenki," as head of the special operations component of the DB of the Republic of Serbia, commanded, directed, or otherwise exercised effective control over agents of the DB who perpetrated crimes specified in this indictment. In addition, he provided arms, funds, training, or other substantial assistance or support to Serb paramilitary units and

police units that were subsequently involved in the crimes charged in this indictment.

19. Radovan Stojicic also known as "Badza" as Deputy Minister of Interior of Serbia and head of Public Security Service, commanded, directed or otherwise exercised effective control over special forces of the Serbian MUP and volunteer units who participated in the crimes specified in this indictment. In addition, he provided arms, funds, training, or other substantial assistance or support to Serb paramilitary units and police units that were subsequently involved in the crimes specified in this indictment.

20. Milan Martic, as "Secretary of the Secretariat of Internal Affairs" of the so-called Serbian Autonomous Region ("SAO") Krajina from 4 January 1991 until 29 May 1991; as "Minister of Defence" of the SAO Krajina from 29 May 1991 to 27 June 1991; and as "Minister of Internal Affairs" for the SAO Krajina (later "Republic of Serbian Krajina") from 27 June 1991 to January 1994, established, commanded, directed, and otherwise exercised effective control over members of his police force (referred to as "Martic's Police," "Martic's Militia," "Marticevci," "SAO Krajina Police" or "SAO Krajina Militia") who were subsequently involved in the crimes specified in this indictment.

21. Zeljko Raznatovic, also known as "Arkan," in 1990 established and commanded the Serbian Volunteer Guard, a paramilitary unit commonly known as "Arkanovci" or "Arkan's Tigers," who during the time relevant to this indictment operated in Bosnia and Herzegovina and were involved in the crimes charged in this indictment. In addition, he maintained a significant military base in Erdut, Croatia, where he functioned as commander. Other paramilitary groups and TO units were trained at this base and were subsequently involved in the crimes charged in this indictment.

22. Vojislav Seselj, as President of the Serbian Radical Party (SRS) from at least February 1991 throughout the time relevant to this indictment recruited or otherwise provided substantial assistance or support to Serb paramilitary units, commonly known as "Seseljevci" or "Seselj's men," who perpetrated crimes as specified in this indictment. In addition, he openly espoused and encouraged the creation of a "Greater Serbia" by violence and other unlawful means, and actively participated in war propaganda and spreading interethnic hatred.

23. From 1987 until late 2000, **Slobodan Milosevic** was the dominant political figure in Serbia and the SFRY/FRY. He acquired control of all facets of the Serbian government, including the police and the state security services. In addition, he gained control over the political leaderships of Kosovo, Vojvodina, and Montenegro.

24. In his capacity as the President of Serbia and through his leading position in the SPS party, **Slobodan Milosevic** exercised effective control or substantial influence over the above listed participants in the joint criminal enterprise and either alone or acting in concert with them and additional known and unknown persons effectively controlled or substantially influenced the actions of the Federal Presidency of the SFRY and later the FRY, the

Serbian Ministry of Internal Affairs ("MUP"), the JNA, the Yugoslav Army ("VJ") and the VRS, as well as Serb paramilitary groups.

25. **Slobodan Milosevic,** acting alone and in concert with other members of the joint criminal enterprise participated in the joint criminal enterprise in the following ways:

a) He exerted effective control over elements of the JNA and VJ which participated in the planning, preparation, facilitation and execution of the forcible removal of the majority of non-Serbs, principally Bosnian Muslims and Bosnian Croats, from large areas of Bosnia and Herzegovina.

b) He provided financial, logistical and political support to the VRS. These forces subsequently participated in the execution of the joint criminal enterprise through the commission of crimes which are in violation of Articles 2, 3, 4 and 5 of the Statute of the Tribunal.

c) He exercised substantial influence over, and assisted, the political leadership of Republika Srpska in the planning, preparation, facilitation and execution of the take-over of municipalities in Bosnia and Herzegovina and the subsequent forcible removal of the majority of non-Serbs, principally Bosnian Muslims and Bosnian Croats, from those municipalities.

d) He participated in the planning and preparation of the take-over of municipalities in Bosnia and Herzegovina and the subsequent forcible removal of the majority of non-Serbs, principally Bosnian Muslims and Bosnian Croats, from those municipalities. He provided the financial, material and logistical support necessary for such take-over.

e) He participated in the formation, financing, supply, support and direction of special forces of the Republic of Serbia Ministry of Internal Affairs. These special forces participated in the execution of the joint criminal enterprise through the commission of crimes which are in violation of Articles 2, 3, 4 and 5 of the Statute of the Tribunal.

f) He participated in providing financial, logistical and political support and direction to Serbian irregular forces or paramilitaries. These forces participated in the execution of the joint criminal enterprise through the commission of crimes which are in violation of Articles 2, 3, 4 and 5 of the Statute of the Tribunal.

g) He controlled, manipulated or otherwise utilised Serbian state-run media to spread exaggerated and false messages of ethnically based attacks by Bosnian Muslims and Croats against Serb people intended to create an atmosphere of fear and hatred among Serbs living in Serbia, Croatia and Bosnia and Herzegovina which contributed to the forcible removal of the majority of non-Serbs, principally Bosnian Muslims and Bosnian Croats, from large areas of Bosnia and Herzegovina.

26. **Slobodan Milosevic** knowingly and wilfully participated in the joint criminal enterprise, while being aware of the foreseeable consequences of this

enterprise. On this basis, he bears individual criminal responsibility for these crimes under Article 7(1) of the Statute of the Tribunal, in addition to his responsibility under the same Article for having planned, instigated, ordered or otherwise aided and abetted in the planning, preparation and execution of these crimes.

Article 7(3) of the Statute of the Tribunal

27. **Slobodan Milosevic,** while holding positions of superior authority, is also individually criminally responsible for the acts or omissions of his subordinates, pursuant to Article 7(3) of the Statute of the Tribunal. A superior is responsible for the criminal acts of his subordinates if he knew or had reason to know that his subordinates were about to commit such acts or had done so, and the superior failed to take the necessary and reasonable measures to prevent such acts or to punish the perpetrators.

28. From at least March 1991 until 15 June 1992, **Slobodan Milosevic** exercised effective control over the four members of the "Serbian Bloc" within the Presidency of the SFRY. These four individuals were Borisav Jovic, the representative of the Republic of Serbia; Branko Kostic, the representative of the Republic of Montenegro; Jugoslav Kostic, the representative of the Autonomous Province of Vojvodina; and Sejdo Bajramovic, the representative of the Autonomous Province of Kosovo and Metohija. **Slobodan Milosevic** used Borisav Jovic and Branko Kostic as his primary agents in the Presidency and through them he directed the actions of the "Serbian Bloc." From 1 October 1991, in the absence of the representatives of the Presidency from Croatia, Slovenia, Macedonia and Bosnia and Herzegovina, the four members of the "Serbian Bloc" exercised the powers of the Presidency, including that of collective "Commander-in-Chief" of the JNA. This "Rump Presidency" acted without dissension to execute **Slobodan Milosevic's** policies. The Federal Presidency had effective control over the JNA as its "Commander-in-Chief" and other units under the supervision of the JNA. Generals Veljko Kadijevic and Blagoje Adzic, who directed and supervised the JNA forces in Bosnia and Herzegovina, were in constant communication and consultation with the accused.

29. On 27 April 1992, the Supreme Defence Council was formed. Throughout the time relevant to this indictment, **Slobodan Milosevic** was a member of the Supreme Defence Council and exercised substantial influence and control over other members of the Council. The Supreme Defence Council and the President of the FRY had *de jure* control over the JNA and later the VJ. In addition to his *de jure* powers, at all times relevant to this indictment, **Slobodan Milosevic** exercised *de facto* control over the JNA and the VJ through his control over the high ranking officers of these armies.

30. **Slobodan Milosevic** is therefore individually criminally responsible, under Article 7(3) of the Statute of the Tribunal, for the participation of the members of the JNA and the VJ and other units under the supervision of the JNA and the VJ in the crimes described in this indictment.

31. From the time **Slobodan Milosevic** came to power in Serbia, he exercised control over key officials in the Serbian MUP, among them Radmilo Bogdanovic and Zoran Sokolovic, who were both, at different times, the Minister

of Internal Affairs of Serbia. He also exercised control over Jovica Stanisic and Franko Simatovic, both high-ranking officials in the DB. Through these officials, **Slobodan Milosevic** exercised effective control over agents of the MUP, including the DB, who directed and supported the actions of the special forces and Serb paramilitary groups operating in Bosnia and Herzegovina. The accused **Slobodan Milosevic** is therefore individually criminally responsible, under Article 7(3) of the Statute of the Tribunal, for the participation of the members of the Serbian MUP, including the DB, in the crimes described in this indictment.

The Charges

Counts 1 and 2: Genocide or Complicity in Genocide

32. From on or about 1 March 1992 until 31 December 1995, **Slobodan Milosevic,** acting alone or in concert with other members of the joint criminal enterprise, planned, instigated, ordered, committed or otherwise aided and abetted the planning, preparation and execution of the destruction, in whole or in part, of the Bosnian Muslim and Bosnian Croat national, ethnical, racial or religious groups, as such, in territories within Bosnia and Herzegovina, including: Bijeljina; Bosanski Novi; Bosanski Samac; Bratunac; Brcko; Doboj; Foca; Sarajevo (Ilijas); Kljuc; Kotor Varos; Sarajevo (Novi Grad); Prijedor; Rogatica; Sanski Most; Srebrenica; Visegrad; Vlasenica and Zvornik. The destruction of these groups was effected by:

   a) The widespread killing of thousands of Bosnian Muslims and Bosnian Croats, during and after the take-over of territories within Bosnia and Herzegovina, including those listed above, as specified in **Schedule A** to this indictment. In many of the territories, educated and leading members of these groups were specifically targeted for execution, often in accordance with pre-prepared lists. After the fall of Srebrenica in July 1995, almost all captured Bosnian Muslim men and boys, altogether several thousands, were executed at the places where they had been captured or at sites to which they had been transported for execution.
   b) The killing of thousands of Bosnian Muslims and Bosnian Croats in detention facilities within Bosnia and Herzegovina, including those situated within the territories listed above, as specified in **Schedule B** to this indictment.
   c) The causing of serious bodily and mental harm to thousands of Bosnian Muslims and Bosnian Croats during their confinement in detention facilities within Bosnia and Herzegovina, including those situated within the territories listed above, as specified in **Schedule C** to this indictment. Members of these groups, during their confinement in detention facilities and during their interrogation at these locations, police stations and military barracks, were continuously subjected to, or forced to witness, inhumane acts, including murder, sexual violence, torture and beatings.

d) The detention of thousands of Bosnian Muslims and Bosnian Croats in detention facilities within Bosnia and Herzegovina, including those situated within the territories listed above, under conditions of life calculated to bring about the partial physical destruction of those groups, namely through starvation, contaminated water, forced labour, inadequate medical care and constant physical and psychological assault.

By these acts and omissions, **Slobodan Milosevic** committed:

Count 1: **GENOCIDE,** punishable under Articles 4(3)(a) and 7(1) and 7(3) of the Statute of the Tribunal; or

Count 2: **COMPLICITY IN GENOCIDE,** punishable under Articles 4(3)(e) and 7(1) and 7(3) of the Statute of the Tribunal.

Count 3: Persecutions

33. From on or about 1 March 1992 until 31 December 1995, **Slobodan Milosevic,** acting alone or in concert with members of the joint criminal enterprise, planned, instigated, ordered, committed or otherwise aided and abetted the planning, preparation or execution of persecutions of non-Serbs, principally Bosnian Muslims and Bosnian Croats, within the territories of [a list of Bosnian towns and cities follows]. . . .

34. Throughout this period, Serb forces, comprised of JNA, VJ, VRS units, local TO units, local and Serbian MUP police units and paramilitary units from Serbia and Montenegro, attacked and took control of towns and villages in these territories. After the take-over, the Serb forces in co-operation with the local Serb authorities established a regime of persecutions designed to drive the non-Serb civilian population from these territories.

35. These persecutions were committed on the discriminatory grounds of political affiliation, race or religion and included:

a) The extermination or murder of thousands of Bosnian Muslim, Bosnian Croat and other non-Serb civilians, including women and the elderly, in those territories listed above, the details of which are set out in **Schedules A and B** to this indictment.

b) The prolonged and routine imprisonment and confinement of thousands of Bosnian Muslim, Bosnian Croat and other non-Serb civilians in detention facilities within and outside of Bosnia and Herzegovina, the details of which are set out in **Schedule C** to this indictment.

c) The establishment and perpetuation of inhumane living conditions against Bosnian Muslim, Bosnian Croat and other non-Serb civilians, within the above mentioned detention facilities. These living conditions were brutal and characterised by inhumane treatment, overcrowding, starvation, forced labour and systematic physical and psychological abuse, including torture, beatings and sexual assault.

d) The prolonged and frequent forced labour of Bosnian Muslim, Bosnian Croat and other non-Serb civilians, from these detention facilities. The forced labour included digging graves and trenches and other forms of manual labour at the frontlines.

e) The cruel and inhumane treatment of Bosnian Muslim, Bosnian Croat and other non-Serb civilians during and after the take-over of the municipalities specified above. Such inhumane treatment included, but was not limited to, sexual violence, torture, physical and psychological abuse and forced existence under inhumane living conditions.

f) The imposition of restrictive and discriminatory measures against Bosnian Muslims, Bosnian Croats and other non-Serbs, such as, the restriction of freedom of movement; removal from positions of authority in local government institutions and the police; dismissal from jobs; arbitrary searches of their homes; denial of the right to judicial process and the denial of the right of equal access to public services, including proper medical care.

g) The beating and robbing of Bosnian Muslim, Bosnian Croat and other non-Serb civilians.

h) The forcible transfer and deportation of thousands of Bosnian Muslim, Bosnian Croat and other non-Serb civilians, from the territories listed above, to locations outside of Serb held territories as described in paragraphs 40 and 41 and **Schedule D** to this indictment.

i) The appropriation and plunder of property belonging to Bosnian Muslim, Bosnian Croat and other non-Serb civilians.

j) The intentional and wanton destruction of homes, other public and private property belonging to Bosnian Muslims and Bosnian Croats, their cultural and religious institutions, historical monuments and other sacred sites, as described in paragraph 42.

k) The obstruction of humanitarian aid, in particular medical and food supplies into the besieged enclaves Bihac, Gorazde, Srebrenica and Zepa, and the deprivation of water from the civilians trapped in the enclaves designed to create unbearable living conditions.

By these acts and omissions, **Slobodan Milosevic** committed:

Count 3: Persecutions on political, racial or religious grounds, a **CRIME AGAINST HUMANITY,** punishable under Articles 5(h) and 7(1) and 7(3) of the Statute of the Tribunal.

Counts 4 to 7: Extermination, Murder and Wilful Killing

36. From on or about 1 March 1992 until 31 December 1995, **Slobodan Milosevic,** acting alone or in concert with other members of the joint criminal enterprise, planned, instigated, ordered, committed or otherwise aided and abetted the planning, preparation or execution of the extermination, murder and wilful killings of non-Serbs, principally Bosnian Muslims and Bosnian Croats living in the territories of [a list of Bosnian towns and cities follows]. . . . The extermination, murder and wilful killings of these groups were effected by:

a) The killing of Bosnian Muslims, Bosnian Croats and other non-Serbs in their towns and villages, during and after the take-over of the territories listed above including those specified in **Schedule A** to this indictment.

b) The killing of Bosnian Muslims, Bosnian Croats and other non-Serbs in detention facilities and during their deportation or forcible transfers, including those specified in **Schedule B** to this indictment.

By these acts and omissions, **Slobodan Milosevic** committed:

Count 4: Extermination, a **CRIME AGAINST HUMANITY,** punishable under Articles 5(b) and 7(1) and 7(3) of the Statute of the Tribunal.

Count 5: Murder, a **CRIME AGAINST HUMANITY,** punishable under Articles 5(a) and 7(1) and 7(3) of the Statute of the Tribunal.

Count 6: Wilful killing, a **GRAVE BREACH OF THE GENEVA CONVENTIONS OF 1949,** punishable under Articles 2(a) and 7(1) and 7(3) of the Statute of the Tribunal.

Count 7: Murder, a **VIOLATION OF THE LAWS OR CUSTOMS OF WAR,** as recognised by Common Article 3(1)(a) of the Geneva Conventions of 1949, punishable under Articles 3 and 7(1) and 7(3) of the Statute of the Tribunal.

Counts 8 to 15: Unlawful Confinement, Imprisonment, Torture, Wilfully Causing Great Suffering, Other Inhumane Acts

37. From on or about 1 March 1992 until 31 December 1995, **Slobodan Milosevic,** acting alone or in concert with members of the joint criminal enterprise, planned, instigated, ordered, committed or otherwise aided and abetted the planning, preparation or execution of the unlawful confinement or imprisonment under inhumane conditions of Bosnian Muslims, Bosnian Croats and other non-Serbs within the territories of [a list of Bosnian towns and cities follows]. . . .

38. Serb military forces, comprised of JNA, VJ, VRS, TO and paramilitary units acting in co-operation with local police staff and local Serb authorities, arrested and detained thousands of Bosnian Muslim, Bosnian Croat and other non-Serb civilians from the territories listed above. These civilians were held in short and long-term detention, of which the major facilities are specified in **Schedule C** to this indictment.

39. The living conditions in these detention facilities were brutal and characterised by inhumane treatment, overcrowding, starvation, forced labour, inadequate medical care and systematic physical and psychological assault, including torture, beatings and sexual assault.

By these acts and omissions, **Slobodan Milosevic** committed:

Count 8: Imprisonment, a **CRIME AGAINST HUMANITY,** punishable under Articles 5(e) and 7(1) and 7(3) of the Statute of the Tribunal.

Count 9: Torture, a **CRIME AGAINST HUMANITY,** punishable under Articles 5(f) and 7(1) and 7(3) of the Statute of the Tribunal.

Count 10: Inhumane acts, a **CRIME AGAINST HUMANITY,** punishable under Articles 5(i) and 7(1) and 7(3) of the Statute of the Tribunal.

Count 11: Unlawful Confinement, a **GRAVE BREACH OF THE GENEVA CONVENTIONS** OF 1949, punishable under Articles 2(g) and 7(1) and 7(3) of the Statute of the Tribunal.

Count 12: Torture, a **GRAVE BREACH OF THE GENEVA CONVEN-TIONS OF 1949,** punishable under Articles 2(b) and 7(1) and 7(3) of the Statute of the Tribunal.

Count 13: Wilfully causing great suffering, a **GRAVE BREACH OF THE GENEVA CONVENTIONS** OF 1949, punishable under Articles 2(c) and 7(1) and 7(3) of the Statute of the Tribunal.

Count 14: Torture, a **VIOLATION OF THE LAWS OR CUSTOMS OF WAR** as recognised by Common Article 3(1)(a) of the Geneva Conventions of 1949, punishable under Articles 3 and 7(1) and 7(3) of the Statute of the Tribunal.

Count 15: Cruel Treatment, a **VIOLATIONS OF THE LAWS OR CUS-TOMS OF WAR** as recognised by Common Article 3(1)(a) of the Geneva Conventions of 1949, punishable under Articles 3 and 7(1) and 7(3) of the Statute of the Tribunal.

Counts 16 to 18: Deportation and Inhumane Acts (Forcible Transfers)

40. From on or about 1 March 1992 until 31 December 1995, **Slobodan Milosevic,** acting alone or in concert with members of the joint criminal enterprise, planned, instigated, ordered, committed or otherwise aided and abetted the planning, preparation or execution of the unlawful forcible transfer, also qualifying as deportation where indicated hereinafter, of tens of thousands of Bosnian Muslim, Bosnian Croat and other non-Serb civilians from their legal domiciles in the territories of Banja Luka (deportation); Bihac; Bijeljina; Bileca (deportation); Bosanska Dubica; Bosanska Gradiska; Bosanska Krupa; Bosanski Novi; Bosanski Petrovac; Bosanski Samac (deportation); Bratunac; Brcko; Cajnice; Celinac; Doboj; Donji Vakuf; Foca; Gacko (deportation); Sarajevo (Hadzici); Sarajevo (Ilidza); Sarajevo (Ilijas); Kljuc; Kalinovik; Kotor Varos; Nevesinje; Sarajevo (Novi Grad); Sarajevo (Novo Sarajevo); Sarajevo (Pale); Prijedor; Prnjavor; Rogatica; Rudo (deportation); Sanski Most; Sekovici; Sipovo; Sokolac; Srebrenica; Teslic; Trebinje; Sarajevo (Trnovo); Visegrad; Vlasenica; Sarajevo (Vogosca) and Zvornik (deportation), to other areas both inside and outside Bosnia and Herzegovina. The details of such acts and omissions are described in **Schedule D**.

41. In order to achieve this objective, Serb forces comprised of JNA, VJ, VRS and TO, paramilitary units acting in co-operation with local police staff, local Serb authorities and special forces of the Serbian Ministry of Internal Affairs under the effective control of **Slobodan Milosevic** or other members of the joint criminal enterprise, subjugated villages and towns in Bosnia and Herzegovina and participated with members of the SDS in the disarming of the non-Serb population. The towns and villages, including areas in which the inhabitants complied and offered no resistance, were then attacked. These attacks were intended to compel the non-Serb population to flee. After taking control of the towns and villages, the Serb forces often rounded-up the remaining non-Serb civilian population and forcibly removed them from the area. On other occasions, the Serb forces in co-operation with the local Serb

authorities imposed restrictive and discriminatory measures on the non-Serb population and engaged in a campaign of terror designed to drive them out of the territory. The majority of non-Serbs that remained were eventually deported or forcibly transferred from their homes.

By these acts and omissions **Slobodan Milosevic** committed:

Count 16: Deportation, a **CRIME AGAINST HUMANITY,** punishable under Articles 5(d) and 7(1) and 7(3) of the Statute of the Tribunal.

Count 17: Inhumane Acts (Forcible Transfers), a **CRIME AGAINST HUMANITY,** punishable under Articles 5(i) and 7(1) and 7(3) of the Statute of the Tribunal.

Count 18: Unlawful Deportation or Transfer, a **GRAVE BREACH OF THE GENEVA CONVENTIONS OF 1949,** punishable under Articles 2(g) and 7(1) and 7(3) of the Statute of the Tribunal.

Counts 19 to 22: Wanton Destruction, Plunder of Public or Private Property

42. From on or about 1 March 1992 until 31 December 1995, **Slobodan Milosevic,** acting alone or in concert with members of the joint criminal enterprise, planned, instigated, ordered, committed or otherwise aided and abetted the planning, preparation or execution of the wanton destruction and plunder of the public and private property of the Bosnian Muslim, Bosnian Croat and other non-Serb populations within the territories of [a list of Bosnian towns and cities follows]. . . .This intentional and wanton destruction and plunder was not justified by military necessity and included:

a) The appropriation and plunder of property belonging to Bosnian Muslim, Bosnian Croat and other non-Serb civilians, including the coerced signing of documents relinquishing property rights.

b) The intentional and wanton destruction of homes and other property owned by Bosnian Muslim, Bosnian Croat and other non-Serb civilians. Such destruction was employed as a means to compel non-Serbs to flee their legal domiciles and to prevent their subsequent return.

c) The intentional and wanton destruction of religious and cultural buildings of the Bosnian Muslim and Bosnian Croat communities including, but not limited to, mosques, churches, libraries, educational buildings and cultural centres.

By these acts and omissions, **Slobodan Milosevic** committed:

Count 19: Extensive destruction and appropriation of property, not justified by military necessity and carried out unlawfully and wantonly, a **GRAVE BREACH OF THE GENEVA CONVENTIONS OF 1949,** punishable under Articles 2(d) and 7(1) and 7(3) of the Statute of the Tribunal.

Count 20: Wanton destruction of villages, or devastation not justified by military necessity, a **VIOLATION OF THE LAWS OR CUSTOMS OF WAR,** punishable under Articles 3(b) and 7(1) and 7(3) of the Statute of the Tribunal.

Count 21: Wilful destruction or wilful damage done to historic monuments and institutions dedicated to education or religion, a **VIOLATION OF THE LAWS OR CUSTOMS OF WAR,** punishable under Articles 3(d) and 7(1) and 7(3) of the Statute of the Tribunal.

Count 22: Plunder of public or private property, a **VIOLATION OF THE LAWS OR CUSTOMS OF WAR,** punishable under Articles 3(e) and 7(1) and 7(3) of the Statute of the Tribunal.

Counts 23 to 29: Murder, Wilful Killing, Wilfully Causing Great Suffering, Cruel Treatment, Attacks on Civilians

43. Between April 1992 and November 1995, **Slobodan Milosevic,** acting alone or in concert with members of the joint criminal enterprise, planned, instigated, ordered, committed, or otherwise aided and abetted the planning, preparation, or execution of a military campaign of artillery and mortar shelling and sniping onto civilian areas of Sarajevo and upon its civilian population, killing and wounding thousands of civilians of all ages and both sexes.

44. In this time period, the Sarajevo Romanija Corps of the VRS, under the effective control of Radovan Karadzic and General Ratko Mladic, launched an extensive, forty-four month shelling and sniping attack on Sarajevo, mostly from positions in the hills surrounding the city with an unobstructed view of Sarajevo.

45. The Sarajevo Romanija Corps conducted a protracted campaign of shelling and sniping upon Sarajevo during which civilians were either specifically targeted or the subject of reckless fire into areas where civilians were known to have been. Among the victims of this campaign were civilians who were, amongst other things, tending vegetable plots, queuing for bread or water, attending funerals, shopping in markets, riding on trams, gathering wood. Specific instances of sniping are described in **Schedule E** attached to this indictment. Specific instances of shelling are set forth in **Schedule F**.

By these acts and omissions, **Slobodan Milosevic** committed:

Count 23: Murder, a **CRIME AGAINST HUMANITY,** punishable under Articles 5(a) and 7(1) and 7(3) of the Statute of the Tribunal.

Count 24: Inhumane acts, a **CRIME AGAINST HUMANITY,** punishable under Articles 5(i) and 7(1) and 7(3) of the Statute of the Tribunal.

Count 25: Wilful killing, a **GRAVE BREACH OF THE GENEVA CONVENTIONS OF 1949,** punishable under Articles 2(a) and 7(1) and 7(3) of the Statute of the Tribunal.

Count 26: Wilfully causing great suffering, a **GRAVE BREACH OF THE GENEVA CONVENTIONS OF 1949,** punishable under Articles 2(c) and 7(1) and 7(3) of the Statute of the Tribunal.

Count 27: Murder, a **VIOLATION OF THE LAWS OR CUSTOMS OF WAR,** as recognised by Common Article 3(1)(a) of the Geneva Conventions of 1949, punishable under Articles 3 and 7(1) and 7(3) of the Statute of the Tribunal.

Count 28: Cruel treatment, a **VIOLATION OF THE LAWS OR CUSTOMS OF WAR,** as recognised by Common Article 3(1)(a) of the Geneva Conventions of 1949, punishable under Articles 3 and 7(1) and 7(3) of the Statute of the Tribunal.

Count 29: Attacks on civilians, a **VIOLATION OF THE LAWS OR CUS-TOMS OF WAR,** as recognised by Article 51 (2) of Additional Protocol I and Article 13 (2) of Additional Protocol II to the Geneva Conventions of 1949, punishable under Articles 3 and 7(1) and 7(3) of the Statute of the Tribunal.

General Legal Allegations

46. All acts and omissions alleged in this indictment occurred on the territory of the former Yugoslavia.

47. At all times relevant to this indictment, a state of international armed conflict and partial occupation existed in Bosnia and Herzegovina.

48. All acts and omissions charged as Grave Breaches of the Geneva Conventions of 1949 occurred during the international armed conflict and partial occupation of Bosnia and Herzegovina. All such acts and omissions were committed against persons protected under the Geneva Conventions.

49. All acts and omissions charged relative to the destruction of property as Grave Breaches of the Geneva Conventions of 1949 involved "protected property" under the relevant provisions of the Geneva Conventions.

50. At all times relevant to this indictment **Slobodan Milosevic** was required to abide by the laws and customs governing the conduct of armed conflicts, including the Geneva Conventions of 1949 and the Additional Protocols thereto.

51. All conduct charged as Crimes against Humanity was part of a widespread or systematic attack directed against the Bosnian Muslim, Bosnian Croat and other non-Serb civilian populations within large areas of Bosnia and Herzegovina.

Additional Facts

52. In November 1990, multi-party elections were held in Bosnia and Herzegovina. At the Republic level, the SDA ("*Stranka Demokratske Akcije*—Party of Democratic Action) the party of the Bosnian Muslims won 86 seats; the SDS, the party of the Bosnian Serbs, won 72 seats and the HDZ (*Hrvatska demokratska zajednica*—Croatian Democratic Community) won 44 seats in the Assembly.

53. The central idea within the SDS political platform, as articulated by its leaders, including Radovan Karadzic, Momcilo Krajisnik and Biljana Plavsic, was the unification of all Serbs within one state. The SDS regarded the separation of Bosnia and Herzegovina from the SFRY as a threat to the interests of the Serbs.

54. On 5 February 1991 the Assembly of the Republic of Serbia passed a "Law on Ministries" submitted by Slobodan MILOSEVIC. This law established twenty "Ministries" of the Serbian government, including the Ministry for Links with Serbs outside Serbia. This Ministry assisted the SDS to establish the Serb Republic of Bosnia and Herzegovina.

55. The results of the November 1990 elections meant that, as time went on, the SDS would be unable through peaceful means to keep the Republic of Bosnia and Herzegovina in what was becoming a Serb-dominated Yugoslavia. As a result, Serb people within certain areas of Bosnia and Herzegovina, with

Serb majorities, began to organise themselves into formal regional structures that they referred to as "Associations of Municipalities." In April 1991 the Association of Municipalities of Bosnian Krajina, centred in Banja Luka, was formed.

56. In March 1991, the collective Presidency of the SFRY reached a deadlock on several issues including the issue of instituting a state of emergency in Yugoslavia. The representatives on the Presidency from the Republic of Serbia, the Republic of Montenegro, the Autonomous Province of Vojvodina, and the Autonomous Province of Kosovo and Metohija all resigned from their posts. In a televised address on 16 March 1991, **Slobodan Milosevic,** in his capacity as President of the Republic of Serbia, declared that Yugoslavia was finished and that Serbia would no longer be bound by decisions of the Federal Presidency.

57. On 25 March 1991, **Slobodan Milosevic** and Franjo Tudman met in Karadjordjevo and discussed the partition of Bosnia and Herzegovina between Serbia and Croatia.

58. On 25 June 1991, Slovenia and Croatia declared their independence. On 26 June, the JNA intervened in Slovenia. In the summer of 1991, fighting broke out in Croatia.

59. In August 1991 Radovan Karadzic instituted a system of secret communication between the local boards of the SDS and the Main Staff and with the Republic of Serbia. This secret communication protocol was declared mandatory for the transmission of reports and orders.

60. From autumn 1991, the JNA began to withdraw its forces out of Croatia. Forces under the control of the JNA began to re-deploy in Bosnia and Herzegovina. Many of these troops were deployed to areas in which there was no garrison or other JNA facility.

61. As the war continued in Croatia it appeared increasingly likely that Bosnia and Herzegovina would also declare its independence from the SFRY. The SDS, realising it could not prevent the secession of Bosnia and Herzegovina from the SFRY, began the creation of a separate Serbian entity within Bosnia and Herzegovina. During the period from September to November 1991, several Serbian Autonomous Regions (SAO) were formed, some of them on the basis of the Associations of Municipalities referred to above.

62. On 12 September 1991, the Serbian Autonomous Region of Herzegovina was proclaimed. On 16 September 1991, the Autonomous Region of Krajina was proclaimed by the Assembly of the Association of Municipalities of Bosnian Krajina. By 21 November 1991, the Serbian Autonomous Regions and Autonomous Regions consisted of the Autonomous Region of Krajina, the SAO Herzegovina, the SAO Romanija-Birac, the SAO Semberija, and SAO Northern Bosnia.

63. On 3 October 1991, the four members of the SFRY Presidency from Serbia and Montenegro (Borisav JOVIC, Jugoslav Kostic, Sejdo BAJRAMOVIC and Branko Kostic) assumed the function of the SFRY Presidency, circumventing the roles and responsibilities of the Presidency members from Slovenia, Croatia, Bosnia and Herzegovina and Macedonia.

64. On 15 October 1991, at the meeting of the SDS Party Council the deci-

sion was reached to form a separate assembly, entitled the "Assembly of the Serbian People of Bosnia and Herzegovina" to secure Serb interests.

65. On or around 22 October 1991, **Slobodan Milosevic,** together with other members of the joint criminal enterprise, continued to advocate for a unitary Serb state governed from Belgrade, Serbia. On the same date the "Rump Presidency" called for the mobilisation of reservists in Serbia and "other regions that want to stay in Yugoslavia."

66. On or about 26 October 1991, Radovan Karadzic declared a full mobilisation of the TO and the formation of field units in the Serb Republic of Bosnia and Herzegovina.

67. On 24 October 1991, the Assembly of the Serbian People in Bosnia and Herzegovina, dominated by the SDS, decided to conduct a "Plebiscite of the Serbian People in Bosnia and Herzegovina" in order to decide whether to stay in the common state of Yugoslavia with Serbia, Montenegro, the Serbian Autonomous Region of Krajina, SAO Western Slavonia and SAO Eastern Slavonia, Baranja and Western Srem.

68. On 9 and 10 November 1991, the Bosnian Serbs held the plebiscite on the issue of whether Bosnia and Herzegovina should stay in Yugoslavia or become an independent state. The results overwhelmingly showed that the Bosnian Serbs wanted to stay in Yugoslavia.

69. On 21 November 1991, the Assembly of the Serbian People of Bosnia and Herzegovina, proclaimed as part of the territory of the federal Yugoslav state all those municipalities, local communities and populated places, in which over 50% of the people of Serbian nationality had voted, during the plebiscite, to remain in that state as well as those places where citizens of other nationalities had expressed themselves in favour of remaining in Yugoslavia.

70. On 11 December 1991, the Assembly of the Serbian People delivered a detailed request to the JNA to protect with all available means as "integral parts of the State of Yugoslavia" the territories of Bosnia and Herzegovina in which the plebiscite of the Serbian people and other citizens on remaining in a joint Yugoslav state had been conducted.

71. On 19 December 1991, the SDS issued instructions for the "Organisation and Activity of the Organs of the Serbian People in Bosnia and Herzegovina in Extraordinary Circumstances" which provided a plan for the SDS take-over of municipalities in Bosnia and Herzegovina.

72. On 9 January 1992, the Assembly of the Serbian People of Bosnia and Herzegovina adopted a declaration on the Proclamation of the Serbian Republic of Bosnia and Herzegovina. The territory of that republic was declared to include "the territories of the Serbian Autonomous Regions and Districts and of other Serbian ethnic entities in Bosnia and Herzegovina, including the regions in which the Serbian people remained in the minority due to the genocide conducted against it in World War Two", and it was declared to be a part of the federal Yugoslav state. On 12 August 1992, the name of the Bosnian Serb Republic was changed to Republika Srpska.

73. From 29 February to 2 March 1992, Bosnia and Herzegovina held a referendum on independence. At the urging of the SDS, the majority of Bosnian

Serbs boycotted the vote. The referendum resulted in a pro-independence majority.

74. On 18 March 1992, during the 11th session of the Assembly of the Serbian People, a conclusion was reached to "prepare for the next session proposals for the take-over of power in the Republic of Serbian People of Bosnia and Herzegovina."

75. From March 1992 onwards, Serb regular and irregular forces seized control of territories within Bosnia and Herzegovina, including those specified in this indictment.

76. On 6 April 1992, the United States and the European Community formally recognized the independence of Bosnia and Herzegovina.

77. On 27 April 1992, Serbia and Montenegro proclaimed a new Federal Republic of Yugoslavia and declared it the successor state of the Socialist Federal Republic of Yugoslavia.

78. On 12 May 1992, at the 16th Assembly of the Serbian People in Bosnia and Herzegovina, Radovan Karadzic announced the six strategic objectives of the Serbian People in Bosnia and Herzegovina. These objectives included the eradication of the Drina River as a border between the Serbian states. During the same session, General Ratko Mladic told the Assembly that it would not be possible to separate Serbs from non-Serbs and have the non-Serbs simply leave the territory. He warned that attempting this process would amount to genocide.

79. On 15 May 1992, the United Nations Security Council in its resolution number 752 demanded that all interference from outside Bosnia and Herzegovina by units of the JNA cease immediately and that those units either be withdrawn, be subjected to the authority of the Government of the Republic, or be disbanded and disarmed. . . .

[Schedules A through F listed specific instances of war crimes referred to in the indictment. **Schedule A** listed "Killings Not Associated with Detention Facilities' and gave the numbers of people killed in various towns and villages in Bosnia. **Schedule B** listed "Killings Associated with Detention Facilities" and listed the numbers of people killed at various prisons and similar facilities. **Schedule C** listed "Detention Facilities" in Bosnia. **Schedule D** listed cases of "Forcible Transfers" of non-Serb displaced persons and refugees in various towns and villages, giving the number of people transferred in each case. **Schedule E** listed forty-seven incidents in which non-Serbs in the Bosnian capital of Sarajevo were killed by snipers. **Schedule F** listed specific incidents in which Serbian and Yugoslav military forces fired artillery shells at Sarajevo.]

PRESIDENT BUSH ON TERRORISM AND THE THREATS POSED BY IRAQ
November 26, 2001

The United States and Iraq, locked in confrontation since the Persian Gulf war of 1991, appeared headed for outright conflict at the end of 2001. In the wake of the September 11 terrorist attacks against the United States, President George W. Bush stepped up rhetorical attacks against Iraqi leader Saddam Hussein, bluntly warning him that he would be "held accountable" for building biological, chemical, and nuclear weapons. Some of Bush's senior aides were lobbying, both publicly and behind the scenes, for firm action against Iraq. The exact nature of that action apparently had not been decided as of year's end, but the options ranged from covert operations to drive Saddam from power to a full-scale military invasion. The vast majority of U.S. allies appeared to be skeptical, at best, or even adamantly opposed to the invasion option. (Terrorist attacks, pp. 614, 624, 637)

In the meantime, Iraq's 22 million people continued to suffer from the consequences of the long-term economic collapse that followed Saddam's failed military adventures during the previous two decades. The country's economic woes were deepened by sanctions imposed by the United Nations following the Persian Gulf war. The UN had eased the sanctions to allow Iraq to use its vast oil exports to buy food for its people, but the United States insisted that Saddam was diverting much of the money to rebuild his army and to maintain himself in power. (Iraq background, Historic Documents of 2000, p. 581; Historic Documents of 1999, p. 144; Historic Documents of 1998, p. 482)

Sanctions on Iraq

George W. Bush's father, then-president George H. Bush, had stopped short of a direct attack on Saddam at the conclusion of the Persian Gulf war in 1991. After ending Iraq's occupation of Kuwait and destroying much of Saddam's army, he had decided against marching the U.S. and allied armies to Baghdad for what almost certainly would have been a bloody struggle to drive Saddam from power. Instead, Bush decided on a policy of containing Saddam in the hopes of preventing him from continuing to threaten his neighbors. The United Nations Security Council passed resolutions imposing sanctions against Iraq (including exercising UN control over the Iraqi oil industry) and requiring Baghdad to destroy its ballistic missiles and stockpiles of biological and chemical weapons and components for nuclear weapons.

During the 1990s UN inspectors succeeded in dismantling most, if not all, of Iraq's missiles and its nuclear weapons program, but Iraq skillfully used deceit and delay to preserve much of its presumed arsenals of biological and chemical weapons. Frustrated by Iraqi recalcitrance, UN inspectors withdrew from Iraq in December 1998. President Bill Clinton ordered a four-day attack by bombs and missiles on Iraqi military installations, but Saddam showed no sign of a willingness to change his ways. The UN Security Council in 1999 voted to establish a new system of weapons inspections and, in return, allow Iraq more freedom to spend its oil revenues. Saddam refused to allow any new inspections and demanded an end to the sanctions. Saddam also sought to circumvent the sanctions by reopening an old oil pipeline to Syria that the UN did not control and by striking secret commercial deals with many of his neighbors.

International support for the sanctions had waned by late 2000, largely because of increasing evidence that the sanctions had contributed to the economic woes that beset the Iraqi people. Saddam's government claimed that more than 1 million Iraqis had starved because of the sanctions. The United States said Saddam was to blame for any hardship in Iraq because he had diverted hundreds of millions of dollars to rebuilding his army and enriching himself and his supporters.

After taking office in January 2001, the new Bush administration attempted to negotiate a new system, which it called "smart" sanctions, that would maintain the pressure on Saddam but ease the negative effect of sanctions on his people. Secretary of State Colin Powell undertook extensive negotiations with U.S. allies. Those talks resulted in a proposal, offered by Britain and the United States to the UN Security Council in May, to lift all prohibitions on exports to Iraq except for weapons and military-related items. In return, the proposal required Iraq to admit the UN weapons inspectors and give them unfettered access to all weapons facilities; the UN would also retained control over Iraqi oil revenues. China, Russia, and other Security Council members blocked consideration of the proposal, however, and so the 1991 sanctions remained in place through the rest of 2001.

Even as the Bush administration was attempting to revise the sanctions policy, it acted to maintain military pressure on Saddam. In the largest attack against Iraq since December 1998, U.S. and British warplanes on February 16 fired missiles at five air defense installations in southern Iraq, just north of the "no fly zone" that covered the southern one-third of the country. That zone was intended to protect Shiites in the area from government repression. U.S. and British planes carried out smaller attacks on Iraq military installations in April, May, and August.

Bush Administration Threats to Iraq

After the September 11 terrorist attacks in the United States, Bush announced the launching of a long-term war against all terrorist groups "of global reach." Initially, the war focused on Afghanistan, the operational base of the al Qaeda network that Bush blamed for the attacks. But Bush made clear, in numerous statements, that the United States would go after terrorist groups elsewhere and the countries that harbored them. In that context, some officials within the administration and numerous experts outside the administration argued after September 11 that, because Saddam continued to pose a major threat to stability in the Middle East, Iraq should be the next target in the war against terrorism. Richard Perle, a Republican defense analyst who chaired a Pentagon advisory panel, was the principal public exponent of this view. Defense Secretary Donald H. Rumsfeld and Deputy Defense Secretary Paul Wolfowitz reportedly were among senior administration officials who agreed with Perle's assessment.

Bush fueled speculation that he had adopted that assessment himself. In an appearance at the White House on November 26, Bush responded to reporters' questions about Iraq with sharp language that categorized Saddam as a terrorist. "If anybody harbors a terrorist, they're a terrorist," he said. "If they fund a terrorist, they're a terrorist. If they house terrorists, they're terrorists. I mean, I can't make it any more clearly to other nations around the world. If they develop weapons of mass destruction that will be used to terrorize nations, they will be held accountable. And as for Mr. Saddam Hussein, he needs to let inspectors back into his country, to show us that he is not developing weapons of mass destruction."

With that statement, Bush appeared to adopt a much broader definition of terrorism than he had in previous remarks since September 11. That statement was the first in which he had equated the possession of weapons of mass destruction with terrorism. In response to a follow-up question, however, Bush denied that he was changing policy by expanding his definition of terrorism: "Have I expanded the definition? I've always had that definition, as far as I'm concerned."

The day after Bush made those remarks, his spokesman, Ari Fleischer, said the president did not mean to imply that military action against Iraq was imminent. "The president is focused on phase one," Fleischer said, referring to the ongoing war in Afghanistan. "Anything that may come subsequent to that would be something the president would discuss at the appropriate time, if and whether that would come to be."

Bush's stepped up rhetoric against Iraq raised widespread concerns among U.S. allies. Few allied leaders chose to confront Bush directly on the matter, but, according to news reports, senior diplomats from Europe and the Middle East suggested to the administration that it needed to be cautious about mounting a major military campaign against Saddam. Among other things, these diplomats reportedly noted that the United States had offered no evidence that Iraq played any role in the September 11 terrorist attacks, so a new war against that country could not be justified as direct retaliation.

851

Allies, including German chancellor Gerhard Schroeder and Egyptian president Hosni Mubarak, also argued that Saddam was a much tougher and more resilient foe than the Taliban regime had been in Afghanistan. Attempting to push him from power, they said, likely would be an expensive and time-consuming operation with no guarantee of success. Cautionary advice also came from the NATO secretary general, Lord Robertson, who suggested in a December 28 interview with the BBC that military force would only be justified if the United States could prove that Iraq played a role in the September 11 attacks, either by sponsoring the terrorists or by harboring "people who were intimately connected with" the terrorists. "Until that happens, I don't think people should jump to conclusions," he said.

Russian president Vladimir Putin said in an interview with London's Financial Times, *published December 17, that he expected to be consulted by Washington before any new military operations were launched outside of Afghanistan. Russia, along with France, was owed billions of dollars by Baghdad from work during the 1970s and 1980s on the Iraqi oil industry. Russian businesses also hoped to expand operations in Iraq once the UN sanctions were lifted.*

According to a report issued in 2000 by the International Institute for Strategic Studies in London, Iraq had rebuilt much of the army that had been heavily damaged during the Persian Gulf war. The report put Iraq's active-duty army strength at 429,000, with another 650,000 in reserves. Even so, that report and other studies said it was unclear whether Iraq had been able to maintain its weaponry and other military equipment. UN sanctions officially blocked all military imports by Iraq, forcing the country to rely on limited domestic production, smuggling, and illegal shipments from other countries for spare parts and new equipment.

Aiding the Opposition

After the Gulf war, the Bush and Clinton administrations had provided covert aid to the Iraqi National Congress (INC), a London-based coalition of groups opposed to Saddam's rule. The INC included former government and military officials who had broken with Saddam and representatives of various groups that Saddam had suppressed. Among the latter were the Kurdish minority in the north of Iraq and the majority Shiite Muslims who were predominant in the southern part of the country. (Saddam and his inner circle were Sunni Muslims, a minority in Iraq but a majority in most other Islamic countries.)

Among other things, U.S. aid during the early 1990s enabled the Iraqi Congress to create a small guerrilla army based in the northern area of Iraq that since 1991 had been protected by a no-fly zone barring Iraqi military flights. But in 1996 Saddam sent his army into that zone to crush the Iraqi opposition, and the Clinton administration withdrew most of its financial support from the opposition, which had proven ineffective. Congress in 1998 attempted to force the administration to step up the aid by passing legislation known as the Iraq Liberation Act (PL 105-338), authorizing $97 million for the Iraqi opposition. According to most reports, the major result of *that legislation was to subsidize the INC office in London, which was headed by its founder, Ahmed Chalabi. Congress acted again in late 2000, appropriating $12 million for "humanitarian" aid in Iraq, which was to be distributed by the INC, and $6 million to enable that organization to set up radio and television broadcasts in Iraq.*

In its final weeks in office, the Clinton administration approved plans for the use of the $12 million in humanitarian aid. After taking office in January, the Bush administration reportedly confirmed that proposal and authorized the Iraqi National Congress to use U.S. aid for additional operations in Iraq, including collecting intelligence information for the United States. The Washington Post *quoted a State Department official as saying, "We're saying to the INC, you're beyond the organizational phase. Now do something." The Bush administration in June approved use of the $6 million for broadcasts, and in August the INC began transmitting anti-Saddam propaganda into Iraq by satellite.*

Despite these aid efforts, some members of Congress pressed for even more aggressive assistance to the INC. In a December 7 letter, nine House and Senate members asked Bush to step up aid for that group's operations inside Iraq. "We believe we must directly confront Saddam, sooner rather than later," the members said. Among the signers were Trent Lott, R-Miss., the Senate minority leader, and Henry J. Hyde, R-Ill., chairman of the House International Relations Committee.

Following are excerpts from remarks November 26, 2001, by President George W. Bush at an event at the White House celebrating the release of two American aid workers who had been held captive in Afghanistan by the Taliban government after the United States launched its military offensive there in October. During that session Bush responded to questions by reporters about his statements concerning Iraq and his proclaimed war against terrorism.

The document was obtained from the Internet at http://www .whitehouse.gov/news/release/2001/11/print/20011126-1 .html.

Question: Mr. President, at Fort Campbell, you said: across the world and across the years, we will fight the evil ones, and we will win—

President Bush: Yes.

Q:—suggesting very strongly that Afghanistan is only the first step. What would you say about Iraq, as you begin to look at the next steps in the campaign against global terrorism? What message would you like to send to them now?

President Bush: Well, my message is, is that if you harbor a terrorist, you're a terrorist. If you feed a terrorist, you're a terrorist. If you develop weapons of mass destruction that you want to terrorize the world, you'll be held accountable. And I also have said, as I recall at the White House, we're going to make sure that we accomplish each mission that we tackle. First things first.

Now having said that, we, the coalition, has arrested over 300 people. I can't wait to thank my friend, President Aznar of Spain, for having arrested eight terrorists in Spain. In other words, there is an international drag—international effort to bring people to justice. And over 300 people that have been involved with al Qaeda have been brought to justice. Terrorism is terrorism. In this country, we'll deal with it. . . .

Q: Does Saddam Hussein have to agree to allow weapons inspectors back into Iraq? Is that an unconditional demand of yours?

President Bush: Saddam Hussein agreed to allow inspectors in his country. And in order to prove to the world he's not developing weapons of mass destruction, he ought to let the inspectors back in.

Q: And if he doesn't, sir?

President Bush: Yes?

Q: And if he does not do that, sir, what will be the consequence? If he does not do that, what will be the consequences?

President Bush: That's up for—he'll find out.

Q: Sir, what is your thinking right now about taking the war to Iraq? You suggested that on Wednesday, when you said Afghanistan was just the beginning.

President Bush: I stand by those words. Afghanistan is still just the beginning. If anybody harbors a terrorist, they're a terrorist. If they fund a terrorist, they're a terrorist. If they house terrorists, they're terrorists. I mean, I can't make it any more clearly to other nations around the world. If they develop weapons of mass destruction that will be used to terrorize nations, they will be held accountable. And as for Mr. Saddam Hussein, he needs to let inspectors back in his country, to show us that he is not developing weapons of mass destruction.

Q: Mr. President, following up on that thought, when you initially made—defined terrorism in your speech before Congress, you did not include them as weapons of mass destruction. Are you now extending this to countries like North Korea, other places where we have had evidence over the years that there's been development of such weapons?

President Bush: Well, clearly, in terms of North Korea, we want North Korea to allow inspectors in, to determine whether or not they are. We've had that discussion with North Korea. I made it very clear to North Korea that in order for us to have relations with them, that we want to know, are they developing weapons of mass destruction? And they ought to stop proliferating.

So part of the war on terror is to deny terrorist weapons getting—I mean, weapons to be used for means of terror getting in the hands of nations that will use them. And so I'm not quite sure of the—

Q: I'm just asking if you've expanded your definition to countries who don't just harbor terrorists, but also develop such weapons.

President Bush: Have I expanded the definition? I've always had that definition, as far as I'm concerned.

December

ENRON CORPORATION ON ITS BANKRUPTCY FILING
December 2, 2001

The Enron Corporation, a Houston-based energy firm that grew quickly during the 1980s and 1990s with creative business and accounting practices, on December 2, 2001, became the largest American company ever to file for bankruptcy. Enron's rapid fall from the heights of the business world briefly roiled the financial markets and set off a mad scramble of recriminations and investigations that seemed certain to have repercussions for months, and possibly years, to come.

The collapse of Enron had political as well as business implications. Enron had been one of the most aggressive corporate contributors to candidates of both political parties, and its chairman, Kenneth Lay, was a longtime friend of President George W. Bush and a major financial supporter of his political campaigns. By year's end no evidence had emerged that anyone in government had done anything improper to aid Enron. But evidence did emerge showing that Enron used its political connections to convince state and federal governments to scale back their regulations effecting the types of business that Enron pioneered. Congressional investigations planned for 2002 appeared likely to result in some corrective legislation.

Enron was often described as a corporate behemoth, based largely on Fortune *magazine's ranking of it as number seven among the country's five hundred largest companies. At the beginning of 2001 Enron's shares were valued at more than $60 billion, and the company reported earnings for 2000 of more than $100 billion, making it bigger than such longtime giants as AT&T or IBM. After Enron filed for bankruptcy, it soon became clear that much of Enron's corporate heft was more hype than substance. The company had used questionable partnerships to disguise billions of dollars in debt and had claimed billions of dollars in revenues that did not exist. Once the wishful thinking was stripped away, Enron was exposed as a shell of the corporate giant that for a time had bedazzled investors, stock analysts, business partners, and government regulators.*

How Enron Grew

Enron was formed in 1985 by the merger of two natural gas pipeline companies, Houston Natural Gas and InterNorth, which was based in Omaha. The combined company controlled approximately 37,000 miles of pipeline. Under Lay's leadership, Enron quickly moved beyond simply selling and delivering natural gas. In 1989 it became a trading company, at first trading natural gas commodities and growing to become the nation's largest seller of natural gas. Enron moved into the electricity field in 1994, eventually becoming the nation's largest seller of electricity. By the late 1990s Enron was brokering deals for just about anything that could be sold in bulk, whether immediately or in the future, including coal, metals, wood pulp, and Internet services. Enron even bought and sold the weather—or at least speculative investments known as "weather derivatives" based on fluctuations in energy usage resulting from the weather. In some cases, Enron actually produced or delivered the products it sold. In other cases Enron traded products made by other companies, making its money by negotiating prices between buyers and sellers; often it set the prices itself and took a cut from both buyers and sellers.

Enron's innovative business practices carried over into the high-technology field, which was booming in the late 1990s. In 1999 Enron introduced EnronOnline, which it described as the world's first Internet-based market for trading commodities. Within a year, Enron claimed that service was one of its most profitable businesses.

The rise of Enron was not totally smooth. The company's stock fell in 1997 after Wall Street analysts cut their projections for the company earnings. Enron's response was to move several partnerships it had created off its books, helping it to inflate its earnings and, more importantly, disguise its debts. That move was part of an Enron innovation that went virtually unnoticed at the time: the use of multiple partnerships to shoulder much of the debt burden that Enron would assume if it lost its bets on the future prices of the commodities it traded. In its required financial reports, Enron gave vague, generally incomprehensible descriptions of these partnerships as "related party entities" or "special purpose entities" and similar titles.

Enron stock rose again in 1998 and kept on soaring. Between 1998 and 2000 its reported revenues more than tripled, from $31 billion to $100 billion. Enron installed a banner in the lobby of its Houston headquarters building: "The World's Leading Energy Company." It promised to pay $100 million over thirty years for the rights to name Houston's new baseball park "Enron Field." Enron's claim that it developed an entirely new business model went unchallenged for years. Fortune *magazine consistently listed Enron among the nation's "Most Admired Companies," and for six years in a row named it the country's "Most Innovative" company. Such glowing reviews, based almost entirely on the company's claims of endless earnings growth, consistently led New York stock analysts to put the word* buy *next to Enron's name. And that is what millions of investors did. Enron stock hit $90 a share in August 2000 and closed that year at just over $88 a share.*

How Enron Fell

Until 2001 few people bothered to question how Enron made its money, or even if it actually made the money it claimed. One of the first important skeptical looks at Enron came early in the year from James Chanos, who headed a New York company, Kynikos Associates, which specialized in betting that company stock prices would fall (a specialized field known as "short-selling"). Chanos questioned Enron's earnings claims and business practices. Among other things, Chanos said Enron was selling some of its physical assets and reporting the income as recurring ordinary revenue, not as a one-time sale. Chanos also questioned Enron's vague reporting of the partnerships and undefined "entities" with which it did business. In particular, Chanos expressed concern that at least one of the "entities" was managed by an unidentified senior Enron executive—an apparent conflict of interest. Those "entities" later turned out to be the off-the-books partnerships that Enron used to hide much of its debt; the biggest of them, using variations on the name LJM, were managed by Andrew Fastow, Enron's chief operating officer (COO), who had personally invested in them.

Because of the nature of his own business, Chanos had a stake in seeing Enron's stock fall, so few people took his questions seriously at the time. One person who did was Fortune *magazine writer Bethany McLean, who queried top Enron executives about the issues Chanos raised, only to be told that she was not capable of understanding the business. McLean said Jeffrey Skilling, recently named the company's chief executive officer, told her: "People who raise questions are people who have not gone through it [company financial reporting] in detail. We have explicit answers, but people want to throw rocks at us."*

McLean's report in Fortune *raised eyebrows on Wall Street, which was beginning to become nervous about energy companies in general because of political controversies stemming from the energy crisis then under way in California. That state's governor, Gray Davis, and other politicians had charged that Enron and other energy firms were manipulating the markets by cutting supplies.* (Energy issues, p. 331)

Enron's stock began to slide, from its $90 peak in 2000 to less than $45 in mid-August 2001. On August 14 Skilling resigned suddenly as Enron CEO, citing personal reasons. Kenneth Lay, the company's chairman, took back the CEO title he had given to Skilling just six months earlier and managed to calm now-jittery nerves on Wall Street. Lay insisted the company was sound, but he acknowledged for the first time that Enron needed to improve its credibility, which had been damaged by its vague financial reports that some people were belatedly reading. Despite these concerns, Enron remained popular on Wall Street. According to a later report by the Motley Fool, *an investment advisory firm in Virginia, sixteen of the seventeen securities analysts who specialized in Enron rated the company a "buy" as late as September. In its August 14, 2001, edition* Fortune *named Enron as one of the top ten "growth stocks" for the first decade of the twenty-first century.*

The public collapse of Enron began on October 16, when it reported a loss of $618 million for the third quarter of 2001. The loss resulted from one-time charges of $1.2 billion resulting from losses in its water-management and telecommunications divisions—but Enron offered no details. The October 16 announcement shook Wall Street and raised many new questions. Saying that company executives had "lost credibility," David Fleischer, an analyst for Goldman, Sachs, told the New York Times: *"They need to convince investors these earnings are real, that the company is for real and that growth will be realized. That has to be proven over time." Fleischer had been one of Enron's strongest supporters on Wall Street, the newspaper said.*

As Enron's stock entered into a free fall, the Wall Street Journal *raised further questions about its financial practices. The* Journal *reported that $35 million of the $1.2 billion write-off had been due to losses by the partnerships managed by Fastow. On October 22, the company announced that the Securities and Exchange Commission (SEC) had opened an "informal inquiry" into the partnerships Fastow had created. Enron stock fell even further, to less than $15 a share, and Lay put in a conference call to investment analysts, assuring them that the company would be making no further announcements about writing off losses. Lay also fired Fastow.*

Despite Lay's soothing words, the bad news continued with the company's announcement on November 1 that the SEC had launched a formal investigation. Moreover, Standard and Poor's and Moody's, the credit-rating services, lowered their rating on Enron debt to just above junk bond ("speculative investment") status. Companies that in the past had eagerly done business with Enron now shied away from any deal in which Enron was accepting risk. That hesitancy to associate with Enron was heightened early in November, when reports emerged that the company was seeking a major investor but not having any luck. The company's stock fell to below $10 a share on November 6.

Another blow came on November 8 when Enron acknowledged that it was reducing its claimed earnings since 1997 by $586 million—contradicting Lay's assurances just two weeks earlier that there would be no further announcements along this line. Even so, Enron found a buyer, rival Houston energy firm Dynegy Inc. That company agreed on November 9 to buy Enron for $7.8 billion in stock, along with the assumption of $13 billion worth of Enron debt. Dynegy's chairman, Chuck Watson, expressed confidence about the union of the two companies, which had been fierce competitors. "We know the company well," he said of Enron. "It's not like we started fresh. I'm confident that it's as solid as we thought it was."

However sincere Watson's expressions of confidence might have been at the time, new disclosures shook that confidence. Enron acknowledged on November 19 that it was unable to make payments on $690 million in outstanding debts. On November 27 Standard and Poor's and Moody' cut Enron's credit rating to junk bond status; that move triggered contractual obligations for Enron to repay more than $3 billion in debt—money the company did not have. Dynegy quickly pulled out of the merger deal, saying

Enron had not disclosed all its debt. "Sometimes, a company's best deals are the very ones they did not do," Watson said. Enron stock fell that day to $3.50 a share, a huge drop from its level of about $90 at the start of the year. One day later, Enron stock sold for just 61 cents.

After struggling unsuccessfully to line up emergency financing, Enron announced on December 2 that it was filing for Chapter 11 bankruptcy protection. The company listed asserts of $50 billion and liabilities of $31 billion, but the latter figure did not include billions of dollars in debts owed by Enron's partnerships. Apparently looking for a silver lining, Enron also announced that it was filing suit against Dynegy for breach of contract and demanding $10 billion in damages. Enron also asked a federal court to block Dynegy from seizing the Northern Natural Gas pipeline. Dynegy said it was entitled to the pipeline, one of Enron's chief assets, in compensation for $1.5 billion it had invested in Enron as part of the merger agreement. Dynegy's own stock prices tumbled in the wake of the Enron collapse, along with those of several other energy firms.

At least nominally, the Enron bankruptcy was the largest in U.S. history. The previous holder of that honor was Texaco, the oil company, which filed for bankruptcy in 1987, listing assets at that time of $36 billion. Texaco later was acquired by Chevron.

Enron on December 3 fired about 4,000 of the 7,500 employees at its Houston headquarters. The firings were the latest blow for Enron employees, who previously had expressed intense pride in their company. Many of Enron's 21,000 employees lost the bulk of their retirement savings, which they had invested in Enron stock based on assurances by Lay and other executives that the company was sound. For nearly a month between October and November, when Enron stock was in its final plunge, Enron barred employees from selling the company shares in their retirement plans. Millions of other Americans also lost money on Enron—although to a far lesser degree than Enron employees—through pension funds and mutual funds that had invested heavily in the company.

Also suffering because of its relationship with Enron was the accounting firm Arthur Andersen & Co., which had been Enron's auditor and financial adviser. Enron's collapse led investors, members of Congress, and others to ask how Arthur Anderson had missed the company's financial irregularities, or if it had not missed then, why it had not reported them to the SEC, as commission regulations required. Testifying on December 12 at the first congressional hearing on Enron, Arthur Anderson's chief executive, Joseph P. Bernardino, said Enron had engaged in "possibly illegal acts" but had withheld information from its auditors.

Many analysts attributed Enron's problems to the fundamental business failings of greed and arrogance. In this view, high-flying company executives simply wanted to make Enron the biggest and richest company in the world—and to enrich themselves along with it. Executives were paid according to a complex formula based on the value of the contracts they delivered—an incentive that almost inevitably led some executives to exaggerate what those contracts would produce, according to a December 24 report by Fortune.

The company's apparent rapid success toward its financial goals led, in turn, to a certain hubris, according to this view. "The story of Enron is the story of unmitigated pride and arrogance," Jeffrey Pfeffer, a professor of behavioral science at Stanford University's Business School told the Washington Post. *"My impression is that they thought they knew everything, which [is] always the fatal flaw. No one knows everything." Ironically, former Enron CEO Skilling later insisted to the* New York Times *that he did not know everything—at least all the facts about the company's financial problems. "We're all trying to figure out what happened," Skilling told the newspaper. "This was a tragedy. I had no idea the company was in anything but excellent shape."*

Avoiding Government Regulations

As they began investigating the Enron collapse, one of the issues that members of Congress and federal agencies considered was whether government itself had played any role in the matter. The most important question involved a number of decisions, at the federal and state levels, that effectively exempted much of Enron's business—along with that of many other companies—from government scrutiny.

During its rise, Enron used its political clout to urge federal agencies and state legislatures to deregulate the energy business, and then it moved in to take advantage of new markets that deregulation offered. California, which deregulated its energy market in 1996, was the biggest prize, and Enron became the state's single biggest supplier of electricity and natural gas. In May 2000 Enron launched The New Power Company, which it described as the first national energy service to provide for residences and small businesses. Among the company's "strategic investors" were IBM and AOL-Time Warner.

Enron also escaped some of the key regulations that the federal government normally imposed on the trading of commodities futures. Late in 1992, near the end of the presidency of George H. Bush, the Commodities Futures Trading Commission (CFTC) exempted power companies, such as Enron, from oversight of trading in futures of energy derivatives (a type of investment based on the value of other stocks and financial instruments). The commission was headed at the time by Wendy L. Gramm. Gramm then stepped down as commission chairman and, just five weeks later, was named a member of Enron's board of directors. Trading in energy derivatives later became one of Enron's most profitable ventures, according to news reports.

During the latter stages of the Clinton administration, the CFTC moved to reconsider its earlier exemption of energy derivatives from regulation. Enron then worked with its allies on Capitol Hill to ensure that a provision preventing such a step was included in the Commodity Future Modernization Act, which was passed in 2000. One of the congressional committees that reviewed the legislation was the Senate Banking Committee, whose chairman at the time was Phil Gramm, R-Texas, the husband of Wendy Gramm. According to the New York Times, *one of the Clinton administration's key representatives in the debate over that legislation was Linda Robertson, the Treasury Department's liaison to Congress. After leaving the government in November 2000, Robertson was named head of Enron's Washington office.*

When the administration of President George W. Bush took office in January 2001, Lay parlayed his friendship with the president into access at the highest levels in Washington. Lay or his aides met several times with Vice President Dick Cheney and other members of a task force Cheney headed on energy policy.

In the wake of the Enron collapse, congressional committees in December began a reexamination of previous government decisions about regulations involving Enron and similar companies. One of the most likely fields for new legislation was pension law. Members of Congress in both parties suggested reforms requiring employers to give their employees better information and limiting the amount of company stock held in employee pension plans.

> *Following are excerpts from a news release issued December 2, 2001, by the Enron Corporation, in which it announced that it was filing for Chapter 11 bankruptcy protection and suing Dynegy Inc. for alleged "breach of contract."*
>
> **The document was obtained from the Internet at http:// www.enron.com/corp/pressroom/releases/2001/ene/Press Release11-12-02-01letterhead.html**

Enron Corp. announced today that it along with certain of its subsidiaries have filed voluntary petitions for Chapter 11 reorganization with the U.S. Bankruptcy Court for the Southern District of New York. As part of the reorganization process, Enron also filed suit against Dynegy Inc. in the same court, alleging breach of contract in connection with Dynegy's wrongful termination of its proposed merger with Enron and seeking damages of at least $10 billion. Enron's lawsuit also seeks the court's declaration that Dynegy is not entitled to exercise its option to acquire an Enron subsidiary that indirectly owns Northern Natural Gas Pipeline. Proceeds from the lawsuit would benefit Enron's creditors.

In a related development aimed at preserving value in its North American wholesale energy trading business, Enron said that it is in active discussions with various leading financial institutions to provide credit support for, recapitalize and revitalize that business under a new ownership structure. It is anticipated that Enron would provide the new entity with traders, back office capabilities and technology from Enron's North American wholesale energy business, and that the new entity would conduct counterparty transactions through EnronOnline, the company's existing energy trading platform. Any such arrangement would be subject to the approval of the Bankruptcy Court.

In connection with the company's Chapter 11 filings, Enron is in active discussions with leading financial institutions for debtor-in-possession (DIP) financing and expects to complete these discussions shortly. Upon the completion and court approval of these arrangements, the new funding will be available immediately on an interim basis to supplement Enron's existing capital and help the company fulfill obligations associated with operating its business, including its employee payroll and payments to vendors for goods and services provided on or after today's filing.

Filings for Chapter 11 reorganization have been made for a total of 14 affiliated entities, including Enron Corp.; Enron North America Corp. , the company's wholesale energy trading business; Enron Energy Services, the company's retail energy marketing operations; Enron Transportation Services, the holding company for Enron's pipeline operations; Enron Broadband Services, the company's bandwidth trading operation; and Enron Metals & Commodity Corp.

Enron-related entities not included in the Chapter 11 filing are not affected by the filing. These non-filing entities include Northern Natural Gas Pipeline, Transwestern Pipeline, Florida Gas Transmission, EOTT, Portland General Electric and numerous other Enron international entities.

To conserve capital, Enron will implement a comprehensive cost-saving program that will include substantial workforce reductions. These workforce reductions primarily will affect the company's operations in Houston, where Enron currently employs approximately 7,500 people.

In addition, the company will continue its accelerated program to divest or wind down non-core assets and operations. Details of the units to be affected will be communicated shortly.

The Dynegy Lawsuit

In its lawsuit filed today in U.S. Bankruptcy Court in New York, Enron alleges, among other things, that Dynegy breached its Merger Agreement with Enron by terminating the agreement when it had no contractual right to do so; and that Dynegy has no right to exercise its option to acquire the entity that indirectly owns the Northern Natural Gas pipeline because that option can only be triggered by a valid termination of the Merger Agreement.

The Chapter 11 Filings

In conjunction with today's petitions for Chapter 11 reorganization, Enron will ask the Bankruptcy Court to consider a variety of "first day motions" to support its employees, vendors, trading counterparties, customers and other constituents. These include motions seeking court permission to continue payments for employee payroll and health benefits; obtain interim financing authority and maintain cash management programs; and retain legal, financial and other professionals to support the company's reorganization actions. In accordance with applicable law and court orders, vendors and suppliers who provided goods or services to Enron Corp. or the subsidiaries that have filed for Chapter 11 protection before today's filing may have pre-petition claims, which will be frozen pending court authorization of payment or consummation of a plan of reorganization.

The Wholesale Energy Trading Business

The discussions currently underway with various leading financial institutions are aimed at obtaining credit support for, recapitalizing and revitalizing Enron's North American wholesale energy trading operations under a new ownership structure in which Enron would continue to have a significant ownership interest.

"If these discussions are successful, they could result in the creation of a new trading entity with a strong and unencumbered balance sheet, the industry's finest trading team, and its leading technology platform, all backed by one or more of the world's leading financial institutions," said Greg Whalley, Enron president and chief operating officer. "We understand that it may take time for counterparties to resume normal trading levels with this entity, but we are confident that this business can be put back on a solid footing. Obviously, our potential partners share our confidence or they would not be at the table with us. We intend to take steps to retain employees who are key to the future success of our wholesale energy trading business and to regain the support and confidence of its trading counterparties."

Comment by Ken Lay

"From an operational standpoint, our energy businesses—including our pipelines and utilities—are conducting normal operations and will continue to do so, " said Kenneth L. Lay, chairman and CEO of Enron. "While uncertainty during the past few weeks has severely impacted the market's confidence in Enron and its trading operations, we are taking the steps announced today to help preserve capital, stabilize our businesses, restore the confidence of our trading counterparties, and enhance our ability to pay our creditors."

Enron's principal legal advisor with regard to the proposed merger with Dynegy, Enron's Chapter 11 filings, the Dynegy lawsuit, and related matters is Weil, Gotshal & Manges LLP. Enron's principal financial advisor with regard to its financial restructuring is The Blackstone Group.

About Enron Corp.

Enron Corp. markets electricity and natural gas, delivers energy and other physical commodities, and provides financial and risk management services to customers around the world. Enron's Internet address is *www.enron.com.*

Forward-looking Statements

This press release contains statements that are forward-looking within the meaning of Section 27A of the Securities Act of 1933 and Section 21E of the Securities Exchange Act of 1934. Investors are cautioned that any such forward-looking statements are not guarantees of future performance and that actual results could differ materially as a result of known and unknown risks and uncertainties, including: various regulatory issues, the outcome of the Chapter 11 process, the outcome of the litigation discussed above, the outcome of the discussions referred to above, general economic conditions, future trends, and other risks, uncertainties and factors disclosed in the Company's most recent reports on Forms 10-K, 10-Q and 8-K filed with the Securities and Exchange Commission.

PRESIDENTIAL PANEL ON HEALTH CARE FOR CANCER PATIENTS
December 3, 2001

While medical, scientific, and pharmaceutical researchers made some headway in their search for causes and treatment of cancers in 2001, others questioned whether cancer patients were benefiting from the results. One damning report came December 3, 2001, from the President's Cancer Panel. "Growing evidence indicates that most people in America receive neither the most appropriate care when faced with a cancer diagnosis, nor adequate cancer prevention and detection services," the advisory panel warned. Other reports issued during the year raised questions about the efficacy of early screening for breast and prostate cancers and about the lack of palliative care for terminally ill cancer patients

Cancer was the second leading cause of death in the United States behind heart disease. An estimated 1,268,000 million new cases of cancer were diagnosed in 2001, and an estimated 553,000 people died, according to figures compiled by the National Cancer Institute (NCI). In 1998 more than half of all new cancers were cancers of the prostate, breast, lung, and colon/rectum, and the incidence of all four cancers appeared to be stable or declining, although lung cancer rates among women were continuing to rise. Cancer of the esophagus and melanoma skin cancer were also increasing. (Women and smoking, p. 222)

The NCI reported that some behaviors known to cause or contribute to cancer were improving. Adult smoking rates, as well as fat and alcohol consumption, had all declined. But youth smoking rates were rising, people were doing less than they once did to protect themselves from the sun, and overweight and obesity, which were linked to some cancers, had risen to epidemic proportions. (Obesity, p. 935)

Improving the Cancer Care Delivery System

The President's Cancer Panel was created by the National Cancer Act of 1971 to monitor the federal cancer program and report to the president and Congress every year on its progress. Much of what the panel had to say in 2001 it had said in earlier reports: the country needed to take steps to remove the barriers that prevented many Americans from receiving the benefits of what the panel described as "the world's most vigorous cancer research program." For its 2001 report, "Voices of a Broken System," the panel decided to illustrate the problems with the actual experiences of cancer patients. "The statistics sometimes mask the human suffering behind them," said the panel's chairman, Harold P. Freeman. "We tend to debate the numbers and forget that every statistic is a human being."

The panel heard comments and complaints about the cancer care delivery system from nearly 400 patients, their families, health care professionals, administrators, and patient advocates at seven regional meetings conducted around the country. What the panel found, Freeman said, was that it "doesn't matter whether you are rich or poor, educated or not. The [health care delivery] system is so complex and fragmented for people who have serious diseases like cancer, they are likely to have difficulties getting through the system. We found that many people had to fight their way through the system while they were trying to fight their cancer." Many of the panel's findings echoed those offered by an Institute of Medicine study issued earlier in the year on problems with the quality of overall health care. (Health care quality, p. 191)

The report said that the current health care system underemphasized cancer prevention and that cancer prevention, education, and screening programs were limited and highly uneven across the country. Treatment for the uninsured was often unavailable, and people who were underinsured often found themselves choosing between bankruptcy and treatment. Appropriate care and treatment facilities were often simply unavailable in rural areas and inner cities. Fear of cancer, sometimes exacerbated by language or cultural barriers, often prevented minority populations from seeking timely treatment of their disease. Similar barriers also affected people in need of treatment for mental illness, according to a surgeon general's report released in August. (Mental health report, p. 575)

The panel made several general recommendations that it said should be acted upon immediately. The first was to provide medical coverage for anyone diagnosed with cancer who did not already have health insurance. It also urged that patients be reimbursed for chemotherapy drugs and pain medication whether it was taken orally or injected. (Insurance companies did not cover many orally administered anticancer or pain relieving drugs.) It also urged funding of community-based programs that would help people obtain information about cancer screening, treatment, and supportive services. Over the long haul, the panel said, the government should develop policies that would minimize racial, ethnic, and cultural biases in the provision of cancer care. Such policies would improve the quality of cancer care by keeping health care providers up to speed on cancer treatments and care and would extend state-of-the-art cancer care to currently underserved areas.

In a separate report, issued in June, the Institute of Medicine's National Cancer Policy Board called on the health care profession to do a better job of controlling pain and relieving other symptoms commonly experienced by cancer patients, especially those who were reaching the end of their life. Advanced cancer patients and their families also needed social and emotional support that they often did not receive, the panel said. "In accepting a single-minded focus on research toward a cure, we have inadvertently devalued the critical need to care for and support patients with advanced disease and their families," the panel wrote. The Institute of Medicine was an arm of the National Academy of Science, an independent organization chartered by Congress to give advice to policymakers on issues of science and technology.

The panel was especially critical of health insurance policies that required cancer patients to choose between continued treatment aimed at prolonging life and hospice care. The panel also said that health care professionals lacked standards and adequate training in treating dying patients and that funding for research in palliative care was too low. It called on the NCI to designate cancer centers that specialized in symptom control and palliative care and to expand its research in this area.

Although cancer patients and their families might want and need support, a major study conducted in Canada found that support groups did not extend the lives of women with advanced breast cancer. The findings, which were published in the New England Journal of Medicine *in December, directly countered a small and inconclusive study in 1989 that indicated involvement with a support group might extend the life of breast cancer patients by as long as eighteen months. The Canadian study found that the median survival time for women attending support groups was 17.9 months, while for women not attending support groups, it was 17.6 months, a statistically insignificant difference.*

Although many in the medical profession thought support groups might offer benefits such as emotional support and information exchange, they questioned whether participation in the groups actually extended life. Although several teams of researchers had tried to study the issue since 1989, so firmly had the support group come to symbolize the power of "mind over matter" that many women refused to participate in the studies. Yet doctors knew that many advanced breast cancer patients did not want to participate in such groups. One cancer specialist told the New York Times *that the findings would come as a big relief for many women. Now, she said, "you don't need to feel your life is shortened if you don't go to a group." Nor should women be made to feel guilty if they chose not to participate, she added.*

Value of Early Detection Questioned

A study, published in the October 20 issue of the British journal Lancet *concluded that there was no evidence that women who had regular mammograms to detect breast cancers in their early stages had any less risk of dying from the disease than women who did not have mammograms. The study also found that women who received mammograms had more aggressive treatment, including more surgeries, than women whose breast cancers*

*were detected in other ways. Previously, women had been told that early de-
tection could reduce their risk of death from breast cancer by as much as
30 percent and help them avoid the invasive surgeries and difficult therapies that treatment of a long-undetected tumor might require. However, because doctors could not tell which tumors would be life threatening and
which might not even develop into cancer, they tended to treat any tumor detected in a mammogram screening.*

*Researchers at the Nordic Cochrane Center in Copenhagen undertook the
study. It analyzed the findings of other large mammography studies and
concluded that five of the seven studies failed to meet accepted standards for
well-designed and reliable studies. The two that did, one in Sweden and one
in Canada, found no statistically significant difference in the rates of death
from breast cancer between women who routinely had mammograms and
those who did not.*

*The findings created confusion and controversy in the United States,
where the federal government recommended that all women over age forty
have a mammogram every one or two years. Many health care professionals and women's health advocates worried about continuing to recommend
mammograms if early detection did not reduce the risk of death but instead
raised the incidence of unnecessary treatment.* (Mammogram screening,
Historic Documents of 1997, p. 142)

*Similar controversies surrounded other screening tests. The PSA test, for
example, led to early detection and treatment for prostate cancer, which was
the second leading cause of cancer death among men. However, a majority
of prostate cancers grew very slowly; autopsy reports showed that as many
as 70 percent of elderly men with undetected prostate tumors died of other
diseases. Yet finding a tumor through PSA testing generally led to aggressive
treatment, which left many patients incontinent or impotent. "I believe in
screening,"* one doctor who had studied the issue told the New York Times.
*"But I think physicians as well as the public tend to overblow the risks of
cancer. And, more important, we overblow the risk reduction conferred by
screening."*

> *Following are excerpts from the executive summary of "Voices of
> a Broken System: Real People, Real Problems," a report issued De-
> cember 3, 2001, by the President's Cancer Panel, recommending
> improvements in the health care delivery system for cancer
> patients.*
>
> **The document was obtained from the Internet at http://
> deainfo.nci.nih.gov/ADVISORY/pcp/video-report.htm.**

The issues of cancer care in America are everyone's issues. Each day, 3,400
people in America are diagnosed with cancer and another 1,500 die from the

disease. Nearly nine million more are living with a cancer history. And every person, regardless of income, education, ethnicity, race, age, or geographic locale, is at risk of developing cancer.

Growing evidence indicates that most people in America receive neither the most appropriate care when faced with a cancer diagnosis, nor adequate cancer prevention and detection services. Factors contributing to this massive failing are many and complex, but the clear and central issue is the failure of our health care system to deliver, in an equitable and timely manner, the cancer care we know is most effective—regardless of a person's insurance status or ability to pay.

The President's Cancer Panel, established by the National Cancer Act of 1971 to monitor implementation of the National Cancer Program, previously reported to the President on this critical "disconnect" between our cancer research discoveries and the type, timeliness, and continuity of cancer care that people actually receive. In 2000 and 2001, the Panel held seven regional meetings to hear firsthand from people with cancer, their families, and the health professionals, administrators, advocates, and volunteers who serve them—393 in all—about problems they experience in accessing and providing cancer care and cancer information. In every corner of the Nation, patients and professionals alike echoed the same moral tenet:

> **No person in America with cancer should go untreated, experience insurance-related diagnosis or treatment delays that jeopardize survival, or be bankrupted by a cancer diagnosis.**

Yet these very things are happening to far too many of us. The problems of cancer care in America are not theoretical, analytic, or abstract—they are real problems affecting real people.

What Is Happening to Real People: Findings

The numerous issues described by meeting participants fall broadly into two categories: access and information. In addition, cancer care can be influenced greatly by behaviors and decision-making by both health care providers and the public that stems from perceived differences among populations and individuals.

Barriers Limiting or Preventing Access to Cancer Care

Access barriers include those related to the organization and operation of the health care system itself, financial barriers to care, and physical barriers that reduce or prevent access. However, these categories are not always mutually exclusive.

System Barriers

The current health care system underemphasizes cancer prevention and often allocates cancer funding by disease site. Both approaches are counterproductive to providing comprehensive cancer care and developing effective cancer control programs. Cancer prevention, education, and screening efforts

are limited at best and highly uneven across the country. Treatment for detected cancer remains unavailable to some of the uninsured unless they are
able to obtain charity care or qualify for medical assistance. In addition, coordination between public payers is poor, and patients often are not informed
of all health benefits for which they may be eligible. Believing they have no
coverage or limited coverage, patients may incur unnecessary out-of-pocket
costs, delay treatment, or even forego care.

System-related barriers to care most often described by people with
employer-sponsored or other private health insurance include fragmentation
of care, gatekeepers who control access to screening and specialists, and limitations or exclusions on specific drugs and services, including clinical trials.
Numerous patients recounted having to fight their insurers to get the care they
needed to save their lives. The current system also discourages appropriate
end-of-life care, resulting in late referral to hospice (or no referral) and causing many terminal cancer patients to die without adequate pain and other
symptom control.

Financial Barriers

Financial Issues Affecting Patient Access to Care. For people with
cancer and their families, health care system issues that can be explained logically by fiscal and economic realities often translate into a personal reality
that includes family bankruptcy, needless suffering, loss of dignity, and loss
of life. Currently, 44 million Americans have no health insurance at all. Uninsured rates are as high as 25 percent of the non-elderly in some states, with
much higher rates in some rural and frontier regions.

Many of the cancer survivors and family caregivers providing testimony
were self-employed—farmers, ranchers, small business owners, and other
independent workers. These speakers explained that they seldom can afford
even basic health insurance, though they make enough money to support
themselves and their families. The working poor may hold two or three jobs,
none offering health benefits. This population is likely to lack both health insurance and the financial reserves to see them through an extended illness.
They often avoid cancer screening or care for suspicious symptoms because
they know they cannot pay for cancer care. Late stage diagnosis is a common
result. When cancer strikes, uninsured workers may find they have too much
income or too many assets to qualify for Medicaid or other medical assistance,
but are too young for Medicare. These patients can quickly amass huge medical debts that will take the family many years to repay. Some are forced into
bankruptcy.

To qualify for Medicaid, patients typically must give up the employment
that provides family support and divest themselves of virtually all assets, including their car, home, business, or farm. In addition, survivors described
such long delays in obtaining Medicaid approval that they were faced with
more advanced disease by the time they were able to begin treatment. Even
after securing a Medicaid card, it sometimes took weeks or months to find a
provider who would accept Medicaid payment. Cancer patients who remain
disabled by their disease for 12 months may qualify for Social Security Income

(SSI) payments; however, this income may exceed Medicaid eligibility ceilings, causing them to lose access to cancer care.

At least 31 million non-elderly insured Americans are underinsured for cancer care costs. Though they pay substantial monthly premiums, many find the combined burden of copayments, deductibles, non-covered services, medical supplies, and drug costs (particularly for oral chemotherapy and supportive medications), slow health plan reimbursements, and additional transportation and child care costs quickly exhausts family savings. This is particularly true when patient income is reduced or lost and/or when a family wage earner must work less in order to care for the cancer patient. Should the patient or spouse lose the job providing health insurance, the family can face a quick descent into indigent care and bankruptcy. Some survivors who return to work but have lapsed insurance coverage may find they are uninsurable, subject to a lengthy waiting period for cancer-related coverage, or eligible only for prohibitively expensive coverage.

Financial Issues Affecting Health Care Providers. As health care payers and purchasers struggle to contain health care costs, financial pressures on health care providers continue to increase, affecting the care available to people with cancer and those in need of screening, diagnostic, and preventive services. Survivors and family members reported widely varied experiences in terms of provider willingness to accommodate patients' lack of insurance or full insurance coverage. Some patients were told to "pay what you can, when you can;" others were able to negotiate reduced rates and payment plans; and some providers donated their time and services. In other cases, however, providers asked for advance payments of $20,000 to $100,000 before initiating treatment. These highly divergent responses to patients in need appear to reflect an extreme and intensifying conflict between some providers' commitment to render care as needed and a range of financial pressures that threaten the solvency, vitality, ethics, and integrity of health care institutions and individual providers alike. . . .

Physical Barriers

Living in rural or frontier areas poses a special set of problems that comprise a vastly underappreciated barrier to cancer care access. Approximately one-fourth of the U.S. population lives in areas designated as rural or frontier, and half of all states have frontier regions (i.e., fewer than 6.6 people per square mile).

Excessive distance from cancer care is due in part to the concentration of health care personnel and resources in urban areas, the lack of public transportation systems in rural and frontier areas, and the fact that many rural and frontier residents lack the resources to travel to care. The scarcity of both primary and specialty care providers in rural and remote areas is a longstanding problem that contributes to late diagnosis of cancer in these populations. Lower reimbursements for care provided in rural settings not related to operating cost differences and limited grant funding to sparsely populated areas continue to hamper efforts to recruit and retain oncologists and other cancer care professionals. Speakers called for incentives to attract health care professionals to these regions and help them sustain careers in underserved areas, including underserved inner cities.

Most rural areas have no public transportation system; patients reported driving up to 300 miles one way for screening or treatment, and some are too ill to do so. Because some services cannot easily be taken to rural areas (e.g., radiation oncology), patients may choose treatment options (e.g., mastectomy versus lumpectomy) that do not require repeated trips to a distant treatment facility. Native Americans, particularly those living on reservations, frequently drive long distances to an Indian Health Service (IHS) hospital or clinic and wait all day to be seen, only to be turned away and told to return the next day. This situation is so discouraging that some avoid seeking care for symptoms until they require emergency care. Many managed care enrollees and Veterans Administration beneficiaries must obtain services from contracted providers distant from the patient's home, sometimes in another state. . . .

Transportation also is an issue for inner city residents who may not own cars or be able to afford bus or subway fares. In addition, some urban cancer patients are too sick to undertake a trip that may cover few miles but involves multiple bus transfers and considerable walking.

Barriers Related to Information or Education

Lack of information or education, not knowing how to find or evaluate information, not believing or acting appropriately on available information, not knowing how to get needed care within the health system—all can constitute barriers to cancer care.

Provider-Related Information and Education Barriers

Lack of information about cancer and cancer care was the provider-related barrier most commonly cited by those providing testimony at the regional meetings. Speakers emphasized strongly the need to better educate primary care providers about cancer. Initial decisions about care can be a critical determinant of patient outcome, and primary care providers, especially in rural and remote areas, often make these crucial referral and treatment choices.

Considerable disagreement exists, even among oncology professionals, about sometimes conflicting published screening and treatment guidelines. More broadly, there is confusion among providers, payers, and patients as to what constitutes quality care for cancer.

Speakers graphically described the serious repercussions to patients when providers lack reliable current information about cancer care or fail to change practice patterns based on new evidence. Most alarming among these were misdiagnoses that caused lengthy treatment delays, resulted in unnecessary surgery or incorrect treatment, and jeopardized patient survival or quality of life. Speakers also noted that providers may miss signs of cancer in patients with other chronic illnesses or fail to detect depression or other serious health problems in cancer patients. Provider education in these areas, on the care and needs of dying patients, and on cultural differences that affect care were listed among the areas of greatest need in provider education.

Finally, the lack of effective medical data and reminder systems in most clinical settings was cited as a significant reason why some patients "fall through the cracks." As one physician observed, *"Medicine currently is less computerized than Wal-Mart."*

Information and Education Barriers Faced by Patients and the Public

The lack of accurate cancer-related information that is readily available, understandable, clear, and delivered in a sensitive and culturally acceptable manner is a major contributor to the inability of patients and the public to obtain the most appropriate cancer prevention, treatment, and supportive care.

Cancer is perhaps the most feared of diseases. As speakers described vividly, fear of cancer is shared by virtually all populations and cultures, and takes the form of fatalism, fear of treatment and its costs, fear of pain and disfigurement, and fear of rejection by one's partner, family, or community. These fears, and enduring myths about cancer, cause many people to reject cancer prevention messages, avoid cancer screening, delay or avoid treatment if diagnosed, and have difficulty understanding and choosing among treatment options or following treatment regimens.

For some Americans, cancer-related information is simply unavailable. Thousands in remote regions and high poverty areas lack telephones and in many areas library access is limited. Some remote areas even lack radio or television reception. . . .

For many other Americans, available cancer information is unusable due to literacy, language, or cultural barriers. . . .

Cancer survivors and health care professionals emphasized repeatedly that regardless of educational level, income, or insurance status, people need help finding and evaluating accurate, up-to-date cancer information and navigating the complex and fragmented health care system. Communities are attempting to address this need by training community members to be outreach workers and cancer educators and by establishing "patient navigator" programs in hospitals and other treatment facilities to help people access medical and financial assistance for which they may qualify and secure the care they need. While the need for such programs for insured and uninsured patients at all educational and socioeconomic levels was unquestioned, the tenuous stability of these often fledgling programs was also underscored.

Finally, speakers indicated that cancer surveillance is grossly underfunded in many areas of the country. Without adequate information on the extent and nature of the cancer burden, states cannot identify high risk groups, focus their planning efforts, develop targeted prevention and cancer control efforts, or evaluate their success. Local data on cancer patterns and trends may take years to accumulate, but these activities should proceed in tandem with action to address readily apparent cancer control problems.

The Impact of Culture and Bias on Cancer Care

Disparities in cancer treatment and disease outcome between various population groups are being documented with increasing frequency and clarity.

A considerable number of speakers recounted experiences in which they or others received—or did not receive—cancer information or care for reasons stemming from cultural or racial differences, and biases these differences engendered. Importantly, bias that results in negative health outcomes can originate from both patients and health care providers.

Issues of Culture and Bias Originating With Patients and the Public

Cultural perspectives or biases may cause individuals to avoid cancer screening or treatment, or otherwise make decisions that may adversely affect their survival and quality of life. These biases can also have a positive impact on health. They affect the ways in which people perceive illness, how they develop and act on medical and caregiver preferences including folk healing methods, how they explain and tolerate pain, and what they perceive to be quality care. As numerous speakers indicated, however, fatalism about cancer remains pervasive in many cultures, though it takes different forms in different cultural groups. Old myths about cancer also persist in many populations.

The grinding circumstances and resulting culture of poverty profoundly affect the information and care-seeking behaviors of the poor. Rural residence and agricultural lifestyle also comprise a distinct culture in which it is rare to seek medical care unless one is in significant pain. Many rural residents, some of whom are poor, are uninsured and do not believe in going to the doctor unless they can pay the bill. In addition, farming women are unlikely to interrupt farm routines to seek medical care, even when they have symptoms. Similarly, speakers suggested that the cultural importance of fulfilling one's role in the family causes many Asian women to minimize their own health needs and avoid out-of-pocket health care expenditures.

Provider-patient relationships built on familiarity and trust are crucial to effective education and medical care for some populations, notably Native Americans and a number of recent immigrant populations. Yet the medical facilities at which these populations typically receive care are staffed by temporary duty doctors who often are of different cultures or lack sensitivity to the cultures of their patients. In some cases, resistance to entering the health care system and difficulty navigating it are undergirded by cultural traditions that consider assertiveness, particularly with authority figures, to be inappropriate or rude. Speakers testified to the critical need for health care providers from minority and under-served populations. In addition, traditions concerning female modesty and the acceptability of female patients being examined by male physicians underscored the need for more female health care providers.

Distrust of the health care system generally is common, particularly among populations that historically have been targets of discrimination. Many people fear being used as "guinea pigs" by medical practitioners. This distrust reinforces the fear of cancer treatment, including clinical trials, and remains a significant barrier to appropriate cancer care.

Secrecy about cancer remains prevalent in some populations, with patients hiding their disease even from partners and other family members. In some

Asian cultures, knowledge of a cancer diagnosis still is withheld from the patient. These cultural prohibitions can make it extremely difficult to reach people with needed cancer information and care.

Issues of Culture and Bias Originating With Health Care Providers

Bias, either overt or unintended, also can originate with health care providers and administrators who may make decisions or recommendations that are not in the patient's best interest. Physicians in particular have a special responsibility to be sensitive to their own cultural mindsets and biases, as well as those of their patients, because of the power and authority many patients confer upon their doctors. Speakers testified to pervasive and often overt provider bias against gay and lesbian patients that causes these patients to avoid screening and care. Patients with disabilities may experience unintended bias when they are not offered screening or other cancer-related care because providers focus only on health issues related to the disability. In other cases, providers may not share clinical information with patients who they assume will not understand it, or may fail to offer treatment regimens they assume patients will be unable to follow.

Numerous speakers indicated that bias at the provider and institutional levels also may occur when assistance, referrals, treatment, and other services are more readily offered to more educated or white patients compared with less educated or minority patients, even when they have equivalent resources, or lack of them. Some disparate behavior may be intentional, but according to speakers, more often reflects biases transparent to the providers themselves.

In addition, presenters described instances in which culturally insensitive behavior on the part of providers reflected a simple lack of education about other cultures and customs or an unwillingness to accommodate non-medical traditional practices that would not interfere with treatment but would comfort the patient.

What Can Be Done to Help People Now: Recommendations

The President's Cancer Panel is acutely aware that the issues and problems described in this report are not being expressed for the first time. Indeed, the very fact that these problems—faced by real people with cancer every day, in every corner of the Nation—remain so prevalent makes concrete, achievable action to resolve them that much more urgent.

Access to appropriate cancer care is the crucial, fundamental step needed to relieve the desperate physical suffering, financial devastation, and loss of dignity so many people endure when cancer is diagnosed. If we lack the political will to craft and implement a National plan to address this unacceptable situation, then incremental steps must be taken to quickly remedy health care financing and delivery system elements that result in so much of the needless distress now experienced by cancer patients and survivors, and their families.

Continued research on the quality and equity of cancer care, outcome disparities, and related health economics and system issues is essential to guide transformation of the health care system in the coming years to better serve the public. But the people with cancer today, and their families, cannot wait for this distant relief. The President's Cancer Panel recommends:

Immediate Action Steps

1. Provide immediate medical coverage for the uninsured—84 percent of whom are workers and their dependents—upon a diagnosis of cancer to help ensure that no person with this disease goes untreated.

2. Address health coverage issues that contribute substantially to the financial devastation of people underinsured for cancer care costs:
   - Provide reimbursement for anti-cancer agents, supportive medications (e.g., antiemetics, pain medications), and proven chemopreventive agents, regardless of method of administration.
   - Within two years, public and private payers should reach consensus on and implement a standard health benefit package for cancer care. This benefit package should be based on the best available medical evidence and should be updated regularly to reflect advances in the standard of care. The reports and deliberations of the Institute of Medicine, other groups, and consumers should be used to inform this effort.

3. Address patient and public needs for cancer information and for assistance in accessing services:
   - Provide funding to help communities coordinate, promote, and support community-based programs, including patient navigator programs, that help people obtain cancer information, screening, treatment, and supportive services.
   - Recognize that the services of non-physician personnel who are trained to conduct cancer screening, and provide cancer education and case management in varied settings are an important component of cancer care that should be reimbursed.

4. Sustain cancer care in the community by providing consistent and realistic health care provider reimbursement across states, and between urban and rural locations within states, for the cost of chemotherapy drugs and their administration.

Longer-Term Solutions

1. Medicare, Medicaid, the Veterans Administration, the Department of Defense, the Indian Health Service, and other public payers should clarify the order of responsibility for payment for cancer care services when individual patients are eligible for benefits under more than one program. This information should be communicated promptly and clearly to those who provide cancer care services and assist patients in navigating the health care system. The existing Quality Interagency Coordination Task Force may provide a forum for accomplishing this important task.

2. Develop Federal policies to minimize bias in the provision of cancer care:
   - Raise awareness of unintended or overt bias through initial and continuing training of health care professionals at all levels, as well as administrators and others who make decisions affecting patient care.

- Establish and implement systems for monitoring treatment equity. In addition, expand quality of care research to include issues of treatment equity.
3. Minimize disparities in the provision of cancer care by:
   - Educating primary care providers about cancer.
   - Educating all cancer care professionals about the nature and application of evidence-based medicine and about clinical trials.
   - Developing and disseminating better tools to assist health care providers in conveying information about cancer and about cancer care options.
4. Address the problems of temporary medical staffing and cultural incompatibility by establishing additional mechanisms to encourage more minorities and members of other underserved populations to enter cancer care professions. Provide incentives to encourage providers to practice in medically underserved areas.
5. Extend state-of-the-art cancer care to rural, frontier, and other underserved areas by expanding the use of telemedicine and providing a reimbursement system that facilitates expansion of telemedicine to geographically underserved areas.
6. Permit more flexible use of categorical funding where appropriate to enable states to fashion more rational and more comprehensive cancer control programs.

AFGHANISTAN LEADERS ON INTERIM GOVERNMENT
December 5, 2001

One of the most conflicted places on Earth for more than two decades, Afghanistan in late 2001 began attempting to build a peaceful, civil society. The hopeful moves in Afghanistan came even as war was still under way: the United States and its allies in December were finishing up the grisly task of eliminating remnants of the Taliban faction that had controlled most of the country since 1995 and the al Qaeda terrorist network that had been based there. That war was the direct outgrowth of the September 11 terrorist attacks in the United States, which President George W. Bush said were sponsored by al Qaeda and its leader, Osama bin Laden.

Leaders of Afghanistan's many ethnic, tribal, and political factions agreed on December 5, 2001, to a complex arrangement for governing the country, starting with the appointment of an interim administration with a six-month assignment. That interim government, headed by Hamid Karzai, a leader of the majority Pashtun ethnic group, took office December 22. It was supported, at least for the time being, by a small United Nations peacekeeping force. That force, headed by Great Britain, had the unenviable task of maintaining some semblance of order in a country recently ruled more by tribal warlords and bandits than by reasoned debate.

The UN and other humanitarian agencies also launched the process of rebuilding a nation that had been battered by war since 1979 and severe drought for nearly four years. The United States and other countries pledged support for a relief and reconstruction effort that the UN projected to cost $10 billion or more. One of the first priorities was helping the estimated 5 million of Afghanistan's 26 million people who were refugees, either within the nation's borders or in neighboring Iran and Pakistan. (Terrorist attacks, p. 614; Afghanistan war, p. 686; previous Afghanistan conflicts, Historic Documents of 1999, p. 524)

Agreement on Interim Government

The United States and Britain on October 7 launched military attacks against the Taliban and al Qaeda with the goal of eliminating their influ-

ence in Afghanistan Within weeks it was apparent that the allied war effort would soon succeed, putting pressure on the United Nations to make arrangements for a new government. UN Secretary General Kofi Annan had appointed Lakhdar Brahimi, a former Algerian foreign minister and a respected UN diplomat, as his special representative with an assignment of reconciling Afghanistan's many factions.

On November 26 more than thirty delegates from nearly every Afghan faction, except the Taliban, began meeting with Brahimi at a historic hotel just outside Bonn, Germany. The delegates represented four major groups: the Northern Alliance, a guerrilla coalition based in the northern part of Afghanistan that had fought the Taliban since it took power and that had seized Kabul, the capital, earlier in November; a "royalist" faction representing exiled king Mohammad Zahir Shah, who had been ousted by a cousin in 1973 and had lived since then in Rome; a so-called Peshawar group composed of Afghan exiles living in Peshawar, Pakistan; and a group from western Pakistan with close ties to Iran. Among the sensitive issues facing the delegates was the future role, if any, of Burhannudin Rabbani, who had been president of Afghanistan before the Taliban took power and was still recognized by the UN and most countries as holding that title. Rabbani made statements during the Bonn conference indicating that he expected a role in the new government, but he had little support among the delegates. In the end, he was supplanted and gave way grudgingly.

Despite strongly conflicting views about Afghanistan's history and future, the factions reached surprisingly rapid agreement on a temporary political settlement, backed by a limited international peacekeeping force. Signed December 5, with Brahimi and German chancellor Gerhard Schroeder as witnesses, the agreement provided for a broad-based transitional government, with Karzai as chairman, to take office December 22. The interim government would be in place for a period of six months, during which a special commission would be formed to call an emergency "loya jirga," a traditional Afghan assembly of provincial and tribal leaders. The former king was to preside over that assembly, which, in turn, would appoint a subsequent "transitional government" to last up to two years. During that two-year period, a "constitutional loya jirga" would meet to draft and approve a new constitution, leading to elections for a permanent government.

Nearly as important as the agreement was the decision by the Afghan representatives to name Karzai as interim chairman. The leader of one of the most prominent families among the Pashtun ethnic group, Karzai was acceptable to a broad range of the county's factions, and he was known and respected in Washington and many other Western capitals. UN officials said no other Afghan leader was as well positioned to unite the country's many factions and get needed international help.

"Afghans have done their bit, they agreed," said Yonus Qanooni, chief delegate of the Northern Alliance. "We believe it is now the international community's turn."

The UN Security Council unanimously endorsed the political agreement on December 6, and Annan pledged that the world body would "try and do our best" to support it. The ink was barely dry on the agreement, however, when it came under heavy criticism from some Afghan leaders who had not been involved in the Bonn negotiations. Perhaps the most threatening remarks came from Abdurrashid Dostum, a powerful Northern Alliance warlord who had repeatedly shifted sides during the country's two decades of war. "This is a humiliation for us," Dostum told the Reuters news agency.

Karzai traveled to Kabul on December 13 to meet with leaders of the Northern Alliance, who controlled the capital. Five days later he flew to Rome to meet with the exiled king, who gave him his blessing and promise of support.

Afghanistan's next big moment came December 22, when Karzai took the oath of office as interim chairman and swore in twenty-nine cabinet members representing a diverse range of the country's ethnic and political life. In hopeful signs, former president Rabbani embraced Karzai, and General Dostum was one of several warlords who appeared and pledged their support. Karzai appealed to all Afghans to contribute to the rebuilding of the country. "In this critical time, when our motherland is watching our actions, let us come together and be brothers and sisters," he said. "Let us be good to each other and be compassionate and share our grief. Let us forget the sad past." Karzai won wide applause with a pledge to rid the country of corruption, which had long been a scourge. Signaling his determination to be inclusive, Karzai spoke both in Pashtu, the language of his own ancestry, and Dari, an Afghan-Persian dialect that was the country's most widely spoken language. Among the invited guests was General Tommy Franks, who as head of the U.S. Central Command was in charge of the still-ongoing war against the Taliban and al Qaeda in Afghanistan.

Karzai held the first meeting of his government the next day, December 23, and ministers agreed to focus their efforts on the few areas of the country controlled by the government, rather than by local warlords. At least for the moment, that meant the government would be limited to Kabul, Kandahar, and a handful of other cities.

Peacekeeping Issues

With a war still under way and thousands of armed men roaming the country, Afghanistan's most urgent need in late December was to establish order so the new government could get to work and international aid agencies could step up deliveries of humanitarian supplies. The first step in that direction was the creation of a limited international peacekeeping force. In an annex to their December 5 political agreement, the Afghanistan representatives asked the United Nations to establish such a force to help protect the new government while it established and trained its own military and police forces. The delegates asked for the peacekeeping force to be stationed in "Kabul and its surrounding areas," but left open the prospect that it could be expanded to "other urban centers and other areas." The delegates pledged that all militias would be withdrawn from Kabul before the peacekeeping force arrived.

The UN Security Council on December 20 approved the new Afghan force, and that same day fifty-three British Royal Marines arrived in Afghanistan as the advance contingent. Britain, which was to command the force, pledged 1,500 troops for it, and twenty other countries agreed to contribute up to 4,000 more troops. The Security Council resolution limited the initial mandate of the peacekeeping force to six months and to the maintenance of security "in Kabul and its surrounding areas." The United States had refused to contribute to the force and insisted on limiting it to the capital city area because it did not want UN peacekeepers interfering with its military operations in much of the rest of the country. At year's end, numerous experts on Afghanistan suggested that the U.S.-imposed limits on the size and mandate of the peacekeeping force ultimately would prove unworkable, given the security dangers in the country.

Humanitarian Situation

The lack of security was just the beginning of Afghanistan's problems after the fall of the Taliban. Battered by two decades of war and mismanagement by successive governments, the country had no functioning economy and virtually no internal resources to establish one. A drought that began in 1998 and continued unabated for the next three years devastated what remained, after the wars, of the once-fertile countryside.

UN and other international relief agencies had been working in Afghanistan even while the repressive Taliban regime was in power, but all foreigners left or were expelled in the days after the September 11 terrorist attacks in the United States. The U.S. military dropped tons of food, medicine, and other supplies during the air war that began October 7. The effectiveness of those aid drops was difficult to gauge, however.

International aid workers began returning to Afghanistan in November as the Taliban withdrew under heavy U.S. bombardment. Summarizing their early findings in a report to the Security Council on December 6, Annan said some 6 million people—nearly one-fourth of the entire population of Afghanistan—likely would be vulnerable during the coming winter to malnourishment, disease, and cold. One million Afghanis were homeless inside their own country, he said, and another 3 million were refugees in Pakistan and 1 million in Iran. "Given the third consecutive year of drought, further internal displacement, continued fighting and, more recently, a breakdown of law and order, it is reasonable to assume, through qualitative and quantitative extrapolations, that thousands of civilian deaths will occur in the winter of 2001/2002 from hunger-related causes, hypothermia and curable diseases," Annan told the council.

In a report issued December 14, the UN High Commissioner on Refugees said Afghanis who had taken refuge in neighboring countries should not "rush back" home, nor should the neighboring countries rush to send them back. "The security situation in many parts of Afghanistan remains tense, and the war- and drought-ravaged country requires an enormous amount of humanitarian relief and reconstruction assistance before large-scale returns can be considered sustainable," the agency said. Among other obstacles facing returning refugees—as well as Afghanis who remained at

home—were the millions of land mines that the Soviet Union and local war-
ring factions had strewn around the countryside.

By year's end aid agencies had launched the full range of relief efforts in
much of the country, and as a result appeared to be heading off the famine
that Annan had predicted just a few weeks earlier. "There will be no fam-
ine in Afghanistan this winter," Catherine Bertini, executive director of the
UN's World Food Program said on December 30. "There will be deaths, be-
cause the country was in a pre-famine condition this summer before the
war started. But it will be isolated, and not large scale."

The relief programs under way in the country included feeding programs
in the hardest-hit areas, especially the northwest, where a survey in one
province showed early in December that about 50 percent of the children
were suffering from malnutrition; restoration of health services, such as in-
oculations of up to 9 million children to head off a measles epidemic; and
the expansion of existing refugee camps to accommodate the millions of
people who had left or been forced from their homes.

At an international donors conference in Washington on November 20,
the United States and nearly two dozen other nations offered tentative
pledges to a UN fund for the reconstruction of Afghanistan. The United
States offered an initial pledge of $320 million; that figure represented about
5 percent of the total U.S. cost for the first three months of the war in
Afghanistan. A UN "needs assessment" being prepared in late December
estimated the rough cost of reconstructing Afghanistan through 2006 at
$10.2 billion; the first-year cost, in 2002, would be $1.3 billion. A follow-up
conference for donor nations to make firm pledges toward the reconstruction
effort was planned for Tokyo in late January 2002.

> *Following are excerpts from the "Agreement on Provisional Ar-*
> *rangements in Afghanistan Pending the Re-Establishment of*
> *Permanent Government Institutions," signed December 5, 2001,*
> *in Bonn, Germany, by representatives of major political, ethnic,*
> *and tribal factions from Afghanistan.*
>
> **The document was obtained from the Internet at http://**
> **www.uno.de/friedwn/afghanistan/talks/agreement.htm.**

The participants in the UN Talks on Afghanistan,

In the presence of the Special Representative of the Secretary-General for
Afghanistan,

Determined to end the tragic conflict in Afghanistan and promote national
reconciliation, lasting peace, stability and respect for human rights in the
country,

Reaffirming the independence, national sovereignty and territorial integrity of Afghanistan,

Acknowledging the right of the people of Afghanistan to freely determine their own political future in accordance with the principles of Islam, democracy, pluralism and social justice,

Expressing their appreciation to the Afghan mujahidin who, over the years, have defended the independence, territorial integrity and national unity of the country and have played a major role in the struggle against terrorism and oppression, and whose sacrifice has now made them both heroes of jihad and champions of peace, stability and reconstruction of their beloved homeland, Afghanistan,

Aware that the unstable situation in Afghanistan requires the implementation of emergency interim arrangements and expressing their deep appreciation to His Excellency Professor Burhanuddin Rabbani for his readiness to transfer power to an interim authority which is to be established pursuant to this agreement,

Recognizing the need to ensure broad representation in these interim arrangements of all segments of the Afghan population, including groups that have not been adequately represented at the UN Talks on Afghanistan,

Noting that these interim arrangements are intended as a first step toward the establishment of a broad-based, gender-sensitive, multi-ethnic and fully representative government, and are not intended to remain in place beyond the specified period of time,

Recognizing that some time may be required for a new Afghan security force to be fully constituted and functional and that therefore other security provisions detailed in Annex I to this agreement must meanwhile be put in place,

Considering that the United Nations, as the internationally recognized impartial institution, has a particularly important role to play, detailed in Annex II to this agreement, in the period prior to the establishment of permanent institutions in Afghanistan,

Have agreed as follows:

THE INTERIM AUTHORITY

I. General provisions

1) An Interim Authority shall be established upon the official transfer of power on 22 December 2001.

2) The Interim Authority shall consist of an Interim Administration presided over by a Chairman, a Special Independent Commission for the Convening of the Emergency Loya Jirga, and a Supreme Court of Afghanistan, as well as such other courts as may be established by the Interim Administration. The composition, functions and governing procedures for the Interim Administration and the Special Independent Commission are set forth in this agreement.

3) Upon the official transfer of power, the Interim Authority shall be the repository of Afghan sovereignty, with immediate effect. As such, it shall,

throughout the interim period, represent Afghanistan in its external relations and shall occupy the seat of Afghanistan at the United Nations and in its specialized agencies, as well as in other international institutions and conferences.

4) An Emergency Loya Jirga shall be convened within six months of the establishment of the Interim Authority. The Emergency Loya Jirga will be opened by His Majesty Mohammed Zaher, the former King of Afghanistan. The Emergency Loya Jirga shall decide on a Transitional Authority, including a broad-based transitional administration, to lead Afghanistan until such time as a fully representative government can be elected through free and fair elections to be held no later than two years from the date of the convening of the Emergency Loya Jirga.

5) The Interim Authority shall cease to exist once the Transitional Authority has been established by the Emergency Loya Jirga.

6) A Constitutional Loya Jirga shall be convened within eighteen months of the establishment of the Transitional Authority, in order to adopt a new constitution for Afghanistan. In order to assist the Constitutional Loya Jirga prepare the proposed Constitution, the Transitional Administration shall, within two months of its commencement and with the assistance of the United Nations, establish a Constitutional Commission.

II. Legal framework and judicial system

1) The following legal framework shall be applicable on an interim basis until the adoption of the new Constitution referred to above:

   i) The Constitution of 1964, a/ to the extent that its provisions are not inconsistent with those contained in this agreement, and b/ with the exception of those provisions relating to the monarchy and to the executive and legislative bodies provided in the Constitution; and

   ii) existing laws and regulations, to the extent that they are not inconsistent with this agreement or with international legal obligations to which Afghanistan is a party, or with those applicable provisions contained in the Constitution of 1964, provided that the Interim Authority shall have the power to repeal or amend those laws and regulations.

2) The judicial power of Afghanistan shall be independent and shall be vested in a Supreme Court of Afghanistan, and such other courts as may be established by the Interim Administration. The Interim Administration shall establish, with the assistance of the United Nations, a Judicial Commission to rebuild the domestic justice system in accordance with Islamic principles, international standards, the rule of law and Afghan legal traditions.

III. Interim Administration

A. Composition

1) The Interim Administration shall be composed of a Chairman, five Vice Chairmen and 24 other members. Each member, except the Chairman, may head a department of the Interim Administration.

2) The participants in the UN Talks on Afghanistan have invited His Majesty Mohammed Zaher, the former King of Afghanistan, to chair the Interim Administration. His Majesty has indicated that he would prefer that a suitable candidate acceptable to the participants be selected as the Chair of the Interim Administration.

3) The Chairman, the Vice Chairmen and other members of the Interim Administration have been selected by the participants in the UN Talks on Afghanistan, as listed in Annex IV to this agreement. The selection has been made on the basis of professional competence and personal integrity from lists submitted by the participants in the UN Talks, with due regard to the ethnic, geographic and religious composition of Afghanistan and to the importance of the participation of women.

4) No person serving as a member of the Interim Administration may simultaneously hold membership of the Special Independent Commission for the Convening of the Emergency Loya Jirga.

B. Procedures

1) The Chairman of the Interim Administration, or in his/her absence one of the Vice Chairmen, shall call and chair meetings and propose the agenda for these meetings.

2) The Interim Administration shall endeavour to reach its decisions by consensus. In order for any decision to be taken, at least 22 members must be in attendance. If a vote becomes necessary, decisions shall be taken by a majority of the members present and voting, unless otherwise stipulated in this agreement. The Chairman shall cast the deciding vote in the event that the members are divided equally.

C. Functions

1) The Interim Administration shall be entrusted with the day-to-day conduct of the affairs of state, and shall have the right to issue decrees for the peace, order and good government of Afghanistan.

2) The Chairman of the Interim Administration or, in his/her absence, one of the Vice Chairmen, shall represent the Interim Administration as appropriate.

3) Those members responsible for the administration of individual departments shall also be responsible for implementing the policies of the Interim Administration within their areas of responsibility.

4) Upon the official transfer of power, the Interim Administration shall have full jurisdiction over the printing and delivery of the national currency and special drawing rights from international financial institutions. The Interim Administration shall establish, with the assistance of the United Nations, a Central Bank of Afghanistan that will regulate the money supply of the country through transparent and accountable procedures.

5) The Interim Administration shall establish, with the assistance of the United Nations, an independent Civil Service Commission to provide the Interim Authority and the future Transitional Authority with shortlists of candidates for key posts in the administrative departments, as well as those of governors and uluswals, in order to ensure their competence and integrity.

6) The Interim Administration shall, with the assistance of the United Nations, establish an independent Human Rights Commission, whose responsibilities will include human rights monitoring, investigation of violations of human rights, and development of domestic human rights institutions. The Interim Administration may, with the assistance of the United Nations, also establish any other commissions to review matters not covered in this agreement.

7) The members of the Interim Administration shall abide by a Code of Conduct elaborated in accordance with international standards.

8) Failure by a member of the Interim Administration to abide by the provisions of the Code of Conduct shall lead to his/her suspension from that body. The decision to suspend a member shall be taken by a two-thirds majority of the membership of the Interim Administration on the proposal of its Chairman or any of its Vice Chairmen.

9) The functions and powers of members of the Interim Administration will be further elaborated, as appropriate, with the assistance of the United Nations.

IV. The Special Independent Commission for the Convening of the Emergency Loya Jirga

1) The Special Independent Commission for the Convening of the Emergency Loya Jirga shall be established within one month of the establishment of the Interim Authority. The Special Independent Commission will consist of twenty-one members, a number of whom should have expertise in constitutional or customary law. The members will be selected from lists of candidates submitted by participants in the UN Talks on Afghanistan as well as Afghan professional and civil society groups. The United Nations will assist with the establishment and functioning of the commission and of a substantial secretariat.

2) The Special Independent Commission will have the final authority for determining the procedures for and the number of people who will participate in the Emergency Loya Jirga. The Special Independent Commission will draft rules and procedures specifying (i) criteria for allocation of seats to the settled and nomadic population residing in the country; (ii) criteria for allocation of seats to the Afghan refugees living in Iran, Pakistan, and elsewhere, and Afghans from the diaspora; (iii) criteria for inclusion of civil society organizations and prominent individuals, including Islamic scholars, intellectuals, and traders, both within the country and in the diaspora. The Special Independent Commission will ensure that due attention is paid to the representation in the Emergency Loya Jirga of a significant number of women as well as all other segments of the Afghan population.

3) The Special Independent Commission will publish and disseminate the rules and procedures for the convening of the Emergency Loya Jirga at least ten weeks before the Emergency Loya Jirga convenes, together with the date for its commencement and its suggested location and duration.

4) The Special Independent Commission will adopt and implement procedures for monitoring the process of nomination of individuals to the Emer-

gency Loya Jirga to ensure that the process of indirect election or selection is transparent and fair. To pre-empt conflict over nominations, the Special Independent Commission will specify mechanisms for filing of grievances and rules for arbitration of disputes.

5) The Emergency Loya Jirga will elect a Head of the State for the Transitional Administration and will approve proposals for the structure and key personnel of the Transitional Administration.

V. Final provisions

1) Upon the official transfer of power, all mujahidin, Afghan armed forces and armed groups in the country shall come under the command and control of the Interim Authority, and be reorganized according to the requirements of the new Afghan security and armed forces.

2) The Interim Authority and the Emergency Loya Jirga shall act in accordance with basic principles and provisions contained in international instruments on human rights and international humanitarian law to which Afghanistan is a party.

3) The Interim Authority shall cooperate with the international community in the fight against terrorism, drugs and organized crime. It shall commit itself to respect international law and maintain peaceful and friendly relations with neighbouring countries and the rest of the international community.

4) The Interim Authority and the Special Independent Commission for the Convening of the Emergency Loya Jirga will ensure the participation of women as well as the equitable representation of all ethnic and religious communities in the Interim Administration and the Emergency Loya Jirga.

5) All actions taken by the Interim Authority shall be consistent with Security Council resolution 1378 (14 November 2001) and other relevant Security Council resolutions relating to Afghanistan.

6) Rules of procedure for the organs established under the Interim Authority will be elaborated as appropriate with the assistance of the United Nations.

This agreement, of which the annexes constitute an integral part, done in Bonn on this 5th day of December 2001 in the English language, shall be the authentic text, in a single copy which shall remain deposited in the archives of the United Nations. Official texts shall be provided in Dari and Pashto, and such other languages as the Special Representative of the Secretary-General may designate. The Special Representative of the Secretary-General shall send certified copies in English, Dari and Pashto to each of the participants. . . .

ANNEX I

INTERNATIONAL SECURITY FORCE

1. The participants in the UN Talks on Afghanistan recognize that the responsibility for providing security and law and order throughout the country resides with the Afghans themselves. To this end, they pledge their commitment to do all within their means and influence to ensure such security,

including for all United Nations and other personnel of international governmental and non-governmental organizations deployed in Afghanistan.

2. With this objective in mind, the participants request the assistance of the international community in helping the new Afghan authorities in the establishment and training of new Afghan security and armed forces.

3. Conscious that some time may be required for the new Afghan security and armed forces to be fully constituted and functioning, the participants in the UN Talks on Afghanistan request the United Nations Security Council to consider authorizing the early deployment to Afghanistan of a United Nations mandated force. This force will assist in the maintenance of security for Kabul and its surrounding areas. Such a force could, as appropriate, be progressively expanded to other urban centres and other areas.

4. The participants in the UN Talks on Afghanistan pledge to withdraw all military units from Kabul and other urban centers or other areas in which the UN mandated force is deployed. It would also be desirable if such a force were to assist in the rehabilitation of Afghanistan's infrastructure.

ANNEX II

ROLE OF THE UNITED NATIONS DURING THE INTERIM PERIOD

1. The Special Representative of the Secretary-General will be responsible for all aspects of the United Nations' work in Afghanistan.

2. The Special Representative shall monitor and assist in the implementation of all aspects of this agreement.

3. The United Nations shall advise the Interim Authority in establishing a politically neutral environment conducive to the holding of the Emergency Loya Jirga in free and fair conditions. The United Nations shall pay special attention to the conduct of those bodies and administrative departments, which could directly influence the convening and outcome of the Emergency Loya Jirga.

4. The Special Representative of the Secretary-General or his/her delegate may be invited to attend the meetings of the interim Administration and the Special Independent Commission on the Convening of the Emergency Loya Jirga.

5. If for whatever reason the Interim Administration or the Special Independent Commission were actively prevented from meeting or unable to reach a decision on a matter related to the convening of the Emergency Loya Jirga, the Special Representative of the Secretary-General shall, taking into account the views expressed in the Interim Administration or in the Special Independent Commission, use his/her good offices with a view to facilitating a resolution to the impasse or a decision.

6. The United Nations shall have the right to investigate human rights violations and, where necessary, recommend corrective action. It will also be responsible for the development and implementation of a programme of human rights Education to promote respect for and understanding of human rights.

ANNEX III

REQUEST TO THE UNITED NATIONS BY THE PARTICIPANTS AT THE UN TALKS ON AFGHANISTAN

The participants in the UN Talks on Afghanistan hereby

1. Request that the United Nations and the international community take the necessary measures to guarantee the national sovereignty, territorial integrity and unity of Afghanistan as well as the non-interference by foreign countries in Afghanistan's internal affairs;

2. Urge the United Nations, the international community, particularly donor countries and multilateral institutions, to reaffirm, strengthen and implement their commitment to assist with the rehabilitation, recovery and reconstruction of Afghanistan, in coordination with the Interim Authority;

3. Request the United Nations to conduct as soon as possible (i) a registration of voters in advance of the general elections that will be held upon the adoption of the new constitution by the constitutional Loya Jirga and (ii) a census of the population of Afghanistan.

4. Urge the United Nations and the international community, in recognition of the heroic role played by the mujahidin in protecting the independence of Afghanistan and the dignity of its people, to take the necessary measures, in coordination with the Interim Authority, to assist in the reintegration of the mujahidin into the new Afghan security and armed forces;

5. Invite the United Nations and the international community to create a fund to assist the families and other dependents of martyrs and victims of the war, as well as the war disabled;

6. Strongly urge that the United Nations, the international community and regional organizations cooperate with the Interim Authority to combat international terrorism, cultivation and trafficking of illicit drugs and provide Afghan farmers with financial, material and technical resources for alternative crop production. . . .

NATO MEMBERS AND RUSSIA ON A "NEW RELATIONSHIP"
December 6 and 7, 2001

Among the many consequences of the September 11, 2001, terrorist attacks against the United States was a sudden warming of relations between Russia and the West—especially the United States. Earlier in the year Moscow and Washington had engaged in rhetorical spats reminiscent of the cold war. But after September 11 the two former enemies found common cause in the fight against terrorism, in particular Islamist terrorism.

By year's end the budding U.S. and Russian cooperation had extended to the NATO alliance, which had been formed in 1949 to keep the Soviet Union out of Western Europe. NATO and Russia on December 7 pledged a "new relationship," including the creation of a joint council that for the first time would give Moscow a voice, but not a veto, in some alliance decisions.

A Rough Start, Then Optimism

During the first half of the year, few would have predicted that 2001 would be a year of positive breakthroughs in relations between Russia and the United States. Russian president Vladimir Putin wrote to U.S. president George W. Bush just after the latter took office in January pledging to work "towards broadening interaction" between the two countries. The Bush administration said it shared that goal, but some of its early words and actions seemed calculated to put more distance between the two countries.

The first verbal blow came from CIA director George J. Tenet, the most senior holdover from the previous administration of President Bill Clinton. Testifying before the Senate Intelligence Committee on February 7, Tenet voiced strong concerns about Putin's domestic and foreign policies. "There can be little doubt that President Putin wants to restore some aspects of the Soviet past—status as a great power, strong and central authority and a stable and predictable society—sometimes at the expense of neighboring states or the civil rights of individual Russians," Tenet said. The Russian foreign ministry objected vigorously to Tenet's remarks, calling them "astonishing."

Secretary of Defense Donald H. Rumsfeld and his deputy, Paul D. Wolfowitz, stepped up the administration's rhetorical attack with statements complaining about Russian decisions, announced on March 12, to resume sales of conventional military equipment to Iran after a lapse of five years and to help Iran finish work on a nuclear power plant. "Russia is an active proliferator," Rumsfeld said in an interview with Britain's Sunday Telegraph *newspaper published March 18. Wolfowitz charged that the Russians "seem to be willing to sell anything to anyone for money." The Russian foreign ministry on March 20 responded by saying such statements were "in the spirit of the cold war."*

During the same period, Washington and Russia were engaged in a dispute over espionage that explicitly echoed the cold war period. The FBI on February 20 arrested a senior FBI counterintelligence agent, Robert Philip Hanssen, on charges of spying for the Soviet Union and then Russia. A month later the State Department announced that it planned to expel more than forty Russian diplomats from the United States, leading to a reciprocal action by Moscow. (Hanssen case, p. 150)

The growing unease between Washington and Moscow broke open after May 1, when Bush announced that he intended to develop a high-technology defense against ballistic missile attacks on the United States. Bush had made no secret of his support for missile defense, which had been a central promise of his presidential campaign the year before. But to pursue such a system, Bush ultimately would have to scrap the 1972 Anti-Ballistic Missile (ABM) treaty, which prohibited either the United States or the Soviet Union (later Russia) from building a missile defense covering its entire national territory. The treaty was widely considered the cornerstone of nuclear arms control during the latter stages of the cold war, and by the turn of the century many Russians viewed it as an important symbol of that country's great power status. Russian officials reacted angrily to Bush's announcement, and Putin later said the decision might force Russia to build its own national missile defense system. Russia had built a small defense system to protect Moscow in the 1970s; that system was allowed under the ABM treaty. (Missile defense, p. 281; ABM treaty, p. 927)

A break in the confrontational rhetoric came June 16 when Bush and Putin met for the first time in Slovenia, one of the countries being considered for membership in NATO. The brief session appeared to be more of a get-acquainted session than one of substance, but the two leaders attempted to project a determination to seek a new relationship based on cooperation. Another brief meeting on July 22 between the two leaders at the Group of Eight summit session in Genoa, Italy, produced talk of linking the planned U.S. missile defense system with a new round of cutbacks in the strategic nuclear arsenals of the United States and Russia. Bush administration officials expressed optimism that a broad agreement on those issues could be reached in coming months, and Bush himself seemed suddenly effusive about the personal relationship that he had developed with Putin. "This is a man with whom I can have an honest dialogue," he said.

Despite the apparently warm personal relations between Bush and Putin, underlying disagreements remained and were on full display in mid-August, when Rumsfeld flew to Moscow for follow-up talks. Rumsfeld made it clear that the United States intended to withdraw from the ABM treaty, which his Russian counterpart, Sergei Ivanov, called "one of the most important elements" of international arms control. The two sides disagreed even over the basic question of whether any subsequent arms control agreements between them should be in the form of a negotiated treaty or merely a handshake deal based on trust. The Russians insisted on a treaty, while Rumsfeld said the era of such formal measures was over and the United States no longer wished to be bound by legal restrictions.

Post-September 11 Events

Just seven weeks after Bush and Putin met in Genoa, the September 11 terrorist attacks created an urgency for the Bush administration to seek the cooperation of other countries. Bush told cheering members of Congress on September 20 that the United States would fight terrorism internationally and would welcome all the support it could get. Implicit in his statement was a new recognition at the highest levels of government that the United States could not defeat terrorism by itself. (Terrorist attacks, p. 614; Bush speech, p. 637; war in Afghanistan, p. 686)

Bush's objective coincided nicely with the plans of Putin, who for two years had battled what he viewed as an Islamist terrorist movement in Chechnya. Putin on September 24 gave a televised address to his nation saying that Russia fully supported the U.S. war against terrorism; Russia would even allow the United States to use Russian air space for "humanitarian" aid flights into Afghanistan, he said. Putin and other Russian officials subsequently said Moscow would not object if the United States used military bases in Central Asian countries adjacent to Afghanistan. These were remarkable concessions for the leader of a country that, in its former guise of the Soviet Union, had controlled Central Asia and had jealously guarded the region as a Russian sphere of influence. The Bush administration immediately took Putin up on that offer, negotiating agreements under which the United States used the air space of several Central Asian republics and rebuilt an airbase in Uzbekistan for U.S. use in the Afghanistan war.

Putin's full-scale support for the United States came with a price: he clearly wanted the Bush administration to acknowledge that Russia also had a legitimate struggle against terrorism in Chechnya. The Clinton and Bush administrations had both been critical of Russia's harsh tactics in suppressing a rebellion in Chechnya by guerrillas wanting to establish an independent Islamist state there; the issue had become a major sore point in relations between Washington and Moscow. Putin got what he wanted on September 26, when White House spokesman Ari Fleischer referred to "international terrorists" in Chechnya and implied that Bush understood the difficulties Putin faced there. Fleischer's statements pleased Russian officials but angered international human rights groups, which accused the

Bush administration of dropping its concerns about Russian repression in Chechnya. (War in Chechnya, Historic Documents of 2000, p. 175)

Putin followed up his new support for the United States on October 8, strongly endorsing the U.S. and British air strikes that had begun the previous day in Afghanistan. Putin said the terrorists had misjudged the willingness of what he called "modern civilization" to fight back. "I think their arrogance and self-confidence has been the terrorists' undoing," he said. "They did not expect the international community to show such cohesion in the face of a common threat."

The new-found allies, Bush and Putin, met twice more in the late fall as the war in Afghanistan was under way. In Shanghai on October 21, during the annual meeting of the Asia Pacific Economic Cooperation forum, the two leaders held an hour-long talk and expressed optimism about resolving their continuing differences over the ABM treaty.

That meeting, and subsequent comments by officials in both Washington and Moscow, led to fevered speculation early in November that the two leaders would be able to sign a significant arms control agreement when Putin visited the president's Texas ranch in mid-November. The two men issued a joint statement November 14 celebrating the "new relationship" between the United States and Russia and calling for the development of a "new strategic framework" to ensure their mutual security and world peace. Bush and Putin each announced plans to reduce nuclear weapons arsenals to levels slightly below those that had been previously agreed: to about 1,500 warheads for Russia and 1,700 to 2,200 warheads for the United States. But the leaders had no formal agreement to announce on arms control measures, and there was no more talk about linking strategic arms reductions to abandonment of the ABM treaty. One month later Bush announced that he was unilaterally pulling out of that treaty.

A Russian Role in NATO

With arms control measures at least temporarily sidetracked, the key remaining issue on the table between the United States and Russia in the closing weeks of 2001 was Russia's relationship with NATO. NATO during the 1990s gradually had been expanding its membership eastward, taking in countries that once had been wards of the Soviet Union, including the Czech Republic, Hungary, and Poland. Russia had viewed that expansion as a threat and had objected even more strongly to NATO plans to offer membership to one or more of the Baltic states (Estonia, Latvia, and Lithuania) immediately adjacent to Russia. Expressing anxieties about such a development, Putin on July 18 had said NATO could resolve Russia's concerns by dissolving itself, by asking Russia to join the alliance, or by working with Russia to create an entirely new organization.

The post-September 11 evolving relationship between Washington and Russia offered a new opportunity to address the questions of NATO and Russia, and diplomats worked busily on the matter throughout November and into early December. A breakthrough of sorts seemed near on November 22 when NATO secretary general Lord Robertson suggested creation of a new "Russia-North Atlantic Council" in which Russia would have an equal voice with the nineteen NATO members in discussions of such matters as peace-keeping and countering terrorism and weapons proliferation. Robertson's statement suggested that Russia might be given an effective veto power over some NATO decisions, which normally were made by consensus. He acknowledged that his proposal would require "major shifts in attitude" on the part of Russia and Western countries. Russia since 1997 had been part of a Joint Permanent Council that served as an adjunct to NATO's decision-making body, the North Atlantic Council. But the joint council had no real power.

Although Robertson said the United States and other key members supported his proposal, it soon became clear that NATO was not quite ready to offer Russia any type of veto power. Meeting in Brussels on December 6, the nineteen NATO foreign ministers adopted a statement pledging closer cooperation with Russia and agreeing to form the new Russia-NATO council that Robertson had suggested. The council would discuss such issues as counterterrorism and "nonproliferation, export control and arms-control matters, arms transparency and confidence-building measures, missile defense, search and rescue at sea, and military-to-military cooperation." But the NATO ministers said Russia would not have a veto over any alliance decisions. Ambassadors said several NATO countries opposed giving Russia any type of veto, especially over the sensitive issue of expanding the alliance membership. Among those reportedly most opposed to a Russian veto were the newest alliance members: the Czech Republic, Hungary, and Poland. The ministers also called on Russia to work toward a "lasting political and peaceful resolution" to the war in Chechnya.

Meeting the next day with Russian foreign minister Igor Ivanov, the NATO ministers formally agreed to proceed with a new, though unnamed council including Russia. In a joint statement, the ministers said the new council should be in place by the time of the NATO ministerial meeting planned for May 2002. "There is no issue more important to the security and stability of the Euro-Atlantic area than the further development of a confident and cooperative relationship between us," Robertson said.

Subsequent news reports revealed that much of the discussion within the Bush administration, and among NATO members, concerned the possible use of the phrase "NATO at 20" to describe the new Russia-NATO council. Rumsfeld and some NATO countries reportedly were reluctant to use the phrase, fearing that it implied full Russian membership. Secretary of State Colin Powell reportedly favored use of the term, rejecting any implication of Russian membership in NATO. The final statements issued by NATO on December 6 and 7 each included one general reference to NATO "at 20."

> *Following are excerpts from a statement issued December 6, 2001, by the foreign ministers of NATO member nations following their meeting in Brussels in which they proposed a "new relationship" with Russia. That statement is followed by the text of*

a joint statement issued December 7, 2001, by the foreign ministers of NATO nations and Russia after a meeting at which it was decided to form a new council giving Russia a greater voice—but not a veto—in the alliance's deliberations.

The documents were obtained from the Internet at http:// www.nato.int/docu/pr/2001/p01-158e.htm; http://www.nato .int/docu/pr/2001/p011207e.htm.

NATO COMMUNIQUÉ

. . . 2. Today we commit ourselves to forge a new relationship with Russia, enhancing our ability to work together in areas of common interest. We re-affirm that a confident and cooperative partnership between the Allies and Russia, based on shared democratic values and the shared commitment to a stable, peaceful and undivided Europe, as enshrined in the NATO-Russia Founding Act, is essential for stability and security in the Euro-Atlantic area. We have decided to give new impetus and substance to our partnership, with the goal of creating, with Russia, a new NATO-Russia Council, to identify and pursue opportunities for joint action at 20. To that end, we have tasked the North Atlantic Council in Permanent Session to explore and develop, in the coming months, building on the Founding Act, new, effective mechanisms for consultation, cooperation, joint decision, and coordinated/joint action. We intend that such cooperative mechanisms will be in place for, or prior to, our next meeting in Reykjavik in May 2002. NATO's fundamental objectives remain as set out in the Washington Treaty, under which provisions NATO will maintain its prerogative of independent decision and action at 19 on all issues consistent with its obligations and responsibilities.

3. We are pleased that Russia stands with us in the struggle against terrorism, and believe this will contribute significantly to our common goal of a strong, stable and enduring NATO-Russia partnership. We are intensifying our cooperation in this and other areas, including non-proliferation, export control and arms control matters, arms transparency and confidence building measures, missile defence, search and rescue at sea, and military-to-military cooperation, which represents a major step towards a qualitatively new relationship. We support Russia's right to protect her territorial integrity, and recognise her right to protect all citizens against terrorism and criminality. We welcome the initial steps Russia has taken towards establishing a political dialogue over the conflict in Chechnya. We urge Russia to build on these steps to find a prompt and lasting political and peaceful resolution to the conflict and to respect and protect the human and legal rights of the population. We call on the Chechen side to cooperate in good faith in seeking a political solution to the conflict, to condemn terrorism and to take actions against it. . . .

NATO-RUSSIA JOINT STATEMENT

1. Today we commit ourselves to forge a new relationship between NATO Allies and Russia, enhancing our ability to work together in areas of common interest and to stand up to new threats and risks to our security. We reaffirm that a confident and cooperative partnership between the Allies and Russia, based on shared democratic values and the shared commitment to a stable, peaceful and undivided Europe, as enshrined in the NATO-Russia Founding Act [of 1997], is essential for stability and security in the Euro-Atlantic area. We have decided to give new impetus and substance to our partnership, with the goal of creating a new council bringing together NATO member states and Russia to identify and pursue opportunities for joint action at 20.

2. We, the Ministers, will continue our dialogue on the process on which we have embarked today. Regular working contacts will also be maintained between the Ministry of Foreign Affairs of the Russian Federation and NATO. The NATO-Russia Permanent Joint Council has also tasked its Ambassadors to explore and develop, in the coming months, building on the Founding Act, new, effective mechanisms for consultation, cooperation, joint decision, and coordinated/joint action. We intend that such cooperative mechanisms beyond the current format will be in place for, or prior to, our meeting in Reykjavik in May 2002.

3. We condemn terrorism in all its manifestations. We reiterate our deepest sympathies to the victims, and their families, of the September 11 and other terrorist attacks. We fully support UN Security Council Resolutions 1368 and 1373, and will spare no efforts in bringing to justice the perpetrators, organisers and sponsors of such acts and in defeating the scourge of terrorism.

4. We are reminded by these tragic events that NATO and Russia face common threats that demand comprehensive, co-ordinated responses. We are encouraged by the strong spirit of partnership and co-operation that has evolved in the NATO-Russia relationship. We are intensifying our cooperation in the struggle against terrorism and in other areas, including crisis management, non-proliferation, arms control and confidence building measures, theatre missile defence, search and rescue at sea, military-to-military cooperation and civil emergencies, which represents a major step towards a qualitatively new relationship.

UN SECRETARY GENERAL ANNAN ON HIS NOBEL PEACE PRIZE
December 10, 2001

The United Nations and its secretary general, Kofi Annan, were awarded the Nobel Peace Prize in 2001, in recognition of their work "for a better organized and more peaceful world." The award was the first for the UN as a whole, although several of its specialized agencies and functions had won earlier peace prizes. Annan was the second secretary general to win the award. The first, Dag Hammarskjold, was awarded the Nobel Prize posthumously in 1961 after he died while attempting to end fighting in the Congo.

Annan, a Ghanian, was the first career UN official to be elected secretary general, effective January 1, 1997. He quickly became the most active UN leader in many years, pressing for peaceful settlements to conflicts in Africa, Asia, and the Middle East, and launching a major campaign to combat the AIDS pandemic. He implemented reforms in the UN bureaucracy, reducing the intensity of a long-running feud between the U.S. Congress and the world body. Annan also issued several hard-hitting but widely praised reports on controversial matters, including one in 1998 calling African leaders to task for failing to stop the continent's wars and to improve the lives of their people and two reports in 1999 documenting the UN's failures to prevent the 1994 genocide in Rwanda and the 1995 mass killing by Serbs of Muslims in the Bosnian town of Srebenica. Annan had headed the UN peacekeeping department at the time of the Rwanda and Bosnia disasters, and he accepted personal as well as institutional responsibility. (Annan speech to African leaders, p. 159; Annan election, Historic Documents of 1996, p. 824; Africa report, Historic Documents of 1998, p. 220; Rwanda report, Historic Documents of 1999, p. 860; Srebenica report, Historic Documents of 1999, p. 735)

Largely because of the UN failures in Rwanda and Bosnia, Annan sought to have the United Nations play a more vigorous role than it had in the past in protecting human rights, even over the opposition of the governments that were violating those rights. He told the UN General Assembly in September 1999 that "massive, systematic violations of human rights—wherever they might take place—should not be allowed to stand." That statement was not welcomed by some world leaders who argued that the world body had no business interfering in the "internal" business of UN member nations.

Annan in 2000 issued what he called a "Millennium report" calling on the UN, other international agencies, and member nations to commit themselves to an ambitious program of reducing poverty, ending conflict, protecting the environment, and fighting AIDS. That report became the basis for the "Millennium Declaration" approved in September 2000 by a large summit meeting of world leaders. (Millennium declaration, Historic Documents of 2000, p. 700)

Annan Nobel Prize Speech

Annan accepted the Nobel Peace Prize at a ceremony in Oslo on December 10, 2001, the anniversary date of the death of the prize's benefactor, Swedish gunpowder manufacturer Alfred Nobel. The 2001 prize marked the one hundredth anniversary of the prestigious award.

In his public statements, Annan often was optimistic and upbeat, expressing hope that the people and nations of the world would somehow find ways to work together to overcome common problems. His speech accepting the prize was uncharacteristically somber, however, perhaps a reflection of the shock the world had received just three months earlier when terrorists attacked the United States. As Annan spoke, an international military force led by the United States was trying to wipe out the remaining resistance in Afghanistan by the al Qaeda terrorist network, which was said to be responsible for the September 11 attacks. (Terrorist attacks, pp. 614, 624)

Annan spoke directly about the consequences of those attacks, which he placed in the context of a larger struggle between those who would divide the people of the world and those who sought to unite them. "We have entered the third millennium through a gate of fire," he said. "If today, after the horror of 11 September, we see better, and we see further we will realize that humanity is indivisible. New threats make no distinction between races, nations, or regimes. A new insecurity has entered every mind, regardless of wealth or status. A deeper awareness of the bonds that bind us all—in pain as in prosperity—has gripped young and old."

Annan seemed especially eager to address the fundamental causes of ethnic and religious disputes that had become the most prevalent sources of national and regional conflict during the last decade of the twentieth century and into the twenty-first. After the end of the cold war, Africa, Eastern Europe, South Asia, and Southeast Asia all experienced numerous wars that stemmed from disputes over ethnicity and religion.

"Each of us has the right to take pride in our particular faith or heritage," Annan said. "But the notion that what is ours is necessarily in conflict with what is theirs is both false and dangerous. It has resulted in endless enmity and conflict, leading men to commit the greatest of crimes in the name of a higher power."

The U.S. and the UN

It had little to do with the Nobel Prize, but 2001 may also have marked the final resolution of a long-running dispute between the United Nations and some members of Congress. During the 1990s congressional conservatives had managed to hold up much of the money owed by the United States to the world body for annual dues, known as "assessments." Congress had deducted most of the money from annual appropriations bills because of complaints that the UN had a bloated bureaucracy, was ineffective, and often was under the control of Third World countries hostile to U.S. interests. By 1999 the UN said that Washington owed more than $1.6 billion; the Clinton administration put the figure at $1.1 billion.

After taking office in 1997, Annan initiated a series of reforms to make the UN more efficient and more accountable to member nations. A polished diplomat, but one not afraid to speak forthrightly, he also managed to win grudging respect from many UN critics on Capitol Hill, notably Jesse Helms, R-N.C., chairman of the Senate Foreign Relations Committee.

The Clinton administration in 1999 negotiated an agreement with Congress providing for the United States to pay $926 million in back dues to the UN in three segments. Clinton made a first payment of $100 million in 1999, but a second payment of $582 million was held up during 2000 because of continuing congressional resistance—especially to the large U.S. share of the world body's peacekeeping budget. Late in 2000 Richard C. Holbrooke, then the U.S. ambassador to the United Nations, negotiated an agreement that lowered the U.S. share of peacekeeping expenses from the existing 30 percent to 28 percent in fiscal 2001 and to 26 percent in 2002; in return, Congress would release the rest of the money that Washington owed. (Dues agreement, Historic Documents of 2000, p. 181)

Holbrooke's deal won backing from Helms, who on February 7, 2001, secured unanimous Senate approval of a bill releasing the pending $582 million. But the money then was held hostage in the House, where Republican leaders were angered by the UN's creation of an International Criminal Court to handle war crimes and severe human rights violations; critics feared the anti-U.S. countries and factions would use the court to prosecute U.S. servicemen stationed overseas. The bill releasing the UN money sat in the House with little prospect for action until after the September 11 terrorist attacks. At that point, the Bush administration realized that the continued dispute over past dues was hindering its attempt to build international diplomatic support for a U.S. war against terrorism. With the administration's support, the bill quickly cleared the House on September 24 and President Bush signed it into law (PL 107–46) on October 5. That left a final tranche of $244 million scheduled to be released in 2002, conditioned on administrative reforms at the UN's World Health Organizations and several other agencies.

Following is the text of a speech delivered December 10, 2001, in Oslo, Norway, by United Nations Secretary General Kofi Annan

*upon his acceptance of the Nobel Peace Prize. The prize was
awarded jointly to Annan and the United Nations.*

**The document was obtained from the Internet at http://
www.un.org/News/ossg/latestsm.htm.**

Your Majesties, Your Royal Highnesses, Excellencies, Members of the Norwegian Nobel Committee, Ladies and Gentlemen,

Today, in Afghanistan, a girl will be born. Her mother will hold her and feed
her, comfort her and care for her—just as any mother would anywhere in
the world. In these most basic acts of human nature, humanity knows no divisions. But to be born a girl in today's Afghanistan is to begin life centuries
away from the prosperity that one small part of humanity has achieved. It is
to live under conditions that many of us in this hall would consider inhuman.
Truly, it is as if it were a tale of two planets.

I speak of a girl in Afghanistan, but I might equally well have mentioned
a baby boy or girl in Sierra Leone. No one today is unaware of this divide between the world's rich and poor. No one today can claim ignorance of the cost
that this divide imposes on the poor and dispossessed who are no less de-
serving of human dignity, fundamental freedoms, security, food and education
than any of us. The cost, however, is not borne by them alone. Ultimately, it is
borne by all of us—North and South, rich and poor, men and women of all
races and religions.

Today's real borders are not between nations, but between powerful and
powerless, free and fettered, privileged and humiliated. Today, no walls can
separate humanitarian or human rights crises in one part of the world from national security crises in another.

Scientists tell us that the world of nature is so small and interdependent
that a butterfly flapping its wings in the Amazon rainforest can generate a violent storm on the other side of the earth. This principle is known as the "Butterfly Effect." Today, we realize, perhaps more than ever, that the world of
human activity also has its own "Butterfly Effect"—for better or for worse.

Ladies and Gentlemen,

We have entered the third millennium through a gate of fire. If today, after
the horror of 11 September, we see better, and we see further—we will realize that humanity is indivisible. New threats make no distinction between
races, nations or regions. A new insecurity has entered every mind, regardless
of wealth or status. A deeper awareness of the bonds that bind us all—in pain
as in prosperity—has gripped young and old.

In the early beginnings of the 21st century—a century already violently dis-
abused of any hopes that progress towards global peace and prosperity is
inevitable—this new reality can no longer be ignored. It must be confronted.

The 20th century was perhaps the deadliest in human history, devastated
by innumerable conflicts, untold suffering, and unimaginable crimes. Time af-

ter time, a group or a nation inflicted extreme violence on another, often driven by irrational hatred and suspicion, or unbounded arrogance and thirst for power and resources. In response to these cataclysms, the leaders of the world came together at mid-century to unite the nations as never before.

A forum was created—the United Nations—where all nations could join forces to affirm the dignity and worth of every person, and to secure peace and development for all peoples. Here States could unite to strengthen the rule of law, recognize and address the needs of the poor, restrain man's brutality and greed, conserve the resources and beauty of nature, sustain the equal rights of men and women, and provide for the safety of future generations.

We thus inherit from the 20th century the political, as well as the scientific and technological power, which—if only we have the will to use them—give us the chance to vanquish poverty, ignorance and disease.

In the 21st Century I believe the mission of the United Nations will be defined by a new, more profound, awareness of the sanctity and dignity of every human life, regardless of race or religion. This will require us to look beyond the framework of States, and beneath the surface of nations or communities. We must focus, as never before, on improving the conditions of the individual men and women who give the state or nation its richness and character. We must begin with the young Afghan girl, recognizing that saving that one life is to save humanity itself.

Over the past five years, I have often recalled that the United Nations' Charter begins with the words: "We the peoples." What is not always recognized is that "we the peoples" are made up of individuals whose claims to the most fundamental rights have too often been sacrificed in the supposed interests of the state or the nation.

A genocide begins with the killing of one man—not for what he has done, but because of who he is. A campaign of 'ethnic cleansing' begins with one neighbour turning on another. Poverty begins when even one child is denied his or her fundamental right to education. What begins with the failure to uphold the dignity of one life, all too often ends with a calamity for entire nations.

In this new century, we must start from the understanding that peace belongs not only to states or peoples, but to each and every member of those communities. The sovereignty of States must no longer be used as a shield for gross violations of human rights. Peace must be made real and tangible in the daily existence of every individual in need.

Peace must be sought, above all, because it is the condition for every member of the human family to live a life of dignity and security.

The rights of the individual are of no less importance to immigrants and minorities in Europe and the Americas than to women in Afghanistan or children in Africa. They are as fundamental to the poor as to the rich; they are as necessary to the security of the developed world as to that of the developing world.

From this vision of the role of the United Nations in the next century flow three key priorities for the future: eradicating poverty, preventing conflict, and promoting democracy. Only in a world that is rid of poverty can all men and women make the most of their abilities. Only where individual rights are respected can differences be channelled politically and resolved peacefully. Only in a democratic environment, based on respect for diversity and dialogue, can individual self-expression and self-government be secured, and freedom of association be upheld.

Throughout my term as Secretary-General, I have sought to place human beings at the centre of everything we do—from conflict prevention to development to human rights. Securing real and lasting improvement in the lives of individual men and women is the measure of all we do at the United Nations.

It is in this spirit that I humbly accept the Centennial Nobel Peace Prize. Forty years ago today, the Prize for 1961 was awarded for the first time to a Secretary-General of the United Nations—posthumously, because Dag Hammarskjöld had already given his life for peace in Central Africa. And on the same day, the Prize for 1960 was awarded for the first time to an African—Albert Luthuli, one of the earliest leaders of the struggle against apartheid in South Africa. For me, as a young African beginning his career in the United Nations a few months later, those two men set a standard that I have sought to follow throughout my working life.

This award belongs not just to me. I do not stand here alone. On behalf of all my colleagues in every part of the United Nations, in every corner of the globe, who have devoted their lives—and in many instances risked or given their lives in the cause of peace—I thank the Members of the Nobel Committee for this high honour. My own path to service at the United Nations was made possible by the sacrifice and commitment of my family and many friends from all continents—some of whom have passed away—who taught me and guided me. To them, I offer my most profound gratitude.

In a world filled with weapons of war and all too often words of war, the Nobel Committee has become a vital agent for peace. Sadly, a prize for peace is a rarity in this world. Most nations have monuments or memorials to war, bronze salutations to heroic battles, archways of triumph. But peace has no parade, no pantheon of victory.

What it does have is the Nobel Prize—a statement of hope and courage with unique resonance and authority. Only by understanding and addressing the needs of individuals for peace, for dignity, and for security can we at the United Nations hope to live up to the honour conferred today, and fulfil the vision of our founders. This is the broad mission of peace that United Nations staff members carry out every day in every part of the world.

A few of them, women and men, are with us in this hall today. Among them, for instance, are a Military Observer from Senegal who is helping to provide basic security in the Democratic Republic of the Congo; a Civilian Police Adviser from the United States who is helping to improve the rule of law in Kosovo; a UNICEF Child Protection Officer from Ecuador who is helping to secure the rights of Colombia's most vulnerable citizens; and a World Food Programme Officer from China who is helping to feed the people of North Korea.

Distinguished guests,

The idea that there is one people in possession of the truth, one answer to the world's ills, or one solution to humanity's needs, has done untold harm throughout history—especially in the last century. Today, however, even amidst continuing ethnic conflict around the world, there is a growing understanding that human diversity is both the reality that makes dialogue necessary, and the very basis for that dialogue.

We understand, as never before, that each of us is fully worthy of the respect and dignity essential to our common humanity. We recognize that we are the products of many cultures, traditions and memories; that mutual respect allows us to study and learn from other cultures; and that we gain strength by combining the foreign with the familiar.

In every great faith and tradition one can find the values of tolerance and mutual understanding. The Qur'an [Koran], for example, tells us that "We created you from a single pair of male and female and made you into nations and tribes, that you may know each other." Confucius urged his followers: "when the good way prevails in the state, speak boldly and act boldly. When the state has lost the way, act boldly and speak softly." In the Jewish tradition, the injunction to "love thy neighbour as thyself," is considered to be the very essence of the Torah.

This thought is reflected in the Christian Gospel, which also teaches us to love our enemies and pray for those who wish to persecute us. Hindus are taught that "truth is one, the sages give it various names." And in the Buddhist tradition, individuals are urged to act with compassion in every facet of life.

Each of us has the right to take pride in our particular faith or heritage. But the notion that what is ours is necessarily in conflict with what is theirs is both false and dangerous. It has resulted in endless enmity and conflict, leading men to commit the greatest of crimes in the name of a higher power.

It need not be so. People of different religions and cultures live side by side in almost every part of the world, and most of us have overlapping identities which unite us with very different groups. We can love what we are, without hating what—and who—we are not. We can thrive in our own tradition, even as we learn from others, and come to respect their teachings.

This will not be possible, however, without freedom of religion, of expression, of assembly, and basic equality under the law. Indeed, the lesson of the past century has been that where the dignity of the individual has been trampled or threatened—where citizens have not enjoyed the basic right to choose their government, or the right to change it regularly—conflict has too often followed, with innocent civilians paying the price, in lives cut short and communities destroyed.

The obstacles to democracy have little to do with culture or religion, and much more to do with the desire of those in power to maintain their position at any cost. This is neither a new phenomenon nor one confined to any particular part of the world. People of all cultures value their freedom of choice, and feel the need to have a say in decisions affecting their lives.

The United Nations, whose membership comprises almost all the States in the world, is founded on the principle of the equal worth of every human being. It is the nearest thing we have to a representative institution that can address the interests of all states, and all peoples. Through this universal, indispensable instrument of human progress, States can serve the interests of their citizens by recognizing common interests and pursuing them in unity. No doubt, that is why the Nobel Committee says that it "wishes, in its centenary year, to proclaim that the only negotiable route to global peace and cooperation goes by way of the United Nations."

I believe the Committee also recognized that this era of global challenges leaves no choice but cooperation at the global level. When States undermine the rule of law and violate the rights of their individual citizens, they become a menace not only to their own people, but also to their neighbours, and indeed the world. What we need today is better governance—legitimate, democratic governance that allows each individual to flourish, and each State to thrive.

Your Majesties, Excellencies, Ladies and Gentlemen,

You will recall that I began my address with a reference to the girl born in Afghanistan today. Even though her mother will do all in her power to protect and sustain her, there is a one-in-four risk that she will not live to see her fifth birthday. Whether she does is just one test of our common humanity—of our belief in our individual responsibility for our fellow men and women. But it is the only test that matters.

Remember this girl and then our larger aims—to fight poverty, prevent conflict, or cure disease—will not seem distant, or impossible. Indeed, those aims will seem very near, and very achievable—as they should. Because beneath the surface of states and nations, ideas and language, lies the fate of individual human beings in need. Answering their needs will be the mission of the United Nations in the century to come.

Thank you very much.

VETERANS AFFAIRS SECRETARY ON ALS IN GULF WAR VETERANS
December 10, 2001

The federal government announced December 10, 2001, that veterans who had served in southwest Asia during the Persian Gulf war were twice as likely as other veterans to suffer from amyotrophic lateral sclerosis (ALS), a fatal neurological illness commonly known as Lou Gehrig's disease. It was the first time that the government had acknowledged a direct link between a specific illness and service in the region during the war against Iraq in 1990–1991. Until the announcement, the government had denied that a host of illnesses and disorders, collectively known as Gulf war syndrome, were caused during service in the region.

"In today's battlefield, we need to recognize that nontraumatic illnesses and injuries can be as deadly as a bullet wound," Anthony J. Principi, secretary of veterans affairs, said in a prepared statement. "And where we can show scientific evidence of an association between service and illness, we must compensate veterans with that illness." Principi said that all veterans who served in the Gulf war operations Desert Storm and Desert Shield who developed ALS would receive disability and medical benefits. He also promised that the department would focus its medical research efforts on finding the cause of and a cure for the disease, which destroyed the nerve cells that controlled muscle function. Victims of ALS suffered severe wasting of their muscles, eventually losing the ability to swallow or breathe. Most died within two to five years of developing the disease. ALS first came to public attention when Lou Gehrig, the great baseball player for the New York Yankees, contracted the disease. He died in 1941.

Gulf War Syndrome

More than 100,000 veterans of the Gulf war had reported a range of illnesses and disorders including chronic fatigue, muscle pain, memory loss, respiratory problems, and sleep disorders. Exposure to chemical weapons, stress, smoke from burning oil wells, depleted uranium used in U.S. anti-tank shells, pesticides, and vaccines against biological and chemical agents had variously been blamed for causing the problems. But after more than

190 studies, at a cost of $155 million, no conclusive link had been shown be-
tween any one of the disorders and any one of the suspected causes. Some
researchers said it was likely that the ailing veterans were suffering the lin-
gering effects of combat stress; some implied that many of the complaints
resulted from a kind of mass hysteria.

The government's refusal to acknowledge that this complex of medical
problems might be related to duty in the Persian Gulf region angered many
Gulf war veterans and their supporters, who said the government was sim-
ply trying to avoid having to pay medical benefits. Congress in 1994 sought
to alleviate some of the problem by authorizing medical and disability bene-
fits for Gulf war veterans with "undiagnosed illnesses." But this did not help
veterans who had been diagnosed with specific illnesses, because no specific
illness had been shown to have a direct connection to service in the Persian
Gulf. (Congressional action, Historic Documents of 1994, p. 264)

The government's credibility was further weakened in 1996 when the De-
fense Department was forced to admit that chemical agents had been pres-
ent at a munitions dump in southern Iraq that had been dismantled by U.S.
military personnel in March 1991. Until that admission, the Pentagon had
insisted that no soldiers had been exposed to any Iraqi chemical agents dur-
ing the war. (Chemical agents exposure, Historic Documents of 1997, p. 740)

Many veterans said the struggle to show that their illnesses were linked to
their service in the Gulf war was reminiscent of Vietnam veterans' struggle
with the government over Agent Orange, a herbicide used to defoliate the
Vietnamese countryside. After years of denying any connection between
the herbicide and various illnesses among Vietnam veterans, the Depart-
ment of Veterans Affairs in the 1990s began paying medical and disability
benefits for certain disorders that studies showed were likely linked to Agent
Orange. These included specific skin, liver, and nerve disorders as well as
several kinds of cancers. In May 2001 the department added Type 2 dia-
betes to the list after the National Academy of Sciences reported "limited/
suggestive" evidence of a link between Agent Orange and the disease. The de-
partment said about 9 percent of the 2.3 million Vietnam veterans still alive
had Type 2 diabetes.

The ALS Study

The joint announcement by the departments of veteran affairs and de-
fense was based on the preliminary findings of a study involving nearly
700,000 soldiers sent to the Persian Gulf between August 2, 1990, and
July 31, 1991, and 1.8 million service members who were not sent to region.
The study found forty veterans with ALS among those who were sent to the
Gulf region, about double the number expected compared with sixty-seven
cases among the veterans who did not serve in the Gulf. Twenty of the forty
had died, Principi said. Although the findings had not yet been peer re-
viewed, Principi said they were being released so that the Veterans Affairs
Department could get benefits to those suffering from the disease. "They need
help now, and we well offer them that help," Principi said.

The study, which was conducted at a veterans hospital in Durham, North Carolina, found that the risk for ALS was 3.5 per million for veterans who were not sent to the Persian Gulf region, and 6.7 per million for veterans who were. The risk for ALS also varied from service to service. Air force veterans were 2.7 times more likely than veterans not deployed to the region to develop ALS, while army veterans were twice as likely to develop the disease. Navy and Marine Corps veterans had the same rate of risk as veterans who were not sent to the region. Principi said additional studies would try to determine what, if anything, the veterans who developed ALS had in common, such as where they were stationed.

The study cost $1.3 million to conduct. Two earlier, smaller studies had found no link between ALS and service in the Persian Gulf during the war.

Veterans' groups and their supporters were pleased with the announcement. "It's just a shame it has taken so long," said Representative Christopher Shays, R-Conn., chairman of a veterans health subcommittee in the U.S. House. "There has been an incredible reluctance on the part of the Defense Department to acknowledge any Gulf war illness. So I consider this a huge announcement." Acknowledging that reluctance, Bill Winkerwerder Jr., assistant secretary of defense for health affairs, said at the news conference that there had been "a maturation of thinking about health risks associated with deployed military service" within the Defense Department.

"We've been proven right, and we're going to be proven right on a lot of other things as well," said Stephen L. Robinson, executive director of the National Gulf War Resource Center. "We want more research and compensation for Gulf War veterans who are sick. For the last 10 years, not much has been done that benefits Gulf War veterans." The head of the association that represented people with ALS also applauded the announcement. "This may give us some insight into an environmental exposure that would have something to do with ALS," said Mike Havlicek. "We are very supportive of the effort to get to the bottom on this."

Related Studies

A study conducted by the Department of Veterans Affairs and researchers at Johns Hopkins University reported that veterans who served in the Persian Gulf were two to three times more likely than other veterans to have children with birth defects. The study, which was reported in the October issue of Annals of Epidemiology, *was based on a survey of Gulf and non-Gulf veterans from all four branches of the military. About 21,000 people answered the questionnaire, which asked about first pregnancies after June 30, 1991.*

The study found that females who served in the Gulf region reportedly were almost three times as likely to recount having a child with birth effects as non-Gulf veteran females, while male Gulf veterans were about twice as likely to report having a child with birth defects as male non-Gulf veterans. The Gulf veterans also reported a higher incidence of miscarriage. The researchers considered such things as heart murmurs, webbed toes or fingers, and chromosomal abnormalities to be birth defects. Developmental disabilities, perinatal complications, and pediatric illnesses were not considered to be birth defects.

Several earlier studies had failed to find any link between service in the Persian Gulf region and birth defects, and several critics questioned the reliability of the study, saying that parents' opinions about their children's birth defects was not an objective measure. A Pentagon spokesman said the findings were worth further investigation but was skeptical that they would hold up. He said it was difficult to believe that the earlier studies would have missed such an increased incidence of birth defects among attributable to service in the Persian Gulf.

A study funded by the British Ministry of Defence and released April 13 found that British Gulf war veterans suffered from twice as many cases of illness as veterans who were not sent to the Gulf, but that none of the illnesses was unique to the Gulf vets. The illnesses included post-traumatic stress disorder, chronic fatigue, and respiratory problems. The researchers looked at several possible causes, including exposure to oil fires, pesticides, depleted uranium, combat stress, and vaccinations against chemical and biological agents, but no one factor emerged as the "single most important" cause. The team of researchers suggested further study of pesticide exposure and vaccinations. About 53,000 British troops served in southwest Asia during the Persian Gulf war.

Following is the text of a prepared statement released December 10, 2001, at a news conference in which Anthony J. Principi, secretary of veterans affairs, announced that instances of amyotrophic lateral sclerosis had been linked to service in the Persian Gulf war and that the department would offer medical and disability benefits to veterans of that war who contracted the disease.

**The document was obtained from the Internet at http://www
.gulflink.osd.mil/news/na_als_remarks_10dec01.html.**

Good afternoon, ladies and gentlemen. Thank you all for coming.

Following the largest epidemiological investigation of its kind—involving studying 2.5 million American veterans—the Department of Veterans Affairs has found preliminary evidence that veterans who served in Operations Desert Shield and Desert Storm are nearly twice as likely as veterans who were not deployed to Southwest Asia to develop amyotrophic (am-ee-o-trow-phic) lateral sclerosis, or ALS—an illness often called Lou Gehrig's disease.

In accomplishing this study, we worked as full partners with the Department of Defense, which provided most of the funding for the project. I want to thank Bill Winkenwerder, the Assistant Secretary of Defense for Health Affairs, for partnering with us—and for all of DoD's help and support on this vital issue.

ALS is a neurological disease that destroys the nerve cells that control muscle movement. Neither a cause nor an effective treatment for ALS is known, and it is a fatal illness.

Our study involved nearly 700,000 service members who were deployed to Southwest Asia during Desert Shield and Desert Storm, and 1.8 million service members who were not deployed. We found 40 cases of ALS among deployed veterans—almost twice as many as we would have expected compared to those who were on active duty during that period but did not serve in the Gulf. About half are now deceased.

This, incidentally, is the third study of ALS our department has accomplished. The first two, which were much smaller in scale than the present study, were inconclusive, but we kept searching in response to requests from veterans and veterans service organizations. They believed that there was an association between service in the Gulf and ALS—and preliminary evidence indicates that they were correct.

The finding that Desert Shield and Desert Storm veterans are at greater risk to develop ALS is of great concern to me, and to our department—as I am sure it is to these veterans and their families. In response to the results of this study, I intend to immediately take three actions.

First, I will insure veterans who served in the Gulf during the period from August 2, 1990 through July 31, 1991 and subsequently develop ALS are compensated. In today's battlefield, we need to recognize that non-traumatic illnesses and injuries can be as deadly as a bullet wound. And where we can show scientific evidence of an association between service and illness, we must compensate veterans with that illness.

Therefore, we will compensate Desert Shield and Desert Storm veterans with ALS—and we will do so quickly. We will immediately contact those who were identified by the study and will help them to file new claims or prosecute existing claims—and we will pay benefits retroactively to the date their claims are filed.

We are providing compensation at this time despite the fact that this study has not yet been peer reviewed because of the progressively fatal nature of ALS. Those veterans who have contracted the disease cannot wait for the peer review process to be completed. They need help now-and we will offer it to them.

Second, I intend to fully focus our medical resources and research capabilities on this issue. VA is an internationally recognized leader in medical research, specializing in studies of illnesses, diseases and injuries are related to military service. In recognition for their work, two VA researchers have won Nobel Prizes.

Our department pioneered the understanding of Post-Traumatic Stress Disorder—a contribution that will serve the entire nation in the aftermath of September 11.

We will now turn our expertise to ALS. We will work with others to pursue a cause, a treatment, and a cure. I am confident that we will make a contribution to this field as we have in so many others—not only veterans but all people—who contract this disease.

And third, we will insure that every veteran with ALS who seeks it will receive the best possible care at VA health care facilities throughout the nation. We will see to it that our patients receive the benefit of any new treatment developed by medical researchers anywhere in the world.

Once again, I thank the Department of Defense for their cooperation in the completion of this study, and for providing the bulk of the funding for the study. I would also like to thank the other federal agencies and researchers who participated.

And I also commend the dedicated and talented VA staff who worked so expeditiously, to complete the study in order to benefit veterans and their families. Their work was in keeping with the great traditions of VA research. . . .

PRESIDENT'S COMMISSION ON SOCIAL SECURITY REFORM
December 11, 2001

A presidential commission directed by President George W. Bush to propose an overhaul of Social Security that would incorporate personal investment accounts offered instead three alternatives. Enactment of any one of the options for allowing workers to invest part of their payroll taxes in stocks and bonds would represent the most profound change ever made in the public retirement system. But each of the options would require some politically unpalatable combination of benefit cuts, tax hikes, or infusion of general tax revenue to make the system fiscally sustainable. The fact that the commission was unable to reach a consensus on any one of the three options only underscored the economic complexity and political sensitivity of revamping what was arguably the most popular federal program on the books.

The commission's final report, released December 11, 2001, was somewhat anticlimactic. Only three weeks earlier the country had been officially declared to be in a mild recession. American troops were fighting terrorist forces in Afghanistan, and Bush was warning that the war on terrorism might have to be expanded to other countries. The recession, the war, and the massive Bush tax cut enacted in June pushed the federal budget, which had been in surplus since 1998, back into deficit, where it was expected to stay for at least three years. Still mindful of the beating Republicans had taken at the polls in 1982 and 1986 when they sought to shore up the ailing Social Security trust fund by cutting benefits, GOP leaders had already let it be known that they would not take up Social Security reform in the months before the crucial 2002 congressional elections. President Bush, who had announced the creation of the commission in May with great fanfare, made no public comment on its final report. Even the commission said policymakers should spend at least a year discussing the options before taking any legislative action. (Bush tax cut, p. 400; Terrorist attacks, p. 614; Economy after September 11, p. 663)

Pushing for Privatization

Social Security was enacted in 1935 to help the elderly and disabled whose pensions and savings had been wiped out by the Great Depression and to provide a minimum income for future retirees. Benefits were financed through a payroll tax, with the taxes that current workers and their employers paid into the fund used to pay current benefits. (In 2001 workers and their employers each paid 6.2 percent of the first $80,400 of the workers' wages.) Since 1935, as life expectancy increased and the birth rate declined, the ratio of workers to retirees had been shrinking and was expected to be about two to one by about 2020 when the last of the baby boom generation would be retiring. Policymakers had known for decades that such a small ratio of workers to retirees could not sustain the system unless benefits were reduced or taxes raised, but those choices were so politically unpopular that Congress and presidents had done little more than tinker with the system at the edges.

In recent years Republicans and a few Democrats began to coalesce behind a broad proposal to privatize a portion of the Social Security system, allowing or requiring individuals to invest a portion of their payroll taxes in the private market. They argued that people might realize greater benefits under this arrangement than they would with the current system. Most Democrats, labor unions, civil rights organizations, and groups representing the elderly opposed privatization, arguing that investing in the stock market was too risky, especially for low-income workers; that the system would be difficult to regulate; and that it would erode the social insurance functions of the current system, which favored low-wage earners, survivors, and the disabled.

With the advent of a budget surplus in 1998, Democratic president Bill Clinton held a White House conference on Social Security reform in an effort to begin to forge a bipartisan consensus to solve the system's long-term funding problems. Attendees of both parties said the initial talks were productive. But with Clinton diverted by his impeachment trial and the Republican majority in Congress more interested in pushing through a tax cut, nothing further happened during the remainder of Clinton's term. (Social Security solvency, Historic Documents of 1998, p. 98)

Following Up on a Campaign Promise

During his campaign for the presidency in 2000, George W. Bush promised to "fix" Social Security by giving younger workers the option to open personal investment accounts, which he said would allow them to maximize their retirement benefits and keep the system from running out of money. But he offered few details about how such a system might work. Bush reiterated his promise in his first address to Congress February 27 and said he soon would name a commission to work out the details of a plan. At a formal ceremony in the White House Rose Garden on May 2, Bush introduced the commission, composed of eight Republicans and eight Democrats, all of whom supported private Social Security accounts. Co-chairs of the com-

mission were former Democratic senator Daniel Patrick Moynihan of New York and Richard D. Parsons, a Republican and co-chief operating officer of AOL Time Warner who later in the year was named chief executive of the communications giant. The other members were economists, business people, politicians, and academicians.

Bush asked the commission to bring him a recommendation for reform that met certain conditions. Among the caveats were that the plan had to include voluntary individual personal accounts; benefits for retirees or for people nearing retirement could not be cut; payroll taxes could not be increased; and the reform had to preserve Social Security's disability and survivors' benefits programs. The administration said Bush had named like-minded individuals to the commission because he did not want the panel to end up in gridlock over competing plans. Bush "wants a commission that results in action," White House spokesman Ari Fleischer said.

Democrats portrayed the selection of the commission as an attempt to foreclose any other options to shoring up the long-run solvency of Social Security, and they vowed to fight any recommendation that privatized the system. "We are not going to stand by and let Social Security be ruined," House Minority Leader Richard A. Gephardt, D-Mo., said after the commission was announced. Democrats and their allies, including the AFL-CIO, advocacy groups for the elderly, and others, had already organized to drum up opposition to private accounts, while business groups and others had rallied their forces to campaign for the changes.

An interim report detailing the weaknesses of the current system provoked even more outrage when it was released July 24. In that report the commission said the existing system, if left unchanged, was "fiscally unsustainable." It said that by 2016, when the last of the baby boom generation was beginning to retire, benefits paid out would begin to exceed payroll taxes taken in. The system would then have to make up the shortfall, first by using interest paid on the Treasury bonds that compose the trust fund, and then by redeeming the bonds themselves. By 2038, under current projections, all the bonds would have been redeemed, and the system would be totally reliant on payroll taxes for revenue, which would cover only about 72 cents for every dollar of benefit owed. The interim report also said the current system was unfair to African American and Hispanic workers, who tended to receive less in total benefits because their life expectancies were shorter than white workers, and to women, whose connection to the labor force was not as strong as men's and who tended to live longer. "Unless we move boldly and quickly," Moynihan and Parsons wrote in a preface to the report, "the promise of Social Security to retirees cannot be met without eventual resort to benefit cuts, tax increases or massive borrowing. The time to act is now."

Opponents immediately assailed the report as alarmist. Its "only purpose," said Representative Robert T. Matsui, D-Calif., "is to frighten the American public and to have the public think the system is about to fall *apart. It's intended to make younger people think they're not going to get their benefits, so they should keep their money and invest it in a private account." John Rother, legislative direction of AARP, an advocacy group for older Americans and one of the most potent lobby organizations in Washington, said the report would further polarize the debate, making it even more difficult to find a consensus for fixing Social Security.*

Unions argued that the privatization push was simply a way for Republicans to throw more business toward investment firms, which stood to make billions of dollars from fees and commissions on individual personal investment accounts. At least one union official said he would urge union members and trustees of union pension funds to boycott any investment firm that actively supported the push for private accounts.

A Menu of Options

By the time the commission released its final report in December, the president and his supporters were already backing away from further action on the issue until at least after the 2002 elections. With the panel acknowledging that virtually any solution including personal accounts would also require benefit cuts, tax hikes, or both, it appeared highly unlikely that Bush would tackle the issue unless the Republicans added substantially to their numbers in the House and Senate.

Meanwhile, policymakers and the public could, as the panel recommended, ponder the three options it proposed:

- *Under the first option, workers would be allowed to invest 2 percent of their taxable wages in personal accounts. Social Security benefits for those workers would be offset by the workers' personal contributions compounded at an interest rate of 3.5 percent above inflation. The panel did not recommend any other changes, so this option did not address the long-term financing problems. The estimated cost was $3.4 trillion over the next seventy-five years to make up for the expected shortfall in the trust fund and $1 trillion in startup costs for the personal accounts.*

- *Under the second option, workers would be allowed to redirect 4 percentage points of their payroll taxes, up to $1,000 annually, in personal accounts. Traditional Social Security benefits would then be offset by the amount of the contribution compounded at an interest rate of 2 percent above inflation. The panel said workers who chose this option "can reasonably expect combined benefits greater than those paid to current retirees; greater than those paid to workers without accounts; and greater than the future benefits payable under the current system should it not be reformed." In addition, traditional Social Security benefits would be reduced by indexing them to inflation, rather than growth in personal wages, which was usually higher and which was how benefits were currently indexed. This option would also establish a guaranteed benefit of at least 120 percent of the federal poverty level for certain low-income workers and survivors. The estimated coast of* *this option was $2 trillion to cover startup costs and any trust fund shortfalls.*

- *The third option would allow workers to shift 2.5 percentage points of their payroll taxes, up to $1,000 a year, to personal accounts if they also contributed an additional 1 percent of their annual earnings to the accounts. Traditional benefits would be offset by the personal account contributions compounded at an interest rate of 2.5 percent above inflation. The option would also slow future traditional benefit increases by adjusting them for life expectancy and would give people who worked longer higher retirement benefits. Survivors and low-income workers would be guaranteed income of at least 100 percent of the poverty line. The changes would require new taxes equal to 0.6 percent of payroll over the entire seventy-five year period and thereafter. The estimated cost of this option was put at $2.25 trillion.*

In their foreword, Moynihan and Parsons offered the outlines of a fourth option, under which workers would contribute an additional 1 percent of their pay into a personal account. That amount would be matched by the government, at an estimated cost of $40 billion a year. The Clinton administration had once offered a similar proposal.

Following are texts of the introduction to and executive summary of "Strengthening Social Security and Creating Personal Wealth for All Americans," the final report of the President's Commission on Strengthening Social Security, issued December 11, 2001. The introduction was signed by the panel's co-chairs, former Democratic senator Daniel Patrick Moynihan of New York and Richard D. Parsons, co-chief operating officer of AOL Time Warner.

The document was obtained from the Internet at http://www .commtostrengthensocsec.gov/reports/Final_report.pdf.

Introduction by the Co-Chairs

From the first, Social Security was a work in progress. It remains so now. In 1939, just four years after enactment, the Administration and Congress added major provisions. FDR called for more. As he signed the 1939 Amendments he stated: "we must expect a great program of social legislation, as such as is represented in the Social Security Act, to be improved and strengthened in the light of additional experience and understanding." He urged an "active study" of future possibilities.

One such possibility—personal retirement accounts that would endow workers with a measure of wealth—has emerged as the central issue in the ongoing national debate over social insurance.

There are a number of reasons for this. The first is the most obvious, if perhaps the least commented upon: Social Security retirement benefits are no longer the bargain they once were. There is nothing sinister about this. Early retirees benefited from the fixed formula of retirement benefits. For years the Social Security Administration would distribute photographs of Ida May Fuller of Ludlow, Vermont, who having paid $24.75 in Social Security taxes lived to age 100 and collected $22,889 in benefits.

In Miss Fuller's time there were almost 42 covered workers for each Social Security beneficiary. We are now down to 3.4 workers per beneficiary. As a result, Social Security as a retirement measure has become a poor investment. It is, even so, an essential *insurance* program. Widows and dependent children are very reliant on dependent benefits. For widows, widowers, singles and children, the monthly check can be a steady, stabilizing factor in life. That said, however, Social Security' actuaries estimate that, for a single male worker born in 2000 with average earnings, the real annual return on his currently-scheduled contributions to Social Security will be only 0.86 percent. This is not what sends savers to savings banks. For workers who earn the maximum amount taxed (currently $80,400, indexed to wages) the real annual return is *minus* 0.72 percent.

This should come as no surprise. Demography is a kind of destiny. The founders of Social Security always assumed it would be supplemented by individual forms of savings. (In his original Message to Congress, President Roosevelt envisioned pensioners owning annuities.) In the first instance, savings took the form of housing; government subsidies were created in the 1930s, followed by the enormous influence of Veterans Administration mortgages following World War II. By 2000, two-thirds—67.4 percent—of Americans owned their homes.

The Crash of '29 left an indelible mark on the generation that lived through it—and for that matter, the one that followed, such that direct investment in markets was slow in returning. But eventually it did.

Partly as a consequence of 1929, we have learned a great deal about how a modern economy works. During the Depression, the Federal government did not even calculate the unemployment rate; it was taken every ten years in the Census. Today, our economic statistics are extraordinary in range and accuracy, and since enactment of the Employment Act of 1946 economic policies have, on balance, been successful. The great swings in economic activity have been radically mitigated. In November 2001, the Dating Committee of the National Bureau of Economic Research gave out its judgment that the period of economic expansion that began in March 1991 ended in March 2001. Such a ten-year period of uninterrupted growth is something never before recorded. There will continue to be ups and downs, and all manner of risks, but in the main the modern market economy appears to have settled down to impressive long-term growth.

The post-World War II growth period was reflected, naturally enough, in the stock market. More important, a new form of investment, the mutual fund, was developed which enabled small savers to "pool" their investments over a range of stocks and bonds. As reported by the Investment Company Institute, "As of May, 2001, 93.3 million individuals, representing 52 percent of all U. S. households owned mutual funds." Further, "Nearly half of mutual fund shareholders have household financial assets below $100,000; 29 percent have less than $50,000."

The surge in mutual fund ownership began in the early 1980s. One of the more notable innovations was the development of a similar fund, the Thrift Savings Plan, as part of the retirement arrangements for Federal employees. The legislation was enacted quietly by Congress and signed by President Reagan in 1986. In terms of the markets, the timing could not have been better. The results have been stunning, as the Commission learned from testimony by the Director of the Federal Retirement Thrift Investment Board, Roger Mehle. Three funds were available, in whatever combination the employee chose. A "G" Fund is invested in short-term non-marketable U. S. Treasury securities specially issued to the TSP. An "F" Fund is invested in a commercial bond index; and a "C" Fund is invested in an equity index fund. The compound rates of return for the closing decade of the last century were as follows:

G Fund	6.7 percent
F Fund	7.9 percent
C Fund	17.4 percent

Actual trading is contracted out and administrative expenses are minimal: 50 cents for every $1,000 of G Fund account balance, 70 cents for the F Fund, and 60 cents for the C Fund. (Additional funds are now being developed and offered.) As of September 2001, 86.6 percent of all Federal employees participated in the program. It is a singular success.

Martha Derthick's classic study *Policy Making for Social Security* begins with a quotation from Arthur Altmeyer, who was chief executive of the program from 1937 to 1953:

> Social Security will always be a goal, never a finished thing because human aspirations are infinitely expandable . . . just as human nature is infinitely perfectible. (p. 17)

This would not quite have been the view of the Founders, who thought human nature to be anything but "infinitely perfectible." Hence checks and balances were needed to make up for the "defect of better motives." And indeed some things, notably demography, proved anything but perfectible. The Social Security tax (F. I. C. A. for Federal Insurance Contribution Act) began at two percent and has been raised more than twenty times, reaching the present 12.4 percent. This is a regressive tax that is paid on the first dollar of income by rich and poor alike. In fact, as of 1997, 79 percent of American households paid more in payroll taxes than in income taxes.

One egregious failing of the present system is its effect on minorities with shorter life spans than the white majority. For black men age 20, only some 65 percent can be expected to survive to age 65. Thus, one of every three black youths will pay for retirement benefits they will never collect. No one intends this; and with time the gap may close. But it is not closed now. And because Social Security provides no property rights to its contributors—the Supreme Court has twice so ruled—a worker could easily work forty years then die and own not a penny of the contributions he has made for retirement benefits he will never collect. There are, to be sure, survivors and dependents benefits, but many workers die before eligibility for these is established. Disability insurance was added during the Eisenhower Administration so that workers are covered during their working years. But far too many never receive any retirement benefits and leave no estate.

Similarly, the present Social Security provision can prove unjust to women, especially divorced women who too often share nothing of the benefits acquired by a previous spouse. It is time we addressed this matter. There are a number of legitimate approaches that simply need to be worked out, with the plain objective of equal treatment.

As the early administrators of Social Security anticipated—and very much hoped for—the program steadily evolved. Health insurance (Medicare) was enacted in the 1960s. By the 1990s, the time had come for Personal Retirement Accounts. (As with much else in social insurance, other nations had preceded us.) In the mode of earlier innovations, the subject was first broached in academic circles, notably by economists such as Harvard's Martin Feldstein. In the fall of 1997, the Clinton Administration began to analyze proposals to create a system of individual retirement accounts, either as part of Social Security or outside of it. By early 1998, working groups were formed within Treasury and other departments to study issues related to such proposals.

A primary issue was how a feasible system of accounts could be administered and what would be the associated costs. In the spring of 1999 the Treasury had contracted a study by the State Street Bank entitled, "Administrative Challenges Confronting Social Security Reform." The sum of it was that the task was feasible—the Thrift Savings Accounts were already in place—and the cost modest. Accenture (formerly known as Andersen Consulting) produced similar findings. In 1998 and 1999 a range of similar measures were introduced in Congress. None were enacted, but there was now a striking new item on the national agenda.

In the course of the Republican presidential primary campaign of 2000, then Governor George W. Bush gave a major address on Social Security, proclaiming it "the single most successful government program in American history . . . a defining American promise." He went on to discuss Personal Retirement Accounts that would, in the words of a Democratic Senator, "take the system to its 'logical completion.' " Then-Governor Bush envisioned a program that would "give people the security of ownership," the opportunity "to build wealth, which they will use for their own retirement and pass on to their children." He cited a range of legislators, Republican and Democrat, who shared this general view, including Senator Bob Kerrey, who had recently stated: "It's very important, especially for those of us who have already accumulated wealth, to write laws to enable other people to accumulate it." Governor Bush then added:

Ownership in our society should not be an exclusive club. Independence should not be a gated community. Everyone should be a part owner in the American dream.

In his address, then-Governor Bush insisted that "personal accounts are not a substitute for Social Security," but a supplement, a logical completion. He proposed several measures necessary to ensure the long-term fiscal viability of Social Security itself. Among them was the following:

Reform should include personal retirement accounts for young people—an element of all the major bipartisan plans. The idea works very simply. A young worker can take some portion of his or her payroll tax and put it in a fund that invests in stocks and bonds. We will establish basic standards of safety and soundness, so that investments are only in steady, reliable funds. There will be no fly-by-night speculators or day trading. And money in this account could only be used for retirement, or passed along as an inheritance.

Personal retirement accounts within Social Security could be designed and financed in a number of ways, some of which are analyzed by the Commission in detail in the pages that follow. To illustrate the power of personal accounts, however, let us offer the following example. This approach would establish an opportunity for all people with earnings to set up a personal retirement account, on a voluntary basis. These accounts could be financed by the individual worker voluntarily adding one percent of his pay on top of the present 6.2 percent employee share of the Social Security payroll tax. The Federal government could match the employee's contribution with a matching one percent of salary, drawn from general revenues. The result would be retirement savings accounts for all participating American workers and their families, which might or might not interact directly with the Social Security system, depending on design choices that are discussed further in Chapter 4. The cost to the Federal government would be approximately $40 billion per year, depending on rates of participation. The magic of compound interest now commences to work its wonders.

To illustrate what a participant might anticipate from setting aside one percent of his or her pay, matched with the government's one percent, we can forecast the situation of a "scaled medium earner" entering the workforce at age 21 and retiring at age 65 in the year 2052. Assume a portfolio choice—there should be choices—roughly that of the current Thrift Savings Plan: 50 percent corporate equity, 30 percent corporate bonds, and 20 percent U. S. Treasury bonds. Real yields are assumed to be 6.5 percent for equities, 3.5 percent for corporate bonds, and 3 percent for Treasury bonds. Also assume that this worker pays 0.3 percent of his account assets for annual administrative costs. At retirement, she or he will have an expected portfolio worth $523,000 ($101,000 in constant 2001 dollars). A two-earner family could easily have an expected net "cash" worth of $1 million.

As the Commission's interim report has shown, Social Security is in need of an overhaul. The system is not sustainable as currently structured. The final report demonstrates that there are several different approaches that national policymakers could take to address the problem, and we hope the pages that follow will provide sufficient analysis and suggestion to prompt a reasoned debate concerning how best to strengthen Social Security.

In the accompanying report, the Commission recommends that there be a period of discussion, lasting for at least one year, before legislative action is taken to strengthen and restore sustainability to Social Security. Regardless of how policymakers come to terms with the underlying sustainability issues, however, one thing is clear to us: the time to include personal accounts in such action has, indeed, arrived. The details of such accounts are negotiable, but their need is clear. The time for our elected officials to begin that discussion, informed by the findings in this report, is now.

Carpe diem!

Daniel Patrick Moynihan and Richard D. Parsons
Co-Chairmen, President's Commission to Strengthen Social Security

Executive Summary

Findings:

Social Security will be strengthened if modernized to include a system of voluntary personal accounts. Personal accounts improve retirement security by facilitating wealth creation and providing participants with assets that they own and that can be inherited, rather than providing only claims to benefits that remain subject to political negotiation. By allowing investment choice, individuals would be free to pursue higher expected rates of return on their Social Security contributions. Furthermore, strengthening Social Security through personal accounts can add valuable protections for widows, divorced persons, low-income households and other Americans at risk of poverty in old age.

Partial advance funding of Social Security should be a goal of any effort to strengthen the system. Advance funding within Social Security can best be accomplished through personal accounts rather than direct government investment. Personal accounts offer numerous economic benefits, including a likely increase in national saving, as well as an improvement in incentives for labor force participation.

Personal accounts can be administered in an efficient and cost effective manner. This report outlines specific measures that would effectively balance the desire for low administrative costs along with consumer choice and efficient financial markets. Accounts should be structured so as to allow inheritability and to strengthen the protection of spouses.

Personal accounts can also contribute towards the fiscal sustainability of the Social Security system. While there are multiple paths to fiscal sustainability that are consistent with the President's principles for Social Security reform, we have chosen to include three reform models in the report that improve the fiscal sustainability of the current system, are costed honestly, and are preferable to the current Social Security system.

Under the current system, benefits to future retirees are scheduled to grow significantly above the level received by today's retirees, even after adjusting for inflation. The cost of paying these benefits will substantially exceed the amount of payroll taxes collected. To bring the Social Security system to a path of fiscal sustainability—an essential task for any reform plan—there are differing approaches. The Commission believes that no matter which approach is taken, personal accounts can increase expected benefits to future participants in the Social Security system.

Each of the three reform plans abides by the President's Principles for reform.

President's Principles

The President directed the Commission to propose Social Security reform plans that will strengthen Social Security and increase its fiscally sustainability, while meeting several principles:

- Modernization must not change Social Security benefits for retirees or near-retirees.
- The entire Social Security surplus must be dedicated to Social Security only.
- Social Security payroll taxes must not be increased.
- Government must not invest Social Security funds in the stock market.
- Modernization must preserve Social Security's disability and survivors components.
- Modernization must include individually controlled, voluntary personal retirement accounts, which will augment the Social Security safety net.

Unifying Elements of the Three Reform Plans

- The Commission has developed three alternative models for Social Security reform that feature personal accounts as a central component. Under all three reform plans, future retirees can expect to receive benefits that are at least as high as those received by today's retirees, even after adjusting for inflation.
- All three models include a voluntary personal retirement account that would permit participants to build substantial wealth and receive higher expected benefits than those paid to today's retirees. Thus, all of the plans would enhance workers' control over their retirement benefits with accounts that they own and can use to produce retirement income, or pass on to others in the form of an inheritance.
- Because the Commissioner believes that the benefits currently paid to low-wage workers are too low, it has included a provision in two of the three plans that would enhance the existing Social Security system's progressivity by *significantly increasing benefits for low-income workers above what the system currently pays*. This provision will raise even more of our low-income elderly—most of whom are women—out of poverty. Two of the three models also boost survivor benefits for below-average income widows and widowers.

- The Commission set a goal of moving the Social Security system toward a fiscally sustainable course that reduces pressure on the remainder of the federal budget and can respond to economic and demographic changes in the future. The three reform models outlined here are therefore transparently scored in terms of plan provisions, effects on workers' expected costs and benefits, and effects on Trust Fund operations as well as the unified federal budget. We also identify clearly how large the personal account assets may be expected to grow as the system evolves.
- All three reform models improve the fiscal sustainability of the program, though some move farther than others. Model 1 would require additional revenues in perpetuity in order to pay scheduled Social Security benefits under the plan. Model 3 prescribes an amount of additional revenues needed to pay scheduled benefits under the plan, an amount smaller than that required under Model 1. Model 2 does not require permanent additional funding.
- All three models also require transitional investments to move to a system that includes Personal Accounts. These transitional investments advance fund future benefits, thus substantially reducing the cost on future generations.
- All three models reduce the long-term need for general revenues as compared to the current, unsustainable, system. In two of the three plans (Models 2 and 3), the system's cash flow needs are met so that the benefits promised by each plan can be paid as retirees need them.
- All three of the models are expected to increase national saving, though some would do so more than others.
- The Commission concludes that building substantial wealth in personal accounts can be and should be a viable component of strengthening Social Security. We commend our three models to the President, the Members of Congress and to the American public in order to enrich national understanding of the opportunities for moving forward.

Three Reform Models

The three models for Social Security reform devised by the Commission demonstrate how alternative formulations for personal accounts can contribute to a strengthened Social Security system.

Reform Model 1 establishes a voluntary personal account option but does not specify other changes in Social Security's benefit and revenue structure to achieve full long-term sustainability.

- Workers can voluntarily invest 2 percent of their taxable wages in a personal account.
- In exchange, traditional Social Security benefits are offset by the worker's personal account contributions compounded at an interest rate of 3.5 percent above inflation.
- No other changes are made to traditional Social Security.
- Expected benefits to retirees rise while the annual cash deficit of Social Security falls by the end of the valuation period.

- Workers, retirees, and taxpayers continue to face uncertainty because a large financing gap remains requiring future benefit changes or substantial new revenues.
- Additional revenues are needed to keep the trust fund solvent starting in the 2030s.

Reform Model 2 enables future retirees to receive Social Security benefits that are at least as great as today's retirees, even after adjusting for inflation, and increases Social Security benefits paid to low-income workers. Model 2 establishes a voluntary personal account without raising taxes or requiring additional worker contributions. It achieves solvency and balances Social Security revenues and costs.

- Workers can voluntarily redirect 4 percent of their payroll taxes up to $1000 annually to a personal account (the maximum contribution is indexed annually to wage growth). No additional contribution from the worker would be required.
- In exchange for the account, traditional Social Security benefits are offset by the worker's personal account contributions compounded at an interest rate of 2 percent above inflation.
- Workers opting for personal accounts can reasonably expect combined benefits greater than those paid to current retirees; greater than those paid to workers without accounts; and greater than the future benefits payable under the current system should it not be reformed.
- The plan makes Social Security more progressive by establishing a minimum benefit payable to 30-year minimum wage workers of 120 percent of the poverty line. Additional protections against poverty are provided for survivors as well.
- Benefits under the traditional component of Social Security would be price indexed, beginning in 2009.
- Expected benefits payable to a medium earner choosing a personal account and retiring in 2052 would be 59 percent above benefits currently paid to today's retirees. At the end of the 75-year valuation period, the personal account system would hold $12.3 trillion (in today's dollars; $1.3 trillion in present value), much of which would be new saving. This accomplishment would need neither increased taxes nor increased worker contributions over the long term.
- Temporary transfers from general revenue would be needed to keep the Trust Fund solvent between 2025 and 2054.
- This model achieves a positive system cash flow at the end of the 75-year valuation period under all participation rates.

Reform Model 3 establishes a voluntary personal account option that generally enables workers to reach or exceed current-law scheduled benefits and wage replacement ratios. It achieves solvency by adding revenues and by slowing benefit growth less than price indexing.

- Personal accounts are created by a match of part of the payroll tax — 2.5 percent up to $1000 annually (indexed annually for wage growth) —

925

for any worker who contributes an additional 1 percent of wages subject to Social Security payroll taxes.

- The add-on contribution is partially subsidized for workers in a progressive manner by a refundable tax credit.
- In exchange, traditional Social Security benefits are offset by the worker's personal account contributions compounded at an interest rate of 2.5 percent above inflation.
- The plan makes the traditional Social Security system more progressive by establishing a minimum benefit payable to 30-year minimum wage workers of 100 percent of the poverty line (111 percent for a 40-year worker). This minimum benefit would be indexed to wage growth. Additional protections against poverty are provided for survivors as well.
- Benefits under the traditional component of Social Security would be modified by:
  - ▸ adjusting the growth rate in benefits for actual future changes in life expectancy,
  - ▸ increasing work incentives by decreasing the benefits for early retirement and increasing the benefits for late retirement, and
  - ▸ flattening out the benefit formula (reducing the third bend point factor from 15 to 10 percent).
- Benefits payable to workers who opt for personal accounts would be expected to exceed scheduled benefit levels and current replacement rates.
- Benefits payable to workers who do not opt for personal accounts would be over 50 percent higher than those currently paid to today's retirees.
- New sources of dedicated revenue are added in the equivalent amount of 0.6 percent of payroll over the 75-year period, and continuing thereafter.
- Additional temporary transfers from general revenues would be needed to keep the Trust Fund solvent between 2034 and 2063.

U.S., RUSSIAN REMARKS ON U.S. WITHDRAWAL FROM ABM TREATY
December 13, 14, and 17, 2001

President George W. Bush announced on December 13, 2001, that the United States intended to withdraw from the Anti-Ballistic Missile (ABM) treaty, effective early in 2002. Signed in 1972 by the United States and the Soviet Union, the treaty barred either cold war superpower from building a national system to protect itself against attack by ballistic missiles. The treaty set the stage for later strategic weapons agreements between Moscow and Washington and had long been considered the cornerstone of international arms control.

Bush said the treaty was an outdated relic of the cold war that hindered his plans to build a missile defense system to protect the United States against new threats from North Korea and other countries that were attempting to build long-range ballistic missiles. On May 1 Bush had announced his intention to build such a system. The president's decision disappointed Vladimir Putin, president of Russia, which had inherited the Soviet Union's strategic weapons arsenal and its arms control responsibilities. Ever since Bush's May 1 announcement, Putin had tried, in vain, to convince the United States to amend, rather than withdraw from, the ABM treaty.

Earlier in the year, when U.S.-Russian relations were at their frostiest level in many years, Bush's withdrawal from the ABM treaty might have precipitated a major diplomatic confrontation with Russia and with many of Washington's European allies, most of whom wanted to keep the treaty intact. But Bush and Putin had established an increasingly warm personal relationship since their meeting in June. Moreover, the September 11 terrorist attacks against the United States enabled Bush to forge a new solidarity with Russia and the U.S. allies. Less than a week before Bush made his announcement, NATO and Russian foreign ministers declared a "new relationship." (Missile defense, p. 281; Terrorist attacks, p. 614; NATO and Russia, p. 892)

The ABM Treaty

The negotiation and signing of the ABM treaty was a landmark event in the phase of the cold war known as détente: a temporary lessening of cold war hostilities in the early 1970s. The treaty was negotiated by President Richard M. Nixon and Soviet leader Leonid Brezhnev. It was an attempt by the two nuclear superpowers to guarantee that nuclear weapons would never be used. The treaty was based on the premise that each country would be less likely to attack the other with nuclear missiles and bombs if it was itself open to a full-scale nuclear retaliation—and therefore vulnerable to total destruction. Building a defense against ballistic missiles would reduce that vulnerability, according to this theory, and thus make using nuclear weapons seem less dangerous. The ABM treaty allowed each country to have one small regional missile defense system. The Soviet Union used this provision to build a system protecting Moscow, and the United States built a system (called "Safeguard") to protect its missile installations in North Dakota but abandoned it after a few months of operation in the mid-1970s.

The ABM treaty set the stage for later negotiations between the United States and the Soviet Union on other agreements intended to curb their race to build nuclear weapons. Negotiations during the 1970s were aimed at producing a Strategic Arms Limitation Treaty (SALT) to reduce the rate of the weapons buildup. Negotiations beginning in the late 1980s and running through the 1990s produced two Strategic Arms Reduction Treaties (START I and START II) that called on both countries to reduce their nuclear weapons arsenals. While not directly related to the ABM treaty, all these negotiations were based on that treaty's underlying logic of the need for nuclear stability. (START I treaty, Historic Documents of 1991, p. 475; START II treaty, Historic Documents of 1993, p. 17)

Missile Defense Proposals

The first serious challenge to the premise of the ABM treaty came in the 1980s, when President Ronald Reagan proposed an elaborate missile defense system that he called the "Strategic Defense Initiative" and that his critics derided as "Star Wars," after the space-age movies. Reagan's dream of a shield protecting all the United States against missiles proved to be extraordinarily expensive and unworkable, and it was abandoned by his successor, George Bush. Bush proposed his own more limited missile defense system but that, too, was abandoned by his successor, Bill Clinton.

Clinton at first avoided the missile defense issue, but under pressure from Congress approved plans to develop a limited system, based in Alaska, that would protect the United States against a small-scale missile attack by a newly emerging power such as North Korea. Clinton administration lawyers determined that the United States would violate the ABM treaty once it began actual construction in Alaska. Russia rejected numerous attempts by the administration to negotiate a revision of the treaty to enable that construction. Meanwhile, the Pentagon encountered numerous technical difficulties during testing of the system, and Clinton announced in Septem-

ber 2000 that he would leave a decision on missile defense to his successor. (Clinton announcement, Historic Documents of 2000, p. 677)

Clinton's successor was George W. Bush, who had made building a missile defense one of the most important planks of his campaign platform. Within days of taking office, Bush's aides began talking about the need to scrap the ABM treaty so the new president could build the missile defense system he wanted. Bush formally announced on May 1 that he was determined to proceed with such a system, but he offered few details about it. Bush also made it clear that he would not allow the ABM treaty to stand in the way of his plans; he said it "enshrines the past."

Bush's announcement was not welcomed in much of the world. Russian president Putin said he believed the ABM remained a necessary arms control "cornerstone" and threatened to build a new generation of multiple-warhead missiles if it was scrapped. China took a similar stand, arguing that the U.S. moves could set off another arms race. Most U.S. allies in Europe expressed dismay, as well, and suggested that Bush should consider carefully any actions that might upset nuclear weapons stability.

Negotiating with Russia

As the inheritor of the Soviet Union's signature on the ABM treaty—as well as the remnants of the Soviet nuclear arsenal—Russia was the party most affected by Bush's declaration that the treaty was out of date. Over the next several months, U.S. and Russian officials, including Bush and Putin themselves, engaged in extended private negotiations and public statements on the matter, but at no point was there any serious indication that Bush would consider backing down.

In early July senior Pentagon officials told Congress that U.S. work on a missile defense system would soon "bump up against" the limitations imposed by the treaty, and so the treaty either would have to be amended or scrapped. Administration diplomats reportedly suggested to their Russian counterparts modifications of the treaty that would have permitted work on the missile defense system to continue while the two countries negotiated more permanent arrangement. Russian diplomats, in turn, reportedly demanded a say in determining what kinds of U.S. missile defense tests would be allowed and what kinds would not. Neither side, according to news reports, was willing to go much beyond these basic positions.

The ABM treaty was a prime topic at meetings between Bush and Putin in June, July, October, and November. The latter two meetings came after the September 11 terrorist attacks, a period when the United States and Russia were moving rapidly toward a more cooperative relationship than at any time in the past. In October diplomats talked about the possibility of crafting an overall agreement that linked a revision of the ABM treaty with at least an informal decision by the two countries to reduce their nuclear arsenals well below the limits required by the pending START II treaty. Speculation that such an agreement could be reached at a mid-November summit meeting at Bush's Texas ranch proved unrealistic, however. Bush announced unilateral plans to cut the U.S. arsenal, and Putin said Russia planned deeper arms cuts as well, but the two sides failed to agree on a grand plan to revise the ABM treaty and cut strategic weapons. News reports later indicated that Bush had told Putin he planned to withdraw from the ABM treaty in any event; that stance offered Putin no bargaining room.

Bush Announces ABM Withdrawal

The diplomatic maneuvering over the ABM treaty came to an end on December 13, when Bush made a brief appearance in the Rose Garden of the White House to announce that he was invoking a provision allowing the United States to withdraw from the treaty with a six-month notice to Russia. "I have concluded that the ABM treaty hinders our government's ability to protect our people from future terrorist or rogue-state missile attacks," he said. The treaty had been signed "at a much different time, in a vastly different world," Bush added. After the September 11 attacks, it was clear that the greatest threats to the United States and Russia came not from each other "but from terrorists who strike without warning, or rogue states who seek weapons of mass destruction." The president insisted that some terrorist groups, which he did not identify, were trying to obtain ballistic missiles. His remark about "rogue states" was a clear reference to North Korea, which according to the CIA was capable of producing one or two nuclear bombs and was developing long-range missiles to deliver them.

In a televised address from his Kremlin office, Putin described Bush's decision as "mistaken," but he indicated that the recent improvement in U.S.-Russian relations was more important than continuing to argue about the ABM treaty. Putin said the U.S. step made it even more urgent than in the past that the two countries work out a new "strategic relationship." Putin's mild reaction was echoed by the Chinese government, which criticized the Bush decision but did not repeat past threats about responding with a new buildup of nuclear weapons.

> *Following are the texts of four statements made December 13, 2001: an announcement by President George W. Bush that the United States intended to withdraw from the 1972 Anti-Ballistic Missile treaty; the diplomatic note sent by the U.S. State Department to Russia, Belarus, Kazakhstan, and Ukraine, formally notifying those countries of the ABM withdrawal (the latter three countries had inherited portions of the Soviet nuclear weapons arsenal but had since disposed of those weapons); a statement by Russian president Vladimir Putin in response to Bush's announcement; and remarks by White House press secretary Ari Fleischer in response to Putin's statement.*

> ***The documents were obtained from the Internet at http://www.state.gov/r/pa/prs/ps/2001/index.cfm?docid=6859; http://www.whitehouse.gov/news/releases/2001/12/***

20011213-4.html; http://www.russianembassy.org; and http://www.whitehouse.gov/news/releases/2001/12/ 20011213-8.html.

BUSH NOTICE OF WITHDRAWAL

Good morning. I've just concluded a meeting of my National Security Council. We reviewed what I discussed with my friend, President Vladimir Putin, over the course of many meetings, many months. And that is the need for America to move beyond the 1972 Anti Ballistic Missile treaty.

Today, I have given formal notice to Russia, in accordance with the treaty, that the United States of America is withdrawing from this almost 30 year old treaty. I have concluded the ABM treaty hinders our government's ability to develop ways to protect our people from future terrorist or rogue state missile attacks.

The 1972 ABM treaty was signed by the United States and the Soviet Union at a much different time, in a vastly different world. One of the signatories, the Soviet Union, no longer exists. And neither does the hostility that once led both our countries to keep thousands of nuclear weapons on hair-trigger alert, pointed at each other. The grim theory was that neither side would launch a nuclear attack because it knew the other would respond, thereby destroying both.

Today, as the events of September the 11th made all too clear, the greatest threats to both our countries come not from each other, or other big powers in the world, but from terrorists who strike without warning, or rogue states who seek weapons of mass destruction.

We know that the terrorists, and some of those who support them, seek the ability to deliver death and destruction to our doorstep via missile. And we must have the freedom and the flexibility to develop effective defenses against those attacks. Defending the American people is my highest priority as Commander in Chief, and I cannot and will not allow the United States to remain in a treaty that prevents us from developing effective defenses.

At the same time, the United States and Russia have developed a new, much more hopeful and constructive relationship. We are moving to replace mutually assured destruction with mutual cooperation. Beginning in Ljubljana, and continuing in meetings in Genoa, Shanghai, Washington and Crawford [Texas—the site of Bush's ranch], President Putin and I developed common ground for a new strategic relationship. Russia is in the midst of a transition to free markets and democracy. We are committed to forging strong economic ties between Russia and the United States, and new bonds between Russia and our partners in NATO. NATO has made clear its desire to identify and pursue opportunities for joint action at 20.

I look forward to visiting Moscow, to continue our discussions, as we seek a formal way to express a new strategic relationship that will last long beyond our individual administrations, providing a foundation for peace for the years to come.

We're already working closely together as the world rallies in the war against terrorism. I appreciate so much President Putin's important advice and cooperation as we fight to dismantle the al Qaeda network in Afghanistan. I appreciate his commitment to reduce Russia's offensive nuclear weapons. I reiterate our pledge to reduce our own nuclear arsenal between 1,700 and 2,200 operationally deployed strategic nuclear weapons. President Putin and I have also agreed that my decision to withdraw from the treaty will not, in any way, undermine our new relationship or Russian security.

As President Putin said in Crawford, we are on the path to a fundamentally different relationship. The Cold War is long gone. Today we leave behind one of its last vestiges.

But this is not a day for looking back. This is a day for looking forward with hope, and anticipation of greater prosperity and peace for Russians, for Americans and for the entire world.

Thank you.

DIPLOMATIC NOTICE OF WITHDRAWAL

The following is the text of diplomatic notes sent to Russia, Belarus, Kazakhstan, and the Ukraine on December 13, 2001:

The Embassy of the United States of America has the honor to refer to the Treaty between the United States of America and the Union of Soviet Socialist Republics (USSR) on the Limitation of Anti-Ballistic Missile Systems signed at Moscow May 26, 1972.

Article XV, paragraph 2, gives each Party the right to withdraw from the Treaty if it decides that extraordinary events related to the subject matter of the treaty have jeopardized its supreme interests.

The United States recognizes that the Treaty was entered into with the USSR, which ceased to exist in 1991. Since then, we have entered into a new strategic relationship with Russia that is cooperative rather than adversarial, and are building strong relationships with most states of the former USSR.

Since the Treaty entered into force in 1972, a number of state and non-state entities have acquired or are actively seeking to acquire weapons of mass destruction. It is clear, and has recently been demonstrated, that some of these entities are prepared to employ these weapons against the United States. Moreover, a number of states are developing ballistic missiles, including long-range ballistic missiles, as a means of delivering weapons of mass destruction. These events pose a direct threat to the territory and security of the United States and jeopardize its supreme interests. As a result, the United States has concluded that it must develop, test, and deploy anti-ballistic missile systems for the defense of its national territory, of its forces outside the United States, and of its friends and allies.

Pursuant to Article XV, paragraph 2, the United States has decided that extraordinary events related to the subject matter of the Treaty have jeopardized its supreme interests. Therefore, in the exercise of the right to withdraw from the Treaty provided in Article XV, paragraph 2, the United States hereby gives notice of its withdrawal from the Treaty. In accordance with the terms of the Treaty, withdrawal will be effective six months from the date of this notice.

PUTIN STATEMENT ON U.S. WITHDRAWAL

The US Administration today announced that it will withdraw from the 1972 ABM Treaty in six months' time.

The Treaty does indeed allow each of the parties to withdraw from it under exceptional circumstances. The leadership of the United States has spoken about it repeatedly and this step has not come as a surprise to us. But we believe this decision to be mistaken.

As is known, Russia, like the United States and unlike other nuclear powers, has long possessed an effective system to overcome anti-missile defense. So, I can say with full confidence that the decision made by the President of the United States does not pose a threat to the national security of the Russian Federation.

At the same time our country elected not to accept the insistent proposals on the part of the US to jointly withdraw from the ABM Treaty and did everything it could to preserve the Treaty. I still think that this is a correct and valid position. Russia was guided above all by the aim of preserving and strengthening the international legal foundation in the field of disarmament and non-proliferation of mass destruction weapons.

The ABM Treaty is one of the supporting elements of the legal system in this field. That system was created through joint efforts during the past decades.

It is our conviction that the development of the situation in the present world dictates a certain logic of actions.

Now that the world has been confronted with new threats one cannot allow a legal vacuum to be formed in the sphere of strategic stability. One should not undermine the regimes of non-proliferation of mass destruction weapons.

I believe that the present level of bilateral relations between the Russian Federation and the US should not only be preserved but should be used for working out a new framework of strategic relations as soon as possible.

Along with the problem of anti-missile defense a particularly important task under these conditions is putting a legal seal on the achieved agreements on further radical, irreversible and verifiable cuts of strategic offensive weapons, in our opinion to the level of 1,500–2,200 nuclear warheads for each side.

In conclusion I would like to note that Russia will continue to adhere firmly to its course in world affairs aimed at strengthening strategic stability and international security.

RESPONSE TO RUSSIAN STATEMENT

The United States welcomes President Putin's statement. We agree with President Putin that the decision taken by the President of the United States presents no threat to the national security of the Russian Federation.

We have worked intensively with Russia to create a new strategic framework for our relationship based on mutual interests and cooperation across a broad range of political, economic, and security issues. Together, the United States and Russia have made substantial progress in our efforts and look forward to even greater progress in the future.

The United States in particular welcomes Russia's commitment to deep reductions in its level of offensive strategic nuclear forces. Combined with the reductions of U.S. strategic nuclear forces announced by President Bush in November, this action will result in the lowest level of strategic nuclear weapons deployed by our two countries in decades. We will work with Russia to formalize this arrangement on offensive forces, including appropriate verification and transparency measures.

Russia's announcement of nuclear reductions and its commitment to continue to conduct close consultations with the United States reflect our shared desire to continue the essential work of building a new relationship for a new century.

SURGEON GENERAL'S CALL
TO ACTION ON OBESITY
December 13, 2001

If current trends continued, obesity among adults and children would reach epidemic proportions in the United States and was poised to cause as much preventable disease and death as cigarette smoking. That was the conclusion of Surgeon General David Satcher, who set forth the first national plan of action to help Americans keep their weight at healthy levels.

According to the report, three-fifths of all American adults were overweight. Of those, nearly half were considered obese—nearly double the proportion in 1980. The proportion of overweight children and adolescents had tripled in the last two decades. Being overweight was linked to a host of serious diseases and conditions, including heart disease, stroke, diabetes, asthma, arthritis, and psychological disorders such as depression. Noting that losing even a few pounds, or simply not gaining more weight, could reduce one's risk for weight-related disease, Satcher urged Americans to eat less, eat healthier foods, and exercise more frequently. "This is not about aesthetics and it's not about appearances," Satcher said at a news conference December 13, 2001. "We're talking about health."

Satcher stressed that weight reduction was not solely an individual responsibility, but one that the entire community shared. "When there are no safe, accessible places for children to play or adults to walk, jog, or ride a bike, that is a community responsibility. When school lunchrooms or office cafeterias do not provide healthy and appealing food choices, that is a community responsibility. . . . When we do not require daily physical education in our schools, that is also a community responsibility," Satcher wrote in a foreword to the report. He called on schools, workplaces, restaurants, and federal, state, and local governments to take part in a campaign to help Americans reach and remain at a healthy weight.

The report drew widespread praise from consumer and health groups. "What's unique is to have the government saying that we need to address nutrition and physical activity as a societal issue, much like we did for tobacco," Margo Wootan of the Center for Science in the Public Interest told the

Washington Post. *"We need to put in place policy and change the environment around people so that it is easier for them to eat well and be active."*

Defining the Problem

Since 1998 the federal government had used a measure called body mass index (BMI) to classify weight. BMI was calculated by multiplying a person's weight in pounds by 703 and then dividing the product by the person's height in inches, squared. A BMI between 18.5 and 25 was considered a healthy weight. People with a BMI in the 25 to 30 range were considered overweight, while those with a BMI above 30 were considered obese. Obesity was further divided into three classes. In children and adolescents, overweight is defined according to an age- and gender-specific BMI. While BMI correlated well with total body fat in most people, it could overestimate body fat in people who were very muscular and underestimate body fat in people, such as the elderly, who had lost muscle mass.

Having a BMI in the overweight or obese range did not in and of itself mean that a person was necessarily unhealthy. Other factors, such as high blood pressure, high cholesterol, smoking, diabetes, and personal medical history needed to be considered to assess overall health. However, a person who was overweight was at higher risk than a healthy person of having high blood pressure, high cholesterol, and diabetes. A government study released in August showed that the loss of ten to fifteen pounds, combined with a regimen of moderate physical exercise, could significantly delay the onset of diabetes in overweight people who had already shown medical signs of being at risk for developing the disease, saving about $58 million a year in treatment costs as well as untold amounts of pain and disability.

The major causes of weight problems in both adults and children were overeating, unhealthy eating, and lack of exercise. According to Department of Agriculture surveys, few Americans met federal dietary guidelines, which emphasized diets high in fruits, vegetables, and grains and low in sugar, salt, fat, and cholesterol. Moreover, Americans had grown more sedentary as jobs became less labor-intensive and as television and other forms of inactive entertainment began to consume more of the average person's leisure hours. According to the surgeon general's report, less than one-third of all adults engaged in thirty minutes or more of physical activity on most days— the recommended amount. Two of five adults did not engage in any physical activity during leisure time. (Dietary guidelines, Historic Documents of 1996, p. 3; Benefits of physical exercise, Historic Documents of 1996, p. 418)

The rapid increase in overweight children was particularly disturbing. Overweight adolescents had a 70 percent risk of becoming overweight or obese adults—and thus at increased risk for a range of serious diseases. Doctors were already reporting a dramatic increase in the incidence of Type 2 diabetes in children and adolescents. Type 2 diabetes accounted for about 95 percent of all diabetes cases and was once considered primarily an adult disease.

Like their parents, children were prone to inactivity and unhealthy eating habits. Television, computers, and video games kept children inside and

*inactive; in an earlier era the same children might have played more ac-
tively outside. Many schools had sharply reduced or even curtailed physical
education classes. Advertising, convenience, and peer pressure lured children to fast food and soft drinks that are generally high in fat, sugar, and
salt. Many schools contracted with candy and soft drink companies to place
vending machines in or near school cafeterias; under many of the contracts,
the higher the vending machine sales, the higher the fees paid to the school.
A report to Congress from the Agriculture Department in January said that
"the availability of foods sold in competition with school meals jeopardizes
the nutritional effectiveness of the [school lunch] programs and may be a
contributor to the trend of unhealthy eating practices among children."*

A Call to Action

*Satcher called on individuals to eat healthier and get more exercise. Adults
should engage in at least thirty minutes of activity on most days; children
should aim for sixty minutes. Physical activity could include common
chores, such as washing and waxing a car, raking leaves, or shoveling snow,
as well as walking, swimming, or dancing. But Satcher also called upon the
greater society to provide an environment that would make it easier for
people to reach and maintain healthy weights. Among the dozens of steps the
surgeon general recommended in his call to action were the following:*

- *Schools should ensure that all students in all grades receive daily physical education.*
- *Employers should make facilities and time for physical exercise available to employees.*
- *Communities should ensure safe and accessible places for people to engage in physical activity.*
- *Schools should emphasize healthy eating by providing more fruits,
  vegetables, and whole-grain foods and reducing access to foods that are
  high in calories, fat, and added sugars. The report said existing federal
  regulations prohibiting use of vending machines during school lunch
  hours should be enforced.*

*Following are excerpts from "The Surgeon General's Call To Ac-
tion To Prevent and Decrease Overweight and Obesity," a report
issued December 13, 2001, by Surgeon General David Satcher.*

**The document was obtained from the Internet at http://
www.surgeongeneral.gov/topics/obesity.**

Foreword

Overweight and obesity may not be infectious diseases, but they have
reached epidemic proportions in the United States. Overweight and obesity

are increasing in both genders and among all population groups. In 1999, an estimated 61 percent of U. S. adults were overweight or obese, and 13 percent of children and adolescents were overweight. Today there are nearly twice as many overweight children and almost three times as many overweight adolescents as there were in 1980. We already are seeing tragic results from these trends. Approximately 300,000 deaths a year in this country are currently associated with overweight and obesity. Left unabated, overweight and obesity may soon cause as much preventable disease and death as cigarette smoking.

Overweight and obesity have been grouped as one of the *Leading Health Indicators in Healthy People 2010*, the Nation's health objectives for the first decade of the 21st century. The Leading Health Indicators reflect the major public health concerns and opportunities in the United States. While we have made dramatic progress over the last few decades in achieving so many of our health goals, the statistics on overweight and obesity have steadily headed in the wrong direction. If this situation is not reversed, it could wipe out the gains we have made in areas such as heart disease, diabetes, several forms of cancer, and other chronic health problems. Unfortunately, excessive weight for height is a risk factor for all of these conditions.

Many people believe that dealing with overweight and obesity is a personal responsibility. To some degree they are right, but it is also a community responsibility. When there are no safe, accessible places for children to play or adults to walk, jog, or ride a bike, that is a community responsibility. When school lunchrooms or office cafeterias do not provide healthy and appealing food choices, that is a community responsibility. When new or expectant mothers are not educated about the benefits of breastfeeding, that is a community responsibility. When we do not require daily physical education in our schools, that is also a community responsibility. There is much that we can and should do together.

Taking action to address overweight and obesity will have profound effects on increasing the quality and years of healthy life and on eliminating health disparities in the United States. With this outcome in mind, I asked the Office of Disease Prevention and Health Promotion, along with other agencies in the Department of Health and Human Services, to assist me in developing this *Surgeon General's Call To Action To Prevent and Decrease Overweight and Obesity*. Our ultimate goal is to set priorities and establish strategies and actions to reduce overweight and obesity. This process begins with our attitudes about overweight and obesity. Recognition of the epidemic of overweight and obesity is relatively recent, and there remain enormous challenges and opportunities in finding solutions to this public health crisis. Overweight and obesity must be approached as preventable and treatable problems with realistic and exciting opportunities to improve health and save lives. The challenge is to create a multifaceted public health approach capable of delivering long-term reductions in the prevalence of overweight and obesity. This approach should focus on health rather than appearance and empower both individuals and communities to address barriers, reduce stigmatization, and move forward in addressing overweight and obesity in a positive and proactive fashion.

Several events have drawn attention to overweight and obesity as public health problems. In 1998, the National Heart, Lung, and Blood Institute in cooperation with the National Institute of Diabetes and Digestive and Kidney Diseases of the National Institutes of Health released the *Clinical Guidelines on the Identification, Evaluation, and Treatment of Obesity in Adults: Evidence Report.* This report was the result of a thorough scientific review of the evidence related to the risks and treatment of overweight and obesity, and it provided evidence-based treatment guidelines for health care providers. In early 2000, the release of *Healthy People 2010* identified overweight and obesity as major public health problems and set national objectives for reduction in their prevalence. The National Nutrition Summit in May 2000 illuminated the impact of dietary and physical activity habits on achieving a healthy body weight and began a national dialogue on strategies for the prevention of overweight and obesity. Finally, a Surgeon General's Listening Session, held in late 2000, and a related public comment period, generated many useful ideas for prevention and treatment strategies and helped forge and reinforce an important coalition of stakeholders. Participants in these events considered many prevention and treatment strategies, including such national priorities as ensuring daily physical education in schools, increasing research on the behavioral and environmental causes of obesity, and promoting breastfeeding.

These activities are just a beginning, however. Effective action requires the close cooperation and collaboration of a variety of organizations and individuals. This *Call To Action* serves to recruit your talent and inspiration in developing national actions to promote healthy eating habits and adequate physical activity, beginning in childhood and continuing across the lifespan. I applaud your interest in this important public health challenge.

David Satcher, M.D., Ph.D.

Section 1: Overweight and Obesity as Public Health Problems in America

This *Surgeon General's Call To Action To Prevent and Decrease Overweight and Obesity* seeks to engage leaders from diverse groups in addressing a public health issue that is among the most burdensome faced by the Nation: the health consequences of overweight and obesity. This burden manifests itself in premature death and disability, in health care costs, in lost productivity, and in social stigmatization. The burden is not trivial. Studies show that the risk of death rises with increasing weight. Even moderate weight excess (10 to 20 pounds for a person of average height) increases the risk of death, particularly among adults aged 30 to 64 years.

Overweight and obesity are caused by many factors. For each individual, body weight is determined by a combination of genetic, metabolic, behavioral, environmental, cultural, and socioeconomic influences. Behavioral and environmental factors are large contributors to overweight and obesity and provide the greatest opportunity for actions and interventions designed for prevention and treatment.

For the vast majority of individuals, overweight and obesity result from excess calorie consumption and/or inadequate physical activity. Unhealthy dietary habits and sedentary behavior together account for approximately 300,000 deaths every year. Thus, a healthy diet and regular physical activity, consistent with the *Dietary Guidelines for Americans*, should be promoted as the cornerstone of any prevention or treatment effort. According to the U.S. Department of Agriculture's 1994–1996 Continuing Survey of Food Intakes by Individuals, very few Americans meet the majority of the Food Guide Pyramid recommendations. Only 3 percent of all individuals meet four of the five recommendations for the intake of grains, fruits, vegetables, dairy products, and meats. Much work needs to be done to ensure the nutrient adequacy of our diets while at the same time avoiding excess calories. Dietary adequacy and moderation in energy consumption are both important for maintaining or achieving a healthy weight and for overall health.

Many adult Americans have not been meeting Federal physical activity recommendations to accumulate at least 30 minutes of moderate physical activity most days of the week. In 1997, less than one-third of adults engaged in the recommended amount of physical activity, and 40 percent of adults engaged in no leisure-time physical activity. Although nearly 65 percent of adolescents reported participating in vigorous activity for 20 minutes or more on 3 or more out of 7 days, national data are not available to assess whether children and adolescents meet the Federal recommendations to accumulate at least 60 minutes of moderate physical activity most days of the week. Many experts also believe that physical inactivity is an important part of the energy imbalance responsible for the increasing prevalence of overweight and obesity. Our society has become very sedentary; for example, in 1999, 43 percent of students in grades 9 through 12 viewed television more than 2 hours per day.

Both dietary intake and physical activity are difficult to measure on either an individual or a population level. More research is clearly necessary to fully understand the specific etiology of this crisis. However, these statistics and the increasing prevalence of overweight and obesity highlight the need to engage all Americans as we move forward to ensure the quality and accessibility of prevention and treatment programs.

Measuring Overweight and Obesity

The first challenge in addressing overweight and obesity lies in adopting a common public health measure of these conditions. An expert panel, convened by the National Institutes of Health (NIH) in 1998, has utilized Body Mass Index (BMI) for defining overweight and obesity. BMI is a practical measure that requires only two things: accurate measures of an individual's weight and height BMI is a measure of weight in relation to height. BMI is calculated as weight in pounds divided by the square of the height in inches, multiplied by 703. Alternatively, BMI can be calculated as weight in kilograms divided by the square of the height in meters.

Studies have shown that BMI is significantly correlated with total body fat content for the majority of individuals. BMI has some limitations, in that it can overestimate body fat in persons who are very muscular, and it can underestimate body fat in persons who have lost muscle mass, such as many elderly. Many organizations, including over 50 scientific and medical organizations that have endorsed the NIH *Clinical Guidelines*, support the use of a BMI of 30 kg/m² or greater to identify obesity in adults and a BMI between 25 kg/m² and 29.9 kg/m² to identify overweight in adults. These definitions are based on evidence that suggests health risks are greater at or above a BMI of 25 kg/m² compared to those at a BMI below that level. The risk of death, although modest until a BMI of 30 kg/m² is reached, increases with an increasing Body Mass Index. . . .

Health Risks

Epidemiological studies show an increase in mortality associated with overweight and obesity. Individuals who are obese (BMI ≥ 30) have a 50 to 100 percent increased risk of premature death from all causes compared to individuals with a BMI in the range of 20 to 25. An estimated 300,000 deaths a year may be attributable to obesity.

Morbidity from obesity may be as great as from poverty, smoking, or problem drinking. Overweight and obesity are associated with an increased risk for coronary heart disease; type 2 diabetes; endometrial, colon, postmenopausal breast, and other cancers; and certain musculoskeletal disorders, such as knee osteoarthritis. Both modest and large weight gains are associated with significantly increased risk of disease. For example, a weight gain of 11 to 18 pounds increases a person's risk of developing type 2 diabetes to twice that of individuals who have not gained weight, while those who gain 44 pounds or more have four times the risk of type 2 diabetes.

A gain of approximately 10 to 20 pounds results in an increased risk of coronary heart disease (nonfatal myocardial infarction and death) of 1.25 times in women and 1.6 times in men. Higher levels of body weight gain of 22 pounds in men and 44 pounds in women result in an increased coronary heart disease risk of 1.75 and 2.65, respectively. In women with a BMI of 34 or greater, the risk of developing endometrial cancer is increased by more than six times. Overweight and obesity are also known to exacerbate many chronic conditions such as hypertension and elevated cholesterol. Overweight and obese individuals also may suffer from social stigmatization, discrimination, and poor body image.

Although obesity-associated morbidities occur most frequently in adults, important consequences of excess weight as well as antecedents of adult disease occur in overweight children and adolescents. Overweight children and adolescents are more likely to become overweight or obese adults; this concern is greatest among adolescents. Type 2 diabetes, high blood lipids, and hypertension as well as early maturation and orthopedic problems also occur with increased frequency in overweight youth. A common consequence of childhood overweight is psychosocial—specifically discrimination.

These data on the morbidity and mortality associated with overweight and obesity demonstrate the importance of the prevention of weight gain, as well as the role of obesity treatment, in maintaining and improving health and quality of life.

Economic Consequences

Overweight and obesity and their associated health problems have substantial economic consequences for the U. S. health care system. The increasing prevalence of overweight and obesity is associated with both direct and indirect costs. Direct health care costs refer to preventive, diagnostic, and treatment services related to overweight and obesity (for example, physician visits and hospital and nursing home care). Indirect costs refer to the value of wages lost by people unable to work because of illness or disability, as well as the value of future earnings lost by premature death.

In 1995, the total (direct and indirect) costs attributable to obesity amounted to an estimated $99 billion. In 2000, the total cost of obesity was estimated to be $117 billion ($ 61 billion direct and $56 billion indirect). Most of the cost associated with obesity is due to type 2 diabetes, coronary heart disease, and hypertension.

Epidemiology

The United States is experiencing substantial increases in overweight and obesity (as defined by a BMI $\geq$ 25 for adults) that cut across all ages, racial and ethnic groups, and both genders. According to self-reported measures of height and weight, obesity (BMI $\geq$ 30) has been increasing in every State in the Nation. Based on clinical height and weight measurements in the 1999 National Health and Nutrition Examination Survey (NHANES), 34 percent of U.S. adults aged 20 to 74 years are overweight (BMI 25 to 29.9), and an additional 27 percent are obese (BMI $\geq$ 30). This contrasts with the late 1970s, when an estimated 32 percent of adults aged 20 to 74 years were overweight, and 15 percent were obese.

The most recent data (1999) estimate that 13 percent of children aged 6 to 11 years and 14 percent of adolescents aged 12 to 19 years are overweight. During the past two decades, the percentage of children who are overweight has nearly doubled (from 7 to 13 percent), and the percentage of adolescents who are overweight has almost tripled (from 5 to 14 percent).

Disparities in Prevalence

Between the second and third National Health and Nutrition Examination Surveys (NHANES II and III), the prevalence of overweight and obesity (BMI $\geq$ 25 for adults and $\geq$ 95th percentile for age and gender in children) increased in both genders, across all races and ethnicities, and across all age groups. Disparities in overweight and obesity prevalence exist in many segments of the population based on race and ethnicity, gender, age, and socioeconomic status. For example, overweight and obesity are particularly common among minority groups and those with a lower family income.

Race and Ethnicity, Gender, and Age

In general, the prevalence of overweight and obesity is higher in women who are members of racial and ethnic minority populations than in non-Hispanic white women. Among men, Mexican Americans have a higher prevalence of overweight and obesity than non-Hispanic whites or non-Hispanic blacks. For non-Hispanic men, the prevalence of overweight and obesity among whites is slightly greater than among blacks.

Within racial groups, gender disparities exist, although not always in the same direction. Based on NHANES III (1988–1994), the proportion of non-Hispanic black women who were overweight or obese (BMI ≥ 25; 69 percent) was higher than the proportion of non-Hispanic black men (58 percent). For non-Hispanic whites, on the other hand, the proportion of men who were overweight or obese (BMI ≥ 25; 62 percent) exceeded the proportion of women (47 percent). However, when looking at obesity alone (BMI ≥ 30), the prevalence was slightly higher in non-Hispanic white women compared to non-Hispanic white men (23 percent and 21 percent, respectively). The prevalence of overweight or obesity (BMI ≥ 25) was about the same in Mexican American men and women (69 percent and 70 percent, respectively). Although smaller surveys indicate a higher prevalence of overweight and obesity in American Indians, Alaska Natives, and Pacific Islander Americans and a lower prevalence in Asian Americans compared to the general population, the number surveyed in NHANES III was too small to reliably report prevalence comparisons of overweight and obesity for these populations.

Racial and ethnic disparities in overweight may also occur in children and adolescents. Data for youth from NHANES III showed a similar pattern to that seen among adults. Mexican American boys tended to have a higher prevalence of overweight than non-Hispanic black and non-Hispanic white boys. Non-Hispanic black girls tended to have a higher prevalence of overweight compared to non-Hispanic white and Mexican American girls. The National Heart, Lung, and Blood Institute Growth and Health Study on overweight in children found a higher mean BMI for black girls aged 9 and 10 years, compared to white girls of the same ages. This racial difference in BMI widened and was even greater at age 19.

In addition to racial and ethnic and gender disparities, the prevalence of overweight and obesity also varies by age. Among both men and women, the prevalence of overweight and obesity increases with advancing age until the sixth decade, after which it starts to decline.

Socioeconomic Status

Disparities in the prevalence of overweight and obesity also exist based on socioeconomic status. For all racial and ethnic groups combined, women of lower socioeconomic status (income ≤ 130 percent of poverty threshold) are approximately 50 percent more likely to be obese than those with higher socioeconomic status (income > 130 percent of poverty threshold). Men are about equally likely to be obese whether they are in a low or high socioeconomic group.

Among children, the relationship between socioeconomic status and overweight in girls is weaker than it is in women; that is, girls from lower income families have not consistently been found to be overweight compared to girls from higher income families. Among Mexican American and non-Hispanic black children and adolescents, family income does not reliably predict overweight prevalence. However, non-Hispanic white adolescents from lower income families experience a greater prevalence of overweight than those from higher income families.

Health Benefits of Weight Loss

The recommendations to treat overweight and obesity are based on two rationales. First, overweight and obesity are associated with an increased risk of disease and death, as previously discussed. Second, randomized controlled trials have shown that weight loss (as modest as 5 to 15 percent of excess total body weight) reduces the risk factors for at least some diseases, particularly cardiovascular disease, in the short term. Weight loss results in lower blood pressure, lower blood sugar, and improved lipid levels. While few published studies have examined the link between weight loss and reduced disease or death in the long-term, current data as well as scientific plausibility suggest this link.

Studies have shown that reducing risk factors for heart disease, such as blood pressure and blood cholesterol levels, lowers death rates from heart disease and stroke. Therefore, it is highly probable that weight loss that reduces these risk factors will reduce the number of deaths from heart disease and stroke. Trials examining the direct effects of weight loss on disease and death are currently under way. For example, one trial shows that weight loss, a healthful diet, and exercise prevent the development of type 2 diabetes among persons who are overweight or obese. The recently completed Diabetes Prevention Program from NIH also confirmed significant reductions in the risk for developing type 2 diabetes among obese subjects with impaired glucose tolerance through similar lifestyle interventions.

Section 2: Posing Questions and Developing Strategies

Current knowledge is clear on many issues: the prevalence of overweight and obesity is high, and that of obesity is increasing rapidly; adolescents who are overweight are at high risk of becoming overweight or obese adults; overweight and obesity increase the risk for serious diseases such as type 2 diabetes, hypertension, and high blood cholesterol; and overweight and obesity are associated with premature death and disability. It is also known that a healthy diet and adequate physical activity aid in maintaining a healthy weight and, among overweight or obese persons, can promote weight loss.

Knowledge is less clear, however, on some very important questions. How can overweight and obesity be prevented? What are the most effective prevention and treatment strategies? How can the environment be modified to promote healthier eating and increased physical activity? Determining the answers to these questions demands a national public health response. Assembling the components of this response has begun.

Developing a Public Health Response

In December 2000, the Surgeon General hosted a public Listening Session on overweight and obesity. The meeting—Toward a National Action Plan on

Overweight and Obesity: The Surgeon General's Initiative—began a developmental process that led to this *Surgeon General's Call To Action To Prevent and Decrease Overweight and Obesity*. A menu of important activities has been assembled from comments received during the Surgeon General's Listening Session, a public comment period, and the National Nutrition Summit. The menu, which is presented in the following section, highlights areas that received significant attention during one or more of these events. Although not meant to be prescriptive, the menu should establish useful starting points as individuals and groups focus their own skills, creativity, and inspiration on the national epidemic of overweight and obesity.

The discussions at the Surgeon General's Listening Session centered on activities and interventions in five key settings: families and communities, schools, health care, media and communications, and worksites. The key actions discussed are presented for each of these settings. Many of these actions overlap the different settings and can be applied in several or all environments.

CARE to Address Overweight and Obesity

The key actions are organized by setting in a framework called CARE: Communication, Action, and Research and Evaluation.

COMMUNICATION: Provision of information and tools to motivate and empower decision makers at the governmental, organizational, community, family, and individual levels who will create change toward the prevention and decrease of overweight and obesity.

ACTION: Interventions and activities that assist decision makers in preventing and decreasing overweight and obesity, individually or collectively.

RESEARCH and EVALUATION: Investigations to better understand the causes of overweight and obesity, to assess the effectiveness of interventions, and to develop new communication and action strategies.

Within the CARE framework, effective actions must occur at multiple levels. Obviously, individual behavioral change lies at the core of all strategies to reduce overweight and obesity. Successful efforts, however, must focus not only on individual behavioral change, but also on group influences, institutional and community influences, and public policy. Actions to reduce overweight and obesity will fail without this multidimensional approach. Individual behavioral change can occur only in a supportive environment with accessible and affordable healthy food choices and opportunities for regular physical activity. Furthermore, actions aimed exclusively at individual behavioral change, while not considering social, cultural, economic, and environmental influences, are likely to reinforce attitudes of stigmatization against the overweight and obese.

Setting 1: Families and Communities

Families and communities lie at the foundation of the solution to the problems of overweight and obesity. Family members can share their own knowledge and habits regarding a healthy diet and physical activity with their children, friends, and other community members. Emphasis should be placed on family and community opportunities for communication, education, and peer support surrounding the maintenance of healthy dietary choices and physical activity patterns.

Communication

- Raise consumer awareness about the effect of being overweight on overall health.
- Inform community leaders about the importance of developing healthy communities.
- Highlight programs that support healthful food and physical activity choices to community decision makers.
- Raise policy makers' awareness of the need to develop social and environmental policy that would help communities and families be more physically active and consume a healthier diet.
- Educate individuals, families, and communities about healthy dietary patterns and regular physical activity, based on the *Dietary Guidelines for Americans*.
- Educate parents about the need to serve as good role models by practicing healthy eating habits and engaging in regular physical activity in order to instill lifelong healthy habits in their children.
- Raise consumer awareness about reasonable food and beverage portion sizes.
- Educate expectant parents and other community members about the potentially protective effect of breastfeeding against the development of obesity.

Action

- Form community coalitions to support the development of increased opportunities to engage in leisure time physical activity and to encourage food outlets to increase availability of low-calorie, nutritious food items.
- Encourage the food industry to provide reasonable food and beverage portion sizes.
- Increase availability of nutrition information for foods eaten and prepared away from home.
- Create more community-based obesity prevention and treatment programs for children and adults.
- Empower families to manage weight and health through skill building in parenting, meal planning, and behavioral management.
- Expand efforts to encourage healthy eating patterns, consistent with the *Dietary Guidelines for Americans*, by nutrition assistance recipients.
- Provide demonstration grants to address the lack of access to and availability of healthy affordable foods in inner cities.
- Promote healthful dietary patterns, including consumption of at least five servings of fruits and vegetables a day.
- Create community environments that promote and support breast-feeding.
- Decrease time spent watching television and in similar sedentary behaviors by children and their families.

- Provide demonstration grants to address the lack of public access to safe and supervised physical activity.
- Create and implement public policy related to the provision of safe and accessible sidewalks, walking and bicycle paths, and stairs.

Research and Evaluation

- Conduct research on obesity prevention and reduction to confirm their effects on improving health outcomes.
- Determine the root causes, behaviors, and social and ecological factors leading to obesity and how such forces vary by race and ethnicity, gender, and socioeconomic status.
- Assess the factors contributing to the disproportionate burden of overweight and obesity in low-income and minority racial and ethnic populations.
- Develop and evaluate preventive interventions that target infants and children, especially those who are at high risk of becoming obese.
- Coordinate research activities to refine risk assessment, to enhance obesity prevention, and to support appropriate consumer messages and education.
- Study the cost-effectiveness of community-directed strategies designed to prevent the onset of overweight and obesity.
- Conduct behavioral research to identify how to motivate people to increase and maintain physical activity and make healthier food choices.
- Evaluate the feasibility of incentives that support healthful dietary and physical activity patterns.
- Identify techniques that can foster community motivation to reduce overweight and obesity.
- Examine the marketing practices of the fast food industry and the factors determining construction of new food outlets.

Setting 2: Schools

Schools are identified as a key setting for public health strategies to prevent and decrease the prevalence of overweight and obesity. Most children spend a large portion of time in school. Schools provide many opportunities to engage children in healthy eating and physical activity and to reinforce healthy diet and physical activity messages. Public health approaches in schools should extend beyond health and physical education to include school policy, the school physical and social environment, and links between schools and families and communities. Schools and communities that are interested in reducing overweight among the young people they serve can consider options listed below. Decisions about which options to select should be made at the local level.

Communication

- Build awareness among teachers, food service staff, coaches, nurses, and other school staff about the contribution of proper nutrition and physical activity to the maintenance of lifelong healthy weight.

- Educate teachers, staff, and parents about the importance of school physical activity and nutrition programs and policies.
- Educate parents, teachers, coaches, staff, and other adults in the community about the importance they hold as role models for children, and teach them how to be models for healthy eating and regular physical activity.
- Educate students, teachers, staff, and parents about the importance of body size acceptance and the dangers of unhealthy weight control practices.
- Develop sensitivity of staff to the problems encountered by the overweight child.

Action

- Provide age-appropriate and culturally sensitive instruction in health education that helps students develop the knowledge, attitudes, skills, and behaviors to adopt, maintain, and enjoy healthy eating habits and a physically active lifestyle.
- Ensure that meals offered through the school breakfast and lunch programs meet nutrition standards.
- Adopt policies ensuring that all foods and beverages available on school campuses and at school events contribute toward eating patterns that are consistent with the *Dietary Guidelines for Americans.*
- Provide food options that are low in fat, calories, and added sugars, such as fruits, vegetables, whole grains, and lowfat or nonfat dairy foods.
- Ensure that healthy snacks and foods are provided in vending machines, school stores, and other venues within the school's control.
- Prohibit student access to vending machines, school stores, and other venues that compete with healthy school meals in elementary schools and restrict access in middle, junior, and high schools.
- Provide an adequate amount of time for students to eat school meals, and schedule lunch periods at reasonable hours around midday.
- Provide all children, from prekindergarten through grade 12, with quality daily physical education that helps develop the knowledge, attitudes, skills, behaviors, and confidence needed to be physically active for life.
- Provide daily recess periods for elementary school students, featuring time for unstructured but supervised play.
- Provide extracurricular physical activity programs, especially inclusive intramural programs and physical activity clubs.
- Encourage the use of school facilities for physical activity programs offered by the school and/or community-based organizations outside of school hours.

Research and Evaluation

- Conduct research on the relationship of healthy eating and physical activity to student health, learning, attendance, classroom behavior, violence, and other social outcomes.

- Evaluate school-based behavioral health interventions for the prevention of overweight in children.
- Develop an ongoing, systematic process to assess the school physical activity and nutrition environment, and plan, implement, and monitor improvements.
- Conduct research to study the effect of school policies such as food services and physical activity curricula on overweight in children and adolescents.
- Evaluate the financial and health impact of school contracts with vendors of high-calorie foods and beverages with minimal nutritional value.

Setting 3: Health Care

The health care system provides a powerful setting for interventions aimed at reducing the prevalence of overweight and obesity and their consequences. A majority of Americans interact with the health care system at least once during any given year. Recommendations by pediatric and adult health care providers can be influential in patient dietary choices and physical activity patterns. In collaboration with schools and worksites, health care providers and institutions can reinforce the adoption and maintenance of healthy lifestyle behaviors. Health care providers also can serve as effective public policy advocates and further catalyze intervention efforts in the family and community and in the media and communications settings.

Communication

- Inform health care providers and administrators of the tremendous burden of overweight and obesity on the health care system in terms of mortality, morbidity, and cost.
- Inform and educate the health care community about the importance of healthy eating, consistent with the *Dietary Guidelines for Americans*, and physical activity and fitness for the promotion of health.
- Educate health care providers and administrators to identify and reduce the barriers involving patients' lack of access to effective nutrition and physical activity interventions.
- Inform and educate the health care community about assessment of weight status and the risk of inappropriate weight change.
- Educate health care providers on effective ways to promote and support breastfeeding.

Action

- Train health care providers and health profession students in effective prevention and treatment techniques for overweight and obesity.
- Encourage partnerships between health care providers, schools, faith-based groups, and other community organizations in prevention efforts targeted at social and environmental causes of overweight and obesity.
- Establish a dialogue to consider classifying obesity as a disease category for reimbursement coding.

- Explore mechanisms that will partially or fully cover reimbursement or include as a member benefit health care services associated with weight management, including nutrition education and physical activity programs.

Research and Evaluation

- Develop effective preventive and therapeutic programs for obesity.
- Study the effect of weight reduction programs on health outcomes.
- Analyze the cost-effectiveness data on clinical obesity prevention and treatment efforts and conduct further research where the data are inconclusive.
- Promote research on the maintenance of weight loss.
- Promote research on breastfeeding and the prevention of obesity.
- Review and evaluate the reimbursement policies of public and private health insurance providers regarding overweight and obesity prevention and treatment efforts.

Setting 4: Media and Communications

The media can provide essential functions in overweight and obesity prevention efforts. From a public education and social marketing standpoint, the media can disseminate health messages and display healthy behaviors aimed at changing dietary habits and exercise patterns. In addition, the media can provide a powerful forum for community members who are addressing the social and environmental influences on dietary and physical activity patterns.

Communication

- Emphasize to media professionals that the primary concern of overweight and obesity is one of health rather than appearance.
- Emphasize to media professionals the disproportionate burden of overweight and obesity in low-income and racial and ethnic minority populations and the need for culturally sensitive health messages.
- Communicate the importance of prevention of overweight through balancing food intake with physical activity at all ages.
- Promote the recognition of inappropriate weight change.
- Build awareness of the importance of social and environmental influences on making appropriate diet and physical activity choices.
- Provide professional education for media professionals on policy areas related to diet and physical activity.
- Emphasize to media professionals the need to develop uniform health messages about physical activity and nutrition that are consistent with the *Dietary Guidelines for Americans.*

Action

- Conduct a national campaign to foster public awareness of the health benefits of regular physical activity, healthful dietary choices, and maintaining a healthy weight, based on the *Dietary Guidelines for Americans.*

- Encourage truthful and reasonable consumer goals for weight loss programs and weight management products.
- Incorporate messages about proper nutrition, including eating at least five servings of fruits and vegetables a day, and regular physical activity in youth-oriented TV programming.
- Train nutrition and exercise scientists and specialists in media advocacy skills that will empower them to disseminate their knowledge to a broad audience.
- Encourage community-based advertising campaigns to balance messages that may encourage consumption of excess calories and inactivity generated by fast food industries and by industries that promote sedentary behaviors.
- Encourage media professionals to utilize actors' influences as role models to demonstrate eating and physical activity lifestyles for health rather than for appearance.
- Encourage media professionals to employ actors of diverse sizes.

Research and Evaluation

- Evaluate the impact of community media advocacy campaigns designed to achieve public policy and health-related goals.
- Conduct consumer research to ensure that media messages are positive, realistic, relevant, consistent, and achievable.
- Increase research on the effects of popular media images of ideal body types and their potential health impact, particularly on young women.

Setting 5: Worksites

More than 100 million Americans spend the majority of their day at a worksite. While at work, employees are often aggregated within systems for communication, education, and peer support. Thus, worksites provide many opportunities to reinforce the adoption and maintenance of healthy lifestyle behaviors. Public health approaches in worksites should extend beyond health education and awareness to include worksite policies, the physical and social environments of worksites, and their links with the family and community setting.

Communication

- Inform employers of the direct and indirect costs of obesity.
- Communicate to employers the return-on-investment (ROI) data for worksite obesity prevention and treatment strategies.

Action

- Change workflow patterns, including flexible work hours, to create opportunities for regular physical activity during the workday.
- Provide protected time for lunch, and ensure that healthy food options are available.
- Establish worksite exercise facilities or create incentives for employees to join local fitness centers.

- Create incentives for workers to achieve and maintain a healthy body weight.
- Encourage employers to require weight management and physical activity counseling as a member benefit in health insurance contracts.
- Create work environments that promote and support breastfeeding.
- Explore ways to create Federal worksite programs promoting healthy eating and physical activity that will set an example to the private sector.

Research and Evaluation

- Evaluate best practices in worksite overweight and obesity prevention and treatment efforts, and disseminate results of studies widely.
- Evaluate economic data examining worksite obesity prevention and treatment efforts.
- Conduct controlled worksite studies of the impact of overweight and obesity management programs on worker productivity and absenteeism.

[Section 3 omitted]

Section 4: Vision for the Future

This *Surgeon General's Call To Action To Prevent and Decrease Overweight and Obesity* underscores the tremendous health impact that overweight and obesity have on the United States. Through widespread action on the part of all Americans, this *Call To Action* aims to catalyze a process that will reduce the prevalence of overweight and obesity on a nationwide scale. Without support and investment from a broad array of public and private partners, these efforts will not succeed. With such support, however, there exist few limitations on the potential of this effort to improve the health of individuals, families, communities, and, ultimately, the Nation as a whole.

Surgeon General's Priorities for Action

The previously discussed CARE framework presents a menu of important activities for the prevention and treatment of overweight and obesity. Building from this menu, the Surgeon General identifies the following 15 activities as national priorities for immediate action. Individuals, families, communities, schools, worksites, health care, media, industry, organizations, and government must determine their role and take action to prevent and decrease overweight and obesity.

Communication

The Nation must take an informed, sensitive approach to communicate with and educate the American people about health issues related to overweight and obesity. Everyone must work together to:

- Change the perception of overweight and obesity at all ages. The primary concern should be one of health and not appearance.
- Educate all expectant parents about the many benefits of breastfeeding.

> —Breastfed infants may be less likely to become overweight as they grow older.
> —Mothers who breastfeed may return to prepregnancy weight more quickly.

- Educate health care providers and health profession students in the prevention and treatment of overweight and obesity across the lifespan.
- Provide culturally appropriate education in schools and communities about healthy eating habits and regular physical activity, based on the Dietary Guidelines for Americans, for people of all ages. Emphasize the consumer's role in making wise food and physical activity choices.

Action

The Nation must take action to assist Americans in balancing healthful eating with regular physical activity. Individuals and groups across all settings must work in concert to:

- Ensure daily, quality physical education in all school grades. Such education can develop the knowledge, attitudes, skills, behaviors, and confidence needed to be physically active for life.
- Reduce time spent watching television and in other similar sedentary behaviors.
- Build physical activity into regular routines and playtime for children and their families. Ensure that adults get at least 30 minutes of moderate physical activity on most days of the week. Children should aim for at least 60 minutes.
- Create more opportunities for physical activity at worksites. Encourage all employers to make facilities and opportunities available for physical activity for all employees.
- Make community facilities available and accessible for physical activity for all people, including the elderly.
- Promote healthier food choices, including at least five servings of fruits and vegetables each day, and reasonable portion sizes at home, in schools, at worksites, and in communities.
- Ensure that schools provide healthful foods and beverages on school campuses and at school events by:
  - —Enforcing existing U. S. Department of Agriculture regulations that prohibit serving foods of minimal nutritional value during mealtimes in school food service areas, including in vending machines.
  - —Adopting policies specifying that all foods and beverages available at school contribute toward eating patterns that are consistent with the *Dietary Guidelines for Americans.*
  - —Providing more food options that are low in fat, calories, and added sugars such as fruits, vegetables, whole grains, and low-fat or nonfat dairy foods.
  - —Reducing access to foods high in fat, calories, and added sugars and to excessive portion sizes.

- Create mechanisms for appropriate reimbursement for the prevention and treatment of overweight and obesity.

Research and Evaluation

The Nation must invest in research that improves our understanding of the causes, prevention, and treatment of overweight and obesity. A concerted effort should be made to:

- Increase research on behavioral and environmental causes of overweight and obesity.
- Increase research and evaluation on prevention and treatment interventions for overweight and obesity, and develop and disseminate best practice guidelines.
- Increase research on disparities in the prevalence of overweight and obesity among racial and ethnic, gender, socioeconomic, and age groups, and use this research to identify effective and culturally appropriate interventions.

Conclusion

This *Call To Action* is for all who can have an impact on overweight and obesity in the United States to take action to create a future where:

- It is widely recognized that overweight and obesity can reduce the length and quality of life.
- The etiology of this complex problem of overweight and obesity is better understood.
- Effective and practical prevention and treatment are widely available and integrated in health care systems.
- Environments have been modified to promote healthy eating and increased physical activity.
- Disparities in overweight and obesity prevalence based on race and ethnicity, socioeconomic status, gender, and age are eliminated.
- The health consequences of overweight and obesity are reduced.
- The social stigmatism associated with overweight and obesity is eradicated.

This vision should be approached vigorously and optimistically but with patience. There is no simple or quick answer to this multifaceted challenge. This *Surgeon General's Call To Action To Prevent and Decrease Overweight and Obesity* calls upon individuals, families, communities, schools, worksites, organizations, government, and the media to work together to build solutions that will bring better health to everyone in this country. Working together, we can make this vision become a reality.

UNICEF DIRECTOR ON SEXUAL EXPLOITATION OF CHILDREN
December 17, 2001

Despite heightened efforts throughout the world in recent years to combat child prostitution, pornography, and trafficking, the executive director of the United Nations Children's Fund (UNICEF) warned that sexual exploitation of children was on the rise. In delivering the keynote address December 17, 2001, in Yokohama, Japan, to the Second World Congress Against the Commercial Sexual Exploitation of Children, Carol Bellamy stated that every year hundreds of thousands of children "are bought and sold like fresh produce, commodities in a global sex industry steeped in greed and unspeakable cruelty."

According to UNICEF, an estimated 1 million children under the age of nineteen were forced into the sex trade every year, the victims of greed, poverty, war, gender discrimination, and weak laws and enforcement. By some estimates, trafficking in women and children was the third largest source of profits for organized crime, behind drugs and weapons. Child victims of sexual exploitation were often condemned to a life of poverty and virtual slavery, put at heightened risk for contracting HIV/AIDS and other sexually transmitted diseases, and vulnerable to lifelong physical, sexual, and emotional damage.

Sexual exploitation was only one of many hardships afflicting the world's children. More than 10 million children under age five died every year, mostly from malnutrition and preventable disease. One of every ten children was disabled. Still, these numbers represented a marked improvement over 1990, when it was estimated that nearly 13 million children under age five died. A major success story in the 1990s, according to UNICEF, was the greatly expanded use of iodized salt: 72 percent of homes in developing countries used iodized salt in 2000, up from just 20 percent in 1990. Iodine deficiency was the single greatest source of preventable mental retardation. The proportion of children enrolled in primary school also increased during the 1990s, rising from 80 percent in 1990 to 85 percent in 2000. About 120 million school-age children, 60 percent of them girls, were not in school, however.

More than 2 million children died as a result of armed conflict in the 1990s, and more than 6 million were seriously injured or disabled. More than 300,000 had been recruited to fight in wars. One particularly gruesome practice occurred in Sierra Leone, where an estimated 5,000 children were kidnapped by rebel forces during the country's ten-year civil war in the 1990s and forced into combat, sometimes into committing atrocities against their own villages and families. Many of these children were branded by the rebel groups so that they would not escape. With the end of war, many were finding that the tattoos were making it even more difficult to return home than it already would have been. "I was branded because they said I would run away, and now I can't even run away from my own self. Evil is with me all the time, imprinted on my body," one child told a reporter for the Christian Science Monitor.

Scope of the Problem

Because trafficking and sexual exploitation of children was illegal and clandestine, accurate statistics were difficult to gather and much of the evidence was anecdotal, but the problems affected virtually every region in the world. According to one UNICEF report, more than 30 percent of all sex workers in the Mekong region of Southeast Asia—Cambodia, Laos, Myanmar, Thailand, Vietnam, and neighboring provinces in China—were between the ages of twelve and seventeen. The International Labor Organization estimated that the sex trade, including children, in Thailand accounted for 14–16 percent of the country's gross domestic product. A survey by the magazine India Today *found that there were about 500,000 child prostitutes in India. Up to 50 percent of the prostitutes in Lithuania were thought to be minors, with some as young as eleven working in brothels.*

The United States was not immune to the problem. A study by a team of researchers at the University of Pennsylvania released in September found that an estimated 325,000 children in the United States were sexually exploited every year. Exploitation ranged from abuse at home, to use in pornography, to working as prostitutes on the street, to selling sex at school to earn cash. "That figure just blew our minds," said Richard Estes, a professor of social work and the author of the study. "We never at the beginning of the study thought we would encounter so many children in this predicament." In a report on sexual health, released June 28, the U.S. surgeon general put the number of sexually abused children at slightly more than 100,000. (Sexual health, p. 456)

Children who ran away from home, often to escape abusive situations there, were the largest group of exploited children, according to the study. An estimated 122,000 children ran away from home, while another 52,000 were thrown out by a parent or guardian. Many of these children ended up on the streets, practicing what Estes called "survival sex" to obtain food, clothing, and shelter. These street children were vulnerable to drug abuse and were often the victims of assault, rape, and murder by their pimps and customers, Estes told the Reuters news service. The researchers also found that about 20 percent of the children who were interviewed were involved with prostitution rings that worked across state lines.

Supply and Demand

Supplying the demand for adolescent and child sex workers was not particularly difficult, given the life situations of many of the victims. Poverty was perhaps the leading contributor to child sexual exploitation. Children growing up in urban slums and rural areas, where education and job opportunities were nearly nonexistent, were often targets of traffickers who lured them away from their homes with promises of a better life elsewhere. In some cases, parents sold their children; in other instances parents willingly sent their children away in hopes that their opportunities would improve. Once in the hands of traffickers, children and adolescents were often trapped—forced into prostitution or pornography, unable to earn enough to buy their freedom, and often isolated in a strange culture.

Armed conflict was another major contributor to the problem, particularly in regional conflicts where one ethnic group was vying for control over another. In those cases combatants used the rape of women and children of the opposing ethnic group as an instrument of war to demoralize and terrorize the enemy. Such tactics were prominent during the wars in Bosnia, Kosovo, and several regional conflicts in Africa, including the Congo. (Milosevic war crimes trial, p. 826)

Child marriage, a common practice in many parts of the world, was also considered a form of sexual exploitation by UNICEF and other organizations advocating children's rights. Early marriages were common in sub-Saharan Africa and in parts of Asia. According to UNICEF, 7 percent of girls in Nepal were married before they were ten and 40 percent were married by age fifteen. "Forcing children, especially girls, into early marriages can be physically and emotionally harmful," Bellamy said in a report issued March 7. Pregnancy-related complications were the leading cause of deaths among girls ages fifteen to nineteen worldwide. UNICEF said that although poor health care was often the primary cause of these deaths, the risks to the health of the girls was increased by their physical immaturity. Girls who ran away from their marriages often became victims of so-called honor killings, committed by male relatives to save face for the family.

On the demand side, a key contributor was "sex tourism," where adults could buy sex as part of a tour package; often the tourists were pedophiles seeking sex with adolescents and children. Sex tourists from North America, Europe, and Australia were said to have contributed significantly to the trafficking of women and children in Latin America and the Caribbean—in part because of a crackdown on the practice in Thailand, Sri Lanka, and other Asian countries where such "tourism" began.

Another contributor was the HIV/AIDS epidemic. Young children were attractive sexual partners for some adults who thought the children were less likely to be infected with the incurable virus. Demand for young girls was particularly high in parts of Asia and Africa because of the mistaken notion that sex with a virgin could cure a person already infected with the human immunodeficiency virus. In many parts of sub-Saharan Africa, where HIV/ AIDS was prevalent, children orphaned by the disease often turned to the streets to earn a living, greatly increasing their vulnerability to sexual exploitation, forced labor, and risk of infection from HIV.

Stopping the Exploitation

These and related problems were the subject of the Second World Congress Against Commercial Sexual Exploitation of Children, held December 17–20 in Yokohama, where more than 3,000 representatives of government, intergovernmental, and nongovernmental organizations, children, the private sector, and the media met to develop global strategies for stopping the exploitation of children. The conference was organized by UNICEF, ECPAT International (End Child Prostitution, Child Pornography, and the Trafficking of Children for Sexual Purposes), and the NGO Group on the Convention on the Rights of the Child. Since the first World Congress, held in Stockholm in 1996, nearly fifty countries had taken steps to combat child sexual exploitation, including reforming their juvenile justice systems, training police and judicial authorities to recognize vulnerable children, creating special agencies to protect children's rights, and cracking down on traffickers and others who abuse children.

Child sex exploitation was a violation of the UN Convention on the Rights of the Child, adopted in 1989 and ratified by 191 nations. That treaty stipulated that every child has the right to be free from abuse, to receive an education, and to play. An Optional Protocol to the Convention on the Rights of the Child was aimed at ending the sale of children, as well as child prostitution and pornography, by holding the traffickers and other adult perpetrators criminally responsible for these activities. The protocol, which had been ratified by ten countries, was scheduled to go into effect in January 2002.

In addition, the conference hoped to expand awareness of the problem and to increase international cooperative efforts to stop the exploitation. "For us, the single most important message to come from this congress is that the demand side of commercial sexual exploitation has to be tackled in a serious way," said Muireann O'Briain, executive director of ECPAT International. UNICEF and other children's organizations also stressed the necessity to educate children how to recognize and avoid high-risk situations and to encourage all societies and cultures to recognize the problem and taken actions to stop it.

Following are excerpts from the keynote address to the Second World Congress against Commercial Sexual Exploitation of Children delivered December 17, 2002, in Yokohama, Japan, by Carol Bellamy, the executive director of UNICEF.

The document was obtained from the Internet at http:// www.unicef.org/exspecches/01esp44.htm.

Mr. President, Excellencies, Distinguished Delegates—and All the Young Participants with us, whose voices are at the heart of the struggle for child rights:

Five years ago in Stockholm, governments and civil society sent a forceful and unequivocal message: that children are not property to be bought and sold; that they have fundamental rights that must be promoted and protected—and that in fulfilling those rights, their views must be heard and acted upon.

Mr. President, we are here today to reaffirm that pledge—and to see it implemented with all possible dispatch.

As the Stockholm Congress acknowledged, there is no one solution to the commercial sexual exploitation and abuse of children, but many—each tailored to the diverse national, local and cultural realities in which these affronts to child rights originate.

But in designing those solutions, let us be clear: the commercial sexual exploitation and abuse of children is nothing less than a form of terrorism—one whose wanton destruction of young lives and futures must not be tolerated for another year, another day, another hour.

Mr. President, the facts are well known to all of us. Each year, millions of children—boys as well as girls—are bought and sold like fresh produce, commodities in a global sex industry steeped in greed and unspeakable cruelty.

Trafficked within and across borders, press-ganged into prostitution, pornography and other intolerable forms of child labour, they are overwhelmingly drawn from the ranks of the most vulnerable—refugees, orphans, abandoned children, child labourers working as domestic servants, children in armed conflict—and those whose sexual abuse began at home or in other familiar surroundings.

Distinguished Delegates, you have before you an historic opportunity to make a frank and honest assessment of how far we have come since Stockholm—and to summon the resources and the political will to end the abuse that continues to strip countless children of their rights, their dignity, their childhood—and often their very lives.

It is fitting that this Second World Congress is being held in Japan, where the efforts of Government and civil society, including NGOs, the media and other elements of the private sector, are together showing how to change the world with children. . . .

Mr. President, because of the Stockholm Declaration and Agenda for Action, there is now greater public awareness of the appalling scale of the commercial sexual exploitation of children, which afflicts every corner of the world, from the richest countries to the most impoverished.

Most importantly, we have seen how the exercise of leadership, by governments as well as by every level of civil society, can advance the cause of child rights—in this case the right of every child to be protected from all forms of sexual exploitation and abuse.

The lion's share of responsibility for ensuring child rights and well-being rests with governments at the highest level—and those obligations are set forth in the 1989 Convention on the Rights of the Child. Ratified by almost every country on Earth, it is a document that proclaims the right of all children to be protected against dangers that hamper their growth and development, from armed conflict and disability to racial and ethnic discrimination and all forms of neglect, cruelty and exploitation.

It is in line with those principles that nearly 50 countries have now moved to draw up national plans of action to combat sexual exploitation and assist victims. Measures range from the establishment of special bodies to protect child rights; reform of juvenile-justice systems; training of police and judicial authorities; and all-out crackdowns on those who sexually exploit children.

Because of such steps, we have seen an increase in police actions growing out of cooperation among national law enforcement groups and Interpol.

We have seen stepped-up involvement by the private sector, particularly in the tourism and Internet-service industries.

And we are seeing the commitment of more resources on a regional basis to combat sexual exploitation, in line with efforts like those of the European Commission.

At the global level, we have seen the adoption of three major treaties that address sexual exploitation and abuse: ILO Convention No. 182, which calls the involvement of children in prostitution and pornography one of the worst forms of child labour; the Protocol on the prevention of trafficking of children and others, part of the UN Convention against Transnational Organised Crime; and the Optional Protocol to the Convention on the Rights of the Child, in this case a measure aimed at ending the sale of children, as well as child prostitution and child pornography. The Protocol will enter into force next month, thanks to the example set by the first 10 countries that have ratified it: Andorra, Bangladesh, Cuba, Iceland, Kazakhstan, Morocco, Norway, Panama, Romania and Sierra Leone.

Finally, Mr. President, we are seeing a greater emphasis on the role of children and young people themselves in ending commercial sexual exploitation and abuse. It is a trend dramatised not only here, but by young people's conferences recently in Manila and Victoria, Canada—and just this week in Kawasaki City.

These are occasions that give exploited youth a voice in the fight to eliminate some of the most difficult and shocking obstacles to the realisation of child rights. Participants are vocal, they are visible—and yet they are not re-victimized or sensationalized. They feel safe in sharing their stories. We need to be guided by such participation, not only because it is a basic right, but because it will help us find ways to repair the deep damage that is done to sexually exploited children. So we are eager to hear what the young people have to say about the outcome of the Kawasaki City proceedings.

And yet, Mr. President, for all these advances since Stockholm, sexual exploitation for profit continues to blight the lives of millions of children.

Indeed, while there is relatively little official data, we have every reason to believe that the commercial sexual exploitation of children is on the rise.

The proliferation of armed conflict and the displacement of whole populations; widening disparities within countries and around the world; increased consumerism, widening of communication networks including roads, air transport and electronic and satellite media and connections between individuals and groups—all help create conditions that fuel rising demand.

There is also mounting evidence of a complex link between child sexual exploitation and the ongoing spread of HIV/AIDS in the developing world and among the countries of eastern Europe and the former Soviet Union.

Children who are forced into the sex trade—which a new UNICEF Report, Profiting From Abuse, puts at a million a year worldwide—are exceptionally vulnerable to contracting the virus that causes AIDS.

The high infection rates among teen-age girls in some hard-hit countries appear to be linked to a belief among HIV-positive men that they can cure themselves by having sex with virgins.

And data presented by African delegates at a recent preparatory meeting in Rabat suggest that a vast number of children who have lost one or both parents to HIV/AIDS become sex workers out of desperation.

Mr. President, it is hard to imagine a more difficult and shocking obstacle to the realisation of human rights than the commercial sexual exploitation of children. Yet it is only one element of the even more pervasive and deeply rooted problem of sexual abuse, which often begins in the home, at the hands of a close relative or friend.

Children who are sexually abused find their world turned upside down. It makes enemies out of the very people children look to for protection—those they know, love and trust. And because it can happen where children live, learn and play, familiar places like home or school can become forbidding and dangerous.

The vast majority are denied their right to education—and even to the briefest moments of leisure and play.

The desperate vulnerability of such children is only heightened by endemic factors like violence, drugs and sexually transmitted diseases. Because they are fearful of further abuse, including abuse by the authorities, such children typically have little recourse to the law. And those who return home may find themselves stigmatised by their own families and communities.

UNICEF's objective in this crisis is two-fold:

- To decrease the risks of sexual abuse and exploitation through full access to education and adequate legislation;
- And to ensure that children trapped in abusive or exploitative situations are not only freed from those situations, but that they have access to legal aid, protection, secure housing, economic assistance, counselling, and health and social services—in short, the services they need to make a physical and psychological recovery from their ordeal.

Above all, Mr. President, they need love and acceptance.

To sustain this kind of work, global partnerships are crucial. To this end, UNICEF supports the global NGO Support Group, which links key NGOs with United Nations partners, including the Committee on the Rights of the Child.

Such partnerships are already helping to improve legislative measures, law enforcement and programmes for the recovery of children through alternative education and employment opportunities.

Mr. President, Excellencies, Distinguished Delegates:

We already know a great deal about what must be done to eliminate sexual trafficking and abuse of children. But to succeed, we must strengthen international cooperation and action at every level of every society.

Governments and media outlets, must have the courage to end, once and for all, the shameful silence that keeps commercial exploitation and abuse a secret. That means shining light on the problem, using public information campaigns, increased media coverage, more sophisticated monitoring and sharing of information, educating children about sexual abuse from an early age at home and in school.

This includes working together to identify and bring to justice culpable individuals—knowing that it is often the very adults entrusted with the care and protection of children who sexually exploit children. And it means moving forcefully against criminal networks, whose global role has been under scrutiny by the UN Office for Drug Control and Crime Prevention.

We must emphasise education and awareness-raising, which can empower children and families to protect themselves.

We must confront gender discrimination in all its forms, for only by ensuring girls and women full equality and opportunity in all spheres of life can we begin to attack the roots of sexual exploitation and abuse.

Although girls are clearly the vast majority of the abused—a consequence of their low status in many societies—boys are also targets of sexual exploitation and abuse—and both need the benefits of education.

Racial inequality and ethnic discrimination must also be confronted, for they are factors that often determine who is sexually exploited and who is spared.

Mr. President, the sustained realisation of the rights of children hinges not only on what governments do, but on the outcome of partnerships involving a broad range of allies in civil society—partnerships based on a shared understanding of the rights of all human beings.

The global movement that produced the Convention on the Rights of the Child has helped generate pressure to protect the rights of all children, including children in war; children performing hazardous or exploitative labour; children exposed to violence; children in extreme poverty; and indigenous and disabled children.

Now it is up to all of us—including governments, law enforcement, international organisations and all levels of civil society—to see to it that the elimination of commercial sexual exploitation is accorded the same urgent priority.

Thank you.

HOME MINISTER OF INDIA ON
THE ATTACK ON PARLIAMENT
December 18, 2001

India and Pakistan stepped perilously close to the brink of war in December. As had been the case for a half-century, the dispute centered on Kashmir, the territory that each country claimed. Five terrorist guerrillas fighting India's control of most of the province attacked the Indian parliament building in New Delhi on December 13, 2001, and killed seven people before dying themselves in the ensuing gunfire. The two countries then massed large armies along their borders, including the "line of control" that had long divided their disputed portions of Kashmir. At year's end the two countries were insisting that they did not want war, and they were under intense pressure from the United States to avoid it.

Since the partition of the Indian subcontinent in 1947, India and Pakistan had fought three wars involving Kashmir. None of those wars resolved the underlying dispute, and the prospect of yet another war was considered especially dangerous because both countries had tested nuclear weapons in 1998. Moreover, the sudden flare-up of tensions on the subcontinent threatened regional support for the ongoing U.S. war against the al Qaeda terrorist network and the remnants of the Taliban government in nearby Afghanistan. India and Pakistan had both supported the Afghanistan war, and Pakistan had provided crucial logistical support, including the use of four military bases by U.S. forces. (Afghanistan war, p. 686; India-Pakistan nuclear tests, Historic Documents of 1998, p. 326)

Another Failed Peace Effort

India claimed Kashmir as a result of political arrangements made when Britain gave up its control of the Indian subcontinent in 1947. Pakistan, an Islamic state, insisted that Kashmir's inhabitants—most of whom were Muslim—should have the right to join Pakistan if they wished, rather than be governed by India, which was dominated by Hindus. Wars in 1947, 1965, and 1971 left India with control over about two-thirds of Kashmir (including the beautiful valley known as the "Vale of Kashmir"); Pakistan controlled most of the rest, but China also had seized a part of the territory in 1962.

Pro-Pakistan militants, armed and aided by the Pakistan government, launched a guerrilla war against Indian control of Kashmir in 1989. The fighting continued on a sporadic basis all through the 1990s, resulting in nearly 40,000 deaths, according to India's official estimate. During the late 1990s India charged that non-Kashmiri guerrillas had escalated the fighting to a greater and more dangerous level. Indian authorities said many of the guerrillas came from Arab countries and Central Asia, were associated with Islamist terrorist groups, and had the full support of Pakistan. Pakistan denied these charges and insisted that the guerrillas were Kashmiri freedom-fighters.

Numerous attempts to negotiate a settlement had always stumbled on such basic questions as whether Kashmir was even a subject of dispute. India argued that Kashmir was rightfully a part of India and, therefore, not a proper topic for negotiation between the two countries. Pakistan argued that Kashmir was the central issue that needed to be resolved before the two countries could deal with any other matters. Talks in February 1999 between Indian prime minister Atal Bihari Vajpayee and Pakistani prime minister Nawaz Sharif ended on an optimistic note, with the leaders promising to "intensify their efforts" to resolve the Kashmir issues. A few weeks later, however, the two countries nearly came to blows when guerrillas backed by the Pakistan army invaded a region of Kashmir known as Kargil and blew up an Indian munitions dump. That crisis was averted in large part through the diplomatic intervention of President Bill Clinton, who pressured Sharif into ordering a withdrawal of Pakistani forces from the Kargil area. Sharif soon paid a heavy price for his concession: in mid-October 1999 he was ousted by the head of the Pakistani armed forces, General Pervez Musharraf.

The general insisted that military rule would be temporary, but by 2001 it appeared that he had adopted an expansive definition of that term. On June 20, twenty months after seizing power, Musharraf had himself sworn in as president of Pakistan, a post that in the past had been largely ceremonial. Musharraf retained his post as head of the military and scheduled parliamentary elections for October 2002 but made no promises about stepping aside himself.

Musharraf's assumption of the presidency came in the context of a move by India to return to the peace table. Vajpayee in May had invited Musharraf to visit India for a new round of talks following up on the February 1999 meeting between Vajpayee and Sharif. Many analysts suggested that Musharraf wished to enter those talks holding the title of president, rather than the more corporate-sounding title of "chief executive" that he had been using.

The meeting between Vajpayee and Musharraf in Agra, in north-central India, began on an upbeat note on July 16, with both leaders expressing optimism about resolving their differences. But Indian officials quickly took offense at Musharraf's remarks to Indian reporters stating that Kashmir was the central dispute between the two countries and comparing the Kashmiri independence fighters to Palestinians who were battling Israel. The summit ended late on July 17 without agreement even on a closing statement, and spokesman for each country accused the other of failing to engage in serious negotiations. Musharraf invited Vajpayee for a follow-up meeting in Pakistan, although no date was set. Vajpayee later criticized Musharraf for focusing solely on Kashmir, and Musharraf responded that real peace between the countries was "certainly not" possible without first settling that issue. A month later, in August 15 ceremonies marking India's fifty-fourth anniversary as an independent nation, Vajpayee pledged to "crush Pakistan-sponsored terrorism" in Kashmir.

On the international stage, the India-Pakistan dispute faded from view after the September 11 terrorist attacks against the United States. The Bush administration rushed to secure support from both countries for its plan to eliminate the al Qaeda terrorist network and the Taliban government that hosted it in Afghanistan. Both countries responded positively to the U.S. request, which afforded them an opportunity to improve relations with Washington that had been strained since the nuclear weapons tests of 1998. (Pakistan support for U.S. war, p. 624)

New Violence over Kashmir

On October 1, just as the United States was readying to open its antiterror war in Afghanistan, the old devils of Kashmiri violence made a sudden reappearance An apparent suicide squad hijacked a van in Srinagar (the summer capital of Indian-held Kashmir), filled it with explosives, and rammed it into the main gate of the provincial headquarters, setting off a large explosion. At least a dozen people, including one of the attackers, died in the explosion and panic that followed it; others died in an ensuing gun battle that lasted for hours. The Indian government put the final death toll at thirty-eight, most of them civilians. Indian officials blamed Musharraf's government for allowing Pakistan-based guerrillas to mount the attack—a charge that Pakistan denied. Numerous Pakistani spokesmen condemned the attack, but at the same time insisted that Muslim Kashmiris had legitimate grievances against India. A Pakistan-based guerrilla movement, Jaish-i-Muhammad ("Army of Muhammad" in Urdu) at first claimed responsibility for the attack but later retracted that claim, reportedly under pressure from Musharraf's government.

Two weeks after the attack in Srinagar, Indian and Pakistani military forces traded artillery fire across the line of control that divided Kashmir. That outbreak of fighting came just as Colin Powell, U.S. secretary of state, was headed to both countries for talks about Afghanistan, where the U.S. war against the al Qaeda and Taliban was just getting under way. In advance of Powell's visit, President George W. Bush called on both countries to "stand down during our activities in Afghanistan, for that matter forever."

Bush's call from Washington for quiet, and Powell's face-to-face diplomacy in Islamabad and New Delhi, may have helped avert a rapid escalation into outright war over Kashmir just as U.S. bombers and missile-firing submarines were getting to work in Afghanistan. But low-intensity fighting continued in Kashmir between the guerrillas and Indian security forces, and the Indian and Pakistani armies kept firing the occasional artillery shell at each other across the line of control.

A dangerous new turning point was reached on December 13 with a repetition of the Srinagar attack, this time in the heart of India. Shortly after the Indian parliament had adjourned its morning session in New Delhi, five heavily armed men stole a car and drove it into a parking lot on the grounds of the parliament building. Firing assault rifles and throwing grenades, the men attacked the building. Guards managed to close the main door to parliament before the attackers could reach it. One of the attackers, armed with explosives, was blown up just outside the main entrance. In a gun battle lasting more than thirty minutes, the four remaining attackers, four policemen, and two guards were killed, as was a gardener caught in the cross-fire. Eighteen people were injured, but no legislators were among them.

Vajpayee, who was not in the parliament building at the time, went on television shortly afterward. "This is a warning to the entire nation," he said. "Our fight against terrorism has been going on for the last two decades and has now entered its final, decisive stage."

The next day, India said it had uncovered evidence that the attack was carried out by a Kashmiri independence group based in Pakistan, the Lashkar-e-Tayyaba ("Army of the Pure"). The Indian foreign secretary summoned Pakistan's ambassador to a meeting and handed him a note protesting the attack on "the seat of Indian democracy and on the sovereignty of the Indian people." The Pakistani government hotly denied any connection with the attack, and a spokesman for Lashkar-e-Tayyaba insisted that Indian intelligence agencies had mounted the attack in a "game plan" to blame Kashmiri separatists. Indian officials later said they had new evidence that the main group behind the attack was Jaish-i-Muhammad — the group generally considered responsible for the earlier attack in Srinagar.

On December 18 India's home minister, L.K. Advani, pointed a finger directly at Pakistan, saying the attack had been carried out by both groups, Jaish-i-Muhammad and Lashkar-e-Tayyaba, with support from the Pakistani intelligence agency. In remarks to parliament during its first session since December 13, Advani offered a detailed description of the attack, which he called "undoubtedly the most audacious, and also the most alarming, act of terrorism in the two-decade-long history of Pakistan-sponsored terrorism in India." Advani was a leader of a hard-line Hindu nationalist factions in the Indian government and was generally considered one of the country's staunchest anti-Pakistan politicians.

In a speech to parliament the following day, Prime Minister Vajpayee said India was trying through diplomatic channels to convince Pakistan to dismantle the Kashmiri guerrilla groups. If that effort failed, he said India would have no choice but to pursue "other options" — suggesting that India was prepared for war.

The rising tension between India and Pakistan put President Bush and his administration in a difficult position. Bush had decreed a worldwide war against terrorism, was fighting what he called the first stage of it in Afghanistan, and could not easily dismiss India's charges that Pakistan— an important U.S. ally in that war—was itself a sponsor of terrorism. But Bush also needed Musharraf's' aid for the Afghanistan war and was limited in how much pressure he could place on the Pakistani leader, whose support was uncertain among the Pakistani people or even among his own military colleagues.

Saying that he wanted to support both India and Pakistan, Bush on December 20 ordered a freeze on any U.S.-based assets of two groups: Lashkar-e-Tayyaba, which he said had sponsored the December 13 attack on the Indian parliament, and Ummah Tameer-e-Nau, a Pakistani charity group headed by two former Pakistani nuclear scientists who, according to U.S. officials, had met at least once with Osama bin Laden, head of the al Qaeda terrorist network that Bush blamed for the September 11 attacks.

Whatever U.S. expectations might have been, Bush's action did not produce an immediate de-escalation of tension in the region. On December 21 India recalled its ambassador from Islamabad and halted bus and train service between the two countries. As periodic gunfire continued across the border, India on December 25 began evacuating villages along the border, and both countries poured thousands of troops into the border areas. Vajpayee gave a fiery speech to the youth wing of his Hindu nationalist party, blaming Pakistan for the crisis and warning: "We do not want war, but war is being thrust upon us, and we will have to face it." Musharraf responded with a speech acknowledging that Pakistan faced many problems, including the "internal challenge" of militants who were damaging the country for their own purposes, and the external challenge of India. "Let me assure my countrymen that your armed forces are fully prepared and capable of defeating all challenges," he said. Musharraf coupled his tough rhetoric with a conciliatory action, however, ordering the arrest of the founder of Jaish-i-Muhammad, the group that might have been involved in the October 1 and December 13 attacks.

Pressure continued to build in the following days as India deployed ballistic missiles near the border areas, the two armies kept firing warning shots at each other, and each country banned flights over its territory by the national airline of the other country. The United States continued to exert pressure on both sides: on India to restrain itself from unleashing its much larger army against Pakistan, and on Pakistan to act more forcefully against the Kashmiri guerrillas.

Musharraf budged on December 28, quietly ordering the arrest of four dozen senior leaders of both Jaish-i-Muhammad and Lashkar-e-Tayyaba. Musharraf also denounced what he called "misguided elements who have spread violence and hatred. They are not Muslims." President Bush followed that step with telephone calls on December 29 to both Musharraf and Vajpayee urging them to back away from war. The calls represented Bush's first direct, personal intervention in the crisis following numerous similar appeals by Powell. U.S. officials said they hoped Bush's personal pressure would help enable both leaders to avoid the war they both said they did not want.

Following are excerpts from a statement to the parliament of India on December 18, 2001, by L.K. Advani, the country's home minister, describing an attack on the parliament building five days earlier and blaming Pakistan for sponsoring "terrorism" against India.

The document was obtained from the Internet at http:// rajyasabha.nic.in/photo/attack/stamentofhm.htm.

The ghastly attack on Parliament House on 13th December, 2001 has shocked the entire nation. This terrorist assault on the very bastion of our democracy was clearly aimed at wiping out the country's top political leadership. It is a tribute to our security personnel that they rose to the occasion and succeeded in averting what could have been a national catastrophe. In so doing they made the supreme sacrifice for which the country would always remain indebted to them.

2. It is now evident that the terrorist assault on the Parliament House was executed jointly by Pak-based [Pakistan] and supported terrorist outfits, namely, Lashkar-e-Taiba and Jaish-e-Mohmmad. These two organizations are known to derive their support and patronage from Pak ISI [the Pakistani Intelligence Service]. The investigation so far carried out by the police shows that all the five terrorists who formed the suicide squad were Pakistani nationals. All of them were killed on the spot and their Indian associates have since been nabbed and arrested.

3. The investigation at this stage indicates that the five Pakistani terrorists entered the Parliament House Complex at about 11.40 A.M. in an Ambassador Car bearing registration No.DL-3CJ-1527 and moved towards Building Gate No. 12 when it encountered the carcade of Vice President of India which was parked at Gate No.11. One of the members of the Parliament House Watch and Ward Staff, Shri Jagdish Prasad Yadav, became suspicious about the identity of the car and immediately ran after it. The car was forced to turn backward and in the process it hit the Vice President's car. When challenged by the security personnel present on the spot all the five terrorists jumped out of the car and started firing indiscriminately. The Delhi Police personnel attached with the Vice-President's security as also the personnel of CRPF and ITBP on duty immediately took their positions and returned the fire. It was at this point that another member of Parliament House Watch and Ward Staff, Shri Matbar Singh, sustained bullet injuries. He rushed inside Gate No.11 and closed it. An alarm was raised and all the gates in the building were immediately closed. The terrorists ran towards Gate No. 12 and then to Gate No.1 of the Parliament House Building. One terrorist was shot dead by the security forces at Gate

No.1 and in the process the explosives wrapped around his body exploded. The remaining four terrorists turned back and reached Gate No.9 of the Building. Three of them were gunned down there. The fifth terrorist ran towards Gate No.5 where he also was gunned down.

4. During the exchange of fire, four Delhi Police personnel, namely, Shri Nanak Chand, Assistant Sub-Inspector, Shri Rampal, Assistant Sub-Inspector, Shri Om Prakash, Head Constable and Shri Ghanshyam, Head Constable attached with the Vice President's security lost their lives on the spot. The other three persons who were also killed were Smt. Kamlesh Kumari, a Woman Constable of CRPF, Shri Jagdish Prasad Yadav, a Security Assistant of Watch and Ward Staff of the Parliament House, who had rushed after the terrorists' car and a civilian employee of CPWD, Shri Desh Raj—18 other persons were injured and they were immediately rushed to Dr. Ram Manohar Lohia Hospital for medical treatment. These included Shri Matbar Singh, Security Assistant, Watch and Ward Staff of the Parliament House who later succumbed to his injuries. The scene of the crime was cordoned off and Investigation Teams including Forensic Experts and Bomb Detection Squads were pressed into service. A number of hand grenades were recovered from the site of the incident and defused. A large quantity of arms and ammunition including explosives was also recovered.

5. The break-through in the investigation of the case was achieved with the arrest of Syed Abdul Rehman Gilani, a Lecturer in a local College, whose interrogation led to the identification of two other accomplices, Afzal and Shaukat Hussain Guru. The wife of the latter disclosed that her husband and Afzal had in the afternoon of 13th December, 2001 left for Srinagar. This information was immediately conveyed to the J&K Police who apprehended both of them. A laptop computer and Rs.10 lakhs in cash were recovered from them. They were later brought to Delhi by a Special Team deputed for the purpose by Delhi Police.

6. Interrogation of the accused persons has revealed that Afzal was the main coordinator who was assigned this task by a Pakistani national, Gazi Baba of Jaish-e-Mohmmad. Afzal had earlier been trained in a camp run by Pak ISI at Muzaffarabad in Pak Occupied Kashmir. The hideouts for the five Pak terrorists were arranged by Shaukat Hussain Guru, two in Mukherjee Nagar and one in Timarpur area in North Delhi. During the subsequent raids, the police recovered from two of these hideouts a lot of incriminating material including a large quantity of Ammonium Nitrate and other ingredients used in preparing Improvised Explosive Devices; a map of Delhi; a sheet of paper carrying a map of Chankyapuri drawn in hand; and three police uniforms. In all, four persons have so far been arrested in connection with this case.

7. This incident once again establishes that terrorism in India is the handiwork of Pakistan-based terrorist outfits known to derive their support and sustenance from Pak ISI. The hijacking of IC-814 Flight to Kandahar, the terrorist intrusion into the Red Fort and attack on J&K [Jammu and Kashmir] Legislative Assembly Complex at Srinagar on 1st October this year were masterminded and executed by militant outfits at the behest of the ISI. Lashkar-e-Taiba and Jaish-e-Mohmmad in particular have been in the forefront in

organizing terrorist violence in our country. The Pakistan High Commissioner in India was summoned to the Ministry of External Affairs and issued a verbal demarche demanding that Islamabad take action against the two terrorist outfits involved in the attack on the Parliament House.

8. Last week's attack on Parliament is undoubtedly the most audacious, and also the most alarming, act of terrorism in the nearly two-decades-long history of Pakistan-sponsored terrorism in India. This time the terrorists and their mentors across the border had the temerity to try to wipe out the entire political leadership of India, as represented in our multi-party Parliament. Naturally, it is time for all of us in this august House, and all of us in the country, to ponder why the terrorists and their backers tried to raise the stakes so high, particularly at a time when Pakistan is claiming to be a part of the international coalition against terrorism.

9. The only answer that satisfactorily addresses this query is that Pakistan —itself a product of the indefensible Two-Nation Theory, itself a theocratic State with an extremely tenuous tradition of democracy—is unable to reconcile itself with the reality of a secular, democratic, self-confident and steadily progressing India, whose standing in the international community is getting inexorably higher with the passage of time.

10. The Prime Minister in his address to the nation on the 13th December, 2001 has declared that the fight against terrorism had reached a decisive phase. The supreme sacrifice made by the security personnel who lost their lives in this incident will not be allowed to go in vain. Those behind the attack on Parliament House should know that the Indian people are united and determined to stamp out terrorism from the country.

CUMULATIVE INDEX, 1997–2001

Foster, Vincent W., Jr.
meeting with attorney James Hamilton, **1998** 393
suicide, **1998** 633
Fox, James Alan, juvenile crime, **1998** 871; **1999** 615
Fox, Vicente
Mexico presidential election, **2000** 963–977
U.S. immigration policy, **2001** 764–765
Framework Convention on Climate Change, **2000** 337
Framework Convention on Tobacco Control, **2000** 537–538, 552
France
Air France flight 4590 crash (Concorde plane) investigations, **2000** 488–493
euro currency, **1998** 271
Frank, Barney (D-Mass.)
House Judiciary Committee impeachment inquiry, **1998** 702
U.S.-China trade relations, **2000** 216
Frankel, Jeffrey, U.S. economic growth, **1999** 88
Franklin, John Hope, presidential advisory panel on race relations, **1997** 314, 316, 322, 323; **1998** 665, 668
Free Access to Clinic Entrances, **1998** 810
Free speech. *See under* Constitution, First Amendment
Free trade. *See* Trade; Trade negotiations
Freedom of Access to Clinic Entrances (FACE) Act, **1998** 810, 814
Freedom Initiative for Americans with Disabilities, **2001** 178
Freeh, Louis J.
Hanssen espionage case, **2001** 150–158
investigations into campaign finance practices, **1997** 824, 830–831
Waco incident investigation, **1999** 481
Wen Ho Lee spy case, **2000** 742–744
Freeman, Harold P., cancer patient care, **2001** 868
Friedman, Leon, Miranda warning, **2000** 386
Friedman, Louis, on Mars exploration, **2000** 93
Friedman, Michael
food recalls, **1997** 691
on tamoxifen trials, **1998** 197
Friedman, Rob, marketing violent entertainment to children, **2000** 731
Friedman, Stanton T., Roswell incident, **1997** 400
Frist, Bill (R-Tenn.)
Clinton State of the Union address, Republican response, **2000** 19–20, 38–40
during shooting of Capitol policemen, **1998** 511
food safety system, **2001** 700
patient safety hearings, **1999** 782
Frohnmayer, David, on ballot initiatives, **1999** 5
Frost, Martin (D-Texas), U.S.-China trade relations, **2000** 215
FTC. *See* Federal Trade Commission (FTC)
Fuhrman, Mark, racist police detective in Simpson trial, **1997** 74
Fujimori, Alberto K.
Peruvian hostage crisis, **1997** 234–236
Peruvian president's accomplishments, **2000** 923–926
Funk v. U.S. **1998** 398, 402

G

Gallegly, Elton (R-Calif.), House Judiciary Committee impeachment inquiry, **1998** 705–706
Gangs
legislation controlling, **1997** 39
youth gangs, Justice Department report on, **2001** 73, 75
Garcia v. San Antonio Metropolitan Transit Authority **1999** 334, 347
Gardner, Neil, death of at Columbine School shooting, **2000** 875–876
Garment, Leonard, Rich presidential pardon, **2001** 90
Garofalo, Lucia, **1999** 499
Garten, Jeffrey E., U.S. economy, **2001** 57
Gartner Group, on year 2000 computer conversion, **1997** 534, 536; **2000** 5
Garvey, Jane E., aviation fuel tank requirements, **1997** 782
Garza, Cutberto, federal nutritional guidelines, **2000** 240
Garza, Juan Raul, death sentencing of, **2000** 990; **2001** 387, 390
Gates, William H., **1999** 655; **2001** 776, 777
Gaviria, Cesar, Haiti political situation, **2001** 396
Gay, Hobart R., Korean War massacre incident, **1999** 556
Gay rights
Clinton speech to Human Rights Campaign, **1997** 760–766
same-sex civil unions, Vermont legislation, **2000** 158–167
same-sex marriages, **1997** 761; **1999** 4
and security clearances, **1997** 761
See also Homosexual rights
Gearhart, John, on embryonic research, **1998** 66
Gebser v. Lago Vista Independent School District **1998** 442; **1999** 222, 228, 229
Gehman, Harold W., USS *Cole* bombing, **2001** 5–6
Gekas, George (R-Pa.), House Judiciary Committee impeachment inquiry, **1998** 703
General Accounting Office (GAO)
aviation safety enforcement, **1998** 169–179
aviation safety report, **1997** 112–121
aviation security, **2001** 650–659
Balkans political situation, **2000** 141–157
bioterrorism preparation, **2001** 672–685
Colombia aid program, **2000** 840–851
computers, security of systems, **1998** 676–686
computers, Y2K (year 2000) conversion, **1997** 534–540; **1998** 543–554
drug-resistant bacteria, **1999** 185–199
federal election system reform, **2001** 526–527
food safety
foodborne illness, **1998** 521–531
threats to food supply, **2001** 698–709
Food Safety Agency proposal, **1997** 693
Gulf War, "smart" weapons effectiveness, **1997** 493–500
Gulf War syndrome, **1997** 741
health insurance coverage, **1998** 139–150
Roswell incident, **1997** 397
Russian nuclear weapons reports, **2001** 19
social security system solvency, **1998** 98–109
terrorism, **1997** 711
UN peacekeeping operations report, **1997** 150–157
United Nations reform, **2000** 179–189
welfare reform, **1998** 354–363; **1999** 257–271
General Agreement on Tariffs and Trade (GATT)
CEA report on, **1998** 83
Uruguay Round, **1997** 53; **1999** 798
See also under its later name World Trade Organization (WTO)
General Electric (GE), and Hudson River pollution, **2001** 218

N

Q

R

S